Company mission

Company profile

Possible?

Desired?

External environment-
operating industry,
and multinational
analyses

Long-term objectives

Grand strategy

Annual objectives

Operating strategies

Policies

Institutionalization
of strategy

Control and evaluation

Feedback

Feedback

Legend

Major impact

Minor impact

STRATEGIC MANAGEMENT

FORMULATION, IMPLEMENTATION, AND CONTROL

STRATEGIC MANAGEMENT

FORMULATION, IMPLEMENTATION, AND CONTROL

JOHN A. PEARCE II

School of Business Administration

George Mason University

RICHARD B. ROBINSON, JR.

College of Business Administration

University of South Carolina

FOURTH EDITION

Homewood, IL 60430   Boston, MA 02116

© RICHARD D. IRWIN, INC., 1982, 1985, 1988, and 1991

Sponsoring editor: Craig S. Beytien
Developmental editor: Kama Brockmann
Project editor: Gladys True
Production manager: Bette K. Ittersagen
Designer: Diane Beasley Design
Artist: Benoit Design
Compositor: J. M. Post Graphics, Corp.
Typeface: 10/12 Times Roman
Printer: R. R. Donnelley & Sons Company

Library of Congress Cataloging-in-Publication Data

Pearce, John A.
    Strategic management: formulation, implementation, and control /
John A Pearce II, Richard B. Robinson, Jr.—4th ed.
      p.   cm.
    Includes index.
    ISBN 0-256-08323-1
    1. Strategic planning.   I. Robinson, Richard B. (Richard Braden),
date. II. Title.
HD30.28.P3395 1991
658.4′012—dc20   90–41993

Printed in the United States of America

2 3 4 5 6 7 8 9 0 DO 7 6 5 4 3 2 1

To
David Donham Pearce, Mark McCartney Pearce,
Katherine Elizabeth Robinson, John Braden Robinson—
wonderful young people and
our much beloved children

PREFACE

The fourth edition of this book is the culmination of 12 years of diligent work by many people. It represents our earnest efforts to further improve a book that has been adopted by over 300 colleges and universities and studied by over a quarter of a million students. This preface will provide you with an overview of the content of this newest edition, and it will give us the opportunity to recognize the many contributors who have aided us in its development.

We have divided the preface into three sections. The first section is for students. It provides a concise overview of the structure and content of the book. The second section is for the instructor. It provides an educator's perspective on what is new in the strategic management field and in this edition. The third section acknowledges the many contributors to this ongoing project.

To the Student

Strategic Management: Strategy Formulation, Implementation and Control, 4th edition, is a book designed to introduce you to the critical business skills of planning and managing strategic activities. It incorporates three teaching approaches: text, cohesion cases, and business case studies.

The text portion provides you with a readable, up-to-date introduction to the management of strategy in the business enterprise. We have integrated the work of strategic management theorists, practitioners, and researchers, with a strong emphasis on real-world applications of strategic management concepts. To further this aim, we have included **Strategy-in-Action** reports throughout all 11 chapters to give you well-known business examples of the key strategy concepts.

The structure of the text material is guided by a comprehensive model of the strategic management process. Perfected by strategic planners and first published by the prestigious journal *California Management Review,* the model will help you acquire an executive-level perspective on strategy formulation, implementation, and control. It provides a visual display of the major components of the entire process and shows both how they are conceptually related and how they are sequenced through the process.

The major components of the model are each discussed in depth in separate chapters, thereby enabling you to acquire detailed knowledge and specific skills within a broad framework of strategic management. The use of the model is also extended to the cohesion cases and to the business case studies, where you will be guided in your case analyses to pursue disciplined, systematic, and comprehensive studies of actual strategic dilemmas.

The **Cohesion Case** offers an innovative and unique feature designed to aid you and the instructor of strategic management and business policy. We have taken a dynamic entrepreneurial firm in the hazardous waste management industry, Bryson Industrial Services, Inc., and used it as the basis of an in-depth case study to illustrate in detail the application of the text material. To do this, we provide a cohesion case section at the end of each chapter that applies the chapter material to the company. The Bryson case offers a clear illustration of the corporate, business, and functional levels of strategy— so important to the understanding of strategic management in today's corporate environment.

The cohesion case will magnify the benefits of your learning efforts in several important ways:

- It provides a continuous illustration of the interdependence of the various parts of the strategic management process by using the same enterprise throughout the chapters.
- It provides a useful aid in understanding the text material when the primary emphasis in the course is to be on case studies or other nontext analysis.
- It provides a useful aid in preparing for the case analysis component of the course, in the event that the instructor prefers to emphasize the conceptual material.
- It offers an in-depth basis for class discussion of strategic management concepts, application, and ideas for any classroom pedagogy.

The **business case studies and industry notes** developed and chosen for this book offer you wide exposure to a systematically selected cross-section of strategic management situations. All 41 cases and industry notes represent pertinent, relevant, factual, and, we hope, interesting and challenging opportunities to develop and test your skills as strategic managers. The rich diversity among these exciting cases and industry notes is described in greater detail later in this preface.

To the Instructor

Strategic Management: Strategy Formulation, Implementation, and Control, 4th edition, provides a thoroughly revised, state-of-the-art treatment of the critical business skills of planning and managing strategic activities. We have reorganized our treatment of strategic management into 11 chapters, added critical pedagogical features, expanded the number of real-world examples, added a totally new and engaging Cohesion Case, and further incorporated the work of contemporary scholars into our coverage of strategic management. We feel confident you will find the material to be well organized, full of current examples, and reflective of new contributions in the strategic management literature while retaining a structure guided by our time-tested and widely accepted model of the strategic management process.

We have selected 41 cases and industry notes for this edition—all 41 are new! Only one of the cases, an updated version of the widely acclaimed "Wendy's International case," pertains to a company studied in our last edition. Our survey of professors confirmed our belief that the most valuable cases are those that review business situations and that reflect the realities of today's dynamic, global, and supercompetitive marketplace. For most of us, and certainly for students, there are no classic cases, just old ones.

The cases are grouped into four sections. Eleven cases introduce students to strategic management and the process of strategy formulation, 9 cases place students in the role of implementing basic strategies, 10 cases allow students to experience the challenges of monitoring and controlling implemented strategies, and 11 cases and industry notes allow you to cover industry analysis and strategic management across an integrated set of competitive business situations. We are very excited about the cases selected for this edition—they are contemporary and interesting situations that students will learn from, recognize, and enjoy.

We have prepared a totally new cohesion case. Few industries have captured the interest and reflected the concerns of managers worldwide as has hazardous waste management. Our new cohesion case from this industry, Bryson Industrial Services, Inc., focuses on a representative firm confronted with the numerous and varied strategic opportunities and challenges. Bryson is entrepreneurial, innovative, growing, and cleverly managed. We think that your students will find it to be an ideal case to study as they perfect their applications of the text material to actual business situations.

The teaching package for this edition has been greatly enhanced. J. Kim Dedee of the University of Wisconsin, Oshkosh, and a longtime Pearce & Robinson user, has completely reorganized and revised the **Instructor's Manual** for this edition. Included in the Instructor's Manual are such standard features as the 1,500-question test bank, text chapter overviews, and transparency masters. However, the most important part of the manual is the Case Teaching Notes. Kim has completely prepared each teaching note to follow a consistent format. This should make your presentation of the material easier to prepare and deliver. Also included is a section of Strategy Design Decision Support Tools and Techniques, as well as suggested classroom handouts. Our package also includes Lotus templates for the financial information provided in the cases, transparency acetates, and a computerized version of the test bank. Each of the components of our teaching package offers the instructor optimal, integrated flexibility in designing and conducting the strategic management course.

Changes to Our Text Material

The literature and research comprising the strategic management field has been developing at a rapid pace in recent years. We have endeavored to create a fourth edition that incorporates major developments in this literature while keeping our focus centered on a straightforward and understandable framework through which students can begin to grasp the complexity of strategic management. Several text revisions or additions that you should be aware of are described below:

- The three chapters on external analysis are strengthened by application examples that give our adopters more information on competitive dynamics than is available in any other text. Separate chapters now cover the nature of external environments and industry analysis, environmental forecasting, and the multinational business setting.

- A revised and concisely focussed section on the issue of designing organizational structures to fit different strategies.
- Clear distinction between strategic alternatives at the corporate versus business level.
- Major emphasis has been placed on the topic of "strategic control." Three basic types of strategic control and ways to use them are highlighted in this material.
- Organizational culture as a central dimension of strategy implementation receives thorough coverage. Several useful analytical concepts and techniques that aid identification and management of the strategy-culture interface are incorporated to aid the student in understanding the cultural concept.

Three useful appendices now accompany our text material. A guide to industry information sources follows Chapter 5, Environmental Forecasting. Students will find it most helpful in rapidly orienting them to where and how to get company and industry data. Also following Chapter 5 is an appendix on strategic planning tools and techniques for forecasting. It offers a practical assessment of each of 20 planning aides, as well as source information on where detailed how-to materials can be found. A revised guide to financial analysis is provided following Chapter 6, Internal Analysis. It provides perhaps the most thorough and easy-to-use guide to quantitative analysis of financial and operating information available in any strategic management text.

We have updated and improved our **Strategy-in-Action Capsules**. The text material contains 37 of these illustration vignettes, 30 of which are new to this edition. Each Strategy-in-Action provides a contemporary business example of a key chapter topic designed to enhance student interest and aid learning.

Our popular **Cohesion Case feature** has received considerable attention this edition. Not only have we prepared a completely new case to illustrate in detail the application of the text material but we also continue to provide cohesion case sections at the end of each chapter, which apply chapter material to the Bryson Industrial Services situation.

Our survey of over 200 adopters and "almost adopters" told us they wanted material to aid students who are unsure about the case method. They wanted us to inform students about what they need to do in preparing a case and in maintaining a strategic point of view. Therefore, we have included a major section in this edition that is solely intended to aid students in understanding case method pedagogy and to prepare them to analyze a case. The first part of this section provides a thorough and detailed description of the case method format; what to expect in each class session; and how to analyze a case, prepare it for class, and participate in class discussion. The second part offers a short case accompanied by a useful example of former students' analysis and preparation of it. These two learning aids, combined with the new cohesion case illustrating each step of strategic analysis, provide the most thorough package available in any strategy textbook to ensure that students understand and benefit from the case method pedagogy.

In conclusion, we are confident you will find the text material in this edition to be organized, concise, filled with current examples, and consistent with the current theory and practice of strategic management.

Cases in the Fourth Edition

We are very excited about the 41 cases and industry notes available in this edition. All 41 are new to this edition! We are confident that you will find this case collection does an excellent job of meeting your classroom needs for several reasons.

The collection offers a rich diversity of recognizable domestic, foreign, and international companies and industries. The cases present very current situations. All of the cases involve situations from 1987 to 1990, and all focus on issues in the forefront of strategic management for the 1990s.

Contemporary, recognizable, interesting situations abound: the resurgence of Wendy's; the reemergence of Harley-Davidson; the dynamic environment of Harcourt Brace Jovanovich; the strategic maneuvering of Polaroid Corporation; survival strategies in mature industries exemplified by General Motors, Chrysler, and American Motors; the explosive growth of global competitor Hazleton Laboratories; and the cases of both male and female entrepreneurs building companies in retailing, software, and entertainment settings—all situations our tests have shown stimulate student interest.

The nature of the firms provides varied exposure. We have included 7 small companies in either family or rapid-growth phases, 2 foreign (non-U.S.) companies, 28 companies with international operations, 12 of the top companies in America, 2 nonprofit organizations, and 3 industry notes providing three companies in competition with each other.

In all, adopters have a variety of domestic and international industry settings at different stages of evolution and that span manufacturing, services, and consumer products. Different cases cover the basic types of business (retail, wholesale, service, manufacturing), of companies in market leadership positions, of companies falling out of leadership, of high-tech companies, and of exporters, importers, and diversifying companies.

We have also given significant attention to case length. A major effort has been made to ensure that a majority of the cases are short to medium in length.

Finally, we have endeavored to ensure a collection of cases that are flexible in their course sequencing, yet able to offer exposure to distinct management challenges associated with strategy formulation, implementation, or control. Because our survey found case flexibility to be one of the key concerns of strategic management professors, the cases were assembled with this need upmost in our minds.

Overall, we think you will find this case collection interesting and motivating for your students, representative and varied in the application of strategic problems and analytical applications, flexible in terms of course sequencing, and teachable.

Acknowledgments

We have repeatedly benefited from the help of many people in the evolution of this book over four editions. Students, adopters, colleagues, and reviewers have provided literally hundreds of insightful comments, suggestions, and contributions that have progressively enhanced this "package." We are indebted to several researchers, writers, and practicing managers who have accelerated the development of the literature on strategic management.

We are likewise indebted to the talented case researchers who have produced several cases used in this book, as well as to the growing network of case researchers encouraging the revitalization of case research as an important academic endeavor. The discipline of strategic management is eminently more teachable when current well-written and well-researched cases are available. We encourage every opportunity to reinforce proper recognition and reward for first-class research—it is a major avenue through which top strategic management scholars should be recognized.

The following strategic management scholars have provided the results of their case research in the creation of this fourth edition:

Robert Anderson, College of Charleston
Bobby Bizzell, University of Houston
Charles Boyd, Southwest Missouri State
Lew Brown, University of North Carolina
James Chrisman, University of South Carolina
Robert Crowner, Eastern Michigan University
Keith Denton, Southwest Missouri State
John Dunkelberg, Wake Forest University
Caroline Fisher, Loyola University
John Grant, Arizona State
Walter Green, Pan American University
Stuart Hinrichs, Iowa State University
Alan Hoffman, Bentley College
Mark Kroll, University of Texas at Tyler
Carol Reeves, University of Arkansas
John Seeger, Bentley College
Neil Snyder, University of Virginia
Joseph Wolfe, University of Tulsa
Shaker Zahra, George Mason University

We have personally ensured that the dean at each of the case author's respective institutions is aware of the value that their case research efforts have added to the professionals' ability to teach strategic management.

The development of this book through four editions has been greatly enhanced by the generous commitment of time, energy, and ideas from the following people:

Sonny Ariss, University of Toledo
Robert Earl Bolick, Metropolitan State University
William Burr, University of Oregon
E. T. Busch, Western Kentucky University
Richard Castaldi, San Diego State University
Bill Crittenden, Northeastern University
Larry Cummings, Harvard University
Ellen Foster Curtis, University of Lowell
William Davig, Auburn University
Peter Davis, Memphis State University
Marc Dollinger, Indiana University

Michael Dowling, University of Georgia
Liam Fahey, Boston University
Elizabeth Freeman, Portland State University
Diane Garsombke, University of Maine
Michael Geringer, Southern Methodist University
Peter Goulet, University of Northern Iowa
Don Hambrick, Columbia University
Richard Hoffman, University of Delaware
Dan Jennings, Han Kamer School of Business
Troy Jones, University of Central Florida
Jon Kalinowski, Mankato State University
Kay Keels, Louisana State University,
Joel Knowles, California State University, Sacramento
Michael Koshuta, Purdue North Central
Myroslaw Kyj, Widener University of Pennsylvania
Joseph Leonard, Miami University, Ohio
Edward McClelland, Roanoke College
Patricia McDougall, George State University
John Maurer, Wayne State University
Carl McKenry, University of Miami
S. Mehta, San Jose State University
Richard Merner, University of Delaware
Bill Middlebrook, Southwest Texas State University
Cynthia Montgomery, Harvard University
Stephanie Newell, York University
Kenneth Olm, University of Texas at Austin
Braimoh Osegahale, Radford University
Benjamin Oviatt, Clemson University
Joseph Paolillo, University of Mississippi
Norris Rath, Shepard College
Paula Rechner, University of Illinois
Carol Reeves, University of Arkansas
Robert Roth, City University
Les Rue, Georgia State University
J. A. Ruslyk, Memphis State University
Jack Scarborough, Berry University
Scott Snell, Michigan State University
Arien Ulman, SUNY at Binghamton
John Valas, Ferris State College
William Waddell, California State University, Los Angeles
Bill Warren, College of William and Mary
Kirby Warren, Columbia University
Michael White, University of Tulsa
Frank Winfrey, Kent State University
Robley Wood, Virginia Commonwealth University

The valuable ideas, recommendations, and support of these outstanding scholars and teachers have added quality to this book.

Because we are affiliated with two separate universities, we have two sets of co-workers to thank.

The growth and dynamic environment at George Mason University have contributed directly to the development of this edition. Valuable critiques and helpful recommendations have been made by strategic management faculty: Jeff Bracker, Keith Robbins, and Shaker Zahra, and Jack's colleagues Debra Cohen, Jon English, Rodger Griffith, Eileen Hogan, Janice Jackson, Ken Kovach, and Bill Schulte. For his gracious support and personal encouragement, we also wish to thank Coleman Raphael, dean of George Mason University's School of Business Administration. For their excellent secretarial assistance, we most sincerely appreciate the work of Virginia Martin and Alesia Gesualdi.

We are especially grateful to LeRoy Eakin, Jr., and his family for their generous endowment of the Eakin Endowed Chair in Strategic Management at George Mason University that Jack holds. The provisions of the chair have enabled Jack to continue his dual involvements with this book and strategic management research.

The stimulating environment at the University of South Carolina has contributed to the development of this book. Thought-provoking discussions with strategy colleagues Alan Bauerschmidt, Carl Clamp, Jim Chrisman, Herb Hand, John Logan, Bob Rosen, Bill Sandberg, and David Schweiger gave us many useful ideas. Likewise, we want to thank James F. Kane, dean of the College of Business Administration; James G. Hilton, associate dean; and Joe Ullman, program director in management, for their interest and support. Our sincere appreciation also goes to Susie Gossage and Sandy Bennett for their help in preparing this manuscript and in solving endless logistical problems.

In using this text, we hope that you will share our enthusiasm both for the rich subject of strategic management and for the learning approach that we have taken. We value your recommendations and thoughts about our materials. Please write Jack at the Department of Management, School of Business Administration, George Mason University, Fairfax, Virginia 22030, (703-323-4361) or Richard at the College of Business Administration, University of South Carolina, Columbia, South Carolina 29208, (803-777-5961).

We wish you the very best as you advance your knowledge in the exciting and rewarding field of strategic management.

Jack Pearce

Richard Robinson

About the Authors

John A. Pearce II, Ph.D., is the holder of the Eakin Endowed Chair in Strategic Management and a State of Virginia Eminent Scholar in the School of Business Administration at George Mason University (Fairfax, VA 22030, 703-323-4361).

Professor Pearce has published more than 130 journal articles, invited book chapters, and professional papers in outlets that include the *Academy of Management Executive, Academy of Management Journal, Academy of Management Review, California Management Review, Journal of Business Venturing, Sloan Management Review,* and the *Strategic Management Journal.* Professor Pearce is also the coauthor or coeditor of 25 texts, proceedings, and supplements for publishers that include Richard D. Irwin, Inc., McGraw-Hill, Random House, and the Academy of Management.

Elected to more than a dozen offices in national and regional professional associations, Professor Pearce has served as Chairman of the Academy of Management's Entrepreneurship Division, Strategic Management and Entrepreneurship Track Chairman for the Southern Management Association, and Strategy Formulation and Implementation Track Chairman for the Decision Sciences Institute. He was the President of the Southern Management Association in 1990.

An active consultant and management trainer, Professor Pearce specializes in helping executive teams to develop and activate their firms' strategic plans.

Richard B. Robinson, Jr., Ph.D., is currently on leave from his position as Professor of Strategy and Entrepreneurship in the College of Business Administration at the University of South Carolina (Columbia, SC 29208, 803-777-5961). Professor Robinson has accepted the position of President of Bryson Industrial Services, Inc.—the cohesion case company. The Board of Directors has asked Professor Robinson to guide the company's transition from being an owner-managed to a manager-managed company. He is also responsible for implementing an aggressive acquisition program in preparation for a potential, mid-1990s public offering.

Professor Robinson has published more than 100 journal articles, invited chapters, and professional papers in outlets that include the *Academy of Management Journal, Strategic Management Journal, Academy of Management Review, Journal of Business Venturing, Journal of Small Business Management, Entrepreneurship: Theory and Practice,* and the

Personnel Administrator. He is also coauthor or coeditor of 16 texts, proceedings, and supplements for publishers that include Richard D. Irwin, Inc., McGraw-Hill, Random House, and the Academy of Management.

Professor Robinson is the recipient of several awards in recognition of his work in strategic management and entrepreneurship. Sponsors of these awards include the Heizer Capital Corporation, the Academy of Management, the Center for Family Business, the National Association of Small Business Investment Companies, the Southern Business Administration Association, the Small Business Administration, the National Venture Capital Association, and Beta Gamma Sigma. He has also held offices in the Academy of Management, the Southern Management Association, and the International Council of Small Business. Professor Robinson is an active consultant in the strategic management of growth-oriented ventures.

CONTENTS

I OVERVIEW OF STRATEGIC MANAGEMENT

The first chapter of this text introduces strategic management, the set of decisions and actions that result in the design and activation of strategies to achieve the objectives of an organization. The chapter provides an overview of the nature, need, benefits, and terminology of strategic management. Subsequent chapters provide greater detail.

The first major section of Chapter 1, "The Nature and Value of Strategic Management," emphasizes the practical value and benefits of strategic management for a firm. It also distinguishes between a firm's strategic decisions and its other planning tasks.

The section stresses the key point that strategic management activities are undertaken at three levels: corporate, business, and functional. The distinctive characteristics of strategic decision making at each of these levels affect the impact of activities at these levels on company operations. Other topics dealt with in this section are the value of formality in strategic management and the alignment of strategy makers in strategy formulation and implementation. The section concludes with a review of the planning research on business, which demonstrates that the use of strategic management processes yields financial and behavioral benefits that justify their costs.

The second major section of Chapter 1 presents a model of the strategic management process. The model which will serve as an outline for the remainder of the text, describes approaches currently used by strategic planners. Its individual components are carefully defined and explained, as is the process for integrating them into the strategic management process. The section ends with a discussion of the model's practical limitations and the advisability of tailoring the recommendations made to actual business situations.

1 STRATEGIC MANAGEMENT

THE NATURE AND VALUE OF STRATEGIC MANAGEMENT

Managing activities internal to the firm is only part of the modern executive's responsibilities. The modern executive must also respond to the challenges posed by the firm's immediate and remote external environment. The immediate external environment includes competitors, suppliers, increasingly scarce resources, government agencies and their ever more numerous regulations, and customers whose preferences often shift inexplicably. The remote external environment comprises economic and social conditions, political priorities, and technological developments, all of which must be anticipated, monitored, assessed, and incorporated into the executive's decision making. However, the executive is often compelled to subordinate the demands of the firm's internal activities and external environment to the multiple and often inconsistent requirements of its stakeholders: owners, top managers, employees, communities, customers, and country. To deal effectively with everything that affects the growth and profitability of a firm, executives employ management processes that they feel will position it optimally in its competitive environment by maximizing the anticipation of environmental changes and of unexpected internal and competitive demands.

Broad-scope, large-scale management processes became dramatically more sophisticated after World War II. These processes responded to increases in the size and number of competing firms; to the expanded role of government as a buyer, seller, regulator, and competitor in the free enterprise system; and to greater business involvement in international trade. Perhaps the most significant improvement in management processes came in the 1970s, when "long-range planning," "new venture management," "planning, programming, budgeting," and "business policy" were blended. At the same time, increased emphasis was placed on environmental forecasting and external considerations in formulating and implementing plans. This all-encompassing approach is known as strategic management or strategic planning.[1]

---

[1]In this text, the term *strategic management* refers to the broad overall process. To some scholars and practitioners, the term connotes only the formulation phase of total management activities.

Strategic management is defined as the set of decisions and actions that result in the formulation and implementation of plans designed to achieve a company's objectives. It comprises nine critical tasks:

1. Formulate the company's mission, including broad statements about its purpose, philosophy, and goals.
2. Develop a company profile that reflects its internal conditions and capabilities.
3. Assess the company's external environment, including both the competitive and general contextual factors.
4. Analyze the company's options by matching its resources with the external environment.
5. Identify the most desirable options by evaluating each option in light of the company's mission.
6. Select a set of long-term objectives and grand strategies that will achieve the most desirable options.
7. Develop annual objectives and short-term strategies that are compatible with the selected set of long-term objectives and grand strategies.
8. Implement the strategic choices by means of budgeted resource allocations in which the matching of tasks, people, structures, technologies, and reward systems is emphasized.
9. Evaluate the success of the strategic process as an input for future decision making.

As these nine tasks indicate, strategic management involves the planning, directing, organizing, and controlling of a company's strategy-related decisions and actions. By *strategy,* managers mean their large-scale, future-oriented plans for interacting with the competitive environment to achieve company objectives. A strategy is a company's "game plan." Although that plan does not precisely detail all future deployments (of people, finances, and material), it does provide a framework for managerial decisions. A strategy reflects a company's awareness of how, when, and where it should compete; against whom it should compete; and for what purposes it should compete.

DIMENSIONS OF STRATEGIC DECISIONS

What decisions facing a business are strategic and therefore deserve strategic management attention? Typically, strategic issues have the following dimensions.

Strategic Issues Require Top-Management Decisions Since strategic decisions overarch several areas of a firm's operations, they require top-management involvement. Usually only top management has the perspective needed to understand the broad implications of such decisions and the power to authorize the necessary resource allocations.

Strategic Issues Require Large Amounts of the Firm's Resources Strategic decisions involve substantial allocations of people, physical assets, or moneys that must be either redirected from internal sources or secured from outside the firm. They also commit the firm to actions over an extended period. For these reasons, they require substantial resources.

Strategic Issues Often Affect the Firm's Long-Term Prosperity   Strategic decisions ostensibly commit the firm for a long time, typically five years; however, the impact of such decisions often lasts much longer. Once a firm has committed itself to a particular strategy, its image and competitive advantages are usually tied to that strategy. Firms become known in certain markets, for certain products, with certain technologies. They would jeopardize their previous gains if they shifted from these markets, products, or technologies by adopting a radically different strategy. Thus, strategic decisions have enduring effects on firms—for better or worse.

Strategic Issues Are Future Oriented   Strategic decisions are based on what managers forecast rather than on what they know. In such decisions, emphasis is placed on the development of projections that will enable the firm to select the most promising strategic options. In the turbulent and competitive free enterprise environment, a firm will succeed only if it takes a proactive (anticipatory) stance toward change.

Strategic Issues Usually Have Multifunctional or Multibusiness Consequences   Strategic decisions have complex implications for most areas of the firm. Decisions about such matters as customer mix, competitive emphasis, or organizational structure necessarily involve a number of the firm's strategic business units (SBU's), divisions, or program units. All of these areas will be affected by allocations or reallocations of responsibilities and resources that result from these decisions.

Strategic Issues Require Considering the Firm's External Environment   All business firms exist in an open system. They affect and are affected by external conditions that are largely beyond their control. Therefore, to successfully position a firm in competitive situations, its strategic managers must look beyond its operations.[2] They must consider what relevant others (e.g., competitors, customers, suppliers, creditors, government, and labor) are likely to do.[3]

Three Levels of Strategy

The decision-making hierarchy of a firm typically contains three levels. At the top of this hierarchy is the corporate level, composed principally of a board of directors and the chief executive and administrative officers. They are responsible for the firm's financial performance and for the achievement of nonfinancial goals, such as enhancing the firm's image and fulfilling its social responsibilities. To a large extent, attitudes at the

---

[2]R. E. Seiler and K. E. Said, "Problems Encountered in Operationalizing a Company's Strategic Plans," *Managerial Planning*, January–February 1983, pp. 16–20.

[3]M. Allen, "Strategic Management of Consumer Services." *Long Range Planning*, December 1988, pp. 20–25.

corporate level reflect the concerns of stockholders and society at large. In a multibusiness firm, corporate-level executives determine the businesses in which the firm should be involved. They also set objectives and formulate strategies that span the activities and functional areas of these businesses. Corporate-level strategic managers attempt to exploit their firm's distinctive competences by adopting a portfolio approach to the management of its businesses and by developing long-term plans, typically for a five-year period.

In the middle of the decision-making hierarchy is the business level, composed principally of business and corporate managers. These managers must translate the statements of direction and intent generated at the corporate level into concrete objectives and strategies for individual business divisions or SBUs. In essence, business-level strategic managers determine how the firm will compete in the selected product/market arena. They strive to identify and secure the most promising market segment within that arena. This segment is the piece of the total market that the firm can claim and defend because of its competitive advantages.

At the bottom of the decision-making hierarchy is the functional level, composed principally of managers of product, geographic, and functional areas. They develop annual objectives and short-term strategies in such areas as production, operations, research and development, finance and accounting, marketing, and human relations. However, their principal responsibility is to implement or execute the firm's strategic plans. Whereas corporate- and business-level managers center their attention on "doing the right things," managers at the functional level center their attention on "doing things right." Thus, they address such issues as the efficiency and effectiveness of production and marketing systems, the quality of customer service, and the success of particular products and services in increasing the firm's market shares.

Figure 1–1 depicts the three levels of strategic management as structured in practice. In alternative 1, the firm is engaged in only one business and the corporate- and business-level responsibilities are concentrated in a single group of directors, officers, and managers. This is the organizational format of most small businesses.

Alternative 2, the classical corporate structure, comprises three fully operative levels—the corporate level, the business level, and the functional level. The approach taken throughout this text assumes the use of alternative 2. Moreover, whenever appropriate, topics are covered from the perspective of each level of strategic management. In this way, the text presents a comprehensive discussion of the strategic management process.

Characteristics of Strategic Management Decisions

The characteristics of strategic management decisions vary with the level of strategic activity considered. As shown in Figure 1–2, decisions at the corporate level tend to be more value oriented, more conceptual, and less concrete than decisions at the business or functional level. Corporate-level decisions are also characterized by greater risk, cost, and profit potential; a greater needs for flexibility; and longer time horizons. Such decisions include the choice of businesses, dividend policies, sources of long-term financing, and priorities for growth.

FIGURE 1–1
Alternative Strategic Management Structures

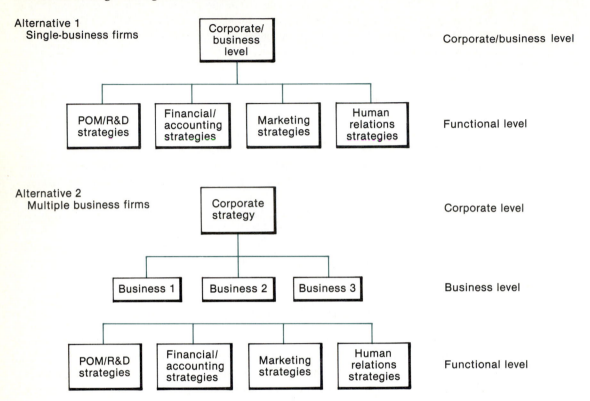

Alternative 1
Single-business firms

| Corporate/business level | | | Corporate/business level |

POM/R&D strategies · Financial/accounting strategies · Marketing strategies · Human relations strategies — Functional level

Alternative 2
Multiple business firms

Corporate strategy — Corporate level

Business 1 · Business 2 · Business 3 — Business level

POM/R&D strategies · Financial/accounting strategies · Marketing strategies · Human relations strategies — Functional level

Functional-level decisions implement the overall strategy formulated at the corporate and business levels. They involve action-oriented operational issues and are relatively short range and low risk. Functional-level decisions incur only modest costs because they are dependent on available resources. They are usually adaptable to ongoing activities, and therefore can be implemented with minimal cooperation. Because such decisions are relatively concrete and quantifiable, they receive critical attention and analysis even though their comparative profit potential is low. Common functional-level decisions include decisions on generic versus brand-name labeling, basic versus applied research and development (R&D), high versus low inventory levels, general-purpose versus specific-purpose production equipment, and close versus loose supervision.

Business-level decisions help bridge decisions at the corporate and functional levels. Such decisions are less costly, risky, and potentially profitable than corporate-level decisions, but they are more costly, risky, and potentially profitable than functional-level

FIGURE 1–2
Hierarchy of Objectives and Strategies

Ends (What is to be achieved?)	Means (How is it to be achieved?)	Strategic Decision Makers			
		Board of Directors	Corporate Managers	Business Managers	Functional Managers
Mission, including goals and philosophy		√√	√√	√	
Long-term objectives	Grand strategy	√	√√	√√	
Annual objectives	Short-term strategies and policies		√	√√	√√
Functional objectives	Tactics			√	√√

Note: √√ indicates a principal responsibility; √ indicates a secondary responsibility.

decisions. Common business-level decisions include decisions on plant location, marketing segmentation and geographic coverage, and distribution channels.

FORMALITY IN STRATEGIC MANAGEMENT

The formality of strategic management systems varies widely among companies. *Formality* refers to the degree to which participants, responsibilities, authority, and discretion in decision making are specified. It is an important consideration in the study of strategic management because greater formality is usually positively correlated with the cost, comprehensiveness, accuracy, and success of planning.

A number of forces determine how much formality is needed in strategic management. The size of the organization, its predominant management styles, the complexity of its environment, its production process, its problems, and the purpose of its planning system all play a part in determining the appropriate degree of formality.[4]

In particular, formality is associated with the size of the firm and with its stage of development. Methods of evaluating strategic success are also linked to formality. Some firms, especially smaller ones, follow an *entrepreneurial* mode. They are basically under the control of a single individual, and they produce a limited number of products or services. In such firms, strategic evaluation is informal, intuitive, and limited. Very large firms, on the other hand, make strategic evaluation part of a comprehensive, formal planning system, an approach that Henry Mintzberg called the *planning mode*. Mintzberg also identified a third mode (the *adaptive mode*), which he associated with medium-sized

[4]M. Goold and A. Campbell, "Managing the Diversified Corporation: The Tensions Facing the Chief Executive," *Long Range Planning*, August 1988, pp. 12–24.

firms in relatively stable environments.[5] For firms that follow the adaptive mode, the identification and evaluation of alternative strategies are closely related to existing strategy. It is not unusual to find different modes within the same organization. For example, Exxon might follow an entrepreneurial mode in developing and evaluating the strategy of its solar subsidiary but follow a planning mode in the rest of the company.

The Strategy Makers

The ideal strategic management team includes decision makers from all three company levels (the corporate, business, and functional levels)—for example, the chief executive officer (CEO), the product managers, and the heads of functional areas. In addition, the team obtains input from company planning staffs, when they exist, and from lower-level managers and supervisors. The latter provide data for strategic decision making and then implement strategies.

Because strategic decisions have a tremendous impact on a company and require large commitments of company resources, top managers must give final approval for strategic action. Figure 1–2 aligns levels of strategic decision makers with the kinds of objectives and strategies for which they are typically responsible.

Planning departments, often headed by a corporate vice president for planning, are common in large corporations. Medium-sized firms often employ at least one full-time staff member to spearhead strategic data-collection efforts. Even in small firms or less progressive larger firms, strategic planning is often spearheaded by an officer or by a group of officers designated as a planning committee.

Precisely what are managers' responsibilities in the strategic planning process at the corporate and business levels? Top management shoulders broad responsibility for all the major elements of strategic planning and management. It develops the major portions of the strategic plan and reviews, evaluates, and counsels on all other portions. General managers at the business level typically have principal responsibilities for developing environmental analysis and forecasting, establishing business objectives, and developing business plans prepared by staff groups.

A firm's president or CEO characteristically plays a dominant role in the strategic planning process. In many ways, this situation is desirable. The CEO's principal duty is often defined as giving long-term direction to the firm, and the CEO is ultimately responsible for the firm's success and therefore for the success of its strategy. In addition, CEOs are typically strong-willed, company-oriented individuals with high self-esteem. They often resist delegating authority to formulate or approve strategic decisions.

However, when the dominance of the CEO approaches autocracy, the effectiveness of the firm's strategic planning and management processes are likely to be diminished. For this reason, establishing a strategic management system implies that the CEO will allow managers at all levels to participate in the strategic posture of the company.

---

[5]Henry Mintzberg, "Strategy Making in Three Modes," *California Management Review*, 16, no. 2 (1973), pp. 44–53.

Benefits of Strategic Management[6]

Using the strategic management approach, managers at all levels of the firm interact in planning and implementing. As a result, the behavioral consequences of strategic management are similar to those of participative decision making. Therefore, an accurate assessment of the impact of strategy formulation on organizational performance requires not only financial evaluation criteria but also nonfinancial evaluation criteria—measures of behavior-based effects. In fact, promoting positive behavioral consequences also enables the firm to achieve its financial goals.[7] However, regardless of the profitability of strategic plans, several behavioral effects of strategic management improve the firm's welfare:

1. Strategy formulation activities enhance the firm's ability to prevent problems. Managers who encourage subordinates attention to planning are aided in their monitoring and forecasting responsibilities by subordinates who are aware of the needs of strategic planning.
2. Group-based strategic decisions are likely to be drawn from the best available alternatives. The strategic management process results in better decisions because group interaction generates a greater variety of strategies and because forecasts based on the specialized perspectives of group members improve the screening of options.
3. The involvement of employees in strategy formulation improves their understanding of the productivity-reward relationship in every strategic plan and thus heightens their motivation.
4. Gaps and overlaps in activities among individuals and groups are reduced as participation in strategy formulation clarifies differences in roles.
5. Resistance to change is reduced. Though the participants in strategy formulation may be no more pleased with their own decisions than they would be with authoritarian decisions, their greater awareness of the parameters that limit the available options makes them more likely to accept those decisions.

Risks of Strategic Management

Managers must be trained to guard against three types of unintended negative consequences of involvement in strategy formulation. First, the time that managers spend on the strategic management process may have a negative impact thus on operational responsibilities. Managers must be trained to minimize that impact by scheduling their duties so as to allow the necessary time for strategic activities.

---

[6]This section was adapted in part from John A. Pearce II and W. A. Randolph, "Improving Strategy Formulation Pedagogies by Recognizing Behavioral Aspects," *Exchange*, December 1980, pp. 7–10, with permission of the authors.

[7]Ann Langely, "The Roles of Formal Strategic Planning," *Long Range Planning*, June 1988, pp. 40–50.

STRATEGY IN ACTION 1–1 — EXECUTIVES' GENERAL OPINIONS AND ATTITUDES

Item	Percent of Respondents Indicating		
	Agreement	Neutral	Disagreement
1. Reducing emphasis on strategic planning will be detrimental to our long-term performance.	88.7	4.9	6.4
2. Our plans today reflect implementation concerns.	73.6	16.9	9.5
3. We have improved the sophistication of our strategic planning systems.	70.6	18.6	10.8
4. Our previous approaches to strategic planning are not appropriate today.	64.2	16.2	19.6
5. Today's systems emphasize creativity among managers more than our previous systems did.	62.6	20.2	17.2
6. Our strategic planning systems today are more consistent with our organization's culture.	55.6	30.7	13.7
7. We are more concerned about the evaluation of our strategic planning systems today.	54.0	29.7	16.3
8. There is more participation from lower-level managers in our strategic planning	56.6	18.0	25.4
9. Our tendency to rely on outside consultants for strategic planning has been on the decrease.	50.8	23.0	26.2
10. Our systems emphasize control more than before.	41.3	33.0	25.7
11. Planning in our company or unit is generally viewed as a luxury today.	15.0	13.0	72.0

Source: Adapted from V. Ramanujam, J. C. Camillus, and N. Venkatraman, "Trends in Strategic Planning," in *Strategic Planning and Management Handbook,* ed. W. R. King and D. I. Cleland (New York: Van Nostrand Reinhold, 1987), p. 619.

Second, if the formulators of strategy are not intimately involved in its implementation, they may shirk their individual responsibility for the decisions reached.[8] Thus, strategic managers must be trained to limit their promises to performance that the decision makers and their subordinates can deliver.

Third, strategic managers must be trained to anticipate and respond to the disappointment of participating subordinates over unattained expectations. Subordinates may ex-

---

[8]George S. Day, "Tough Questions for Developing Strategies," *Journal of Business Strategy,* Winter 1986, pp. 60–68.

pect their involvement in even minor phases of total strategy formulation to result in both acceptance of their proposals and an increase in their rewards, or they may expect a solicitation of their input on selected issues to extend to other areas of decision making.

Sensitizing managers to these possible negative consequences and preparing them with effective means of minimizing such consequences will greatly enhance the potential of strategic planning.

Executives' Views of Strategic Management

How do managers and corporate executives view the contribution of strategic management to the success of their firms? To answer this question, a survey was conducted that included over 200 executives from the Fortune 500, Fortune 500 Service, and INC 500 companies.[9] Their responses are summarized in Strategy in Action 1–1.

Overall, these responses indicate that corporate America sees strategic management as instrumental to high performance, evolutionary and perhaps revolutionary in its ever-growing sophistication, action oriented, and cost effective. Clearly, the responding executives view strategic management as critical to their individual and organizational success.

THE STRATEGIC MANAGEMENT PROCESS

Businesses vary in the processes they use to formulate and direct their strategic management activities. Sophisticated planners, such as General Electric, Procter & Gamble, and IBM have developed more detailed processes than less formal planners of similar size. Small businesses that rely on the strategy formulation skills and limited time of an entrepreneur typically exhibit more basic planning concerns than those of larger firms in their industries. Understandably, firms with multiple products, markets, or technologies tend to use more complex strategic management systems. However, despite differences in detail and the degree of formalization, the basic components of the models used to analyze strategic management operations are very similar.[10]

---

[9]V. Ramanujam, J. C. Camillus, and N. Venkatraman, "Trends in Strategic Planning," in *Strategic Planning and Management Handbook,* ed. W. R. King and D. I. Cleland (New York: Van Nostrand Reinhold, 1987), pp. 611–28.

[10]Models by academics that reflect such similarity, typically developed from consulting experience and intended for either business or educational use, include those of Stevenson (1976), Rogers (1975), and King and Cleland (1978). Models recommended for use by small firms, for example, those published by Gilmore (1971) and Steiner (1970) are almost identical to those recommended for larger firms. Finally, models that describe approaches for accomplishing strategic options contain elements similar to those included in general models; see, for example, Pryor (1964) on mergers, Steiner (1964) on diversification, and TenDam (1986) for governmental agencies. The bibliography at the end of this chapter contains complete citations.

Because of the similarity among the general models of the strategic management process, it is possible to develop an eclectic model representative of the foremost thought in the strategic management area. Such a model is shown in Figure 1–3. It serves three major functions. First, it depicts the sequence and the relationships of the major components of the strategic management process. Second, it is the outline for this text. This chapter provides a general overview of the strategic management process, and the major

FIGURE 1–3
Strategic Management Model

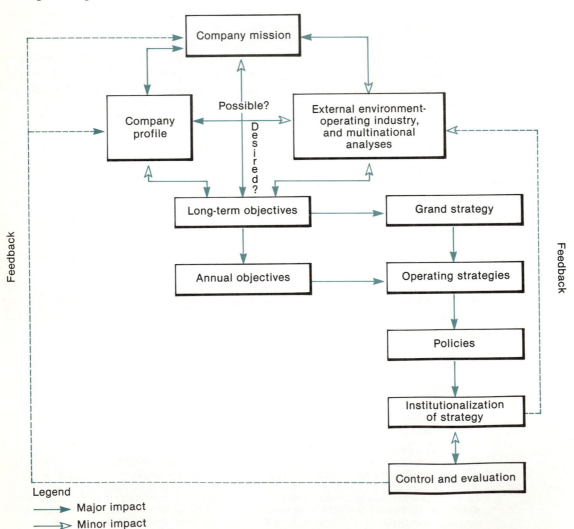

components of the model will be the principal theme of subsequent chapters. Finally, the model offers one approach for analyzing the case studies in this text and thus helps the analyst develop strategy formulation skills.

COMPONENTS OF THE STRATEGIC MANAGEMENT MODEL

This section will define and briefly describe the key components of the strategic management model. Each of these components will receive much greater attention in a later chapter. The intention here is simply to introduce them.

Company Mission

The mission of a company is the unique purpose that sets it apart from other companies of its type and identifies the scope of its operations. In short, the mission describes the company's product, market, and technological areas of emphasis in a way that reflects the values and priorities of the strategic decision makers.

Company Profile

The company profile depicts the quantity and quality of the company's financial, human, and physical resources. It also assesses the strengths and weaknesses of the company's management and organizational structure. Finally, it contrasts the company's past successes and traditional concerns with the company's current capabilities in an attempt to identify the company's future capabilities.

External Environment

A firm's external environment consists of all the conditions and forces that affect its strategic options but are typically beyond its control. The strategic management model shows the external environment as three interactive segments: the operating, industry, and remote environments.

Strategic Analysis and Choice

Simultaneous assessment of the external environment and the company profile enables a firm to identify a range of possibly attractive interactive opportunities. These opportunities are *possible* avenues for investment. However, they must be screened through the criterion of the company mission to generate a set of possible and *desired* opportunities. This screening process results in the selection of options from which a *strategic choice* is made. The process is meant to provide the combination of long-term objectives and grand strategy that will optimally position the firm in its external environment to achieve the company mission.

Long-Term Objectives

The results that an organization seeks over a multiyear period are its *long-term objectives*.[11] Such objectives typically involve some or all of the following areas: profitability, return on investment, competitive position, technological leadership, productivity, employee relations, public responsibility, and employee development.

Grand Strategy

The comprehensive, general plan of major actions through which a firm intends to achieve its long-term objectives in a dynamic environment is called the *grand strategy*. This *statement of means* indicates how the objectives are to be achieved.[12] Although every grand strategy is, in fact, a unique package of long-term strategies, 12 basic approaches can be identified: concentration, market development, product development, innovation, horizontal integration, vertical integration, joint venture, concentric diversification, conglomerate diversification, retrenchment/turnaround, divestiture, and liquidation. Each of these grand strategies will be covered in detail in Chapter 7.

Annual Objectives

The results that an organization seeks to achieve within a one-year period are *annual objectives* or short-term objectives. Such objectives involve areas similar to those entailed in long-term objectives. The differences between short-term objectives and long-term objectives stem principally from the greater specificity possible and necessary in short-term objectives.

Functional Strategies

Within the general framework of the grand strategy, each business function or division needs a specific and integrative plan of action. Most strategic managers attempt to develop an operating strategy for each related set of annual objectives. Operating strategies are detailed statements of the *means* that will be used to achieve objectives in the following year.[13]

Policies

Policies are broad, precedent-setting decisions that guide or substitute for repetitive managerial decision making. They guide the thinking, decisions, and actions of managers and their subordinates in implementing the organization's strategy. Policies provide guidelines for establishing and controlling the ongoing operating process of the firm in a manner

---

[11]Five years is the normal, but largely arbitrary, period of time identified as long term.

[12]James A. Belohlav and Karen Giddens-Ering, "Selecting a Master Strategy," *Journal of Business Strategy*, Winter 1987, pp. 76–82.

[13]Bob Powers, "Developing an Operational Plan for Better Performance Results," *Management Solutions*, September 1986, pp. 27–30.

consistent with the firm's strategic objectives. Policies often increase managerial effectiveness by standardizing routine decisions and limit the discretion of managers and subordinates in implementing operation strategies.

The following are examples of the nature and diversity of company policies:

A requirement that managers have purchase requests for items costing more than $500 cosigned by the controller.

The minimum equity position required for all new McDonald's franchises.

The standard formula used to calculate return on investment for the 43 strategic business units of General Electric.

A decision that employees have their annual performance review on the anniversary of their hiring date.

Institutionalizing the Strategy

Annual objectives, functional strategies, and specific policies provide important means of communicating what must be done to implement the firm's overall strategy. By translating long-term intentions into short-term guides to action, they make that strategy operational. But the overall strategy must also be *institutionalized*. That is, it must permeate the day-to-day life of the company if it is to be effectively implemented.[14]

Three organizational elements provide the fundamental, long-term means for institutionalizing the firm's strategy: (1) structure, (2) leadership, and (3) culture. Successful implementation requires effective management and integration of these three elements to ensure that the strategy "takes hold" in the daily life of the firm.

Control and Evaluation

An implemented strategy must be monitored to determine the extent to which its objectives are achieved.[15] Despite efforts at objectivity, the process of formulating a strategy is largely subjective. Thus, the first substantial test of a strategy comes only after implementation.[16] Strategic managers must watch for early signs of marketplace response to their strategies. They must also provide monitoring and controlling methods to ensure that their strategic plan is followed.[17]

---

[14]Roy Wernham, "Bridging the Awful Gap between Strategy and Action." *Long Range Planning*, December 1984, pp. 34–42.

[15]Scott P. Scherrer, "From Warning to Crisis: A Turnaround Primer," *Management Review*, September 1988, pp. 30–36; and Don Collier, "How to Implement Strategic Plans," *Journal of Business Strategy* 4, no. 3, (1984), pp. 92–96.

[16]Alex F. DeNoble, Loren T. Gustafson, and Michael Hergert, "Planning for Post-Merger Integration— Eight Lessons for Merger Success," *Long Range Planning*, August 1988, pp. 82–85.

[17]A. C. Kelley, "Auditing the Planning Process," *Managerial Planning*, 32, no. 4, January–February 1984, pp. 12–14 and 27; and Peter Lorange and Declan Murphy, "Consideration in Implementing Strategic Control," *Journal of Business Strategy*, Spring 1984, pp. 27–35.

STRATEGIC MANAGEMENT AS A PROCESS

A *process* is the flow of information through interrelated stages of analysis toward the achievement of an aim. Thus, the strategic management model in Figure 1-3 depicts a process. In the strategic management process, the flow of information involves historical, current, and forecast data on the operations and environment of the business. Managers evaluate these data in light of the values and priorities of influential individuals and groups—often called *stakeholders*—that are vitally interested in the actions of the business. The interrelated stages of the process are the 12 components discussed in the last section. Finally, the aim of the process is the formulation and implementation of strategies that work, achieving the company's long-term mission and near-term objectives.

Viewing strategic management as a process has several important implications. First, a change in any component will affect several or all of the other components. Most of the arrows in the model point two ways, suggesting that the flow of information is usually reciprocal. For example, forces in the external environment may influence the nature of a company's mission, and the company may in turn affect the external environment and heighten competition in its realm of operation. A specific example is a power company that is persuaded, in part by governmental incentives, to include a commitment to the development of energy alternatives in its mission statement. The company might then promise to extend its R&D efforts in the area of coal liquefaction. The external environment has affected the company's mission, and the revised mission signals a competitive condition in the environment.

A second implication of viewing strategic management as a process is that strategy formulation and implementation are sequential. The process begins with development or reevaluation of the company mission. This step is associated with, but essentially followed by, development of a company profile and assessment of the external environment. Then follow, in order, strategic choice, definition of long-term objectives, design of the grand strategy, definition of short-term objectives, design of operating strategies, institutionalization of the strategy, and review and evaluation.

The apparent rigidity of the process, however, must be qualified. First, a firm's strategic posture may have to be reevaluated in response to changes in any of the principal factors that determine or affect its performance. Entry by a major new competitor, the death of a prominent board member, replacement of the chief executive officer, or a downturn in market responsiveness are among the thousands of changes that can prompt reassessment of a firm's strategic plan. However, no matter where the need for a reassessment originates, the strategic management process begins with the mission statement.

Second, not every component of the strategic management process deserves equal attention each time planning activity takes place. Firms in an extremely stable environment may find that an in-depth assessment is not required every five years.[18] Companies are

---

[18]Formal strategic planning is not necessarily done on a rigid five-year schedule, although this is the most common approach. Some planners advocate planning on an irregular time basis to keep the activity from being overly routine.

often satisfied with their original mission statements even after decades of operation and spend only a minimal amount of time in addressing this subject. In addition, while formal strategic planning may be undertaken only every five years, objectives and strategies are usually updated each year, and rigorous reassessment of the initial stages of strategic planning is rarely undertaken at these times.

A third implication of viewing strategic management as a process is the necessity of feedback from institutionalization, review, and evaluation to the early stages of the process. *Feedback* can be defined as the collection of postimplementation results to enhance future decision making. Therefore, as indicated in Figure 1–3, strategic managers should assess the impact of implemented strategies on external environments. Thus, future planning can reflect any changes precipitated by strategic actions. Strategic managers should also analyze the impact of strategies on the possible need for modifications in the company mission.

A fourth implication of viewing strategic management as a process is the need to regard it as a dynamic system. The term *dynamic* characterizes the constantly changing conditions that affect interrelated and interdependent strategic activities.[19] Managers should recognize that the components of the strategic process are constantly evolving but that formal planning artificially freezes those components, much as an action photograph freezes the movement of a swimmer. Since change is continuous, the dynamic strategic planning process must be monitored constantly for significant shifts in any of its components as a precaution against implementing an obsolete strategy.

Changes in the Process

The strategic management process undergoes continual assessment and subtle updating. Although the elements of the basic strategic management model rarely change, the relative emphasis that each element receives varies with the decision makers who use the model and with the environments of their companies.

Strategy in Action 1–2 is an update on general trends in strategic management, summarizing the responses of over 200 corporate executives. This update shows that there has been an increasing companywide emphasis on and appreciation for the value of strategic management activities. It also provides evidence that practicing managers have given increasing attention to the need for frequent and widespread involvement in the formulation and implementation phases of the strategic management process. Finally, it indicates that as managers and their firms gain knowledge, experience, skill, and understanding in how to design and manage their planning activities, they become better able to avoid the potential negative consequences of instituting a vigorous strategic management process.

---

[19]N. Tichy, "The Essentials of Strategic Change Management," *Journal of Business Strategy,* Spring 1983, pp. 55–67.

STRATEGY IN ACTION 1–2 · GENERAL TRENDS IN STRATEGIC MANAGEMENT

Item	Percent of Respondents Indicating		
	Increase	No Change	Decrease
1. Overall emphasis on strategic planning systems.	81.2	7.7	11.1
2. Perceived usefulness of strategic planning.	82.0	10.2	7.8
3. Involvement of line managers in strategic planning activities.	75.2	21.4	3.4
4. Time spent by the chief executive in strategic planning.	78.7	17.8	3.5
5. Acceptance of the outputs of the strategic planning exercise by top management.	74.0	20.6	5.4
6. Perceived usefulness of annual planning.	53.9	38.7	7.4
7. Involvement of staff managers in the annual planning exercise.	52.9	39.3	7.8
8. Involvement of the board of directors in strategic planning.	51.4	47.0	1.6
9. Resources provided for strategic planning.	62.9	23.9	13.2
10. Consistency between strategic plans and budgets.	53.4	38.2	8.3

Source: Adapted from V. Ramanujam, J. C. Camillus, and N. Venkatraman, "Trends in Strategic Planning," in *Strategic Planning and Management Handbook,* ed. W. R. King and D. I. Cleland (New York: Van Nostrand Reinhold, 1987), p. 614.

SUMMARY

Strategic management is the set of decisions and actions that result in the formulation and implementation of plans designed to achieve a company's objectives. Because it involves long-term, future-oriented, complex decision making and requires considerable resources, top-management participation is essential.

Strategic management is a three-tier process involving corporate-, business-, and functional-level planners, and support personnel. At each progressively lower level, strategic activities were shown to be more specific, narrow, short term, and action oriented, with lower risks but fewer opportunities for dramatic impact.

The strategic management model presented in this chapter will serve as the structure for understanding and integrating all the major phases of strategy formulation and implementation. The chapter provided a summary account of these phases, each of which is given extensive individual attention in subsequent chapters.

The chapter stressed that the strategic management process centers on the belief that a firm's mission can be best achieved through a systematic and comprehensive assessment

Item	Percent of Respondents Indicating		
	Increase	No Change	Decrease
11. Use of annual plans in monthly performance review.	42.3	55.6	2.1
12. Overall satisfaction with the strategic planning system.	57.4	24.5	18.1
13. Number of planners (that is, those management personnel whose primary task is planning).	52.9	24.8	22.3
14. Attention to stakeholders other than stockholders.	32.8	63.0	4.2
15. Use of planning committees.	40.9	46.1	13.1
16. Attention to societal issues in planning.	33.2	59.8	7.0
17. The planning horizon (that is, the number of years considered in the strategic plan).	28.8	56.6	14.6
18. The distance between the CEO and the chief of planning.	13.3	45.1	41.5
19. Threats to the continuation of strategic planning.	12.0	47.0	41.0
20. Resistance to planning in general.	10.2	31.7	58.0

of both its internal capabilities and its external environment. Subsequent evaluation of the firm's opportunities leads, in turn, to the choice of long-term objectives and grand strategies and, ultimately, to annual objectives and operating strategies, which must be implemented, monitored, and controlled.

QUESTIONS FOR DISCUSSION

1. Find a recent copy of *Business Week* and read the "Corporate Strategies" section. Was the main decision discussed strategic? At what level in the organization was the key decision made?

2. In what ways do you think the subject matter in this strategic management/business policy course will differ from that of previous courses you have taken?

3. After graduation, you are not likely to move directly to a top-level management position. In fact, few members of your class will ever reach the top-management level. Why, then, is it important for all business majors to study the field of strategic management?

4. Do you expect outstanding performance in this course to require a great deal of memorization? Why or why not?

5. You have undoubtedly read about individuals who have seemingly given singled-handed direction to their corporations. Is a participative strategic management approach likely to stifle or suppress the contributions of such individuals?

6. Think about the courses you have taken in functional areas such as marketing, finance, production, personnel, and accounting. What is the importance of each of these areas to the strategic planning process?

7. Discuss with practicing business managers the strategic management models used in their firms. What are the similarities and differences between these models and the one in the text?

8. In what ways do you believe the strategic planning approach of not-for-profit organizations would differ from that of profit-oriented organizations?

9. How do you explain the success of firms that do not use a formal strategic planning process?

10. Think about your postgraduation job search as a strategic decision. How would the strategic management model be helpful to you in identifying and securing the most promising position?

BIBLIOGRAPHY

Agor, W. H. "How Top Executives Use Their Intuition to Make Important Decisions." *Business Horizons,* January–February 1986, pp. 49–53.

Allen, M. G. "Strategic Management Hits Its Stride." *Planning Review,* September 1985, pp. 6–9.

Brache, A. "Taking the Strategic Planning Initiative." *Management Solutions,* June 1986, pp. 36–42.

Cook, Deborah, and Ferris Gerald. "Strategic Human Resource Management and Firm Effectiveness in Industries Experiencing Decline." *Human Resource Management,* Fall 1986, pp. 441–457.

Diffenbach, J., and R. B. Higgins, "Strategic Credibility Can Make a Difference." *Business Horizons,* May–June 1987, pp. 13–18.

Drucker, P. F. "Keeping U.S. Companies Productive." *Journal of Business Strategy,* Winter 1987, pp. 12–15.

Eastlack, Joseph, Jr., and Philip McDonald. "CEO's Role in Corporate Growth." *Harvard Business Review,* May–June 1970, pp. 150–63.

Gilmore, Frank. "Formulating Strategy in Smaller Companies." *Harvard Business Review,* May–June 1971, pp. 75–85.

Glueck, William F. *Business Policy and Strategic Management.* 3rd ed. New York: McGraw-Hill, 1980.

Goold, Michael, and Andrew Campbell. "Many Best Ways to Make Strategy." *Harvard Business Review,* November–December 1987, pp. 70–76.

Gray, Daniel H. "Uses and Misuses of Strategic Planning." *Harvard Business Review,* January–February 1986, pp. 89–96.

Greenley, Gordon E. "Does Strategic Planning Improve Company Performance?" *Long Range Planning* April 1986, pp. 101–9.

Hamermesh, R. E. "Making Planning Strategic." *Harvard Business Review,* July–August 1986, pp. 114–20.

Hegarty, W. H., and R. C. Hoffman, "Who Influences Strategic Decisions?" *Long Range Planning,* April 1987, pp. 76–85.

Hofer, C. W., and D. Schendel. *Strategy Formulation: Analytical Concepts.* St. Paul, Minn.: West Publishing, 1978.

Hornaday, R. W., and W. J. Wheatley. "Managerial Characteristics and the Financial Performance of Small Business." *Journal of Small Business Management.* April 1986, pp. 1–7.

Ireland, R. D.; M. A. Hitt; R. A. Bettis; and D. A. de Porras. "Strategy Formulation Process: Differences in Perceptions of Strength and Weakness Indicators and Environmental Uncertainty by Managerial Level." *Strategic Management Review,* September–October 1987, pp. 469–86.

Jauch, L. R., and K. L. Kraft. "Strategic Management of Uncertainty." *Academy of Management Review,* October 1986, pp. 777–90.

King, William R., and David I. Cleland. *Strategic Planning and Policy*. New York: Van Nostrand Reinhold, 1978.

Kudja, R. J. "Elements of Effective Corporate Planning." *Long Range Planning,* August 1976, pp. 82–93.

Lorange, P. *Corporate Planning: An Executive Viewpoint*. Englewood Cliffs, N.J.: Prentice-Hall, 1980.

McKinney, George W., III. "An Experimental Study of Strategy Formulation Systems." Ph.D. dissertation Graduate School of Business, Stanford University, 1969.

MacMillan, K. "Strategy: An Introduction." *Journal of General Management,* Spring 1986, pp. 75–94.

Malik, Zafar, and Delmar Karger. "Does Long-Range Planning Improve Company Performance?" *Management Review,* September 1975, pp. 27–31.

Mason, J. "Developing Strategic Thinking." *Long Range Planning,* June 1986, 72–80.

Mintzberg, Henry, "Strategy Making in Three Modes." *California Management Review,* Spring 1973, pp. 44–53.

Ohmae, K. "In Praise of Planning." *Planning Review,* September 1985, p. 4.

Pearce, John A., II. "An Executive-Level Perspective on the Strategic Management Process." *California Management Review,* Spring 1982, pp. 39–48.

Pearce, J. A., II, and W. A. Randolph. "Improving Strategy Formulation Pedagogies by Recognizing Behavioral Aspects." *Exchange,* December 1980, pp. 7–10.

Peters, Thomas P. *Thriving on Chaos*. New York: Alfred A. Knopf, 1987.

Pryor, Millard H., Jr. "Anatomy of a Merger." *Michigan Business Review,* July 1964, pp. 28–34.

Ramamurti, R. "Strategic Planning in Government-Dependent Business." *Long Range Planning,* June 1986, pp. 62–71.

Reimann, B. C. "Personal Computers Empower Strategic Management." *Planning Review,* November–December 1986, pp. 28–34.

Ring, P. S., and J. L. Perry. "Strategic Management in Public and Private Organizations: Implications of Distinctive Contexts and Constraints." *Academy of Management Review* 10, no. 2 (1985), pp. 276–86.

Rogers, David D. C. *Essentials of Business Policy*. New York: Harper & Row, 1975.

Rue, Leslie, and Robert Fulmer. "Is Long-Range Planning Profitable?" *Academy of Management Proceedings,* 1972.

Schwaninger, M. "A Practical Approach to Strategy Development." *Long Range Planning* October 1987, pp. 74–85.

Stagner, Ross. "Corporate Decision Making." *Journal of Applied Psychology,* February 1969, pp. 1–13.

Steiner, G. A. "Why and How to Diversity." *California Management Review,* Summer 1964, pp. 11–18.

————. "The Rise of the Corporate Planner." *Harvard Business Review,* September–October 1970, pp. 133–39.

Stevenson, Howard H. "Defining Corporate Strengths and Weakneses." *Sloan Management Review,* Spring 1976, pp. 51–68.

TenDam, H. "Strategic Management in a Government Agency." *Long Range Planning,* August 1986, pp. 78–86.

Vancil, R. F. ". . . So You're Going to Have a Planning Department!" *Harvard Business Review,* May–June 1967, pp. 88–96.

Waterman, Robert H., Jr. *The Renewal Factor: How the Best Get and Keep the Competitive Edge*. New York: Bantam Books, 1987.

Wood, D. Robley, Jr., and R. Lawrence LaForge. "The Impact of Comprehensive Planning on Financial Performance." *Academy of Management Journal* 22, no. 3 (1979) pp. 516–26.

Yoo, Sanglin, and Lester Digman. "A Fresh Look at Strategic Management." *Journal of Business Strategy,* Fall 1985, pp. 4–19.

————. "Decision Support System: A New Tool for Strategic Management." *Long Range Planning,* April 1987, pp. 114–124.

CHAPTER 1 COHESION CASE

BRYSON INDUSTRIAL SERVICES AND THE HAZARDOUS WASTE INDUSTRY

Nothing about the business of handling, cleaning-up, and treating hazardous wastes seems attractive. It deals with dangerous and repulsive gunk. It reeks with economic, legal, political, and technological perils. Even as politicians and enraged citizens scream ever louder for a cleanup, engineers are finding that decontaminating toxic sites is a lot harder than they thought. Companies that try must contend with confusing laws and a sluggish bureaucracy at the Environmental Protection Agency. And they must work with practically no insurance protection against almost unlimited liability.

Yet for a lot of companies the sheer scale of the potential business dwarfs the dangers. The Office of Technology Assessment, a research arm of Congress, expects cleanup in the United States alone will last 50 years and cost over $500 billion (in 1986 dollars), not including the costs of handling ongoing generation of toxic wastes."

—Jeremy Main, reporter, *FORTUNE* magazine

In 1978, eight-year South Carolina Department of Health and Environmental Control employee Charles Kelly was convinced that recent federal legislation to rigidly and aggressively regulate hazardous wastes would create the need for new businesses to help U.S. companies manage their hazardous wastes. He placed a call to a longtime friend from his college days, Joel Stevenson, to propose that they consider starting a company specializing in handling and transporting hazardous substances. Joel Stevenson was co-owner of an Alabama-based company providing specialized industrial cleaning services to steel mills in the Birmingham, Alabama, area. Charles Kelly reasoned that his experience with hazardous waste regulation, combined with Joel Stevenson's experience selling cleaning services to manufacturers, provided a sound basis from which to start such a company.

Within a year the two had started a hazardous waste transportation company outside of Columbia, South Carolina, as a branch of the Alabama company, Bryson Environmental Services, of which Joel Stevenson was a co-owner. Shortly thereafter the South Carolina branch was sold to Kelly and Stevenson as their own separate company and the two entered the 1980s as Bryson Industrial Services—a company specializing in hazardous waste transportation services. By early 1990, Bryson was a $13 million a year hazardous waste management company providing transportation, remediation, and recycling services through three locations in the southeastern United States.

This case provides you with the opportunity to join the Bryson board of directors as strategic managers planning the company's development in the 1990s. You will first be provided with information about the hazardous waste management industry, followed by a detailed description of Bryson Industrial Services, Inc., to aid you in this endeavor. Additional information will be provided in subsequent cohesion case modules to further assist you in this process.

THE HAZARDOUS WASTE INDUSTRY

What Is Hazardous Waste?

Hazardous materials are transported every day on the nation's highways, railroads, and waterways. Gasoline and other petroleum products make up half of this traffic. Many familiar substances, such as paint and dry cleaning fluid, must also be handled with caution to ensure human safety and environmental protection.

Hazardous materials become wastes after they have been used and are discarded. Depending upon the products involved, they may be toxic (poisonous), corrosive, ignitable, or explosive. In contrast to pure chemicals, hazardous wastes often contain a mixture of different compounds, as well as dirt, water, and other contaminants. Such mixtures represent the unavoidable byproduct of virtually *every* modern manufacturing and industrial process. To pick one familiar example, your neighborhood dry cleaner uses chemicals that must be shipped to special disposal facilities. Putting the color in paints and fabrics also generates potentially harmful wastes. Even computer chips must be washed in toxic solvents that cannot be completely recycled.

In addition to these regularly generated hazardous wastes, numerous sites exist around the country where hazardous wastes have been disposed of in ways that we now know represent environmental threats. Before the threat to groundwater and other environmental elements was fully understood, many industrial and governmental/military concerns throughout the United States would discharge waste residues in "pits, ponds, or lagoons" where the liquids would "settle out" and the process repeated. Similarly, this formerly uninformed approach to handling hazardous wastes also resulted in contaminated buildings, dump sites, and other areas (e.g., spraying petroleum residues on dirt roads to control dust) throughout the country. These hazardous "sites" represent another source of hazardous wastes that must be cleaned up at a cost Jeremy Main of *Fortune* magazine estimated will exceed $300 billion. It is estimated that there are between 110,000 (U.S. Congress GAO) and 425,000 (state officials) such sites in the United States alone. In addition, there are an estimated 2 million plus underground storage tanks, many of which now or may leak hazardous substances into the soil and groundwater.

Key Driving Force: Federal Legislation and EPA Regulation

In 1976, Congress passed the Resource Conservation and Recovery Act (RCRA), whereby the EPA was authorized to set standards for generators and transporters of hazardous wastes and for owners and operators of hazardous waste treatment, storage, and disposal facilities (TSDFs). RCRA's cradle-to-grave system of liability for environmental damage identified 52,864 wastes generators, 12,000 transporters, and about 5,000 TSDFs as falling under its regulations. RCRA established any waste material that is either ignitable, corrosive, reactive, flammable, or toxic as a hazardous waste subject to RCRA regulation.

RCRA was reauthorized in 1984 and again in 1989. New and far-reaching federal requirements were imposed. Most notably, 200,000 enterprises that generate small amounts (220 pounds or more per month) of hazardous waste were no longer exempt, and waste oil, previously classified as nonhazardous, was defined as hazardous waste. Finally, businesses owning an estimated 2 million underground storage tanks came under RCRA regulation and were required to register their tanks, monitor them, and remove any that are leaking to include restoring the soil and groundwater to its normal state. Criminal as well as civil liability was imposed on companies and their managers for violations of RCRA guidelines.

The Comprehensive Environmental Response, Compensation, and Liability Act (CERCLA), which became law in 1981, was spurred by such incidents as Love Canal in New York. CERCLA established a program known as "Superfund" to identify sites from which releases of hazardous substances into the environment might occur or have occurred. Funds were set aside to study and identify sites and to aid in their cleanup. Perhaps of greater concern as a driving force, CERCLA established the concept of "primary responsible parties (PRPs)" to share in the liability associated with the cleanup of any such sites and the restoration of the health to the environment and individuals affected by the site. PRPs were any individuals or entities generating, handling, transporting, or treating wastes that had ended up at the site and was part of the damage to the environment. Liability was retroactive and applied to any future sites as well. As a result, a company generating waste that had allowed a waste company to handle it and unknowingly the waste ended up at such a site would be considered a PRP. CERCLA was extended in 1986 by SARA (the Superfund Amendments and Reauthorization Act) and PRP liability extended to include leaking underground storage tanks.

State regulation was spurred by this federal legislation, in part because federal funds available to states to aid in implementing these regulations were contingent on state regulatory action. Led by California, New Jersey, and South Carolina, virtually all 50 states now have hazardous waste regulations and personnel to enforce federal and state guidelines.

Federal and state regulations have laid the foundation for driving forces behind the growth of the hazardous waste industry. Key ways this has been accomplished include:

1. A mandatory EPA-manifest system whereby every shipment of hazardous waste that leaves a generating facility is recorded and signed by persons releasing it for the company (generator), transporting it to a disposal site, and the person receiving it at an approved disposal facility. Specific composition, amounts and times are also required, and failure to comply with this manifesting system results in stiff fines and potential additional liabilities if lack of compliance is proven intentional.

2. The 90-day rule and the 10-day rule that apply to offsite transportation and disposal. Companies that generate hazardous waste and do not have onsite treatment or disposal capability are required under RCRA to remove that waste from their facility within 90 days of generation. The current manifesting system for tracking the movement of hazardous waste also requires that waste leaving a generator must be de-

livered to a disposal facility or be returned to the generator within 10 days. This 10-day rule put considerable pressure on the transporting/handler of the waste and places a premium of having a Part-B facility (or TSDF—see point 4 below) which allows waste to be received and become the TSDF's responsibility, terminating the 90-day and 10-day requirements and thus relieving the generator of worry about violating either rule.

3. The EPA and its state counterparts have the right to inspect industrial sites at any time. Industrial sites are required to report their annual hazwaste generation by types and amounts as well as progress in efforts to reduce their levels of waste generation.

4. Any facility involved in handling, treating, or disposing of hazardous substances must have an EPA-issued permit to operate. Without this permit (the primary one is called a Part-B permit), a hazardous waste treatment or disposal facility (TSDF) cannot operate. Over 6,000 such treatment, incineration, or land disposal facilities are currently under review in the United States and must either comply with EPA operation requirements (usually high capital expenditures plus posting bonds to cover potential accidents) and complete public hearings to receive their permit or close their facility and incur the cost of cleaning it up by November 1992.

5. Numerous state regulations have arisen related to real estate transactions wherein prior and future owners of property can be held liable for the cleanup of the impact of any release of hazardous substances on that property. In several states, owners must assure the state EPA that no such release has occurred.

6. The result of all of these regulatory efforts has created perhaps the principal driving force—the growing awareness by corporations and individuals of the liabilities of not protecting our nation's soil and groundwater. For example, identification of corporations as PRPs associated with potential Superfund Sites is forcing accountants to ask CFOs about potential environmental liabilities. Corporations are learning that they will receive less for property sales or have to establish escrow accounts to remediate [cleanup] property when buying or selling it. Awareness that neglecting or delaying action may result in punitive damages is contributing to a change in attitude.

Buyers of Hazardous Waste Services

Industrial plants are the primary generators (by volume) of hazardous wastes in the United States. Approximately 15,000 plants were registered with EPA as large waste generators in 1989, with some industry analysts saying the number should be closer to 55,000. Most of these plants handle their wastes onsite, with 6 percent of the plants shipping their wastes offsite to commercial treatment or disposal facilities. An additional 175,000 business entities are registered small quantity generators. Table 1 describes the U.S. generators of hazardous waste as of 1987 on a regional basis. A 1987 study by Frost & Sullivan (New York City) says almost 350,000 sites will be generating toxic wastes in sizable quantities by 1991 . . . from large chemical plants to local golf courses (waste pesticides) to photo processors (spent solvents).

TABLE 1
Hazwaste by Geographic Sector of the United States: 1987

Sector	Quantity of RCRA Waste Managed (MMTons)	
Northeast	63	million metric tons
Southwest	84	
Southwest	58	
Midwest	64	
Rocky Mountains	1	
Far West	5	
Total	275	million metric tons

Treatment and Disposal

The generators identified in Table 1 create the demand for one of four major segments of the hazardous waste industry—offsite treatment and disposal services. Approximately 6 percent of the waste identified in Table 1 is handled offsite. The remainder is handled by the generator at the plant site (often treated and disposed or burned for energy). Offsite treatment and disposal services is estimated at between $3 to $5 billion in 1990 revenue and is expected to grow at an annual rate of 30 percent or more through the 1990s.

Offsite disposal of hazardous waste has traditionally been handled by one of three methods: landfills, incineration, and deep well injection. A rapidly growing fourth alternative is treatment. Treatment involves a method of neutralizing the hazardous wastes that are part of liquid residues from manufacturing processes. The predominant form of this waste is wastewater, with treatment focusing on neutralizing the hazardous contaminants and discharging the waterous liquid into a local sewer system. Other forms of liquid waste, such as spent solvents, are treated via recycling methods or resource recovery methods whereby the liquid wastes are run through a distillation process and clean, recycled solvents are reclaimed while impurities are segregated and typically sent as fuel for cement kilns or neutralized and landfilled.

Arthur D. Little, Inc., (Cambridge, Massachusetts), predicts hazardous waste treatment and disposal companies will reach $10 billion in revenue by 1996. The firm projects a 25 percent plus annual growth in hazardous waste landfill revenues to $2.4 billion by 1995. Higher profitability and prices are predicted as demand sharpens for increasingly scarce RCRA-permitted landfills. Incineration is predicted to experience 30 percent plus annual growth to $.5 billion in 1995. Slower growth (18 percent) is predicted for deep well injection to about $3 billion by 1995.

One of the factors driving the treatment and disposal market is the currently ongoing RCRA-permitting process going on for every disposal and treatment site in the United States. Every site has had to make a choice with the EPA about its future intentions to either (a) enter EPA's "Permit Track" and seek approval to operate after 1992 as an EPA-approved site or (b) enter EPA's "Closure Track" wherein the site is to be examined for present contamination and a remediation plan to cleanup the site submitted to and approved by EPA and completed before the current facility owner can be free of any liability associated with the facility.

Transportation

Offsite transportation of hazardous wastes, while not matching the dramatic 40 percent annual growth of the whole hazardous waste industry, is predicted to grow at 20 to 25 percent annually through 1996, according to Neil Nunn, CEO of a consulting firm working with transporters and the hazardous waste industry. The many events driving this growth into the foreseeable future include natural market growth; the inability to quickly shift the waste industry's focus from disposal and treatment to waste minimization; costs associated with alternative onsite disposal and treatment options; introduction of small quantity generators (who do not have means to contain their wastes onsite); and the increasing appeal of landfill stabilization and solidification or treatment practices before disposal.

Two factors determine the need for transportation capacity: volume and distance. Approximately 4 to 5 percent of the estimated 275 million metric tons of 1987 hazardous waste was shipped offsite, requiring the equivalent of about 550,000 truckloads or 157,000 railcar loads. Current industry trends, particularly stringent controls on the RCRA-permitting of treatment, storage, and disposal facilities (TSDFs) wherein an estimated 1,161 out of 1,538 or 75 percent of the total land disposal facilities are closing, creates a wider geographic dispersion among fewer destination sites requiring greater transportation distances. EPA's continual addition of wastes and amounts generated to the "hazardous" category significantly expands the volume of waste to be handled—usually for businesses without existing waste handling capability. The 1989 classification of waste oil as hazardous means over 100,000 automotive and machine servicing businesses are now hazardous waste generators in need of waste management (usually including transportation) services. When waste-to-energy and coal-fired plants' ash residues are classified as hazardous by 1991, over 85 million tons annually will be added to the hazardous waste volume in the United States.

Remediation

A third segment served by the hazardous waste industry is remediation—cleanup of sites contaminated by hazardous wastes or hazardous substances. Jeffrey Klein, ranked number 1 research analyst in environmental services by *Institutional Investor* for 13 years, says of this segment:

> The sector most likely to show rapid (albeit occasionally volatile) growth over the next five years is the remediation services sector—the actual containment and cleanup of the 30-year legacy of improper waste treatment and disposal. There are now 1,177 sites on the Superfund's National Priority List; thousands of DOD, DOE, and RCRA facilities that require corrective action which will entail cleanup; onsite, and offsite treatment, transportation, and disposal; and well over 1 million pits, ponds, lagoons, and underground storage tanks at industrial sites nationwide that will require some form of remediation to meet new EPA standards intended to eliminate groundwater contamination.

EPA alone paid $1.24 billion to private contractors in 1989 for Superfund-related cleanup activities at only 500 Superfund sites. Dan Beardsley, special assistant in EPA's

Policy Office, says the total cleanup bill for RCRA sites alone could reach $250 billion in the 1990s. And Marcia Williams, former director of EPA's Office of Solid Waste, expects that RCRA laws will eventually apply to as many as 100,000 large chemical and other industrial facilities and 6,000 solid waste landfills in the United States requiring significant remediation attention. When you add in the need to remediate contamination associated with millions of pits, ponds, lagoons, and underground fuel storage tanks at large-to-small industrial sites all the way to corner gas stations, an overall annualized market growth to exceed 45 percent (*Waste Age* estimate) seems realistic. When EPA estimates that Superfund sites alone could generate $26 billion in costs by 1996 and DOD cleanups another $10 billion, the addition of numerous private sector sites suggests $50 billion plus in expenditures for remediation services by the late 1990s. The typical costs associated with different types of remedial service jobs are shown below:

Types and Sizes of Remediation Projects

Type of Project	Typical Size	"Typical" Description
Leaking Underground Storage Tank (LUST) and typical pits, ponds, and lagoons	$50,000 to $500,000	Removal of a tank and cleanup of contaminated soil or groundwater, or both.
Corrective action of active RCRA facility	$100,000 to several million	Cleanup of tanks, ponds, or surface impoundments to remove contamination on a portion of an active site.
Closure of RCRA facility	$500,000 to more than $10 million	Cleanup of storage areas of old pits, ponds, lagoons, usually involving treatment onsite.
Large Superfund cleanup	$1 million to more than $50 million	Extensive investigation and design work followed by onsite treatment or disposal or offsite treatment or disposal.

Source: Kidder, Peabody & Co., Inc., estimates.

Engineering and Consulting

By 1992, the market for environmental analysis, consulting, and engineering alone will be worth $2.1 billion, according to a study released by EnviroQuest (San Diego). *Chemicalweek*'s estimates are even higher, claiming a 1990 market of $2.5 billion already and growth at 25 percent or higher at least through 1995. An even higher growth rate could occur after 1992 if members of the new European Economic Community adopt strict environmental regulations, as many expect them to do.

Competition

As an emerging industry, the hazardous waste industry is experiencing a lot of change among competitors within the industry. Over 200 environmental services companies have gone public since 1986. Major companies that are well known hazardous waste generators, like Westinghouse and Du Pont, are diversifying "backward" into the industry. Westinghouse has acquired Haztech (a remediation firm), Soil & Materials Engineering (engineering and consulting), and Aptus (a joint venture with National Electric to provide testing, transportation, and incineration) in 1988 creating a $300 million hazwaste subsidiary virtually overnight. Du Pont was reportedly following a similar acquisition and joint venture program as 1990 approached, and Phillips Petroleum is yet another entrant with joint ventures and its own proprietary technology.

While many entrants have jointed the industry, two firms that are the major garbage collection firms have set an early imprint as industry leaders: Waste Management (through its Chemical Waste Management spinoff) and Browning Ferris Industries (BFI). Waste Management is probably the largest player in waste services, with garbage collection and disposal revenues in excess of $3.5 billion in 1989. Chemical Waste Management generated an additional $1 billion in 1989 focused exclusively on the hazardous waste segment. BFI generated over $2 billion in 1989 garbage collection and disposal revenue but also included almost $600 million in hazardous waste-related services. Of only 20 RCRA-approved and permitted hazardous waste landfills in the United States, Waste Management owned eight and BFI owned four. Waste Management is also well positioned with several incineration sites. Citing compelling opportunities in solid waste and recycling when compared to the uncertainty in the hazwaste industry, BFI surprised the industry when it announced its decision to exit the hazwaste business in mid-1990.

In addition to these two industry leaders, several other firms have emerged as early, significant players in selected segments of the hazardous waste industry. Table 2 lists several firms in each segment that analysts consider established competitors. Yet, while several participants already exist, analysts agree that there is plenty of room given the industry's continued growth for many players, particularly on a region-by-region basis. This appears particularly true in transportation, TSDF recycling/recovery facilities, and remediation services.

BRYSON INDUSTRIAL SERVICES, INC.

History

After becoming the sole owners of Bryson Industrial Services in 1979, Joel Stevenson and Charles Kelly paid a visit to Bill Stillwell, a former associate of Kelly's at South Carolina DHEC and then the president of SCA (forerunner of GSX). SCA was a Pinewood, South Carolina, based hazardous waste landfill—one of only two EPA-sanctioned hazardous waste landfills in the Southeast. The purpose of the visit was to discuss their new company. The result of the meeting was an agreement with Stillwell that Bryson would provide transportation services on behalf of SCA with hazardous waste generators using the Pinewood landfill.

The SCA agreement provided the impetus for Bryson's early growth. Starting in 1980, Bryson saw its annual revenues grow from $250,000 the previous year to $1 million and reach $1.9 million by 1983. Over 85 percent of this revenue was associated with Bryson's services as a contract transporter for SCA. Stevenson and Kelly initially saw this as providing an added advantage, because SCA handled all marketing and customer contact

TABLE 2
Selected Companies in the Hazardous Waste Industry

Company	Sales (In million $) 1988	1989	Stock Price 9/27/88	Earnings/Share Fiscal '88	Fiscal '89*	Fiscal '90*	Outstanding Shares (In millions)
Allwaste	$127	$170	$21.13	$0.68	$0.80	$1.07	14.3
Browning-Ferris Industries	210	260	41.38	1.51	1.75	2.10	150.7
Calgon Carbon	226	264	42.25	1.47	1.75	2.20	20.3
Chemical Waste Management	700	945	43.25	1.17	1.49	1.90	100.5
Clean Harbors	100	135	16.50	0.66	0.33	0.62	9.0
ENSR	123	170	7.25	0.21	0.05	0.45	10.4
Geraghty & Miller	34	53	14.00	0.41	0.60	0.90	5.7
Hander	20	34	18.75	0.61	0.87	1.10	5.1
Roline Environmental	200	175	10.63	0.55	(0.36)	0.50	60.3
Roy F. Weston	137	170	12.38	0.71	0.70	1.00	8.3

*Estimated

Source: Alex Brown & Sons (estimate)

Principal Players in the Remediation Sector

	Clean Harbors	Canonie Env't	Chemical Waste Mgmt (EN-RAC)	ENSR	Env't Systems	Env't Treat & Tech.	Int'l Tech.	Groundwater Tech.	Geraghty Miller	Harding Associates	Riedel Env't	Rollins Env't	Roy F. Weston	Private
Leaking Underground Storage Tank (LUST), and pits, ponds, and lagoons	X			X		X	X	X	X	X			X	Many
Corrective action of active RCRA facility	X	X		X		X	X	X		X	X		X	Many
Closure of RCRA facility		X	X			X	X				X			Many
Large Superfund cleanup		X	X		X	X	X				X	X		Many

Source: Kidder, Peabody & Co., Inc.

while Kelly and Stevenson concentrated solely on operating transportation services and administrative activities necessary to support them.

As 1983 drew to close, Bryson management began to reassess their competitive posture. After much internal discussion, they decided to inform SCA in 1984 that Bryson would sell transportation services directly to southeastern generators. As they expected, SCA management decided to terminate Bryson's special transportation relationship, because Bryson had in effect become a competitor with SCA. And while the termination of Bryson's relationship with SCA threatened 85 percent of Bryson's revenue, the long-term advantages of being in control of their own marketing efforts necessitated Bryson taking the risk.

Bryson found the SCA risk worthwhile, with many SCA customers for whom Bryson had provided transportation service switching to Bryson and with Bryson arranging disposal while providing their regular transportation services. By 1985, Bryson management decided to expand into remediation services. Bryson's transportation and remediation sales continued to grow and 1987 saw a new location opened in Memphis, Tennessee. During 1988 and 1989, Bryson's management placed a major emphasis on developing a strong middle management team to significantly reduce the company's dependence on its original founders and secondly to develop opportunities to expand the company beyond its current service scope. The result was a new venture providing medical waste handling/transportation services in early 1988 and a mid-1989 acquisition of a small Alabama handler of dry cleaner waste in line for RCRA-TSDF permit. Table 3 shows a summary of Bryson's growth and development from 1983 through 1989.

In January 1990, Bryson's board of directors faced several strategic decisions:

1. Whether to make a serious commitment to involvement in the recycling/treatment segment of the hazwaste industry and do so by merging a small recycling/treatment facility in Memphis, Tennessee into Bryson. The facility, Wall Chemical, was under RCRS–TSDF permit review status in Tennessee.

TABLE 3
Strategic Financial Summary of Bryson from 1983–1989

Dollars (000s)	1983	1984	1985	1986	1987	1988	1989
Transp. rev.	$ 1,819	$ 2,228	$ 3,463	$ 4,399	$ $ 5,124	$ 5,472	$ 7,569
Remd'l rev.	$ 489	$ 829	$ 979	$ 1,014	$ 1,357	$ 1,978	$ 1,469
Total revenue	$ 2,308	$ 3,057	$ 4,442	$ 5,413	$ $ 6,481	$ 7,450	$ 9,038
Total costs	$ 2,285	$ 3,006	$ 4,283	$ 5,137	$ 6,050	$ 7,263	$ 8,691
Profit bef. tax	$ 23	$ 51	$ 159	$ 276	$ 431	$ 187	$ 347
No. of people	36	47	46	57	67	77	85
No. of tractors	12	13	15	19	23	30	33
Current ratio	1.4	1.4	1.4	1.4	2	2	1.6
Debt/asset ratio	1.2	1.2	1.2	1.2	1.5	1	1

Source: Author estimates.

2. The best corporate strategy for managing Bryson involvement in four base businesses (transportation, remediation, Cleanway, and medical waste) and perhaps a fourth (number 1 above).

Once the corporate strategy decision is made, then what should be the appropriate competitive strategy for each business?

3. Level of commitment to make to the Alabama acquisition in its dry cleaner thrust, given the importance of Safety Kleen (the dominant competitor nationally to dry cleaners) to Bryson (approximately 35 percent of Bryson's transportation revenue in November 1989) and its long-term intent for the Alabama facility.

4. Best way to organize the company—should it be organized as two separate geographic divisions or in a simple functional manner?

5. Marketing, operations, and financial strategies to support each of Bryson's businesses?

6. Compensation and stock plan for key managers and employees?

The remainder of this case provides you with information about Bryson and the southeastern hazardous waste market. Using this information, along with the earlier provided description of the U.S. hazardous waste industry, you are asked to join the Bryson board of directors in addressing these strategic decisions.

Southeastern Market for Hazwaste Services

From Table 1 provided earlier in this case, we saw that the southeastern region of the United States was a significant generator of hazardous waste (84 million metric tons). At the same time the southeastern market is dispersed over 10 states—compared to the highly concentrated midwestern and northeastern markets. While geographically dispersed across and within 10 states, the Southeast is home to a lot of industrial plants that have operational processes generating hazardous waste residues.

Another interesting facet of the southeastern market is that two major EPA-approved landfills for hazardous waste east of the Mississippi River are in the southeast—Emille, Alabama, (Chemical Waste Management), and Pinewood, South Carolina, (GSX). These facilities, as well as several incineration and treatment facilities, frequently receive hazardous wastes from throughout the United States—particularly the eastern half of the United States.

Competitors

Several firms compete in each of the four segments of the hazardous waste industry within the southeastern region. Each of the two major nationals, Chemical Waste and BFI, are active in the southeastern region. These and other key competitors in four industry sectors across states currently important to Bryson are summarized in Table 4.

A survey examining the needs and opinions of generators of waste in Georgia, North Carolina, and South Carolina conducted in late 1989 is summarized in Table 5. In response to questions seeking to identify the image of different competitors, GSX, Bryson, and

TABLE 4
Selected Hazardous Waste Competitors in the Southeast: 1990
(according to Bryson management)

Major Market Segments by Nature of Service

State	Trans-port'n	Remedial Services	Treatment Recycling	Engr'g & Consult.	Landfill or Incin.
S.C.	GSX Bryson Wilms	GSX Bryson Haztech Wilms [GSX] Fenn-Vac Four Seasons	So'Eastern M&J (Atl.)	Sirrine ETE W'house ATE RMT	GSX
N.C.	GSX Bryson	GSX Bryson Four Seasons Haztech	So'Eastern	Law ETE W'house RH Weston	GSX
Ga.	GSX Barton (Alwst) St.Josp Bryson	Haztech Enrac Bryson Ensite OH Matls	M&J Allworth	Law RH Weston Waytec all others	GSX ChmWst
Tenn.	OSCO ChmWst GSX Bryson	OSCO W'house Enrac	GSX Allworth Earth Rineco	Law W'house	ChmWst
Ala.	Suttles ChmWst	ChemWst. ????	Allworth	???	ChmWst
Fla.	ChemCon ChmWst GSX	ChemWst. ???	GSX ???	???	ChmWst

1. GSX—South Carolina based owner of Pinewood hazwaste landfill; 250+ tractor fleet providing transportation services; acquisitions in transportation (Wilms.–Charleston, S.C.), treatment, and incineration in North Carolina and Tennessee; major recent California acquisition; over $300 million annual revenue; a subsidiary of Laidlaw, in turn, a subsidiary of Canadian Pacific. GSX-Remedial in Greensboro, North Carolina.

2. Barton—Atlanta HW transporter, acquired by Allwaste; $5 million annual revenue. Allwaste a $150 million OTC company.

3. St. Joseph—Atlanta based, southeastern LTL carrier that also provides hazwaste transportation ($3 million in hazwaste)

4. Haztech—Atlanta based remediation firm focusing on large remediation jobs; $25 million annual revenues; owned by Westinghouse.

5. Four Seasons—Greensboro, North Carolina, based remediation firm; $12 million in annual revenue; all types of jobs.

6. Fenn-Vac—Charleston, South Carolina based vacuum tanker and small-scale remediation firm ($1 million annual rev.).

7. Wilms Trucking—Charleston, South Carolina, gravel and hazwaste transportation company; also does tank and lagoon remedial services; $14 million annual rev.

8. Enrac—remedial services arm of ChemWaste; Atlanta based; $25 million; focuses on large remedial jobs.

9. Ensite—remedial services arm of Law engineering and Law Environmental; big job focus.

10. O&H Materials—Ohio and Atlanta based; large remedial services contractor; $100 million; mostly Superfund contractor.

11. OSCO—Columbia, Tennessee, based recycler; also provides limited transportation and active in remediation; $15 million annual rev.

12. Large to medium-sized environmental engineering firms: Westinghouse; Law; R. H. Weston; RMT (Greenville, S.C.); ETE (Columbia, S.C.—70 percent of business with GSX); Atlanta Testing & Engineering (ATE); virtually every national firm has representation in Atlanta.

Descriptions were provided by one Bryson manager, along with this comment; "we are certain that others exist, but we aren't sure who they are if the customer doesn't tell us about them."

TABLE 5

1989 Survey of Southeastern Hazwaste Generators

Waste generators were asked to identify the two companies that come to mind when they think about (1) highest quality service, (2) lowest price, and (3) best price/quality value as it applies to transportation services and remediation services in Georgia, South Carolina, and North Carolina.

Transportation Services			Remediation Services		
Company Mentioned	**Percentage of Time Mentioned**		**Company Mentioned**	**Percentage of Time Mentioned**	
	First	**Second**		**First**	**Second**
1. High-quality Service			**1. High-quality Service**		
GSX	30	18	GSX	21	14
ChemWaste Mgmt.	11	5	O&H Materials	8	1
Bryson	10	3	ChemWaste Mgmt.	6	1
Safety Kleen	5	5	Van Waters	5	3
Oldover	4	0	Bryson	1	4
Omni	4	1	Four Seasons	0	0
Rollins	1	3	No response	30	42
No response	6	30			
2. Lowest price			**2. Lowest price**		
GSX	6	8	GSX	6	4
ChemWaste Mgmt.	4	0	O&H Materials	1	1
Bryson	3	0	ChemWaste Mgmt.	1	0
Safety Kleen	1	4	Van Waters	0	0
Oldover	4	0	Bryson	0	1
Omni	1	3	Four Seasons	4	3
Rollins	4	1	No response	63	73
No response	44	64			
3. Best price/quality value			**3. Best price/quality value**		
GSX	11	13	GSX	14	9
ChemWaste Mgmt.	3	5	O&H Materials	4	3
Bryson	6	3	ChemWaste Mgmt.	1	5
Safety Kleen	5	4	Van Waters	0	0
Oldover	4	0	Bryson	4	3
Omni	1	3	Four Seasons	1	4
Rollins	3	0	No response	49	59
No response	39	55			

A large number of additional companies were mentioned but at very low percentages.

Chemical Waste emerged as the most frequently mentioned companies in transportation and GSX, Chemical Waste, O&H Materials, and Four Seasons in remedial services. Perhaps the most noticeable statistic in the overall responses to this survey are the number of nonresponses to selected questions—suggesting that a lot of generators are still uncertain about who all the firms in the industry are and what their differences might be. In other words, the southeastern industry is an emerging industry with many participants, and new entrants are attracted by the potential for high profits yet uncertain about clear "rules" in the industry about pricing, rivalry, and so on.

Bryson Services and Markets

HW Transportation

Bryson was founded as a hazardous waste transportation company. Transportation remained a major portion of Bryson's revenue through 1989.

Different types of hazardous waste requires different pieces of transportation equipment. Vans are used to carry wastes in 55-gallon drums. Tankers are used to carry waste that is in liquid form, usually in 5,500-gallon loads per tanker. Many manufacturers with hazardous waste in solid (sludge) form, while formerly using 55-gallon drums, have moved to the use of 6,000-gallon "rolloff containers" that collect sludge residues onsite until full, and then the containers are lifted onto a "rolloff frame" with a wench device and transported away to a disposal site. Finally, large cleanup sites where a lot of contaminated dirt is being moved often require the use of large dump trailers.

Bryson has provided all these types of equipment. The rolloffs are usually provided on a five-year lease effectively tying the customer to Bryson for that time period. Other vehicles are provided on an as-needed basis, with a long-term contract seldom in place. Bryson usually receives about $1.50 per mile for transportation services (versus about $1.00 for normal commodity transporters) and experiences costs of about $1.24 per mile. A brief summary of Bryson's transportation business is provided below:

	1983	1986	1987	1988	1989
Transportation revenue:					
Vans	$1,316,009	$1,680,955	$ 847,677	$ 678,400	$ 815,525
Tankers	243,208	897,403	1,218,540	950,021	2,389,382
Rolloffs	—	220,444	329,716	459,756	1,198,222
Eqmt. rental	47,234	135,621	454,770	495,004	512,432
Total (includes other*)	1,869,217	4,399,000	5,123,978	5,471,854	7,569,191

* Other is mgt. assistance, eqmt. sales, and disposal

	1983	1986	1987	1988	1989
Disposal revenue: (gross with markup—included in above)	410,000	1,112,555	1,000,928	1,216,874	2,354,082
Number of:					
Vans	12	30	20	33	27
Tankers	2	14	27	23	34
Rolloff boxes	0	9	70	53	88
Tractors	14	19	30	23	33
Drivers	14	19	30	23	30
Sales personnel	3	6	11	11	9
Other personnel	34	41	48	46	53
Est. no. of miles	884,094	1,701,727	1,896,059	1,795,156	2,364,587

Bryson has endeavored to move more into tankers and out of vans as the profit margins are higher, perhaps because many more companies can provide vans to haul drums. Tankers and rolloffs also cut generator costs of handling hazardous waste. Bryson also offers to arrange a generator's disposal and handle it for a 10 percent to 15 percent markup. Disposal revenue above reflects gross disposal fees handled through Bryson.

Bryson initially sold transportation services using outside salespersons in different states to represent Bryson. These people regularly called on generators and represented a cost to Bryson of approximately $75,000 per salesperson annually plus travel expenses. They also sold remedial services. In 1986, Bryson eliminated its three outside sales personnel (described in the "Organization" section) in favor of using "inside" telemarketers/telemanagers to solicit and manage generators' waste. While only seeing generators "over the phone," Bryson's four inside salespersons represented a cost to Bryson of approximately $25,000 annually with very little travel involved. They were also located in a room directly next to the transportation dispatchers, who was responsible for all equipment scheduling.

HW Remediation

Started in 1985, Bryson's remedial services group has become a significant part of its overall business. A review of this development is summarized below. Table 6 lists some of the many cleanup jobs Bryson's work crews have undertaken since starting this division. Exhibit 1 shows remedial service project sites.

	1987	1988	1989
Remedial services revenue:			
Lexington office	$ 657,388	$1,655,100	$1,136,797
Memphis office	130,295	218,439	323,685
TOTAL (includes other)	1,357,220	1,978,000	1,469,062
Disposal revenue (gross with markup—included in above)	78,463	278,401	390,838
Number:			
Management personnel	1	2	3
Field superintendents	1	3	4
Work crews (4 people)	1	3	4

Jim Ullery left South Carolina DHEC in 1987 to join Bryson as the head of remedial services. A chemical engineer from Georgia Tech with 15 years at DHEC, including being EPA Superfund director for South Carolina, Ullery brought impressive credentials to Bryson. Within one year, two former DHEC technicians who worked for Ullery had joined Bryson to help manage remedial services.

Selling remedial services is a challenging task. Remedial service cleanup can easily range from $50,000 to $500,000 for rather simple jobs and much higher for complicated ones. These expenditures often require multiple levels of approval and take time to work into a budget. Seasonality also comes into play as most of the work is done outside,

TABLE 6
Selected Remedial Cleanup Jobs Done by Bryson: 1988–89

Client/Location/Date	Description of Services Rendered
Atlanta Testing & Engineering South Carolina April–August 1989	Delivery of drums to all Atlanta. Testing drilling sites in South Carolina (approximtely 185 sites).
Stone Container Corp. Florence, SC July, 1989	Emergency response. Project consisted of cleanup of a spill of 4,000 gallons of 98 percent H2SO4. The project required removal of a 100-foot section track of railway (on plant property) and the removal of soil, containerization, and backfill associated with the spill area.
IT Corporation Columbia, SC January–June 1989	Subcontracted by IT Corporation to assist with well installation, drum removal, decontamination of equipment, and transportation of contaminated groundwater at the SCRDI Bluff Road Superfund Site.
Firestone Wilson, NC May 1989	Project involved the bulk repackaging of over 400 drums into rolloff containers. We also solidified the material to allow it to be land disposed.
Landspan, Inc. Aiken, SC April 1989	Emergency response. Bryson responded to an intransit spill of Ethylene Diamine. This emergency temporarily closed I-20 and required all personnel to use Level B protection. We repackaged the drums involved and later transported them for disposal.
Mack Truck Winnsboro, SC April 1989	Emergency response. Cleanup of xylene spill near their tank farm. Project required removal of concrete, contaminated soil, extensive soil analysis, and then transportation and disposal of all contaminated materials.
Plasticos Intern'l Columbia, SC April 1989	Emergency response. After a warehouse fire, Bryson responded on Easter Sunday to remove 240 cubic yards of shredded wire insulation as requested by SCDHEC and the fire department. The material in question proved to be hazardous waste and was bulk containerized and transported for disposal.
Highland Industries Kernersville, NC March, 1989	Removal of hardened rubber/toluene mixture from a reactor vessel.
Safety Kleen Holly Hill, SC March, 1989	Cleaned two 40,000-gallon aboveground storage tanks that contained various solvents. Project required vacuum removal of thick sludge, hydroblasting interior tank walls, scaffolding inside the tank to allow cleaning of higher places, and finally steam cleaning to remove potentially explosive vapors from the tanks' interiors.
ITT Thompson Adel, GA March, 1989	Cleaned, cut, and disposed of a 500-gallon gasoline tank (and contents).
Allied Fibers Moncure, NC March, 1989	Cleanout of mist towers and containerization of all sludge, mildew, and solids. Also, transportation of sludge to secure landfill.
Columbus Foundries Columbus, GA February, 1989	Recontainerization for transportation, then transportation and disposal of PCB capacitors.

EXHIBIT 1
Bryson Industrial Services, Inc., Engineering and Remedial Service Project Locations

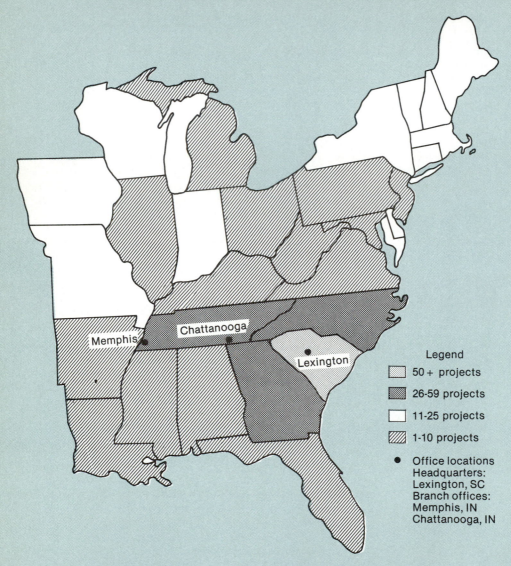

Legend

- ☐ 50 + projects
- ■ 26-59 projects
- ☐ 11-25 projects
- ▨ 1-10 projects
- ● Office locations
  Headquarters:
  Lexington, SC
  Branch offices:
  Memphis, IN
  Chattanooga, IN

making winter months traditionally lean ones. Bryson has traditionally handled this by switching remedial personnel into driver roles rather frequently during November through February. This flexibility is diminishing, however, as regulatory requirements impose training levels that force Bryson to have better qualified field personnel available year 'round. Schematically, remedial jobs involve several steps, depending on their size:

	Steps		
	Site Analysis and Engineering	Job Scope and General Contractor	Work at Site by Gen'l and Subcontractors
Large jobs (over $250K)	**Large, bonded Engineering and Hazwaste Management Cos.**		+ +Bryson as a trns. & reml sub-ctr. + + + +
Small jobs (less than $100k)	+ + + +Bryson doing everything & arr'g disposal + + + + +		

Selling was originally handled by Bryson's outside salespersons before their dismissal (see Organization section). All have engineering or technical backgrounds. Sales responsibility then transferred to the telemarketers as lead generators, with Ullery or other staff members serving as deal closers. Sells are now primarily Ullery's responsibility, with some help from the telemarketers/telemanagers. Jim Ullery commented on sales and remedial services within Bryson:

Since I have been at Bryson we have had some confusion in the selling of our remedial services. First, we have historically relied on salespeople (outside and inside) whose primary sales affiliation is the transportation division. Thus, their customer contact is first from a transportation perspective and perhaps with a lower-level decision-maker. Result—we are seen as a transporter and not as a remedial services firm as, I think, the recent survey bears out. Second, getting work is traditionally a bid-oriented process—we need to know when to bid and be invited to the table early. Often we're approached as transportation contractors before we get into the large bidding projects. Then there is the need to be bonded for the big jobs; and the issue of conflict of interest if you try to offer all services (engineer the job *and* do the work). Some of our best customers are the big engineering firms. We also continue to focus on the smaller, $25k to $200k jobs. But I'm concerned about the need to communicate our image and have a better sales effort.

Charles Kelly offered these comments about remedial services:

I am proud of Jim Ullery and John Cain. Jim's degree, his Superfund role, and being a PE [registered professional engineer] help our image. I'm concerned about their efforts to sell— just sitting back waiting on bids may not work. I used to work in government. Government folks watch the clock, leave at five P.M., and wait for things to happen. You have to be entrepreneurial in this business. I'm not sure we're there yet.

Memphis

Bryson's decision to open an office in Memphis was essentially based on the idea that this location provided Bryson with a position on the west side of the southeastern market and positioned Bryson to serve points west. Roger Woolbright, a former University of South Carolina football player and trusted protege of Stevenson and Kelly as a remedial services superintendent, was moved to Memphis to start the operation in 1987. Woolbright was put in charge of the total Memphis office: sales, operations, and administration. Commenting of the development of the Memphis office, Woolbright said:

chemicals and separates out dirt and waste residues, resales the clean chemicals, and mixes the waste residues (usually flammable) with other types of solid or sludge wastes (e.g., paint residues) to create a fuel that can be sent to cement kilns and burned as fuel. As an interim Part B facility, Wall can also take title to wastes (thus eliminating the 10-day rule), mix wastes from various SQGs onsite to ship off for disposal or fuel, and store up to 200 drums of waste indefinitely.

Commenting on Wall and its relationship with Bryson, Paul Lynes (Wall president) said:

> We started on a shoestring, but we knew if we can get a Part B that Wall would be worth something. Working with Roger and the Bryson people has generally worked well for us. We originally tried to do all our transportation, but that was a hassle and a money loser for us. We've subcontracted all transportation through Bryson. We also share leads—in fact, much of our growth has come through their sales efforts. Bryson uses our facility advantageously for them to handle waste over here, which they are not permitted to do.
>
> An investment by a Bryson stockholder of $900,000 in 1988 in Wall virtually rescued us from bankruptcy. We're still not home free. We've got to spend $500,000 to $700,000 for additional equipment, tank farms, and land to be a fully operational facility. We've agreed to propose a merger with Bryson on a net book value basis—there are pros and cons for each of us, but I think our stockholders will approve it and I hope Bryson's will, as we cannot borrow any more money—yet we must have the additional investment to make Wall a true reality. I also think there is some sales synergy and operating synergy to be gained.

Commenting on the Wall relationship, several Bryson managers shared their thoughts:

Woolbright: "Having access to Wall really helped us with the 10-day rule and allowed us to come up with a way to service small generators—a big part of the Memphis [300-mile radius] market. Paul Lynes is also very knowledgeable and serves as a good resource. We get to sell a lot of disposal through Wall, which builds our revenue [plus Crowley and Woolbright's commission]. I hope they can work out some way to merge."

Kelly: "We didn't research the Memphis-area market, but we learned fast that access to a Wall-type facility sure helps. In fact, it seems as if we can do a better job of selling Wall than can Wall itself. I like what Wall represents to us if it becomes a part of Bryson—a chance for us to be a real full-service player with one or more Part Bs versus just a transporter. Paul is a smart guy and Gary can be led."

Crowley: "I've known about Wall since its inception. It allows us to sell things and accounts we couldn't otherwise serve. Heck, I generate 70 percent of Wall's business—I think I know the marketplace better than they do. Wall needs to hurry up and get finished. I turn down business or send it elsewhere, because they aren't really able to do what they say."

Stevenson: "I like how Wall has helped our business in Memphis. But I'm concerned, too. I don't want us to overly depend on Wall until it is stable. Getting Wall stable may be a challenge, when you consider that more needs to be invested; a Bryson stockholder already invested $900k, and their management team is unproven. We're looking at a proposed merger based on net book value—essentially a 70/30 split of a new company. I agree with Charles that it can put us in a new league, but the operative word is *can* and there is a lot to be done before it *will*. I'm not sure what to recommend to our stockholders without further evaluation."

Cleanway

Cleanway is a small start-up company in Montgomery, Alabama, providing hazardous waste management services to dry cleaners in parts of Alabama and central Tennessee. Founded in 1987 by Donnie Davis, son of the owner of a 12-location dry cleaning chain in Alabama, Cleanway sends out route trucks to its approximately 275 customer sites to pick up chlorinated solvents and dirty filters used in their cleaning plants and classified as hazardous wastes. These are brought back to Montgomery, separated, and sent to recycling sites for reclamation and/or Chemical Waste Management (Emile, Alabama) for disposal. Safety Kleen is the dominant competitor, serving most of the dry cleaners in Cleanway's current markets and over 50 percent of dry cleaners nationwide on a weekly pickup program.

"Dry cleaners are mostly small businesses, cost sensitive, frustrated with their dependence on Safety Kleen, and open to any alternative as long as the price is right," offered Donnie Davis. "We think we can beat Goliath Safety Kleen. "We've just got to have financial support and a good recycling outlet for our chlorinated solvents." The chlorine mixed with solvents by dry cleaners in their cleaning process is nonflammable. Therefore, recyclers handling it must be careful to manage the amount of chlorinated solvents they take in, because only small amounts of residue (chlorinated) can be mixed with wastes as fuel before it lowers its BTU level (flammability) too low.

Cleanway operates in an old building rented from a family friend. Like Wall, Cleanway is operating under interim status while its RCRA permit application awaits Alabama EPA review in 1990–1991. The application calls for Cleanway to move to a new, clean, five-acre site outside Montgomery.

Bryson acquired the stock of Cleanway in the fall of 1989 (see Table 8) and put Donnie Davis on a two-year employment contract. Davis stands to receive an additional $150,000 bonus if the permit application is successful. Davis felt, in selling to Bryson, that "an association with Bryson may help my application process, and Bryson can help me finance development of the dry cleaner business if persuaded it is viable." Bryson acquired the stock of Cleanway, according to Charles Kelly. "Cleanway affords us the opportunity to get a RCRA-permitted facility in Alabama that would be built on a clean piece of property [no cleanup problems] and allow us to have a place to route hazardous waste in Georgia and the Carolinas through as state restrictions on the amount of waste in those states get tighter. It allows us to have a place to consolidate waste and remanifest waste [take title to it, terminating the 10-day rule] that is in the center of the southeastern marketplace."

Medical Waste

Robin Martin-Scott, a young woman with a B.A. degree in nursing from the University of North Carolina five years previous, was working as a Bryson hazardous waste telemarketer in January 1987 when Charles Kelly asked her to read some materials he had been reviewing about the AIDS-prompted emergence of medical and infectuous waste as a potentially hazardous waste. Three months and several meetings later, Kelly and Scott persuaded the Bryson board to allow them to reassign her to work under Kelly and seek to build a medical waste business with Bryson. By May 1987, they had talked to several

TABLE 8
Cleanway's Financial History and the Bryson Purchase

	1987	1988	1989
1. Cleanway P&Ls			
Revenue	$94,577	$161,259	$212,348
Cost of sales (includes disposal)	20,017	46,449	55,169
Opr Expenses:			
Salaries	23,250	48,105	46,800
Insurance	4,513	13,941	23,394
Rent	8,500	12,964	8,002
Travel	13,893	17,410	16,793
Other	25,446	24,162	58,829
Total	75,602	116,582	153,818
Profit before taxes	(1,042)	(1,772)	3,361
2. Cleanway balance sheet			
Current assets	1,070	3,561	4,536
Equipment & vehicles	19,385	12,435	35,304
Other	2,594	1,946	6,797
Total assets	23,049	17,947	46,637
Current liabilities	9,530	14,896	27,171
Long-term liabilities	13,561	4,860	17,919
Stockholders' equity	(42)	(1,814)	(1,547)

3. **Terms of the Cleanway purchase**
   A. Pay Donnie Davis $67,000, all legal expenses, and accounting expenses for 100 percent of the stock of Cleanway.
   B. Agree to pay Donnie Davis $150,000 upon receipt of the final RCRA Part B permit.
   C. Set up a Cleanway SQG subsidiary in which Bryson owns 60 percent of the stock; D. Davis owns 40 percent of the stock; to serve dry cleaners. Once the RCRA permit is generated, parties can choose to (1) allocate 40 percent of the permitted site's capabilities to Cleanway SQG for development of an expanded drycleaner servicing business or (2) purchase D. Davis' 40 percent for $50,000 and use the whole site as Bryson sees fit.
   D. Donnie Davis signs a two-year employment contract to manage Cleanway and pursue the permit like he is now doing on a part-time basis (he works in his dad's business, and runs a farm as well as Cleanway).

hospitals, attended numerous seminars, hired Kelly's nephew who was scheduled to graduate from North Georgia College in June as a salesman, and hired a driver to serve the two hospitals that they had persuaded to let Bryson Medical Waste Management (BMWM) handle their waste.

Two major events during the summer of 1987 brought infectious wastes to the forefront of public attention—exciting Charles Kelly about the business potential. First, in Indianapolis, 12 children were found playing with vials of blood—two of which were infected with the AIDS virus—that came from an unlocked dumpster outside several doctors' offices. Next, some 30 miles of New Jersey shoreline had to be closed by local officials after a 60-mile-long slick of hypodermic needles, refuse, and infectious wastes washed up on the state's beaches. Charles Kelly was heard to say, "Medical waste will be to the 90s what hazardous waste was to the 80s."

Several major players shared his view. By the end of 1987, BFI had a medical waste division, with several incinerators around the country and over 5,000 clients nationwide. Med-X, a large medical waste company in Florida, was rapidly expanding via acquisition with the backing of its British parent company, Attwood. Chemical Waste was belatedly but rapidly entering the industry. Other major regionals, often spinoffs from regional solid waste companies, were already pursuing business. These companies all seemed to be seeking market recognition and position in anticipation of greater regulation. Each saw the potential for high volumes of waste (15 pounds per bed per day, according to one estimate) to burn at their incinerators plus high-margin services to doctors' offices, clinics, and veterinary clinics.

Regulation RCRA was the driving force behind hazardous waste, but few regulations existed for medical waste. And many hospital associations were fighting legislation as reactionary when the problem, bacteria and viruses in waste, was already solved the old fashion way—steaming, exposure to oxygen, and antiseptics. The result was an EPA and 50 state legislatures locked in a battle between groups reacting to highly publicized beach spills and experts saying that regular solid waste approaches will work—create legislation to create a new medical waste industry and you just add costs to health care.

In the states with initial regulations or where hospitals and doctors offices wanted greater comfort, medical wastes was becoming a competitive business. Most medical facilities preferred incineration as a disposal method, which suited the major entrants very well. About 80 percent of every dollar spent on medical waste went for disposal (usually incineration) with a remaining 12 percent for transportation and 8 percent for supplies and handling. Regional and national incinerators often subcontracted "hauling" to local transporters, keeping the high value-added portion in the incineration charge. Siting new incinerators was increasingly difficult (public pressure) and time consuming.

Ms. Scott and young Tom Kelly worked hard to build an initial South Carolina clientele for Bryson Medical Waste. They were gradually successful in winning over selected hospitals to let Bryson handle and transport the waste and arrange incineration services. One major strategy Ms. Scott used was to try to get the contract for the largest hospital in the area at the lowest possible price and then make up lost margin with higher prices to doctors' offices and clinics in the vicinity. This occasionally resulted in break-even pricing (25 cents per pound where she had to pay 21 cents for incineration), and many hesitant doctors offices awaiting clearer regulations.

By late 1989, sales had reached $25–$30,000 per month, as the following figures show. A telemarketer was added and two drivers, Ms. Scott took over marketing/sales, and Tom Kelly was moved to the hazardous waste operation. Ms. Scott had these thoughts in anticipation of the 1989 planning meeting:

> I'm real proud of what we've done and the reputation we've built. I know I'm well respected in this business [several customers and associations regularly seek her advice and counsel]. But I'm frustrated at our slow growth. I know its part legislation, but I'm also not sure that Bryson wants to make a firm commitment to us. Sometimes I feel like the stepchild business in Bryson.

Charles Kelly, offering reassurance to Ms. Scott on several occasions, had these thoughts in late 1989:

Robin has really built a base for our medical waste business. I'm convinced that it's going to be a major market, but I'm concerned about the lack of regulation. Without legislation, many hospitals and most doctors' offices will not choose to handle their waste as other than regular trash like they are used to doing. We may be ahead of our time.

Tom Kelly, having joined the hazardous waste side of Bryson three months earlier, noticed some other differences:

The medical waste pickups are different from the hazardous side. One pickup at an industrial site for hazardous wastes can easily generate $3,000 to $5,000 in transportation and disposal revenue. Most medical waste clients (except the biggest hospitals) involve one pickup a week of approximately 100 pounds [4 boxes] for a $50 minimum charge. Now that's quite a difference. I'm not sure we can make money here without being in incineration, if then.

Joel Stevenson, hearing Tom Kelly's comments, added:

And I'm getting concerned about the amount of management time we have to allocate across this company. Medical Waste is an exciting business, as are three others we are committed to as well. I'm concerned that Charles is overcommitted, or we are overcommitted. We've got to take a good look. We're in on the ground floor. Robin is well known throughout the Carolinas; analysts say Medical Waste could become a $3 billion market within a few years. We've got decisions that challenge our management expertise.

The results of Bryson Medical Waste Management through 1989 are provided below. Capital needs for 1990 are estimated as well.

	1987	1988	1989
Revenues:			
Transportation	$ 11,123	$ 29,269	$ 66,450
Supplies	7,301	9,942	19,630
Consulting	2,955	9,087	17,300
Disposal (gross cost plus markup)	24,531	74,211	142,700
Total	$ 45,909	$122,509	$245,080
Costs:			
Variable	$ 37,822	67,380	$134,794
Fixed	33,457	105,680	147,330
Other	1,210	7,245	13,756
Total	$ 72,489	$180,305	$295,880
Profit or (loss)	$(26,580)	$(57,796)	$(50,800)
Personnel	2.5	3.5	5.0
Equipment	$ 32,450	$110,250	$162,410
Estimated capital investment needed for 1990			$154,500

Organization and Management

Joel Stevenson, talking to Charles Kelly and the case writer, said, "It's amazing that just 10 years ago there was just me, Charles and Frances—now there are over 80 people and even more, counting seasonal temporaries and subcontractors as we move into the 1990s. They're all great people, talented and dedicated, but that represents a much bigger management challenge than what we grew up with! We certainly can't run the company like we used to, and we're *all* going to have to grow in our management capabilities to rise to the challenge of the 1990s."

Bryson's organizational structure has evolved through several forms during those 10 years. In the early 1980s, when it was primarily serving as a transporter for the SCA hazwaste landfill in Pinewood, Bryson had the following organization:

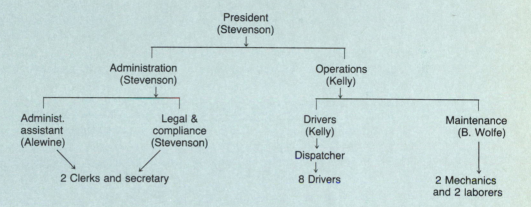

While Stevenson and Kelly had different roles, they frequently overlapped in supervising and directing people.

When Bryson decided to add its own marketing functions to become less dependent on SCA and to build its "own" customer base, the organization was changed, as follows:

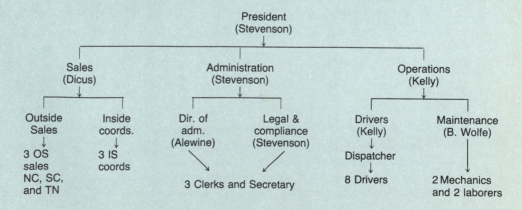

One major addition in this new structure was Ron Smith. A neighbor of Joel Stevenson, Smith was a territorial salesman for the health care products division of 3M Corporation. In this capacity, he called on hospitals and doctors' offices for 11 years throughout the Carolinas and east Tennessee. Smith attended East Tennessee State University and he was 33 years old when he joined Bryson in 1984.

In 1985, Bryson entered the remedial services business providing field superintendents and work crews to do hazwaste cleanup at industrial sites in South and North Carolina. These personnel reported to the operations manager, Charles Kelly.

By mid-1986, Bryson was experiencing several problems as it continued steady gowth. First, sales personnel were increasingly vocal about their frustration with the operations group. An important part of transportation sales was ensuring that the customer experienced punctual service from Bryson drivers. A customer would arrange with a salesperson to have a load of waste picked up at a certain time (usually 8 AM) on a specific day. But Bryson drivers were often late, as they would encounter logistical difficulties getting from one location the previous day (e.g., eastern Tennessee) to another at 8 AM the next morning (e.g., south Georgia). Related, sales people found that remediation jobs they sold as being done in one way were done differently by operations personnel that came to do the job.

These problems were temporarily put aside as Bryson's top management determined that its sales volume did not justify the costs of three outside salespersons. Within six months after letting them go, the problems had become more intense. So, in early 1987, Bryson moved to a modified-divisional form, as follows:

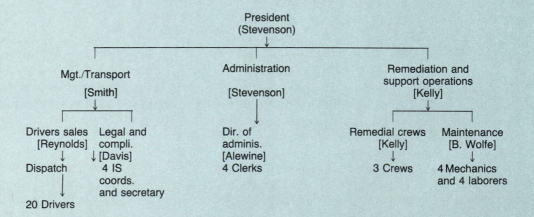

The remainder of 1987 saw Bryson add an office in Memphis and enter the medical waste business. Both entities initially reported to Kelly. But conflicts between the transportation division and Memphis-based operations, as well as issues regarding the sales focus of the Memphis office manager, led to the transfer of the Memphis operations under the transportation division by early 1988. In summer 1988, the differences between

Bryson's top managers over the future direction of the company led to the departure of Smith, who, along with Bryson's transportation dispatcher and four drivers, joined a newly established branch of a Florida transportation company seeking to enter the hazardous waste transportation business, locating in Columbia, South Carolina. Smith was replaced by Joel Stevenson as head of the transportation division, and Dick Robinson, a business professor on leave from a local university, replaced Stevenson as head of administration and secretary to the board of directors.

Mid-1989 saw Bryson restructure along geographic lines. With Memphis operations increasing in volume and scope, and a special relationship emerging between Bryson-Memphis and a Memphis-based RCRA treatment/recycling facility (Wall Chemical), the company was divided into Bryson East and Bryson West as follows:

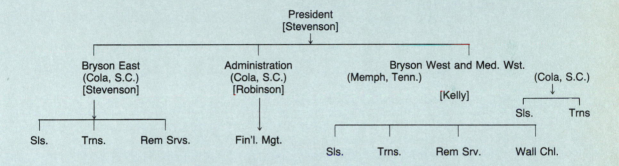

The rationale behind this organization was the need to have self-contained operations responding to the unique and often different market needs in two geographic markets. Furthermore, it was seen as a way to focus top management attention. During fall 1989, Robinson moved exclusively to the role of secretary to the board and coordinator of the top management team and was replaced in administration by a 30-year old controller (Don Boan, CPA) with several years of financial management experience at Chem-Nuclear's transportation division. Responsibility for the newly added dry cleaning treatment operation in Montgomery, Alabama, was placed under Kelly.

A list of key management-level personnel at Bryson in 1989 is provided in Table 9. Some key changes were underway during this time. First, the pressure on ensuring legal operations was increasing, given the growing size of the company, the number of loads transporting, and sites cleaned, each representing a potential for mistakes. Legal and compliance remained under Stevenson, with Jerry Davis (B.A., M.B.A.) responsible for this function. Davis informed Stevenson of his desire to seek employment elsewhere in October 1989. Second, Wall Chemical's financial condition was deteriorating and its sales success was declining, which was putting stronger pressure on the need to consider merging the two companies as a means to help Wall's financial/sales situations and to maintain Bryson's advantageous access to a RCRA facility. Third, reports that one Memphis salesperson was independently deciding what substances would be handled at

TABLE 9
Key Managers at Bryson in Late 1989

Joel Stevenson—B.S. industrial mgt. 1970; Ga. Tech, captain of Tech football team, 1968; banking two years [Atl.]; industrial sales two years Continental Can; co-owner, industrial cleaning business six years [Ala.; Penn.; Colorado]; founder, Bryson.

Charles Kelly—B.S. geology 1969, Univ. of Georgia; member of Georgia baseball team; staff and hazwaste coordinator, South Carolina DHEC, eight years; owner, sporting goods store, 1 year; founder, Bryson.

Don Boan—B.S. accounting, Univ. of South Carolina 1981; CPA; Columbia CPA firm two years; controller, ChemNuclear Transp. Division three years; controller, Carolina Forklift three years; controller, Bryson one year.

Dick Robinson—B.S. Ga. Tech, 1970; MBA and Ph.D., Univ. of Ga., 1979; manager, Holiday Inns three years; consultant eight years; professor eight years; consultant to Bryson six years; V.P. and board mbr. Bryson.

Jim Ullery—B.S. chem engr. Ga. Tech, 1976; staff & Superfund director, SC DHEC 12 years; dir. of Remedial Services, Bryson three years; P.E.

Evon Reynolds—B.A. Midlands Tech, 1975; clerical, Southeastern Freight Lines, eight years; clerical, Bryson two years; sales coord., Bryson two years; asst dir., Trans. Div., Bryson three years.

Robin Martin-Scott—B.S. nursing, Univ. of North Carolina, 1982; nurse two years; retailing four years; telemarketing Bryson one year; manager, Bryson Medical Waste Mgt. three years.

John Cain—B.S. chemistry, Univ. of S. Carolina, 1979; environmental quality mgr., S.C. DHEC nine years; asst. dir. Remd'l Services, Bryson two years.

Roger Woolbright—B.S. education, Univ. of South Carolina, 1978; teacher and coach five years; Remdl. supt. Bryson three years; manager—Memphis, Bryson three years.

Donnie Davis (Cleanway)—B.S. Auburn, 1982; 14 years in family dry cleaning and farming business; founder, Cleanway 1987.

At Wall Chemical

Paul Lynes—B.S., M.S., and ABD chem engr, Vanderbilt 1980; chem engr, various companies; consultant five years; president Wall Chemical three years; P.E.

Gary Rimer—B.S. chem engr., Vanderbilt, 1972; engr., Memphis Water and Elect., 10 years; sales, Wall Brother Oil Co. four years; founder and sales, Wall Chemical three years.

the Wall facility reached Stevenson as part of a complaint that there was no control over the sales function in Memphis. These were accompanied by repeated disputes between other Bryson locations and Memphis operations about just what they did and did not do. Fourth, Stevenson received a call about this time from a vice president for Dry Cleaner Services at Safety Kleen that he had video tapes of Cleanway (new Alabama acquisition) personnel splitting dry cleaning filters, improperly spilling hazardous waste over the ground, and was considering talking to EPA and the Alabama-EPA official responsible for evaluating Cleanway's RCRA Permit application. Finally, the manager of the Medical Waste Division was complaining to Kelly that her division was being neglected by Bryson's top management while also facing intense price-cutting competition from two national firms, BFI and Med-X, seeking to enter South Carolina.

APPENDIX 1

Bryson Financial Information [$000s]

	Year Ending			
	1986	**1987**	**1988**	**1989**
A. Balance Sheet [000s]				
Current assets:				
Cash	$ 97	$ 290	$ 77	$ 0
Acct recvble	785	1,021	1,315	1,920
Inventory	49	21	41	22
Prepaid exps.	27	0	31	48
Total	957	1,332	1,464	1,990
Property, plant, eq.	1,321	1,515	2,125	2,435
Other assets	16	16	17	59
Current liabilities	677	1,043	1,325	1,695
Long-term liabs.	536	489	804	1,301
Deferred taxes	162	235	293	253
Stockholders' equity	920	1,096	1,182	1,234

B. Estimated Capital Expenditure Needs for Next Few Years [000s]

	1990	**1991**	**1992**
1. Bryson hazwaste:			
Plant & equipment	$400	$500	$300
Vehicles	14	750	750
Trailers/tanks	647	400	400
2. Bryson Medical Waste	155	325	250
3. Cleanway	100	{200 to 1,500} w/Part B	
4. Wall Chemical	610	400	400

II STRATEGY FORMULATION

Strategy formulation guides executives in defining the business their firm is in, the aims it seeks, and the means it will use to accomplish those aims. The approach of strategy formulation is an improvement over that of traditional long-range planning. As discussed in the following seven chapters, in developing a firm's competitive plan of action, strategy formulation combines a future-oriented perspective with concern for the firm's internal and external environments.

The process of strategy formulation begins with definition of the company mission, as discussed in Chapter 2. In that chapter, the purpose of business is defined to reflect the values of a wide variety of interested parties.

Chapter 3 deals with the principal factors in a firm's external environment that strategic managers must assess so they can anticipate and take advantage of future business conditions. It emphasizes the importance to a firm's planning activities of factors in the firm's remote, industry, and operating environments. A key theme of the chapter is the problem of deciding whether to accept environmental constraints or to maneuver around them.

Chapter 4 describes the key differences in strategic planning and implementation among domestic, multinational, and global firms. It gives special attention to the new vision that a firm must communicate in a revised company mission when it multinationalizes.

Chapter 5 focuses on the environmental forecasting approaches currently used by strategic managers in assessing and anticipating changes in the external environment.

Chapter 6 shows how firms evaluate their internal strengths and weaknesses to produce a company profile. Strategic managers use such profiles to target competitive advantages they can emphasize and competitive disadvantages they should correct or minimize.

Chapter 7 examines the types of long-range objectives strategic managers set and specifies the qualities these objectives must have to provide a basis for direction and evaluation. The chapter also examines the 12 grand strategies that firms use to achieve long-range objectives.

Comprehensive approaches to the evaluation of strategic opportunities and to the final strategic decision are the focus of Chapter 8. The chapter shows how a firm's strategic options can be compared in a way that allows selection of the best available option.

2 DEFINING THE COMPANY MISSION

WHAT IS A COMPANY MISSION?

Whether a firm is developing a new business or reformulating direction for an ongoing business, it must determine the basic goals and philosophies that will shape its strategic posture. This *company mission* is defined as the fundamental purpose that sets a firm apart from other firms of its type and identifies the scope of its operations in product and market terms. As discussed in Chapter 1, the company mission is a broadly framed but enduring statement of a firm's intent. It embodies the business philosophy of the firm's strategic decision makers, implies the image the firm seeks to project, reflects the firm's self-concept, and indicates the firm's principal product or service areas and the primary customer needs the firm will attempt to satisfy. In short, it describes the firm's product, market, and technological areas of emphasis, and it does so in a way that reflects the values and priorities of the firm's strategic decision makers. An excellent example is the company mission statement of NICOR, Inc., shown in Strategy in Action 2–1.

The Need for an Explicit Mission

No external body requires that the company mission be defined, and the process of defining it is time-consuming and tedious. Moreover, it contains broadly outlined or implied objectives and strategies rather than specific directives. Characteristically, it is a statement, not of measurable targets, but of attitude, outlook, and orientation.

What is that statement designed to accomplish? According to King and Cleland, the objectives of the company mission are

1. To ensure unanimity of purpose within the organization.
2. To provide a basis for motivating the use of the organization's resources.
3. To develop a basis, or standard, for allocating organizational resources.
4. To establish a general tone or organizational climate; for example, to suggest a businesslike operation.

MISSION STATEMENT OF NICOR, INC.

Preamble

We, the management of Nicor, Inc., here set forth our belief as to the purpose for which the company is established and the principles under which it should operate. We pledge our effort to the accomplishment of these purposes within these principles.

Basic purpose

The basic purpose of Nicor, Inc., is to perpetuate an investor-owned company engaging in various phases of the energy business, striving for balance among those phases so as to render needed satisfactory products and services and earn optimum, long-range profits.

What we do

The principal business of the company, through its utility subsidiary, is the provision of energy through a pipe system to meet the needs of ultimate consumers. To accomplish its basic purpose, and to ensure its strength, the company will engage in other energy-related activities, directly or through subsidiaries or in participation with other persons, corporations, firms, or entities.

All activities of the company shall be consistent with its responsibilities to investors, customers, employees, and the public and its concern for the optimum development and utilization of natural resources and for environmental needs.

Where we do it

The company's operations shall be primarily in the United States, but no self-imposed or regulatory geographical limitations are placed upon the acquisition, development, processing, transportation, or storage of energy resources, or upon other energy-related ventures in which the company may engage. The company will engage in such activities in any location where, after careful review, it has determined that such activity is in the best interest of its stockholders.

Utility service will be offered in the territory of the company's utility subsidiary to the best of its ability, in accordance with the requirements of regulatory agencies and pursuant to the subsidiary's purposes and principles.

5. To serve as a focal point for those who can identify with the organization's purpose and direction and to deter those who cannot do so from participating further in its activities.
6. To facilitate the translation of objectives and goals into a work structure involving the assignment of tasks to responsible elements within the organization.
7. To specify organizational purposes and the translation of these purposes into goals in such a way that cost, time, and performance parameters can be assessed and controlled.[1]

[1]William R. King and David I. Cleland, *Strategic Planning and Policy* (New York: Van Nostrand Reinhold, 1978), p. 124.

FORMULATING A MISSION

The process of defining the company mission for a specific business can perhaps be best understood by thinking about the business at its inception. The typical business begins with the beliefs, desires, and aspirations of a single entrepreneur. Such an owner-manager's sense of mission is usually based on the following fundamental beliefs:

1. The *product* or *service* of the business can provide benefits at least equal to its price.
2. The product or service can satisfy a *customer need* of specific market segments that is currently not being met adequately.
3. The *technology* that is to be used in production will provide a cost- and quality-competitive product or service.
4. With hard work and the support of others, the business can not only *survive* but also *grow* and be *profitable*.
5. The *management philosophy* of the business will result in a favorable *public image* and will provide financial and psychological rewards for those who are willing to invest their labor and money in helping the business to succeed.
6. The entrepreneur's *self-concept* of the business can be communicated to and adopted by employees and stockholders.

As the business grows or is forced by competitive pressures to alter its product/market/technology, redefining the company mission may be necessary. If so, the revised mission statement will contain the same components as the original. It will state the basic type of product or service to be offered, the primary markets or customer groups to be served, and the technology to be used in production or delivery; the firm's fundamental concern for survival through growth and profitability; the firm's managerial philosophy; the public image the firm seeks; and the self-concept those affiliated with the firm should have of it. This chapter will discuss in detail these components. The examples shown in Strategy in Action 2–2 provide insights into how some major corporations handle them.

Basic Product or Service; Primary Market; Principal Technology

Three indispensable components of the mission statement are specification of the basic product or service, specification of the primary market, and specification of the principal technology for production or delivery. These components are discussed under one heading because only in combination do they describe the company's business activity. A good example of the three components is to be found in the business plan of ITT Barton, a division of ITT. Under the heading of business mission and area served, the following information is presented:

> The unit's mission is to serve industry and government with quality instruments used for the primary measurement, analysis, and local control of fluid flow, level, pressure, temperature, and fluid properties. This instrumentation includes flow meters, electronic readouts, indicators, recorders, switches, liquid level system, analytical instruments such as titrators, integrators, controllers, transmitters, and various instruments for the measurement of fluid properties (den-

---

**STRATEGY
IN ACTION
2–2**

IDENTIFYING MISSION STATEMENT COMPONENTS: A COMPILATION OF EXCERPTS FROM ACTUAL CORPORATE MISSION STATEMENTS

1. Customer/ market	We believe our first responsibility is to the doctors, nurses, and patients, to mothers and all others who use our products and services. (Johnson & Johnson)
	To anticipate and meet market needs of farmers, ranchers, and rural communities within North America. (CENEX)
2. Product/ service	AMAX's principal products are molybdenum, coal, iron ore, copper, lead, zinc, petroleum and natural gas, potash, phosphates, nickel, tungsten, silver, gold, and magnesium. (AMAX)
3. Geographic domain	We are dedicated to the total success of Corning Glass Works as a worldwide competitor. (Corning Glass)
4. Technology	Control Data is in the business of applying microelectronics and computer technology in two general areas: computer-related hardware and computing-enhancing services, which include computation, information, education, and finance. (Control Data)
	The common technology in these areas relates to discrete particle coatings. (NASHUA)
5. Concern for survival	In this respect, the company will conduct its operation prudently, and will provide the profits and growth which will assure Hoover's ultimate success. (Hoover Universal)
6. Philosophy	We are committed to improve health care throughout the world. (Baxter Travenol)
	We believe human development to be the worthiest of the goals of civilization and independence to be the superior condition for nurturing growth in the capabilities of people. (Sun Company)
7. Self-concept	Hoover Universal is a diversified, multi-industry corporation with strong manufacturing capabilities, entrepreneurial policies, and individual business unit autonomy. (Hoover Universal)
8. Concern for public image	We are responsible to the communities in which we live and work and to the world community as well. (Johnson & Johnson)
	Also, we must be responsive to the broader concerns of the public, including especially the general desire for improvement in the quality of life, equal opportunity for all, and the constructive use of natural resources. (Sun Company)

Source: John A. Pearce II and F. R. David "Corporate Mission Statements: The Bottom Line," *Academy of Management Executive,* May 1987, pp. 109–16.

sity, viscosity, gravity) used for processing variable sensing, data collecting, control, and transmission. The unit's mission includes fundamental loop-closing control and display devices, when economically justified, but excludes broadline central control room instrumentation, systems design, and turnkey responsibility.

Markets served include instrumentation for oil and gas production, gas transportation, chemical and petrochemical processing, cryogenics, power generation, aerospace, government and marine, as well as other instrument and equipment manufacturers.

In only 129 words, this segment of the mission statement clearly indicates to all readers—from company employees to casual observers—the basic products, primary markets, and principal technologies of ITT Barton.

Often the most referenced public statement of a company's selected products and markets appears in "silver bullet" form in the mission statement; for example, "Dayton-Hudson Corporation is a diversified retailing company whose business is to serve the American consumer through the retailing of fashion-oriented quality merchandise."[2] Such an abstract of company direction is particularly helpful to outsiders who value condensed overviews.

Company Goals: Survival, Growth, Profitability

Three economic goals guide the strategic direction of almost every business organization. Whether the mission statement explicitly states these goals, it reflects the firm's intention to secure *survival* through *growth* and *profitability*.

A firm that is unable to survive will be incapable of satisfying the aims of any of its stakeholders. Unfortunately, the goal of survival, like the goals of growth and profitability, is often taken for granted to such an extent that it is neglected as a principal criterion in strategic decision making. When this happens, the firm may focus on short-term aims at the expense of the long run. Concerns for expediency, a quick fix, or a bargain may displace the assessment of long-term impact. Too often, the result is near-term economic failure owing to a lack of resource synergy and sound business practice. For example, Consolidated Foods, maker of Shasta soft drinks and L'eggs hosiery, sought growth through the acquisition of bargain businesses. However, the erratic sales patterns of its diverse holdings forced it to divest itself of more than four dozen companies. This process cost Consolidated Foods millions of dollars and hampered its growth.

Profitability is the mainstay goal of a business organization. No matter how profit is measured or defined, profit over the long term is the clearest indication of a firm's ability to satisfy the principal claims and desires of employees and stockholders. The key phrase here is "over the long term." Obviously, basing decisions on a short-term concern for profitability would lead to a strategic myopia. Overlooking the enduring concerns of customers, suppliers, creditors, ecologists, and regulatory agents may produce profit in the short term, but over time, the financial consequences are likely to be detrimental.

The following excerpt from the Hewlett-Packard statement of mission ably expresses the importance of an orientation toward long-term profit:

> To achieve sufficient profit to finance our company growth and to provide the resources we need to achieve our other corporate objectives.
>
> In our economic system, the profit we generate from our operation is the ultimate source of the funds we need to prosper and grow. It is the one absolutely essential measure of our corporate performance over the long term. Only if we continue to meet our profit objective can we achieve our other corporate objectives.

---

[2]See W. Ouchi, *Theory Z* (Reading, Mass.: Addison-Wesley Publishing, 1981). Ouchi presents more complete mission statements of three of the companies discussed in this chapter: Dayton-Hudson, Hewlett-Packard, and Intel.

A firm's growth is inextricably tied to its survival and profitability. In this context, the meaning of growth must be broadly defined. Although the product impact market studies (PIMS) have shown that growth in market share is correlated with profitability, other important forms of growth do exist. For example, growth in the number of markets served, in the variety of products offered, and in the technologies used to provide goods or services frequently leads to improvements in a firm's competitive ability. Growth means change, and proactive change is essential in a dynamic business environment. Hewlett-Packard's mission statement provides an excellent example of corporate regard for growth:

> Objective: To let our growth be limited only by our profits and our ability to develop and produce technical products that satisfy real customer needs.
>
> We do not believe that large size is important for its own sake; however, for at least two basic reasons, continuous growth is essential for us to achieve our other objectives.
>
> In the first place, we serve a rapidly growing and expanding segment of our technological society. To remain static would be to lose ground. We cannot maintain a position of strength and leadership in our field without growth.
>
> In the second place, growth is important in order to attract and hold high-caliber people. These individuals will align their future only with a company that offers them considerable opportunity for personal progress. Opportunities are greater and more challenging in a growing company.

The issue of growth raises a concern about the definition of the company mission. How can a firm's product, market, and technology be specified sufficiently to provide direction without precluding the exercise of unanticipated strategic options? How can a firm define its mission so that it can consider opportunistic diversification while maintaining the parameters that guide its growth decision? Perhaps such questions are best addressed when a firm's mission statement outlines the conditions under which the firm might depart from ongoing operations. The growth philosophy of Dayton-Hudson embodies this approach:

> The stability and quality of the corporation's financial performance will be developed through the profitable execution of our existing businesses, as well as through the acquisition or development of new businesses. Our growth priorities, in order, are as follows:
>
> 1. Development of the profitable market preeminence of existing companies in existing markets through new store development or new strategies within existing stores.
> 2. Expansion of our companies to feasible new markets.
> 3. Acquisition of other retailing companies that are strategically and financially compatible with Dayton-Hudson.
> 4. Internal development of new retailing strategies.

Capital allocations to fund the expansion of existing Dayton-Hudson operating companies will be based on each company's return on investment (ROI), in relationship to its ROI objective and its consistency in earnings growth and on the ability of its management to perform up to the forecasts contained in its capital requests. Expansion via acquisition or new venture will occur when the opportunity promises an acceptable rate of long-term growth and profitability, an acceptable degree of risk, and compatibility with Dayton-Hudson's long-term strategy.

Company Philosophy

The statement of a company's philosophy, often called the company creed, usually accompanies or appears within the mission statement. It reflects or specifies the basic beliefs, values, aspirations, and philosophical priorities to which strategic decision makers are committed in managing the company. Fortunately, the philosophies vary little from one firm to another. Owners and managers implicitly accept a general, unwritten, yet pervasive code of behavior that governs business actions and permits them to be largely self-regulated. Unfortunately, statements of company philosophy are so similar and so platitudinous that they read more like public relations handouts than the commitment to values they are meant to be.

Despite the similarity of these statements, the intentions of the strategic managers in developing them do not warrant cynicism. Company executives attempt to provide a distinctive and accurate picture of the firm's managerial outlook. One such statement of company philosophy is that of Dayton-Hudson Corporation. As Strategy in Action 2–3 shows, Dayton-Hudson's board of directors and executives have established especially clear directions for company decision making and action.

Perhaps most noteworthy in the Dayton-Hudson statement is its delineation of responsibility at both the corporate and business levels. In many ways, the statement could serve as a prototype for the three-tier approach to strategic management. This approach implies that the mission statement must address strategic concerns at the corporate, business, and functional levels of the organization. Dayton-Hudson's management philosophy does this by balancing operating autonomy and flexibility on the one hand with corporate input and direction on the other.

Public Image

Both present and potential customers attribute certain qualities to particular businesses. Gerber and Johnson & Johnson make safe products; Cross Pen makes high-quality writing instruments; Aigner Étienne makes stylish but affordable leather products; Corvettes are power machines; and Izod Lacoste stands for the preppy look. Thus, mission statements should reflect the public's expectations, since this makes achievement of the firm's goals more likely. Gerber's mission statement should not open the possibility for diversification into pesticides, and Cross Pen's should not open the possibility for diversification into 39-cent brand-name disposables.

On the other hand, a negative public image often prompts firms to reemphasize the beneficial aspects of their mission. For example, in response to what it saw as a disturbing trend in public opinion, Dow Chemical undertook an agressive promotional campaign to fortify its credibility, particularly among "employees and those who live and work in [their] plant communities." Dow described its approach in its annual report:

> All around the world today, Dow people are speaking up. People who care deeply about their company, what it stands for, and how it is viewed by others. People who are immensely proud

MANAGEMENT PHILOSOPHY OF DAYTON-HUDSON CORPORATION

The corporation will:
Set standards for return on investment (ROI) and earnings growth.
Approve strategic plans.
Allocate capital.
Approve goals.
Monitor, measure, and audit results.
Reward performance.
Allocate management resources.

The operating companies will be accorded the freedom and responsibility:
To manage their own business.
To develop strategic plans and goals that will optimize their growth.
To develop an organization that can ensure consistency of results and optimum growth.
To operate their businesses consistent with the corporation's statement of philosophy.

The corporate staff will provide only those services that are:
Essential to the protection of the corporation.
Needed for the growth of the corporation.
Wanted by operating companies and that provide a significant advantage in quality or cost.

The corporation will insist on:
Uniform accounting practices by type of business.
Prompt disclosure of operating results.
A systematic approach to training and developing people.
Adherence to appropriately high standards of business conduct and civic responsibility in accordance with the corporation's statement of philosophy.

of their company's performance, yet realistic enough to realize it is the public's perception of that performance that counts in the long run.

Firms seldom address the question of their public image in an intermittent fashion. Although public agitation often stimulates greater attention to this question, firms are concerned about their public image even in the absence of such agitation. The following excerpt from the mission statement of Intel Corporation is an example of this attitude:

We are sensitive to our *image with our customers and the business community*. Commitments to customers are considered sacred, and we are upset with ourselves when we do not meet our commitments. We strive to demonstrate to the business world on a continuing basis that we are credible in describing the state of the corporation, and that we are well organized and in complete control of all things that determine the numbers.

Company Self-Concept

A major determinant of a firm's success is the extent to which the firm can relate functionally to its external environment. To its proper place in a competitive situation, the firm must realistically evaluate its competitive strengths and weaknesses. This idea—that the firm must know itself—is the essence of the company self-concept. The idea is not commonly integrated into theories of strategic management; its importance for individuals has been recognized since ancient times. As one scholar writes, "Man has struggled to understand himself, for how he thinks of himself will influence both what he chooses to do and what he expects from life. Knowing his identity connects him both with his past and with the potentiality of his future."[3]

Both individuals and firms have a crucial need to know themselves. The ability of either to survive in a dynamic and highly competitive environment would be severely limited if they did not understand their impact on others or of others on them.

In some senses, then, firms take on personalities of their own. Much behavior in firms is organizationally based; that is, a firm acts on its members in ways other than their individual interactions. Thus, firms are entities whose personality transcends the personalities of their members. As such, they can set decision-making parameters based on aims different and distinct from the aims of their members. These organizational considerations have pervasive effects.

> Organizations do have policies, do and do not condone violence, and may or may not greet you with a smile. They also manufacture goods, administer policies, and protect the citizenry. These are organizational actions and involve properties of organizations, not individuals. They are carried out by individuals, even in the case of computer-produced letters, which are programmed by individuals—but the genesis of the actions remains in the organization.[4]

The characteristics of the corporate self-concept have been summarized as follows:

1. It is based on management's perception of the way in which others (society) will respond to the company.
2. It directs the behavior of people employed by the company.
3. It is determined in part by the responses of others to the company.
4. It is incorporated into mission statements that are communicated to individuals inside and outside the company.[5]

Ordinarily, descriptions of the company self-concept per se do not appear in mission statements. Yet such statements often provide strong impressions of the company self-concept. The following excerpts from the Intel Corporation mission statement describes the corporate persona that its top management seeks to foster:

> Management is *self-critical*. The leaders must be capable of recognizing and accepting their mistakes and learning from them.

---

[3] J. Kelly, *Organizational Behavior* (Homewood, Ill.: Richard D. Irwin, 1974), p. 258.

[4] R. H. Hall, *Organization-Structure and Process* (Englewood Cliffs, N.J.: Prentice-Hall, 1972), p. 13.

[5] E. J. Kelley, *Marketing Planning and Competitive Strategy* (Englewood Cliffs, N.J.: Prentice-Hall, 1972), p. 55

Open (*constructive*) *confrontation is encouraged* at all levels of the corporation and is viewed as a method of problem solving and conflict resolution.

Decision by *consensus* is the rule. Decisions once made are supported. Position in the organization is not the basis for quality of ideas.

A *highly communicative, open management* is part of the style.

Management must be ethical. Managing by telling the truth and treating all employees equitably has established credibility that is ethical.

We strive to provide an *opportunity for rapid development.*

Intel is a *results-oriented* company. The focus is on *substance* versus form, *quality* versus quantity.

We believe in the principle that *hard work, high productivity* is something to be proud of.

The concept of *assumed responsibility* is accepted. (If a task needs to be done, assume you have the responsibility to get it done.)

Commitments are long term. If career problems occur at some point, reassignment is a better alternative than termination.

We desire to have *all employees involved and participative* in their relationship with Intel.

OVERSEEING THE STRATEGY MAKERS

Who is responsible for determining the firm's mission? Who is responsible for acquiring and allocating resources so that the firm can thoughtfully develop and implement a strategic plan? Who is responsible for monitoring the firm's success in the competitive marketplace to determine whether that plan was well designed and activated? The answer to all of these questions is "strategic decision makers." As you saw in Figure 1–3, most organizations have multiple levels of strategic decision makers; typically, the larger the firm, the more levels it will have. The strategic managers at the highest level are responsible for decisions that affect the entire firm, commit the firm and its resources for the longest periods, and declare the firm's sense of values. In other words, this group of strategic managers is responsible for overseeing the creation and accomplishment of the company mission. The term that describes the group is *board of directors*.

In overseeing the management of a firm, the board of directors operates as the representatives of the firm's stockholders. Elected by the stockholders, the board has these major responsibilities:

1. To establish and update the company mission.
2. To elect the company's top officers, the foremost of whom is the CEO.
3. To establish the compensation levels of the top officers, including their salaries and bonuses.
4. To determine the amount and timing of the dividends paid to stockholders.
5. To set broad company policy on such matters as labor-management relations, product or service lines of business, and employee benefit packages.

6. To set company objectives and to authorize managers to implement the long-term strategies that the top officers and the board have found agreeable.
7. To mandate company compliance with legal and ethical dictates.

This chapter considers the board of directors because the board's greatest impact on the behavior of a firm results from its determination of the company mission. The philosophy espoused in the mission statement sets the tone by which the firm and all of its employees will be judged. As logical extensions of the mission statement, the firm's objectives and strategies embody the board's view of proper business demeanor. Through its appointment of top executives and its decisions about their compensation, the board reveals its priorities for organizational achievement.

Board Success Factors

Shaker A. Zahra and his research colleagues have reviewed an extensive body of writings and research on the behavior of boards.[6] They conclude that boards are judged to be most successful when

1. They represent the interests of stockholders and carefully monitor the actions of senior executives to promote and protect those interests.[7]
2. They link the firm to influential stakeholders in its external environment, thereby promoting the company mission while ensuring attention to important societal concerns.[8]
3. They are composed of 8 to 12 highly qualified members.
4. They exercise independent and objective thinking in appraising the actions of senior executives and in introducing strategic changes.[9]
5. They pay special attention to their own composition to ensure an appropriate mix of inside and outside directors and the inclusion of minority representatives.[10]

---

[6]S. A. Zahra and W. W. Stanton, "The Implications of Board of Directors' Composition for Corporate Strategy and Performance," *International Journal of Management* 5, no. 2 (1988), pp. 229–36; and S. A. Zahra and J. A. Pearce II, "Boards of Directors and Corporate Financial Performance: A Review and Integrative Model," *Journal of Management* 15 (1989), pp. 291–334.

[7]P. L. Rechner and D. R. Dalton, "Board Composition and Shareholders' Wealth: An Empirical Assessment," *Strategic Management Journal,* in press.

[8]M. S. Mizruchi, "Who Controls Whom?: An Examination of the Relation between Management and Board of Directors in Large American Corporations," *Academy of Management Review,* August 1983, pp. 426–35.

[9]T. M. Jones and L. D. Goldberg, "Governing the Large Corporation: More Arguments for Public Directors," *Academy of Management Review* 7 (1982), pp. 603–11.

[10]I. F. Kesner, "Directors' Characteristics and Committee Membership: An Investigation of Type, Occupation, Tenure, and Gender," *Academy of Management Journal,* 31 (1988), pp. 66–84; and J. A. Pearce II, "The Relationship of Internal versus External Orientations to Financial Measures of Strategic Performance," *Strategic Management Journal* 4 (1983), pp. 297–306.

6. They have a well-developed structure; that is, they are organized into appropriate committees to perform specialized tasks, (e.g., to review executive compensation and to audit the company's financial transactions).[11]
7. They meet frequently to discuss progress in achieving organizational goals and to provide counsel to executives.[12]
8. They evaluate the CEO's performance at least annually to provide guidance on issues of leadership style.[13]
9. They conduct strategy reviews to determine the fit between the firm's strategy and the requirements of its competitive environment.[14]
10. They formulate the ethical codes that are to govern the behavior of the firm's executives and employees.[15]
11. They promote a future-oriented outlook on the company mission by challenging executives to articulate their visions for the firm and for its interface with society.

These criteria can enable board members, CEOs, and stockholders to judge board behavior. The question "What should boards do?" can be largely answered by studying the criteria.

THE STAKEHOLDER APPROACH TO COMPANY RESPONSIBILITY

In defining or redefining the company mission, strategic managers must recognize the legitimate rights of the firm's claimants. These include not only stockholders and employees but also outsiders affected by the firm's actions. Such outsiders commonly include customers, suppliers, governments, unions, competitors, local communities, and the general public. Each of these interest groups has justifiable reasons for expecting, and often for demanding that the firm satisfy their claims in a responsible manner. In general, stockholders claim appropriate returns on their investment; employees seek broadly de-

---

[11]R. Molz, "Managerial Domination of Boards of Directors and Financial Performance," *Journal of Business Research* 16 (1988), pp. 235–50.

[12]A. Tashakori and W. Boulton "A Look at the Board's Role Planning," *Journal of Business Strategy* 3, no. 3 (1985), pp. 64–70.

[13]R. Nader, "Reforming Corporate Governance," *California Management Review,* Winter 1984, pp. 126–32.

[14]J. R. Harrison, "The Strategic Use of Corporate Board Committees," *California Management Review* 30 (1987), pp. 109–25; and J. W. Henke, Jr., "Involving the Board of Directors in Strategic Planning," *Journal of Business Strategy* 7, no. 2 (1986), pp. 87–95.

[15]K. R. Andrews, *The Concept of Corporate Strategy* (Homewood, Ill.: Dow Jones-Irwin, 1987).

fined job satisfactions; customers want what they pay for; suppliers seek dependable buyers; governments want adherence to legislation; unions seek benefits for their members; competitors want fair competition; local communities want the firm to be a responsible citizen; and the general public expects the firm's existence to improve the quality of life.

However, when a firm attempts to incorporate the interests of these groups into its mission statement, broad generalizations are insufficient. These steps need to be taken:

1. Identification of the stakeholders.
2. Understanding the stakeholders' specific claims vis-à-vis the firm.
3. Reconciliation of these claims and assignment of priorities to them.
4. Coordination of the claims with other elements of the company mission.

Identification   The left-hand column of Figure 2–1 lists the commonly encountered stakeholder groups, to which the executive officer group is often added. Obviously, though, every business faces a slightly different set of stakeholder groups, which vary in number, size, influence, and importance. In defining the company, strategic managers must identify all of the stakeholder groups and weight their relative rights and their relative ability to affect the firm's success.

Understanding   The concerns of the principal stakeholder groups tend to center on the general claims listed in the right-hand column of Figure 2–1. However, strategic decision makers should understand the specific demands of each group. They will then be better able to initiate actions that satisfy these demands.

Reconciliation and Priorities   Unfortunately, the claims of various stakeholder groups often conflict. For example, the claims of governments and the general public tend to limit profitability, which is the central claim of most creditors and stockholders. Thus, claims must be reconciled in a mission statement that resolves the competing, conflicting, and contradictory claims of stakeholders. For objectives and strategies to be internally consistent and precisely focused, the statement must display a single-minded, though multidimensional, approach to the firm's aims.

There are hundreds, if not thousands, of claims on any firm—high wages, pure air, job security, product quality, community service, taxes, occupational health and safety regulations, equal employment opportunity regulations, product variety, wide markets, career opportunities, company growth, investment security, high ROI, and many, many more. Although most, perhaps all, of these claims may be desirable ends, they cannot be pursued with equal emphasis. They must be assigned priorities in accordance with the relative emphasis that the firm will give them. That emphasis is reflected in the criteria that the firm uses in its strategic decision making; in the firm's allocation of its human, financial, and physical resources; and in the firm's long-term objectives and strategies.

FIGURE 2–1
A Stakeholder View of Company Responsibility

Stakeholder	Nature of the Claim
Stockholders	Participation in distribution of profits, additional stock offerings, assets on liquidation; vote of stock; inspection of company books; transfer of stock; election of board of directors; and such additional rights as have been established in the contract with the corporation.
Creditors	Legal proportion of interest payments due and return of principal from the investment. Security of pledged assets; relative priority in event of liquidation. Management and owner prerogatives if certain conditions exist with the company (such as default of interest payments).
Employees	Economic, social, and psychological satisfaction in the place of employment. Freedom from arbitrary and capricious behavior on the part of company officials. Share in fringe benefits, freedom to join union and participate in collective bargaining, individual freedom in offering up their services through an employment contract. Adequate working conditions.
Customers	Service provided with the product; technical data to use the product; suitable warranties; spare parts to support the product during use; R&D leading to product improvement; facilitation of credit.
Suppliers	Continuing source of business; timely consummation of trade credit obligations; professional relationship in contracting for, purchasing, and receiving goods and services.
Governments	Taxes (income, property, etc.); adherence to the letter and intent of public policy dealing with the requirements of fair and free competition; discharge of legal obligations of businesspeople (and business organizations); adherence to antitrust laws.
Unions	Recognition as the negotiating agent for employees. Opportunity to perpetuate the union as a participant in the business organization.
Competitors	Observation of the norms for competitive conduct established by society and the industry. Business statesmanship on the part of peers.
Local communities	Place of productive and healthful employment in the community. Participation of company officials in community affairs, provision of regular employment, fair play, reasonable portion of purchases made in the local community, interest in and support of local government, support of cultural and charitable projects.
The general public	Participation in and contribution to society as a whole; creative communications between governmental and business units designed for reciprocal understanding; assumption of fair proportion of the burden of government and society. Fair price for products and advancement of the state-of-the-art technology that the product line involves.

Source: William R. King and David I. Cleland, *Strategic Planning and Policy.* © 1978 by Litton Educational Publishing Inc., p. 153. Reprinted by permission of Van Nostrand Reinhold Company.

Coordination with Other Elements The demands of stakeholder groups constitute only one principal set of inputs to the company mission. The other principal sets are the managerial operating philosophy and the determinants of the product-market offering. Those determinants constitute a reality test that the accepted claims must pass. The key question is: How can the firm satisfy its claimants and at the same time optimize its success in the marketplace?

Social Responsibility

As indicated by Figure 2–2, the various stakeholders of a firm can be divided into inside stakeholders and outside stakeholders. The insiders are the individuals or groups that are stockholders or employees of the firm. The outsiders are all the other individuals or groups that the firm's actions affect. The extremely large and often amorphous set of outsiders makes the general claim that the firm be socially responsible.[16]

Perhaps the thorniest issues faced in defining a company mission are those that pertain to responsibility. The stakeholder approach offers the clearest perspective on such issues. Broadly stated, outsiders often demand that insiders' claims be subordinated to the greater good of the society, that is, to the greater good of outsiders. They believe that such issues as pollution, the disposal of solid and liquid wastes, and the conservation of natural resources should be principal considerations in strategic decision making. Also broadly stated, insiders tend to believe that the competing claims of outsiders should be balanced against one another in a way that protects the company mission. For example, they tend to believe that the need of consumers for a product should be balanced against the water pollution resulting from its production if the firm cannot eliminate that pollution entirely and still remain profitable. Some insiders also argue that the claims of society, as expressed in government regulation, provide tax money that can be used to eliminate water pollution and the like if the general public wants this to be done.

The issues are numerous, complex, and contingent on specific situations. Thus, rigid rules of business conduct cannot deal with them. Each firm must decide how to meet its perceived social responsibility. Different approaches adopted by different firms reflect differences in competitive position, industry, country, environmental and ecological pressures, and a host of other factors. In other words, they will reflect both situational factors and differing priorities in the acknowledgment of claims.

FIGURE 2–2
Inputs to the Development of the Company Mission

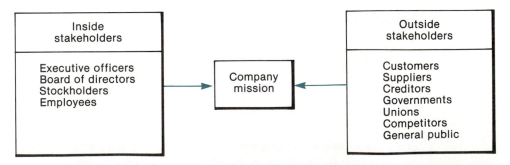

---

[16]Jeffrey S. Bracker and Angelo J. Kinicki, "Strategic Management, Plant Closings, and Social Responsibility: An Integrative Process Model," *Employee Responsibilities and Rights Journal* 1, no, 3 (1988), pp. 201–13.

Despite differences in their approaches, most American firms now try to assure outsiders that they attempt to conduct business in a socially responsible manner. Many firms, including Abt Associates, Dow Chemical, Eastern Gas and Fuel Associates, Exxon, and the Bank of America, conduct and publish annual social audits. Elements of the social audit published in Exxon's 1988 annual report are given in Strategy in Action 2–4. Such audits attempt to evaluate the firm from the perspective of social responsibility. Private consultants often conduct them for the firm and offer minimally biased evaluations on what are inherently highly subjective issues.

Guidelines for a Socially Responsible Firm

After decades of public debate on the social responsibility of business, the individual firm must still struggle to determine its own orientation. However, public debate and business concern have led to a jelling of perspectives. Sawyer has provided an excellent summary of guidelines for a socially responsible firm that is consistent with the stakeholder approach:

1. The purpose of the business is to make a profit; its managers should strive for the optimal profit that can be achieved over the long run.
2. No true profits can be claimed until business costs are paid. This includes all social costs, as determined by detailed analysis of the social balance between the firm and society.
3. If there are social costs in areas where no objective standards for correction yet exist, managers should generate corrective standards. These standards should be based on the managers' judgment of what ought to exist and should simultaneously encourage individual involvement of firm members in developing necessary social standards.
4. Where competitive pressure or economic necessity precludes socially responsible action, the business should recognize that its operation is depleting social capital and, therefore, represents a loss. It should attempt to restore profitable operation through either better management, if the problem is internal, or by advocating corrective legislation, if society is suffering as a result of the way that the rules for business competition have been made.[17]

SUMMARY

Defining the company mission is one of the most often slighted tasks in strategic management. Emphasizing the operational aspects of long-range management activities comes much more easily for most executives. But the critical role of the mission statement is repeatedly demonstrated by failing firms whose short-run actions have been at odds with their long-run purposes.

[17]G. E. Sawyer, *Business and Society: Managing Corporate Social Impact* (Boston: Houghton Mifflin, 1979), p. 401.

STRATEGY
IN ACTION
2–4

EQUAL EMPLOYMENT OPPORTUNITY/ CONTRIBUTION AT EXXON

STEADY PROGRESS FOR WOMEN AND MINORITIES

The percentage of women in Exxon's U.S. work force grew from 25.3 to 25.9 percent, while minority groups increased from 22.5 to 22.9 percent.

At year-end, minorities held 11.4 percent of managerial assignments compared with 10.3 percent, while minority groups increased from 11.5 to 11.7 percent.

Women employees held 10 percent of managerial posts, compared with 8.9 percent last year, while the women's share of professional jobs rose from 18.9 to 19.5 percent.

The focus on recruitment of minorities and women was expanded through summer jobs, co-op assignments, and scholarships.

EXXON GRANTED $49 MILLION TO NON-PROFIT ORGANIZATIONS, INCLUDING $35 MILLION IN THE UNITED STATES

Educational institutions and programs accounted for 59 percent of total U.S. grants. To encourage support for higher education for minority students, the Exxon Education Foundation amended its matching gift program. Employees and annuitants may now make gifts to three organizations with

Source: Exxon 1988 annual report to stockholders.

The principal value of the mission statement is its specification of the firm's ultimate aims. A firm gains a heightened sense of purpose when its board of directors and its top executives address these issues: "What business are we in?" "What customers do we serve?" "Why does this organization exist?" However, the potential contribution of the company mission can be undermined if platitudes or ambiguous generalizations are accepted in response to these questions. It is not enough to say that Lever Brothers is in the business of "making anything that cleans anything" or that Polaroid is committed to businesses that deal with "the interaction of light and matter." Only if a firm clearly articulates its long-term intentions can its goals serve as a basis for shared expectations, planning, and performance evaluation.

A mission statement that is developed from this perspective provides managers with a unity of direction transcending individual, parochial, and temporary needs. It promotes a sense of shared expectations among all levels and generations of employees. It consolidates values over time and across individuals and interest groups. It projects a sense of worth and intent that can be identified and assimilated by outside stakeholders that is, customers, suppliers, competitors, local committees, and the general public. Finally, it asserts the firm's commitment to responsible action in symbiosis with the preservation which the donors or their families may have had no prior affiliation. Those educational fits will be matched three-to-one by the Foundation. The three organizations are the United Negro College Fund, the American Indian College Fund, and the Hispanic Association of Colleges and Universities.

A solid grounding in mathematics is a critical asset in many careers in industry. The Exxon Education Foundation began a program in 1988 with these main goals: To foster use of college-level math teaching resources and to address major national math education policy issues.

In its elementary school program, the Foundation's initial 1988 K–3 (kindergarten through third grade) math specialist Planning Grants went to some 50 school districts across America, representing a cross-section of rural, suburban, and inner-city schools. Grantees are now seeking more effective approaches for improving math teaching and learning in these early, formative years.

Of the 24 percent of Exxon's U.S. contributions that were directed to health, welfare, and community serve programs, a number addressed problems common to the nation's inner cities. A $50,000 grant was made to the Institute on Black Chemical Abuse in St. Paul, Minnesota, to help develop a national technical assistance, training, and information center.

A $200,000 grant was made to the Environmental and Occupational Health Sciences Institute, a joint program of Rutgers University and the University of Medicine and Dentistry of New Jersey. This grant will contribute to a better understanding of how the environment affects human health.

and protection of the essential claims of insider stakeholders—survival, growth, and profitability.

QUESTIONS FOR DISCUSSION

1. Reread Nicor, Inc.'s mission statement in Strategy in Action 2–1. List five insights into Nicor that you feel you gained from knowing its mission.

2. Locate the mission statement of a company not mentioned in the chapter. Where did you find it? Was it presented as a consolidated statement, or were you forced to assemble it yourself from various publications of the firm? How many of the mission statement elements outlined in this chapter were discussed or revealed in the statement you found?

3. Prepare a one- or two-page typewritten mission statement for your school of business or for a firm selected by your instructor.

4. List five potentially vulnerable areas of a firm without a stated company mission.

5. The partial social audit shown in Strategy in Action 2–4 included only a few of the possible indicators of a firm's social responsibility performance. Name five other potentially valuable indicators, and describe how company performance in each could be measured.

6. Define the term *social responsibility*. Find an example of a company action that was legal but not socially responsible. Defend your example on the basis of your definition.

BIBLIOGRAPHY

Ackoff, R. "Mission Statements." *Planning Review,* July–August 1987, pp. 30–32.

Alexander, G., and R. Bucholtz. "Corporate Social Responsibility and Stock Market Performance." *Academy of Management Journal* 21 (1978), pp. 479–86.

Andrews, K. R. *The Concept of Corporate Strategy*. Homewood, Ill.: Dow Jones-Irwin, 1987.

Aupperle, K.; A. Carroll; and J. Hatfield. "An Empirical Examination of the Relationship between Corporate Social Responsibility and Profitability." *Academy of Management Journal* 28 (1985), pp. 446–63.

Bracker, J. S., and A. J. Kinicki. "Strategic Management, Plant Closings, and Social Responsibility: An Integrative Process Model." *Employee Responsibilities and Rights Journal* 1, no. 3 (1988), pp. 201–13.

Byars, L. "Organizational Philosophy and Mission Statements." *Planning Review,* July–August 1987, pp. 32–36.

Cadbury, A. "Ethical Managers Make Their Own Rules." *Harvard Business Review,* September–October 1987, pp. 69–73.

Carroll, A. B. "In Search of the Moral Manager." *Business Horizons,* March–April 1987, pp. 7–15.

Castaldi, R., and M. S. Wortman. "Board of Directors in Small Corporations: An Untapped Resource." *American Journal of Small Business* 9, no. 2 (1984), pp. 1–11.

Chaganti, R.; V. Mahajan; and S. Sharman. "Corporate Board Size, Composition and Corporate Failures in Retailing Industry." *Journal of Management Studies* 22 (1985), pp. 400–416.

Gellerman, S. W. "Why 'Good' Managers Make Bad Ethical Choices." *Harvard Business Review,* July–August 1986, pp. 85–90.

Hall, R. H. *Organization–Structure and Process*. Englewood Cliffs, N.J.: Prentice-Hall, 1972.

Harrison, J. R. "The Strategic Use of Corporate Board Committees." *California Management Review* 30 (1987), pp. 109–25.

Henke, J. W., Jr. "Involving the Board of Directors in Strategic Planning." *Journal of Business Strategy* 7, no. 2 (1986), pp. 87–95.

Hunter, J. C. "Managers Must Know the Mission: 'If It Ain't Broke, Don't Fix It.' " *Managerial Planning,* January–February 1985, pp. 18–22.

Jones, T. M. and L. D. Goldberg. "Governing the Large Corporation: More Arguments for Public Directors." *Academy of Management Review* 7 (1982), pp. 603–11

Kerr, J., and R. A. Bettis. "Boards of Directors, Top Management Compensation, and Shareholder Returns." *Academy of Management Journal* 30 (1987), pp. 645–64.

Kesner, I. F. "Directors' Characteristics and Committee Membership: An Investigation of Type, Occupation Tenure, and Gender." *Academy of Management Journal* 31 (1988), 66–84.

Kesner, I. F.; B. Victor; and B. Lamont. "Board Composition and the Commission of Illegal Acts: An Investigation of Fortune 500 Companies." *Academy of Management Journal* 29 (1986), pp. 789–899.

King, W. R., and D. I. Cleland. *Strategic Planning and Policy*. New York: Van Nostrand Reinhold, 1978.

Litzinger, W. D., and T. E. Schaefer. "Business Ethics Bogeyman: The Perpetual Paradox." *Business Horizons,* March–April 1987, pp. 16–21.

Loucks, V. R., Jr. "A CEO Looks at Ethics." *Business Horizons,* March–April 1987, pp. 2–6.

McGinnis, V. J. "The Mission Statement: A Key Step in Strategic Planning." *Business,* November–December 1981, pp. 39–43.

Mizruchi, M. S. "Who Controls Whom?: An Examination of the Relation between Management and Board of Directors in Large American Corporations." *Academy of Management Review* 8, no. 3 (1983), pp. 426–35.

Molz, R. "Managerial Domination of Boards of Directors and Financial Performance." *Journal of Business Research* 16 (1988), pp. 235–50.

Nader, R. "Reforming Corporate Governance." *California Management Review,* Winter 1984, pp. 126–32.

Ouchi, W. *Theory Z.* Reading, Mass.: Addison-Wesley Publishing, 1981.

Pearce, J. A., II. "The Relationship of Internal versus External Orientations of Financial Measures of Strategic Performance." *Strategic Management Journal* 4 (1983), pp. 297–306.

Pearce, J. A., II, and F. R. David. "Corporate Mission Statements: The Bottom Line." *Academy of Management Executive,* (May 1987), pp. 109–16.

Pearce, J. A., II; R. B. Robinson, Jr.; and Kendall Roth. "The Company Mission as a Guide to Strategic Action." In *Strategic Planning and Management Handbook,* ed. William R. King and David I. Cleland. New York: Van Nostrand Reinhold, 1987.

Rechner, P. L. and D. R. Dalton, "Board Composition and Shareholders' Wealth: An Empirical Assessment." *Strategic Management Journal,* in press.

Rosenstein, J. "Why Don't U.S. Bonds Get More Involved in Strategy?" *Long Range Planning,* June 1987, pp. 20–34.

Sawyer, G. E. *Business and Society: Managing Corporate Social Impact.* Boston: Houghton Mifflin, 1979.

Schoorman, F. D.; M. H. Brazerman; and R. S. Atkin, "Interlocking Directories: A Strategy for Reducing Environmental Uncertainty." *Academy of Management Review* 6 (1981), pp. 243–51.

Tashakori, A., and W. Boulton. "A Look at the Board's Role Planning." *Journal of Business Strategy* 3, no. 3 (1985), pp. 65–70.

Venkatraman, N., and V. Ramanujam. "Measurement of Business Performance in Strategy Research: A Comparison of Approaches." *Academy of Management Review* 11 (1986), pp. 801–14.

Want, J. H. "Corporate Mission: *Management Review,* August 1986, pp. 46–50.

Zahra, S. A., and J. A. Pearce II. "Boards of Directors and Corporate Financial Performance: A Review and Integrative Model." *Journal of Management* 15 (1989), pp. 291–334.

Zahra, S. A., and W. W. Stanton. "The Implications of Board of Directors' Composition for Corporate Strategy and Performance." *International of Management* 5, no. 2 (1988), pp. 229–36.

CHAPTER 2 COHESION CASE

DEVELOPING A COMPANY MISSION STATEMENT

In 1986, Bryson's president, Joel Stevenson, was concerned that Bryson needed a clear vision of what the company intended to be that could be used to communicate the company's purpose to a growing number of employees and areas of company activity. After several meetings with a company advisor and executives of other companies, Stevenson decided to develop a company mission statement. Stevenson had two priorities:

1. To provide a concise statement of the market focus of Bryson Industrial Services, Inc.
2. To provide broad direction for Bryson employees about their roles and priorities as they moved the company in the direction the market focus called for.

Several discussions and drafts of a mission statement ensued. In September 1986, Stevenson produced the mission statement shown below, which he promptly had reproduced as a plaque to hang on the wall of every Bryson manager's office.

The *Mission* of Bryson Industrial Services, Inc.

Bryson exists to assist businesses and selected public organizations in effectively managing their hazardous wastes and their hazardous waste-related problems.
Bryson People will always *emphasize three basic priorities as they pursue this mission:*

Serve Bryson Customers in the Safest Manner to all concerned.

Serve Bryson Customers in a manner that is within all applicable Legal Guidelines.

Serve Bryson Customers in a quality manner that maintains customer loyalty and is profitable to Bryson.

Bryson People are committed to a level of profitable, rapid growth that leads the Hazardous Waste Management Industry.

Three years later, as Bryson's managers prepared to go to their December 1989 strategic planning retreat, Dick Robinson was preparing the *Bryson Planning Handbook* for every attendee. In a questionnaire sent out two months earlier, Robinson asked each Bryson manager to evaluate Bryson's strengths and weaknesses. One response offered from several managers was the need to have a clear picture of the future direction of Bryson. Dick Robinson sought to respond to this concern within the planning notebook by editing Bryson's initial mission statement to reflect what he saw as Bryson's future direction and including it in the 1989 planning notebook. The revised mission statement Dick Robinson created follows.

The *Mission* of Bryson Industrial Services, Inc. (revised)

Bryson exists to assist businesses and selected public organizations in the South and Midwest to effectively manage their hazardous wastes and their hazardous waste-related problems where transportation, remediation, recovery, recycling, or management/engineering services provide an appropriate solution.

BRYSON PEOPLE will *always* emphasize three basic priorities as they pursue this mission:

Serve BRYSON CUSTOMERS in the SAFEST MANNER to all concerned.

Serve BRYSON CUSTOMERS in a manner that is within all applicable legal guidelines.

Serve BRYSON CUSTOMERS in a quality manner that maintains customer loyalty and is profitable to BRYSON.

BRYSON PEOPLE are committed to a level of profitable, rapid growth that establishes BRYSON as a major, southern-based competitor in the Hazardous Waste Management/Environmental Services Industry.

Now that you have seen two Bryson mission statements, we want you to evaluate them. Evaluate the initial and the revised mission statements for Bryson as a source of decision-making guidance for managers into the 1990s. Based on what you have read in Chapter 2, use the following questions to guide your evaluation:

1. You have heard the company mission defined as "a broadly framed but enduring statement of company intent. It embodies the business philosophy of strategic decision makers, implies the image the company seeks to project, reflects the company's self-concept, and indicates the principal product or service, technological approach, and primary customer needs the company will satisfy."

Evaluate each version of Bryson's mission statement for consistency with this definition.

2. Bryson's mission statements' development was essentially accomplished by two individuals. What is your evaluation of this developmental approach?

3. Write a new Bryson mission statement that you think would improve on the latest version and recommend a process to Bryson's management to have it developed and approved.

Economic Factors

Economic factors concern the nature and direction of the economy in which a firm operates. Because consumption patterns are affected by the relative affluence of various market segments, in its strategic planning each firm must consider economic trends in the segments that affect its industry. On both the national and international level, it must consider the general availability of credit, the level of disposable income, and the propensity of people to spend. Prime interest rates, inflation rates, and trends in the growth of the gross national product are other economic factors it must consider.

Until recently, the potential impact of international economic forces appeared to be severely restricted and was largely discounted. However, the emergence of new international power brokers has changed the focus of economic environmental forecasting. Among the most prominent of these power brokers are the European Economic Community (EEC or Common Market), the Organization of Petroleum Exporting Countries (OPEC), and coalitions of developing countries.

The EEC, whose members include most of the West European countries, was established by the Treaty of Rome in 1957. It has eliminated quotas and established a tariff-free trade area for industrial products among its members. By fostering intra-European economic cooperation, it has helped its member countries compete more effectively in non-European international markets.

Vying with the opening of Eastern European borders to commerce as the most significant marketplace occurrence of the 1990s has been the opening of protected markets by the European Community. Commonly referred to as EC 92, the stated goal of this cooperative effort is the elimination of all technical, physical, and fiscal barriers to the conduct of international trade in Europe by 1992. While pragmatists see the EC 92 as a concept and not a deadline, significant progress is being made each year toward the attainment of aims of the collaboration. As of early 1990, 125 of the 265 directives related to 1992 had become EC law.

Much of the excitement over EC 92 stems from the size of the market in Europe, which exceeds 320 million consumers. As Europeans' incomes rise and their tastes become less geocentric, a booming market is expected for consumer goods, from appliances to soft drinks. As evidence of their enthusiasm for the EC 92 marketplace, U.S. companies spent $20.9 billion in 1987 alone to build plants and buy companies in Europe, an amount 28 times greater than their expenditures in 1982.

Among the U.S. firms that invested heavily and early in Europe in the hope of profiting from the EC 92 developments were:

American Express, which projected a 20 percent annual growth rate in Europe in the 1990s owing to weak competition from "mom-and-pop" travel agencies.

AT&T, which completed a five-year, $27 billion deal with Italy's state-owned telephone equipment maker to overhaul the country's aging telephone system.

Federal Express, which was among the early organizers of warehousing and distribution services for European companies. Its $200 million-a-year business in Europe is forecasted to grow 80 percent annually during this decade.

Following the original EEC initiative of economic cooperation, the United States, Canada, Japan, the EEC, and other countries conducted multilateral trade negotiations in 1979 to establish rules for international trade and conduct. Those negotiations had a profound effect on almost every aspect of U.S. business activity.

In terms of impact on the United States, OPEC is at present among the most powerful international economic force. This cartel includes most of the world's major oil and gas suppliers. Its drastic price increases impeded U.S. recovery from the recession of the early 1970s and fueled inflationary fires throughout the world. Those price increases affected the U.S. automobile industry in particular by raising the fuel costs of automobile users and by giving rise to legislation on engine design and performance standards.

Third World and Fourth World countries have recently assumed a greater role in international commerce as a source of both threats and opportunities. Following OPEC's success, these countries found it economically beneficial to directly confront the established powers. Since 1974, producers of primary commodities in the developing countries have formed or greatly strengthened trade organizations to enforce higher prices and achieve larger real incomes for their members. Even developing countries not desiring or unable to form cartels now exhibit an aggressive attitude in their international economic relations. On the other hand, developing countries offer U.S. firms huge new markets for foodstuffs and capital equipment.

> The intense nationalism of the developing countries, with nearly three fourths of the world's population, represents perhaps the greatest challenge our industrialized society and multinational corporations will face in the next two decades. As one Third World expert puts it, "the vastly unequal relationship between the rich and poor nations is fast becoming the central issue of our time."[2]

All of these international forces can affect the economic well-being of—for better or worse—the U.S. business community. Consequently, firms must try to forecast the repercussions of major actions taken in both the domestic and international economic arenas. Such forecasting is a critical part of the strategic management process.

Social Factors

The social factors that affect a firm involve the beliefs, values, attitudes, opinions, and lifestyles of persons in the firm's external environment, as developed from cultural, ecological, demographic, religious, educational, and ethnic conditioning. As social attitudes change, so too does the demand for various types of clothing, books, leisure activities, and so on. Like other forces in the remote external environment, social forces are dynamic, with constant change resulting from the efforts of individuals to satisfy their desires and needs by controlling and adapting to environmental factors.

One of the most profound social changes in recent years has been the entry of large

---

[2]R. Steade, "Multinational Corporations and the Changing World Economic Order," *California Management Review,* Winter 1978, p. 5.

numbers of women into the labor market. This has not only affected the hiring and compensation policies and the resource capabilities of their employers; it has also created or greatly expanded the demand for a wide range of products and services necessitated by their absence from the home. Firms that anticipated or reacted quickly to this social change offered such products and services as convenience foods, microwave ovens, and day-care centers.

A second profound social change has been the accelerating interest of consumers and employees in quality-of-life issues. Evidence of this change is seen in recent contract negotiations. In addition to the traditional demand for increased salaries have been worker demands for such benefits as sabbaticals, flexible hours or four-day workweeks, lump-sum vacation plans, and opportunities for advanced training.

A third profound social change has been the shift in the age distribution of the population. Changing social values and a growing acceptance of improved birth control methods are expected to raise the mean age of the U.S. population, which was 27.9 in 1970, to 34.9 by the end of the 20th century. This trend will have an increasingly unfavorable impact on most producers of predominantly youth-oriented goods and will necessitate a shift in their long-range marketing strategies. Producers of hair- and skin-care preparations have already begun to adjust their research and development to reflect anticipated changes in demand.

A consequence of the changing age distribution of the population has been a sharp increase in the demands made by a growing number of senior citizens. Constrained by fixed incomes, these citizens have demanded that arbitrary and rigid policies on retirement age be modified and have successfully lobbied for tax exemptions and increases in social security benefits. Such changes have significantly altered the opportunity-risk equations of many firms—often to the benefit of firms that anticipated the changes.

Translating social change into forecasts of business effects is a difficult process at best. Nevertheless, informed estimates of the impact of such alterations as geographic shifts in populations and changing work values, ethical standards, and religious orientations can only help a strategizing firm in its attempts to prosper.

Political Factors

The direction and stability of political factors is a major consideration for managers in formulating company strategy. Political factors define the legal and regulatory parameters within which firms must operate. Political constraints are placed on firms through fair-trade decisions, antitrust laws, tax programs, minimum wage legislation, pollution and pricing policies, administrative jawboning, and many other actions aimed at protecting employees, consumers, the general public, and the environment. Since such laws and regulations are most commonly restrictive, they tend to reduce the potential profits of firms. However, some political actions are designed to benefit and protect firms. Such actions include patent laws, government subsidies, and product research grants. Thus, political factors may either limit or benefit the firms they influence.

In addition, political activity may have a significant impact on three governmental functions that influence the remote environment of firms.

Supplier Function   Government decisions regarding the accessibility of private businesses to government-owned natural resources and national stockpiles of agricultural products will profoundly affect the viability of the strategies of some firms.

Customer Function   Government demand for products and services can create, sustain, enhance, or eliminate many market opportunities. For example, in the same way that the Kennedy administration's emphasis on landing a man on the moon spawned a demand for thousands of new products, the Carter administration's emphasis on developing synthetic fuels created a demand for new skills, technologies and products, and the Reagan administration's strategic defense initiative (the "Star Wars" defense) sharply accelerated the development of laser technologies.

Competitor Function   The government can operate as an almost unbeatable competitor in the marketplace. Thus, knowledge of government's strategies gained through assessment of the remote environment can help a firm avoid unfavorable confrontation with the government as a competitor. For example, forecasts that the government will increase the number of its nuclear power plants or communications facilities might serve both as a retreat signal to direct private competitors and as an invitation to private producers of such plants and facilities.

Firms are greatly affected by government decisions, as shown in Strategy in Action 3–1. Thus, continual assessment of government strategizing will help individual firms develop complementary plans that anticipate and optimize environmental opportunities.

Technological Factors

The fourth set of factors in the remote environment involves technological change. To avoid obsolescence and promote innovation, a firm must be aware of technological changes that might influence its industry. Creative technological adaptations can suggest possibilities for new products, for improvements in existing products, or in manufacturing and marketing techniques.

A technological breakthrough can have a sudden and dramatic effect on a firm's environment. It may spawn sophisticated new markets and products or significantly shorten the anticipated life of a manufacturing facility. Thus, all firms, and most particularly those in turbulent growth industries, must strive for an understanding both of the existing technological advances and the probable future advances that can affect their products and services. This quasi science of attempting to foresee advancements and estimate their impact on an organization's operations is known as *technological forecasting*.

Technological forecasting can help protect and improve the profitability of firms in growing industries. It alerts strategic managers to both impending challenges and promising opportunities. As examples: (1) advances in xerography were a key to Xerox's success but caused major difficulties for carbon paper manufacturers and (2) the perfection of transistors changed the nature of competition in the radio and television industry, helping such giants as RCA while seriously weakening smaller firms whose resource commitments required that they continue to base their products on vacuum tubes.

A Major Threat in the Environment of Accounting Firms

"These are our own ideas and opinions, our private notes," says Robert Hermann, a tax manager with the accounting firm of Deloitte Haskins & Sells. "They are none of the IRS's business."

The Internal Revenue Service disagrees, however, and the result is a bitter controversy.

The notes in question are those in which auditors spell out any doubts they have about a client's tax position. Accountants have always considered these confidential. But now, they say, recent IRS aggressiveness in seeking these papers has undermined their relationships with their corporate clients and has threatened to damage the quality of financial reports.

Says William Raby, a partner in Touche Ross & Co., "We've seen a drying up of the willingness of clients to discuss or even show data to their auditors. And the bottom line is that it isn't leading to good financial reporting."

When preparing and auditing financial statements, accountants include a reserve for taxes that might be payable if the IRS investigates. A company may take an investment tax credit, for instance, although it realizes that the IRS could disagree. [The company's] memos, and those of its auditors, would spell out the arguments on each side.

Source: "Auditors Say IRS Demand for Documents Is Poisoning Relations with Client Firms." Reprinted by permission of *The Wall Street Journal,* © Dow Jones & Company, Inc., January 15, 1981. All rights reserved.

The key to beneficial forecasting of technological advancement lies in accurately predicting future technological capabilities and their probable impacts. A comprehensive analysis of the effect of technological change involves study of the expected impact of new technologies on the remote environment, on the competitive business situation, and on the business-society interface. In recent years, forecasting in the last area has warranted particular attention. For example, as a consequence of increased concern over the environment, firms must carefully investigate the probable effect of technological advances on quality-of-life factors, such as ecology, and public safety.

Ecological Factors

As strategic managers forecast the 1990s, the most prominent factor in the remote environment is often the reciprocal relationship between business and the ecology. The term *ecology* refers to the relationships among humans and other living things and the air, soil, and water that supports them. Threats to our life-supporting ecology caused principally by human activities in an industrial society are commonly referred to as *pollution*.

Air pollution is created by dust particles and gaseous discharges that contaminate the air. Acid rain, or rain contaminated by sulfur dioxide, which can destroy aquatic and plant life, is believed to result from coal-burning factories in 70 percent of all cases. A

But the tax credit would likely be just one of many such items, and the IRS typically sees only the grand total reserve. If [the IRS] had access to the internal documents, it could see a breakdown of all the uncertain areas.

"It's a trail to the sensitive issues on the tax return," says William T. Holloran, a New York City lawyer and accountant. He says accountants try to dream up the worst possible scenarios, but "if the IRS sees that you wondered about something, they may just say, 'Gee, there must be something wrong with it.'"

An IRS official takes a different view: "We feel that the information might throw light on the correctness of a taxpayer return." He says the memos are necessary because corporations usually are more open with accountants than with the government, "and we can't stay with a company for an unlimited period of time" ferreting out information. "The tax system shouldn't be viewed as a game of hide and seek. If we can get the papers, we can make a determination [of tax liability] much quicker, and not waste the taxpayers' money."

Most experts say that the only answer may rest with the IRS. "We can only hope that the IRS won't go bananas in this area," says Holloran. "On a normal audit, they have to show restraint."

health-threatening "thermal blanket" is created when the atmosphere traps carbon dioxide emitted from unscrubbed smokestacks in factories burning fossil fuels. This "greenhouse effect" can have disastrous consequences, making the climate unpredictable and raising temperatures. Finally, airborne carcinogens resulting from manufacturing processes have been linked to approximately 20,000 deaths each year.[3]

Water pollution occurs principally when industrial toxic wastes are dumped or leak into the nation's waterways. Since fewer than 50 percent of all municipal sewer systems are in compliance with Environmental Protection Agency requirements for water safety, contaminated waters represent a substantial present threat to public welfare.

Land pollution is most frequently caused by the disposal of industrial toxic wastes in underground sites. With approximately 90 percent of the annual U.S. output of 500 million metric tons of hazardous industrial wastes being placed in underground dumps, it is evident that land pollution and its resulting endangerment of the ecology will be a major item on the political agenda for the 1990s.

As a major contributor to ecological pollution, business is now being held responsible for eliminating the toxic by-products of its current manufacturing processes and for

---

[3]"How the EPA Plans to Live with Cancer Risks," *Business Week*, August 8, 1982, p. 84.

cleaning up the environmental damage that it did previously. Increasingly, managers are being required by the government or expected by the public to incorporate ecological concerns into their decision making.[4] Steel companies and public utilities have invested billions of dollars in costlier but cleaner-burning fuels and pollution control equipment. The automobile industry has been required to install expensive emission controls in cars. The gasoline industry has been forced to formulate new low-lead and no-lead products. And thousands of companies have found it necessary to direct their R&D resources into the search for ecologically superior products such as Sears' phosphate-free laundry detergent and Pepsi-Cola's biodegradable plastic soft-drink bottle. One company that has made major commitments to the elimination of waste from its production is Dow Chemical, whose proecology efforts are described in Strategy in Action 3–2.

Despite cleanup efforts to date, the job of protecting the ecology will continue to be a top strategic priority—usually because corporate stockholders and executives choose it, increasingly because the public and the government require it. As evidenced by Figure 3–2, the government has made numerous interventions into the conduct of business for the purpose of bettering the ecology. Such interventions will undoubtably escalate.

INDUSTRY ENVIRONMENT

Harvard professor Michael E. Porter's book *Competitive Strategy* propelled the concept of industry environment into the foreground of strategic thought and business planning. The cornerstone of the book is an article form the *Harvard Business Review* in which Porter explains the five forces that shape competition in an industry. His well-defined analytic framework helps strategic managers to link the impact of remote factors to the resulting effects on a firm's operating environment.

With the special permission of Professor Porter and the *Harvard Business Review,* we present in this section of the chapter his seminal article on the industry environment and its impact on strategic management.[5]

OVERVIEW

The nature and degree of competition in an industry hinge on five forces: the threat of new entrants, the bargaining power of customers, the bargaining power of suppliers, the threat of substitute products or services (where applicable), and the jockeying among current contestants. To establish a strategic agenda for dealing with these contending currents and to grow despite them, a company must understand how they work in its industry and how they affect the company in its particular situation. This chapter will

---

[4]Philip Kotler, *Marketing Management* (Englewood Cliffs, N.J.: Prentice-Hall, 1989), p. 98.

[5]Michael E. Porter, "How Competitive Forces Shape Strategy," *Harvard Business Review,* March–April 1979, pp. 137–45.

STRATEGY IN ACTION 3–2 — DOW'S COMMITMENT TO ECOLOGY

The following excerpt from Dow Chemical's annual report to stockholders provides evidence of Dow's concern for ecological factors. Clearly, Dow understands the impact that failure to deal with ecological issues could have on the future of its operations.

All companies exist to reward the people who invest in them, beginning with their shareholders. Yet their responsibilities extend to being good neighbors and responsible citizens.

In 1988, Dow continued to meet these broader responsibilities. In the United States alone, contributions totaled more than $20 million. About 60 percent was earmarked for educational efforts, while the remainder was largely devoted to community improvement and health programs. One of the company's single largest awards was a five-year, $2 million commitment to improve public awareness of the value of chemistry in daily life.

Dow has also demonstrated continuing worldwide concern for the environment. Since the 1960s, its policy has been to prevent waste whenever possible so that less material requires treatment and disposal. In the United States, these efforts are united under the name Waste Reduction Always Pays. It does. In 1988, the company learned that it will receive the World Environment Center's 1989 Gold Medal for International Corporate Environmental Achievement. In its award citation praising Dow's leadership in waste reduction and community involvement, the selection panel noted that Dow serves as a model for industry in protecting "the global environment for future generations."

One way to protect the environment is through recycling, and Dow is committed to showing that recycling can pay. In 1988, it signed a joint venture agreement with Montreal-based Domtar, Inc., to recycle plastics commonly found in containers for soft drinks and milk. A full-scale commercial plant, using technology licensed from Dow, could be in operation as early as 1990. Waste reduction and recycling are not Dow's only contributions to environmental quality, however. Employees have participated actively in efforts ranging from household hazardous waste collection days to bird counts. In Joliet, Illinois, the company is working to enhance its relationship with a wetlands wildlife sanctuary near one of its plants.

Dow displays the same commitment around the world. The company's largest European facility, Terneuzen, recently received the Dutch government's Environmental Award for Industry. In Portugal, the Friends of the Earth presented a similar award to Dow's Isopor plant in Estarreja.

Source: Dow Chemical 1988 annual report to stockholders.

detail how these forces operate and suggest ways of adjusting to them, and, where possible, of taking advantage of them.

HOW COMPETITIVE FORCES SHAPE STRATEGY

The essence of strategy formulation is coping with competition. Yet it is easy to view competition too narrowly and too pessimistically. While one sometimes hears executives complaining to the contrary, intense competition in an industry is neither coincidence nor bad luck.

Moreover, in the fight for market share, competition is not manifested only in the

FIGURE 3-2
Federal Ecological Legislation

CENTERPIECE LEGISLATION

National Environmental Policy Act, 1969 Established Environmental Protection Agency; consolidated federal environmental activities under it. Established Council on Environmental Quality to advise president on environmental policy and to review environmental impact statements.

AIR POLLUTION

Clean Air Act, 1963 Authorized assistance to state and local governments in formulating control programs. Authorized limited federal action in correcting specific pollution problems.

Clean Air Act Amendments (Motor Vehicle Air Pollution Control Act), 1965 Authorized federal standards for auto exhaust emission. Standards first set for 1968 models.

Air Quality Act, 1967 Authorized federal government to establish air quality control regions and to set maximum permissible pollution levels. Required states and localities to carry out approved control programs or else give way to federal controls.

Clean Air Act Amendments, 1970 Authorized EPA to establish nationwide air pollution standards and to limit the discharge of six principal pollutants into the lower atmosphere. Authorized citizens to take legal action to require EPA to implement its standards against undiscovered offenders.

Clean Air Act Amendments, 1977 Postponed auto emission requirements. Required use of scrubbers in new coal-fired power plants. Directed EPA to establish a system to prevent deterioration of air quality in clean areas.

SOLID WASTE POLLUTION

Solid Waste Disposal Act, 1965 Authorized research and assistance to state and local control programs

Resource Recovery Act, 1970 Subsidized construction of pilot recycling plants; authorized development of nationwide control programs.

Resource Conservation and Recovery Act, 1976 Directed EPA to regulate hazardous waste management, from generation through disposal.

Surface Mining and Reclamation Act, 1976 Controlled strip mining and restoration of reclaimed land.

WATER POLLUTION

Refuse Act, 1899 Prohibited dumping of debris into navigable waters without a permit. Extended by court decision to industrial discharges.

---

other players. Rather, competition in an industry is rooted in its underlying economics, and competitive forces exist that go well beyond the established combatants in a particular industry. Customers, suppliers, potential entrants, and substitute products are all competitors that may be more or less prominent or active depending on the industry.

The state of competition in an industry depends on five basic forces, which are diagramed in Figure 3–3. The collective strength of these forces determines the ultimate profit potential of an industry. It ranges from intense in industries like tires, metal cans,

FIGURE 3–2 (concluded)

Federal Water Pollution Control Act, 1956   Authorized grants to states for water pollution control. Gave federal government limited authority to correct specific pollution problems.

Water Quality Act, 1965   Provided for adoption of water quality standards by states, subject to federal approval.

Water Quality Improvement Act, 1970   Provided for federal cleanup of oil spills. Strengthened federal authority over water pollution control.

Federal Water Pollution Control Act Amendments, 1972   Authorized EPA to set water quality and effluent standards; provided for enforcement and research.

Safe Drinking Water Act, 1974   Set standards for drinking water quality.

Clean Water Act, 1977   Ordered control of toxic pollutants by 1984 with best available technology economically feasible.

OTHER POINTS

Federal Insecticide, Fungicide and Rodenticide Act, 1947   To protect farmers, prohibited fraudulent claims by salespersons. Required registration of poisonous products.

Federal Insecticide, Fungicide, and Rodenticide Amendments, 1967, 1972   Provided new authority to license users of pesticides.

Pesticide Control Act, 1972   Required all pesticides shipped in interstate commerce to be certified as effective for their stated purposes and harmless to crops, animal feed, animal life, and humans.

Noise Control Act, 1972   Required EPA to set noise standards for major sources of noise and to advise Federal Aviation Administration on standards for airplane noise.

Federal Environmental Pesticide Control Act Amendments, 1975   Set 1977 deadline (not met) for registration, classification, and licensing of many pesticides.

Toxic Substances Control Act, 1976   Required testing of chemicals; authorized EPA to restrict the use of harmful substances.

Comprehensive Environmental Response, Compensation, and Liability Act, 1980   Commonly called "Superfund Act"; created a trust fund (paid for in part by toxic-chemical manufacturers) to clean up hazardous waste sites.

and steel, where no company earns spectacular returns on investment, to mild in industries like oil-field services and equipment, soft drinks, and toiletries, where there is room for quite high returns.

In the economists' "perfectly competitive" industry, jockeying for position is unbridled and entry to the industry very easy. This kind of industry structure, of course, offers the worst prospect for long-run profitability. The weaker the forces collectively, however, the greater the opportunity for superior performance.

FIGURE 3–3
Forces Driving Industry Competition

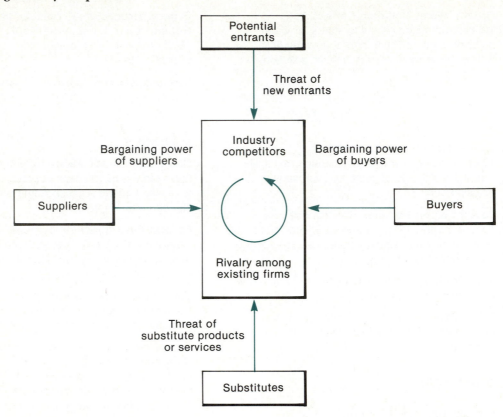

Whatever their collective strength, the corporate strategist's goal is to find a position in the industry where his or her company can best defend itself against these forces or can influence them in its favor. The collective strength of the forces may be painfully apparent to all the antagonists; but to cope with them, the strategist must delve below the surface and analyze the sources of competition. For example, what makes the industry vulnerable to entry? What determines the bargaining power of suppliers?

Knowledge of these underlying sources of competitive pressure provides the groundwork for a strategic agenda of action. They highlight the critical strengths and weaknesses of the company, animate the positioning of the company in its industry, clarify the areas where strategic changes may yield the greatest payoff, and highlight the places where industry trends promise to hold the greatest significance as either opportunities or threats.

Understanding these sources also proves to be of help in considering areas for diversification.

CONTENDING FORCES

The strongest competitive force or forces determine the profitability of an industry and so are of greatest importance in strategy formulation. For example, even a company with a strong position in an industry unthreatened by potential entrants will earn low returns if it faces a superior or a lower-cost substitute product—as the leading manufacturers of vacuum tubes and coffee percolators have learned to their sorrow. In such a situation, coping with the substitute product becomes the number one strategic priority.

Different forces take on prominence, of course, in shaping competition in each industry. In the oceangoing tanker industry the key force is probably the buyers (the major oil companies), while in tires it is powerful OEM buyers coupled with tough competitors. In the steel industry the key forces are foreign competitors and substitute materials.

Every industry has an underlying structure, or a set of fundamental economic and technical characteristics, that gives rise to these competitive forces. The strategist, wanting to position his company to cope best with its industry environment or to influence that environment in the company's favor, must learn what makes the environment tick.

This view of competition pertains equally to industries dealing in services and to those selling products. To avoid monotony in this article, I refer to both products and services as "products." The same general principles apply to all types of business.

A few characteristics are critical to the strength of each competitive force. They will be discussed in this section.

Threat of Entry

New entrants to an industry bring new capacity, the desire to gain market share, and often substantial resources. Companies diversifying through acquisition into the industry from other markets often leverage their resources to cause a shape-up, as Philip Morris did with Miller beer.

The seriousness of the threat of entry depends on the barriers present and on the reaction from existing competitors that the entrant can expect. If barriers to entry are high and a newcomer can expect sharp retaliation from the entrenched competitors, obviously he will not pose a serious threat of entering.

There are six major sources of barriers to entry:

1. Economies of Scale   These economies deter entry by forcing the aspirant either to come in on a large scale or to accept a cost disadvantage. Scale economies in production, research, marketing, and service are probably the key barriers to entry in the mainframe computer industry, as Xerox and GE sadly discovered. Economies of scale can also act as hurdles in distribution, utilization of the sales force, financing, and nearly any other part of a business.

2. Product Differentiation   Brand identification creates a barrier by forcing entrants to spend heavily to overcome customer loyalty. Advertising, customer service, being first in the industry, and product differences are among the factors fostering brand identifi-

THE EXPERIENCE CURVE AS AN ENTRY BARRIER

In recent years, the experience curve has become widely discussed as a key element of industry structure. According to this concept, unit costs in many manufacturing industries (some dogmatic adherents say in all manufacturing industries) as well as in some service industries decline with "experience," or a particular company's cumulative volume of production. (The experience curve, which encompasses many factors, is a broader concept than the better-known learning curve, which refers to the efficiency achieved over a period of time by workers through much repetition.)

The causes of the decline in unit costs are a combination of elements, including economies of scale, the learning curve for labor, and capital-labor substitution. The cost decline creates a barrier to entry because new competitors with no "experience" face higher costs than established ones, particularly the producer with the largest market share, and have difficulty catching up with the entrenched competitors.

Adherents of the experience curve concept stress the importance of achieving market leadership to maximize this barrier to entry, and they recommend aggressive action to achieve it, such as price cutting in anticipation of falling costs in order to build volume. For the combatant that cannot achieve a healthy market share, the prescription is usually, "Get out."

Is the experience curve an entry barrier on which strategies should be built? The answer is: not in every industry. In fact, in some industries, building a strategy on the experience curve can be potentially disastrous. That costs decline with experience in some industries is not news to corporate executives. The significance of the experience curve for strategy depends on what factors are causing the decline.

A new entrant may well be more efficient than the more experienced competitors; if it has built the newest plant, it will face no disadvantage in having to catch up. The strategic prescription,

cation. It is perhaps the most important entry barrier in soft drinks, over-the-counter drugs, cosmetics, investment banking, and public accounting. To create high fences around their business, brewers couple brand identification with economies of scale in production, distribution, and marketing.

3. Capital Requirements   The need to invest large financial resources in order to compete creates a barrier to entry, particularly if the capital is required for unrecoverable expenditures in up-front advertising or R&D. Capital is necessary not only for fixed facilities but also for customer credit, inventories, and absorbing start-up losses. While major corporations have the financial resources to invade almost any industry, the huge capital requirements in certain fields, such as computer manufacturing and mineral extraction, limit the pool of likely entrants.

4. Cost Disadvantages Independent of Size   Entrenched companies may have cost advantages not available to potential rivals, no matter what their size and attainable economies

"You must have the largest, most efficient plant," is a lot different from "You must produce the greatest cumulative output of the item to get your costs down."

Whether a drop in costs with cumulative (not absolute) volume erects an entry barrier also depends on the sources of the decline. If costs go down because of technical advances known generally in the industry or because of the development of improved equipment that can be copied or purchased from equipment suppliers, the experience curve is not an entry barrier at all—in fact, new or less experienced competitors may actually enjoy a cost advantage over the leaders. Free of the legacy of heavy past investments, the newcomer or less experienced competitor can purchase or copy the newest and lowest-cost equipment and technology.

If, however, experience can be kept proprietary, the leaders will maintain a cost advantage. But new entrants may require less experience to reduce their costs than the leaders needed. All this suggests that the experience curve can be a shaky entry barrier on which to build a strategy.

While space does not permit a complete treatment here, I want to mention a few other crucial elements in determining the appropriateness of a strategy built on the entry barrier provided by the experience curve:

The height of the barrier depends on how important costs are to competition compared with other areas like marketing, selling, and innovation.

The barrier can be nullified by product or process innovations leading to a substantially new technology and thereby creating an entirely new experience curve. New entrants can leapfrog the industry leaders and alight on the new experience curve, to which those leaders may be poorly positioned to jump.

If more than one strong company is building its strategy on the experience curve, the consequences can be nearly fatal. By the time only one rival is left pursuing such a strategy, industry growth may have stopped and the prospects of reaping the spoils of victory long since evaporated.

of scale. These advantages can stem from the effects of the learning curve (and of its first cousin, the experience curve), proprietary technology, access to the best raw materials sources, assets purchased at preinflation prices, government subsidies, or favorable locations. Sometimes cost advantages are legally enforceable, as they are through patents. (For analysis of the much-discussed experience curve as a barrier to entry, see Strategy in Action 3–3.)

5. Access to Distribution Channels   The new boy on the block must, of course, secure distribution of his product or service. A new food product, for example, must displace others from the supermarket shelf via price breaks, promotions, intense selling efforts, or some other means. The more limited the wholesale or retail channels are and the more that existing competitors have these tied up, obviously the tougher that entry into the industry will be. Sometimes this barrier is so high that, to surmount it, a new contestant must create its own distribution channels, as Timex did in the watch industry in the 1950s.

6. Government Policy   The government can limit or even foreclose entry to industries with such controls as license requirements and limits on access to raw materials. Regulated industries like trucking, liquor retailing, and freight forwarding are noticeable examples; more subtle government restrictions operate in fields like ski-area development and coal mining. The government also can play a major indirect role by affecting entry barriers through controls such as air and water pollution standards and safety regulations.

The potential rival's expectations about the reaction of existing competitors also will influence its decision on whether to enter. The company is likely to have second thoughts if incumbents have previously lashed out at new entrants or if:

> The incumbents possess substantial resources to fight back, including excess cash and unused borrowing power, productive capacity, or clout with distribution channels and customers.

> The incumbents seem likely to cut prices because of a desire to keep market shares or because of industrywide excess capacity.

> Industry growth is slow, affecting its ability to absorb the new arrival and probably causing the financial performance of all the parties involved to decline.

Powerful Suppliers and Buyers

Suppliers can exert bargaining power on participants in an industry by raising prices or reducing the quality of purchased goods and services. Powerful suppliers can thereby squeeze profitability out of an industry unable to recover cost increases in its own prices. By raising their prices, soft-drink concentrate producers have contributed to the erosion of profitability of bottling companies because the bottlers, facing intense competition from powdered mixes, fruit drinks, and other beverages have limited freedom to raise their prices accordingly. Customers likewise can force down prices, demand higher quality or more service, and play competitors off against each other—all at the expense of industry profits.

The power of each important supplier or buyer group depends on a number of characteristics of its market situation and on the relative importance of its sales or purchases to the industry compared with its overall business.

A *supplier* group is powerful if:

> It is dominated by a few companies and is more concentrated than the industry it sells to.

> Its product is unique or at least differentiated, or if it has built up switching costs. Switching costs are fixed costs buyers face in changing suppliers. These arise because, among other things, a buyer's product specifications tie it to particular suppliers, it has invested heavily in specialized ancillary equipment or in learning how to operate a supplier's equipment (as in computer software), or its production lines are connected to the supplier's manufacturing facilities (as in some manufacturing of beverage containers).

> It is not obliged to contend with other products for sale to the industry. For in-

stance, the competition between the steel companies and the aluminum companies to sell to the can industry checks the power of each supplier.

It poses a credible threat of integrating forward into the industry's business. This provides a check against the industry's ability to improve the terms on which it purchases.

The industry is not an important customer of the supplier group. If the industry is an important customer, suppliers' fortunes will be closely tied to the industry, and they will want to protect the industry through reasonable pricing and assistance in activities like R&D and lobbying.

A *buyer* group is powerful if:

It is concentrated or purchases in large volumes. Large-volume buyers are particularly potent forces if heavy fixed costs characterize the industry—as they do in metal containers, corn refining, and bulk chemicals, for example—which raise the stakes to keep capacity filled.

The products it purchases from the industry are standard or undifferentiated. The buyers, sure that they can always find alternative suppliers, may play one company against another, as they do in aluminum extrusion.

The products it purchases from the industry form a component of its product and represent a significant fraction of its cost. The buyers are likely to shop for a favorable price and purchase selectively. Where the product sold by the industry in question is a small fraction of buyers' costs, buyers are usually much less price sensitive.

It earns low profits, which create great incentive to lower its purchasing costs. Highly profitable buyers, however, are generally less price sensitive (that is, of course, if the item does not represent a large fraction of their costs).

The industry's product is unimportant to the quality of the buyers' products or services. Where the quality of the buyers' products is very much affected by the industry's product, buyers are generally less price sensitive. Industries in which this situation exists include oil-field equipment, where a malfunction can lead to large losses; and enclosures for electronic medical and test instruments, where the quality of the enclosure can influence the user's impression about the quality of the equipment inside.

The industry's product does not save the buyer money. Where the industry's product or service can pay for itself many times over, the buyer is rarely price sensitive; rather, he is interested in quality. This is true in services like investment banking and public accounting, where errors in judgment can be costly and embarrassing, and in businesses like the logging of oil wells, where an accurate survey can save thousands of dollars in drilling costs.

The buyers pose a credible threat of integrating backward to make the industry's product. The Big Three auto producers and major buyers of cars have often used the threat of self-manufacture as a bargaining lever. But sometimes an industry engenders a threat to buyers that its members may integrate forward.

Most of these sources of buyer power can be attributed to consumers as a group as well as to industrial and commercial buyers; only a modification of the frame of reference is necessary. Consumers tend to be more price sensitive if they are purchasing products that are undifferentiated, expensive relative to their incomes, and of a sort where quality is not particularly important.

The buying power of retailers is determined by the same rules, with one important addition. Retailers can gain significant bargaining power over manufacturers when they can influence consumers' purchasing decisions, as they do in audio components, jewelry, appliances, sporting goods, and other goods.

Substitute Products

By placing a ceiling on prices it can charge, substitute products or services limit the potential of an industry. Unless it can upgrade the quality of the product or differentiate it somehow (as via marketing), the industry will suffer in earnings and possibly in growth.

Manifestly, the more attractive the price-performance trade-off offered by substitute products, the firmer the lid placed on the industry's profit potential. Sugar producers confronted with the large-scale commercialization of high-fructose corn syrup, a sugar substitute, are learning this lesson today.

Substitutes not only limit profits in normal times, they also reduce the bonanza an industry can reap in boom times. In 1978 the producers of fiberglass insulation enjoyed unprecedented demand as a result of high energy costs and severe winter weather. But the industry's ability to raise prices was tempered by the plethora of insulation substitutes, including cellulose, rock wool, and styrofoam. These substitutes are bound to become an even stronger force once the current round of plant additions by fiberglass insulation producers has boosted capacity enough to meet demand (and then some).

Substitute products that deserve the most attention strategically are those that *(a)* are subject to trends improving their price-performance trade-off with the industry's product or *(b)* are produced by industries earning high profits. Substitutes often come rapidly into play if some development increases competition in their industries and causes price reduction or performance improvement.

Jockeying for Position

Rivalry among existing competitors takes the familiar form of jockeying for position—using tactics like price competition, product introduction, and advertising slugfests. Intense rivalry is related to the presence of a number of factors:

Competitors are numerous or are roughly equal in size and power. In many U.S. industries in recent years, foreign contenders, of course, have become part of the competitive picture.

Industry growth is slow, precipitating fights for market share that involve expansion-minded members.

The product or service lacks differentiation or switching costs, which lock in buyers and protect one combatant from raids on its customers by another.

Fixed costs are high or the product is perishable, creating strong temptation to cut prices. Many basic materials businesses, like paper and aluminum, suffer from this problem when demand slackens.

Capacity is normally augmented in large increments. Such additions, as in the chlorine and vinyl chloride businesses, disrupt the industry's supply-demand balance and often lead to periods of overcapacity and price cutting.

Exit barriers are high. Exit barriers, like very specialized assets or management's loyalty to a particular business, keep companies competing even though they may be earning low or even negative returns on investment. Excess capacity remains functioning, and the profitability of the healthy competitors suffers as the sick ones hang on. If the entire industry suffers from overcapacity, it may seek government help—particularly if foreign competition is present.

The rivals are diverse in strategies, origins, and "personalities." They have different ideas about how to compete and continually run head-on into each other in the process.

As an industry matures, its growth rate changes, resulting in declining profits and (often) a shakeout. In the booming recreational vehicle industry of the early 1970s, nearly every producer did well; but slow growth since then has eliminated the high returns, except for the strongest members, not to mention many of the weaker companies. The same profit story has been played out in industry after industry—snowmobiles, aerosol packaging, and sports equipment are just a few examples.

An acquisition can introduce a very different personality to an industry, as has been the case with Black & Decker's takeover of McCullough, the producer of chain saws. Technological innovation can boost the level of fixed costs in the production process, as it did in the shift from batch to continuous-line photo finishing in the 1960s.

While a company must live with many of these factors—because they are built into the industry economics—it may have some latitude for improving matters through strategic shifts. For example, it may try to raise buyers' switching costs or increase product differentiation. A focus on selling efforts in the fastest-growing segments of the industry or on market areas with the lowest fixed costs can reduce the impact of industry rivalry. If it is feasible, a company can try to avoid confrontation with competitors having high exit barriers and can thus sidestep involvement in bitter price cutting.

INDUSTRY ANALYSIS AND COMPETITIVE ANALYSIS

Designing viable strategies for a firm requires a thorough understanding of the firm's industry and competition. The firm's executives need to address four questions: (1) What are the boundaries of the industry? (2) What is the structure of the industry? (3) Which firms are our competitors? and (4) What are the major determinants of competition? The answers to these questions provide a basis for thinking about the appropriate strategies that are open to the firm.

Industry Boundaries

An industry is a collection of firms that offer similar products or services. (By "similar products," we mean products that customers perceive to be substitutable for one another.) Consider, for example, the brands of personal computers (PCs) that are now being marketed. The firms that produce these PCs, such as ATT, IBM, Apple, and Compaq form the nucleus of the microcomputer industry.

Suppose a firm competes in the microcomputer industry. Where do the boundaries of this industry begin and end? Does the industry include desktops? Laptops? These are the kinds of questions that executives face in defining industry boundaries.

Why is a definition of industry boundaries important? First, it helps executives determine the arena in which their firm is competing. A firm competing in the microcomputer industry participates in an environment very different from that of the broader electronics business. The microcomputer industry comprises several related product families, including personal computers, inexpensive computers for home use, and workstations. The unifying characteristic of these product families is the use of a central processing unit (CPU) in a microchip. On the other hand, the electronics industry is far more extensive; it includes computers, radios, supercomputers, superconductors, and many other products.

The microcomputer and electronics industries differ in their volume of sales, their scope (some would consider microcomputers a segment of the electronics industry), their rate of growth, and their competitive makeup. The dominant issues faced by the two industries are also different. Witness, for example, the raging public debate being waged on the future of the "high-definition TV." U.S. policymakers are attempting to ensure domestic control of that segment of the electronics industry. They are also considering ways to stimulate "cutting-edge" research in superconductivity. These efforts are likely to spur innovation and stimulate progress in the electronics industry. In contrast, the same policymakers are attempting to ensure that microcomputer technology does not reach Eastern Bloc countries. These efforts will restrict the scope of international markets for microcomputer producers.

Second, a definition of industry boundaries focuses attention on the firm's competitors. Defining industry boundaries enables the firm to identify its competitors and producers of substitute products. This is critically important to the firm's design of its competitive strategy.

Third, a definition of industry boundaries helps executives determine key factors for success. Survival in the premier segment of the microcomputer industry requires skills that are considerably different from those required in the lower end of the industry. Firms that compete in the premier segment need to be on the cutting edge of technological development and to provide extensive customer support and education. On the other hand, firms that compete in the lower end need to excel in imitating the products introduced by the premier segment, to focus on customer convenience, and to maintain operational efficiency that permits them to charge the lowest market price. Defining industry boundaries enables executives to ask these questions: Do we have the skills it takes to succeed here? If not, what must we do to develop these skills?

Finally, a definition of industry boundaries gives executives another basis on which to evaluate their firm's goals. Executives use that definition to forecast demand for their firm's products and services. Armed with that forecast, they can determine whether those goals are realistic.

Problems in Defining Industry Boundaries

Defining industry boundaries requires both caution and imagination. Caution is necessary because there are no precise rules for this task and because a poor definition will lead to poor planning. Imagination is necessary because industries are dynamic—in every industry important changes are under way in such key factors as competition, technology, and consumer demand.

Defining industry boundaries is a very difficult task. The difficulty stems from three sources:

1. The evolution of industries over time creates new opportunities and threats. Compare the financial services industry as we know it today with that of the 1970s and 1980s, and then try to imagine how different the industry will be in the year 2000.
2. Industrial evolution creates industries within industries. The electronics industry of the 1960s has been transformed into many "industries"—TV sets, transistor radios, micro- and macrocomputers, supercomputers, superconductors, and so on. Such transformation allows some firms to specialize and others to compete in different, related industries.
3. Industries are becoming global in scope. Consider the civilian aircraft manufacturing industry. For nearly three decades, U.S. firms dominated world production in that industry. But, small and large competitors were challenging their dominance by 1990. At that time, Airbus Industries (a consortium of European firms) and Brazilian, Korean, and Japanese firms were actively competing in the industry.

Developing a Realistic Industry Definition

Given the difficulties outlined above, how do executives draw accurate boundaries for an industry? The starting point is a definition of the industry in global terms, that is, in terms that consider the industry's international components as well as its domestic components.

Having developed a preliminary concept of the industry (e.g., computers), executives flush out its current components. This can be done by defining its product segments, as illustrated in Figure 3–4. Executives need to select the scope of their firm's potential market from among these related but distinct areas.

To understand the makeup of the industry, executives adopt a longitudinal perspective.

FIGURE 3–4
Computer Industry Product Segments

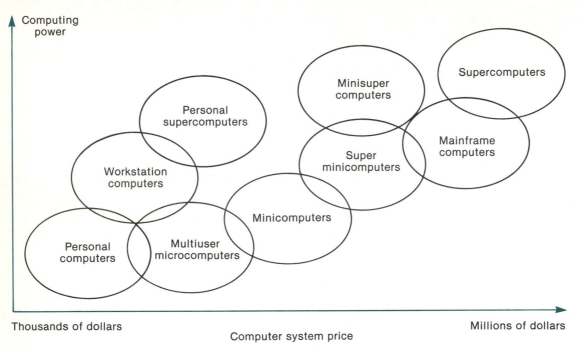

Source: Egil Juliussen and Karen Juliussen, *The Computer Industry Almanac* (New York: Simon & Schuster, 1988), p. 1.11.

They examine the emergence and evolution of product families. Why did these product families arise? How and why did they change? The answers to such questions provide executives with clues about the factors that drive competition in the industry.

Executives also examine the companies that offer different product families, the overlapping or distinctiveness of customer segments, and the rate of substitutability among product families.

To realistically define their industry, executives need to examine five issues:

a. Which part of the industry corresponds to our firm's goals?
b. What are the key ingredients of success in that part of the industry?
c. Does our firm have the skills needed to compete in that part of the industry? If not, can we build those skills?
d. Will the skills enable us to seize emerging opportunities and deal with future threats?
e. Is our definition of the industry flexible enough to allow necessary adjustments to our business concept as the industry grows?

INDUSTRY STRUCTURE

Defining an industry's boundaries is incomplete without an understanding of its structural attributes. *Structural attributes* are the enduring characteristics that give an industry its distinctive character. Consider the cable television and financial services industries. Both industries are competitive, and both are important for our quality of life. But these industries have very different requirements for success. To succeed in the cable television industry, firms require vertical integration, which helps them lower their operating costs and ensures their access to quality programs; technological innovation, to enlarge the scope of their services and deliver them in new ways; and extensive marketing, using appropriate segmentation techniques to locate potentially viable niches. To succeed in the financial services industry, firms need to meet very different requirements, among which are extensive orientation of customers and an extensive capital base.

How can we explain such variations among industries? The answer lies in examining the four variables that industry comprises: (1) concentration, (2) economies of scale, (3) product differentiation, and (4) barriers to entry.

Concentration

This variable refers to the extent to which industry sales are dominated by only a few firms. In a highly concentrated industry, that is, an industry whose sales are dominated by a handful of companies, the intensity of competition declines over time. High concentration serves as a barrier to entry into an industry because it enables the firms that hold large market shares to achieve significant economies of scale, (e.g., savings in production costs due to increased production quantities) and thus to lower their prices in order to stymie attempts of new firms to enter the market.

The U.S. aircraft manufacturing industry is highly concentrated. In 1988, its concentration ratio—the percent of market share held by the top four firms in the industry—was 67 percent. Competition in the industry has not been vigorous. Firms in the industry have been able to deter entry through proprietary technologies and the formation of strategic alliances (e.g., joint ventures).

Economies of Scale

This variable refers to the savings that companies within an industry achieve due to increased volume. Simply put, when the volume of production increases, the long-range average cost of a unit produced will decline.

Economies of scale result from technological and nontechnological sources. The technological sources are a higher level of mechanization or automation and a greater up-to-dateness of plant and facilities. The non-technological sources include better managerial coordination of production functions and processes, long-term contractual agreements with suppliers, and enhanced employee performance arising from specialization.

Economies of scale are an important determinant of the intensity of competition in an industry. Firms that enjoy such economies can charge lower prices than their competitors. They can also create barriers to entry by reducing their prices temporarily or permanently to deter new firms from entering the industry.

Product Differentiation

This variable refers to the extent to which customers perceive products or services offered by firms in the industry as different.

The differentiation of products can be real or perceived. The differentiation between Apple's Macintosh and IBM's PS/2 Personal Computer is a prime example of real differentiation. These products differ significantly in their technology and performance. Similarly, the civilian aircraft models produced by Boeing differ markedly from those produced by Airbus. The differences result from the use of different design principles and different construction technologies. For example, the newer Airbus planes follow the principle of "fly by wire," whereas Boeing planes utilize the laws of hydraulics. Thus, in Boeing planes, wings are activated by mechanical handling of different parts of the plane, whereas in the newer Airbus planes, this is done almost automatically.

Perceived differentiation results from the way in which firms position their products and from their success in persuading customers that their products differ significantly from competing products. Marketing strategies provide the vehicles through which this is done. Witness, for example, the extensive advertising campaigns of the automakers, each of which attempts to convey an image of distinctiveness. BMW ads highlight the excellent engineering of the BMW and its symbolic value as a sign of achievement. Some automakers focus on roominess and durability, which are desirable attributes for the family segment of the automobile market.

Real and perceived differentiation often intensify competition among existing firms. On the other hand, successful differentiation poses a competitive disadvantage for firms that attempt to enter an industry.

Barriers to Entry

As Porter noted earlier in this chapter, barriers to entry are the obstacles that a firm must overcome to enter an industry. They can be tangible or intangible. The tangible barriers include capital requirements, technological know-how, resources, and the laws regulating entry into an industry. The intangible barriers include the reputation of existing firms, the loyalty of consumers to existing brands, and access to the managerial skills required for successful operation in an industry.

Entry barriers both increase and reflect the level of concentration, economies of scale, and product differentiation in an industry, and such increases make it more difficult for new firms to enter the industry. Therefore, when high barrier levels exist in an industry, competition in that industry declines over time.

In summary, analysis of concentration, economies of scale, product differentiation, and barriers to entry in an industry enables a firm's executives to understand the forces that determine competition in an industry and sets the stage for identifying the firm's competitors and how they position themselves in the marketplace.

COMPETITIVE ANALYSIS

Competitive analysis usually has these objectives: (1) to identify current and potential competitors, (2) to identify potential moves by competitors, and (3) to help the firm devise effective competitive strategies.

How to Identify Competitors

In identifying their firm's current and potential competitors, executives consider several important variables:

How do other firms define the scope of their market? The more similar the definitions of firms, the more likely it is that the firms will view each other as competitors.

How similar are the benefits customers derive from the products and services that other firms offer? The more similar the benefits of products or services, the higher the level of substitutability between them. High substitutability levels force firms to compete fiercely for customers.

How committed are other firms to the industry? Although this question may appear to be far removed from the identification of competitors, it is in fact one of the most important questions that competitive analysis must address because it sheds light on the long-term intentions and goals. To size up the commitment of potential competitors to the industry, reliable intelligence data are needed. Such data may relate to potential resource commitments (e.g., planned facility expansions).

Common Mistakes in Identifying Competitors

Identifying competitors is a milestone in the development of strategy. But it is a process laden with uncertainty and risk, a process in which executives sometimes make costly mistakes. Examples of these mistakes are:

Overemphasizing current, known competitors while giving inadequate attention to potential entrants.

Overemphasizing large competitors while ignoring small competitors.

Overlooking potential international competitors.

Assuming that competitors will continue to behave in the same way they have behaved in the past.

Misreading signals that may indicate a shift in the focus of competitors or a refinement of their present strategies or tactics.

Overemphasizing competitors' financial resources, market position, and strategies while ignoring their intangible assets, such as a top management team.

Assuming that all of the firms in the industry are subject to the same constraints or open to the same opportunities.

Believing that the purpose of strategy is to outsmart the competition rather than to satisfy customer needs and expectations.

OPERATING ENVIRONMENT

The operating environment, also called the competitive or task environment, comprises factors in the competitive situation that affect a firm's success in acquiring needed resources or in profitably marketing its goods and services. Among the most important of these factors are the firm's competitive position, the composition of its customers, its reputation among suppliers and creditors, and its ability to attract capable employees. The operating environment is typically much more subject to the firm's influence or control than the remote environment. Thus, firms can be much more proactive (as opposed to reactive) in dealing with the operating environment than in dealing with the remote environment.

Competitive Position

Assessing its competitive position improves a firm's chances of designing strategies that optimize its environmental opportunities.[6] Development of competitor profiles enables a firm to more accurately forecast both its short- and long-term growth and its profit potentials. Although the exact criteria used in constructing a competitors's profile are largely determined by situational factors, the following criteria are often included:

1. Market share.
2. Breadth of product line.
3. Effectiveness of sales distribution.
4. Proprietary and key-account advantages.
5. Price competitiveness.
6. Advertising and promotion effectiveness.
7. Location and age of facility.
8. Capacity and productivity.
9. Experience.
10. Raw materials costs.
11. Financial position.
12. Relative product quality.

---

[6]M. Lauenstein, "The Strategy Audit," *Journal of Business Strategy*, Winter 1984, pp. 87–91.

13. R&D advantages/position.
14. Caliber of personnel.
15. General image.[7]

Once appropriate criteria have been selected, they are weighted to reflect their importance to a firm's success. Then the competitor being evaluated is rated on the criteria, the ratings are multiplied by the weight, and the weighted scores are summed to yield a numerical profile of the competitor, as shown in Figure 3–5.

This type of competitor profile is limited by the subjectivity of its criteria selection, weighting, and evaluation approaches. Nevertheless, the process of developing such profiles is of considerable help to a firm in defining its perception of its competitive position. Moreover, comparing the firm's profile with those of its competitors can aid its managers in identifying factors that might make the competitors vulnerable to strategies that the firm might choose to implement.

Customer Profiles

Perhaps the most valuable result of analyzing the operating environment is the understanding of a firm's customers that this provides.[8] Developing a profile of a firm's present and prospective customers improves the ability of its managers to plan strategic operations, to anticipate changes in the size of markets, and to reallocate resources so as to support forecast shifts in demand patterns. The principal types of information used in constructing customer profiles are geographic, demographic, psychographic, and buyer behavior information, as illustrated in Figure 3–6.

Geographic   It is important to define the geographic area from which customers do or could come. Almost every product or service has some quality that makes it variably attractive to buyers from different locations. Obviously, a Wisconsin manufacturer of snow skis should think twice about investing in a wholesale distribution center in South Carolina. On the other hand, advertising in the *Milwaukee Sun-Times* could significantly expand the geographically defined customer market of a major Myrtle Beach (South Carolina) hotel.

Demographic   Demographic variables are most commonly used to differentiate groups of present or potential customers. Demographic information (such as information on sex, age, marital status, income, and occupation) is comparatively easy to collect, quantify, and use in strategic forecasting, and such information is the minimum basis for a customer profile.

---

[7]These items were selected from a matrix for assessing competitive position proposed by Charles W. Hofer and Dan Schendel, *Strategy Formulation: Analytical Concepts* (St. Paul, Minn.: West Publishing, 1978), p. 76.

[8]R. McGill, "Planning for Strategic Performance in Local Government," *Long Range Planning*, October 1988, pp. 77–84.

FIGURE 3–5
Competitor Profile

Key Success Factors	Weight	Rating†	Weighted Score
Market share	.30	4	1.20
Price competitiveness	.20	3	0.60
Facilities location	.20	5	1.00
Raw materials costs	.10	3	0.30
Caliber of personnel	.20	1	0.30
	1.00*		3.30

*The total of the weights must always equal 1.00.

†The rating scale suggested is as follows: very strong competitive position (5 points), strong (4), average (3), weak (2), very weak (1).

Psychographic   Personality and lifestyle variables are often better predictors of customer purchasing behavior than geographic or demographic variables. In such situations, a psychographic study is an important component of the customer profile. Recent advertising campaigns by soft-drink producers—Pepsi-Cola ("the Pepsi generation"), Coca-Cola ("catch the wave"), and 7UP ("America's turning 7UP")—reflect strategic management's attention to the psychographic characteristics of their largest customer segment—physically active, group-oriented nonprofessionals.

Buyer Behavior   Buyer behavior data can also be a component of the customer profile. Such data are used to explain or predict some aspect of customer behavior with regard to a product or service. As Figure 3–6 indicates, information on buyer behavior (such as usage rate, benefits sought, and brand loyalty) can provide significant aid in the design of more accurate and profitable strategies.

SUPPLIERS AND CREDITORS: SOURCES OF RESOURCES

Dependable relationships between a firm and its suppliers and creditors are essential to the firm's long-term survival and growth. A firm regularly relies on its suppliers and creditors for financial support, services, materials, and equipment. In addition, it is occasionally forced to make special requests for such favors as quick delivery, liberal credit terms, or broken-lot orders. Particularly at such times, it is essential for a firm to have had an ongoing relationship with its suppliers and creditors.

In assessing a firm's relationships with its suppliers and creditors, several factors other than the strength of that relationship should be considered. With regard to its competitive position with its suppliers, the firm should address the following questions:

Are the suppliers' prices competitive? Do the suppliers offer attractive quantity discounts? How costly are their shipping charges?

FIGURE 3–6
Customer Profile Considerations

Type of Information	Typical Breakdowns
Geographic:	
Region	Pacific, Mountain, West North Central, West South Central, East North Central, East South Central, South Atlantic, Middle Atlantic, New England
County size	A, B, C, D
City or SMSA size*	Under 5,000, 5,000–19,999, 20,000–49,999, 50,000–99,999, 100,000–249,999, 250,000–499,999, 500,000–999,999, 1,000,000–3,999,999, 4 million or over
Density	Urban, suburban, rural
Climate	Northern, southern
Demographic:	
Age	Under 6, 6–11, 12–17, 18–34, 35–49, 50–64, 65+
Sex	Male/female
Family size	1–2, 3–4, 5+ persons
Family life cycle	Young, single; young, married, no children; young, married, youngest child under 6; young married, youngest child 6 or over; older, married, with children; older, married, no children under 18; older, single; other
Income	Under $5,000, $5,000–$10,000, etc.
Occupation	Professional and technical; managers, officials, and proprietors; clerical, sales; craft workers, supervisors; operatives; farmers; retired; students; homemakers; unemployed
Education	Grade school or less, some high school, graduated from high school, some college, graduated from college
Religion	Catholic, Protestant, Jewish, other
Race	Caucasian, Negro, Oriental, other
Nationality	American, British, French, German, East European, Scandinavian, Italian, Spanish, Latin American, Middle Eastern, Japanese, and so on
Social class	Lower-lower, upper-lower, lower-middle, middle-middle, upper-middle, lower-upper, upper-upper
Psychographic:	
Compulsiveness	Compulsive/noncompulsive
Gregariousness	Extrovert/introvert
Autonomy	Dependent/independent
Conservatism	Conservative/liberal/radical
Authoritarianism	Authoritarian/democratic
Leadership	Leader/follower
Ambitiousness	High achiever/low achiever
Buyer behavior:	
Usage rate	Nonuser, light user, medium user, heavy user
Readiness stage	Unaware, aware, interested, intending to try, trier, regular buyer
Benefits sought	Economy, status, dependability
End use	Varies with the product
Brand loyalty	None, light, strong
Marketing-factor sensibility	Quality, price, service, advertising, sales promotion

*SMSA stands for standard metropolitan statistical area.
Source: Adapted from Philip Kotler, *Marketing Management* (Englewood Cliffs, N.J.: Prentice-Hall, 1972), p. 170.

Are the suppliers competitive in terms of production standards? In terms of deficiency rates?

Are the suppliers' abilities, reputations, and services competitive?

Are the suppliers reciprocally dependent on the firm?

With regard to its competitive position with its creditors, among the most important questions that the firm should address are the following:

Do the creditors fairly value and willingly accept the firm's stock as collateral?

Do the creditors perceive the firm as having an acceptable record of past payment? A strong working capital position? Little or no leverage?

Are the creditors' loan terms compatible with the firm's profitability objectives?

Are the creditors' able to extend the necessary lines of credit?

The answers to these and related questions help a firm forecast the availability of the resources it will need to implement and sustain its competitive strategies. Because the quantity, quality, price, and accessibility of financial, human, and material resources are rarely ideal, assessment of suppliers and creditors is critical to an accurate evaluation of a firm's operating environment.

HUMAN RESOURCES: NATURE OF THE LABOR MARKET

A firm's ability to attract and hold capable employees is essential to its success. However, a firm's personnel recruitment and selection alternatives are often influenced by the nature of its operating environment. A firm's access to needed personnel is affected primarily by three factors: the firm's reputation as an employer, local employment rates, and the ready availability of people with the needed skills.

Reputation   A firm's reputation within its operating environment is a major element of its ability to satisfy its personnel needs. A firm is more likely to attract and retain valuable employees if it is seen as permanent in the community, competitive in its compensation package, and concerned with the welfare of its employees and if it is respected for its product or service and appreciated for its overall contribution to the general welfare.

Employment Rates   The readily available supply of skilled and experienced personnel may vary considerably with the stage of a community's growth. A new manufacturing firm would find it far more difficult to obtain skilled employees in a vigorous industrialized community than in an economically depressed community in which similar firms had recently cut back operations.

Availability   The skills of some people are so specialized that relocation may be necessary to secure the jobs and the compensation that those skills commonly command. People with such skills include oil drillers, chefs, technical specialists, and industry executives.

A firm that seeks to hire such a person is said to have broad labor market boundaries; that is, the geographic area within which the firm might reasonably expect to attract qualified candidates is quite large. On the other hand, people with more common skills are less likely to relocate from a considerable distance in order to achieve modest economic or career advancements. Thus, the labor market boundaries are fairly limited for such occupational groups as unskilled laborers, clerical personnel, and retail clerks.

EMPHASIS ON ENVIRONMENTAL FACTORS

This chapter has described the remote, industry, and operating environments as encompassing five components each. While that description is generally accurate, it may give the false impression that the components are easily identified, mutually exclusive, and equally applicable in all situations. In fact, the forces in the external environment are so dynamic and interactive that the impact of any single element cannot be wholly disassociated from the impact of other elements. For example, are increases in OPEC oil prices the result of economic, political, social, or technological changes? Or are a manufacturer's surprisingly good relations with suppliers a result of competitors', customers', or creditors' activities or of the supplier's own activities? The answer to both questions is probably that a number of forces in the external environment have combined to create the situation. Such is the case in most studies of the environment.

In a recent study involving more than 200 company executives, the respondents were asked to identify key planning issues in terms of their increasing importance to strategic success. As shown in Figure 3–7, domestic competitive trends, customer or end-user preferences, and technological trends were the issues they selected most often.

Strategic managers are frequently frustrated in their attempts to anticipate the environment's changing influences. Different external elements affect different strategies at different times and with varying strengths. The only certainty is that the impact of the remote and operating environment will be uncertain until a strategy is implemented. This leads many managers, particularly in less powerful, smaller firms, to minimize long-term planning, which requires a commitment of resources. Instead, they favor allowing managers to adapt to new pressures from the environment. While such a decision has considerable merit for many firms, there is an associated trade-off, namely that absence of a strong resource and psychological commitment to a proactive strategy effectively bars a firm from assuming a leadership role in its competitive environment.

There is yet another difficulty in assessing the probable impact of remote, industry, and operating environments on the effectiveness of alternative strategies. Assessment of this kind involves collecting information that can be analyzed to disclose predictable effects. Except in rare instances, however, it is virtually impossible for any single firm to anticipate the consequences of a change in the environment, for example, the precise effect on alternative strategies of a 2 percent increase in the national inflation rate, a 1 percent decrease in statewide unemployment, or the entry of a new competitor in a regional market.

FIGURE 3–7
Key Planning Issues

	Percent of Respondents Indicating		
Issue	Increase	No Change	Decrease
1. Competitive (domestic) trends	83.6%	13.5%	2.9%
2. Customer or end-user preferences	69.0	29.1	2.0
3. Technological trends	71.4	25.6	3.0
4. Diversification opportunities	61.7	30.3	8.0
5. Worldwide or global competition	59.4	34.4	6.3
6. Internal capabilities	55.4	40.2	4.4
7. Joint venture opportunities	56.6	36.7	6.6
8. Qualitative data	55.9	38.1	5.9
9. General economic and business conditions	46.4	47.3	6.3
10. Regulatory issues	42.8	51.2	6.0
11. Supplier trends	26.0	69.1	5.0
12. Reasons for past failures	27.6	62.3	10.1
13. Quantitative data	36.8	40.7	22.5
14. Past peformance	27.3	51.2	21.5

Source: Adapted from V. Ramanujam, J. C. Camillus, and N. Venkatraman, "Trends in Strategic Planning," in *Strategic Planning and Management Handbook,* ed. W. R. King and D. I. Cleland (New York: Van Nostrand Reinhold, 1987), p. 615.

Still, assessing the potential impact of changes in the external environment offers a real advantage. It enables decision makers to narrow the range of the available options and to eliminate options that are clearly inconsistent with the forecast opportunities. Environmental assessment seldom identifies the best strategy, but it generally leads to the elimination of all but the most promising options.

SUMMARY

A firm's external environment consists of three interrelated sets of factors that play a principal role in determining the opportunities, threats, and constraints that the firm faces. The remote environment comprises factors originating beyond, and usually irrespective of, any single firm's operating situation—economic, social, political, technological, and ecological factors. Factors that more directly influence a firm's prospects originate in the environment of its industry, including entry barriers, competitor rivalry, the availability of substitutes, and the bargaining power of buyers and suppliers. The operating environment comprises factors that influence a firm's immediate competitive situation—competitive position, customer profiles, suppliers and creditors, and the labor market. These three sets of factors provide many of the challenges that a particular firm faces in its attempts to attract or acquire needed resources and to profitably market its goods and services. Environmental assessment is more complicated for multinational corporations

(MNCs) than for domestic firms because multinationals must evaluate several environments simultaneously.

Thus, the design of business strategies is based on the conviction that a firm able to anticipate future business conditions will improve its performance and profitability. Despite the uncertainty and dynamic nature of the business environment, an assessment process that narrows, even if it does not precisely define, future expectations is of substantial value to strategic managers.

QUESTIONS FOR DISCUSSION

1. Briefly describe two important recent changes in the remote environment of U.S. business in each of the following areas:
   a. Economic.
   b. Social.
   c. Political.
   d. Technological.
   e. Ecological.

2. Describe two major environmental changes that you expect to have a major impact on the wholesale food industry in the next 10 years.

3. Develop a competitor profile for your college and the one geographically closest to it. Next, prepare a brief strategic plan to improve the competitive position of the weaker of the two colleges.

4. Assume the invention of a competitively priced synthetic fuel that could supply 25 percent of U.S. energy needs within 20 years. In what major ways might this change the external environment of U.S. business?

5. With your instructor's help, identify a local firm that has enjoyed great growth in recent years. To what degree and in what ways do you think that this firm's success resulted from taking advantage of favorable conditions in its remote, industry, and operating environments?

6. Choose a specific industry and, relying solely on your impressions, evaluate the impact of the five forces that drive competition in that industry.

7. Choose an industry in which you would like to compete. Use the five-forces method of analysis to explain why you find that industry attractive.

8. Many firms neglect industry analysis. When does this hurt them? When does it not?

9. The model below depicts industry analysis as a funnel that focuses on remote-factor analysis to better understand the impact of factors in the operating environment. Do you find this model satisfactory? If not, how would you improve it?

10. Who in a firm should be responsible for industry analysis? Assume that the firm does not have a strategic planning department.

BIBLIOGRAPHY

Aaker, D. A. "Managing Assets and Skills: The Key to a Sustainable Competitive Advantage." *California Management Review,* Winter 1989, pp. 91–106.

Allen, M. G. "Competitive Confrontation in Consumer Services." *Planning Review,* January–February 1989, pp. 4–9.

Amit, R.; I. Damowitz; and C. Fershtman. "Thinking One Step Ahead: The Use of Conjectures in Competitor Analysis." *Strategic Management Journal,* September–October 1988, pp. 431–42.

Attanasio, D. B. "The Multiple Benefits of Competitor Intelligence." *Journal of Business Strategy,* May–June 1988, pp. 16–19.

Ball, R. "Assessing Your Competitor's People and Organization." *Long Range Planning,* April 1987, pp. 32–41.

Brewton, C. "A Model for Analyzing the Lodging Industry." *Cornell Hotel and Restaurant Administration Quarterly,* August 1987, pp. 10–12.

Bush, R. F.; P. H. Bloch; and S. Dawson. "Remedies for Product Counterfeiting." *Business Horizons,* January–February 1989, pp. 59–65.

Calori, R. "Designing a Business Scanning System." *Long Range Planning,* February 1989, pp. 69–82.

Capon, N.; J. Farley, Jr.; and J. Hulbert. "International Diffusion of Corporate and Strategic Planning Practices." *Columbia Journal of World Business,* Fall 1980, pp. 5–13.

Caves, R. E., and M. E. Porter. "From Entry Barriers to Mobility Barriers: Conjectural Decisions and Contrived Deterrence to New Competition." *Quarterly Journal of Economics* 91 (1976), pp. 421–34.

Cespedes, F. V. "Channel Management Is General Management." *California Management Review,* Fall 1988, pp. 98–120.

Conner, K. R. "Strategies for Product Cannibalism." *Strategic Management Journal,* Summer 1988, pp. 9–26.

Cooper, P. D., and G. Miaoulis. "Altering Corporate Strategic Criteria: The Role of Life Satisfaction and the Growth of the Senior Market." *California Management Review,* Fall 1988, pp. 87–97.

Covin, J. G., and D. P. Slevin. "Strategic Management of Small Firms in Hostile and Benign Environments." *Strategic Management Journal,* January–February 1989, pp. 75–87.

Cowley, R. R. "Market Structure and Business Performance: An Evaluation of Buyer/Seller Power in the PIMS Database." *Strategic Management Journal,* May–June 1988, pp. 271–78.

Cravens, D. W. "Gaining Strategic Marketing Advantage." *Business Horizons,* September–October 1988, pp. 44–54.

Cvitkovic, E. "Profiling Your Competitors." *Planning Review,* May–June 1989, pp. 28–31.

deVasconcellos e Sa', J. A. S., and D. C. Hambrick. "Key Success Factors: Test of a General Theory in the Mature Industrial Product Sector." *Strategic Management Journal,* July–August 1989, pp. 367–82.

DeMingo, E. "The Fine Art of Positioning." *Journal of Business Strategy,* March–April 1988, pp. 34–38.

Eisenhardt, K. M., and L. J. Bourgeois III. "Politics of Strategic Decision Making in High-Velocity Environments: Toward a Midrange Theory." *Academy of Management Journal,* December 1988, pp. 737–70.

Filho, P. V. "Environmental Analysis for Strategic Planning." *Managerial Planning,* January–February 1985, pp. 23–30.

Gilbert, X., and P. Strebel. "Strategies to Outpace the Competition." *Journal of Business Strategy,* Summer 1987, pp. 28–35.

Goldsmith, H. "Members Only Fashions a Unique Selling Strategy." *Journal of Business Strategy,* May–June 1989, pp. 8–11.

Gottliebsen, D. "How to Live and Prosper among the Giants." *Journal of Business Strategy,* March–April 1989, pp. 9–13.

Harvel G., and C. K. Prahalad. "Strategic Intent." *Harvard Business Review,* May–June 1989, pp. 63–76.

Hill, C. W. L. "Differentiation versus Low Cost of Differentiation and Low Cost: A Contingency Framework." *Academy of Management Review,* July 1988, pp. 401–12.

Hlvacek, J. D., and B. C. Ames. "Segmenting Industrial and High-Tech Markets." *Journal of Business Strategy,* Fall 1986, pp. 39–50.

Hofer, C. W., and D. Schendel. *Strategy Formulation: Analytical Concepts.* St. Paul, Minn.: West Publishing, 1978.

Hout, T.; M. Porter; and E. Rudden. "How Global Companies Win out." *Harvard Business Review,* September–October 1982, pp. 98–108.

Kane, C. L. "Overcome the 'Me Too' Product Syndrome." *Journal of Business Strategy,* March–April 1989, pp. 14–16.

Keats, B. W., and M. A. Hitt. "A Causal Model of Linkages among Environmental Dimensions, Macro Organizational Characteristics, and Performance." *Academy of Management Journal,* September 1988, pp. 570–98.

Kiser, J. W. "Tapping Eastern Bloc Technology." *Harvard Business Review,* March–April 1982, pp. 85–93.

Koch, J. V. "Industry Market Structure and Industry Price-Cost Margins." *Industrial Organization Review* (1974), pp. 186–93.

Kotler, P. *Marketing Management.* Englewood Cliffs, N.J.: Prentice-Hall, 1989.

Lambkin, M. "Order of Entry and Performance in New Markets." *Strategic Management Journal,* Summer 1988, pp. 127–40.

Lauenstein, M. "The Strategy Audit." *Journal of Business Strategy,* Winter 1984, pp. 87–91.

Leigh, T. W. "Case Study: Competitive Assessment in Service Industries." *Planning Review,* January–February 1989, pp. 10–19.

Leonard-Barton, D., and J. J. Sviokla. "Putting Expert Systems to Work." *Harvard Business Review,* March–April 1988, pp. 91–98.

Lieberman, M. B. "The Learning Curve, Technology Barriers to Entry, and Competitive Survival in the Chemical Processing Industries." *Strategic Management Journal,* September–October 1989, 431–47.

Lieberman, M. B., and D. B. Montgomery. "First-Mover Advantages." *Strategic Management Journal,* Summer 1988, pp. 41–58.

MacMillan, I. C. "Controlling Competitive Dynamics by Taking Strategic Initiative." *Academy of Management Executive,* May 1988, pp. 111–18.

Mahmood, S. T., and M. M. Moon. "Competitive Analysis from a Strategic Planning Perspective." *Managerial Planning,* July–August 1984, pp. 37–63.

Mascarenhas, B., and D. A. Aaker, "Mobility Barriers and Strategic Groups." *Strategic Management Journal,* September–October 1989, pp. 475–85.

Mayer, R. "Winning Strategies for Manufacturers in Mature Industries." *Journal of Business Strategy,* Fall 1987, pp. 23–31.

Miles, R. E. "Adapting to Technology and Competition: A New Industrial Relations System for the 21st Century." *California Management Review,* Winter 1989, pp. 9–28.

Miller, D. "Relating Porter's Business Strategies to Environment and Structure: Analysis and Performance Implications." *Academy of Management Journal,* June 1988, pp. 280–308.

Murray, A. I. "A Contingency View of Porter's Generic Strategies." *Academy of Management Review,* July 1988, pp. 390–400.

Nemetz, P. L., and L. W. Fry. "Flexible Manufacturing Organizations: Implications for Strategy Formulation and Organization Design." *Academy of Management Review,* October 1988, pp. 627–38.

Peters, T. "Restoring American Competitiveness: Looking for New Models of Organizations." *Academy of Management Executive,* May 1988, pp. 103–9.

Porter, M. E. "From Competitive Advantage to Corporate Strategy." *Harvard Business Review,* May–June 1987, pp. 43–59.

"How Competitive Forces Shape Strategy." *Harvard Business Review,* March–April 1979, pp. 137–45.

"The Structure within Industries' and Companies' Performance." *Review of Economics and Statistics,* May 1979, 61 (1979) pp. 214–227.

Prescott, J. E., and J. H. Grant. "A Manager's Guide for Evaluating Competitive Analysis Techniques." *Interfaces,* May–June 1988, pp. 10–22.

Rafferty, J. "Exit Barriers and Strategic Position in Declining Markets." *Long Range Planning,* April 1987, pp. 86–91.

Reimann, B. C. "Sustaining the Competitive Advantage." *Planning Review,* March–April 1989, pp. 30–39.

Rothschild, W. E. "Who Are Your Future Competitors?" *Journal of Business Strategy,* May–June 1988, pp. 10–14.

Scherer, F. M. *Industrial Market Structure and Economic Performance.* 2nd ed. Skokie, Ill.: Rand McNally, 1980.

Smith, D. C., and J. Prescott. "Demystifying Competitive Analysis." *Planning Review,* September–October 1987, pp. 8–13.

Stroup, M. A. "Environmental Scanning at Monsanto." *Planning Review,* July–August 1988, pp. 24–27.

Svatko, J. E. "Analyzing the Competition." *Small Business Reports,* January 1989, pp. 21–28.

Ulrich, D., and F. Wiersema. "Gaining Strategic and Organizational Capability in a Turbulent Business Environment." *Academy of Management Executive,* May 1988, pp. 115–22.

Yoffie, D. B. "How an Industry Builds Political Advantage." *Harvard Business Review,* May–June 1988, pp. 82–89.

CHAPTER 3 COHESION CASE

ASSESSING THE EXTERNAL ENVIRONMENT

As Bryson's managers planned for their year-end strategic planning retreat, they placed critical importance on assessing the external environment. Each manager was given at least one dimension of the external environment to assess. Their assignment was twofold: identify critical factors in this dimension and assess their strategic implications for Bryson or relevant parts of its operations. Key parts of their assessments are provided below.

ECONOMIC

1990–92 appear to be years of modest growth in business activity in the national economy. Eight years have passed since the last U.S. recession. Economists are mixed in their predictions—some saying a stable, "muddled" U.S. economy, and others predicting a slowdown into a recession.

(*Implications for Bryson*: Bryson's customers are mostly industrial plants. "Muddled" slow growth would mean a continued growth in the demand for Bryson's services. Bryson management must continually monitor economic trends, however, because a slowdown or recession would cause many target customers to cut back on the scope of remediation projects to include postponing them whenever possible to control their costs.)

Interest rates are predicted to experience a gradual rise over the next three years. A rapid acceleration in interest rates would be detrimental to Bryson's ability to finance expansion of its equipment base.

(*Implications for Bryson*: Bryson's CFO should seek to lock in rates of equipment purchases, rather than letting the rate float with prime.)

POLITICAL/REGULATORY

A key driving force behind the growth potential for the hazardous waste services industry remains public concern about cleaning up the environment and, perhaps equally important, enhanced corporate awareness of the need to reduce the potential liabilities of being a "poor corporate citizen." The recent publicity of several oil spills and intense publicity in each southeastern state about the citing of hazardous waste disposal facilities have focused public attention on the environment's fragility. Recent clean air legislation proposed by the Bush administration and its recommendation to grant cabinet status to the

EPA suggest that the Bush administration is sensitive to this growing public awareness and is intent on extending the impact of hazardous waste regulations.

(*Implications for Bryson*: Increased public awareness and expanded regulatory pressure should have a favorable impact on the demand for Bryson's services. Management should be active in industry associations that influence proposed legislation. A. G. Edwards and Kidder, Peabody predict that hazardous wastes services will grow by 25 percent to 30 percent annually over the next three to five years as a result of these driving forces. Bryson should stay abreast of the latest regulatory developments and convey that awareness to current and potential customers. And Bryson should promote a public image in the communities it has locations as being a company that is involved in solving hazardous waste problems, rather than one creating them. This is particularly true where it is involved in treatment services.)

DEMOGRAPHIC/SOCIAL

Heightened awareness of problems with hazardous wastes as well as solid wastes in general will bring increased attention to the hazwaste industry, what it does, and the demand for its services. The baby boomers are moving into their highest earning years, fueling the demand for consumer goods whose manufacture generates more hazardous waste.

(*Implications for Bryson*: Fuels the growth in demand for Bryson's services but also increases public awareness of hazwaste companies and scrutiny of what they do and the potential liability they represent.)

BUYERS

Buyers are numerous and increasing, with new RCRA guidelines covering small-quantity generators. They are becoming increasingly aware of their hazwaste-related obligations and potential liabilities, and they understand what hazwaste service companies can do. This makes them less dependent on any one supplier, and switching costs are low. The larger generators, like Du Pont, are seriously reviewing the possibility of backward integration. The costs of hazwaste services for these firms is still a low percentage of overall costs, but it is a rapidly rising cost and, with liabilities figured in, an increasingly significant one. Small generators are overwhelmed by RCRA regulatory impact, and the costs *are* significant for them—an unexpected reduction in their overall profit margins.

(*Implications for Bryson*: Buyers are increasing in power, which will manifest itself by increased price sensitivity, demand for quality service, knowledge of alternative suppliers, and willingness to switch when disappointed with Bryson. Bryson must focus in more specialized areas with hard-to-handle substances to maintain high profit potential.)

SUPPLIERS

Bryson's key suppliers include landfill and incineration disposal companies, equipment companies, insurance companies, labor (skilled, technical), and capital (capital intensive). Disposal companies are essential to transportation and to remediation and treatment companies. They are highly concentrated, able to forward integrate (a few already have—ChemWaste and BFI), and a major cost (20 percent to 35 percent of sales) to companies like Bryson. Equipment companies are smaller, more numerous, and cooperative but don't view transportation and remediation companies as a large part of their business. Only two or three insurance companies are willing to serve the hazwaste industry, and it is a small part of their overall revenue. Skilled personnel at virtually every level are in high demand, because the industry is both new and rapidly growing. Sources of capital are attracted to the industry's profit and growth potential, but they are increasingly concerned about the significant liability.

(*Implication for Bryson*: Supplier power is very high, particularly among those without whom Bryson couldn't operate—disposal companies, insurance, and skilled personnel. Bryson needs to seek long-term contractual relationships, maintain high standards and sound profitability, and join with other rivals to deal with disposal and insurance suppliers whenever possible to reduce their impact on industry profitability.)

SUBSTITUTES

The main substitute for the industry's services is for generators to provide it themselves. Only the largest firms are able to do this, as discussed under "buyers."

(*Implications for Bryson*: Substitutes do not represent a source of competitive pressure for the foreseeable future.)

NEW ENTRANTS

Several barriers to entry are present—permits, capital requirements, insurance costs, reputation, and expertise. At the same time, the attractive industry growth is fueling numerous entrants attempting to overcome these barriers. This is particularly true in areas with minimal permit requirements, like transportation and remediation. In these areas, the hazwaste arena represents a higher profit alternative to traditional transportation or construction-oriented (remedial services) firms.

(*Implications for Bryson*: Bryson can expect frequent new competitors in transportation and remedial services. These entrants can be expected to interrupt the industry's ability to establish a stable pricing structure as they enter with lower overhead or fight for business on a contract-by-contract basis. Long-term contracts and focused differentiation are Bryson's main competitive weapons.)

RIVALRY

Industry growth is substantial, leaving room for many players. Fixed costs are high for personnel and equipment. Seasonal fluctuations in work, particularly remediation, cause intermittent overcapacity. Switching costs are low. Brand identification (reputation and name recognition) accrues primarily to the few large players and selected regional competitors (Bryson in transportation). Full service and financial strength are important factors influencing "brand" reputation. Exit barriers are low for transportation and remediation, high for disposal and treatment. There is a wide diversity of competitors with varied technology. A consolidation trend is underway with numerous acquisitions by medium to larger companies.

(*Implications for Bryson*: Because of rapid industry growth, Bryson is in a position to establish itself without intense rivalry. However, several trends suggest increased future rivalry—consolidation, low exit barriers in transportation and remediation, and need to build name recognition. And as larger, full-service rivals emerge, they will be in a position to increase competitive pressures on specialized providers of basic services. Bryson needs to press its name recognition advantage in transportation. It must decide whether to become full service, compete on a low cost basis, or differentiate itself in terms of the types of waste it handles and the geographic areas it serves.)

Bryson's managers concluded their environmental assessment with the determination that their strategy for the 1990s must:

1. Be based in RCRA-regulated areas and sensitive to future RCRA changes.
2. Posture Bryson as a handler and reducer of waste, not a disposer.
3. Focus on buyers with hard-to-handle substances, preferably medium-sized manufacturers who would need Bryson's expertise and create ways to tie buyers to Bryson with higher switching costs.
4. Within a narrow focus, create a way to make Bryson provide a full line of services that certain generators may need.

What is your assessment of Bryson's environmental analysis? What factors should have been included that were omitted? Do you agree with Bryson's interpretation of the factors they examined? What conclusions do you draw, in addition to the four they reached?

4 Evaluating the Multinational Environment

Strategic Considerations for Multinational Firms

Special complications confront a firm involved in international operations. Multinational corporations (MNCs) headquartered in one country with subsidiaries in other countries experience difficulties that are understandably associated with operating in two or more distinctly different competitive arenas.

Awareness of the strategic opportunities faced by MNCs and of the threats posed to them is important to planners in almost every domestic U.S. industry. Among corporations headquartered in the United States that receive more than 50 percent of their annual profits from foreign operations are Citicorp, Coca-Cola, Exxon, Gillette, IBM, Otis Elevator, and Texas Instruments. In fact, the 100 largest U.S. MNCs earn an average of 37 percent of their operating profits abroad. Equally impressive is the impact of foreign-based MNCs that operate in the United States. Their "direct foreign investment" in the United States now exceeds $90 billion, with Japanese, West German, and French firms leading the way. The extent of this foreign influence is evident in Figure 4–1.

Understanding the myriad and sometimes subtle nuances of competing in international markets or against MNCs is rapidly becoming a required competence of strategic managers. Therefore, this section will focus on the nature, outlook, and operations of MNCs.

Development of an MNC

The evolution of an MNC often entails progressively involved strategy levels. The first level, which entails export-import activity, has minimal effect on the existing management orientation or on existing product lines. The second level, which involves foreign licensing and technology transfer, requires little change in management or operation. The third level is characterized by direct investment in overseas operations, including manufacturing plants. This level requires large capital outlays and the development of international management skills. Although the domestic operations of a firm at this level continue to

FIGURE 4-1
Multinational Corporation Ownership Test

In this test, you go down the alphabet and pick out the products that are foreign owned.

A Airwick, Alka-Seltzer antacid, Aim toothpaste
B Baskin Robbins ice cream, Bactine antiseptic, Ball Park Franks
C Certain-Teed, Capitol records, Castrol oils.
D Deer Park sparkling water, Dove soap, Dunlop tires.
E ENO antacids, Eureka vacuum cleaners, Ehler spices.
F Four Roses whisky, French's mustard, First Love dolls.
G Good Humor ice cream, Garrard turntables, Grand Trunk Railroad.
H *Humpty Dumpty* magazine, Hires Root Beer, Hills Brothers coffee.
I Imperial margerine, Instant potato mix, Indian Head textiles.
J Juvena cosmetics, Jaeger sportswear, Jade cosmetics.
K Knox gelatine, Kool cigarettes, Keebler cookies.
L Libby's fruits and vegetables, *Look* magazine, Lifebuoy soap.
M Magnavox, Massey-Ferguson tractors, Mr. Coffee.
N Norelco appliances, Nescafé coffee, New Yorker Hotel.
O Ovaltine drink mix, One-a-Day vitamins.
P Panasonic, Pop Shoppes, Pepsodent toothpaste.
Q Nestlé Quik chocolate mix, Quasar television sets, Quadra-Bar sedatives.
R Ray-O-Vac batteries, Rinso, Rona Barrett's gossip magazines.
S Scripto pens, Seven Seas salad dressings, Slazenger tennis balls.
T Tetley tea, Tic Tac breath fresheners, Taster's Choice instant coffee.
U Underwood typewriters, Urise antiseptics, Ultra Tears eye lotion.
V Valium tranquilizers, Vogue pipe tobacco, Vim detergent.
W Wish-Bone salad dressings, Wisk detergent, White Motor trucks.
X Xam clock radios, Xylocaine salves, Xylee plastics.
Y Yardley cosmetics, Yale locks, Yashica cameras.
Z Zesta crackers, Zig-Zag cigarette papers, Zestatabs vitamins.

Answer: All of the companies (A through Z) are foreign owned.

dominate its policy, such a firm is commonly categorized as a true MNC. The most involved strategy level is characterized by a substantial increase in foreign investment, with foreign assets comprising a significant portion of total assets. At this level, the firm begins to emerge as a global enterprise with global approaches to production, sales, finance, and control.

Some firms downplay their multinational nature (so as never to appear distracted from their domestic operations), whereas others highlight it. For example, General Electric's formal statement of mission and business philosophy includes the following commitment:

> To carry on a diversified, growing, and profitable worldwide manufacturing business in electrical apparatus, appliances, and supplies, and in related materials, products, systems, and services for industry, commerce, agriculture, government, the community, and the home.

A similar worldwide orientation is evident at IBM, which operates in 125 countries, conducts business in 30 languages and more than 100 currencies, and has 23 major manufacturing facilities in 14 countries.

Why Firms Internationalize

The technological advantage once enjoyed by the United States has declined dramatically during the past 30 years. In the late 1950s, over 80 percent of the world's major technological innovations were first introduced in the United States. By 1990, the figure had declined to less than 50 percent. In contrast, France is making impressive advances in electric traction, nuclear power, and aviation. West Germany leads in chemicals and pharmaceuticals, precision and heavy machinery, heavy electrical goods, metallurgy, and surface transport equipment. Japan leads in optics, solid-state physics, engineering, chemistry, and process metallurgy. Eastern Europe and the Soviet Union, the so-called CO-MECON (Council for Mutual Economic Assistance) countries, generate 30 percent of annual worldwide patent applications. However, the United States can regain some of its lost technological advantage. Through internationalization, U.S. firms can often reap benefits from industries and technologies developed abroad. Even a relatively small service firm that possesses a distinctive competitive advantage can capitalize on large overseas operations. One such firm that has done this is Domino's Pizza, as described in Strategy in Action 4–1.

In many situations, multinational development makes sense as a competitive weapon. Direct penetration of foreign markets can drain vital cash flows from a foreign competitor's domestic operations. The resulting lost opportunities, reduced income, and limited production can impair the competitor's ability to invade U.S. markets. A case in point is IBM's move to establish a position of strength in the Japanese mainframe computer industry before two key competitors, Fiyitsue and Hitachi, could dominate it. Once IBM had achieved a substantial share of the Japanese market, it worked to deny its Japanese competitors the vital cash and production experience they needed to invade the U.S. market.[1]

Considerations prior to Internationalization

To begin their internationalizing activities, firms are advised to take four steps.[2]

Scan the International Situation   Scanning includes reading journals and patent reports and checking other printed sources—as well as meeting people at scientific-technical conferences and in-house seminars.

Make Connections with Academia and Research Organizations   Firms active in overseas R&D often pursue work-related projects with foreign academics and sometimes enter into consulting agreements with them.

---

[1]C. M. Watson, "Counter Competition Abroad to Protect Home Markets," *Harvard Business Review,* January–February 1982, p. 40.

[2]R. Ronstadt and R. Kramer, "Getting the Most out of Innovation Abroad," *Harvard Business Review,* March–April 1982, pp. 94–99.

D omino's Pizza International, adding stores in Japan at an astounding rate of one every four weeks, had 10 in operation by mid-October 1987. By the end of 1988, another 16 stores were to be added. A good reason exists for this expansion. Sales in Japan average $25,000 per store each week, compared with an average of $8,000–8,500 in the United States.

Domino's works through the Y. Higa Corporation under a licensing agreement to set up pizza franchises. Donald K. Cooper, controller of Domino's Pizza International, has said: "The key to success is spending a lot of time training the workers. It takes a year and a half for a driver to move up to manager-in-training and eventually become a store manager. Early on, managers-in-training learn how to complete a profit and loss statement every four weeks, and, after six months, they know their inventories and how to run a business."

Another reason for Domino's success is the attention it gives to standards. The International stores of Domino's Pizza are kept as close to the U.S. version as possible. Employee uniforms, outdoor signs, and logos are the same as those in the United States. Delivery in 30 minutes or $3 off the price is guaranteed no matter where in the world a Domino's is located, and the menu is always kept simple. Each store must limit the number of toppings it offers, and only two pizza sizes are available.

Domino's operates 200 stores worldwide. It hopes to double that number of stores each year. Cooper said, "Everyone realizes that International is going to be the force in the future."

Source: Adapted from Andrea Chancellor, "Domino's Finds Japanese Sales as Easy as Pie," *Journal of Commerce,* October 13, 1987, p. 1A; and M. R. Czinkota, P. Rivoli, and I. A. Ronkainen, *International Business* (Hinsdale, Ill.: Dryden Press, 1989).

Increase the Firm's International Visibility   Common methods that firms use to attract international attention include participating in trade fairs, circulating of brochures on their products and inventions, and hiring technology-acquisition consultants.

Undertake Cooperative Research Projects   Some firms engage in joint research projects with foreign firms to broaden their contacts, reduce expenses, diminish the risk for each partner, or forestall the entry of competitors into their markets.

In a similar vein, external and internal assessments may be conducted before a firm enters international markets.[3] External assessment involves careful examination of critical features of the international environment, particular attention being paid to the status of the host nation in such areas as economic progress, political control, and nationalism. Expansion of industrial facilities, favorable balances of payments, and improvements in technological capabilities over the past decade are gauges of the host nation's economic progress. Political status can be gauged by the host nation's power in and impact on international affairs.

[3]J. Fayweather and A. Kapoor, *Strategy and Negotiation for the International Corporation* (Cambridge, Mass.: Ballinger, 1976).

CHECKLIST OF FACTORS TO CONSIDER IN CHOOSING A FOREIGN MANUFACTURING SITE

The following considerations were drawn from an 88-point checklist developed by Business International Corporation.

Economic factors:
1. Size of GNP and projected rate of growth.
2. Foreign exchange position.
3. Size of market for the firm's products; rate of growth.
4. Current or prospective membership in a customs union.

Political factors:
5. Form and stability of government.
6. Attitude toward private and foreign investment by government, customers, and competition.
7. Practice of favored versus neutral treatment for state industries.
8. Degree of antiforeign discrimination.

Geographic factors:
9. Efficiency of transport (railways, waterways, highways).
10. Proximity of site to export markets.
11. Availability of local raw materials.
12. Availability of power, water, gas.

Labor factors:
13. Availability of managerial, technical, and office personnel able to speak the language of the parent company.
14. Degree of skill and discipline at all levels.
15. Presence or absence of militant or Communist-dominated unions.
16. Degree and nature of labor voice in management.

Tax factors:
17. Tax rate trends (corporate and personal income, capital, withholding, turnover, excise, payroll, capital gains, customs, and other indirect and local taxes).
18. Joint tax treaties with home country and others.
19. Duty and tax drawbacks when imported goods are exported.
20. Availability of tariff protection.

Capital source factors:
21. Cost of local borrowing.
22. Local availability of convertible currencies.
23. Modern banking systems.
24. Government credit aids to new businesses.

Business factors:
25. State of marketing and distribution system.
26. Normal profit margins in the firm's industry.
27. Competitive situation in the firm's industry; do cartels exist?
28. Availability of amenities for expatriate executives and their families.

Internal assessment involves identification of the basic strengths of a firm's operations. These strengths are particularly important in international operations because they are often the characteristics of a firm that the host nation values most and thus offer significant bargaining leverage. The firm's resource strengths and global capabilities must be analyzed. The resources that should be analyzed include, in particular, technical and managerial skills, capital, labor, and raw materials. The global capabilities that should be analyzed include the firm's product delivery and financial management systems.

A firm that gives serious consideration to internal and external assessment is Business International Corporation, which recommends that seven broad categories of factors be considered. As shown in Strategy in Action 4–2, these categories include economic, political, geographic, labor, tax, capital source, and business factors.

COMPLEXITY OF THE MULTINATIONAL ENVIRONMENT

Multinational strategic planning is more complex than such purely domestic planning. There are at least five factors that contribute to this increase in complexity:

1. Multinationals face multiple political, economic, legal, social, and cultural environments as well as various rates of changes within each of them.
2. Interactions between the national and foreign environments are complex because of national sovereignty issues and widely differing economic and social conditions.
3. Geographic separation, cultural and national differences, and variations in business practices all tend to make communication between headquarters and the overseas affiliates difficult.
4. Multinationals face extreme competition because of differences in industry structures.
5. Multinationals are restricted in their selection of competitive strategies by various international organizations, such as the European Economic Community, the European Free Trade Area, and the Latin American Free Trade Area.

Indications of how these factors contribute to the increased complexity of multinational strategic management are provided in Figure 4–2.

CONTROL PROBLEMS OF THE MULTINATIONAL FIRM

An inherent complicating factor for many multinational firms is that their financial policies are typically designed to further the goals of the parent company and pay minimal attention to the goals of the host countries. This built-in bias creates conflict between the different parts of the multinational firm, between the whole firm and its home and host countries, and between the home and host countries themselves. The conflict is accentuated by the

FIGURE 4–2
Differences between U.S. and Multinational Operations That Affect Strategic Management

Factor	U.S. Operations	International Operations
Language	English used almost universally	Use of local language required in many situations
Culture	Relatively homogeneous	Quite diverse, both between countries and within countries
Politics	Stable and relatively unimportant	Often volatile and of decisive importance
Economy	Relatively uniform	Wide variations among countries and among regions within countries
Government interference	Minimal and reasonably predictable	Extensive and subject to rapid change
Labor	Skilled labor available	Skilled labor often scarce, requiring training or redesign of production methods
Financing	Well-developed financial markets	Poorly developed financial markets; capital flows subject to government control
Market research	Data easy to collect	Data difficult and expensive to collect
Advertising	Many media available; few restrictions	Media limited; many restrictions; low literacy rates rule out print media in some countries
Money	U.S. dollar used universally	Must change from one currency to another; problems created by changing exchange rates and government restrictions
Transportation/ communication	Among the best in the world	Often inadequate
Control	Always a problem, but centralized control will work	A worse problem—centralized control won't work; must walk a tightrope between overcentralizing and losing control through too much decentralizing
Contracts	Once signed, are binding on both parties even if one party makes a bad deal	Can be avoided and renegotiated if one party becomes dissatisfied
Labor relations	Collective bargaining; layoff of workers easy	Layoff of workers often not possible; may have a mandatory worker participation in management; workers may seek change through political process rather than collective bargaining
Trade barriers	Nonexistent	Extensive and very important

Source: R. G. Murdick, R. C. Moor, R. H. Eckhouse, and T. W. Zimmerer, *Business Policy: A Framework for Analysis,* Adapted from 4th ed. (Columbus, Ohio: Grid, 1984), p. 275.

Globalization refers to the strategy of approaching worldwide markets with standardized products. Such markets are most commonly created by end consumers that prefer lower-priced, standardized products over higher-priced, customized products and by MNCs that use their worldwide operations to compete in local markets.[7] *Stakeholder activism* refers to demands placed on the multinational firm by the foreign environments in which it operates, principally by foreign governments. This section provides a basic framework for the analysis of strategic decisions in this complex setting.

Multidomestic Industries and Global Industries

Michael E. Porter has developed a framework for analyzing the basic strategic alternatives of a firm that competes internationally.[8] The starting point of the analysis is an understanding of the industry or industries in which the firm competes. International industries can be ranked along a continuum that ranges from multidomestic to global.

Multidomestic Industries

A multidomestic industry is one in which competition is essentially segmented from country to country. Thus, even if MNCs are in the industry, competition in one country is independent of competition in other countries. Examples of such industries include retailing, insurance, and consumer finance.

In a multidomestic industry, an MNC's subsidiaries should be managed as distinct entities; that is, each subsidiary should be rather autonomous, having the authority to make independent decisions in response to local market conditions. Thus, the international strategy of such an industry is the sum of the strategies developed by subsidiaries operating in different countries. The primary difference between a domestic firm and a multinational firm competing in a multidomestic industry is that the latter makes decisions related to the countries in which it competes and to how it conducts business abroad.

Factors that increase the degree to which an industry is multidomestic include:[9]

—The need for customized products to meet the tastes or preferences of local customers.

—Fragmentation of the industry, with many competitors in each national market.

—A lack of economies of scale in the functional activities of firms in the industry.

—Distribution channels unique to each country.

—A low technological dependence of subsidiaries on R&D provided by the multinational firm.

---

[7]T. Levitt, "The Globalization of Markets," *Harvard Business Review,* September–October 1982, p. 91; and T. Hout, M. E. Porter, and E. Rudden, "How Global Companies Win Out," *Harvard Business Review,* September–October, 1982, pp. 98–108.

[8]Michael E. Porter, "Changing Patterns of International Competition," *California Management Review,* Winter 1986, pp. 9–40.

[9]Y. Doz and C. K. Prahalad, "Patterns of Strategic Control within Multinational Corporations," *Journal of International Business Studies,* Fall 1984, pp. 55–72.

Global Industries

A global industry is one in which competition crosses national borders. In fact, it occurs on a worldwide basis. In such an industry, a firm's strategic moves in one country can be significantly affected by its competitive position in another country. The very rapidly expanding list of global industries includes commercial aircraft, automobiles, mainframe computers, and electronic consumer equipment. Many authorities are convinced that almost all product-oriented industries will soon be global.

The international business scholars Donald A. Ball and Wendell H. McCulloch, Jr., believe that corporate planning must be global for six reasons:[10]

1. *The increased scope of the multinational management task.* Growth in the size and complexity of multinational firms made management virtually impossible without a coordinated plan of action detailing what is expected of whom during a given period. The common practice of management by exception is impossible without such a plan.

2. *The increased internationalization of firms.* Three aspects of international business make global planning necessary: (1) differences among the environmental forces in different countries, (2) greater distances, and (3) the interrelationships of international operations.

3. *The information explosion.* It has been estimated that the world's stock of knowledge is doubling every 10 years. Without the aid of a formal plan, executives can no longer know all that they must know to solve the complex problems they face. A global planning process provides an ordered means for assembling, analyzing, and distilling the information required for sound decisions.

4. *The increase in international competition.* Because of the rapid increase in international competition, firms must constantly adjust to changing conditions or lose markets to competitors. The increase in international competition also spurs managements to search for methods of increasing efficiency and economy.

5. *The rapid development of technology.* Rapid technological development has shortened product life cycles. Planning is necessary to ensure the replacement of products that are moving into the maturity stage, with fewer sales and declining profits. Planning gives management greater control of all aspects of new product introduction.

6. *Planning breeds managerial confidence.* Like the motorist with a road map, managers with a plan for reaching their objectives know where they are going. Such a plan breeds confidence because it spells out every step along the way and assigns responsibility for every task. The plan simplifies the managerial job.

The multinational firm in a global industry must maximize its capabilities through a worldwide strategy. Such a strategy necessitates a high degree of centralized decision making in corporate headquarters so as to permit trade-off decisions across subsidiaries.

Among the factors that made for the creation of a global industry are

Economies of scale in the functional activities of firms in the industry.

A high level of R&D expenditures on products that require more than one market to recover development costs.

---

[10]D. A. Ball and W. H. McCulloch, Jr., *International Business* (Plano, Tex.: Business Publications, 1988), p. 775.

The presence in the industry of predominantly multinational firms that expect consistency of products and services across markets.

The presence of homogeneous product needs across markets, which reduces the requirement of customizing the product for each market.

The presence of a small group of global competitors.

A low level of trade regulation and of regulation regarding foreign direction investment.[11]

The Multinational Challenge

Although industries can be characterized as global or multidomestic, few "pure" cases of either type exist. A multinational firm competing in a global industry must, to some degree, be responsive to local market conditions. Similarly, a multinational firm competing in a multidomestic industry cannot totally ignore opportunities to utilize intracorporate resources in competitive positioning. Thus, each multinational firm must decide which of its corporate functional activities should be performed where and what degree of coordination should exist among them.

Location and Coordination Functional Activities

Typical functional activities of a firm include purchases of input resources, operations, research and development, marketing and sales, and after-sale service. An MNC has a wide range of possible location options for each of these activities and must decide which sets of activities will be performed in how many and which locations. An MNC may have each location perform each activity, or it may center an activity in one location to serve the organization worldwide. For example, research and development centered in one facility may serve the entire organization.

An MNC must also determine the degree to which functional activities are to be coordinated across locations. Such coordination can be extremely low, allowing each location to perform each activity autonomously, or extremely high, tightly linking the functional activities of different locations. Coca-Cola tightly links its R&D and marketing functions worldwide to offer a standardized brand name, concentrate formula, market positioning, and advertising theme. However, its operations function is more autonomous, with the artificial sweetener and packaging differing across locations.[12]

Location and Coordination Issues

Figure 4–4 presents some of the issues related to the critical dimensions of location and coordination in international strategic planning. It also shows the functional activities that the firm performs with regard to each of these dimensions. For example, in connection

---

[11]G. Harvel and C. K. Prahalad, "Managing Strategic Responsibility in the MNC," *Strategic Management Journal,* October–December 1983, pp. 341–51.

[12]J. A. Quelch and E. J. Hoff, "Customizing Global Marketing," *Harvard Business Review,* May–June 1986, pp. 59–68.

FIGURE 4–4
Location and Coordination Issues by Functional Activity

Functional Activity	Location Issues	Coordination Issues
Operations	Location of production facilities for components	Networking of international plants
Marketing	Product line selection Country (market) selection	Commonality of brand name worldwide
		Coordination of sales to multinational accounts
		Similarity of channels and product positioning worldwide
		Coordination of pricing in different countries
Service	Location of service organization	Similarity of service standards and procedures worldwide
Research and development	Number and location of R&D centers	Interchange among dispersed R&D centers
		Developing products responsive to market needs in many countries
		Sequence of product introductions around the world
Purchasing	Location of the purchasing function	Managing suppliers located in different countries
		Transferring market knowledge
		Coordinating purchases of common items

Source: Adapted from Michael E. Porter, "Changing Patterns of International Competition," *California Management Review,* Winter 1986, p. 18.

with the service function, a firm must decide where to perform after-sale service and whether to standardize such service.

How a particular firm should address location and coordination issues depends on the nature of its industry and on the type of international strategy that the firm is pursuing. As discussed earlier, an industry can be ranked along a continuum that ranges between multidomestic at one extreme and global at the other. Little coordination of functional activities across countries may be necessary in a multidomestic industry since competition occurs within each country in such an industry. However, as its industry becomes increasingly global, a firm must begin to coordinate an increasing number of functional activities in order to effectively compete across countries.

International Strategy Options

Figure 4–5 presents the basic international strategy options that have been derived from a consideration of the location and coordination dimensions. Low coordination and geographic dispersion of functional activities are implied if a firm is operating in a multidomestic industry and has chosen a country-centered strategy. This allows each subsidiary

FIGURE 4–5
International Strategy Options

Coordination of activities	Geographically dispersed	Geographically concentrated
High	High foreign investment with extensive coordination among subsidiaries	Global strategy
Low	Country-centered strategy by multinationals with a number of domestic firms operating in only one country	Export-based strategy with decentralized marketing

Location of activities

Source: Adapted from Michael E. Porter, "Changing Patterns of International Competition," *California Management Review,* Winter 1986, p. 19.

to closely monitor the local market conditions it faces and to respond freely to those conditions.

High coordination and geographic concentration of functional activities result from the choice of a pure global strategy. Although some functional activities, such as after-sale service, may need to be located in each market, tight control of those activities is necessary to ensure standardized performance worldwide. For example, IBM expects the same high level of marketing support and service for all of its customers, regardless of their location.

Two other strategy options are shown in Figure 4–5. High foreign investment with extensive coordination among subsidiaries would describe the choice of remaining at a particular growth stage such as that of an exporter. Export-based strategy with decentralized marketing would describe the choice of moving toward globalization, which a multinational firm might make.

MULTINATIONALIZATION OF THE COMPANY MISSION[13]

Few strategic decisions bring about a more radical departure from the existing direction and operations of a firm than the decision to expand internationally. Multinationalization subjects a firm to a radically different set of environmentally determined opportunities,

[13]The material in this section is taken from John A. Pearce II and Kendall Roth, "Multinationalization of the Corporate Mission," *Advanced Management Journal,* Summer 1988, pp. 39–44.

constraints, and risks. To prevent these external factors from dictating the firm's direction, top management must reassess the firm's fundamental purpose, philosophy, and strategic intentions before multinationalization in order to ensure their continuation as decision criteria in proactive planning.

Caterpillar Tractor reversed its decline in market share and profitability in part by multinationalizing its mission. The reversal in 1988–89 can be attributed primarily to the strength of the U.S. dollar, which made Caterpillar's products relatively more expensive in the global market. However, Caterpillar had forecasted the impact of the dollar on its operations in declaring its long-term commitments. Caterpillar's mission states:

1. "Caterpillar prefers to locate facilities wherever in the world it is most economically advantageous to do so from a long-term standpoint."
2. "Facility operations should be planned with the long term in mind in order to minimize the impact of sudden changes in the local work force and economy."

The MNC Mission Statement

Expanding across national borders to secure new market or production opportunities may be initially viewed as consistent with the growth objectives outlined in a firm's existing mission statement. However, a firm's direction is inherently altered as multinationalization occurs. For example, as a firm expands overseas, its operations are physically relocated in foreign operating environments. Since strategic decisions are made in the context of some understanding of the environment, management will absorb information from new sources into its planning processes as the environment becomes pluralistic, with a revised corporate direction as a probable and desirable result. Thus, before reconsidering the firm's strategic choices, management must reassess its mission and institute the changes required as the appropriate environmental information is defined, collected, analyzed, and integrated into existing data bases.

Management must also provide a mission that continues to serve as a basis for evaluating strategic alternatives as this information is incorporated into the firm's decision-making processes. Consider the financial component of Zale Corporation's mission statement from this standpoint:

> Our ultimate responsibility is to our shareholders. Our goal is to earn an optimum return on invested capital through steady profit growth and prudent, aggressive asset management. The attainment of this financial goal, coupled with a record of sound management, represents our approach toward influencing the value placed on our common stock in the market.

From a U.S. perspective, this component seems quite reasonable. In a global context, however, it could be unacceptable. Research has shown that corporate financial goals vary in different countries.[14] The clear preference of French, Japanese, and Dutch ex-

---

[14]A. Stonehill, T. Beekhuisen, R. Wright, L. Remmers, N. Toy, P. Pares, A. Shapiro, D. Egan, and T. Bates, "Financial Goals and Debt Ratio Determinants: A Survey of Practice in Five Countries," *Financial Management*, Autumn 1975, pp. 27–40.

ecutives has been to maximize growth in after-tax earnings, and that of Norwegian executives has been to maximize earnings before interest and taxes. In contrast, these executives have assigned a low priority to the maximization of stockholder wealth. Thus, from a global perspective, a mission statement specifying that a firm's ultimate responsibility is to its stockholders may be an inappropriate basis for its financial operating philosophy. This example illustrates the critical need to review and revise the mission statement prior to international expansion so that it will maintain its relevance in the new situations confronting the firm.

Components of the Company Mission Revisited

The mission statement must be revised to accommodate the changes in strategic decision making, corporate direction, and strategic alternatives mandated by multinationalization and must encompass the additional strategic capabilities that will result from internationalizing operations. Therefore, each of its basic components needs to be analyzed in light of specific considerations that accompany multinationalization.

Product or Service, Market, and Technology

The mission statement defines the basic market need that the firm aims to satisfy. This definition is likely to remain essentially intact in the MNC context since competences acquired in the firm's home country can be exploited as competitive advantages when they are transferred to other countries. However, confronted with a multiplicity of contexts, the firm must redefine its primary market to some extent.

The firm could define its market as global, which would necessitate standardization in product and company responses, or it could pursue a "market concept" orientation by focusing on the particular demands of each national market. The mission statement must provide a basis for strategic decision making in this trade-off situation. For example, the directive in Hewlett-Packard's mission statement, "HP customers must feel that they are dealing with one company with common policies and services," implies a standardized approach designed to provide comparable service to all customers. In contrast, Holiday Inns' mission statement reflects the marketing concept: "Basic to almost everything Holiday Inns, Inc., does is its interaction with its market, the consumer, and its consistent capacity to provide what the consumer wants, when, and where it is needed."

Company Goals: Survival, Growth, and Profitability

The mission statement specifies the firm's intention of securing its future through growth and profitability. In the United States, growth and profitability are considered essential to corporate survival. These goals are also acceptable in other countries that are supportive of the free enterprise system. Following international expansion, however, the firm may operate in countries that are not unequivocally committed to the profit motive. As Figure 4–6 suggests, many countries are committed to state ownership of industries that they view as critical to domestic prosperity. A host country may view social welfare and development goals as taking precedence over the goals of free market capitalism. In Third World countries, for example, employment and income distribution goals often take precedence over rapid economic growth.

FIGURE 4–6
State-Owned Industries in the Multinational Marketplace

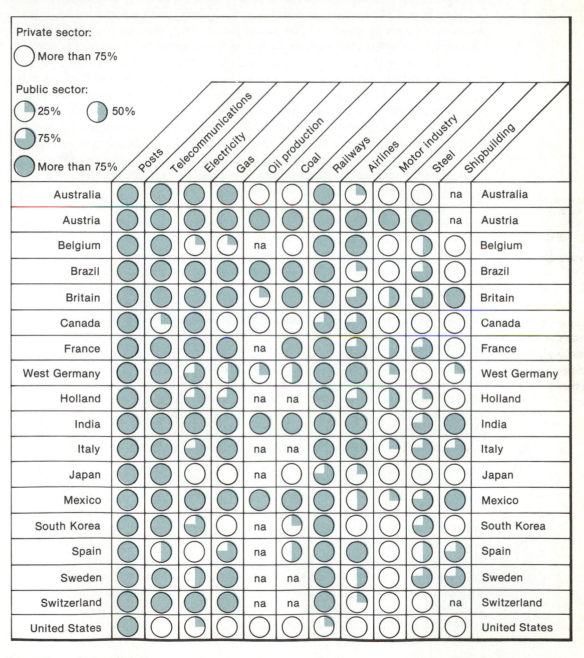

Source: *Economist*, December 21, 1985, p. 72.

Moreover, even countries that accept the profit motive may oppose the profit goals of MNCs. In such countries, the flow of MNC profits is often viewed as unidirectional. At the extreme, the multinational is seen as a tool for exploiting the host country for the exclusive benefit of the parent company's home country, and its profits are regarded as evidence of corporate atrocities. This means that in a multinational context, a corporate commitment to profits may increase the risk of failure rather than help secure survival.

Therefore, the mission statement of an MNC must reflect the firm's intention of securing its survival through dimensions that extend beyond growth and profitability. An MNC must develop a corporate philosophy that embodies its belief in a bidirectional flow of benefits among the firm and its multiple environments. The mission statement of Gulf & Western Americas Corporation expresses this view deftly: "We believe that in a developing country, revenue is inseparable from mandatory social responsibility and that a company is an integral part of the local and national community in which its activities are based."[15] This statement maintains a commitment to profitability yet acknowledges the firm's responsibility to the host country.

The growth dimension of the mission statement remains closely tied to survival and profitability even in the MNC context. Multinationalization disperses corporate resources and operations. This implies that strategic decision makers are no longer located exclusively at corporate headquarters and that they are less accessible for participation in collective decision-making processes. To maintain the firm's cohesiveness in these circumstances, some mechanism is required to record its commitment to a unifying purpose. The mission statement can provide such a mechanism. It can provide the MNC's decision makers with a common guiding thread of understanding and purpose.

Company Philosophy

Within the domestic setting, implicit understandings result in a general uniformity of corporate values and behavior even if a firm's philosophy goes unstated. Few domestic events challenge a firm to properly formulate and implement its implied or expressed philosophy. Multinationalization, however, is clearly such an event. A corporate philosophy developed from a singular perspective is inadequate for a firm that functions in variant cultures. A firm's values and beliefs are primarily culturally defined, reflecting the general philosophical perspective of the society in which the firm operates. Thus, when a firm extends its operations into another society, it encounters a new set of accepted corporate values and beliefs, which it must assimilate and incorporate into its own.

For example, numerous U.S. multinational corporations have been subjected to considerable criticism with regard to the policies of their South African, Namibian, and Dominican Republic subsidiaries. In general, violations of corporate social responsibility pertaining to working standards have been alleged, not by coalitions within host countries but by coalitions within the United States, such as the Interfaith Center on Corporate Responsibility. Thus, if an MNC tailors its values and beliefs to those of interest groups in various host countries, it will generate domestic opposition to which it must respond. Consequently, in adopting a company philosophy, an MNC must recognize its accountability to such opposition.

---

[15]See O. Williams, "Who Cast the First Stone?" *Harvard Business Review*, September–October 1984, pp. 151–61.

DOES DIRECT FOREIGN INVESTMENT "COST" JOBS?

Between 1980 and 1985, Japanese direct investment in the United States tripled, and it is expected to grow 14.2 percent each year until 2000. Japan's Ministry of Industry and Trade estimates that such investment will create 840,000 jobs in the United States directly, and millions of additional jobs indirectly.

Many U.S. experts disagree. They cite as examples the construction contracts for Fujitsu's $30 million magnetic disc plant and Hattori Seiko's $10 million printer assembly plant that were awarded to Shimizu America Corporation, the local arm of Tokyo's $4.7 billion Shimizu Construction Company. The same contractor was also designated as the prime subcontractor on the Toyota/GM plant in Fremont, California, and the Sharp electronics plant in Memphis, Tennessee.

Many national development experts additionally argue that the arrival of Japanese builders has disturbing implications for U.S. producers of the hardware and software to be purchased for the new plants. GE's manager of planning and development, Robert W. Baeder, said, "The brick and the mortar isn't the critical end; it's the systems and the software." A central concern is that Japanese general contractors will put Japanese-produced computers, robots, and numerically controlled machine tools into the factories they build in the United States.

Similar fears are being expressed by suppliers to the major domestic producers. American auto-parts makers have become vulnerable to competition by the foreign-affiliated suppliers who have followed Japanese automakers into Kentucky, Ohio, and Tennessee. "They are not creating jobs," said William A. Raftery, president of the Motor and Equipment Manufacturers Association, "they are stealing them."

Source: Mark Beauchamp, "Close the Door, They Are Coming through the Windows," *Forbes*, January 27, 1986, pp. 81–84; and "Japan, U.S.A.," *Business Week*, July 14, 1986, pp. 45–55.

Direct investment by U.S. firms in foreign countries can also give rise to unintended and unexpected consequences that cool the hospitality of host nations. For example, as shown in Strategy in Action 4–3, such investment can have results that contradict the intentions and philosophies of all the concerned parties.

Self-Concept

The multinationalized self-concept of a firm is dependent on management's understanding of the firm's strengths and weaknesses as a competitor in each of its operating arenas. The firm's ability to survive in multiple dynamic and highly competitive environments is severely limited if its management does not understand the impact it has or can have on those environments, and vice versa.

Public Image

Domestically, a firm's public image is often shaped from a marketing viewpoint. That image is managed as a marketing tool whose objective is customer acceptance of the firm's product. Although this consideration remains critical in the multinational environment, in that environment it must be balanced with consideration of organizational claimants other than the customer. In many countries, the MNC is a major user of national resources and a major force in socialization processes. Thus, it must broaden its image so as to clearly convey its recognition of the additional internal and external claimants resulting from multinationalization. The following excerpt from Hewlett-Packard's mission statement exemplifies such an image: "As a corporation operating in many different communities throughout the world, we must assure ourselves that each of these communities is better for our presence. . . . Each community has its particular set of social problems. Our company must help to solve these problems." These words convey an image of Hewlett-Packard's responsiveness to claimants throughout the world.

SUMMARY

To understand the strategic planning options available to a multinational corporation, its managers need to recognize that different types of industry-based competition exist. Specifically, they must identify the position of their industry along the global versus multidomestic continuum and then consider the implications of that position for their firm. This is the first step in developing a multinational strategy.

The differences between global and multidomestic industries with regard to the location and coordination of functional corporate activities necessitate differences in strategic emphasis. As an industry becomes global, managers of firms within that industry must increase the coordination and concentration of functional activities.

The appendix at the end of this chapter lists many components of the environment with which MNCs must contend. This list is useful in understanding the issues that confront MNCs and in evaluating the thoroughness of MNC strategies.

As a starting point for international expansion, the firm's mission statement needs to be reviewed and revised. As multinational operations fundamentally alter the direction and strategic capabilities of a firm, its mission statement, originally developed from a domestic perspective, must be multinationalized.

The multinationalized mission statement provides the firm with a unity of direction that transcends the divergent perspectives of geographically dispersed managers. It provides a basis for strategic decisions in situations where strategic alternatives may appear to conflict. It promotes corporate values and commitments that extend beyond single cultures and satisfies the demands of the firm's internal and external claimants in different countries. Finally, it ensures the survival of the MNC by asserting the MNC's legitimacy with respect to support coalitions in a variety of operating environments.

QUESTIONS FOR DISCUSSION

1. How does environmental analysis at the domestic level differ from a multinational analysis?
2. Which factors complicate environmental analysis at the multinational level? Which factors are making such analysis easier?
3. Do you agree with the suggestion that soon all industries will need to evaluate global environments?

4. Which industries operate almost devoid of international competition? Which inherent immunities do they enjoy?

BIBLIOGRAPHY

Aggarwal, R. "The Strategic Challenge of the Evolving Global Economy." *Business Horizons,* July–August 1987, pp. 38–44.

Allio, R. J. "Formulating Global Strategy." *Planning Review,* March–April 1989, pp. 22–29.

Alston, J. P. "Wa, Guanxi, and Inhwa: Managerial Principles in Japan, China, and Korea." *Business Horizons,* March–April 1989, pp. 26–31.

Amsden, A. H. "Private Enterprise: The Issue of Business-Government Control." *Columbia Journal of World Business,* Spring 1988, pp. 37–42.

Barnlund, D. C. "Public and Private Self in Communicating with Japan." *Business Horizons,* March–April 1989, pp. 32–40.

Bolt, J. F. "Global Competitors: Some Criteria for Success." *Business Horizons,* May–June 1988, pp. 62–72.

Bunke, H. C. "Lessons from Singapore." *Business Horizons,* May–June 1989, pp. 2–10.

Calantone, R. J., and C. A. di Benedetto. "Defensive Marketing in Globally Competitive Industrial Markets." *Columbia Journal of World Business,* Fall 1988, pp. 3–14.

Carter, J. R., and J. Gagne. "The Dos and Don'ts of International Countertrade." *Sloan Management Review,* Spring 1988, pp. 31–37.

Chankin, W., and R. A. Mauborgne. "Becoming an Effective Global Competitor." *Journal of Business Strategy,* January–February 1988, pp. 33–37.

Chaudhuri, A. "Multinational Corporations in Less-Developed Countries: What Is in Store?" *Columbia Journal of World Business,* Spring 1988, pp. 57–63.

Fannin, W. R., and C. B. Gilmore. "Developing a Strategy for International Business." *Long Range Planning,* June 1986, pp. 81–85.

Franko, L. G. "Global Corporate Competition: Who's Winning, Who's Losing, and the R&D Factor as One Reason Why." *Strategic Management Journal,* September–October 1989, pp. 449–74.

Friedmann, R., and J. Kim. "Political Risk and International Marketing." *Columbia Journal of World Business,* Fall 1988, pp. 63–74.

Garsombke, D. "International Competitors Analysis," *Planning Review,* May–June 1989, pp. 42–47.

Godiwalla, Y. H. "Multinational Planning—Developing a Global Approach." *Long Range Planning,* April 1986, pp. 110–16.

Gomes-Casseres, B. "Joint Ventures in the Face of Global Competition." *Sloan Management Review,* Spring 1989, pp. 17–26.

Higgins, J. M., and T. Santalainen. "Strategies for Europe, 1992." *Business Horizons,* July–August 1989, pp. 54–58.

Hitt, M. A., and R. D. Ireland. "Building Competitive Strength in International Markets." *Long Range Planning,* February 1987, pp. 115–22.

Hout, T.; M. E. Porter; and E. Rudden. "How Global Companies Win Out." *Harvard Business Review,* September–October 1982, pp. 98–108.

Kashani, K. "Beware of the Pitfalls of Global Marketing." *Harvard Business Review,* September–October 1989, pp. 91–98.

Kedia, B. L., and R. S. Bhagat. "Cultural Constraints on Transfer of Technology across Nations: Implications for Research in International and Comparative Management." *Academy of Management Review,* October 1988, pp. 558–71.

Kim, W. C. "Global Diversification Strategy and Corporate Profit Performance." *Strategic Management Journal*, January–February 1989, pp. 45–57.

Knotts, R. "Cross-Cultural Management: Transformations and Adaptations." *Business Horizons*, January–February 1989, pp. 29–33.

Koch, J. V. "An Economic Profile of the Pacific Rim." *Business Horizons*, March–April 1989, pp. 18–25.

Koepfler, E. R. "Strategic Options for Global Market Players." *Journal of Business Strategy*, July–August 1989, pp. 46–50.

Kogut, B. "Designing Global Strategies: Profiting from Operational Flexibility." *Sloan Management Review*, Fall 1985, pp. 27–38.

Kuhn, R. L. "Japanese-American Strategic Alliances." *Journal of Business Strategy*, March–April 1989, pp. 51–53.

Larson, M. R. "Exporting Private Enterprise to Developing Communist Countries." *Columbia Journal of World Business*, Spring 1988, pp. 79–90.

Levy, B. "Korean and Taiwanese Firms as International Competitors." *Columbia Journal of World Business*, Spring 1988, pp. 43–51.

Magee, J. F. "1992: Moves Americans Must Make." *Harvard Business Review*, May–June 1989, pp. 78–84.

Metzger, R. O., and A. Ginsburg. "Lessons from Japanese Global Acquisitions." *Journal of Business Strategy*, May–June 1989, pp. 32–36.

———. "The Global Logic of Strategic Alliances." *Harvard Business Review*, March–April 1989, pp. 143–54.

———. "Managing in a Borderless World." *Harvard Business Review*, May–June 1989, pp. 152–61.

———. "Planting for a Global Harvest." *Harvard Business Review*, July–August 1989, pp. 136–45.

Onkvisit, S., and J. J. Shaw. "Marketing Barriers in International Trade." *Business Horizons*, May–June 1988, pp. 64–72.

O'Reilly, A. J. F. "Establishing Successful Joint Ventures in Developing Nations: A CEO's Perspective." *Columbia Journal of World Business*, Spring 1988, pp. 65–71.

Schmidt, W. G. "Heinz Covers the Globe." *Journal of Business Strategy*, March–April 1989, pp. 17–20.

Schwartz, H. "The Potential Role of Behavioral Analysis in the Promotion of Private Enterprise in Developing Countries." *Columbia Journal of World Business*, Spring 1988, pp. 53–56.

Shanks, D. "Strategic Planning for Global Competition." *Journal of Business Strategy*, Winter 1985, pp. 80–89.

Webster, D. R. "International Joint Ventures with Pacific Rim Partners." *Business Horizons*, March–April 1989, pp. 65–71.

West, P. "Cross-Cultural Literacy and the Pacific Rim." *Business Horizons*, March–April 1989, pp. 3–17.

White, B. J. "The Internationalization of Business." *Academy of Management Executive*, February 1988, pp. 29–32.

White, M. I. "Learning and Working in Japan." *Business Horizons*, March–April 1989, pp. 41–47.

Whitehall, A. M. "American Executives through Foreign Eyes." *Business Horizons*, May–June 1989, pp. 42–48.

Wright, P. "Strategic Management within a World Parameter." *Managerial Planning*, January–February 1985, pp. 33–36.

Yamaguchi, T. S. "The Challenge of Internationalization: Japan's Kokusaika." *Academy of Management Executive*, February 1988, pp. 33–36.

Yip, G. S.; P. M. Loewe; and M. Y. Yoshino. "How to Take Your Company to the Global Market." *Columbia Journal of World Business*, Winter 1988, pp. 37–48.

APPENDIX

COMPONENTS OF THE MULTINATIONAL ENVIRONMENT

Multinational firms must operate within an environment that has numerous components. These components include:

I. Government, laws, regulations, and policies of home country (United States, for example).
  A. Monetary and fiscal policies and their effect on price trends, interest rates, economic growth, and stability.
  B. Balance-of-payment policies.
    1. Mandatory controls on direct investment.
    2. Interest equalization tax and other policies.
  C. Commercial policies, especially tariffs, quantitative import restrictions, and voluntary import controls.
  D. Export controls and other restrictions on trade with East European and other communist nations.
  E. Tax policies and their impact on overseas business.
  F. Antitrust regulations, their administration, and their impact on international business.
  G. Investment guarantees, investment surveys, and other programs to encourage private investments in less developed countries.
  H. Export-import and governmental export expansion programs.
  I. Other changes in government policy that affect international business.

II. Key political and legal parameters in foreign countries and their projection.
  A. Type of political and economic system, political philosophy, national ideology.
  B. Major political parties, their philosophies, and their policies.
  C. Stability of the government.
    1. Changes in political parties.
    2. Changes in governments.
  D. Assessment of nationalism and its possible impact on political environment and legislation.
  E. Assessment of political vulnerability.
    1. Possibilities of expropriation.
    2. Unfavorable and discriminatory national legislation and tax laws.
    3. Labor laws and problems.

Source: W. A. Dymsza, *Multinational Business Strategy* (New York: McGraw-Hill, 1972), pp. 83–85.

F. Favorable political aspects.
   1. Tax and other concessions to encourage foreign investments.
   2. Credit and other guarantees.
G. Differences in legal system and commercial law.
H. Jurisdiction in legal disputes.
 I. Antitrust laws and rules of competition.
 J. Arbitration clauses and their enforcement.
K. Protection of patients, trademarks, brand names, and other industrial property rights.

III. Key economic parameters and their projection.
   A. Population and its distribution by age groups, density, annual percentage increase, percentage of working age, percentage of total in agriculture, percentage in urban centers.
   B. Level of economic development and industrialization.
   C. Gross national product, gross domestic product, or national income in real terms and also on a per capita basis in recent years and projections over future planning period.
   D. Distribution of personal income.
   E. Measures of price stability and inflation, wholesale price index, consumer price index, other price indexes.
   F. Supply of labor, wage rates.
   G. Balance-of-payments equilibrium or disequilibrium, level of international monetary reserves, and balance-of-payments policies.
   H. Trends in exchange rates, currency stability, evaluation of possibility of depreciation of currency.
    I. Tariffs, quantitative restrictions, export controls, border taxes, exchange controls, state trading, and other entry barriers to foreign trade.
    J. Monetary, fiscal, and tax policies.
   K. Exchange controls and other restrictions on capital movements, repatriation of capital, and remission of earnings.

IV. Business system and structure.
   A. Prevailing business philosophy: mixed capitalism, planned economy, state socialism.
   B. Major types of industry and economic activities.
   C. Numbers, size, and types of firms, including legal forms of business.
   D. Organization: proprietorships, partnerships, limited companies, corporations, cooperatives, state enterprises.
   E. Local ownership patterns: public and privately held corporations, family-owned enterprises.
   F. Domestic and foreign patterns of ownership in major industries.
   G. Business managers available: their education, training, experience, career patterns, attitudes, and reputations.
   H. Business associations and chambers of commerce and their influence.
    I. Business codes, both formal and informal.

    J. Marketing institutions: distributors, agents, wholesalers, retailers, advertising agencies, advertising media, marketing research and other consultants.

    K. Financial and other business institutions: commercial and investment banks, other financial institutions, capital markets, money markets, foreign exchange dealers, insurance firms, engineering companies.

    L. Managerial processes and practices with respect to planning, administration, operations, accounting, budgeting, control.

V. Social and cultural parameters and their projections.

    A. Literacy and educational levels.

    B. Business, economic, technical, and other specialized education available.

    C. Language and cultural characteristics.

    D. Class structure and mobility.

    E. Religious, racial, and national characteristics.

    F. Degree of urbanization and rural-urban shifts.

    G. Strength of nationalistic sentiment.

    H. Rate of social change.

    I. Impact of nationalism on social and institutional change.

CHAPTER 4 COHESION CASE

EVALUATING THE MULTINATIONAL ENVIRONMENT

Bryson's management group decided to take a global look at hazardous waste management, with two main purposes in mind:

1. To become more familiar with hazardous waste management practices around the world to detect trends and procedures that might become a part of the U.S. experience.

2. To be more aware of opportunities that Bryson may be in a position to take advantage of by being familiar with hazwaste management practices in other industrialized nations.

Working in conjunction with a student in the international business program of a nearby university, the following internal report was assembled.

A GLOBAL LOOK AT HAZARDOUS WASTES

Hazardous waste management is not strictly a U.S. issue. Throughout the world, nations—industrialized and developing—know that they must be concerned with the management of these wastes and the means to improve their practices. This concern is so great, in fact, that the International Solid Waste and Public Cleansing Association (ISWA) established a working group on hazwastes to compare and contrast the status of hazwaste management practices around the world.

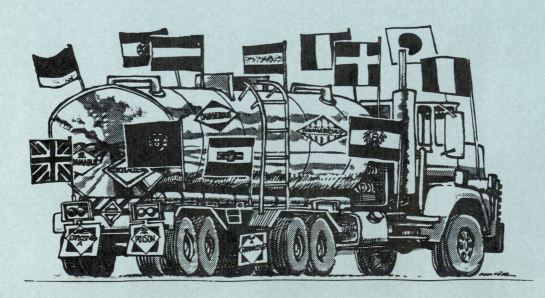

Establishment of a national regulatory control program—with appropriate legislation, regulations, ordinances, and licenses—is probably the singular most important step to protect human health and the environment from mismanagement of hazwaste, as well as the best impetus for services provided by a hazwaste management industry. There are 12 countries with a national regulatory program similar to the U.S. program. Their programs are summarized in the Table 1.

Countries without regulatory control (most developing and Third World countries) experience indiscriminant dumping of hazardous wastes or insufficient codisposal with municipal wastes. Alternative methods of treatment, like incineration, are not adequately developed, and frequently these nations have become a dumping ground for imported wastes—Mexico has received wastes from U.S. companies and Morocco wastes from several European companies, wherein local business people legally take title to the wastes and simply dispose of it on the ground at a cost to the U.S. and European generators significantly less than they would have to pay domestically.

(*Bryson management interpretation*: Be sensitive to the possibility that some generators in southeastern markets, particularly those served through Memphis, may be using such an approach with existing or fictitious Mexican companies. Report these if found, as well as the one known incident where untrained and ill-equipped Mexican nationals were brought in to do the labor on a Louisiana remediation job—at very low costs—without being RCRA-trained, equipped, and certified. Take every opportunity to disassociate Bryson with such practices.)

Focusing on the 12 developed countries with national regulation, these comparisons were of particular interest:

1. **Hazardous wastes are defined differently in each country.** Some countries, like Denmark and the United Kingdom, define hazwastes very broadly, covering all industrial wastes and many household wastes. Others, like the United States, define hazwastes much narrower, meaning federal legislation applies only to specific hazwastes.

(*Bryson management interpretation*: Monitor the moves in progressive states to add wastes to their hazwaste list and similar moves in the household wastes area to assess their implications for Bryson's long-term services in the Southeast.)

2. **Notification and defined responsibilities of waste generators.** Every country has required generator reporting systems to properly identify and to assure proper packaging and labeling, as well as tracking wastes to their final destination. In the Netherlands, each generator is also required to orally notify regulatory authorities of every hazwaste transfer.

3. **Specified responsibilities for waste transporters,** including requirements for safe transport and a manifest or trip-ticket system, that provides a record for identifying and locating lost or misdirected shipments.

4. **Required facility license permits** are similar in all 12 countries for any hazwaste treatment, storage, or disposal facility. Licenses impose design, operation, and maintenance conditions as a basis for permission to operate.

(*Bryson management interpretation*: These requirements appear similar across every country. Special administrative programs, like computer programs, for monitoring waste handling should be investigated to see if an effective alternative to Bryson's current one is available.)

TABLE 1
Elements in National Control Systems

	Austria	Denmark	FRG	France	Italy	Japan	Netherlands	Spain	Sweden	Southern Africa	UK	USA
State of progress												
Date of main legislation	1983	1972	1972	1975	1982/84	1970	1979	no system yet enacted	1975	proposed (1)	1972/74	1976/84
Registration/ licensing (2)												
Collectors/ transporters	L	(3)	L	R	L	L	No	—	L	No	No	R
Treatment/ disposal contractors	L	L	L	R	No	L	L	—	L	No	No	R
Control over transport												
Manifest system	Yes	Yes	Yes	New	Yes	No	Yes	—	Soon	No	Yes	Yes
Control over import	Yes	Yes	Yes	Yes	Yes	Yes	Yes	—	Yes	by sea	Soon	Yes
Control over export	No	Yes	Yes	Soon	Yes	Yes	Yes	—	Yes	by sea	Soon	Yes
Permitting of facilities												
Storage	Yes(4)	Yes	Yes	Yes	Yes	Yes	Yes	—	Yes	Soon	Soon	Yes
Treatment	Yes	Yes	Yes	Yes	Yes	Yes	Yes	—	Yes	Soon	Yes	Yes
Disposal	Yes	Yes	Yes	Yes	Yes	Yes	Yes	—	Yes	Soon	Yes	Yes
Have all operating sites now been permitted?	No	Yes	Yes	Yes	No	Yes	Yes	—	Yes	No	Yes	No
Planning and establishment of facilities												
Is there a national strategy/plan?	Yes	Yes	No	No	No	No	Yes	—	No	No	No	No
Are authorities required to produce a plan?	Yes	Yes	Yes	No	Yes	Yes	Yes	—	No	Yes	Yes	No
Has this been done?	Yes	Yes	Yes	No	No	Partial	Yes	—	No	No	Partial	No
Old or abandoned hazardous waste sites												
Is there a national inventory	New	Yes	Yes	Yes	No	No	Yes	—	Yes	No	No	Yes
Is there a clean-up program?	No	Yes	(5)	(5)	No	No	Yes	—	Yes	No	No	Yes

(1) In Southern Africa, the situation varies between countries. In most cases, control is presently informal, in the absence of formal legislation.

(2) L = licensing scheme, implying investigation by the authorities; R = registration, implying simply being listed in a register.

(3) Partial, from the central collection points to the treatment plant.

(4) Mainly under the Trade Act, not under the Hazardous Waste Act.

(5) Although there is no formal, nationwide clean-up program, the clean-up of individual sites is proceeding.

144

5. **Old and abandoned industrial facilities.** Italy and Spain appear to be countries with significant numbers of sites needing remediation. Surprisingly, only the United States has a comprehensive national program currently in existence (Superfund) to deal with old and abandoned sites in need of environmental cleanup.

(*Bryson management interpretation*: A significant demand for remediation worldwide will emerge over the next 10 years. The probable implication is that it will fuel the growth of the largest U.S. remediation firms and their focus on large-scale remediation technologies. It may well aid Bryson by its being able to focus on smaller—less than $250,000—remediation jobs that these larger players are less inclined to bother with.)

6. **Treatment, disposal, and recycling facilities.** European countries stress incineration and treatment as their means for handling about 80 percent of their hazwaste. The United Kingdom is an exception, with over 85 percent of all hazwastes disposed of in landfills. There is no rotary kiln (incineration) in the U.K. The use of landfills, surface impoundments, and deep well injection are also methods of choice in the United States.

Several European countries—Denmark, Sweden, Netherlands—have large, centralized disposal facilities serving industry throughout their countries. West Germany has several onsite treatment and incineration facilities built by their larger chemical companies, which also sell capacity to other companies. France places primary emphasis on commercial treatment and incineration facilities at the same site, and it also has a major national program that invests in programs/businesses developing improvements in methods for treating and recycling hazwastes.

(*Bryson management interpretation*: We should increase our ability to monitor what is happening in France and to look for ways to develop recycling efforts we will be involved with in Alabama and possibly at Wall Chemical. The West German practice could foretell a U.S. trend we already see at Du Pont—large waste producers getting into the waste treatment/incineration/disposal business. Bryson should monitor this with its key big customers to preplan handling potential loss of this business and hopefully be in a position to joint venture or preferred vend services to them if they do so.)

1. Having read Bryson's effort to evaluate the multinational environment, what is your assessment of their interpretations?
2. If you were advising Bryson, what would you suggest they change about the global environmental assessment approach? Why would you suggest this and how would you justify it?

5 ENVIRONMENTAL FORECASTING

IMPORTANCE OF FORECASTING

Change was rapid in the 1980s, with even greater changes and challenges forecast for the 1990s. The crucial responsibility for managers will be ensuring their firm's capacity for survival. This will be done by anticipating and adapting to environmental changes in ways that provide new opportunities for growth and profitability. The impact of changes in the remote industry and task environments must be understood and predicted.[1]

Even large firms in established industries will be actively involved in transitions. The $5.5 billion loss in the U.S. auto industry in the early 1980s is a classic example of what can happen when firms fail to place a priority on environmental forecasting. The preceding decade saw a 20 percent penetration of the U.S. new car market by foreign competition, a nation-crippling oil embargo, rapidly climbing fuel prices, and uncertain future supplies of crude oil. Yet the long-range implications of these predictable factors on future auto sales were largely ignored by U.S. automakers. Because it was not open to changes in technology, Detroit was left without viable, fuel-efficient, quality-made alternatives for the American market. On the other hand, Japanese automakers anticipated the future need for fuel efficiency, quality, and service through careful market research and environmental forecasting. As a result, they gained additional market share at Detroit's expense.

In retaliation, American automakers spent $80 billion over a three-year period on product and capital-investment strategies that were meant to recapture their lost market share. They realized that success in strategic decisions rests not solely on dollar amounts but also on anticipation of and preparation for the future.

Accurate forecasting of changing elements in the environment is an essential part of

---

[1]S. C. Sufrin and G. S. Odiorne, "The New Strategic Planning Boom: Hope for the Future or/a Bureaucratic Exercise?" *Managerial Planning*, January 1985, pp. 4–46; and C. Starry and N. McGaughey, "Growth Industries: Here Today, Gone Tomorrow," *Business Horizons*, July 1988, pp. 69–74.

STRATEGY IN ACTION 5–1 THE FUTURE OF RETAILING

Small retailers striving to remain competitive in the new year may want to heed the projections of a new study on the retailing industry from the Harris Bank in Chicago.

The study focuses on such topics as demographics, the labor force, pricing concerns, and acquisitions.

Among the study's forecasts:

Retailers will dedicate more resources to training all employees, not only about merchandise but also about the significance of quality service.

Wage levels will increase. This, combined with the expected rise in training costs and increased levels of health-care expenditures, will bring about a substantial rise in employment costs for retailers.

The current shortage of entry-level employees will continue to grow because of the decreasing number of people in the 18–24 age group. A possible solution to this problem, according to the study, is the growing employment of retirees as part-time workers. Older workers are proving to be a boon to retailers' efforts to improve customer service.

The use of state-of-the-art technology will gain increased importance among retailers because such technology is the key to maintaining high levels of customer service and controlling costs.

Vertically integrated merchandisers will continue to shift manufacturing operations to Asian countries now in the early stages of industrialization. Substantial cost savings should be realized because of the labor-intensive nature of such manufacturing operations and the lower labor costs in these countries.

In the future, acquisition activity will not be limited to domestic companies.

More retailers will look to the Far East, Canada, and Europe for buying opportunities.

The study is based on extensive research of the retailing industry, including an in-depth review of the financial performance of 55 retailing concerns.

Source: *Nation's Business*, October 1989, p. 8.

strategic management.[2] A specific example is the retailing study conducted by the Harris Bank in Chicago. As described in Strategy in Action 5–1, in 1988 Harris Bank undertook to forecast the future of retailing in 1990 as a basis for advising its corporate customers on their strategic planning activities.

Forecasting and business environment for the 1990s led many firms to diversify. For example, USX Corporation (formerly U.S. Steel) purchased Marathon Oil so as to have a profit generator whose proceeds could be used to turn USX into a low-cost steel producer.

---

[2]S. C. Jain, "Environmental Scanning in U.S. Corporations," *Long Range Planning*, April 1984, pp. 117–28; and A. H. Mesch, "Developing an Effective Environmental Assessment Function," *Managerial Planning*, March 1984, pp. 17–22.

Other firms have forecast a need for massive retrenchment. One such firm is Chrysler Corporation, which laid off 9,000 employees in 1987 and 1988 to streamline its cost of doing business. Still other firms have cut back in one area of operations to underwrite growth in another. For example, CBS sold its Records Division to Sony in 1988 for $2 billion to raise the capital it needed for its planned expansion in television stations in the 1990s.

These and many other examples indicate that strategic managers need to develop skill in predicting significant environmental changes. To aid in the search for future opportunities and constraints, they should take the following steps:

1. Select the environmental variables that are critical to the firm.
2. Select the sources of significant environmental information.
3. Evaluate forecasting techniques.
4. Integrate forecast results into the strategic management process.
5. Monitor the critical aspects of managing forecasts.

SELECT CRITICAL ENVIRONMENTAL VARIABLES

Management experts have argued that the most important cause of the turbulent business environment is the change in population structure and dynamics. This change, in turn, produced other major changes in the economic, social, and political environments.

Historically, population shifts tended to occur over 40–50 year periods and therefore had little relevance to business decisions. During the second half of the 20th century, however, population changes have become radical, erratic, contradictory, and therefore of great importance.

For example, the U.S. baby boom between 1945 and the mid-1960s has had and will have a dramatic impact on all parts of society—from maternity wards and schools to the labor force and the marketplace. This population bulge is facing heavy competition for jobs, promotions, and housing, despite a highest-ever educational level. Compounding the problem are the heightened expectations of women and racial minorities. The lack of high-status jobs to fit these expectations poses a potential for major social and economic changes. In addition, an increasingly aging labor force finds it difficult to give up status, power, and employment when retirement programs are either not financially attractive or not available at the traditional age of 65. (See Figure 5–1 for work force projections through the year 2000.)

Obviously, the demands of these groups will have important effects on social and political changes in terms of lifestyle, consumption patterns, and political decisions. In economic terms, the size and potential affluence of these groups suggest increasing markets for housing, consumer products, and leisure goods and services.

Interestingly, the same shifts in population, life expectancy, and education have occurred in many developed nations. However, developing nations face the opposite population configurations. Although birthrates have declined, high survival rates resulting from medical improvements, have created a large population of people who will reach adulthood in the 1990s. Jobs and food are expected to be in short supply. Therefore,

FIGURE 5–1
The New Work Force

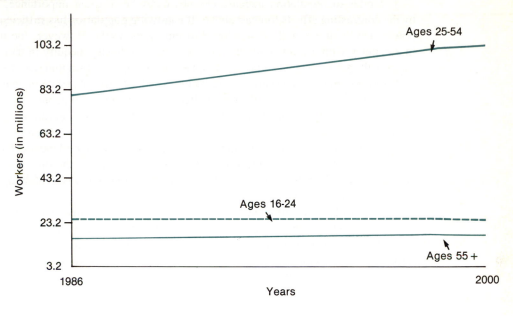

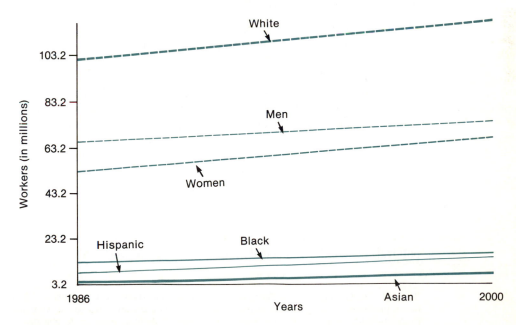

Source: *American Demographics.*

1. Include all variables that would have a significant impact although their probability of occurrence is low (e.g., trucking deregulation). Also include highly probable variables regardless of their impact (e.g., a minimal price increase by a major supplier). Delete others with little impact and low probabilities.[6]
2. Disregard major disasters, such as nuclear war.
3. When possible, aggregate variables into gross variables (e.g., a bank loan is based more on the dependability of a firm's cash flow than on the flow's component sources).
4. If the value of one variable is based on the value of another, separate the dependent variable for future planning.

Limits of money, time, and forecasting skill prevent a firm from predicting many variables. The task of predicting even a dozen is substantial. Firms often try to select a set of key variables by analyzing the environmental factors in the industry that are most likely to foster sharp growth or decline in the marketplace. For the furniture, appliance, and textiles industries, housing starts are a key variable. Housing starts, in turn, are greatly affected by interest rates.

Figure 5–2 identifies some issues that may have critical impacts on a firm's future success.

SELECT SOURCES OF SIGNIFICANT ENVIRONMENTAL INFORMATION

Before formal forecasting can begin, appropriate sources of environmental information should be identified. Casual gathering of strategic information—through reading, interactions, and meetings—is part of the normal course of executive behavior but is subject to bias and must be balanced with alternative viewpoints. Although *The Wall Street Journal, Business Week, Fortune, Harvard Business Review, Forbes,* and other popular trade and scholarly journals are important sources of forecasting information, formal, deliberate, and structured searches are desirable. Appendix 5–A to this chapter lists published sources that strategic managers can use to meet their specific forecasting needs. If the firm can afford the time and expense, it should also gather primary data in such areas as market factors, technological changes, and competitive and supplier strategies.

EVALUATE FORECASTING TECHNIQUES

Debate exists over the accuracy of quantitative versus qualitative approaches to forecasting (see Figure 5–3), with most research supporting quantitative models. However, the differences in the predictions derived from these approaches are often minimal. Moreover, subjective or judgmental approaches are often the only practical method of forecasting political, legal, social, and technological trends in the remote external environment. The

---

[6]M. A. Stromp, "Questioning Assumptions: One Company's Answer to the Planner's Nemesis," *Planning Review,* September 1986, pp. 10–15.

FIGURE 5–3
Popular Approaches to Forecasting

Technique	Short Description	Cost	Popularity	Complexity	Association with Life-Cycle Stage
Quantitative/Causal models					
Econometric models	Simultaneous systems of multiple regression equations	High	High	High	Steady state
Single and multiple regression	Variations in dependent variables are explained by variations in one or more independent variables	High/ medium	High	Medium	Steady state
Times series models	Linear, exponential, S-curve, or other types of projections	Medium	High	Medium	Steady state
Trend extrapolation	Forecasts obtained by linear or exponential smoothing or averaging of past actual values	Medium	High	Medium	Steady state
Qualitative or judgmental models					
Sales force estimate	A bottom-up approach aggregating salespersons' forecasts	Low	High	Low	All stages
Juries of executive opinion	Forecasts jointly prepared by marketing, production, finance, and purchasing executives	Low	High	Low	Product development
Customer surveys; market research	Learning about intentions of potential customers or plans of businessess	Medium	Medium	Medium	Market testing and early introudction
Scenario development	Impacts of anticipated conditions imagined by forecasters	Low	Medium	Low	All stages
Delphi method	Experts guided toward a consensus	Low	Medium	Medium	Product development
Brainstorming	Idea generation in a noncritical group situation	Low	Medium	Medium	Product development

same is true of several factors in the task environment, especially customer and competitive considerations.

Ultimately, the choice of technique depends not on the environmental factor under review but on such considerations as the nature of the forecast decision, the amount and accuracy of available information, the accuracy required, the time available, the importance of the forecast, the cost, and the competence and interpersonal relationships of the managers and forecasters involved.[7] Frequently, assessment of such considerations leads to the selection of a combination of quantitative and qualitative techniques, thereby strengthening the accuracy of the ultimate forecast.[8]

[7]S. C. Wheelwright and C. G. Clarke, "Corporate Forecasting: Promise and Reality," *Harvard Business Review*, November–December 1976, p. 42.

[8]R. S. Clark, "The Strategic Planner's Toolbox," *CA Magazine*, July 1987, pp. 24–34.

Techniques Available

Economic Forecasts

At one time, only forecasts of economic variables were used in strategic management. The forecasts were primarily concerned with remote factors, such as general economic conditions, disposable personal income, the consumer price index, wage rates, and productivity. Derived from government and private sources, these economic forecasts served as the framework for industry and company forecasts, which dealt with task-environment concerns, such as sales, market share, and other pertinent economic trends.

Econometric Models

With the advent of sophisticated computers, the government and some wealthy firms contracted with private consulting firms to develop "causal models," especially models involving econometrics. These *econometric models* utilize complex simultaneous regression equations to relate economic occurrences to areas of corporate activity. They are especially useful when information on causal relationships is available and large changes are anticipated. During the relatively stable decade of the 1970s, econometrics was one of the nation's fastest-growing industries. In the 1980s, however, the three biggest econometric firms—Data Resources (McGraw-Hill), Chase Econometrics (Chase Manhattan Bank), and Wharton Econometric Forecasting Associates (Ziff-Davis Publishing)—fell on hard times. The explosion of oil prices, inflation, and the growing interdependence of the world economy created problems that fell beyond the inherent limits of econometric models. And despite enormous technological resources, such models still depend on the often undependable judgment of the model builders.[9]

Two more widely used and less expensive forecasting techniques are *time series models* and *judgmental models*. Time series models attempt to identify patterns based on combinations of historical trends and seasonal and cyclical factors. This technique assumes that the past is a prologue to the future. Time series techniques, such as exponential smoothing and linear projections, are relatively simple, well known, inexpensive, and accurate.

Of the time series models, *trend analysis* models are the most frequently used. Such models assume that the future will be a continuation of the past, following some long-range trend. If sufficient historical data, such as annual sales, are readily available, a trend analysis can be done quickly and inexpensively.

In the trend analysis depicted in Figure 5–4, concern should focus on long-term trends, such as Trend C, which is based on 11 years of fluctuating sales. Trend A, which is based on three excellent years is much too optimistic. Similarly, Trend B, which is based on four bad years, is much too pessimistic.

The major limitation of trend analysis is the assumption that all of the relevant conditions will remain relatively constant. Sudden changes in these conditions falsify trend predictions.

Judgmental models are useful when historical data are unavailable or hard to use. *Sales*

---

[9]"Where the Big Economometric Models Go Wrong," *Business Week,* March 30, 1981, pp. 70–73.

FIGURE 5-4
Interpretations in Trend Analysis

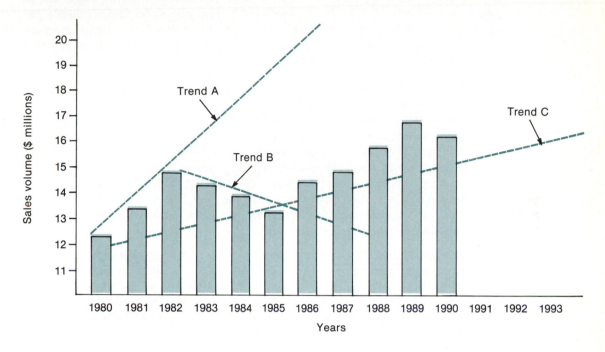

force estimates and *juries of executive opinion* are examples of such models. Sales force estimates consolidate salespeople's opinions of customer intentions regarding specific products. These estimates can be relevant if customers respond honestly and their intentions remain consistent. Juries of executive opinion average the estimates made by executives from marketing, production, finance, and purchasing. No elaborate math or statistics are required.

Customer surveys are conducted by means of personal interviews or telephone questionnaires. The questions must be well stated and easily understood. The respondents are a random sample of the relevant population. Custom surveys can provide valuable in-depth information. Although they are often difficult to construct and time-consuming to administer, many marketing research firms use them.

Social Forecasts

If strategic forecasting relies only on economic indicators, social trends that can have a profound impact may be neglected. Some firms have recognized this and identify social trends and underlying attitudes as part of their environmental scanning. Recent social forecasting efforts have involved analysis of such areas as population, housing, social security and welfare, health and nutrition, education and training, income, and wealth and expenditures.

A variety of approaches are used in social forecasting, including time series analysis and the judgmental techniques described earlier. However, *scenario development* is probably the most popular approach. Scenarios, imagined stories that integrate objective and subjective parts of other forecasts, are designed to help prepare strategic managers for alternative possibilities, thus enabling them to develop contingency plans.[10] Because scenarios can be presented in easily understood forms, they are often used in social forecasting. They can be developed by the following process:

1. Prepare the background by assessing the overall social environment under investigation (such as social legislation).
2. Select critical indicators, and search for future events that may affect them (e.g., growing distrust of business).
3. Analyze the reasons for the past behavior of each indicator (e.g., perceived disregard for air and water quality).
4. Forecast each indicator in three scenarios—showing the least favorable environment, the likely environment, and the most favorable environment.
5. Write the scenarios from the viewpoint of someone at a given future time.
6. Condense each scenario to a few paragraphs.

Strategy in Action 5–2 presents two scenarios that were developed in 1987 for Georgia Power Company. Their purpose was to determine how the future environment might influence the firm's load and energy growth to the year 1995.

With the help of Battelle Columbus Division, a consulting firm, Georgia Power identified five broad areas of influence—the same areas you studied in Chapter 3 as the constituents of the remote external environment. From these areas, 15 key factors were isolated for investigation, of which 5 were judged to be critical to Georgia Power's planning. The scenarios in Strategy in Action 5–2 were built on forecasts regarding these five factors. Several scenarios were developed, of which the two presented in Strategy in Action 5–2 show the great contrast between futures with high versus low economic growth.

Political Forecasts

Some strategic planners want to give political forecasts the same serious consideration that is given to economic forecasts. They believe that business success can be profoundly affected by shifts in a broad range of political factors, such as the size of government budgets, tariffs, tax rates, defense spending, the growth of regulatory bodies, and the extent of business leaders' participation in government planning.

Political forecasts for foreign countries are also important. Political risks in those countries affect firms that are in any way dependent on international subsidiaries, suppliers for customers, or critical resources. Increasing worldwide interdependence makes it imperative for firms of all sizes to consider the international political implications of their strategies.

---

[10]W. Whipple III, "Evaluating Alternative Strategies Using Scenarios," *Long Range Planning,* June 1989, pp. 82–86.

GEORGIA POWER PLANNING SCENARIOS FOR 1995

HIGH ECONOMIC GROWTH SCENARIO

The average annual growth rate of the real U.S. gross national product (GNP) will exceed 3.2 percent between now and the year 2010. This growth rate is about the same as the growth rate of 3.4 percent experienced during the post–World War II era but is greater than the average growth rate for the 1980s. Economic growth in Georgia will exceed that of the nation as a whole by as much as one percentage point. This growth pattern is expected to result from a continuation of the Sunbelt phenomenon that drove Georgia's strong growth over the past two decades. With higher economic growth elsewhere, net migration to Georgia will slow down.

Higher productivity growth and lower real interest rates will be associated with higher U.S. economic growth. Higher productivity growth will occur as the baby boom generation matures and the work experience of its members increases. Interest rates will remain lower as long as inflationary pressures do not reemerge.

The average price of oil in 1985 dollars will remain under $18 per barrel as a result of the transformation of the OPEC-dominated world oil market into a commodity-based market. The surplus of natural gas will diminish, but not until the middle-1990s. Industrial demand for natural gas will dampen, as lower oil prices encourage substitution to oil. Coal prices will increase more slowly. Real electricity prices will decline if the free market energy policy pursued by the Reagan administration continues. Emissions will remain essentially stable through 1995.

Real U.S. GNP will grow at an annual rate of less than 2.7 percent, a rate lower than the average growth rate experienced so far in the 1980s. This decline will result from a worsening trade imbalance and from large deficit spending that exerts an upward pressure on interest rates. Georgia's personal income growth will exceed that of the United States as a whole by over one percentage point. Higher levels of net migration into Georgia will occur as economic circumstances worsen elsewhere. This will accelerate growth in the state.

The annual increase in U.S. productivity will be less than 1.5 percent, an increase consistent with the slow growth of the 1970s. The low growth rate will result from a decline in demand for most goods and services as the population ages. Taxes will increase to support the aged population. Both higher taxes and higher interest rates will accelerate the shift from a manufacturing to a service economy.

By 1995, oil prices will average over $30 per barrel in 1985 dollars. The current world surplus will erode quickly in the early years as the current strong economic growth increases oil demand. This will cause a return to OPEC price controls. Deregulation will free natural gas prices to adjust rapidly to supply and demand imbalances. Exploration and development will be dampened by the initial lower prices and by inconsistent and unpredictable government energy policy. Real electricity prices will decline. Some acid rain legislation will be passed, but not enough to discourage significantly growth in the utility industry.

Source: D. L. Goldfarb and W. R. Huss, "Building Scenarios for an Electric Utility," *Long Range Planning*, June 1988, pp. 78–85.

Because of the billions of U.S. dollars lost in the last two decades as a result of revolutions, nationalization, and other manifestations of political instability, multinational firms and consultants have developed a variety of approaches to international forecasting. Some of the better known are:

Haner's Business Environmental Risk Index, which monitors 15 economic and political varibles in 42 countries.

Frost and Sullivan's World Political Risks Forecasts, which predict the likelihood of various catastrophes befalling an individual firm.

Probe International's custom reports for specific firms, which examine broad social trends.

The developmental forecasts of Arthur D. Little, which examine a country's progress from the Stone Age to the computer age.[11]

Of all the approaches in use, those of ADL may be the most ambitious and sophisticated. With computer assistance, ADL follows the progress of each country by looking at five criteria: social development, technological advancement, abundance of natural resources, level of domestic tranquility, and type of political system. When a country's development in any of one of these areas gets too far ahead of its development in the other areas, tension builds and violence often follows. Using this system, ADL forecast political turbulence in Iran eight years before the U.S. hostage crisis. ADL foresees that uneven development will probably produce similar turmoil in 20 other countries, such as Peru, Chile, Malaysia, and the Philippines. It believes the world is highly predictable if the right questions are asked. Unfortunately, too many executives fail to use the same logic in analyzing political affairs that they use in other strategic areas. Political analysis should be routinely incorporated into economic analyses. Ford, General Motors, PepsiCo, Singer, Du Pont, and United Technologies are among the many firms that follow ADL's advice.

Technological Forecasts

Such rapidly developed and revolutionary technological innovations as lasers, nuclear energy, satellites and other communication devices, desalination of water, electric cars, and miracle drugs have prompted many firms to invest in technological forecasts. Knowledge of probable technological development helps strategic managers prepare their firms to benefit from change. Except for econometrics, all of the previously described techniques can be used to make technological forecasts. However, uncertainty of information favors the use of scenarios and two additional forecasting approaches: brainstorming and the Delphi technique.

Brainstorming helps a group generate new ideas and forecasts. With this technique, analysis or criticisms of participants' contributions is postponed so that creative thinking is not stifled or restricted. Because there are no interruptions, group members are encouraged to offer original ideas and to build on one another's innovative thoughts. The most promising ideas generated in this way are thoroughly evaluated at a later time.

[11]N. Howard, "Doing Business in Unstable Countries," *Dun's Review,* March 1980, pp. 49–55.

The *Delphi method* is a systematic procedure for obtaining consensus among a group of experts. The method includes:

1. A detailed survey of opinions of experts, usually obtained through a mail questionnaire.
2. Anonymous evaluation of the responses by the experts involved.
3. One or more revisions of the experts' answers until convergence has been achieved.

The Delphi method is expensive and time-consuming, but it can be successful in social and political forecasting.

At the end of this chapter, Appendix 5–B briefly describes the 20 most frequently used forecasting approaches and provides references containing more details about their derivation and application.

Integrate Forecast Results into the Strategic Management Process

Once the forecasting techniques have been selected and the forecasts made, the results must be integrated into the strategic management process. For example, the economic forecast must be related to analyses of the industry, suppliers, the competition, and key resources. Figure 5–5 presents a format for displaying interrelationships between forecast remote environment variables and the influential task environment variables. The resulting predictions become a part of the assumed environment in formulating strategy.

It is critical that strategic decision makers understand the assumptions on which environmental forecasts are based. The experience of Itel, a computer-leasing firm, illustrates the consequences of a failure to understand these assumptions. Itel had been able to lease 200 plug-in computers made by Advance Systems and by Hitachi largely because IBM could not deliver its newest AT systems. Consequently, Itel bullishly forecast that it would place 430 of its systems in the following year—despite the rumor that IBM would announce a new line of aggressively priced systems in the first quarter of that year. Even Itel's competitors felt that customers would hold off their purchasing decisions until IBM made the announcement. However, Itel signed long-term purchase contracts with its suppliers and increased its marketing staff by 80 percent. Itel's forecasting mistake and its failure to examine its sales forecasts in relationship to the actions of competitors and suppliers were nearly disastrous. It slipped close to bankruptcy within less than a year.

Forecasting external events enables a firm to identify its probable requirements for future success, to formulate or reformulate its basic mission, and to design strategies for achieving its goals and objectives. If the forecast identifies any gaps or inconsistencies between the firm's desired position and its present position, strategic managers can respond with plans and actions.

Dealing with the uncertainty of the future is a major function of strategic managers. The forecasting task requires systematic information gathering coupled with the utilization of a variety of forecasting approaches. A high level of insight is also needed to integrate

FIGURE 5–5
Task and Remote Environment Impact Matrix

Remote Environments	Task Environments			
	Key Customer Trends	Key Competitor Trends	Key Supplier Trends	Key Labor Market Trends
Economic	*Example:* Trends in inflation and unemployment rates		*Example:* Annual domestic oil demand and worldwide sulfur demand through the year 2000.	
Social	*Example:* Increasing numbers of single-parent homes			*Example:* Rising education level of U.S. population
Political	*Example:* Increasing numbers of punitive damage awards in product liability cases		*Example:* Possibility of Arab oil boycotts	
Technological		*Example:* Increasing use of superchips and computer-based instrumentation for synthesizing genes	*Example:* Use of cobalt 60 gamma irradiation to extend shelf life of perishables.	
Ecological		*Example:* Increased use of biodegradable fast-food packaging		*Example:* Increasing availability of mature workers with experience in "smokestack" industries

risks and opportunities in formulating strategy. However, intentional or unintentional delays or the inability to understand certain issues may prevent a firm from using the insights gained in assessing the impact of broad environmental trends. Sensitivity and openness to new and better approaches and opportunities are therefore essential.

MONITOR THE CRITICAL ASPECTS OF MANAGING FORECASTS

Although almost all aspects of forecast management may be critical in specific situations, three aspects are critical over the lifetime of a firm.

The first is the identification of the environmental factors that deserve forecasting. Hundreds of factors may affect a firm, but often the most important of these factors are a few of immediate concern, such as sales forecasts and competitive trends. The time and resources needed to completely understand all the environmental factors that might be critical to the success of a strategy are seldom available. Therefore, executives must depend on their collective experience and perception to determine which factors are worth the expense of forecasting.

The second aspect is the selection of reputable, cost-efficient forecasting sources outside the firm that can expand its forecasting database. Strategic managers should identify federal and state government agencies, trade and industry associations, and individuals or other groups that can provide data forecasts at reasonable costs.

The third aspect is the selection of forecasting tasks that are to be done in-house. Given the great credence that is often accorded to formally developed forecasts—despite the inherent uncertainty of the database—the selection of forecasting techniques is indeed critical. A firm beginning its forecasting efforts is well advised to start with less technical methods, such as sales force estimates and the jury of executive opinion, rather than highly sophisticated forecasting techniques, such as econometrics, and to add approaches requiring greater analytic sophistication as its experience and understanding increase. In this way, its managers can learn how to deal with the varied weaknesses and strengths of forecasting techniques.

SUMMARY

Environmental forecasting starts with the identification of critical factors external to the firm that might provide opportunities or pose threats in the future. Both quantitative and qualitative strategic forecasting techniques are used to project the long-range direction and impact of these factors in the remote and task environments. To select the forecasting techniques that are most appropriate for the firm, the strengths and weaknesses of the various techniques must be understood. To offset the potential biases or errors individual techniques involve, employment of more than one technique is usually advisable.

Critical aspects in forecast management include the identification of the environmental factors that deserve forecasting, the selection of forecasting sources outside the firm, and the selection of forecasting tasks that are to be done in-house.

QUESTIONS FOR DISCUSSION

1. Identify five changes in the remote environment that you believe will affect major U.S. industries over the next decade. What forecasting techniques could be used to assess the probable impact of these changes?

2. Construct a matrix with forecasting techniques on the horizontal axis and at least five qualities of forecasting techniques across the vertical axis. Indicate the relative strengths and weaknesses of each technique.

3. Develop three rules of thumb for guiding strategic managers in their use of forecasting.

4. Develop a typewritten two-page forecast of a variable that you believe will affect the prosperity of your business school over the next 10 years.

5. Using prominent business journals, find two examples of firms that either benefited or suffered from environmental forecasts.

6. Describe the background, skills, and abilities of the individual you would hire as the environmental forecaster for a firm with $500 million in annual sales. How would the qualifications of such an individual differ for a much smaller firm? For a much larger firm?

BIBLIOGRAPHY

Allaire, Y., and M. E. Firsirotu. "Coping with Strategic Uncertainty." *Sloan Management Review,* Spring 1989, pp. 7–16.

Ansoff, H. I. "Strategic Management of Technology." *Journal of Business Strategy,* Winter 1987, pp. 40–48.

Asher, M. G. "Recent Tax Reforms in the New Industrial Economics of East Asia and Their Implications." *Business Horizons,* March 1989, pp. 72–79.

Barrett, F. D. "Strategies for the Use of Artificial and Human Intelligence." *Business Quarterly,* Summer 1986, pp. 18–27.

Briggs, W. "Software Tools for Planning: DSS and AI/Expert Systems." *Planning Review,* September 1985, pp. 36–45.

Clark, R. S. "The Strategic Planner's Toolbox." *CA Magazine,* July 1987, pp. 24–34.

Coccari, R. L. "How Quantitative Business Techniques Are Being Used." *Business Horizons,* July 1989, pp. 70–74.

Cohen, B. G. "A New Approach to Strategic Forecasting." *Journal of Business Strategy,* September 1988, pp. 38–42.

Coplin, W. D., and M. K. O'Leary. "World Political/Business Risk Analysis for 1987." *Planning Review,* January 1987, pp., 34–40.

Daft, R. L.; J. Sormunen; and D. Parks. "Chief Executive Scanning. Environmental Characteristics, and Company Performance: An Empirical Study." *Strategic Management Journal,* March 1988, pp. 123–39.

Drucker, Peter M. *Managing in Turbulent Times.* New York: Harper & Row, 1980.

ElSawy, O. A., and T. C. Pauchant. "Triggers, Templates, and Twitches in the Tracking of Emerging Strategic Issues." *Strategic Management Journal,* September 1988, pp. 455–73.

Fahey, L., and W. R. King. "Environmental Scanning for Corporate Planning." *Business Horizons*, August 1977, pp. 61–71.

Ghoshal, S., and S. K. Kim. "Building Effective Intelligence Systems for Competitive Advantage." *Sloan Management Review*, Fall 1986, pp. 49–58.

Ginsberg, A. "Measuring and Modelling Changes in Strategy: Theoretical Foundations and Empirical Directions." *Strategic Management Journal*, November 1988, pp. 559–75.

Howard, N. "Doing Business in Unstable Countries." *Dun's Review*, March 1980, pp. 49–55.

Jain, S. C. "Environmental Scanning in U.S. Corporations." *Long Range Planning*, April 1984, pp. 117–28.

Kast, F. "Scanning the Future Environment: Social Indications." *California Management Review*, Fall 1980, pp. 22–32.

Keiser, B. "Practical Competitor Intelligence." *Planning Review*, September 1987, pp. 14–19.

La Bell, D., and O. J. Krasner. "Selecting Environmental Forecasting Techniques from Business Planning Requirements." *Academy of Management Review*, July 1977, pp. 373–83.

Linneman, R. E. *Short-Sleeve Approach to Long-Range Planning: For the Smaller, Growing Corporation.* Englewood Cliffs, N.J.: Prentice-Hall, 1980.

Linneman, R. E., and J. D. Kennell. "Shirt-Sleeve Approach to Long-Range Plans." *Harvard Business Review*, March–April 1977, pp. 141–50.

McConkey, D. D. "Planning for Uncertainty." *Business Horizons*, January 1987, pp. 40–45.

Madridakis, S., and S. Wheelwright. "Forecasting: Issues and Challenges for Marketing Management." *Journal of Marketing*, October 1977, pp. 24–38.

Meredith, J. "The Strategic Advantages of New Manufacturing Technologies for Small Firms." *Strategic Management Journal*, May 1987, pp. 249–58.

Mesch, A. H. "Developing an Effective Environmental Assessment Function." *Managerial Planning*, March 1984, pp. 17–22.

Morris, E. "Vision and Strategy: A Focus for the Future." *Journal of Business Strategy*, Fall 1987, pp. 51–58.

Prescott, J. E., and D. C. Smith. "A Project-Based Approach to Competitive Analysis." *Strategic Management Journal*, September 1987, pp. 411–24.

Schnaars, S. P. "How to Develop and Use Scenarios." *Long Range Planning*, February 1987, pp. 105–14.

Starry, C., and N. McGaughey. "Growth Industries: Here Today, Gone Tomorrow." *Business Horizons*, July 1988, pp. 69–74.

Stromp, M. A. "Questioning Assumptions: One Company's Answer to the Planner's Nemesis." *Planning Review*, September 1986, pp. 10–15.

Sufrin, S. C., and G. S. Odiorne. "The New Strategic Planning Boom: Hope for the Future or/a Bureaucratic Exercise?" *Managerial Planning*, January 1985, pp. 4–46.

Vandermerwe, S., and M. L'Huillier. "Euro-Consumers in 1992." *Business Horizons*, January 1989, pp. 34–40.

Weiss, E. "Future Public Opinion of Business." *Management Review*, March 1978, pp. 8–15.

Wheelwright, S. C., and D. G. Clarke. "Corporate Forecasting: Promise and Reality." *Harvard Business Review*, November–December 1976, pp. 40–64.

"Where the Big Econometric Models Go Wrong." *Business Week*, March 30, 1981, pp. 70–73.

Whipple, W. III. "Evaluating Alternative Strategies Using Scenarios." *Long Range Planning*, June 1989, pp. 82–86.

Zenger, T. R., and B. S. Lawrence. "Organizational Demography: The Differential Effects of Age and Tenure Distributions on Technical Communication." *Academy of Management Journal*, June 1989, pp. 353–76.

APPENDIX 5–A

SOURCES FOR ENVIRONMENTAL FORECASTS

REMOTE ENVIRONMENT

A. Economic considerations
1. *Predicasts* (most complete and up-to-date review of forecasts).
2. National Bureau of Economic Research.
3. *Handbook of Basic Economic Statistics.*
4. *Statistical Abstract of the United States* (also includes industrial, social, and political statistics).
5. Publications by Department of Commerce agencies.
    a. Office of Business Economics (e.g., *Survey of Business).*
    b. Bureau of Economic Analysis (e.g., *Business Conditions Digest).*
    c. Bureau of the Census (e.g., *Survey of Manufacturers* and various reports on population, housing, and industries).
    d. Business and Defense Services Administration (e.g., *United States Industrial Outlook).*
6. Securities and Exchange Commission (various quarterly reports on plant and equipment, financial reports, working capital of corporations).
7. The Conference Board.
8. *Survey of Buying Power.*
9. *Marketing Economic Guide.*
10. *Industrial Arts Index.*
11. U.S. and national chambers of commerce.
12. American Manufacturers Association.
13. *Federal Reserve Bulletin.*
14. *Economic Indicators*, annual report.
15. *Kiplinger Newsletter.*
16. International economic sources:
    a. *Worldcasts.*
    b. Master key index for business international publications.

Sources: Adapted with numerous additions from C. R. Goeldner and L. M. Kirks, "Business Facts: Where to Find Them," *MSU Business Topics,* Summer 1976, pp. 23–76, reprinted by permission of the publisher, Division of Research, Graduate School of Business Administration, MSU; F. E. deCarbonnel and R. G. Donance, "Information Source for Planning Decisions," *California Management Review,* Summer 1973, pp. 42–53; and A. B. Nun, R. C. Lenz, Jr., H. W. Landford, and M. J. Cleary, "Data Source for Trend Extrapolation in Technological Forecasting," *Long Range Planning,* February 1972, pp. 72–76.

Industrial Outlook

       c. Department of Commerce.
          (1) Overseas business reports.
          (2) Industry and Trade Administration.
          (3) Bureau of the Census—*Guide to Foreign Trade Statistics*.
    17. *Business Periodicals Index*.

B. Social considerations.
    1. Public opinion polls.
    2. Surveys such as *Social Indicators* and *Social Reporting,* the annals of the American Academy of Political and Social Sciences.
    3. Current controls: Social and behavioral sciences.
    4. Abstract services and indexes for articles in sociological, psychological, and political journals.
    5. Indexes for *The Wall Street Journal, New York Times,* and other newspapers.
    6. Bureau of the Census reports on population, housing, manufacturers, selected services, construction, retail trade, wholesale trade, and enterprise statistics.
    7. Various reports from groups such as the Brookings Institution and the Ford Foundation.
    8. World Bank Atlas (population growth and GNP data).
    9. Work Bank—World Development Report.

C. Political considerations
    1. *Public Affairs Information Services Bulletin*.
    2. CIS Index (Congressional Information Index).
    3. Business periodicals.
    4. Funk & Scott (regulations by product breakdown).
    5. Weekly compilation of presidential documents.
    6. *Monthly Catalog of Government Publications*.
    7. *Federal Register* (daily announcements of pending regulations).
    8. *Code of Federal Regulations* (final listing of regulations).
    9. Business International Master Key Index (regulations, tariffs).
    10. Various state publications.
    11. Various information services (Bureau of National Affairs, Commerce Clearing House, Prentice-Hall).

D. Technological considerations.
    1. *Applied Science and Technology Index*.
    2. *Statistical Abstract of the United States*.
    3. Scientific and Technical Information Service.
    4. University reports, congressional reports.
    5. Department of Defense and military purchasing publishers.
    6. Trade journals and industrial reports.
    7. Industry contacts, professional meetings.
    8. Computer-assisted information searches.
    9. National Science Foundation annual report.
    10. *Research and Development Directory* patent records.
    11. Industry considerations
       a. *Concentration Ratios in Manufacturing* (Bureau of the Census).

    b. *Input-Output Survey* (productivity ratios).

    c. *Monthly Labor Review* (productivity ratios).

    d. *Quarterly Failure Report* (Dun & Bradstreet).

    e. *Federal Reserve Bulletin* (capacity utilization).

    f. *Report on Industrial Concentration and Product Diversification in the 1,000 Largest Manufacturing Companies* (Federal Trade Commission).

    g. Industry trade publications.

    h. Bureau of Economic Analysis, Department of Commerce (specialization ratios).

OPERATING ENVIRONMENT

A. Competition and supplier considerations.
   1. Target Group Index.
   2. U.S. Industrial Outlook.
   3. Robert Morris annual statement studies.
   4. Troy, Leo Almanac of Business & Industrial Financial Ratios.
   5. Census of Enterprise Statistics.
   6. Securities and Exchange Commission (10-K reports).
   7. Annual reports of specific companies.
   8. *Fortune 500 Directory, The Wall Street Journal, Barron's, Forbes, Dun's Review.*
   9. Investment services and directories: Moody's, Dun & Bradstreet, Standard & Poor's, Starch Marketing, Funk & Scott Index.
   10. Trade association surveys.
   11. Industry surveys.
   12. Market research surveys.
   13. *Country Business Patterns.*
   14. *Country and City Data Book.*
   15. Industry contacts, professional meetings, salespeople.
   16. *NFIB Quarterly Economic Report for Small Business.*

B. Customer profile.
   1. *Statistical Abstract of the United States,* first source of statistics.
   2. *Statistical Sources* by Paul Wasserman (a subject guide to data—both domestic and international).
   3. *American Statistics Index* (Congressional Information Service Guide to statistical publications of U.S. government—monthly).
   4. Office to the Department of Commerce.
      a. Bureau of the Census reports on population, housing, and industries.
      b. *U.S. Census of Manufacturers* (statistics by industry, area, and products).
      c. *Survey of Current Business* (analysis of business trends, especially February and July issues).

5. Market research studies (*A Basic Bibliography on Market Review,* compiled by Robert Ferber et al., American Marketing Association).
6. *Current Sources of Marketing Information: A Bibliography of Primary Marketing Data* by Gunther & Goldstein, AMA.
7. *Guide to Consumer Markets,* The Conference Board (provides statistical information with demographic, social, and economic data—annual).
8. *Survey of Buying Power.*
9. *Predicasts* (abstracts of publishing forecasts of all industries, detailed products, and end-use data).
10. *Predicasts Basebook* (historical data from 1960 to present, covering subjects ranging from population and GNP to specific products and services; series are coded by Standard Industrial Classifications).
11. *Market Guide* (individual market surveys of over 1,500 U.S. and Canadian cities; includes population, location, trade areas, banks, principal industries, colleges and universities, department and chain stores, newspapers, retail outlets, and sales).
12. *County and City Data Book* (includes bank deposits, birth and death rates, business firms, education, employment, income of families, manufacturers, population, savings, wholesale and retail trade).
13. *Yearbook of International Trade Statistics* (UN).
14. *Yearbook of National Accounts Statistics* (UN).
15. *Statistical Yearbook* (UN—covers population, national income, agricultural and industrial production, energy, external trade and transport).
16. *Statistics of (Continents): Sources for Market Research* (includes separate books on Africa, America, Europe).

C. Key natural resources.
1. *Minerals Yearbook, Geological Survey* (Bureau of Mines, Department of the Interior).
2. *Agricultural Abstract* (Department of Agriculture).
3. Statistics of electric utilities and gas pipeline companies (Federal Power Commission).
4. Publications of various institutions: American Petroleum Institute, Atomic Energy Commission, Coal Mining Institute of America, American Steel Institute, and Brookings Institution.

APPENDIX 5–B

STRATEGIC PLANNING FORECASTING TOOLS AND TECHNIQUES

1. Dialectical Inquiry.
    Development, evaluation, and synthesis of conflicting points of view by (1) having separate assigned groups use debate format to formulate and refine each point of view and then (2) bringing two groups together for presentation of debate between and synthesis of their points of view.
    R. O. Mason and I. I. Mitroff, *Strategic Assumptions Surfacing and Testing* (New York: John Wiley & Sons, 1981)

2. Nominal Group Technique.
    Development, evaluation, and synthesis of individual points of view through an interactive process in a group setting.
    A. L. Delbecq, A. H. Van de Ven, and D. H. Gustafson, *Group Techniques for Program Planning: A Guide to Nominal Group and Delphi Processes* (Glenview, Ill.: Scott, Foresman, 1975).

3. Delphi Method.
    Development, evaluation, and synthesis of individual points of view by systematically soliciting and collating judgments on a particular topic through a set of carefully designed sequential questionnaires interspersed with summarized information and feedback of opinions derived from earlier responses.
    A. L. Delbecq, A. H. Van de Ven, and D. H. Gustafson, *Group Techniques for Program Planning: A Guide to Nominal Group and Delphi Processes* (Glenview, Ill: Scott, Foresman, 1975).

4. Focus Groups.
    Bringing together recognized experts and qualified individuals in an organized setting to develop, evaluate, and synthesize their individual points of view on a particular topic.
    D. L. Johnson and A. H. Mendelson, *Using Focus Groups in Marketing Planning* (St. Paul, Minn.: West Publishing, 1982).

5. Simulation Technique.
    Computer-based technique for simulating future situations and then predicting the outcome of various courses of action against each of these situations.

Source: Excerpted from J. Webster, W. Reif, and J. Bracker, "The Manager's Guide to Strategic Planning Tools and Techniques," *Planning Review*, November–December 1989, pp. 4–13, 48.

G. D. Craig, "A Simulation System for Corporate Planning," *Long Range Planning,* October 1980, pp. 43–56.

6. PIMS Analysis.

   Application of the experiences of a diverse sample of successful and unsuccessful firms.

   S. R. Schoeffler, R. D. Buzzell, and D. F. Heaney, "Impact of Strategic Planning on Profit Performance," *Harvard Business Review,* March–April 1974, pp. 137–45.

7. Market Opportunity Analysis.

   Identification of markets and market factors in the economy and the industry that will affect the demand for and marketing of a product or service.

   D. Silverman, "Consultants' Concepts—Field Analysis: A 3–D Look at Opportunities," *Planning Review,* September 1984, pp. 22–24.

8. Benchmarking.

   Comparative analysis of competitor programs and strategic positions for use as reference points in the formulation of organizational objectives.

   L. J. Mennon and D. W. Landers, *Advanced Techniques for Strategic Analysis* (Hindsale, Ill.: Dryden Press, 1987).

9. Situational Analysis (SWOT or TOWS).

   Systematic development and evaluation of past, present, and future data to identify internal strengths and weaknesses and external threats and opportunities.

   H. Weihrich, "The TOWS Matrix—A Tool for Situational Analysis," *Long Range Planning,* April 1982, pp. 54–66.

10. Critical Success Factors/Strategic Issues Analysis.

    Identification and analysis of a limited number of areas in which high performance will ensure a successful competitive position.

    A. C. Boynton and R. W. Zmud, "An Assessment of Critical Success Factors," *Sloan Management Review,* Summer 1984, pp. 17–24.

11. Product Life Cycle Analysis.

    Analysis of market dynamics in which a product is viewed according to its position within distinct stages of its sales history.

    G. S. Day, *Analysis for Strategic Market Decisions* (St. Paul, Minn.: West Publishing 1986).

12. Future Studies.

    Development of future situations and factors based on agreement of a group of "experts," often from a variety of functional areas within a firm.

    S. W. Edmunds, "The Role of Futures Studies in Business Strategic Planning," *Journal of Business Strategy,* Fall 1982, pp. 40–46.

13. Multiple Scenarios.

    Smoothly unfolding narratives that describe an assumed future expressed through a sequence of time frames and snapshots.

    K. Nair and R. Sarin, "Generating Future Scenarios—Their Use in Strategic Planning," *Long Range Planning,* June 1979, pp. 57–61.

14. SPIRE (Systematic Procedure for Identification of Relevant Environments).
    A computer-assisted, matrix-generating tool for forecasting environmental
    changes that can have a dramatic impact on operations.
    H. Klein and W. Newman, "How to Use SPIRE: A Systematic Procedure for
    Identifying Relevant Environments for Strategic Planning," *Journal of Business
    Strategy,* Summer 1980, pp. 32–45.
15. Environmental Scanning, Forecasting, and Trend Analysis.
    Continuous process, usually computer based, of monitoring external factors,
    events, situations, and projections of forecasts of trends.
    L. Fahey, William R. King, and V. K. Narayanan, "Environmental Scanning
    and Forecasting in Strategic Planning—The State of the Art," *Long Range
    Planning,* February 1981, pp. 32–39.
16. Experience Curves.
    An organizing framework for dynamic analyses of cost and price for a product,
    a company, or an industry over an extended period.
    P. Ghemawat, "Building Strategy on the Experience Curve," *Harvard Business
    Review,* March–April 1985, pp. 143–49.
17. Portfolio Classification Analysis.
    Classification and visual display of the present and prospective positions of
    firms and products according to the attractiveness of the market and the ability
    of the firms and products to compete within that market.
    G. S. Day, *Analysis for Strategic Market Decisions* (St. Paul, Minn.: West
    Publishing, 1986).
18. Metagame Analysis.
    Arriving at a strategic direction by thinking through a series of viewpoints on a
    contemplated strategy in terms of every competitor and every combination of
    competitive responses.
    B. K. Dutta and William R. King, "Metagame Analysis of Competitive Strat-
    egy," *Strategic Management Journal,* October 1980, pp. 357–70.
19. Strategic Gap Analysis.
    Examination of the difference between the extrapolation of current performance
    levels (e.g., current sales) and the projection of desired performance objectives
    (e.g., a desired sales level).
    H. I. Ansoff, *Corporate Strategy* (New York: McGraw-Hill, 1972).
20. Sustainable Growth Model.
    Financial analysis of the sales growth rate that is required to meet market share
    objectives and the degree to which capacity must be expanded to achieve that
    growth rate.
    P. Varadarajan, "The Sustainable Growth Model: A Tool for Evaluating the
    Financial Feasibility of Market Share Strategies," *Strategic Management Jour-
    nal,* October 1984, pp. 353–67.

CHAPTER 5 COHESION CASE

ENVIRONMENTAL FORECASTING

"I guess it probably started when we kept seeing so many of our vans sit on the yard in South Carolina in the mid-1980s," said president Joel Stevenson discussing Bryson's approach to environmental forecasting. "We realized that the reason was that the way waste generators wanted to have their waste handled was apparently changing, and the impact was further accelerated by so many small 'truckers' trying to get into the hazwaste transportation business using their vans to try and haul drums of waste. We were paying for vans we weren't using and losing business with generators needing to have their wastes handled in bulk tankers or rolloff boxes. So we knew we needed to do a better job of forecasting future trends to avoid this happening in the future!"

Stevenson quickly adapted a "delphi" approach to forecast the need for different types of equipment in handling hazardous wastes being transported for disposal. He assigned Jim Ullery, head of Bryson's remedial service division and very familiar with RCRA regulations, to research the impact of RCRA/EPA regulations on future waste handling options. Both he and Ullery identified six "experts" around the country that were active in the hazardous waste industry or were hazardous waste managers in companies known to be progressive in their waste management practices. They then called these people to obtain their opinions about transportation equipment-related trends affecting the industry.

"We found several useful insights," recalled Jim Ullery. "EPA regs were requiring waste minimization, and companies were becoming more sensitive to approaches that would reduce both costs and risks in handling."

"EPA regs," added Stevenson, "were also increasing the number of waste streams, with more being liquid or semiliquid in nature. The result was that waste handling equipment that was volume-oriented and also liquid-oriented would be more appropriate than drum-oriented traditional vans."

So Bryson's delphi technique suggested that Bryson move more into tankers and rolloff boxes while phasing out of drum-oriented vans in serving large generators. Acting on this forecast, Bryson's transportation revenues for the last of the 1980s evolved as follows:

	1983	1986	1989
Vans	$1,316,009	$1,680,955	$ 815,525
Tankers	243,208	897,403	2,389,382
Rolloffs (transp. rev)	—	220,444	1,198,222
Eqmt rental (r'offs & tankers)	47,234	135,621	512,432

These numbers reflect Bryson management's decision to move more into tanker and rolloff-related transportation services in response to these environmental forecasts.

FIGURE 6–2
SWOT Analysis Diagram

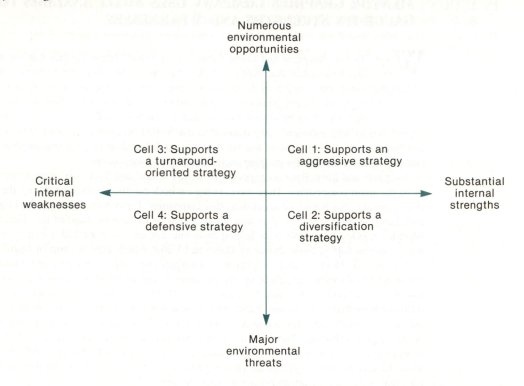

between strengths in reputation and resources and an opportunity for impressive market growth. Cell 4 is the least favorable situation, with the firm facing major environmental threats from a position of relative weakness. This situation clearly calls for strategies that reduce or redirect involvement in the products markets examined by means of SWOT analysis. Chrysler Corporation's successful turnaround from the verge of bankruptcy in the early 1980s is an example of such a strategy.

In cell 2, a firm with key strengths faces an unfavorable environment. In this situation, strategies would use current strengths to build long-term opportunities in other products-markets. Greyhound, possessing many strengths in intercity bus transportation, still faced an environment dominated by fundamental, long-term threats, such as airline competition and high costs. The result was product development into nonpassenger (freight) services, followed by diversification into other businesses (e.g., financial services). A firm in cell 3 faces impressive market opportunity but is constrained by internal weaknesses. The focus of strategy for such a firm is eliminating the internal weaknesses so as to more effectively pursue the market opportunity. Apple's redirection of its Lisa technology to multiple products was an attempt to reformulate its technology-based strategy across several new product offerings in the microcomputer industry.

Overall, SWOT analysis highlights the central role that the identification of internal strengths and weaknesses plays in a manager's search for effective strategies. The careful matching of a firm's opportunities and threats with its strengths and weaknesses is the essence of sound strategy formulation.

Although SWOT analysis highlights the role of internal analysis in identifying sound strategies, it does not explain how managers identify internal strengths and weaknesses. The next section explains the process of internal analysis.

VIEWING INTERNAL ANALYSIS AS A PROCESS

Figure 6–3 diagrams the development of a company profile as a four-step process that you should find useful in guiding internal analysis.

In step 1, managers examine key aspects of the firm's operation, targeting key areas for further assessment. The areas targeted are those deemed central to the firm's strategic direction. As such, they are called "strategic internal factors."

In step 2, managers evaluate the firm's status on these factors by comparing their current condition with their past condition. This is where most managers start their planning efforts. How do we compare with last year? Have we improved over the last year? Are we better able to do key things this year than we were last year? Does the condition of the strategic internal factors represent a favorable or an unfavorable situation?

The third step is very critical. In this step, managers seek some comparative basis—linked to key industry/market or product-market conditions—against which to more accurately determine whether the condition of a strategic internal factor represents a potential strength or a potential weakness. Managers use three perspectives to do this: (1) the key requirements for success at the relevant stages of product-market evolution, (2) the capabilities of key competitors, and (3) the key requirements for success in the industry-market sectors being considered.

The third step should result in a determination of whether the strategic internal factors are:

a. *Competitive advantages*—factors that provide the firm with a competitive edge and are therefore factors around which the firm's strategy should be built.

b. *Basic business requirements*—factors that are important capabilities of both the firm and its competitors and therefore do not represent a potential source of strategic advantage.

c. *Key vulnerabilities*—factors on which the firm currently lacks the skill, knowledge, or resources needed to compete effectively. Managers will want to avoid strategies that depend on such factors, and they will usually target these factors as areas requiring remediation.

In the final step, the company profile that results from the earlier steps becomes input into the strategic management process. This input is vital during the early, strategy formulation phase in the strategic management process.

FIGURE 6–3
Steps in the Development of a Company Profile*

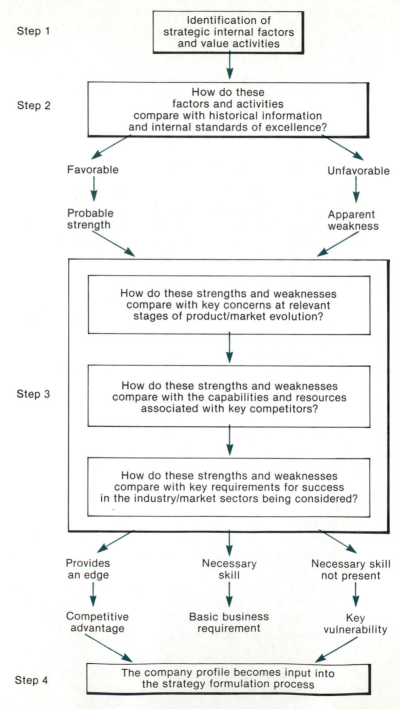

*The work of Leslie Rue and Phyllis Holland, *Strategic Management* (New York: McGraw-Hill, 1989), p. 133, provided an important foundation for the portrayal of these steps.

FIGURE 6–4
Key Internal Factors: Potential Strengths or Weaknesses

Marketing

Firm's products/services: breadth of product line.
Concentration of sales in a few products or to a few customers.
Ability to gather needed information about markets.
Market share or submarket shares.
Product/service mix and expansion potential: life cycle of key products; profit/sales balance in product/service.
Channels of distribution: number, coverage, and control.
Effective sales organization; knowledge of customer needs.
Product/service image, reputation, and quality.
Imaginativeness, efficiency, and effectiveness of sales promotion and advertising.
Pricing strategy and pricing flexibility.
Procedures for digesting market feedback and developing new products, services, or markets.
After-sale service and follow-up.
Goodwill/brand loyalty.

Financial and Accounting

Ability to raise short-term capital.
Ability to raise long-term capital; debt/equity.
Corporate-level resources (multibusiness firm).
Cost of capital relative to that of industry and competitors.
Tax considerations.
Relations with owners, investors, and stockholders.
Leverage position; capacity to utilize alternative financial strategies, such as lease or sale and leaseback.
Cost of entry and barriers to entry.
Price-earnings ratio.
Working capital; flexibility of capital structure.
Effective cost control; ability to reduce cost.
Financial size.
Efficiency and effectiveness of accounting system for cost, budget, and profit planning.

Production/Operations/Technical

Raw materials cost and availability; supplier relationships.
Inventory control systems; inventory turnover.
Location of facilities; layout and utilization of facilities.
Economies of scale.
Technical efficiency of facilities and utilization of capacity.
Effectiveness of subcontracting use.
Degree of vertical integration; value added and profit margin.
Efficiency and cost/benefit of equipment.
Effectiveness of operation control procedures: design, scheduling, purchasing, quality control, and efficiency.
Costs and technological competences relative to those of industry and competitors.
Research and development/technology/innovation.
Patents, trademarks, and similar legal protection.

Personnel

Management personnel.
Employees' skill and morale.
Labor relations costs compared to those of industry and competitors.
Efficiency and effectiveness of personnel policies.
Effectiveness of incentives used to motivate performance.
Ability to level peaks and valleys of employment.
Employee turnover and absenteeism.
Specialized skills.
Experience.

(continued)

FIGURE 6–4 (concluded)

Organization of General Management

Organizational structure.
Firm's image and prestige.
Firm's record in achieving objectives.
Organization of communication system.
Overall organizational control system (effectiveness and utilization).
Organizational climate; organizational culture.
Use of systematic procedures and techniques in decision making.
Top-management skill, capabilities, and interest.
Strategic planning system.
Intraoganizational synergy (multibusiness firms).

Step 1: Identification of Strategic Internal Factors

What are the firm's specific internal factors? How and where do they originate? How do we decide which of them must be carefully evaluated? These are questions that managers might consider as they identify a firm's key internal factors as strengths or weaknesses and as possible bases for the firm's future strategy.

A Function Approach

Key internal factors are a firm's basic capabilities, limitations, and characteristics. Figure 6–4 lists typical factors of this kind, some of which would be the focus of internal analysis in most firms. The list is broken down along functional lines.

Firms are not likely to evaluate all of the factors listed in Figure 6–4 as potential strengths or weaknesses. To develop or revise a strategy, managers would prefer to identify the few factors on which its success is most likely to depend. Equally important, a firm's reliance on particular internal factors will vary by industry, market segment, product life cycle, and the firm's current position. Managers are looking for what Chester Barnard calls "the strategic factors," those internal capabilities that are most critical for success in a particular competitive area. The strategic factors of firms in the oil industry, for example, will be quite different from those of firms in the construction industry or the hospitality industry. Strategic factors can also vary among firms within the same industry. In the mechanical writing industry, for example, the strategies of BIC and Cross, both successful firms, are based on different internal strengths: BIC's on its strength in mass production, extensive advertising, and mass distribution channels; Cross's on high quality, image, and selective distribution channels.

Strategists examine a firm's past performance to isolate key internal contributors to favorable (or unfavorable) results. What did we do well, or poorly, in marketing, operations, and financial management that had a major influence on our past results? Was our sales force effectively organized? Were we in the right channels of distribution? Did we have the financial resources needed to support our past strategy? The same examination can be applied to a firm's current situation, with particular emphasis on changes in the

| STRATEGY IN ACTION 6–2 | MONSANTO CHARTS A NEW STRATEGY BASED ON IDENTIFICATION OF ITS TRADITIONAL STRENGTHS AND ITS POTENTIAL WEAK PRODUCTS |

In 1979, Monsanto's *Annual Report* stated that its operations included "more than 180 manufacturing plants, laboratories and technical centers in 20 nations. The company's products [were] sold in 123 nations." According to the April 30, 1984, issue of *Fortune,* "Monsanto hit its nadir in 1980; though sales increased 6 percent to $6.57 billion, earnings plunged 55 percent to $149 million. . . . [The firm] lost over $300 million on old-line businesses, with fibers and styrene proving the worst performers." Its return on stockholder equity was 5.3 percent.

Along with most of the other major chemical firms, Monsanto started to move away from low-margin commodity products toward higher-margin, patent-protected specialty products. However, instead of merely joining the "me-too" rush from commodities to specialties, Monsanto decided to take stock of its inherent strengths and weaknesses as a springboard to capitalizing on the future evolution of the chemical industry.

Based on that internal scrutiny, Monsanto concluded that its major corporate strength lay in its ability to apply chemical technology to the life sciences, as evidenced by its strong positions in plant herbicides, growth regulators, plant breeding, and certain pharmaceuticals. However, its major weakness in those areas was that it lacked a significant pharmaceutical marketing organization.

With this assessment complete, Richard J. Mahoney, Monsanto's chairman and CEO, sold off many of Monsanto's mainstay businesses representing $4 billion in annual sales and over 3,000 employees. He acquired the G. D. Searle pharmaceutical company, boosting Monsanto's sales force by 2,500 people in pharmaceutical markets, and the Belgium drugmaker Centinental Pharma. Finally, Monsanto created venture capital firms in the United States and Europe that had invested over $1.5 billion by 1990 in a portfolio of small entrepreneurial companies focused on agribusiness, biotechnology, and the life sciences, electronic chemicals, process control, and instrumentation. Although these generated an annual return on invested capital of about 20 percent, Mahoney said, "The exposure [to new products and technologies] . . . gained through these investments is more important than financial return."

Has it worked? In 1988, Monsanto's earnings rose 36 percent to $591 million. At the same time, Monsanto's return on equity hit 15.6 percent, its best since 1947. Monsanto's price-earnings ratio was 50 percent higher than that of Dow Chemical. Obviously, many investors felt that its managers had done a good job of identifying its strengths and developing a good strategy based on them.

importance of key dimensions over time. For example, heavy advertising, mass production, and mass distribution were strategic internal factors in BIC's initial strategy for ballpoint pens and disposable lighters. With the product life cycle fast reaching maturity, BIC later determined that cost-conscious mass production was a strategic factor, whereas heavy advertising was not. Strategy in Action 6–2 describes how Monsanto reoriented itself based on identification of its key internal strengths and weaknesses.

Analysis of past trends in a firm's sales, costs, and profitability is of major importance in identifying its strategic internal factors. And that identification should be based on a clear picture of the nature of the firm's sales. An anatomy of past sales trends broken down by product lines, channels of distribution, key customers or types of customers, geographic region, and sales approach should be developed in detail. A similar anatomy should be developed on costs and profitability. Detailed investigation of the firm's performance history helps isolate the internal factors that influence its sales, costs, and profitability or their interrelationships. For example, one firm may find that 83 percent of its sales result from 25 percent of its products, and another firm may find that 30 percent of its products (or services) contribute 78 percent of its profitability. On the basis of such results, a firm may determine that certain key internal factors (e.g., experience in particular distribution channels, pricing policies, warehouse location, technology) deserve major attention in the formulation of future strategy.

The identification of strategic internal factors requires an external focus. A strategist's efforts to isolate key internal factors are assisted by analysis of industry conditions and trends and by comparisons with competitors. BIC's identification of mass production and advertising as key internal factors was based as much on analysis of industry and competitive characteristics as on analysis of its own past performance. Changing conditions in an industry can lead to the need to reexamine a firm's internal strengths and weaknesses in light of newly emerging determinants of success in that industry. Furthermore, strategic internal factors are often evaluated in depth because firms are contemplating expansion of products or markets, diversification, and so forth. Clearly, scrutinizing the industry under consideration and potential competitors is a key means of identifying strategic factors if a firm is evaluating its capability to move into an unfamiliar market.

The "Value Chain" Approach

Diagnosing a firm's key strengths and weaknesses requires the adoption of a disaggregated view of the firm. Examining the firm across distinct functional areas, as suggested above and in Figure 6–4, is one way to disaggregate the firm for purposes of internal analysis. Another way is to use the "value chain" approach. Developed by Michael Porter in his book *Competitive Advantage,* this approach is a way of systematically viewing the series of activities a firm performs to provide its customers with a product.[2] Figure 6–5 diagrams a typical value chain. The value chain disaggregates a firm into its strategically important activities in order to understand the behavior of the firm's cost and the firm's existing or potential sources of differentiation. A firm gains competitive advantage by performing these strategically important activities—what we have called *key internal factors*—more cheaply or better than its competitors.

Every firm can be viewed (disaggregated) as a collection of value activities that are performed to design, produce, market, deliver, and support its product. As portrayed in Figure 6–5, these activities can be grouped into nine basic categories for virtually any firm at the business unit level. Within each category, a firm typically performs a number of discrete activities that may represent key strengths or weaknesses for it. Service activities, for example, may include such discrete activities as installation, repair, parts distribution, and upgrading—any of which could be a major source of competitive advantage or disadvantage. Through the systematic identification of these activities, man-

---

[2]Michael E. Porter, *Competitive Advantage* (New York: Free Press, 1985).

FIGURE 6–5
A Typical Value Chain

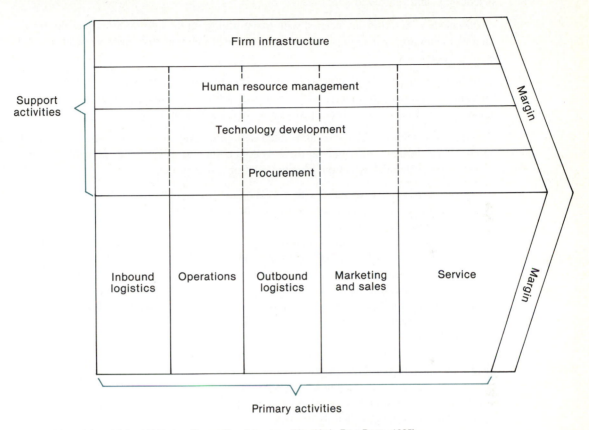

Source: Adapted from Michael E. Porter, *Competitive Advantage* (New York: Free Press, 1985).

agers using the value chain approach can target potential strengths and weaknesses for further evaluation.

The basic categories of activities can be grouped into two broad types. *Primary* activities are those involved in the physical creation, marketing, delivery, and after-sale support of the firm's product or service. Overarching all of these activities are *support* activities, which provide infrastructure or inputs that allow them to take place on an ongoing basis.

Identifying Primary Activities   Identifying primary value activities requires the isolation of activities that are technologically and strategically distinct. Each of the five basic categories of primary activities is divisible into a number of distinct activities, such as the following:[3]

---

[3]Ibid.

Inbound Logistics   Activities associated with receiving, storing, and disseminating inputs to the product, such as material handling, warehousing, inventory control, vehicle scheduling, and returns to suppliers.

Operations   Activities associated with transforming inputs into the final product form, such as machining, packaging, assembly, equipment maintenance, testing, printing, and facility operations.

Outbound Logistics   Activities associated with collecting, storing, and physically distributing the product to buyers, such as finished goods warehousing, material handling, delivery vehicle operation, order processing, and scheduling.

Marketing and Sales   Activities associated with providing a means by which buyers can purchase the product and inducing them to do so, such as advertising, promotion, sales force quoting, channel selection, channel relations, and pricing.

Service   Activities associated with providing service to enhance or maintain the value of the product, such as installation, repair, training, parts supply, and product adjustment.

The primary activities most deserving of further analysis depend on that particular industry. For example, Holiday Inns may be much more concerned about operations activities—it provides its service instantaneously at each location—and marketing/sales activities than about outbound logistics. For a distributor, such as the food distributor PYA, inbound and outbound logistics are the most critical areas. After-sale service is becoming increasingly critical to automotive dealerships. In any firm, however, all of the primary activities are present to some degree and deserve attention in a systematic internal analysis.

Identifying Support Activities   Support value activities arise in one of four categories and can be identified or disaggregated by isolating technologically or strategically distinct activities. Often overlooked as sources of competitive advantage, these four categories can typically be distinguished as follows:[4]

Procurement   Activities involved in obtaining purchased inputs—raw materials, purchased services, machinery, and so on. Procurement stretches across the entire value chain because it supports every activity—every activity uses purchased inputs of some kind. Many discrete procurement activities are typically performed within a firm, often by different people.

Technology Development   Activities involved in designing the product as well as in creating and improving the ways in which the various activities in the value chain are performed. We tend to think of technology in terms of the product or manufacturing process. In fact, every activity a firm performs involves a technology or technologies, which may be mundane or sophisticated, and every firm has a stock of know-how for performing each of these activities. Technology development typically involves a variety of discrete activities, some of which are performed outside the R&D department.

---

[4]Michael E. Porter, "Changing Pattern of International Competition," *California Management Review,* Winter 1986, p. 14.

Human Resource Management   Activities necessary to ensure the recruiting, training, and development of personnel. Every activity involves human resources, and thus human resource management activities cut across the entire value chain.

Firm Infrastructure   Such activities as general management, accounting, legal, finance, and strategic planning and all others that are decoupled from specific primary or support activities but are essential to the operation of the entire value chain.

Using the Value Chain in Internal Analysis   The value chain approach provides a useful means for guiding a systematic internal analysis of the firm's existing or potential strengths and weaknesses. By systematically disaggregating a firm into its distinct value activities across the nine activity categories, the strategist is able to identify key internal factors for further examination as potential sources of competitive advantage.

Whether using the value chain approach or an examination of functional areas, or both approaches, the strategist's next step in a systematic internal analysis is to compare the firm's status with meaningful standards to determine which of its value activities are strengths or weaknesses. Four sources of meaningful standards for evaluating internal factors and value activities are discussed in the next section.

Steps 2 and 3: Evaluation of Strategic Internal Factors

Identification and evaluation of key internal factors have been separated for discussion, but in practice they are not separate and distinct steps. The objective of internal analysis is to carefully determine a firm's strategic strengths and weaknesses. An internal analysis that generates a long list of resources and capabilities is of little help in strategy formulation. Instead, internal analysis must identify and evaluate a limited number of strengths and weaknesses relative to the opportunities targeted in the firm's current and future competitive environment.

What are potential strengths and weaknesses? A factor is considered a strength if it is a distinctive competence or competitive advantage. It is more than merely what the firm has the competence to do. It is something the firm does (or has the capacity to do) particularly well relative to the abilities of existing or potential competitors. A distinctive competence (strength) is important because it gives a firm a comparative advantage in the marketplace. For example, Apple's Macintosh computer and its publishing software were two of its distinctive competences.

A factor is considered a weakness if it is something the firm does poorly or lacks the capacity to do although key competitors have that capacity. Decentralized production facilities and management structures were major weaknesses of Apple Computers in its efforts to compete with IBM in the PC industry.

There are four basic perspectives strategists should use in evaluating strategic internal factors: (1) comparison with the firm's past performance, (2) stage of industry evolution, (3) comparison with competitors, and (4) comparison with key success factors in the firm's industry.

Comparison with Past Performance

Strategists use the firm's historical experience as a basis for evaluating internal factors. Managers are most familiar with the internal capabilities and problems of their firm because they have been immersed in its financial, marketing, production, and R&D activities. Not surprisingly, a manager's assessment of whether a certain internal factor—such as production facilities, sales organization, financial capacity, control systems, or key personnel—is a strength or a weakness will be strongly influenced by his or her experience in connection with that factor. In the capital-intensive airline industry, for example, debt capacity is a strategic internal factor. Delta Airlines managers view Delta's debt/equity ratio of less than 0.6, which is comparable to its past debt/equity ratio, as a continued strength, representing significant flexibility for supporting decisions to invest in facilities or equipment. American Airlines managers, on the other hand, view American's much higher 1.8 debt/equity ratio as a growing strength because it is down 50 percent from its 3.5 level in the mid-1980s.

Although historical experience can provide a relevant evaluation framework, strategists must avoid tunnel vision in making use of it. Texaco's management, for example, long considered its large number of service stations (27,000 in the 1980s) a key strength, believing that this "strength" (along with other perceived strengths) had "worked so well for so long [at Texaco] that even the thought of changing them was heretical."[5] But Shell, with just over 6,280 service stations, sold slightly more gasoline than Texaco.[6] Clearly, using only historical experience as a basis for identifying strengths and weaknesses can prove dangerously inaccurate.

Stage of Industry Evolution

The requirements for success in industry segments change over time. Strategists can use these changing requirements, which are associated with different stages of industry evolution, as a framework for identifying and evaluating the firm's strengths and weaknesses.

Figure 6–6 depicts four stages of industry evolution and the typical changes in functional capabilities that are often associated with business success at each of these stages. The early development of a product-market, for example, entails minimal growth in sales, major R&D emphasis, rapid technological change in the product, operating losses, and a need for sufficient resources or slack to support a temporarily unprofitable operation. Success at this introduction stage may be associated with technical skill, with being first in new markets, or with having a marketing advantage that creates widespread awareness. Radio Shack's initial success with its TRS–80 home computer was based in part on its ability to gain widespread exposure and acceptance in the ill-defined home computer market via the large number of existing Radio Shack outlets throughout the country.

The strengths necessary for success change in the growth stage. Rapid growth brings new competitors into the product-market. At this stage, such factors as brand recognition, industry differentiation, and the financial resources to support both heavy marketing

---

[5]"Texaco: Restoring Luster to the Star," *Business Week,* December 22, 1980, p. 54; and "Inside the Shell Oil Company," *Newsweek,* June 15, 1981, p. 74.

[6]"Texaco," p. 60.

FIGURE 6–6
Sources of Distinctive Competence at Different Stages of Industry Evolution

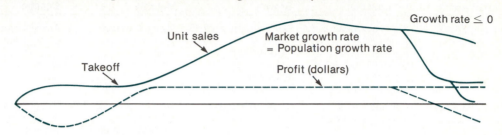

Functional Area	Introduction	Growth	Maturity	Decline
Marketing	Resources/skills to create widespread awareness and find acceptance from customers; advantageous access to distribution	Ability to establish brand recognition, find niche, reduce price, solidify, strong distribution relations, and develop new channels	Skills in aggressively promoting products to new markets and holding existing markets; pricing flexibility; skills in differentiating products and holding customer loyalty	Cost-effective means of efficient access to selected channels and markets; strong customer loyalty or dependence; strong company image
Production operations	Ability to expand capacity effectively, limit number of designs, develop standards	Ability to add product variants, centralize production, or otherwise lower costs; ability to improve product quality; seasonal subcontracting capacity	Ability to improve product and reduce costs; ability to share or reduce capacity; advantageous supplier relationships; subcontracting	Ability to prune product line; cost advantage in production, location or distribution; simplified inventory control; subcontracting or long production runs
Finance	Resources to support high net cash overflow and initial losses; ability to use leverage effectively	Ability to finance rapid expansion, to have net cash outflows but increasing profits; resources to support product improvements	Ability to generate and redistribute increasing net cash inflows; effective cost control systems	Ability to reuse or liquidate unneeded equipment; advantage in cost of facilities; control system accuracy; streamlined management control
Personnel	Flexibility in staffing and training new management; existence of employees with key skills in new products or markets	Existence of and ability to add skilled personnel; motivated and loyal work force	Ability to cost effectively, reduce work force, increase efficiency	Capacity to reduce and reallocate personnel; cost advantage

(continued)

FIGURE 6–6 (concluded)

Functional Area	Introduction	Growth	Maturity	Decline
Engineering and research and development	Ability to make engineering changes, have technical bugs in product and process resolved	Skill in quality and new feature development; ability to start developing successor product	Ability to reduce costs, develop variants, differentiate products	Ability to support other grown areas or to apply product to unique customer needs
Key functional area and strategy focus	Engineering; market penetration	Sales; consumer loyalty; market share	Production efficiency; successor products	Finance; maximum investment recovery

Source: Adapted from Peter Doyle, "The Realities of the Product Life Cycle," *Quarterly Review of Marketing,* Summer 1976, pp. 1–6; Harold Fox, "A Framework for Functional Coordination," *Atlantic Economic Review,* November–December 1973; Charles W. Hofer, *Conceptual Constructs for Formulating Corporate and Business Strategy* (Boston: Intercollegiate Case Clearing House, 1977), p. 7; Philip Kotler, *Marketing Management* (Englewood Cliffs, N.J.: Prentice-Hall, 1988); and Charles Wasson, *Dynamic Competitive Strategy and Product Life Cycles* (Austin, Tex.: Austin Press, 1978).

expenses and the effect of price competition on cash flow can be key strengths. IBM entered the personal computer market in the growth stage and was able to rapidly become the market leader with a strategy based on its key strengths in brand awareness and possession of the financial resources needed to support consumer advertising.

As the industry moves through a shakeout phase and into the maturity stage, industry growth continues, but at a decreasing rate. The number of industry segments expands, but technological change in product design slows considerably. As a result, competition usually becomes more intense, and promotional or pricing advantages and differentiation become key internal strengths. Technological change in process design becomes intense as the many competitors seek to provide the product in the most efficient manner. Where R&D was critical in the introduction stage, efficient production is now crucial to continued success in the broader industry segments. Chrysler has found efficiency to be a key strength in the maturing auto industry.

When the industry moves into the decline stage, strengths and weaknesses center on cost advantages, superior supplier or customer relationships, and financial control. Competitive advantage can exist at this stage, at least temporarily, if a firm serves gradually shrinking markets that competitors are choosing to leave.

Figure 6–6 is a rather simple model of the stages of industry evolution. These stages can and do vary from the model. What should be borne in mind is that the relative importance of various determinants of success differs across the stages of industry evolution. Thus, the state of that evolution must be considered in internal analysis. Figure 6–6 suggests dimensions that are particularly deserving of in-depth consideration when a company profile is being developed.

Comparison with Competitors

A major focus in determining a firm's strengths and weaknesses is comparison with existing (and potential) competitors. Firms in the same industry often have different marketing skills, financial resources, operating facilities and locations, technical know-how, brand images, levels of integration, managerial talent, and so on. These different internal capabilities can become relative strengths (or weaknesses) depending on the strategy a firm chooses. In choosing a strategy, managers should compare the firm's key internal capabilities with those of its rivals, thereby isolating its key strengths and weaknesses.[7]

In the home appliance industry, for example, Sears and General Electric are major rivals. Sear's principal strength is its retail network. For GE, distribution—through independent franchised dealers—has traditionally been a relative weakness. GE's possession of the financial resources needed to support modernized mass production has enabled it to maintain both cost and technological advantages over its rivals, particularly Sears. This major strength for GE is a relative weakness for Sears, which depends solely on subcontracting to produce its Kenmore appliances. On the other hand, maintenance and repair service are important in the appliance industry. Historically, Sears has had strength in this area because it maintains a fully staffed service components and spreads the costs of that component over numerous departments at each retail location. GE, on the other hand, has had to depend on regional service centers and on local contracting with independent service firms by its independent local dealers.

Among the internal factors that Sears and GE must consider in developing a strategy are distribution network, technological capabilities, operating costs, and service facilities. Comparison with key competitors can prove useful in ascertaining whether their internal capabilities on these and other factors are strengths or weaknesses. Significant favorable differences (existing or expected) from competitors are potential cornerstones of a firm's strategy. Moreover, through comparison with major competitors, a firm may avoid strategic commitments that it cannot competitively support. Strategy in Action 6–3 shows how SAS used competitor comparison to assess its strengths and weaknesses.

Comparison with Success Factors in the Industry

Industry analysis involves identifying the factors associated with successful participation in a given industry. As was true for the evaluation methods discussed above, the key determinants of success in an industry may be used to identify a firm's internal strengths and weaknesses. By scrutinizing industry competitors, as well as customer needs, vertical industry structure, channels of distribution, costs, barriers to entry, availability of substitutes, and suppliers, a strategist seeks to determine whether a firm's current internal capabilities represent strengths or weaknesses in new competitive arenas. The discussion in Chapter 3 provides a useful framework—five industry forces—against which to examine a firm's potential strengths and weaknesses. General Cinema Corporation, the largest U.S. movie theater operator, determined that its internal skills in marketing, site analysis, creative financing, and management of geographically dispersed operations were key strengths relative to major success factors in the soft-drink bottling industry. This

---

[7]Michael E. Porter, *Competitive Strategy: Techniques for Analyzing Industries and Competitors* (New York: Free Press, 1980), offers broad, in-depth coverage of numerous techniques for evaluating the strengths and weaknesses of a firm and its competitors. Chapter 7 presents key aspects underlying Professor Porter's analytical approaches.

STRATEGY IN ACTION 6–3
SAS USES COMPETITOR COMPARISON TO IDENTIFY ITS STRENGTHS AND WEAKNESSES

For many years, Scandinavian Airline System (SAS) was a premier European airline. Benefiting from Internation Airline Transportation Association (IATA), a protective European airline industry trade organization, SAS was profitable for 17 straight years. But changes in the global airline industry caused its earnings to plummet in the last few years. When SAS was on the verge

We've got some tough competition. Like the "street fighters" from the rough-and-tumble American domestic

market. Efficient. In shape. Like Delta...

Or European companies which have pursued more consistent and purposeful policies than we have.

And who keep making money, hard times or not.

assessment proved accurate. Within 10 years after it entered the soft-drink bottling industry, General Cinema became the largest franchised bottler of soft drinks in the United States, handling Pepsi, 7UP, Dr Pepper, and Sunkist.

The use of industry-level analysis to evaluate a firm's capacity for success and to help devise future strategy has become a popular technique. The relevance of this technique to comprehensive internal analysis is discussed more fully in the appendix at the end of this chapter.

STRATEGY
IN ACTION   **concluded**
6–3

of folding, its new CEO undertook an extensive competitor comparison as a basis for finding a strategy to turn it around. The CEO shared the following assessment in an employee pamphlet communicating the firm's new strategy and the rationale behind it.

Look at the differences:

Key figures*	Swissair International	SAS International
Cabin Factor	63.6	59.3
Load Factor	59.2	47.6
Passenger revenue (USD)/RPK	0.09	0.08
Cargo revenue (USD)/RFTK	0.37	0.31
Total revenue (USD)/RTK	0.79	0.73
Operating cost (USD)/ATK	0.45	0.42
Revenue-Cost Relationship (Over 100-profit)	103.5	99.7
Average flight leg/km	1051	967

*USD-U.S. Dollars, RPK-Revenue Passenger-kilometers, RFTK-Revenue Freight Tonne-kilometers, RTK-Revenue Tonne-kilometers, ATK-Available Tonne-kilometers.
Exchange rate: one USD - 4.65 Swedish kronor.

Delta has:

o 40% more revenue tonne-kms per employee

o 120% more passengers per employee

o 14% more available tonne-kms per pilot

o 40% more passenger-kms per cabin attendant

o 35% more passenger-kms per passenger sales employee

It is difficult to make similar comparisons in the technical and maintenance fields, but even in these areas Delta has a substantially higher productivity than SAS.

The final step in internal analysis is to provide its results—the company profile—as input into the strategic management process. That input is vital during the early, strategy formulation phase of the process.

While this discussion and Figure 6–3 explain internal analysis in a stepwise fashion, it is important to remember that the steps in the process often overlap. Separating the steps helps explain the process of internal analysis, but efforts to distinguish the steps are seldom emphasized in practice because the process is very interactive.

SUMMARY

This chapter has examined the role and nature of internal analysis as part of the strategic management process. The results of an internal analysis, often called the company profile, identify a firm's key strengths and weaknesses. Strengths are factors that represent potential competitive advantages in targeted markets; weaknesses are factors that represent potential competitive disadvantages. These strengths and weaknesses are compared with external opportunities and threats as a basis for generating strategic alternatives—a process that is often called SWOT analysis.

The process by which managers identify and assess internal capabilities can be conceptualized as three basic steps. Managers first identify strategic internal factors and value activities. They then compare these factors with historical information and internal standards of excellence. Finally, they use stages of industry evolution, key competitors, and industry success factors to segment strengths and weaknesses into a strategic context for input into the strategy formulation process.

When matched with management's environmental analyses and mission priorities, the process of internal analysis provides the critical foundation for strategy formulation. Armed with an accurate, thorough, and timely internal analysis, managers are in a better position to formulate effective strategies. The next chapter describes basic strategy alternatives that any firm may consider.

QUESTIONS FOR DISCUSSION

1. Describe how key internal factors are identified in a firm's strategic management process. Why does such identification appear to be an important part of the strategic management process?

2. Apply the two broad steps of internal analysis to yourself and your career aspirations. What are your major strengths and weaknesses? How might you use your knowledge of these strengths and weaknesses to develop your future career plans?

3. Select one firm in your area that appears to be doing well and another that appears to be doing poorly. Form two small teams with the help of your instructor. Have each team schedule a brief interview with a key manager of one of the firms and obtain a *specific* assessment of the firm's internal strengths and weaknesses. Compare the results in a subsequent class. Are there substantial differences? Is one assessment more comprehensive and specific than the other? From the results of the interviews, would you conclude that strengths and weaknesses vary by type of business? Why or why not?

BIBLIOGRAPHY

Aaker, David A. "Managing Assets and Skills: The Key to a Sustainable Competitive Advantage." *California Management Review,* Winter 1989, pp. 91–106.

Barton, Sidney L., and Paul J. Gordan, "Corporate Strategy: Useful Perspective for the Study of Capital Structure?" *Academy of Management Review,* January 1987, p. 67.

Boag, D. A., and A. Dastmalchian. "Market Vulnerability and the Design and Management of the Marketing Function." *Journal of Small Business Management,* October 1988, pp. 37–43.

Bukszar, Ed, and Terry Connolly. "Hindsight Bias and Strategy Choice." *Academy of Management Journal*, September 1988, p. 828.

Cvitkovic, Emillo. "Profiling Your Competitors." *Planning Review*, May–June 1989, pp. 28–31.

De Geus, A. P. "Planning as Learning." *Harvard Business Review*, March 1988, pp. 70–74.

Dilts, J. C., and G. E. Prough. "Strategic Options for Environmental Management." *Journal of Small Business Management*, July 1989, pp. 31–38.

Fann, G. L., and L. R. Smittzer. "The Use of Information from and about Competitors in Small Business Management." *Entrepreneurship: Theory and Practice*, Summer 1989, pp. 35–46.

Feinman, B. C. "Sustaining the Competitive Market Advantage." *Planning Review*, March 1989, pp. 30–39.

Fifer, R. M., "Cost Bench Marking Approach: Functions in the Value Chain." *Planning Review*, May 1989, pp. 18–27.

Furey, Timothy R. "Benchmarking: The Key to Developing Competitive Advantage in Mature Markets." *Planning Review*, September–October 1987, p. 30.

Gale, B. T., and D. J. Swire. "Business Strategies that Create Wealth." *Planning Review*, March 1988, pp. 6–13.

Gale, B. T., and R. D. Buzzel. "Market Perceived Quality: Key Strategic Concept." *Planning Review*, March 1989, pp. 6–15.

Gomes, Glen M. "Excess Earnings, Competitive Advantage, and Goodwill Value." *Journal of Small Business Management*, July 1988, p. 22.

Hergert, M., and D. Morris. "Accounting Data for Value Chain Analysis." *Strategic Management Journal*, March 1989, pp. 175–88.

Kazanjian, Robert K. "Relation of Dominant Problems to Stages of Growth in Technology-Based New Ventures." *Academy of Management Journal*, September 1988, p. 628.

Langley, A. "The Roles of Formal Strategic Planning." *Long Range Planning*, June 1988, pp. 40–50.

Leigh, T. W. "Competitive Assessment in Service Industries." *Planning Review*, January 1989, pp. 10–19.

Mackay, H. B. "Humanize Your Selling Strategy." *Harvard Business Review*, March 1988, pp. 36–47.

Medley, G. J. "Strategic Planning for the World Wildlife Fund." *Long Range Planning*, February 1988, pp. 46–54.

Mitchell, D. E., "Growth Strategy for Start-Up Businesses." *Journal of Business Strategy*, July 1988, pp. 45–58.

Namiki, N. "Export Strategy for Small Business." *Journal of Small Business Management*, April 1988, pp. 32–37.

Naugle, David G., and Garret A. Davies. "Strategic-Skill Pools and Competitive Advantage." *Business Horizons*, November–December 1987, p. 35.

Payne, Adrian F. "Developing a Marketing-Oriented Organization." *Business Horizons*, May–June 1988, p. 46.

Porter, Michael E. "From Competitive Advantage to Corporate Strategy." *Harvard Business Review*, May–June 1987, p. 43.

Potts, G. W. "Exploit Your Product's Service Life Cycle." *Harvard Business Review*, September 1988, pp. 32–39.

Quinn, J. B. "Strategic Change: Logical Incrementalism." *Sloan Management Review*, Summer 1989, pp. 45–60.

Raymond, M. A., and H. C. Barksdale. "Corporate Strategic Planning and Corporate Marketing: Toward an Interface?" *Business Horizons*, September 1989, pp. 49–55.

Rosenbloom, Richard S., and Michael A. Cusamaro. "Technological Pioneering and Competitive Advantage: The Birth of the VCR Industry." *California Management Review*, Summer 1987.

Schmidt, J. A. "The Strategic Review," *Planning Review*, July 1988, pp. 14–19.

Steiner, M. P., and O. Solem. "Factors for Success in Small Manufacturing Firms." *Journal of Small Business Management*, January 1988, pp. 51–56.

Stoner, Charles R. "Distinctive Competence and Competitive Advantage." *Journal of Small Business Management,* April 1987, p. 33.

Waddock, S. "Core Strategy: End Result of Restructuring?" *Business Horizons,* May 1989, pp. 49–55.

Weigelt, K., and C. Camerer. "Reputation and Corporate Strategy: A Review of Recent Theory." *Strategic Management Journal,* September 1988, pp. 443–54.

USING FINANCIAL ANALYSIS

One of the most important tools for assessing the strength of an organization within its industry is financial analysis. Managers, investors, and creditors all employ some form of this analysis as the beginning point for their financial decision making. Investors use financial analyses in making decisions about whether to buy or sell stock, and creditors use them in deciding whether or not to lend. They provide managers with a measurement of how the company is doing in comparison with its performance in past years and with the performance of competitors in the industry.

Although financial analysis is useful for decision making, there are some weaknesses that should be noted. Any picture that it provides of the company is based on past data. Although trends may be noteworthy, this picture should not automatically be assumed to be applicable to the future. In addition, the analysis is only as good as the accounting procedures that have provided the information. When making comparisons between companies, one should keep in mind the variability of accounting procedures from firm to firm.

There are four basic groups of financial ratios: liquidity, leverage, activity, and profitability.

Depicted in Exhibit 6–1 are the specific ratios calculated for each of the basic groups. Liquidity and leverage ratios represent an assessment of the risk of the firm. Activity and profitability ratios are measures of the return generated by the assets of the firm. The interaction between certain groups of ratios is indicated by arrows.

Typically, two common financial statements are used in financial analyses: the balance sheet and the income statement. Exhibit 6–2 is a balance sheet and Exhibit 6–3 an income statement for the ABC Company. These statements will be used to illustrate the financial analyses.

LIQUIDITY RATIOS

Liquidity ratios are used as indicators of a firm's ability to meet its short-term obligations. These obligations include any current liabilities, including currently maturing long-term debt. Current assets move through a normal cash cycle of inventories—sales—accounts receivable—cash. The firm then uses cash to pay off or reduce its current liabilities. The

Prepared by Elizabeth Gatewood, University of Houston. © Elizabeth Gatewood, 1990. Reprinted by permission of Elizabeth Gatewood.

EXHIBIT 6–1
Financial Ratios

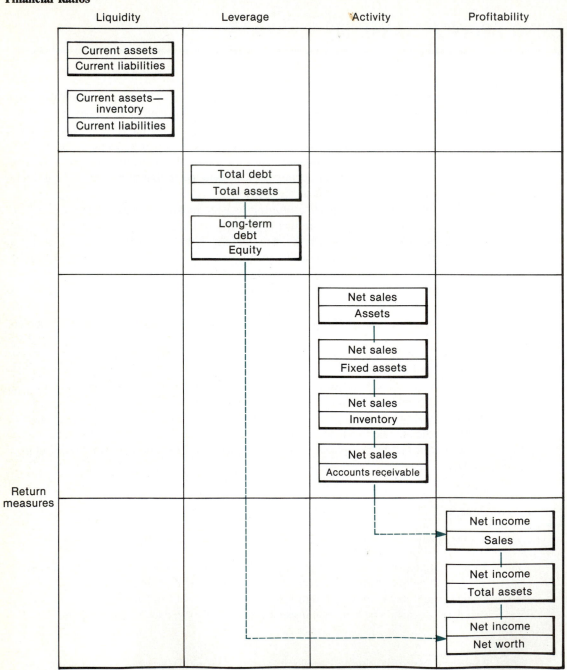

EXHIBIT 6-2

ABC COMPANY
Balance Sheet
As of December 31

	1991		1990
Assets			
Current assets:			
Cash	$ 140,000		$ 115,000
Accounts receivable	1,760,000		1,440,000
Inventory	2,175,000		2,000,000
Prepaid expenses	50,000		63,000
Total current assets	4,125,000		3,618,000
Fixed assets:			
Long-term receivable	1,255,000		1,090,000
Property and plant	$2,037,000	$2,015,000	
Less: Accumulated depreciation	862,000	860,000	
Net property and plant	1,175,000		1,155,000
Other fixed assets	550,000		530,000
Total fixed assets	2,980,000		2,775,000
Total assets	$7,105,000		$6,393,000
Liabilities and Stockholders' Equity			
Current liabilities:			
Accounts payable	$1,325,000		$1,225,000
Bank loans payble	475,000		550,000
Accured federal taxes	675,000		425,000
Current maturities (long-term debt)	17,500		26,000
Dividends payable	20,000		16,250
Total current liabilities	2,512,500		2,242,250
Long-term liabilities	1,350,000		1,425,000
Total liabilities	3,862,000		3,667,250
Stockholders' equity:			
Common stock (104,046 shares outstanding in 1989; 101,204 shares outstanding in 1988)	44,500		43,300
Additional paid-in capital	568,000		372,450
Retained earnings	2,630,000		2,310,000
Total stockholders' equity	3,242,500		2,725,750
Total liabilities and stockholders' equity	$7,105,000		$6,393,000

EXHIBIT 6–3

ABC COMPANY
Income Statement
For the Years Ending December 31

		1991		1990
Net sales		$8,250,000		$8,000,000
Cost of goods sold	$5,100,000		$5,000,000	
Administrative expenses	1,750,000		1,680,000	
Other expenses	420,000		390,000	
Total		7,270,000		7,070,000
Earnings before interest and taxes		980,000		930,000
Less: Interest expense		210,000		210,000
Earnings before taxes		770,000		720,000
Less: Federal income taxes		360,000		325,000
Earnings after taxes (net income)		$ 410,000		$ 395,000
Common stock cash dividends		$ 90,000		$ 84,000
Addition to retained earnings		$ 320,000		$ 311,000
Earnings per common share		$ 3.940		$ 3.90
Dividends per common share		$ 0.865		$ 0.83

best-known liquidity ratio is the current ratio: current assets divided by current liabilities. For the ABC Company, the current ratio is calculated as follows:

$$\frac{\text{Current assets}}{\text{Current liabilities}} = \frac{\$4,125,000}{\$2,512,500} = 1.64 \ (1991)$$

$$= \frac{\$3,618,000}{\$2,242,250} = 1.61 \ (1990)$$

Most analysts suggest a current ratio of 2 to 3. A large current ratio is not necessarily a good sign; it may mean that an organization is not making the most efficient use of its assets. The optimum current ratio will vary from industry to industry, with the more volatile industries requiring higher ratios.

Since slow-moving or obsolescent inventories could overstate a firm's ability to meet short-term demands, the quick ratio is sometimes preferred to assess a firm's liquidity. The quick ratio is current assets minus inventories, divided by current liabilities. The quick ratio for the ABC Company is calculated as follows:

$$\frac{\text{Current assets} - \text{Inventories}}{\text{Current liabilities}} = \frac{\$1,950,000}{\$2,512,500} = 0.78 \ (1991)$$

$$= \frac{\$1,618,000}{\$2,242,250} = 0.72 \ (1990)$$

A quick ratio of approximately 1 would be typical for American industries. Although there is less variability in the quick ratio than in the current ratio, stable industries would be able to operate safely with a lower ratio.

LEVERAGE RATIOS

Leverage ratios identify the source of a firm's capital—owners or outside creditors. The term *leverage* refers to the fact that using capital with a fixed interest charge will "amplify" either profits or losses in relation to the equity of holders of common stock. The most commonly used ratio is total debt divided by total assets. Total debt includes current liabilities and long-term liabilities. This ratio is a measure of the percentage of total funds provided by debt. A total debt/total assets ratio higher than 0.5 is usually considered safe only for firms in stable industries.

$$\frac{\text{Total debt}}{\text{Total assets}} = \frac{\$3,862,500}{\$7,105,000} = 0.54 \text{ (1991)}$$

$$= \frac{\$3,667,250}{\$6,393,000} = 0.57 \text{ (1990)}$$

The ratio of long-term debt to equity is a measure of the extent to which sources of long-term financing are provided by creditors. It is computed by dividing long-term debt by the stockholders' equity.

$$\frac{\text{Long-term debt}}{\text{Equity}} = \frac{\$1,350,000}{\$3,242,500} = 0.42 \text{ (1991)}$$

$$= \frac{\$1,425,000}{\$2,725,750} = 0.52 \text{ (1990)}$$

ACTIVITY RATIOS

Activity ratios indicate how effectively a firm is using its resources. By comparing revenues with the resources used to generate them, it is possible to establish an efficiency of operation. The asset turnover ratio indicates how efficiently management is employing total assets. Asset turnover is calculated by dividing sales by total assets. For the ABC Company, asset turnover is calculated as follows:

$$\text{Asset turnover} = \frac{\text{Sales}}{\text{Total assets}} = \frac{\$8,250,000}{\$7,105,000} = 1.16 \text{ (1991)}$$

$$= \frac{\$8,000,000}{\$6,393,000} = 1.25 \text{ (1990)}$$

The ratio of sales to fixed assets is a measure of the turnover on plant and equipment. It is calculated by dividing sales by net fixed assets.

$$\text{Fixed asset turnover} = \frac{\text{Sales}}{\text{Net fixed assets}} = \frac{\$8,250,000}{\$2,980,000} = 2.77 \ (1991)$$

$$= \frac{\$8,000,000}{\$2,775,000} = 2.88 \ (1990)$$

Industry figures for asset turnover will vary with capital-intensive industries, and those requiring large inventories will have much smaller ratios.

Another activity ratio is inventory turnover, estimated by dividing sales by average inventory. The norm for American industries is 9, but whether the ratio for a particular firm is higher or lower normally depends on the product sold. Small, inexpensive items usually turn over at a much higher rate than larger, expensive ones. Since inventories are normally carried at cost, it would be more accurate to use the cost of goods sold in place of sales in the numerator of this ratio. Established compilers of industry ratios such as Dun & Bradstreet, however, use the ratio of sales to inventory.

$$\text{Inventory turnover} = \frac{\text{Sales}}{\text{Inventory}} = \frac{\$8,250,000}{\$2,175,000} = 3.79 \ (1991)$$

$$= \frac{\$8,000,000}{\$2,000,000} = 4 \ (1990)$$

The accounts receivable turnover is a measure of the average collection period on sales. If the average number of days varies widely from the industry norm it may be an indication of poor management. A too low ratio could indicate the loss of sales because of a too restrictive credit policy. If the ratio is too high, too much capital is being tied up in accounts receivable, and management may be increasing the chance of bad debts. Because of varying industry credit policies, a comparison for the firm over time or within an industry is the only useful analysis. Because information on credit sales for other firms is generally unavailable, total sales must be used. Since not all firms have the same percentage of credit sales, there is only approximate comparability among firms.

$$\begin{array}{c}\text{Accounts}\\\text{receivable turnover}\end{array} = \frac{\text{Sales}}{\text{Accounts receivable}} = \frac{\$8,250,000}{\$1,760,000} = 4.69 \ (1991)$$

$$= \frac{\$8,000,000}{\$1,440,000} = 5.56 \ (1990)$$

$$\text{Average collection period} = \frac{360}{\text{Accounts receivable turnover}}$$

$$= \frac{360}{4.69} = 77 \text{ days } (1991)$$

$$= \frac{360}{5.56} = 65 \text{ days } (1990)$$

PROFITABILITY RATIOS

Profitability is the net result of a large number of policies and decisions chosen by an organization's management. Profitability ratios indicate how effectively the total firm is being managed. The profit margin for a firm is calculated by dividing net earnings by sales. This ratio is often called return on sales (ROS). There is wide variation among industries, but the average for American firms is approximately 5 percent.

$$\frac{\text{Net earnings}}{\text{Sales}} = \frac{\$410,000}{\$8,250,000} = 0.0497 \ (1991)$$

$$= \frac{\$395,000}{\$8,000,000} = 0.0494 \ (1990)$$

4.949°

A second useful ratio for evaluating profitability is the return on investment—or ROI, as it is frequently called—found by dividing net earnings by total assets. The ABC Company's ROI is calculated as follows:

$$\frac{\text{Net earnings}}{\text{Total assets}} = \frac{\$410,000}{\$7,105,000} = 0.0577 \ (1991)$$

5.77°

$$= \frac{\$395,000}{\$6,393,000} = 0.0618 \ (1990)$$

The ratio of net earnings to net worth is a measure of the rate of return or profitability of the stockholders' investment. It is calculated by dividing net earnings by net worth, the common stock equity and retained earnings account. ABC Company's return on net worth, also called ROE, is calculated as follows:

$$\frac{\text{Net earnings}}{\text{Net worth}} = \frac{\$410,000}{\$3,242,500} = 0.1264 \ (1991)$$

$$= \frac{\$395,000}{\$2,725,750} = 0.1449 \ (1990)$$

It is often difficult to determine causes for lack of profitability. The Du Pont system of financial analysis provides management with clues to the lack of success of a firm. This financial tool brings together activity, profitability, and leverage measures and shows how these ratios interact to determine the overall profitability of the firm. A depiction of the system is set forth in Exhibit 6–4.

The right side of the exhibit develops the turnover ratio. This section breaks down total assets into current assets (cash, marketable securities, accounts receivable, and inventories) and fixed assets. Sales divided by these total assets gives the turnover on assets.

The left side of the exhibit develops the profit margin on sales. The individual expense

EXHIBIT 6–4
Du Pont's Financial Analysis

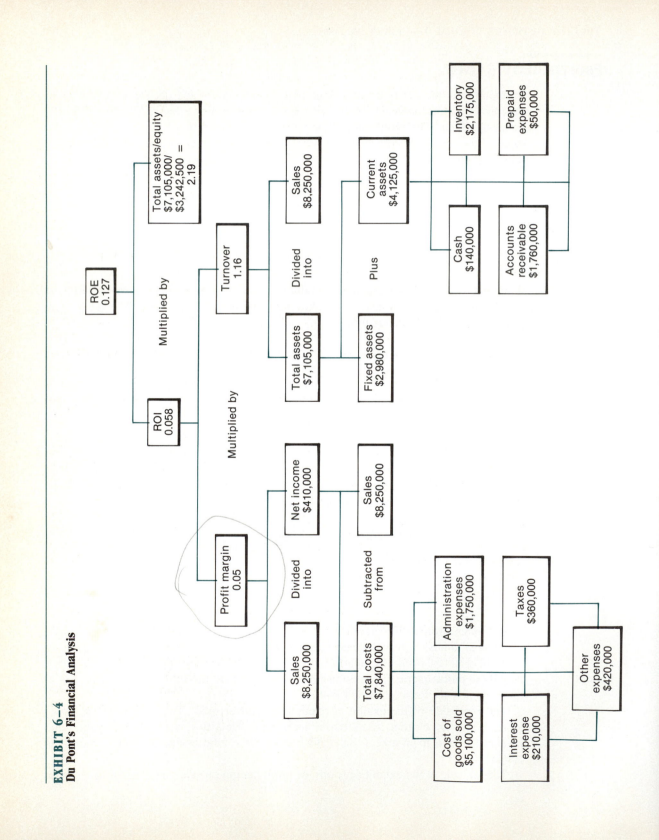

items plus income taxes are subtracted from sales to produce net profits after taxes. Net profits divided by sales gives the profit margin on sales. When the asset turnover ratio on the right side of Exhibit 6–4 is multiplied by the profit margin on sales developed on the left side of the exhibit, the product is the return on assets (ROI) for the firm. This can be shown by the following formula:

$$\frac{\text{Sales}}{\text{Total assets}} \times \frac{\text{Net earnings}}{\text{Sales}} = \frac{\text{Net earnings}}{\text{Total assets}} = \text{ROI}$$

The last step in the Du Pont analysis is to multiply the rate of return on assets (ROI) by the equity multiplier, which is the ratio of assets to common equity, to obtain the rate of return on equity (ROE). This percentage rate of return could, of course, be calculated directly by dividing net income by common equity. However, the Du Pont analysis demonstrates how the return on assets and the use of debt interact to determine the return on equity.

The Du Pont system can be used to analyze and improve the performance of a firm. On the left, or profit, side of the exhibit, attempts to increase profits and sales could be investigated. The possibilities of raising prices to improve profits (or lowering prices to improve volume) or seeking new products or markets, for example, could be studied. Cost accountants and production engineers could investigate ways to reduce costs. On the right, or turnover, side, financial officers could analyze the effect of reducing investment in various assets as well as the effect of using alternative financial structures.

There are two basic approaches to using financial ratios. One approach is to evaluate the corporation's performance over several years. Financial ratios are computed for different years, and then an assessment is made as to whether there has been an improvement or deterioration over time. Financial ratios can also be computed for projected, or pro forma, statements and compared with present and past ratios.

The other approach is to evaluate a firm's financial condition and compare it with the financial conditions of similar firms or with industry averages in the same period. Such a comparison gives insight into the firm's relative financial condition and performance. Financial ratios for industries are provided by Robert Morris Associates, Dun & Bradstreet, and various trade association publications. (Associations and their addresses are listed in the *Encyclopedia of Associations* and the *Directory of National Trade Associations*.) Information about individual firms is available through *Moody's Manual*, Standard & Poor's manuals and surveys, annual reports to stockholders, and the major brokerage houses.

To the extent possible, accounting data from different companies must be standardized so that companies can be compared or so that a specific company can be compared with an industry average. It is important to read any footnotes of financial statements, since various accounting or management practices can have an effect on the financial picture of the company. For example, firms using sale-leaseback methods may have leverage pictures that are quite different from what is shown as debts or assets on the balance sheet.

ANALYSIS OF THE SOURCES AND USES OF FUNDS

The purpose of this analysis is to determine how the company is using its financial resources from year to year. By comparing balance sheets from one year to the next, one may determine how funds were obtained and how these funds were employed during the year.

To prepare a statement of the sources and uses of funds, it is necessary to (1) classify balance sheet changes that increase and decrease cash, (2) classify from the income statement those factors that increase or decrease cash, and (3) consolidate this information on a sources and uses of funds statement form.

Sources of funds that increase cash are as follows:

1. A net decrease in any asset other than a depreciable fixed asset.
2. A gross decrease in a depreciable fixed asset.
3. A net increase in any liability.
4. Proceeds from the sale of stock.
5. The operation of the company (net income, and depreciation if the company is profitable).

Uses of funds include:

1. A net increase in any asset other than a depreciable fixed asset.
2. A gross increase in depreciable fixed assets.
3. A net decrease in any liability.
4. A retirement or purchase of stock.
5. Payment of cash dividends.

We compute gross changes to depreciable fixed assets by adding depreciation from the income statement for the period to net fixed assets at the end of the period and then subtracting from the total net fixed assets at the beginning of the period. The residual represents the change in depreciable fixed assets for the period.

For the ABC Company, the following change would be calculated:

Net property and plant (1991)	$1,175,000
Depreciation for 1991	+ 80,000
	$1,255,000
Net property and plant (1990)	−1,155,000
	$ 100,000

To avoid double counting, the change in retained earnings is not shown directly in the funds statement. When the funds statement is prepared, this account is replaced by the earnings after taxes, or net income, as a source of funds and dividends paid during the year as a use of funds. The difference between net income and the change in the retained-earnings account will equal the amount of dividends paid during the year. The accompanying sources and uses of funds statement was prepared for the ABC Company.

A funds analysis is useful for determining trends in working-capital positions and for demonstrating how the firm has acquired and employed its funds during some period.

ABC COMPANY
Sources and Uses of Funds Statement
For 1991

Sources:	
Prepaid expenses	$ 13,000
Accounts payable	100,000
Accrued federal taxes	250,000
Dividends payable	3,750
Common stock	1,200
Additional paid-in capital	195,500
Earnings after taxes (net income)	410,000
Depreciation	80,000
Total sources	$1,053,500
Uses:	
Cash	$ 25,000
Accounts receivable	320,000
Inventory	175,000
Long-term receivables	165,000
Property and plant	100,000
Other fixed assets	20,000
Bank loans payable	75,000
Current maturities of long-term debt	8,500
Long-term liabilities	75,000
Dividends paid	90,000
Total uses	1,053,500

CONCLUSION

It is recommended that you prepare a chart such as that shown in Exhibit 6–5 so that you can develop a useful portrayal of these financial analyses. The chart allows a display of the ratios over time. The "Trend" column could be used to indicate your evaluation of the ratios over time (for example, "favorable," "neutral," or "unfavorable"). The "Industry Average" column could include recent industry averages on these ratios or those of key competitors. These would provide information to aid interpretation of the analyses. The "Interpretation" column could be used to describe your interpretation of the ratios for this firm. Overall, this chart gives a basic display of the ratios that provides a convenient format for examining the firm's financial condition.

Finally, Exhibit 6–6 is included to provide the quick reference summarizing the calculation and meaning of the ratios discussed earlier.

EXHIBIT 6–5
A Summary of the Financial Position of a Firm

Ratios and Working Capital	1987	1988	1989	1990	1991	Trend	Industry Average	Interpre-tation
Liquidity: Current								
Quick								
Leverage: Debt/assets								
Debt/equity								
Activity: Asset turnover								
Fixed asset ratio								
Inventory turnover								
Accounts receivable turnover								
Average collection period								
Profitabilty: ROS								
ROI								
ROE								
Working-capital position								

EXHIBIT 6–6
A Summary of Key Financial Ratios

Ratio	Calculation	Meaning
Liquidity ratios:		
Current ratio	$$\frac{\text{Current assets}}{\text{Current liabilities}}$$	The extent to which a firm can meet its short-term obligations.
Quick ratio	$$\frac{\text{Current assets} - \text{Inventory}}{\text{Current liabilities}}$$	The extent to which a firm can meet its short-term obligations without relying on the sale of its inventories.
Leverage ratios:		
Debt-to-total-assets ratio	$$\frac{\text{Total debt}}{\text{Total assets}}$$	The percentage of total funds that are provided by creditors.
Debt-to-equity ratio	$$\frac{\text{Total debt}}{\text{Total stockholders' equity}}$$	The percentage of total funds provided by creditors versus the percentage provided by owners
Long-term-debt-to-equity ratio	$$\frac{\text{Long-term debt}}{\text{Total stockholders' equity}}$$	The balance between debt and equity in a firm's long-term capital structure.
Times-interest-earned ratio	$$\frac{\text{Profits before interest and taxes}}{\text{Total interest charges}}$$	The extent to which earnings can decline without the firm becoming unable to meet its annual interest costs.
Activity ratios:		
Inventory turnover	$$\frac{\text{Sales}}{\text{Inventory of finished goods}}$$	Whether a firm holds excessive stocks of inventories and whether a firm is selling its inventories slowly compared to the industry average.
Fixed assets turnover	$$\frac{\text{Sales}}{\text{Fixed assets}}$$	Sales productivity and plant and equipment utilization.
Total assets turnover	$$\frac{\text{Sales}}{\text{Total assets}}$$	Whether a firm is generating a sufficient volume of business for the size of its assets investment.
Accounts receivable turnover	$$\frac{\text{Annual credit sales}}{\text{Accounts receivable}}$$	In percentage terms, the average length of time it takes a firm to collect on credit sales.
Average collection period	$$\frac{\text{Accounts receivable}}{\text{Total sales/365 days}}$$	In days, the average length of time it takes a firm to collect on credit sales.
Profitability ratios:		
Gross profit margin	$$\frac{\text{Sales} - \text{Cost of good sold}}{\text{Sales}}$$	The total margin available to cover operating expenses and yield a profit.
Operating profit margin	$$\frac{\text{Earnings before interest and taxes (EBIT)}}{\text{Sales}}$$	Profitability without concern for taxes and interest.

(continued)

EXHIBIT 6–6 (concluded)

Ratio	Calculation	Meaning
Net profit margin	$\dfrac{\text{Net income}}{\text{Sales}}$	After-tax profits per dollar of sales.
Return on total assets (ROA)	$\dfrac{\text{Net income}}{\text{Total assets}}$	After-tax profits per dollar of assets; this ratio is also called return on investment (ROI).
Return on stockholders' equity (ROE)	$\dfrac{\text{Net income}}{\text{Total stockholders' equity}}$	After-tax profits per dollar of stockholders' investment in the firm.
Earnings per share (EPS)	$\dfrac{\text{Net income}}{\text{Number of shares of common stock outstanding}}$	Earnings available to the owners of common stock.
Growth ratio:		
Sales	Annual percentage growth in total sales	Firm's growth rate in sales.
Income	Annual percentage growth in profits	Firm's growth rate in profits.
Earnings per share	Annual percentage growth in EPS	Firm's growth rate in EPS.
Dividends per share	Annual percentage growth in dividends per share	Firm's growth rate in dividends per share.
Price-earnings ratio	$\dfrac{\text{Market price per share}}{\text{Earnings per share}}$	Faster-growing and less risky firms tend to have higher price-earnings ratios.

CHAPTER 6 COHESION CASE

INTERNAL ANALYSIS AND COMPANY PROFILE

December 1989 was the month for a three-day strategic planning retreat of Bryson's key managers. As part of the preparation for this meeting, each manager was asked to assess Bryson's key strengths and weaknesses. Their assessments suggested the following strengths and weaknesses.

Strengths as Assessed by Memphis-based Managers

1. Full-service company.
2. Environmental and engineering knowledge.
3. Geographic locations.
4. Loyal customers.
5. Reputation and name recognition.
6. Transportation department.
7. Family atmosphere.
8. Relationships with regulatory agencies.
9. Longevity in the marketplace.
10. Financial resources relative to other smaller companies.
11. Acceptance of materials into numerous TSDF facilities.

Strengths as Assessed by South Carolina-based Managers

1. Flexibility; ability to adapt to different and difficult situations.
2. Maximum utilization of personnel and equipment.
3. Customer service orientation; Bryson people put customers number 1.

Strengths as Assessed by Board of Directors

1. Established reputation and position in the southeastern marketplace as a quality provider of hazwaste transportation services.
2. Loyal management team and operating personnel.
3. Name recognition in selected areas of the Southeast.
4. Relationship with regulators in Southeast.
5. Sound core management team with several years of experience in the industry and working together.
6. Low-cost structure; nonunion; strong work ethic.
7. Ten years without a major accident; low insurance costs.
8. Transportation permits in 40 states, including hard states.
9. Ability to compete profitably in smaller remedial service projects.
10. Personnel in Medical Waste Division—loyal and low cost.

7 FORMULATING LONG-TERM OBJECTIVES AND GRAND STRATEGIES

The company mission was described in Chapter 2 as encompassing the broad aims of the firm. The most specific statement of aims presented in that chapter appeared as the goals of the firm. However, these goals, which commonly dealt with profitability, growth, and survival, were stated without specific targets or time frames. They were always to be pursued but could never be fully attained. They gave a general sense of direction but were not intended to provide specific benchmarks for evaluating the firm's progress in achieving its aims.[1] Providing such benchmarks is the function of objectives.[2]

The first part of this chapter will focus on long-term objectives. These are statements of the results a firm seeks to achieve over a specified period of time, typically five years. The second part will focus on the formulation of grand strategies. These provide a comprehensive general approach guiding major actions designed to accomplish the firm's long-term objectives.

The chapter has two major aims: (1) to discuss in detail the concept of long-term objectives, the topics they cover, and the qualities they should exhibit and (2) to discuss in detail the concept of grand strategies and to describe the 12 principal grand strategy options that are available to firms singly or in combination.

LONG-TERM OBJECTIVES

Strategic managers recognize that short-run profit maximization is rarely the best approach to achieving sustained corporate growth and profitability. An often repeated adage states that if impoverished people are given food, they will eat it and remain impoverished; however, if they are given seeds and tools and shown how to grow crops, they will be

---

[1] Max D. Richards, *Setting Strategic Goals and Objectives,* 2nd ed. (St. Paul, Minn: West Publishing, 1986). p. 22.

[2] Throughout this text, the terms *goals* and *objectives* are each used to convey a special meaning, with *goals* being the less specific and more encompassing concept. Most authors follow this usage; however, some use the two words interchangeably, while others reverse the usage.

able to improve their condition permanently. A parallel choice confronts strategic decisions makers:

1. Should they eat the seeds by laying off workers during periods of slack demand by selling off inventories and cutting back on research and development so as to improve the near-term profit picture and make large dividend payments?
2. Or should they sow the seeds by reinvesting profits in growth opportunities, committing resources to employee training, or increasing advertising expenditures?

For most strategic managers, the solution is clear—distribute a small amount of profit now but sow most of it to increase the likelihood of a long-term supply. This is the most frequently used rationale in selecting objectives.

To achieve long-term prosperity, strategic planners commonly establish long-term objectives in seven areas:

Profitability   The ability of any firm to operate in the long run depends on attaining an acceptable level of profits. Strategically managed firms characteristically have a profit objective, usually expressed in earnings per share or return on equity.

Productivity   Strategic managers constantly try to improve the productivity of their systems. Firms that can improve the input-output relationship normally increase profitability. Thus, firms almost always state an objective for productivity. Commonly used productivity objectives are the number of items produced or the number of services rendered per unit of input. However, productivity objectives are sometimes stated in terms of desired cost decreases. For example, objectives may be set for reducing defective items, customer complaints leading to litigation, or overtime. Achieving such objectives increases profitability if unit output is maintained.

Competitive Position   One measure of corporate success is relative dominance in the marketplace. Larger firms often establish an objective in terms of competitive position, often using total sales or market share as measures of their competitive position. An objective with regard to competitive position may indicate a firm's long-term priorities. For example, Gulf Oil set a five-year objective of moving from third to second place as a producer of high-density polypropylene. Total sales were the measure.

Employee Development   Employees value growth and career opportunities. Providing such opportunities, often increases productivity and decreases turnover. Therefore, strategic decision makers frequently include an employee development objective in their long-range plans. For example, PPG has declared an objective of developing highly skilled and flexible employees and thus providing steady employment for a reduced number of workers.

Employee Relations   Whether or not they are bound by union contracts, firms actively seek good employee relations. In fact, proactive steps in anticipation of employee needs and expectations are a characteristic concern of strategic managers. Strategic managers believe that productivity is linked to employee loyalty and perceived management interest in workers' welfare. They therefore set objectives to improve employee relations. Among the outgrowths of such objectives are safety programs, worker representation on management committees, and employee stock option plans.

Technological Leadership   Firms must decide whether to lead or follow in the marketplace. Either approach can be successful, but each requires a different strategic posture. Therefore, many firms state an objective with regard to technological leadership. For example, Caterpillar Tractor Company, established its early reputation and dominant position in its industry by being in the forefront of technological innovation in the manufacture of large earthmovers.

Public Responsibility   Firms recognize their responsibilities to their customers and to society at large. In fact, many firms seek to exceed the demands made by government. They work not only to develop reputations for fairly priced products and services but also to establish themselves as responsible corporate citizens. For example, they may establish objectives for charitable and educational contributions, minority training, public or political activity, community welfare, or urban renewal.

Qualities of Long-Term Objectives

What distinguishes a good objective from a bad one? What qualities of an objective improve its chances of being attained? Perhaps these questions are best answered in relation to seven criteria that should be used in preparing long-term objectives: acceptable, flexible, measurable over time, motivating, suitable, understandable, and achievable.

Acceptable   Managers are most likely to pursue objectives that are consistent with their preferences. They may ignore or even obstruct the achievement of objectives that offend them (e.g., promoting a nonnutritional food product) or that they believe to be inappropriate or unfair (e.g., reducing spoilage to offset a disproportionate allocation of fixed overhead. In addition, long-term corporate objectives are frequently designed to be acceptable to groups external to the firm. An example is efforts to abate air pollution that are undertaken at the insistence of the Environmental Protection Agency.

Flexible   Objectives should be adaptable to unforeseen or extraordinary changes in the firm's competitive or environmental forecasts. However, such flexibility is usually increased at the expense of specificity. Moreover, employee confidence may be tempered because adjustment of flexible objectives may affect their jobs. One way of providing flexibility while minimizing its negative effects is to allow for adjustments in the level rather than in the nature of objectives. For example, the personnel department objective of providing managerial development training for 15 supervisors per year over the next five-year period might be adjusted by changing the number of people to be trained. In contrast, changing the personnel department's objective of "assisting production supervisors in reducing job-related injuries by 10 percent per year" after three months had gone by would understandably create dissatisfaction.

Measurable   Objectives must clearly and concretely state what will be achieved and when it will be achieved. Thus, objectives should be measurable over time. For example, the objective of "substantially improving our return on investment" would be better stated as "increasing the return on investment on our line of paper products by a minimum of 1 percent a year and a total of 5 percent over the next three years."

Motivating   Studies have shown that people are most productive when objectives are set at a motivating level—one high enough to challenge but not so high as to frustrate or so low as to be easily attained. The problem is that individuals and groups differ in their perceptions of what is high enough. A broad objective that challenges one group frustrates another and minimally interests a third. One valuable recommendation is that objectives be tailored to specific groups. Developing such objectives requires time and effort, but objectives of this kind are more likely to motivate.

Suitable   Objectives must be suited to the broad aims of the firm, which are expressed in its mission statement. Each objective should be a step toward the attainment of overall goals. In fact, objectives that do not coincide with the company mission can subvert the firm's aims. For example, if the mission is growth oriented, the objective of reducing the debt-to-equity ratio to 1.00 would probably be unsuitable and counterproductive.

Understandable   Strategic managers at all levels must understand what is to be achieved. They must also understand the major criteria by which their performance will be evaluated. Thus, objectives must be stated so that they are as understandable to the recipient as they are to the giver. Consider the misunderstandings that might arise over the objective of "increasing the productivity of the credit card department by 20 percent within five years." What does this objective mean? Increase the number of outstanding cards? Increase the use of outstanding cards? Increase the employee workload? Make productivity gains each year? Or hope that the new computer-assisted system, which should improve productivity, is approved by year five? As this simple example illustrates, objectives must be clear, meaningful, and unambiguous.

Achievable   Finally, objectives must be possible to achieve. This is easier said than done. Turbulence in the remote and operating environments affects a firm's internal operations, creating uncertainty and limiting the accuracy of the objectives set by strategic management. For example, the wildly fluctuating prime interest rates in 1980 made objective setting extremely difficult for the years 1981 to 1985, particularly in such areas as sales projections for producers of consumer durable goods like General Motors and General Electric.

   An especially fine example of long-term objectives is provided in CACI, Inc.'s strategic plan for 1990. Shown in Strategy in Action 7–1 are CACI's major financial objectives for the period. The firm's approach is wholly consistent with the list of desired qualities for long-term objectives. In particular, CACI's objectives are flexible, measurable over time, understandable, and suitable for a high-technology and professional services organization.

CACI's Long-Term Objectives, 1990

REVENUE

Increase revenue range to $167–176M or better in FY 90 (FY 90 bookings at $170M).

FY 91: Revenue in the $193–202M range; bookings at $195–205M range.

Increase company revenue 15–20 percent per year *steadily* over next decade.

Consistently increase revenues to $500M per annum by 1997 or earlier. Steady manageable and consistent profitable growth.

PROFITABILTY

Achieve 4 percent NAT or better as an annual corporate target for return on revenues, moving to 5 percent NAT by mid-90s.

Individual departments and divisions must target NAT percentage profits at 50–100 percent above company levels, i.e., 6–8 percent moving to 7.5–10 percent.

SHAREHOLDERS' VALUE

Increase stock price (market value) to $20 per share or better by 1997 (current share basis).

GENERIC STRATEGIES

Many planning experts believe that the general philosophy of doing business declared by the firm in the mission statement must be translated into a holistic statement of the firm's strategic orientation before it can be further defined in terms of a specific long-term strategy. In other words, a long-term or grand strategy must be based on a core idea about how the firm can best compete in the marketplace.

The popular term for this core idea is *generic strategy*. From a scheme developed by Michael Porter, many planners believe that any long-term strategy should derive from a firm's attempt to seek a competitive advantage based on one of three generic strategies:

1. Striving for overall *low-cost leadership* in the industry.
2. Striving to create and market unique products for varied customer groups through *differentiation*.
3. Striving to have special appeal to one or more groups of consumer or industrial buyers, *focusing* on their cost or differentiation concerns.

Advocates of generic strategies believe that each of these options can produce above-average returns for a firm in an industry. However, they are successful for very different reasons.

FIGURE 7-1
Requirements for Generic Competitive Strategies

Generic Strategy	Commonly Required Skills and Resources	Common Organizational Requirements
Overall cost leadership	Sustained capital investment and access to capital Process engineering skills Intense supervision of labor Products designed for ease in manufacture Low-cost distribution system	Tight cost control Frequent, detailed control reports Structured organization and responsibilities Incentives based on meeting strict quantitative targets
Differentiation	Strong marketing abilities Product engineering Creative flair Strong capability in basic research Corporate reputation for quality or technological leadership Long tradition in the industry or unique combination of skills drawn from other businesses Strong cooperation from channels	Strong coordination among functions in R&D, product development, and marketing Subjective measurement and incentives instead of quantitative measures Amenities to attract highly skilled labor, scientists, or creative people
Focus	Combination of the above policies directed at the particular strategic target	Combination of the above policies directed at the regular strategic target

Source: Reprinted with permission of the Free Press, a Division of Macmillan, Inc. from *COMPETITIVE STRATEGY: Techniques for Analyzing Industries and Competitors* by Michael E. Porter, pp. 40–41. Copyright © 1980 by The Free Press.

Low-cost leaders depend on some fairly unique capability to achieve and sustain their low-cost position. Examples of such capabilities are: having secured suppliers of scarce raw materials, being in a dominant market share position, or having a high degree of capitalization. Low-cost producers usually excel at cost reductions and efficiencies. They maximize economies of scale, implement cost-cutting technologies, stress reductions in overhead and administrative expenses, and use volume sales techniques to propel themselves up the earning curve. The commonly accepted requirements for successful implementation of the low-cost and other two generic strategies is overviewed in Figure 7–1.

A low-cost leader is able to use its cost advantage to charge lower prices or enjoy higher profit margins. By so doing the firm can effectively defend itself in price wars, attack competitors on price to gain market share, or if dominant in the industry already, simply benefit from exceptional returns. As an extreme case, it has been argued that National Can Company, a corporation in an essentially stagnant industry, is able to generate attractive and improving profits by being the low-cost producer.

Strategies dependent on differentiation are designed to appeal to customers with a special sensitivity for a particular product attribute. By stressing the attribute above other product qualities, the firm attempts to build customer loyalty. Often such loyalty translates into a firm's ability to charge a premium price for its product. Cross brand pens, Brooks Brothers suits, Porsche automobiles, and Chivas Regal Scotch whiskey are all examples.

FIGURE 7–2
Risks of the Generic Strategies

Risks of Cost Leadership	Risks of Differentiation	Risks of Focus
Cost leadership is not sustained: • Competitors imitate. • Technology changes. • Other bases for cost leadership erode.	Differentiation is not sustained: • Competitors imitate. • Bases for differentiation become less important to buyers	The focus strategy is imitated. The target segment becomes structurally unattractive: • Structure erodes. • Demand disappears.
Proximity in differentiation is lost.	Cost proximity is lost.	Broadly targeted competitors overwhelm the segment: • The segment's differences from other segments narrow. • The advantages of a broad line increase.
Cost focusers achieve even lower cost in segments.	Differentiation focusers achieve even greater differentiation in segments.	New focusers sub-segment the industry.

Source: Michael E. Porter, *Competitive Advantage: Creating and Sustaining Superior Performance* Copyright © 1985 by Michael E. Porter. Reprinted with permission of The Free Press, a Division of Macmillan, Inc.

The product attribute can also be the marketing channels through which it is delivered, its image for excellence, the features it includes, and the service network that supports it. As a result of the importance of these attributes, competitors often face "perceptual" barriers to entry when customers of a successfully differentiated firm fail to see largely identical products as being interchangeable. For example, General Motors hopes that customers will accept "only genuine GM replacement parts."

A focus strategy, whether anchored in a low-cost base or a differentiation base, attempts to attend to the needs of a particular market segment. Likely segments are those that are ignored by marketing appeals to easily accessible markets, to the "typical" customer, or to customers with common applications for the product. A firm pursuing a focus strategy is willing to service isolated geographic areas; to satisfy the needs of customers with special financing, inventory, or servicing problems; or to tailor the product to the somewhat unique demands of the small- to medium-sized customer. Focusing firms profit from their willingness to serve otherwise ignored or under-appreciated customer segments. The classic example is cable television. An entire industry was born because of a willingness of cable firms to serve isolated rural locations that were ignored by traditional television services. Brick producers that typically service a radius of less than 100 miles and commuter airlines that serve regional geographic areas are other examples of industries where a focus strategy frequently yields above-average industry profits.

While each of the generic strategies enables a firm to maximize certain competitive advantages, each one also exposes the firm to a number of competitive risks. For example, a low-cost leader fears a new low-cost technology being developed by a competitor; a differentiating firm fears imitators; and a focused firm fears invasion by a firm that largely targets customers. As Figure 7–2 suggests, each generic strategy presents the firm with a number of risks.

GRAND STRATEGIES[3]

While the need for firms to develop generic strategies remains an unresolved debate, designers of planning systems agree about the critical role of *grand strategies*. Grand strategies, often called *master* or *business* strategies, provide basic direction for strategic actions. They are the basis of coordinated and sustained efforts directed toward achieving long-term business objectives.

The purpose of this section is twofold: (1) to list, describe, and discuss 12 grand strategies that strategic managers should consider and (2) to present approaches to the selection of an optimal grand strategy from the available alternatives.

Grand strategies indicate how long-range objectives will be achieved. Thus, a grand strategy can be defined as a comprehensive general approach that guides a firm's major actions. As an example, Strategy in Action 7–2 presents the grand strategy of CSX, the $8 billion conglomerate that decided to concentrate on its railroad.

The 12 principal grand strategies are concentrated growth, market development, product development, innovation, horizontal integration, vertical integration, joint venture, concentric diversification, conglomerate diversification, retrenchment/turnaround, divestiture, and liquidation. Any one of these strategies could serve as the basis for achieving the major long-term objectives of a single firm. But a firm involved with multiple industries, businesses, product lines, or customer groups—as many firms are—usually combines several grand strategies. For clarity, however, each of the principal grand strategies is described independently in this section, with examples to indicate some of its relative strengths and weaknesses.

Concentrated Growth[4]

Many of the firms that fell victim to merger mania were once mistakenly convinced that the best way to achieve their objectives was to pursue unrelated diversification in the search for financial opportunity and synergy. By rejecting that "conventional wisdom," such firms as Martin-Marietta, Kentucky Fried Chicken, Compaq, Avon, Hyatt Legal Services, and Tenant have demonstrated the advantages of what is increasingly proving to be sound business strategy.

---

[3]Portions of this section were adapted from John A. Pearce II, "Selecting among Alternative Grand Strategies," *California Management Review,* Spring 1982, pp. 23–31.

[4]Portions of this section were adapted from John A. Pearce II and J. Harvey, "Risks and Rewards of a Concentrated Growth Strategy," *Academy of Management Executive,* February 1990, pp. 62–69.

STRATEGY
IN ACTION   CSX's GRAND STRATEGY
7-2

West Virginia's palatial Greenbrier Hotel looms behind a dapper horseman in a 1987 ad for CSX Corporation. The headline asks: "Is This Any Way to Run a Railroad?" For CSX, the answer was yes. Now, its maybe.

It's possible that the $8 billion railroad conglomerate will find a way to keep some financial interest in the resort hotel, which has sheltered various aristocrats, presidents, and captains of industry for almost 80 years. But on September 19, 1988, CSX put the Greenbrier and a string of other hotels on the block, along with a natural gas pipeline and a gas-liquids processing business. Simultaneously, CSX announced that it would buy as much as $1.9 billion worth of its stock.

That was quite a reversal for the company, which under Chairman Hays T. Watkins went on a buying binge. An accountant by training and a railroad executive all his life, Watkins helped merge the Chessie System RRS and the Seaboard System RR in 1980. Later, as CSX's new chief, he embarked on the acquisition trail. In 1983 he paid $1.1 billion for an oil and gas company and its midwestern barge subsidiary. Three years later, he bought Roskresort, Inc., a collection of posh hotels developed by Laurance S. Rockefeller. In the same year he picked up Sea-Land Corporation, a big container shipping company, for $803 million.

With his purchases, Watkins intended to transform CSX, which is based in Richmond, Virginia, from a mere railroad into a "one-stop" transporter of global dimensions. The new CSX would allow shippers to turn their goods over to a single company and not sweat the details of how they moved across land or sea. The rest of CSX—the real estate development branch, a fiber-optic

These firms are just a few of the majority of American firms that pursue a concentrated growth strategy by focusing on a specific product and market combination. Concentrated growth is the strategy of the firm that directs its resources to the profitable growth of a single product, in a single market, with a single dominant technology. The main rationale for this approach, sometimes called a market penetration or concentration strategy, is that the firm thoroughly develops and exploits its expertise in a delimited competitive arena.[5]

Rationale for Superior Performance

Why do concentrated growth strategies lead to enhanced performance? A study of product successes and failures across multiple industries suggests several reasons. This study shows that the greatest influences on market success are those characteristic of firms that implement a concentrated growth strategy.[6]

---

[5]For a more detailed and comprehensive description of alternative business strategies, refer to Pearce, "Selecting among Alternative Grand Strategies."

[6]Robert G. Cooper, "Identifying Industrial New Product Success: Project NewProd," *Industrial Marketing Management,* April 1979, pp. 124–35.

venture, the oil and gas operations, and the hotels—would help churn out earnings even when shipping hit a slump.

Somehow, the grand vision has failed to produce superior profits. Negotiations with the railway unions for wage reforms and more worker cutbacks fell through. The barge business, hurt in 1987 by low shipping rates, scraped bottom in the drought of 1988. In June 1988 the CSX board adopted a poison-pill measure that was to go into effect if anyone amassed 20 percent or more of the firm's stock. "We looked like a prime target," says CSX board member Steven Muller, president of Johns Hopkins University.

The announced buyback returned some zip to CSX shares, producing a 3-point jump, to over 30, and giving the stock a small gain for the year. The move was expected to sharply raise earnings per share without adding too much new debt to the balance sheet, since selling most of the gas and resort properties would just about cover the cost of repurchasing shares.

Most analysts think that unless there is a recession, earnings should pick up for both Sea-Land and the railroad in 1989. Higher demand this summer for chemicals and fertilizers shipped on CSX's railroad has already produced much stronger earnings in the third quarter.

Investors, however, are not happy with Watkins' performance. Says James Severance, an investment director at the Wisconsin Investment Board, which manages pension funds for that state and which holds 2.7 million CSX shares: "More can be wrung out of this company and should be. They have to be more cold-blooded."

These influences include the ability to assess market needs, knowledge of buyer behavior, customer price sensitivity, and effectiveness of promotion. Further underscoring the importance of concentrated growth-based company skills, the study also shows that these core capabilities are a more important determinant of competitive market success than are the environmental forces faced by the firm. The high success rates of new products are also tied to avoiding situations that require undeveloped skills, such as serving new customers and markets, acquiring new technology, building new channels, developing new promotional abilities, and facing new competition.[7]

A major misconception about the concentrated growth strategy is that the firm practicing it will settle for little or no growth. This is certainly not true for a firm that correctly utilizes the strategy. A firm employing concentrated growth grows by building on its competences and achieves a competitive edge by concentrating in the product-market segment it knows best. A firm employing this strategy is aiming for the growth that results from increased productivity, better coverage of its actual product-market segment, and more efficient use of its technology.

[7]Robert G. Cooper, "The Impact of New Product Strategies," *Industrial Marketing Management*, October 1983, pp. 243–56.

Conditions That Favor Concentrated Growth

Specific conditions in the firm's environment are favorable to the concentrated growth strategy. The first is a condition in which the firm's industry is resistant to major technological advancements. This is usually the case in the late growth and maturity stages of the product life cycle and in product-markets where product demand is stable and industry barriers, such as capitalization, are high. Machinery for the paper manufacturing industry, in which the basic technology has not changed for more than a century, is a good example.

An especially favorable condition is one in which the firm's targeted markets are not product saturated. Markets with competitive gaps leave the firm with alternatives for growth other than taking market share away from competitors. The successful introduction of traveler services by All-State and Amoco demonstrates that even an organization as entrenched and powerful as the AAA could not build a defensible presence in all segments of the automobile club market.

A third condition that favors concentrated growth exists when the firm's product-markets are sufficiently distinctive to dissuade competitors in adjacent product-markets from trying to invade the firm's segment. John Deere scrapped its plans for growth in the construction machinery business when mighty Caterpillar threatened to enter Deere's mainstay, the farm machinery business, in retaliation. Rather than risk a costly price war on its own turf, Deere scrapped these plans.

A fourth favorable condition exists when the firm's inputs are stable in price and quantity and are available in the amounts and at the times needed. Maryland-based Giant Foods is able to concentrate in the grocery business largely due to its stable long-term arrangements with suppliers of its private-label products. Most of these suppliers are makers of the national brands that compete against the Giant labels. With a high market share and aggressive retail distribution, Giant controls the access of these brands to the consumer. Consequently, its suppliers have considerable incentive to honor verbal agreements, called bookings, in which they commit themselves for a one-year period with regard to the price, quality, and timing of their shipments to Giant.

The pursuit of concentrated growth is also favored by a stable market, a market without the seasonal or cyclical swings that would encourage a firm to diversify. Night Owl Security, the Washington-based District of Columbia market leader in home security services commits its customers to initial four-year contracts. In a city were affluent consumers tend to be quite transient, the length of this relationship is remarkable. Night Owl's concentrated growth strategy has been reinforced by its success in getting subsequent owners of its customers' homes to extend and renew the security service contracts.

A firm can also grow while concentrating, if it enjoys competitive advantages based on efficient production or distribution channels. These advantages enable the firm to formulate advantageous pricing policies. More efficient production methods and better handling of distribution also enable the firm to achieve greater economies of scale or, in conjunction with marketing, result in a product that is differentiated in the mind of the consumer. Graniteville Company, a large South Carolina textile manufacturer, enjoyed decades of growth and profitability by adopting a "follower" tactic as part of its concentrated growth strategy. By producing fabrics only after market demand had been well established and by featuring products that reflected its expertise in adopting manufacturing innovations and in maintaining highly efficient long production runs, Graniteville prospered through concentrated growth.

Finally, the success of market generalists creates conditions favorable to concentrated growth.[8] When generalists succeed by using universal appeals, they avoid making special appeals to particular groups of customers. The net result is that many small pockets are left open in the markets dominated by generalists and that specialists emerge and thrive in these pockets. For example, hardware store chains such as Stanbaugh-Thompsons and Hechinger focus primarily on routine household repair problems and offer solutions that can be easily sold on a self-service, do-it-yourself basis. This approach leaves gaps at both the "semiprofessional" and "neophyte" ends of the market—in terms of the purchaser's skill at household repairs and the extent to which available merchandise matches the requirements of individual homeowners.

Risk and Rewards of Concentrated Growth

Under stable conditions, concentrated growth poses lower risk than any other grand strategy, but in a changing environment, a firm committed to concentrated growth faces high risks. The greatest risk is that concentrating in a single product-market makes a firm particularly vulnerable to changes in that segment. Slowed growth in the segment would jeopardize the firm because its investment, competitive edge, and technology are deeply entrenched in a specific offering. It is difficult for the firm to attempt sudden changes if its product is threatened by near-term obsolescence, a faltering market, new substitutes, or changes in technology or customer needs. For example, the manufacturers of IBM clones faced such a problem when IBM adopted the OS/2 operating system for its personal computer line. That change made existing clones out of date.

The concentrating firm's entrenchment in a specific industry makes it particularly susceptible to changes in the economic environment of that industry. For example, Mack Truck, the second-largest truck maker in America, lost $20 million as a result of an 18-month slump in the truck industry.

Entrenchment in a specific product-market tends to make a concentrating firm more adept than competitors at detecting new trends. However, any failure of such a firm to properly forecast major changes in its industry can result in extraordinary losses. Numerous makers of inexpensive digital watches were forced to declare bankruptcy because they failed to anticipate the competition posed by Swatch, Guess, and other trendy watches that emerged from the fashion industry.

A firm pursuing a concentrated growth strategy is also vulnerable to the high opportunity costs that result from remaining in a specific product-market and ignoring other options that could employ the firm's resources more profitably. Overcommitment to a specific technology and product-market can hinder a firm's ability to enter a new or growing product-market that offers more attractive cost-benefit trade-offs. Had Apple Computers maintained its policy of making equipment that did not interface with IBM equipment, it would have missed out on what have proved to be its most profitable strategic opinions.

---

[8]Glenn R. Carroll, "The Specialist Strategy," *California Management Review*, Spring 1984, pp. 126–37.

Concentrated Growth Is Often the Most Viable Option

Examples abound of firms that have enjoyed exceptional returns on the concentrated growth strategy. Such firms as McDonald's, Goodyear, and Apple Computers have used firsthand knowledge and deep involvement with specific product segments to become powerful competitors in their markets. The strategy is associated even more often with successful smaller firms that have steadily and doggedly improved their market position.

The limited additional resources necessary to implement concentrated growth, coupled with the limited risk involved, also make this strategy desirable for a firm with limited funds. For example, through a carefully devised concentrated growth strategy, medium-sized John Deere & Company was able to become a major force in the agricultural machinery business even when competing with such firms as Ford Motor Company. While other firms were trying to exit or diversify from the farm machinery business, Deere spent $2 billion in upgrading its machinery, boosting its efficiency, and engaging in a program to strengthen its dealership system. This concentrated growth strategy enabled it to become the leader in the farm machinery business despite the fact that Ford was more than 10 times its size.

The firm that chooses a concentrated growth strategy directs its resources to the profitable growth of a narrowly defined product and market, focusing on a dominant technology. Firms that remain within their chosen product-market are able to extract the most from their technology and market knowledge and thus are able to minimize the risk associated with unrelated diversification. The success of a concentration strategy is founded on the firm's use of superior insights into its technology, product, and customer to obtain a sustainable competitive advantage. Superior performance on these aspects of corporate strategy has been shown to have a substantial positive effect on market success.

A grand strategy of concentrated growth allows for a considerable range of action. Broadly speaking, the firm can attempt to capture a larger market share by increasing the usage rates of present customers, by attracting competitors' customers, or by selling to nonusers. In turn, each of these options suggests more specific options, some of which are listed in the top section of Figure 7–3.

When strategic managers forecast that their current products and their markets will not provide the basis for achieving the company mission, they have two options that involve moderate costs and risk: market development and product development.

Market Development

Market development commonly ranks second only to concentration as the least costly and least risky of the 12 grand strategies. It consists of marketing present products, often with only cosmetic modifications, to customers in related market areas by adding channels of distribution or by changing the content of advertising or promotion. Several specific approaches are listed under this heading in Figure 7–3. Thus, as suggested by the figure, firms that open branch offices in new cities, states, or countries are practicing market development. Likewise, firms are practicing market development if they switch from advertising in trade publications to advertising in newspapers or if they add jobbers to supplement their mail-order sales efforts.

FIGURE 7–3
Specific Options under the Grand Strategies of Concentration,
Market Development, and Product Development

Concentration (increasing use of present products in present markets):
1. Increasing present customers' rate of use:
   a. Increasing the size of purchase.
   b. Increasing the rate of product obsolescence.
   c. Advertising other uses.
   d. Giving price incentives for increased use.
2. Attracting competitors' customers.
   a. Establishing sharper brand differentiation.
   b. Increasing promotional effort.
   c. Initiating price cuts.
3. Attracting nonusers to buy the product.
   a. Inducing trial use through sampling, price incentives, and so on.
   b. Pricing up or down.
   c. Advertising new uses.

Market development (selling present products in new markets):
1. Opening additional geographic markets.
   a. Regional expansion.
   b. National expansion.
   c. International expansion.
2. Attracting other market segments.
   a. Developing product versions to appeal to other segments.
   b. Entering other channels of distribution.
   c. Advertising in other media.

Product development (developing new products for present markets):
1. Developing new product features.
   a. Adapt (to other ideas, developments).
   b. Modify (change color, motion, sound, odor, form, shape).
   c. Magnify (stronger, longer, thicker, extra value).
   d. Minify (smaller, shorter, lighter).
   e. Substitute (other ingredients, process, power).
   f. Rearrange (other patterns, layout, sequence, components).
   g. Reverse (inside out).
   h. Combine (blend, alloy, assortment, ensemble; combine units, purposes, appeals, ideas).
2. Developing quality variations.
3. Developing additional models and sizes (product proliferation).

Source: Adapted from Philip Kotler. *Marketing Management Analysis, Planning, and Control,* 6th ed., 1987. Reprinted by permission of Prentice-Hall, Inc., Englewood Cliffs, N.J.

Market development allows firms to practice a form of concentrated growth by identifying new uses for existing products and new demographically, psychographically, or geographically defined markets. Frequently, changes in media selection, promotional appeals, and distribution are used to initiate this approach. Du Pont used market development when it found a new application for Kevlar, an organic material police, security, and military personnel had used primarily for bulletproofing. Kevlar is now being used to refit and maintain wooden-hulled boats, since it is lighter and stronger than glass fibers and has 11 times the strength of steel.

The medical industry provides other examples of new markets for existing products. The National Institutes of Health's report of a study showing that the use of aspirin may lower the incidence of heart attacks is expected to boost sales in the $2.2 billion analgesic market. It has been predicted that the expansion of this market will lower the market share of nonaspirin brands, such as industry leaders Tylenol and Advil. Product extensions currently planned include Bayer Calendar Pack, 28-day packaging to fit the once-a-day prescription for the prevention of a second heart attack.

Product Development

Product development involves the substantial modification of existing products or the creation of new but related products that can be marketed to current customers through established channels. The product development strategy is often adopted either to prolong the life cycle of current products or to take advantage of a favorable reputation or brand name. The idea is to attract satisfied customers to new products as a result of their positive experience with the firm's initial offering. The bottom section in Figure 7–3 lists some of the options available to firms undertaking product development. A revised edition of a college textbook, a new car style, and a second formula of shampoo for oily hair are examples of the product development strategy.

The product development strategy is based on the penetration of existing markets by incorporating product modifications into existing items or by developing new products with a clear connection to the existing product line. The telecommunications industry provides an example of product extension based on product modification. To increase its estimated 8–10 percent share of the $5–6 billion corporate user market, MCI Communication Corporation extended its direct-dial service to 146 countries, the same as those serviced by AT&T, at lower average rates than those of AT&T. MCI's recent addition of 79 countries to its network underscores its belief in this market, which it expects to grow 15–20 percent annually. Another example of expansions linked to existing lines is Gerber's decision to engage in general merchandise marketing. Gerber's recent introduction included 52 items that ranged from feeding accessories to toys and children's wear.

Innovation

In many industries, it has become increasingly risky not to innovate. Both consumer and industrial markets have come to expect periodic changes and improvements in the products offered. As a result, some firms find it profitable to make innovation their grand strategy. They seek to reap the initially high profits associated with customer acceptance of a new or greatly improved product. Then, rather than face stiffening competition as the basis of profitability shifts from innovation to production or marketing competence, they search for other original or novel ideas. The underlying rationale of the grand strategy of innovation is to create a new product life cycle and thereby make similar existing products obsolete. Thus, this strategy differs from the product development strategy of extending an existing product's life cycle.

While most growth-oriented firms appreciate the need to be innovative occasionally, a few firms use it as their fundamental way of relating to their markets. An outstanding example is Polaroid, which heavily promotes each of its new cameras until competitors

FIGURE 7–4
Decay of New Product Ideas (51 Companies)

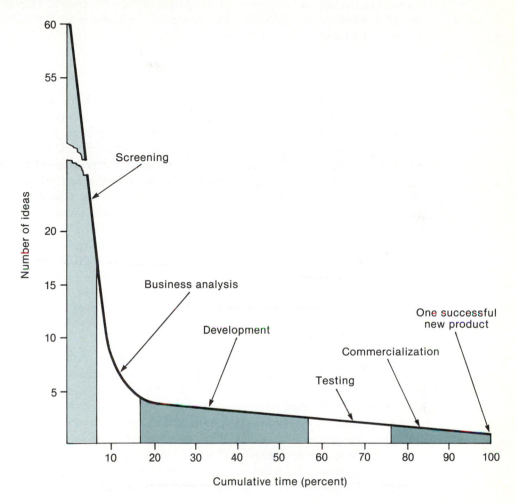

are able to match its technological innovation. By this time, Polaroid is normally prepared to introduce a dramatically new or improved product. For example, it introduced consumers in quick succession to the Swinger, the SX-70, the One Step, and the Sun Camera 660.

Few innovative ideas prove profitable because the research, development, and premarketing costs of converting a promising idea into a profitable product are extremely high. A study by the Booz Allen & Hamilton management research department provides some understanding of the risks. As shown in Figure 7–4, Booz Allen & Hamilton found that less than 2 percent of the innovative projects initially considered by 51 companies eventually reached the marketplace. Specifically, out of every 58 new product ideas, only 12 pass an initial screening test that finds them compatible with the firm's mission and long-term objectives, only 7 remain after an evaluation of their potential, and only 3 survive development attempts. Of the three survivors, two appear to have profit potential after test marketing and only one is commercially successful. In fact, other studies show that the failure rate is far higher. For example, one study found the failure rates for commercial products to be as high as 89 percent.[9]

Horizontal Integration

When a firm's long-term strategy is based on growth through the acquisition of one or more similar firms operating at the same stage of the production-marketing chain, its grand strategy is called *horizontal integration*. Such acquisitions eliminate competitors and provide the acquiring firm with access to new markets.[10] One example is Warner-Lambert's acquisition of Parke Davis, which reduced competition in the ethical drugs field for Chilcott Laboratories, a firm that Warner-Lambert had previously acquired. Another example is the long-range acquisition pattern of White Consolidated Industries, which expanded in the refrigerator and freezer market through a grand strategy of horizontal integration by acquiring Kelvinator Appliance, the Refrigerator Products Division of Bendix Westinghouse Automotive Air Brake, and Frigidaire Appliance from General Motors. More recently, Nike's acquisition in the dress shoes business and N. V. Homes' purchase of Ryan Homes have vividly exemplified the success that horizontal integration strategies can bring.

Vertical Integration

When a firm's grand strategy is to acquire firms that supply it with inputs (such as raw materials) or are a customer for its outputs (such as warehousers for finished products), *vertical integration* is involved. For example, if a shirt manufacturer acquires a textile producer—by purchasing its common stock, buying its assets, or exchanging ownership interests, the strategy is vertical integration. In this case, it is *backward* vertical integration since the firm acquired operates at an earlier stage of the production-marketing process. If the shirt manufacturer had merged with a clothing store, it would have been *forward* vertical integration—the acquisition of a firm nearer to the ultimate consumer.

Amoco emerged as North America's leader in natural gas reserves and products in 1988 as a result of its acquisition of Dome Petroleum. This backward integration by Amoco was made in support of its downstream businesses in refining and gas stations, whose profits made the acquisition possible.

Figure 7–5 depicts both horizontal and vertical integration. The principal attractions of a horizontal integration grand strategy are readily apparent. The acquiring firm is able to greatly expand its operations, thereby achieving greater market share, improving econ-

---

[9]Burt Schorr, "Many New Products Fizzle, Despite Careful Planning, Publicity," *The Wall Street Journal*, April 5, 1961.

[10]Martin K. Perry and Robert H. Porter, "Oligopoly and the Incentive for Horizontal Merger," *American Economic Review*, March 1985, pp. 219–27.

FIGURE 7–5
Vertical and Horizontal Integrations

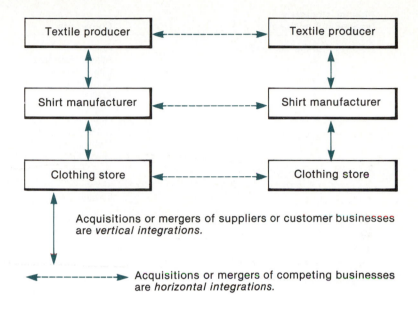

Acquisitions or mergers of suppliers or customer businesses are *vertical integrations.*

Acquisitions or mergers of competing businesses are *horizontal integrations.*

omies of scale, and increasing the efficiency of capital use. In addition, these benefits are achieved with only moderately increased risk, since the success of the expansion is principally dependent on proven abilities.

The reasons for choosing a vertical integration grand strategy are more varied and sometimes less obvious.[11] The main reason for backward integration is the desire to increase the dependability of the supply or quality of the raw materials used as production inputs. That desire is particularly great when the number of suppliers is small and the number of competitors is large. In this situation, the vertically integrating firm can better control its costs and thereby improve the profit margin of the expanded production-marketing system. Forward integration is a preferred grand strategy if great advantages accrue to stable production. A firm can increase the predictability of demand for its output through forward integration, that is, through ownership of the next stage of its production-marketing chain.

Some increased risks are associated with both types of integration. For horizontally integrated firms, the risks stem from increased commitment to one type of business. For vertically integrated firms, the risks result from the firm's expansion into areas requiring strategic managers to broaden the base of their competences and to assume additional responsibilities.

---

[11]Kathryn Rudie Harrigan, "Formulating Vertical Integration Strategies," *Academy of Management Review,* October 1984, pp. 638–52.

FIGURE 7-6
Joint Ventures in the Oil Pipeline Industry

Pipeline Company (assets in $ millions)	Co-owners	Percent Held by Each
Colonial Pipeline Co. ($480.2)	Amoco	14.3%
	Atlantic Richfield	1.6
	Cities Service	14.0
	Continental	7.5
	Phillips	7.1
	Texaco	14.3
	Gulf	16.8
	Sohio	9.0
	Mobil	11.5
	Union Oil	4.0
Olympic Pipeline Co. ($30.7)	Shell	43.5
	Mobil	29.5
	Texaco	27.0
West Texas Gulf Pipeline Co. ($19.8)	Gulf	57.7
	Cities Service	11.4
	Sun	12.6
	Union Oil	9.0
	Sohio	9.2
Texas–New Mexico Pipeline Co. ($30.5)	Texaco	45.0
	Atlantic Richfield	35.0
	Cities Service	10.0
	Getty	10.0

Source: Testimony of Walter Adams in *Horizontal Integration of the Energy Industry,* hearings before the Subcommittee on Energy of the Joint Economic Committee, 94th Congress. 1st sess. (1975), p. 112.

Joint Venture

Occasionally two or more capable firms lack a necessary component for success in a particular competitive environment.[12] For example, no single petroleum firm controlled sufficient resources to construct the Alaskan pipeline. Nor was any single firm capable of processing and marketing all of the oil that would flow through the pipeline. The solution was a set of *joint ventures*. As shown in Figure 7–6, these cooperative arrangements could provide both the funds needed to build the pipeline and the processing and marketing capacity needed to profitably handle the oil flow.

The particular form of joint venture discussed above is joint ownership.[13] In recent years, it has become increasingly appealing for domestic firms to join foreign firms by means of this form. For example, Bethlehem Steel acquired an interest in a Brazilian

---

[12]Godfrey Devlin and Mark Bleackley, "Strategic Alliances—Guidelines for Success," *Long Range Planning,* October 1988, pp. 18–23.

[13]Other forms of joint ventures (such as leasing, contract manufacturing, and management contracting) offer valuable support strategies. They are not included in the categorization, however, because they are seldom employed as grand strategies.

STRATEGY IN ACTION 7–3

JOINT VENTURE IN HUNGARY

Schwarzkopf, a West German cosmetics producer, marked its 10th-anniversary in the Hungarian market with a milestone: production in Hungary with a majority Western ownership. Schwarzkopf proposed a series of appealing arrangements to the Hungarians, and the result was an unusual mix of capital, know-how, and marketing expertise in which both sides perceived advantages.

Schwarzkopf first entered the Hungarian market in 1975 through a licensing arrangement with KHV/Caola; this worked out quite well. When Hungarian authorities began to actively promote joint ventures with Western firms, Schwarzkopf decided that it could improve its position in the Hungarian market. In particular, it decided that a joint venture would give it greater opportunity to apply its marketing skills and increase its sales. Having made this decision, Schwarzkopf began negotiations to transform its relationship with KHV/Caola into a full joint venture. The partners in the joint venture were Schwarzkopf, with 51 percent, Caola, with 45 percent; and Chemo-Caola, itself a joint venture between Caola and FTO Chemoplex, with the remaining 4 percent.

To gain this advantage, Schwarzkopf provided more than two thirds of the needed $600,000 capital in the form of licenses, know-how, machinery, and equipment. Caola's staff was used for administration, purchasing, and other operational functions. This was an advantage because the average income of Hungarian workers was $142. Meanwhile, Caola could sell Western-quality merchandise in its foreign and domestic markets without investing in scarce hard currency.

The major stumbling blocks in the first two years of the joint venture's operation were currency, market, and confidence. The West German partner was reluctant to export products made in Hungary to its Western markets. But it had trouble selling those products to Caola's East European clients because they lacked convertible currency. The Hungarians, on their part, were willing to participate in the joint venture only if export sales matched the costs of imported raw materials. That translated into an artificially small operation. Laszlo Sperber, the on-site manager of the joint venture's plant, said, "We could sell 20 times as much, but then we would have problems of equilibrium."

Source: "Hungary Grants First Joint Venture with Western Majority," *Business Eastern Europe*, April 19, 1985, p. 123; "East Bloc Ventures Face Uncertainties," *Washington Post*, March 1, 1987, p. H3; and S. H. Robock and K. Simmonds, *International Business and Multinational Enterprises* (Homewood, Ill: Richard D. Irwin, 1989), p. 218.

mining venture to secure a raw material source. The stimulus for this joint ownership venture was grand strategy, but such is not always the case. Certain countries virtually mandate that foreign firms entering their markets do so on a joint ownership basis. India and Mexico are good examples. The rationale of these countries is that joint ventures minimize the threat of foreign domination and enhance the skills, employment, growth, and profits of local firms.

It should be noted that strategic managers in the typical firm rarely seek joint ventures. Admittedly, joint ventures present new opportunities with risks that can be shared. On the other hand, joint ventures often limit the discretion, control, and profit potential of partners while demanding managerial attention and other resources that might be directed toward the firm's mainstream activities. Nevertheless, increasing globalization in many industries may require greater consideration of the joint venture approach, if historically national firms are to remain viable.[14] Advantages and disadvantages of an international joint venture are highlighted in Strategy in Action 7–3.

Concentric Diversification

Grand strategies involving diversification represent distinctive departures from a firm's existing base of operations, typically the acquisition or internal generation (spin-off) of a separate business with synergistic possibilities counterbalancing the strengths and weaknesses of the two businesses. For example, Head Ski initially sought to diversify into summer sporting goods and clothing to offset the seasonality of its snow business. However, diversifications are occasionally undertaken as unrelated investments because of their high profit potential and their otherwise minimal resource demands.

Regardless of the approach taken, the motivations of the acquiring firms are the same:

Increase the firm's stock value. In the past, mergers have often led to increases in the stock price or the price-earnings ratio.

Increase the growth rate of the firm.

Make an investment that represents better use of funds than plowing them into internal growth.

Improve the stability of earnings and sales by acquiring firms whose earnings and sales complement the firm's peaks and valleys.

Balance or fill out the product line.

Diversify the product line when the life cycle of current products has peaked.

Acquire a needed resource quickly (e.g., high-quality technology or highly innovative management).

Achieve tax savings by purchasing a firm whose tax losses will offset current or future earnings.

Increase efficiency and profitability, especially if there is synergy between the acquiring firm and the acquired firm.[15]

Concentric diversification involves the acquisition of businesses that are related to the acquiring firm in terms of technology, markets, or products. With this grand strategy, the new businesses selected possess a high degree of compatibility with the firm's current businesses. The ideal concentric diversification occurs when the combined company profits increase strengths and opportunities and decrease weaknesses and exposure to risk. Thus, the acquiring firm searches for new businesses whose products, markets, distribution channels, technologies, and resource requirements are similar to but not identical with its own, whose acquisition results in synergies but not complete interdependence.

---

[14]Benjamin Gomes-Casseres, "Joint Ventures in the Face of Global Competition," *Sloan Management Review,* Spring 1989, pp. 17–26.

[15]William F. Glueck, *Business Policy and Strategic Management* (New York: McGraw-Hill, 1980), p. 213.

Conglomerate Diversification

Occasionally a firm, particularly a very large one, plans to acquire a business because it represents the most promising investment opportunity available. This grand strategy is commonly known as *conglomerate diversification*. The principal concern, and often the sole concern, of the acquiring firm is the profit pattern of the venture. Unlike concentric diversification, conglomerate diversification gives little concern to creating product-market synergy with existing businesses. What conglomerate diversifiers such as ITT, Textron, American Brands, Litton, U.S. Industries, Fuqua, and I.C. Industries seek is financial synergy. For example, they may seek a balance in their portfolios between current businesses with cyclical sales and acquired businesses with countercyclical sales, between high-cash/low-opportunity and low-cash/high-opportunity businesses, or between debt-free and highly leveraged businesses.

The principal difference between the two types of diversification is that concentric diversification emphasizes some commonality in markets, products, or technology, whereas conglomerate diversification is based principally on profit considerations.

Retrenchment/Turnaround

For any of a large number of reasons, a firm can find itself with declining profits. Among these reasons are economic recessions, production inefficiencies, and innovative break-throughs by competitors. In many cases, strategic managers believe that such a firm can survive and eventually recover if a concerted effort is made over a period of a few years to fortify its distinctive competences. This grand strategy is known as *retrenchment*. It is typically accomplished in one of two ways, employed singly or in combination:

1. *Cost reduction*. Examples include decreasing the work force through employee attrition, leasing rather than purchasing equipment, extending the life of machinery, and eliminating elaborate promotional activities.
2. *Asset reduction*. Examples include the sale of land, buildings, and equipment not essential to the basic activity of the firm and the elimination of "perks," such as the company airplane and executives' cars.

If these methods fail to achieve their purpose, more drastic action may be necessary. It is sometimes essential to lay off employees, to drop items from a production line, and even to eliminate low-margin customers.

Since the underlying purpose of the retrenchment strategy is to reverse current negative trends, it is often referred to as a *turnaround* strategy. Interestingly, the turnaround most commonly associated with this approach is in management positions. In a study of 58 large firms, researchers Shendel, Patton, and Riggs found that turnaround was almost always associated with changes in top management.[16] Bringing in new managers was believed to introduce needed new perspectives on the firm's situation, to raise employee

---

[16]Dan G. Schendel, G. Richard Patton, and James Riggs, "Corporate Turnaround Strategies: A Study of Profit Decline and Recovery," *Journal of General Management* 3 (1976), pp. 3–11.

morale, and to facilitate drastic actions, such as deep budgetary cuts in established programs.

Divestiture

A *divestiture strategy* involves the sale of a firm or a major component of a firm. When retrenchment fails to accomplish the desired turnaround, strategic managers often decide to sell the firm. However, because the intent is to find a buyer willing to pay a premium above the value of a going concern's fixed assets, the term *marketing for sale* is more appropriate. Prospective buyers must be convinced that because of their skills and resources or because of the firm's synergy with their existing businesses, they will be able to profit from the acquisition.

The reasons for divestiture vary. They often arise because of partial mismatches between the acquired firm and the parent corporation. Some of the mismatched parts cannot be integrated into the corporation's mainstream activities and thus must be spun off. A second reason is corporate financial needs. Sometimes the cash flow or financial stability of the corporation as a whole can be greatly improved if businesses with high market value can be sacrificed.[17] The result can be a balancing of equity with long-term risks or of long-term debt payments to optimize the cost of capital.[18] A third, less frequent reason for divestiture is government antitrust action when a firm is believed to monopolize or unfairly dominate a particular market.[19]

Although examples of the divestiture grand strategy are numerous, CBS, Inc., recently provided an outstanding example. From 1986 to 1988, the once diverse entertainment and publishing giant sold its Records Division to Sony, its magazine publishing business to Diamandis Communications, its book publishing operations to Harcourt Brace Jovanovich, and its music publishing operations to SBK Entertainment World. Other firms that have recently pursued this type of grand strategy include Esmark, which divested Swift & Company, and White Motors, which divested White Farm.

An example of the value of divestiture is shown in Strategy in Action 7–4. As discussed, Gulf & Western used the proceeds of divestitures together with savings from selective retrenchments to create tax write-offs and reduce its huge level of long-term debt.

Liquidation

When *liquidation* is the grand strategy, the firm is typically sold in parts, only occasionally as a whole, but for its tangible asset value and not as a going concern. In selecting liquidation, the owners and strategic managers of a firm are admitting failure and recognize that this action is likely to result in great hardships to themselves and their employees.

---

[17]Richard J. Schmidt, "Corporate Divestiture: Pruning for Higher Profits," *Business Horizons,* May 1987, pp. 26–31.

[18]Christopher Clarke and Francois Gall, "Planned Divestment—A Five-Step Approach," *Long Range Planning,* February 1987, p. 17.

[19]Clark E. Chastain, "Divestiture: Antidote to Merger Mania," *Business Horizons,* November 1987, pp. 43–49.

STRATEGY IN ACTION 7–4   GULF & WESTERN SLIMS DOWN?

Charles Bluhdorn was one of the earliest and flashiest conglomerateurs, a master of the unfriendly takeover. Starting with a small auto-parts company in 1958, he assembled an incredible array of disparate businesses into Gulf & Western Industries (1982 sales; $5.3 billion). Bluhdorn eventually bought some 100 companies large and small, ranging from Paramount Pictures to publisher Simon & Schuster to New York City's Madison Square Garden. In one six-year period, he brought 80 firms into what became jokingly known as "Engulf and Devour." Bluhdorn died in February 1983, at 56, after a heart attack, and his successors were in no mood to keep up that pace. They contracted Gulf & Western almost as fast as Bluhdorn had expanded it.

In 1983, a new management team headed by Vice Chairman and Chief Executive Martin Davis, 56, announced a major streamlining program to rid the company of low-profit operations. Among the cast-offs: Arlington Park race track near Chicago and Roosevelt Raceway in New York, manufacturer E. W. Bliss, and Sega's video-game unit. The moves saved the company about $470 million in tax write-offs but produced a loss of $215 million in the first year.

The divestitures were just the latest ordered by Davis, who went to Gulf & Western from Paramount in 1969 and took over immediately after Bluhdorn's death. Davis had earlier moved to sell off $650 million of company-owned stock in 30 companies, leaving the conglomerate with some $150 million in such holdings. The money was used to bring down the company's mountain of debt to $1.2 billion. Davis then also sold Gulf & Western's 21.4 percent stake in Brunswick, the sports equipment manufacturer, for $97 million. Davis likewise chopped away at the company's work force, reducing it by about 10,000 to 47,000.

Pointless mixing of dissimilar firms seemed finished at Gulf & Western. Said Shearson/American Express analyst Scott Merlis: "Few of their businesses were related to their other businesses." Instead, the company now seemed determined to focus sharply on a few areas: consumer products (apparel, Kayser-Roth; home furnishing, Simmons), entertainment (Paramount), and financial services (Associates Corp.).

Gulf & Western was only one of several companies to follow the newly fashionable divestiture route. Such firms as Beatrice Foods, Quaker Oats, and General Electric all sold off major holdings during 1982–1983.

Source: "The Big Sell-Off," *Time*, August 29, 1983, p. 45.

For these reasons, liquidation is usually seen as the least attractive of the grand strategies. As a long-term strategy, however, it minimizes the losses of all the firm's stakeholders. Faced with bankruptcy, the liquidating firm usually tries to develop a planned and orderly system that will result in the greatest possible return and cash conversion as the firm slowly relinquishes its market share.

Planned liquidation can be worthwhile. For example, Columbia Corporation, a $130 million diversified firm, liquidated its assets for more cash per share than the market value of its stock.

SELECTION OF LONG-TERM OBJECTIVES AND GRAND STRATEGY SETS

At first glance, the strategic management model, which provides the framework for study throughout this book, seems to suggest that strategic choice decision making leads to the *sequential* selection of long-term objectives and grand strategies. In fact, however, strategic choice is the *simultaneous* selection of long-range objectives and grand strategies. When strategic planners study their opportunities, they try to determine which are most likely to result in achieving various long-range objectives. Almost simultaneously, they try to forecast whether an available grand strategy can take advantage of preferred opportunities so that the tentative objectives can be met. In essence, then, three distinct but highly interdependent choices are being made at one time. Several triads or sets of possible decisions are usually considered.

A simplified example of this process is shown in Figure 7–7. In this example, the firm has determined that six strategic choice options are available. These options stem from three interactive opportunities (e.g., West Coast markets) that present little competition. Because each of these interactive opportunities can be approached through different grand strategies—for options 1 and 2, the grand strategies are horizontal integration and market development—each offers the potential for achieving long-range objectives to varying degrees. Thus, a firm can rarely make a strategic choice only on the basis of its preferred opportunities, long-range objectives, or grand strategy. Instead, these three elements must be considered simultaneously because only in combination do they constitute a strategic choice.

In an actual decision situation, the strategic choice would be complicated by a wider variety of interactive opportunities, feasible company objectives, promising grand strategy options, and evaluative criteria. Nevertheless, Figure 7–7 does partially reflect the nature and complexity of the process by which long-term objectives and grand strategies are selected.

In the next chapter, the strategic choice process will be fully explained. However, knowledge of long-term objectives and grand strategies is essential to understanding that process.

SEQUENCE OF OBJECTIVES AND STRATEGY SELECTION

The selection of long-term objectives and grand strategies involves simultaneous rather than sequential decisions. While it is true that objectives are needed to prevent the firm's direction and progress from being determined by random forces, it is equally true that objectives can be achieved only if strategies are implemented. In fact, long-term objectives and grand strategies are so interdependent that some business consultants do not distinguish between them. Long-term objectives and grand strategies are still combined under the heading of company strategy in most of the popular business literature and in the thinking of most practicing executives.

However, the distinction has merit. Objectives indicate what strategic managers *want* but provide few insights as to *how* this will be achieved. Conversely, strategies indicate what types of *actions* will be taken but do not define what *ends* will be pursued or what criteria will serve as constraints in refining the strategic plan.

FIGURE 7–7
A Profile of Strategic Choice Options

	Six Strategic Choice Options					
	1	2	3	4	5	6
Interactive opportunities	West Coast markets present little competition		Current markets sensitive to price competition		Current industry product lines after too narrow a range of markets	

Appropriate long-range objectives (limited sample):
  Average 5-year ROI
  Company sales by year 5
  Risk of negative profits
	15%
	+50%
	.30
		19%
		+40%
		.25
			13%
			+20%
			.10
				17%
				+0%
				.15
					23%
					+35%
					.20
						15%
						+25%
						.05

Grand strategies	Horizontal integration	Market development	Concentration	Selective retrenchment	Product development	Concentration

The view of objectives as constraints on strategy formulation rather than as ends toward which strategies are directed has been stressed by several prominent management experts.[20] They argued that strategic decisions are designed (1) to satisfy the minimum requirements of different company groups, for example, the production department's requirement for an increase in inventory capacity or the marketing department's requirement for an increase in the sales force and (2) to create the synergistic profit potential given these constraints.

Does it matter whether strategic decisions are made to achieve objectives or to satisfy constraints? No, because constraints are themselves objectives. The constraint of increased inventory capacity is a desire (an objective), not a certainty. Likewise, the constraint of an increase in the sales force does not assure that the increase will be achieved, given such factors as other company priorities, labor market conditions, and the firm's profit performance.

SUMMARY

Before learning how strategic decisions are made, it is important to understand the two principal components of any strategic choice, namely long-term objectives and the grand strategy. The purpose of this chapter was to convey that understanding.

Long-term objectives were defined as the results a firm seeks to achieve over a specified period of time, typically five years. Seven common long-term objectives were discussed:

---

[20]See, for example, Peter M. Drucker, *The Practice of Management* (New York: Harper & Row, 1954); R. M. Cyert and J. G. March, *A Behavioral Theory of the Firm* (Englewood Cliffs, N.J.: Prentice-Hall, 1963); H. A. Simon, "On the Concept of Organizational Goals," *Administrative Science Quarterly* 9 (1964), pp. 1–22; and M. D. Richards, *Organizational Goal Structures* (St. Paul, Minn.: West Publishing, 1978).

profitability, productivity, competitive position, employee development, employee relations, technological leadership, and public responsibility. These, or any other long-term objectives, should be acceptable, flexible, measurable over time, motivating, suitable, understandable, and achievable.

Grand strategies were defined as comprehensive approaches guiding the major actions designed to achieve long-term objectives. Twelve grand strategy options were discussed: concentrated growth, market development, product development, innovation, horizontal integration, vertical integration, joint ventures, concentric diversification, conglomerate diversification, retrenchment/turnaround, divestiture, and liquidation.

QUESTIONS FOR DISCUSSION

1. Identify firms in the business community nearest to your college or university that you believe are using each of the 12 grand strategies discussed in this chapter.
2. Identify firms in your business community that appear to rely principally on 1 of the 12 grand strategies. What kind of information did you use to classify the firms?
3. Write a long-term objective for your school of business that exhibits the seven qualities of long-term objectives described in this chapter.
4. Distinguish between the following pairs of grand strategies:
   a. Horizontal and vertical integration.
   b. Conglomerate and concentric diversification.
   c. Product development and innovation.
5. Rank each of the 12 grand strategy options discussed in this chapter on the following three scales:

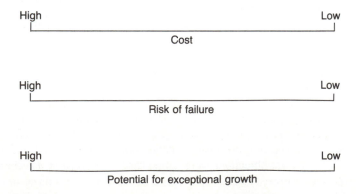

6. Identify firms that use one of the eight specific options shown in Figure 7–1 under the grand strategies of concentration, market development, and product development.

BIBLIOGRAPHY

Amit, Raphael, and Joshua Livnat. "Diversification Strategies, Business Cycles, and Economic Performance." *Strategic Management Journal,* March 1988, pp. 99–100.

"Concept of Conglomerate Diversification." *Journal of Management,* December 1988, pp. 593–604.

Ansoff, H. I. "Strategies for Diversification." *Harvard Business Review,* September–October 1957, pp. 113–24.

Corporate Strategy. New York: McGraw-Hill, 1965.

Strategic Management. New York: John Wiley & Sons, 1979.

Baba, Yasunori. "The Dynamics of Continuous Innovation in Scale-Intensive Industries." *Strategic Management Journal,* January 1989, pp. 89–100.

Bailey, George, and Julia Szerdy. "Is There Life after Downsizing?" *Journal of Business Strategy,* January 1988, pp. 8–11.

Balakrishnan, Srinivasan. "The Prognostics of Diversifying Acquisitions." *Strategic Management Journal,* March 1988, pp. 155–96.

Barreyre, P. Y. "The Concept of 'Impartition' Policies: A Different Approach to Vertical Integration Strategies." *Strategic Management Journal,* July 1988, pp. 319–32.

Bart, Christopher K. "New Venture Units: Use Them Wisely to Manage Innovation." *Sloan Management Review,* Summer 1988, pp. 35–43.

Bassin, Sue. "Innovative Packaging Strategies." *Journal of Business Strategy,* January 1988, pp. 28–32.

Batts, W. L. "Dart & Kraft from Merger to Strategic Management." *Planning Review,* November 1985, pp. 12–17, 44.

Baysinger, Barry, and Robert E. Hoskisson. "Diversification Strategy and R&D Intensity in Multiproduct Firms." *Academy of Management Journal,* June 1989, pp. 310–32.

Block, Zenas. "Damage Control for New Corporate Ventures." *Journal of Business Strategy,* March 1989, pp. 22–28.

Butler, John E. "Theories of Technological Innovation as Useful Tools for Corporate Strategy." *Strategic Management Journal,* January 1988, pp. 15–29.

Clarke, C. J., and E. Gall. "Planned Divestment—A Five-Step Approach." *Long Range Planning,* February 1987, pp. 17–24.

Cyert, R. M., and J. G. March. *A Behavioral Theory of the Firm.* Englewood Cliffs, N.J.: Prentice-Hall, 1963.

Davidson, K. M. "Do Megamergers Make Sense?" *Journal of Business Strategy,* Winter 1987, pp. 49–51.

De Souza, G. "The Best Strategies for Corporate Venturing." *Planning Review,* March 1986, pp. 12–14.

"Now Service Businesses Must Manage Quality." *Journal of Business Strategy,* May 1989, pp. 21–25.

DiPrimio, Anthony. "When Turnaround Management Works." *Journal of Business Strategy,* January 1988, pp. 61–64.

Drucker, Peter M. *The Practice of Management.* New York: Harper & Row, 1954.

"Creating Strategies of Innovation." *Planning Review,* November 1985, pp. 8–11.

Duncan, W. Jack; Peter M. Ginter; Andrew C. Rucks; and T. Douglas Jacobs. "Entrepreneurship and the Reinvention of the Corporation." *Business Horizons,* May 1988, pp. 16–21.

Framerman, Robert. "How to Avoid Technical Traps in Product Development." *Planning Review,* November 1988, pp. 20–27.

Gilbert, X., and P. Strebel. "Strategies to Outpace the Competition." *Journal of Business Strategy,* Summer 1987, pp. 28–35.

Glueck, William F. *Business Policy and Strategic Management.* New York: McGraw-Hill, 1980.

Goold, Michael, and Andrew Campbell. "Many Best Ways to Make Strategy." *Harvard Business Review,* November–December 1987, pp. 70–76.

Gray, D. H. "Uses and Misuses of Strategic Planning." *Harvard Business Review,* January–February 1986, pp. 89–96.

Greenhalgh, Leonard; Anne T. Lawrence; and Robert I. Sutton. "Determinants of Work Force Reduction Strategies in Declining Organizations." *Academy of Management Review,* April 1988, pp. 241–54.

Grosack, I., and D. A. Heenan. "Cooperation, Competition, and Antitrust: Two Views." *Business Horizons,* September 1986, pp. 24–28.

Hardy, Cynthia. "Investing in Retrenchment: Avoiding the Hidden Costs." *California Management Review,* Summer 1987, pp. 111–25.

Harrigan, K. R. "Matching Vertical Integration Strategies to Competitive Conditions." *Strategic Management Journal,* November–December 1986, pp. 535–55.

"Joint Ventures: Linking for a Leap Forward." *Planning Review,* July 1986, pp. 10–14.

"Joint Ventures and Competitive Strategy." *Strategic Management Journal,* March 1988, pp. 141–58.

Heenan, David A. "Is Big Business Heading for Small Town, U.S.A.? *Journal of Business Strategy,* July 1989, pp. 4–9.

Higgins, J. M. *Organizational Policy and Strategic Management.* Hinsdale, Ill.: Dryden Press, 1979.

Hopkins, H. D. "Acquisition Strategy and the Market Position of Acquiring Firms." *Strategic Management Journal,* November 1987, pp. 535–48.

Jemison, D. B., and S. B. Sitkin. "Corporate Acquisitions: A Process Perspective." *Academy of Management Review,* January 1986, pp. 145–63.

Kanter, Rosabeth Moss. "Swimming in New Streams: Mastering Innovation Dilemmas." *California Management Review,* Summer 1989, pp. 45–69.

Kelso, Louis, and Patricia Kelso. "Leveraged Buyouts Good and Bad." *Management Review,* November 1987, pp. 28–31.

King, William R., and David I. Cleland. *Strategic Planning and Policy.* New York: Van Nostrand Reinhold, 1978.

Kogut, Bruce. "Joint Ventures: Theoretical and Empirical Perspectives." *Strategic Management Journal,* July 1988, pp. 319–32.

Kumpe, Ted, and Piet T. Bolwijn. "Manufacturing: The New Case for Vertical Integration." *Harvard Business Review,* March–April 1988, pp. 75–81.

LaRusso, Anthony C. "Shifting It Down: A Test for Management." *Business Horizons,* July 1989, pp. 59–62.

Leonard-Barton, Dorothy. "The Case for Integrative Innovation: An Expert System at Digital." *Sloan Management Review,* Fall 1987, pp. 7–19.

Locke, Edwin A.; Gary P. Latham; and Miriam Erez. "The Determinants of Goal Commitment." *Academy of Management Review,* January 1988, pp. 23–39.

Luck, D. J., and A. E. Prell. *Market Strategy.* New York: Appleton-Century-Crofts, 1968.

Porter, M. E. *Competitive Strategy: Techniques for Analyzing Industries and Competitors.* New York: Free Press, 1980.

Competitive Advantage: Creating and Sustaining Superior Performance. New York: Free Press, 1985.

Mansfield, Edwin. "Technological Creativity: Japan and the United States." *Business Horizons,* March 1989, pp. 48–53.

Morone, Joseph. "Strategic Use of Technology." *California Management Review,* Summer 1989, pp. 91–110.

Nahauandi, Afsaneh, and Ali R. Malekzadeh. "Acculturation in Mergers and Acquisitions." *Academy of Management Review,* January 1988, pp. 79–90.

Nielson, R. P. "Cooperative Strategies." *Planning Review,* March 1986, pp. 16–20.

Olsen, Richard J. "Niche Shock: And How to Survive It." *Planning Review,* July 1988, pp. 6–13.

Osborn, A. F. *Applied Imagination.* 3rd rev. ed. New York: Charles Scribner's Sons, 1968.

Pearce, J. A., II. "An Executive-Level Perspective on the Strategic Management Process." *California Management Review,* Summer 1981, pp. 39–48.

_____. "Selecting Among Alternative Grand Strategies." *California Management Review,* Spring 1982, pp. 23–31.

Pearce, J. A., II; D. K. Robbins; E. B. Freeman; R. B. Robinson, Jr. "The Impact of Grand Strategy and Planning Formality on Financial Performance." *Strategic Management Journal,* March 1987, pp. 125–34.

Pearson, Andrall E. "Tough-Minded Ways to Get Innovative." *Harvard Business Review,* May–June 1988, pp. 75–81.

Pekar, P. "Joint Venture: A New Information System Is Born." *Planning Review,* July 1986, pp. 15–19.

Richards, M. D. *Organizational Goal Structures.* St. Paul, Minn.: West Publishing, 1978.

Roberts, E. B., and C. A. Berry. "Entering New Businesses: Selecting Strategies for Success." *Sloan Management Review,* Spring 1985, pp. 3–17.

Rule, Erik G., and Donald W. Irwin. "Fostering Entrepreneurship: The New Competitive Edge." *Journal of Business Strategy,* May 1988, pp. 44–47.

Schendel, Dan G.; G. R. Patton; and J. Riggs. "Corporate Turnaround Strategies: A Study of Profit Decline and Recovery." *Journal of General Management,* Fall 1976, pp. 3–11.

Schillaci, Carmela, "Designing Successful Joint Ventures." *Journal of Business Strategy,* Fall 1987, pp. 59–62.

Schmidt, R. J., "Corporate Divestiture: Pruning for Higher Profits." *Business Horizons,* May 1987, pp. 26–31.

Schorr, B. "Many New Products Fizzle, Despite Careful Planning, Publicity." *The Wall Street Journal,* April 5, 1961.

Schroeder, Dean M., and Robert Hopley. "Product Development Strategies for High-Tech Industries." *Journal of Business Strategy,* May 1988, pp. 38–43.

Shortell, Stephen M., and Edward J. Zajac, "Internal Corporate Joint Ventures: Development Processes and Performance Outcomes." *Strategic Management Journal,* November 1988, pp. 527–42.

Shostack, G. Lynn. "A Turnaround Is a Delicate Operation." *Journal of Business Strategy,* March 1988, pp. 59–61.

Shrivastava, P. "Postmerger Integration." *Journal of Business Strategy,* Summer 1986, pp. 65–76.

Simon, H. A. "On the Concept of Organizational Goals." *Administrative Science Quarterly* 9 (1964), pp. 1–22.

Smith, Clayton G., and Arnold C. Cooper. "Established Companies Diversifying into Young Industries: A Comparison of Firms with Different Levels of Performance." *Strategic Management Journal,* March 1988, pp. 111–21.

Steiner, G. A. *Strategic Planning.* New York: Free Press, 1979.

Steiner, G. A., and J. B. Miner. *Management Policy and Strategy.* New York: Macmillan, 1977.

Sutton, Robert I., and Anita L. Callahan. "The Stigma of Bankruptcy: Spoiled Organizational Image and Its Management." *Academy of Management Journal,* September 1987, pp. 405–36.

Sutton, Robert I., and Thomas D. D'Anno. "Decreasing Organizational Size: Untangling the Effects of Money and People." *Academy of Management Review,* April 1989, pp. 194–212.

Varadarajan, P. R., and V. Ramanujam. "Diversification and Performance: A Reexamination Using a New Two-Dimensional Conceptualization of Diversity in Firms." *Academy of Management Journal,* June 1987, pp. 380–93.

Weidenbaum, Murray, and Stephen Vogt. "Takeovers and Stockholders: Winners and Losers. *California Management Review,* Summer 1987, pp. 157–68.

Wheelwright, Steven C., and W. Earl Sasser, Jr. "The New Product Development Map." *Harvard Business Review,* May 1989, pp. 112–25.

Williams, Jeffrey R.; Betty Lynn Paez; and Leonard Saunders. "Conglomerates Revisited." *Strategic Management Journal,* September 1988, pp. 507–20.

Woo, Carolyn Y.; Gary E. Willard; and Stephen M. Beckstead. "Spin-Offs: What Are the Gains?" *Journal of Business Strategy,* March 1989, pp. 29–32.

CHAPTER 7 COHESION CASE

LONG-TERM OBJECTIVES AND STRATEGY OPTIONS

As Bryson managers sought to weigh their strengths and weaknesses with environmental/industry forces facing their firm, they generated these initial long-term objectives:

1. Bryson will have an annual sales volume of $45 million by the beginning of 1995.

2. Bryson's profitability as a percent of sales will reach a minimum of 15 percent of sales (before taxes) by 1993.

3. Bryson will clearly have established itself as one of the three largest firms in the Southeast in the services which it chooses to provide by 1993.

4. Bryson will be known throughout the Southeast as a leader in safety and the quality of its services among firms that have had dealings with Bryson by 1991.

5. Bryson's key employees will become stockholders in the company by 1991.

As Bryson's managers continued to discuss objectives and their SWOT analysis, they identified the following potential strategies for Bryson.

Corporate Strategy Alternatives

1. Full-service company, providing transportation, remedial services, and recycling services (with acqusition/merger of Wall) to hazardous waste companies and medical waste transportation services to hospitals and doctors in the southeastern United States.
2. Narrow the focus of the company to transportation and remedial services, the areas most known to company personnel, and exit recycling and medical waste to generate resources.
3. Merge the company with one or more similar companies in the eastern United States to build a larger business base.
4. Rapidly expand Bryson's involvement in recycling facilities (TSDFs) in logistically coordinated locations around the Southeast that can also serve as a center around which to expand the market for transportation and remedial services.

Business Strategy Alternatives

1. *Focus strategies*.

Numerous focus strategies are possible in each line of business. Bryson managers were rather strongly committed to focus in the Southeast (plus a 300-mile radius of Memphis) in each of its businesses. Further focus could certainly be appropriate for Bryson's businesses—transportation could focus on selected types of equipment or customers; remedial services could focus on certain types of cleanup situations or level of costs; medical waste could focus on selected types of customers and narrow the scope of services (handling, audits, and so on) it might offer.

2. *Low costs strategies.*

Within the region Bryson serves, one or more of its businesses could attempt to become the low-cost provider of that business's basic services. Transportation could, for example, strive for long-term contracts servicing large generators of regular waste streams as the basis for building a volume-based low-cost business. Remedial services could focus on a narrow range of services (like removing underground tanks) and concentrate on scheduling and accomplishing jobs in an unusually efficient manner. Others could be pursued as a means to create a low cost-based competitive strategy. But the reality of three large rivals—GSX, BFI, and Chemical Waste—make this business strategy a challenging one to successfully develop.

As you review Bryson's situation, what are the most reasonable long-term objectives for Bryson? Which objectives would you change or add to those suggested by Bryson managers?

Critique Bryson managers' basic options for corporate strategy, which have been briefly described above. Are any corporate strategies appropriate for Bryson that are not included above? Bryson's business strategy options are described above in general terms. Take a few minutes and list one detailed business strategy option for each Bryson business that is a focus strategy and one that is a low-cost strategy.

8 STRATEGIC ANALYSIS AND CHOICE

Strategic analysis and choice is the step in the strategic management process whereby managers consider alternative strategies and choose those that the firm will pursue. This step usually involves the choice of a corporate-level strategy identifying the businesses that the firm will be involved in and then the choice of the competitive strategy that each of these businesses will pursue.

Holiday Corporation, a multibusiness firm that included motels (Holiday Inns and Hampton Inns), casino gaming (Harrah's), steamships (Delta), restaurants (Perkins Family Restaurants), and bus lines (Trailways), faced a corporate strategy decision regarding which businesses it should remain in looking toward the 1990s and what level of resources it should commit to each of these businesses. Each of Holiday's businesses required a choice of strategy to guide its competitive posture. As McDonald's Corporation moved into the 1990s, the highly successful fast-food chain faced a corporate strategy decision regarding whether to remain in a single business—the fast-food industry—or to expand into other businesses via vertical integration, horizontal integration, or diversification. With that decision, McDonald's managers had to choose the competitive strategy its single-line business or multiple lines of businesses would pursue. At both Holiday Corporation and McDonald's Corporation, strategists had to analyze and choose corporate- and business-level strategies. Such are the decisions that strategists in any firm must face as they chart their firm's future.

This chapter examines the analysis and choice of corporate and business strategies. First, it looks at corporate strategy, examining how corporate managers choose among alternative grand strategies and analyze a diversified portfolio of businesses. Then it turns to analysis and choice among alternative business strategies—to the factors that managers consider in choosing among competitive strategies and to the influence of different types of industries on business strategy choices.

252

CORPORATE STRATEGY ANALYSIS AND CHOICE

The analysis and choice of corporate strategy varies according to the complexity of the business involvements of the overall firm. For firms that are predominantly in one line of business, such as McDonald's, corporate strategy is concerned with deciding whether to concentrate solely on that line of business or to become involved in other lines of business that are either related or unrelated to it. For firms that are already involved in several lines of business, such as Holiday Inns, corporate strategy is concerned with deciding whether to increase or reduce the resources committed to the current lines of business and whether to become involved in other lines that are either related or unrelated to them.

An Evolutionary Perspective

One way to view the analysis and choice of corporate strategy is to look at the typical evolution of corporate strategy in American firms. Figure 8–1 portrays that evolution. Like McDonald's, most American firms start by concentrating on a single line of business. This corporate strategy offers compelling advantages. It enhances unity of purpose throughout the firm. It is typically headed by top managers who have come up "through the ranks" and clearly appreciate what makes the firm successful. It makes the firm sensitive to changes in customer needs and industry conditions and thus enables it to build strong competitive advantages.

Concentration on a single business is also subject to certain risks. All of the firm's "eggs" are in one industry "basket." As the firm's industry matures, growth becomes more difficult and pressures on profit margins increase. Moreover, technological innovation can rapidly change the industry, as computers changed the typewriter industry and digital electronics changed the watch industry.

One response to these risks is a corporate strategy of vertical integration. Depending on where the firm's business is concentrated in the product chain, that strategy would have the firm undertake "backward" integration or "forward" integration. Backward integration allows a firm to stabilize its sources of supply previously paid to its suppliers and to absorb the profit margins. Forward integration increases a firm's access to customers, thus enabling it to increase its sales and to acquire the profit margins associated with "downstream" markups. Vertical integration is usually appropriate when downstream or upstream profit margins are attractive, when corporate managers feel comfortable about taking on new areas of business activity, and when it can yield competitive advantages in the pricing or quality areas of the core business.

Related diversification is typically the next move in corporate strategy. As expertise in various aspects of the core business is refined, corporate strategists look for ways to apply that expertise in other businesses or to shore up weaknesses by becoming involved in other businesses. Figure 8–2 provides a typical relatedness checklist that managers might use to pursue a corporate strategy of related diversification. As an example, Holiday Corporation's move into casino gaming and family restaurants was based on the synergies

FIGURE 8–1
Typical Evolution of Corporate Strategy in American Firms

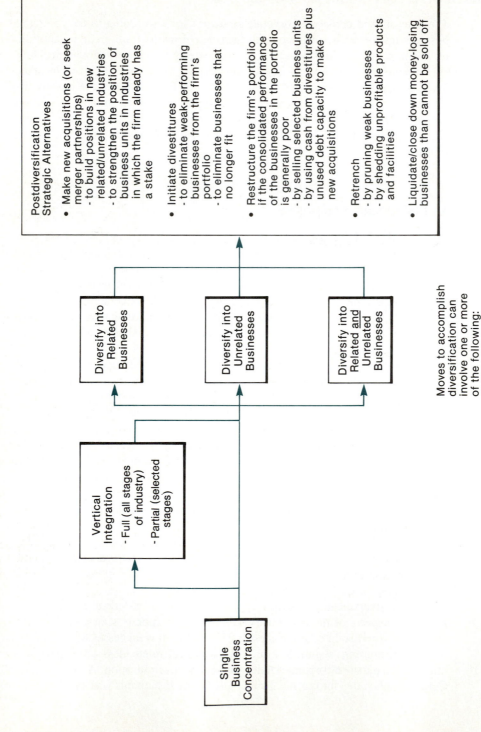

Source: Arthur Thompson, Jr., and A. J. Strickland III, *Strategic Management*, 4th ed. (Homewood, Ill.: Business Publications, 1987), p. 179.

FIGURE 8–2

Checklist of Types of Strategic Fit, Their Competitive Advantage Potentials, and the Impediments to Achieving Their Benefits in Related Diversification

Types of Strategic Fit and Opportunities for Sharing	Potential Competitive Advantages	Impediments to Achieving the Benefits of Fit
Market-related strategic fits		
Shared sales force activities and/or shared sales offices	• Lower selling costs • Better market coverage • Stronger technical advice to buyers • Enhanced convenience for buyers (can buy from single source) • Improved access to buyers (have more products to sell)	• Buyers have different purchasing habits toward the products. • Different salespersons are more effective in representing the product. • Some products get more attention than others. • Buyers prefer to multiple source rather than single source their purchases.
Shared after-sale service and repair work	• Lower servicing costs • Better utilization of service personnel (less idle time) • Faster servicing of customer calls	• Different equipment and/or different labor skills are needed to handle repairs. • Buyers may do some in-house repairs.
Shared brand name	• Stronger brand image and company reputation • Increased buyer confidence in the brand	• Company reputation is hurt if quality of one product is lower.
Shared advertising and promotional activities	• Lower costs • Greater clout in purchasing ads	• Appropriate forms of messages are different. • Appropriate timing of promotions is different.
Common distribution channels	• Lower distribution costs • Enhanced bargaining power with distributors and retailers to gain shelf space, shelf positioning, stronger push and more dealer attention, and better, profit margins	• Dealers resist being dominated by a single supplier and turn to multiple sources and lines. • Heavy use of the shared channel erodes willingness of other channels to carry or push the firm's products.
Shared order processing	• Lower order processing costs • One-stop shopping for buyer enhances service and thus differentiation	• Differences in ordering cycles disrupt order processing economies.
Operating fits		
Joint procurement of purchased inputs	• Lower input costs • Improved input quality • Improved service from suppliers	• Input needs are different in terms of quality or other specifications. • Inputs are needed at different plant locations, and centralized purchasing is not responsive to separate needs of each plant.
Shared manufacturing and assembly facilities	• Lower manufacturing/assembly costs • Better capacity utilization because peak demand for one product correlates with valley demand for other • Bigger scale of operation improves access to better technology and results in better quality	• Higher changeover costs in shifting from one product to another. • High-cost special tooling or equipment is required to accommodate quality differences or design differences.

(continued)

FIGURE 8–2 (concluded)

Types of Strategic Fit and Opportunities for Sharing	Potential Competitive Advantages	Impediments to Achieving the Benefits of Fit
Shared inbound or outbound shipping and materials handling	• Lower freight and handling costs • Better delivery reliability • More frequent deliveries such that inventory costs are reduced	• Input sources and/or plant locations are in different geographic areas. • Needs for frequency and reliability of inbound/outbound delivery differ among the business units.
Shared product and/or process technologies and/or technology development	• Lower product and/or process design costs because of shorter design times and transfers of knowledge from area to area • More innovative ability, owing to scale of effort and attraction of better R&D personnel	• Technologies are the same, but the applications in different business units are different enough to prevent much sharing of real value.
Shared administrative support activities	• Lower administrative and operating overhead costs	• Support activities are not a large proportion of cost, and sharing has little cost impact (and virtually no differentiation impact).
Management Fits Shared management know-how, operating skills, and proprietary information	• Efficient transfer of a distinctive competence—can create cost savings or enhance differentiation • More effective management as concerns strategy formulation, strategy implementation, and understanding of key success factors	• Actual transfer of know-how is costly and/or stretches the key skill personnel too thinly. • Increased risks that proprietary information will leak out.

Source: Adapted from Michael E. Porter, *Competitive Advantage* (New York: Free Press, 1985) pp. 337–51; and Arthur A. Thompson, Jr., and A. Strickland III, *Strategic Management,* 4th ed. (Homewood, Ill.: Business Publications, 1987), pp. 167–68.

that its managers expected from applying its knowledge of running hotels and hotel restaurants in these two related businesses.

Finally, unrelated diversification occurs in firms whose strategies feel that resources generated by current businesses can be better invested in other business activities. Such firms may engage in unrelated diversification for various reasons: (1) a "cash-rich, opportunity-poor" firm may acquire opportunity-rich, cash-poor businesses; (2) a firm in a seasonal core business may acquire businesses that provide it with counterseasonal financial balance; or (3) a highly leveraged firm may acquire a debt-free business so as to balance its overall capital structure. ITT is perhaps the best known pioneer of unrelated diversification. Among the many businesses in which it became involved were telephone equipment, Sheraton hotels, Scott lawn products, Wonder Bread, and Hartford Insurance.

The patterns of strategic evolution that researchers have found among American firms provide one perspective on the analysis and choice of corporate strategy. The challenge for corporate strategists using this perspective is to decide when corporate conditions call for movement to a new strategy. The next section provides guidelines that help corporate strategists make such decisions.

Choosing among Grand Strategy Alternatives

Strategists in single-business or dominant-business firms face a choice among 12 grand strategies (described in Chapter 7) as they seek strategy alternatives that offer a stronger fit with a firm's overall situation. This section describes two ways of analyzing this situational fit.

Grand Strategy Selection Matrix

One valuable guide to the selection of a promising grand strategy is the matrix shown in Figure 8–3. The basic idea underlying the matrix is that two variables are of central concern in the selection process: (1) the principal purpose of the grand strategy and (2) the choice of an internal or external emphasis for growth and/or profitability.

In the past, planners were advised to follow certain rules or prescriptions in their choice of strategies. Now, most experts agree that strategy selection is better guided by the conditions of the planning period and by company strengths and weaknesses. It should be noted, however, that even the early approaches to strategy selection sought to match a concern over internal versus external growth with a desire to overcome weaknesses or maximize strengths.

The same considerations led to the development of the grand strategy selection matrix. A firm in quadrant I, with "all its eggs in one basket," often views itself as over committed to a particular business with limited growth opportunities or high risks. One reasonable solution is *vertical integration,* which enables the firm to reduce risk by reducing uncertainty about inputs or access to customers. Another is *conglomerate diversification,* which provides a profitable investment alternative without diverting management attention from the original business. However, the external approaches to overcoming weaknesses usually result in the most costly grand strategies. Acquiring a second business demands large investments of time and sizable financial resources. Thus, strategic managers considering these approaches must guard against exchanging one set of weaknesses for another.

More conservative approaches to overcoming weaknesses are found in quadrant II. Firms often choose to redirect resources from one internal business activity to another. This approach maintains the firm's commitment to its basic mission, rewards success, and enables further development of proven competitive advantages. The least disruptive of the quadrant II strategies is *retrenchment,* pruning the current activities of a business. If the weaknesses of the business arose from inefficiencies, retrenchment can actually serve as a *turnaround* strategy—that is, the business gains new strength from the streamlining of its operations and the elimination of waste. However, if those weaknesses are a major obstruction to success in the industry and the costs of overcoming them are unaffordable or are not justified by a cost-benefit analysis, then eliminating the business must be considered. Strategy in Action 8–1 illustrates a systematic divestiture and refocus strategy at Honeywell. *Divestiture* offers the best possibility for recouping the firm's investment, but even *liquidation* can be an attractive option if the alternatives are bankruptcy or an unwarranted drain on the firm's resources.

A common business adage states that a firm should build from strength. The premise of this adage is that growth and survival depend on an ability to capture a market share

FIGURE 8–3
Grand Strategy Selection Matrix

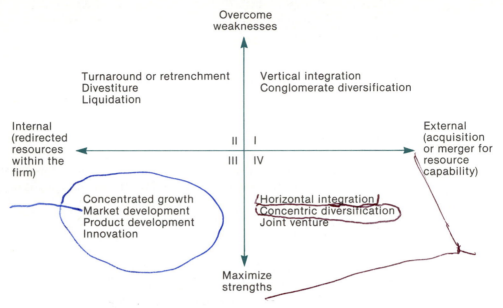

Source: John A. Pearce II, "Selecting among Alternative Grand Strategies," *California Management Review,* Spring 1982, p. 29.

that is large enough for essential economies of scale. If a firm believes that this approach will be profitable and prefers an internal emphasis for maximizing strengths, four grand strategies hold considerable promise. As shown in quadrant III, the most common approach is *concentrated growth, that is, market penetration.* The firm that selects this strategy is strongly committed to its current products and markets. It strives to solidify its position by reinvesting resources to fortify its strengths.

Two alternative approaches are *market development* and *product development.* With these strategies, the firm attempts to broaden its operations. Market development is chosen if the firm's strategic managers feel that its existing products would be well received by new customer groups. Product development is chosen if they feel that the firm's existing customers would be interested in products related to its current lines. Product development may also be based on technological or other competitive advantages. The final alternative for quadrant III firms is *innovation.* When the firm's strengths are in creative product design or unique production technologies, sales can be stimulated by accelerating perceived obsolescence. This is the principle underlying the innovative grand strategy.

Maximizing a firm's strengths by aggressively expanding its base of operations usually requires an external emphasis. The preferred options in such cases are shown in quadrant IV. *Horizontal integration* is attractive because it makes possible a quick increase in output capability. Moreover, in horizontal integration, the skills of the managers of the original business are often critical in converting newly acquired facilities into profitable

---

STRATEGY IN ACTION 8–1   **HONEYWELL CREATES A NEW STRATEGY**

One of the "BUNCH" left the mainframe computer business in 1986. After a phased withdrawal that started three years earlier, Honeywell, one of the five mainframe manufacturers known as the BUNCH (Burroughs, Univac, NCR, Control Data, Honeywell), will concentrate on factory automation, in which its century-old expertise gives it a chance for leadership.

When Honeywell started in the computer business in 1955, it decided to compete directly with IBM. Believing size to be critical, it bought GE's computer business in 1970 and Xerox's computer business in 1976. But by 1986, IBM controlled 71 percent of the mainframe computer business versus 3 percent for Honeywell.

Honeywell decided to concentrate on its strengths. As a manufacturer of torpedoes and navigational equipment, it has a $1.9 billion aerospace and defense business. It also has a $2.8 billion controls business, being the leading manufacturer of heating and air-conditioning controls for buildings and process controls for industry. Along the way, Honeywell withdrew from the mainframe computer business.

Now, Honeywell wants to concentrate on factory automation as its next growth vector. It is pursuing this opportunity through logical development of its core control business, not through merger. It is focusing on the "brain" segment of automation, as opposed to the "muscle" end (robots and machine tools). The brain segment involves sensors, programmable controllers, software, and minicomputers—all of which are conveniently similar to Honeywell's control competencies. This segment now yields $10 billion in annual sales and is growing at an annual rate of 15 percent.

Source: Based on "Strategic Withdrawal," *Forbes,* February 10, 1986, p. 42; Honeywell, *1989 Annual Report.*

---

contributors to the parent firm; this expands a fundamental competitive advantage of the firm—its management.

Concentric diversification is a good second choice for similar reasons. Because the original and newly acquired businesses are related, the distinctive competences of the diversifying firm are likely to facilitate a smooth, synergistic, and profitable expansion.

The final alternative for increasing resource capability through external emphasis is a *joint venture*. This alternative allows a firm to extend its strengths into competitive arenas that it would be hesitant to enter alone. A partner's production, technological, financial, or marketing capabilities can reduce the firm's financial investment significantly and increase its probability of success.

Model of Grand Strategy Clusters

A second guide to selecting a promising grand strategy is shown in Figure 8–4. The figure is based on the idea that the situation of a business is defined in terms of the growth rate of the general market and the firm's competitive position in that market. When these factors are considered simultaneously, a business can be broadly categorized in one of four quadrants: (I) strong competitive position in a rapidly growing market, (II) weak

FIGURE 8–4
Model of Grand Strategy Clusters

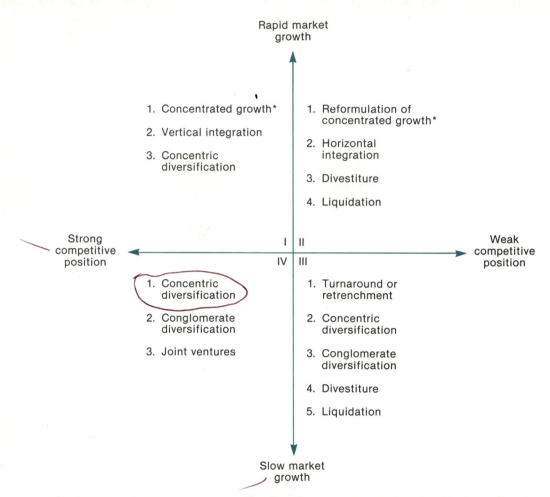

Note: The grand strategy of innovation was omitted from this model. Apparently, the authors felt that the notion of market growth was incompatible with the assumptions underlying that strategy.
Note: Grand strategies are listed in probable order of attractiveness.
*In this model, the grand strategy of concentrated growth was meant to encompass market development and product development.
Source: Adapted from R. Christensen, N. A. Berg, and M. S. Salter, *Policy Formulation and Administration* (Homewood, Ill.: Richard D. Irwin, 1976), pp. 16-18.

position in a rapidly growing market, (III) weak position in a slow-growth market, or (IV) strong position in a slow-growth market. Each of these quadrants suggests a set of promising possibilities for the selection of a grand strategy.

Firms in quadrant I are in an excellent strategic position. One obvious grand strategy for such firms is continued concentration on their current business as it is currently defined.

Because consumers seem satisfied with the firm's current strategy, shifting notably from it would endanger the firm's established competitive advantages. However, if the firm has resources that exceed the demands of a concentrated growth strategy, it should consider vertical integration. Either forward or backward integration helps a firm protect its profit margins and market share by ensuring better access to consumers or material inputs. Finally, to diminish the risks associated with a narrow product or service line, a quadrant I firm might be wise to consider concentric diversification; with this strategy, the firm continues to invest heavily in its basic area of proven ability.

Firms in quadrant II must seriously evaluate their present approach to the marketplace. If a firm has competed long enough to accurately assess the merits of its current grand strategy, it must determine (1) why that strategy is ineffectual and (2) whether it is capable of competing effectively. Depending on the answers to these questions, the firm should choose one of four grand strategy options: formulation or reformulation of a concentrated growth strategy, horizontal integration, divestiture, or liquidation.

In a rapidly growing market, even a small or relatively weak business is often able to find a profitable niche. Thus, formulation or reformulation of a concentrated growth strategy is usually the first option that should be considered. However, if the firm lacks either a critical competitive element or sufficient economies of scale to achieve competitive cost efficiencies, then a grand strategy that directs its efforts toward horizontal integration is often a desirable alternative. A final pair of options involve deciding to stop competing in the market or product area of the business. A multiproduct firm may conclude that it is most likely to achieve the goals of its mission if the business is dropped through divestiture. This grand strategy not only eliminates a drain on resources but may also provide funds to promote other business activities. As an option of last resort, a firm may decide to liquidate the business. This means that the business cannot be sold as a going concern and is at best worth only the value of its tangible assets. The decision to liquidate is an undeniable admission of failure by a firm's strategic management and is thus often delayed—to the further detriment of the firm.

Strategic managers tend to resist divestiture because it is likely to jeopardize their control of the firm and perhaps even their jobs. Thus, by the time the desirability of divestiture is acknowledged, businesses often deteriorate to the point of failing to attract potential buyers. The consequences of such delays are financially disastrous for firm owners because the value of a going concern is many times greater than the value of its assets.

Strategic managers who have a business in quadrant III and expect a continuation of slow market growth and a relatively weak competitive position will usually attempt to decrease their resource commitment to that business. Minimal withdrawal is accomplished through retrenchment; this strategy has the side benefits of making resources available for other investments and of motivating employees to increase their operating efficiency. An alternative approach is to divert resources for expansion through investment in other businesses. This approach typically involves either concentric or conglomerate diversification because the firm usually wants to enter more promising arenas of competition than forms of integration or development would allow. The final options for quadrant III businesses are divestiture, if an optimistic buyer can be found, and liquidation.

Quadrant IV businesses (strong competitive position in a slow-growth market) have a basis of strength from which to diversify into more promising growth areas. These businesses have characteristically high cash flow levels and limited internal growth needs. Thus, they are in an excellent position for concentric diversification into ventures that utilize their proven acumen. A second option is conglomerate diversification, which spreads investment risk and does not divert managerial attention from the present business. The final option is joint ventures, which are especially attractive to multinational firms. Through joint ventures, a domestic business can gain competitive advantages in promising new fields while exposing itself to limited risks.

Managing Diversified Corporate Portfolios

When a single- or dominant-business firm is transformed into a collection of numerous businesses across several industries, strategic analysis becomes much more complex. One of the early methods that attempted to aid corporate strategists in this task was the portfolio approach.

The *portfolio approach* involves examining each of the firm's separate "businesses" as elements of its total *portfolio* of businesses. In a broad sense, corporate strategy is concerned with the generation and allocation of corporate resources. The businesses in the firm's portfolio are, to varying degrees, the generators and recipients of these resources. Thus, the portfolio approach provides a simple, visual way of identifying and evaluating alternative strategies for the generation and allocation of corporate resources.

The BCG Growth/Share Matrix

One of the earliest portfolio approaches to corporate strategic analysis was the growth/share matrix, pioneered by the Boston Consulting Group (BCG) and illustrated in Figure 8–5. This matrix facilitates the strategic analysis of likely "generators" and optimum "users" of corporate resources.

To use the BCG matrix, each of the firm's businesses is plotted according to market growth rate (percentage growth in sales) and relative competitive position (market share). Market growth rate is the projected rate of sales growth for the market being served by a particular business. Usually measured as the percentage increase in a market's sales or unit volume over the two most recent years, this rate serves as an indicator of the relative attractiveness of the markets served by each business in the firm's portfolio of businesses. Relative competitive position is usually expressed as the market share of a business divided by the market share of its largest competitor. Thus, relative competitive position provides a basis for comparing the relative strengths of the businesses in the firm's portfolio in terms of their positions in their respective markets.

The positions of businesses on the BCG matrix are based on their market growth rates and their relative competitive positions. Figure 8–5 represents the BCG matrix for a firm with nine businesses. Each circle represents a business. The size of the circle represents the proportion of corporate revenue generated by that business.

Market growth rates are frequently separated into "high" and "low" areas by an arbitrary 10 percent growth line. The dividing point between "high" and "low" competitive positions is usually set between 1.0 and 1.5, since any amount above 1.0 signifies a market share

FIGURE 8–5
BCG's Growth/Share Matrix

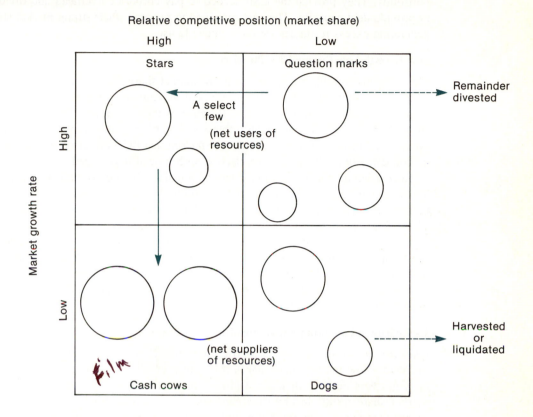

greater than that of the largest competitor. The positions of businesses on the BCG matrix will be in one of four cells, with differing implications for their role in corporate-level strategy.

High-Growth/High Competitive Position

The *stars*, as the BCG matrix labeled them, are businesses in rapidly growing markets with large market shares. These businesses represent the best long-run opportunities (growth and profitability) in the firm's portfolio. They require substantial investment to maintain (and expand) their dominant position in a growing market. This investment requirement is often in excess of the funds that they can generate internally. Therefore, these businesses are often short-term, priority consumers of corporate resources.

Low-Growth/High Competitive Position

Cash cows are businesses with a high market share in low-growth markets or industries. Because of their strong positions and their minimal reinvestment requirements, these businesses often generate cash in excess of their needs. Therefore, they are selectively

FIGURE 8–6
Underlying Relationship between ROI and Market Share in the New BCG Matrix

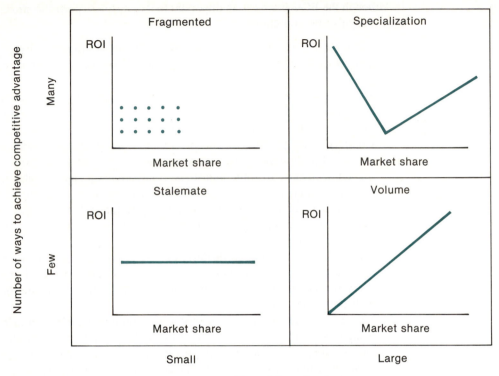

for every business was as follows: Higher market share leads to higher accumulated volume, which leads to lower unit cost and higher profitability.

A new approach proposed by the Boston Consulting Group for the 1990s is a matrix with two dimensions: the size of a business's competitive advantage and the number of ways in which that advantage can be achieved. The matrix, shown in Figure 8–6, recognizes four categories of businesses: Volume, Stalemate, Fragmented, and Specialization.

1. Only in the volume businesses are the previous strategies of market-share leadership and cost reduction still meaningful. In this category, a close association between market share and profitability can still be observed. A typical example of such businesses would be the American automakers prior to the emergence of foreign competitors.

2. The stalemate businesses are in industries where profitability is low for all competitors and unrelated to the size of the business. The difference between the most profitable and the least profitable business is relatively small. The American steelmakers provide an illustration of businesses in this category.

3. The profitability of businesses in the fragmented category is uncorrelated with market share. There are poor and good performers among both large and small businesses. The performance of businesses in this category depends on how they exploit the very many ways in which they can achieve competitive advantage. A typical example of such businesses would be restaurants.

4. Finally, the specialization category shows that the most attractive profitability may be enjoyed by the smallest businesses if they are able to distinguish themselves among their competitors by pursuing a focused strategy. The Japanese automakers pursued that strategy to enter the American automobile industry.

In this matrix, the horizontal axis, pertaining to the size of the advantage, is definitively linked to the barriers of entry, because it is only with high entry barriers that a business can sustain a long-term defensible advantage over its competitors. Likewise, the number of ways to achieve advantages seems to be strongly linked to the issue of differentiation. At the extremes of the differentiation range, we encounter the commodity and specialty products. The overall contribution of the new BCG matrix is its recognition that requirements for business success vary across industry settings and that a strategy based solely on gaining market share is not always effective in building a high return on investment.

The GE Nine-Cell Planning Grid

General Electric popularized the nine-cell planning grid (Figure 8–7), an adaptation of the BCG approach that attempts to overcome some of the limitations mentioned above. First, the GE grid uses multiple factors to assess industry attractiveness and business strength, rather than the single measures (market share and market growth, respectively) employed in the BCG matrix. Second, GE expanded the matrix from four cells to nine—replacing the high/low axes with high/medium/low axes to make finer distinctions among business portfolio positions.

To use the GE planning grid, each of the firm's businesses is rated on multiple strategic factors within each axis of the grid, such as those suggested in Figure 8–8. The position of a business within the planning grid is then calculated by "subjectively" quantifying the two dimensions of the grid.

To measure the attractiveness of an industry, the strategist first selects the factors that contribute to it. Each attractiveness factor is then assigned a weight that reflects its perceived importance relative to the others. Favorable to unfavorable future conditions for those factors are forecast and rated, based on some scale (a 0-to-1 scale is illustrated in Figure 8–9). A weighted composite score is then obtained for the overall attractiveness of an industry, as shown in Figure 8–9.

To assess business strength, a similar procedure is followed. Factors are selected, and weights are assigned to them, and then the business is rated on those dimensions, as illustrated in Figure 8–9.

These examples illustrate how one business within a corporate portfolio might be assessed using the GE planning grid. It is important to remember that what factors should be included or excluded, as well as how they should be rated and weighted, is primarily a matter of managerial judgment and that several managers are usually involved in the planning process. The result of the ratings is a high, medium, or low classification for

FIGURE 8–7
The GE Nine-Cell Planning Grid

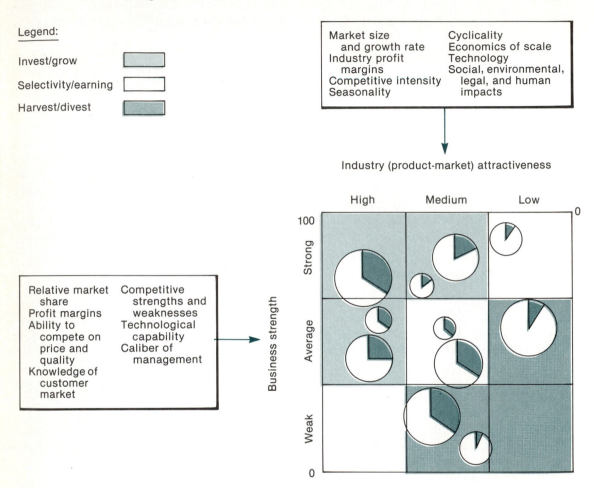

Legend:

Invest/grow

Selectivity/earning

Harvest/divest

Market size and growth rate
Industry profit margins
Competitive intensity
Seasonality

Cyclicality
Economics of scale
Technology
Social, environmental, legal, and human impacts

Industry (product-market) attractiveness

Relative market share
Profit margins
Ability to compete on price and quality
Knowledge of customer market

Competitive strengths and weaknesses
Technological capability
Caliber of management

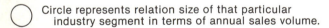
Circle represents relation size of that particular industry segment in terms of annual sales volume.

Pie wedge represents the firm's market share as defined by sales volume with that industry segment.

both the projected strength of the business and the projected attractiveness of the industry, as shown in Figure 8–9.

Depending on the location of a business within the grid, one of the following strategic approaches is suggested: (1) invest to grow, (2) invest selectively and manage for earnings, or (3) harvest or divest for resources. The resource allocation decisions remain quite similar to those of the BCG approach.

FIGURE 8–8

Factors Contributing to Industry Attractiveness and Business Strength

Industry Attractiveness	Business Strength
Market Factors	
Size (dollars, units, or both)	Your share (in equivalent terms)
Size of key segments	Your share of key segments
Growth rate per year:	Your annual growth rate:
Total	Total
Segments	Segment
Diversity of market	Diversity of your participation
Sensitivity to price, service features, and external factors	Your influence on the market
Cyclicality	Lags or leads in your sales
Seasonality	
Bargaining power of upstream suppliers	Bargaining power of your suppliers
Bargaining power of downstream suppliers	Bargaining power of your customers
Competition	
Types of competitors	Where you fit, how you compare in terms of products, marketing capability, service, production strength, financial strength, management
Degree of concentration	
Changes in type and mix	
Entries and exits	Segments you have entered or left
Changes in share	Your relative share change
Substitution by new technology	Your vulnerability to new technology
Degrees and types of integration	Your own level of integration
Financial and Economic Factors	
Contribution margins	Your margins
Leveraging factors, such as economies of scale and experience	Your scale and experience
Barriers to entry or exit (both financial and nonfinancial)	Barriers to your entry or exit (both financial and nonfinancial)
Capacity utilization	Your capacity utilization
Technological Factors	
Maturity and volatility	Your ability to cope with change
Complexity	Depths of your skills
Differentiation	Types of your technological skills
Patents and copyrights	Your patent protection
Manufacturing process technology required	Your manufacturing technology
Sociopolitical Factors in Your Environment	
Social attitudes and trends	Your company's reponsiveness and flexibility
Laws and government agency regulations	Your company's ability to cope
Influence with pressure groups and government representatives	Your company's aggressiveness
Human factors, such as unionization and community acceptance	Your company's relationships

Source: Derek F. Abell and John S. Hammond, *Strategic Market Planning: Problems and Analytical Approaches.* © 1979, p. 214. Reprinted by permission of Prentice-Hall, Inc., Englewood Cliffs, New Jersey.

FIGURE 8–9
An Illustration of Industry Attractiveness and Business Strength Computations

	Weight	Rating (1–5)	Value
Industry Attractiveness			
Overall market size	0.20	4.00	0.80
Annual market growth rate	0.20	5.00	1.00
Historical profit margin	0.15	4.00	0.60
Competitive intensity	0.15	2.00	0.30
Technological requirements	0.15	3.00	0.45
Inflationary vulnerability	0.05	3.00	0.15
Energy requirements	0.05	2.00	0.10
Environmental impact	0.05	1.00	0.05
Social/political/legal	Must be acceptable		
	1.00		3.45
Business Strength			
Market share	0.10	4.00	0.40
Share growth	0.15	4.00	0.60
Product quality	0.10	4.00	0.40
Brand reputation	0.10	5.00	0.50
Distribution network	0.05	4.00	0.20
Promotional effectiveness	0.05	5.00	0.25
Productive capacity	0.05	3.00	0.15
Productive efficiency	0.05	2.00	0.10
Unit costs	0.15	3.00	0.45
Material supplies	0.05	5.00	0.25
R&D performance	0.10	4.00	0.20
Managerial personnel	0.05	4.00	0.20
	1.00		4.30

Source: Philip Kotler, *Marketing Management: Analysis, Planning, and Control,* 5th ed. Copyright © 1984, p. 56. Reprinted by permission of Prentice-Hall, Inc., Englewood Cliffs, New Jersey. Slightly modified from La Rue T. Hormer, *Strategic Management* (Englewood Cliffs, N.J.: Prentice-Hall, 1982), p. 310.

Although the strategic recommendations generated by the GE grid are similar to those generated by the BCG matrix, the GE grid improves on the BCG matrix in three fundamental ways. First, the terminology associated with the GE grid is preferable because it is less offensive and more understandable. Second, the multiple measures associated with each dimension of the GE grid tap many factors relevant to business strength and market attractiveness besides market share and market growth. And this, in turn, makes for broader assessment during the planning process, bringing to light considerations of importance in both strategy formulation and strategy implementation.

One criticism of the portfolio approaches is their static quality—they portray businesses as they exist at one point in time rather than as they evolve over time. To overcome this problem and better identify "developing winners" or "potential losers," Hofer proposed

FIGURE 8–10
The Life-Cycle Portfolio Matrix

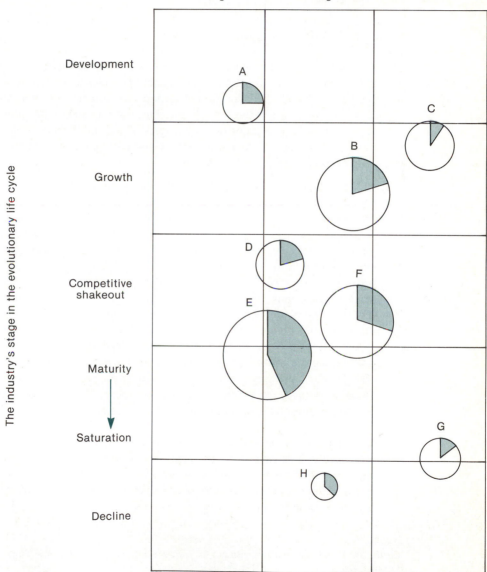

Source: Adapted from Charles W. Hofer, "Conceptual Constructs for Formulating Corporate and Business Strategies" (Boston: Harvard Case Services, #9–378–754, 1977), p. 3.

a 15-cell matrix like that shown in Figure 8–10.[5] As before, the circles represent industry size and the wedges represent market share. Referring to Figure 8–10, business A appears to be a *developing winner;* business C, a *potential loser;* business E, an *established winner;* business F, a cash cow; and business G, a loser or a dog. The value of Hofer's life-cycle matrix lies in the story it tells about the distribution of the firm's businesses across the stages of industry evolution.

Beyond the Portfolio Matrix

Constructing business portfolio matrixes can be a useful first step in appraising the strategic situation of a diversified firm. But at best it merely provides a basis for further discussion of corporate strategy and the allocation of corporate resources. Corporate strategists must become thoroughly aware of the status of each business unit and of the industry conditions that give rise to the expectations of its managers. Hofer and Schendel have summarized the types of awareness that corporate strategists must pursue to complete the task of evaluating corporate strategy alternatives:

1. Constructing a summary profile of the industry and competitive environment of each business unit.
2. Appraising the strength and competitive position of each business unit. Understanding how each business unit ranks against its rivals on the key factors for competitive success affords corporate managers a basis for judging its chances for real success in its industry.
3. Identifying the external opportunities, threats, and strategic issues peculiar to each business unit.
4. Determining how much corporate financial support is needed to fund each unit's business strategy and what corporate skills and resources could be deployed to boost the competitive strength of the various business units.
5. Comparing the relative attractiveness of the businesses in the corporate portfolio. This includes not only industry attractiveness/business strength comparisons but also comparisons of the businesses on various historical and projected performance measures—sales growth, profit margins, return on investment, and the like.
6. Checking the corporate portfolio to ascertain whether the mix of businesses is adequately "balanced"—not too many losers or question marks, not so many mature businesses that corporate growth will be slow, enough cash producers to support the stars and the developing winners, enough dependable profit performers, and so on.[6]

---

[5]Charles W. Hofer, "Conceptual Constructs for Formulating Corporate and Business Strategies," (Boston: Harvard Case Services, #9-378-754, 1977), p. 3.

[6]Charles W. Hofer and Dan G. Schendel, *Strategy Formulation: Analytical Concepts,* (St. Paul, Minn: West Publishing, 1978) p. 84–93; and Arthur A. Thompson, Jr., and A. A. Strickland III, *Strategic Management,* 4th ed., (Homewood, Ill: Richard D. Irwin, 1988), p. 273–74.

EVALUATING AND CHOOSING BUSINESS-LEVEL STRATEGY[7]

Chapter 7 identified three generic strategies from which business strategists choose one overriding competitive strategy—low cost, differentiation, or focus. This section examines key factors that business strategists must consider as they choose among these strategies. Managers must first determine whether their business possesses the requirements of each strategy—skills, resources, and organizational assets. Second, they must carefully weigh the risks associated with each strategy. Finally, they must consider the requirements for strategic success emanating from the type of industry in which the business competes.

Requirements for the Success of Each Generic Strategy

Strategists choosing among the three generic strategies must be confident that the business possesses the basic requirements necessary to pursue a particular strategy. Figure 8–11 summarizes these requirements for each of the generic strategies in two categories: (1) skills and resources needed to make the strategy work and (2) organizational requirements necessary to implement the strategy.

The strategy of being the low-cost leader requires that the business have a sustainable cost advantage. It must be capable of providing products or services similar to those of its competitors at a distinct price advantage over those competitors. Through the skills or resources identified in Figure 8–11, it must either be able to accomplish one or more steps in its value chain (see Chapter 6)—procuring raw materials, processing them into products, marketing the products, and distributing the products—in a more cost-effective manner than that of its competitors or it must be able to reconfigure its value chain so as to achieve a cost advantage. Strategy in Action 8–2 shows how Iowa Beef Packers and Federal Express reconfigured their value chains to create a sustainable cost advantage in their respective industries.

The business strategy of differentiation requires that the business have sustainable advantages that allow it to provide buyers with something uniquely valuable to them. A successful differentiation strategy allows the business to provide a product or service of perceived higher value to buyers at a differentiation cost below the value premium to the buyers. Differentiation usually arises from one or more activities in the value chain that create a unique value important to buyers. Perrier's control of a carbonated water spring in France, Stouffer's frozen food packaging and sauce technology, Apple's highly integrated chip designs in its Macintosh Computers, American Greeting Card's automated inventory system for retailers, and IBM's customer service capabilities are all examples of sustainable advantages around which successful differentiation strategies have been built. A business can achieve differentiation by performing its existing value activities or reconfiguring in some unique way. And the sustainability of that differentiation will

---

[7]This section is based on Michael E. Porter, *Competitive Strategy,* (New York: Free Press, 1980), chap. 2; and Michael Porter, *Competitive Advantage,* (New York: Free Press, 1985), chap. 3.

FIGURE 8–11
**Skill, Resource, and Organizational Requirements of the
Three Generic Business Strategies**

Generic Strategy	Commonly Required Skills and Resources	Common Organizational Requirements
Overall cost leadership	Sustained capital investment and access to capital Process engineering skills Intense supervision of labor Products designed for ease in manufacture Low-cost distribution system	Tight cost control Frequent, detailed control reports Structured organization and responsibilities Incentives based on meeting strict quantitative targets
Differentiation	Strong marketing abilities Product engineering Creative flair Strong capability in basic research Corporate reputation for quality or technological leadership Long tradition in the industry or unique combination of skills drawn from other businesses Strong cooperation from channels	Strong coordination among functions in R&D, product development, and marketing Subjective measurement and incentives instead of quantitative measures Amenities to attract highly skilled labor, scientists, or creative people
Focus	Combination of the above policies directed at the particular strategic target	Combination of the above policies directed at the particular strategic target

Source: Micheal E. Porter, *Competitive Strategy* (New York: Free Press, 1980), pp. 40–41.

depend on two things—a continuation of its high perceived value to buyers and a lack of imitation by competitors.

A focus strategy must be able to achieve a cost or differentiation advantage targeted to a niche market that is a distinct subset of the overall market served by the industry of which the business is a part. For this strategy to work, the business must possess the required skills and organizational capacity and a distinct subgroup of buyers must be identified. Wendy's implemented a highly successful focus strategy by targeting young adults and selling fresh-meat hamburgers in pleasing surroundings that created high perceived value at a sustainable premium above its costs.

To make an informed choice among the generic strategies, strategists must be sensitive to the risks inherent in each of them. Figure 8–12 summarizes the key risks that must be considered. The concern central to all of these risks is whether the business will be able to sustain the cost or differentiation advantage on which its strategy is based. Thus, before choosing the generic strategy, strategists must determine the likelihood of these risks.

RESTRUCTURING VALUE CHAINS TO BUILD A SUCCESSFUL COST ADVANTAGE AT IOWA BEEF PACKERS AND FEDERAL EXPRESS

Iowa Beef Packers and Federal Express have been able to build strong competitive advantages by restructuring the traditional activity-cost chains in their respective industries. In beef packing, the traditional value chain was based on raising cattle on isolated ranches and then shipping them live to labor-intensive, unionized slaughterhouses in major rail centers such as Chicago and Kansas City. Butchers at these centers slaughtered the cattle and cut them into sides of beef that were shipped to markets where retailers cut them into smaller pieces. Iowa Beef Packers changed this traditional chain by building large automated plants near the cattle sources, at which the meat was processed into smaller, "boxed" cuts. This significantly reduced transportation costs and raised yields by avoiding the weight loss that occurred when live animals were shipped. Iowa Beef also cut its operational costs by using cheaper, nonunion labor in the rural areas where its plants were located.

Federal Express creatively redefined the value chain for express delivery of small packages. Traditional firms such as Airborne and Emery Freight collected freight of all sizes, used regular airlines to ship it, and then delivered it with their own trucks. Federal Express limited its focus to small packages, which it flew on company-owned planes to its central Memphis hub, where the parcels were sorted. The parcels were then reloaded on the same planes, which returned to their original locations, where company-owned trucks delivered the parcels to local addresses the next morning.

Source: Adapted from Michael E. Porter, *Competitive Advantage* (New York: Free Press, 1985), p. 191.

FIGURE 8–12
Risks Associated with the Generic Business Strategies

Risks with Low-Cost Leadership

Technological change that nullifes past investments or learning.

Low-cost learning by industry newcomers or followers, through imitation or through their ability to invest in state-of-the-art facilities

Inability to make required product or marketing changes because of the attention placed on cost.

Inflation in costs that narrows the ability of the business to maintain enough of a price differential to offset competitors' brand images or other approaches to differentiation.

Risks with Differentiation

The cost differential between low-cost competitors and the differentiated business becomes too great for differentiation to hold brand loyalty. Buyers thus sacrifice some of the features, services, or image possessed by the differentiated business for large cost savings.

Buyers' need for the differentiating factor falls. This can occur as buyers become more sophisticated.

Imitation narrows perceived differentiation, a common occurrence as industries mature.

Risks with Focus

The cost differential between broad-range competitors and the focused business widens to eliminate the cost advantages of serving a narrow target or to offset the differentiation achieved by focus.

The differences between the products or services desired by the strategic target and those desired by the market as a whole narrow.

Competitors find submarkets *within* the strategic target and outfocus the focuser.

Source: Michael E. Porter, *Competitive Strategy*; (New York: Free Press, 1980), pp. 45–46.

GENERIC INDUSTRY ENVIRONMENTS AND STRATEGIC CHOICES[8]

The analysis and choice of business strategies can be enhanced by taking industry conditions into account. Chapters 3 through 5 discussed ways to do this in detail. The purpose of this section is to summarize business strategy concepts that increase the likelihood of generating competitive advantage in five "generic" industry settings. The success that business strategists experience in their analysis and choice of a business strategy will be enhanced if they apply these concepts during that process.

Strategy in Fragmented Industries[9]

A fragmented industry is one in which no firm has a significant market share and can strongly influence industry outcomes. Fragmented industries are found in many areas of the economy and are common in such areas as professional services, retailing, distribution, wood and metal fabrication, and agricultural products.

There are a number of strategic alternatives for coping with a fragmented industry that should be considered when business strategy alternatives are being examined. These are specific approaches to the pursuit of the low-cost, differentiation, or focus strategies discussed above.

Tightly Managed Decentralization

Fragmented industries are characterized by a need for intense local coordination, a local management orientation, high personal service, and local autonomy. Recently, however, successful firms in such industries have introduced a high degree of professionalism into the operations of local managers.

"Formula" Facilities

This alternative, related to the previous one, introduces standardized, efficient, low-cost facilities at multiple locations. Thus, the firm gradually builds a low-cost advantage over localized competitors. Fast-food and motel chains have applied this approach with considerable success.

Increased Value Added

The products or services of some fragmented industries are difficult to differentiate. In this case, an effective strategy may be to add value by providing more service with the sale or by engaging in some product assembly that is of additional value to the customer.

Specialization

Focus strategies that creatively segment the market can enable firms to cope with fragmentation. Specialization can be pursued by:

---

[8]This section benefits from the ideas of Porter, *Competitive Strategy*, Chapter 11.

[9]Ibid., chap. 9.

Product Type: The firm builds expertise focusing on a narrow range of products or services.

Customer Type: The firm becomes intimately familiar with and serves the needs of a narrow customer segment.

Type of Order: The firm handles only certain kinds of orders, such as small orders, custom orders, or quick turnaround orders.

Geographic Area: The firm blankets or concentrates on a single area.

Although specialization in one or more of these ways can be the basis for a sound focus strategy in a fragmented industry, each of these types of specialization risks limiting the firm's potential sales volume.

Bare Bones/No Frills

Given the intense competition and low margins in fragmented industries, a "bare bones" posture—low overhead, minimum wage employees, tight cost control—may build a sustainable cost advantage in such industries.

Strategy in Emerging Industries[10]

Emerging industries are newly formed or re-formed industries that are typically created by technological innovation, newly emerging customer needs, or other economic or sociological changes. Among the emerging industries of the last two decades have been the personal computer, fiber optic, video game, solar heating, and cellular telephone industries.

From the standpoint of strategy formulation, the essential characteristic of an emerging industry is that there are no "rules of the game." The absence of rules presents both a risk and an opportunity—a wise strategy positions the firm to favorably shape the emerging industry's rules.

Business strategies must be shaped to accommodate the following characteristics of markets in emerging industries:[11]

Technologies that are mostly proprietary to the pioneering firms and technological uncertainty as to how product standardization will unfold.

Competitor uncertainty because of inadequate information about competitors, buyers, and the timing of demand.

High initial costs but steep cost declines as the experience curve takes effect.

Few entry barriers, which often spurs the formation of many new firms.

First-time buyers requiring initial inducement to purchase and customers confused by the availability of a number of nonstandard products.

---

[10]Ibid., chap. 10.

[11]Ibid., pp. 216–21.

Inability to obtain raw materials and components until suppliers gear up to meet the industry's needs.

Need for high-risk capital because of the industry's uncertainty prospects.

For success in this industry setting, business strategies require one or more of these features:

1. The ability to *shape the industry's structure* based on the timing of entry, reputation, success in related industries or technologies, and role in industry associations.
2. The ability to *rapidly improve product quality* and performance features.
3. *Advantageous relationships* with key suppliers and promising distribution channels.
4. The ability to *establish the firm's technology as the dominant one* before technological uncertainty decreases.
5. The early acquisition of *a core group of loyal customers* and then the expansion of that customer base through model changes, alternative pricing, and advertising.
6. The ability to *forecast future competitors* and the strategies they are likely to employ.

A firm that has had repeated successes with business in emerging industries is 3M Corporation. In each of the last 20 years, over 25 percent of 3M's annual sales have come from products that did not exist 5 years earlier.[12] Start-up companies enhance their success by having experienced entrepreneurs at the helm, a knowledgeable management team and board of directors, and patient sources of venture capital.

Strategy in the Transition to Industry Maturity[13]

As an industry evolves, its rate of growth eventually declines. This "transition to maturity" is accompanied by several changes in its competitive environment:

Competition for market share becomes more intense as firms in the industry are forced to achieve sales growth at one another's expense.

Firms in the industry selling increasingly to experienced, repeat buyers that are now making choices among known alternatives.

Competition becomes more oriented to cost and service as knowledgeable buyers expect similar price and product features.

Industry capacity "tops out" as sales growth ceases to cover up poorly planned expansions.

New products and new applications are harder to come by.

---

[12]"Masters of Innovation," *Business Week,* April 10, 1989, p. 56.

[13]This section benefits from the ideas of Porter, *Competitive Strategy,* chap. 11.

International competition increases as cost pressures lead to overseas production advantages.

Profitability falls, often permanently, as a result of pressure to lower prices and the increased costs of holding or building market share.

These changes necessitate a fundamental strategic reassessment. Strategy elements of successful firms in maturing industries often include:

1. *Pruning the product line* by dropping unprofitable product models, sizes, and options from the firm's product mix.
2. *Emphasis on process innovation* that permits low-cost product design, manufacturing methods, and distribution synergy.
3. *Emphasis on cost reduction* through exerting pressure on suppliers for lower prices, switching to cheaper components, introducing operational efficiencies, and lowering administrative and sales overhead.
4. *Careful buyer selection* to focus on buyers that are less aggressive, more closely tied to the firm, and able to buy more from the firm.
5. *Horizontal integration* to acquire rival firms whose weaknesses can be used to gain a bargain price and are correctable by the acquiring firms.
6. *International expansion* to markets where attractive growth and limited competition still exist and the opportunity for lower-cost manufacturing can influence both domestic and international costs.

Business strategists in maturing industries must avoid several pitfalls. First, they must make a clear choice among the three generic strategies and avoid a middle-ground approach, which would confuse both knowledgeable buyers and the firm's personnel. Second, they must avoid sacrificing market share too quickly for short-term profit. Finally, they must avoid waiting too long to respond to price reductions, retaining unneeded excess capacity, engaging in sporadic or irrational efforts to boost sales, and placing their hopes on "new" products rather than aggressively selling existing products.

Strategies for Mature and Declining Industries[14]

Declining industries are those that make products or services for which demand is growing slower than demand in the economy as a whole or is actually declining. This slow growth or decline in demand is caused by technological substitution (such as the substitution of electronic calculators for slide rules), demographic shifts (such as the increase in the number of older people and the decrease in the number of children), and shifts in needs (such as the decreased need for red meat).

Firms in a declining industry should choose strategies that emphasize one or more of the following themes:

1. *Focus* on segments within the industry that offer a chance for higher growth or a higher return.

---

[14]Ibid., chap. 12.

2. *Emphasize product innovation and quality improvement,* where this can be done cost effectively, to differentiate the firm from rivals and to spur growth.
3. *Emphasize production and distribution efficiency* by streamlining production, closing marginal productions facilities and costly distribution outlets, and adding effective new facilities and outlets.
4. *Gradually harvest the business*—generate cash by cutting down on maintenance, reducing models, and shrinking channels and make no new investment.

Strategists who incorporate one or more of these themes into the strategy of their business can anticipate relative success, particularly where the industry's decline is slow and smooth and some profitable niches remain. At the same time, three pitfalls must be avoided: (1) being overly optimistic about the prospects for a revival of the industry, (2) getting trapped in a profitless war of attrition, (3) and harvesting from a weak position.

Strategies in Global Industries[15]

A global industry is one that comprises firms whose competitive positions in major geographic or national markets are fundamentally affected by their overall global competitive positions. To avoid strategic disadvantages, firms in global industries are virtually required to compete on a worldwide basis. Oil, steel, automobiles, apparel, motorcycles, televisions, and computers are examples of global industries.

Global industries have four unique strategy-shaping features:

Differences in prices and costs from country to country due to currency exchange, fluctuations, differences in wage and inflation rates, and other economic factors.

Differences in buyer needs across different countries.

Differences in competitors and ways of competing from country to country.

Differences in trade rules and governmental regulations across different countries.

These unique features and the global competition of global industries require that two fundamental components be addressed in the business strategy: (a) the approach used to gain global market coverage and (b) the generic competitive strategy.

Three basic options can be used to pursue global market coverage:

1. *License* foreign firms to produce and distribute the firm's products.
2. *Maintain a domestic production base* and export products to foreign countries.
3. *Establish foreign-based plants and distribution* to compete directly in the markets of one or more foreign countries.

Along with the market coverage decision, strategists must scrutinize the condition of the global industry features identified earlier to choose among four generic global competitive strategies:

---

[15]Ibid., chap. 13.

1. *Broad-line global competition*—directed at competing worldwide in the full product line of the industry, often with plants in many countries, to achieve differentiation or an overall low-cost position.
2. *Global focus* strategy—targeting a particular segment of the industry for competition on a worldwide basis.
3. *National focus* strategy—taking advantage of differences in national markets that give the firm an edge over global competitors on a nation-by-nation basis.
4. *Protected niche* strategy—seeking out countries in which governmental restraints exclude or inhibit global competitors and/or allow concessions that are advantageous to localized firms.

Competing in global industries is an increasing reality for many U.S. firms. Strategists must carefully match their skills and resources with global industry structure and conditions in selecting the most appropriate strategy option.

In conclusion, the analysis and choice of business strategy involves three basic considerations. First, strategists must recognize that their overall choice revolves around three generic options and that once one of them has been chosen, it will require total, consistent commitment. Second, strategists must carefully weigh the skills, resources, organizational requirements, and risks associated with each generic business strategy. Finally, strategists must consider the unique influence that the generic industry environment most similar to the firm's situation will have on the desired features of the generic strategy they choose.

BEHAVIORAL CONSIDERATIONS AFFECTING STRATEGIC CHOICE

Strategic choice is a decision. At both the corporate and business levels, that decision determines the future strategy of the firm.

After alternative strategies have been examined, a strategic choice is made. This is a decision to adopt one of those strategies. If the examination identified a clearly superior strategy or if the current strategy will clearly meet future company objectives, then the decision is relatively simple. Such clarity is the exception, however, so the decision is usually judgmental and difficult. After comprehensive strategy examination, strategic decision makers are often confronted with several viable alternatives rather than the luxury of a clear-cut, obvious choice. Under these circumstances, several factors influence the strategic choice. Some of the more important are:

1. Role of past strategy.
2. Degree of the firm's external dependence.
3. Attitudes toward risk.
4. Internal political considerations.
5. Timing.
6. Competitive reaction.

Role of Past Strategy

Current strategists are often the architects of past strategies. If they have invested substantial time, resources, and interest in those strategies, they would logically be more comfortable with a choice that closely parallels them or represents only incremental alterations to them.

Such familiarity with and commitment to past strategy permeate the entire firm. Thus, lower-level managers reinforce the top managers' inclination toward continuity with past strategy during the choice process. In one study, during the planning process, lower-level managers suggested strategic choices that were consistent with current strategy and likely to be accepted while withholding suggestions with less probability of approval.[16]

Research by Henry Mintzberg suggests that past strategy strongly influences current strategic choice.[17] The older and more successful a strategy has been, the harder it is to replace. Similarly, once a strategy has been initiated, it is very difficult to change because organizational momentum keeps it going. Strategy in Action 8–3 illustrates just this situation at Holiday Inn.

Mintzberg's work and research by Barry Staw found that even as a strategy begins to fail due to changing conditions, strategists often increase their commitment to it.[18] Thus, firms may replace top executives when performance has been inadequate for an extended period because replacing these executives lessens the influence of unsuccessful past strategy on future strategic choice.

Degree of the Firm's External Dependence

A comprehensive strategy is meant to effectively guide a firm's performance in its external environment. Owners, suppliers, customers, government, competitors, and unions are elements in that environment, as elaborated on in Chapters 3 through 5. A major constraint on strategic choice is the power of environmental elements over this decision. If a firm is highly dependent on one or more environmental elements, its strategic alternatives and its ultimate strategic choice must accommodate that dependence. The greater a firm's external dependence, the lower its range and flexibility in strategic choice.

Two examples highlight the influence of external dependence on strategic choice. For many years, Whirlpool sold most of its major appliance output to one customer—Sears. With its massive retail coverage and its access to alternative suppliers, Sears was a major external dependence for Whirlpool. Whirlpool's strategic alternatives and ultimate choice

---

[16]Eugene Carter, "The Behavioral Theory of the Firm and Top-Level Corporate Decisions," *Administrative Science Quarterly* 16, no. 4 (1971), pp. 413–28.

[17]Henry Mintzberg, "Research on Strategy Making," *Proceedings of the Academy of Management* (Minneapolis: 1972).

[18]Barry M. Staw, "Knee-Deep in the Big Muddy: A Study of Escalating Commitment to a Chosen Course of Action," *Organizational Behavior and Human Performance*, June 1976, pp. 27–44; Mintzberg, "Research on Strategy Making."

| STRATEGY IN ACTION 8–3 | THE ROLE OF PAST STRATEGY AND POLITICAL CONSIDERATIONS IN HOLIDAY INNS' RESPONSE TO BUDGET MOTELS |

When Kemmons Wilson started Holiday Inns as his response to a need he perceived for medium-priced, standardized motel accommodations, little did he realize that Holiday Inns would become the dominant creator of a worldwide lodging industry. By the early 1980s, 5 out of every 22 U.S. travelers stayed at a Holiday Inn each night. One of every three hotel rooms being built worldwide was part of a Holiday Inn.

This success led Holiday Inns to think that it *was* the lodging industry. Holiday Inn University trained thousands of lodging personnel each month. Holiday Inn's rapid growth enabled its executives to build very successful and lucrative careers. Their strategy of providing business and recreational travelers with quality operations at upper-middle-price levels had a strong following and was supported by an entrenched culture and an entrenched way of running a motel/hotel property. So when Days Inn started in the 1970s as an efficient, budget-conscious alternative focused on business people, government employees, retirees, and young families in need of inexpensive lodging alternatives, Holiday Inn strategists expressed little concern.

By the 1980s, Days Inn was one of several chains that had pioneered the most profitable and fastest-growing segment of the lodging industry—budget motels. Holiday Inns' strategy remained unchanged, allowing these new entrants to draw away numerous former businesspeople and retirees.

Eventually, Holiday Inns' executives decided to start an entirely new chain—Hampton Inns—to compete in the budget segment. The influence of Holiday Inns' past strategy and the culture and power relationships built around it necessitated the creation of an entirely new chain with a new strategy that responded to the needs of budget travelers.

---

of strategy were limited and strongly influenced by Sears's demands. Whirlpool carefully narrowed its grand strategy and important related decisions in areas such as research and development, pricing, distribution, and product design with its critical dependence on Sears in mind.

Chrysler Corporation's dependence on federal loan guarantees and financial concessions by labor considerably limited the strategic choices available to it in the early 1980s. Lee Iacocca's decision to pay off several of Chrysler's federal obligations before they were due was partially meant to increase Chrysler's flexibility by reducing one restrictive external dependence.

These examples show that increased environmental dependence lessens a firm's flexibility in strategic choice. If dependence on an external element is critical, firms may include representatives of that element (government, union, supplier, bank) in the strategic choice process. In 1980, for example, Chrysler took the unprecedented action of including Leonard Woodcock, president of the United Auto Workers, on its board of directors.

Attitudes toward Risk

Attitudes toward risk exert considerable influence on strategic choice. These attitudes, which may vary from eager risk taking to strong aversion to risk, influence the range of available strategic choices. Where attitudes favor risk, the range of the strategic choices expands and high-risk strategies are acceptable and desirable. Where management is risk averse, the range of strategic choices is limited and risky alternatives are eliminated before strategic choices are made. Risk-oriented managers prefer offensive, opportunistic strategies. Risk-averse managers prefer defensive, safe strategies. Past strategy exerts far more influence on the strategic choices of risk-averse managers than on the strategic choices of risk-oriented managers.

Industry volatility influences the propensity of managers toward risk. Top managers in highly volatile industries absorb and operate with greater amounts of risk than do their counterparts in stable industries. Therefore, top managers in volatile industries consider a broader, more diverse range of strategies in the strategic choice process.

Industry evolution is another determinant of managerial propensity toward risk. A firm in the early stages of the product-market cycle must operate with considerably greater risk than a firm in the later stages of that cycle.

In making a strategic choice, risk-oriented managers lean toward opportunistic strategies with higher payoffs. They are drawn to offensive strategies based on innovation, company strengths, and operating potential. Risk-averse managers lean toward safe, conservative strategies with reasonable, highly probable returns. They are drawn to defensive strategies that minimize a firm's weaknesses, external threats, and the uncertainty associated with innovation-based strategies.

A recent study of strategic business units (SBUs) examined the relationship between SBU performance and the willingness of SBU managers to take risks. The study found a link between risk taking and strategic choice. Looking first at SBUs that had been assigned build or star strategic missions within a corporate portfolio, it found that the general managers of the higher-performing SBUs were *more willing to take risks* than their counterparts in the lower-performing SBUs. Looking next at SBUs that had been assigned harvest missions, it found that the general managers of the high-performing SBUs were *less willing to take risks* than the general managers of the lower-performing SBUs.[19]

This study supports the idea that managers make different decisions depending on their willingness to take risks. Perhaps most important, the study suggests that being either risk prone or risk averse is not inherently good or bad, that which risk orientation is more effective depends on the strategic mission of the SBU. Although this single study is not the final word on the influence of risk orientation on strategic choice, it illustrates the importance of risk orientation in the process of making and implementing strategic decisions.

---

[19]Gupta and Govindarajan, "Build, Hold, Harvest."

Internal Political Considerations

Power/political factors influence strategic choice. The use of power to further individual or group interests is common in organizational life. An early study by Ross Stagner found that strategic decisions in business organizations were frequently settled by power rather than by analytical maximization procedures.[20]

A major source of power in most firms is the chief executive officer (CEO). In smaller firms, the CEO is consistently the dominant force in strategic choice, and this is also often true in large firms, particularly those with a strong or dominant CEO. When the CEO begins to favor a particular choice, it is often selected unanimously.

Cyert and March identified another power source that influences strategic choice, particularly in larger firms.[21] They called this the *coalition* phenomenon. In large firms, subunits and individuals (particularly key managers) have reason to support some alternatives and oppose others. Mutual interest often draws certain groups together in coalitions to enhance their position on major strategic issues. These coalitions, particularly the more powerful ones (often called *dominant coalitions*), exert considerable influence on the strategic choice process. Numerous studies confirm the frequent use of power and coalitions in strategic decision making. Interestingly, one study found that managers occasionally tried to hide their preference for judgmental/political bargaining over systematic analysis and that when politics was a factor, it slowed decision making.[22]

Figure 8–13 illustrates the focus of political action across the phases of strategic decision making. It shows that the *content* of strategic decisions and the *processes* of arriving at such decisions are politically intertwined. Each phase in the process of strategic choice presents an opportunity for political action intended to influence the outcome. The challenge for strategists lies in recognizing and managing this political influence. If strategic choice processes are not carefully overseen, managers can bias the content of strategic decisions in the direction of their own interests.[23] For example, selecting the criteria used to compare alternative strategies or collecting and appraising information regarding those criteria may be particularly susceptible to political influence. This possibility must be recognized and, where necessary "managed" to avoid dysfunctional political bias. Relying on different sources to collect and appraise information might serve this purpose.

Rather than simply being denoted as "bad" or "inefficient," organizational politics must be viewed as an inevitable dimension of organizational decision making that strategic

---

[20]Ross Stagner, "Corporate Decisions Making," *Journal of Applied Psychology* 53, no. 1 (1969), pp. 1–13.

[21]Richard M. Cyert and James G. March, *A Behavioral Theory of the Firm* (Englewood Cliffs, N.J.: Prentice-Hall, 1963).

[22]See, for example, Henry Mintzberg, D. Raisinghani, and Andre Theoret, "The Structure of Unstructured Decision Process," *Administrative Science Quarterly*, June 1976, pp. 246–75; and William Guth, "Toward a Social System Theory of Corporate Strategy," *Journal of Business*, July 1976, pp. 374–88.

[23]Liam Fahey and V. K. Naroyanan, "The Politics of Strategic Decision Making," in *The Strategic Management Handbook*, ed. Kenneth J. Albert (New York: McGraw-Hill, 1983), p. 21–18.

FIGURE 8–13
Political Activities in Phases of Strategic Decision Making

Phases of Strategic Decision-Making	Focus of Political Action	Examples of Political Activity
Identification and diagnosis of strategic issues	Control of: Issues to be discussed Cause-and-effect relationships to be examined	Control agenda Interpretation of past events and future trends
Narrowing the alternative strategies for serious consideration	Control of alternatives	Mobilization Coalition formation Resource commitment for information search
Examining and choosing the strategy	Control of choice	Selective advocacy of criteria Search and representation of information to justify choice
Initiating implementation of the strategy	Interaction between winners and losers	Winners attempt to "sell" or co-opt losers Losers attempt to thwart decisions and trigger fresh strategic issues
Designing procedures for the evaluation of results	Representing oneself as successful	Selective advocacy of criteria

Source: Adapted from Liam Fahey and V. K. Naroyanan, "The Politics of Strategic Decision Making," in *The Strategic Management Handbook,* ed. Kenneth J. Albert (New York: McGraw-Hill, 1983), p. 21–20.

management must accommodate. Some authors argue that politics is a key ingredient in the "glue" that holds an organization together. Formal and informal negotiating and bargaining between individuals, subunits, and coalitions are indispensable mechanisms for organizational coordination.[24] Accommodating these mechanisms in the choice of strategy will result in greater commitment and more realistic strategy. The costs of doing so, however, are likely to be increased time spent on decision making and incremental (as opposed to drastic) change.

Timing

The time issue can have considerable influence on strategic choice. Consider the case of Mech-Tran, a small manufacturer of fiberglass piping that found itself in financial difficulty. At the same time that it was seeking a loan guarantee through the Small Business Administration (SBA), KOCH Industries (a Kansas City–based supplier of oil field supplies) approached it with a merger offer. The offer involved a 100 percent sale of Mech-Tran's stock and a two-week response deadline. The SBA loan procedure, on the other

---

[24]Ibid.

hand, could take three months. Obviously, Mech-Tran's strategic decision was heavily influenced by external time constraints that limited analysis and evaluation. Research by Peter Wright indicates that under such time constraints, managers put greater weight on negative than on positive information and prefer defensive strategies.[25] The Mech-Tran owners decided to accept KOCH's offer rather than risk losing the opportunity and subsequently being turned down by the SBA. Thus, consistent with Wright's findings, they opted for a defensive strategy.

Another aspect of the time issue is the timing of a strategic decision. A good strategy may be disastrous if it is undertaken at the wrong time. Winnebago was the darling of Wall Street in 1970, when its stock rose from $3 to $44 per share. Winnebago's 1972 strategic choice, enlarging its centralized production facility, was a continuation of the strategy that had successfully differentiated it in the recreational vehicle industry. As a result of that choice, the dismal effects of the 1973 Arab oil embargo on Winnebago were intensified. The strategic choice was good, but its timing proved disastrous. On the other hand, IBM's decision to hold off entering the rapidly growing personal computer market until 1982 appeared to be perfectly timid. Welcomed by Apple with a full-page advertisement in *The Wall Street Journal*, IBM assumed the market share lead by early 1983.

A final aspect of the time issue is the relationship between the lead time required for alternative choices and the time horizon contemplated by management. Management's primary attention may be on the short or long run, depending on circumstances. Logically, strategic choice will be strongly influenced by the match between management's current time horizon and the lead time (or payoff time) associated with different choices. In a move toward vertical integration, Du Pont went heavily into debt to acquire Conoco in 1982. By 1983, the worldwide oil glut would have enabled Du Pont to buy raw materials on more favorable terms in the open market. This short-term perspective was not of great concern to Du Pont's management, however, because the acquisition was part of a strategy to stabilize Du Pont's long-term position as a producer of numerous petroleum-based products.

Competitive Reaction

In weighing strategic choices, top management frequently incorporates perceptions of likely competitor reactions to those choices. For example, if it chooses an aggressive strategy directly challenging a key competitor, that competitor can be expected to mount an aggressive counterstrategy. In weighing strategic choices, top management must consider the probable impact of such reactions on the success of the chosen strategy.

The beer industry provides a good illustration. In the early 1970s, Anheuser-Busch dominated the industry, and Miller Brewing Company, recently acquired by Philip Morris, was a weak and declining competitor. Miller's management decided to adopt an expensive,

---

[25]Peter Wright, "The Harassed Decision Maker," *Journal of Applied Psychology* 59, no. 5 (1974), pp. 555–61.

advertising-oriented strategy that challenged the big three (Anheuser-Busch, Pabst, and Schlitz) head-on because it assumed that their reaction would be delayed due to Miller's current declining status in the industry. This assumption provided correct, and Miller was able to reverse its trend in market share before Anheuser-Busch countered with an equally intense advertising strategy.

Miller's management took another approach in its next major strategic decision. In the mid-1970s, it introduced (and heavily advertised) a low-calorie beer—Miller Lite. Other industry members had introduced such products without much success. Miller chose a strategy that did not directly challenge its key competitors and was not expected to elicit immediate counterattacks from them. This choice proved highly successful because Miller was able to establish a dominant share of the low-calorie beer market before those competitors decided to react. In this case, as in the preceding case, expectations regarding the reactions of competitors were a key determinant of the strategic choice made by Miller's management.

SUMMARY

This chapter has examined several considerations in strategic analysis and choice. The first concern of strategic analysis and choice is with an overall corporate strategy that answers the questions of what businesses to be in and what basic brand strategy to adopt. To understand the evolving role of corporate strategy, it is important to recognize how firms typically evolve from single-business to multibusiness operations. When a firm moves from a single-business or dominant-business posture to a multibusiness posture, its managers usually choose among 12 grand strategies. As single-business firms become multibusiness firms, they also use a portfolio-type approach to their corporate strategy.

At the business level, strategic analysis and choice is concerned with the competitive posture of a single business. Strategists must choose among three generic strategies. This choice is accomplished by matching the skill, resource, and organizational requirements of each strategy with the capabilities of the business. In choosing the generic strategy most appropriate to their business, strategists must also consider five generic industry environments.

Strategic analysis often limits alternatives to several viable strategic choices. The luxury of making what is obviously the best strategic choice is seldom available. Nonetheless, a choice must be made. Strategic choice is influenced by several factors that are outside the realm of purely analytic consideration, such as propensity for risk, past strategy, and coalitions.

The strategic management process does not end with the choice of corporate- and business-level strategies. Functional strategies and organizational systems and processes to initiate and control daily activities in a manner consistent with those must be identified and implemented. The next part of this book examines the implementation phase of the strategic management process.

QUESTIONS FOR DISCUSSION

1. How does strategic analysis at the corporate level differ from strategic analysis at the business level? How are they related?
2. When would multiindustry firms find the portfolio approach to strategy evaluation useful?
3. Explain the role of a tool facilitating strategic choice within the grand strategy selection matrix and the model of grand strategy clusters of corporate strategy.
4. Define each of the generic business strategies, and explain their skills, resource, and organizational requirements.
5. Select two generic industry environments, and state the strategic alternatives that are most likely to succeed in them.
6. What role does politics play in the development and evaluation of alternative strategies? Please explain.
7. Explain and illustrate the role of three behavioral considerations in strategy examination and choice.

BIBLIOGRAPHY

Aaker, A. David, and Robert Jacobson. "The Role of Risk in Explaining Differences in Profitability." *Academy of Management Journal,* June 1987, p. 227.

Allaire, Yvon, and Michaela E. Firsirotu. "Coping With Strategic Uncertainty." *Sloan Management Review,* Spring 1987, p. 7.

Bart, K. Christopher "Implementing 'Growth' And 'Harvest' Product Strategies." *California Management Review,* Summer 1987, p. 139.

Barwise, Patrick; Paul R. Marsh; and Robin Wensley. "Must Finance and Strategy Clash?" *Harvard Business Review,* September–October 1989, p. 85.

Bitner, Larry N., and Judith D. Powell. "Expansion Planning for Small Retail Firms." *Journal of Small Business Management,* April 1987, p. 47.

Chaganti, Rajeswararao, and Vijay Mahajan, "Profitable Small Business Strategies under Different Types of Competition." *Entrepreneurship: Theory And Practice,* Spring 1989, p. 21.

Cohen, B. G. "A New Approach to Strategic Forecasting." *Journal of Business Strategy,* September–October 1988, pp. 38–42.

Cravens, David W. "Gaining Strategic Marketing Advantage." *Business Horizons,* September–October 1988, p. 44.

Dess, Gregory G., and Nancy K. Orizer. "Environment, Structure, and Consensus in Strategy Formulation." *Academy of Management Review,* April 1987, p. 313.

Eynn, P. J. "Avoid the Seven Deadly Sins of Strategic Risk Analysis." *Journal of Business Strategy,* September 1988, pp. 18–23.

Fulmer, William E., and Jack Goodwin. "Differentiation: Begin with the Consumer." *Business Horizons,* September–October 1988, p. 55.

Govindarajan, Vijay. "A Contingency Approach to Strategy Selection at the Business Unit Level." *Academy of Management Journal,* December 1988, p. 828.

Henderson, Bruce D. "The Origin of Strategy." *Harvard Business Review,* November–December 1989, p. 139.

Hill, Charles W. L., and Robert E. Hoskisson. "Strategy and Structure in the Multi-Product Firm" *Academy of Management Review,* April 1987, p. 331.

Hoskinson Robert E. "Multidivisional Structure and Performance: The Contingency of Diversification Strategy." *Academy of Management Journal*, December 1987, p. 621.

Jones, T., and G. Seiler. "The Rapidly Growing Pump Company: Marketing for Competitive Advantage." *Planning Review*, May–June 1988, pp. 30–35.

Kennedy, C., "Planning Global Strategies for 3M." *Long Range Planning*, February 1988, pp. 9–17.

Krubasik, E. G. "Customize Your Product Development." *Harvard Business Review*, September–October 1988, pp. 46–53.

McConkey, Dale D. "Planning in a Changing Environment." *Business Horizons*, September–October 1988, p. 64.

Mason, David H., and Robert G. Wilson. "Future-Mapping: A New Approach to Managing Strategic Uncertainty." *Planning Review*, May–June 1987, p. 20.

Pelham, A. M., and D. E. Clayson. "Receptivity to Strategic Planning Tools." *Journal of Small Business Management*, January 1988, pp. 43–50.

"The Pluralization of Consumption." Editorial. *Harvard Business Review*, May 1988, pp. 7–8.

Schofield, M., and D. Arnold. "Strategies for Mature Businesses." *Long Range Planning*, October 1988, pp. 69–76.

Schrage, Michael. "A Japanese Firm Rethinks Globalization: Interview with Yoshihisa Tabuchi." *Harvard Business Review*, July–August 1989, p. 70.

Stalk, G., "Time—The Next Source of Competitive Advantage." *Harvard Business Review*, July–August 1988, pp. 41–53.

Ulrich David. "Tie The Corporate Knot: Gaining Complete Customer Commitment." *Sloan Management Review*, Summer 1987, p. 139.

CHAPTER 8 COHESION CASE

STRATEGIC ANALYSIS AND CHOICE

Bryson's top management group spent considerable time at the strategic planning retreat concluding discussions that had been going on for some time about the appropriateness and way it should be involved in the four basic businesses we have discussed. A summary of their assessment of each business is provided below (5 = very favorable . . . 0 = unfavorable):

Dimension Evaluated	Bryson Businesses			
	Trns.	Reml.	Recy.	Mwst.
A. Industry attractiveness				
1. Size of market	4	5	4	3
2. Growth rate of our segment	3	5	5	4
3. Margins we can expect	2	4	4	1
4. Buyer power—size and cooperation	2	3	2	1
5. Potential entrants	2	2	5	2
6. Suppliers—disposal and othrs	2	2	4	1
7. Rivals—size and reputation	3	2	4	1
8. Substitutes	4	4	4	2
9. Strong regulation	5	4	5	2
10. Liability	3	3	2	4
11. Technological—chance of change	4	3	3	2
Overall industry attractiveness...	34	38	42	23
	Med.	High	High	Low
B. Business strength				
1. Market share or relative position	4	3	2	1
2. Growth Rate of our business	4	3	2	2
3. Margins we have generated & expect	3	5	4	1
4. Advantages relative to Competitors	4	3	3	1
5. Strength of our Name Recognition	5	4	2	2
6. Experience & depth of personnel	5	4	2	1
7. Liklihood & impact of new tech	4	4	4	2
8. Experience of top mgt in business	5	4	2	1
9. Existing or pot'l level of intgr	4	4	4	2
10. Operation Advantages	4	4	4	2
11. Strong customer base	4	4	2	2
Overall business strength...	46	42	31	17
	Strg.	Strg.	Avg.	Weak

These assessments made by Bryson's managers could be portrayed in a corporate planning grid, as shown in the illustration of business strengths on the following page.

This corporate-level strategy analysis would suggest that Bryson consider "harvesting" its medical waste business; manage its transportation business as a stable source of resources that first maintain that business's favorable market position, and then channel its excess resources to build other businesses; invest to ensure the strong position in remedial services as a potential source of excess resources; and make a final decision whether to invest resources to build the opportunity in recycling/recovery or to exit this

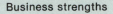

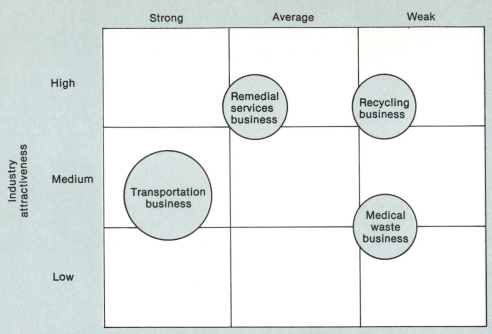

business as a source of resources for the remedial services business. Bryson's management decided to pursue these basic business missions, including a decision to merge Wall Chemical into Bryson so as to build that business, because of its potential synergy with the other two hazardous waste businesses.

Bryson managers chose to pursue focused differentiation strategies in each of their three remaining businesses. They felt like they had strong marketing skills, creative abilities to "engineer" and adapt each business's services as needed, a reputation for quality and a long tradition of safety, and strong cooperative relations with key "channels" for potential business, like large engineering firms, several large existing customers, and regulatory officials. Each of these key strengths, in their view, supported the logic of pursuing a differentiation strategy in the southeast while a low-cost approach would be more risky, given the capital available to the three larger industry rivals.

Their differentiation strategies in each business were further specified, as follows.

1. *Transportation*.

Bryson sought to build its already strong position as a bulk liquid waste specialist requiring specialized (capital-intensive) tanker equipment and expertise in operating that equipment. As the Wall and Cleanway facilities are developed, Bryson can bring to bear the integrated synergy that these facilities offer bulk liquid waste streams, so Bryson transportation will be positioned to overcome a key differentiation strategy risk as the industry matures: the risk that the cost differential between low-cost competitors and the differentiated firm could become too great for differentiation to hold brand loyalty.

Bryson also included in this strategy a very active profile in trade associations influencing legislation and regulation that would allow Bryson to position its permits and extensive driver training efforts as increasing barriers to entry facing marginal competitors or bulk tank transporters considering entry into hazardous waste.

2. *Remedial services.*

Bryson sought to pursue a differentiation strategy in this business by focusing on smaller remediation jobs ($50k to $250k) needed by industrial clientele served by Bryson's other two businesses and engineering firms that "engineer" larger cleanup jobs for industrial and government clients but are forced by conflict of interest considerations to solicit outside contractors (like Bryson) to actually do the work. In each of these markets, Remedial Services takes advantage of Bryson's overall strong marketing abilities (outside sales and telemarketing/telemanagement), a well-trained group of onsite creative work crews, and an exceptionally qualified business management team (engineers, chemist, former EPA-type regulators) that represent value at relatively small costs to routine Bryson customers and someone engineering customers can easily "talk to" in a technical way that would be understood.

3. *Recycling and recovery.*

Bryson's managers decided to merge Wall into Bryson, building on the Cleanway acquisition so as to create a core or base position in the recycling/recovery business (in the Southeast) that also allowed the company to have two interim Part B TSDF facilities, with good prospects that they ultimately would be permanently approved. Bryson sought to differentiate itself in these businesses by first investing to complete each facility (since both were new locations) with state-of-the-art equipment. As the managers were doing this, they sought to integrate it with the other two businesses to take advantage of their existing customer bases. Finally, they sought to gradually specialize in hard-to-handle wastes as a source of differentiation.

While most recycling sites currently operating or under EPA review are existing facilities that have provided recycling services for some time, Bryson's two locations were both new sites. Therefore, while most others faced contamination from handling practices that likely contaminated their soil and groundwater before these were regulated and were therefore required to clean them up as part of permitting, Bryson did not face this problem. That, in turn, could be used in Bryson's management opinion as a significant source of differentiation in the minds of waste generators increasingly sensitive about their "cradle-to-grave" liability for wastes taken from their operations.

Bryson management viewed each of its businesses as being in emerging industries— really segments of the emerging hazardous waste management industry. Therefore, at a corporate level, maximum emphasis was placed on doing things that help shape the emerging industry's "game rules." The president and key managers were positioned to be very active in industry trade associations regularly solicited for input about future legislation and regulation. Bryson regularly created special ways to maintain a core group of loyal customers that would support Bryson as the industry began to mature. Bryson's business and operations managers were focused on constantly seeking opportunities to rapidly improve service quality. And corporate management regularly sought contractual and "special" relationships with key suppliers (disposal companies) and distribution channels (like engineering firms and waste brokers) to strengthen Bryson's position as the markets began to mature.

What is your assessment of Bryson's corporate strategy choices and the business strategies they chose to pursue in their three basic businesses? What alternatives do you think represent equally appropriate or even better choices?

III STRATEGY/ IMPLEMENTATION

The last part of this book examines what is often called the action phase of the strategic management process: implementation of the chosen strategy. Up to this point, three phases of that process have been covered—strategy formulation, analysis of alternative strategies, and strategic choice. Although important, these phases alone cannot ensure success. To ensure success, the strategy must be translated into carefully implemented action. This means that

1. The strategy must be translated into guidelines for the daily activities of the firm's members.
2. The strategy and the firm must become one—that is, the strategy must be reflected in the way the firm organizes its activities and in the firm's values, beliefs and tone.
3. In implementing the strategy, the firm's managers must direct and control actions and outcomes and adjust to change.

The three chapters of this part discuss these issues.

Organizational action is successfully initiated in three interrelated steps:

1. Identification of measurable, mutually determined *annual objectives*.
2. Development of specific *functional strategies*.
3. Development and communication of concise *policies* to guide decisions.

Annual objectives guide implementation by converting long-term objectives into short-term goods. Functional strategies translate the firm's grand strategy into action plans for its units. Policies provide operating managers and their subordinates with specific guidelines for executing strategies. Chapter 9 examines how to operationalize a strategy through the use of annual objectives, functional strategies, and policies.

To be effectively implemented, a strategy must be institutionalized—must permeate the firm's day-to-day life. Chapter 10 discussed four organizational elements that provide fundamental, long-term means for institutionalizing the firm's strategy:

1. The firm's *structure*.
2. The *leadership* provided by the firm's CEO and key managers.
3. The fit between the strategy and the firm's *culture*.
4. The firm's *reward systems*.

Since the firm's strategy is implemented in a changing environment, successful implementation requires that execution be controlled and evaluated. The control and evaluation process must include at least these dimensions:

1. *Strategic controls* that "steer" execution of the strategy.
2. *Operations control systems* that monitor performance, evaluate deviations, and initiate corrective action.

Chapter 11 examines the dimensions of the control and evaluation process.

Implementation is "where the action is." It is the arena that most students enter at the start of their business careers. It is the strategic phase in which staying close to the customer, achieving competitive advantage, and pursuing excellence become realities. The chapters in this part will help you understand how this is done.

9 IMPLEMENTING STRATEGY THROUGH THE BUSINESS FUNCTIONS

Even after the grand strategies have been determined and the long-term objectives set, the strategic management process is far from complete. Strategic managers now move into a critical new phase of that process—translating strategic thought into organizational action. In the words of two well-worn phrases, they move from "planning their work" to "working their plan" as they shift their focus from strategy formulation to strategy implementation. This shifting gives rise to three interrelated concerns:

1. Identifying measurable, mutually determined annual objectives.
2. Developing specific functional strategies.
3. Communicating concise policies to guide decisions.

Annual objectives translate long-range aspirations into this year's budget. If well developed, these objectives provide clarity, a powerful motivator and facilitator of effective strategy implementation. This chapter shows how to develop annual objectives that maximize implementation-related payoffs.

Functional strategies translate grand strategy at the level of the firm as a whole into activities for the firm's units. Operating managers participate in the development of these strategies, and their participation, in turn, helps clarify what their units are expected to do in implementing the grand strategy.

Policies are specific guides for operating managers and their subordinates. Although often misunderstood and misused, policies can be powerful tools for strategy implementation if they are clearly linked to functional strategies and long-term objectives. This chapter explains how to use policies in the implementation and control of the firm's strategies.

ANNUAL OBJECTIVES

Chapter 7 dealt with the importance of long-term objectives as benchmarks for corporate strategies. Such objectives as market share, return on investment (ROI), return on equity (ROE), stock price, and new market penetration provide guidance in assessing the ultimate effectiveness of a chosen grand strategy. While objectives of this kind clarify the long-range purposes of a grand strategy and the bases for judging its success, they are less useful in guiding the daily operating activities that implement a grand strategy. Short-term (usually annual) objectives provide key mechanisms to aid managers in guiding such activities toward the accomplishment of their firm's long-term objectives.[1] Accomplishing these objectives adds up to successful execution of the firm's long-term plan.

Qualities of Effective Annual Objectives

Annual objectives are specific, measurable statements of what organization units are expected to contribute to the accomplishment of the firm's grand strategy. Problems in the implementation of grand strategies often stem from poorly conceived or stated annual objectives. The contribution of these objectives will be maximized if they possess certain basic qualities.

Link to Long-Term Objectives

Each annual objective must be clearly linked to one or more long-term objectives of the firm's grand strategy. To accomplish this, it is important to understand the three basic ways in which annual objectives differ from long-term objectives:

1. *Time frame.* Long-term objectives are usually focused five years or more into the future. Annual objectives are more immediate, usually involving one year or less.
2. *Specificity.* Long-term objectives are broadly stated companywide ends. Annual objectives are very specific and are directly linked to a project or to a functional area or a unit of the firm.
3. *Measurement.* Although both long-term and annual objectives are quantifiable, long-term objectives are stated in broad, relative terms (for example, 20 percent market share), whereas annual objectives are stated in absolute terms (for example, a 15 percent increase in sales in the next year).

Annual objectives add breadth and specificity in identifying *what* must be accomplished in order to achieve long-term objectives. For example, Wal-Mart's top management recently set forth "to obtain 30 percent market share in five years" as a long-term objective.[2] Achieving that objective can be greatly enhanced if a series of specific annual

---

[1] An *annual* time frame is the most popular short-term planning horizon in most firms. Short-term objectives, particularly for a key project, program, or activity, may involve a shorter time horizon (e.g., a three- or six-month horizon). The discussion in this section accommodates such shorter horizons.

[2] Wal-Mart annual report, 1990.

FIGURE 9–1
The Role of Short-Term Objectives in the Integration/Coordination of Activities in a Manufacturing Firm

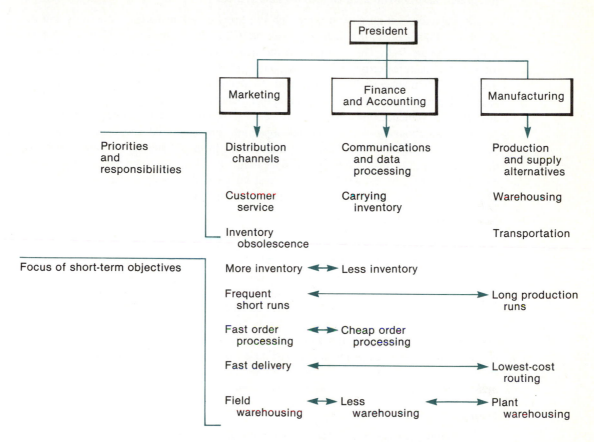

objectives identify what must be accomplished each year in order to do so. If Wal-Mart's market share is now 15 percent, then one likely annual objective might be "to have each regional office achieve a minimum 3 percent increase in market share in the next year." "Open two regional distribution centers in the Southeast in 1990" might be an annual objective that Wal-Mart's marketing and production managers consider essential if the firm is to achieve a 30 percent market share in five years. "Conclude arrangements for a $1 billion line of credit at 1/4 percent above prime in 1991" might be an annual objective of Wal-Mart's financial managers to support the operation of new distribution centers and the purchase of increased inventory in reaching the firm's long-term objective.

The link between short-term and long-term objectives should resemble cascades through the firm from basic long-term objectives to specific annual objectives in key operating areas. Thus, long-term objectives are segmented and reduced to annual objectives. The cascading effect has the added advantage of providing a clear reference for communication and negotiation, which may be necessary to integrate and coordinate objectives and activities at the operating level.[3]

Integrated and Coordinated Objectives and Activities

As the objective-setting cascades through the firm, it should force discussions and negotiations among operating managers with often conflicting priorities. Consider the example in Figure 9–1. The priorities of the marketing function can easily conflict with those of the manufacturing or finance/accounting function. As a result of these priorities, manufacturing managers might set annual efficiency objectives that only long production runs and plant warehousing can accomplish, whereas marketing managers might set customer convenience objectives that are better served by frequent, short production runs and field warehousing. Unless annual objectives are integrated and coordinated, each operating unit might pursue activities that detract from the success of other operating units and this might result in the failure of the long-term objectives (and the grand strategy). Thus, the setting of annual objectives must be viewed as a focal point for resolving conflicts between organizational units that might impede strategic performance.

Measurable Objectives

Annual objectives are more consistent when they each clearly state *what* is to be accomplished, *when* it will be accomplished, and *how* its accomplishment will be *measured*. These objectives can then be used to monitor both the effectiveness of each operating unit and the collective progress of all operating units toward the firm's long-term objectives. Figure 9–2 illustrates several effective and ineffective annual objectives. Measurable objectives make misunderstanding less likely among the interdependent operating managers who must implement the grand strategy. It is far easier to quantify the objectives of *line* units (e.g., production) than of certain *staff* areas (e.g., personnel). Difficulties in quantifying objectives can often be overcome by initially focusing on *measurable activity* and then identifying *measurable outcomes*.

Priorities

Due to timing considerations and the varying impact of annual objectives on strategic success, these objectives often have *relative priorities*.

Timing considerations often necessitate initiating or completing one activity before another is started. Figure 9–3 shows how a failure to take adequate account of such considerations hindered Citibank's implementation of a program designed to expand its credit card base as part of an ambitious market development strategy in the financial services industry. Citibank did not give sufficient priority to establishing the accounting procedures needed to support its marketing program.

Although all annual objectives are important, some deserve priority because of their particular impact on a strategy's success. If such priorities are not established, conflicting assumptions about the relative importance of annual objectives may inhibit progress toward

---

[3]Lawrence G. Hrebiniak and William F. Joyce, *Implementing Strategy* (New York: Macmillan, 1984), p. 110.

FIGURE 9–2

Operationalizing Measurable Annual Objectives

Examples of Deficient Annual Objectives	Examples of Annual Objectives with Measurable Criteria for Performance
To improve morale in the division (plant, department, etc.)	To reduce turnover (absenteeism, number of rejects, etc.) among sales managers by 10 percent by January 1, 1992 *Assumption:* Morale is related to measurable outcomes (i.e., high and low morale are associated with different results).
To improve support of the sales effort	To reduce the time lapse between order data and delivery by 8 percent (two days) by June 1, 1992 To reduce the cost of goods produced by 6 percent to support a product price decrease of 2 percent by December 1, 1992 To increase the rate of before- or on-schedule delivery by 5 percent by June 1, 1992
To develop a terminal version of the SAP computer program	To develop a terminal version of SAP capable of processing X bits of information in time Y at cost not to exceed Z per 1,000 bits by December 1, 1992 *Assumption:* There is virtually an infinite number of "terminal" or operational versions. Greater detail or specificity defines the objective more precisely
To enhance or improve the training effort	To increase the number of individuals capable of performing X operation in manufacturing by 20 percent by April 15, 1992 To increase the number of functional heads capable of assuming general management responsibility at the division level by 10 percent by July 15, 1992 To provide sales training to X number of individuals, resulting in an average increase in sales of 4 percent within six months after the training session
To improve the firm's image	To conduct a public opinion poll using random samples in the five largest U.S. metropolitan markets to determine average scores on 10 dimensions of corporate responsibility by May 15, 1992. To increase our score on those dimensions by an average of 7.5 percent by May 1, 1993

Source: Adapted from Laurence G. Hrebiniak and William F. Joyce, *Implementing Strategy* (New York: Macmillan, 1984), p. 116.

strategic effectiveness.[4] Facing the real possibility of bankruptcy in 1989 as it confronted an extended strike of pilots and machinists, Eastern Air Lines formulated a retrenchment strategy with several important annual objectives in labor relations, routes, fleet, and financial condition. But its highest priority was to maintain the integrity of selected debt-related measures so as to satisfy key creditors that might otherwise move to force bankruptcy.

[4]Ibid., p. 119.

STRATEGY IN ACTION 9–1

ANNUAL OBJECTIVES AND FUNCTIONAL STRATEGIES AT THE NATIONAL BASKETBALL ASSOCIATION

By the mid-1980s, a safe bet around sport circles was that the NBA would not survive to the 1990s. Of the NBA's 23 teams, 16 were losing money; the NBA's TV ratings were dropping; and buyers of "for sale" NBA franchises were nowhere to be found. In 1987 NBA Commissioner David J. Stern identified three annual objectives and five functional strategies to turn the situation around.

Annual Objectives for the NBA

Stern set three objectives for 1988:

1. Gross league revenues will be $325 million.
2. All 23 teams will generate a profit.
3. The NBA's TV ratings will increase by 10 percent.

Functional Strategies for the NBA

Stern used five functional strategies to accomplish these objectives:

1. *Stop overspending for players.* Selected NBA teams had courted bankruptcy by overspending for players. The new salary strategy set a salary pool beyond which a team

---

Source: Based on "Basketball: Business Is Booming," *Business Week*, October 28, 1986.

Priorities are established in various ways. A simple *ranking* may be based on discussion and negotiation during the planning process. However, this does not necessarily communicate the real difference in the importance of objectives, so such terms as *primary, top* and *secondary* may be used to indicate priority. Some firms assign *weights* (for example, 0–100 percent) to establish and communicate the relative priority of objectives. Whatever the method, recognizing priorities is an important dimension in the implementing action of annual objectives.

The qualities of good objectives discussed in Chapter 7—acceptable, flexible, suitable, motivating, understandable, and achievable—also apply to annual objectives. They will not be discussed again here, but the reader should review the discussion in Chapter 7 to appreciate these qualities common to all good objectives.

Benefits of Annual Objectives

One benefit of annual objectives is that they give operating personnel a better understanding of their role in the firm's mission. "Achieve $2.5 million in 1991 sales in the Chicago territory," "Develop an OSHA-approved safety program for handling acids at all Georgia Pacific plants in 1991," and "Reduce Ryder Truck's average age of accounts receivable to 31 days by the end of 1991" are examples of how annual objectives clarify the role of particular personnel in their firm's broader mission. Such *clarity of purpose*

STRATEGY IN ACTION 9–1   concluded

could not (normally) spend. The figure was arrived at by apportioning 53 percent of total NBA revenues equally among the 23 teams.

2. *Recruit businesspersons to buy sagging franchises.* Stern took charge of targeting and recruiting successful businesspeople to acquire problem NBA franchises. He felt such owners would understand, appreciate, and restore financial sanity to these franchises.

3. *Reduce overexposure on TV.* In 1984, over 200 NBA games were televised nationally on cable and network TV. This avalanche of games depressed NBA ratings, which reduced its advertising rates and revenues. Stern reduced the number of televised games to 55 regular season games and 20 playoff games. This strategy raised NBA ratings and increased its revenues.

4. *Institute a league MIS system.* An MIS system was developed that offered each team an item-by-item revenue-and-expense comparison with other teams and with NBA averages.

5. *Institute an antidrug program.* The NBA took the forefront among professional sports in fighting the drug problem. It developed a comprehensive drug program for its athletes that generated sizable goodwill toward the NBA.

can be a major force in effectively mobilizing a firm's "people assets."[5] Strategy in Action 9–1 illustrates how annual objectives were used to reverse the decline of the National Basketball Association (NBA).

A second benefit of annual objectives comes from the process of developing them. If the managers responsible for the accomplishment of the annual objectives have participated in their development, these objectives provide valid basis for addressing and accommodating conflicting concerns that might interfere with strategic effectiveness. Meetings to set annual objectives become the forum for raising and resolving conflicts between strategic intentions and operating realities.

A third benefit of annual objectives is that they provide *a basis for strategic control*. The control of strategy will be examined in detail in Chapter 11; but it is important to recognize here that annual objectives provide a clear, measurable basis for developing budgets, schedules, trigger points, and other mechanisms for controlling the implementation of strategy.

A fourth benefit of annual objectives is their *motivational payoffs*. Annual objectives that clarify personal and group roles in a firm's strategies and are also measurable, realistic,

[5]One recent book that supports this point is Thomas J. Peters and Robert H. Waterman, Jr., *In Search of Excellence* (New York: Harper & Row, 1982). Extensive literature on one of the best-known management techniques, management by objectives (MB), supports the value of objective setting in achieving desired performance. For a useful discussion of MBO, see Karl Albrecht, *Successful Management by Objectives* (Englewood Cliffs, N.J.: Prentice-Hall, 1978).

and challenging can be powerful motivators of managerial performance—particularly when these objectives are linked to the firm's reward structure.

Although annual objectives are a powerful tool for implementing a firm's strategy, other tools are necessary. Successful implementation also requires functional strategies, the *means* to accomplish the annual objectives.

DEVELOPING FUNCTIONAL STRATEGIES

Functional strategies are the short-term activities that each functional area *within* a firm must undertake in order to implement the grand strategy. Such strategies must be developed in the key areas of marketing, finance, production/operations, R&D and human resource management. They must be consistent with the long-term objectives and the grand strategy. They help implement the grand strategy by organizing and activating specific units of the firm (marketing, finance, production, etc.) to pursue that strategy in daily activities. In a sense, functional strategies translate thought (grand strategy) into action designed to accomplish specific annual objectives. For every major unit of a company, functional strategies identify and coordinate actions that support the grand strategy and help accomplish annual objectives. Strategy in Action 9–1 illustrates key functional strategies that were used to implement the NBA's turnaround in the late 1980s.

Figure 9–4 illustrates the important role of functional strategies in implementing corporate and business strategy. The corporate strategy defined General Cinema Corporation's general posture in the broad economy. The business strategy outlined the competitive posture of its operations in the movie theater industry. To increase the likelihood that these strategies would be successful, more specific strategies were needed for the firm's operating components. These functional strategies clarified the business strategy, giving specific, short-term guidance to operating managers. Figure 9–4 shows possible functional strategies in the areas of marketing, operations, and finance. Additional functional strategies were necessary, most notably in the personnel area.

Differences between Grand and Functional Strategies

To better understand the role of functional strategies within the strategic management process, they must be differentiated from grand strategies. Three basic characteristics differentiate functional strategies from grand strategies:

1. Time horizon covered.
2. Specificity.
3. Participants in strategy development.

Time Horizon

Functional strategies identify activities that are to be undertaken now or in the immediate future. Grand strategies focus on the firm's posture 3–5 years out. Sears, for example, might implement a spring 1991 marketing strategy of increasing price discounts and sales bonuses in its appliance division to reduce excess appliance inventory. This functional strategy focuses on immediate activities, whereas Sears's grand strategy focuses on its market posture as a full-line retail merchandiser in 1995.

FIGURE 9-3
A Case of Misplaced Priorities

CITIBANK
Citibank (New York State), N.A.
P.O. Box 227
Cheektowaga, New York 14225

January 18, 1988

Dear Silver Card Customer:

Several months ago we at Citibank began issuing The Silver Card to Goodyear customers.

The Silver Card revolving loan plan was established and offered by Citibank to provide a more effective nationwide tire and auto service credit card for customers of Goodyear's retail outlets.

As a national credit card, The Silver Card will offer you far more convenience than previously available. Our objective is to make The Silver Card the best credit card available anywhere.

Providing The Silver Card to over a million customers was an ambitious and complex effort, and it resulted in account processing problems for some account holders. We understand how frustrating these types of problems can be for you. We are working around the clock to assure that any problems will be corrected promptly.

In the meantime, we trust that you will continue to patronize your Goodyear retail outlet as they will render you the finest products and service available anywhere.

We apologize for any inconvenience we may have caused you, and we thank you for your patience and understanding.

Sincerely,

CITIBANK

Source: Mailed to the author, a Goodyear credit customer.

The shorter time horizon of functional strategies is critical to the successful implementation of the grand strategy for two reasons. First, it focuses the attention of functional managers on what needs to be done *now* to make the grand strategy work. Second, it allows functional managers to adjust to changing current conditions.

Specificity

Functional strategies are more specific than grand strategies. Grand strategies provide general direction. Functional strategies identify the specific activities that are to be undertaken in each functional area and thus show operating managers *how* they are expected to pursue annual objectives.

Figure 9–4 illustrates the difference in the specificity of grand and functional strategies.

FIGURE 9–4
Role of Functional Strategies at General Cinema Corporation

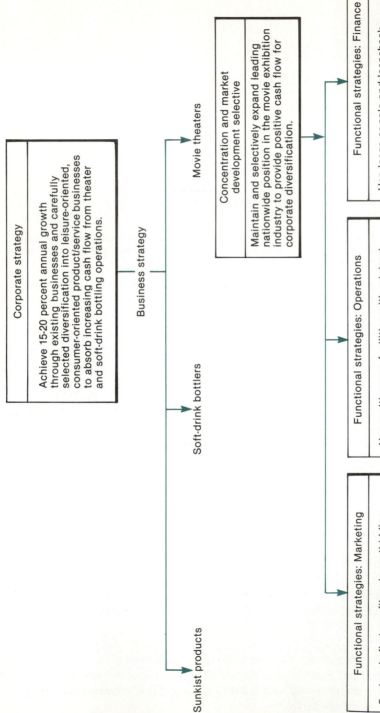

Sunkist products

Soft-drink bottlers

Movie theaters

Business strategy

Corporate strategy

Achieve 15-20 percent annual growth through existing businesses and carefully selected diversification into leisure-oriented, consumer-oriented product/service businesses to absorb increasing cash flow from theater and soft-drink bottling operations.

Concentration and market development selective

Maintain and selectively expand leading nationwide position in the movie exhibition industry to provide positive cash flow for corporate diversification.

Functional strategies: Marketing

Seek only first-run films by outbidding competition in each local market; provide primarily family-oriented movies, and maintain an admission price only slightly above that of local competition.

Offer concurrent movies of varying ratings (P, PG, R) at multiscreen locations to attract different audiences at the same location.

Functional strategies: Operations

Use multiscreen facilities with minimal maintenance requirements and a joint service area to serve each minitheater.

Locate movie theaters in popular regional shopping centers; selectively dominate theater locations in local markets to allow flexibility across areas in bidding for first-run films.

Functional strategies: Finance

Use lease or sale and leaseback arrangements of each theater to maximize cash flow for corporate expansions; seek profitability through volume, not higher ticket prices.

Selectively underwrite the production of quality films to ensure an adequate supply of first-run movies.

General Cinema's grand strategy gives its movie theater division broad direction on how to pursue a concentration and selective market development strategy. Two functional strategies in the marketing area give managers specific direction on what types of movies (first-run, primarily family-oriented, P, PG, R) should be shown and what pricing strategy (competitive in the local area) should be followed.

Specificity in functional strategies contributes to successful implementation for several reasons. First, it adds substance, completeness, and meaning to what a specific unit of the firm must do. The existence of specific functional strategies helps ensure that managers know what needs to be done and can focus on accomplishing results.[6] Second, specific functional strategies clarify for top management how functional managers intend to accomplish the grand strategy. This increases top management's confidence in and sense of control over the grand strategy. Third, specific functional strategies facilitate coordination among operating units *within* the firm by clarifying areas of interdependence and potential conflict.

Participants

Different people participate in strategy development at the functional and business levels. Business strategy is the responsibility of the general manager of a business unit. That manager typically delegates the development of functional strategy to subordinates charged with running the operating areas of the business. The manager of a business unit must establish long-term objectives and a strategy that corporate management feels contributes to corporate-level goals. Similarly, key operating managers must establish annual objectives and operating strategies that contribute to business-level goals. Just as business strategies and objectives are approved through negotiation between corporate managers and business managers, so too are annual objectives and functional strategies approved through negotiation between business managers and operating managers.[7]

Involving operating managers in the development of functional strategies improves their understanding of what must be done to achieve annual objectives and thus contributes to successful implementation. And perhaps more important, it increases the commitment of operating managers to the strategies developed.

The next several sections will indicate the key decision variables that should receive attention in the functional strategies of the various functional areas.

Functional Strategies in Production/Operations

The functional strategies of production operations management (POM) must be coordinated with the functional strategies of marketing if the firm is to succeed. Careful coordination of POM strategy with components of financial strategy (such as capital budgeting and investment decisions) and of personnel strategy is also necessary. Figure 9–5 illustrates the importance of such coordination by showing the different POM concerns

---

[6]While a company typically has one grand strategy, it should have a functional strategy for each major subunit and several operating strategies within the subunit. For example, a business may specify distinct pricing, promotion, and distribution strategies as well as an overall strategy to guide marketing operations.

[7]Arthur A. Thompson, Jr., and A. J. Strickland III, *Strategy Formulation and Implementation,* 2nd ed. (Plano, Tex.: Business Publications, 1983), p. 77.

FIGURE 9–5
Concerns Associated with Different Elements of a POM Strategy

Possible Elements of Strategy	Concomitant Conditions that May Affect or Place Demands on the Operations Activities
1. Compete as low-cost provider of goods or services	Broadens market. Requires longer production runs and fewer product changes. Requires special-purpose equipment and facilities.
2. Compete as high-quality provider	Often possible to obtain more profit per unit, and perhaps more total profit from a smaller volume of sales. Requires more quality-assurance effort and higher operating cost. Requires more precise equipment, which is more expensive. Requires highly skilled workers, necessitating higher wages and greater training efforts.
3. Stress customer service	Requires broader development of servicepeople and service parts and equipment. Requires rapid response to customer needs or changes in customer tastes, rapid and accurate information system, careful coordination. Requires a higher inventory investment.
4. Provide rapid and frequent introduction of new products	Requires versatile equipment and people. Has higher research and development costs. Has high retraining costs and high tooling and changeover costs. Provides lower volumes for each product and fewer opportunities for improvements due to the learning curve.
5. Strive for absolute growth	Requires accepting some projects or products with lower marginal value which reduces ROI. Diverts talents to areas of weakness instead of concentrating on strengths.

continued

that arise when different marketing/financial/personnel strategies are required as elements of the grand strategy.

Production/operations management is the core function of firms. That function converts inputs (raw materials, supplies, machines, and people) into value-enhanced output. The function is most easily associated with manufacturing firms, but it also applies to all other types of businesses (service and retail firms, for example).

The functional strategies of POM must guide decisions regarding (1) the basic nature of the firm's POM system, seeking an optimum balance between investment input and production/operations output and (2) location, facilities design, and process planning on a short-term basis. Figure 9–6 illustrates these concerns by highlighting key decision areas in which the POM strategies should provide guidance.

The facilities and equipment component of POM strategy involves decisions regarding plant location, size, equipment replacement, and facilities utilization that should be consistent with grand strategy and other operating strategies. In the mobile home industry for example, the facilities and equipment strategy of Winnebago was to locate one large, centralized, highly integrated production center (in Iowa) near its raw materials. On the other hand, Fleetwood, Inc., a California-based competitor, located dispersed, decentralized production facilities near markets and emphasized maximum equipment life and

FIGURE 9–5 (concluded)

Possible Elements of Strategy	Concomitant Conditions that May Affect or Place Demands on the Operations Activities
6. Seek vertical integration	Enables firm to control more of the process.
	May not have economies of scale at some stages of process.
	May require high capital investment as well as technology and skills beyond those currently available within the firm.
7. Maintain reserve capacity for flexibility	Provides ability to meet peak demands and quickly implement some contingency plans if forecasts are too low.
	Requires capital investment in idle capacity.
	Provides capability to grow during the lead time normally required for expansion.
8. Consolidate processing (centralize)	Can result in economies of scale.
	Permits location near one major customer or supplier.
	Vulnerability—entire operation can be halted by one strike, fire, or flood.
9. Disperse processing of service	Permits location near several market territories.
	Requires more complex coordination network, perhaps expensive data transmission, and duplication of some personnel and equipment at each location.
	If each location produces one product in the line, then other products still must be transported to be available at all locations.
	If each location specializes in a type of component for all products, the company is vulnerable to strike, fire, flood, etc.
	If each location provides the total product line, then economies of scale may not be realized.
10. Stress the use of mechanization, automation, robots	Requires high capital investment.
	Reduces flexibility.
	May affect labor relations.
	Makes maintenance more crucial.

less integrated, labor-intensive production processes. Both firms are leaders in the mobile home industry.

The purchasing component of POM strategy should address such questions as the following: Are the cost advantages of using only a few suppliers outweighed by the risk of overdependence? What criteria (for example, payment requirements) should be used in selecting vendors? Which vendors can provide "just-in-time" inventory and how can the business provide it to our customers? How can operations be supported by the volume and delivery requirements of purchases?

The planning and control component of POM strategy provides guidelines for ongoing production operations. These guidelines are intended to match production/operations resources to long-range, overall demand. The planning and control component often dictates whether production/operations will be demand oriented, inventory oriented, or subcontracting oriented. POM strategy may have to ensure that production/operations processes are geared to a cyclical or seasonal demand pattern. A bathing suit manufacturer, for example, would seek to maximize inventories in the early spring. If demand is less

FIGURE 9–6
Key Functional Strategies in POM

Functional Strategy	Typical Questions that the Functional Strategy Should Answer
Facilities and equipment	How centralized should the facilities be? (One big facility or several small facilities?)
	How integrated should the separate processes be?
	To what extent should further mechanization or automation be pursued?
	Should size and capacity be oriented toward peak or normal operating levels?
Purchasing	How many sources are needed?
	How should suppliers be selected, and how should relationships with suppliers be managed over time?
	What level of forward buying (hedging) is appropriate?
Operations planning and control	Should work be scheduled to order or to stock?
	What level of inventory is appropriate?
	How should inventory be used (FIFO/LIFO), controlled, and replenished?
	What are the key foci for control efforts (quality, labor cost, downtime, product use, other)?
	Should maintenance efforts be oriented to prevention or to breakdown?
	What emphasis should be placed on job specialization? Plant safety? The use of standards?

cyclical, POM strategy may aim at a steady level of production and inventories. Given unpredictable fluctuations in demand, idle capacity and excess capital investment may be avoided by using subcontractors to handle sudden increases.

Functional Strategies in Marketing

The role of the marketing function is to achieve the firm's objectives by bringing about the profitable sale of products/services in target markets. Functional marketing strategies should guide marketing managers in determining who will sell what, where, to whom, in what quantity, and how. These strategies typically entail four components: products, price, place, and promotion. Figure 9–7 illustrates the types of questions that the strategies must address in terms of these four components. Strategy in Action 9–2 shows how marketing strategies implemented a new business strategy at Peachtree Software.

The functional strategy for the *product component* of the marketing function should clearly identify the customer needs that the products/services are intended to meet. This strategy should provide a comprehensive statement of the product/service concept and of the target markets that the firm is seeking to serve. Such a statement fosters consistency and continuity in the daily activity of the marketing function.

The functional strategy for the *place component* identifies where, when, and by whom

FIGURE 9–7
Key Functional Strategies in Marketing

Functional Strategy	Typical Questions that the Functional Strategy Should Answer
Product (or service)	Which products do we emphasize?
	Which products/services contribute most to profitability?
	What product/service image do we seek to project?
	What consumer needs does the product/service seek to meet?
	What changes should be influencing our customer orientation?
Price	Are we competing primarily on price?
	Can we offer discounts or other pricing modifications?
	Are our pricing policies standard nationally, or is there regional control?
	What price segments are we targeting (high, medium, low, etc.)?
	What is the gross profit margin?
	Do we emphasize cost/demand or competition-oriented pricing?
Place	What level of market coverage is necessary?
	Are there priority geographic areas?
	What are the key channels of distribution?
	What are the channel objectives, structure, and management?
	Should the marketing managers change their degree of reliance on distributors, sales reps, and direct selling?
	What sales organization do we want?
	Is the sales force organized around territory, market, or product?
Promotion	What are the key promotion priorities and approaches?
	Which advertising/communication priorities and approaches are linked to different products, markets, and territories?
	Which media would be most consistent with the total marketing strategy?

the products/services are to be offered for sale. The primary concern here is the channels of distribution—the combination of marketing institutions through which the products/services flow to the final user. This component of marketing strategy guides decisions regarding channels (for example, single versus multiple channels) to ensure consistency with the total marketing effort.

The functional strategy for the *promotion component* defines how the firm will communicate with the target markets. This strategy should provide marketing managers with basic guides for the use and mix of advertising, personal selling, sales promotion, and media selection. It must be consistent with the other components of the marketing strategy, and due to its cost requirements, it should be closely integrated with the financial strategy.

The functional strategy for the *price component* is perhaps the single most important consideration in marketing. That strategy directly influences demand and supply, profitability, consumer perception, and regulatory response. The approach to pricing strategy may be cost oriented, market oriented, or competition (industry) oriented. With a cost-oriented approach, pricing decisions center on the total cost and usually involve an

STRATEGY
IN ACTION   **CHANGING FUNCTIONAL MARKETING STRATEGIES AT**
9–2   **PEACHTREE SOFTWARE**

Founded as an Atlanta-based retail computer store, Peachtree Software took off as a software company in the early 1980s, when IBM selected it to develop a high-end, PC-based accounting software program. Peachtree's grand strategy was to focus on the high-end user of PC-based accounting software via product and market development. Buoyed by the IBM connection, its optimistic management implemented functional strategies similar to those of other growing software companies:

1. The Peachtree Complete, the firm's flagship product, was priced at $4,760 to reflect development costs, customer support costs, and a quality image.
2. The number of employees increased from 21 in 1980 to 140 in 1986 as sales persons, customer support personnel, and new product development programmers were hired.
3. The product was sold direct to business users, mostly smaller companies.
4. A sizable block of common stock was sold to finance start-up costs.

The early results were exciting. Sales grew from $1.5 million in 1980 to $3 million in 1981, $6.2 million in 1982, and a high of $15.8 million in 1983. Unfortunately, after achieving a slight profit in 1981, Peachtree had continuous operating losses starting in 1982, including a $12 million operating loss in 1983.

By 1986, Peachtree's management had decided that major changes in strategy were necessary to save the firm. Sales had dropped to $2 million 1985. Management chose a new grand strategy—concentration on low-end accounting software and market development. It made these change in Peachtree's functional strategies:

1. Drop the price of Peachtree Complete from $4,760 to $199—a 96 percent reduction.
2. Cut the product line from 62 to 3.
3. Reduce employment from 140 to 29.
4. Eliminate direct selling and all but minimal customer support.
5. Increase borrowing to provide capital.
6. Focus almost exclusively on Peachtree's main product—Peachtree Complete.

The results have been impressive. Sales grew from $2 million in 1985 to $15 million in 1989, with operating profits a steady 30 percent of sales.

---

acceptable markup or target price ranges. With a market-oriented approach, pricing is based on consumer demand (e.g., gasoline pricing in a deregulated oil industry). With a competition-oriented approach, pricing decisions center on those of the firm's competitors. The discount pricing that occurred in the U.S. automobile industry in 1989–90, with several domestic and foreign producers usually following Chrysler's discount pricing initiatives, is an example of competition-oriented pricing. While one of these orientations may predominate in a firm's pricing strategy, that strategy is always influenced to some degree by the other orientations.

Functional Strategies in Finance and Accounting

While most functional strategies guide implementation in the immediate future, the time frame for functional strategies in the area of finance varies because these strategies direct the use of financial resources in support of the business strategy, long-term goals, and annual objectives. Functional financial strategies with longer time perspectives guide financial managers in long-term capital investment, debt financing, dividend allocation, and leveraging. Functional financial strategies designed to manage working capital and short-term assets have a more immediate focus. Figure 9–8 highlights some key questions that functional financial strategies must answer.

Capital acquisition is usually guided by long-term financial strategies since priorities in capital acquisition usually change infrequently over time. The desired level of debt versus equity versus internal long-term financing of business activities is a common issue in capital acquisition strategy. For example, Delta Airlines has a long-standing functional strategy that seeks to minimize the level of debt in proportion to equity and to fund capital needs internally, whereas General Cinema Corporation has a long-standing functional strategy of expanding its theater and soft-drink bottling facilities through long-term leasing. The debt-to-equity ratios of these two firms are approximately 0.50 and 2.0, respectively. Both firms have had similar records of steady profitable growth over the last 20 years, yet they represent two very different functional strategies for capital acquisition.

Capital allocation, like capital acquisition, is a functional financial strategy of major importance. Growth-oriented grand strategies generally require numerous major investments in facilities, projects, acquisitions, and people. Since it is usually neither possible nor desirable to make these investments immediately, the capital allocation strategy sets priorities and timing for them. This also helps manage conflicting priorities for capital resources among operating managers.

Retrenchment or stability often require a financial strategy that focuses on the reallocation of existing capital resources. This could necessitate pruning product lines and reallocating production facilities or personnel. Under the best of circumstances, the overlapping careers and aspirations of key operating managers create a politically charged organizational setting. With retrenchment, a functional strategy that clearly delineates capital allocation priorities becomes particularly important for effective implementation in such a setting.

Capital allocation strategy frequently defines the level of capital expenditure that is to be delegated to operating managers. If a firm is pursuing a strategy of rapid growth, timely responses to an evolving market may be facilitated by flexibility in making capital expenditures at the operating level. On the other hand, if a firm is pursuing a strategy of retrenchment, it may carefully control capital expenditures at the operating level.

Dividend management is an integral part of a firm's financing. Lower dividends increase the internal funds available for growth, and internal financing reduces the need for external, often debt, financing. However, stable dividends often enhance the market price of a firm's stock. Therefore, the strategy guiding dividend management must support the firm's posture toward equity markets.

Working capital is critical to the daily operation of firms, and the working capital requirements of a firm are influenced by seasonal and cyclical fluctuations, the size of

FIGURE 9–8
Key Functional Strategies in Finance

Key Functional Strategy	Typical Questions that the Functional Strategy Should Answer
Capital acquisition	What is an acceptable cost of capital?
	What is the desired proportion of short- and long-term debt? Preferred and common equity?
	What balance is desired between internal and external funding?
	What risk and ownership restrictions are appropriate?
	What level and forms of leasing should be used?
Capital allocation	What are the priorities for capital allocation projects?
	On what basis should the final selection of projects be made?
	What level of capital allocation can be made by operating managers without higher approval?
Dividend and working capital management	What portion of earnings should be paid out as dividends?
	How important is dividend stability?
	Are things other than cash appropriate as dividends?
	What are the cash flow requirements? The minimum and maximum cash balances?
	How liberal/conservative should the credit policies be?
	What limits, payment terms, and collection procedures are necessary?
	What payment timing and procedure should be followed?

the firm, and the pattern of the firm's receipts and disbursements. The working capital component of financial strategy must be built on accurate projections of cash flow and must provide cash management guidelines for conserving and rebuilding the cash balances required for daily operation.

Functional Strategies in Research and Development

With the increasing rate of technological change in most competitive industries, research and development (R&D) has assumed a key functional role in many firms. In the technology-intensive computer and pharmaceutical industries, for example, firms typically spend between 4 and 6 percent of their sales dollars on R&D. In other industries, such as the hotel/motel and construction industries, R&D spending is less than 1 percent of sales. Thus, functional R&D strategies may be more critical instruments of the business strategy in some industries than in others.

Figure 9–9 illustrates the types of questions addressed by functional R&D strategies. First, R&D strategy should clarify whether basic research or product development research will be emphasized. Several major oil companies now have solar energy subsidiaries in which basic research is emphasized, while the smaller oil companies emphasize product development research.

Directly related to the choice of emphasis between basic research and product devel-

FIGURE 9–9
Key Functional Strategies in R&D

R&D Decision Area	Typical Questions that the Functional Strategy Should Answer
Basic research versus product development	To what extent should innovation and breakthrough research be emphasized? In relation to the emphasis on product development, refinement, and modification? What new projects are necessary to support growth?
Time horizon	Is the emphasis short term or long term? Which orientation best supports the business strategy? The marketing and production strategy?
Organizational fit	Should R&D be done in-house or contracted out? Should R&D be centralized or decentralized? What should be the relationship between the R&D units and product managers? Marketing managers? Production managers?
Basic R&D posture	Should the firm maintain an offensive posture, seeking to lead innovation in its industry? Should the firm adopt a defensive posture, responding to the innovations of its competitors?

opment is the time horizon for R&D efforts. Should these efforts be focused on the near term or the long term? The solar energy subsidiaries of the major oil companies have long-term perspectives, while the smaller oil companies want to establish a competitive niche in the growing solar industry.

Functional R&D strategies should also guide organization of the R&D function. For example, should R&D work be conducted solely within the firm, or should portions of that work be contracted out? A closely related issue is whether R&D should be centralized or decentralized.

Decisions on all of the above questions are influenced by the firm's basic R&D posture, which can be offensive or defensive, or both. If that posture is offensive, as is true for small, high-technology firms, the firm will emphasize technological innovation and new product development as the basis for its future success. This orientation entails high risks (and high payoffs) and demands considerable technological skill, forecasting expertise, and the ability to quickly transform innovations into commercial products.

A defensive R&D posture emphasizes product modification and the ability to copy or acquire new technology. American Motors (AMC) is a good example of a firm with such an R&D posture. Faced with the massive R&D budgets of General Motors, Ford, and foreign competitors, AMC placed R&D emphasis on bolstering the product life cycle of its prime products (particularly Jeeps).

Large companies with some degree of technological leadership often use a combination of offensive and defensive R&D strategy. GE in the electrical industry, IBM in the computer industry, and Du Pont in the chemical industry all have a defensive R&D posture for currently available products *and* an offensive R&D posture in basic, long-term research.

FIGURE 9–10
Key Functional Strategies in HRM

Functional Strategy	Typical Questions that the Functional Strategy Should Answer
Recruitment, selection, and orientation	What key human resources are needed to support the chosen strategy?
	How do we recruit these human resources?
	How sophisticated should our selection process be?
	How should we introduce new employees to the organization?
Career development and training	What are our future human resource needs?
	How can we prepare our people to meet these needs?
	How can we help our people develop?
Compensation	What levels of pay are appropriate for the tasks we require?
	How can we motivate and retain good people?
	How should we interpret our payment, incentive, benefit, and seniority policies?
Evaluation, discipline, and control	How often should we evaluate our people? Formally or informally?
	What disciplinary steps should we take to deal with poor performance or inappropriate behavior?
	In what ways should we "control" individual and group performance?
Labor relations and equal opportunity requirements	How can we maximize labor-management cooperation?
	How do our personnel practices affect women/minorities?
	Should we have hiring priorities?

Functional Strategies in Human Resource Management (HRM)

The strategic importance of functional strategies in the HRM has become more widely accepted in recent years. HRM management aids in accomplishing the grand strategy by ensuring the development of managerial talent and competent employees and the presence of systems to manage compensation and regulatory concerns. Functional HRM strategies should guide the effective utilization of human resources to achieve both the firm's annual objectives and employees' satisfaction and development. These strategies involve the areas shown in Figure 9–10. The recruitment, selection, and orientation component of functional personal strategies should establish the basic parameters for bringing new people into a firm and adapting them to "the way things are done" in the firm. The career development and training component should guide the actions that personnel takes to meet the future human resource needs of the grand strategy. Merrill Lynch, a major brokerage firm whose long-term corporate strategy is to become a diversified financial service institution, has moved into such areas as investment banking, consumer credit, and venture capital. In support of its long-term objectives, it has incorporated extensive early-career training and ongoing career development programs to meet its expanding need for personnel with multiple competences.

Larger organizations need functional HRM strategies that guide decisions regarding labor relations, EEOC requirements, and employee compensation, discipline, and control.

To summarize, functional strategies specify how each major activity of a firm contributes to the implementation of the firm's grand strategy. The specificity of functional strategies and the involvement of operating managers in their development help ensure understanding of and commitment to the chosen strategy. A related step in implementing that strategy is the development of policies that guide and control the decisions of operating managers and their subordinates.

DEVELOPING AND COMMUNICATING CONCISE POLICIES

Policies are directives designed to guide the thinking, decisions, and actions of managers and their subordinates in implementing a firm's strategy. Policies provide guidelines for establishing and controlling ongoing operations in a manner consistent with the firm's strategic objectives. Often referred to as standard operating procedures, policies increase managerial effectiveness by standardizing many routine decisions and controlling the discretion of managers and subordinates in implementing functional strategies. Logically, policies should be derived from functional strategies (and, in some instances, from corporate or business strategies) with the key purpose of aiding strategy execution.[8] Strategy in Action 9–3 illustrates selected policies of several well-known firms.

The Purpose of Policies

Policies communicate specific guides to decisions. They are designed to control and reinforce the implementation of functional strategies and the grand strategy, and they do this in several ways:

1. *Policies establish indirect control over independent action* by clearly stating how things are to be done *now*. By limiting discretion, policies in effect control decisions and the conduct of activities without direct intervention by top management.
2. *Policies promote uniform handling of similar activities*. This facilitates the coordination of work tasks and helps reduce friction arising from favoritism, discrimination, and the disparate handling of common functions.

---

[8]The term *policy* has various definitions in management literature. Some authors and practitioners equate policy with strategy. Others do this inadvertently by using "policy" as a synonym for company mission, purpose, or culture. Still other authors and practitioners differentiate policy in terms of "levels" associated respectively with purpose, mission, and strategy. "Our policy is to make a positive contribution to the communities and societies we live in" and "our policy is not to diversify out of the hamburger business" are two examples of the breadth of what some call policies. This book defines *policy* much more narrowly as specific guides to managerial action and decisions in the implementation of strategy. This definition permits a sharper distinction between the formulation and implementation of functional strategies. And, of even greater importance, it focuses the tangible value of the policy concept where it can be most useful—as a key administrative tool to enhance effective implementation and execution of strategy.

3. *Policies ensure quicker decisions* by standardizing answers to previously answered questions that would otherwise recur and be pushed up the management hierarchy again and again.

4. *Policies institutionalize basic aspects of organization behavior.* This minimizes conflicting practices and establishes consistent patterns of action in attempts to make the strategy work.

5. *Policies reduce uncertainty in repetitive and day-to-day decision making,* thereby providing a necessary foundation for coordinated, efficient efforts.

6. *Policies counteract resistant to or rejection of chosen strategies by organization members.* When major strategic change is undertaken, unambiguous operating policies clarify what is expected and facilitate acceptance, particularly when operating managers participate in policy development.

7. *Policies offer predetermined answers to routine problems.* This greatly expedites dealing with both ordinary and extraordinary problems—with the former, by referring to these answers; with the latter, by giving managers more time to cope with them.

8. *Policies afford managers a mechanism for avoiding hasty and ill-conceived decisions in changing operations.* Prevailing policy can always be used as a reason for not yielding to emotion-based, expedient, or temporarily valid arguments for altering procedures and practices.[9]

Policies may be written and formal or unwritten and informal. Informal, unwritten policies are usually associated with a strategic need for competitive secrecy. Some policies of this kind, such as "promotion from within," are widely known (or expected) by employees and implicitly sanctioned by management. Managers and employees often like the latitude "granted" by unwritten and informal policies. However, such policies may detract from the long-term success of a strategy. Formal, written policies have at least seven advantages:

1. They required managers to think through the policy's meaning, content, and intended use.

2. They reduced misunderstanding.

3. They make equitable and consistent treatment of problems more likely.

4. They ensured unalterable transmission of policies.

5. They communicate the authorization or sanction of policies more clearly.

6. They supply a convenient and authoritative reference.

7. They systematically enhanced indirect control and organizationwide coordination of the key purposes of policies.[10]

The strategic significance of policies can vary. At one extreme are such policies as travel reimbursement procedures, which are really work rules and may not be linked to

---

[9]These eight points are adapted from related discussion by Richard H. Buskirk, *Business and Administrative Policy* (New York: John Wiley & Sons, 1971), pp. 145–55; Thompson and Strickland, *Strategy Formulation,* pp. 377–79; Milton J. Alexander, *Business Strategy and Policy* (Atlanta: University Publications, 1983), chap. 3.

[10]Adapted from Robert G. Murdick, R. Carl Moor, Richard H. Eckhouse, and Thomas W. Zimmerer, *Business Policy: A Framework for Analysis* (Columbus, Ohio: Grid, 1984), p. 65.

SELECTED POLICIES THAT AID STRATEGY IMPLEMENTATION

3M Corporation has a *personnel policy*, called the 15 percent rule, that allows virtually any employee to spend up to 15 percent of the workweek on anything that he or she wants to, as long as it's product related.

(This policy supports 3M's corporate strategy of being a highly innovative manufacturer, with each division required to have a quarter of its annual sales come from products introduced within the past five years.)

Wendy's has a purchasing policy that gives local store managers the authority to buy fresh meat and produce locally rather than from regionally designated or company-owned sources.

(This policy supports Wendy's functional strategy of having fresh, unfrozen hamburgers daily.)

General Cinema has a *financial policy* that requires annual capital investment in movie theaters not to exceed annual depreciation.

(By seeing that capital investment is no greater than depreciation, this policy supports General Cinema's financial strategy of maximizing cash flow—in this case, all profit—to its growth areas. The policy also reinforces General Cinema's financial strategy of leasing as much as possible.)

IBM had a *marketing policy* of not giving free IBM personal computers (PCs) to any person or organization.

(This policy attempted to support IBM's image strategy by maintaining its image as a professional, high-value, service business as it sought to dominate the PC market.)

Crown, Cork, and Seal Company has an *R&D policy* of not investing any financial or people resources in basic research.

(This policy supports Crown, Cork and Seal's functional strategy, which emphasizes customer service, not technical leadership.)

Citizen & Southern's Bank of South Carolina has an *operating policy* that requires annual renewal of the financial statement of all personal borrowers.

(This policy supports C&S's financial strategy, which seeks to maintain a loan-to-loss ratio below the industry norm.)

the implementation of a strategy. At the other extreme are organizationwide policies that are virtually functional strategies, such as Wendy's requirement that every location invest 1 percent of its gross revenue in local advertising.

Policies can be externally imposed or internally derived. Policies regarding equal employment practices are often developed in compliance with external (government) requirements, and policies regarding leasing or depreciation may be strongly influenced by current tax regulations.

Regardless of the origin, formality, and nature of policies, the key point to bear in mind is the valuable role that they can play in strategy implementation. Existing policies should be examined with a view to ensuring their guidance and control of operating activities in a manner consistent with current business and functional strategies. Communicating specific policies will help overcome resistance to strategic change and foster commitment to successful strategy implementation.

SUMMARY

The first concern in the implementation of a grand strategy is to translate that strategy into action throughout the organization. This chapter discussed three important tools for accomplishing this: annual objectives, functional strategies, and policies.

Annual objectives are derived from long-term objectives, which they translate into current targets. They differ from long-term objectives in time frame, specificity, and measurement. To be effective in strategy implementation, they must be integrated and coordinated. They must also be consistent, measurable, and prioritized.

Functional strategies are derived from the business strategy. They identify the specific, immediate actions that must be taken in key functional areas to implement the grand strategy.

Policies provide another means for directing and controlling behavior, decisions, and actions at the firm's operating levels in a manner consistent with its business and functional strategies. Effective policies channel actions, behavior, decisions, and practices to promote strategic accomplishment.

Annual objectives, functional strategies, and policies represent only the start of the strategy implementation. The strategy must be institutionalized—must permeate the firm. The next chapter examines this phase of strategy implementation.

QUESTIONS FOR DISCUSSION

1. How does the concept "Translate thought into action" bear on the relationship between grand strategy and operating strategy? Between long-term and short-term objectives?

2. How do functional strategies differ from corporate and business strategies?

3. What key concerns must functional strategies address in marketing? Finance? POM? Personnel?

4. How do policies aid strategy implementation? Illustrate your answer.

5. Illustrate a policy, an objective, and a functional strategy in your personal career strategy.

6. Why are annual objectives needed when long-term objectives are already available?

BIBLIOGRAPHY

Allio, R. J. "Formulating Global Strategy," *Planning Review,* March–April 1989, pp. 22–29.

Boag, David A., and Ali Dastmalchian. "Market Vulnerability and the Design and Management of the Marketing Function in Small Firms." *Journal of Small Business Management,* October 1988, p. 37.

Charalambides, L. C., "Designing Communication Support Systems for Strategic Planning." *Long Range Planning,* December 1988, pp. 93–100.

Coates, N. "The Globalization of the Motor Vehicle Manufacturing Industry." *Planning Review,* January–February 1989, pp. 34–39.

David, F. R. "How Companies Define Their Mission." *Long Range Planning,* February 1989, pp. 90–97.

Drucker, Peter M. *The Practice of Management.* (New York: Harper & Row, 1954).

Freund, Y. P. "Critical Success Factors." *Planning Review,* March–April 1988, pp. 20–23.

Kazanjian N. and Jay Golbraith, *Strategy Implementation: Structure, Systems, and Process,* (St. Paul, Minn.: West Publishing, 1986).

"Inside Met Life's Growth Strategy." Interview with CEO J. Creedon. *Journal of Business Strategy,* January–February 1988, pp. 23–27.

Miller, J. G., and W. Hayslip. "Implementing Manufacturing Strategic Planning." *Planning Review,* July–August 1989, pp. 22–29.

Nielson, Richard P. "Cooperative Strategy in Marketing." *Business Horizons,* July–August 1987, p. 61.

Ohmae, K. "Getting Back to Strategy." *Harvard Business Review,* September–October 1988, pp. 149–56.

Peterson, R. T. "An Analysis of New Product Ideas." *Journal of Small Business Management,* April 1988, pp. 25–31.

————."The Marketing Concept vs. Other Strategies." *Journal of Small Business Management,* January 1989, pp. 38–46.

Randolph, W. A., and B. Z. Posner. "What Every Manager Needs to Know about Project Management." *Sloan Management Review,* Summer 1988, pp. 65–74.

Shank, J. K., and V. Govindarajan. "Making Strategy Explicit in Cost Analysis." *Sloan Management Review,* Spring 1988, pp. 19–30.

Stern, Joel. "Think Cash and Risk—Forget ESP." *Planning Review,* January–February 1988, p. 6.

Stonich, Paul. *Implementing Strategy: Making Strategy Happen.* (New York: Ballinger, 1982).

Wheelwright, S., and N. S. Langowitz. "Plus Development Corporation: Joint Venturing A Breakthrough Product." *Planning Review,* July–August 1989, pp. 6–21.

"Winning Turnaround Strategies at Black and Decker." Interview with Marketing Executive G. DiCamillo. *Journal of Business Strategy,* March 1988, pp. 30–33.

CHAPTER 9 COHESION CASE

IMPLEMENTATION: ORGANIZING FOR ACTION

Bryson's managers moved quickly to set a few key annual objectives to guide the efforts of their subordinates. After discussing their corporate and business strategies within each unit, the following annual objectives were established.

1. *Safety*: complete the year without any accidents or spills of hazardous materials.
2. *RCRA facility*: conclude the merger of Wall Chemical into Bryson.
3. *Revenues*: Achieve the following revenues at the end of 1990:

	Columbia	Memphis	Cleanway	Total
Transp. & management srvs.	$6,651	$1,578	$ 0	$ 8,769
Remedial services	1,765	277	0	2,042
Recycling & recovery srvs.	0	3,093	0	3,093
Cleanway dry cleaner srvs.	0	0	465	465
	8,416	4,948	465	14,369

4. *Profit*: Achieve the following revenues at the end of 1990:

	Columbia	Memphis	Cleanway	Total
Transp. & management srvs.	$ 606	$ 162	$ 0	$ 768
Remedial services	465	(31)	0	434
Recycling & recovery srvs.	0	668	0	668
Cleanway dry cleaner srvs.	0	0	183	183
	1,071	799	183	2,053

5. *Memphis*: the Memphis-area operations have the following annual objectives during 1990:
   a. Complete the initial construction of the Wall Chemical facility, to be called "Bryson Recovery Systems," at a cost of $600,000 no later than May 1, 1990.
   b. Establish an effective, three-person telemarketing organization serving Bryson's three revenue streams in Memphis (transportation, remedial services, and recycling/recovery) by June 30, 1990.
   c. Create an easily functioning administrative process and coordination with the remedial group in the Columbia headquarters.
6. *Columbia*: the Columbia-area operations established the following 1990 objectives:
   a. Develop a remedial services management group capable of managing remedial services across every Bryson location during 1990.
   b. Develop a transportation and management services management group capable of managing transportation and management services across every Bryson location during 1990.

    c. Complete the creation of a computer-based management information system to support the management of every unit of Bryson by December 1, 1990.

    d. Train a new sales manager for the eastern area that Bryson serves and train an operations manager to oversee all of Bryson's transportation operations.

7. *Cleanway*: expand the Cleanway customer base by establishing at least 30 Cleanway customers in the Atlanta market by August 1, 1990.

Bryson managers then established the following functional strategies to guide the implementation of its competitive strategies.

1. *Sales*. Create a strong outside sales group supported by a well-trained, aggressive telemarketing and telemanagement group at Columbia and Memphis that work effectively as a team to build Bryson's base business and to uncover timely opportunities for remedial service jobs. The sale of remedial services would involve remedial services' managers (Ullery, Cain, and Woolbright) early in the sales process once a potential customer need is identified.

2. *Operations*. Create a centralized (Columbia-based) computer-based management of daily transportation services coordinated with each location to manage transportation equipment utilization in the most efficient manner. Develop an increasingly centralized (Columbia-based) remedial services group that has remedial teams capable of responding to requests for remedial services throughout the Bryson market areas, while keeping a core group of teams closest to the main activity center so they can be used in other activities when remedial business is slow. Cleanway will seek to automate its dry cleaner filter handling process (separating the metal casing from the inner paper filter) early in 1990 so overall volume can increase without increasing personnel at the Montgomery site until 1991, when the pending Part B permit's approval should be more predictable.

3. *Administration and finance*. Expand the current computer system to serve as a companywide management information system informing managers in each division, unit, and location of the information they need on a weekly (or whatever time interval needed) basis to manage their area of responsibility. Increase current lines of credit, providing working capital from $1 million to $2 million in 1990, and prepare for similar increases annually the following three years. Monitor cash flow on a daily basis and initiate actions to improve it—particularly in collecting receivables and credit checks on new customers.

4. *Marketing*. Set up a generator data base using information collected by each states' EPA office and update it quarterly. Incorporate it in an ongoing target market program integrated with the planning of monthly sales activities. Assign a "know competitor" to each manager, with the responsibility of developing full information about that competitor one month later and continuously updating that information. Add a new competitor to each manager's "special group" on a regular basis until all key competitors are well monitored.

5. *Human resource management*. Expand the current hazwaste training program to ensure modules appropriate to each job assignment are provided on a regular basis. Create a position of safety director, responsible for introductory, ongoing, and special update training of all operating and sales personnel.

Bryson managers also established several policies intended to support the objectives and strategies to which Bryson's managers committed the organization in their planning meetings. Examples include the following.

1. All operating personnel must have an annual physical exam to monitor their health and possible problems associated with working around hazardous materials.
2. All Bryson personnel are subject to random drug testing at least four times per year.
3. Every driver on the road in Bryson equipment must call in to dispatch between 4 P.M. and 6 P.M. daily and again between 7 A.M. and 9 A.M. daily so transportation schedulers know your exact location at the start and the end of each day.
4. No piece of Bryson equipment and no transportation or remedial service job can be operated or worked on unless you have completed all of Bryson's RCRA-certified training programs.
5. New customer credit checks through Dun & Bradstreet must be completed and approved before services can commence for that customer.
6. Sales commissions will be paid to sales personnel responsible for the territory within which the customer is located.

You have seen examples of annual objectives, functional strategies, and policies Bryson's managers have designed to implement their corporate, business, and competitive strategies. What is your evaluation of them? Where would you make improvements or additions? What would they be?

10 IMPLEMENTING STRATEGY THROUGH STRUCTURE, LEADERSHIP, AND CULTURE

Say "IBM" to European or Japanese executives, and they are likely to nod knowingly and respectfully. Technologically powerful, active in more than 130 countries, the world's fifth-largest industrial corporation is emblematic of America's hopes for winning on the rugged fields of global competition. Yet IBM faltered as it moved into the 1990s. In the late 1980s, annual sales growth, usually over 15 percent, dropped below 3 percent.

John Akers, IBM's chairman and CEO, responded to the situation with candor. "We took our eye off the ball," he observed "We decided to be careful instead of aggressive, and we were trying to solve some problems that were more IBM's than the customer's." He concluded that IBM's strategy of product development for the 1990s was basically sound, that IBM's fundamental problems lay in the way its 387,000 people were organized.[1]

Akers set out to remedy those problems by reinventing the firm. To reorganize IBM's bureaucratic management structure into a structure designed to address customer needs, he divided IBM into seven autonomous business units and an eighth unit that handled marketing for all of the others. He systematically pushed responsibility down the ranks by putting the firm's fate in the hands of the general managers of these autonomous business units. Sales had been the sole route to the top at IBM, but Akers added many top executives with strong technological backgrounds. This he believed, would change IBM's longtime practice of telling customers what it thought was good for them to one in which technologically capable executives listened to customers and became problem solvers. To sanction this new "culture," he took the unprecedented step of having several key customers participate in IBM's annual strategic planning conferences. And finally, Akers changed IBM's reward system, in which bonuses had been based on sales of existing products, to emphasize the varied challenges facing each of the autonomous business units.[2]

---

[1]"Restructuring IBM," *Business Week*, August 8, 1989, p. 22.

[2]Ibid., p. 24.

FIGURE 10–1
McKinsey 7–S Framework

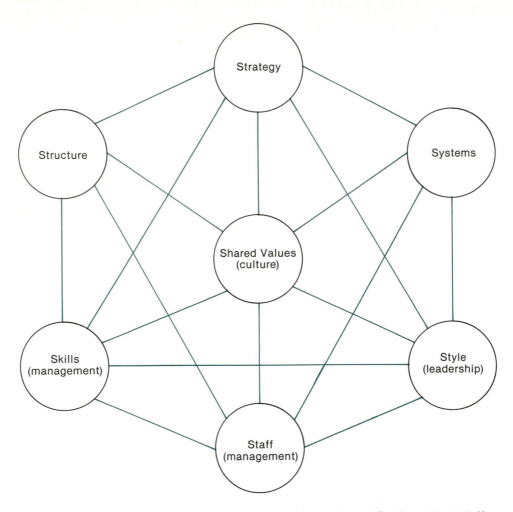

Source: Adapted from Thomas J. Peters and Robert H. Waterman, Jr., *In Search of Excellence*, (New York: Harper & Row, 1982), p. 11.

The IBM example shows that a firm must be properly *organized for action* if its strategy is to be successful. Although annual objectives, functional strategies, and specific policies provide important means of communicating what must be done to implement the firm's strategy, more is needed to implement that strategy successfully. To be successfully implemented, the strategy must also be *institutionalized*—must permeate the firm's day-to-day life. Four organization elements provide the fundamental, long-term means for institutionalizing the firm's strategy: (1) structure, (2) leadership, (3) culture, and (4) rewards.

IBM's John Akers focused on these four elements as he prepared IBM for global competiveness in the 21st century. He revamped IBM's *organizational structure,* allowing autonomous business units to position the firm close to appropriate customer groups. He brought in a new type of *leadership,* giving technical people greater access to top positions. He sought to transform IBM's inwardly focused *culture* into a customer-driven culture. And he revised IBM's *reward systems* to reinforce these strategic changes.

In the 1980s these topics received considerable attention from executives, authors, and researchers seeking to understand the reasons behind the superior performance among the "best" American companies. *In Search of Excellence* is perhaps the best known of these efforts. It offers a framework identifying the key factors found in the research of authors Tom Peters and Robert Waterman to best explain superior performance. That framework, known as the McKinsey 7–S Framework, is provided in Figure 10–1. This framework provides a useful visualization of the key components managers must consider in succesffully institutionalizing a strategy—making sure it permeates the day-to-day life of the firm.

Once the strategy has been designed, the McKinsey Framework suggests managers focus on six components to ensure effective execution: structure, systems, shared values (culture), skills, style, and staff. This chapter organizes these six components into four basic elements through which managers can implement strategy. The first is *structure*—the basic way the firm's different activities are organized. Second is leadership, encompassing the need to establish an effective *style* as well as the necessary *staff* and *skills* to execute the strategy. The third element is culture—the *shared values* that create the norms of individual behavior and the tone of the organization. The final elements are the *systems* for rewarding performance as well as monitoring and controlling organizational action. Reward systems are examined in this chapter, while a discussion of systems for monitoring and controlling organizational action is reserved for Chapter 11.

This chapter has these major aims as it introduces you to these four elements: (1) to examine the advantages and disadvantages of structural alternatives and their role in strategy implementation; (2) to discuss the leadership dimensions that are important in strategy implementation; (3) to explain how the organizational culture influences organizational life and to examine ways of managing the strategy-culture relationship; and (4) to show how reward systems can be used to institutionalize a strategy.

STRUCTURING AN EFFECTIVE ORGANIZATION

Successful strategy implementation depends in large part on the firm's primary organizational structure. That structure identifies key activities within the firm and the manner in which they will be coordinated to achieve the firm's strategic purpose. The preceding IBM example referred to a change from a highly centralized, functional structure to a highly decentralized, strategic business unit structure that IBM's top managers viewed as more consistent with the firm's product development strategy.

A primary organizational structure comprises the firm's major elements, components, or differentiated units. Such a structure portrays how key tasks and activities have been divided to achieve efficiency and effectiveness.

The primary structure is not the only means for getting "organized" to implement the strategy. Reward systems, coordination terms, planning procedures, and information and budgetary systems are among the other means that often become necessary. However, it is through the primary structure that strategists attempt to position the firm so as to execute its strategy in a manner that balances internal efficiency and overall effectiveness.

Primary Organizational Structures and Their Strategy-Related Pros and Cons

Matching the structure to the strategy is a fundamental task of company strategists. To understand how that task is handled, we must first review the five basic primary structures. We will then turn to guidelines for matching structure to strategy.

The five basic primary structures are: (1) functional organization, (2) geographic organization, (3) divisional organization, (4) strategic business units, and (5) matrix organization. Each of these structures has advantages and disadvantages that strategists must consider when choosing an organization form.

Functional Organizational Structure

Functional structures predominate in firms with a single or narrow product focus. Such firms require well-defined skills and areas of specialization in order to build competitive advantages in providing their products or services. Dividing tasks into functional specialties enables the personnel of these firms to concentrate on only one aspect of the necessary work. This allows use of the latest technical skills and develops a high level of efficiency.

Product, customer, or technology considerations determine the identity of the parts in a functional structure. A hotel business might be organized around housekeeping (maids), the front desk, maintenance, restaurant operations, reservations and sales, accounting, and personnel. An equipment manufacturer might be organized around production, engineering/quality control, purchasing, marketing, personnel, and finance/accounting. Two examples of functional organizations are illustrated in Figure 10–2.

The strategic challenge presented by the functional structure is effective coordination of the functional units. The narrow technical expertise achieved through specialization can lead to limited perspectives and to differences in the priorities of the functional units. Specialists may see the firm's strategic issues primarily as "marketing" problems or "production" problems. The potential conflict among functional units makes the coordinating role of the chief executive critical. Integrating devices (such as project teams or planning committees) are frequently used in functionally organized firms to enhance coordination and to facilitate understanding across functional areas.

Geographic Organizational Structure

Firms often grow by expanding the sale of their products or services to new geographic areas. In these areas, they frequently encounter differences that necessitate different approaches in producing, providing, or selling their products or services. Structuring by geographic areas is usually required to accommodate these differences. Thus, Holiday

FIGURE 10–2
Functional Organization Structures

A "typical" functional structure:

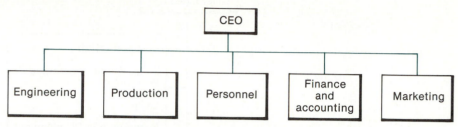

A process-oriented functional structure (an electronics distributor):

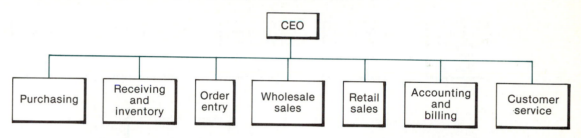

Strategic Advantages	Strategic Disadvantages
1. Achieves efficiency through specialization.	1. Promotes narrow specialization and functional rivalry or conflict.
2. Develops functional expertise.	2. Creates difficulties in functional coordination and interfunctional decision making.
3. Differentiates and delegates day-to-day operating decisions.	
4. Retains centralized control of strategic decisions.	3. Limits development of general managers.
5. Tightly links structure to strategy by designating key activities as separate units.	4. Has a strong potential for interfunctional conflict—priority placed on functional areas, not the entire business.

Inns is organized by regions of the world because of differences among nations in the laws, customs, and economies affecting the lodging industry. And even within its U.S. organization, Holiday Inns is organized geographically because of regional differences in traveling requirements, lodging regulations, and customer mix.

The key strategic advantage of geographic organizational structures is their responsiveness to local market conditions; this increases revenue or lowers costs. Figure 10–3 illustrates a typical geographic organizational structure and itemizes the strategic advantages and disadvantages of such structures.

FIGURE 10-3
A Geographic Organizational Structure

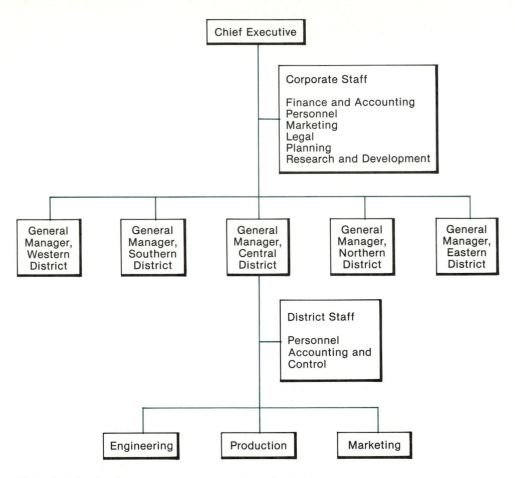

Strategic Advantages

1. Allows tailoring of strategy to needs of each geographic market.
2. Delegates profit/loss responsibility to lowest strategic level.
3. Improves functional coordination within the target market.
4. Takes advantage of economies of local operations.
5. Provides excellent training grounds for higher-level general managers.

Strategic Disadvantages

1. Poses problem of deciding whether headquarters should impose geographic uniformity or geographic diversity should be allowed.
2. Makes it more difficult to maintain consistent company image/reputation from area to area.
3. Adds layer of management to run the geographic units.
4. Can result in duplication of staff services at headquarters and district levels.

Source: Arthur A. Thompson, Jr., and A. J. Strickland III, *Strategic Management: Concepts and Cases* (Homewood, Ill.: 1987, Richard D. Irwin), p. 208.

FIGURE 10–4
Divisional Organization Structure

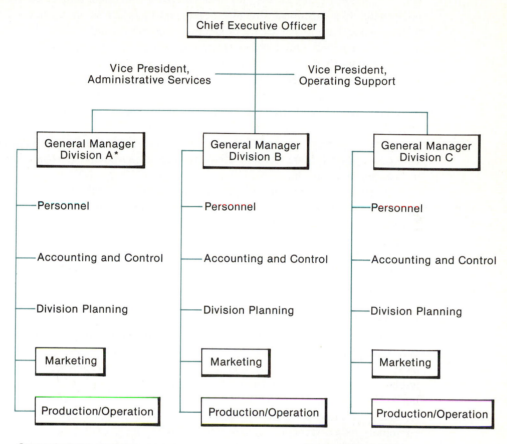

Strategic Advantages

1. Forces coordination and necessary authority down to the appropriate level for rapid response.
2. Places strategy development and implementation in closer proximity to the unique environments of the divisions.
3. Frees chief executive officer for broader strategic decision making.
4. Sharply focuses accountability for performance.
5. Retains functional specializaiton within each division.
6. Provides good training grounds for strategic managers.

Strategic Disadvantages

1. Fosters potentially dysfunctional competition for corporate-level resources.
2. Presents the problem of determining how much authority should be given to division managers.
3. Creates a potential for policy inconsistencies among divisions.
4. Presents the problem of distributing corporate overhead costs in a way that's acceptable to division managers with profit responsibility.

Divisional Organizational Structure

When a firm diversifies its product/service lines, utilizes unrelated market channels, or begins to serve heterogeneous customer groups, a functional structure rapidly becomes inadequate. If a functional structure is retained under these circumstances, production managers may have to oversee the production of numerous and varied products or services, marketing managers may have to create sales programs for vastly different products or sell through vastly different distribution channels, and top management may be confronted with excessive coordination demands. A new organizational structure is often necessary to meet the increased coordination and decision-making requirements that result from increased diversity and size, and the divisional organizational structure is the form often chosen.

For many years, Ford and General Motors have used divisional structures organized by product groups. Manufacturers often organize sales into divisions based on differences in distribution channels.

A divisional structure allows corporate management to delegate authority for the strategic management of distinct business entities—the divisions. This expedites decision making in response to varied competitive environments and enables corporate management to concentate on corporate-level strategic decisions. The divisions are usually given profit responsibility, which facilitates accurate assessment of profit and loss.

Figure 10–4 illustrates a divisional oganizational structure and specifies the strategic advantages and disadvantages of such structures.

Strategic Business Units

Some firms encounter difficulty in evaluating and controlling the operations of their divisions as the diversity, size, and number of these units continues to increase. Under these conditions, a firm may add another layer of management to improve strategy implementation, promote synergy, and gain greater control over the firm's diverse business interests. This can be accomplished by creating groups that combine various divisions (or parts of some divisions) in terms of common strategic elements. These groups, commonly called strategic business units (SBUs), are usually based on the independent product-market segments served by the firm.[3] Figure 10–5 illustrates an SBU organizational structure.

General Electric, faced with massive sales growth but little profit growth in the 1960s, was a pioneer in establishing the SBU structure. It converted over 48 divisions into six (sector) SBUs. For example, it merged three divisions that made food preparation appliances into a single SBU serving the housewares market. General Foods, whose SBUs were originally defined along product lines (and thus served overlapping markets), restructured its SBUs along menu lines. SBUs for breakfast foods, beverages, main meals, desserts, and pet foods allowed the firm to target specific markets.[4]

---

[3]William K. Hall, "SBUs: Hot, New Topic in the Management of Diversification," *Business Horizons*, February 1978, p. 19.

[4]Ibid.

FIGURE 10–5

Strategic Business Unit Organizational Structure

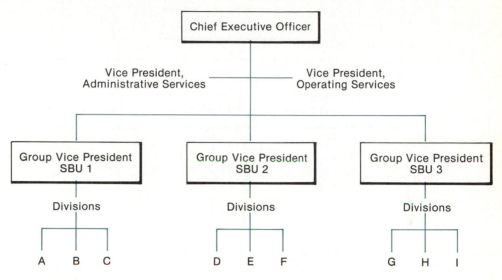

Strategic Advantages

1. Improves coordination between divisions with similar strategic concerns and product-market environments.
2. Tightens the strategic management and control of large, diverse business enterprises.
3. Facilitates distinct and in-depth business planning at the corporate and business levels.
4. Channels accountability to distinct business units.

Strategic Disadvantages

1. Places another layer of management between the divisions and corporate management.
2. May increase dysfunctional competition for corporate resources.
3. May present difficulties in defining the role of the group vice president.
4. May present difficulties in defining how much autonomy should be given to the group vice presidents and division managers.

Matrix Organization

In large companies, increased diversity leads to numerous product and project efforts of major strategic significance. The result is a need for an organizational form that provides skills and resources where and when they are most vital. The matrix organization has been used increasingly to meet this need. Among the firms that now use some form of matrix organization are Citicorp, Digital Equipment, General Electric, Shell Oil, Dow Chemical, and Texas Instruments.

The matrix organization provides dual channels of authority, performance responsibility, evaluation, and control, as shown in Figure 10–6. Essentially, subordinates are assigned both to a basic functional area and to a project or product manager. The matrix

FIGURE 10–6
Matrix Organizational Structure

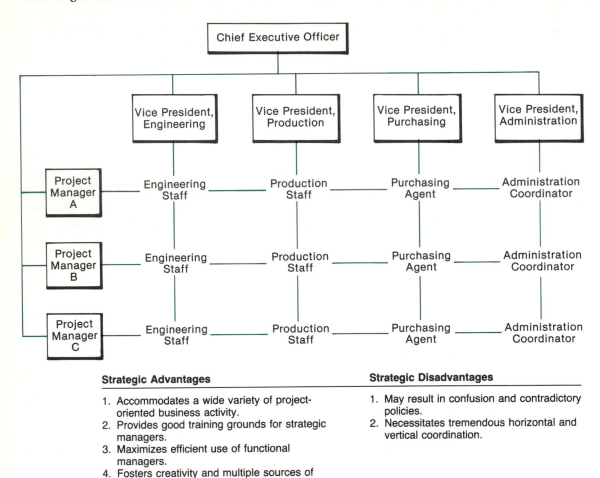

Strategic Advantages

1. Accommodates a wide variety of project-oriented business activity.
2. Provides good training grounds for strategic managers.
3. Maximizes efficient use of functional managers.
4. Fosters creativity and multiple sources of diversity.
5. Gives middle management broader exposure to strategic issues.

Strategic Disadvantages

1. May result in confusion and contradictory policies.
2. Necessitates tremendous horizontal and vertical coordination.

form is intended to make the best use of talented people within a firm by combining the advantages of functional specialization and product-project specialization.

The matrix structure also increases the number of middle managers who exercise general management responsibilities (through the project manager role) and thus broaden their exposure to organizationwide strategic concerns. In this way, the matrix structure overcomes a key deficiency of functional organizations while retaining the advantages of functional specialization.

Although the matrix structure is easy to design, it is difficult to implement. Dual chains of command challenge fundamental organizational orientations. Negotiating shared responsibilities, the use of resources, and priorities can create misunderstanding or confusion among subordinates.

To avoid the deficiencies that might arise from a permanent matrix structure, some firms are accomplishing particular strategic tasks, by means of a "temporary" or "flexible" *overlay structure*. This approach, used recently by such firms as General Motors, IBM, and Texas Instruments, is meant to take *temporary* advantage of a matrix-type team while preserving an underlying divisional structure.[5] Thus, the basic idea of the matrix structure—*to simplify and amplify the focus of resources on a narrow but strategically important product, project, or market*—appears to be an important structural alternative for large, diverse organizations.

Choosing an Effective Organizational Structure[6]

Which organizational structure is best? Considerable research has been done on this question, and the collective answer is that this depends on the strategy of the firm. Since the structural design ties together key activities and resources of the firm, it must be closely aligned with the demands of the firm's strategy.

Alfred Chandler conducted a landmark study of structural choice as a function of strategy.[7] In examining 20 large corporations over an extended period, Chandler found a common strategy-structure sequence:

1. The choice of a new strategy.
2. Administrative problems and a decline in performance.
3. A shift to an organizational structure more in line with the strategy's needs.
4. Improved profitability and strategy execution.

The logic underlying this sequence was that firms changed their growth strategy in response to environmental changes but that the new strategy created administrative problems that resulted in a decline in performance. These problems arose because the existing structure was ineffective in organizing and coordinating the activities required by the new strategy. To resolve the problems and improve performance, the structure was redesigned. Chandler implied that a failure to redesign structure would eventually cause a decline in performance. Strategy in Action 10–1 presents a description of the evolving organizational structure at Procter & Gamble. The description, offered by John Smale, P&G's chairman and CEO, vividly illustrates Chandler's findings.

Chandler also observed a common sequence of evolution in strategy and structure among American firms. The sequence reflected their increasing scope. Most firms began as simple functional units operating at a single site (e.g., a plant, a warehouse, or a sales office) and within a single industry. The initial growth strategy of such firms was *volume expansion,* which created a need for an administrative office to manage the increased

[5]Robert H. Waterman, Jr., Thomas J. Peters, and J. R. Phillips, "Structure Is Not Organization," *Business Horizons,* June 1980, p. 20.

[6]This section benefited from several thoughts and ideas shared with the authors by Professor David Sweiger, University of South Carolina.

[7]Alfred D. Chandler, *Strategy and Structure* (Cambridge, Mass: MIT Press, 1962).

STRATEGY
IN ACTION
10–1
PROCTER & GAMBLE'S CEO TALKS ABOUT P&G'S ORGANIZATIONAL STRUCTURE

John Smale, P&G's chairman and CEO, recently made the following remarks about P&G's changing organizational structure:

Many students take notice of *Fortune* magazine's ranking of the 500 largest industrial corporations in the United States, which show Procter & Gamble advancing over the last few years to the 15th position on that list.

While we have no objectives with respect to Procter & Gamble's position on such lists, it underscores the point that Procter & Gamble is a very large business which grows ever larger.

Procter & Gamble has always planned for growth. In that planning, there is perhaps nothing more fundamental than sound organizational structuring.

Recently, in a move to position P&G for strengthened performance, three major changes were made in the way we are organized to manage our U.S. consumer business—first, a move to management of this business on a strategic business unit basis; second, the combination of our manufacturing, engineering, purchasing, and distribution functions into a simple product supply function; and, finally, the initial steps of restructuring our sales organization. I want to tell you about the first, our move to SBUs.

Some history will be helpful. At the end of the Second World War, P&G's business in the United States was based on five product categories—toilet soaps, laundry detergents, hard surface cleaners, shortening, and shampoo.

In the decade that followed the war, P&G's energy was importantly directed toward the growth of its business within these categories, particularly the laundry category. But by 1955, P&G had entered new businesses—dentifrice, peanut butter, and home permanent waves among them—and was looking to even more growth through more product diversity in the future.

In order to prepare itself to manage a broader-based consumer goods business, P&G then created the *division organizational structure*—centering profit responsibility with the divisions. It is that concept which we followed until a year ago, when core profit center responsibility within P&G was moved a notch down from the division level. This was done with the creation of strategic business units.

Why this change?

Source: Adapted from Procter & Gamble, *Annual Meeting of Stockholders*, October 11, 1988.

volume. The next growth strategy was *geographic expansion,* which required multiple field units, still performing the same function but in different locations. Administrative problems with regard to standardization, specialization, and interunit coordination then gave rise to the need for geographic units and for a central administrative unit to oversee them. *Vertical integration* was usually the next growth strategy. Firms remained within the same industry but performed additional functions. Problems associated with the flow of information and materials among the various functions led to the functional organization, in which staff personnel developed forecasts and schedules that facilitated overall coordination.

The final growth strategy was *product diversification.* Firms entered other industries in which they could use their existing resources. Problems in managing diverse product

STRATEGY IN ACTION 10–1 concluded

The fundamental reason is simply the growth in the size and complexity of our business, which has in turn created the need for sharper focus on each of the business categories in which P&G is competing.

When P&G divisionalized its structure in 1955, we were engaged in 10 categories in our U.S. consumer goods business.

That number had grown to 26 categories by 1980.

But in the first nine years of the 1980s, our rate of entry into new businesses accelerated. Seventeen additional categories of business have been entered since 1980.

Growth in the number of categories in which P&G competes had, of course, been accommodated over the years by expanding the number of divisions.

Our divisions themselves, however, had grown over the years to the point that some are larger than P&G's total U.S. business was when the divisional structure was established. Also, the volume in several of our business categories surpasses the volume of some of our original divisions.

But quite apart from any measure based on the size of our business units, growth in the diversity of our businesses has multiplied the amount of change that needs to be effectively managed somewhere in P&G at any given instant.

All of this led to the decision to manage the U.S. business by SBUs and to locate core profit center responsibility at the SBU management level.

The move to strategic business units has been accomplished, by and large, without adding people or layers to the organization. Rather, our previous structures have been rearranged to create business units—each headed by a general manager—with product supply and financial analysis resources.

These SBU teams are lean. They bring sharp focus to each of P&G's varied businesses, and we are already beginning to see the results.

There is a common thread to all of our organization changes. They are designed to simplify what we do—to flatten our organization, to drive decisions and responsibility for those decisions down in the organization, to bring increased focus to each of our businesses, and to move closer to our customers.

And in the final analysis, the moves that have been taken over the last year to restructure Procter & Gamble's organization and governance will strengthen our ability to continue the growth that has been characteristic of this company since its inception 151 years ago.

divisions and evaluating their capital investment proposals led to the multidivisional structure in which similar activities were grouped. Separate divisions handled independent products and were responsible for short-run operating decisions. General managers (i.e., group managers) at a central office were responsible for long-term strategic decisions. These managers had to relate divisional decisions and performance to strategic direction and to balance divisional autonomy against central control.

Larry Wrigley built on Chandler's work by examining how a firm's degree of diversification from its core business affected its choice of structure. He identified four growth strategies: (1) *single-product businesses;* (2) *single dominant businesses,* with one business accounting for 70–95 percent of sales; (3) *related diversified businesses* based on a common distribution channel or technology, with more than 30 percent of sales outside the primary business; and (4) *unrelated diversified businesses,* with more than 30 percent of sales outside the primary business.[8]

Wrigley's major finding was that greater diversity led to greater divisionalization. Specifically, single-product businesses used a functional structure; related and unrelated businesses used a divisionalized structure; and single dominant businesses used a functional structure in the dominant business and a divisional structure in the remaining businesses.

Richard Rumelt extended Chandler's and Wrigley's work by using a more detailed classification scheme.[9] His findings generally confirmed those of Chandler and Wrigley. The greater the diversity in a firm's businesses, the greater was the likelihood that the firm would employ a multidivisional structure. Rumelt also found that from 1949 to 1969 the use of the single-product and single dominant business strategies declined and the use of the multidivisional strategy increased. Finally, Rumelt's research suggested that the fit between strategy and structure affected performance. Table 10–1 summarizes the strategy-structure recommendations emanating from this stream of research.

More recent research has extended our understanding of the strategy-structure fit.[10] This research continues to suggest that in smaller firms with a single product or product line, the functional structure significantly outperforms the multidivisional structure. In larger firms, however, the roles of corporate- and lower-level staffs significantly affect performance. The greater the diversity among a firm's businesses, the more desirable it is to have strong, decentralized staffs within the businesses (or divisions); with less diversity, firms having strong staffs at higher organizational levels are more effective. In other words, the greater the diversity among the businesses in multibusiness firms, the greater is the necessary degree of decentralization and self-containment. On the other hand, where the diversity among a firm's businesses is low and the interdependence of these businesses is high, more integration at the corporate level is needed.

Four significant conclusions can be drawn from this research:[10]

1. *A single-product firm or single dominant business firm should employ a functional structure.* This structure allows for strong task focus through an emphasis on specialization and efficiency while providing opportunity for adequate controls through centralized review and decision making.

2. *A firm in several lines of business that are somehow related should employ a multidivisional structure.* Closely related divisions should be combined into groups within this structure. When synergies (i.e., shared or linked activities) are possible within such

---

[8]Larry Wrigley, *Divisional Autonomy and Diversification.* Doctoral dissertation, Harvard Business School, 1970.

[9]Richard Rumelt, *Diversification strategy and Performance, Strategic Management Journal* 3 (January–February 1982), pp. 359–69; Richard Rumelt, *Strategy, Structure and Economic Performance* (Boston: HBS Press, 1986).

[10]D. A. Nathanson and J. S. Cassano, "Organization, Diversity, and Performance," *Wharton's Magazine* 6 (1982), pp. 19–26.

[11]V. R. Galbraith and R. K. Kazanjian, *Strategy Implementation: Structure, Systems & Processes* (St. Paul, Minn: West Publishing, 1986).

TABLE 10–1
Choosing a Primary Structure to Fit Different Strategies

Strategic Conditions, Product and Market Factors, and Other Key Variables	Strategies	Primary Structure
I. Commodity-type products Small numbers of products and services High degree of production and market relatedness Need to focus on efficiency criteria, cost reduction, or economies of scale	Volume expansion (horizontal growth) Geographic expansion	Functional organization (process specialization) Geographic organization with central administration
II. As in I above, plus High stability or low demand volatility for products Prospect of adding new products with high production or technological relatedness High proportion of potential new productive capacity being absorbed by existing or new products	As in I above, plus vertical integration	As in I above, plus More sophisticated functional structures (usually special coordination teams, planning councils, and staff coordination roles)
III. Large numbers of products or services Low production relatedness Low market relatedeness Excess productive capacity (distinctive competence) Slack resources Need to reduce coordination costs	Product diversification	Multidivisional organization (purpose specialization by product, customer, or geography) Strategic business units (discrete units, highly self-contained)
IV. Need for dual focus—products and functions Scarcity of resources, with opportunity for cross-fertilization or synergy across products or projects High uncertainty, complexity, and interdependence, increasing need to process information and make decisions more efficiently	As in I, II, or III above	Matrix organization

Source: Adapted from L. G. Hrebiniak and W. F. Joyce, *Implementing Strategy* (New York: Macmillan, 1984), pp. 88–89.

a group, the appropriate location for staff influence and decision making is at the group level, with a lesser role for corporate-level staff. The greater the degree of diversity across the firm's businesses, the greater should be the extent to which the power of staff and decision-making authority is lodged within the divisions.

3. *A firm in several unrelated lines of business should be organized into strategic business units*. Although the stategic business unit structure resembles the multidivisional structure, there are significant differences between the two. With a strategic business unit structure, finance, accounting, planning, legal, and related activities should be centralized at the corporate office. Since there are no synergies across the firm's businesses, the corporate office serves largely as a capital allocation and control mechanism. Otherwise, its major decisions involve acquisitions and divestitures. All operational and business-level strategic plans are delegated to the strategic business units.

4. *Early achievement of a strategy-structure fit can be a competitive advantage*. A competitive advantage is obtained by the first firm among competitors to achieve an appropriate strategy-structure fit. That advantage will disappear as the firm's competitors also attain such a fit. Moreover, if the firm alters its strategy, its structure must obviously change as well. Otherwise, a loss of fit will lead to a competitive disadvantage for the firm.

The description in Strategy in Action 10–1 of Procter & Gamble's organizational structures over a 50-year period provides a good illustration of these conclusions.

ORGANIZATIONAL LEADERSHIP

Organizational structure provides the overall framework for strategy implementation, but an appropriate organizational structure is not in itself sufficient to ensure successful implementation. Within the organizational structure, individuals, groups, and units are the mechanisms of organizational action. And the effectiveness of that action is a major determinant of successful implementation. Three basic factors encourage or discourage effective action—leadership, culture, and rewards.[12] This section examines leadership as a key element of strategy implementation; the next section explains the role of organizational culture; and a final section considers the importance of reward systems.

Leadership, a seemingly vague and esoteric concept, is an essential element of effective strategy implementation. In this regard, two leadership issues are of fundamental importance: (1) the role of the chief executive officer (CEO) and (2) the assignment of key managers.

---

[12]Leadership and organizational culture are interdependent phenomena. Each aspect of leadership ultimately helps shape organizational culture. Conversely, the prevailing organizational culture can profoundly influence a leader's effectiveness. The richness of this interdependence will become apparent. The topics are addressed in separate sections because it is important to develop an appreciation of the role of each in strategy implementations.

Role of the CEO

The chief executive officer is a key catalyst in strategic management. This individual is most closely identified with and ultimately accountable for a strategy's success. CEOs spend up to 80 percent of their time in developing and guiding strategy.

The CEO's role in strategy implementatiron is both *symbolic* and *substantive*. First, the CEO is a symbol of the new strategy. This individual's actions and the perceived seriousness of his or her commitment to the chosen strategy, particularly if that strategy represents a major change, significantly influence the intensity of subordinate managers' commitment to implementation. In the 1980s, Lee Iacocca's highly visible role as spokesperson for the "new Chrysler Corporation" on television, in Chrysler factories and offices, and before securities analysts was intended to provide a strong symbol of the workability of Chrysler's desperate turnaround strategy.

Second, the personal goals and values of the CEO strongly influence the firm's mission, strategy, and key long-term objectives. To the extent that the CEO invests time and effort in the chosen strategy, he or she represents an important source for clarification, guidance, and adjustment during implementation.

Major changes in strategy are often preceded or quickly followed by a change in CEO. This suggests that different strategies require different CEOs. L. M. Clymer's resignation as CEO of Holiday Inns clearly illustrates this point. Holiday Inns's executive group was convinced that casinos provided a key growth area for the firm. Clymer chose to resign because a move into this area was not consistent with his personal values and with his perception of what Holiday Inns should be. Research has concluded that a successful turnaround strategy "will require almost without exception either a change in top management or a substantial change in the behavior of the existing management team."[13] Strategy in Action 10–2 describes such a change at Corning Glass Works. Clearly, successful strategy implementation is directly linked to the characteristics, orientation, and actions of the CEO.

Assignment of Key Managers

A major concern of top management in implementing a strategy, particularly if it involves a major change, is that the right managers be in the right positions for the new strategy. Of all the means for ensuring successful implementation, this is the one that CEOs mention first. Confidence in the individuals occupying pivotal managerial positions is directly correlated with top-management expectations that a strategy can be successfully executed.

This confidence is based on the answers to two fundamental questions:

1. Which persons hold the leadership positions that are especially critical to execution of the strategy?
2. Do these persons have the characteristics needed to ensure effective implementation of the strategy?

---

[13]Charles W. Hofer, "Turnaround Strategies," *Journal of Business Strategy*, January–February 1980, p. 25.

| STRATEGY IN ACTION 10–2 | NEW LEADERSHIP AT CORNING GLASS WORKS |

James R. Houghton, 52, chief executive of Corning Glass Works, is a model of how to develop and communicate a leader's vision. He has repeatedly stated his goals and how he plans to reach them. In 1980 Corning was carrying unproductive divisions and earning meager profits when Houghton, great-great-grandson of the firm's founder, took over as its CEO. He quickly shed the losers and set the following long-term financial objectives for the 1990s: a return on equity of over 17 percent (he isn't there yet), annual inflation-adjusted revenue growth above 5 percent (not there yet either), a debt-to-capital ratio below 25 percent (he's there), and an average dividend payout of 33 percent of earnings (he's met that goal over the past five years). Houghton's overall aim—which he has tirelessly communicated to his employees—is to head one of the 10 most admired U.S. corporations in the annual poll that *Fortune* magazine publishes. According to Houghton, "*Fortune*'s criteria match Corning's values, and being one of these companies means you're living your values."

Houghton has established concern for quality as the firm's central long-term value. "The cynics at first said 'quality' was like the flavor of the month and would go away," he says. "But people buy it here now, and I believe companies that don't buy into quality are doomed." Houghton's chief reason for stressing the issue is economic; he estimates that the costs of preventing, detecting, and paying for errors comes to 20–30 percent of sales. He believes that a motivated work force attuned to quality can slice those costs fast, so he harps on the subject. He preaches this gospel on 40 to 50 annual trips to Corning's far-flung divisions. and all new Corning employees take courses that emphasize the firm's commitment to quality. By 1991, every Corning employee will spend more than two weeks a year on additional training. Houghton says, "Quality applies to everything we do. This is a lifelong journey, not a destination."

Houghton's quality campaign has helped engender a cultural change at Corning. Suggestion boxes used to be scattered around the firm's plants, and employees who made useful suggestions would receive small checks months later. The system led to considerable backbiting and jealousy as employees bickered over whose suggestion most merited rewards. Worse, it failed to produce anything like a steady stream of good ideas. Now, Corning's managers repeatedly encourage the troops to make suggestions. Good ideas are adopted more quickly, and with the suggester's help. As a result, far more employees have been piping up, and they have found their satisfaction sufficient reward. "There is a much more open atmosphere," says Houghton. "We get 5 times as many suggestions; we act on 40 times as many of them—and we don't give money."

Source: "At Corning, a Vision of Quality," *Fortune*, October 24, 1988, p. 64.

Although it is impossible to specify the characteristics that are most important in this context, they probably include (1) ability and education, (2) previous track record and experience, and (3) personality and temperament. An individual's suitability on these counts, combined with top managers' gut feelings about the individual, provides the basis for top management's confidence in the individual.

Recently, numerous studies have attempted to match "preferred" managerial charac-

FIGURE 10–7
Using Existing Executives versus Bringing in Outsiders in Managerial Assignments to Implement a New Strategy

	Advantages	Disadvantages
Using existing executives to implement a new strategy	Existing executives already know key people, practices, and conditions.	Existing executives are less adaptable to major strategic changes because of their knowledge, attitudes, and values.
	Personal qualities of existing executives are better known and understood by associates.	Past commitments of existing executives hamper the hard decisions required in executing a new strategy.
	Existing executives have established relationships with peers, subordinates, suppliers, buyers, etc.	Existing executives have less ability to become inspired and credibly convey the need for change.
	Use of existing executives symbolizes organizational commitment to individual careers.	
Bringing in outsiders to implement a new strategy	Outsiders may already believe in and have "lived" the new strategy.	Bringing in outsiders is often, costly in terms of both compensation and "learning-to-work-together" time.
	Outsiders are unencumbered by internal commitments to people.	Candidates suitable in all respects (i.e., exact experience) may not be available, leading to compromise choices.
	Outsiders come to the new assignment with heightened commitment and enthusiasm.	Uncertainty exists in selecting the right outsiders to bring in.
	Bringing in outsiders can send powerful signals throughout the organization that change is expected.	"Morale costs" are incurred when an outsider takes a job that several insiders want.
		The "what to do with poor ol' Fred" problem arises when outsiders are brought in.

Source: Adapted from Boris Yavitz and William H. Newman, *Strategy in Action* (New York: Free Press, 1982), chap. 10; and Paul J. Stonich, *Implementing Strategy* (Cambridge, Mass.: Ballinger, 1982), chap. 4.

teristics with different grand strategies.[14] These studies are meant to capsulize, for example, the behavioral characteristics appropriate for a manager responsible for implementing an "invest to grow" strategy in contrast to those appropriate for a manager implementing a "harvest" strategy. One of the studies found that three managerial characteristics—years of experience in marketing/sales, willingness to take risks, and tolerance for ambiguity—positively related to managerial effectiveness for divisions pursuing a

---

[14]See, for example J. G. Wisseman, H. W. Van der Pol, and H. M. Messer, "Strategic Management Archetypes," *Strategic Management Journal* 1, no. 1 (1980), pp. 37–45; William F. Glueck and Lawrence R. Jauch, *Strategic Management and Business Policy* (New York: McGraw-Hill, 1984), p. 365; Boris Yavitz and William H. Newman, *Strategy in Action* (New York: Free Press, 1982), p. 167; and "Wanted, a Manager to Fit Each Strategy," *Business Week,* February 25, 1980, p. 166.

build strategy and negatively related to mangerial effectiveness for divisions being harvested. Despite widespread theoretical discussion of this idea, a study comprising a broad sample of firms failed to find a single firm that matched managerial characteristics to strategic mission in a formal manner. However, the study did find several firms that addressed such considerations as an informal, intuitive manner.[15] The following comment summarizes these findings:

> Despite the near unanimity of belief that, for effective implementation, different strategies require different skills . . . many corporate executives avoid too rigid an approach to matching managerial characteristics and strategy [for three reasons]: (1) exposure to and experience at managing different kinds of strategies and businesses is viewed as an essential component of managerial development; (2) too rigid a differentiation is viewed as much more likely to result in some managers being typecast as "good builders" and some others as "good harvesters," thereby creating motivational problems for the latter; and (3) a "perfect match" between managerial characteristics and strategy is viewed as more likely to result in overcommitment [or] self-fulfilling prophecies (a harvester becoming only a harvester) as compared with a situation where there was some mismatch.[16]

One practical consideration in making key managerial assignments when implementing strategy is whether to utilize current (or promotable) executives or bring in new personnel. This is obviously a difficult, sensitive, and strategic issue. Figure 10–7 highlights the key advantages and disadvantages of these alternatives.

ORGANIZATIONAL CULTURE

Organizational culture is the set of important assumptions (often unstated) that members of an organization share in common. Every organization has its own culture. An organization's culture is similar to an individual's personality—an intangible yet ever-present theme that provides meaning, direction, and the basis for action. In much the same way as personality influences the behavior of an individual, the shared assumptions (beliefs and values) among a firm's members influence opinions and actions within that firm.

Shared Assumptions: Internalized Beliefs and Values that Organizational Members Hold in Common

A member of an organization can simply be aware of the organization's beliefs and values without sharing them in a personally significant way. Those beliefs and values have more personal meaning if the member views them as a guide to appropriate behavior in the organization and therefore complies with them. The member becomes fundamentally committed to the beliefs and values when he or she internalizes them, that is, comes to

---

[15]Anil K. Gupta and V. Govindarajan, "Build, Hold, Harvest: Converting Strategic Intentions into Reality," *Journal of Business Strategy,* Winter 1984, p. 41; Peter Lorange, "The Human Resources Dimension in the Strategic Planning Process," (Cambridge, Mass: Sloan School, MIT, 1983, mimeographed), p. 13.

[16]Gupta and Govindarajan, "Build, Hold, Harvest," p. 41.

hold them as personal beliefs and values. In this case, the corresponding behavior is *intrinsically rewarding* for the member—the member derives personal satisfaction from his or her actions in the organization because those actions are congruent with corresponding personal beliefs and values. *Assumptions become shared assumptions through internalization among an organization's individual members*. And those shared, internalized beliefs and values shape the content and account for the strength of an organization's culture.

Understanding the relevance of an organization's culture to strategic success is facilitated by examples from a classic series of reports on America's best-managed companies initiated by Peters and Waterman.[17] Some examples include:[18]

The cultures of excellent companies are seen in key themes that guide members' behavior and orientation. At IBM, the key themes include respect for the individual and services to the customer. At Procter & Gamble (P&G), the overarching value is product quality. McDonald's uncompromising emphasis on QSCV—quality, service, cleanliness, and value—through meticulous attention to detail is legendary. Delta Airlines is driven by the "family feeling" theme, which builds a team spirit and nurtures each employee's cooperative attitude toward others. cheerful outlook toward life, and pride in a job well done. Du Pont's safety orientation—a report of every accident must be on the chairman's desk within 24 hours—has resulted in a safety record that was 17 times better than the chemical industry average and 68 times better than the all-manufacturing average in the mid-1980s.

Companies with strong cultures are enthusiastic collectors and tellers of stories, anecdotes, and legends in support of basic beliefs. Frito-Lay's zealous emphasis on customer service is reflected in frequent stories about potato chip route salesmen who have slogged through sleet, mud, hail, snow, and rain to uphold the 99.5 percent service level to customers in which the entire company takes great pride. Milliken (a textile leader) holds "sharing" rallies once every quarter at which teams from all over the company swap success stories and ideas. Typically, more than 100 teams make five-minute presentations over a two-day period. Every rally is designed around a major theme such as quality, cost reduction, or customer service. No criticisms are allowed, and awards are given to reinforce this institutionalized approach to storytelling. L. L. Bean tells customers service stories; 3M tells innovation stories; P&G, Johnson & Johnson, IBM, and Maytag tell quality stories. These stories are very important in developing an organizational culture because organization members identify strongly with them and come to share the beliefs and values they support.

---

[17]Thomas J. Peters and Robert H. Waterman, Jr., *In Search of Excellence,* New York; Harper & Row, 1982); and Thomas J. Peters and Nancy Austin, *A Passion for Excellence* New York; Random House, 1985).

[18]Adapted from Peters and Waterman, *In Search of Excellence,* pp. xxi, 73–78, 280–86; Peters and Austin, *A Passion for Excellence,* pp. 279–86; and Arthur A. Thompson, Jr., and A. A. Strickland III, *Strategic Management,* 4th ed. (Homewood, Ill,: Business Publications, 1987), pp. 241–2.

Companies with strong cultures are clear on what their beliefs and values need to be and take the process of shaping those beliefs and values very seriously. Most important, the values these companies espouse undergird the strategies they employ. For example, McDonald's has a yearly contest to determine the best hamburger cooker in its chain. First, there is a competition to determine the best hamburger cooker in each store; next, the store winners compete in regional championships; finally, the regional winners compete in the "All-American" contest. The winners, who are widely publicized throughout the company, get tropies and All-American patches to wear on their McDonald's uniforms.

The most typical beliefs that shape organizational culture include (1) a belief in being the best (or, as at GE, "better than the best"); (2) a belief in superior quality and service; (3) a belief in the importance of people as individuals and a faith in their ability to make a strong contribution; (4) a belief in the importance of the details of execution, the nuts and bolts of doing the job well; (5) a belief that customers should reign supreme; (6) a belief in inspiring people to do their best, whatever their ability; (7) a belief in the importance of informal communication; and (8) a belief that growth and profits are essential to a company's well-being. Every company implements these beliefs differently (to fit its particular situation), and every company's values are the handiwork of one or two legendary figures in leadership positions. Accordingly, every company has a distinct culture that it believes no other company can copy successfully. And in companies with strong cultures, managers and workers either accept the norms of the culture or opt out from the culture and leave the company.

The stronger a company's culture and the more that culture directed toward customers and markets, the less the company uses policy manuals, organization charts, and detailed rules and procedures to enforce discipline and norms. The reason is that the guiding values inherent in the culture convey in crystal-clear fashion what everybody is supposed to do in most situations. Poorly performing companies often have strong cultures. However, their cultures are dysfunctional, being focused on internal politics or operating by the numbers as opposed to emphasizing customers and the people who make and sell the product.

Content of Culture

The content of a firm's culture ultimately derives from three sources. First, the influence of the business environment in general, and the industry in particular, is an important determinant of shared assumptions. For example, firms in industries characterized by rapid technological change, such as computer and electronics firms, normally have cultures that strongly value innovation. At high-technology firms such as IBM, GE, and 3M, top executives deliberately make "champions" out of individuals who believe so strongly in their ideas that they take it upon themselves to hurdle the bureaucracy, maneuver their projects through the system, and turn them into improved services, new products, or even new businesses. In these firms, "product champions" are given high visibility, room to push their ideas, and strong executive support. Champions whose ideas prove out are usually handsomely rewarded; those whose ideas don't pan out still have secure jobs and are given chances to try again.[19]

Second, founders, leaders, and employees bring a pattern of assumptions with them when they join a firm. Such assumptions often depend on the experiences of these individuals in the cultures of the national, regional, ethnic, religious, occupational, and professional communities from which they came. For example, some firms with otherwise low-paying jobs upgrade the importance and status of individual employees by referring to them as cast members (Disney), crew members (McDonald's), or associates (Wal-Mart and J. C. Penney). Such firms as Tupperware and McDonald's actively seek out reasons and opportunities for giving pins, buttons, badges, and medals to honor good showings by average performers—the idea being to show appreciation and help give a boost to the "middle 60 percent" of the work force.[20]

Third, shared assumptions are molded by the actual experiences that people in the firm have had in working out solutions to the basic problems it encounters. Consider the example of the manager of a New York area sales office who rented the Meadowlands Stadium (home field of the New York Giants) for an evening. On that evening, all the salesmen of the New York office were assembled at the stadium and were asked to run one at a time through the player's tunnel onto the field. As each emerged, the electronic scoreboard flashed his name to those gathered in the stands—executives from corporate headquarters, employees from the sales office, family, and friends—so that they could cheer loudly in honor of his sales accomplishments. The firm involved was IBM. The action was intended to reaffirm IBM's commitment to satisfy the need of individuals to be part of something great and to reiterate IBM's concern for championing individual accomplishment as IBM's problem-solving approach.[21]

The above examples help demonstrate the crucial role of culture in institutionalizing a firm's strategy. As a consequence, managing culture to successfully implement a strategy is a critical issue—an issue that is easy to state yet exceedingly difficult to manage. The critical issue that must be managed is ensuring that the culture "fits" with the implementation requirements of the chosen strategy.

Managing the Strategy-Culture Relationship

Managers find it difficult to think through the relationship between a firm's culture and the critical factors on which strategy depend. They quickly recognize, however, that key components of the firm—structure, staff, systems, people, style—influence the ways in which key managerial tasks are executed and critical management relationships are formed. And implementation of a new strategy is largely concerned with adjustments in these

---

[19]Peters and Waterman, *In Search of Excellence*, p. 240; and Thompson and Strickland, *Strategic Management*, p. 245.

[20]Ibid.

[21]Peters and Austin, *A Passion for Excellence*, p. 305; and Thompson and Strickland, *Strategic Management*, p. 245.

FIGURE 10–8
Managing the Strategy-Culture Relationship

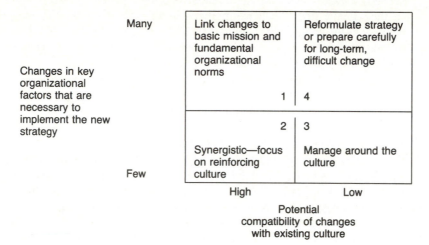

components to accommodate the perceived needs of the strategy. Consequently, managing the strategy-culture relationship requires sensitivity to the interaction between the changes necessary to implement the new strategy and the compatibility or "fit" between those changes and the firm's culture. Figure 10–8 provides a simple framework for managing the strategy-culture relationship by identifying four basic situations a firm might face.

Link to Mission

A firm in cell 1 is faced with a situation in which implementing a new strategy requires several changes in structure, systems, managerial assignments, operating procedures, or other fundamental aspects of the firm. However, most of the changes are potentially compatible with the existing organizational culture. Firms in this situation usually have a tradition of effective performance and are either seeking to take advantage of a major opportunity or attempting to redirect major product-market operations consistent with proven core capabilities. Such firms are in a very promising position: they can pursue a strategy requiring major changes but still benefit from the power of cultural reinforcement.

Four basic considerations should be emphasized by firms seeking to manage a strategy-culture relationship in this context. First, *key changes should be visibly linked to the basic company mission*. Since the company mission provides a broad official foundation for the organizational culture, top executives should use all available internal and external forums to reinforce the message that the changes are inextricably linked to it. Second, *emphasis should be placed on the use of existing personnel* where possible to fill positions created to implement the new strategy. Existing personnel embody the shared values and norms that help ensure cultural compatibility as major changes are implemented. Third, *care should be taken if adjustments in the reward system are needed*. These adjustments should be consistent with the current rewarded system. If, for example, a new product-market thrust requires significant changes in the way sales are made, and therefore in incentive compensation, common themes (e.g., incentive oriented) should be emphasized. In this way, current and future reward approaches are related and the changes in the reward sytem are justified (encourage development of less familiar markets). Fourth, *key attention should be paid to the changes that are least compatible with the current culture,* so that current norms are not disrupted. For example, a firm may choose to subcontract an important step in a production process because that step would be incompatible with the current culture.

IBM's strategy in entering the personal computer market is an illustration. Serving this radically different market required numerous organizational changes. To maintain maximum compatibility with its existing culture while doing so, IBM went to considerable public and internal effort to link its new PCs with its long-standing mission. Numerous messages relating the PCs to IBM's tradition of top-quality service appeared on television and in magazines, and every IBM manager was given a PC. Where feasible, IBM personnel were used to fill the new positions created to implement the strategy. But because the PC's production requirements were not compatible with IBM's current operations, virtually all manufacturing of the PC was subcontracted.

Maximize Synergy

A firm in cell 2 needs only a few organizational changes to implement its new strategy, and those changes are potentially quite compatible with its current culture. A firm in this situation should emphasize two broad themes: (1) *take advantage of the situation to reinforce and solidify the current culture and* (2) *use this time of relative stability to remove organizational roadblocks to the desired culture.* Holiday Inns's move into casino gambling required a few major organizational changes. Holiday Inns saw casinos as resort locations requiring lodging, dining, and gambling/entertainment services. It only had to incorporate gambling/entertainment expertise into its management team, which was already capable of managing the lodging and dining requirements of casino (or any other) resort locations. It successfully inculcated this single major change by selling the change internally as completely compatible with its mission of providing high-quality accommodations for business and leisure travelers. The resignation of Roy Clymer, its CEO, removed an organizational roadblock, legitimizing a culture that placed its highest priority on quality service to the middle-to-upper-income business traveler rather than a culture that placed its highest priority on family-oriented service. The latter priority was fast disappearing from Holiday Inns's culture, with the encouragement of most of the firm's top management, but its disappearance had not yet been fully sanctioned because of Clymer's personal beliefs. His voluntary departure helped solidify the new values that top management wanted.

Manage around the Culture

A firm in cell 3 must make a few major organizational changes to implement its new strategy, but these changes are potentially inconsistent with the firm's current organizational culture. The critical question for a firm in this situation is whether it can make the changes with a reasonable chance of success.

TRANSFORMING ORGANIZATIONAL CULTURE AT UNITED TECHNOLOGIES

It was with some urgency that Robert F. Daniell, the newly appointed CEO of United Technologies Corporation, summoned his top executives. Just weeks after taking the reins from Harry J. Gray, Daniell called a management powwow at the Jupiter Beach Hilton in Florida. The subject? UTC's shaky future. Customers of its Pratt & Whitney jet engines, outraged by lousy service, were defecting in droves to archrival General Electric Company. Market shares at UTC's once dominant Otis elevator unit and Carrier air-conditioning company were evaporating. Profits had hit a 13-year low. "Things had to change," says Daniell.

Unlike the iron-fisted Gray, however, Daniell did not lecture at management meetings. Instead, a Boston consultant moderated a roiling discussion in which managers put forth their remedies: dump divisions wholesale, diversify, pump up research-and-development spending. "Just the fact that we went through all of that yelling and screaming was unusual," says one executive who attended. After two days, Daniell and his team decided to remake UTC—to level its autocratic structure and bring more of its 186,800 employees into the decision-making process. *The ultimate goal: To get UTC's haughty culture to take marching orders from its customers.*

Worker empowerment. Team building. Getting close to your customer. While a lot of companies are just starting to talk about such methods, Bob Daniell is already proving that they can work wonders on the bottom line. The changes are nowhere more apparent than at jet-engine maker Pratt & Whitney, which pulls in more than half of UTC's operating profit. Orders have increased eightfold, to nearly $8 billion, since 1987.

When Daniell finally became CEO, he inherited a divided, argumentative management. Executives were too frightened to admit mistakes, and they directed their staffs like armies. All the way down the line, staffers refused to take responsibility for errors.

At the same time, Daniell was working on a long-term goal: changing Pratt's by-the-book structure. Dictatorial management and a Byzantine approval process made employees feel powerless. Take the case of an airplane builder who wants to mount an engine a fraction of a millimeter closer

Source: "Changes at United Technologies," *Forbes*, August 28, 1989, pp. 42–46.

Consider, for example, a multibillion-dollar industry leader that is faced with major threats to its record of outstanding growth and profitability. To meet those threats, it makes considerable effort to design a new organizational structure around major markets. After formally assessing the "cultural risks" of this change, it rejects the change as too inconsistent with its functional culture. In this situation, a positive alternative is available. The firm can increase planning and coordination personnel to *manage around the culture* in implementing the new strategy.[22] This means of implementation can be important if a firm has to change a factor inextricably linked to its culture (such as structure).

A firm can manage around the culture in various ways: create a separate firm or

[22]Howard Schwartz and Stanley M. Davis, "Matching Corporate Culture and Business Strategy," *Organizational Dynamics*, Summer 1981, p. 43

to the wing than the blueprint specifies. Normally, a good engineer at Pratt could just eyeball the blueprint and give the customer the nod for such a change. But until Pratt changed the system in February 1988, the request would wind through nine departments, including a committee that met only once a week.

Now, the design engineer makes the decision and only needs to get three signatures. Says Garvey: "It's all part of quality—taking responsibility." As a result, average response time has gone from 82 days to 10, and the request backlog has shrunk from 1,900 cases to fewer than 100.

Daniell went further with this campaign to improve service. He increased the number of service representatives in the field by nearly 70 percent—despite 30 percent staff cuts in the rest of the company.

Overall, Daniell's effort to change the culture is based on four approaches:

Flatten the hierarchy. Daniell leveled a Byzantine corporate structure by cutting many layers of decision making. At Pratt & Whitney, for instance, he cut eight levels of management to as few as four.

Empower your workers. Managers pushed decision making down. For instance, field representatives at Pratt & Whitney now make multimillion-dollar decisions about reimbursing customers on warranty claims. Before, they would have to wait for approvals from numerous layers above.

Get close to your customers. This is Daniell's battle cry. Worker empowerment helps, but the imperative goes even further than that. For instance, Pratt & Whitney lends some of its top engineers to customers for a year—and pays their salaries.

Train, train, train. Daniell uses training to revamp the corporate culture. More than 5,000 senior and middle managers are getting at least 40 hours of classroom work. In some classes, customers are brought in for gripe sessions and a problem-solving team gathered from many different departments must come up with solutions.

division; use task forces, teams, or program coordinators; subcontract; bring in an outsider; or sell out. These are a few of the available options, but the key idea is to create a method of achieving the change desired that avoids confronting the incompatible cultural norms. As cultural resistance diminishes, the change may be absorbed into the firm.

In the 1970s, Rich's was a highly successful, quality-oriented department store chain that served higher-income customers in several southeastern locations. With Sears and K mart experiencing rapid growth in the sale of mid- to low-priced merchandise, Rich's decided to serve this market as well. Finding such merchandise inconsistent with the successful values and norms of its traditional business, it created a separate business called Richway to tap this growth area in retailing. Through a new store network, it was able to *manage around its culture*. Both Rich's and Richway have since flourished, though their cultures are radically different in some respects.

Reformulate the Strategy

A firm in cell 4 faces the most difficult challenge in managing the strategy-culture relationship. To implement its new strategy, such a firm must make organizational changes that are incompatible with its current, usually entrenched, values and norms. A firm in this situation faces the complex, expensive, and often long-term challenge of changing its culture. According to numerous consultants on organizational culture, it is a challenge that borders on impossibility.[23] Strategy in Action 10–3 describes the challenge faced by Robert Daniell, CEO of United Technologies, as he attempted to change the culture of his firm.

When a stategy requires massive organizational change and engenders cultural resistance, a firm should determine whether reformulation of the strategy is appropriate. Are all of the organizational changes really necessary? Is there any real expectation that the changes will be acceptable and successful? If the answer to these questions is no, the firm should reformulate its strategic plan so as to make it more consistent with established organizational norms and practices.

Merrill Lynch faced the challenge of strategy-culture incompatibility in 1982. Seeking to remain number one in the newly deregulated financial services industry, it chose to pursue product development strategy in its brokerage business. Under this strategy, Merrill Lynch would sell a broader range of investment products to a more diverse customer base and would integrate other financial services, such as real estate sales, into the Merrill Lynch organization. The new strategy could succeed only if Merrill Lynch's traditionally service-oriented brokerage network became sales and marketing oriented. Initial efforts to implement the strategy generated substantial resistance from Merrill Lynch's highly successful brokerage network. The strategy was fundamentally inconsistent with long-standing cultural norms at Merrill Lynch that emphasized personalized service and very close broker-client relationships. Merrill Lynch divested its real estate operation and focused its brokers more narrowly on basic client investment needs.

Reward Systems: Motivating Strategy Execution

The execution of strategy ultimately depends on individual organizational members, particularly key managers. And motivating and rewarding good performance by individuals and organizational units are key ingredients in effective strategy implementation. If strategy accomplishment is a top priority, then the reward system must be clearly and tightly linked to strategic performance. Motivating and controlling managerial personnel in the execution of strategy are accomplished through a firm's reward mechanisms—compensation, raises, bonuses, stock options, incentives, benefits, promotions, demotions, recognition, praise, criticism, more (or less) responsibility, group norms, performance appraisal, tension, and fear. These mechanisms are positive and negative, short run and long run.

A firm's reward system should align the actions and objectives of individuals and units with the objectives and needs of the firm's strategy. And reward systems, like strategies,

---

[23]"The Corporate Culture Vultures," *Fortune,* October 17, 1983, p. 66.

vary greatly across different firms. For example, Harold Geneen, former CEO of ITT, purportedly used an interesting combination of money (compensation and incentives), tension (strict accountability for results), and fear to reward individual managers' efforts toward strategy implementation. According to one author:

> Geneen provides his managers with enough incentives to make them tolerate the system. Salaries all the way through ITT are higher than average—Geneen reckons 10 percent higher—so that few people can leave without taking a drop. As one employee put it: "We're all paid just a bit more than we think we're worth." At the very top, where the demands are greatest, the salaries and stock options are sufficient to compensate for the rigors. As someone said, "He's got them by their limousines."
>
> Having bound his men to him with chains of gold, Geneen can induce the tension that drives the machine. "The key to the system," one of his men explained, "is the profit forecast. Once the forecast has been gone over, revised, and agreed on, the managing director has a personal commitment to Geneen to carry it out. That's how he produces the tension on which the success depends." The tension goes through the company, inducing ambition, perhaps exhilaration, but always with some sense of fear: what happens if the target is missed?[24]

BIC Pen Company takes a different approach. Its reward structure involves incentive systems, wide latitude for operating managers, and clearly specified objectives to motivate and control individual initiative. All employees are invited to participate in a stock purchase plan whereby up to 10 percent of their salary can be used to purchase stock at a 10 percent discount from the market price. Functional managers are given wide rein in operational decisions while being held strictly accountable for results. The director of manufacturing, for example, is free to spend up to $500,000 for a cost-saving machine as long as profit margin objectives are maintained. Commenting on his approach to rewarding executives, Robert Adler, BIC's president, said:

> We have a unique bonus system, which I'm sure the Harvard Business School would think is crazy. Each year I take a percentage of profits before tax and give 40 percent to sales, 40 percent to manufacturing, and 20 percent to the treasurer to be divided up among executives in each area. Each department head keeps some for himself and gives the rest away. We never want bonuses to be thought of as salaries because they would lost their effect. So we change the bonus day each year so that it always comes as a pleasant surprise, something to look forward to.[25]

These two examples illustrate several generalizations about the use of rewards and sanctions to control individuals, particularly managers, in strategy execution. Financial incentives are important reward mechanisms. They are particularly useful in encouraging managerial success when they are directly linked to specific activities and results. Intrinsic, nonfinancial rewards, such as flexibility and autonomy in the job and visible control over performance, are important managerial motivators. And negative sanctions, such as the withholding of financial and intrinsic rewards or the tensions emanating from possible consequences of substandard performance, are necessary ingredients in encouraging managers' efforts.

---

[24]Anthony Sampson, *The Sovereign State of ITT,* (New York: Steig & Day, 1973), p. 132.

[25]C. R. Christensen, K. R. Andrews, and J. L. Bower, *Business Policy: Text and Cases* (Homewood, Ill.: Richard D. Irwin, 1978), p. 318.

The time horizon on which rewards and sanctions are based is a major consideration in linking them to strategically important activities and results. Numerous authors and business leaders have expressed concern about incentive systems based on short-term (typically annual) performance. They fear that short-term reward structures can result in actions and decisions that undermine the long-term position of firms. A marketing director whose rewards are based on the cost effectiveness of the sales generated by the marketing staff might place significantly greater emphasis on established distribution channels than on "inefficient" nurturing and development of new channels. A reward system based on maximizing current profitability can shortchange the future in terms of current investments (in time, people, and money) in the areas from which the primary return is intended to come.[26] If the firm's grand strategy is growth through, among other means, horizontal integration of current products into new channels and markets, the reward structure may be directing the marketing director's efforts in ways that thwart the ultimate success of the strategy. And the marketing director, having performed notably within the current reward structure, may have moved on to other responsibilities before the shortcomings emerge.

Short-term executive incentive schemes typically focus on last year's (or last quarter's) profits. In terms of promoting a new strategy, this exclusive concentration on the bottom line has four weaknesses:

1. It is backward looking. Reported results reflect past events and, to some extent, past strategy.
2. The focus is short term, though many of the recorded transactions have effects over longer periods.
3. Strategic gains or losses are not considered due to, among other things, basic accounting methods.
4. Investment of time and money in future strategy can have a negative impact. Since such outlays and efforts are usually intermingled with other expenses, a manager can improve his or her bonus by *not* preparing for the future.[27]

Although incentive systems encourage short-run thinking and neglect the longer term, there is real danger in hastily condemning short-term measures. It is a mistake to conclude that short-term concerns are not important or that they are necessarily counterproductive to the strategic needs of the organization. In an effectively implemented strategy, short-term aims support, and are critical to, the attainment of long-term strategic objectives. The real problem is not the short- versus long-term concerns of management but the failure to achieve consistency between long- and short-term plans and objectives in the control system.[28] The critical ingredients for achieving such consistency are appropriate rewards and incentives.

---

[26]William R. King and David I. Cleland, *Strategic Planning and Policy* (New York: Van Nostrand Reinhold, 1978), p. 364.

[27]B. Yavitz and W. H. Newman, *Strategy in Action* (New York: Free Press, 1982), p. 207.

[28]Lawrence G. Hrebiniak and William F. Joyce, *Implementing Strategy* (New York: Macmillian, 1984), pp. 204–9.

FIGURE 10–9
Annual Incentive System with Long-Term Perspective

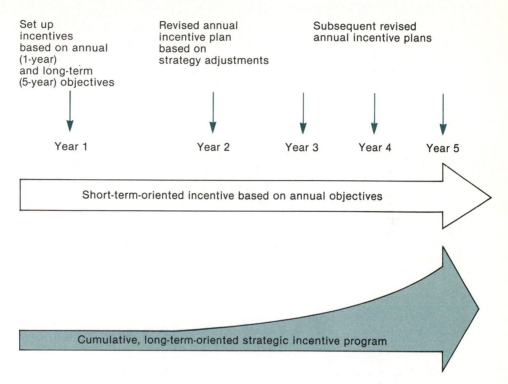

To integrate long- and short-term concerns, reward systems must be based on the assessment and control of both the short-run and long-run (strategic) contributions of key managers. An effective reward system should provide payoffs that control and evaluate the creation of *potential* future performances as well as last year's results. Figure 10–9 illustrates a management reward system that is tied to a five-year cycle of strategy implementation. Review and evaluation in a specific year include *both* an assessment of performance during that year and an evaluation of progress toward the five-year strategic objectives. Each year's objectives and incentives can reflect the adjustments necessary for successful implementation of the strategy. This helps integrate short- and long-term considerations in strategy implementation by linking the adjustments necessitated by revised, long-term considerations to next year's reward structure. A component of the management reward system shown in Figure 10–9 is an incentive based on cumulative progress toward strategic objectives. It is shown as increasing over time, which reinforces the long-term, strategic perspective. This reward component could be structured through such incentives as stock options, deferred bonuses, or cumulative compensation indexed to future performance indicators. The key ingredient is an incentive system linked to longer-term progress toward strategic goals. This approach reinforces the interdependence of performance over the five-year period.

FIGURE 10–10

Perceived Importance of Various Performance Dimensions in Determination of SBU General Manager's Incentive Bonus

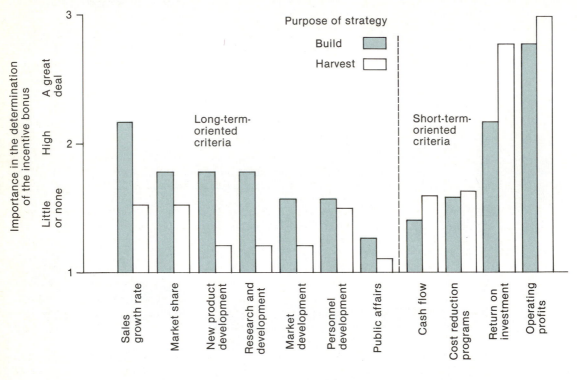

Source: Anil K. Gupta and V. Govindarajan, "Build Hold, Harvest: Converting Strategic Intentions into Reality," *Journal of Business Strategy*, Winter 1984, p. 43.

Long-term versus short-term incentive priorities should vary depending on the nature of the strategy. Figure 10–10 provides the results of a study illustrating this point. Comparing the importance of 11 criteria used in determining bonuses for SBU managers, the researchers found that long-term criteria were more important determinants of bonuses in SBUs with "build-oriented" strategies than in SBUs with "harvest-oriented" strategies. Although short-term criteria were important in both types of SBUs, they were much more important in harvest-oriented SBUs than in build-oriented SBUs. Strategy in Action 10–4 illustrates how the compensation of the two top executives at Disney and Gulf & Western was linked to strategic success.

Another means for constructing incentive systems that reward both long-term (strategic) and short-term thinking is the use of *strategic budgets*.[29] These budgets are employed

---

[29]Peter Lorange, *Implementation of Strategic Planning* (Englewood Cliffs, N.J.: Prentice-Hall, 1982); and "Strategic Control: Some Issues in Making It Operationally More Useful," in *Latest Advances in Strategic Management*, ed. R. Lamb Warren (Englewood Cliffs, N.J.: Prentice-Hall, 1986).

STRATEGY IN ACTION 10–4

TOP MANAGEMENT COMPENSATION IN TWO ENTERTAINMENT COMPANIES

An intriguing dynamic scene gets played out in the boardroom when it is time to set the CEO's pay. Consider the story behind the $12.6 million in restricted stock that Martin S. Davis, chairman of Gulf & Western, Inc., got in 1988. In 1983, after the death of Charles G. Bluhdorn, Davis was named chairman. In offering Davis a new contract, the board's compensation committee toyed with the idea of granting him 250,000 shares of restricted stock. The committee eventually settled on 150,000 shares, then valued at $4 million.

But a year later, after Disney upped the ante for top entertainment executives by awarding Michael Eisner and Frank Wells very lucrative contracts, the committee added an extra 100,000 shares to Davis's kitty. "A new plateau was established for us competitively," explained Samuel J. Silberman, the chairman of G&W's compensation committee. "You have to be in the ballpark. Everybody seems to worry about overpaying executives, but it would scare the hell out of me to underpay."

Compensation committees often fail to grasp how fast the rewards of complicated long-term packages can escalate if all goes well. When Eisner and Wells were recruited to Disney in 1984, the company's compensation committee was ready to pay them the going rate for entertainment executives—about $2 million a year. Instead, both executives proposed taking smaller base salaries—$750,00 for Eisner and $400,000 for Wells—in exchange for lucrative bonuses and a spate of stock options.

With earnings down and raiders circling, the board was eager to entice the pair. It offered contracts that included a piece of the action—for Eisner, an annual cash bonus equal to 2 percent of Disney's net income in excess of a 9 percent return on equity. That clause alone resulted in a $6.8 million 1988 bonus when Disney's return on equity hit 25 percent.

"I had no idea that it would turn out like it has." admitted Raymond L. Watson, former company chairman and a Disney director. "But then I didn't think that our stock would be trading at four or five times what it was when they came in, either."

Even so, couldn't Eisner and Wells have been recruited to Disney without offering carrots bigger than Mickey Mouse's ears? "If you're asking whether we could have gotten them for a 1 percent bonus instead of 2 percent or fewer stock options, I don't really know," said Watson. "But I know that no one is complaining." Not even Scrooge McDuck.

Source: "Is the Boss Getting Paid Too Much?" *Business Week*, May 1, 1989, pp. 46–53.

simultaneously with operating budgets, but the objectives and plans associated with the two types of budgets vary greatly. The focus of the operating budget is control and evaluation of business as usual, whereas the strategic budget specifies resources (and targets) for key programs or activities that are integral to the long-term strategy. To give more explicit weight to strategic activities in executive incentive plans, proponents of strategic budgets suggest three basic steps:

1. Measure progress toward strategic targets separately from the results of established operations.

2. Determine incentive awards separately for established operations and for progress toward strategic targets.

3. Devise a long-term stock option equivalent to encourage revisions of strategy and entrepreneurial risk taking.[30]

Common to the various reward and sanction approaches to implementing strategy is growing recognition of the need for an incentive system linked to both short-run and long-run considerations. The relative emphasis given to these considerations should be determined by the focus of the strategy. For firms with growth-oriented strategies, incentive systems weighted toward long-term payoffs are more appropriate. For firms pursuing more immediate strategic goals, the incentive emphasis should shift accordingly. In harvest business units of large firms, for example, greater emphasis on short-term, easily quantified performance indicators appears to be the basis for reward systems designed to evaluate strategic results.

SUMMARY

This chapter examined the idea that a key aspect of implementing a strategy is the *institutionalization* of the strategy so that it permeates daily decisions and actions in a manner consistent with long-term strategic success. Four fundamental elements must be managed to "fit" a strategy if the strategy is to be effectively institutionalized: *organizational structure, leadership, culture,* and *rewards.*

Five fundamental organizational structures were examined, and the advantages and disadvantages of each were identified. Institutionalizing a strategy requires a good strategy-structure fit. This chapter dealt with how this requirement is often overlooked until performance becomes inadequate and indicated the conditions under which the various structures would be appropriate.

Organizational leadership is essential to effective strategy implementation. The CEO plays a critical role in this regard. Assignment of key managers, particularly within the top-management team, is an important aspect of organizational leadership. Deciding whether to promote insiders or hire outsiders is often a central leadership issue in strategy implementation. This chapter showed how this decision could be made in a manner that would best institutionalize the new strategy.

In recent years, organizational culture has been recognized as a pervasive influence on organizational life. Organizational culture, the shared beliefs and values of an organization's members, may be a major help or hindrance to strategy implementation. This chapter discussed an approach to managing the strategy-culture fit. It identified four fundamentally different strategy-culture situations and provided recommendations for managing the strategy-culture fit in each of these situations.

The reward system is a key ingredient in motivating managers to execute a firm's strategy. Firms should emphasize incentive systems that ensure adequate attention to strategic thrusts. This usually requires a concerted effort to emphasize long-term strategic

---

[30]Yavitz and Newman, *Strategy in Action*, p. 179.

performance as well as short-term measures of performance. Short- and long-term performance considerations must be integrated to ensure performance consistent with a firm's strategy.

QUESTIONS FOR DISCUSSION

1. What key structural considerations must be incorporated into strategy implementation? Why does structural change often lag a change in strategy?

2. Which organizational structure is most appropriate for successful strategy implementation? Explain how state of development affects your answer.

3. Why is leadership an important element in strategy implementation? Find an example in a major business periodical of the CEO's key role in strategy implementation.

4. Under what conditions would it be more appropriate to fill a key management position with someone from outside the firm when a qualified insider is available?

5. What is organizational culture? Why is it important? Explain two different situations a firm might face in managing the strategy-culture relationship.

6. How would you vary an incentive system for a growth-oriented versus a harvest-oriented business?

7. Why do strategists prefer reward systems similar to the one shown in Figure 10–9? What are the advantages and disadvantages of such a system?

BIBLIOGRAPHY

Bailey, G., and J. Szerdy. "Is There Life after Downsizing?" *Journal of Business Strategy*, January 1988, pp. 8–11.

Barney, J. B. "Organizational Culture: Can It Be a Source of Sustained Competitive Advantage?" *Academy of Management Review*, July 1986, p. 656.

Block, Barbara. "Creating A Culture All Employees Can Accept," *Management Review*, July 1989, p. 41.

Bower, Joseph Lyon, and Martha Wagner Weinberg. "Statecraft, Strategy, and Corporate Leadership." *California Management Review*, Winter 1988, p. 107.

Byles, C. M., and R. J. Keating. "Strength of Organizational Culture and Performance: Strategic Implications." *Journal of Business Strategy*, Spring 1989, pp. 45–55.

Chapman, P. "Changing the Corporate Culture of Rank Xerox." *Long Range Planning*, April 1988, pp. 23–28.

Cowherd, D. M., and R. H. Luchs. "Linking Organization Structures and Processes to Business Strategy." *Long Range Planning*, October 1988, pp. 47–53.

"Cultural Transition at AT&T." *Sloan Management Review*, Fall 1983, pp. 15–26.

Daft, R. L.; J. Sormunen; and D. Parks. "Chief Executive Scanning." *Strategic Management Journal*, March 1988, pp. 123–140.

Drake, Bruce H., and Eileen Drake. "Ethical and Legal Aspects of Managing Corporate Cultures." *California Management Review*, Winter 1988, p. 107.

Forman, R. "Strategic Planning and the Chief Executive." *Long Range Planning*, August 1988, pp. 57–64.

Fredrickson, James W.; Donald C. Hambrick; and Sara Bawmrin. "A Model of CEO Dismissal." *Academy of Management Review*, April 1988, p. 255.

Freund, York P. "Critical Success Factors." *Planning Review,* July–August 1988, p. 20.

Gomez-Mejia, Luis R.; Henri Tose; and Timothy Hinkin. "Managerial Control, Performance, and Executive Compensation." *Academy of Management Journal,* March 1987, p. 51.

Gupta, Anil K. "SBU Strategies, Corporate-SBU Relations, and SBU Effectiveness in Strategy Implementation." *Academy of Management Journal,* September 1987, p. 477.

Hosking, D. M. "Organizing, Leadership and Skillful Process." *Journal of Management Studies,* March 1988, pp. 147–66.

Koch, D. L., and D. W. Steinhauser. "Changing the Corporate Culture." *Datamotion,* October 1983, pp. 247–52.

Larson, Erik W., and David H. Gobeli. "Matrix Management: Contradictions and Insights." *California Management Review,* Summer 1987, p. 126.

Liden, Robert C., and Terence R. Mitchell. "Ingratiatory Behavior in Organizational Settings." *Academy of Management Review,* October 1988, p. 572.

Main, John G., and John Thackray. "The Logic of Restructuring." *Planning Review,* May–June 1987, p. 5.

Meindl, James R., and Sanford B. Ehrlich. "The Romance of Leadership and Evaluation of Organizational Performance." *Academy of Management Journal,* March 1987, p. 91.

Miller, Danny. "Strategy Making and Structure: Analysis and Implications for Performance." *Academy of Management Journal,* March 1987, p. 7.

Nichols, Don. "Bottom-up Strategies." *Management Review,* December 1989, p. 44.

Reed, R., and M. Reed. "CEO Experience and Diversification Strategy Fit." *Journal of Management Studies,* March 1988, pp. 251–70.

Reimann, Bernard C., and Yoash Wiener. "Corporate Culture: Avoiding the Elitist Trap." *Business Horizons,* March–April 1988, p. 36.

Saffold, Guy S., III. "Culture Traits, Strength, and Settings." *Academy of Management Review,* October 1988, p. 546.

Spector, Bert A. "From Bogged-Down to Fired-Up: Inspiring Oranizational Change." *Sloan Management Review,* Summer 1989, p. 29.

"Strategic Leaders and Leadership." *Strategic Management Journal,* special issue, Summer 1989.

Vancil, Richard F. "A Look at CEO Succession." *Harvard Business Review,* March–April 1987, p. 107.

Vincent, D. R. "Understanding Organization Power." *Journal of Business Strategy,* March 1988, pp. 40–44.

Wagner, John A., III and Richard Z. Gooding. "Shared Influence and Organizational Behavior: A Meta-Analysis of Situational Variables Expected to Moderate Participation-Outcome Relationships," *Academy of Management Review,* September 1987, p. 524.

Webber, Alvin M. "The CEO Is the Company." *Harvard Business Review,* January–February 1987, p. 114.

Zabriskie, N., and A. Huellmantel. "Implementing Strategies for Human Resources." *Long Range Planning,* April 1989, pp. 70–77.

CHAPTER 10 COHESION CASE

IMPLEMENTATION: INSTITUTIONALIZING THE STRATEGY

The next issue Bryson's managers addressed in implementing their strategies for the 1990s was that of organizational structure. What was the best organizational structure to meet the needs of their new strategy?

Bryson's structure in 1989 as described in the cohesion case was basically a geographically based structure. The company was divided into Bryson-East and Bryson-West. Each geographical unit operated as a highly autonomous division of the company.

There were sound reasons for this structure. Customers in the two locations tended to be somewhat different. Most eastern customers, with routine waste disposal needs, generated large quantities regularly. They were also in an area of the country that had become very sensitive to the need to cleanup past contaminated areas. Mixed with a few larger-quantity generators were many smaller-quantity generators within 500 miles of Memphis, Tennessee. The level of cleanup activity and EPA scrutiny was less than the East. So many "west" managers argued that the differences in their marketplace required that "things be done differently" and to do so required significant regional autonomy.

Other reasons managers felt a geographically based structure was appropriate included the different types of business activities in each region (Memphis was heavily involved with the Wall Chemical recycling facility, while no such facility existed in Bryson's eastern organization; Lexington included a medical waste operation, while no such business was anticipated for Memphis for some time) and a sense that Memphis was a newer, entrepreneurial outpost, while the eastern operations were more mature and established.

While reasons were available to justify keeping a geographically based, divisional organization, Bryson's board of directors had several reasons to change the structure to accommodate the new strategy. First, the directors were concerned about a lack of control over geographically dispersed operations. Second, the decision to sell the medical waste business reduced their diversity of businesses. Third, the decision to merge Wall Chemical into Bryson was based primarily on the potential synergy across Bryson's other two types of business with recycling and a Part B facility—a synergy that could be better achieved with a more centralized organization. Fourth, Wall was in a financially weak position and, along with Memphis, represented a major financial risk over which corporate management needed greater control. Fifth, Bryson's two core businesses—transportation and remedial services—both had key resources (equipment and service crews, respectively] that were not always in use. Consequently, a more central management of each business had the potential to more efficiently deploy them across multiple locations as the need for them shifted back and forth. Sixth, Bryson realized it was located at the two "outside ends" of the southeastern market it targeted. The largest concentration of potential southeastern clients resided in Georgia, a fact that had not gone unnoticed by some of Bryson's larger national competitors who made sure to have an Atlanta-based office. So Bryson's board felt that again a centralized sales organization, with salespeople assigned to different territories but centrally controlled, would allow greater flexibility in allocating or shifting salespeople and resources to more aggressively penetrate the Georgia/central southeastern market. Finally, Bryson was still a relatively small company, compared to several prominent competitors. As such, it could not afford serious financial mistakes. Therefore, centralized control of finance and administration would increase control and lessen the risk of a serious financial mistake.

The board of directors decided to adopt a functional organization at Bryson for the 1990s. Their initial organization was as follows:

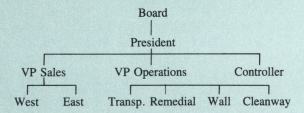

After four months into 1990, that structure was simplified even further to look like:

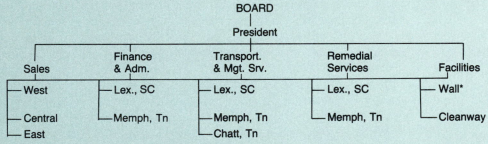

*Name changed to "Bryson Recovery Services" in mid-1990.

What is your evaluation of the revised Bryson structure? Does it fit the strategy for the 1990s? What reasons support your answer?

Assignments of key management personnel became a second major concern of the Bryson board of directors. The board was comfortable with the current placement of two Bryson managers—Don Boan as controller and Jim Ullery as director of remedial services. The other positions remained somewhat of a question mark moving into 1990. Initially, Joel Stevenson served the dual role of president and V.P. for sales. Charles Kelly accepted the position of V.P. for Operations, overseeing each of the core businesses at Bryson.

These assignments began to produce problems. Essentially, Stevenson and Kelly were spread rather broadly. The role of president required serious attention to organizational issues and creating a precedent for delegation. The V.P. for sales position needed to focus attention on creating a sales organization that rationalized and integrated multiple locations and the role of outside salespeople versus inside salespeople. Coverage of three types of businesses in multiple locations was a remaining challenge, requiring highly developed organizational skills.

The result was a change in organizational structure, as shown above, where the structure had a president and five executive managers. After much consideration, Joel Stevenson stepped down as president to focus exclusively on managing the sales organization. Charles Kelly was put in charge of facilities, because of his initial involvement with personnel in each facility operation. Jim Ullery and Don Boan held their current positions but were placed on a par with Kelly and Stevenson in daily organizational decision making.

Two major management assignments remained. The first was president. After much consideration of seeking outside versus inside people, the board decided that an inside person known to all key personnel would be more appropriate during this change period. The board then offered the position of president to Dr. Richard Robinson, who had been consultant to the company for six years. Robinson, in turn, placed a high priority on hiring a new director of management and transportation. After interviews with several experienced managers with outside transportation firms, Dr. Robinson decided to offer the position to an internal person—Evon Reynolds—who had grown up within the Bryson business, assisting two male managers of transportation sales and operations. While her formal education included some post-high school technical college training, Ms. Reynolds was highly respected among Bryson's drivers for her stern fairness and work ethic.

The last area of concern to the board was management of the culture of Bryson. Essentially, Bryson had evolved as a "trucking" company, with an attendant culture. It was not actively involved in "more sophisticated" activities associated with engineers and specialists in remedial services and recycling. A careful blend of the cultures associated with each activity was something the board of Bryson considered a major challenge in pursuing the new strategies into the 1990s.

A second "culture" issue identified by Bryson's board was the need to change Bryson from essentially an "owner-managed" company into a "manager-managed" company. The board felt this change was essential to make the 1990s strategy with multiple revenue streams and multiple locations work and to provide an environment attractive to talented "middle" management personnel that will be essential additions to make this strategy work. The change of the president of the company and the reassignment of two key owner-managers, Stevenson and Kelly, were considered by the board to be major first steps to reinforce this new, manager-managed culture.

What is your assessment of the management changes and culture sensitivity pursued by the Bryson board? Are they supportive of the new strategy? What additional or alternative changes you would suggest?

11 STRATEGIC CONTROL: GUIDING AND EVALUATING THE STRATEGY

Strategies are forward looking, designed to be accomplished several years into the future, and based on management assumptions about numerous events that have not yet occurred. How should managers control a strategy? The traditional approach to control compares actual results against a standard. After work is done, the manager evaluates it and then uses that evaluation as input to control further work. Although this approach has its place, it is inappropriate as a means for controlling a strategy. The full execution of a strategy often takes five or more years, during which many changes occur that have major ramifications for the strategy's ultimate success. Consequently, the traditional approaches to control must be replaced by an approach that recognizes the unique control needs of long-term strategies.

Strategic control is concerned with tracking a strategy as it is being implemented, detecting problems or changes in its underlying premises, and making necessary adjustments. In contrast to postaction control, strategic control is concerned with guiding action in behalf of the strategy as that action is taking place and when the end result is still several years off. Managers responsible for the success of a strategy are typically concerned with two sets of questions:

1. Are we moving in the proper direction? Are key things falling into place? Are our assumptions about major trends and changes correct? Are we doing the critical things that need to be done? Should we adjust or abort the strategy?
2. How are we performing? Are objectives and schedules being met? Are costs, revenues, and cash flows matching projections? Do we need to make operational changes?

Strategic controls, augmented by certain operational controls, are designed to answer these questions.

ESTABLISHING STRATEGIC CONTROLS

The control of strategy can be characterized as a form of "steering control."[1] Ordinarily, a good deal of time elapses between the initial implementation of a strategy and achievement of its intended results. During that time, investments are made and numerous projects and actions are undertaken to implement the strategy. Also during that time, changes are taking place in both the environmental situation and the firm's internal situation. Strategic controls are necessary to steer the firm through these events. They must provide the basis for adapting the firm's actions and directions in implementing its strategy to these developments and changes.

Prudential Insurance Company provides a useful example of the proactive, steering nature of strategic control. Several years ago, Prudential adopted a long-term market development strategy in which it sought to attain the top position in the life insurance industry by differentiating its level of service from those of its competitors. It decided to achieve a differential service advantage by establishing regional home offices. Exercising strategic control, its managers used the experience of the first regional offices to reproject the overall expenses and income associated with this strategy. The predicted expenses were so high that the original schedule for establishing other regional offices had to be modified. And on the basis of other early feedback, the restructuring of the services performed at Prudential's corporate headquarters was sharply revised. Thus, the steering control (or strategic control) exercised by Prudential managers significantly altered the firm's strategy. In this case, the major objectives of the strategy remained in place; in other cases, strategic control has led to changes in the major strategic objectives.

The four basic types of strategic control are:

1. Premise control.
2. Implementation control.
3. Strategic surveillance.
4. Special alert control.

The nature of these four types is summarized in Figure 11–1.

Premise Control

Every strategy is based on certain planning premises—assumptions or predictions. *Premise control is designed to check systematically and continuously whether the premises on which the strategy is based are still valid.* If a vital premise is no longer valid, the strategy may have to be changed. The sooner an invalid premise can be recognized and rejected, the better are the chances that an acceptable shift in the strategy can be devised.

Which Premises Should Be Monitored?

Planning premises are primarily concerned with environmental and industry factors. These are described next.

---

[1] B. Yavitz and W. H. Newman, *Strategy in Action* (New York: Free Press, 1982), p. 207.

Monitoring Strategic Thrusts

As a means of implementing broad strategies, narrow strategic projects are often undertaken—projects that represent part of what needs to be done if the overall strategy is to be accomplished. These strategic thrusts provide managers with information that helps them determine whether the overall strategy is progressing as planned or needs to be adjusted.

Although the utility of strategic thrusts seems readily apparent, it is not always easy to use them for control purposes. It may be difficult to interpret early experience or to evaluate the overall strategy in light of such experience. One approach is to agree early in the planning process on which thrusts or which phases of thrusts are critical factors in the success of the strategy. Managers responsible for these implementation controls single them out from other activities and observe them frequently. Another approach is to use stop/go assessments that are linked to a series of meaningful thresholds (time, costs, research and development, success, etc.) associated with particular thrusts. A program of regional development via company-owned inns in the Rocky Mountain area was a monitoring thrust that Days Inn used to test its strategy of becoming a nationwide motel chain. Problems in meeting time targets and unexpectedly large capital needs led Days Inn's executives to abandon the overall strategy and sell the firm.

Milestone Reviews

Managers often attempt to identify significant milestones that will be reached during the time a strategy is being implemented. These milestones may be critical events, major resource allocations, or simply the passage of a certain amount of time. The milestone reviews that then take place usually involve a full-scale reassessment of the strategy and of the advisability of continuing or refocusing the firm's direction.

A useful example of implementation control based on milestone review is offered by Boeing's product development strategy of entering the supersonic transport (SST) airplane market. Boeing had invested millions of dollars and years of scarce engineering talent during the first phase of its SST venture, and competition from the British/French Concorde effort was intense. Since the next phase represented a billion-dollar decision, Boeing's management established the initiation of the phase as a milestone. The milestone reviews greatly increased the estimates of production costs; predicted relatively few passengers and rising fuel costs, thus raising the estimated operating costs; and noted that the Concorde, unlike Boeing, had the benefit of massive government subsidies. These factors led Boeing's management to scrap its SST strategy in spite of high sunk costs, pride, and patriotism. Only an objective, full-scale strategy reassessment could have led to such a decision.[2]

In this example, a milestone review occurred at a major resource allocation decision point. Milestone reviews may also occur concurrent when a major step in a strategy's implementation is being taken or when a key uncertainty is resolved. Managers may even set an arbitrary period, say two years, as a milestone review point. Whatever the basis for selecting that point, the critical purpose of a milestone review is to thoroughly scrutinize the firm's strategy so as to control the strategy's future.

---

[2]Ibid.

Strategic Surveillance

By their nature, premise control and implementation control are focused controls; strategic surveillance, however, is unfocused. *Strategic surveillance is designed to monitor a broad range of events inside and outside the firm that are likely to affect the course of its strategy.*[3] The basic idea behind strategic surveillance is that important yet unanticipated information may be uncovered by a general monitoring of multiple information sources.

Strategic surveillance must be kept as unfocused as possible. It should be a loose "environmental scanning" activity. Trade magazines, *The Wall Street Journal,* trade conferences, conversations, and intended and unintended observations are all subjects of strategic surveillance. Despite its looseness, strategic surveillance provides an ongoing, broad-based vigilance in all daily operations that may uncover information relevant to the firm's strategy. Citicorp benefited significantly from a Peruvian manager's strategic surveillance of political speeches by Peru's president, as discussed in Strategy in Action 11–1.

Special Alert Control

Another type of strategic control, really a subset of the other three, is special alert control. *A special alert control is the thorough, and often rapid, reconsideration of the firm's strategy because of a sudden, unexpected event.* A political coup in the Middle East, an outside firm's sudden acquisition of a leading competitor, an unexpected product difficulty

TABLE 11–1
Characteristics of the Four Types of Strategic Control

Basic Characteristics	Types of Strategic Control			
	Premise Control	Implementation Control	Strategic Surveillance	Special Alert Control
Objects of control	Planning premises and projections	Key strategic thrusts and milestones	Potential threats and opportunities related to the strategy	Occurrence of recognizable but unlikely events
Degree of focusing	High	High	Low	High
Data acquisition:				
Formalization	Medium	High	Low	High
Centralization	Low	Medium	Low	High
Use with:				
Environmental factors	Yes	Seldom	Yes	Yes
Industry factors	Yes	Seldom	Yes	Yes
Strategy-specific factors	No	Yes	Seldom	Yes
Company-specific factors	No	Yes	Seldom	Seldom

Source: Adapted from G. Schreyogg and H. Steinmann, "Strategic Control: A New Perspective," *Academy of Management Review* 12, no. 1 (1987), p. 91–103.

---

[3]G. Schreyogg and H. Steinmann, "Strategic Control: A New Perspective," *Academy of Management Review* 12, no. 1 (1987), p. 101.

EXAMPLES OF STRATEGIC CONTROLS

PREMISE CONTROL AT MOBIL CORPORATION

Mobil Corporation, which has been operating in South Africa since 1895, is withdrawing from the country and selling its assets to General Mining Union Corporation of South Africa. The transaction will include a refinery and 1,150 gasoline stations.

The decision was based on a change in the U.S. tax law that forbids U.S. companies from taking credit for taxes paid to South Africa on their U.S. operations in that country. As a result, Mobil claims their profit generated in South Africa is doubly taxed at an effective rate of 72 percent. A major *premise* of Mobil's overseas business strategy is that the U.S. tax liability will be reduced by the amount of tax paid in the host country. Disinvestment of U.S. companies now in South Africa could be intensified in light of possible U.S. legislation completely banning any U.S. companies from operating in that country.

IMPLEMENTATION CONTROL AT DAYS INN

When Days Inns pioneered the budget segment of the lodging industry, its strategy placed primary emphasis on company-owned facilities and it insisted on maintaining a roughly 3-to-1 company-owned/franchise ratio. This ratio ensured the parent company's total control over standards, rates, and so forth.

As other firms moved into the budget segment, Days Inns saw the need to expand rapidly throughout the United States and therefore reversed its conservative franchise posture. This reversal would rapidly accelerate its ability to open new locations. Longtime executives, concerned about potential loss of control over local standards, instituted *implementation controls* requiring both franchise evaluation and annual milestone reviews. Two years into the program, Days Inn's executives were convinced that a high franchise-to-company ratio was manageable, and so they accelerated the growth of franchising by doubling the franchise sales department.

STRATEGIC SURVEILLANCE AT CITICORP

Citicorp has been pursuing an aggressive product development strategy intended to achieve an annual earnings growth of 15 percent while it becomes an institution capable of supplying clients

Source: Adapted from "Citicorp: What the New Boss Is up to," *Fortune*, February 17, 1986, p. 40; conversations with selected Days Inns executives; Peter M. Drucker, *Innovation and Entrepreneurship* (New York: Harper & Row, 1986); and "How Companies Prepare for the Worst," *Business Week*, December 23, 1985, p. 74.

such as the poisoned Tylenol capsules—events of these kinds can drastically alter the firm's strategy.

Such an event should trigger an immediate and intense reassessment of the firm's strategy and its current strategic situation. In many firms, crisis teams handle the firm's initial response to unforeseen events that may have an immediate effect on its strategy. Increasingly, firms have developed contingency plans along with crisis teams to respond to circumstances such as those illustrated in Strategy in Action 11–1.

STRATEGY IN ACTION 11–1   **concluded**

with any kind of financial service anywhere in the world. A major obstacle to the achievement of this earnings growth is Citicorp's exposure to default because of its extensive earlier loans to troubled Third World countries. Citicorp is sensitive to the wide variety of predictions about impending Third World defaults.

Citicorp's long-range plan assumes an annual 10 percent default on its Third World loans over any five-year period. Yet it maintains active *strategic surveillance control* by having each of its international branches monitor daily announcements from key governments and from inside contacts for signs of changes in a host country's financial environment. When that surveillance detects a potential problem, management attempts to adjust Citicorp's posture. For example, when Peru's president, Alan Garcia, stated that his country would not pay interest on its debt as scheduled, Citicorp raised its annual default charge to 20 percent of its $100 million Peruvian exposure.

SPECIAL ALERT CONTROL AT UNITED AIRLINES

The sudden impact of an airline crash can be devastating to a major airline. United Airlines has made elaborate preparations to deal with this contingency. Its executive vice president, James M. Guyette, heads a crisis team that is permanently prepared to respond. Members of the team carry beepers and are always on call. If United's Chicago headquarters receives word that a plane has crashed, for example, they can be in a "war room" within an hour to direct the response. Beds are set up nearby so that team members can catch a few winks; while they sleep, alternates take their places.

Members of the team have been carefully screened through simulated crisis drills. "The point is to weed out those who don't hold up well under stress." says Guyette. Although the team was established to handle flight disasters, it has since assumed an expanded role. The crisis team was activated when American Airlines launched a fare war. And according to Guyette, "We're brainstorming about how we would be affected by everything from a competitor who had a serious problem to a crisis involving a hijacking or taking a United employee hostage."

Table 11–1 summarizes the major characteristics of the four types of strategic control. All four types share a common purpose: to assess whether the strategic direction should be altered in light of unfolding events. Unlike operational controls, which are concerned with the control of action, strategic controls are designed to continuously and proactively question the basic direction of the strategy. Both operational and strategic controls are needed to manage the strategic process effectively. The next section examines key types of operational control systems used to aid the strategic management process.

OPERATIONAL CONTROL SYSTEMS

Operational control systems guide, monitor, and evaluate progress in meeting annual objectives. While strategic controls attempt to steer the company over an extended period (usually five years or more), operational controls provide postaction evaluation and control over short periods—usually from one month to one year. To be effective, operational control systems must take four steps common to all postaction controls:

1. Set standards of performance.
2. Measure actual performance.
3. Identify deviations from standards set.
4. Initiate corrective action.

Three types of operational control system are *budgets, schedules,* and *key success factors.* The nature and use of these three types of systems are described in the next sections.

Budgets

The budgetary process was the forerunner of strategic planning. A budget is a resource allocation plan that helps managers coordinate operations and facilitates managerial control of performance. Budgets themselves do not control anything. They simply set standards against which action can be measured. They also provide a basis for negotiating short-term resource requirements to implement strategy at the operating level.

Most firms employ a budgeting system rather than a singular budget. Figure 11–2 represents a typical budgeting system for a manufacturing business. A budgeting system incorporates a series of different budgets fitting the organization's unique characteristics. Because organizations differ, so do their budgets. Yet most firms include three general types of budgets—revenue, capital, and expenditure—in their budgetary control system.

Revenue Budgets

Most firms employ some form of revenue budget to monitor their sales projections (or expectations) because sales are a key objective of the chosen strategy. The revenue budget provides important information for the daily management of financial resources and key feedback as to whether the strategy is working. For example, most hotel/motel operators emphasize daily revenue as compared to revenue for the same day in the previous year as a monitor of sales effectiveness.

A revenue budget is particularly important as a means of obtaining early warnings about the effectiveness of the firm's strategy.

Capital Budgets

Capital budgets outline specific expenditures for plant, equipment, machinery, inventories, and other capital items needed during the budget period. For effective control, a capital budget that carefully plans the timing of the acquisition and expenditure of funds is essential.

Two additional budgets—a cash budget and a balance sheet budget—are often developed to control the use of capital resources. A *cash budget* forecasts receipts and

FIGURE 11–2
A Typical Budgeting System for Controlling Strategy Implementation

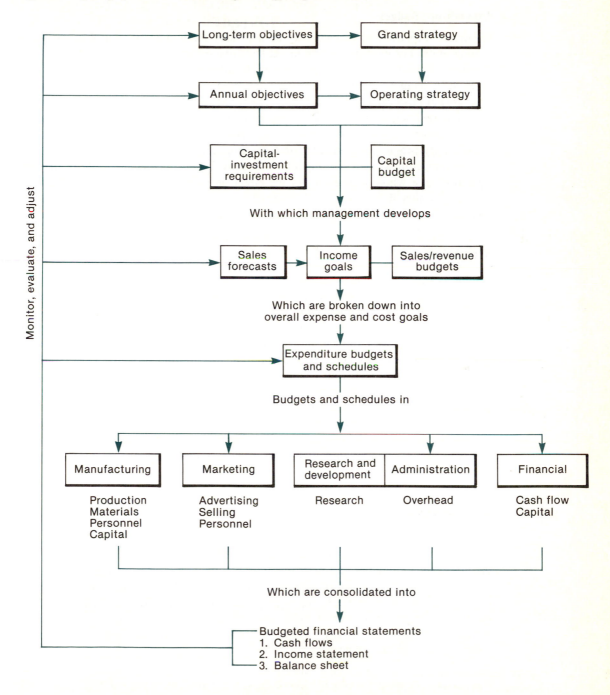

Guide to Strategic Management Case Analysis

The Case Method

Case analysis is a proven educational method that is especially effective in a strategic management course. The case method complements and enhances the text material and your professor's lectures by focusing attention on what a firm has done or should do in an actual business situation. Use of the case method in the strategic management course offers you an opportunity to develop and refine analytical skills. It can also provide exciting experience by allowing you to assume the role of the key decision maker for the organizations you will study.

When assuming the role of the general manager of the organization being studied, you will need to consider all aspects of the business. In addition to drawing on your knowledge of marketing, finance, management, production, and economics, you will be applying the strategic management concepts taught in this course.

The cases in this book are accounts of real business situations involving a variety of firms in a variety of industries. To make these opportunities as realistic as possible, the cases include a variety of quantitative and qualitative information in both the presentation of the situation and the exhibits. As the key decision maker, you will need to determine which information is important, given the circumstances described in the case. Keep in mind that the results of analyzing one firm will not necessarily be appropriate for another since every firm is faced with a different set of circumstances.

Preparing for Case Discussion

The case method requires an approach to class preparation that differs from the typical lecture course. In the typical lecture course, you can still benefit from each class session even if you did not prepare, by listening carefully to the professor's lecture. This approach will not work in a course using the case method. For such a case course, proper preparation is essential.

Suggestions for Effective Preparation

1. *Allow adequate time in preparing a case.* Many of the cases in this text involve complex issues that are often not apparent without careful reading and purposeful reflection on the information in the cases.

This guide was developed by John A. Pearce II, Richard B. Robinson, Jr., and William R. Bayer.

2. *Read each case twice.* Because many of these cases involve complex decision making, you should read each case at least twice. Your first reading should give you an overview of the firm's unique circumstances and the issues confronting the firm. Your second reading allows you to concentrate on what you feel are the most critical issues and to understand what information in the case is most important. Make limited notes identifying key points during your first reading. During your second reading, you can add details to your original notes and revise them as necessary.

3. *Focus on the key strategic issue in each case.* Each time you read a case you should concentrate on identifying the key issue. In some of the cases, the key issue will be identified by the case writer in the introduction. In other cases, you might not grasp the key strategic issue until you have read the case several times. (Remember that not every piece of information in a case is equally important.)

4. *Do not overlook exhibits.* The exhibits in these cases should be considered an integral part of the information for the case. They are not just "window dressing." In fact, for many cases you will need to analyze financial statements, evaluate organizational charts, and understand the firm's products, all of which are presented in the form of exhibits.

5. *Adopt the appropriate time frame.* It is critical that you assume the appropriate time frame for each case you read. If the case ends in 1985, that year should become the present for you as you work on that case. Making a decision for a case that ends in 1985 by using data you could not have had until 1986 defeats the purpose of the case method. For the same reason, although it is recommended that you do outside reading on each firm and industry, you should not read material written after the case ended unless your professor instructs you to do so.

6. *Draw on all of your knowledge of business.* As the key decision maker for the organization being studied, you will need to consider all aspects of the business and industry. Do not confine yourself to strategic management concepts presented in this course. You will need to determine if the key strategic issue revolves around a theory you have learned in a functional area, such as marketing, production, finance, or economics, or in the strategic management course.

PARTICIPATING IN CLASS

Because the strategic management course uses the case method, the success and value of the course depend on class discussion. The success and value of the class discussion, in turn, rely on the roles both you and your professor perform. Following are aspects of your role and your professor's, which, if kept in mind, will enhance the value and excitement of this course.

The Student as Active Learner

The case method requires your active participation. This means you role is no longer one of sitting and listening.

1. *Attend class regularly*. Not only is your grade likely to depend on your involvement in class discussions, but the benefit you derive from this course is directly related to your involvement in and understanding of the discussions.

2. *Be prepared for class*. The need for adequate preparation has already been discussed. You will benefit more from the discussions, will understand and participate in the exchange of ideas, and will avoid the embarrassment of being called on when not prepared. By all means, bring your book to class. Not only is there a good chance you will need to refer to a specific exhibit or passage from the case, you may need to refresh your memory of the case (particularly if you made notes in the margins while reading).

3. *Participate in the discussion*. Attending class and being prepared are not enough; you need to express your views in class. You can participate in a number of ways: by addressing a question asked by your professor, by disagreeing with your professor or your classmates (by all means, be tactful), by building on an idea expressed by a classmate, or by simply asking a relevant question.

4. *Participate wisely*. Although you do not want to be one of those students who never raises his or her hand, you should also be sensitive to the fact that others in your class will want to express themselves. You have probably already had experience with a student who attempts to dominate each class discussion. A student who invariable tries to dominate the class discussion breeds resentment.

5. *Keep a broad perspective*. By definition, the strategic management course deals with the issues facing general managers or business owners. As already mentioned, you need to consider all aspects of the business, not just one particular functional area.

6. *Pay attention to the topic being discussed*. Focus your attention on the topic being discussed. When a new topic is introduced, do not attempt to immediately introduce another topic for discussion. Do not feel you have to have something to say on every topic covered.

Your Professor as Discussion Leader

Your professor is a discussion leader. As such, he or she will attempt to stimulate the class as a whole to share insights, observations, and thoughts about the case. Your professor will not necessarily respond to every comment you or your classmates make. Part of the value of the case method is to get you and your classmates to assume this role as the course progresses.

The professor in a strategic management case course performs several roles:

1. *Maintaining focus*. Because multiple complex issues need to be explored, your professor may want to maintain the focus of the class discussion on one issue at a time. He or she may ask you to hold your comment on another issue until a

previous issue is exhausted. Do not interpret this response to mean your point is unimportant; your professor is simply indicating there will be a more appropriate time to pursue that particular comment.

2. *Getting students involved.* Do not be surprised if your professor asks for input from volunteers and nonvolunteers alike. The value of the class discussion increases as more people share their comments.

3. *Facilitating comprehension of strategic management concepts.* Some professors prefer to lecture on strategic management concepts on a "need-to-know" basis. In this scenario, a lecture on a particular topic will be followed by an assignment to work on a case that deals with that particular topic. Other professors will have the class work through a case or two before lecturing on a topic to give the class a feel for the value of the topic being covered and for the type of information needed to work on cases. Still other professors prefer to cover all of the theory in the beginning of the course, thereby allowing uninterrupted case discussion in the remaining weeks of the term. All three of these approaches are valid.

4. *Playing devil's advocate.* At times your professor may appear to be contradicting many of the comments or observations being made. At other times your professor may adopt a position that does not immediately make sense, given the circumstances of the case. At other times your professor may seem to be equivocating. These are all examples of how your professor might be playing devil's advocate. Sometimes the professor's goal is to expose alternative viewpoints. Sometimes he or she may be testing your resolve on a particular point. Be prepared to support your position with evidence from the case.

ASSIGNMENTS

Written Assignments

Written analyses are a critical part of any strategic management course. In fact, professors typically put more weight on written analyses than on exams or quizzes. Each professor has a preferred format for these written analyses, but a number of general guidelines will prove helpful to you in your written assignments.

1. *Analyze.* Avoid merely repeating the facts presented in the case. Analyze the issues involved in the case and build logically toward your recommendations.

2. *Use headings or labels.* Using headings or labels throughout your written analysis will help your reader follow your analysis and recommendations. For example, when you are analyzing the weaknesses of the firm in the case, include the heading Weaknesses. Note the headings in the sample case analysis that follows.

3. *Discuss alternatives.* Follow the proper strategic management sequence by (1) identifying alternatives, (2) evaluating each alternative, and (3) recommending the alternative you feel is best.

4. *Use topic sentences.* You can help your reader more easily evaluate your analysis by putting the topic sentence first in each paragraph and following with statements directly supporting the topic sentence.

5. *Be specific in your recommendations.* Develop specific recommendations logically and be sure your recommendations are well defended by your analysis. Avoid using generalizations, clichés, and ambiguous statements. Remember that any number of answers are possible, and so your professor is most concerned about how your reasoning led to your recommendations and how well you develop and support your ideas.

6. *Do not overlook implementation.* Many good analyses receive poor evaluations because they do not include a discussion of implementation. Your analysis will be much stronger when you discuss how your recommendation can be implemented. Include some of the specific actions needed to achieve the objectives you are proposing.

7. *Specifically state your assumptions.* Cases, like all real business situations, involve incomplete information. Therefore, it is important that you clearly state any assumptions you make in your analysis. Do not assume your professor will be able to fill in the missing points.

Oral Presentations

Your professor is also quite likely to ask you and your classmates to make oral presentations on a particular case. Oral presentations are usually done by groups of students. In these groups, each member will typically be responsible for one aspect of the overall case. Keep the following suggestions in mind when you are faced with an oral presentation:

1. *Use your own words.* Avoid memorizing a presentation. The best approach is to prepare an outline of the key points you want to cover. Do not be afraid to have the outline in front of you during your presentation, but do not just read the outline.

2. *Rehearse your presentation.* Do not assume you can simply read the outline you have prepared or that the right words will come to you when you are in front of the class making your presentation. Take the time to practice your speech, and be sure to rehearse the entire presentation with your group.

3. *Use visual aids.* The adage "a picture is worth a thousand words" contains quite a bit of truth. The people in your audience will more quickly and thoroughly understand your key points—and will retain them longer—if you can use visual aids. Think of ways you and your team members can use the blackboard in the classroom; a graph, chart, or exhibit on a large posterboard; or, if you will have a number of these visual aids, a flip chart.

4. *Be prepared to handle questions.* You will probably be asked questions by your classmates. If questions are asked during your presentation, try to address those that require clarification. Tactfully postpone more elaborate questions until you have completed the formal phase of your presentation. During your rehearsal, try to anticipate the types of questions that you might be asked.

Working as a Team Member

Many professors assign students to groups or teams for analyzing cases. This adds more realism to the course, since most strategic decisions in business are addressed by a group of key managers. If you are a member of a group assigned to analyze a case, keep in mind that your performance is tied to the performance of the other group members, and vice versa. The following are some suggestions to help you be an effective team member:

1. *Be sure the division of labor is equitable*. It is not always easy to decide how the workload can be divided equitably, since it is not always obvious how much work needs to be done. Try breaking the case down into the distinct parts that need to be analyzed to determine if having a different person assume responsibility for each part is equitable. All team members should read and analyze the entire case, but different team members can be assigned primary responsibility for each major aspect of the analysis. Each team member with primary responsibility for a major aspect of the analysis will also be the logical choice to write that portion of the written analysis or to present it orally in class.

2. *Communicate with other team members*. This is particularly important if you encounter problems with your portion of the analysis. Since, by definition, the team members are dependent on each other, it is critical that you communicate openly and honestly with each other. It is therefore essential that your team members discuss problems, such as some members not doing their fair share of work or members insisting that their point of view dominate the team's report.

3. *Work as a team*. Since a group's output should reflect a combined effort, the whole group should be involved in each part of the analysis, even if different individuals assume primary responsibility for different parts of the analysis. Avoid having the marketing major do the marketing portion of the analysis, the production major handle the production issues, and so forth. This will both hamper the group's aggregate analysis and do all of the team members a disservice by not giving each member exposure to decision making involving the other functional areas. The strategic management course provides an opportunity to look at all aspects of the business situation, to develop the ability to see the big picture, and to integrate the various functional areas.

4. *Plan and structure team meetings*. When working with a group on case analysis, it is impossible to achieve the team's goals and objectives without meeting outside of class. As soon as the team is formed, establish mutually convenient times for regular meetings, and be sure to keep this time available each week. Be punctual in going to the meetings, and manage the meetings so they end at a predetermined time. Plan several shorter meetings, as opposed to one longer session right before the case is due. (This, by the way, is another way realism is introduced in the strategic management course. Planning and managing your time is essential in business, and working with others to achieve a common set of goals is a critical part of life in the business world.)

SUMMARY

The strategic management course is your opportunity to assume the role of a key decision maker in a business organization. The case method is an excellent way to add excitement and realism to the course. To get the most out of the course and the case method, you need to be an active participant in the entire process.

The case method offers you the opportunity to develop your analytical skills and to understand the interrelationships of the various functional areas of business; it also enables you to develop valuable skills in time management, group problem solving, creativity, organization of thoughts and ideas, and human interaction. All of these skills will prove immensely valuable when you enter the job market and begin your career.

SAMPLE CASE

PENNSYLVANIA MOVIE THEATRES, INC.

THE CORPORATE PERSPECTIVE

1   Pennsylvania Movie Theatres, Inc. (PMT), was an organization of largely autonomous and previously independent theatres located throughout Pennsylvania. Seven years ago, 28 manager-owners of privately held corporations exchanged their theatre ownership for PMT stock and the right to continue as theatre managers with the newly formed corporation. At their first annual meeting, the managers voted to select a five-member board of directors from their ranks to coordinate theatre operations and to oversee all corporate activities. Further, they determined that one new director would be elected each year to fill a scheduled vacancy. Each director would serve in a part-time capacity for a four-year term at $3,000 per year.

2   The PMT managers believed that as a corporation they would have better opportunities and capabilities than were available to them when they owned their theatres separately. Because of their system of cooperative exchange, they would be able to minimize film rental and advertising costs. They could also offer better opportunities for advancement to their assistant managers. Additionally, the corporate form enabled the managers to provide support to weaker member theatres because of their collective managerial experience and collective financial strength. Taking a long-term perspective, the managers believed that this consolidation arrangement would result in a more profitable operation for all theatres.

3   The PMT managers wished to offer their communities a safe, inexpensive, and pleasurable leisure-time activity. By satisfying these and other societal needs, they believed they could achieve their basic corporate objectives of survival and profitability. Among other pertinent societal needs, the managers saw the desire for:

1. A safe, inexpensive form of entertainment.
2. A wholesome, imaginative, and stimulating children's diversion.
3. A forum for social debate.
3. An opportunity for family activity.
5. A source for employment of local labor forces.
6. An escape from demanding realities.
7. An opportunity for educational and cultural enhancement.

4   Because of their concern for satisfying these needs, the managers chose their films carefully, attempting to offer high-quality movies at the peak of their popularity. They were also concerned with appealing to an audience that included people of all ages and descriptions. The managers saw the corporation as a group of family theatres, so they wanted to ensure that, with few exceptions, a family unit could attend any show at a PMT theatre without totally sacrificing the enjoyment of

---

This case was prepared by John A. Pearce II of George Mason University.

any single member. Since their incorporation, PMT theatres had, therefore, restricted their film offerings primarily to those movies rated G (general audience), PG (parental guidance suggested), and R (restricted to persons over 18). With rare exceptions, X-rated, but never hard-core pornographic films had been shown.

5   The managers also wanted to ensure that the family could enjoy a movie in pleasant surroundings. They attempted to maintain a future-oriented perspective in supervising the daily operations of the theatres as well as in selecting films to be shown. Theatre facilities were periodically renovated, and employees were well trained. All of these efforts were expended in order to provide the most comfortable of theatre experiences and to ensure continued audience patronage.

6   PMT gauged its corporate performance in a number of different ways, among which were ticket sales by type, show time, and moving rating; quarterly revenues; and quarterly profits. Last year, PMT's seventh in operation, the net profits of the PMT theatres dropped almost 7 percent from the year before, even though during the same period, the theatre industry at large had reached all-time-high profit levels. Two years ago, the return on investment achieved by PMT had been 11.7 percent, while the industry average was 11.3 percent. Last year, the return on investment for PMT was down to 10.1 percent, while the industry average climbed to 11.8 percent. The industry average return on investment for the past five years was 10.9 percent.

7   In reviewing the performance of individual films shown during the past year, the PMT directors found that the few X-rated films they had offered far and away resulted in the greatest profit per film, followed by those rated R. They also noted that on dates when their competitors had shown pornographic-type films, they had appeared to outdraw PMT theatres. Further, since adult ticket sales were the most profitable, the loss of these customers probably represented an associated loss in net income.

AN ALTERNATIVE

8   A major film distributor recently approached the PMT directors with an offer to supply them with a selection of good-quality X-rated and pornographic-type films for the minimum contract period of 12 months. If ordered, these films would constitute approximately one third of the movies shown at any single theatre during the year, with the remaining two thirds being supplied by the corporation's present distributor.

9   While a revised movie offering would not require any major technological changes for PMT (for example, the present projection screens and sound system would be adequate), it would have a potentially strong psychological impact on both the PMT employees and their audiences.

10   Thus, the directors realized that a large and varied set of factors needed to be taken into consideration prior to any contractual commitment to the second distributor.

11   One such factor was the possible consequence of a bill, currently before the Pennsylvania state legislature, that would ban the showing of pornographic films within the state. Although the bill was being hotly debated, it was given only a 10 percent chance of being passed. The directors were also watching the upcoming gubernatorial election in the state with particular interest. One of the declared candidates was running as a morality candidate, and a major plank in his platform was the banning of all X-rated films in Pennsylvania theatres. While he was given only a 5 percent chance of being elected, the news media had given great attention to the morality issues raised by this candidate, as they had to the pending legislation.

12   On the other hand, the directors perceived a widespread belief among the general population that sexual explicitness in any medium had some value. They also sensed growing support for the individual's right to decide what did or did not possess redeeming social value.

13   Another factor the directors considered was that as the nation's affluence increases, so does its leisure time and its demand for leisure-time activities, such as movie theatre entertainment. They were uncertain, however, about the effects that current economic conditions would have on their operations. They expected an economic recession but were unsure whether the accompanying period of tight money would bring more people to the theatre in lieu of more expensive forms of entertainment or, alternatively, whether all entertainment businesses would suffer.

14   Another consideration affecting the directors' decision was the fact that the majority of PMT theatres were located in small- to medium-sized towns with an average population of 23,569 people. All of the theatres were in downtown business districts, and all theatre fronts opened onto main shopping streets. In nearly every case, however, the PMT theatres had a competitor within two city blocks. These facts concerned the directors since they believed trends toward liberalism were relatively slow to develop in small towns and any failure on their part would be to the immediate advantage of their competitors.

15   The possible impacts on price policies and theatre hours were also considered. The average price for an adult movie ticket at a PMT theatre in the past year was $3.68, while the average price for PMT competitors was estimated at $3.83. Should the second contract be approved, PMT estimated that its average could rise to $3.77, reflecting the corporation's ability to increase its rate for the X-rated movie audiences.

16   Although show hours varied slightly among PMT theatres, the pattern for weekdays includes a matinee at 2 P.M. and two evening shows at 7:30 P.M. and 9:30 P.M. On weekends, a late-afternoon performance at 5:30 P.M. was added. On Saturdays, the matinee was often reserved for the showing of children's films, which were scheduled by the individual managers especially for this purpose. Although these films contributed no profit to the corporation—because of their low ticket prices— the managers felt this policy developed goodwill between the theatre and the community. No change in the theatre hours was anticipated by the directors in the event the second supplier contract was signed.

17   In addition to price policies (selective rate increases needed) and modifications in theatre hours (no changes required), the directors considered the possible effects of showing X-rated films on other facets of the theatres' operations, for example, media advertising and in-theatre promotion.

18   PMT theatres advertised through the radio and newspaper media. Whether or not the new contract with the supplier of the X-rated films was signed, these two media would continue to be used, with the expectation that neither costs nor potential audiences would change significantly.

19   Concession stand operations were not expected to be affected, since on previous occasions when X-rated movies were shown, managers did not notice any changes in concession volume or item preference. The directors believed the concession stand would continue to yield approximately 93 cents (gross) per customer regardless of the movie being shown.

20   PMT's distribution channels should be unaffected in the event that a contract with the second film supplier was approved. No additional distribution costs were expected, therefore, but some inventory control changes would be necessary. The main change would be that the two different brands of film would need to be kept separate in the film depository, which would be possible through the initiation of a second numerical filing system. The PMT managers recognized the difficulties commonly associated with such a new system but felt the required adjustments could be quickly overcome

21   No attempt had yet been made to determine how nonmanagerial PMT employees would feel about an increase in the number of X-rated films being shown in their theatres. Of central concern was the impact the change might have on the employees' interest in union membership. To management's knowledge, no attempt had ever been made by its employees to bring in a union. The directors attributed this desired situation to its employee relations effort and to the high turnover rate among its teenage employees. To date, there had been only one incident, involving a 55-year-

old female street booth ticket clerk who objected to "dirty films," to indicate the employees might reactive negatively to any increase in X-rated offerings.

CONSOLIDATED PROJECTIONS

22   After conducting the broad-based assessment of the impact that offering X-rated and pornographic films might have on PMT's profits, the directors reached the following projection for three years from now, assuming the second contract was signed:

Likelihood of reaching or exceeding industry average	30%
Likelihood of equaling their own performance of last year	30
Likelihood of a 10 percent decrease in the PMT return on investment from the previous year	20
Likelihood of a 20 percent (or greater) decrease in the PMT return on investment from the previous year	20

23   Overall, the directors foresaw an opportunity to increase business by attracting a new segment of moviegoers. Additionally, the prospective new supplier argued that regular adult PMT customers would attend the theatre more often. Thus, the directors believed a revised film offering would enable them to better meet the interests of an enlarged segment of the population and, in return, these customers would help ensure PMT's long-term survival.

24   Should they contract with the second supplier, the directors planned to monitor the corporate performance carefully. Among their targets would be the following:

1. Adult ticket sales per movie for all but X-rated films should remain stable or increase slightly.
2. Children's ticket sales should remain stable or increase slightly.
3. Adult ticket sales per movie on X-rated films should exceed adult ticket sales per movie for films of any other rating.
4. Quarterly profits, adjusted for seasonal variations, should reflect an upward trend.

In the event any of these targets were not being met, it would signal a need to reassess the wisdom of the revised film offering.

25   Although the PMT directors had the responsibility of proposing corporate strategy, the success of the strategy rested on the commitment of the managers in carrying it out. The question arose for the directors as to the extent to which the managers would give the films of the second supplier a real chance. Although, or since, a manager's bonus reflected the degree of profit of his theatre, he may be reluctant to fully implement a new strategy regardless of the directors' judgment. A recent straw vote of managers to the question "Do you favor an increased offering of X-rated and pornographic-type films?" showed 12 in favor, 5 against, and 11 undecided.

26   It appeared that the results of the straw vote somewhat paralleled the performance of the voting managers' theatres. Managers who were experiencing increasing revenues tended to vote against the second supplier, those with relatively level sales seemed to be undecided, while those with decreasing or typically low sales favored the proposal. Such voting tendencies might have been a reflection of the managers' bonus system. Each manager-owner received an annual bonus equal to 60 percent of the pretax net income of their individual theatre and a $1/_{28}$ share of a pool composed of 25 percent of the pretax net income of all theatres.

27   In two months, the annual stockholders' meeting would take place. The managers all anticipated that the main order of business would be a discussion of the directors' proposal regarding a contract with the second distributor.

SAMPLE CASE ANALYSIS

PENNSYLVANIA MOVIE THEATRES, INC.

Pennsylvania Movie Theatres, Inc. (PMT), was formed in 1978 when 28 independent motion picture houses scattered throughout Pennsylvania joined together primarily to obtain economic efficiencies garnered through mutual cooperation and control. A five-member board of directors (costing the corporation $15,000 a year) will be proposing to its members in two months the regular showing of quality X-rated or pornographic films in numbers far in excess of current practice. The board believed the exhibition of this type film in this quantity would

> increase business by attracting a new segment of moviegoers. Additionally, . . . regular adult PMT cus- tomers would attend the theatre more often. Thus, the directors believed a revised film offering would enable them to better meet the interests of an enlarged segment of the population and, in return, these customers would help ensure PMT's long-term survival [23].[1]

Taken in these terms, the board will be proposing a major policy change that will be of strategic importance to the chain should the results of the decision be either a success or a failure. The following is an analysis of the situation facing motion picture exhibitors in general and, more specifically, of PMT as an exhibitor in the state of Pennsylvania, with a recommended plan of action given the described circumstances.

HISTORY AND BACKGROUND INFORMATION

A motion picture exhibitor is just one of many entities competing for the public's time and dollars. Inexpensive mass entertainment has always been part of the American scene—tent and wandering minstrel shows first entertained the masses, followed by vaudeville shows mounted in any number of theatre chains strung across the country. By the early 1920s, the motion picture had become the country's major form of mass entertainment, and this form dominated until the early 1950s. Today this industry is in a state of decline as its overall growth rate is less than the population's, and it exhibits many of the other characteristics of an industry in decline—many motion picture studios have either gone out of business (Republic, Monogram, PRC), merged (United Artists/MGM, Universal/International), or become part of a larger conglomerate (Paramount Studios, Warner Brothers, Columbia Pictures). Fewer and fewer films are being produced solely for theatre distri- bution each year; and in-theatre motion picture viewing is being substituted by videocassette recorder (VCR) and broadcast and cable television viewing. Although under these conditions of overall

---

This analysis has been prepared by Professor Joseph Wolfe of the University of Tulsa for class demonstra- tion purposes and does not constitute the only analyses, observations, and conclusions that could be drawn from the case.

[1]The bracketed numbers refer to the numbered paragraphs in the case.

decline "success" is only comparative and may entail a holding action until the organization can switch its resources and capabilities to more profitable and growth-oriented markets or industries, survival depends on the building of efficient market access, strong customer loyalty, a strong theatre image, simplified inventory controls, efficient operations, streamlined management control, and the elimination of excess labor or a change from labor-intensive to capital-intensive operations. The key functional area in this situation should be that of finance, and the business's strategic focus must be placed on financial strength and maximum investment recovery. It is not clear whether PMT realizes the strategic requirements of its situation. The chain was created to reduce expenses in film rentals and advertising, and PMT managers wished to provide career opportunities for their assistant managers [2]. PMT also wished to help its weaker theatres with collective financial strength, but it is not explained how this was to be realized. Additionally, it is not known to what degree PMT has (1) made its theatres more accessible to the public, (2) caused its present customers to be more loyal to *PMT* than to its inevitable competitor [14] only two blocks away, (3) created a strong and readily identifiable image in the marketplace, (4) simplified and made more rational the booking of films for 28 theatres rather than just 1, (5) made its operations more automated and capital intensive, and (6) put into place management controls, which yield valuable operational and strategic information.

Not only does PMT face difficulties due to the declining nature of its industry, the chain faces the problems of survival in a state or geographic area that is experiencing low or negative growth in addition to a general population that is moving toward those age categories least likely to attend a motion picture theatre. As shown in Exhibit 1, American's population is growing the fastest in

---

EXHIBIT 1
Selected Demographic Data

Population Age Mix Changes, 1980–1990*

Under age 20	+2.1%
Age 20–29	−4.3
Age 30–39	+28.5
Age 40–49	+37.4
Age 50–64	−2.0
Age 65 and over	+19.6

Geographic Population Shifts, 1970–1990†

Pennsylvania, 1970–80 (+71,000)	+0.06%
Pennsylvania, 1980–90	−1.0
New York, 1980–90	−6.2
Oklahoma, 1980–90	+15.8
Texas, 1980–90	+23.0
Nevada, 1980–90	+59.6

Interpretations:

1. Population growth will be the greatest in the 40–49 age class and impressive in the 30–39 and over-65 age groups. These groups are the least likely to attend a motion picture theatre.

2. Pennsylvania's population is basically flat or falling during the case's time period, and this trend can be expected to continue in the future. America's population growth lies in states other than in the Northeast.

* U.S. Department of Commerce, "Note on the U.S. Lodging Industry," *Casebook,* 1982, p. 865.

† U.S. Bureau of Census, 1982.

the 40- to 49-year-old category, followed by the 30 to 39 and 65-and-over age groups. Over the past 10 years, the state of Pennsylvania's population grew only 0.06 percent, and its population for the next decade is expected to fall 1.00 percent. While this decrease is not as great as that for other "rustbelt" states, such as New York, this nation's growth states and cities are far from Pennsylvania and therefore inaccessible to PMT as it is currently structured. It must also be assumed that the small towns in which PMT has its theatres are losing their populations at a greater rate than for the state of Pennsylvania in general, as these small towns offer the fewest economic opportunities for their younger citizens.

A Porter competitive forces-type analysis (refer to Chapter 5) highlights the formidable problems facing PMT's board of directors. Although a number of barriers to entry exist, these barriers provide little solace at this time since most firms are attempting to leave rather than enter the industry. Economies of scale, however, do not appear to exist, and the products (the theatre itself and the films it shows) are basically nondifferentiated; although a theatre's structure is somewhat unique, its capital requirements are low and the technology to run a theatre is easily obtained. On the supply side of the Porter model, the theatre owner's potential attendance figures are largely controlled by the quantity, quality, and diversity of new and old films available for showing. Additionally, as a buying/renting group of theatres, PMT is in a relatively weak bargaining position as it represents the interests of small theatres with consequently low rental revenue yields per screening. The threat of substitutes also plays an important factor in this industry. As already stated, numerous substitutes for motion picture theatre viewing exist. On a broader level, however, the public in general can pursue any number of different diversions—both active (jogging, sailing, gardening, reading, games of chance) and passive (record listening, sporting event attendance, television viewing).

The most important factors shaping the nature of competition in the motion picture theatre industry, however, are those factors encouraging a high degree of rivalry between those already in the industry. Exhibit 2 summarizes those factors. PMT faces a motion picture theatre of its same type and size in almost every small town; the industry's growth is not only slow but also negative; it is very difficult to physically differentiate one theatre from another or to make its offerings unique if the house classifies itself as a first-run theatre [4] a customer can easily attend one theatre over another, given they are only two blocks away from each other; fixed costs are relatively high if a mortgage exists on the building and/or its property; the product is perishable (a customer missing from the theatre is gone forever for that particular film in a PMT theatre); and exit barriers are high since few other businesses can use the configuration typically employed by a motion picture theatre.

Although PMT has not created a formal mission statement, such a statement can be derived from its belief in the societal needs fulfilled by motion picture viewing [3]. A switch to a greater emphasis on X-rated films would appear to violate the following desirable ends in its derived mission statement—an opportunity for family activity and an opportunity for educational and cultural enhancement. Alternatively, the change in programming, if successful, would enhance PMT's desires to be a forum for social debate, provide an escape from demanding realities, and be a source for the employment of the local labor force. More problematical for PMT is its desire to provide a safe, inexpensive form of entertainment, as many consider pornography to be mentally and spiritually unsafe for the viewer and physically unsafe for those who may be subjected to the passions and mental states incited by the subject matter. The provision of a wholesome, imaginative, and stimulating children's diversion may or may not be impunged since the films would be shown only during evening screenings, although children could be exposed to PMT's X-rated advertisements, marquee displays, and lobby posterboards.

Of greater import concerning the use of X-rated films, however, is the impact of their use on the screening times allowed for regular fare, given the board's assumption that additional screening times (and hence no additional labor costs) would not be created. Exhibit 3 shows that PMT's

EXHIBIT 2
Factors Causing Intense Rivalry among an Industry's Participants

1. Numerous, equally sized companies.
2. Slow industry growth.
3. Low differentiation and switching costs.
4. High fixed costs; product is perishable.
5. Capacity increases in large increments.
6. Exit barriers are high.
7. Rivals are diverse in their strategies, origins/histories, and personalities.

EXHIBIT 3
Change in Product Mix per Theatre with X-rated Films

Rating	Estimated Current Mix		Estimated Future Mix	
	Percent	Number	Percent	Number
G	10.0%	5	6.7%	3
PG	49.0	25	33.7	18
R	38.0	20	26.3	14
X	3.0	2	33.3	17*
Total	100.0%	52†	100.0%	52

* Assumes all X-rated films will be supplied by the new distributor.

† Assumes PMT theatres operate all year and are single screened; also assumes a number of films will run for more than one week, but many children's matinee films only show on Saturday. Although almost 100 new films are produced each year for the American market, at least one third of them will receive little commercial exposure, while only about 20 percent of "Hollywood's" output receives an extended run.

current product mix exhibits 5 G-rated films, 25 PG-rated films, and 20 R-rated films. One could immediately question how family-oriented a theatre chain could be when approximately 38 percent of its films are of the R-rated (*Scarface, Rambo, Terminator*) variety, but PMT's future mix would employ 17 R-rated films while sacrificing 15 films acceptable to larger audiences. Additionally, even though PMT's new distributor promises a supply of high-quality pornographic films, the quality of these films, although suitable to a certain type of clientele, may not be superior to the intrinsic quality of the general-interest films they would have to replace.

As part of their preparation for PMT's annual stockholders' meeting, the directors generated ROI likelihood estimates associated with the chain exhibiting X-rated films for three years. By their X-rated decision, the board is attempting to reverse the negative long-term trend shown in Exhibit 4. PMT's current ROI has fallen 13.8 percent from 1984 to 1985. Its average two-year performance and its most recent year's performance are both below and counter to the industry's ROI performance. This negative trend would not be reversed by their X-rated film decision, based on the expected value of the events anticipated both by the board and by the set of alternative optimistic and pessimistic scenarios presented in Exhibit 5. Additionally, the results they anticipated will only occur after two years of ROI experiences that will be inferior to the results they have historically obtained.

EXHIBIT 4
PMT versus Industry ROI Performance

	1984	1985	Average	Change
PMT	11.7%	10.1%	10.9%	−13.8%
Industry*	11.3	11.8	11.6	+4.4

* Five-year industry average ROI was 10.9 percent; 1985's results were an 8.3 percent improvement over the five-year historical average.

EXHIBIT 5
Alternate ROI Likelihood Estimates after Three Years*

Estimate Category	ROI	Board Estimate	Optimistic Estimate	Pessimistic Estimate
Likelihood of reaching or exceeding industry average	11.8%	30.0%	50.0%	10.0%
Likelihood of equaling own performance of last year	10.1	30.0	35.0	15.0
Likelihood of a 10 percent decrease in PMT ROI from the previous year	9.1	20.0	10.0	60.0
Likelihood of a 20 percent (or greater) decrease in PMT ROI from the previous year	8.1	20.0	5.0	15.0
Estimated ROI		10.0%	10.8%	9.4%

* ROI used in all calculations, although PMT desires an increase in *profits;* open-ended points beyond extremities were not calculated (i.e., exceeding industry average of 11.8 percent or a greater than 20 percent decrease in ROI).

Interpretation: PMT's ROI projection after three years of X-rated films is 10 percent, which is not an improvement over its current return of 10.1 percent; comparatively optimistic estimates (which probably cannot be obtained due to the falling trend experienced by PMT for the past two years) produce an ROI of only 10.8 percent, which is not a significant improvement given the three years needed to obtain it; comparatively pessimistic estimates produce an ROI of 9.4 percent, which is a decline of 7.2 percent from 1985's results (the decline from 1984 to 1985 was 13.8 percent).

PROBLEM STATEMENT

It would appear at first glance that PMT's problem or decision in this case is one of determining if the showing of X-rated films is advisable given the risk and opportunities incurred by this decision. In a larger sense, however, the use of X-rated films is only a decision element within PMT's basic desire to change the strategic direction of its theatre chain in the name of greater profits [2] and long-term survival [23]. PMT could follow a number of routes toward the accomplishment of these ends; and the showing of X-rated films, with the directors' belief that this type of film would "increase business by attracting a new segment of moviegoers," [23] is merely the implementation of a grand strategy of either product development or concentric diversification, depending on how markets and products are defined. As the implementation of a grand strategy

EXHIBIT 6
Grand Strategies

1. Concentration
2. Market development
3. Product development
4. Innovation
5. Horizontal integration
6. Vertical integration
7. Joint venture
8. Concentric diversification
9. Conglomerate diversification
10. Retrenchment/turnaround
11. Divestiture
12. Liquidation

of product development, PMT is attempting to sell a new concentration of products (X-rated films) to a new market (the adult, usually male, customer). As the implementation of a grand strategy of concentric diversification, the exhibit of X-rated films represents a distinctive departure from PMT's existing operations base (a significant divergence from its family theatre orientation) for both customer type and product while simultaneously obtaining synergies through the use of the same projection technology.

Exhibit 6 lists 12 grand strategies outlined in Chapter 9. The problem in this case is to pick which grand strategy, given PMT's resource and resource acquisition position, is the strategy most likely to accomplish the profit and survival criteria PMT has established for itself. Once the grand strategy has been chosen, the board must then outline the components of the grand strategy so that it can be implemented in a timely and correct fashion. In the final analysis, the showing of X-rated films may or may not be included as part of this grand strategy.

ALTERNATIVE CHOICES

The "correct" strategy for any organization is a function of the salient characteristics of the organization's internal and external environments. A grand strategy cluster analysis, which considers these factors, will therefore be employed to prioritize the alternative grand strategies that could be used by PMT (refer to Chapter 9).

As shown in Exhibit 7, grand strategy cluster analysis requires the classification of PMT's (1) markets as experiencing rapid or slow growth and (2) relative strength of a competitive position. Based on our previous analysis, PMTs markets are growing slowly or are actually shrinking in size. It cannot be determined precisely from the case whether PMT's individual theatres are strong or weak in their specific geographic areas, but it is assumed PMT as a corporation does not face a comparably sized chain and therefore possesses a relatively strong competitive position. On this basis, PMT finds itself in cell IV, which indicates the employment of the grand strategies of concentric diversification, conglomerate diversification, and joint ventures, in order of their level of decreasing attractiveness.

EXHIBIT 7
Model of Grand Strategy Clusters

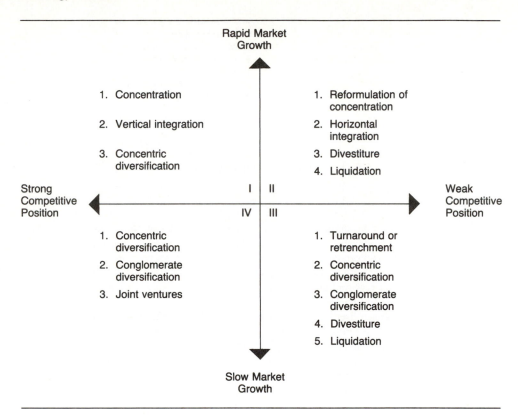

Rapid Market
Growth

1. Concentration

2. Vertical integration

3. Concentric
   diversification

1. Reformulation of
   concentration

2. Horizontal
   integration

3. Divestiture

4. Liquidation

Strong
Competitive
Position   I | II   Weak
                                                         Competitive
                            IV | III   Position

1. Concentric
   diversification

2. Conglomerate
   diversification

3. Joint ventures

1. Turnaround or
   retrenchment

2. Concentric
   diversification

3. Conglomerate
   diversification

4. Divestiture

5. Liquidation

Slow Market
Growth

Concentric Diversification

In a general sense, this grand strategy involves a distinctive departure "from a firm's existing base of operations, typically the acquisition or internal generation of a separate business with synergistic possibilities counterbalancing the two businesses' strengths and weaknesses."[2] For PMT this strategy could take the specific form of (1) a greater offering of X-rated films (a distinct move away from a family orientation and toward the cultivation of a male audience), (2) the showcasing or special treatment of other types of films (classics, recent rereleases, and documentaries), or (3) the expansion of similar theatres in larger towns or cities.

Alternative 1—Concentric Diversification via X-Rated Films

Although the PMT board of directors appears to favor this alternative, many negative features are associated with the decision. Based on the board's estimates, the ROI generated by the decision is not an improvement in the performance already being obtained by the chain. Additionally, all

[2]John A. Pearce II and Richard B. Robinson, Jr., *Strategic Management,* 3rd ed. (Homewood, Ill.: Richard D. Irwin, 1988).

EXHIBIT 8
Disadvantages (or down-side risks) Associated with the Decision to Exhibit X-rated Films

1. The innovation is easily copied—any advantage gained from the decision to exhibit X-rated films would be temporary, as it could be easily duplicated by other theatre chains if the innovation is successful, and therefore is of little long-term value. The innovation does not generate customer loyalty or a preferable supplier relationship, as it is assumed other distributors of "quality" X-rated films exist. Additionally, the contract period is only for a 12-month period, and all ROI projections are based on a continuous supply of quality pornographic films for a 36-month period.

2. Many of the planning premises employed by the board are not viable, or the factors that would make them viable are not completely under the control of the theatre chain.

3. No clear mandate for X-rated films has come from the chain, as its individual members appear to be voting their pocketbooks (or bottom-line profits)—the degree of enthusiasm for implementing the decision is variable and could produce mixed results.

4. Given the long-term negative repercussions should the innovation be unacceptable to the public, the weighted-ROI results are not substantial enough to warrant the risk involved—the expected monetary value of the investment is not positive enough to risk the likelihood of failure.

EXHIBIT 9
Derived Planning Premises

1. Adult ticket sales per movie for all but X-rated films should remain stable or increase slightly (current average ticket for last year was $3.68)
2. Children's ticket sales should remain stable or increase slightly.
3. Adult ticket sales per movie on X-rated films should exceed adult ticket sales per movie for films of any other rating. (X-rated ticket prices would have to average $3.96 per adult if overall average ticket sold is to climb to its estimated $3.77. See Appendix for calculations.)
4. Quarterly profits, adjusted for seasonal variations, should reflect an upward trend.

their estimates have not considered competitive reactions by other motion picture theatres. Exhibit 8 outlines the substantial downside or negative elements associated with the decision—the innovation is easily copied if successful but could easily backfire if it failed; many of the planning premises employed by the board are not viable, or the factors that would make them viable are not completely under the control of the board (see Exhibit 9); no clear mandate for X-rated films has come from the chain, and the board has recognized [25] that the "success of the strategy rested on the commitment of the managers in carrying it out."

On the pro side of the debate, the showing of X-rated films would at least temporarily allow ticket prices to be increased, additional concession stand revenues would be generated, and no new media costs would be involved. From the board's point of view, they would be showing that they are able to make decisions and are doing something to reverse the chain's downward slide in profitability and rate of return.

Alternative 2—Concentric Diversification via Showcased Films

This alternative would entail the scheduling of special films, or series of films built around themes ("Great Actors, Great Faces," a Cary Grant commemorative, "The World's Greatest Adventure Films"), or films appealing to special audiences (films of social conscience, past and near-present elaborate musical fantasies, those great silent comedians). The advantages of this alternative are product differentiation and lowered costs. These special films could be scheduled on a theatre's off-night, or at specific times for senior citizens, or for social clubs with unique interests in conjunction with a meal (as in a dinner theatre operation). Rather than merely displaying the normal fare created by Hollywood, the theatre itself could create its own distinctive personality by the films it selects to supplement the regular diet being fed to the masses. Film rental costs would be very low or nonexistent as many of the films are in the public domain, and ticket prices could be sold at a premium because of the showing's unusual nature or could be sold in blocks, thereby guaranteeing revenues for each series. The disadvantages of this alternative are increased planning and creativity. Under this alternative, PMT would have to do more than just "throw something on the screen," and it would also have to understand the entertainment needs of each town in which it operates a theatre. It would also have to obtain the (part-time) services of a film historian to compile the film series, introduce each film to the audience, or prepare a descriptive catalog for each series.

Alternative 3—Concentric Diversification via Selective Geographic Relocation

This alternative would entail the establishment of theatres in towns (1) with greater populations or larger disposal incomes, (2) where direct competition does not exist, or (3) where the direct competition is weak. Under option 1 above, PMT would be dealing with larger potential audiences or audiences with more money to spend. Thus they would possess the ability either to afford motion picture entertainment or to pay a higher price for the entertainment they purchase. Under option 2, PMT would obtain a monopolostic position within its market area. Under option 3, PMT would not have a monopolostic position but would have a comparative advantage over its rival. Taken in total, these options would take PMT's operations out of areas that are not conducive to economic well-being, while placing itself in areas or situations that are potentially more profitable. The disadvantages of alternative 3 are the costs of relocation or the building of a new theatre if an older one is not available for renovation, the need to become established as a viable entertainment entity in the new community, and the probable capital loss on the sale of the old theatre being vacated.

SOLUTION CHOICE

Depending on the time frame allowed by the PMT board of directors, the organization should implement alternatives 2 or 3. If the board wishes to engage in an effort that would cost very little to implement and would cost very little if it failed, PMT should choose alternative 2. No capital costs are involved; excess capacity probably already exists within its theatres, so few paying customers would be pushed aside for the special showings; and a different type of clientele with outstanding public relations value would be created. If the board takes a longer-term point of view, it should implement alternative 3—after thoroughly researching the competitive position facing each of its theatres and the competitive situation existing in alternative towns and cities in Pennsylvania. Based on the voting pattern on the X-rated film issue, 12 theatres appear to be experiencing decreasing or low sales, while 11 theatres appear to be experiencing level ticket sales. Accordingly, theatre owners in this group are candidates for relocation decisions. Under no circumstances should

PMT exhibit X-rated films as a strategy of concentric diversification. Any advantage obtained by this move would be temporary, and the long-term consequences of failure are too high.

In addition to the implementation of either alternatives 2 or 3 and depending on the time horizon for action chosen by PMT, the board should seek to obtain the advantages of cooperation mainly in the areas of financial control and reporting, capital expenditures, and the sharing of management expertise, since these are the strategic imperatives of an organization operating in the decline stage of its industry's life cycle. At this time, it appears PMT is only a nominally organized confederation, rather than an integrated organization, and the board has yet to deal with those basic issues of industrial decline.

APPENDIX: CALCULATIONS FOR NEW AVERAGE X-RATED TICKET PRICE

Current condition:

Film Category	Proportion of Total	Ticket Price	Weighted Component
G, PG, and R	0.97	$3.68	$3.57
X	0.03	3.68	3.68
Total	1.00	$3.68	$3.68

Proposed condition:

Film Category	Proportion of Total	Ticket Price	Weighted Component
G, PG, and R	0.67	$3.68	$2.45
X	0.33	3.96	1.32
Total	1.00	$3.77	$3.77

Assumptions:

1. Attendance roughly approximates the product mix.
2. Prices for G, PG, and R films will remain stable.

Interpretations:

1. PMT believes the use of X-rated films will enable it to increase its overall ticket prices by 7.6 percent.
2. PMT's forecasted average ticket price is 3.2 percent above what its competition is currently obtaining.
3. PMT must be assuming the competition will not exhibit X-rated films, or the competition will not cut prices in an attempt to hold customers attracted to the X-rated films shown by PMT.

contributed by the stockholders and a $35,000 operating loan from a local bank. RACKES, Inc., hired a part-time employee in October 1976 fiscal year to a total of three, and this part-time employee completed her 13th year with RACKES, Inc., in 1989.

3   Ms. Rackes purchased Ms. Whitten's stock in Rackes and Whitten, Inc., in 1977 and changed the corporate charter to RACKES, Inc. Due to adverse parking conditions, RACKES, Inc., was forced to consider a change in location in 1978. Ms Rackes sought alternate locations within a six-block radius. The only available and possibly suitable location was an abandoned A&P grocery store at the corner of Devine Street and Sims Avenue. The prospective new location was 10,000 square feet in size, five times the size of Rackes' present location.

4   In order to make the best possible use of this location, Ms. Rackes created a concept of complimentary, noncompeting specialty businesses under one roof. This concept became a reality under the name "Shandonshop." The five specialty stores which joined together—a men's clothing store; a fine jewelry and gift store; a bed, bath, and kitchen shop; a glass and china shop; and RACKES, Inc., selling women's apparel and accessories—operated together with moderate success for the first year after its June 1978 opening. After that first year, the lack of business acumen on the part of some of the Shandonshop entrepreneurs created escalating problems among all merchants doing business in this close situation.

5   Determined to succeed as a company, RACKES, Inc., quietly and gradually took over the leases of less-successful tenants, and, by September 1980, RACKES occupied more than 5,000 square feet of space and employed 14 people. As of February 1981, RACKES was the only tenant remaining and utilized approximately 8,500 square feet for retail sales and support. Having access to only personal funds, Ms. Rackes was forced to finance the majority of this unplanned expansion with funds gained by the sale of her personal residence. Additionally, Ms. Rackes was able to persuade

one commercial bank to increase RACKES' operating loan by a small amount. In order to maintain the positive relationship with its landlord, RACKES assumed the obligation for unpaid rent of previous Shandonshop businesses.

6   In 1981, five years after it first opened its doors, RACKES virtually began again. The drain on the company's income and assets caused by rapid expansion and the assumption of former associates' debts was over. RACKES' owner and managers and tenured staff concluded the struggle to merely survive, and they embarked on the challenge of creating a stable and profitable business.

7   Ms. Rackes enlisted the help of the School of Business Administration, University of South Carolina, to assist in creating the first profile of a RACKES' customer. That profile clearly defined a RACKES' customer as a busy woman, either professionally or within community activities. She had a shortage of time, an expanding need to look good, and a stable income providing her the means to maintain that image. She was between the ages of 25 and 45, had a stable family life, and was more interested in quality and value than in bargain price. Based upon that profile, RACKES developed the following store mission statement in 1982, a mission which has guided nearly every planned devised and action taken since that time:

> To make RACKES the specialty store best known throughout the Southeast for excellent and courteous service and quality merchandise at price points affordable to middle and upper income persons by the year 1992.

8   RACKES' Total Concept program, the precursor to the RSP (RACKES Special Person) wardrobing service, was implemented on a test basis in spring 1982. RACKES Total Concept wardrobe director selected 25 current RACKES customers and offered them the service of going into their home, organizing their closet, and creating a wardrobe plan allowing for the most efficient use of the apparel dollars available. Careful attention was paid to the customers' budget, lifestyle, physical proportions, and personal preferences. These 25 test customers were so pleased with the comprehensive and coordinating wardrobe created with minimal time and reasonable financial investment that the program grew, by word of mouth, to an overwhelming 100-plus customers in the personal wardrobe service provided by one RACKES' counselor.

9   1983 was devoted to broadening the wardrobe program to more of RACKES' growing customer base; to revising the merchandising areas of the store, so they provided ease of selection and coordination; to training additional sales counselors in the skills required to create efficient ward-

robing packages; to revising the buying procedures, so merchandise appropriate to professional wardrobes was available 12 months of the year.

10   Rackes' wardrobing program is the only organized and professionally administered service program of this nature in the greater Columbia area. It is perceived by Barbara Rackes to be the key to RACKES' present and future success, in that it provides a valuable service to RACKES' busy customer, who no longer has the time to devote to leisurely wardrobe-building.

11   RACKES' sales have grown at a rate of 20 to 30 percent per year since 1980. RACKES' sales in fiscal year 1980 were slightly over $400,000. RACKES' sales for the fiscal year ending January 31, 1990, were just over $4.25 million, a 10 fold increase in nine years. Employment has increased from the level of 14 in 1981 to 30 by the end of fiscal 1985, 36 in 1986, to 63 in 1989.

On Devine History

12   In December 1977, Ms. Rackes contracted for an option on the property located at the corner of Devine Street and Sims Avenue, the future site of Shandonshop. The site was and is within two miles of Columbia, South Carolina's prestigious downtown neighborhoods. After applying with all commercial and mortgage lending institutions in Columbia, Ms. Rackes was forced to accept a lease on the property with an option to buy, the price of which option accelerated substantially for each year of the lease in which it was not exercised. In 1983, the final year of the option, Ms. Rackes was finally able to obtain financing and purchased the acre and half of property on which Ms. Rackes' abandoned A&P-turned-apparel store was located. In 1985, Ms. Rackes created, financed, and constructed the On Devine Center, a plaza of retail specialty stores. It is the refinement of the initial Shandonshop concept: a group of complimentary and noncompeting specialty stores offering quality merchandise and service at one location. The On Devine Center, anchored by RACKES, consisted of a Northern Italian restaurant and five related specialty shops in 1986. By 1989, Rackes had taken over two of the sites, a Carribean restaurant had replaced the Italian one, and two new tenants (Prestige Travel and Hamilton Jewelers) occupied the On Devine Center. Ms. Rackes owns the On Devine Center and all tenants, including RACKES, lease space from Ms. Rackes.

Community Involvement

13   Ms. Rackes and the company bearing her name are actively involved within the community in which they reside and do business. Ms. Rackes contributes more than 20 percent of her working hours to organizations which enhance either the community or the well-being of its residents. Those hours are spent in board of directors meetings, fundraising endeavors, or just plain being there.

14   RACKES, Inc.,'s community commitments center around areas of specific interest to its predominantly female staff and customer base. The corporate support is dedicated to those causes or organizations which directly improve the lives of women and children. RACKES, Inc.,'s owner and managers have further resolved to concentrate company contributions toward a few chosen organizations to which a substantive contribution may be made. The many available choices were divided into quadrants: children, health, equal/civil rights, the arts. The four organizations in which RACKES invests substantively are: Children's Hospital at Richland Memorial, the Arthritis Foundation of South Carolina, the South Carolina Sickle Cell Foundation, and the Columbia City Ballet. Each full-time staff member at RACKES is encouraged to participate in a community organization of her or his choosing. That requested participation is presented at the hiring interview and is included as part of RACKES, Inc.,'s six-week review.

THE RACKES' CONCEPT

15   RACKES' concept is intended to eliminate the need for the professional or active woman to invest extensive amounts of time visiting numerous clothing retailers to assemble a unique and fashionable wardrobe. Barbara Rackes described this idea in a 1987 presentation to business school students about her business:

> I was working in Washington, D.C., as an aid to a South Carolina congressman and needed to buy several outfits that were professional in appearance. Unless I wanted to buy the woman's version of the gray suit, I had to spend several days going back and forth from several stores to assemble the right garments to create the wardrobe I wanted. It was almost impossible to assemble even one professional, fashionable, unique outfit at one store. It occurred to me that this was a problem that presented a real business opportunity, and I stored it away in my mind to act on when I returned to South Carolina. When I returned to Columbia, I set about putting it into reality. It took almost six years to perfect, but the RACKES' concept began to emerge structured around these 10 dimensions:

1. Have fashion-sensitive, fashion-trained sales personnel that are developed as wardrobing consultants who serve a concentrated group of repeat clients with their clothing needs.

2. Focus on developing a strong personal relationship with each client, wherein the RACKES' consultant becomes intimately familiar with each customer's wardrobe, keeps a detailed record of every item purchased, and seeks to build an interchangeable, fashion-conscious wardrobe of outfits to serve that customer's clothing needs. Rather than viewing each purchase as an item sold, the RACKES' consultant and customer work as a team to so integrate items that multiple interchangeable outfits are created. This creates value for the customer who buys quality garments but achieves cost-effective interchangeable outfits.

3. The RACKES' consultant does most of the customers' initial shopping for them. RACKES' customers are welcome to come into the store to browse; but consultants emphasize prearranged appointments with customers, wherein the consultant preselects numerous clothing items that the customers will choose from when they visit the store. This reduces the time investment for the customers, allows the consultant to plan their sales time, and ties the customers to RACKES' wardrobing services over time. RACKES' consultants will even visit a customer's closet to use it as a starting point to build a wardrobe of varied, integrated outfits with "what she has" as a starting point. This approach, in turn, allows RACKES to generate a sales per square foot of two to three times the national average, because floor-time emphasizes consultation about and the sale of preselected garments, rather than salespeople standing around waiting for potential purchasers to walk into the store.

4. RACKES' buying and merchandising is guided by an effort to buy limited quantities of a wide variety of upscale apparel that reflect current but stable fashion trends. This approach allows RACKES' consultants to create unique outfits for their customers, where the customer can expect not to see several other women with the same outfit. It also enhances store appearance, wherein there are no racks with row after row of virtually the same garment—rather, a wide variety of colors and designs that are visually appealing dominates the store.

5. Roomy dressing rooms with private viewing areas interspersed throughout the store reinforce the private, professional relationship RACKES desires between its clothing consultants and their customers (clients).

6. RACKES has its own charge program and RACKES Special Person (RSP) accounts to lend an air of professionalism and convenience to the customer's purchasing process.

7. RACKES provides well-planned seasonal promotional programs to support its consultants in their selling efforts. A major emphasis is placed on fall and spring invitation-only fashion shows at evening time slots.

8. RACKES targets middle and upper-income women as customers, regularly communicating via attractive direct mail pieces to support the required quarterly contact by RACKES' consultants.

9. RACKES maintains a detailed file on the clothing purchases, preferences, sizes, and purchase patterns of each customer to support the consultants' sales efforts.

10. Every RACKES employee (e.g., accounting, janitor, receiving clerks, alterations) receives a bonus based on the sales success of RACKES' consultant sales group. This is intended to build a true team commitment, wherein everyone is attentive to RACKES' image as a service intensive and sensitive wardrobing store to its valued clientele.

CONFIRMING THE CONCEPT

16 "We conducted several market studies during the early days of RACKES, Inc., but we needed clear confirmation that the idea was working relative to Columbia competitors as we refined what we did," said Ms. Rackes, recalling some early frustration trying to get credible market research. She continued, "So I was fortunate to work with a few groups of USC-business students that helped me evaluate the RACKES' concept. They developed a series of perceptual maps, based on surveys of RACKES' customers and their neighbors that didn't shop at RACKES, which were real helpful in understanding the impact of our concept in the Columbia marketplace in 1986. They followed up a year later with focus groups. Let me share some of their findings with the following perceptual maps."

MAP 1
Respondent Perceptions of Stores on Customer Service and Variety Factors

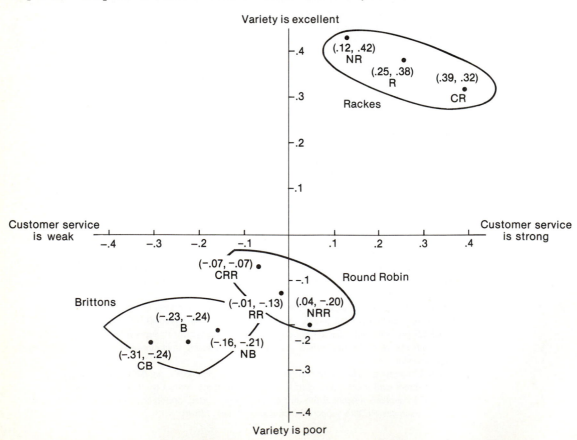

Perceptual Maps

17   The perceptual maps, alluded to in Ms. Rackes' comments, examine RACKES relative to two key Columbia competitors: Brittons and Round Robin. Brittons is a long-standing specialty clothing store in Columbia, with a strong tradition in men's clothing and later offering comparable quality clothing to women. Round Robin is a smaller specialty retailer to women, frequently mentioned as another place where some RACKES' customers shop—with a Devine Street area location and a location in a large regional mall on the northeast side of Columbia, far away from the Devine Street location.

18   The maps are two-dimensional, factor analysis-based interpretations of the answers of approximately 100 RACKES' customers (more than one purchase) and their closest neighbor never purchasing from RACKES (100 respondents). These differences are reflected by the codes "C" and "N" in each map. Each map contains the letters "B," reflecting comments about Brittons; "R,"

MAP 2
Respondent Perceptions of Stores on Variety and Price Factors

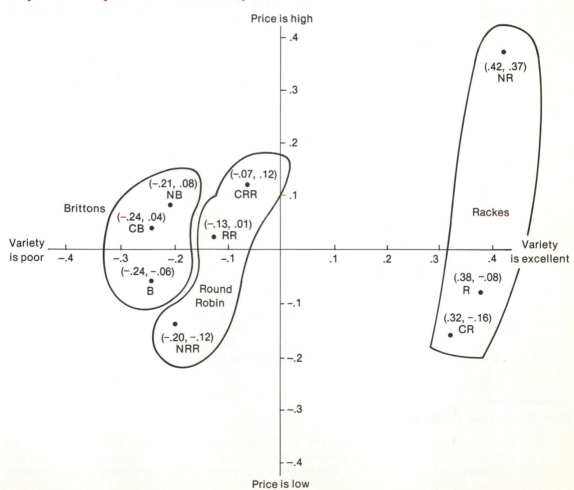

MAP 3
Respondent Perceptions of Stores on Customer Service and Price Factors

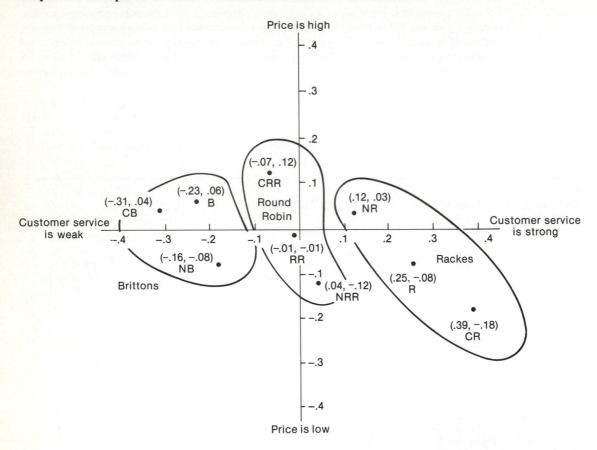

reflecting comments about RACKES; and "RR," reflecting comments about Round Robin. When preceded by "C," for example, "CB," this point refers to the mean response of the RACKES' customer group (in this case about Brittons). If preceded by "N," this refers to the neighbor group. And when no letter precedes the store code, the overall sample mean is referred to.

19   There are three maps. Map 1 plots customer service and variety of merchandise. Map 2 plots variety and price. Map 3 plots customer service and price. The maps suggest Ms. Rackes was successful in creating and implementing a concept that is perceived as distinct from key competitors.

BUILDING THE BASE

20   With a successful concept underway, Ms. Rackes turned her attention to building the base of her business from a marginally profitable one with around $2 million in sales to a more profitable operation with a larger sales base. Central to this desire was the development of a sophisticated,

creative management group to help her oversee a larger, complex operation and also a group that would understand the subtleties and customer service sacrifices associated with making the RACKES' concept work.

21   This meant salespeople who understood working weekends, calling customers, fashion, remembering every one of their clients and what they wore/bought/look best in/and so on. It meant administrative people excited about the computer age—ready to adapt new retailing programs and create their own. Financial people who understood credit selling, coordinating finance with a heavy customer services emphasis, and payroll-intensive service—all with a low profit margin and low margin for error. It meant operations and merchandising that moved merchandise onto the floor, kept up with thousands of items daily, creatively coordinated the floor with buyers, and avoided costly overstocked situations. While several people who started with RACKES in 1980 were still there, what this really meant for Barbara Rackes was that many of the "managers" with whom she grew the concept were no longer capable or willing to perform in a manner necessary to accommodate the next level to which she wanted to take the business. So Ms. Rackes had to experience (usually effect) the departure, often after months of agonizing trial by error, of dedicated people who were her key managers in sales, merchandising, operations, administration, and marketing—virtually her whole first generation of managers—because they could not rise to the next level. As someone fiercely loyal to what she calls her "Rackes family," membership in which was based on loyal service to RACKES, facing the need to grow in each member including herself, and having that lead to some "family members" departure was a painful challenge for Barbara Rackes. She also faced the challenge of attracting managerial talent that would challenge traditional compensation levels within RACKES. As she faced these hard challenges, Ms. Rackes received the accolades of many observers of her initial success with the RACKES' concept, as evidenced by selected news and magazine clippings in Appendix B.

22   Ms. Rackes' challenge was twofold. First, she had to attract or develop managers who could take over decisions across every level of the Columbia store that she was still involved in every day. Second, once a level of confidence was built, this group (or yet another management generation) had to redesign what it did to accommodate her vision (confirmed in a study by a USC–M.B.A. field study group in 1987) of adding additional stores in other southeastern cities by becoming the corporate management staff overseeing multiple stores or the multisite expansion of RACKES. The challenge of building this team, or trying to let go but knowing unnoticed mistakes would diminish profitability (and thus her ability to develop) proved a time-consuming, difficult, but exciting challenge for Ms. Rackes between 1987 and 1989.

1987 AND 1988: SEEKING A MANAGEMENT TEAM TO SUSTAIN GROWTH

23   Ms. Rackes focused during these two years on establishing a management team capable of building her RACKES' vision and of relieving her of direct involvement in every key activity of the store. She quickly added Tom Schultz, USC M.B.A., to the staff for financial management purposes. While young, Tom had been exposed to RACKES through several M.B.A. projects and had done some financial consulting for Ms. Rackes after he took a position with NCR in Columbia.

24   Shortly before adding Schultz, Ms. Rackes had hired an experienced merchandising manager (16 years) who had worked with such firms as Embry's, Associated Dry Goods, and Miller & Rhodes. He moved to Columbia from the Northeast and attempted to professionalize RACKES' merchandising and buying practices. True to his reputation, he proved to be an experienced "numbers man," with an uncanny ability to keep his own personalized manual recording system for balancing, buying, receiving, and floor stock in a $2+ million store like RACKES was at the time. Ms.

Rackes also hired a series of knowledgeable sales managers to run floor selling operations and to assure the continuity and growth of the RACKES "culture."

25   Next, Ms. Rackes turned to computerization. Her vision was to create a totally automated, integrated system for managing RACKES' daily transactions and linking that information into and with all other store activities instantaneously. Two computer systems and one computer manager later, Ms. Rackes and Tom Schultz had adapted such a system at RACKES by early 1989.

26   By mid-1988, with these changes underway, Ms. Rackes pulled out the 1987 USC–M.B.A. field study that had examined 12 southeastern cities for their appropriateness as future RACKES' locations and reviewed the conclusions about the top three sites: Charlotte, North Carolina; Richmond, Virginia; and Raleigh, North Carolina. She started to plan (or plan to plan) the move to her next location, which she thought should be Charlotte. She also announced to her management staff the desire to build a "corporate office" building onto the rear of her RACKES building to house a growing corporate and administrative staff.

27   By late 1988, Ms. Rackes was dissatisfied with the progress she, with some managers' involvement, had made with this planning effort. She sought to improve this situation by bringing all of RACKES' top managers into a more systematic planning process. "We had a long tradition of management meetings at RACKES. Those meetings helped coordinate day-to-day activities, facilitate communication, and make key decisions. But I wanted to go further: to get my key managers intimately involved in long-range planning and the multistore issue. After all, they would be managing the multistore company," she rationalized.

28   By the spring of 1989, Ms. Rackes was again frustrated. The team had endured numerous meetings, but only marginal progress had been made. Now she was not only frustrated with the slow planning progress but was alarmed at something else she saw. "I realized that while we had several good people [managers], they were essentially a good team at managing the Columbia location," she recalled, "and they (or we) were not functioning as a good corporate management team focusing on the management implications of a multistore operation." This realization alarmed Ms. Rackes as she further noticed that 1989 first quarter sales were not only below their growth targets but were actually below the previous year (price increase adjusted) and income was 30 percent below target!

29   Known for her propensity to make a decision and act quickly, Ms. Rackes hired (on a six-month contract basis) an experienced manager and management consultant (former military officer and recent USC–M.B.A. graduate), Sid Britt, to join her staff as executive vice president, with the responsibility of addressing and solving this problem. His initial assignment was twofold:

1. Create a training program to improve the management skills of RACKES' management team.
2. Coordinate the multistore planning process.

Mr. Britt described the situation as follows:

> Rackes was a 12-year-old women's specialty retail firm, emphasizing service, quality, and convenience in fashion wardrobing. The owner had successfully positioned the company's product lines in the Columbia metropolitan market area for appeal to a market segment that included working women who had well-defined tastes for the updated classic image and who had the money but not the time to shop for the clothing they wanted.
>
> The owner's success in communicating the RACKES' image of quality merchandise and specialized service has earned the company and its owner local, regional, and national acclaim.
>
> The RACKES' merchandising program was effective but heavily dependent on the president for buying decisions. Capitalization of the company was adequate to secure financing for immediate operational needs and limited capital investments, but not for major expansion.

The managerial team consists of talented, experienced individuals who have not developed their full potential as an executive team and who are focused more on improving the performance of the Columbia store than building management systems for a multistore corporation. During the past year, the president has made a series of decisions that are placing pressure on the management team:

The construction of a two-story corporate headquarters behind the main store, which has lowered the corporate net income position and raised 1989 sales goals.

The purchase of a high-capacity computer system, which requires training for all personnel to ensure rapid adjustment to new methods of processing information.

The opening of a new store in Charlotte, North Carolina, not later than August 1990.

The institution of a credit center to reduce the costs of credit.

The potential hiring of a permanent executive vice president [interviews to start in one month] to help integrate operational programs with expansion projects and improve the management of both.

As these decisions began to be implemented, sales began to decline. Even without considering the additional salary of an executive vice president (and other unprogrammed hires), the corporation was experiencing a 33 percent net income shortfall only two months into the fiscal year. These events represented a significant challenge and considerable pressure on an essentially untested and inexperienced corporate management group. My challenge was to help Barbara develop the top management team into a well-functioning "corporate" management group.

30   By the fall of 1989, significant progress had been made in the ability of the top management team to function as a forward looking and planning-oriented group. Along the way, however, Ms. Rackes and Mr. Britt faced some difficult challenges realizations. For example, they reached the difficult but necessary conclusion that two members of the management group were capable of managing their responsibilities within a one "relatively small" store environment quite well, but their ability to cope with broader challenges, change, and the need to develop and delegate to subordinates was not consistent with the needs of the multistore company RACKES was becoming.

31   "Both managers were good, loyal people whom I respected very much," said Ms. Rackes. "They contributed to the early development of RACKES. But their skills and management approach were generally effective in a small store setting. The increased size of RACKES and the planning for new locations placed much greater pressure on them, as did the demand to change rapidly and the need to move into automation and computer-based decisions. Reluctantly, we agreed that their future was better pursued in settings other than Rackes. This was a hard but necessary decision for Rackes. Fortunately," said Ms. Rackes, "Bonita Scarborough, who worked for one of these managers in merchandising, has proven to have the skills we needed—they were just not used. She is a leader, a people person and she is not afraid of change."

32   As 1989 drew to a close, the new management team was making significant progress toward developing a five-year plan.

33   The management team then began to turn toward expansion. In terms of an entry strategy, one of the team members was a strong advocate for a "franchising approach." She felt that the "RACKES System" of wardrobing services, buying coordination, and its highly developed computer/administrative system could be packaged and transferred to Charlotte and other cities by locating and selling a RACKES' franchise and supporting services to a preferred store (carefully screened) in each location or even two or three locations in larger areas. Equally appropriate, she argued, would be to use the franchise concept to sell to experienced area retailers (with capital and local knowledge and contacts) to start entirely new RACKES stores, rather than converting part or all of their existing one. All of this, in turn, could be accomplished with lower capital requirements, the generation of an upfront fee ($10k–$50k), a regular percentage (3 to 10 percent) of sales, and also afford RACKES the opportunity to move quickly to more locations, thus preempting

TABLE 1
RACKES' Franchising Plan ($000s)

	(Current) FY End'g 1/31/90	FY End'g 1/31/91	FY End'g 1/31/92	FY End'g 1/31/93	FY End'g 1/31/94	FY End'g 1/31/95
1. Current Stores						
Missy (RACKES Cola)	$3,732.0	$4,200.0	$4,400.0	$4,590.0	$4,780.0	$4,975.0
Petite (RACKES P. Cola)	525.0	550.0	580.0	615.0	650.0	725.0
2. Franchise Assumptions						
a. Number of franchises						
Missy (Big RACKES)	0	3	7	10	10	10
Petite (Little RKES)	0	3	7	10	10	10
b. Franchise fee						
Missy (Big RACKES)	$0.0	$30.0	$50.0	$50.0	$50.0	$50.0
Petite (Little RKES)	0.0	15.0	25.0	25.0	25.0	25.0
c. Estimated sales/frch.						
Missy (Big RACKES)	0.0	750.0	1,500.0	1,650.0	1,815.0	2,000.0
Petite (Little RKES)	0.0	300.0	350.0	400.0	450.0	500.0
d. Estimated frch. sales	0.0	1,575.0	6,450.0	14,800.0	25,072.5	36,427.5
3. Projections						
Revenues						
Existing stores (Cola)	$4,257.0	$4,750.0	$4,980.0	$5,205.0	$5,430.0	$5,700.0
1. Franchise fees	0.0	135.0	525.0	750.0	750.0	750.0
2. Mandatory store remodeling consult'g	0.0	24.0	56.0	80.0	80.0	80.0
3. Sales royalty (3%)	0.0	47.3	193.5	444.0	752.2	1,092.8
4. Adv. charge (1.5%)	0.0	23.6	96.8	222.0	376.1	546.4
5. Buying & merch. fee (3%–10% dependg.)	0.0	102.4	419.3	962.0	1,629.7	2,367.8
6. Extras ($5k/M;$2k/P)	0.0	21.0	70.0	140.0	210.0	280.0
Total revenues	$4,257.0	$5,103.3	$6,340.5	$7,803.0	$9,228.0	$10,817.0
Direct costs:						
Cola stores	$2,349.9	$2,622.0	$2,749.0	$2,873.2	$2,997.4	$3,146.4
Franchising srvs.	$0.0	173.1	660.4	1,205.2	1,685.2	2,212.8
Gross profit	1,907.1	2,308.2	2,931.1	3,724.6	4,545.4	5,457.8
Expenses:						
Cola M & P	1,822.0	2,033.0	2,131.4	2,227.7	2,324,0	2,439.6
Franchising (C. O'hd)	0.0	70.7	272.1	519.6	759.6	1,023.4
Net profit b. tax	85.1	204.5	527.6	977.3	1,461.8	1,994.8

"copiers" of the RACKES' concept. "RACKES' corporate management team could then focus on training franchisees, merchandise services, administrative support, and regular quality control," she argued, "and not get bogged down in the day-to-day people hassles associated with running a retail store." She continued, "What we would be doing is what Century 21 did in real estate or Best Western did in lodging, plus think of the value and expediency of linking up with skilled retailers with contacts/people/knowledge of the local situation, not to mention the eventual cost savings in areas like quantity purchases—of everything from garments to employee benefits—as we rapidly build the number of outlets!" The net result, she argued (see her estimates in Table 1), would be a quicker buildup of "value" in RACKES, value that Barbara had intimated all corporate managers would somehow participate in.

TABLE 2
RACKES' Inc., Five-Year Financial Plan ($000)

Store	(Current) FY Ending 1/31/90	FY Ending 1/31/91	FY Ending 1/31/92	FY Ending 1/31/93	FY Ending 1/31/94	FY Ending 1/31/95
Missy	$3,732.0	$4,200.0	$4,400.0	$4,590.0	$4,780.0	$4,975.0
Petite	525.0	550.0	580.0	615.0	650.0	725.0
Charlotte	—	750.0	1,500.0	1,650.0	1,815.0	2,000.0
Raleigh	—	—	750.0	1,500.0	1,650.0	1,815.0
Richmond	—	—	—	750.0	1,500.0	1,650.0
Next	—	—	—	—	750.0	1,500.0
Next	—	—	—	—	—	750.0
Total all	$4,257.0	$5,500.0	$7,230.0	$9,105.0	$11,145.0	$13,415.0
Cost of goods sold	$2,264.7	$2,926.0	$3,846.4	$4,843.9	$5,929.1	$7,136.8
Other cost of goods	85.1	110.0	144.6	182.1	222.9	268.3
Gross margin	$1,907.1	$2,464.0	$3,239.0	$4,079.0	$4,993.0	$6,009.9
Expenses	$1,822.1	$2,319.0	$3,034.0	$3,809.0	$4,643.0	$5,559.9
Net income before tax	85.0	145.0	205.0	270.0	350.0	450.0
Percent of sales		2.6%	2.8%	3.0%	3.1%	3.4%
Net income after tax	61.2	98.6	133.3	167.4	210.0	265.5
Beginning equity	380.0	441.2	539.8	673.1	840.5	1,050.5
Plus ret earnings	61.2	98.6	133.3	167.4	210.0	265.5
Ending equity	441.2	539.8	673.1	840.5	1,050.5	1,316.0
Return on equity	13.9%	18.3%	19.8%	19.9%	20.0%	20.2%

34   The second approach, strongly preferred by two members of the management team, was a more traditional "RACKES-owned and managed" selection and development of each new location. The proponent of this approach argued that this was the usual way to expand to new locations, that it gave RACKES greater control over the store and its people, and that RACKES stood to make more money in the long run this way. The main proponent of this approach argued that the RACKES' concept could not be franchised, that it was too unique. "The only way to expand RACKES," he argued, "is one store at a time—just one per year for the first few years. Otherwise, we could blow it!"

35   The second proponent interrupted. "It is possible that we could find and acquire an existing women's clothier, or similar retailer for that matter, and acquire it if the price is right to gain people and the right location. Then we could close, train our people, and reopen as 'Rackes.' " It was clear she thought this would have to be the perfect situation, otherwise the fully RACKES-developed store was best. See Table 2 for estimates associated with this approach.

36   The management group faced these and other issues as 1990 arrived. Tom Schultz, RACKES' controller, commented: "We're ready! It would be a crime not to go on to the next location!"

37   Another team member commented: "I'm sure the multistore idea can work. But I'm not sure that the management team has developed the proven track record to let Barbara feel confident that she can let go of the decisions and responsibilities that she must let go of if the multistore concept is to work. It could be very hard for her to let go of many decisions as they arise, because she's

clearly the most talented, knowledgeable person in the management team. This, in turn, could present problems as Barbara takes on the additional challenges of a multistore CEO."

38   "I've got a lot of developing to do to be a 'corporate' CEO, a 'manager of managers!' But I've also got a responsibility to people that work here and to myself to make sure that this business is run right," Ms. Rackes said about her delegation practices: "It's a complicated, fast-changing business, and my managers are better able to understand that than any group so far; but I've still got to be able to oversee their decisions in key ways or in more involved ways when I think they're in an area which they don't fully understand yet."

39   Turning to the issue of going to Charlotte and other cities, Barbara Rackes was equally ready to move, although her enthusiasm was tempered with several concerns. "Regardless of the approach we choose," Ms. Rackes said, "I've got several questions or issues I would like answers for: (1) I'm concerned about our ability to transfer a highly developed culture into another area [store and town] without a history like RACKES'; (2) I'm concerned about our ability to keep high and consistent standards 'long distance'; (3) I'm concerned for RACKES or any store in terms of its ability to develop human resources to our high standard and grow rapidly at the same time; (4) is our culture strong enough to carry us in these challenges, or will I dilute the culture I've spent 12 years creating in pursuit of rapid growth?; (5) money—how to maintain that delicate balance between credit worthiness in an unstable new market situation, while needing money there and elsewhere to fuel growth; (6) tying good people to the company—both to create career paths and earning/value-building opportunities that will keep them."

40   When asked if "tying good people" meant sharing stock in the company, now 100 percent owned by Ms. Rackes, she said: "I think I will need to give stock in RACKES to key people that make growth happen. I am real concerned about how to do this—I don't want to give away too much, want to be sure it is linked to growth, and that it keeps good people around—and must proceed cautiously." When asked how much stock she thought she would have to "give away," Ms. Rackes replied: "I think by the end of year 2 of our expansion plan, 20 percent of the RACKES stock will be in others—my managers—hands."

41   Asked to elaborate on issues associated with expansion to Charlotte and beyond, controller Tom Schultz had these remarks:

> I think we're ready to go, and we should do so with our own store. The idea of acquiring an existing operation is a good one, but candidly, I don't think that is 'really' an available option in the minds of key decision makers. Concerning stock, Barbara has talked about setting up each store as a separate corporation and allocating 20 percent of its stock to key corporate and store people that will make it a success. I'm concerned about multiple sets of stock [i.e., a different corporation for each store]. I think just one set of stock [RACKES stock] would be better. And if we successfully meet my projections, she may never need to share stock as a means of 'additional compensation.' Anyway, I'm excited about what we're developing. We're going to be a multistore management team and I'm soon to be a multistore CFO in a company that is on the *leading edge* for retail companies nationwide. Just think about it—Neiman Marcus is just moving to commission on sales compensation; we've refined that approach for over 10 years now and are in the eighth generation of doing it! All the star firms are talking about customer service; we've put our money where our mouth is and are in about the fifth cycle refining our understanding (that's my job) of the financial management of intense and extensive customer service! I've just finished running all the buying plans for spring—we were temporarily without a merchandising manager, and I did so on our system I helped design! Can you image that: Tom Schultz generating all the spring buying plans for RACKES. It certainly helps Bonnie Scarborough do more, and shows again the leading edge. Yes, I'm on the leading edge in financial/retailing management with a company that is on the leading edge and a CEO driven by that commitment. We're the most sophisticated retailer in Columbia, and throughout the industry we're developing that reputation.

APPENDIX A

FINANCIAL INFORMATION

Statements of Income and Retained Earnings
for the years ended January 31, 1989 and 1988
(see accountant's Compilation Report)

	1989	1988
Sales	$3,483,609	$2,932,887
Cost of goods sold	1,833,859	1,563,657
Gross margin	1,649,750	1,369,230
Operating expenses:		
Payroll	883,049	704,420
Fringe benefits	112,132	92,564
Advertising	152,136	133,563
Taxes	7,351	5,530
Supplies	86,068	58,584
Services purchased	87,717	84,209
Miscellaneous	20,772	16,743
Travel	54,239	29,316
Communications	24,434	13,630
Insurance	21,300	9,507
Depreciation	62,908	51,229
Professional services	15,708	25,718
Bad debts	2,353	9,963
Equipment rentals	10,664	9,288
Repairs and maintenance	15,671	9,857
Property rentals	90,947	71,899
Management fee, RACKES Petite, Inc.	(44,457)	
Miscellaneous credits	(4,158)	(4,218)
Total operating expenses	1,598,834	1,321,802
Net operating income	50,916	47,428
Other income	27,275	10,081
Income before income taxes	78,191	57,509
Income taxes	21,495	10,243
Net income	56,696	47,266
Retained earnings, beginning of year	114,168	66,902
Retained earnings, end of year	$ 170,864	$ 114,168

RACKES, INC.
BALANCE SHEETS
January 31, 1989 and 1988
(see accountants' Compilation Report)

	1989	1988
Assets		
Current assets:		
Cash	$ 63,881	$132,119
Accounts receivable, trade, and employees	78,196	38,616
Amounts due from RACKES Petite, Inc.	88,670	
Inventories, at lower of first-in, first-out cost or market	330,023	293,752
Prepaid expenses	13,066	8,416
Total current assets	573,836	472,903
Leasehold improvements and equipment, at cost:		
Leasehold improvements	225,980	189,692
Furniture and fixtures	284,111	212,194
	510,091	401,886
Accumulated depreciation	(251,450)	(186,093)
Net leasehold improvements and equipment	258,641	215,793
Other assets	29,692	1,500
Total assets	$862,169	$690,196
Liabilities and Shareholders' Equity		
Current liabilities:		
Accounts payable	$348,316	$228,898
Accrued expenses	89,260	53,686
Income taxes payable	15,100	4,906
Current portion of notes payable, banks	30,000	47,225
Total current liabilities	482,676	334,715
Deferred income taxes	4,700	
Notes payable, banks		37,384
Total liabilities	487,376	372,099
Shareholders' equity:		
Common stock	14,000	14,000
Paid-in capital	189,929	189,929
Retained earnings	170,864	114,168
Total shareholders' equity	374,793	318,097
Total liabilities and shareholders' equity	$862,169	$690,196

APPENDIX B

MAGAZINE CLIPPING: POSTCONCEPT SUCCESS

Desperately Seeking USA

42 Think specialty store accounts are small change? Want only those big accounts because they mean large orders and fat bottom lines? Take another look. Retailers such as Barbara Rackes, President and CEO of RACKES specialty store in Columbia, SC, could make the difference tomorrow, as one apparel manufacturer ruefully learned.

43 Several years ago, long before RACKES located to its current posh location, she placed a reorder with one of her manufacturers for 100 skirts in one color. The shipment never came; the manufacturer had shipped it to one of his volume customers. Ms. Rackes dropped the supplier and, years later, when he wanted her business back, it was her turn to say "No."

44 Today, this energetic 36-year-old entrepreneur owns a 20,000 sq. ft. retail specialty plaza consisting of six other stores in addition to RACKES. She also makes a point of getting what she wants, when she wants it. "Now I can go into the market and say I want those goods delivered between August 15 and September 30. In almost every situation, I can be guaranteed that kind of delivery," she says, admitting she's wiser now.

45 "The other side of it is we now buy large enough quantities and are able to persuade them to make better arrangements for us because we are worthy of their attention." Actually, for the last five years, RACKES has been "worthy." With 30 percent annual sales increases during that time, the store's annual sales figure now stands at around $3 million.

46 Ms. Rackes is the first to admit she's come a long way since those early days, 11 years ago to be exact. This former law student and congressional aide in Washington, D.C., began her retailing career in 1976 as the co-owner of Rackes and Whitten, a women's specialty clothing store whose initial stock consisted of 13 blouses, two pairs of pants, and 23 dresses. Eventually, she became the sole owner, achieving her initial goal of earning a living while being autonomous and creative.

47 The roots for such a step, she says, had been established long before. Her mother owned a clothing store in Michigan for more than 30 years. But even with such a foundation, she says retailing—which someone once described to her as "pretty guerrilla warfare"—has been quite a learning experience. However, just a casual walk through her chic, well-managed, artfully displayed store is evidence of her successful retailing tactics.

48 Her tactics, though they appear basic, form the blueprint for many successful retailers these days, and are ones that manufacturers should probably commit to memory if they want to be the domestic resources for specialty stores across the country. The manufacturer must meet the retailers' challenge of delivering unusual goods demanded by the specialty store customer. The formula consists of quality, fabrics, and exclusivity, she emphasizes.

49 "RACKES has a specialty customer, as does Macys and Bloomingdale's," Ms. Rackes says. "We're not talking about main floor department; we're talking about better Missy bridge-type of departments where the customer understands a very, very high quality of fabric. They want to be different from the other people on the street; they don't want to have in their apparel the same thing that somebody else is buying on the first floor."

50 As for quality, she points out that both domestic and offshore production is not as good as it used to be five years ago. "Some of it has to do with manufacturers who have grown so large that

they're using a lot of subcontractors and are not controlling the quality of the goods produced for them.

51   "Part of it has to do with cutting corners, not finishing seams, not having inspectors who discover defects either in fabrication or in the manufacturing process. Part of it is just sloppiness, perhaps an increasing level of it."

52   Besides price, another area she says the domestic manufacturer comes up short, an area which is a must-have for her customer, is fabric. The offering of top-quality fine fabrics are all part of the exclusivity she requires for her customer.

53   "We just have not been able to get that from as many domestic manufacturers," she says. "We've been able to get price domestically on a lot of basic goods, gabardine, doeskins, even worsteds to some extent, but not on the light novelty fabrics, the very fine challis, obviously not silks, a lot of the twills and patterns and unusual fabrics."

54   The problem, according to Rackes' suppliers, is that the mills are unwilling to take the risk to make smaller quantities of unusual fabrics or they're not able to make the shorter runs.

55   "If I bring in a swatch that I got from someplace else, they'll bring out four alternate fabrics and say, 'We don't have access to that fabric, but this is what we do have.' And I'll say, 'That's not the fineness that I want in this fabric.' To which they reply, 'That's what we're able to get domestically.' "

56   Because of this, she is importing most of her fabrics from Italy and Germany for her private label program. She also purchases imports through a 17-member buying office in New York.

57   Although she profits by these methods, she would prefer to buy domestically. "The relationship with vendors all the way down the hierarchy, whether it's me with my cut-and-sew manufacturer, my woven man, and they, in turn, with the piece goods manufacturer, is simplified God knows what percent. With having it all here within the Continental U.S., it is a phone call away; it is all in a language and done on a fit model that everybody understands. You're dealing with like banking systems, like currency; you don't have quotas or anything sitting on the docks for six months."

58   Despite her list of advantages, she comes back to her primary reason for not buying more domestically: Not being able to get the fabrics, the colors, and the price, in that order. Fifty percent of her inventory is purchased from domestic resources. Of that, she says, 25 percent represents U.S. goods made from foreign fabrics, which supports the importance she places on fabric. And obviously, the pending trade bill in Congress, which limits imports of goods and textiles is of great concern to her now.

59   Ms. Rackes' own demeanor and style indicate the type of customer she is targeting. Impeccably dressed in clothes made of fine fabrics, she is a walking example of what she means when she says, "Our customer wants more unusual clothes. The businesswoman who comes to see us doesn't want a navy blue suit; she comes in to buy something that is a lot more updated, still functional and classic, but doesn't look like she walked out of the AT&T boardroom 10 years ago."

60   This successful retail executive believes that "manufacturers who have stayed close to their customers have grown and changed." The ones who haven't, she notes, based on her experiences, are "in Chapter 11s and 13s."

61   In a voice textured by experience, Ms. Rackes is also quick to credit those manufacturers who do serve her well. She cites Bowdon Manufacturing Co., Bowdon, Ga, as an example. "I can send Tom Plunkett, the president, a jacket or another item that is a wonderful seller for us and he can make it up in 45 days for a considerably lower price and in the color that I want. He has been wonderful for us to work with; he's a good stylist and the fit is always right.

62   In fact, Ms. Rackes does so much of the store's private label program, both in suits and sportswear, with Bowdon, that at Plunkett's suggestion, she is considering using a consistent bar code to be on-line with them in order to allow processing of their goods in a quicker and more accurate way.

63   She has always recognized the importance of keeping abreast of change. Rackes already has a computer network throughout the store, and its customer service terminal is online with their inventory system. "At any second during the day, I can tell you what our cost of retail inventory is and what our sales to date to the hour of the day, for the day, week, month, year, department, and classification is," she says.

64   Sophistication pervades the RACKES operation, from stock to inventory control to marketing. Take demographics: "We capture our customer demographics at the cash register." Savvy is no stranger here. "We have a little card customers fill out with name, address, telephone number, general size, and two categories of color ranges they would prefer to buy in. When they make a purchase, the department they shopped is automatically registered."

65   Rackes adds about eight new customers a day, "which adds up at the end of the year," she explains, knowing the advantage it affords them in stockkeeping units.

66   Taking these marketing efforts one step further, she says, "We do semiannual customer profiles, and also track 15 service and quality categories on a 100-point scale twice a year to see how we're doing in comparison with ourselves." A local university sends out mailers and does a statistical analysis of the results.

67   They learn who their customers are—by occupation, activities, income, etc.—and test themselves on such categories as merchandise, service, and price. "We judge what is important to them at a particular period of time. If we find out that either we're slipping or they're changing, we try to go in a different direction."

68   Over the last five years, the city of Columbia, which she describes as "once a much more conservative, sleepy community," has moved more and more into the world of fashion. This makes such marketing procedures invaluable in terms of sales for Rackes. As additional proof, she says, "We have remarkably low markdowns. Our markdowns last year on retail were about 13.5 percent."

69   Yet, her marketing efforts do not stop there. "We hire very skilled professionals, who know how to sell and what to sell, which is the answer to a lot of the problems other retailers are having," she says with conviction.

70   This year, Ms. Rackes' business acumen was recognized across the board. She was awarded trophies and plaques by the Greater Columbia Chamber of Commerce and the June 1987 issue of *Cosmopolitan*.

71   As Barbara Rackes continues to make a name for herself, whether through media coverage or her retailing abilities, it is certain that her manufacturers will try to keep pace with her. After all, Bloomingdale's, Neiman-Marcus, and the like weren't built in a day. . . . Her expressed goal is to make RACKES a specialty store best known throughout the Southeast for excellent courteous service and quality merchandise at price points affordable to middle and upper income persons," and they'll probably want to be there racking up the sales with her.

CASE 2

AMERICAN COMPUTER PROFESSIONALS

HISTORY

1   American Computer Professionals (ACP) was founded in 1979. In 1982, the company was losing money on billings of approximately $400,000. That same year, Jack Rinehart, the president and owner of a large local recruiting firm for engineers, purchased ACP as a "good business investment." Rinehart sold his recruiting business in 1984 and took complete control of ACP at that time.

THE MARKET

2   ACP is a contractor of programming and systems design services to industrial users of mini- and mainframe computer information systems. By 1987, ACP was regularly a member of the INC. magazine's 500 fastest growing, new companies. The market nationwide for such services in 1988 was estimated by Rinehart to be $17 billion. Approximately $1 billion of the market, Rinehart estimates, is in the area including South Carolina, Georgia, North Carolina, and east Tennessee. With the exception of isolated incidents beyond these borders, all of ACP's efforts are directed at this geographic region.

3   The market for contractor services is broken down into four levels. The first is systems planning and design. The next is the systems integration level. The third level, which is the market ACP serves, is the custom/contract programming stage. The final stage is facilities maintenance and training. Each level represents a different stage in service delivery. Most contractors in the business concentrate their efforts on only one segment of the market. Rinehart estimates that 25 percent of the money spent on contractor services is spent at the third level.

ACP'S COMPETITION

4   ACP's competition is composed of firms that either provide exclusive service on the same level as ACP or that provide service on all of the levels. Contracts for services are let out in phases. Consequently, there is competition among all vendors that serve a given level regardless of their involvement at previous levels.

This case was developed by Richard Robinson and Allen Amason, University of South Carolina. Copyright © by Richard Robinson, 1990.

Key Competitors at Each Level

Level one Systems planning & design	IBM; DEC; Anderson Consulting; "Big Eight" accounting firms; PMS (Policy Management Systems)
Level two Systems integration	IBM; DEC; Anderson Consulting; "Big Eight" accounting firms; many small "specialists"; PMS
Level three Custom/contractor programming	Computer Task Group (CTG); AGS (a division of NYNEX); CGA; PMS; same as levels one & two
Level four Facilities maintenance & training	"In House"; same as levels one & two

5   To some degree the market is dominated by a few very large firms, such as Digital, IBM, or EDS, Ross Perot's former company. Anderson Consulting, formerly a division of Arthur Anderson, had over $1.5 billion in billings in 1988. Between 35 percent and 40 percent of the entire market is served by these few leviathans. The majority of firms serving the third level are of comparable size and orientation as ACP. CGA is a French company, with approximately $200 million in revenues, that has a large U.S. presence and is seeking to expand into the Southeast by acquisition of a firm like ACP. (CGA has recently made offers to acquire ACP.) AGS, a firm with revenues of approximately $150 million, was purchased by NYNEX, thus becoming a competitor with tremendous resources. Computer Task Group is a publicly held company with $250 million in revenue, which competes in many of the areas ACP serves. In addition, each new market has numerous small competitors that have a reputation locally. There are also many small firms that serve users of micro- and mini-computer customers. Firms such as these are not direct competitors of ACP.

6   ACP's management has made the decision to further segment its target market by concentrating only on those organizations with the potential to spend more than $1 million a year on contractor services. Initial efforts are concentrated on customers that ACP already serves in some capacity. This does not imply that such potential customers would spend that amount or any amount with ACP.

STRATEGIC POSITION

7   ACP's current market goal is to increase market share 30% annually in the geographic area it serves (South Carolina, North Carolina, Tennessee, Georgia). ACP currently has approximately 3 percent of the programming market in the states in which it operates. The national programming market is growing at a 22 percent annual rate. ACP's current profit margin is 8–10 percent. Management desires that such a margin be maintained, regardless of growth.

8   To accomplish this goal within the boundaries of its market, ACP managers feel that they must cultivate relationships with their existing customers so their contracts are extended for longer periods. They feel that they must also generate new business among customers with the potential for spending a million dollars or more on such services. The strategy for accomplishing this focuses on two areas.

9   The first is to recruit and supply the best systems engineers and programming technicians for work in the field. Often a contract for service is extended beyond that for which the contract was

let, because of the value that is placed on having that individual in the organization. ACP has been quite successful in this area. Rinehart cited examples where ACP systems engineers had been reassigned within an organization, thus having their contracts renewed because of their expertise in a given area. This is a competitive advantage for ACP. Many of their competitors prefer to hire recent college graduates, whom they provide with intensive training. ACP, taking advantage of Rinehart's recruiting background, hires only recognized experts for specific applications.

Partial Customer List

Customer Name	% of ACP's Revenue	Associated Since	Prospect
TVA	Historically—43%	1984	None
SRP	1989—36%	1984	Slow
DuPont	(His.)—10.5% 1989—14.2%	1985	Good
Westinghouse	(His.)—4.3% 1989—1.1%	1983	Slow
SCE&G (South Carolina Electric and Gas Co.)	(His.)—15% 1989—22%	1983	Good
Westvaco			
Fed Land Bank			

10   The only problem with this portion of the strategy is that often contracts are for a fixed price. W. M. Morris, the general manager of ACP, pointed out that a fixed price contract becomes less profitable each year as the personnel on a job get higher salaries.

11   ACP has been less successful in expanding its customer list. Customers hire contractors, such as ACP, to work on matters of importance. "Trust is essential," according to Rinehart. Customers will work only with those individuals that they can trust. The reputation of the firm is overshadowed by the relationship of the salesperson with the potential customer. Such a relationship may take many years to develop. Consequently, sales develop slowly. ACP has experienced excessive turnover in its sales force. This has caused some interruption in coverage of some areas. Each time a new person is brought into an area, the effort in that area is set back. "Consistency is the key to increased sales," said Morris.

12   As mentioned earlier, ACP's goal is to expand within its market by 30 percent annually. Implementation of a strategy to achieve this goal requires overcoming the slowing growth in sales. Even with their technical proficiency, two of ACP's "super customers" will be leaving at the end of 1989. These two customers, the Tennessee Valley Authority and the Savannah River Plant, were satisfied with the service but lost funding for the contracts. These budget cuts were beyond ACP's control. They did, however, demonstrate the need for an aggressive sales force. The national average of a contract's duration is about one year. Morris believes that it is difficult to maintain a suitable profit margin in the contract much beyond that.

OPTIONS

13   ACP has been somewhat successful in its early effort to secure longer contracts with appropriate price adjustments. However, the problem with sales and the growth that they would bring has been "frustrating" for Rinehart. ACP has several options for expanding its operation.

14   The first is simply to continue on the current course. Revenue has increased in each of the years since 1982 without sacrificing profit margins (see Exhibit 1). This effort could be bolstered by

EXHIBIT 1

AMERICAN COMPUTER PROFESSIONALS
Operating Summary 1983–1989
(dollars in thousands)

	1983	1984	1985	1986	1987	1988	1989-Q3
Revenues	$790	$1,451	$3,776	$4,208	$5,991	$6,595	$5,196
Direct sal'y	419	893	2,159	2,597	3,491	3,897	2,922
Direct fringe	36	72	139	167	336	420	314
per diem/rel'n	19	53	105	135	284	233	118
Direct total	474	1,018	2,404	2,899	4,111	4,550	3,354
Gross profit	$316	$433	$1,372	$1,309	$1,880	$2,045	$1,842
Percent of sales	40.0%	29.8%	36.3%	31.1%	31.4%	31.0%	35.5%
VP salaries	84	5	30	76	144	213	141
Sales salaries	4	57	111	304	332	413	233
Recruiting sal.	27	28	98	82	62	72	180
Adm./acct. sal.	10	43	62	74	106	159	99
Indir. fringe	12	19	37	48	71	93	62
Indirect total	137	152	338	584	715	950	715
Overhead exp.	103	113	336	373	484	651	486
Depreciation	1	5	10	14	25	44	23
Interest	15	29	63	26	23	11	36
Operat'g income	$ 60	$ 134	$ 625	$ 312	$ 633	$ 389	$ 582
Percent of sales	7.6%	9.2%	16.6%	7.4%	10.6%	5.9%	11.2%
Allocation:							
Owner salary	15	26	78	130	115	360	90
Amortization*	84	0	203	165	32	0	0
Transfer†	0	34	36	0	0	0	0
Income tax‡	0	0	4	0	19	0	0
Net income	(39)	74	304	17	467	29	492

Figures are unaudited and taken from company operating records on an accrual basis.

* Amortization of acquisitions in 1982 and 1985.

† Payment of consulting fees to another company held by owner.

‡ Income taxes largely paid at stockholders personal level. Corporation converted to "S" status in 1989.

additional junior salespeople. On average, ACP's first year salesperson generates between $300,000 and $400,000. The extra personnel would not cover new geographic territory, but they would work with the existing staff of seven salespersons and managers in better penetrating the market. New sales staff could be added easily with the help of an employment agency. A potential problem exists here. As mentioned earlier, sales develop slowly. Even with ACP's compensation package, which combines a straight salary with bonus provisions based on earnings, it has proven difficult for ACP to retain personnel.

15   Another option would involve the recruiting of what Rinehart calls a "Rainmaker" or super-salesperson. Such an individual would already be in the business, with an established identity and client list. With a high profile in the trade and a proven reputation, the individual would be easy to recognize. A "head-hunter" type of agency could be used in the recruiting process. This has been tried by ACP. ACP hired a tremendously successful salesman, who worked the Dallas area, to come and generate the same type of volume in Atlanta. A six-figure salary, a company Jaguar, and the title of VP produced only low morale in the organization. The rainmaker was with the

company for less than a year. Rinehart does not believe the idea was necessarily bad, but is cautious, given the potential price of failure. The reward could also be quite high. In return for a large salary and generous bonus package, ACP would expect production of several millions of dollars of new business over the first two or three years.

16   A third possibility is acquisition. Many advantages could be gained through the acquisition of an existing business in the field. Such an acquisition could potentially provide additional market penetration, as well as an experienced sales leader. Acquisition is not uncommon in this business. Morris believes that most growth by individual firms is accomplished through acquisition. CTG has made 19 acquisitions in the past decade. CGA has made approximately the same number. A firm that ACP would consider for acquisition would be in the business at the same level as ACP. ACP has considered some deals. All of the firms that have been courted have been less than half the size of ACP and have been within the geographic area that ACP serves. *Contract stability* is the most important factor to consider, according to Morris. There is a substantial amount of risk involved in a business where personal relationships are so important. Consequently ACP has been cautious. "It sounds good right up to the point where we write the check," said Morris. ACP currently has approximately $2 million in capital for such an undertaking. Rinehart is not opposed to seeking bank financing, or perhaps even venture capital, to facilitate a deal if appropriate. Rinehart pointed out that there are tax advantages to acquisitions, in that the purchase can be amortized over the life of the contracts acquired. This is rarely over three years.

17   Although always a possibility, being acquired by a firm such as CGA is not something that ACP management has pursued. Management desires that its role be unchanged following any sort of acquisition or merger.

18   A fourth possibility is specialization. Many of the customers that are served by ACP have become specialized to the point that the technical expertise required by the vendors is not transferrable to other industries. After a contract expires, ACP is in a position of locating customers that need such specific knowledge if they intend to keep the engineers. Examples of industries where contractors like ACP have specialized are nuclear, banking, insurance, and state and federal governments. In each area there have been success stories. ACP has developed a superior reputation in the nuclear field through its efforts at the Savannah River Plant and other nuclear installations. A nationwide marketing effort in a single, highly specialized field could be very profitable. There is risk in identifying the right industry. ACP management believes that should it concentrate on only the nuclear industry, which accounted for 30 percent of billings in 1989, ACP would lose 100 percent of its nonnuclear business when the current contracts expired. Morris believes that a firm should "dance with the one who brought you to the party."

19   The last option currently under consideration would be to expand into all levels of the computer services contracting business. Other firms, such as the large firms mentioned earlier, have entered all of the levels and have experienced tremendous growth. This would involve expansion into areas that are foreign to ACP. Expertise in the areas of hardware and software delivery, as well as initial consultation and needs evaluation, would be required. Rinehart is confident in ACP's recruiting ability and believes that such expertise could be added. Morris believes that ACP's objectivity about hardware and software products would allow the firm to give excellent service. The new services would need a new sales force that would call initially on ACP's customers in an effort to build a reputation. Name recognition would be essential in the effort to compete against the large firms that dominate the full-service landscape. Rinehart, however, questions whether service at all levels is necessarily a competitive advantage when bidding for work. Contracts at each level are let independently and with respect only to a specific need. He is, however, impressed with the growth and profit margins of multilevel firms, like EDS and Anderson Consulting. Morris is concerned that ACP would need more "muscle" before expanding its scope in so broad a fashion. There would have to be some investment in product inventories as well as additional staff. Morris

estimates that the expansion would require $250,000, and that new business from the expanded service would take at least a year to develop.

EVALUATION

20 Management has been active in its evaluation and research of these options. The management team consists of Rinehart; W. M. Morris, the general manager, who has three years with ACP, over 20 years' experience with a recently sold software company, Digital Systems, as well as an early career with IBM; and an outside marketing consultant, who knows the business well. All have been active in the discussions. They perceive substantial potential for growth regardless of the course that is chosen. As mentioned earlier, they see a growing market (20 percent per year) for data processing/systems design service that they peg at $17 billion nationally and $1 billion regionally in 1988. The dollar volume in the market is distributed nearly equally across the four levels. Rinehart expects growth of the industry to accelerate both nationally and regionally. ACP's predictions are for a $34 billion national market by 1993. Of that $34 billion, the southeastern portion would be $3 billion.

21 A complicating factor in the decision is the matter of Rinehart's participation in the firm's operation. After achieving a respectable degree of success, Rinehart, at the age of 58, is admittedly reluctant to "throw himself" into a position that would require a great deal more active participation on his part. He is a knowledgeable owner who sees himself in the role of investor, rather than of aggressive entrepreneur. This is the role that he prefers. Thus, the question of future strategy is influenced by Rinehart's dilemma of "what to do with the company." Continued growth would provide the opportunity to take ACP public. There have also been offers from other firms in the business to purchase ACP. Rinehart and other family members currently hold 100 percent of the stock.

22 ACP's management team has shared this information with you—expecting your help in decision making about the future direction of the company. While they are not desperate for a decision,

Industry Projections (input: 1989)

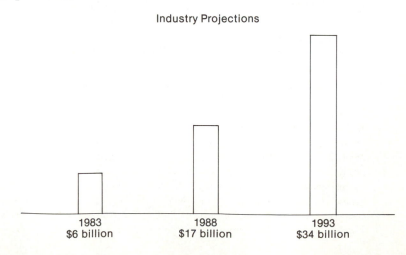

Industry Projections

| 1983 | 1988 | 1993 |
| $6 billion | $17 billion | $34 billion |

management believes that ACP is in an excellent position now to capitalize and build on its success, and feel that time may soon be a concern. The management team will meet again in about a week. The team is expecting a recommendation from you about the course that ACP should pursue, and your rationale for the recommendation versus other possible courses of action.

ACP's Management

Jack Rinehart

Age, 58
University of Kentucky, 1954

Career:

U.S. Air Force		to 1957
Methods coordinator,	Sonoco Products Company	to 1960
Vice president,	S. J. Fecht and Associates (consulting engineering)	to 1965
President/owner	Continental Consultants (chemical engineering recruiting)	to 1985
President/owner	American Computer Professionals	

W. M. (Moose) Morris

Age, 60
University of South Carolina

Career:

Regional manager, sales manager	IBM Atlanta
Executive vice president president	Digital Systems Software Company (utility industry)
Marketing vice president, executive vice president, general manager	American Computer Professionals

American Computer Professionals, Inc. (ACP) is a professional services firm providing software design, analysis and implementation capabilities for commercial and government organizations. Headquartered in Columbia, South Carolina, ACP provides client support from offices in Georgia, North Carolina, South Carolina, and Tennessee with a staff of well over 100 systems engineers.

Founded in 1979, ACP has grown to be the premier southeastern based company in this industry. ACP has been listed in the INC. 500 fastest growing companies of America for the past three years.

ACP SUPPORT AREAS

- Systems Analysis
- Requirements Definition
- Software/Hardware Evaluation
- Project Management
- Systems Design
- Systems Implementation
- Systems Testing
- Applications Programming
- Systems Conversion
- User Training
- Systems Documentation

CAPABILITIES

Despite the sophistication of today's computer hardware and software, the major challenge facing today's user is turning them into workable solutions. As new applications and technologies are multiplying, progressive companies are increasingly calling on consulting firms such as ACP to help provide those solutions.

ACP's ten years of experience in many environments give clients the use of the most advanced technology in user-specific situations. Individualized support services are provided from complete project planning to programming, networking, conversions and technical writing.

ACP's Training Division is also available for state of the art software, data base and language instruction including classroom programs for first-time personal computer users.

Individually, ACP's consultants average ten years or more experience in large information systems, encompassing a variety of software, hardware and applications. Clients have access to the skills of the entire ACP team, as well as to ACP's unique ability to quickly recruit specific talent when needed from across the country.

TYPICAL ENGAGEMENTS

MANUFACTURING

A team of 6 ACP systems engineers achieved the installation and implementation of a multi-million dollar real-time process control system for automating the manufacture of a sophisticated component. An inventory control subsystem and some 500 other programs were developed under this three year contract.

BANKING

A team of 12 ACP systems engineers supported a five year development program for a major national bank, providing analysis, design, programming and project management. Involved were a variety of financial systems and a major conversion.

UTILITIES

A team of 16 analysts, designers, programmers, and training specialists assisted in applications including power usage analysis, time reporting, environmental information for a nuclear power plant.

FEDERAL GOVERNMENT

A team of 30 senior analysts, systems programmers, technical writers, and project managers are supporting a long-term contract for business, scientific, environmental, and telecommunications applications at a large southeastern site.

STATE GOVERNMENT

A team of 15 systems engineers is bringing online a new sophisticated social services program to reduce cost and improve services delivery.

PARTIAL CLIENT LISTING

American General Life Insurance
Barnett Computing Company
Blue Cross and Blue Shield
Chrysler Corporation
Collins & Aikman Corp.
Colonial Life & Accident
E.I. du Pont de Nemours & Company
Engelhard Corporation
Federal Land Bank
Georgetown Steel Corporation
Gold Bond Building Products
L-TEC Welding & Cutting Systems
Memphis Light, Gas and Water Co.
Nuclear Fuel Services, Inc.
Opryland USA, Inc.
Policy Management Systems
Provident Life & Accident
R. J. Reynolds Tobacco Company
State of South Carolina
South Carolina Electric & Gas Co.
Tennessee Valley Authority
Textron Aerostructures
U. S. Department of Energy
Westinghouse Electric Corporation
Westvaco Corporation

ACP OFFICE LOCATIONS

American Computer Professionals, Inc.
(Corporate Office)
1777 St. Julian Place, Second Floor
Post Office Box 5125
Columbia, South Carolina 29250
803-256-2343
800-332-0555 (out SC)
800-327-1066 (in SC)

American Computer Professionals, Inc.
946 Millbrook Avenue, Suite D
Aiken, South Carolina 29801
803-649-2802

American Computer Professionals, Inc.
1100 Circle 75 Parkway, Suite 800
Atlanta, Georgia 30339
404-933-1555

American Computer Professionals, Inc.
5250 77 Center Drive, Suite 350
Charlotte, North Carolina 28217
704-529-0150

American Computer Professionals, Inc.
One Northgate Park, Suite 305
Chattanooga, Tennessee 37415
615-875-6791

American Computer Professionals, Inc.
3200 West End Avenue, Suite 405
Nashville, Tennessee 37203
615-292-1113

AMERICAN COMPUTER
PROFESSIONALS, INC.

Case 3

Doorstep Video, Inc.

Background

1   The growth of the video and electronic industry had always interested 21-year old Clay Lindsay. Clay was more than one year away from finishing his education, and he planned to start and run his own business after graduation. He constantly thought about different business ventures which he felt could be profitable. He also wanted to start a business that had never been tried before. While on Christmas break, Clay came up with an idea for what he thought could be a very successful business venture—a video rental store that delivered movies, similar to the established pizza delivery service.

2   Clay discussed this idea with his parents and close friends. They criticized the concept and doubted that such a business could be profitable. Clay's father, who had owned and operated a drug store in downtown Salisbury, North Carolina, for over 30 years, was one of those who doubted its profitability. He thought that Clay should finish his education before becoming involved in a new, time-consuming business venture. Clay, however, did find support from a couple of friends. One, Brent Snipes, whom Clay had known for about eight years, was very interested and recommended that they pursue the idea as a team. Brent would graduate from college that May, although Clay would not finish for another year.

3   Brent and Clay planned to start the business in June, with Brent controlling the everyday operations; Clay could come home when necessary since there was only a 45-minute drive between college and home.

Name and Logo

4   The two budding entrepreneurs immediately began to brainstorm for ideas on what to name the business, and Clay came up with the name Doorstep Video. After discussing other possibilities, they adopted Doorstep Video as a name that was easy to remember and one that conveyed the concept of what the business would be.

5   The next step, the design of a logo, took the two planners a little longer. They wanted a logo that would stick in the minds of their customers and one they would be proud to display. They decided that red and white would be the store colors as they felt these very dominant colors would demand attention. The design they finally adopted is shown below. Brent and Clay felt details like this were necessary to project a professional image. In particular, Clay wanted this store to be an independent store that operated with the efficiency of a chain store.

This case was prepared by John Dunkelberg, Wake Forest University, and Robert Anderson, College of Charleston.

"FROM OUR STORE TO YOUR DOOR" ®

LOCATION

6   The next order of business was to determine where to locate the business. Brent and Clay had lived in Salisbury, North Carolina, all of their lives and felt that the contacts they had established in the area would be a major factor in the success of their planned business. Clay's father owned the building in the downtown shopping district which housed his drug store. Clay was able to convince his father to rent them a small vacant space in the back of the store that was completely separate from the drug store.

7   Brent and Clay knew that they must establish a basic plan of operation, including name, location, and a business plan, in order to gain the support of their parents. This would be a key to the success of their new business. After evaluating the preliminary steps the two had taken, Clay's parents seemed a little more positive about the idea than they had been at first. Brent's parents, however, remained very skeptical, and Brent decided not to pursue the business venture.

8   Clay, who strongly believed in the idea, continued to develop a business plan by learning more about the video industry. He conducted an extensive search of the existing literature using a computer data-based search program located at the college library. Although the number of existing articles on the video tape rental industry were few in number, Clay found several articles that gave him some ideas about the industry, the competition, and what the future might be like. A capsule summary and his findings indicated that the industry was passing from the pioneering stage into the fast-growth stage, and the future seemed to belong to the large, well-funded chain stores that would contain thousands of titles. In addition, he spent many hours visiting existing video stores to see what features they had that he liked.

9   About two months later, during his spring semester, Clay mentioned his idea to a fraternity brother, Garret Barnes, whom he had known for about two years. Garret thought the idea was worthwhile and something with which he would like to become associated. Like Brent, Garret would graduate in May and would be able to begin work on a full-time basis. Clay had already developed a preliminary business plan that included an estimate of the startup costs. These figures indicated that an investment of approximately $14,000 was required to open the doors. After talking with their parents, Garret and Clay decided to explore the business venture further.

THE ENTREPRENEURS

10   Clay Lindsay, from Salisbury, was a business major at a nearby private university. He was active in his fraternity and had always been interested in assuming leadership positions. His goals were to be self-employed and to start a business that offered a better product or service than its competitors. He also wanted to establish a business that was interesting and that had the potential for rapid growth. Clay's business experience involved working at his father's retail drug store and gift shop.

He began janitorial work there when he was 12. He was soon handling everyday functions, such as personnel management, special promotions, the purchasing of imported goods, and advertising. Clay later managed the gift shop for his father during the Christmas season.

11   Garret Barnes, a 22-year old native of Florida, was active in the student legislature and intra-murals, and he served in leadership positions within his fraternity. Garret's interests included competitive sports and other extracurricular activities. His goal was to start his own company, which he could develop and nurture to a point that it would yield healthy returns for his future.

12   Prior to his involvement with Clay, Garret had no business experience; however, he was completing his bachelor of science degree in business. Garret thought this opportunity suited his needs perfectly and that it had the potential for a good career. He made friends easily and worked hard to make a good first impression on the people he met. In his fraternity, Garret was known as a hard worker and one who handled public relations very well.

VIDEO INDUSTRY

13   During the latter part of the 1970s, video cassette recorders (VCRs) became popular. By the end of 1980, approximately 2 million homes had VCRs. At that time, the national sales rate of video cassette recorders was only 17,000 units per month; but, by 1981, VCR sales rose to over 140,000 units per month. In 1984, nearly 7.5 million VCRs were sold, and by the end of that year VCRs were in 20 percent of the homes in America. By the end of 1987, 52 percent of American homes had at least one VCR.[1]

14   The rise in VCR sales was enhanced by an increase in the availability of prerecorded cassettes. In the late 1970s, the thought of selling prerecorded cassettes to consumers frightened the major movie and television studios in the United States. Many were afraid revenues from both television and movie theaters would be greatly decreased as viewers turned from movies and television to cassette tapes. However, a small number of studios decided to gamble on the idea of selling prerecorded cassettes to the home viewer. In the spring of 1978, there were only about 100 prerecorded cassettes available through studio distributors.

15   After some thorough market research, several other studios decided to enter the market. The market research indicated that consumers preferred renting prerecorded cassette tapes to buying by a margin of 7 to 1. At that time, cassette tapes sold for about $50 and rented for about $5 per day. Since then the cost of renting video tapes has dropped from $5 per day to as low as $1 per day. This, of course, was caused by the increased competition within the industry. On the other hand, the price of prerecorded cassettes has risen to as much as $70 and sometimes even higher for the biggest hits.

16   The home video market changed rapidly. Rental and sales outlets seemed to pop up in every shopping area. The industry enjoyed incredible growth over the next five years, but with growth came change. When home video first started, there were two formats available, beta and VHS. Beta and VHS competed with each other in software and hardware and neither was interchangeable with the other—if you bought a beta VCR then you could only show beta tapes and vice versa. However, over the past several years, the VHS format became the dominant choice of consumers, and beta now accounts for only a small percentage of the market. At first, many video stores handled both the VHS and beta software; however, today it is almost impossible to find a beta rental store.

---

[1]Subrata Chakravarty, "Give 'em Variety," *Forbes*, May 2, 1988, pp. 54–57.

17   In 1983, 11 million prerecorded video cassettes were sold to retailers. By 1984 that number rose 100 percent to 22 million cassette tapes. As a result, rental stores can offer a large selection of titles. The smaller stores carry as few as 500 titles while the superstores may have 10,000 or more titles for the consumer to select from. Today, the average video specialty store carries about 2,600 different titles.[2]

18   The prerecorded cassettes are divided into two categories, "A" and "B" titles. The "A" titles are the "hit" videos and the most costly to produce. The "B" titles are those that are lesser known and are considered budget films. Examples of "A" titles would be *Top Gun* or *Fatal Attraction*; "B" titles would include *Creepoziods* or *The Curse*. Since the "B" titles were less expensive than the "A" titles, video rental stores did not have to rent them as often as the "A" titles to earn a profit. In the United States, the average number of rentals (per tape) for an "A" title was 108 and 62 rentals for "B" titles.

19   The video tape rental industry was one of the nation's fastest growing and one of the most fragmented. Nationwide, there were over 25,000 video rental stores, mostly small entrepreneurial type operations. In addition, there were about 32,000 rental outlets, such as convenience stores, that rented video tapes as a sidelight to their major business. These rental outlets usually carried only the newer movies, which they received 3–4 weeks after the release date, and stocked less than 250 titles.

20   As often happens in fast-growth industries, a shakeout seemed inevitable. Chain stores had started to exert pressure on the smaller and undercapitalized stores, and the growth of the superstore chains, carrying more than 6,500 titles, seemed to be just around the corner.[3]

Business Plan

21   Clay and Garret planned to operate their business in the back of a warehouse owned by Clay's father. Since they planned to take telephone orders for rental tape deliveries, the only space requirement was space of the storage of tapes and enough room for the order taker and the driver. The existing warehouse area would require the construction of some walls to create a separate area for Doorstep Video's operations. (For store layout see Exhibit 1) The rental business would operate much like a pizza delivery service, with customers calling and placing orders for video tapes which would be delivered in 30 minutes or less. The planned hours of operation were Monday through Friday from 4 P.M. until 12 A.M. and Saturday and Sunday from 12 noon until midnight.

22   Clay and Garret also planned to deliver popcorn and cokes along with the videos to allow customers to receive some of the full effect of a movie theater without leaving their homes. Videos would be returned by the customer to one of four return boxes positioned strategically throughout the town. The videos would be delivered by part-time drivers, who could make approximately seven deliveries per hour. Drivers (students from a local small private college) would be paid the minimum wage of $3.35 per hour plus an incentive rate of 40 cents per delivery. Clay and Garret thought that, by delivering the videos, the possibility for theft should decrease since they would actually know the customers' correct address.

---

[2]"Video Marketing" published by *Video Store,* Hollywood, Calif., 1987.

[3]Ron Stodghill, "Will Video Chains Push Small Stores Out of the Picture?" *The Charlotte Observer,* February 15, 1988, pp. 1 and 13C.

EXHIBIT 1
Doorstep Video Floor Plan

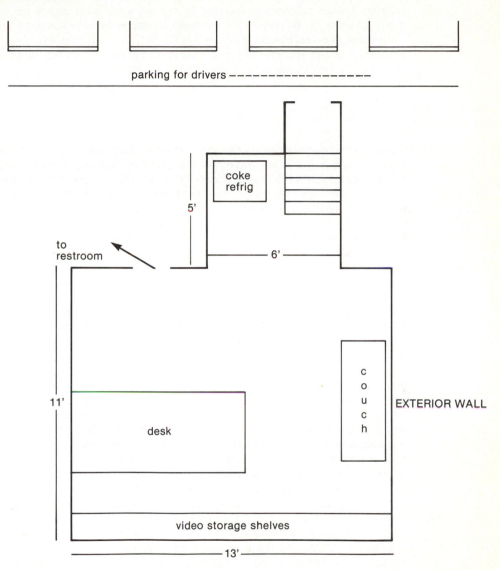

Note: All interior walls will be added by Clay and Garret to minimize cost. Total cost of the project will be $400.00.

23   Although they did not attempt any marketing research, Clay and Garret saw the potential for rapid growth in rental video tape delivery. Their goal was to test the concept in Salisbury, and if successful, expand to locations in other relatively small cities. The reason for operating in small cities was that major chains only located in larger cities, and Doorstep Video could gain strength in the video industry through growth in the less-comptetitive markets.

SALISBURY'S VIDEO MARKET

24   Salisbury, a small city located in the center of North Carolina, had a population of about 25,000. Doorstep Video's delivery area included the city and a few areas outside the city, with a total market of about 28,000 people. The per capita income in this area was approximately $10,000, while the average total household income was $28,000. Currently there were 14 video rental stores in Salisbury and an additional 14 convenience stores and other outlets that rented a small selection of videos. No major video chains had located in Salisbury.

PURCHASING

25   A major factor to consider in any business is where to obtain merchandise. Since he was interested in buying used as well as new video cassettes, Clay contacted several sources across the country. One source, International Movie Merchants (IMM) in Dallas, Oregon, was a used video distributor, and it agreed to supply Doorstep Video. IMM sent Clay a list of 500 used videos that would be available and suitable to the needs of Doorstep Video. IMM quoted a price of $13,000 for the 500 videos, for an average cost of $26. After several changes, the list was approved. According to Clay, you never settle for paying what the seller is asking; therefore, the bargaining process began. After a short time the cost was finally agreed upon and set at $20.30 per video.

26   Doorstep Video also needed a source for new releases. Baker and Taylor Video, a major nationwide distributor, soon became that source. Baker and Taylor provided weekly catalogs, which included all the new releases scheduled for the next several weeks. The average cost of a new release was $65 plus shipping, which usually added another $3. Garret later found another source, Schwartz Brothers, which offered savings of $1 to $2 per video, but shipping costs remained approximately $3. Schwartz Brothers also offered weekly catalogs, which included all the new releases and some special deals.

27   A key to buying new releases is knowing how many of each title to purchase. Garret took on this task, which included a lot of guess work. The only thing he could do was base purchases on how similar titles had sold in the past and on how popular the title had been in the theater. Interestingly, Garret's research indicated that what was popular in the theater was not always a popular renter. On the other hand, some titles that were sleepers in the theater were in high demand in the rental stores. There seemed to be no real formula to use when buying new releases. However, there is a lot of gut feeling involved in the selection process. Doorstep Video set its new release budget at $1,500 per month. Since there are no returns on opened merchandise, if Doorstep Video bought too many of a new release it could only sell the used video to a used video distributor like IMM. Unfortunately, these distributors purchase the video for about one third of its original cost.

28   Doorstep Video also needed a source for the purchase of VCRs suitable for renting and for the plastic cases, which were needed as protective carrying cases for the videos. Commtron, a major distributor in Atlanta, was contacted, and it offered to sell Doorstep Videos the rental type VCRs for $239 each. The plastic cases could be purchased at prices that ranged from $0.49 to $0.55 each, depending on the quantity ordered.

INVENTORY SYSTEM

29   The inventory system used by Doorstep Video would be an index card system. Each video would have a card, which would be placed in the out file when the movie was rented. The customer's number would be written on the card as well as the date rented. This was not the most advanced or efficient system; however, due to lack of funds, a computer system seemed out of the question.

30   As should be expected in a new technology oriented industry, several very complete computer software inventory programs were available for video rental stores. Interestingly, one of the best in the nation was produced and sold by a firm located in Salisbury. These systems are capable of handling 40,000 members and 100,000 videos. All transactions are handled by a bar code reader, which makes the system efficient and accurate. The systems created statistics, such as customers with debit balances; rentals per day, month, and year; rentals by customer; rentals per title; and many other management features. The cost for a system, including the computer and printer, was about $5,500.

FINANCING, LEGAL, AND INSURANCE

31   The total startup cost for Doorstep Video was estimated to be about $15,500 (see Exhibit 2). Based on an estimate of daily rentals, Clay and Garret estimated weekly rentals of 513 titles over the first three months (see Exhibit 3). Rental price was $2.99 for one title and $2.50 each for two or more titles. Based on what they had observed in other stores and from what they had read in *Video Store,* a trade magazine, Clay estimated that the revenue from the average rental would be $2.63. In addition, they estimated that they could rent the VCRs on an average of seven times per week, at $5 per day. Monthly expenses were estimated to be $3,635 (see Exhibit 4). During the first year of operation, Garret, who would be managing the store, would receive $700 a month salary, and Clay, who would be only working part-time, would not receive any compensation. Any profits would be used to purchase additional inventory. To finance the startup and leave funds available to cover any possible cash flow problems over the startup period, Clay and Garret each agreed to put up $10,400 from their personal savings.

32   Due to the potential liability problem, Clay and Garret thought they should organize Doorstep Video as an S corporation. This form of business allows small businesses to enjoy the limited liability benefits of the corporate form of organization yet obtain the benefits of being taxed as a

EXHIBIT 2
Startup Costs—Doorstep Video

Inventory:	
500 Used videos	$10,150
22 New videos	1,500
Rental VCRs 2 at $239	478
Opening advertising:	
Flyer insert	450
Printing	416
Newspaper ads	198
Furniture and equipment	900
Leasehold improvements	400
Return boxes 4 at $50	200
Insurance	300
Shirts for employees	170
Telephone installation	95
Office supplies	60
Plastic cases for videotapes	73
Licenses	60
Legal and professional	49
Total startup costs	$15,499

EXHIBIT 3

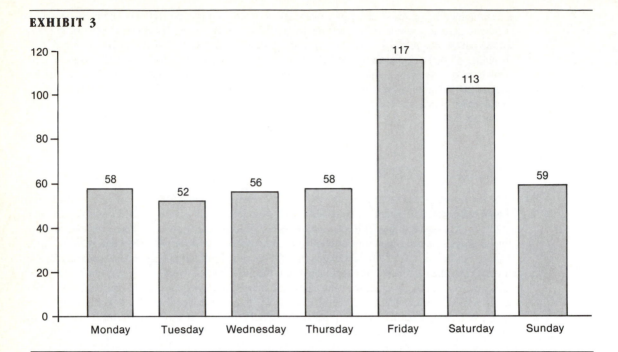

EXHIBIT 4
Projected Monthly Expenses

Videos	$1,500
Gross payroll	1,100
Advertising	300
Taxes	370
Telephone	115
Rent and utilities	100
Misc. expenses	120
Insurance	30
Total projected monthly expenses	$3,635

partnership. They talked to an attorney, who agreed to handle the necessary incorporation paperwork for only $49. In addition, a membership application form was designed to provide a measure of protection for Doorstep Video and serve as a contract between Doorstep and its customers (see Exhibit 5).

33   Clay talked to a local insurance agent about the coverage that would be needed by Doorstep Video. The agent recommended a comprehensive policy that would cover the contents of the store in the amount of $30,000 in case of fire or water damage. Theft insurance was not included. In addition, the drivers were covered by a rider, which provided Doorstep Video with liability insurance for any claim that was in excess of the liability coverage from the driver's own insurance—since the drivers would use their own cars for deliveries.

EXHIBIT 5

"FROM OUR STORE TO YOUR DOOR".

(for office use only)
APPROVAL#_____/_____
TYPED_____
VERIFIED_____
MEMBERSHIP #_____

APPLICATION FOR MEMBERSHIP

DATE:_____

(PLEASE PRINT)
NAME_____
             (LAST)   (FIRST)   (MIDDLE INITIAL)

STREET
ADDRESS_____

_____

CITY_____STATE_____ZIP CODE_____

TELEPHONE: HOME_____OFFICE_____

DRIVER'S LICENSE: STATE _____NUMBER_____ EXP. DATE_____

SOCIAL SECURITY#_____

EMPLOYER_____ DEPT._____

RELATIVE NAME_____TELEPHONE_____
(NOT LIVING AT SAME ADDRESS AS ABOVE)

ADDITIONAL FAMILY MEMBERS ALLOWED TO RENT VIDEO TAPES AND/OR EQUIPMENT ON THIS MEMBERSHIP:
            (MEMBER IS RESPONSIBLE FOR ACTIVITY OF ADDITIONAL RENTERS)

ADULTS

_____

_____

CHILDREN   **AGE**

_____ _____

_____ _____

_____

ARE CHILDREN ALLOWED TO RENT "R" (OR NR) MOVIES?   YES   NO

TOTAL NUMBER OF CARDS REQUESTED_____(MAXIMUM 4)

APPLICANTS SIGNATURE:_____
BEFORE SIGNING THIS APPLICATION SEE REVERSE SIDE FOR TERMS AND CONDITIONS.

ACCEPTED FOR DOORSTEP VIDEO:_____

EXHIBIT 5 (concluded)

AGREEMENT & CONDITIONS OF MEMBERSHIP

AFTER DOORSTEP VIDEO, INC. ACCEPTS APPLICATION FOR MEMBERSHIP THIS APPLICATION CONSTITUTES AN AGREEMENT BETWEEN DOORSTEP VIDEO, INC. AND MEMBER REGARDING MEMBER'S ACCOUNT.

MEMBER AGREES:

TO PAY ALL PROPERLY AUTHORIZED CHARGES ON MEMBER'S ACCOUNT WHEN THEY BECOME DUE.
TO RETURN ALL RENTED TAPES AND/OR EQUIPMENT TO THE DOORSTEP VIDEO FROM WHICH THEY WERE RENTED, ON TIME, OR PAY THE APPROPRIATE LATE CHARGES.
TO REWIND ALL RENTED TAPES OR PAY THE APPROPRIATE REWIND FEE - OUR NORMAL POLICY IS TO PERMIT ONE OR TWO UNREWOUND TAPES AT NO CHARGE - AFTER THAT WE ASSESS REWIND CHARGES ON THE MEMBER'S ACCOUNT.
TO RETURN VIDEO CASSETTES IN THE SAME CONDITION AS WHEN THEY WERE OBTAINED. IF, WHEN RETURNED, THE CARTRIDGE OF A "SALE OR RENT" VIDEO CASSETTE, IN WHICH THE TAPE IS ENCLOSED, IS BROKEN OR SMASHED, THE MEMBER WILL BE REQUIRED TO PAY THE RENTAL FEE AND THEN BUYING THE VIDEO CASSETTE BY PAYING THE PRICE SHOWN ON THE INVENTORY IN THE CASE OF A RENTAL ONLY VIDEO CASSETTE RETURNED WITH A BROKEN CARTRIDGE THE MEMBER WILL PAY THE COST AMOUNT FOR THE CASSETTE AS DAMAGES, THE RENTAL FEES & RETURN THE VIDEO CASSETTE TO THE STORE.
IF A VIDEO CASSETTE HAS BEEN TAMPERED WITH i.e., CARTRIDGE CASE OPENED, MANUFACTURER'S TAPE REMOVED AND/OR REPLACED, MANUFACTURER'S MARKINGS, LABELS OR IDENTIFICATION IS EITHER MISSING OR ASKEW, THE MEMBER IS RESPONSIBLE FOR THE FULL PAYMENTOF THE CASSETTE.
IF THE VIDEO CASSETTE IS LOST, STOLEN OR DESTROYED - IF THE MEMBER IS UNABLE TO RETURN A VIDEO CASSETTE BECAUSE IT HAS BEEN LOST, STOLEN OR DESTROYED, THE MEMBER WILL BE RESPONSIBLE FOR PURCHASING THE VIDEO CASSETTE BY PAYING THE RENTAL FEE AND THEN BUYING THE VIDEO CASSETTE BY PAYING THE PRICE SHOWN IN THE INVENTORY.
THE VIDEO CASSETTE MAY BE SHOWN ONLY IN A PRIVATE HOME, WITHOUT ADMISSION OR OTHER CHARGES. IN THE PRESENCE OF THE MEMBER, HIS FAMILY, AND HIS PERSONAL GUESTS. THE MEMBER MAY NOT LOAN THE VIDEO CASSETTE TO ANYONE ELSE FOR ANY REASON WHATSOEVER.
VIDEO CASSETTE PLAYER/RECORDER AND CAMERA AND ACCESSORY RENTAL - MEMBER MUST RETURN VIDEO PLAYER AND CAMERA IN THE SAME CONDITION AS IT WAS RECEIVED AND TO THE SAME LOCATION FROM WHICH IT WAS RENTED. IF THE RENTED ITEMS ARE RETURNED IN A DAMAGED CONDITION, MEMBER SHALL PAY THE RENTAL FEE AND THE COST OF REPAIRING THE DAMAGE. DAMAGE REFERS TO NEGLIGENCE OR MISUSE OF THE RENTED ITEMS. SUCH NEGLIGENCE OR MISUSE SHALL INCLUDE, DROPPING OR THROWING THE RENTED ITEMS PERMITTING OR INSERTING OBJECTS OR OTHER MATERIALS (OTHER THAN VIDEO TAPES) INTO THE WORKING PARTS OF THE PLAYER.
THE MEMBER IS RESPONSIBLE FOR ANY VISIBLE DAMAGE WHILE THE PLAYER IS IN THEIR POSSESSION. VISIBLE DAMAGE REFERS TO CRACKED OR DENTED CASE, BROKEN OR LOST KNOBS, ANY MISSING OR BROKEN EXTERNAL PARTS, MISSING CONNECTOR CORDS, WIRES OR ADAPTERS.
IN THE CASE OF A PLAYER/RECORDER RETURNED IN A DAMAGED CONDITION, THE STORE WILL ADVISE MEMBER OF THE REPAIR COSTS.
FAILURE OF THE MEMBER TO RETURN A RENTED ITEM SHALL SUBJECT THE MEMBER TO ADDITIONAL RENTAL FEES AT THE BASIC RENTAL CHARGE AS PROVIDED IN THEIS AGREEMENT UNTIL THE RENTAL ITEMS ARE RETURNED. AT NO TIME DOES THE MEMBER OBTAIN OWNERSHIP OF THE RENTAL PROPERTY.
IN ADDITION MEMBER UNDERSTANDS THAT DOORSTEP VIDEO, INC. HAS THE RIGHT TO CANCEL MEMBER'S MEMBERSHIP PRIVILEGES AND/OR PURSUE OTHER CIVIL AND CRIMINAL LEGAL REMEDIES PROVIDED BY THE STATE OF NORTH CAROLINA UNDER ITS GENERAL STATUTES IF, IN DOORSTEP'S SOLE OPINION, THE NEED ARISES - -ALL WITHOUT ADDITIONAL NOTICE TO MEMBER, EXCEPT AS MAY BE REQUIRED BY NORTH CAROLINA LAW.

Decision Time

34   During the last week in April, with the spring semester almost complete, Clay and Garret must make a decision on whether to go ahead with the startup of Doorstep Video or abandon their plans. They have contacted students at a local college and found several who are willing to work on a part-time basis. In addition, the local telephone company agreed to give them a local number that helped describe the purpose of their business—636-FAST.

35   They both feel that the idea of home delivery of rental videos is a good one and one that they can build into a profitable business. Clay, however, does have one more year of college before he can devote full time to the business. To further complicate the decision, Garret received a job offer in sales with a nationally known firm. They agree that they must make a decision no later than the first week in May.

CASE 4

METIS SYSTEMS CORPORATION: NEW VENTURE BUSINESS PLAN

1   Jim Kilpatrick left the meeting feeling somewhat frustrated. This was the third venture capitalist he had met in the last month and not one had demonstrated much enthusiasm for the Metis Systems Concept.

2   Jim had started this venture well aware of most venture capitalists' reluctance to fund start-up operations, but, nonetheless, he had expected at least greater initial interest in the proposal. Clearly, he felt, Metis addressed an extraordinary opportunity in a huge market. The management team he had assembled was far superior to those found in the vast majority of new companies. Initial contacts with representatives of his proposed customer base had been extremely encouraging. All advisors to the project were confident that Metis was a major "winner."

3   As a result, Jim began to wonder whether the investors who had turned him down were being entirely candid. Each of them had known that Metis was a start-up operation when they originally agreed to meet with him. Two possibilities occurred to Jim. One, he was simply visiting the wrong venture capitalists for a deal of this type. Two, perhaps there was some flaw in his presentation of the opportunity, such that his message was not getting across. Altering the presentation and business concept, if the actual problem were the choice of investor, would clearly be a mistake to avoid. On the other hand, if there were a problem Jim had missed, he wanted to catch it as soon as possible.

4   As a midcourse reality check, Jim and his management team have decided to hire you to give them an honest third-party critique of the written business plan they have been using in their capital search. As an independent management consultant, you have until tomorrow morning to prepare your critique of the Metis Business Plan for presentation to Kilpatrick and his team. Metis's actual business plan that was shared with several venture capitalists follows.

OVERVIEW

5   Metis Systems Corporation is a computer software and services company that specializes in developing and servicing knowledge-based business systems for the financial services industry. The company expects to obtain a competitive advantage over other software and service companies through a unique approach to systems development, which integrates an emerging technology known as *expert systems* with more traditional computer technologies.

6   The initial target markets for the company's products and services are commercial banks and savings and loans (S&Ls). With deregulation, nationwide banking, competition from nonbanking

sources, and mergers and acquisitions, these markets are developing into a new generation of "financial supermarkets," where only the financially strong will survive. The company plans to provide a new generation of software products and services that focus on the primary needs and problems of these evolving markets: (1) loan quality and (2) the management of assets and liabilities. The company's initial products will focus on these critical issues and will provide new and improved solutions using technology that has only recently matured.

7 To support the need for improved loan quality, the company is developing a series of products, *The Lending Series,* that use expert systems techniques and focus on lending functions. The first product, *The Policy Manual,* will have a knowledge base containing the lending rules and policies that are normally found in policy and procedure manuals. A follow-on product, *The Loan Instructor,* is an automated tutorial, which supports the training of lending and credit personnel. Its knowledge base includes the policies and procedures obtained from policy manuals, as well as basic lending principles and lending regulations. Supplemental products will support specialty areas of lending, such as asset lending, commercial construction lending, agricultural lending, small business lending, adjustable rate mortgages, consumer leasing plans, and other specific lending types. Professional services will be provided to assist customers in installing and implementing the company's products.

8 The company is working with the consulting firm of Sebastian, Clegg, Sloan & Creighton, Inc., to investigate the potential for an expert system, the *Chief Financial Officer,* which will assist in improving asset/liability planning and management. Ed Sebastian, one of the principals of the firm, was formerly the vice chairman of the board and the chief financial officer of Bankers Trust of South Carolina (now NCNB of South Carolina). He had previously been with Price Waterhouse specializing in bank asset/liability management.

9 The company's management believes that there is an immediate need for these products. One of the reasons for the current need is the generally recognized shortage of the lending expertise required to meet the growing demands of the financial services industry. The advent of new segments of the industry (such as traditional savings and loan institutions) further dilutes the already limited supply of expertise. Another reason is the additional requirements for consistency in lending operations and policies. These requirements are believed to result from the increasing number of bank mergers and acquisitions and the increased attention from regulatory agencies. Also, there are new demands being placed on lending managers, because of interstate banking and sophisticated financing alternatives. In summary, there is a need for the product and the technology that is required for its development exists today.

10 The development of *The Loan Manager* will consist of three phases: (1) a demonstrable prototype of product [nine months], (2) development of a deliverable product and implementation of an initial version [18 months], and (3) implementation of the product in multiple financial institutions and will produce continuing enhancements.

11 An innovative commercial lending organization known for the quality of its lending program is being sought as a participant during the first phase. This initial customer will be asked to provide some funding during this phase, as well as access to its expertise, use of onsite office facilities, and use of data processing resources. It is expected that this customer will receive special considerations in pricing for the future use of the product.

12 The company's management believes that there are definite advantages to an organization for participating with Metis Systems in the development of *The Loan Manager.* Not only does the company have highly skilled and experienced professionals, but it can also offer a fresh outlook on the design of such systems.

13 The concepts and plans for *The Loan Manager* have been presented to senior managers of three major commercial banks: (1) Republic Bank Corporation, Dallas, Texas; (2) Bank One, Columbus, Ohio; and (3) First Union National Bank, Charlotte, North Carolina. These presentations were given to verify the market potential for *The Loan Manager,* to validate the soundness of the

product concepts, and to sell each bank on participating as a development customer. The company's management found the responses to be encouraging about the concepts, ideas, and people involved, but concern was expressed with the company's current level of capitalization. The implication was that there would be more interest in participating with Metis Systems if the company had a more solid financial base. For this reason, a major priority for the company's management is to obtain sufficient start-up capital.

14   Based upon current cash-flow projections (see the financial summary section at the end of this case), a total capitalization of $2.4 million, as well as the revenue from the initial customers, will be required to cover the expenses of developing, selling, and servicing the initial product. This amount should provide sufficient funds until the revenue from the sale of *The Loan Manager* exceeds the operational expenses.

COMPANY'S PROFILE

15   Metis Systems Corporation was incorporated in the state of South Carolina in September 1986. The company is headquartered in Columbia, South Carolina. It specializes in developing and servicing knowledge-based business systems for the financial services industry. The principal individuals associated with the company provide a collection of skills and experience in the areas of management, development, and servicing of successful commercial software products; expert systems applications; integrated micro-processor applications; micro-processor, lending-support systems; and education and training systems. The following is a summary of the experience and qualifications of the key individuals that will participate in executing the company's business plan.

James H. Kilpatrick, President

16   Prior to his involvement with Metis Systems, Kilpatrick was a senior vice president of Policy Management Systems Corporation (PMSC) for four years. He was responsible for the development and maintenance of PMSC's software products, which consisted of managing approximately 600 people and a budget of about $35 million. He was also responsible for mergers and acquisitions for PMSC, which added approximately $60 million to PMSC's annual revenue. Prior to joining PMSC, Kilpatrick was a vice president responsible for the operations center, MasterCard International, in St. Louis, Missouri. At MasterCard, he was responsible for the initial design of BankNet. Prior to MasterCard, he was a senior vice president of the Merchants National Bank of Mobile, Alabama, responsible for data processing, proof, and bookkeeping. Other prior positions include vice president of computer services for Central Bancshares of the South, and a systems engineer for Electronic Data Systems.

17   He holds a bachelor of science degree from the University of Alabama and has attended the ABA's Stonier Graduate School of Banking at Rutger's University.

Camille Nuzum, Vice President, Knowledge Systems Engineering

18   Ms. Nuzum was a systems architect with PMSC for 7 years. She managed the development of the current version of the PMS product and PMSC's initial workstation development projects. Prior to PMSC, Ms. Nuzum held various positions in the property and casualty insurance industry.

19   She also holds a bachelor of arts degree from the University of South Carolina.

William Kirby, Vice President, Software Systems Engineering

20   Kirby has over 20 years experience in working with systems software at PMSC and Blue Cross/Blue Shield of South Carolina. Kirby's most recent experience is in the development of systems support software for the IBM PC.

21   Kirby attended Newberry College and holds the Registered Business Programmers Certificate and the Certificate in Computer Programming.

Larry M. Stephens, Vice President, Expert Systems Technology

22   Dr. Stephens is currently an associate professor in the Department of Electrical and Computer Engineering at the University of South Carolina. He has been a member of the Center for Machine Intelligence and has been actively participating in research projects involving the application of expert systems and related techniques to office automation problems for 10 years.

23   He holds a bachelor of science degree in electrical engineering from the University of South Carolina.

Earl P. Andrews, Marketing and Lending Advisor

24   Andrews is currently president of Market Analysis and Research Services, Inc., management consultants. For the 25 years prior to 1979, he held various banking positions, including 8 years as a lending officer and 10 years as the head of the marketing division. He has taught numerous courses in bank marketing and management at the American Institute of Banking, at the Stonier Graduate School of Banking at Rutger's University, and at the School of Banking of the South at Louisiana State University. Andrews provides marketing and banking experience and guidance to the Company.

25   Andrews holds a bachelor of science degree from Auburn University.

Larry H. Roelofs, Technical Advisor

26   Roelofs is currently the lead knowledge engineer at NASA Goddard Space Flight Center's Laboratory for Applied Intelligent Database Research. Roelofs has over 20 years experience in the development and implementation of high-technology systems.

27   He holds a bachelor of science and a master's degree in physics from the American University.

John S. Williamson III: Financial Advisor

28   Williamson is president of Williamson and Associates, Inc., a business and tax consulting firm franchised with General Business Services. He serves as the principal financial advisor to over 100 business and professional organizations.

29   He holds a law degree from the University of Virginia School of Law, an industrial engineering degree from Virginia Tech, and is a Certified Financial Planner. Williamson provides financial guidance to the company.

John C. Wyatt, Business Advisor

30   Wyatt is currently self-employed, providing consulting and planning services to businesses and local government. From 1980 to August 1985, he was with PMSC, serving as vice president and general counsel, and was responsible for management of PMSC's legal affairs and contract negotiation with PMSC's customers and suppliers.

31   He holds degrees in economics and law from the University of North Carolina at Chapel Hill.

Edward J. Sebastian

32   Sebastian is chairman of the board and chief executive officer of First Sun Capital Corporation, which engages in business combinations with banks, bank holding companies, and other financial institutions. He is also chairman of E. J. Sebastian Group, Inc., which provides financial consulting and related services to banks.

33   From July 1974 to January 1986, Sebastian served as vice chairman of the board, secretary, cashier and chief financial officer with Bankers Trust of South Carolina before its merger with North Carolina National Bank. Prior to this, he was the acting manager for Price Waterhouse in Columbia, South Carolina.

34   He received a bachelor of science degree from Pennsylvania State University. He is a certified public accountant, certified review appraiser, certified manufactured housing appraiser, international certified appraiser, certified mortgage underwriter, and a certified industrial engineer.

35   The company is participating with E. J. Sebastian Associates in several applications of expert systems technology. The primary application being pursued would provide expertise to support the management of the assets and liabilities of banks, savings and loans, and other businesses.

Walter R. Creighton, Jr.

36   Creighton is the chief financial officer of E. J. Sebastian Group and affiliated companies. He is also a member of the board of directors of First South Savings Bank, a $100 million stock savings institution in Columbia, South Carolina. Prior to joining the Sebastian Group, Creighton was a senior audit manager with Price Waterhouse in Columbia for 12 years.

37   Creighton holds a bachelor of science degree in economics from North Carolina State University and a M.B.A. in finance and masters of accountancy from the University of South Carolina.

ORGANIZATION AND OWNERSHIP

38   The following represents a pro forma distribution of the initial ownership of the company. It is intended to reflect management's current thinking with regard to the company's present value and relative percentage of ownership.

39   It is intended that the company be authorized by its articles of incorporation to issue 10,000,000 shares of common stock, par value $0.01 per share, and 5 million shares of preferred stock, par value $1.00 per share. After incorporation, 1.2 million shares of the preferred stock are to be sold at a par value of $1 per share to venture investors to obtain sufficient capitalization for starting the company. The company intends to offer 1.8 million shares of the common stock at a purchase price of $0.01 per share to the individuals and in the amounts as shown below.

Number of Owner of Issued Shares	Number of Shares	Number with Restrictions	Percent Ownership
Preferred stock	1,200,000	0	40.00%
James H. Kilpatrick	450,000	360,000	15.00
James E. Connors	150,000	120,000	5.00
William Kirby	150,000	120,000	5.00
Camille Nuzum	150,000	120,000	5.00
Larry M. Stephens	150,000	120,000	5.00
John C. Wyatt	150,000	120,000	5.00
Earl P. Andrews	7,500	0	0.25
Edward Lott	7,500	0	0.25
Larry H. Roelofs	7,500	0	0.25
Dewey Crim	5,000	0	0.17
Arthur S. Kranzley	5,000	0	0.17
David V. Lakes	5,000	0	0.17
W. Thomas Lavender, Jr.	5,000	0	0.17
John S. Williamson, Jr.	5,000	0	0.17
Reserved for options	552,500		18.40
Total	3,000,000	960,000	100.00%

COMPANY'S MARKETS

40   There are many reasons for having selected the commercial lending area of the financial services industry as the initial market to be served by Metis Systems. It is a market that has a real need for expert-system solutions to significant business problems. The severe shortage of experienced and qualified lending managers is generally considered to be one of the major problems facing the industry today. Recent deregulation of the industry has introduced new competitors and more sophisticated financing alternatives, and it has diluted the already scarce supply of expertise.

41   According to *Polk's World Bank Directory,* the following represents the number of institutions and locations that could be potential installation sites for the product in the United States.

Type of Institution	Number	Locations
National banks	4,827	19,918
State or trust	9,481	17,217
Mutual savings	397	2,745
Private banks	10	142
Other	212	389
Total target market	14,927	40,411

42   The statistics above show that the market potential for *The Loan Manager* in the United States is nearly 15,000 different organizations providing over 40,000 possible installation sites for the product, as well as a potential market in English-speaking countries outside of the United States.

43   There are 300 commercial banks and 50 mutual savings banks that have assets of over 750 million dollars in the United States. While it would be entirely feasible to meet the market projections presented in this plan by making a conservative penetration into this base of large organizations alone, it is believed that the largest portion of Metis Systems revenue will come from a reasonable penetration of the medium and smaller size companies, which represent over 90 percent of the

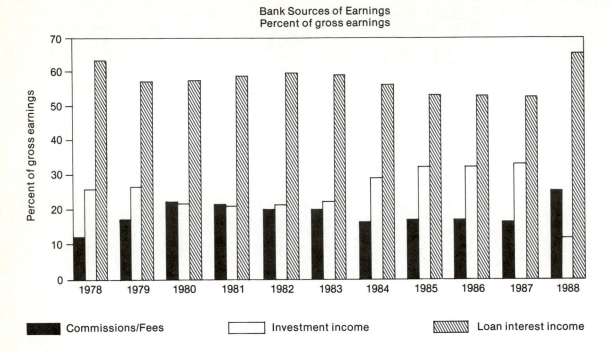

Bank Sources of Earnings
Percent of gross earnings

Percent of gross earnings

Years: 1978, 1979, 1980, 1981, 1982, 1983, 1984, 1985, 1986, 1987, 1988

■ Commissions/Fees   ☐ Investment income   ▨ Loan interest income

organizations and locations in the market. The company will develop and service products that are needed by all of the above potential customers.

COMPANY'S PRODUCTS

44   The key to success in commercial lending continues to be the availability of skilled and knowledgeable lending managers. Surveys of corporate treasurers indicate that to remain competitive, commercial lenders need to become increasingly more sophisticated in identifying and proposing more creative financing alternatives. At the same time, deregulation has broadened the base of financial service institutions competing for the available commercial lending expertise, As with other areas of the financial services industry, there is a positive correlation between the potential profitability of a lending organization and the degree to which systems give it an advantage over its competitors. The use of knowledge-based expert systems that embody the expertise of experienced lending managers can provide this advantage.

45   Expert systems are computer programs that use symbolic reasoning to solve programs well. They differ from traditional computer application software in that they:

1. Use specialized knowledge about a particular problem area, rather than just general purpose knowledge that would apply to all problems.
2. Use symbolic reasoning, rather than just numerical calculations.
3. Perform at a level of competence that is better than that of nonexpert humans.
4. Use heuristic reasoning.
5. Attack problems that are too complex to be solved perfectly.
6. Provide good but not necessarily optimum answers.

The evolution of the knowledge base
for **The Lending Series** of products

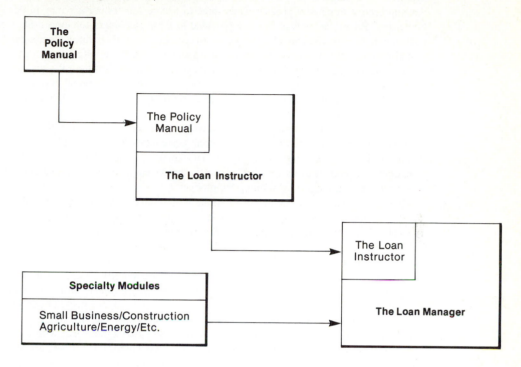

The Lending Series

46   The company's initial products are a series that focus upon the lending area of financial services organizations. They are expected to support widely applicable lending and credit functions and to become strategic to lending administration and training. They include:

47   **The Policy Manual**   A knowledge-based system that automates lending policies that are normally found in policy and procedure manuals.

48   **The Loan Instructor**   A knowledge-based system to be used for training lending and credit personnel on existing and new financing alternatives.

49   **The Loan Manager**   A loan-platform automation solution, based on an intelligent workstation system with an expanded expert knowledge base.

50   Each product in the progression of the series includes the functions of the previous product and its knowledge base.

MARKETING STRATEGY

51   Because of the differences in the complexity and pricing strategy for each of the individual products in *The Lending Series,* the approach to marketing the individual products also differs.

52   *The Policy Manual* will be marketed initially through executive calls by the company's management. The purpose of these calls will be to sign up customers who will participate in the
development of this initial product. Only three to five customers participating in this manner will
be needed. Pricing advantages will be provided to these customers to compensate them for their
contribution of expertise and other resources. Access and use of their current lending policy manuals
will also be of value to the company. The arrangement with these initial customers will be for the
company to produce an automated policy manual, which embodies the rules and procedures contained in their current manuals for a fixed price. Marketing to additional customers will be done
using direct mail and telemarketing techniques and by advertising in trade magazines and participating in trade shows.

53   *The Loan Instructor*, because of its relatively low price, will be marketed through the mail,
through telemarketing, and through remarketing agreements with other vendors. Direct marketing
will be used for the very large organizations. The American Bankers Association (ABA) has agreed
to market this product to its members, assist in the development of this, and allow the company
to use its name and logo in marketing the product.

54   *The Loan Manager* will be marketed primarily through direct sales by experienced professional
sales representatives employed by the company. Each sales representative will be expected to close
from 800 thousand to about $1.2 million in new business each year.

55   The company plans to work very closely with IBM and intends to apply for a Value-Added-
Dealer (VAD) agreement for IBM products. There are currently written and verbal commitments
by key individuals involved in bank automation with Unisys (Burroughs), which provide for the
company to use this vendor's hardware in developing this product to insure compatibility. It is
believed that this involvement will lead to joint marketing arrangements with this vendor, who has
a significant share of the commercial banking and savings and loan markets.

56   The company will also evaluate establishing cooperative agreements with the major lending
software vendors, such as Hogan Systems, Uccel, Systematics, Cullinet, Marshall and Ilsley,
and Florida Software to provide transaction and information interchange between systems. They
may also provide an opportunity for sales representatives of each company to sell the other's
products.

57   The *Chief Executive Officer* will be marketed initially by the Sebastian Group to its clients.
The marketers will be able to use their relationship with these financial organizations to propose
their participation in the joint development and funding of the product. The company will later
begin direct marketing of the product using its own sales staff. It will be marketed in a similar
manner to *The Loan Manager*. Efforts will be made to establish joint marketing relationships with
hardware vendors and major accounting firms that provide services to the financial industry.

PRICING STRATEGY

58   Two important pricing objectives are (1) to value-price the products and (2) to generate increasing
and recurring revenue.

The Policy Manual

59   Priced at $30,000, with 40 percent collected at the execution of the usage agreement and the
remaining $18,000 collected at the time the system is delivered to the customer. Professional
services will also be able to assist the customers in modifying and tailoring the generic manual
using a fixed price for the particular job or on a time and materials basis. The initial, prototype
customers for this product will be charged a fixed price of $50,000.

The Loan Instructor

60 Priced at $5,000 per a single copy order, maintenance and telephone assistance can be renewed by the customer after the first year for a fee equal to 20 percent of the initial purchase price of the product.

61 Pricing for *Specialty Modules* focusing on specific aspects of lending is expected to range from $200 to around $500 per copy.

62 Large organizations are expected to buy multiple copies of the products in order to have them available at many of their locations. To make large multicopy purchases more attractive, discounts will be provided. As a result of the relatively low cost per copy for large quantities, there will be less possibility of significant numbers of unauthorized copies being made.

Discount Range	Discount Percent
1 copy	0%
2 to 5	5
6 to 10	15
11 to 25	63
26 to 50	90
51 to 100	94
101 to 200	98
Over 200	99

63 An average number of copies sold per license agreement is assumed to be five copies. The discounting scheme is designed to encourage the purchase of large numbers of copies. For five copies, the total value of the license agreement will be $24,000.

1st copy	=	$ 5,000
Next 4	=	19,000
Total	=	24,000

64 The total contract value for various other quantities is illustrated in the graph below. Notice the rapidly flattening curve at 30 to 50 copies.

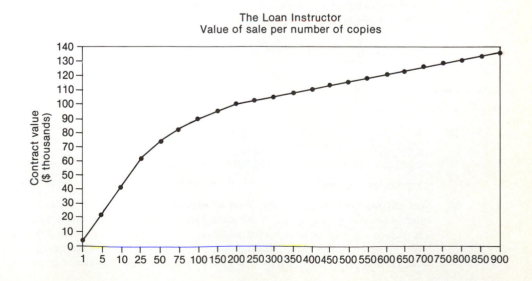

The Loan Instructor
Value of sale per number of copies

65   With the proposed discounting scheme, the price per copy of *The Loan Instructor* drops rapidly. From a single copy value of $5,000, the average price per copy for 30 copies drops to $2,516 and for 100 copies to $913. Copies in excess of 200 are $50 per copy, which brings down the average cost per copy rapidly. The cost per copy for various quantities is illustrated in the graph below.

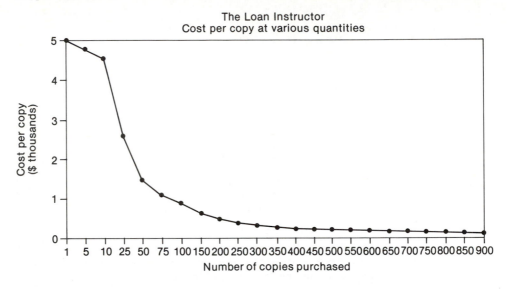

The Loan Instructor
Cost per copy at various quantities

The Loan Manager

66   This product's basic price will be determined by multiplying a factor by the value of the customer's loan portfolio. Initially 30 percent or more of the value of a license agreement will be paid on a monthly basis over a period of 36 months. For a projected average contract value of $250,000, the amount paid at the execution of the usage agreement would be $175,000 and the amount paid on a monthly basis would be about $2,100. Monthly usage fees will include maintenance and will be required for as long as the customer uses the product.

67   The following table provides anticipated prices for *The Loan Manager,* based upon the dollar value of an organization's outstanding loans:

Value of Loans	Amount Piad at Closing	Monthly Payment Amount	Total Value
$ 10,000,000	$ 7,000	$ 83	$ 10,000
100,000,000	15,400	184	22,000
500,000,000	45,500	542	65,000
750,000,000	78,400	933	112,000
1,000,000,000	108,500	1,292	155,000
2,000,000,000	175,000	2,083	250,000
6,000,000,000	350,000	4,167	500,000
10,000,000,000	525,000	6,250	750,000

68   Specialty modules and knowledge bases for specific loan types, such as asset lending, energy, small business, agriculture, and construction loans, will be priced similarly to the base product. The license value of these additional modules will range from $30,000 to $75,000 and will be based upon the complexity of the knowledge base and the value of the customer's outstanding loans for that particular loan type. The average value of these modules is estimated at $45,000.

Charges for professional services and implementation support services will be based on current, prevailing hourly rates.

69   A special pricing strategy will be used for the development customers. This strategy will allow these customers to receive a discounted price for their participation in the development of the product. The training system development customer will receive a 25 percent discount from the regular price. Development customers who sign up after the prototype phase will receive an 18 percent discount. This discount will be decreased by 2 percent each month after the beginning of the product development phase.

Chief Financial Officer

70   It is expected that this product's primary customers will be the medium to larger financial organizations. The price of the product is set at about the level as the annual salary of an individual with the expertise that will be provided by the system. However, the price will be for the use of the system for three years, instead of the employment of the expert for one year. Thus, the expertise provided by the system will be at a third of the cost of the expert, assuming the organization could recruit and retain such an individual. The amount paid at the execution of the usage agreement is expected to be $130,000. In addition to the up-front usage fee, the customer will also be charged a recurring fee for ongoing enhancements and maintenance to the product. These recurring fees will be invoiced on a quarterly basis over a period of three years and are expected to be for an amount of $4,500 ($1,500 per month). The total value of a sale over the 36-month period will be $184,000. An additional source of revenue from this product is expected to result from professional services provided to the customer in support of the product.

SALES PROJECTIONS

71   The sales volumes presented in this plan are considered to be reasonable for the types of products, the market, and the pricing strategy. The number of sales per quarter are based upon the experience of other software companies with products for the same market and price range as the company's products. The sales of each of the products are expected to grow to a peak over a period of about 18 to 24 months and then decline at a somewhat slower rate.

The Policy Manual

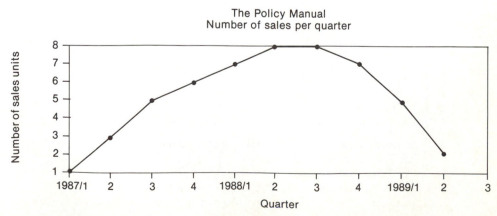

The Policy Manual
Number of sales per quarter

The Loan Instructor

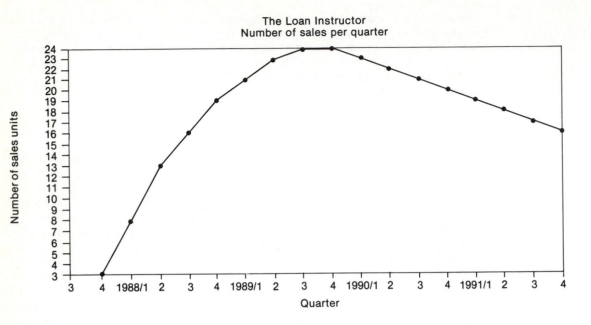

The Loan Manager

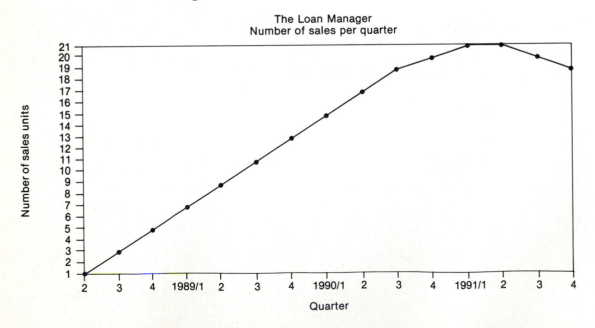

Chief Financial Officer

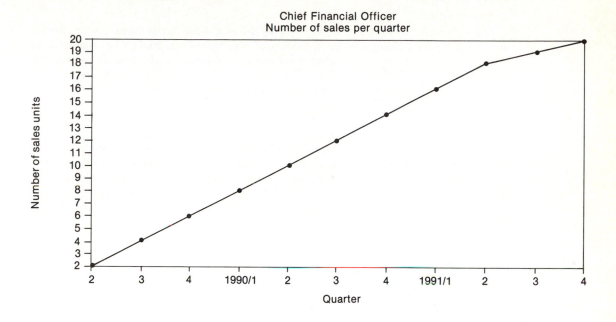

THE COMPETITION

72   There are no other companies known to be taking a similar technology approach and developing similar products as Metis Systems. This has been confirmed in recent conversations with individuals close to the industry and considered to be informed on recent developments and activities. The only other company known to be developing products in the same application area is Syntelligence. There are major differences in the approach being taken.

73   Syntelligence, Inc., Sunnyvale, California, is a privately held company of 100 employees established in 1981. Founded by AI pioneers from Stanford Research International, the company has recently begun development of a commercial lending product with Wachovia Bank in Winston-Salem, North Carolina, and Wells Fargo Bank in California participating in the development of Syntelligence's product. This product seems to focus more on the expert system and less on the office automation functions that are to be an important part of the company's products.

74   Syntelligence is currently actively marketing its commercial lending product and indicates that the support for retail, wholesale, and manufacturing for middle-market commercial loans is complete and deliverable. It is selling these pieces and some amount of custom support for one-half of a million dollars. Revenues mostly from the sale of an insurance product are estimated to have been about $3 million this year and are expected to be $10 million next year.

The Difference in Development Strategies

75   Syntelligence's development strategy is to use the Xerox 11XX machines and Interlisp-D for development and to port it to IBM mainframes under PL-1 and C. Syntelligence built the following tools to support its development environment:

1. A knowledge representation language called *Syntel*.
2. A table manager.
3. User interfaces.

76   Metis Systems' development strategy is quite different from that of Syntelligence. Metis's products will take advantage of the techniques of expert-system technology, as well as more traditional computer technologies, including mainframe, microprocessor, data base, and networking. The proper integration of these technologies provides a distinct advantage over the method taken by Syntelligence. Syntelligence's key personnel are oriented to a more academic approach to expert-systems technology.

77   The principal individuals associated with Metis Systems provide a collection of skills and experience in areas significant to the development of a system for the automation of the lending platform. Their skills include the management, development, and servicing of successful commercial software products; expert-systems applications; integrated microprocessor applications; microprocessor-assisted, lending-support systems; and education and training systems. They are a group of data processing professionals that have already developed systems similar to those being developed by Syntelligence. Metis Systems' personnel have solved many of the problems encountered by Syntelligence in the development of large complex systems.

78   What the difference between Metis Systems and Syntelligence means:

1. Development time:
    a. Micro-based systems require less programming time, because compile and test times can be shortened due to the single-user environment.
    b. Traditional microprogrammers are easier to find than Lisp programmers, because there are more of them.
    c. Development on the machine that will run the product will eliminate the time to re-code for another environment, such as from a Xerox 11XX to an IBM mainframe.
    d. Use of existing software such as screen handlers, data bases, expert-systems tools, and spreadsheets eliminates the substantial development time that would be necessary to code these.
    e. Use of people who have already done projects such as this will eliminate a great deal of trial and error.

2. Development cost:
    a. Microcomputers are much less expensive than mainframe computers and symbolic processors.
    b. Traditional programmers are more experienced and are less expensive than the available Lisp programmers.
    c. Because the amount of development time is less, the total resource cost will be substantially less.
    d. Purchasing or licensing existing software products is much less expensive than hiring programmers and doing the development in house.
    e. Elimination of much of the trial and error will save development cost.

3. Pricing:
    a. Because the development time and cost is less, Metis will be able to sell its products at a substantial savings over the competition.
    b. Because the price is less, the market is greater.
    c. Because the required hardware is less expensive, the product will be more attractive to potential customers.

79   Other companies that are involved in expert systems technology and may in the future provide competition to Metis Systems, but are not currently known to be developing products in the same application area, include the following:

80   **Applied Expert Systems (APEX), Cambridge, Massachusetts**   A privately held company of 50 employees established in August 1982, developing knowledge-based systems in the Financial Systems area. Revenues are estimated to be about $4 million this year and about $10 million next year.

81   **Palladian Corporation, Cambridge, Massachusetts**   A privately held company of 30 employees established in July 1984, developing expert systems for use within the financial services industry. Revenues were less than $1 million this year and are projected to exceed $3 million next year.

82   **Cognitive Systems, New Haven, Connecticut**   A privately held company of 25 employees established in 1983 to develop investment advisory systems for banks in Europe and the United States. The company is also evaluating at small-business and consumer-oriented financial systems. Projected revenues for this year were $2 million.

83   Many of the AI expert-systems tool or framework builders are beginning to approach the knowledge-based applications market as well. Some of these AI companies are receiving grants or buy-in ownership positions by large corporations. For example, General Motors has invested at least $3 million in the Teknowledge Corporation; Ford Motor Company has contracted with the Carnegie Group and Inference Corporation for $14 million each in applied research in the manufacturing area. The AIG Insurance Company and several other major insurance companies are funding the development of underwriting expert systems at Syntelligence Corporation.

84   The large traditional application software firms, such as Management Science America (MSA), Cullinet, Computer Associates Incorporated (CAI), and Pansophic are not rushing into expert-systems technology. These companies have products and installations under existing maintenance contracts and license agreements and cannot turn to new products. Large investments are also required for any major revision of these software application systems.

85   The company's competition could also come from in-house development projects. The 1st National Bank of Chicago is developing an expert system for the lending area. Other industries have in-house groups evaluating and developing knowledge-based systems, Projects are already formed at Litton Industries, Martin-Marietta, Lockheed, General Telephone and Electronics, American International Insurance, and Security Pacific Bank. Any of these in-house projects may produce an expert system that could compete with the company's products.

PROPRIETARY RIGHTS

86   In the software industry, companies must think about protecting their products from pirating by competition or from the unauthorized reproduction within the target market. Some considerations are outlined below.

Patent Protection

87   This registration and protection is probably not available for the company's software and services products, since a general rule of patent law is that software and data are not patentable.

Copyright

88 This protection of the company's products is available and is commercially valuable. Metis Systems intends to vigorously and systematically pursue appropriate copyright protection of its software products and knowledge bases. However, the company may not register its products with the United States Copyright Office if, in the opinion of its counsel, to do so would diminish the company's ability to protect its products as its trade secrets under applicable state laws or would otherwise compromise its proprietary rights in those products.

Trade Secret

89 Metis Systems believes that the unique knowledge and expertise of its employees will prove to be its most valuable asset. The company intends to focus on the protection of its proprietary rights in this knowledge and expertise. The company intends to establish its software, data bases, knowledge bases, and business information generally as confidential, proprietary, and trade secret information and to vigorously and systematically protect them as such. Therefore, Metis Systems will license rights to use its software and knowledge bases and does not intend to sell these products or grant exclusive rights to them. The company's software products will be provided to customers in object code format only. Where required, the company will provide interface software, including source code for the interface, to facilitate data exchange between the company's software and a customer's software or third-party software installed by a customer.

90 Metis Systems will require written license agreements with all third parties who are permitted to use its software. The company will enter into written confidentiality and "works for hire agreements" with all its employees and, to the extent necessary, any third party who is permitted access to the software.

POTENTIAL RISKS

91 The development of commercially successful knowledge-based systems is a high-risk venture. Although there are few commercially viable knowledge-based systems in existence today, the consensus among industry professionals is that these systems will constitute a major segment of the market within three to five years. There is, however, some debate about whether the technology or the markets can be successfully exploited now. As is the case with any new technology, premature entry into the marketplace is a financial risk. Nevertheless, a company that is first in entering an emerging market can realize great rewards.

92 The following items should be considered:

93 1. Existing expert-systems development tools may not be powerful enough to produce applications that have sufficient expertise to be successfully marketed.

94 Metis Systems considers that the expert system shells evaluated to date are powerful enough to develop *The Loan Manager*. Metis Systems personnel have already produced a feasibility prototype which has the essential features of the expert-system portion of the product. The development tool was *M.1* by Teknowledge; an improved version of *M.1*, which is faster and can accommodate a more extensive rule base, is now being released. Metis Systems will continue to evaluate M.1 and other development tools.

95 2. Applications of significant expertise to be successfully marketed may require expensive end-user hardware systems.

96   This statement was true early in 1985; however, the rapidly developing industry has moved from the need for specialized artificial intelligence workstations to the wider markets based on the personal computer. There are many PC-based products that are now available; in particular, the recently announced IBM PC/RL, which has a high-speed processor and a multitasking operating system, improves the market potential for PC-based expert systems.

97   3. Better-capitalized competitors may enter the market once the company has demonstrated the market acceptance of the product.

98   Although this is always a possibility, the initial market leader, with an attractive product, can always benefit from competition. Acknowledged competitors are already in the marketplace; Syntelligence Corporation is currently evaluating a financial-systems application. The company's advantage is the degree of integration and office automation planned for its products. Firms already established in the target market with traditional systems may enter the field and acquire a substantial technological advantage in addition to their existing marketing advantage.

99   It is possible that software firms that offer traditional data processing systems will incorporate expert-system technology into their products. However, this would be a major shift of business emphasis and would entail the risk of changing a proven product. This approach has been done successfully by only a few companies.

100   4. Potential customers may determine that any advantage offered by using the product are overshadowed by its cost.

101   Metis Systems executives have validated the product concept with representatives of major regional banks. These banking personnel have reacted very favorably to the proposed product and recognize that it offers the potential of controlling costs and increasing profits.

102   5. Customers may demand that the product be customized to their particular needs. If these changes are extensive, the advantages of a standardized software package will be lost.

103   Those parameters that vary from customer to customer will be clearly identified; each user may adjust these values interactively during installation of the system.

104   6. Expert-systems technology is relatively untested; therefore, there is a risk the tools and application languages that Metis Systems selects may prove unsatisfactory. Competitors who enter the market at a later time may have access to more powerful and less-expensive development tools.

105   This is always a risk in a high-technology industry. However, the status of current development tools and planned enhancements to them have been carefully assessed by the company. In fact, the main reason that expert-systems technology is gaining such rapid acceptance is that existing development tools are very good.

106   7. The company may not be able to develop an adequate service and support capability if the product gains wide acceptance quickly.

107   The management personnel of the company have in-depth experience in software product development and marketing. Metis Systems will establish a controlled growth environment as its corporate policy.

108   8. Recruitment and training of the required technical personnel and knowledge engineers may unaccountably delay or increase the cost of product development.

109   Because of the intense interest in expert-systems technology, many companies have developed and offer excellent education and training courses. Metis Systems will use these courses, as well as the expertise of its founders, for training new employees. In addition, the company has established close ties with AI educators and researchers at the University of South Carolina. These faculty members are available for consulting on problems that may arise. There are also many undergraduate and graduate students at the university who are studying AI, as well as traditional computer engineering and computer science subjects. Some of these students may wish to work on a part-time basis to gain practical experience, which will complement their formal education. These students are candidates for later full-time employment with the company. As a new venture company in a leading-edge technology, Metis Systems will be able to attract the best of these students, as well as experienced professionals from other regions of the country.

110   9. Metis Systems may not be able to maintain proprietary rights for its software or knowledge bases if the market does not accept the company's assertion of proprietary interest in the products.

111   The distribution technique outlined previously in this plan will insure that the software is protected. The proprietary interest will be clearly identified in all contracts or agreements.

SUMMARY PROJECTIONS

Profit and Loss Projection—Year 1 to Year 5

Factor	Projection (in thousands of dollars)					
	Year 1	Year 2	Year 3	Year 4	Year 5	Total
Development funding	120	180	0	0	0	300
Initial license fees	0	0	4,077	9,875	21,109	35,061
Recurring revenue	0	0	108	701	2,957	3,766
Service revenue	0	0	154	583	908	1,645
Net revenue	120	180	4,339	11,159	24,974	40,772
General expenses	613	1,899	3,294	4,989	7,227	18,022
Profit (loss) b/tax	(493)	(1,719)	1,045	6,170	17,747	22,750
Profit margin (%)			24	55	71	56
Tax expense	0	0	103	2,962	9,051	12,116
Net profit (loss)	(493)	(1,719)	942	3,208	8,696	10,634
After-tax margin (%)			22	29	35	26
Earnings per share*			0.18	0.60	1.63	

Break-Even Analysis (in thousands of dollars)

Periods	Year 1	Year 2	Year 3	Year 3	
				1st Q	2nd Q
Total revenue	120	180	4,338	1,837	2,372
Cumulative		300	4,638	6,475	8,847
Total expenses	613	1,899	3,294	1,080	1,188
Cumulative		2,512	5,806	6,886	8,074
Net total	(493)	(1,719)	1,044	757	1,184
Net cumulative		(2,212)	(1,168)	(411)	773
Break-even quarter					●

* Assuming 5.4 million shares outstanding.

Cash Flow Projection—Year 1 to Year 5

Factors	Projection (in thousands of dollars)					
	Y1	Y2	Y3	Y4	Y5	Total
Source of funds:						
Common stock sales	18	0	0	0	0	18
Preferred stock sales	1,200	1,200	0	0	0	2,400
Initial license fees	0	0	4,077	9,875	21,109	35,061
Recurring revenue	0	0	108	700	2,956	3,764
Interest income	181	81	308	980	3,430	4,980
Other receipts	0	0	154	583	908	1,645
Development funding	120	180	0	0	0	300
Total cash in	1,519	1,461	4,647	12,138	28,403	48,168
Use of funds:						
Capital purchases	138	250	370	410	734	1,902
Payroll expense	434	1,409	2,484	3,726	5,487	13,540
General expense	173	466	753	1,172	1,657	4,221
Income taxes	0	0	103	2,962	9,051	12,116
Total cash out	745	2,125	3,710	8,270	16,929	31,779
Net cash available	774	(635)	937	3,868	13,971	18,915
Cumulative cash*		1,313	2,250	6,118	20,089	

* A major portion of the cash generated is expected to be used to fund the development of additional products to support the long-term growth of the company.

Sales and Revenue Projection—Year 1 to Year 5

Year	Projection (in thousands of dollars)					
	Y1	Y2	Y3	Y4	Y5	Total
Product—*The Loan Manager*						
Percent of new sales	1	0	19	36	81	137
Initial lic. $	0	0	3,591	6,804	12,960	23,355
Number of customers	1	1	20	56	137	
Recurring rev $	0	0	92	367	1,215	1,674
Devlop funds	120	180	0	0	0	300
Product—*Specialty Modules*						
Percent of new sales	0	0	18	68	154	240
Initial lic. $	0	0	486	1,836	3,388	5,710
Number modules sold	0	0	18	86	240	
Recurring rev $	0	0	15	319	1,606	1,940
Product—*New Vertical Product*						
Percent of new sales	0	0	0	19	88	107
Initital lic. $	0	0	0	1,235	4,761	5,996
Number of customers	0	0	0	19	107	
Recurring rev $	0	0	0	15	136	151
Totals						
Initial lic. $	0	0	4,077	9,875	21,109	35,061
Recurring rev $	0	0	107	701	2,957	3,765
Product rev $	120	180	4,184	10,576	24,066	39,126
Service revenue	0	0	154	583	908	1,645
Total revenue	120	180	4,338	11,159	24,974	40,771

Operating Expense Projection—Year 1 to Year 5

Accounts	Projection (in thousands of dollars)					
	Y1	Y2	Y3	Y4	Y5	Total
Number of personnel	12	28	42	54	72	
Salaries	336	1,092	1,704	2,352	3,108	8,592
Salary overhead	37	120	187	259	342	945
Fringe benfits	60	197	307	423	559	1,547
Commissions—bonus	0	0	285	691	1,478	2,454
Personnel expense	433	1,409	2,483	3,725	5,487	13,538
Travel expense	24	68	107	147	194	540
Entertainment	5	9	18	17	40	88
Education/training	6	14	17	21	26	84
Equipment rental	9	13	17	20	24	82
Depreciation expense	7	24	58	93	142	324
Software costs	18	17	10	24	44	112
Office space rental	67	218	341	470	622	1,718
Office supplies	11	14	21	31	44	120
Postage—express	2	4	9	13	34	62
Telephone expense	6	14	21	39	60	139
Publications—dues	6	14	16	22	29	87
Printing—advertising	7	57	147	332	416	959
Business insurance	3	5	6	8	8	30
Computer time	10	19	23	29	57	138
Total nonpersonnel	180	490	811	1,264	1,740	4,484
Total expenses	613	1,899	3,294	4,989	7,227	18,021
Capital expense	138	250	370	410	639	1,807

Projections—Year 3 to Year 5: Sensitivity Analysis

Years of*	Projection (in thousands of dollars)			
	Yr 3	Yr 4	Yr 5	Total
Most likely: plan forecast				
Initial license fees	4,077	9,875	21,109	35,061
Recurring revenues	108	701	2,957	3,766
Service revenues	154	583	908	1,645
Total revenue	4,339	11,159	24,974	40,472
Operating expense	3,294	4,989	7,227	15,510
Profit before tax	1,045	6,170	17,747	24,976
Best case: +20% revenue and −10% expense				
Initial license fees	4,892	11,850	25,331	42,073
Recurring revenues	130	841	3,548	4,519
Service revenues	185	700	1,090	1,974
Total revenue	5,207	13,391	29,969	48,566
Operating expense	2,965	4,490	6,504	13,959
Profit before tax	2,242	8,901	23,465	34,607

(concluded)	Projection (in thousands of dollars)			
Years of*	Yr 3	Yr 4	Yr 5	Total
Worst case: −30% revenue and +10% expense				
Initial license fees	2,854	6,913	14,776	24,543
Recurring revenues	76	491	2,070	2,636
Service revenues	108	408	636	1,152
Total revenue	3,037	7,811	17,482	28,330
Operating expense	3,623	5,488	7,950	17,061
Profit before tax	−586	2,323	9,532	11,269

* Years 1 and 2 were omitted, because revenue was not sufficient to project a best case/worst case.

CASE 5

WENDY'S: BEATING THE ODDS

1   In just 11 years, Wendy's International grew from one store to over 1,800 company-owned and franchised outlets. Between 1974 and 1979, Wendy's growth was explosive with sales, including company-owned and franchised units, growing 4,200 percent ($24 million to $1 billion). In the same period, revenues from company-owned store sales and from franchise royalties grew 726 percent ($38 million to $274 million). Net income increased 2,091 percent in this period from $1.1 million to $23 million. Earnings per share made substantial gains from $.12 in 1974 to $1.54 in 1979, a 1,283 percent rise. Wendy's grew to a position of being the third-largest fast-food hamburger restaurant chain in the United States, ranking behind Burger King and McDonald's, the leading U.S. hamburger chain.

2   Wendy's entry and amazing growth in the hamburger segment of the fast-food industry shocked the industry and forced competitors within it to realize that their market positions are potentially vulnerable. Wendy's flourished in the face of adversities plaguing the industry. Throughout the 1970's, experts said the fast-food industry was rapidly maturing. Analysts for *The Wall Street Journal* and *Business Week*, citing a "competitively saturated fast-food hamburger industry," predicted in the early 1970s that the Wendy's venture would not succeed. As they saw it, market saturation, rising commodity prices, fuel costs, and labor costs were already plaguing the fast-food industry.

3   Clearly unconcerned about such commentary, R. David Thomas pushed Wendy's relentlessly. It opened an average of one restaurant every two days through 1979 and became the first hamburger chain to top $1 billion in sales in its first 10 years.

HISTORY

4   R. David Thomas had an idea. He knew Americans love hamburgers. If he could develop a hamburger better than those currently offered, he believed he could use it to establish a leadership position in the competitive fast-food hamburger market.

5   In November 1969, Thomas, an experienced restaurant operator and Kentucky Fried Chicken franchisee, began to put his idea into reality when he opened Wendy's first unit in downtown Columbus, Ohio. A year later, in November 1970, Wendy's opened its second unit in Columbus, this one with a drive-through pickup window. In August 1972, Wendy's sold L. S. Hartzog the franchise for the Indianapolis, Indiana, market, kicking off Wendy's rapid expansion into the chain hamburger business. Later the same year, Wendy's Management Institute was formed to develop management skills in managers, supervisors, area directors, and franchise owners. After five years, company revenues exceeded $13 million with net income in excess of $1 million. Sales for both company-owned and franchised units topped $24 million for the same period. In June 1975, the

This revised version of an earlier case was prepared by Richard Robinson of the University of South Carolina. Copyright © by Richard Robinson, 1990.

100th Wendy's opened in Louisville, Kentucky. Three months later, Wendy's went public. December 1976 saw Wendy's 500th open in Toronto, Canada. In 1977, Wendy's went national with its first network television commercial, making it the first restaurant chain with less than 1,000 units to mount a national advertising campaign. Eleven months later, Wendy's broke yet another record by opening its 1,000th restaurant in Springfield, Tennessee, within 100 months of opening the first Wendy's in Columbus. In 1979, Wendy's signed franchise agreements for eight European countries and Japan and opened the first European restaurant, company-owned, in Munich, West Germany. Also 1979 saw test marketing of a limited breakfast menu, a children's menu, and salad bars.

WENDY'S DEVELOPMENTAL CONCEPT: THE LAST 10 YEARS

The Menu

6   Wendy's management team believes that its limited menu has been a key factor contributing to Wendy's success. The idea was to concentrate on doing only a few things, but to do them better than anyone else. As a result, the aim was to provide the customer with a Cadillac hamburger that could be custom-made to meet individual preferences.

7   The basic menu item was the quarter-pound hamburger made of only fresh, 100 percent beef hamburger meat converted into patties daily. This kept Wendy's out of head-on competition with McDonald's and Burger King's $1/10$ pound hamburger. If people desired a bigger hamburger, they could order a double (two patties on a bun) or a triple (three patties on a bun). Besides having just one basic menu item, the hamburger, Wendy's also decided to differentiate itself by changing their hamburger's design. Instead of the traditional round patty found in competing fast-food outlets, Wendy's patty was square and sized so its edges would stick out over the edge of the round bun. The unique design alleviated the frequent complaint by most people that they were eating a breadburger. Other menu decisions included the following:

1. To offer different condiments to the customers—cheese, tomato, catsup, onion, lettuce, mustard, mayonnaise, and relish.
2. To provide a unique dairy product, the frosty—a cross between chocolate and vanilla flavors that borders between soft ice cream and a thick milk shake.
3. To serve a product that was unique in the fast-food market—chili.
4. To sell french fries because the public expected a hamburger outlet to offer them.

Facilities

8   Under Thomas's direction, the exterior style and interior decor of all Wendy's restaurants conformed to company specifications. The typical outlet was a freestanding one-story brick building constructed on a 25,000-square-foot site that provided parking for 35 to 45 cars (see Exhibits 1 and 2). There were some downtown storefront-type restaurants, which generally adhered to the standard red, yellow, and white decor and design. Most of the freestanding restaurants contained 2,100 square feet, had a cooking area, dining room capacity for 92 persons, and a pickup window for drive-in service (see Exhibit 3). The interior decor featured table tops printed with reproductions of 19th century advertising, Tiffany-styled lamps, bentwood chairs, colorful beads, and carpeting.

9   Generally, the strategy was to build a functionally modern building that would reflect the old-fashioned theme. Another plus for their building design was its flexibility. With only minor changes,

1. Site approval procedures for locations.
2. On-site inspection and evaluation by staff representative.
3. Counseling in business planning.
4. Drawings and specifications for buildings.
5. Training for franchisees at Wendy's headquarters.
6. Advice on supplies from suppliers selected by Wendy's and assistance in establishing quality-control standards and procedures for supplies.
7. Staff representatives to help in the opening of each restaurant.
8. Assistance in planning opening promotion and continuing advertising, public relations, and promotion.
9. Operations manual with information necessary to operate a Wendy's restaurant.
10. Research and development in production and methods of operations.
11. Information on policies, developments, and activities by means of bulletins, brochures, reports, and visits of Wendy's representatives.
12. Paper-goods standards.
13. National and regional meetings.

18   The criteria used by Wendy's for franchise selection is basically simple but strictly adhered to. They look for good proven business ability. The applicant must demonstrate that he or she is interested in making profits and does not mind getting involved. Wendy's did not make their profits by selling goods and services to their franchisees. Their income came from the restaurants' sales volume. Therefore, the franchisee must be able to build sales.

19   Wendy's operates company-owned restaurants in 26 markets around the following cities:

Columbus, Ohio	33	Indianapolis, Indiana	15
Cincinnati, Ohio	20	Dallas/Ft. Worth, Texas	26
Dayton, Ohio	26	Houston, Texas	25
Toledo, Ohio	12	Oklahoma City, Oklahoma	12
Atlanta, Georgia	35	Tulsa, Oklahoma	12
Tampa, Sarasota		Memphis, Tennessee	13
St. Petersburg		Louisville, Kentucky	14
Clearwater, Florida	22	Syracuse, New York	10
Jacksonville, Florida	15	Harrisburg, Pennsylvania	22
Daytona Beach, Florida	4	Philadelphia, Pennsylvania	20
Detroit, Michigan	20	Virginia Beach, Virginia	15
Portland, Oregon	10	Charleston, West Virginia	14
Reno, Nevada	6	Parkersburg, West Virginia	20
Greensboro, North Carolina	10	Munich, West Germany	2

Other than Detroit, no franchises exist in these markets.

20   At the end of 1979, there were 1,385 franchised restaurants operated by 161 franchise owners in 47 states and 3 foreign countries.

21   In a report to the Securities and Exchange Commission, Wendy's discussed the current state of its franchise program and described the franchise owners' relationship with the company:

Although franchised areas exist in all states except three, areas of some states remain unfranchised. In addition, most franchise owners have the right to build more units in their franchised areas than had been constructed at December 31, 1979. At that date, no franchise owner had more than 88 stores in operation. Several franchise owners operate restaurants in more than one state.

EXHIBIT 4

	Acquisition Date	Company Acquired	Restaurants In Operation	Location	Accounting Treatment	Common Shares Issued/ Purchase Price
1.	7/31/76	Wendy's Management, Inc., and subsidiaries	40	Atlanta, Georgia Indianapolis, Indiana Louisville, Kentucky Jacksonville, Florida Syracuse, New York	Purchase	733,195
2.	10/1/77	Wendy's Old Fashioned Hamburgers of New York, Inc.	5		Purchase	Immaterial
3.	6/30/78	Wendy's of West Virginia, Inc.	33	West Virginia Eastern Kentucky Southeast Ohio	Pooling	535,000
4.	9/30/78	Springfield Managment Company, Inc., and Dakota Land Corporation	6	Springfield, Ohio Richmond, Indiana	Pooling	39,294
5.	5/26/59	1620 South Atlantic, Inc. Forsyth, Inc. RR&WW, Inc. Reaves & Reaves Restaurants, Inc.	14	Greensboro, North Caroloina Winston-Salem, North Carolina Daytona Beach, Florida	Pooling	268,900
6.	5/30/79	Wendcorp of Nevada, Inc. Wendcorp of Portland, Inc.	16	Reno, Nevada Portland, Oregon	Pooling	245,815
7.	8/31/79	Susquehanna Food Services, Inc.	40	Southeastern Pennsylvania and northern Delaware	Pooling	508,861
8.	11/30/79	Wendy's of Virginia, Inc.	14	Southeastern Virgina	Purchase	$5,520,000

475

The rights and franchise offered by the company are contained in two basic documents. A franchise owner first executes a development agreement. This document gives the franchise owner the exclusive right to select proposed sites on which to construct Wendy's Old Fashioned Hamburgers restaurants within a certain geographic area (the franchised area), requires the submission of sites to the company for its acceptance, and, upon acceptance of a proposed site by the company, provides for the execution of a unit franchise agreement with the company to enable the franchise owner to construct, own, and operate a Wendy's Old Fashioned Hamburgers restaurant upon the site. The development agreement provides for the construction and opening of a fixed number of restaurants within the franchised area in accordance with a development or performance schedule. Both the number of restaurants and the development and performance schedules are agreed upon by the franchise owner and the company prior to the execution of the development agreement. The development agreement also grants a right of first refusal to the franchise owner with respect to the construction of any additional restaurants in the franchised area beyond the initially agreed-to number.

The development agreement requires that the franchise owner pay the company a technical assistance fee. The technical assistance fee required by newly executed development agreement is currently $15,000 for each franchise restaurant which the franchise owner has agreed to construct. Under earlier forms of the development agreement or franchise agreements, this fee was either $5,000, $7,500, or $10,000. However, approximately 12 existing franchise owners have the right under certain circumstances to receive additional franchise areas on the basis of the earlier $10,000 fee.

The technical assistance fee is used to defray the cost to the company of providing to its franchise owners site selection assistance; standard construction plans, specifications, and layouts; company review of specific restaurant site plans; initial training in the company's restaurant systems; and such bulletins, brochures, and reports as are from time to time published regarding the company's plans, policies, research, and other business activities.

22   From time to time, the company has reacquired franchised operations. A summary of these acquisitions is presented in Exhibit 4. In 1979, the company adopted a rather aggressive approach to franchise acquisition. Of 145 new company-owned operations in 1979 (representing a 50 percent increase during the year), 84 were acquired from franchisees. This major shift to company-owned restaurant growth away from franchised growth reflects the concern for systemwide control of quality as well as the increasing competition for available locations. Exhibit 5 illustrates the emphasis on company-owned growth since 1974. Granting large territorial franchises rather than single-outlet franchises was similarly practiced by Burger King in its formative stages. At Burger King, this led to franchise empires that were bigger than parent-company operations. Wendy's emphasis on company-owned growth may well be intended to avoid the problem that led to Burger King's decline in the late 1960s.

Finances

23   Wendy's revenues (see Exhibit 6) increased steadily between 1975 and 1980. Net income dropped in 1979 compared to 1978, but Thomas explains:

During 1979, we were informed by the U.S. Department of Labor that a review of company labor practices for a three-year period indicated that certain company policies had not been uniformly adhered to, and, as a result, the company was not in full compliance with the Fair Labor Standards Act.

Based on this review and the company's own investigation, we have determined that $3,800,000 should be accrued and charged against 1979 pretax income. Had this charge not been made, 1979 net income would have been $25,096,000, an increase of 8 percent over the $23,215,000 originally reported a year earlier. We believe company labor practices now comply with both company policy and the act, and, in addition, future compliance will not materially affect net income in 1980 and ensuing years.

EXHIBIT 5
Growth in Company-Operated Restaurants

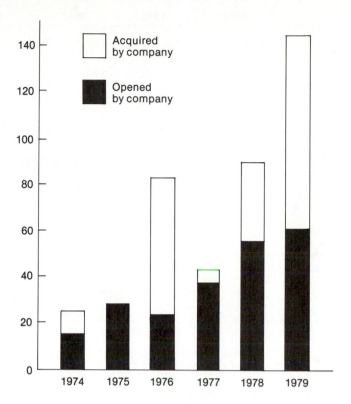

24   Whether the cost of labor compliance was the only cause of the abrupt slowdown in Wendy's steady increase in revenue and profit is questionable. Several factors suggest that Wendy's, after a decade of rapid growth, was reaching the limits of its current capabilities.

25   The heart of Wendy's success has been its streamlined, limited menu with primary emphasis on a quality hamburger. Since 1977, beef prices have soared, as shown in Exhibit 7. And while Wendy's has responded with tighter controls and a series of price increases just under 15 percent for 1979 alone (see Exhibit 8), this has still contributed to a decline in profitability.

26   Further evidence suggests that Wendy's may have been reaching a plateau in its historical pattern of growth. The average sales per restaurant, which climbed steadily from $230,000 in 1970 to $688,800 in 1978, declined significantly in 1979 at both company-owned and franchised restaurants, as shown in Exhibit 9. The impact on the parent company was felt in every revenue category, as shown in Exhibit 10. Wendy's continued to experience increased retail revenue (company-owned stores) and royalties (from franchises based on a percent of sales) but at a drastically slower rate. And for the first time, Wendy's experienced a decrease in technical assistance (franchise) fees.

27   Other evidence of a slowdown in Wendy's growth can be seen in the rate of new store openings. For the first time in its history, Wendy's experienced a decline in the rate of new store openings, as shown in Exhibit 11.

EXHIBIT 6

WENDY'S INTERNATIONAL, INCORPORATED
Consolidated Statement of Income
For the Years Ended December 31, 1975–1979

	1979	1978	1977	1776	1975
Revenue:					
Retail operations	$237,753,097	$198,529,130	$130,667,377	$71,336,626	$35,340,665
Royalties	30,564,613	23,396,211	11,810,277	4,655,432	1,567,008
Technical assistance fees	2,822,500	3,540,000	2,510,000	1,560,000	622,500
Other, principally interest	2,903,261	2,685,909	1,802,691	965,521	246,901
Total revenues	274,043,471	228,151,250	146,790,345	78,517,579	37,777,074
Costs and expenses:					
Cost of sales	146,346,806	113,812,874	72,482,010	40,509,285	19,629,179
Company restuarant operating costs	51,193,050	43,289,285	28,088,460	14,348,150	7,292,391
Department of labor compliance review	3,800,000				
Salaries, travel, and associated expenses of franchise personnel	4,187,399	3,148,532	1,936,877	1,156,493	622,879
General and administrative expenses	15,741,592	13,292,845	8,191,394	4,137,226	2,581,166
Depreciation and amortization of property and equipment ..	7,355,818	5,444,092	3,767,259	2,240,215	799,876
Interest	4,357,973	3,771,878	3,215,432	2,583,876	995,410
Total expenses	232,982,638	182,759,506	117,681,432	64,975,245	31,920,901
Income before incomes taxes ...	41,060,833	45,391,744	29,108,913	13,542,334	5,856,173
Income taxes:					
Federal:					
Current	15,583,700	18,324,600	12,052,200	5,784,600	2,926,700
Deferred	1,303,200	1,020,800	323,700	(19,600)	(501,900)
	16,886,900	19,345,400	12,375,900	5,765,000	2,424,800
State and local taxes	1,077,500	1,559,700	1,296,200	694,400	298,800
Total income taxes	17,964,400	20,905,100	13,672,100	6,459,400	2,723,600
Net income	$ 23,096,433	$ 24,486,644	$ 15,436,813	$ 7,082,934	$ 3,132,373
Net income per share	$1.54	$1.63	$1.04	$.57	$.29
Weighted average number of common shares outstanding	14,970,526	15,017,708	14,855,503	12,525,294	10,645,694
Dividends per common share ...	$0.40	$0.14	$0.125	$0.004	$0.001

Source: Wendy's International, Form 10-K, 1979.

EXHIBIT 7
Yearly Average Meat Price Per Pound for Company-owned Stores

1969	$0.59	1975	$0.69
1970	0.62	1976	0.72
1971	0.64	1977	0.72
1972	0.67	1978	1.02
1973	0.90	1979	1.29
1974	0.74		

EXHIBIT 8
Percentage Price Increases for Hamburgers

1/1/77	0.6%	10/22/78	0.15%
3/1/77	0.3	10/29/78	0.10
12/10/77	6.0	12/17/78	3.40
3/19/78	3.0	1/14/79	3.06
4/16/78	2.5	2/25/79	3.60
5/21/78	1.8	4/8/79	0.10
7/23/78	1.2	4/15/79	0.03
10/1/78	1.7	12/16/79	4.45

EXHIBIT 9
Average Sales per Restaurant

	1979		1978	
	Amount	Percent Change*	Amount	Percent Change*
Company	$624,000	(2.9)%	$624,900	14.3%
Franchise	618,800	(12.4)	706,000	11.7
Systemwide	620,000	(10.0)	688,800	13.0

* Percent increase (or decrease) over the same figure for the previous year.

EXHIBIT 10
Changes in Revenue from 1978 to 1979

	1979		1978	
	Amount*	Percent†	Amount	Percent
Retail operations	$39,224,000	19.8%	$67,862,000	51.9
Royalties	7,168,000	30.6	11,586,000	98.1
Technical assistance fees	(718,000)	(20.3)	1,030,000	41.0
Other, principally interest	(217,000)	(8.1)	883,000	49.0

* Absolute dollar increase (or decrease) over the previous year.

† Percent increase (or decrease) over the previous year.

28   While revenue and profitability growth slowed in 1979, Thomas was confident this was only temporary. Feeling strongly that Wendy's was in a good position to finance continued growth, Thomas offered the following observation:

> While construction money is more difficult to obtain than in the last few years, lines of credit already arranged guarantee financing of 1980 company plans to open 60 or more restaurants. We also anticipate exploring avenues of long-term debt to finance our growth beyond 1980. We believe that with $25 million of long-term debt, exclusive of capitalized lease obligations, and over $100 million in shareholders' equity, we have substantial untapped borrowing power.

Exhibit 12 summarizes Wendy's balance sheet for 1978 and 1979.

EXHIBIT 11
New Restaurant Openings: 1979 versus 1978

	Company*		Franchise		Systemwide	
	1979	1978	1979	1978	1979	1978
Open at beginning of year	348	271	1,059	634	1,407	905
Opened during the year	71	77	340	425	411	502
Purchased from franchise owners	14	—	(14)	—	—	—
Total open at end of year	433	348	1,385	1,059	1,818	1,407
Average open during year	381	309	1,235	828	1,616	1,137

* Restaurants acquired from franchise owners in poolings of interest have been included since date of opening.

EXHIBIT 12

WENDY'S INTERNATIONAL INCORPORATED
Consolidated Balance Sheets
For the Years Ended December 31, 1978, and 1979

	1979	1978
Assets		
Current assets:		
Cash	$ 2,285,180	$ 1,021,957
Short-term investments, at cost, which approximates market, including accrued interest	12,656,352	27,664,531
Accounts receivable	4,902,746	3,248,789
Inventories and other	2,581,528	1,855,313
Total current assets	22,425,806	33,790,590
Property and equipment, at cost Schedule 5:		
Land	30,916,049	23,906,365
Buildings	40,784,581	30,049,552
Leasehold improvements	16,581,947	8,954,392
Restaurant equipment	34,052,952	24,461,860
Other equipment	9,722,666	8,413,363
Construction in progress	1,751,788	2,027,570
Capitalized leases	21,865,829	18,246,427
Total property and equipment before depreciation	155,675,812	116,059,529
Less: Accumulated depreciation and amortization	(20,961,702)	(13,543,473)
Total property and equipment	134,714,110	102,516,056
Cost in excess of net assets acquired, less amortization of $699,410 and $481,162, respectively	8,408,788	5,207,942
Other assets	7,152,131	2,377,648
Total cost over net assets and other assets	15,560,919	7,585,590
Total assets	$172,700,835	$143,892,236

EXHIBIT 12 *(concluded)*

	1979	1978
Liabilities and Shareholders' Equity		
Current liabilities:		
Accounts payable, trade	$ 10,174,980	$ 11,666,272
Federal, state, and local income taxes		7,839,586
Accrued expenses:		
Administrative fee		664,770
Salaries and wages	2,368,244	1,970,977
Interest	433,540	369,603
Taxes	1,932,192	1,498,521
Department of Labor compliance review	3,800,000	
Other	1,576,851	739,588
Current portion, term debt, and capitalized lease		
obligations	3,891,247	2,781,671
Total current liabilities	24,177,054	27,530,988
Term debt, net of current portion	25,097,688	15,308,276
Capital lease obligations, net of current portion	18,707,838	15,130,617
	43,805,526	30,438,893
Deferred technical assistance fees	1,995,000	2,117,500
Deferred federal income taxes	2,027,604	664,300
Shareholders' equity:		
Common stock, $.10 stated value; authorized:		
40,000,000 shares; issued and outstanding:		
14, 882,614 and 14,861,877 shares, respectively	1,488,261	1,486,188
Capital in excess of stated value	34,113,173	33,962,916
Retained earnings	65,094,217	47,691,451
Total shareholders' equity	100,695,651	83,140,555
Total liabilities and shareholders' equity	$172,700,835	$143,892,236

Source: Wendy's International, Form 10-K, 1979.

WENDY'S FUTURE

29   Addressing Wendy's stockholders in early 1980, R. David Thomas offered the following assessment of Wendy's first 10 years:

> We are proud to be marking the 10th anniversary of Wendy's International, Inc. Just 10 years ago, in November 1969, we opened the first Wendy's Old Fashioned Hamburgers restaurant in downtown Columbus, Ohio. Now, after a decade of explosive growth, there are Wendy's quick-service restaurants in 49 of the 50 states and in Canada, Puerto Rico, Germany, and Switzerland.
>
> At year-end 1979, there were 1,818 Wendy's restaurants in operation, 411 more than at the close of 1978. Of the 433 company-operated restaurants, 84 were acquired from franchise owners during 1979. It was a year of progress for our international expansion program as we opened our first restaurants in Europe and entered into agreements for development of Japan, France, Belgium, Luxembourg, the Netherlands, Switzerland, Spain, Germany, and the United Kingdom.
>
> During 1979, the company established a research and development department, which is testing a number of potential menu items. The salad bar, which was tested in our Columbus, Ohio, market, had been introduced into 171 restaurants by year-end.

In 1979, our industry was faced with major challenges, such as inflation and energy problems. Higher labor costs and rising beef prices affected Wendy's profitability and depressed profits for our entire industry. The minimum wage, which affects 90 percent of our employees, increased in January 1979 and January 1980. Ground beef prices increased to an average of $1.29 per pound in 1979, 79 percent higher than the 1977 average price. During 1979, we minimized our retail price increases, with the goal of increasing our market share. This strategy, coupled with more aggressive marketing, helped rebuild customer traffic in the latter part of the year. Although holding back on price increases affected our margins, we believe it was appropriate and that margins benefited by our cost efficiencies, especially in purchasing and distribution.

During 1979, we remained flexible and open to changing customer needs and attitudes, and we continued to take the steps necessary to achieve and support future growth and profitability as we—

Tested and implemented a highly successful salad bar concept.

Tested a breakfast concept and other menu items.

Began development of the European and Japanese markets.

Initiated a new marketing program designed to increase dinner and weekend business.

Prepared to open another 250 to 300 Wendy's restaurants systemwide in 1980.

30   And, setting the tone for Wendy's in the 1980s, Thomas said:

We are aware, as we enter our second decade, that we have achieved a unique position in a highly competitive industry. It was no less difficult and competitive 10 years ago than it is today, we believe, than it will be 10 years from now. We intend to build further on our achievement of being recognized as a chain of high-quality, quick-service restaurants. We will continue to produce fresh, appealing, high-quality food; price it competitively; and serve it in a clean, attractive setting with employees who are carefully selected, well trained, and responsive to our customers.

31   Similar to the way they questioned R. David Thomas's venture into the hamburger jungle in 1970, several business writers once again began to question Wendy's future. Illustrative of this is the following article, which appeared in *The Wall Street Journal*:

Wendy's International, Inc., is making changes it once considered unthinkable.

Wendy's faced the choice confronting many companies when the initial burst of entrepreneurial brilliance dims: Should it stick with the original concept and be content with a niche in a bigger market, or should it change and attempt to keep growing? Wendy's chose to revamp its operations. It is adding salad bars, chicken and fish sandwiches, and a children's meal to its menu, adopting a new advertising strategy, and considering whether to alter the appearance of its restaurants.

Some observers predict Wendy's will regret the quick changes. "This is a company that was able to convince a certain segment of the country it had a different taste in hamburgers," says Carl De Biase, an analyst with Sanford C. Bernstein & Co. in New York. "They've achieved their mandate, and anything they do now is just going to screw up the concept."

But Robert Barney, Wendy's president and chief executive officer, says the company is "in some very difficult times right now." Among the problems: discontented franchise holders and the likelihood that beef prices will rise sharply again in the second half. Barney says Wendy's doesn't even "have the luxury of waiting to see" how each change works before moving to the next one.

This spring, shortly after the changes began, Thomas resigned as chief executive, saying he wanted more time for public relations work and community affairs. Thomas, who is 47 years old and will continue as chairman, had been closely identified with the old ad campaign and with company resistance to broadening the menu.

The company has been doing a little better so far this year, and franchisees say they're much more optimistic. The menu changes, they say, were long overdue. "It had been suggested to everyone in the company," says Raymond Schoenbaum, who operates 33 Wendy's outlets in Alabama and Georgia. "But the mentality wouldn't allow menu diversification before. It had to be forced on them."

Barney concedes that prior to last year "we never did a lot of planning." But that has been remedied, he says, partly with a "research and development department" that will examine new menu prospects.

Not everyone believes that tinkering with the menu will bring back customers and profits. Edward H. Schmitt, president of McDonald's, predicts an image problem for Wendy's and maintains that the company will loose the labor advantage it held over other fast-food outlets. He adds that McDonald's tried and abandoned salad bars. "It's practically a no-profit item," he says, "and it's a high-waste item."

Some franchisees complain that the new children's meal, called Fun Feast, will draw the company into a can't-win competition with McDonald's and Burger King for the children's market, which Wendy's has avoided so far. "Every survey we have says we shouldn't go after that market," a franchisee reports. "Our chairs aren't designed for kids to climb on, and our carpet isn't designed for kids to spill ketchup on."

But Barney insists that Fun Feast isn't intended to attract children. He says Wendy's is trying to remove the adults' reason for not coming to the restaurant. "Where we tested it," he says, "we didn't sell so many of them but we did see an increase in adult traffic."

Wendy's may evolve from a sandwich shop into a more generalized quick-service restaurant that doesn't compete as directly with McDonald's and Burger King. "We're going to be between" McDonald's and quick-service steakhouses, says Schoenbaum, the Georgia and Alabama franchise holder.

To this end, Schoenbaum says, Wendy's will reduce the abundance of plastic fixtures in its restaurants and perhaps cut down on the amount of glass. He says the glass makes Wendy's a pleasant, brightly lit lunch spot but doesn't create a good atmosphere for dinner.

Wendy's officials confirm that they are considering altering the appearance of their restaurants, but they aren't specific. And as for whom Wendy's competes with, Barney says: "We're in competition with anywhere food is served, including the home."[2]

EPILOGUE: 1980–1990

Focusing on a long-term growth strategy of continued U.S. penetration, international growth, and concentric diversification into the chicken segment, Wendy's management team reached 4,000 Wendy's restaurants by 1990. Several things have happened, including numerous changes at Wendy's, since 1979. This section provides 29 observations to help you see what happened at Wendy's between 1979 and 1989.

Product/Market Developments

32 The R&D department has helped develop quality products that will help Wendy's growing in the future. The department develops new products within these guidelines:

Any product additions must reinforce their quality image.

They must be profitable.

They must expand a market base.

They must increase frequency of visits.

They must merge easily into their system of operations.

They must help reduce vulnerability to beef price.

---

[2]"Its Vigor Lost, Wendy's Seeks a New Niche," *The Wall Street Journal,* July 8, 1980, p. 29.

33   Wendy's developed and introduced in the 1980's the following products:

The "Garden Spot" Salad Bar and Baked Potatoes for weight-conscious people.

The Chicken Breast Sandwich to respond to high beef price and to provide variety.

The Wendy's Kids' Fun Pack for family with children.

Breakfast to attack McDonald's lack of variety.

34   The core of the strategic role of R&D is to increase sales up to $1 million a year per restaurant. In 1989, the average net sales per domestic restaurant was $789,000, representing a 28 percent increase in 10 years.

Financial

35   Wendy's revenues result primarily from sales by company-operated restaurants. Royalties and technical-assistance fees from franchisees make up the other major source of revenues. In 1989, 91 percent of the $1.07 billion revenues came from retail sales, 7 percent from royalties, and 2 percent from others.

36   With the exception of the buns sold by New Bakery Company of Ohio, Inc., Wendy's does not sell food or supplies to the franchise owners. The New Bakery Company of Ohio, Inc., was acquired by Wendy's in 1981 and now supplies about 1,000 restaurants with buns.

37   Revenues went up to reach a peak in 1986 with $1.15 billion, then decreased to $1.06 billion in 1987 and 1988, and gained 1 percent in 1989 to reach $1.07 billion. After 1979, net income increased steadily until 1985, when it reached $76 million. Wendy's suffered from a loss of $4.6 million the next year, but its profits became positive and increasing again the following years. In 1989, net income was $30.4 million. The dip in net income of 1986 is reflected in the lower pretax profit margin, which dropped from 11.9 percent to 1.3 percent in one year.

38   Out of the capital expenditures in the beginning of the 80s, about 50 percent were for new domestic restaurants, 25 percent for the new subsidiary Sisters and international restaurants, and 25 percent for costs associated with the image-enhancement program, restaurant refurbishing, and computerized registers. After reaching a peak in 1985, with $222 million capital expenditures, Wendy's decreased gradually its investments to $39 million in 1989. In this last year, Wendy's spent $24 million for improvements to existing restaurants and $15 million to others' additions.

39   Exhibits 13–18 contain additional financial information.

Operations

40   Wendy's marketing strategy has been to target the high-quality end of the quick-service market with primary appeal among young middle-age adults, and its philosophy of quality, service, cleanliness, and value was aimed at this key segment of the population.

41   The population of the baby boomers matures. The age range of this segment will be from 35 to 54 years old from 1980 to 1995. Also, currently 50 percent of Wendy's orders are eaten away from the restaurant. Therefore, the maturing population and the increasing demand for convenience and portability will shape Wendy's products in the future.

42   Wendy's is moving its exterior image further away from the brightly colored, plastic fast-food atmosphere with a new, upgraded image, which features copper-colored roof panels and decorative awnings and lightings. The company spent 18 million on remodeling restaurants in 1989.

EXHIBIT 13
Wendy's Revenues (millions)

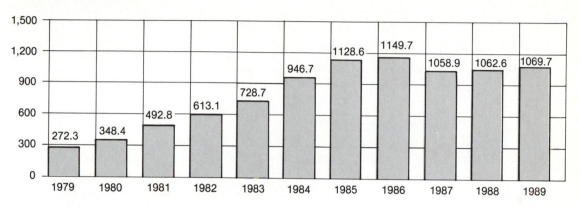

EXHIBIT 14
Wendy's Net Income (millions)

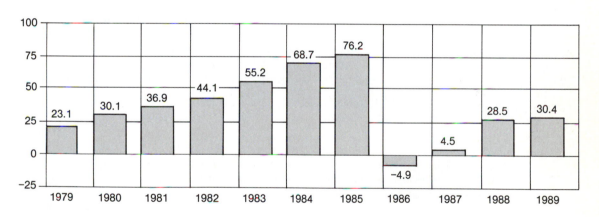

EXHIBIT 15
Wendy's Debt to Equity Ratio

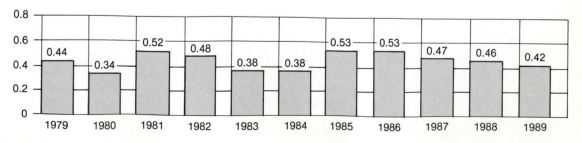

EXHIBIT 16
Wendy's Pretax Profit Margin (%)

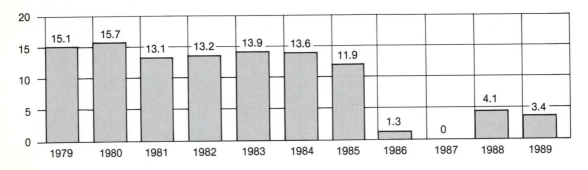

EXHIBIT 17
Wendy's Capital Expenditures (millions)

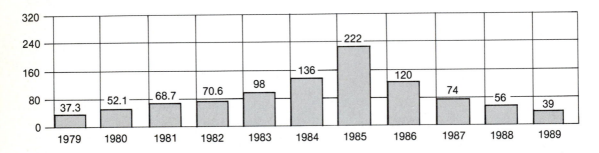

43   Advertising spending has been increased. Franchise owners, in addition to spending 3 percent of their gross receipts for local advertising and promotions, have increased their contribution to Wendy's National Advertising Program (WNAP) from 1 percent in 1980 to 1.5 percent in 1985, and to 2 percent in 1989. This same year, WNAP spent 55 million on advertising and promotion expenses, a 4 percent increase over 1988 spending levels.

44   Advertising in the fast-food burger chain industry has become more fierce since Burger King launched its now-famous comparative advertising campaign.

45   In the second half of 1985 and into 1986, the company's efforts and advertising were focused on implementing the breakfast program systemwide. During that period, Wendy's major competitors also began to more aggressively advertise their hamburger products. Wendy's began to see some sales erosion in its products and dayparts. As a result, the challenges Wendy's faced were intensified.

46   Management took decisive action in response to these issues. The breakfast program was made optional for franchise owners and retained by the company only where economically viable. Also, the company launched a realignment program in mid-1986, intended to substantially improve its operating and financial performance. The major portion of the plan involved the disposition of all marginal or unprofitable company-operated restaurants, including international restaurants and Sisters as well as domestic restaurants. The company intends to franchise the majority of the domestic restaurants, and the remaining restaurants have been closed.

Franchising

47 Two main thrusts appear to characterize Wendy's franchising emphasis for the 1980s: (1) enhanced operational control and support of domestice franchises and (2) expansion through international locations.

48 The systemwide number of restaurants reached 3,755 in 1989. But as a result of the realignment program, the number of company-owned restaurants kept decreasing from 1986 to 1989, while the number of franchises increased during the same period. However, Wendy's continues to buy franchises from time to time.

49 To stimulate growth, the company announced a unit franchise strategy in the early 1980s. This concept enabled individuals who could not develop a multiunit franchise to join the Wendy's family. To avoid the problem that led Burger King to a decline in the 1960s, Wendy's spends an increasing time in assessing and selecting the franchised locations and managers and also provides the personnel an increasing amount of training. This reflects the concern for systemwide control of quality.

International

50 Wendy's established an international division in 1979, and, by 1989, there were 265 restaurants in foreign countries—87 of them were company-owned. The top 5 international markets and number of restaurants were Canada (131 restaurants), Japan (26), Spain (17), Korea (14), and the Philippines (13).

51 Of the fast-food industry, McDonald's is the best established internationally, with approximately 1,500 units in 32 countries (data of 1983). They are heavily concentrated in Canada, Japan, Australia, and various parts of Europe. It is expecting to develop this international market at a rate of 150 additional units a year. Burger King had in 1983 about 300 units abroad.

52 There are numerous pitfalls and high risks to overseas expansion since, for instance, European per capita spending on "fast-food" is only $3.50 a year, compared to approximately $150 for each American in 1982. Also capital investment—land and buildings—and labor consume a large part of revenues in some countries, such as West Germany. As a matter of fact, after having opened about 30 restaurants in West Germany, Wendy's decided to terminate those operations in 1987.

53 Wendy's strategy in international market is to be flexible in order to be successful in the face of differing eating habits and tastes. It consistently opens new international restaurants but it does not hesitate to terminate any unprofitable operations.

Sisters' Development

54 Thinking that the fast-food burger industry might be over-saturated, Wendy's decided to apply the principles that built its success to other segments of the industry, particularly the one of chicken restaurant industry.

55 Wendy's initially owned 20 percent of Sisters International and, in 1981, exercised its option to purchase then remaining 80 percent. The Sisters' concept, to combine the self-service of the quick-food industry with the full menu and warmth of comfortable dining facilities of the traditional family restaurant, is designed to appeal specifically to the maturing, value-conscious consumer.

56 There were 79 Sisters open at the end of 1985. The company operated 38 of these. However. in 1987, as a result of the realignment program Wendy's sold its subsidiary to SIS CORP, Sisters' largest franchisee for $14.5 million in cash and notes.

EXHIBIT 18
Selected Financial Data
Wendy's International, Inc. & Subsidiaries

	1989	1988	1987	1986	1985	1984	1983	1982	1981	1980	1979
Operations (in millions)											
Systemwide Wendy's sales	$3,036.1	2,901.6	2,868.9	2,747.2	2,694.8	2,423.0	1,922.9	1,632.4	1,424.2	1,209.3	1,001.9
Retail sales	$ 973.1	976.6	987.2	1,039.3	1,033.0	877.3	671.6	565.4	450.9	310.1	237.8
Revenues	$1,069.7	1,062.6	1,059.8	1,149.7	1,128.6	946.7	728.7	613.1	492.8	348.4	272.3
Company restaurant operating profit	$ 84.1	107.1	81.8	136.6	176.8	166.4	129.6	104.3	76.8	54.4	36.4
Income (loss) before income taxes	$ 36.9	43.8	(11.6)	14.9	134.7	128.4	101.4	80.7	64.7	54.7	41.0
Net income (loss)*	$ 30.4	28.5	4.5	(4.9)	76.2	68.7	55.2	44.1	36.9	30.1	23.1
Capital expenditures	$ 38.9	56.0	73.9	120.3	221.9	153.5	87.4	81.6	74.9	52.6	38.2
Financial Position (in millions)											
Total assets	$ 779.6	777.0	786.2	814.2	853.3	656.1	542.5	485.0	387.4	220.3	172.8
Property and equipment, net	$ 579.6	593.1	610.2	643.8	704.9	518.2	405.4	348.3	291.9	175.6	135.6
Long-term obligations	$ 178.9	192.6	195.4	223.2	235.5	139.0	115.7	128.2	105.6	43.1	43.9
Shareholders' equity	$ 428.9	419.6	412.2	424.7	443.5	364.5	308.3	264.7	201.7	125.6	100.7
Per Share Data											
Net income (loss)*	$ .32	.30	.05	(.05)	.82	.75	.61	.51	.46	.40	.31
Dividends	$ .24	.24	.24	.21	.17	.15	.12	.09	.08	.08	.08
Shareholders' equity	$ 4.44	4.36	4.29	4.45	4.65	3.98	3.40	2.92	2.37	1.68	1.35
Market price at year-end	$ 4.63	5.75	5.63	10.25	13.38	10.00	9.38	6.63	4.25	2.88	2.63
Ratios											
Company restaurant operating profit margin	% 8.6	11.0	8.3	13.1	17.1	19.0	19.3	18.4	17.0	17.5	15.3
Pretax profit margin	% 3.4	4.1	—	1.3	11.9	13.6	13.9	13.2	13.1	15.7	15.1
Return on average assets†	% 7.9	8.5	2.1	4.8	21.7	24.7	23.5	22.7	24.9	31.1	28.7
Return on average equity	% 7.2	6.9	1.1	—	19.3	20.4	19.3	19.5	22.0	26.6	25.1
Current	.95	1.00	.75	.81	.44	.56	.69	.81	.61	.54	.93
Debt to equity	% 42	46	47	53	53	38	38	48	52	34	44
Debt to total capitalization	% 29	31	32	34	35	28	27	33	34	26	30

Restaurant Data

Domestic Wendy's open at year-end											
Company	**1,031**	1,076	1,114	1,206	1,135	1,014	887	802	734	502	431
Franchise	**2,459**	2,445	2,468	2,290	2,106	1,801	1,633	1,503	1,386	1,450	1,332
International Wendy's open at year-end											
Company	**87**	97	115	129	122	43	35	25	14	4	2
Franchise	**178**	144	119	102	79	134	118	100	95	78	53
Total Wendy's	**3,775**	3,762	3,816	3,727	3,442	2,992	2,673	2,430	2,229	2,034	1,818
Average net sales per domestic Wendy's restaurant (in thousands)											
Company	**$ 808**	793	786	765	850	874	749	687	679	650	608
Franchise	**$ 781**	744	721	748	846	870	769	712	670	634	619
Total domestic	**$ 789**	759	741	754	847	871	762	704	672	638	616
Other Data											
Weighted average shares outstanding (*in thousands*)	**96,378**	96,168	95,783	95,879	92,828	91,903	91,168	87,034	80,990	75,702	74,853
Shareholders of record at year-end	**55,000**	58,000	52,000	48,000	41,000	31,000	25,000	20,000	19,000	18,000	18,000
Number of employees at year-end	**39,000**	42,000	45,000	50,000	48,000	43,000	36,000	29,000	26,000	18,000	16,000

* Net income in 1989 includes the cumulative effect of change in accounting for income taxes of $5.2 million ($0.05 per share) and a $1 million ($0.01 per share) extraordinary gain on early extinguishment of debt, respectively; 1989 and 1987 reflect a $1.6 million ($0.02 per share).

† Return on average assets is computed using income before income taxes and interest charges.

Management Reorganization

57 For the first 11 years of its history, Wendy's was guided by an entrepreneurial spirit that gave the company the fastest growth record in the history of this industry. However, with the pressure of soaring beef prices, inflation, and recession, founder and former chairman R. David Thomas, who presently serves as senior chairman of the board, took the first step in 1980, when he recommended to the board that president Robert L. Barney be named chief executive officer. Barney implemented the remainder of the management reorganization program.

58 In 1989, James W. Near has the functions of CEO, president, and chief operating officer. He replaced Ronald Faye, president from 1980 to 1986, and Barney, former CEO and chairman of the board, who retired in 1989.

59 A new regional structure was also instituted for the Company Operations and Franchising Department, along with the Franchise Advisory Council, in order to increase communication and cooperation between company management and franchisees.

60 The company had 50,000 employees in 1986, but, as part of the realignment program, this number in 1989 decreased to reach 39,000 people.

CASE 6

CROSSLAND SAVINGS, FSB

1   After a decade of upheaval, 1990 was expected to be a watershed in history of the U.S. thrift industry. Declining profit spreads because of rising competition, combined with high level of savings withdrawals, were anticipated to force more thrifts out of business. Of the 3,000 federally insured thrift institutions that existed in 1989, only 1,200 were expected to survive by the year 1993.

2   This case focused on CrossLand Savings, FSB, and its search for a sustainable competitive advantage in the volatile environment of the savings and loans segment of the thrift industry. The case described the profile of the thrift industry and the evolution of CrossLand's strategy. The case highlighted the challenge that even the most innovative thrift organizations must address: How can an institution develop and maintain a distinctive competence to insulate itself from the evergrowing adversity of the competitive environment?

3   In 1988, CrossLand Savings and its consolidated subsidiaries ("CrossLand") was the 11th largest thrift institution in the United States, with $14.8 billion in assets. CrossLand consisted of a savings bank insured by the Federal Deposit Insurance Corporation (FDIC) located in New York, with 41 branches throughout New York ("CrossLand (FDIC)"); a savings bank insured by the Federal Savings and Loan Insurance Corporation (FSLIC) headquartered in Utah, with 50 branches in Florida, Utah, Oregon, Virginia, California, Washington, and New Jersey ("CrossLand (FSLIC)") and a mortgage banking company with offices throughout the United States ("CrossLand Mortgage").

THE U.S. THRIFT INDUSTRY

4   CrossLand's predominant operations were in the thrift industry. This industry, which was created by the Home Owner's Loan Act in 1933 to provide a source of funding for mortgage housing, has undergone many changes in the 1970s and 1980s. Prior to this time, thrift institutions primarily obtained funds from savers at fixed interest rates and lent the money to home owners at rates that guaranteed them a profit. Inflation and rising interest rates in the 1960s and 1970s made thrift institutions unable to retain the funding necessary for liquidity. In the 1970s, this loss of funds became even greater with the creation of money market funds, which paid investors the going market yields with only little additional risk.

5   Reacting to rising losses, in 1978 Congress allowed thrifts to offer money market certificates tied to Treasury bill rates. In 1980, Congress passed the Depository Institutions Deregulation and Monetary Control Act (DIDMCA), which provided for the phasing out of ceilings on deposit rates within six years. Responding to intensifying competition from the money market funds and to the inability of the thrifts to earn market rates on their loan portfolios, Congress passed the Garn-St. Germain Act in 1982. This act empowered thrifts to offer money market accounts, thereby sig-

This case was prepared by Karen Jones and Shaker A. Zahra of George Mason University.

nificantly broadening the investment powers of thrifts. The act also allowed thrifts to make adjustable rate loans.

6   This new economic environment and the resulting deregulation altered the thrift industry significantly. For the first time, thrifts were forced to compete for funds and for investments. Profits were no longer guaranteed, and interest rate risk and credit risk had to be better managed. Many thrifts failed during the 1980 through 1982 recession as interest rates skyrocketed and thrifts were unable to earn enough on their assets to cover the cost of their liability. Under the increased investment powers permitted by the Garn-St. Germain Act, and allowed by some states to the state chartered thrifts, some institutions increased the level of their investment in riskier commercial loans to earn higher rates. Largely as a result of the excess risk and the subsequent collapse of the economy in certain areas of the country, thrifts were increasingly failing at the highest rate in their history.

7   The current historical level of failing thrift institutions and the insolvency of FSLIC has attracted considerable attention to the industry. In February 1989, President George Bush proposed a plan to rescue the industry. This plan included bringing the Federal Home Loan Bank Board (FHLBB) under the control of the Treasury Department. The plan also required the FDIC to take control over the FSLIC. These actions were expected to result in stricter regulations over the thrift industry, which under the FHLBB and the FSLIC, has enjoyed more freedom than commercial banks have under the FDIC. Furthermore, President Bush's plan called for the raising of $50 billion to cover the costs of shutting down insolvent thrifts.

8   There were three additional major issues the industry had to address: regulation, undifferentiated products, and sensitivity of earnings to interest rates. Historically, the industry had been subject to many regulations that were intended to ensure efficiency of operations and institutional stability. The Federal Home Loan Bank Board (FHLBB) and FSLIC played a major role in this regard. FHLBB, for instance, functioned as a policeman, central banker, and deposit insurance administrator. FSLIC, on the other hand, supervised compliance with capital requirements of the federal bank board. FSLIC had the authority to manage those institutions that failed to meet these standards.

9   In terms of the second issue, undifferentiated products, some considered the industry's products to be commodities. These products were distinguishable only in their terms and interest rates. While some innovations, such as adjustable mortgage rates, were introduced, product offerings in the 1980s remained the same.

HISTORY

10   CrossLand was chartered as a New York savings bank in 1860 under the name East Brooklyn Savings Bank. Later, it changed its name to Metropolitan Savings Bank. In 1985, the name CrossLand was adopted to reflect the bank's expanding nationwide scope of the business.

11   The bank grew by acquiring two financial institutions in 1970 and 1978. But, until 1981, the institution operated as a home mortgage lender and deposit gatherer primarily in its own backyard.

12   In 1981, CrossLand began an aggressive strategy of growth through acquisitions by acquiring three local savings banks, which nearly tripled its size. This strategy continued throughout the 1980s, with an acquisition of a mortgage banking company in 1982 (which was sold in 1985), acquisitions of two Florida thrifts, and two Virginia thrifts in 1983, a mortgage banking company and a commercial credit company in 1986, a Utah savings and loan in 1987 (which had licenses to operate in ten states), and a New Jersey savings and loan in 1988.

13   All of the thrift acquisitions, which, with the exception of two in 1981 and a 1983 Florida thrift purchase, were completed in regulatory assisted transactions. For instance, the acquisition of one of the New York banks in 1981 and one of the Florida banks and the two Virginia banks in 1983

EXHIBIT 1
CrossLand Savings, FSB
Significant Acquisition and Financing Activities

Year	Event	Increase* in Assets	Total Assets† at Year End
1981	Acquired Greenwich Savings Bank in New York in an FDIC assisted merger	$2,015	
	Merged with the Brooklyn Savings Bank in New York	1,558	$ 5,712
1983	Acquired one Florida thrift and two Virginia thrifts in FSLIC assisted merger	247	
	Acquired First City Federal in Florida	897	7,432
1985	Sold mortgage banking subsidiary for a net profit	90	
	Sold common stock	116	
	Sold two issues of callable preferred stock (2)	150	
	Sold collateralized floating rate notes	100	8,023
1986	Acquired a mortgage banking company	339	
	Acquired a finance company	99	
	Sold preferred stock	123	
	Sold two issues of callable preferred stock (2)	150	
	Sold senior subordinated capital notes	169	10,096
1987	Acquired Western Savings and Loan Association in a FSLIC assisted merger	445	
	Sold preferred stock	238	
	Sold two issues of callable preferred stock (1)	150	13,775
1988	Acquired Reliance Savings and Loan Association in a FSLIC assisted merger	82	15,144

* All figures are in $ million.

† Represents Dutch Auction Rate Transferable Securities, a form of adjustable rate preferred stock sold through finance subsidiaries and fully collateralized. Although they do not qualify as capital, their high credit rating makes them a cheap form of financing.

were accompanied by subsidies and yield coverage provided by regulators. Likewise, the acquisitions of the Utah and New Jersey institutions in 1986 and 1987 were also regulatory assisted transactions, but little assistance was provided. CrossLand acquired these institutions primarily as a way to enter markets forbidden to them under the limitations on interstate banking. Later, the New York institutions were merged into one institution that was insured by the FDIC, and all other institutions were regrouped into one institution that was insured by the FSLIC.

14   In 1985, CrossLand (FDIC) became a federally chartered institution and went public, thereby raising $116 million. Subsequent offerings to the public of preferred stock and debt raised additional capital in excess of $1 billion. Because 5.5 percent capital (as a percentage of assets) had been maintained to meet FDIC requirements, these funds also represented capital that CrossLand was able to use to leverage its growth.

15   Exhibit 1 summarizes the growth of CrossLand as a result of its acquisitions and financing activities since November 1981.

16   Data in Exhibit 1 indicated that CrossLand had the following annual compound growth rates of various balance sheet line items: 19 percent assets; 25 percent net loans; 65 percent borrowing; and 37 percent common shareholders equity.

CROSSLAND'S FINANCIAL POSITION

17   Exhibit 2 presents a summary of CrossLand's financial performance for the five year period ending December 31, 1988.

18   Operating earnings (income before income taxes, extraordinary items, cumulative effects of accounting changes, and gains on sales of assets) were considered a key measure of ongoing profitability from operations. Data in Exhibit 2 shows that CrossLand's operating earnings has steadily improved during the period from 1984 through 1988. During the same period, operating earnings (loss) were ($78), $0, $92, $92 and $100 million, respectively. In 1986 and 1987, CrossLand's operating earnings (or core earnings) to average assets well exceeded the industry and CrossLand's peer groups averages, as shown in Exhibit 3.

19   The operating losses in 1984 and 1985 were directly attributed to the excess of interest bearing liabilities over interest earning assets. Further, as Exhibit 4 shows, the interest rate spread—defined as the difference between the yield earned on interest-earning assets over the rate paid on interest-bearing liabilities—was generally positive. However, the net yield earned on interest-earning assets was significantly lower than the interest rate spread in 1984 and 1985. This was due, perhaps, to the fact that the level of interest-bearing liabilities significantly exceeded the level of interest earning assets (i.e., although the rate paid on liabilities was 2.44 percent lower than the rate earned on assets in 1985, only 1.64 percent was actually earned on the assets, because there were fewer assets earning interest than liabilities that interest was paid on). The differential between interest-earning assets and interest liabilities improved significantly in 1986 and thereafter, as equity funds were raised and earnings were reinvested. Exhibit 4 displays this improvement.

20   The long-term industry average for return on average assets (net income divided by average assets) was 65 to 70 basis points (a basis point equals one hundredth of a percent). CrossLand compared favorably to this measure of performance over time, even in 1988, when the cumulative effect of accounting change was not considered. CrossLand's return on average assets was 0.75 percent. This was due in part to CrossLand's low level of operating expenses to average assets. Operating expenses to average assets, measuring operating efficiency has declined, on average, over time and have consistently remained below the industry average, as shown in Exhibit 5.

21   Despite these strengths, there were weaknesses in CrossLand's financial position. First, other revenues than interest income were desirable, because they helped to insulate a thrift from the narrowing spreads earned on assets and from interest rate risk. Although CrossLand's other income increased sufficiently to keep up with the growth in assets, the level of other operating income was well below that of the industry and its peer group, as shown in Exhibit 6.

22   In addition, CrossLand had traditionally expected a low effective income tax rate, due to the availability of net operating loss carryforwards (NOLs) to offset income tax expense. As of December 31, 1988, CrossLand had $260 million of NOLs remaining. However, of these, $208 million represented acquired NOLs which, under *Statement of Financial Accounting Standards No. 96* "Accounting for Income Taxes" (*SFAS 96*), would be reflected as a reduction of goodwill and not as a reduction of income tax expense in the income statement. Therefore, it was expected that income rate would increase significantly and net income would decline.

23   Still, a third weakness was the high level of dividends that CrossLand must pay. Because of the preferred stock Crossland issued dividends had increased significantly and net income available

EXHIBIT 2
CrossLand Savings, FSB
Five-Year Summary Financial and Other Data

Statements of Operations Data	As of December 31 (dollars in millions)				
	1988	1987	1986	1985	1984
Interest income	$ 1,251	$ 952	$ 803	$ 753	$ 747
Interest expense	977	709	599	637	707
Net interest income	274	243	204	116	40
Provision for possible loan losses	25	18	8	8	3
Other operating income:					
Gains on asset sales	26	26	25	156	119
Other	97	65	47	52	48
Other operating expenses	245	199	152	160	162
Income before taxes, cumulative effect, and extraordinary items	127	117	116	156	43
Income tax provision (benefit) (1)	22	21	75	49	(1)
Extraordinary items (1)	—	—	58	34	1
Cumulative effect of accounting change (2)	(90)	—	—	—	—
Net income	15	96	100	141	44
Preferred dividends	41	21	8	—	—
Net income available to common shareholders	(26)	75	92	141	44
State of Condition Data					
Total assets	15,143	13,747	10,073	8 001	7,932
Loans—net	13,109	11,709	8,298	5,996	5,005
Investment securities	500	645	556	737	1,308
Goodwill	445	540	512	540	573
Deposits	8,791	7,748	6,876	6,971	7,262
Borrowing	4,785	4,268	1,962	411	392
Senior subordinated capital notes	170	170	169	—	—
Callable preferred stock	300	450	300	150	—
Stockholders' equity	874	922	620	400	139

(1) Net operating loss carryforwards (NOLs) used to offset the income tax provision was recorded as extraordinary items for fiscal years 1986 and prior and was netted against the income tax provision in 1987 and 1988 (due to the adoption of SFAS 96).

(2) Represents the NOLs realized in 1987 and 1988, which arose from the sale of assets acquired in business combinations. Under SFAS 96, these NOLs must be applied as a reduction of goodwill instead of the income tax provision.

to common stockholders had declined. These preferred stock dividends were expected to remain at the 1988 level of $41 million unless some of the outstanding shares were liquidated or additional shares were issued. The payment of these dividends, combined with the low level of net income and the dividends paid on common stock in 1988, caused the first decline in CrossLand's stockholders equity since 1983.

24   Another factor that has kept CrossLand's earnings from being even greater was CrossLand's increasing reliance on borrowing as a source of funds. Borrowing—including the senior subordinate debt and the callable preferred stock—as a percentage of liabilities increased from 5.0 percent in 1984 to 36.8 percent at the end of 1988. In addition, CrossLand's cost of borrowing was 125,

EXHIBIT 3
Profitability: Core Earnings to Average Assets (in percent)
Most Recent Four Years

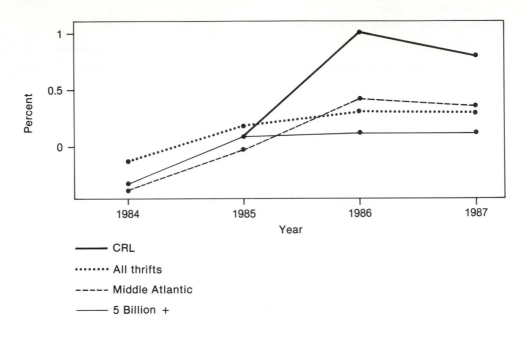

EXHIBIT 4
Spread: Net Interest Income to Average Assets (in percent)
Most Recent Four Years

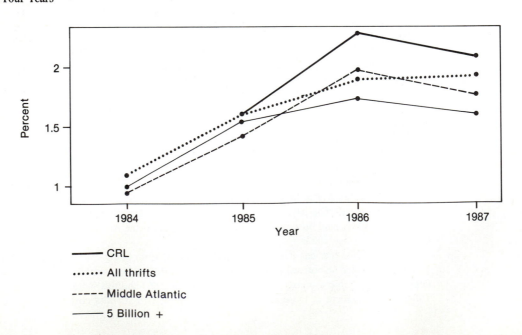

EXHIBIT 5
Overhead: Operating Expense to Average Assets (in percent)
Most Recent Four Years

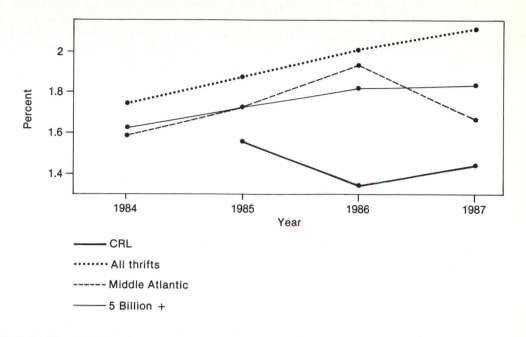

EXHIBIT 6
Loan Fees and Other Income to Average Assets (in percent)
Most Recent Four Years

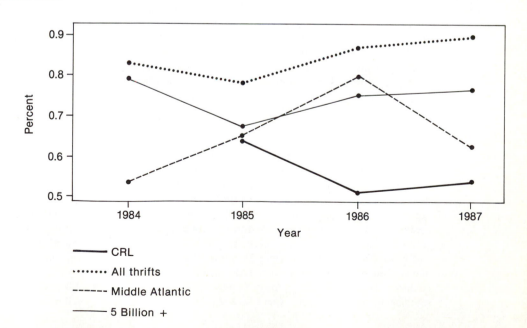

157, and 172 basis points higher than its cost of deposits in 1988, 1987, and 1986, respectively. This relatively high level of borrowing, combined with the greater cost, was a major cause of the decline in the net yield earned during this period. But CrossLand had one of the lowest cost of funds of any public thrift. This was primarily due to its strong presence in Brooklyn and Queens, where depositors continued to invest in low interest bearing passbook accounts.

25   CrossLand's long-term strength was reflected in its equity position. CrossLand (FDIC) was insured by the FDIC and was required to maintain 5.5 percent primary capital requirements (6.0 percent in total capital must also be maintained). In determining whether the capital requirement was met, the FDIC required that any goodwill be deducted from total capital. For CrossLand, this greatly influenced the level of capital as goodwill as significant as a result of its acquisitions. Despite this, CrossLand had always been in compliance with the requirement. In addition to meeting FDIC capital requirements, CrossLand was subject to FHLBB regulations and also had to meet the FHLBB capital requirements. The FHLBB capital requirements were substantially less stringent than those of the FDIC, primarily because goodwill did not have to be deducted from capital and the percent of capital that had to be maintained was lower. As of December 31, 1988, CrossLand exceeded its FHLBB capital requirements of $465 million by $606 million.

CROSSLAND'S INTEREST RATE RISK AND CREDIT RISK EXPOSURE

26   One of the most significant risks that thrift institutions faced in the 1980s was interest rate risk. This occurred as risk when interest-earning assets matured or "repriced" (i.e., the interest rate was adjusted) at other times than interest-bearing liabilities. The gap position, which measured the difference in the repricing of assets and liabilities during select time periods as a percentage of an institution's total assets, was a widely used measure of the level of interest rate risk. A gap that was close to zero signaled a lower level of risk. Yet, generally, a small negative gap position was expected to allow enough positive interest rate spread for the thrift to operate profitably.

27   CrossLand's management established as its target an annual 20 percent negative gap position. CrossLand's gap position declined from 52.8 percent at the end of 1985 to 19.6 percent at the end of 1988. CrossLand succeeded in lowering its gap position through the implementation of an interest rate risk management program, which included the origination of loans with adjustable rates or short-term maturities, increasing the maturities of borrowing, and using hedging activities to extend the repricing term of its liabilities. Despite its success in meeting its 20 percent annual target position, CrossLand's executives believed that the gap position was still significantly greater than that of its peers and of the industry. In fact, CrossLand expected to reprice nearly $3 billion more liabilities than assets in 1989.

28   Industry-wide effort to minimize interest rate risk had been at the cost of net interest income. Earlier in the 1980s, the industry enjoyed higher interest rate spreads, because thrifts received a premium for accepting longer-term assets and holding shorter-term liabilities. This trend changed in the late 1980s. To counteract the narrowing spreads earned on their investments, thrifts increased the credit risk they would accept in return for greater yields. As Exhibit 7 shows, CrossLand did not assume a significant amount of risks, with the great majority of its loan portfolio—over 70 percent in 1988—being concentrated in residential real estate mortgages or in mortgage backed securities. Furthermore, on December 31, 1988, over 25 percent of CrossLand's total loan portfolio was in government insured loans. Also, CrossLand's nonaccrual and renegotiated loans for which interest had been reduced totalled $209 million or 1.5 percent of the net loan portfolio. This compared favorably to the industry average of more than 3 percent. Likewise, CrossLand had significantly increased its allowance for loan losses over recent years, totalling $45 million or 0.34

EXHIBIT 7
CrossLand Savings, FSB
Select Financial Ratios

	As of December 31 (in percent)				
Item	1988	1987	1986	1985	1984
Interest rate spread	2.19%	2.50%	2.83%	2.44%	1.66%
Net yield	2.06	2.34	2.53	1.64	0.59
Return on average equity	1.61	12.79	18.21	61.12	32.35
Return on average assets	0.10	0.84	1.10	1.79	0.58
Equity to assets	5.77	6.71	6.16	5.00	1.76
Operating expense to average assets	1.61	1.73	1.68	2.02	2.12
Operating income to average assets	0.63	0.57	0.52	0.66	0.62

percent of outstanding loans and 0.46 percent of "at-risk" loans (total loans less government insured loans) at the end of 1988. This too, compared favorably to the level of loan chargeoffs as a percentage of average loans, which were 0.08 percent, 0.15 percent, and 0.10 percent in 1988, 1987, and 1986, respectively. Overall, it appeared that CrossLand's relatively low level of credit risk helped to keep its earnings high because there was not a significant level of nonearning loans or loan losses.

CROSSLAND'S PRODUCTS AND MARKETS

29   The 1988 annual report stated:

> CrossLand is a group of financial service companies managed to enhance stockholder value through sustained profitability. We expect to accomplish this by generating quality assets, particularly real estate loans and interest, using least cost funding sources, and carefully controlling operating costs. Lines of business and geographic diversification will be emphasized as strategies to achieve these objectives. CrossLand will seek to enhance its profitability, maintain a strong capital base, and pursue a national presence as a premier banking institution.

30   CrossLand's primary operations were in the thrift industry, as shown in Exhibit 8. Its major source of funds was deposits and it primarily invested these funds in loans. CrossLand's thrift operations were located throughout the country, as shown in Exhibit 9.

31   CrossLand's average outstanding deposits per branch of $97 million was well above the industry average. This was attributable to the high deposit base in the New York branches; the other states had average deposit levels that were below the industry average. The Florida branches included seven full service "mini-branches," which operated in Winn Dixie supermarkets. The bank had plans to open 28 additional supermarket branches in Oregon and Washington. The bank originated commercial real estate and construction loans through the New York branch offices and through 13 offices in 10 states; in addition, residential mortgages were originated through 34 offices in 16 states.

32   Despite its nationwide retail presence, as indicated by its high level of mortgage backed securities and borrowing, CrossLand operated much more as a wholesale bank than the average thrift. Mortgage backed securities represented 29 percent of assets, and borrowing constituted almost 35

EXHIBIT 8
CrossLand Savings, FSB
Composition of Loan Portfolio

	As of December 31 (in percent)		
Item	1988	1987	1986
Residential mortgages	37.6%	26.0%	36.5%
Commercial or industrial loans	22.1	22.7	17.7
Mortgage backed securities	33.0	45.5	38.5
Consumer loans	2.5	2.3	2.9
Commercial business loans	2.9	3.4	4.4
High-yield securities	1.9	0.1	—
Gross loan portfolio	100.0%	100.0%	100.0%

EXHIBIT 9
Dispersion of CrossLand's Operations

State	No. of Branches	Outstanding Deposits ($ million)	Average Deposits per Branch ($ million)
New York	41	$7,256	$177
Florida	33	1,069	32
Oregon	6	154	26
Utah	4	130	32
New Jersey	2	75	37
Virginia	2	26	13
Washington	2	56	28
California	1	24	24
Total	91	$ 8,790	$ 97

percent of assets. Also, a significant part of CrossLand's loan activity was in the purchase and sale of loans. Exhibit 10 shows CrossLand's loan activities for 1986, 1987, 1988. CrossLand's high level of wholesale operations had contributed, in part, to its low operating cost ratio (the cost of obtaining funds was less); but interest rate spreads were typically less on wholesale funds, due to transaction costs.

33   CrossLand also provided nontraditional thrift services directly to depositors and through its subsidiaries, which included the following:

CrossLand Mortgage Corporation.   This was the mortgage banking subsidiary that originated and sold loans for CrossLand and others, serviced loans for CrossLand and others, and conducted secondary mortgage marketing activities.

CrossLand Premium Funding Corporation.   This subsidiary financed insurance premiums for corporate customers.

CrossLand Credit Corporation.   This finance company made equipment leasing loans and wholesale floor plan loans.

Specialized Management Support, Inc.   This data processing company provided accounting, tax reporting, and other financial services to real estate attorneys and brokers, title insurance companies, and other businesses.

EXHIBIT 10
CrossLand Savings, FSB
Loan Activity*

Type	1988	1987 (in millions)	1986
Loans originated	$4,095	$3,061	$1,682
Loans purchased	1,579	5,512	5,129
Loans acquired through merger	42	249	426
Loans sold	1,749	2,914	2,946
Loans satisfactions and amortization	2,560	2,533	2,038
Net loan activity	$1,407	$3,375	$2,253

* Data for the year ended December 31.

Crossland Insurance Agency, Inc. This company provided life, health, accident, property, and casualty insurance and tax-deferred annuities to customers.

34   Perhaps, the largest source of noninterest income from subsidiaries came from CrossLand Mortgage Corporation loan servicing fees. With a loan servicing portfolio of $3.9 billion, $1.1 billion of which was for other banks than CrossLand, such as CrossLand Mortgage which was in the top 20 percent of mortgage banking companies in the United States.

35   CrossLand also offered life insurance in New York through Savings Bank Life Insurance Fund of New York and offered discount brokerage in five branches in New York and Florida in a joint venture with First Institutional Securities Corporation. In addition, CrossLand had entered into joint ventures engaged in real estate activities. All of these activities contributed to noninterest income, which helped to lessen CrossLand's reliance on interest income, and were in line with CrossLand's strategy to expand fee-based services. This expansion was evidenced by the increase in other operating income of 40 percent in 1987 and of 48 percent in 1988.

36   CrossLand's attempt to cross sell its services have been successful, for 74 percent of its savings customers had some other relationship with the bank. Nevertheless, CrossLand's primary focus was on its retail operations. In the 1988 annual report, CrossLand indicated that its strength was in the retail banking and lending franchise, and that its primary focus was to expand this franchise with a focus on cross selling products and services to the retail customers. CrossLand intended to develop a full menu of diversified offerings, providing product and sales training to employees, using incentive programs for branches that met or exceeded sales goals, and by offering new products. One of the first new products was introduced in 1988. Known as CrossLand, it represented a package of services that tied the checking, savings, and loan products.

CrossLand's Competition

37   Over the past decade, competition in the thrift industry increased significantly. This was due to the introduction of money market mutual funds, the effects of deregulation, the advent of interstate banking, the increased marketability of mortgage backed securities, and the increasing sophistication of the typical thrift customer.

38   CrossLand competed for its deposits with other thrift institutions, commercial banks, money market funds, and credit unions. This competition was primarily based on the deposit rates it offered, the service provided, and the convenience of its retail locations. More directly, CrossLand competed with other thrift institutions in the areas in which it had its retail locations.

39   In New York, CrossLand faced stiff competition from five major savings banks: American, Apple, Carteret, CityFed, and Dime. These New York institutions were financially healthy and thus could afford to compete more heavily on rates. To avoid direct competition with these banks, CrossLand concentrated its branches outside Manhattan. Of its 41 New York branches, 14 were in Brooklyn, 9 were in Long Island, 10 were in Manhattan, 3 were in Queens, 2 were in Westchester County, 2 were in Rockland County, and 1 was in Staten Island. In particular, the Brooklyn and Queens branches have a high concentration of passbook savings accounts, which are low cost at 5.5 percent, and have stable deposits.

40   The competition within Florida had a wider range, because many of the larger California and New York thrifts had operations in Florida. In response, CrossLand increased convenience by opening the supermarket branches.

41   CrossLand's competition for real estate, commercial business, and consumer loans came from other thrift institutions, commercial banks, mortgage banking companies, insurance companies, and other institutional lenders. The introduction of mortgage backed securities increased the market for mortgages, because the liquidity of the securities allowed nonfinancial institutions to own mortgages. In addition, the increased lending powers granted to the thrift institutions in 1980 and 1982 made the distinction between thrifts and banks narrower and increased the competition for commercial loans. Because CrossLand originated loans throughout the United States, it has no significant direct competitors. Competition for loans is primarily based on rates and availability.

CROSSLAND'S MANAGEMENT

42   CrossLand's chairman of the board and chief executive officer until October 1988 was Luke Baione, who served with the company for 42 years. Baione was credited for initiating and leading the changes that took place in CrossLand in the 1980s, which made the company among the top thrifts in the United States.

43   In 1988, Baione was replaced by Maurice Reissman, 42, the then president and chief operating officer. Reissman has been with the bank 21 years and served as the president since 1985.

44   Other key members of the top management team and their functions (following a reorganization in 1989) were:

Frank Dellomo, 55, was the vice chairman of the board and was responsible for retail banking, consumer lending, administrative services, and marketing. He joined Brooklyn Savings Bank in 1951 and was its president when it was merged into CrossLand in December 1981.

Thomas Eschmann, 52, was an executive vice president and chief lending officer. Eschmann joined CrossLand in 1985. He served with Chase Manhattan Bank for 10 years (1975–85).

Ramesh Gupta, 41, was the executive vice president and chief financial officer, having previously served as the chief investment officer. Gupta joined CrossLand in 1984 and previously was employed by Goldome Savings Bank.

Donald White, 47, was the executive vice president in charge of bank operations, having previously served as the chief financial officer. White joined CrossLand in June 1983, when the bank acquired Ralph C. Sutro Company, where he served as senior vice president and chief financial officer for the previous six years.

45   The management team had considerable experience in the thrift and financial services industry, and a significant portion of that experience had been with CrossLand itself. Baione, Reissman, and Dellomo, basically spent their careers with the bank. This was noteworthy because, while many of competitors' management teams were unable to adapt successfully to the rapidly changing thrift environment brought about by deregulation, CrossLand enjoyed long-term stability among its highly skilled and innovative senior executives.

MAJOR OPPORTUNITIES AVAILABLE TO CROSSLAND

46   Because of the intense level of competition and the nature of operations within the financial services industry, it was difficult for CrossLand to be distinctive. Yet, two aspects of CrossLand's operations provided it with major opportunities that were not available to competitors.

47   CrossLand had a significant advantage through its retail network. CrossLand operated in several states. This advantage did not extend, however, to all markets in which CrossLand participated. CrossLand did not have a significant presence in New York and Florida and suffered from a lack of name recognition. In addition, because of the high cost of participating in local automated teller machine (ATM) networks, it was not worthwhile for CrossLand to join these local networks until a sufficient number of branches were open. By not being able to provide convenience through a large number of branches, nor by belonging to a local ATM network, deposits in these areas did not reach their potential.

48   The retail network not only provided CrossLand with its major source of funds but also provided opportunities for cross selling and nondeposit related services. CrossLand took advantage of this somewhat by offering, to a limited extent, discount brokerage and insurance services.

49   Another strength of CrossLand was its mortgage banking company. Having offices throughout the United States enabled CrossLand to obtain loans from different areas, therefore, it could minimize its exposure to any one area. The impact of this was significant when considering the effect of the recession in the "energy" states that caused many thrifts to fail. In addition, the mortgage company provided a major source of CrossLand's noninterest revenues by earning service fees on its service portfolio. The service portfolio also had significant value that was not reflected on the balance sheet and could easily be sold.

MAJOR THREATS FACING CROSSLAND

50   Perhaps the major threat facing CrossLand was a threat that afflicted its entire industry. Although 89 percent of thrift institutions holding 90 percent of total industry assets were solvent, there had been a significant amount of press coverage of the remaining thrift that were not solvent. Also, the industry as a whole lost $9.4 billion in the first three quarters of 1988, and FSLIC, the industry insurer, itself was reported to be solvent. This resulted in a campaign for stricter regulations and monitoring of the industry; the Bush Plan was proposed in response to this campaign. If the Bush Plan was adopted, it was expected to increase the capital requirements for CrossLand and its competitors, not only under FSLIC but also under FDIC standards. These increased requirements potentially could cause CrossLand to shrink to meet the minimum capital requirements.

51   A more direct threat to CrossLand was its high level of borrowing, which caused the cost of funds to be higher than it would be expected. In fact, on December 31, 1988, CrossLand's borrowings were equal to 60 percent of deposits, as shown in Exhibit 11. The average cost of these borrowings was 8.42 percent, as opposed to the average cost of deposits of 7.11 percent. In addition, CrossLand's major source of borrowing, Federal Home Loan Bank advances, was not without limit. Dollar repurchase agreements and securities sold under agreements to repurchase, the second largest source of borrowing, were collateralized financing transactions, whereby CrossLand sold mortgage backed securities and agreed to repurchase the same or substantially identical securities. Because the transaction was collateralized, these borrowing arrangements typically were cheaper than other borrowing sources; however, they generally had terms of one month or less and, therefore, were very sensitive to interest rate changes.

52   Still, CrossLand's overall exposure to interest rate changes posed another threat. On December 31, 1988, the level of interest-bearing liabilities, due to reprice within a year, exceeded the level

EXHIBIT 11
CrossLand Savings, FSB
Outstanding Borrowing

Items	Balance* (in millions)	Percent of Total*
Federal Home Loan Bank advanced	$2,762	52.6%
Repurchase agreements	1,695	32.2
Callable preferred stock	300	5.7
Senior subordinated debt	170	3.2
Other borrowing	328	6.3
Total borrowing	$5,255	100.0%

* As of December 31, 1988.

of interest-earning assets, due to reprice by $3 billion. This was expected to result in nearly a $30 million reduction in net interest income for every 1 percent increase in rates. This was particularly significant in light of the increasing interest rates in the first part of 1989. As a result of the Federal Reserve Board increasing its discount rate—intended to control inflation—the prime rate was increased from 10.50 percent on January 1, 1989, to 11.50 percent on April 30, 1989. Although the Federal Reserve Board was not expected to raise the discount rate further, this possibility could not be eliminated.

53   CrossLand was not able to cover its dividend payments with earnings in 1988, primarily due to the cumulative effect of changes in accounting procedures. But the bank was experiencing financial difficulties. For instance, CrossLand's paid dividends in 1988 of $52.5 million, and of these $41.3 million were fixed dividends on preferred stock. Given the effect of rising interest rates, causing narrowing spreads, and the effect of SFAS 96, limiting the NOLs used against income tax expense, CrossLand's net income was expected to decline and may not be sufficient enough to cover dividends.

THE FUTURE

54   CrossLand's executives were well aware that the thrift industry was fraught with risk. With the industry-wide risk of insolvency rising, these executives were pondering options to create and sustain a distinctive competence for CrossLand. Still, they felt compelled to examine the bank's very concept of business. As they reflected on their potential choices, executives recognized the fact that there were four types of thrift institutions. The first was the "traditional" thrift, which originated single-family residential lonas and obtained funds from retail deposits. The second group consisted of thrifts whose strategy centered on investing in mortgage backed securities and obtaining funds from the wholesale markets. The third group included thrifts that elected to become more like commercial banks, with investments in nonresidential loans and a heavier emphasis on commercial checking. The final and fourth group included thrifts that branched into alternative serivces, such as mortgage banking. CrossLand's executives felt pressured to reposition their bank to take advantage of the many opportunities in the 1990s.

55   With their growing geographic expansion, CrossLand's executives faced another crucial choice. How can branches be integrated economically? Did CrossLand have the appropriate organizational structure and managerial expertise to deal with demands of this geographic dispersion? Should the bank continue its expansion? Has the firm reached its optimal size? CrossLand was being challenged to rethink the very foundation of the strategy that has served it so well over the past turbulent decade.

CASE 7

THE AUDUBON ZOO

"AN URBAN EDEN"

1   The Audubon Zoo was the focus of national concern in the early 1970s, with well-documented stories of animals kept in conditions that were variously termed an "animal ghetto,"[1] "the New Orleans antiquarium," and even "an animal concentration camp."[2] In 1971, the Bureau of Governmental Research recommended a $5.6 million zoo improvement plan to the Audubon Park Commission and the City Council of New Orleans. The local *Times-Picayune* commented on the new zoo: "It's not going to be quite like the *Planet of the Apes* situation in which the apes caged and studied human beings but something along those broad general lines."[3] The new zoo confined people to bridges and walkways while the animals roamed amidst grass, shrubs, trees, pools, and fake rocks. The gracefully curving pathways, generously lined with luxuriant plantings, gave the visitor a sense of being alone in a wilderness, although crowds of visitors might be only a few yards away.

THE DECISION

2   The Audubon Park Commission launched a $5.6 million development program, based on the Bureau of Governmental Research plan for the zoo in March 1972. A bond issue and a property tax dedicated to the zoo were put before the voters, with renovations to begin the day following passage. The New Orleans City Planning Commission finally approved the master plan for the Audubon Park Zoo in September 1973. But the institution of the master plan was far from smooth.

The Zoo Question Goes Public

3   A revenue generating proposal was put to the voters by Mayor Moon Landrieu on November 7, 1972. When it passed by an overwhelming majority, serious discussions began about what should be done. Over two dozen special interests were ultimately involved in choosing whether to reno-

This case was prepared by Claire J. Anderson and Caroline M. Fisher, both of Loyola University in New Orleans.

© 1987, Claire J. Anderson and Caroline Fisher, Loyola University, New Orleans.

The authors wish to acknowledge the contributions of graduate students Martha McGraw Hamilton and Debbie Longo, who aided in the research and who contributed many helpful suggestions in the development of the case.

The case was designed for classroom discussion only. It was not meant to depict effective or ineffective handling of administrative situations.

[1]*Times-Picayune,* January 20, 1976.

[2]*Times-Picayune,* March 30, 1975.

[3]Millie Ball, "The New Zoo of '82" *Dixie Magazine, Sunday Times-Picayune,* June 24, 1979.

EXHIBIT 1
The Audubon Park Zoo

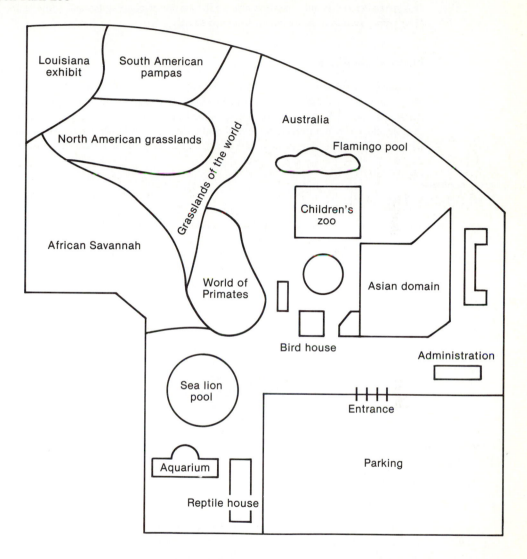

vate/expand the existing facilities or move to another site. Expansion became a major community controversy. Some residents opposed the zoo expansion, fearing "loss of green space" would affect the secluded character of the neighborhood. Others opposed the loss of what they saw as an attractive and educational facility.

4   Most of the opposition came from the zoo's affluent neighbors. Zoo director John Moore ascribed the criticism to "a select few people who have the money and power to make a lot of noise." He went on to say "[T]he real basis behind the problem is that the neighbors who live around the edge

of the park have a selfish concern because they want the park as their private back yard."[4] Legal battles over the expansion plans continued until early 1976. At that time, the Fourth Circuit Court of Appeals ruled that the expansion was legal.[5] An out-of-court agreement with the zoo's neighbors (The Upper Audubon Association) followed shortly.

Physical Facilities

5   The expansion of the Audubon Park Zoo took from 14 to 58 acres. The zoo was laid out in geographic sections: the Asian Domain, World of Primates, World's Grasslands, Savannah, North American Prairie, South American Pampas, and Louisiana Swamp, according to the Zoo Master Plan developed by the Bureau of Governmental Research. Additional exhibits included the Wisner Discovery Zoo, Sea Lion exhibit, and Flight Cage. See Exhibit 1 for a map of the new zoo.

PURPOSE OF THE ZOO

6   The main outward purpose of the Audubon Park Zoo was entertainment. Many of the promotional efforts of the zoo were aimed at creating an image of the zoo as an entertaining place to go. Obviously such a campaign was necessary to attract visitors to the zoo. Behind the scenes, the zoo also preserved and bred many animal species, conducted research, and educated the public.

NEW DIRECTIONS

7   One of the first significant changes made was the institution of an admission charge in 1972. Admission to the zoo had been free to anyone prior to the adoption of the renovation plan. Ostensibly the initial purpose behind instituting the admission charge was to prevent vandalism,[6] but the need for additional income was also apparent. Despite the institution of and increases in admission charges, admissions increased dramatically (see Exhibit 2).

OPERATIONS

Friends of the Zoo

8   The Friends of the Zoo was formed in 1974 and incorporated in 1975, with 400 original members. The stated purpose of the friends was to increase support and awareness of the Audubon Park Zoo. Initially the Friends of the Zoo tried to increase interest and commitment to the zoo, but its activities increased dramatically over the following years to where it was involved in funding, operating, and governing the zoo.

---

[4]*Times-Picayune*, March 30, 1975.

[5]*Times-Picayune*, January 20, 1976.

[6]*Times-Picayune*, April 29, 1972.

EXHIBIT 2
Increase in Admissions

Admission Charges		
Year	Adult	Child
1972	$0.75	$0.25
1978	1.00	0.50
1979	1.50	0.75
1980	2.00	1.00
1981	2.50	1.25
1982	3.00	1.50
1983	3.50	1.75
1984	4.00	2.00
1985	4.50	2.00
1986	5.00	2.50

Admissions		
Year	Number of Paid Admissions	Number of Member Admissions
1972	163,000	
1973	310,000	
1974	345,000	
1975	324,000	
1976	381,000	
1977	502,000	
1978	456,000	
1979	561,000	
1980	707,000	
1981	741,000	
1982	740,339	78,950
1983	835,044	118,665
1984	813,025	128,538
1985	854,996	144,060
1986	915,492	187,119
1987	439,264*	93,327*

* Through the end of the second quarter.
Source: The Audubon Zoo.

9   The Friends of the Zoo had a 24-member governing board. Yearly elections were held for six members of the board who served four-year terms. The board oversaw the policies of the zoo and set guidelines for memberships, concessions, fund raising, and marketing. Actual policymaking and operations were controlled by the Audubon Park Commission, which set zoo hours, admission prices, and the like.

10   Through its volunteer programs, the Friends of the Zoo staffed many of the zoo's programs. Volunteers from members of the Friends of the zoo served as "edZOOcators," education volunteers who were specially trained to conduct interpretive education programs, and "Zoo Area Patrollers," who provided general information about a geographic area of the zoo and helped with crowd control. Other volunteers assisted in the Commissary, Animal Health Care Center, and Wild Bird Rehabilitation Center or helped with membership, public relations, graphics, clerical work, research, or horticulture.

Fund Raising

11   The Audubon Park Zoo and the Friends of the Zoo raised funds through five major types of activities: Friends of the Zoo Membership, concessions, Adopt an Animal, Zoo-To-Do, and capital fund drives. Zoo managers from around the country came to the Audubon Park Zoo for tips on fund raising.

12   *Membership.* Membership in the Friends of the Zoo was open to anyone. The membership fees increased over the years, as summarized in Exhibit 3. Yet the number of members increased steadily, from the original 400 members in 1974 to 33,000 members in 1987. Membership allowed free entry to the Audubon Park Zoo and to many other zoos around the United States. Participation in Zoobilation (annual members-only evenings at the zoo) and the many volunteer programs described earlier were other benefits of membership.

13   Increasing membership required a special approach to marketing the zoo. Chip Weigand, director of marketing for the zoo, stated:

14   [I]n marketing memberships we try to encourage repeat visitations, the feeling that one can visit as often as one wants, the idea that the Zoo changes from visit to visit and that there are good reasons to make one large payment or donation for a membership card, rather than paying for each visit. . . . [T]he overwhelming factor is a good zoo that people want to visit often, so that a membership makes good economical sense.

15   In 1985, the zoo announced a new membership designed for businesses, the Audubon Zoo Curator Club, with four categories of membership: Bronze, $250; Silver, $500; Gold, $1,000; and Platinum, $2,500 and more.

16   *Concessions.* The Friends of the Zoo took over the Audubon Park Zoo concessions for refreshments and gifts in 1976, through a public bidding process. The concessions were run by volunteer members of the Friends of the Zoo and all profits went directly to the zoo. Prior to 1976, concession rentals brought in $15,000 in a good year. Profits from operation of the concessions by the Friends of the Zoo brought in $400,000 a year by 1980 and were budgeted to bring in over $900,000 in profits for 1987.

17   *Adopt an Animal.* Zoo Parents paid a fee to "adopt" an animal, the fee varying with the animal chosen. Zoo Parents' names were listed on a large sign inside the zoo. They also had their own celebration, Zoo Parents Day, held at the zoo yearly.

18   *Zoo-To-Do.* Zoo-To-Do was a black-tie fund raiser held annually, with live music, food and drink, and original high-class souvenirs, such as posters or ceramic necklaces. Admission tickets,

EXHIBIT 3
Membership Fees and Membership

Year	Family Membership Fees	Individual Membership Fees	Number of Memberships
1979	$20	$10	1,000
1980	20	10	7,000
1981	20	10	11,000
1982	25	15	18,000
1983	30	15	22,000
1984	35	20	26,000
1985	40	20	30,000
1986	45	25	32,000
1987	45	25	33,000

Source: The Audubon Zoo.

limited to 3,000 annually, were priced starting at $100 per person. A raffle was conducted in conjunction with the Zoo-To-Do, with raffle items varying from an opportunity to be Zoo Curator for a day, to the use of a Mercedes Benz for a year. Despite the rather stiff price, the Zoo-To-Do was a popular sellout every year. Local restaurants and other businesses donated most of the necessary supplies, decreasing the cost of the affair. In 1985 the Zoo-To-Do raised almost $500,000 in one night, more money than any other nonmedical fund raiser in the country.[7]

Advertising

19   The Audubon Zoo launched impressive marketing campaigns in the 1980s. The zoo received ADDY awards from the New Orleans Advertising Club year after year.[8] In 1986, the film *Urban Eden,* produced by Alford Advertising and Buckholtz Productions, Inc., in New Orleans, finished first among 40 entries in the "documentary films, public relations" category of the 8th Annual Houston International Film Festival. The first-place gold award recognized the film for vividly portraying Audubon Zoo as a conservation, rather than a confining environment.

20   During the same year, local television affiliates of ABC, CBS, and NBC produced independent TV spots using the theme: "One of the World's Greatest Zoos Is in Your Own Back Yard . . . Audubon

EXHIBIT 4
Public Relations Budgets

Category	1987 Percent
Salaries and overtime	24.3%
Education, travel, and subscriptions	1.1
Printing and duplicating	2.4
Professional services	1.5
Tourist brochures for hotel rooms	3.6
Special events	24.1
News releases	0.4
Entertainment	0.7
Photography	0.9
Miscellaneous supplies	0.6
Advertising	40.3

Media Budgets

Media	1986 Percent	1987 Percent
TV and Radio	28.0%	46.3%
Special Promotion Contingency	32.3	13.2
Tourist Publications	10.5	9.2
Streetcar and Bus	6.9	7.3
Magazines	4.2	5.0
Newspaper	—	1.1
Production	18.1	17.8

Source: The Audubon Zoo.

[7]*Jefferson Business*, August 1985.

[8]Ibid.

Zoo!". Along with some innovative views of the Audubon Zoo being in someone's "backyard," local news anchor personalities enjoyed "monkeying around" with the animals and the zoo enjoyed some welcome free exposure.[9]

21   In 1986 and 1987, the advertising budgets were just over $150,000, the total public relations budgets were over $300,000, and the total marketing budgets were over $1 million each year, including salaries. The marketing budgets included development or fund raising and membership, as well as public relations and advertising. Percentage breakdowns of the public relations budget for 1987 can be found in Exhibit 4.

22   The American Association of Zoological Parks and Aquariums reported that most zoos found that the majority of their visitors live within a single population center in close proximity to the park.[10] Thus, to sustain attendance over the years, zoos must attract the same visitors repeatedly. A large number of the zoo's promotional programs and special events were aimed at just that.

23   Progress was slow among nonnatives. For example, Simon & Schuster, a reputed publishing firm, in its 218-page 1983–84 *Guide to New Orleans,* managed only a three-word allusion to a "very nice zoo." A 1984 study found that only 36 percent of the visitors were tourists, and even this number was probably influenced to some extent by an overflow from the World's Fair.

Promotional Programs

24   The Audubon Park Zoo and the Friends of the Zoo conducted a multitude of very successful promotional programs. The effect was to have continual parties and celebrations going on, attracting a variety of people to the zoo and raising additional revenue. Exhibit 5 lists the major annual promotional programs conducted by the zoo.

25   In addition to these annual promotions, the zoo scheduled concerts of well-known musicians, such as Irma Thomas, Pete Fountain, The Monkeys, and Manhattan Transfer, and other special events throughout the year. As a result, a variety of events occurred each month.

26   Many educational activities were conducted all year long. These included (1) a Junior Zoo Keeper program for seventh and eighth graders; (2) a Student-Intern program for high school and college students; and (3) a ZOOmobile, which took live animals to such locations as special education classes, hospitals, and old age homes.

Admission Policy

27   The commission recommended the institution of an admission charge. Arguments that generally advanced against such a charge held that it results in an overall decline in attendance and a reduction of nongate revenues. Proponents held that gate charges control vandalism, produce greater revenues, and result in increased public awareness and appreciation of the facility. In the early 1970s, no major international zoo failed to charge admission and 73 percent of the 125 United States zoos charged admission.

28   The commission argued that there is no such thing as a free zoo; someone must pay. If the zoo is tax supported, then locals carry a disproportionate share of the cost. At the time, neighboring Jefferson Parish was growing by leaps and bounds and surely would bring a large nonpaying

---

[9]*Advertising Age,* March 17, 1986.

[10]Karen Sausmann, ed., *Zoological Park and Aquarium Fundamentals* (Wheeling, W.V.: American Association of Zoological Parks and Aquariums, 1982), p. 111.

EXHIBIT 5
Audubon Park Zoo Promotional Programs

Title (activity)	Month(s)
Photography Contest	January
Fit for Life (aerobics)	March
Zoo-To-Do for Kids	April
Easter Family Days	April
Zoo-To-Do	May
Musical Zoo Revue (symphony concert)	May
Summer Concert Series	April to August
Breakfast with the Beasts	June
Ice Cream Sunday	June
Zoobilation (members party)	June
Play-Doh Invitational (Architects compete with Play-Doh designs)	June
Teddy Bear Affair (teddy bear contests)	August
Press Party	September
Symphony Run	September
Louisiana Swamp Festival	October
Halloween	October
Beast Ballet (ballet performance)	November
Annual Essay Contest	November
Holiday Celebration	December
Annual Members' Christmas Sale	December

Source: The Audubon Zoo.

constitution to the new zoo. Further, as most zoos are tourist attractions, tourists should pay since they contribute little to the local tax revenues.

29   The average yearly attendance for a zoo may be estimated by using projected population figures multiplied by a "visitor generating factor." The average visitor generating factor of 14 zoos similar in size and climate to the Audubon Zoo was 1.34, with a rather wide range from a low of 0.58 in the cities of Phoenix and Miami to a high of 2.80 in Jackson, Mississippi.

Attracting More Tourists and Other Visitors

30   A riverboat ride on the romantic paddle-wheeled *Cotton Blossom* took visitors from downtown to the zoo. Originally, the trip began at a dock in the French Quarter, but it was later moved to a dock immediately adjacent to New Orleans' newest attraction, the Riverwalk, a Rouse development, on the site of the 1984 Louisiana World Exposition. Not only was the riverboat ride great fun, it also lured tourists and conventioneers from the downtown attractions of the French Quarter and the new Riverwalk to the zoo, some six miles upstream. A further allure of the riverboat ride was a return trip to downtown on the New Orleans Streetcar, one of the few remaining trolley cars in the United States. The Zoo Cruise not only drew more visitors but generated additional revenue through landing fees paid by the New Orleans Steamboat company and kept traffic out of uptown New Orleans.[11]

---

[11]*Times-Picayune*, November 30, 1981.

EXHIBIT 6
Operating Budget

Year	Operating Budget	Gov't. Support	Self-Generated
1978	$1,700,000	$700,000	$1,000,000
1980	2,800,000	840,000	1,960,000
1986	4,469,000	460,000	4,009,000

Source: The Audubon Zoo.

FINANCIAL

31   The zoo's ability to generate operating funds has been ascribed to the dedication of the Friends of the Zoo, continuing increases in attendance, and creative special events and programs. A history of adequate operating funds allowed the zoo to guarantee capital donors that their gifts would be used to build and maintain top-notch exhibits. See Exhibit 6 for sources of operating budgets over the years. The 1986 combined balance sheet and statement of revenue and expense for the Park Commission are in Exhibits 7 and 8.

Capital Fund Drives

32   The Audubon Zoo Development Fund was established in 1973. Corporate/industrial support of the zoo has been very strong—many corporations have underwritten construction of zoo displays and facilities. A partial list of major corporate sponsors is in Exhibit 9. A sponsorship was considered to be for the life of the exhibit. The development department operated on a 12 percent overhead rate, which meant 88 cents of every dollar raised went to the projects. By 1987, the master plan for development had been 75 percent completed. The fund-raising goal for 1987 was $1,600,000.

MANAGEMENT

The Zoo Director

33   Ron Forman, Audubon Zoo director, was called a "zoomaster extraordinaire" and was described by the press as a "cross between Doctor Doolittle and the Wizard of Oz," as a "practical visionary," and as "serious, but with a sense of humor."[12] A native New Orleanian, Forman quit an MBA program to join the city government as an administrative assistant and found himself doing a business analysis project on the Audubon Park. Once the city was committed to a new zoo, Forman was placed on board as an assistant to the zoo director, John Moore. In early 1977, Moore gave up the battle between the "animal people" and the "people-people"[13] and Forman took over as park and zoo director.

34   Forman was said to bring an MBA-meets-menagerie style to the zoo, which was responsible for transforming it from a public burden into an almost completely self-sustaining operation. The

---

[12]Steve Brooks, "Don't Say 'No Can Do' to Audubon Zoo Chief," *Jefferson Business*, May 5, 1986.

[13]Ross Yuchey, "No Longer Is Heard a Discouraging Word at the Audubon Zoo," *New Orleans*, August 1980, p. 53.

EXHIBIT 7

AUDUBON PARK COMMISSION
Combined Balance Sheet
December 31, 1986

	Operating Fund	Enterprise Fund	Designated Funds	Total
Assets				
Current assets:				
Cash—Noninterest bearing	$ 12,108	$ 0	$ 131,411	$ 143,519
—Interest bearing	306,483	0	0	306,483
Time certificates of deposit	301,493	0	107,402	408,895
Investments	100	0	0	100
Accounts receivable:				
Friends of the Zoo, Inc.	321,774	0	1,177	322,951
Other	13,240	7,842	75,698	96,780
Due from Operating Fund	0	309,208	320,463	629,671
Due from Enterprise Fund	0	0	300,000	300,000
Due from Designated Funds	0	0	66,690	66,690
Prepaid expenses	166,862	3,371	0	170,233
Total current assets	1,122,060	320,421	1,002,841	2,445,322
Fixed assets:				
Equipment	0	159,455	0	159,455
Less: Accumulated depreciation	0	75,764	0	75,764
Total fixed assets	0	83,691	0	83,691
Total assets	$1,122,060	$404,112	$1,002,841	$2,529,013
Liabilities				
Cash overdraft	$ 39,700	$ 0	$ 0	$ 39,700
Accounts payable:				
City of New Orleans	267,185	0	0	267,185
Friends of the Zoo, Inc.	0	72,658	0	72,658
Other	68,805	7,099	0	75,904
Payroll taxes payable	14,337	0	0	14,337
Accrued salaries	7,973	1,579	0	9,552
Due to Operating Fund	0	0	46,899	46,899
Due to Enterprise Fund	309,208	0	0	309,208
Due to Designated Funds	273,564	300,000	0	573,564
Due to other Designated Funds	0	0	66,690	66,690
Total liabilities	980,722	381,336	113,589	1,475,697
Fund equities:				
Fund balances	141,288	0	889,252	1,030,540
Retained earnings	0	22,776	0	22,776
Total fund equitites	141,288	22,776	889,252	1,053,316
Total liabilities and fund equities	$1,122,060	$404,112	$1,002,841	$2,529,013

EXHIBIT 8

AUDUBON PARK COMMISSION
Statement of Revenue, Expenditures, and Changes in
Operating Fund Balance—Actual and Budgeted
Year Ended December 31, 1986

	Annual Budget	Actual	Percent of Budget
Revenues:			
Intergovernmental:			
City of New Orleans	$ 600,000	$ 450,000	75.0%
State of Louisiana	25,000	10,913	43.7
Other governmental	25,000	0	0.0
Total intergovernmental	650,000	460,913	70.9
Charges for services:			
Animal rides	115,000	127,671	111.0
Binocular receipts	4,000	2,604	65.1
Education programs	10,000	930	9.3
Events	10,000	4,701	47.0
Food and drink	458,000	569,259	124.3
Gift shops	140,000	136,369	97.4
Mombasa Railroad	40,000	40,030	100.1
Race fees	30,000	30,844	102.8
Swimming pool	17,000	15,992	94.1
Tennis	0	10,167	0.0
Train	10,000	0	0.0
Travel program	14,000	5,508	39.3
Zoo admissions	2,420,000	2,718,254	112.3
Total charges for services	3,268,000	3,662,329	112.1
Interest income	10,000	34,867	348.7
Miscellaneous:			
Animal sales	10,000	38,446	384.5
Aquarium campaign	0	124	0.0
Friends of the Zoo	525,000	640,869	122.1
Miscellaneous	12,000	8,569	71.4
Riverboat	35,000	36,278	103.7
Stables	8,400	7,887	93.9
Total miscellaneous	590,400	732,173	124.0
Total revenue	4,518,400	4,890,282	108.2
Expenditures			
Personal services:			
Life insurance	2,000	23,106	1,155.3
Medical insurance	100,000	103,321	103.3
Pension	150,000	160,543	107.0
Payroll taxes	198,000	155,961	78.8
Salaries—Regular	1,883,652	1,959,205	104.0
Salaries—Overtime	59,570	61,937	104.0
Terminal leave	10,000	1,169	11.7
Uniform allowance	19,900	17,287	86.9
Workmen's compensation	50,000	38,779	77.6
Total personal services	2,473,122	2,521,308	101.9

EXHIBIT 8 (*continued*)

	Annual Budget	Actual	Percent of Budget
Expenditures (continued):			
Contractual Services:			
Advertising	$ 131,200	$ 111,863	85.3%
Aquarium	90,000	248,082	275.6
Building repairs	5,400	18,790	348.0
Communications	100	166	166.0
Convention and travel	29,950	32,445	108.3
Delivery and parking	10,850	12,639	116.5
Dues and subscriptions	7,910	7,636	96.5
Duplicating services	14,500	5,021	34.6
Entertainment	5,800	12,350	212.9
Equipment rental	22,750	12,215	53.7
Insurance	260,000	254,079	97.7
Laboratory services	8,100	9,762	120.5
License fees	550	1,108	201.5
Minor repairs	10,300	12,265	119.1
News releases	6,000	1,551	25.9
Penguins	0	10,957	0.0
Personal contracts	46,200	0	0.0
Postage and freight	40,350	33,322	82.6
Printing	18,700	9,207	49.2
Professional services	342,890	362,050	105.6
Swimming pool	48,000	42,835	89.2
Telephone	40,000	50,634	126.6
Utilities	40,000	41,902	104.8
Vehicle repairs	10,000	12,307	123.1
Waste removal	18,800	18,011	95.8
Total contractural services	1,208,350	1,321,197	109.3
Supplies and materials:			
Amphitheater	3,400	2,264	66.6
Art and essay	900	518	57.6
Artifacts	1,000	0	0.0
Building supplies	57,750	63,151	109.4
Display supplies	32,100	17,172	53.5
Educational supplies	10,050	49,626	493.8
Electrical supplies	10,300	25,283	245.5
Events	50,200	45,989	91.6
Feed and forage	187,780	172,398	91.8
Fuel	38,000	23,874	62.8
Graphics supplies	4,500	8,152	181.2
Hand tools	4,000	3,120	78.0
Horticultural supplies	20,000	17,788	88.9
Hospital and laboratory supplies	15,300	13,711	89.6
Janitorial and cleaning	51,500	50,018	97.1
Junior keeper	500	817	163.4
Medical supplies	1,750	1,300	74.3
Minor equipment	28,950	30,384	105.0
Motor vehicle supplies	30,000	10,285	34.3
Office supplies	34,150	29,768	87.2
Photographic supplies	5,150	6,138	119.2
Plants, shrubs and trees	18,300	16,574	90.6
Police supplies	1,500	3,128	208.5
Public information	0	638	0.0

(*continued*)

EXHIBIT 8 (*concluded*)

	Annual Budget	Actual	Percent of Budget
Expenditures (continued):			
Supplies and materials (continued):			
Read the Zoo	$ 7,000	$ 7,675	109.6
Safari carts	3,000	1,136	37.9
Special education	10,000	12,731	127.3
Teacher in-service	6,000	2,562	42.7
Uniforms	5,060	4,329	85.6
ZOOmobile	3,000	1,138	37.9
Total supplies and materials	641,140	621,667	97.0
Equipment:			
Animals	22,400	14,359	64.1
Automotive	40,000	56,722	141.8
Communications	1,150	847	73.7
Construction projects	50,000	32,418	64.8
Educational and recreational	0	96	0.0
General plant	7,000	5,621	80.3
Hospital and medical	4,200	2,947	70.2
Office furniture and equipment	8,500	35,897	422.3
Total equipment	133,250	148,907	111.8
Other expenditures:			
Claims	12,000	10,385	86.5
Miscellaneous	1,000	19,461	1,946.1
Total other expenditures	13,000	29,846	229.6
Total expenditures	4,468,862	4,642,925	103.9
Excess of revenue over expenditures	49,538	247,357	499.3
Other financing uses:			
Operating transfers out	49,538	150,000	302.8
Excess of revenue and other financing sources over expenditures and other uses	$ 0	97,357	
Operating fund balance at beginning of year		43,931	
Operating fund balance at end of year		$ 141,288	

result not only benefited the citizens of the city but also added a major tourist attraction to the economically troubled city of the 1980s.

Staffing

35   The zoo used two classes of employees: civil service, through the Audubon Park Commission, and noncivil service. The civil service employees included the curators and zoo keepers. They fell under the jurisdiction of the city civil service system. Employees who worked in public relations, advertising, concessions, fund raising, and so on were hired through the Friends of the Zoo and were not part of the civil service system. See Exhibit 10 for further data on staffing patterns.

EXHIBIT 9
Major Corporate Sponsors

Amoco Corporation
American Express
J. Aron and Company
Breaux Mart
Chevron USA, Inc.
Conoco, Inc.
Consolidated Natural Gas Corporation
D.H. Holmes, Ltd.
Dr. G.H. Tichenor Antiseptic Company
Exxon Corporation
First National Bank of Commerce
Freeport-McMoRan, Inc.
Frischhertz Electric Company

Goudchaux/Maison Blanche
Hibernia National Bank
Kentwood Spring Water
Louisiana Coca-Cola Bottling Company, Ltd.
Louisiana Land and Exploration Company
McDonald's Operations of New Orleans
William B. Reily and Company
Texaco USA
Trammell Crow Company
Wendy's of New Orleans
Whitney National Bank
Frank B. Williams and Company

Source: The Audubon Zoo.

EXHIBIT 10
Employee Structure

Year	Percent of Paid Employees	Number of Volunteers
1972	36%	
1973	49	
1974	69	
1975	90	
1976	143	
1977	193	
1978	184	
1979	189	
1980	198	
1981	245	
1982	305	
1983	302	56
1984	419	120
1985	454	126
1986	426	250
1987	358*	287*

* Through the end of the second quarter.
Source: The Audubon Zoo.

THE ZOO IN THE LATE 1980s

36   A visitor to the new Audubon Zoo could quickly see why New Orleanians were so proud of their zoo. In a city that was termed among the dirtiest in the nation, the zoo was virtually spotless. This was a result of adequate staffing and the clear pride of both those who worked at and those who visited the zoo. One of the first points made by volunteers guiding school groups was that anyone seeing a piece of trash on the ground must pick it up.[14] A 1986 city poll showed that 93 percent of the citizens surveyed gave the zoo a high approval rating—an extremely high rating for any public facility.

37   Kudos came from groups outside the local area as well. Delegates from the American Association of Zoological Parks and Aquariums ranked the Audubon Zoo as one of the three top zoos of its size in America. In 1982, the American Association of Nurserymen gave the zoo a Special Judges Award for its use of plant materials. In 1985, the Audubon Park Zoo received the Phoenix Award from the Society of American Travel Writers for its achievements in conservation, preservation, and beautification.

38   By 1987, the zoo was virtually self-sufficient. The small amount of money received from government grants amounted to less than 10 percent of the budget. The master plan for the development of the zoo was 75 percent complete and the reptile exhibit was scheduled for completion in the fall. The organization had expanded with a full complement of professionals and managers. (See Exhibit 11 for the organizational structure of the zoo).

39   While the zoo made great progress in 15 years, all was not quiet on the political front. In a court battle, the city won over the state on the issue of who wielded ultimate authority over Audubon Park and Zoo. Indeed, the zoo benefited from three friendly mayors in a row, starting with Moon Landrieu, who championed the new zoo, to Ernest "Dutch" Morial, to the mayor in 1987, Sidney Barthelemy, who threw his support to both the zoo and a proposed aquarium, championed by Ron Forman.

THE FUTURE

New Directions for the Zoo

40   Zoo director, Ron Forman, demonstrated that zoos have almost unlimited potential. A 1980 *New Orleans* magazine article cited some of Forman's ideas, ranging from a safari train to a breeding center for rare animals. The latter has an added attraction as a potential money maker since an Asiatic lion cub, for example, sells for around $10,000. This wealth of ideas was important because expanded facilities and programs are required to maintain attendance at any public attraction. The most ambitious of Forman's ideas was for an aquarium and riverfront park to be located at the foot of Canal Street.

41   Although the zoo enjoyed political support in 1987, New Orleans was suffering from a high unemployment rate and a generally depressed economy, resulting from the depression in the oil industry. Some economists were predicting the beginning of a gradual turn-around in 1988, but any significant improvement in the economy was forecasted to be years away. In addition, the zoo operated in a city where many attractions competed for the leisure dollar of citizens and visitors. The Audubon Zoological Garden had to vie with the French Quarter, Dixieland jazz, the Superdome, and even the greatest of all attractions in the city—Mardi Gras.

---

[14]Yuchey, p. 49.

EXHIBIT 11

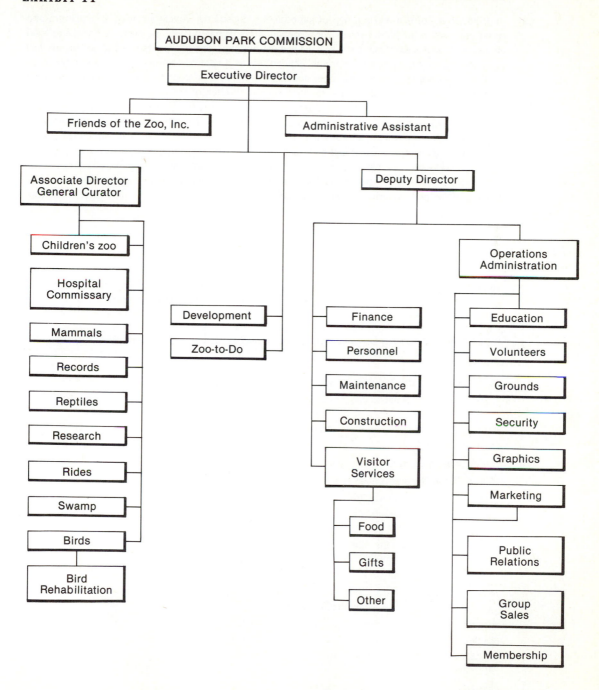

The New Orleans Aquarium

42   In 1986, Ron Forman and a group of supporters proposed the development of an aquarium and riverfront park to the New Orleans City Council. In November 1986, the electorate voted to fund an aquarium and a riverfront park by a 70 percent margin—one of the largest margins the city has ever given to any tax proposal. Forman[15] hailed this as a vote of confidence from the citizens, as well as a mandate to build a world-class aquarium that would produce new jobs, stimulate the local economy, and create an educational resource for the children of the city.

43   Even after the approval of the bond proposal by the voters, the New Orleans City Council had many decisions to make. Up for grabs was the management structure of the aquarium. Should it be placed within the same organization as the Audubon Zoo or under a separate structure? Where should the aquarium be located and how large should it be?

44   A feasibility study prepared by Harrison Price Company[16] projected a probable 863,000 visitors by the year 1990, with 75 percent of the visitors coming from outside the metropolitan area. The location of the new aquarium was to be adjacent to the Riverwalk, providing a logical pedestrian

---

EXHIBIT 12
Chronology of Events for the New Zoo

1972   The Audubon Zoological Society asked the Audubon Park Commission to institute an admission charge "in an amount sufficient to reduce the possibility of vandalism but not so great as to inhibit visits by family groups and less affluent members of the community" (*Times-Picayune,* April 29, 1972).

1973   The City Planning Commission approved a master plan for the Audubon Park Zoo calling for $3.4 million for upgrading. Later phases called for an additional $2.1 million to be completed by 1978.

1974   Friends of the Zoo formed, with 400 members, to increase support and awareness of zoo.

1975   Phase I renovations began—$25 million public and private funds—14 acres to be expanded to 58 acres.

1977   John Moore went to Albuquerque, Ron Forman took over as park and zoo director.

1978   Phase II began.

1980   Phase III began.

1980   First full-time education staff on duty at the zoo.

1980   Last animal removed from antiquated cage—a turning point in zoo history.

1981   Contract signed allowing New Orleans Steamboat Company to bring passengers from downtown to the park.

1981   Delegates from the American Association of Zoological Parks and Aquariums ranked the Audubon Zoo as one of the top three zoos of its size in America.

1981   Zoo accredited.

1982   The Audubon Park Commission reorganized under Act 352, which required the commission to contract with a nonprofit organization for the daily management of the park.

---

[15]*At the Zoo,* Winter 1987.

[16]Feasibility Analysis and Conceptual Planning for a Major Aquarium Attraction, prepared for the City of New Orleans, March 1985.

link for visitors between the New Orleans major attractions of the Riverwalk and the Jax Brewery, a shopping center in the French Quarter.

45   The aquarium would face major confrontations from several interest groups: riverfront developers, the Vieux Carre Commission (preservationists of the old French Quarter), the Dock Board (responsible for river front property usage), the National Park Service, and businesses from downtown and other parts of the City. Several of these groups argued that the proposed site was not safe from river accidents. One counterplan was for the aquarium to be located on the west bank of the Mississippi River. The west bank, while a part of metropolitan New Orleans, was accessible from downtown only by two major bridges and ferry boats. The east bank of the city contained the major tourist and visitor attractions of the French Quarter, Convention Center, Lakefront (Lake

EXHIBIT 13
Respondent Characteristics of Zoo Visitors According to Visitation Frequency (in percent)

	Number of Zoo Visits over Past Two Years			
Respondent Characteristic	Four or More	Two or Three	One or None	Never Visited Zoo
Age:				
Under 27	26%	35%	31%	9%
27 to 35	55	27	15	3
36 to 45	48	32	11	9
46 to 55	18	20	37	25
Over 55	27	29	30	14
Marital status:				
Married	41	28	20	11
Not married	30	34	24	13
Children at home:				
Yes	46	30	15	9
No	34	28	27	12
Interest in visiting the Orleans aquarium:				
Very, with emphasis	47	26	18	9
Very, without emphasis	45	24	23	12
Somewhat	28	37	14	11
Not too	19	32	27	22
Vote-intention on aquarium:				
For, with emphasis	46	33	16	5
For, without emphasis	39	31	16	14
Against or don't know	11	40	32	17
Member of FOTZ:				
Yes	67	24	5	4
No, but heard of it	35	30	24	12
No, and never heard of it	25	28	35	13
Would you be interested in joining FOTZ (nonmembers only):				
Very/somewhat	50	28	14	8
No/don't know	33	29	26	12

EXHIBIT 14
Relative Importance of Seven Reasons on Why Respondent Does not
Visit the Zoo More Often (in percent)

Reason (close-ended) Characteristic	Very Imp. w/ Emphasis	Very Imp. w/o Emphasis	Somewhat Important	Unimportant
The distance of the zoo's location from where you live	7%	11%	21%	60%
The *cost* of a zoo visit	4	8	22	66
Not being all that interested in zoo animals	2	12	18	67
The parking problem on weekends	7	11	19	62
The idea that you get tired of seeing the same exhibits over and over	5	18	28	49
It's too hot during the summer months	25	23	22	30
Just not having the idea occur to you	8	19	26	48

Pontchartrain) restaurants and lake facilities, the historic Garden District, and major shopping areas. A different downtown site was pushed by an opposing political group.

46   Meanwhile, the Audubon Zoo had its own future to plan. The new physical facilities and professional care paid off handsomely in increased attendance and new animal births. But the zoo could not expand at its existing location because of lack of land within the city. Forman and the zoo staff considered several alternatives. One was incorporating the new aquarium. Another was little "neighborhood" zoos to be located all over the city. A third was a separate breeding area to be located outside the city boundaries where land was available. With the zoo running smoothly, the staff seemed to need new challenges to tackle and the zoo needed new facilities or programs to continue to increase attendance.

REFERENCES

Beaulieu, Lovell. "It's All Happening at the Zoo." *The Times-Picayune,* Sunday January 28, 1978.

Ball, Millie. "The New Zoo of '82." *Dixie Magazine, Sunday Times-Picayune,* June 24, 1979.

Brooks, Steve. "Don't Say "No Can Do" to Audubon Zoo Chief." *Jefferson Business,* May 5, 1986.

Bureau of Governmental Research, City of New Orleans. *"Audubon Park Zoo Study, Part I, Zoo Improvement Plan," August 1971.* New Orleans: Bureau of Governmental Research.

Bureau of Governmental Research, City of New Orleans. *Audubon Park Zoo Study, Part II, An Operational Analysis, August 1971.* New Orleans: Bureau of Governmental Research.

Donovan, S. "The Audubon Zoo: A Dream Come True." *New Orleans,* May 1986, pp. 52–66.

Feasibility Analysis and Conceptual Planning for a Major Aquarium Attraction, prepared for the City of New Orleans, March 1985.

Forman, R.; J. Logsdon; and J. Wilds. *Audubon Park: An Urban Eden*. New Orleans: The Friends of the Zoo, 1985.

Poole, Susan. *Frommer's 1983–84 Guide to New Orleans*. New York: Simon & Schuster, 1983.

Sausmann, K., ed. *Zoological Park and Aquarium Fundamentals*. Wheeling, W.V.: American Association of Zoological Parks and Aquariums, 1982.

Yuchey, R. "No Longer Is Heard a Discouraging Word at the Audubon Zoo." *New Orleans,* August 1980, pp. 49–60.

Zuckerman, S., ed. *Great Zoos of the World*. Colorado: Westview Press, 1980.

CASE 8

CHAPARRAL STEEL

COMPANY HISTORY

1   In 1973, Texas Industries, Inc., of Dallas, also known as TXI, a construction materials (cement, aggregates, and concrete products) company, and Co-Steel International Ltd., of Canada determined to build a steel mill as a joint venture. The initial attraction of a small town, 25 miles south of Dallas, to the constructors of a steel "mini-mill" was its promixity to a major population center, large power supplies, highways, and railroads. At the time, Midlothian, Texas, seemed an unlikely choice, but, as the story goes, Co-Steel chairman Gerald Heffernan saw a Midlothian Chamber of Commerce bulletin board notice which read, "Need money? Try working," and he was finally convinced that they had found the sought-after site for the new mill. The farm and ranch lands in the area are peopled with a hardworking stock deeply embued with the work ethic that management was seeking. Few of the locals had ever worked in a steel mill, and, as one manager observed, "We didn't want people who had learned bad work habits."

2   TXI's decision to start its own steel company sprang rather naturally from its building materials business, since steel reinforcement is required in so much of construction. Forecasting a reinforcing bar shortage that never developed, the new TXI venture, christened Chaparral Steel Company, had its initial steel production greeted by a glut in the rebar market. Observed one member of Chaparral's top management: "We had to diversify, and fast." Fortunately for the new manufacturer, flexibility, a trait that has virtually eluded domestic "Big Steel" firms, is one of the drawing cards within the mini-mill segment of the steel industry. Unlike the bigger, more complex "integrated" mills, the mini-mills are basically recycling plants, albeit technologically sophisticated ones. Having scaled-down operations and including fewer steps in the manufacturing process provides the mini-mill with significantly more margin for error and, therefore, more flexibility than exists in the typical integrated mill.

3   The town of Midlothian (current pop. 3,219) has achieved no small degree of acclaim as the setting for a very successful player in the nation's steel industry. Indeed, Chaparral has proven it possible to be profitable and competitive in an industry facing perhaps the most difficult period in its history. For example, when U.S. Steel (now USX) lost $2.5 billion in 1982, Chaparral had a profit of $11 million. While USX was losing $1.8 billion in 1986, the Midlothian enterprise earned $8.9 million on $297 million sales for its parent, TXI, which became the 100 percent owner in November 1985. This represented 46 percent of TXI's $648 million sales and 40 percent of its net profits of $22.1 million in fiscal 1986, ended May 31. Last fiscal year, Chaparral produced and shipped a company record of over 1.2 million tons of steel, and, for the first time, over half of TXI's sales were represented by Chaparral. In excess of $318 million of TXI's $589 million sales were produced by the steel subsidiary. Pursuing market share amid its efforts to be the low-cost producer in the marketplace, Chaparral, in fiscal 1987, produced and sold more tonnage in a greater

This case was prepared by John W. Simmons and Mark Kroll, both of the Department of Management and Marketing, University of Texas at Tyler.

variety and over a wider geographic market than in any previous year. This record production was achieved in the face of what TXI's president and CEO Robert D. Rogers (referring to Texas and surrounding states, TXI's locus of operations) called "the most stagnant economic growth since before Texas Industries was founded in 1951." In his letter to shareholders, dated July 15, 1987, Rogers announced that initial shipments of steel were made that same month to Western Europe and noted that Chaparral's impressive results were accomplished in "only an average market for structural products and a declining market during the year for bar products." Chaparral is one of the most productive steel firms in the world in terms of labor, and it is the nation's 10th largest steelmaker, providing steel products to 44 states, Canada, and now Western Europe. The firm has been the only U.S. mini-mill to lower costs enough to make a profit in foreign markets. Efforts have also been made to crack the Japanese market, with a 1988 target date having been set.

4   Since the first day of operations, May 5, 1975, Chaparral has used unorthodox managerial methods to achieve and maintain its competitiveness. According to Tom Peters: "If you wrote down the 10 most widely believed principles about managing in this century, you would find that Chaparral violates every one of them." Peters, one of the authors of *In Search of Excellence,* writes that some business savants consider Gordon Forward, Chaparral's president and CEO, to be "the most advanced thinker in American management today." Notwithstanding such hyperbole, the Midlothian steel firm is ever-watchful of its competitive environment and looks to the future, rather than resting on its impressive early accomplishments. Noting that this 10th largest U.S. steel producer is "one of the few profitable ones," Peters explains that Forward manages his firm "more as a laboratory than as a factory." Forward, a native of Canada, armed with a Ph.D. in metallurgy from M.I.T. and a healthy distaste for the traditional inefficiencies of Big Steel, has directed his company with managerial acumen, perceptive marketing, and a drive toward technological innovation. Company executives credit Chaparral's success to three major areas of concentration: "a marketing strategy sympathetic to customer needs, an insatiable thirst for technological improvement, and, perhaps, most significantly, the application of participatory management techniques that encourage employee creativity."

5   At start-up in 1975, Chaparral operated with only the basics of a mini-mill plant: a single electric arc furnace, a continuous billet caster, and a rolling mill, with an annual capacity of just over 400,000 tons. By 1978, the firm was a leader in mini-mill technology. From 1978 to 1981, Chaparral earned an average of $18 million per year pretax. Again, this was at a time when the U.S. steel industry as a whole was in the doldrums. Early in 1982, Chaparral's second phase of expansion brought on-line a second electric arc furnace, another continuous billet caster, and a larger rolling mill. This $180 million, largely debt-financed, expansion could not have become operational at a worse time, paralleling the start of the worst steel recession in 50 years. Steel prices tumbled 20–50 percent, the industry's operating rate fell below 40 percent of capacity, and much of Chaparral's debt, at floating rates, floated to the outer reaches of the biosphere. Fueled by high interest rates, the dollar climbed to new heights, imported steel flooded domestic markets, and Chaparral, due to merciless economic conditions, faced losses between 1982 and 1984, returning to profitability in mid-1985. Maintaining a long-term vision of its industry, the highly automated mini-mill tripled its annual capacity between 1982 and 1987. Richard T. Jaffre, VP–Raw Materials, expects the firm to complete its current new product development program by 1988, a time when plant capacity should reach an estimated 1.4 million tons.

6   From the outset, TXI and Co-Steel wanted to build the most modern mini-mill that they possibly could. Not suffering from the myopia that has diminished Big Steel, Chaparral has changed and grown constantly, if only in incremental steps. The attitude at TXI and Chaparral is that it is possible to make money in nongrowth industries if you are good enough. As a result of its vision and diligence, the Midlothian firm currently produces more tonnage than any U.S. steel mill constructed in the past 30 years. Although future growth in the mini-mill segment is expected to

slow somewhat from what it has been within the past decade or so, industry experts still see opportunities for additional mini-mill market growth. The "minis" are expected to retain an advantage because of lower raw material costs, utilization of new technology, efficient operation, plant location, perceptive marketing, flexible work rules, and consequent higher productivity; but saturated markets and cheap imports are forcing the mini-mills to continue seeking new ways to grow. Prior to 1982, Chaparral was a part of the much-publicized mini-mill phenomenon; but the future holds ever-greater challenges. In 1985, four Sun Belt mini-mills closed their doors, and global overcapacity portends a continued threat of industry shake-out. Older, less technologically competent minis are particularly vulnerable. Producers of steel are differentiated nowadays mostly by price, product mix, and service. State-of-the-art technology is so accessible around the world that quality is no longer optional. The challenge which Chaparral has successfully faced in the past and will continue to face in the foreseeable future is to maintain its responsive managerial style, marketing sensitivity, and technological currency and consequent productivity gains. It appears that Chaparral is not striving to become the new Big Steel but rather desires to maintain its status as a highly competitive niche-player.

NATURE OF THE INDUSTRY

Big Steel

7   The term *Big Steel* generally refers to the large traditional "integrated" steel mills, so named because they have the capability of processing coke and iron ore into a number of steel products of a wide range of size and shape. Steel mill products are consumed by industries touching virtually every aspect of daily life, principally transportation, construction, machinery, and containers. Prior to 1970, the United States was still the world's leading steel producer; but, by that time, the domestic steel industry had been declining for over 20 years. Most U.S. steel mills were of pre-World War II vintage; and, despite periodic renovation, the mills lacked the efficient layouts, the economies of scale, and the more productive technologies utilized in the "greenfield" mills of Japan and Western Europe. As Big Steel U.S.A. became less cost-efficient, the competitive foreign producers became more cost-efficient; and as Big Steel U.S.A. became less price-competitive in domestic and world markets, their market-astute foreign rivals were only too happy to compete on the basis of price.

8   After World War II, domestic steel negotiations with the United Steelworkers began an upward spiral of wage rates disproportionate to the growth of labor productivity, thereby increasing unit labor costs. Wishing to reduce escalating wage increases, which averaged 6.6 percent annually between 1947–57, a period of relatively low inflation, Big Steel accepted a long strike (July–November 1959). Foreign producers consequently filled the gap, and the United States became a net importer of steel in 1959. Imports grew to an average 15 percent of consumption in the 1970s, 19 percent in 1981, and over 20 percent in 1982.

9   The world steel industry was becoming much more competitive and internationalized as world exports of finished steel products increased dramatically during the 1960s, prompted by declining raw material and shipping costs, and powered by foreign investment in modern facilities. U.S. steel exports tumbled as Japanese and Western European exports skyrocketed. State-of-the-art technology became available to any producer willing to pay for it, and product quality became essentially uniform across geopolitical boundaries. During the 1970s, domestic steel production grew only modestly, profits remained depressed as competition from imports grew, and, as a result,

the U.S. industry's ability to add new capacity was severely constrained. Domestic industry employment began a steady decline in 1972 and, in 1982, reached the lowest levels since data collection began during the Great Depression. The industry employment roster shrank from 500,000 in 1975 to fewer than 200,000 in 1987. This decline included a drop from 453,000 in 1979 to 247,000 at the end of 1982, a fall of 45 percent in three years.

10   In March 1982, testifying before the U.S. Senate, Dr. Donald F. Barnett, speaking for the American Iron and Steel Institute (AISI) regarding international competitiveness in the domestic steel industry, stated:

11   Perhaps the most significant determinant of international competitiveness is labor productivity. Companies and industries compete directly in terms of price and cost. Labor productivity is one important factor affecting costs. However, even if labor productivity is low, a product can still be competitive if there are other compensating advantages, e.g., lower labor rates as persist in many developing countries. Alternately, an investment which raises productivity can actually decrease cost competitiveness, if the capital cost of the investment outweighs the labor savings. Hence, improved labor productivity cannot be the ultimate goal in and of itself. International competitiveness in the steel industry, therefore, must also look at capital efficiency, e.g., capacity use, labor costs, raw material costs, yield rates, and energy efficiency . . . (U.S. Dept. of Commerce, 1983).

12   Other factors which determine industry competitiveness include regulatory costs and materials availability. According to the AISI, the domestic integrated mills have increased their productivity in the last decade considerably vis-à-vis the Japanese mills (see Table 1). By 1986, AISI reported that the U.S. steel industry had become the most efficient in the world. Generally speaking, while the domestic steel industry is competitive in energy and materials costs and use, it is less competitive in terms of labor costs and productivity, compared to foreign competitors.

13   In 1982, the U.S. steel industry lost a record $3.2 billion. By mid-1987, the industry's operating losses had amounted to $6 billion. However, the integrated mills were attempting to respond to the changing market conditions, as indicated by improved productivity rates. The big mills have gradually improved their marketing techniques by specializing in limited ranges of higher-quality, cost-competitive products. In a word, the Big Steel firms are no longer able to function as steel "supermarkets." The emphasis in recent years has been on "restructuring," what one industry executive referred to as "a state of accelerating self-liquidation." Yet, the "great shake-out" has had a positive side—that is, corporate reorganizations, steel unit spinoffs, forced mergers, management or employee buyouts, and Chapter 11 bankruptcies have required firms to pare costs and exit from unprofitable markets. In 1987, the domestic integrated mills began to emerge from this period of price-war activity, as the dollar declined in relation to other currencies prices firmed for the first time in years, earnings improved amid productivity gains, and export activity began awakening.

14   The hard times which domestic steel has been facing have many causes, including: poor management, labor squabbles, obsolete technology, foreign competition, and such product substitutes as aluminum and fiber-reinforced plastics. The growth of U.S. production is projected to remain relatively low, due to trends in consumption and output. Projections of world steel production indicate a continuing malaise in the industrialized nations, contrasted with rapid growth in the developing countries. Steel production capacity, by one estimate, is expected to have increased by 20 percent in developing countries and to have eroded by 3 percent in the United States by the year 1990. The stock market crash of October 19, 1987, occurred just as the moribund steel industry was reviving. Despite the 33 percent drop in steel stocks, analysts predict sharp increases in earnings, due to a falling dollar and steel import quotas legislated through September 1989. Despite recent difficulties in earning, attracting, and borrowing sufficient investment capital, the domestic integrated firms have retained a large share of the U.S. market.

TABLE 1
Average Man-Hours to Produce One Ton of Steel

	1977	1986
U.S. integrated mills	10.04	6.91
Japanese integrated mills	8.94	8.61
U.S. mini-mills	—	2.00
Chaparral	—	1.60

15   Many of the U.S. Big Steel's problems can be attributed to their own sluggishness and complacency in technology and marketing matters, but the problems of integrated mills are proving to be somewhat systematic as the industries in Japan and Europe have begun to face problems similar to their American counterparts. As Barnett foresaw, developing countries are entering the steel industry with relative ease and success, and some experts doubt whether the large, inflexible integrated mills will survive the 20th century.

Mini-Mills

16   The steel industry can be divided into three segments of different economic and technical profiles: the integrated mills, the mini-mills, and the specialty steel mills. One authority makes a distinction between the traditional major mills (USX, Bethlehem, Inland, National, and Armco) and the restructured/restructuring mills (LTV, Wheeling-Pittsburgh, Weirton). Domestically, the minis are the chief competitors of the integrated mills. The specialty steel mills account for only 5 percent of U.S. output, but they manufacture much more expensive products than do the minis and account for a much higher percentage of total revenues. The minis and specialty steel mills have avoided the worst of the recent industry turmoil, but it is the mini-mills that are expected to make the greatest gains in the domestic market into the 1990s, at the expense of the integrated mills.

17   The mini-mill concept was relatively slow in arriving in the United States. The method had thrived in Japan and Western Europe for over 20 years when Chaparral was founded as one of the U.S. first operations of the kind in 1973. Interestingly, North America's first mini-mill was established in Canada in 1962 by a former manager of Co-Steel, the Canadian holding company that played a seminal role in the creation of Chaparral. Unlike Big Steel, the mini-mills hungrily await new technological developments globally, which they can then adapt to suit their individual purpose. Consequently, since the 1960s, when 10–12 mini-mills shared roughly 2 percent of the domestic steel market, the number of domestic mini-mills is now around 55, with a market share just over 20 percent.

18   The mini-mill segment has been able to remain relatively profitable by restricting product range and, therefore, the level of capitalization required, by utilizing locally generated scrap and, thereby, lowering transportation costs, and by marketing in the vicinity of the mill. The mini-mills have typically concentrated on relatively high-volume, low-cost steels. To increase productivity, the minis have relied on innovative processing technology, much of which comes from abroad. In addition, such firms as Chaparral, Nucor, and Birmingham Steel have much lower base wage rates but provide generous bonus programs for high levels of team productivity.

19   In contrast, the specialty steel industry has typically developed its new technologies in-house. Whereas the specialty steel mill invests in its own R&D and the integrated mill is constrained by relatively larger capital investment requirements and must work under restrictive, union labor contracts. The mini-mill is more able to invest capital in new technology, and by so doing, the

mini-mills have recaptured markets that Big Steel had abandoned to imports. The significance of potential foreign competition in the mini-mill segment is mitigated by the dominant role played by transportation costs. On this topic, Gordon Forward has said of Chaparral:

20   We adopt certain goals. In our beams, for instance, the Koreans are the most efficient producers. So we just adapt so that we will have a lower labor content than the shipping costs of beams from Korea to the West Coast. If they have zero labor costs, we'll still have a competitive advantage.

Furthermore, as mentioned earlier, the minis have the advantage of relatively low raw material costs and flexible work rules.

21   The "mini-mill" is so-named not so much because it is small, but because its operations entail only a part of the integrated steelmaking process. See Exhibit 1. The mini-mill avoids almost entirely the integrated mill's energy- and capital-intensive "front end" of steelmaking—that is, the iron-smelting process, including the mining and preparation of raw materials and the blast-furnace operation. The mini-mill begins with steel scrap, flux, and occasionally directly-reduced iron. The scrap is melted in an electric furnace, poured into ladles, and then transferred to a continuous-casting machine. Continuous casting is the casting of billets, blooms, or slabs directly from the molten steel. The success of domestic minis is due in part to the use of continuous billet-casting, which has been standard practice in minis since around 1970 and which increases yield 18 percent over ingot casting, common to conventional steel mills. Only about half of the domestic integrated mills utilize continuous casters. Continuing to emphasize innovation, Chaparral has a recently commissioned horizontal casting machine expected to come on line in 1988, which should add materially to productivity. See Exhibit 2.

22   Recycling scrap, or the processing of secondary materials, results in less waste and reduces overall raw materials requirements. All three segments of the domestic industry use scrap to one degree or another, but only the mini-mills are almost wholly dependent on it. The United States was estimated to have had a scrap inventory of 620 billion metric tons in 1982, and, with annual accumulations, supply is expected to meet demand for at least several decades. Chaparral processes some 300,000 cars per year, or one every 20 seconds, and this provides roughly 30 percent of the firm's raw material. The use of steel substitutes (plastic, and the like) in automobiles is cause for some concern in the industry, but Forward maintains a sense of humor:

23   There is a possibility we may have to go back to an iron ore base some day. For the moment, however, we are all right. We keep on importing Toyotas, which have a seven-year life. It takes us seven years to get a new Toyota into our furnace.

In the meantime, there is what some call a "ubiquitous availability" of domestically generated scrap. Another dimension of the problem concerns the impurity content of the scrap, which prevents production of certain high-quality grades of steel.

24   The mini-mill products of the recent past have been simple and limited in variety. They have included wire rods, reinforcing rods, and various bar products. The bar forms, classified by cross-sectional shape, include flats, rounds, and squares. Mini-mills may also manufacture light I beams, T beams, angles (with 90 degree cross section), and channels (with a shallow "U" in cross section). A product is a light section if the longest part of a shape viewed in cross section is 75mm or less; a heavy section measures greater than 75mm. Merchant bars are bars made of carbon steel and rolled hot. An alloy steel is made when small amounts of manganese, chromium, nickel, and so on, singly or in combination, are added to the melt. A product made increasingly by mini-mills is termed SBQ (special bar quality) grade. Recently, mini-mills have been venturing into lines of higher-grade products. These items are mainly for the construction industry, but Chaparral and other minis also sell such products to the automakers.

EXHIBIT 1

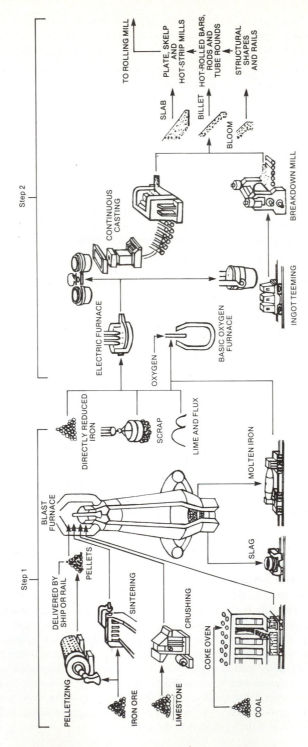

Note: Integrated steel mills produce steel using both steps 1 and 2; beginning with iron ore, coal, and limestone, they go through most of the steps presented here. Mini-mills use scrap as their raw material, and complete step 2, using either an electric furnace or a basic-oxygen furnace. Most recently built mini-mills use an electric furnace and continuous-casting technology.

EXHIBIT 2
Horizontal Continuous Caster, Baltimore Works, Armco.

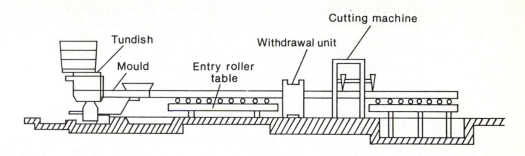

EXHIBIT 3
Mini-Mill Sites in the United States

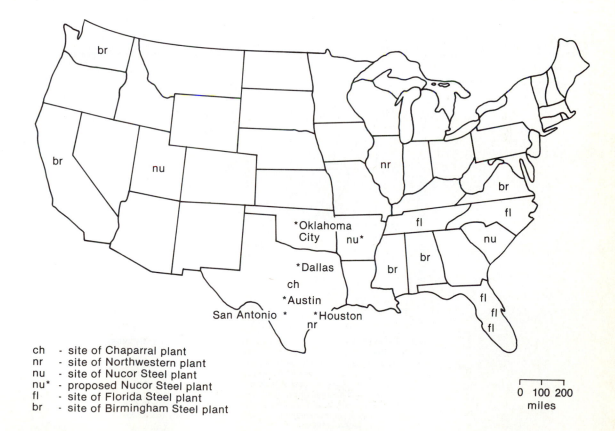

ch - site of Chaparral plant
nr - site of Northwestern plant
nu - site of Nucor Steel plant
nu* - proposed Nucor Steel plant
fl - site of Florida Steel plant
br - site of Birmingham Steel plant

0 100 200
miles

25   Steel sheet and large structural girders have long been the mainstay of integrated steelmakers and out of the province of the minis. Until now, mini-mills haven't been able to manufacture sheet, but Nucor Corporation, the most successful of the minis, is building a sheet mill that will use a new technology to make sheet in mini-mill quantities and of mini-mill thicknesses. Furthermore, Nucor, which already owns a number of mini-mills, has announced a joint venture with Yamato Kogyo Company, a large Japanese steelmaker, to build a mill in Arkansas that will manufacture large structural girders. Similarly, Chaparral has voiced an interest in buying or building a plant that can turn out large structural beams. With continued adaptation of new technologies, the mini-mill segment of the industry is expected to continue to increase market share at the expense of the less efficient, older mills. Estimates for the mini-mill share a range as high as 40% of domestic output by the end of the century. The locations of many of the larger mini-mills are presented in Exhibit 3.

26   Clearly, mini-mills have natural cost advantages over the integrated mills. Indeed, minis are sometimes referred to as "money-mills." The capital cost of building an integrated plant is approximately $1,600 per ton of annual capacity, whereas for a mini-mill it is only $200–300. The capital outlay for an integrated steel plant can easily approach several billion dollars. As mentioned, the man-hours per ton are also substantially different (Table 1). Likewise, raw materials costs and energy costs favor the minis. For a comparison of mini-mill and integrated steel mill cost structures, see Exhibit 4.

EXHIBIT 4
Comparison of Cost Structures

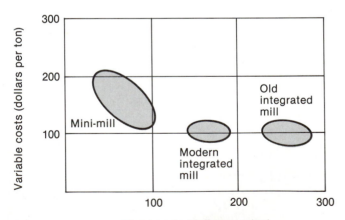

Note: Typical range of costs per ton of annual capacity for an old integrated mill, a modern integrated mill, and a mini-mill can be expressed in terms of fixed and variable costs. Fixed costs are expenditures for such items as capital, manpower, and maintenance, which do not vary significantly once a plant is operating. Variable costs include expenditures for raw materials, other supplies, and energy, which may change from year to year. Since mini-mills do not have to wait as long as integrated mills to recoup the investment in setting up operations, they can consider replacing old equipment with new sooner. (1984)

CHAPARRAL MANAGEMENT

Robert D. Rogers, President and CEO, TXI

27 Robert Rogers, a graduate of Yale and of Harvard Business School, has been with TXI for 25 years. Rogers, a TXI director since 1970, is chairman of the board for the Dallas Chamber of Commerce, the immediate past chairman of the 11th Federal Reserve District, and has numerous additional professional and community associations. Another TXI director, Edward W. Kelley, Jr., went to the Board of Governors of the Federal Reserve System in 1987.

28 In an interview, Rogers reflected back on the unlikely success of an upstart company in a declining steel industry:

29 We went into the carbon steel business when everyone else was going out of it. The biggest advantage we had was that we didn't have any plant, didn't have any customers, didn't have any employees or management, and we didn't really know anything about how to make steel. We're still learning. Once we learn it, we're going to be in big trouble.

30 Pondering further the benefit of being the new kid on the block, Rogers observed:

31 If we would have known the steel business, we would have known that the only way you could go forth with a company of any size would be to be unionized. Not knowing the steel business and being the largest nonunion cement company in the United States, we felt it was far better to represent the legitimate interests of employees ourselves rather than turn it over to some outside partner.

32 Concluding his remarks on Chaparral's unorthodox approach, Rogers said:

33 Another thing was to hire employees who by and large did not come from industrial backgrounds. They came from rural backgrounds. The steel plant is next door to our largest cement plant and we have the same type of employees there. We knew they were hard-working and imaginative, so they didn't know

TABLE 2
Selected Financial Data, TXI and Subsidiaries
(dollars in thousands, except for per share)

	1987	1986	1985	1984	1983	1982	1981	1980
Results of operations:								
Net sales	589,061	648,230	343,688	335,381	321,468	282,713	285,003	278,114
Net income	1,253	22,114	17,597	12,300	18,691	18,332	30,411	41,400
Return on common equity	0.6%	11.9%	9.9%	7.2%	11.4%	11.9%	22.4%	38.9%
Per share information:								
Net income (primary)	—	2.35	2.01	1.37	2.08	2.04	3.35	4.61
Cash dividends	0.80	0.76	0.73	0.70	0.67	0.64	0.62	0.50
Stock dividends and distributions	4%	4%	4%	4%	4%	4%	4%	4%
Other information:								
Average common shares outstanding (000s)	9,653	9.206	8.725	8,928	8,941	8,980	9,064	8,995
Number of common stockholders	5,975	5,508	5,811	6,111	6,286	6,605	6,785	6,892
Common stock prices (high-low)	33–23	32–24	30–22	40–26	38–16	32–14	32–19	19–12

TABLE 3
TXI Business Segment Information (dollars in thousands)

	1987	1986	1985
Net sales:			
Concrete products	$270,639	$351,357	$343,688
Steel	318,422	296,873	—
Total	589,061	648,230	343,688
Operating profit:			
Concrete products	14,104	32,520	37,755
Steel	42,467	37,089	—
Total	56,571	69,609	37,755
Corporate expense (income):			
Administrative and general	17,162	14,836	12,174
Interest expense	38,740	41,880	15,505
Other income	(2,262)	(14,107)	(11,441)
Income before taxes and other items	2,931	27,000	21,517
Depreciation, depletion, and amortization:			
Concrete products	31,347	33,321	30,948
Steel	23,317	22,434	—
Corporate	760	789	710
Total	55,424	56,444	31,658
Capital expenditures:			
Concrete products	14,475	40,969	33,868
Steel	14,228	7,019	—
Corporate	403	573	1,245
Total	29,106	48,561	35,113
Identifiable assets:			
Concrete products	299,874	323,510	324,196
Steel	310,063	298,666	—
Corporate	68,836	86,607	90,611
Total	678,773	708,783	414,807

you were supposed to spend three to four man-hours per ton of steel. When we got to 1.8 or 1.6 and were working to get down substantially less than that, they didn't know that there's a limit on how many tons of steel you can get per man-hour.

34   Despite recent economic setbacks for TXI as a whole, Chaparral remains strong and is moving forward, and Rogers and the TXI board of directors are still planning for the long term. Fiscal 1987 was the 25th consecutive year of increased cash dividends to TXI shareholders. Not withstanding the virtual absence of earnings, due in large part to the regional construction slump and the dumping in TXI markets of imported cement, the directors maintained cash dividends at the annual rate of $0.80 per year, with a year-end stock dividend of 4 percent (see Tables 2 and 3).

Texas Industries, Inc., Board of Directors

35   The TXI board provides a wealth of educational, professional, and cultural experience. Past and present directors have served as university trustees and in other capacities of institutional leadership. Co-Steel chairman Heffernan, who is involved with several Canadian mining and metallurgical

professional groups, has been a TXI director since 1986. Ian Wachtmeister, a director since 1977, is chairman and CEO of a Swedish industrial corporation and is involved with various Swedish professional organizations. All of the board members are involved in community activities to one degree or another and most have other corporate affiliations. Director Ralph B. Rogers, TXI's founder and chairman of the board, is credited with providing the vision and values which have inspired the company.

Gordon E. Forward, President and CEO, Chaparral Steel Company

36   Gordon Forward is described as the architect of the winning Chaparral formula and has received from various quarters, the lion's share of credit for making the formula a success. After leaving a successful career with Big Steel, Forward has come up through the ranks of the mini-mill industry and has displayed a great willingness to undertake managerial experiments. Forward claims the legendary Captain Bill "Scrap Heap" Jones, a 19th-century steel mill superintendent, is a role model for his approach. Of Jones, Forward says:

37   If there was a better machine to do a job, the old one went quickly on the scrap heap. He also fought for his men's welfare and inspired them to set world steel production records. And they loved him for it. I think the industry ought to take a new look at Capt. Jones' ideas.

38   The operating philosophy at Chaparral of concentrating on technological improvement, marketing, and participatory management emerged as early as 1974.

39   Forward, a native of Vancouver, B.C., has been referred to as "a refugee from Big Steel bureaucracy." He was hired as Chaparral's executive vice president in 1974. A vocal critic of the stagnated domestic steel industry, Forward, in an interview, remarked:

40   U.S. steel producers had no real competition after the war. Every time the unions demanded more wages or whatever, the managers said, "Fine, we'll simply pass the costs on to the consumer." Well, this went on for more than 20 years and had a real effect on how managers thought about staying on top technologically. . . . Of course, they spent money on improvement. But they went about it the way that bureaucracies are likely to go about something like that: they kept tacking new things on to their established operations.

41   As steel labor costs rose in the 1970s, the mini-mills, quickly adopting foreign technological improvements, were able to seize new markets, and Chaparral was a leader of the pack. Says Forward: "In our end of the business, we can't afford to act like fat cats."

THE CHAPARRAL WAY OF RUNNING A PROFITABLE BUSINESS

Technological Currency

42   A scientist by training, Forward views his mill as a laboratory and encourages experimentation. Saying that research is too often mistakenly isolated as a staff position, Forward explains:

43   We've tried to bring research right into the factory and make it a line function. We make the people who are producing the steel responsible for keeping their process on the leading edge of technology worldwide. If they have to travel, they travel. If they have to figure out what the next step is, they go out and find the places where people are doing interesting things. They visit other companies. They work with universities.

44   According to the AISI, the integrated steel industry spends an average of 4–7 percent of annual sales on modernizing plant and equipment. Chaparral, by contrast, spends 15 percent. As a matter of policy, the Midlothian firm has an annual summer shutdown to make other necessary capital improvements. Having labor costs at 9–10 percent of sales, compared with an integrated steel industry average of 40 percent, is another factor that makes technology funding an easier task for Chaparral.

45   Chaparral has fought to maintain a work environment that nourishes people, innovation, and accomplishment. The total involvement of the work force is critical, because, as one writer notes:

46   This is really the heart of the matter, because high tech is something people create, implement, and maintain. You can't just go out and buy it. Bodies and dollar bills aren't enough. Big Steel went out and hired thousands of researchers, industrial engineers, corporate planners, and staff specialists and the world still passed them by.

47   What are typically staff functions at other mills are dovetailed with line functions at Chaparral. For example:

48   When there's a need for new production equipment, a line manager is put in charge of the entire project, including conceptual design, budgeting, purchasing, construction, installation, and start-up. Maintenance people are also included in the conceptual design stage, with the result that the equipment is easier to maintain. We've found that when forces shaping the design come from our production managers—when their egos get hooked—the odds of success are greatly enhanced. They make it work.

49   People who are involved in the decision process are more likely to be committed to the decision when reached.

50   Naturally, computers are a major technology which any efficient steel mill will utilize. According to Richard Jaffre, VP–Raw Materials, Chaparral uses computers in "planning, forecasting, inventory management, control of receipts, control of purchase orders, issuance of purchase orders, extensions, payables . . . the whole nine yards." Because the Chaparral operation consumes 100 million tons of junk automobiles, refrigerators, stoves, and so on, per year, Jaffre notes that the computers are most useful as repositories of historical cost-trend information. Like most firms, Chaparral tries to minimize its investment of cash in inventory, but the mini-mill must buy many lots of scrap, and frequently; therefore, observes Jaffre: "We're bound by the market." In conclusion, Jaffre states: ". . . in the main, the computer is for short-term, medium- and long-term planning. It's the data base for our formal planning—the corporate financial forecast, done typically once a year with quarterly updates." The firm not only relies on a talented, motivated work force but also on its investment in sophisticated computerized systems and production facilities.

Market Responsiveness

51   In 1987, Gordon Forward set forth Chaparral's marketing goal: to become the "easiest steel company to buy from." The strategy for accomplishing that objective is to provide service by developing new products, raising quality levels, and extending shipping capabilities. Flexibility and responsiveness to changing customer needs is key. As a recent example, Forward recalls how the company quality control department introduced a micro-alloy steel production capability and began marketing the resultant product in an unconventional way and, thereby, expanded the firm's SBQ customer base. As an additional service, Chaparral customers have full access to the marketing and quality control departments. Furthermore, the Midlothian firm offers flexible rolling schedules and newly developed remote shipping points.

52   The classic mini-mill concept is grounded in the strategy of locating where the mill can take advantage of locally available markets and sources of labor and scrap. Subcategories of mini-mills include the "neighborhood mill," the strategy of which is to locate in an area where the demand for steel is expected to grow; and the "market mill," which concentrates on one or two specific products to meet a given market. When Chaparral began operations 13 years ago, it was essentially a market mill, producing rebar for the regional construction market. Jaffre, noting that domestic and global mini-mill capacity was being overbuilt in the late 1970s, has written:

53   It became clear that if Chaparral was to continue to prosper and grow, we had to rethink our place in the market. From the beginning, our focus has always been on steel. We had no interest in diversifying into oil, insurance, or whatever. We believe the steel business can and should be both profitable and fun. So, in 1979, Chaparral decided that our primary opportunity for growth was to expand our product mix and transcend the traditional mini-mill size range (structural shapes up to six inches in cross-section). The problem with this strategy is that the cost of building a facility for larger shapes can flatten a mini-mill's wallet. The price of steel mill equipment tends to rise exponentially with the cross-sectional dimensions of its products.

54   Nevertheless, the perception of Chaparral as a market mill persisted at least through the mid-1980s, but a recent comment by Forward is quite revealing in this respect:

55   Although Chaparral is classified as a mini-mill, this year we began producing a range of steels traditionally supplied only by larger, integrated steel mills. And when the recently commissioned horizontal casting machine comes on line in 1988, Chaparral will have even greater opportunities to serve customers more completely.

56   Indeed, the horizontal caster is expected to facilitate getting Chaparral down to "micro-mill" size. Rejecting the prospect of making the Midlothian plant bigger or increasing its 950-member employee roster, Forward asserts that his firm is steadfast in its intent to remain relatively flat organizationally, acknowledging that small is better in today's steel industry. After looking hard at microtechnology and studying how McDonald's does what it does, Forward claims: "We figured out how to build something small enough you could literally put it on a barge and run it with only 40 people." Says Forward: "We could almost franchise it."

Participatory Management

57   During the 1970s, U.S. Steel had as many as 11 layers of management. A key Chaparral decision was to create only four layers. U.S. Steel subsequently "evolved down" to four layers. Decision making at Chaparral is forced down to the shop floor, where the actual production takes place. It has been said of Gordon Forward that he is "a man of many slogans," including: "Participatory management means taking decision making to the lowest competent level—and making the lowest level competent." Says Chaparral's CEO: "We believe that people want to work and do a good job if you give them some responsibility and reward them with more than a paycheck." Chaparral's pioneering participatory management strategies appear to bear fruit for the firm as well as the employees. A clear indication is the fact that a 1977 attempt by the United Steelworkers of America to unionize the mill was soundly rejected by 73 percent out of the 98 percent of the work force voting. A former worker at U.S. Steel's South Works mill in Chicago was quoted as saying: "At the other mill I was stuck in a craft line. I couldn't help somebody in a different job, and he couldn't help me. That was because of the union. Here we do what we have to do to get the job done."

58   Described by some in the business literature as a "maverick mini-mill," the "us" versus "them" mentality that haunts so many of the older mills is largely absent from the Midlothian firm. Rather than "steelworkers," some employees prefer to refer to themselves as "Chaparral people." One business reporter, amazed by the enthusiasm of Chaparral employees ("In the fall of 1984, when the steel business was still in a slump, these people were having fun making steel!"), lamented her earlier reportage being perhaps too exuberant:

59   This company is so exciting that it is about unbelievable. Everything I want to say about them sounds corny, or exaggerated: that they give one hope for the future of North American-style capitalist democracies; that they have bested the Japanese in participatory management; that they have proven that the United States can compete with anyone if we take full advantage of our strengths and believe in our people; that they are bright, enthusiastic people dedicated to sustaining all this and continuing to move forward; that these very people believe that one should have fun at one's work.

60   After more circumspect analysis, the same reporter concluded that Chaparral is quite simply a people-oriented firm, whether dealing with employees or with customers.

61   The Chaparral work force is governed by an *esprit de corps* that is hospitable to risk taking and forgiving of setbacks. Although such incidents are not unique to Chaparral nor common there, one $15,000 mistake, which at a less dynamic firm might have cost the melt shop superintendent his job, has been stoically dubbed a "$15,000 paper-weight." Along these lines, the company has a no-layoff policy and claims never to have laid off an employee, not even during the difficult 1982–84 period. In fact, during that time, employees with construction skills were loaned to the construction of Chaparral's second mill, rather than bringing in outside builders and having to sack superfluous steelmakers.

62   Numerous other policies and programs distinguish Chaparral as a steelmaker. For instance, the seniority system, common at Big Steel mills, was never adopted at the Midlothian firm, and promotions are made based upon job performance. There are no time clocks to punch, and all Chaparral employees have been salaried since 1981. Furthermore, there are no assigned parking spots, no dress codes or color-coded hard hats, and no executive lunchroom. Claims one Chaparral manager: "We've eliminated every barrier to communication, every barrier to identification with management and company goals." Of Chaparral, Tom Peters writes:

63   Imagine a $300-million company where the vice president of administration fills in on the switchboard, where there are no formal personnel and purchasing departments, and no personal secretaries. There isn't much for secretaries to do because executives are discouraged from writing memos. For that matter, there aren't that many executives. (*On Achieving Excellence,* 1987)

64   Moreover, Peters declares, "You won't find a corporate organization chart like that in any business text." Team spirit is further promoted by the company-wide practice of communication on a first-name basis, decentralized offices, and the minimization of formalized meetings.

65   Although Chaparral workers have not been paid extravagant wages, job security and other benefits take up the slack. Bonuses and profit sharing were introduced from the start and together have run as high as 20 percent of wages. Management further shows its trust in labor by delegating to every member of the firm responsibility for quality control and sales, thus removing what they see in their company as two inessential managerial layers. Says Forward:

66   Everyone in the company pays attention to our customers. Everyone in the company is a member of the sales department. Literally. About four years ago, we made everyone in the company a member of the sales department. That means people in security, secretaries, everyone.

67   Actually, at Chaparral there is a conscious effort to "bash barriers between jobs." Security guards, for example, are paramedics, run the company ambulance, administer employee hearing tests, and enter safety and quality-control data in the computer. Foremen remain responsible for hiring, education, training, and benefits. To prevent employee burnout, Chaparral has a compulsory annual sabbatical program that permits people at the front-line supervisor level to visit other mills, customers, and so on for a period from two weeks to six months.

THE FUTURE OUTLOOK FOR CHAPARRAL

68   Asked if Chaparral would "swallow hard and scrap unamortized equipment and put in new technology—even if [the firm] didn't feel competition nipping at (its) heels," Forward responded:

69   Absolutely. We simply can't wait until we've been forced into a corner and have to fight back like alley cats. In our end of the business, we can't afford to act like fat cats. We have a system that's tough by its own definition. If we succeed in making our business less capital-intensive, we'd be naive not to expect a lot of others will want to get into it. If we succeed at what we are trying to do as a mini-mill, we'll also lower the price of entry. So we have to go like hell all the time. If the price of what we sell goes up too high, if we start making too much money on certain parts of our product line, all of a sudden lots of folks will be jumping in. And they can get into business in 18 months or so. They can hire our people away. They can wave all kinds of incentives under their noses—just as the new software companies do. This makes us our own worst enemy. We constantly chip away the ground we stand on. We have to keep out front all the time. Our advantages are the part of the industry we're in, but also the kind of organization we have. We have built a company that can move fast and that can run full out. We're not the only ones—there are others like us. Nucor does many of the same things, but it has a slightly different personality. And there's Florida Steel. There are a number of quality mini-mills. We are all a bit different, but we all have to run like hell. (*Harvard Business Review,* 1986)

70   And today's steel industry is increasingly dichotomized into two segments: the quick and the dead. Forward likens firms that don't utilize ever-improved technologies with Forest Lawn: "Not because there are no good ideas there, but because the good ideas are dying there all the time."

71   Observing that mini-mills are no longer very labor-intensive, Forward, taking a cue from Dr. Barnett, believes that the next big step for Chaparral is to use new technology to drastically cut energy use. Technological developments in the forging process are also receiving close scrutiny. Jaffre states that Chaparral maintains a competitive edge:

72   . . . by never forgetting the magnitude and strength of international competition; by maintaining our capacity to anticipate and manage change; by continuously developing our skills in the application of new technology and the service of our markets; by providing an environment that taps our greatest natural resource—our people.

73   Furthermore, Jaffre asserts that Chaparral has aggressively chosen not to be a part of any "deindustrialization" but rather to be a forceful player in the new "industrial renaissance."

74   The question before Chaparral management now is: "How do we grow in the future?" Do they keep expanding the Texas facility or expand into a new area and attempt to duplicate their success? With the opening of the Nucor plant in Arkansas, obviously the competition in both the structural steel and scrap markets in the North Texas, Eastern Oklahoma, Arkansas area will heat up. This is especially true given the reopening of a Houston plant by Northwestern Steel. The regional market may be reaching saturation with these additions.

75   On the other hand, with the dollar declining against other major currencies, both a greater share of the domestic market and export opportunities will be expanding. For all of these reasons, the possibility of a new mill will have to be addressed. Problems may develop if Chaparral continues expanding the present plant. The firm will have to go further and further for scrap. More important, Chaparral's management feels that their success formula is susceptible to diseconomies of scale. As Forward has pointed out, small is beautiful in terms of the Chaparral formula. The firm cannot continue to grow and stay small indefinitely. By the same token, it may not be able to reproduce its magic everywhere it goes. At this juncture the real question facing Chaparral is: "Which way to grow?"

REFERENCES

Carey, David. "Forecast: Industry Analysis—Metals." *Financial World*. January 5, 1988, p. 40.

"Chaparral Steel Company." *Making America Competitive: Corporate Success Formulas*. Bureau of National Affairs Special Report. Washington, D.C.: BNA, n.d.

Eichenwald, Kurt. "America's Successful Steel Industry." *Washington Monthly*. February 1985, pp. 40–44.

The Elements of Leadership: Texas Industries, Inc., 1987 Annual Report. July 15, 1987.

Flint, Jerry. "Help Wanted: Stakhanovites Only." *Forbes*. September 7, 1987, p. 82+.

Forward, Gordon E. "Wide-Open Management at Chaparral Steel." Interview by Alan M. Kantrow. *Harvard Business Review* 64.3 (1986), pp. 96–102.

Freeze, Karen. "From a Casewriter's Notebook." *HBS Bulletin*. June 1986, pp. 54–63.

Jaffre, Richard T. "Chaparral Steel Company: A Winner in a Market Decimated by Imports." *Planning Review*. July 1986, p. 20+.

Keefe, Lisa M. "Forward's March." *Forbes*. April 20, 1986, p. 20+.

Lee, Robert E. "How They Buy Scrap at Chaparral." *Purchasing*. August 22, 1985, pp. 98A1–98A4.

May, Todd, Jr. "The Economy: Surprising Help from the Crash." *Fortune*. January 18, 1988, pp. 68–87.

McManus, George J. "Horizontal Casting: A New Direction for Steel." *Iron Age*. April 5, 1985, p. 29+.

McManus, George J. "Mini-Mill Report: The Honeymoon Is Over." *Iron Age*. March 1, 1986, p. 26+.

Melloan, George. "Making Money Making Steel in Texas." *The Wall Street Journal*. January 26, 1988, southwest ed., p. 29.

Miller, Jack Robert. "Steel Mini-Mills." *Scientific American*. May 1984, pp. 32–39.

"Mini-Mills Up the Heat on the Maxis." *Fortune*. April 13, 1987, pp. 8–9.

Peters, Tom. *On Achieving Excellence*. Monthly Newsletter. San Francisco: TPG. May 1987.

Robert Morris Associates. *RMA '87 Annual Statement Studies*. Philadelphia: RMA, 1987.

Stundza, Tom. "Steel: Making More with Less." *Purchasing*. February 12, 1987, pp. 50–57.

Szekely, Julian. "Can Advanced Technology Save the U.S. Steel Industry?" *Scientific American*. July 1987, pp. 34–41.

United States Department of Commerce. Critical Materials *Requirements of the U.S. Steel Industry*. Washington, D.C.: GPO, March 1983.

CASE 9

CON-WAY CENTRAL EXPRESS

1   Jerry Detter finished the last session of the New Employee Orientation Seminar at the Sheraton in Ann Arbor standing in front of a banner with TEAM on it, in the Con-Way Central Express (CCX) colors of orange and brown likening CCX to bailing twine. "Each strand in bailing twine," he said, "is very weak but when you twist all of the strands together you have a twine that is very strong and not easily broken." The acronym TEAM stands for Together Each Accomplishes Much. Thus, TEAM sums up Jerry's belief about why, by any measure, CCX has been so successful since its inception in 1983.

2   In 1986, CCX, a subsidiary of Consolidated Freightways, Inc., provided short-haul overnight freight service to points in the Midwest, including the states of Michigan, Illinois, Indiana, Iowa, Kentucky, Ohio, Pennsylvania, Minnesota, and Wisconsin. Its headquarters was now located in a 7,600-square-foot office on the south side of Ann Arbor, Michigan, in a commercial/light industry park. The company was founded on June 20, 1983, in a farmhouse nicknamed Tara, which looked like it had barely survived the Civil War. CCX, which began operations in 1983 with 72 employees and 11 terminals, had 1,500 employees at 38 locations in 1986 just three and a half years later. During this same period, revenues increased over 25 times, which is even more amazing given the shakeout in the trucking industry that was causing many firms to go bankrupt.

THE PARENT

3   Consolidated Freightways, Inc. (CFI), the parent of CCX, is a large freight handler operating worldwide with five principal business lines of long-haul trucking, regional trucking of which CCX is one of three subsidiaries: air freight, international ocean container service, and specialized truckload and forwarding service. CFI's balance sheets for 1984 through 1986 are shown in Exhibit 1, and its income statements for 1983 through 1986 are shown in Exhibit 2.

4   CFI pioneered many innovations in the transportation industry that today are standard in the less-than-truckload (LTL) transportation business, such as the use of double trailers. The latest innovation was the establishment in 1983 of the Con-Way regional freight companies, Con-Way Eastern Express (CEX), Con-Way Western Express (CWX), and CCX. The opportunity to begin the regional businesses was ripe, due to the deregulation of the trucking industry, which began with the passage of the Motor Carrier Act of 1980. Con-Way Eastern Express was begun by purchasing an existing carrier, while CCX and Con-Way Western were formed as new companies.

EXHIBIT 1

CONSOLIDATED FREIGHTWAYS, INC.
AND SUBSIDIARIES
Balance Sheet
(dollars in thousands)

	1984	1985	1986
Current assets:			
Cash	$ 34,185	$ 31,176	$ 41,372
Marketable securities	107,409	77,599	94,041
Net accounts receivable	198,640	226,484	249,522
Notes receivable	11,511	13,556	24,891
Operating supplies	23,897	22,470	27,485
Prepaid expenses	37,476	46,567	48,066
Prepaid income taxes	14,478	7,845	14,057
Total current assets	427,596	425,697	499,434
Other assets:			
Marketable securities for investment	120,300	123,056	151,685
Notes receivable due through 1990	10,149	9,525	7,053
Operating rights and goodwill, net	19,689	18,915	20,447
Investment in tax benefit leases	8,042	7,460	5,999
Investment in CF financial services		4,986	5,267
Deferred charges and other assets	9,159	6,275	12,463
Total other assets	167,339	170,217	202,914
Property, plant, and equipment:			
Land	48,660	54,235	63,818
Buildings and improvements	204,918	234,694	249,577
Motor carrier equipment	446,492	515,945	574,153
Other equipment & leasehold improvements	106,699	118,889	129,335
Total	806,769	923,763	1,016,883
Less accumulated depreciation	(341,130)	(386,104)	(443,791)
Total net property	465,639	537,659	573,092
Total assets	$1,060,574	$1,133,573	$1,275,440
Current liabilities:			
Accounts payable & accrued liabilities	$ 229,926	$ 226,574	$ 290,810
Federal & other income taxes	5,800	584	
Accrued claims cost	38,823	35,983	47,049
Current maturities of long-term debt	19,347	9,971	6,688
Total current liabilities	293,896	273,112	344,547
Long-term debt	62,645	62,539	58,700
Deferred items	151,197	194,128	207,145
Total liabilities	507,738	529,779	610,392
Shareholders' equity:			
Common stock, $0.625 par value	17,579	17,647	26,570
Capital in excess of par value	61,863	63,622	57,758
Cumulative translation adjustment	(5,839)	(8,176)	(7,120)
Retained earnings	520,183	571,926	630,228
Less treasury stock	(40,950)	(41,225)	(42,388)
Total shareholders' equity	552,836	603,794	665,048
Total liabilities & shareholders' equity	$1,060,574	$1,133,573	$1,275,440

EXHIBIT 2

CONSOLIDATED FREIGHTWAYS, INC.
AND SUBSIDIARIES
Income Statement
(dollars in thousands)

	1983	1984	1985	1986
Revenues:				
Surface transportation	$1,173,866	$1,480,156	$1,616,567	$1,843,177
Air freight	181,229	224,753	265,575	281,290
Total	1,355,095	1,704,909	$1,882,142	2,124,467
Costs and expenses:				
Surface transportation:				
Operating expenses	864,599	1,121,968	1,215,678	1,353,368
Selling & adm. expenses	159,512	192,076	213,519	262,648
Depreciation	58,934	65,420	79,096	86,875
Total	1,083,045	1,379,464	1,508,293	1,702,891
Air freight:				
Operating expenses	137,235	168,361	214,589	238,781
Selling & adm. expenses	33,077	35,889	43,423	43,825
Depreciation	2,243	2,993	3,602	3,925
Total	172,555	207,243	261,614	286,531
Operating income:				
Surface transportation	90,821	100,692	108,274	140,286
Air freight	8,674	17,510	3,961	(5,241)
Total	99,495	118,202	112,235	135,045
Other income:				
Investment income	23,618	20,991	22,446	16,203
Interest expense	(9,893)	(7,379)	(6,159)	(7,298)
Miscellaneous, net	(162)	(3,079)	(1,103)	3,440
Total	13,563	10,533	15,184	12,345
Income before taxes	113,058	128,735	127,419	147,390
Income taxes	47,594	54,270	48,128	58,281
Net Income	$ 65,464	$ 74,465	$ 79,291	$ 89,109
Net income per share	$1.62	$1.88	$2.06	$2.31

By the end of 1986, CFI had invested $50 million in CCX and, in turn, had a subsidiary that was growing very rapidly and returning excellent profits. In September 1986, *Forbes* estimated that the three regional companies of CFI would generate $15 million in profits on sales of $150 million for 1986.

5   Consolidated Freightways Motor Freight (CFMF), the long-haul division of CFI, accounted for about $1.5 billion in revenue in 1986. It has terminals and operates in many of the same cities as the regional subsidiaries; but CFMF sells to different markets, since the average length of its haul is 1,000 miles. Thus, the regional units do not directly compete with CFMF.

INTRAPRENEURING

6   To say that Jerry Detter, the president of CCX, has charisma seems trite when one sees him in action, for he epitomizes the word. All of the employees agree he was and continues to be the driving force that created and sustains CCX. Jerry was 38 years old when CFI asked him to start CCX. He figured he was "young enough to start over" if the project failed, but he was confident it would succeed.

7   Jerry joined CFI as a terminal dock worker immediately after graduating in the bottom third of his high school class. He said he was only reading at the fifth grade level at the time and realized quickly he needed to improve himself. By the time he was 23 he was a terminal manager and by 28 he managed the largest terminal in the United States with 1,200 employees, which he was able to reduce to 900 five years later. He had been with CFI for 18 years and was a division manager responsible for 23 terminals at the time he was selected to start CCX.

8   Originally, CFI proposed to buy a company, rather than start a new regional carrier from scratch. The accountants said it would cost $11 million to turn the proposed acquisition around, but Jerry thought it would take four times as much. Jerry convinced CFI to start a new company, and the proposed acquisition went out of business within 90 days affirming his judgment. The original concepts for the company were simple and remain so today. Overnight delivery service was to be provided at least 95 percent of the time at a competitive cost, using union-free labor with superior efficiency and flexibility, and with team work and profit sharing stressed. Jerry likened CCX to a speedboat that can make quick turns and adjust rapidly to the marketplace and competitors. Not only are the management concepts and style at CCX atypical of the industry, but they are also unique at CFI.

9   At an employee orientation seminar in February 1987, which covered a two and a half day period, a number of comments were made by the employees regarding the company and Jerry's leadership.

10   It's great to talk to the president personally and think he really cares about your ideas.

I like the honesty of this company.

The company takes care of its equipment and provides good equipment.

The company pays above average wages with profit sharing.

CCX is intense but I like it.

There is real team work here. Everyone tries to help. The spirit and profit sharing are great.

11   Ninety-five percent of the drivers are former union members. Jerry encourages this, because they have something to compare CCX to and are appreciative of the different climate. The employees in turn say they appreciate the union-free environment.

THE TRUCKING INDUSTRY

12   The U.S. trucking industry can be segmented in several different ways. First, there is the for-hire carrier versus the private carrier. For-hire carriers are considered part of the trucking industry, while private carriers are not, since they are solely owned by individual companies and only transport that company's freight. Private carriers are typically not subject to the same detailed regulations as for-hire carriers. By 1980, private carriers probably numbered 100,000.

13   For-hire carriers can, in turn, be divided into intracity truckers and over-the-road truckers. Expenditures for local cartage in 1986 still represented 40 percent of all expenditures on motor freight service. Intrastate cartage represented 60 percent of the tonnage carried. Intracity carriers are subject to state regulation.

14   Over-the-road carriers are subject to federal regulation and to intermodal competition. Regulated carriers can, in turn, be divided into common carriers, who provide service to the general public, and into contract carriers, who do not haul for the general public but provide specialized service to individual shippers. There were an estimated 193,000 self-employed truckers (contract carriers) in 1980. There were three classes of regulated carriers in 1980, based upon the annual amount of revenue they handled, as shown below.

15   Class I—In excess of $3 million.

Class II—Between $500,000 and $3 million.

Class III—Less than $500,000.

16   The common carriers can be regular route carriers or irregular route carriers. Regular route carriers of general freight operate through terminals where less-than-truckload (LTL) cargoes are received, sorted, and consolidated into truckload lots for subsequent movement to other terminals, where the same process is reversed. Such terminals also serve as points for switching cargoes between carriers. Thus, regular route carriers are in the distribution business, and the terminal network required to perform this service requires a much larger capital investment than is necessary for contract carriers. In addition, their terminal operations make them more labor intensive and, therefore, more costly and dependent upon good terminal management.

17   The trucking industry from 1978 through 1984 was relatively stable in regard to ton-miles carried and employment, as shown in Table 1.

18   Regulation of the trucking industry was established by the Motor Carrier Act of 1935 during the Great Depression to overcome destructive competition, chaotic price structures, and market forces that were thought to be unreliable for producing satisfactory results. It was a movement away from the free market. The lack of stability in the industry was thought to be due to the ease of entry with little capital required, that owners were free to send their trucks anywhere they wished, and that each operator set his own rates.

19   The act provided for the Interstate Commerce Commission to control entry into the interstate market, define and limit operations within the market, and control the rates charged. The control of entry was accomplished by requiring a "certificate of public convenience and necessity" for any carrier that sought new or extended routes. This certificate required a hearing in which existing competitors in the market could contest the need for the new carrier. As might be expected, the

TABLE 1

Year	Intercity Ton-Miles (billions)		Employment (000s)
	Number	Percent of U.S. Total	
1978	599	24.3	1212
1979	608	23.6	1249
1980	555	22.3	1189
1981	527	21.7	1168
1982	520	23.1	1128
1983	548	23.7	1133
1984	602	23.6	1212

Source: Transportation Policy Associates, *Transportation in America Regulation of the Trucking Industry*.

majority of the operating rights by the mid-1970s were obtained under the grandfather clause of the act. The protective nature of regulatory policy reduced the risk that would have been encountered in a competitive industry and provided a good opportunity to grow with the general economy.

20   The ICC's limitation of operations was provided by requiring the commission to specify the nature and extent of authorized service that individual carriers could offer. As a result of this power, a congressional study in 1945 showed that 62 percent of intercity certificates had been limited to special commodities and only 32 percent of intercity carriers had general commodity authority, which was subject to numerous exceptions. Furthermore, over one third of the intercity carriers were limited in obtaining income-generating backhauls and one 10th were prohibited from taking return loads for compensation. Route restrictions forced carriers to travel unnecessary distances often partially or totally empty. Of regular route carriers, only 30 percent had full authority to serve all intermediate points on their routes and 10 percent had no such authority.[1]

21   To facilitate the massive job of controlling rates in the interstate trucking industry, the commission encouraged regulated carriers to use rate bureaus to jointly make rates. By 1980, 10 major general freight rate bureaus were operating in different parts of the country. These rate bureaus from their beginning clearly involved price fixing, which was illegal under U.S. antitrust laws. Although this dilemma was resolved by the Reed-Bullwinkle Act of 1948, which theoretically preserved the right to make individual rates, in practice the delays and litigation caused by the requirement that the proposing carrier show that the proposed rate was just, reasonable, and compensatory effectively precluded individual rate making.

Deregulation of the Trucking Industry

22   Deregulation of the trucking industry began in 1977, with some administrative changes, and culminated in the Motor Carrier Act of 1980. This act altered all of the three factors involved in regulation: entry policy, operating authority, and rate making. Ease of entry was facilitated in two ways: the burden of proof of public convenience and necessity was eased, and the basis for protest by existing carriers was constrained. These changes caused the number of applications for operating authority to grow from 12,700 in 1979 to 22,735 in 1980 and to over 29,000 in the 12 months following passage of the act. Grants of authority to new entrants grew from 690 in 1979 to 1,423 in 1980 and to 2,452 in the following 12 months. Two years after the passage of the act, applications were averaging about 1,100 per month, 43,000 new certificates had been issued, and about 8,000 new carriers had been granted operating authority.[2]

23   Rate making was altered by the act to permit carriers to take independent rate actions without the potential procedural obstacles previously put up by the rate bureaus. These obstacles included the power to delay filing the proposal and the right to notify other members of the proposed rate change prior to action being taken.

24   Deregulation served to weaken the elaborate set of barriers to competition among existing carriers. It also produced another incentive, which enhanced competition—added capacity. The operating restrictions previously in place had tied up capacity through inefficiencies. Elimination of the restrictions freed this capacity for productive use.

25   Although the rate bureaus continue to operate, a shakeout occurred in the trucking industry in the three years following the passage of the act, which was caused by the economic climate as well as the increased competition made possible by the act. Rate reductions became more common,

---

[1]Charles R. Perry, *Deregulation and the Decline of the Unionized Trucking Industry* (Philadelphia: Industrial Research Unit, The Wharton School, University of Pennsylvania, 1986), p. 27.

[2]Ibid., p. 76.

TABLE 2
Average Annual Pay and Productivity per Employee
for Class I Carriers 1983

	Union	Lightly Unionized	Nonunion	Union/ Nonunion
Wages	$27,293	$21,734	$18,630	1.46
Benefits	4,096	1,365	897	4.57
Compensation	31,389	23,099	19,527	1.61
Revenues	52,555	57,219	81,097	0.65
Ratio of revenue to compensation	1.67	2.48	4.15	0.40

Source: ICC databank of trucking industry statistics.

EXHIBIT 3
Components of 1986 U.S. Logistics Cost

Distribution Service		Cost ($ billions)	
Inventory carrying/holding:			
Carrying		98	
Warehousing			
Public	6		
Private	50		
Total		56	
Total carrying/holding			154
Transportation:			
Motor carriers:			
Public carriers	54		
Private and shipper affiliated carriers	75		
Local freight carriers	76		
Total		205	
Railroads	29		
Water carriers	18		
Oil pipelines	9		
Air carriers	6		
Forwarders, brokers, and agents (net)	1		
Total nonmotor carriers		63	
Shipper-related services		3	
Total transportation			271
Distribution administration			18
Total			443

Source: Robert V. Delaney, "The Disunited States: A Country in Search of an Efficient Transportation Policy," *CATO Policy Analysis* 84 (March 10, 1987), p. 3.

and carriers had stronger incentives to control costs including wages negotiated with the Teamsters Union. Management could no longer afford to minimize confrontation with the Teamsters.

26   The trend toward nonunion carriers that had begun to develop prior to the 1980 act was accentuated after the passage of the act. In 1983, nonunion employees were 44 percent of the drivers and helpers, 42 percent of the vehicle maintenance personnel, and 69 percent of the cargo handlers. In 1983, Class I nonunion carriers were able to generate 2.5 times as much revenue per

dollar of compensation as the unionized carriers. Table 2 summarizes the costs and revenue relationships.

27   The LTL motor freight industry has higher rates than the truckload segment, because it is a distribution network and, as such, is more labor-intensive. Rate increases over time have brought LTL rates to the point where they reflect the full cost of handling such freight. The competitive advantage has gone to those firms with the lowest labor-productivity costs. Many anticipate a further shakeout of the weak firms in the industry, which will make those least able to control and reduce their labor costs the first to go.

28   The economic benefits from deregulation exceed the original government estimates by a factor of 10, ranging from $56 to $90 billion annually. Not only have transportation costs themselves been reduced but, more important, much of the increased efficiency is due to better management of inventory and delivery systems. In effect, "just-in-time" inventory concepts were facilitated. Exhibit 3 shows the Components of 1986 U.S. Logistics Costs. The performance of transportation services must be consistent and dependable if investments in inventory are to be controlled. Prior to deregulation, producers and distributors either built excessive inventory or operated their own trucks to overcome the poor service provided by many carriers. The competition fostered by deregulation has forced better service.

MARKETING

29   The marketing activities of CCX are managed by Bryan Millican, who is 37 years old. He graduated from the University of Waterloo in Canada with a bachelor's degree in mathematics and computer science and later received his MBA degree from the University of Western Ontario. He began working in the trucking industry in Canada when he was 16 and has had extensive experience in data processing and marketing. He accepted the job at CCX after talking to Jerry Detter without even knowing his salary, because he liked the opportunity and the fact that CCX was open for new thoughts. He normally spends 50 percent of his 60-hour week on the road seeing how customers perceive the marketing programs, and how employees use the programs. Because of his background in computers, Bryan personally wrote many of the programs that are used locally by CCX.

30   CCX uses a three-phase marketing strategy. The first phase is to get awareness in the market as a regional carrier. CCX began with terminals in the 11 major cities in the central states region. Jerry Detter wanted to get the "biggest bang for the buck." Next, more key cities were added, followed by secondary cities, and finally the network was spread out to encompass the entire area. One of the key factors stressed is on-time service, with the goal of 96 percent of the freight being delivered the next day; CCX was operating at 97 percent in late 1986. Regional trucking is much more sensitive to time than national trucking. Another factor is the coverage between major freight centers within the region. Finally, financial stability or staying power is emphasized. Exhibit 4 shows how terminals were added from 1983 through 1986 to carry out these policies.

31   The second phase is the penetration of the market area. CCX is at this point now, being in the top 25 in the country in terms of tonnage handled and is proceeding into the third phase, which is domination of the Midwest market with *the* premier service and coverage. CCX began with 700 points of service, is now at 6,500 points, and is looking forward to an expansion of 15 more terminals to include 10,000 points of service in 1987. CCX's present market share in the region is over 10 percent, and Bryan Millican's goal is to have 20 percent of the market by June 1988. Jerry Detter sees a 45 percent growth in revenue in 1987, which would put CCX among the top 20 in the country, and a 25 percent share of the market by 1990. All of this is to be accomplished with a tight administrative and selling expense budget, which was 5.5 percent of revenues in 1986.

EXHIBIT 4
CCX Terminal Locations in the Year Added

	1983	1984	1985	1986
Michigan				
Detroit	X			
Grand Rapids	X			
Battle Creek		X		
Pontiac			X	
Holland				X
Flint				X
Jackson				X
Ohio				
Toledo	X			
Cleveland	X			
Columbus	X			
Cincinnati	X			
Dayton			X	
Akron			X	
Findlay				X
Pennsylvania				
Pittsburgh	X			
Sharon/Newcastle			X	
Erie			X	
Indiana				
Indianapolis	X			
South Bend		X		
Fort Wayne		X		
Kokomo			X	
Evansville			X	
Illinois				
Chicago	X			
Palatine		X		
Aurora			X	
DesPlaines				X
Bloomington				X
Danville				X
Wisconsin				
Milwaukee	X			
Janesville		X		
Green Bay			X	
Fond Du Lac				X
Minnesota				
Minneapolis	X			
Iowa				
Quad Cities	X			
Kentucky				
Louisville			X	
Lexington				X
Missouri				
St. Louis				X

EXHIBIT 7
Con-Way Central Express Loading Manifest

LOADING MANIFEST	TRAILER NUMBER	MID	LOADING LOC. SIC	RESP RDC	TRAILER NUMBER	DEST SIC
		TCON			—	

DESTINATION	DATE	TOTAL WEIGHT	% CUBE	BILLS	TIME/DATE CLOSED	LOAD RELEASE NUMBER
ORIGIN	SWEPT / NAILS PULLED / HOLES REPAIRED / WHEELS CHOCKED	/	/			841501

	CUBE	BILLS	SPECIAL INSTRUCTIONS/REMARKS	(38 CHARACTER LIMIT)
WEIGHT CARRIED FORWARD				

LINE NO.	PIECES	WEIGHT	ID	H/M	PRO NUMBER	LINE NO.	PIECES	WEIGHT	ID	H/M	PRO NUMBER
1						23					
2						24					
3						25					
4						26					
5						27					
6						28					
7						29					
8						30					
9						31					
10						32					
11						33					
12						34					
13						35					
14						36					
15						37					
16						38					
17						39					
18						40					
19						41					
20						42					
21						43					
22						44					
SUB TOTAL ▶						SUB TOTAL ▶					

TOTAL ▶		CUBE	BILLS

LOADING DIAGRAM (IDENTIFY MARKS)

TOP VIEW / SIDE VIEW

N O S E — R E A R   N O S E — R E A R

SIDE / BOTTOM

MARKS
1. C/ _____ D/ _____
2. C/ _____ D/ _____

DO NOT LOAD CLASS A OR B POISONS IN A TRAILER CONTAINING MATERIAL THAT IS MARKED AS OR KNOWN TO BE FOODSTUFF, FEED OR ANY OTHER EDIBLE MATERIAL INTENDED FOR CONSUMPTION BY HUMANS OR ANIMALS.

SEAL NUMBER	CHANGED SEAL NUMBER

HEATER: ☐ YES ☐ NO   UNIT NO.

PLACARDS: ☐ YES ☐ NO   TYPE

AUTHORITY:

SPECIAL INSTRUCTIONS (TYPES OF HAZARDOUS MATERIAL) INFORMATION USEFUL TO UNLOADER CONCERNING LOAD, ETC.

basis, rather than by staging the material by delivery sequence on the dock prior to loading. The driver salesman making deliveries to customers the next day determines the final delivery sequence.

58   The control of line haul activities is the responsibility of Norm Wallace, the freight flow supervisor. He has three employees working for him at the central office in Ann Arbor. They develop, with the aid of the computer, the line haul report, which is used to control truck operations transferring freight overnight. They balance pounds and linear feet of space, regardless of how high the freight is stacked, on each trailer in and out of each terminal by each "lane," which is the path between the terminals and centers. In case of an imbalance in one direction, an empty trailer will be sent along or carried back as circumstances may require. One of the key reports used in controlling shipments is the loading manifest, shown in Exhibit 7. In 1987, 20.6 percent of revenues was line haul costs and 54.5 percent was terminal costs.

Operations Control

59   Operations are controlled by a number of reports. The production report, known as the "244" is submitted daily, as shown in Exhibit 8, and weekly by each terminal and is done by hand by the terminal manger or an assistant manager. This report goes to the regional managers, to Dick Palazzo, and to CF's Portland, Oregon, computer center. The two operations assistants supervised by Tom Gerstenlauer, senior operations assistant, check the calculations, highlight substandard items, and send a rebuttal back to the regional managers about errors and problems. This activity shows that the reports are actively being used. A monthly "244" report is submitted by each terminal manger within three days from the end of the month, along with a trial income and expense statement. By the 13th to 15th of the month a computer recap of the "244" is received by Dick Palazzo and, in turn, is transmitted to the terminals with comments.

60   Dick daily monitors the morning report, which includes revenue, wages, labor/wages, percent overtime, equipment out of service, number of shipments that did not move, any shipments not billed, and any bills that were brought back because they were not delivered. He also monitors the empty miles report, which shows the empty trailers and in which lanes they occurred. The actual payroll figures are checked versus the various reports and the service factor checked on a weekly basis showing the on-time statistics. Annually, Dick sets goals for all terminals, including revenue, productivity, labor, and claims.

61   Another element of Dick Palazzo's job is handling new terminal expansion. The regional managers do a lot of the leg work, but Dick personally makes the final decisions and arranges for leases of purchases. A terminal is usually 50 feet wide and is leased by the door. The cost of leasing is about $150 per month per door. The cost of building a terminal is $18,000 per door. Originally, all terminals were leased, but now nine are owned through CFI.

62   The operations assistants conduct audits at each terminal, with a goal of two per terminal per year. The audits cover all aspects of operations and operating statistics. The audits are written by hand in the field and are later typed with references to the master manual. The operations assistants also conduct seminars for clerical and supervisory personnel on a semiannual or quarterly basis on such topics as handling hazardous materials, outbound loading, and handling OS&D (over, short, and damaged) freight. Another assistant is to be added in 1987.

63   Claims control is another function of the operations department. In 1985, there were 3,580 claims for loss or damage paid, for a total of $506,827. The ratio of paid claims to shipments was 1/164. The projected claims and payments for 1986 were expected to be 5,350 and $905,000, respectively. This projection, if attained, would actually be only 1 per 177 shipments since the total business of CCX is increasing rapidly.

EXHIBIT 8
Con-Way Central Express Production Report ("244")

WEEKLY TERMINAL PRODUCTION and COST REPORT
0424.20 (3/83)

Terminal: Cleveland OH. Code: XCL Week Ending: 5-16-87

HAND WRITTEN PREFERABLE (LEGIBLE)

FREIGHT HANDLING

FUNCTION		A Std. Hrs.	B Hrs. Worked	C Prem. Hrs.	D P/R Cost	E Inbound CWT	F Outbound CWT	G Reship CWT	H Total CWT	I Std. Lbs./M.H.	J Lbs./M.H.	K Cost/CWT	L $ Variance
1. Direct P&D	266	128	141	12 (24)	1904	3617	4720	xxxx	8337	6500	5913	.23	(310)
2. Cross Dock	379	541	582	16 (31)	6895	14718	14956	4229	34063	6300	5853	.20	(657)
3. City Liner P&D	262	933	1062	50 (98)	1355	14278	14956	xxxx	29463	3200	2810	.47	(246)
4. Direct Peddle		xxxx	xxxx	xxxx	xxxx			xxxx		xxxx	xxxx	xxxx	xxxx
5. LTL Peddle	239							xxxx					
6. Frt. Not Handled		xxxx	xxxx	xxxx	xxxx			xxxx		xxxx	xxxx	xxxx	xxxx
7. Vol. Tsfr (Over 10M)		xxxx	xxxx	xxxx	xxxx					xxxx	xxxx	xxxx	xxxx
8. Weekly Total		1602	1985	78 (153)	22754	18495	19676	4229	42400	xxxx	xxxx	.54	xxxx
9. LTL		xxxx	xxxx	xxxx	xxxx			xxxx		xxxx	xxxx	xxxx	xxxx

% OF CITY LINER AND PEDDLE CWT TO LTL CWT _____   % OF I/B AND O/B CROSS DOCK CWT TO LTL CWT _____   % DIRECT TONNAGE _____

OTHER TERMINAL ACTIVITIES

FUNCTION		B Hrs. Worked	C Prem. Hrs.	D P/R Cost	H Total Hooks	I Std. Hks./Hrs.	J Hooks/Hrs	K Cost/Hooks
10. Hosting - Term Yard	382	15	-	177	98	6.5	1.81	
11. Hosting - Pig/Pike	236							
12. Dispatch – L/H	212		xxxx					
13. Dispatch – P&D	226							
14. Term. & Bldg. Repairs	392							
15. Other Term. Labor *								
16. Weekly Total		15	-	177				

22. Explanation and Comments

(* Hours entered on line 15 must be explained in this section.)

CITY LINER P&D STOPS: 2565   2.13 sph

V. LOAD FACTOR

No. of Trailers	Trailer Type	Avg. Load
237	SEMI'S	
	DUBS	1142 1
	2706674	

OFFICE

Std. Bills/M.H. _____

FUNCTION		B Hrs. Worked	C Prem. Hrs.	D P/R Cost	H Bill/M.H.	J	K Cost/Bills
17. Billing	321 322	50	4 (8)	443	35		.26
18. Cashiering	325 361	170	10 (16)	1476	xxxx		xxxx
& Other	359 363						
19. Sub Total		220	14 (24)	1919	15		.57
20. Sales Clerical–Terminal	422				xxxx		xxxx
21. Weekly Total		220	14 (24)	1919	xxxx		xxxx

NUMBER OF BILLS

E Inbound Bills	1600	
F Outbound Bills	1736	
G Billed for Other Term.	0	
Total Outbound Bills	1736	
H Total In & Out Bills	3336	
U Reship Bills	404	

MARKETING

REVENUE	E Total I/B Rev.	F Total O/B Rev.	Total I/O
Wkly.Ttl.Rev.	131936	130592	262528
Wkly.Qual.Rev	129390	130592	xxxx
Qual. Rev. Quota	126206	124529	xxxx
Qual. % Quota	102.5	104.9	xxxx
Ttl. Rev. Cwt	7.13	6.64	
Ttl. Rev. Pr. Yr.	104982	104904	211886

% OVERTIME HOURS TO HOURS WORKED

FUNCTION	HRS. WORKED	O.T. HOURS	%
Frt. Handling	1785	153	8.6
Oth. Term. Act.	15	1	0
Office	220	24	10.9

PAYROLL TO REVENUE SUMMARY

		CURRENT WEEK	WEEK OF PRIOR YR.
N	Mean Revenue	128715	105562
P	Total Terminal Payroll	24850	19850
R	% P/R to Mean Revenue	19.3	18.8
	Std. % P/R to Rev.	20.0	-

RECEIVED MAY 19 1987 CON-WAY CENTRAL EXPRESS

BY _____

TABLE 4

	1983	1986
Tractors	43	621
Trailers	127	1,524
Dollies	40	410
Fork lifts	11	113
Hostlers	0	10

EQUIPMENT AND MAINTENANCE

64 CCX's investment in equipment has grown substantially from the beginning in 1983 as shown in Table 4.

65 Each tractor costs about $40,000 and each trailer about $12,000. A tractor lasts about 750,000 miles or five years and requires a new engine at 400,000 miles. A dolly carries the front part of the double trailer much like the tractor does to the lead trailer. A hostler is a small tractor type vehicle that is used to move trailers around a freight assembly center instead of using a road tractor.

66 At the end of 1986, CCX had 10 service shops employing 33 mechanics to service the fleet of vehicles shown above. Paul Applegate, the director of maintenance, manages the maintenance activities through two field maintenance managers, who do extensive traveling. Maintenance expenditures are distributed as follows: tractors—56.1 percent, trailers—33.3 percent, washing—7.3 percent, and fork lifts—3.3 percent.

67 Three maintenance meetings, held each year for the whole system, are moved to different shops. A preventive maintenance program is carried out. Maintenance expenditures over $500 must be approved by Paul Applegate. Warranty claims are controlled and administered through a warranty clerk. Tractors are in use about 20 hours per day, except when they are in the shop for major maintenance.

PERSONNEL AND SAFETY

68 Brian Tierney is the manager of personnel and safety. He is 33 years old and has a degree in political science from Loyola University in New Orleans. He began working for CF after graduation at the York, Pennsylvania, consolidation center in a training program that lasted 45 weeks, followed by nine months as office manager in Philadelphia and four years in Portland, Oregon, as a member of the internal audit staff. He first met Jerry Detter in October 1977, and Jerry had kept in touch until he asked him to join CCX. Brian did the preliminary interviewing, for the terminal personnel recruited from blind ads and recommendations from CF. Brian described the organization on June 20, when the first freight was hauled, as a "25-year-old trucking company with one day of experience."

69 One of Brian's key responsibilities is maintaining the personnel policy manual up to date. One copy of the manual is kept in each terminal, where employees can read it but not take it from the terminal. When changes are made to the manual, all copies are returned to Ann Arbor and are updated simultaneously. These measures are taken to insure accuracy and to prevent the manual falling into unfriendly hands, such as the Teamsters. CCX retains the services of an Atlanta law firm that specializes in giving advice to nonunion companies.

70   About 70 percent of Brian's time is spent on "crisis management," including such things as terminations and major accidents. The balance of his time is spent on planning, including such things as training sessions and the driver championship contest.

71   Safety is very important to CCX, considering that 50 million miles are driven each year. The Department of Transportation as well as state agencies have jurisdiction over trucking companies and do perform random inspections. Weekly comparisons are made by CCX regarding preventable accidents. Safety achievement awards are given yearly. The low accident frequency for 1986 is quite impressive: one per 750,000 road miles, one per 4,200 city driving hours, and 8,300 hours worked per industrial injury. The safety program is carried out by two managers reporting to Brian Tierney.

72   CCX has a mandatory drug testing program. Each employee is tested once a year and is given 30 days' notice of the test. Less than 3 percent of new employees and less than 1 percent of present employees test positive. Rehabilitation is stressed for those who are using drugs, and an unpaid leave is given to undergo rehabilitation.

73   About 80 percent of the work force for CCX are regular employees. The balance of the work force is supplemental employees. Since the trucking business is seasonal, with July and late December being the slowest periods, most companies lay off employees during these slow times. CCX does not lay off regular employees but rather discontinues supplemental employees. Supplemental employees usually move into regular employee status after six to nine months, since CCX is expanding rapidly. This period gives CCX a good opportunity to evaluate each employee and, in turn, for the supplemental employee to evaluate CCX as a permanent employer.

74   The pay levels are evaluated each June and changes made as indicated by competitive factors. Supplemental workers make $10.30 per hour. The hourly pay schedule for regular employees is shown in Table 5.

75   Overtime is not paid for line haul driving, since the driver is paid by the mile. Overtime is paid for work in excess of 8 hours per day and 40 hours per week for local operations employees even though government regulations do not require it. Employee benefits include comprehensive health insurance, covering major medical, dental, vision, and hospitalization, group life insurance, pension plan, tuition refund plan, stock purchase plan, a vacation plan of two weeks per year rising to three weeks at 8 years and four weeks at 15 years, nine paid holidays, sick leave, funeral leave, and jury duty leave. Uniforms for all employees are provided by CCX, which is also a valuable marketing tool, since it is not common in the industry. Probably the most important benefit from the employee's standpoint is the incentive compensation plan. Under this plan, CCX paid bonuses of $700,000 in 1984, $2,000,000 in 1985, and $3,200,000 in 1986, with individual employees receiving the maximum or close to the maximum provided for their wage level. The 1986 incentive amounted to approximately 10 percent of each employee's total wages. Unionized workers in 1986

TABLE 5

	Drivers	Mechanics
Initial rate	$10.80	$12.40
After 6 months		13.50*
After 12 months	11.70	
After 24 months	12.40	
After 36 months	13.50	

* A $0.50 premium is paid to lead men.

represented by the Teamsters and working for other companies received $10.09 per hour as a starting wage and received yearly increases for three years to a final wage of $14.41.

76   Supplemental employees are screened for drugs, their driving records are checked, a road test is given, and three interviews are held before they are hired. Each new employee is given one week's training working with four drivers and a supervisor. Upon attaining regular status, employees attend an orientation seminar for three days, which is conducted by Jerry Detter and his executive group and designed to familiarize employees with the personnel policies, procedures, and company benefits in addition to establishing an effective avenue for communications.

77   Regular employees are reviewed for job performance at intervals of 30, 60, 90, and 180 days, and yearly thereafter. The seven categories that are evaluated are job knowledge, work execution, job relationships, meeting job demands, dependability, job conduct, and safety. The evaluations are held privately on a face-to-face basis by the immediate supervisor.

78   CCX believes one of the key differences between itself and others in the industry is its emphasis on communication with its employees at all levels. CCX has an Employee Involvement Committee made up of Dick Palazzo, Paul Applegate, Brian Tierney, and three drivers from each region. This committee meets four times per year to discuss any subject of interest. CCX has an annual meeting for all sales and management personnel—about 200 attend—to review the year's performance. Regional meetings are held four times each year, including a reception and dinner on Saturday night and a Sunday breakfast, followed by a four-hour meeting for all regular employees of the region. About every six weeks a Saturday morning breakfast, followed by a two-hour discussion, is held for the employees of each terminal. Attendance at these latter meetings is voluntary but usually about 80 percent of the employees attend. All of these meetings are designed to maintain the open communications needed in a union-free environment. In addition, Jerry Detter has a uniform and works on a dock or truck about every eight weeks to maintain a first-hand contact with the work force.

FINANCE

79   Kevin Schick is the controller for CCX. He is 35 years old and has a degree in accounting and finance from Marquette University and an MBA with an accounting major from Northwestern University. Before joining CCX in April 1983, he had worked in various accounting positions for Motorola, Evans Products' transportation division (Monon Trailer), and MDSI in Ann Arbor.

80   Since the accounting activities for CCX are handled by CF in Portland on their main frame computer, Kevin has a major liaison activity between CCX and Portland. He has a small staff of two clerks; one does accounts payable and the other does capital expenditure appropriations and analysis work on spreadsheets using a PC computer, thereby freeing Kevin's time for longer-term planning. He does a one-year detailed financial plan, plus four additional years of a strategic plan showing projected revenues, costs, capital expenditures, and net working capital. The input for this plan comes from regional and terminal managers, with Jerry Detter and his executive staff setting basic parameters, such as tonnage and competitors' reactions. Kevin then puts in the detail assumptions, working with Jerry, and to some extent with Dick Palazzo, on a one-to-one basis. The plans have worked out well, since about 80 percent to 90 percent of the costs can be nailed down easily. The final review of the strategic plan is with Jerry before submitting it to CF.

81   Kevin says he has an entrepreneurial taste and fulfills the role of a "corporate wet blanket," which is the role often taken by the financial executive. He submits a weekly forecast compiled from various internal reports to Portland computer center, which, in turn, submits it to CF's home office in Palo Alto. He also submits a "week that was" management report to Palo Alto, which is

really an exception report. Each month after the books are closed he prepares a monthly analysis for Jerry's signature to be sent to Palo Alto. He also does a quarterly forecast on a rolling four-quarter basis.

82 Kevin prepares the narrative for the capital expenditure report. One of the advantages CCX has had was easy access to capital through CFI. Both the payback method, using two to three years, and the net present value, using 15 percent, are utilized in evaluating capital expenditures. CCX remitted 5.1 percent of its revenues to CFI in 1986 to cover the "interest on funds used." He sees some tightening of capital availability from CFI occurring, because other entities of CFI are requiring capital also. After all, CCX has become quite well established and must compete with other divisions.

83 When commenting on Jerry's leadership, Kevin sees him as the "spiritual leader of the drivers who can crawl inside the driver's mind." He believes Jerry's biggest value to CCX is an operational mind who can visualize the future. Kevin anticipates the shakeout in the trucking industry will continue for another three or four years. The service factor will be of prime importance to the customer.

THE FUTURE

84 When thinking about the future, Jerry Detter is just as enthusiastic as he is in describing the path of CCX thus far. Plans are under way to lease a new building being constructed near the present home office. Phase one will include 14,000 square feet, with phase two expanding to 20,000 square feet over a one and a half year period. The new facility will include a training center for 72 people and a cafeteria and kitchen. CCX is paying the local Sheraton hotel so much for the frequent training sessions that a center for CCX can be justified. Thus far, over 1,300 employees have been trained. Proposed capital expenditure needs for 1987 are $20 million. He is looking for a 25 percent market share of the Midwest trucking market within a few years. After that goal is reached? Well, Jerry Detter is never short of ideas!

CASE 10

NORTHROP CORPORATION: DILEMMA OF THE TIGERSHARK

1   LOS ANGELES, May 15, 1985—Thomas V. Jones, chairman and chief executive of the Northrop Corporation, said that Tuesday's crash of an F-20 Tigershark jet fighter would not deter the company from promoting the plane to prospective buyers, including the Air Force. The crash, which killed the pilot, David Barnes, was the second of an F-20 in eight months and leaves only one Tigershark in operation. "Our belief in it (the F-20) has not changed," Mr. Jones said at a news conference after Northrop's annual shareholders' meeting in Hawthorne, California. Northrop has not received any orders for the plane, which has cost the company more than $800 million to produce. . . . *The New York Times.*

2   The second fatal crash of an F-20 fighter plane was unfortunate, but such crashes were hardly unexpected. Test pilots often flew new planes at the limits of their capabilities and many times serious accidents were the result. Indeed, pilot error would be ruled the cause of both Tigershark crashes, rather than problems with the plane itself.

3   However, his confident comments to the stockholders aside, Northrop's CEO had other reasons to worry. Northrop developed the Tigershark F-20 for export to Third World and European allies. Despite high praise from the aviation press and pilots alike, not one had been sold. The plane was Thomas Jones's brainchild, but the program's costs were being borne solely by the company and were approaching a staggering $1 billion.

4   Late in 1970s, the Carter Administration put out a call for an inexpensive, easy to maintain aircraft to be produced primarily for export and to be designed and built without Department of Defense funding. The F-20 was Northrop's answer to that call, but, by 1985, the political sands had shifted and the F-20 was facing competition from frontline U.S. fighters previously reserved for domestic use. It was becoming increasingly apparent that sales to foreign customers were going to be contingent upon either getting the Tigershark into the inventory of some branch of the U.S. military, a purpose for which it was not designed, or competing with some of the world's finest and best-known fighter planes in the international marketplace. The questions for Jones were easily stated if the answers were not. Should he continue costly development of a potentially profitable program or should he close the project and divert the funds to other uses?

COMPANY BACKGROUND

5   The Northrop Corporation was founded in 1939 by John K. Northrop, who was previously an engineer at Douglas Aircraft. There he became a preeminent designer doing most of the work on the Lockheed Vega, which aviator Wiley Post flew around the world. While at Douglas, Northrop also did pioneering work on the DC-1, DC-2, and the popular DC-3 passenger planes. As would be expected, his new company manufactured aircraft, producing several lesser known and unexceptional designs prior to World War II. Although it was not a manufacturer of any of the glamor

This case was prepared by Thad Munnerlyn and James J. Chrisman, College of Business Administration, University of South Carolina. Direct all correspondence to James J. Chrisman, University, Columbia, S.C. 29208; ph. (803)777-5972.

This case was prepared for classroom discussion and was not intended to illustrate either ineffective or effective handling of administrative situations.

planes of the wartime period, such as the P-51 Mustang or P-38 Lightning, Northrop did produce the P-61 Black Widow that appeared late in the Pacific Theater. Painted all-black and designed to fly at night with the aid of radar, the sleek aircraft was technologically advanced for its time, but was built in limited numbers. Northrop also produced one of the world's first production jet fighters, the F-89 Scorpion. It enjoyed moderate success in the Korean War era as an all-weather fighter.

6   During the early 1960s, the company developed and manufactured the Snark intercontinental ballistic missile, before advancing technology soon rendered it obsolete. More important, however, was the B-35 Flying Wing program that was started shortly after the end of World War II. Extraordinarily daring in design, the bomber was a culmination of many of John Northrop's ideas and dreams. The company invested heavily in the boomerang-shaped plane only to have the program canceled in favor of the B-36 developed by Convair, a forerunner of General Dynamics. The Air Force ordered all the remaining prototypes destroyed in what became a bitter loss for Northrop. The cancellation left Northrop near bankruptcy in 1953.

7   It was in 1953 that Thomas V. Jones joined the company as a planner and assistant to the chief engineer. Five years later, he was senior vice president of development planning. By 1960, he was CEO, and in 1963, he was named chairman of the board. During his early tenure as CEO, Jones began returning Northrop to profitability with the F-5 Tiger series, a relatively unsophisticated and inexpensive fighter plane that Jones correctly saw as filling a need for Third World countries. Dismissed by one critic as "toys for sheiks," the F-5 was nevertheless one of the premier success stories in aviation manufacturing history.

8   The F-5 and its variations became the most widely used fighter plane in the world, with more than 2,500 planes sold to nearly 30 countries. The F-5 essentially dominated the export fighter market from its inception in the early 60s and through the late 70s. Its trainer derivative, the T-38 Talon, became extremely successful as well, with 1,000 sold worldwide. Used by tens of thousands of aspiring pilots, it became the most widely used jet trainer in history. Although Northrop had remained afloat after the B-35 cancellation, it was the cash revenues generated by the F-5 program that rallied the company to its current level of success. Using these funds, Northrop entered into more advanced aerospace research and development, and expanded its operations into several areas of military electronics.

9   Northrop made two other attempts to build military aircraft in the 1970s. Bidding against other companies for domestic business, it first lost a battle with Fairchild Aviation's A-10 Thunderbolt to produce an anti-tank aircraft for the Air Force. Northrop then competed for a share of the domestic fighter plane market, but had its F-17 prototype rejected by the Air Force in favor of rival General Dynamic's F-16. The F-17 project was later turned over to McDonnell Douglas and became the Navy's F-18 strike fighter. Subsequently, during the late 70s and through the 80s, Northrop became McDonnell Douglas's main subcontractor for the fuselage assembly of the F-18. Boeing Aviation also designated Northrop as the main subcontractor for its 747 airliner in 1966, and Northrop continued to build the fuselage center section through 1985. Despite the financial success of these programs, however, Northrop was still known primarily as a subcontractor for other companies and as a builder of the F-5, the only modern-day plane the company had built in its entirety.

ENVIRONMENT

10   Late in the 1970s, the Carter Administration was becoming alarmed at the number of foreign requests for frontline military aircraft, particularly fighters. Nations with severe domestic problems were clamoring for planes that were costly and whose capabilities greatly exceeded their security needs. These planes often presented maintenance problems that taxed the Air Force support crews

on U.S. bases and would likely present even greater problems to Third World owners. Sales to such countries were seen as politically and economically destabilizing. As a consequence, President Carter approached the defense industry and asked for a privately funded and developed aircraft specifically designed for foreign customers. It was to be simpler, less expensive, and less capable than the top of the line U.S. fighters. In return, the administration would refuse to license the top shelf planes for sales overseas and virtually force the potential buyers toward the foreign export fighter, or FX as it was known.

11   The details were worked out and the program was put into place in late 1979. With a ready-made customer base of previous F-5 users and substantially improved performance, Northrop executives figured to have a "hot" aircraft in their new F-20. Less than a year later, however, Carter lost his reelection bid to Ronald Reagan and a new administration took office. Within two years, the Reagan Administration, walking a political tightrope between Red China and the Nationalist Chinese, had blocked the sale of approximately 150 F-20s ordered by the Taiwan government. The reason given was that the capabilities of F-20 were too good and, therefore, the plane would be destabilizing for the region. Three years later that would still be the only firm order for the Tigershark. Similarly, negotiations with India were quashed on the grounds that the plane and its advanced electronics would be too close to "too many Russians," a reference to India's relations with the Soviet Union.

12   In 1982, The Reagan Administration, reacting to what it believed to be an increased threat from Russian military presence in Third World areas, overturned long-standing U.S. policy and began to sell U.S. inventory fighters to less-developed countries. The exports included some of McDonnell Douglas's F-15s and F-18s but consisted primarily of the General Dynamics F-16. An American fighter became a highly charged symbol of friendship and support, and the Reagan Administration dangled the planes like political bait to sway Third World countries. Countries with U.S. planes were dependent for parts and technical support. Also, the necessary advisors provided an important American presence. The FX policy for which the F-20 was built was all but officially dead.

COMPETITION

13   The domestic defense industry was made up of approximately 10 major companies. These consisted of aerospace concerns as well as nonaerospace companies with large defense divisions (Exhibit 1). Like its counterparts, Northrop competed for a limited number of large long-term contracts (e.g., aircraft) as well as more numerous smaller short-term projects, such as in the electronics field. The industry was monopsonistic, with the U.S. government the only buyer in one form or another (all branches of the armed forces, NASA, and the like). With military policies changing from administration to administration, the President and his views on defense and international politics were of critical importance. The interplay between Congress and administration, in regard to the proposed defense budget, obviously had great impact on the contractors. Northrop, however, at the outset of the FX program, believed it had few competitors in its effort to sell the F-20 to the export market and was relatively free of political problems at home.

14   The least troublesome competition in the "affordable" fighter market were foreign, although some had been improving their position. Dassault of France, with its Mirage 2000, had made the most notable inroads into the Third World markets but was considered to be an also-ran in the industry, behind the competing U.S. firms. Perceived as not having the glamor or performance of an American fighter, the Mirage was more expensive to fly and lacked the large support network that American companies had worldwide. Still, the French plane was a choice for countries that found it politically expedient to appear neutral in terms of Soviet or American influence.

EXHIBIT 1
Top 10 Defense Aerospace Companies
Financial Information (all data for 1980—dollars in millions)

Company	Ranking in Value of Defense Contracts	Value of Defense Contracts	Federal Sales	Net Income	ROE (in percent)	Assets	Major Defense Products
General Dynamics	1	$3,518	$ 4,645	$195	21.0%	$2,242	F-16, Trident subs, SSN-668 subs, Tomahawk missiles
McDonnell Douglas	2	3,247	6,086	145	9.9	3,900	F-18, F-15, KC-10 planes, Trident II missiles
United Technologies	3	3,109	12,324	393	17.5	7,326	UH-60 helicopters, jet fighter engines
Boeing	4	2,386	9,426	601	28.8	5,931	AWACS, Stealth bomber, B-52 modifications
Lockheed	6	2,037	5,396	28	7.5	2,443	C-5A, C-5B cargo planes Trident II missiles
Hughes*	7	1,819	2,610	NA	NA	NA	AH-64 helicopters, defense electronics
Raytheon	8	1,745	5,002	282	22.7	2,929	Hawk missiles, defense electronics
Grumman	10	1,322	1,729	31	9.5	906	F-14, A-6E planes, aircraft carriers
Northrop	11	1,227	1,655	86	19.0	1,234	F-20, F-18, F-5G, Stealth bomber
Rockwell	14	969	6,907	280	17.3	4,431	B-1 bomber

* Privately held.

Source: Chrisman, James J., "Note on the Defense Electronics Industry," in Zimmerer, et al., *Strategic Management: An Entrepreneurial Approach* (St. Paul, Minn.: West Publishing, 1987).

15   McDonnell Douglas had two frontline domestic aircraft that were being exported: the F-15, an extremely sophisticated and expensive air superiority fighter, and the F-18 strike fighter that was built with the assistance of Northrop. These planes were considered too sophisticated and prohibitively expensive for all but the most well-heeled allies. Canada, Australia, and Spain were examples of friendly nations who were interested in these planes.

16   Northrop's main competition in the export fighter market was the General Dynamics Corporation and its well-received F-16. General Dynamics was the nation's largest defense contractor, and the F-16 was its biggest aviation success, having dominated the U.S. inventory in numbers since its introduction in the 1970s. In performance, it was nearly the equal of the F-15, the United States most capable fighter. It was priced considerably lower than the F-15, although at approximately $14 million it was not inexpensive. General Dynamics responded to President Carter's FX request early but without much enthusiasm. In 1980, it offered a version of the F-16 known as the F-16/J79, so named because it had an older and less-sophisticated engine. In addition, it had fewer electronic refinements. The F-16/J79 suffered from comparison to the U.S. Air Force version of the F-16, whose availability had made the F16/J79 almost extraneous. By 1984, General Dynamics made a request to designate its current series of F-16s as FX fighters and essentially abandoned the F-16/J79. The F-16 was lower in price than the F15 and F-18 but had excellent performance and had the prestige of being a first-rate U.S. inventory fighter.

F-20 versus F-16

17   While the F-16/J79 was an old plane with "detuned" technology, Northrop's export fighter was a completely new aircraft. Although initially built for the FX market, the F-20 was the first fighter plane to be designed with 1980s technology. Even the newer F-15s and F-16s were built with 60s and 70s hardware. The F-20 bore little resemblance to its forerunner, the F-5, and was a legitimate rival to the top U.S. inventory planes. Despite costing at least $2.5 million less per plane, the Tigershark was equal in most areas and actually superior in others to the top line F-16 (Exhibit 2).

EXHIBIT 2
Aircraft Characteristics and Performance Estimates

	F-16	F-20
Empty weight (lbs.)	18,496	12,049
Internal fuel	6,972	5,050
Engine thrust	25,400	18,000
Thrust/weight ratio	1.13	1.19
Number of weapons pylons (air to air missiles)	6	6
Max. external weapons carriage (lbs.)	12,000	10,000
Scramble time (seconds)	60	120+
Sortie rate*		
Maneuverability	Essentially equivalent	
Weapons delivery accuracy	Essentially equivalent	
Range ratio F-16/F-20	GD estimate (1.34/1.56/1.0)	Northrop estimate (1.12/1.0)

* F-20: 12 sorties in 12 hours. Exact data on F-16 unavailable.
Sources: Congressional Budget Office, General Dynamics Corp. (GD),
Northrop Corp.

18   Northrop had built the new plane from the ground up, starting with the engine. Its engineers used General Electric's new F404 engine, which sacrificed a small amount of power in exchange for increased reliability and repairability, as well as an uncanny ability to recover from stalls. The F-16 was powered by the Pratt and Whitney F100, a powerful engine but problematic and expensive to maintain. The F-20 engine held one more advantage. It could start in under 20 seconds, less than half the time of the F-16. In terms of electronics the F-20 was, in many respects, superior to any other American fighter, including the super-sophisticated F-15. The radar, equal to the F-16 in performance, had twice the reliability of the unit used by General Dynamics. The Tigershark also had the fastest scramble time (the time an aircraft needed to become airborne after an alert) of any fighter in the world. The Tigershark could be in the air in less than 60 seconds, at least twice as fast as the F-16 or any other top line fighter. That was owed in large part to a new laser-guided inertial guidance system that replaced the typical mechanical gyroscopes, as well as the faster starting engine. In other areas of performance the two planes were essentially equivalent. Maneuverability and weapons accuracy were approximately equal. The F-16 did hold a slight edge in sustained turns, although the F-20's smaller size could offset the advantage in aerial combat. The F-20 was designed primarily as a defensive aircraft and, as a consequence, did have less payload capability than the F-16. (Payload refers to the amount of armament or missiles and bombs that the plane can carry aloft on one mission.) The F-20 also had a shorter flight range than the F-16, a fact that prompted one General Dynamics salesman to say, "[the F-20 is] a good plane if you want to bomb the end of your runway." Northrop countered by explaining that the F-20 was designed for Third World countries whose enemies were nearby, making range less critical but scramble time of far greater consequence. In test flights the F-20 set records for the number of

---

EXHIBIT 3
Comparative Costs

Annual Operating and Support Costs (including fuel) Flying per Month	
F-20	$ 5.7 million
F-16C	$12.2 million

Costs per Aircraft Flying Hour Including Operating Operating/Support Costs	
F-20	$1,575
F-16C	$3,497

Maintenance Personnel Required by Squadron of 20 Aircraft	
F-20	180
F-16C	380

Procurement Costs per Aircraft (in flyaway condition) for 20 Aircraft		
	w/out spares	w/spares
F-20	$11.4 million	$15.75 million
F-16C	$14 million	$21 million

Amounts expressed in 1985 $U.S.
Figures given for 1985 F-16 model.
Sources: *International Defense Review* (12–85), U.S. Defense Dept.—1986, Northrop bid to Congress—1985.

missions that could be performed in a day, presumably an important point to nations with a limited number of planes and manpower.

19   Just as significant to Third World countries as performance, in the view of the F-20's designers, was the Tigershark's ease of maintenance and its reliability (Exhibit 3). Air Force data estimated that the planes' mean number of hours in the air between failures was 4.2 for the F-20 and 3.2 for the F-16. The F-20 required slightly less than half the man hours of routine maintenance per hour of flight than the F-16. These figures would take on more significance to countries with small numbers of trained personnel working under Third World conditions. According to Northrop's figures, lower fuel consumption and lower maintenance requirements reduced the cost per hour of the F-20 to $1,575, while the F-16 cost $3,497. The other savings in terms of support and maintenance were highly in favor of the F-20.

20   Its lower price had a strategic advantage as well as an economic one, since more planes could be bought for the same amount of money. During the Arab-Israeli war, the Israeli air force had found that a high density of aircraft offset the performance differences between adversary aircraft during aerial combat.

MARKET

21   Initially, the FX policy was not meant to apply to all overseas customers, and the export market was divided into two segments. The first or "high" segment included NATO allies as well as some other countries, such as Israel and Japan. Countries in this group usually had State Department approval for top line aircraft. The second or "low" segment consisted of all remaining countries. It was this second group to which the FX program applied. With the death of the Carter policy, a third subgroup of countries previously included in the FX group emerged as a "medium" segment. These nations wanted and could afford first line fighters like the F-16 and were felt to have legitimate defense threats. Examples were Pakistan, Afghanistan's border neighbor and tacit ally to that country's anticommunist guerilas; and South Korea, whose border was with North Korea, the recent benefactor of Soviet air technology.

22   Three years after the FX policy went into effect, approximately 1,100 planes were sold to foreign customers. Not one was a F-20. In fact, not one was an FX fighter. Nations seen as potential customers for the Tigershark opted for the Air Force issue F-16 after it became apparent that it would be available to them. Pakistan, one of the poorest nations in the world, bought 40 F-16s at a cost of $1 billion. Venezuela, another potential F-20 customer, purchased 24 F-16s. Turkey, viewed by the Reagan Administration as a defense against a growing Warsaw Pact threat to NATO's southern flank, received special political considerations. A request on behalf of the Turkish government for $755 million for aid was put before Congress for consideration in 1985. The loans were earmarked for military hardware and included specific mention of F-16s. Thailand was originally tagged as an FX country, but the threat from Viet Nam had it arguing for F-16s with a large number of regional neighbors anxiously awaiting the results before making their own decisions. Thailand had the potential to purchase up to 225 planes. Saudi Arabia, the best hope for a large order, was high on the F-20 but insisted that Northrop have the plane in production and that the plane be in the U.S. armed forces system before it placed an order. It already owned F-15s and some F-16s in its inventory.

23   It was an all too familiar refrain for Northrop executives. Despite their plane's high performance, the Tigershark had what one expert called a "training wheels" image and was still associated with the concept of an underpowered FX fighter, lacking the aura of a U.S. Air Force or Navy plane. Technological glamor and political prestige of owning a frontline U.S. fighter were paramount

EXHIBIT 4
Potential F-20 Sales

Country	Market Segment	Remarks
Australia	Medium/high	Never classified as FX country. Entitled to front line equipment as major Pacific ally. Received F-18s and F-16s.
Austria	Medium	Neutrality stance led to purchase French of Mirages.
Canada	Medium/high	Traditional ally entitled to front line planes, such as F-15s and F-18s.
Egypt	Medium	Initially seen as big F-20 purchaser but was allowed F-16s by Reagan Administration. Northrop still hoped for some sales.
European Participating Group	Medium/high	European allies entitled to front line fighters. Involvement with successful co-production agreement for previous F-16s made reorders likely.
Greece	Medium	Greece's status as NATO ally allowed front line purchases. Indicated interest in F-16s.
India	Medium	U.S. government prohibited sales talks, due to possibility of F-20 technology falling into hands of India's Soviet military advisors. Bought Russian MIGs.
Indonesia	Low/medium	Strong possibility for F-20 order, but national economy delayed any purchase plans.
Israel	Medium/high	Close relationship to United States allowed access to front line fighters coupled with substantial foreign aid. Ordered F-16s and F-15s.
Jordan	Medium	Sale of F-16s to other Middle Eastern countries created pressure to sell to Jordan, which was needed in Middle Eastern peace process. F-20s still a possibility.
Malaysia	Low/medium	Potential buyer of 50 planes. Would strongly consider F-20 but is strongly cautious and would not be a likely lead buyer in the region.
Pakistan	Medium	One of first FX countries to get approval for F-16s. Proximity to Afghanistan figured in administration's decision.
Portugal	Medium	NATO ally but favored French Mirage 2000 fighters.
Singapore	Medium	FX country considered F-20 and F-16/J79, but Thailand's purchase of F-16s caused reconsideration.
South Korea	Medium	Previously FX country seen as F-20 customer, but Reagan Administration allowed F-16 sales due to North Korean threat.
Spain	Medium	Potential member of NATO would probably seek F-16s for commonality with other NATO members.
Taiwan	Medium	Seen as first buyer for F-20, but potential sale of 150–200 planes stopped by Reagan Administration to avoid upsetting Red China.
Thailand	Low/medium	Previously FX country was given clearance to purchase F-16s due to threat from North Viet Nam. Important country in terms of setting precedent for region.
Turkey	Medium	NATO member and receivng large military aid from United States with specific mention of F-16s.
Venezuela	Medium	One of first FX countries to be allowed front line fighters. Purchased F-16s.

Sources: *International Defense Review,* Sanford C. Bernstein & Co.

concerns for Third World countries, despite the price and their inability to keep the complex planes in the air. As California Congressman Mervyn Dymally noted, "They want the best. It doesn't matter if it works."

24   The remaining countries that made up the lower segment of the export market consisted of smaller, even less-affluent nations, which could afford only limited orders or whose needs dictated fewer planes. The tiny kingdom of Bahrain wanted four Tigersharks, but had to settle for F-5s because the F-20 was not in production. A significant problem now faced Northrop. The company had stated that it would have to have firm orders for 300 to 400 planes before the F-20 could be put in actual production. These smaller countries could not afford a top line U.S. fighter, but it was unclear whether or not this low segment of the FX market could collectively support the F-20 program. While analysts believed that the lower segment might ultimately hold sales potential for 300 or more planes over a period of years, it remained to be seen whether enough of the countries could place sufficient initial orders to justify the start-up of the F-20 production line.

25   The newly created medium segment of previously FX-only fighter buyers, such as Venezuela, South Korea, and Pakistan, was even more substantial, because of the State Department's eagerness to facilitate sales. Countries whose income made them borderline FX customers could purchase higher level fighters, due to the United States direct aid programs, consisting of grants and long-term low-interest loans that reduced immediate costs. Linked with other foreign aid packages, these arrangements often meant that a Third World country paid for its military aircraft with the money provided by the seller, in this case, the United States. An extreme example was Israel's purchase of 150 F-16s worth $3.3 billion. Through 1984, Israel had actually paid $22 million, or roughly the price of one F-16. In fact, over half of the $8.1 billion dollars worth of F-16 sales to foreign countries through 1984 were paid for by grants from the United States or by loans that were later forgiven.

26   It was clear that substantial sales would have to come from the middle segment, the one contested by General Dynamics (Exhibit 4). Nearly all of these countries, as well as some potential NATO customers, were now considering F-16s or had already placed some orders. It was also becoming clearer and clearer to Thomas Jones and his staff that F-20, designed and built as an export fighter, might have to be sold to their own country's air force before anyone else would buy it.

CURRENT OPERATIONS

27   In 1985, Northrop was a diversified company that had numerous operating elements in the fields of aviation and aerospace, electronics, and technical and management support. The company was strategically divided into three major groups—Aircraft, Electronics, and Services, each with its own divisions (Exhibit 5).

Aircraft Group

28   The Aircraft Group's Aircraft Division handled production of the F-5s and the prototype F-20s. The division's F-18 subcontract agreement with McDonnell Douglas brought substantial cash flow into the company and appeared secure, with approximately $623 million in 1984 sales and a backlog of future orders of over $1.1 billion. Once thought politically vulnerable, the program had substantial backing in Congress and was far enough along in its production curve to survive. Northrop had been involved with the assembly of the fuselage midsection of Boeing's 747 airliner since the beginning of the plane's production in 1966. Sales had reached $125 million by 1984 and were expected to have modest increases into the 1990s.

29   In 1981, Northrop had been awarded the development contract for the Air Force's top-secret Advanced Technology Bomber, better known as the Stealth bomber. Although the exact figures were classified, analysts believed that the contribution to revenues from the development contract was near $1 billion in 1984 and would increase in 1985. While Northrop had not officially been awarded a production contract, such a contract could be immensely lucrative. Perhaps as profitable would be the contract for the Air Force's Advanced Technology Fighter. The production contract would be awarded after competition between prototypes. A final decision on the winning company

EXHIBIT 5

Northrop Aircraft Group

Advanced Systems Division: Pico Rivera, California
- Stealth bomber
- ATF development

Aircraft Division: Hawthorne, California
- F-20 fighters
- F-18 fighters
- F-5 fighters
- T-38 trainers
- 747 mid-sections
- Aerospace R&D

Venture Division: Newbury Park, California
- Aeronautical target systems
- Aeronautical tactical systems
- Aircraft subassemblies

Northrop Services Group

Aircraft Services Division: Hawthorne, California
- Training and technical support in maintenance
- Logistics and on-the-job training

Northrop Services, Inc.: Anaheim, California*
- Managerial and technical support services

Northrop Worldwide Aircraft Services, Inc.: Lawton, Oklahoma*
- Military base operations and aircraft maintenance specialist
- Helicopter and aircraft maintenance contractor

Defense Systems Division: Rolling Meadows, Illinois
- Electronic countermeasures
- Infrared countermeasures
- Laser warning receivers

Electro-Mechanical Division: Anaheim, California
- Sensor systems
- Tracking systems
- Tactical missile systems
- Fabricated products

Electronics Division: Hawthorne, California
- Guidance system for Peacekeeper missile
- Navigation systems for AWACS

Precision Products Division: Norwood, Massachusetts
- Gyroscopes
- Accelorometers
- Inertial guidance and control subsystems

* Wholly owned subsidiary.
Source: 1983 Northrop annual report.

would be made in the early 1990s. Along with Lockheed, Rockwell Industries, and Boeing, Northrop was among those being considered and had started preliminary research and development without the benefit of government funding. Both of these projects were being conducted by the Aircraft Group's Advanced Systems Division.

30   The Aircraft Group also included the Ventura Division, which was involved with the production of unmanned drones, or self-propelled targets. Basically small monoplanes driven by turbojets, the drones were typically used to train pilots and anti-aircraft crews in the operation of various weapon systems. A derivative of these drones had also been used by the U.S. Navy as a remotely piloted reconnaissance vehicle, with infrared or high resolution television. Several different variants had been produced. The Northrop UMVs (unmanned vehicle) and RPVs (remotely piloted vehicle) were being used by every branch of the U.S. armed forces and numerous NATO countries as well. The experience gained with unmanned flight vehicles helped land the Ventura Division a contract for a joint U.S. Air Force/Navy radar suppression missile system, known as Tacit Rainbow. Designed to seek out and attack enemy radar warning systems, it had the capability to loiter over a target until a transmitter activated and presented itself as a target. Northrop dominated the target drone market, and the Ventura Division had contributed healthy sales in the amount of $350 million in 1984.

31   The standard-bearer of Northrop, the Aircraft Group, earned over $2.5 billion in sales during 1984, but the figures were deceiving (Exhibit 6–A). The sales of the F-5 were dwindling, notwithstanding a brief flurry of final orders. The final sales would have to be used to cover the costs of the write-down of inventory as the F-5 program came to an end. The overall figures were boosted by the development contract for the Stealth bomber, a program that had not proven its longevity.

EXHIBIT 6–A
Results of Operations by Industry Segment
Northrop Corporation and Subsidiaries (dollars in millions)

Year Ended December 31	1986	1985	1984	1983	1982
Revenue:					
Aircraft:					
Net sales to customers	$4,233.8	$3,830.5	$2,563.9	$2,119.9	$1,452.5
Intersegment sales	1.9	2.3	0.7	3.3	0.3
Other income (deductions)	2.7	53.0	(2.5)	0.1	4.4
Total	4,238.4	3,885.8	2,562.1	2,123.3	1,457.2
Electronics:					
Net sales to customers	1,124.9	828.1	702.4	669.2	525.0
Intersegment sales	121.8	109.2	55.5	16.2	5.6
Other income (deductions)	1.2	1.0	0.6	(0.2)	(0.6)
Total	1,247.9	938.3	758.5	685.2	530.0
Services:					
Net sales to customers	249.7	398.0	421.5	457.7	454.8
Intersegment sales	0.8	1.5	0.3	0.1	0.2
Other income	3.7	1.4	0.2	0.3	—
Total	254.2	400.9	422.0	458.1	455.0
Construction:					
Net sales to customers				13.8	40.6
Other deductions				(6.7)	—
				7.1	40.6
Intersegment eliminations	(124.5)	(113.0)	(56.5)	(19.6)	(6.1)
Total revenue	$5,616.0	$5,112.0	$3,686.1	$3,254.1	$2,476.7

(continued)

EXHIBIT 6–A (*concluded*)

Year Ended December 31	1986	1985	1984	1983	1982
Operating Profit (Loss)					
Aircraft	$ 66.0	$ 348.3	$ 203.3	$ 90.0	$ (114.9)
Electronics	99.7	84.0	81.7	77.3	54.1
Services	21.5	58.5	62.8	68.6	49.2
Construction	—	—	—	(22.7)	(0.4)
Total operating profit (loss)	187.2	490.8	347.8	213.2	(12.0)
Less:					
Other income (deductions) included in total revenue	7.6	55.4	(1.7)	(6.5)	3.8
State and local income taxes	1.2	29.5	18.3	11.4	2.2
General corporate expenses	107.6	98.1	87.8	67.8	48.6
Operating margin (loss)	$ 70.8	$ 307.8	$ 243.4	$ 140.5	$ (66.6)

EXHIBIT 6–B
Net Sales by Geographic Area
Northrop Corporation and Subsidiaries (dollars in millions)

Year Ended December 31	1986	1985	1984	1983	1982
United States					
United States government:					
Domestic agencies	$4,644.7	$3,770.7	$2,670.5	$2,185.9	$1,429.4
Foreign military sales (FMS)	383.9	510.4	434.2	450.5	443.8
	5,028.6	4,281.1	3,104.7	2,636.4	1,873.2
Other domestic sales	364.4	312.3	210.7	247.0	219.8
Total	5,393.0	4,593.4	3,315.4	2,883.4	2,093.0
Near/Middle East					
FMS	176.6	310.6	276.1	264.8	336.1
Direct foreign sales	27.5	29.0	35.7	43.1	28.4
Total	204.1	330.6	311.8	307.9	364.5
Other Areas					
FMS	207.3	208.8	158.1	185.7	107.7
Direct foreign sales	187.9	434.2	336.7	334.1	351.5
Total	395.2	643.0	494.8	519.8	459.2
FMS eliminations	(383.9)	(510.4)	(434.2)	(450.5)	(443.8)
Net sales	$5,608.4	$5,056.6	$3,687.8	$3,260.6	$2,472.9

EXHIBIT 6-C
Net Sales by Major Customer
Northrop Corporation and Subsidiaries (dollars in millions)

Year Ended December 31	1986	1985	1984	1983	1982
United States government (including FMS)					
Aircraft	$3,689.3	$3,092.9	$2,018.6	$1,575.7	$ 946.9
Electronics	1,092.4	799.8	675.4	626.1	486.1
Services	246.9	388.4	410.7	434.6	440.1
Construction	—	—	—	—	0.1
Total	$5,028.6	$4,281.1	$3,104.7	$2,636.4	$1,873.2
Kingdom of Saudi Arabia (mainly FMS)					
Aircraft	$ 61.7	$ 80.6	$ 64.4	$ 30.9	$ 20.7
Electronics	—	0.3	0.2	7.1	29.3
Services	45.9	210.3	221.5	254.8	274.4
Total	$ 107.6	$ 291.2	$ 286.1	$ 292.8	$ 324.4

EXHIBIT 6-D
Consolidated Statements of Financial Position
Northrop Corporation and Subsidiaries (dollars in millions)

December 31	1986	1985	1984	1983	1982
Assets:					
Current assets:					
Cash and cash items	$ 4.8	$ 7.1	$ 3.7	$ 60.2	$ 124.6
Accounts receivable	620.3	492.8	306.7	205.4	137.6
Inventoried costs	505.9	405.9	418.0	301.0	238.6
Prepaid expenses	29.5	24.9	15.0	10.7	10.8
Total current assets	1,160.5	930.7	743.4	577.3	511.6
Property, plant, and equipment at cost:					
Land and land improvements	114.4	111.2	105.6	78.6	70.6
Buildings	666.1	615.9	575.5	479.8	375.4
Machinery and other equipment	1,561.7	1,282.1	981.5	777.9	610.8
Leasehold improvements	45.9	36.5	19.3	16.6	17.8
	2,388.1	2,045.7	1,681.9	1,352.9	1,074.6
Accumulated depreciation and amortization	(901.0)	(694.4)	(510.9)	(379.5)	(278.0)
	1,487.1	1,351.3	1,171.0	973.4	796.6
Other assets:					
Investments in and advances to affiliates	35.0	31.2	22.7	11.9	16.9
Net investment in aircraft direct financing leases	12.7	15.0	17.1	19.2	17.9
Notes and accounts receivable	3.5	4.5	2.3	14.2	9.5
Total other assets	51.2	50.7	42.1	45.3	44.3
Total assets	$2,698.8	$2,332.7	$1,956.5	$1,596.0	$1,352.5

EXHIBIT 6–E
Consolidated Statements of Changes in Financial Position
Northrop Corporation and Subsidiaries (dollars in millions)

Year ended December 31	1986	1985	1984	1983	1982
Operating activities					
Sources of cash:					
Sales, net of change in accounts receivable	$5,480.9	$4,870.5	$3,586.5	$3,192.8	$2,528.3
Other income (deductions), net	5.4	55.5	(1.5)	19.6	13.5
Increase (decrease) in progress payments	(62.5)	40.6	125.6	(95.3)	$146.1
Increase (decrease) in advances on contracts	(24.1)	(142.9)	(5.7)	33.7	65.9
Cash provided by operating activities	5,399.7	4,823.7	3,704.9	3.150.8	2,753.8
Uses of cash:					
Cost of sales, net of changes in inventoried costs, payables and accruals	5,502.7	4,704.1	3,583.5	3,010.1	2,508.8
Depreciation and amortization	(225.6)	(193.4)	(138.1)	(109.8)	(60.9)
Amortization of unvested employee restricted award shares	(4.0)	(4.8)	(13.7)	(6.4)	(5.8)
Income taxes	30.3	(9.9)	2.9	(1.7)	(6.1)
Cash used in operating activities	5,303.4	4,496.0	3,434.6	2,892.2	2.436.0
Net cash provided by operating activities	96.3	327.7	270.3	258.6	317.8
Investment activities					
Additions to property, plant, and equipment	(364.2)	(384.0)	(345.3)	(293.1)	(376.8)
Carrying value of disposals of property, plant, and equipment	2.8	10.3	9.6	6.5	9.6
Decrease (increase) in other assets	(.5)	(8.6)	3.2	(1.0)	(3.4)
Net cash used in investment activities	(361.9)	(382.3)	(332.5)	(287.6)	(370.6)
Financing activities					
Increase in indebtedness	335.9	120.6	44.1	1.4	1.9
Issuance of common stock	10.3	10.6	8.6	3.4	2.9
Net interest income (expense)	(26.7)	(15.2)	0.1	(7.4)	16.4
Repayment of long-term debt	(0.4)	(2.4)	(5.8)	(5.3)	(10.9)
Net cash provided by (used in) financing activities	319.1	113.6	47.0	(7.9)	10.3
Cash dividends	(55.8)	(55.6)	(41.3)	(27.5)	(27.2)
Increase (decrease) in cash and cash items	$ (2.3)	$ 3.4	$ (56.5)	$ (64.4)	$ (69.7)

EXHIBIT 6–F
Consolidated Statements of Income
Northrop Corporation and Subsidiaries (dollars in millions, except per share)

Year Ended December 31	1986	1985	1984	1983	1982
Net sales	$5,608.4	$5,056.6	$3,687.8	$3,260.6	$2,472.9
Cost of sales:					
Operating costs	4,985.9	4,205.4	3,005.5	2,725.0	2,260.2
Administrative and general expenses	551.7	543.4	438.9	395.1	279.3
Operating margin (loss)	70.8	307.8	243.4	140.5	(66.6)
Other income (deductions):					
Claim settlement	—	50.0	—	—	—
Interest income	2.2	2.2	7.6	6.9	19.5
Other, net	5.4	5.5	(1.5)	19.6	13.5
Interest expense	(28.9)	(17.4)	(7.5)	(14.3)	(3.1)
Income (loss) before income taxes	49.5	348.1	242.0	152.7	(36.7)
Federal and foreign income taxes (benefit)	8.3	133.7	75.1	52.0	(42.1)
Net income	$ 41.2	$ 214.4	$ 166.9	$ 100.7	$ 5.4
Weighted average common shares outstanding	46.5	46.3	45.9	45.6	45.3
Earnings per share	$ 0.89	$ 4.63	$ 3.63	$ 2.21	$ 0.12

EXHIBIT 6–G
Consolidated Statements of Changes in Shareholders' Equity
Northrop Corporation and Subsidiaries (in millions, except per share)

Year Ended December 31	1986	1985	1984	1983	1982
Paid-in capital:					
At beginning of year	$161.6	$150.7	$133.3	$128.0	$116.2
Employee stock awards and options exercised, net of forfeitures	15.2	10.9	17.4	5.3	11.8
At end of year	176.8	161.6	150.7	133.3	128.0
Retained earnings:					
At beginning of year	755.5	596.7	471.1	397.9	419.7
Net income	41.2	214.4	166.9	100.7	5.4
Cash dividends	(55.8)	(55.6)	(41.3)	(27.5)	(27.2)
At end of year	740.9	755.5	596.7	471.1	397.9
Unvested employee restricted award shares:					
At beginning of year	(18.1)	(22.6)	(27.5)	(32.0)	(28.9)
Grants, net of forfeitures	(4.9)	(.3)	(8.8)	(1.9)	(8.9)
Amortization	4.0	4.8	13.7	6.4	5.8
At end of year	(19.0)	(18.1)	(22.6)	(27.5)	(32.0)
Total shareholders' equity	$898.7	$899.0	$724.8	$576.9	$493.9
Book value per share	$19.29	$19.42	$15.72	$12.64	$10.87
Cash dividends per share	1.20	1.20	0.90	0.60	0.60

EXHIBIT 6–H

Year Ended December 31	Dollars in Millions				
	1986	1985	1984	1983	1982
Contract acquisitions:					
Aircraft	$3,796.1	$4,259.4	$2,903.6	$2,719.3	$1,513.9
Electronics	1,189.3	1,083.9	1,335.7	715.9	591.1
Services	179.3	339.5	194.8	288.0	828.0
Construction	—	—	(2.8)	3.0	8.7
Total acquisitions	5,164.7	5,682.8	4,431.3	3,726.2	2,941.7
Funded order backlog:					
Aircraft	2,483.6	2,921.3	2,492.4	2,152.7	1,553.3
Electronics	1,593.8	1.529.4	1,273.6	640.3	593.6
Services	89.4	159.8	218.3	445.0	614.7
Construction	—	—	—	2.8	13.6
Total backlog	4,166.8	4,610.5	3,984.3	3,240.2	2,775.2
Identifiable assets:					
Aircraft	1,808.7	1,555.8	1,306.5	1,001.9	783.5
Electronics	574.9	454.1	370.4	264.1	223.6
Services	79.8	89.0	49.6	41.6	31.9
Construction	—	—	—	8.7	7.5
Operating assets	2,463.4	2,098.9	1,726.5	1,316.3	1,046.5
General corporate	235.4	233.8	230.0	279.7	306.0
Total assets	2,698.8	2,332.7	1,956.5	1,596.0	1,352.5
Capital expenditures:					
Aircraft	243.5	282.5	232.6	201.2	246.9
Electronics	100.9	83.6	68.0	40.9	59.7
Services	4.9	4.9	3.5	2.3	1.9
Construction	—	—	—	—	0.1
General corporate	14.9	13.0	41.2	48.7	68.2
Total expenditures	364.2	384.0	345.3	293.1	376.8
Depreciation and amortization:					
Aircraft	164.6	142.6	105.8	75.2	33.3
Electronics	45.2	34.3	22.9	19.8	12.2
Services	3.3	2.8	2.3	1.6	1.6
Construction	—	—	—	—	0.2
General corporate	12.5	13.7	7.1	13.2	13.6
Total depreciation and amortization	225.6	193.4	138.1	109.8	60.9

Electronics Group

32 Northrop had used its cash inflows to build the Electronics Group into an business that, standing alone, would have ranked in the top 300 industrial companies compiled by *Fortune* magazine in 1984. By 1985, the Defense Systems Division of the Electronics Group was on its way to becoming the nation's largest producer of airborne jamming equipment. Broadly defined as electronic countermeasures (ECM), this equipment protected aircraft and crew by confusing and disrupting enemy radar stations and radar guided weapons systems. Enormously successful for a program of its type,

Northrop's ECM equipment was typically installed on various manufacturers' aircraft, such as McDonnell Douglas's F-15 fighter and Boeing's B-52 bomber. In addition, the division had attracted some foreign customers. Overseas, Northrop contracted with Denmark, Spain, and Canada to provide jamming systems for their armed forces. Another sale was to Britain for several components in the ECM group used by their Harrier aircraft.

33   The Electro-Mechanical and Precision Products Divisions performed research and development in several areas that had led to contracts for Northrop. The Electro-Mechanical Division had become an important producer of passive sensor devices. These components used electro-optical television and infrared technology to enable pilots and anti-aircraft crews to locate targets without the telltale emissions of a radar. Both the Army and Navy had placed orders. The Navy refitted its F-14 Tomcat fighter squadrons with Northrop TV systems, which permitted visual identification at distances 10 times greater than what was normally possible. Another field pioneered by Northrop was in its Precision Products Division's "strapdown" guidance and navigation systems. The name was derived from the method of bolting the systems' gyroscopes to a vehicle's frame, rather than mounting the devices in complex gimbals as was previously done. The design had applications in multiple areas, including tactical missiles, airplanes, helicopters, spacecraft, and torpedoes, and was already being used on the F-20. Northrop was expected to receive guidance system contracts for the U.S. Air Force/Navy advanced medium range air to air missile (AMRAAM) guidance system, as well as the Navy Harpoon and Tomahawk anti-ship missiles.

34   The other major division in the Electronics Group, the Electronics Division, was involved in two projects. The first was the development and manufacture of the navigational system for the air forces' AWACS (early warning) plane. The other project involved a long-term contract to produce the Advanced Inertial Reference Sphere, or AIRS, the primary element of the MX Peacekeeper missile's internal guidance system. The size of a basketball, the AIRS contained nearly as many parts as an entire fighter plane and had to be built to exacting tolerances. The program had the potential to last into the early 1990s and was estimated to be worth in excess of a billion dollars in future sales revenues. It was a program, however, that was politically unstable, as budget deficits and arms control talks made its long-term future unclear.

35   Northrop's policy of reinvestment and diversification had paid off handsomely, particularly in the field of electronics, which had accounted for approximately 20 percent of the sales in 1984 and approximately 25 percent of the operating profit. Although the revenues were boosted by the unstable MX missile program, the Electronics Division was considered a growth area for the future and had $750 million dollars in sales in 1984 (Exhibit 6–A).

Services Group

36   The Services Group consisted of three subsidiaries and was the smallest group in terms of growth and earnings potential, but had been profitable throughout the 1980s. The Aircraft Services Division provided on the job training in management and support for civil and military aviation personnel. The Northrop Services, Inc., provided environmental studies and general consulting to a number of federal agencies, such as NASA and the Environmental Protection Agency. Northrop Worldwide Aircraft Services, Inc., provided maintenance, support, and property management for military bases and received a continuing maintenance contract for the famed U.S. Navy "Top Gun" fighter pilot school. A large portion of the Services Group's operating profit was derived from Peace Hawk/ATTS, a project for support services to the Saudi Arabian Air Force that was scheduled to end in 1986. The Service Group was a no-growth field and lacked the excitement of the more illustrious divisions. However, it accounted for $422 million in revenues in 1984 based on the strength of the Peace Hawk contracts (Exhibits 6–A, C).

MANAGEMENT

37   With Thomas Jones leading the company, Northrop had engaged in a strategy with aspects that distinguished it from many of its defense competitors. Much of this strategy related to the F-20 program and how it was formulated.

38   1. *High level of spending in R & D.* Research into radar avoidance won Northrop a profitable development contract for the Stealth bomber. Research in electronics, reinvestment, and purchases of existing companies, such as the Hallicrafters Electronics Company, made Northrop the industry leader in ECM and other military electronics. The Tigershark became the first fighter with 1980s technology. By using avionics and electronics garnered from company research, the F-20 had some abilities beyond those of its competitors including the F-15, F-16, and F-18.

39   2. *Use of own funds to improve productivity.* Northrop owned an unheard of 94 percent of its plants and was above the industry average in capital spending as a percentage of sales. The Defense Department owned half of all other aerospace manufacturing facilities. Northrop's ownership of its own plants allowed more flexibility and made the F-20 project possible without government funding.

40   3. *Conservative financial and accounting practices.* Northrop had employed a financial policy, described by one analyst as reactionary, choosing to expense development costs as they occur. All of the costs of the F-20 program, including fixtures and tools, were charged off as incurred.

41   4. *Focus on defense aerospace and electronics.* Exclusive of its 747 subcontract work, Northrop had no significant contracts outside the defense industry, a problem it had in common with many of its competitors. Northrop's F-5 export sales to foreign governments did give it a degree of protection from domestic budget cuts and political swings, which might affect defense spending. Northrop hoped to keep this advantage with sales of the F-20.

42   5. *Competing for major first line contracts.* In 1985, Northrop was competing for major domestic contracts and was building prototypes of the sophisticated and high performance F-20. Prior to the mid-80s, Northrop had no experience with modern first line aircraft besides its subcontract work on the F-18 and building the unsophisticated F-5.

43   6. *Willing to take risks and reinvest cash flow.* Jones was adamant in his belief that private contractors should accept the risks inherent in developing new technology. The F-20 was the most visible symbol of Jones's entrepreneurial beliefs and was the only modern fighter ever developed solely with private funds and no government contract.

FINANCIAL INFORMATION

44   The current financial situation was not a desperate one, despite the cash drain of the F-20 program. Total sales for all the company's divisions were nearing a $5 billion year by 1985, an almost fivefold increase since 1979 (Exhibits 6–A and 7). High profits had not followed, however. Northrop's policy of heavy reinvestment into its plants and machinery, and the commitment to research and development had depressed profits somewhat, but the F-20 write-offs were the most visible burden. So far the write-offs had amounted to $258.5 million in 1982, $168.1 million in 1983, $148.5 million in 1984, and a like amount was expected in 1985. Northrop had netted a paltry $5 million on $2.5 billion in sales in 1982. That had risen to $167 million on sales of $3.7 billion in 1984, but the F-20 program was still consuming a substantial percentage of operating profit (Exhibit 7).

EXHIBIT 7

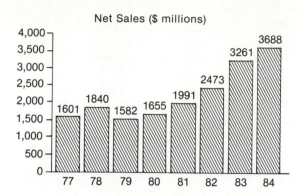

Net Sales ($ millions)

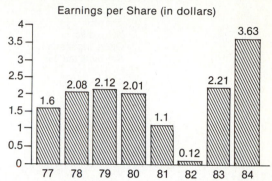

Earnings per Share (in dollars)

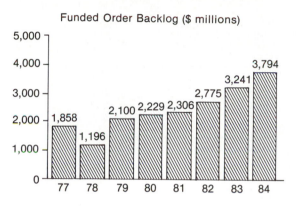

Funded Order Backlog ($ millions)

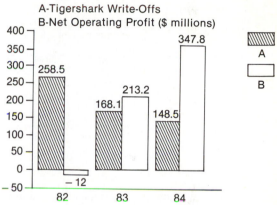

A-Tigershark Write-Offs
B-Net Operating Profit ($ millions)

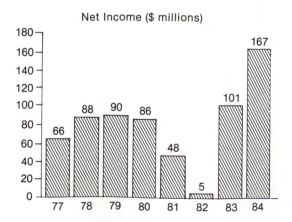

Net Income ($ millions)

EXHIBIT 8
Profitability Statistics and Ratios, 1982–84

	1984	1983	1982
Net profits	166.9	100.7	5.4
Operating margin	10.4%	7.7%	(loss)
Net profit margin	4.5%	3.1%	0.2%
ROI	9.4%	6.8%	0.4%
Asset turnover	1.88	2.04	1.83
ROE	25.6%	18.8%	1.1%

EXHIBIT 9
Capital Statistics and Ratios

	1984	1983	1982
Long-term debt	7.7	10.5	14.5
Short-term debt	233.7	214.1	177.3
Capital expenditures	345.3	293.1	376.8
Current ratio	0.6	0.6	0.7
Quick ratio	0.27	0.46	0.34
Debt/equity	1.63	1.68	1.65
Debt/capital	1.0	1.7	2.7

Sources: Northrop, 1986 Annual Report and *Value Line.*

45   Northrop's short-term debt had increased steadily while long-term debt continued to decline to $7.7 million in 1984. Short-term debt had risen for several years and was expected to approach $300 million by the end of 1985. The current debt/equity ratio stood at 1.63 by the beginning of 1985, and the quick ratio had fallen to 0.27 (Exhibit 8). These ratios were a reflection of Northrop's policy of reinvestment, as well as heavy spending on the F-20. The major profitability indexes sent mixed messages in 1984. Several indicators showed an increase over the previous two years. The return on equity reached 25.6 percent, up from 1.1 percent in 1982. The net profit margin was 4.5 percent in 1984 and return on investment was 9.4 percent, both higher than the figures from the two past years (see Exhibit 9). Even the earlier figures were not indicative of a company in trouble but demonstrated capital investments in several programs, the most costly of which was the F-20. The funded order backlog had steadily increased. This showed that many of Northrop's programs were secure through the near future. However, the apparent increase in several of the 1984 statistics was influenced by the revenues from the Stealth development contract, and Northrop could not risk overdependence on the uncertain program.

46   In the short term, there was little doubt that some Wall Street analysts would be happier if the Tigershark were scrapped. Their predictions were that a decision to drop the program would add as much as $1.55 to the value of a share. They also felt that the company would benefit from not being forced to make a big investment in manufacturing equipment for the F-20's production at a time when the company's profitability indexes were recovering from earlier capital expenditures.

OTHER CONSIDERATIONS

47   Ultimately, to a greater degree than any of its defense competitors, the future of the Northrop's aircraft business rested on risky and uncertain programs. In this case, the programs were the Advanced Technology Bomber (ATB) or Stealth, the Advanced Technical Fighter (ATF), and the F-20 Tigershark. The Stealth was widely discussed, although little was actually known about the secret plane. A large strategic bomber with a radical shape and technology to render it undetectable to radar, it would cost nearly $500 million a plane, making it the mostly costly aircraft ever built—if it were put into production. Northrop, known as a subcontractor and the manufacturer of the unsophisticated F-5, won the development bid—to the surprise of the industry. Capable of producing sales of up to $35 billion in sales revenue over the next decade, the Stealth was politically vulnerable, its astounding price a liability in Congress.

48   The ATF was as much of a gamble in some respects. Designed to be a "superfighter" for the 21st century, the ATF would replace the current F-16s and F-15s as America's top fighter. The competition for the contract, however, could prove long and costly. Teams consisting of prime contractors and subcontractors were required to put in bids to build the plane. The two winning teams would each construct a prototype of their own design. Ultimately, after a competition, one of the prototypes would be chosen for a full-scale production by the team that created it. Northrop was the prime contractor on its team. Along with its subcontractor, McDonnell Douglas, Northrop had an excellent chance of receiving a bid. Financial analysts saw it as a mixed blessing. Each winning team would receive $691 million from the Defense Department but would probably have to contribute several times that amount again to complete a prototype. The stakes would be high, with the winner having potential sales of $35 to $45 billion into the next century. The loser could come away with nothing but substantial research and development costs.

49   As for the F-20 program, one Prudential-Bache security analyst felt the F-20 program could "yield higher profits than any other major weapons production program in history," with pre-tax margins of 15 percent to 20 percent. Despite Northrop's early setbacks, Thomas Jones still believed a potential market of over 2,000 planes existed, because numerous countries were going to have to replace aging F-5s and other outmoded aircraft. In the export market, the F-20 would be free of domestic budgetary pressures and could produce a windfall for the company. Without it or the uncertain Stealth bomber, Northrop would be without a plane to call its own in the very near future.

CONCLUSION

50   Northrop was clearly not prepared for the change in policy that came in with the Reagan Administration, nor did it comprehend the political symbolism Third World countries would attach to having a top quality U.S. Air Force inventory plane. Relegating itself to the foreign market, Northrop had managed to avoid most of the political infrastructure that often marked the domestic defense market. It was doubtful this approach would continue to be possible. Northrop's main competitor, General Dynamics, had the largest share of the industry, but many believed it had an intangible competitive advantage beyond its research and development prowess. General Dynamics built the F-16 in Texas, the home of Senate Armed Services Committee chairman John Tower, and within the district of Jim Wright, the House majority leader, both of whom controlled key votes concerning foreign military aid packages. As one anonymous Air Force officer joked, "It rolls off the assembly line faster if it's built in Texas."

51   Another obstacle Northrop had to overcome was the Defense Department itself. All export sales were handled with the Pentagon acting in a middleman role. Furthermore, information and per-

formance data on competing planes was disseminated through the Pentagon. Defense Department officials had privately stated that both the Air Force and the Navy preferred to promote the sales of their own fighters overseas "to amortize costs and to keep production lines open." Other officials allowed that the Pentagon "procurement community" preferred planes it had initially ordered to privately designed aircraft, like the F-20, even if the aircraft were capable. In addition, the Air Force received $745,000 for each F-16 sold for export to cover flight preparation and testing. Northrop officials had complained that comparison data between the F-16 and the F-20 had not been given to prospective buyers, and the State Department in general had done little to represent their fighter. In fact, Thomas Jones publicly asked that the Air Force be ordered to inform other governments of the low cost and high performance of the F-20.

52   The current success of Northrop was due in large part to the cash flows generated by the F-5 Tiger program. For decades, it had bankrolled Northrop's emergence into military electronics and higher levels of research and development in aerospace and aviation. The F-5 had virtually created the export fighter market and had claimed the lion's share for Thomas Jones and his company. Now, American and foreign export fighters alike were outperforming the Tiger, and the majority of the aging F-5 fleet was reaching obsolescence. To fail with the Tigershark would be tantamount to wiping out the market for export planes that Northrop had exploited for so long.

53   The Stealth project and the ATF bid held the promise of great if uncertain potential, and Jones wondered if Northrop would be in a better position if the board of directors wrote off the F-20 program and diverted the development costs toward these new projects. On the other hand, a successful F-20 program could help fund these projects and more, as the F5 had before it. In 1981, CEO Thomas Jones had said, "If we didn't make this investment [in the Tigershark], I would be telling you our future in fighter planes is less secure. It's riskier to do nothing." Four years later, with no orders in hand, Thomas Jones had to decide if that was still true.

BIBLIOGRAPHY

"High Roller." *Forbes*. March 2, 1981, pp. 38–39.

"General Dynamics." Sanford C. Bernstein & Co. publication. August 6, 1981, pp. 22–23.

"Look Who's Heading for No. 1 in Defense: Northrop." *Business Week*. April 19, 1982, pp. 70–75.

"Aerospace/Defense Outlook." Shearson/American Express publication. March 17, 1983.

"U.S. Will Assist Turkey in Improving Air Defense." *Aviation Week and Space Technology*. February 20, 1984, p. 68.

"Northrop's F-20 Goes Begging." *Newsweek*. March 26, 1984, p. 71.

"Northrop's Campaign to Get a New Fighter Flying in the Third World." *Business Week*. June 18, 1984, pp. 74–75.

"The Airplane That Doesn't Cost Enough." *The Atlantic Monthly*. August 1984, pp. 46–55.

"Tigershark Tour Raises Sales Hopes." *Flight International*. October 6, 1984.

"The Affordable Fighter Market." *Interavia*. January 1985, pp. 23–26.

"Trials of the Tigershark." *Air Force Magazine*. January 1985, pp. 72–77.

"A Cloudy Future for Northrop Corp." *Financial World*. February 20, 1985, pp. 38–39.

"Dispute over Fighter Imports." *New York Times*. April 5, 1985.

"Northrop Backs Tigershark Jet." *New York Times*. May 15, 1985.

"Northrop Aims for a Killing With the Tigershark." *Fortune*. June 24, 1985.

"East Asian Tactical Fighter Markets." *International Defense Review*. December 1985.

"Northrop: The Rewards of Risk." *Dun's Business Month*, December 1985, p. 36.

"Revving Up for the Big Flyoff: F-20 vs. F-16." *Asian Defence Journal*. April 1986, pp. 1–7.

"Northrop Corporation: The Sky's the Limit." *Air Cal*. May 1986.

"Northrop Uses Spit and Polish to Keep an Untarnished Image." *Insight*. June 16, 1986.

"Stealth Specialists Win ATF Contracts." *Flight International*. November 8, 1986, p. 2.

Northrop Corporation Annual Report 1986. Northrop Corporation, March 7, 1987.

"Northrop News." Northrop Corporation Public Relations. 1989.

CASE 11

WAL-MART

THE NEW WAL-MART

1   Growth in sales . . . growth in profitability . . . growth in customers . . . growth in number of stores . . . growth in distributions centers . . . growth in markets . . . growth in associates . . . growth in market share . . . growth in shareholders . . . growth in suppliers . . . growth in financial strength.

History

2   No word better describes Wal-Mart than growth. Wal-Mart Stores, Inc., had its beginning in the small-town variety store business in 1945, when Sam Walton opened his first Ben Franklin franchise operating in Newport, Arkansas. Based in rural Bentonville, Arkansas, Walton, his wife, Helen, and brother, Bud, were the nation's most successful Ben Franklin franchisees. "We were a small chain," says Walton of his 16-store operation. "Things were running so smoothly we even had time for our families."[1] What more could a man want? A great deal, as it turned out.

3   Sam Walton felt he wasn't as secure as he seemed to be. "I could see that the variety store was gradually dying, because there were giant supermarkets and then discounters coming into the picture," explains Walton.[2] Far from being secure, Sam Walton knew he was under siege. He decided to counterattack. Walton first tried to convince the top management of Ben Franklin to enter discounting. After their refusal, Walton made a quick trip around the country in search of ideas. Walton then began opening his own discount stores in small Arkansas towns like Bentonville and Rogers.

4   The company did not open its first discount department store (Wal-Mart) until November 1962. In 1974, at his induction ceremony with Alpha Kappa Psi Chapter Beta Zeta, he announced the opening of his 50th store. The early stores had bare tile floors and pipe racks, and Wal-Mart did not begin to revamp its image significantly until the mid-1970s.

5   Growth in the early years was slow. However, once the company went public in 1970, sales began to increase rapidly. If one had purchased 100 shares of the stock in 1970, he or she would have been worth $350,000 in 1985. The stock traded between $24\frac{1}{4}$ and $33\frac{7}{8}$ in the fiscal year ending January 31, 1988.

6   Such retailers as Target, Venture, and K mart provided the examples that Wal-Mart sought to emulate in its growth. The old Wal-Mart store colors, dark blue and white (too harsh), were dumped

---

This case was prepared by Walter E. Greene, Pan American University, Edinburg, Texas. The case is designed for classroom discussion, not to demonstrate effective or ineffective management practices. Copyright © 1989.

[1]Howard Rudnitsky, "How Sam Walton Does It," *Forbes*, August 1982, p. 42.

[2]Ibid.

in favor of a three-tone combination of light beige, soft blue, and burnt orange. Carpeting, which had been long discarded on apparel sales floors, was put back. New racks were put into use that displayed the entire garment instead of only an edge of it. In 1987, Sam Walton named David G. Glass as the new CEO of Wal-Mart Stores, Inc., while he remained chairman of the board.

Growth in Profitability

7   In 1988, Wal-Mart had 1,247 discount stores in 25 contiguous states, mainly in the Sunbelt and the Midwest. Wal-Mart, with 16 billion in annual revenues, is one of most profitable companies in all of U.S. retailing and second only to K mart as a discounter. While most discounters would gladly settle for 2.5 percent net margins, Wal-Mart's run closer to 3.5 percent. Its return on equity between 1980 and 1985 was 35 percent. Profits have grown at a rate of 33 percent since 1975 (see Exhibit 1, Ten-Year Financial Summary).

8   Growth? In 1981, Wal-Mart racked up 50 percent gains in sales and earnings. In part, the increases came from opening 69 new stores, but Wal-Mart's same-store sales were up a remarkable 15 percent as well. Through June 1982—a brutal period for most retailers—same-store sales were ahead 12 percent, while first-half earnings for 1983 rose by an estimated 35 percent. Same-store sales for fiscal year 87–88 rose 11 percent over previous year. Sales growth of 35 percent per year is normal for Wal-Mart.[3] Sales for the three month period ending April 30, 1988, rose 33 percent. Margins narrowed and pretax income increased 28 percent.[4]

Growth in Markets

9   Wal-Mart stores carry a variety of merchandise, including soft lines, hard lines, domestics, housewares, electronics, and leased departments. Soft lines consist of clothing for the whole family. Hard lines are comprised of hardware, paints, automotives, sporting goods, lawn and garden supplies, and pet supplies. Domestics include furniture, crafts, and linens. Housewares consist of small appliances, detergents, food, picnic supplies, health and beauty aids, and toys. Electronics are comprised of records, tapes, stereos, televisions, and accessories. Leased departments include jewelry and shoes.

10   In his larger Wal-Mart stores, Walton added other departments, including pharmacies, automotive centers, beauty shops, and restaurants. For example, in Bonham, Texas, which has a population of 8,000, the Wal-Mart store includes a pharmacy.

Growth in Number of Stores

11   Of approximately 1,250 stores spanning the Sunbelt from South Carolina through Texas, most are located in towns of 5,000 to 25,000, although a few are located in and around a metropolitan area within the chain's regional trade territory (see Exhibit 2, map of USA). There are still smaller stores for communities of 5000 and under. Table 1 shows the number of stores operated on January 31 for the years 1974 through 1988.

12   There is yet another way for Walton to expand: by taking over failing chains and "Waltonizing" them. In July 1981, Walton picked up ailing Kuhn's Big-K stores—one warehouse and 92 loca-

---

[3]Jane Carmichael, "General Retailers," *Forbes*, January 1982, p. 226.

[4]*Standard & Poor's*, August 3, 1988, p. 2413–14.

EXHIBIT 1
Ten-Year Financial Summary, Wal-Mart Stores, Inc., and Subsidiaries
(dollar amounts in thousands, except per share data)

	1988	1987	1986	1985	1984	1983	1982	1981	1980	1979
Earnings										
Net sales	$15,959,255	$11,909,076	$8,451,489	$6,400,861	$4,666,909	$3,376,252	$2,444,997	$1,643,199	$1,248,176	$900,298
Licensed department rentals and other income—net	104,783	84,623	55,127	52,167	36,031	22,435	17,650	12,063	10,092	9,615
Cost of sales	12,281,744	9,053,219	6,361,271	4,722,440	3,418,025	2,458,235	1,787,496	1,207,802	919,305	661,062
Operating, selling, and general and administrative expenses	2,599,367	2,007,645	1,485,210	1,181,455	892,887	677,029	495,010	331,524	251,616	182,365
Interest costs:										
Debt	25,262	10,442	1,903	5,207	4,935	20,297	16,053	5,808	4,438	3,119
Capital leases	88,995	76,367	54,640	42,506	29,946	18,570	15,351	10,849	8,621	6,595
Taxes on income	441,027	395,940	276,119	230,653	160,903	100,416	65,943	43,597	33,137	27,325
Net income	627,643	450,086	327,473	270,767	196,244	124,140	82,794	55,682	41,151	29,447
Per share of common stock:										
Net income	1.11	0.79*	0.58*	0.48*	0.35*	0.23*	0.16*	0.11*	0.08*	0.06*
Dividends	0.12	0.085*	0.07*	0.0525*	0.035*	0.0225*	0.0163*	0.0125*	0.0095*	0.007*
Stores in operation at the end of the period:										
Wal-Mart stores	1,114	980	859	745	642	551	491	330	276	229
Sam's Wholesale Clubs	84	49	23	11	3					

Financial position

Current assets	$ 2,905,145	$ 2,353,271	$1,784,275	$1,303,254	$1,005,567	$ 720,537	$ 589,161	$ 345,204	$ 266,617	$191,860
Net property, plant, equipment, and capital leases	2,144,852	1,676,282	1,303,450	870,309	628,151	457,509	333,026	245,942	190,562	131,403
Total assets	5,131,809	4,049,092	3,103,645	2,205,229	1,652,254	1,187,448	937,513	592,345	457,879	324,666
Current liabilities	1,743,763	1,340,291	992,683	688,968	502,763	347,318	339,961	177,601	170,221	98,868
Long-term debt	185,672	179,234	180,682	41,237	40,866	106,465	104,581	30,184	24,862	25,965
Long-term obligations under capital leases	866,972	764,128	595,205	449,886	339,930	222,610	154,196	134,896	97,212	72,357
Preferred stock with mandatory redemption provisions	—	—	4,902	5,874	6,411	6,861	7,438	—	—	—
Common shareholders' equity	2,257,267	1,690,493	1,277,659	984,672	737,503	488,109	323,942	248,309	164,844	127,476
Financial ratios										
Current ratio	1.7	1.8	1.8	1.9	2.0	2.1	1.7	1.9	1.6	1.9
Inventories/working capital	2.3	2.0	1.8	1.8	1.5	1.5	2.0	1.7	2.4	1.9
Return on assets†	15.5	14.5	14.8	16.4	16.5	13.2	14.0	12.2	12.7	11.7
Return on shareholders' equity†	37.1	35.2	33.3	36.7	40.2	38.3	33.3	33.8	32.3	30.5

* Adjusted to reflect 100 percent common stock dividend paid July 10, 1987.
† On beginning of year balances.

EXHIBIT 2

JOIN AMERICA'S FASTEST GROWING RETAIL CHAIN

- Operates over 1200 stores in 25 states
- Second largest discount chain in America
- Plans to open over 125 stores per year in each of the next 5 years
- Annually places 400 to 500 college graduates

Wal-Mart Stores, Inc., Bentonville, Arkansas 72716
An Equal Opportunity Employer

Let's Talk About Your Future

A Wal-Mart representative will be on campus recruiting

Contact the placement office for details. A Wal-Mart career information binder is available in the placement office.

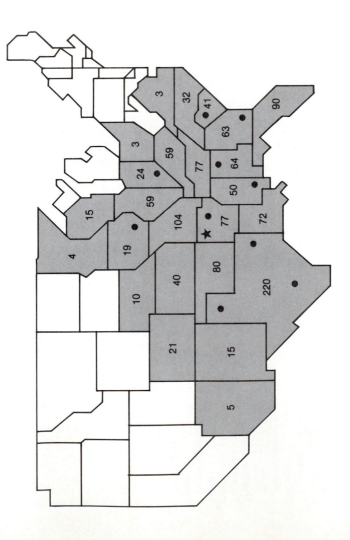

★ General Office
Bentonville, Arkansas (and three Distribution Centers)

● Distribution Centers
(present under construction and proposed)

☐ Projected territory for fiscal year 1988, this trade area includes 1247 stores with projected sales of 20 billion.

▨ Numbers indicate existing and proposed stores for the fiscal year 1988.

TABLE 1

Year	Wal-Mart	Sam's Discount
1974	78	
1975	104	
1976	125	
1977	153	
1978	195	
1979	229	
1980	276	
1981	330	
1982	491	
1983	551	
1984	642	3
1985	745	11
1986	859	23
1987	980	49
1988	1114	84
1989 (estimated)	1247	102

tions—in effect acquiring cheap leases at a discount price. Wal-Mart assumed $19 million in debt and issued $7.5 million worth of preferred stock. Now Kuhn's has a new management team and $60 million in cash for a major facelift. Profits may pour in, as they did after Wal-Mart's only previous acquisition—the 1977 purchase of Mohr Value Stores. "We fixed them up and retrained the people, and now they're our best group," says Walton.[5]

13   Wal-Mart implemented two new concepts: the Hypermarkets, 200,000 square foot stores that sell everything including food, in 1987; and it introduced "Super Centers" (a scaled-down supermarket) in 1988.[6]

Growth in Sales

14   Growth in administrative and support functions was required to maintain sales growth through new stores and existing stores. However, a strong rein was held on operations and expense controls to permit required flexibility in reacting to change in sales trends. Wal-Mart's expense structure, measured as a percentage of sales, continued to be among the lowest in the industry, as reported in Cornell University's Annual Study on Discount Retailers. Within the expense constraints imposed by the company's strategy of selling merchandise at low margins, these support functions have grown at a controlled rate. Sam's management ability came through with a sales volume of $15.9 billion in 1988, up from $11.9 billion in 1987 and from $8.5 billion in 1986 (see Exhibit 3, Income Statement).

15   Though Walton watches expenses, he didn't stint on rewarding sales managers. Sales figures were available to every employee. Monthly figures for each department were ranked and made available throughout the organization. Employees who were "doing better than average, they get rewarded with raises, bonuses, and a pat on the back. If they're doing poorer, we have to talk with

---

[5]Rudnitsky, "How Sam," p. 44.

[6]Alice Bredin, "Hypermarkets: Successful at Last?" *Chain Store Age Executive* 64 (January 1988), p. 15 (3).

EXHIBIT 3–A
Consolidated Statements of Income, Wal-Mart Stores, Inc., and Subsidiaries
(amounts in thousands, except per share data)

| | Fiscal Year Ended January 31 | | |
	1988	1987	1986
Revenues:			
Net sales	$15,959,255	$11,909,076	$8,451,489
Rentals from licensed departments	9,215	10,779	13,011
Other income—net	95,568	73,844	42,116
Total	16,064,038	11,993,699	8,506,616
Costs and expense:			
Cost of sales	12,281,744	9,053,219	6,361,271
Operating, selling, and general and administrative expenses	2,599,367	2,007,645	1,485,210
Interest cost:			
Debt	25,262	10,442	1,903
Capital leases	88,995	76,367	54,640
Total	14,995,368	11,147,673	7,903,024
Income before income taxes	1,068,670	846,026	603,592
Provision for federal and state income taxes:			
Current	432,133	373,508	258,197
Deferred	8,894	22,432	17,922
	441,027	395,940	276,119
Net income	$ 627,643	$ 450,086	$ 327,473
Net income per share	$ 1.11	$ 0.79*	$ 0.58*

*Adjusted to reflect 100% common stock dividend paid on July 10, 1987.

them to find out why and correct it. This leads to greater productivity."[7] Repeated failure will not likely result in dismissal, although demotions were possible.

16   All employees (called "associates") have a stake in the financial performance of the company. Store managers could earn as much as $100,000 to $150,000 per year. Part-time clerks even qualified for profit sharing and stock purchase plans. Millionaires among middle managers were not uncommon. Ideas were also solicited from all employees. Executives frequently asked employees if they had ideas for improving the organization. These ideas were noted and often put into use.

Growth in Financial Strength

17   With his stock selling at 20 to 30 times earnings—an almost incredible price—Walton presided over a sizable fortune. Wal-Mart stock was 39 percent held by the Walton family. Analysts projected the family holdings to be worth nearly $8 billion. Wal-Mart's long-term debt of $1,052,644,000 included 867 million of capital lease obligations. New stores were funded primarily through the sale of common stock and retained earnings or leaseback arrangements.

[7]Rudnitsky, "How Sam," p. 43.

EXHIBIT 3–B
Net Income (millions of dollars)

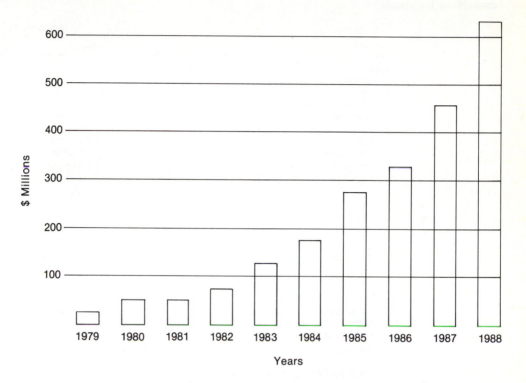

18   Like most discounters, Wal-Mart fills the aisles with tables displaying sales items backed by heavy promotion—an Electronic Bug Killer for $44.96, for example, or an RCA black-and-white 12-inch TV for $79.88. Here, however, was where the chain's competitive edge came in. According to a survey by *Discount Store News,* each Wal-Mart sale table generated twice as much revenue as competitors' (see Exhibits 4, Balance Sheet; 5, Shareholders Equity; and 6, Changes in Financial Positions).

Growth in Shareholders

19   Original investors have been rewarded spectacularly. Those 1970 Wal-Mart shares cost $16.50 and were worth some $900 in 1982. Since then, Walton has tapped the equity markets five times, raised a total of $123 million, and kept his overall capital costs well below those of competitors. In December 1981, Wal-Mart sold $60 million worth of convertible debentures at 9.5 percent. Wal-Mart, in July 1982, announced its intention to sell 2 million shares of additional common. During periods of high interest rates, it's a lot cheaper to sell stock at a 20-times-earnings multiple than borrowing—and it's money you never have to pay back. Wal-Mart stock has split numerous times, the last split was in 1987.

20   Wal-Mart became a Wall Street darling, with the number of stockholders on January 31, 1988, totaling approximately 79,777 with 564 million shares. During the period 1982–83, its stock price

EXHIBIT 4
Consolidated Balance Sheets, Wal-Mart Stores, Inc., and Subsidiaries
(amounts in thousands)

	January 31	
	1988	**1987**
Assets		
Current assets:		
Cash	$ 11,325	$ 8,527
Short-term money market investments	—	157,018
Receivables	95,928	90,380
Recoverable costs from sale/leaseback	126,917	47,160
Inventories	2,651,760	2,030,772
Prepaid expenses	19,215	19,214
Total current assets	2,905,145	2,353,271
Property, plant, and equipment, at cost:		
Land	209,211	134,351
Buildings and Improvements	621,023	402,845
Fixtures and equipment	855,926	655,253
Transportation equipment	46,301	45,346
	1,732,461	1,237,795
Less accumulated depreciation	374,193	267,722
Net property, plant, and equipment	1,358,268	970,073
Property under capital leases	952,305	832,337
Less accumulated amortization	165,721	126,128
Net property under capital leases	786,584	706,209
Goodwill	47,034	—
Other assets and deferred charges	34,778	19,539
Total assets	$5,131,809	$4,049,092
Liabilities and shareholder's equity		
Current liabilities:		
Notes payable	$ 104,382	$ —
Accounts payable	1,099,961	924,654
Accrued liabilities:		
Salaries	89,118	62,774
Taxes, other than income	81,064	46,496
Other	229,921	159,985
Accrued federal and state income taxes	120,773	132,833
Long-term debt due within one year	2,046	1,448
Obligations under capital leases due within one year	16,498	12,101
Total current liabilities	1,743,763	1,340,291
Long-term debt	185,672	179,234
Long-term obligations under capital leases	866,972	764,128
Deferred income taxes	78,135	74,946
Common shareholders equity:		
Common stock (shares outstanding, 565,112 in 1988; and 282,182 in 1987)	56,511	28,218
Capital in excess of par value	170,440	191,857
Retained earnings	2,030,316	1,470,418
Total common shareholders' equity	2,257,267	1,690,493
Total liabilities and shareholders' equity	$5,131,809	$4,049,092

EXHIBIT 5
**Consolidated Statements of Common Shareholders' Equity, Wal-Mart
Stores, Inc., and Subsidiaries (amounts in thousands)**

	Number of Shares	Common Stock	Capital in Excess of Par Value	Retained Earnings	Total
Balance—January 31, 1985	140,223	$14,022	$189,907	$ 780,743	$ 984,672
Net income				327,473	327,473
Cash dividends:					
Common stock ($0.07* per share)				(39,302)	(39,302)
Preferred stock ($2.00 per share)				(396)	(396)
Accretion of preferred stock redemption premium				(70)	(70)
Exercise of stock options	65	7	334		341
Conversion of preferred stock	86	9	997		986
100% common stock dividend	140,374	14,038	(14,038)		
Exercise of stock options	288	28	954		982
Tax benefit from stock options			3,352		3,352
Conversion of preferred stock	9	1	54		55
Other			(434)		(434)
Balance—January 31, 1986	281,045	28,105	181,106	1,068,448	1,277,659
Net income				450,086	450,086
Cash dividend:					
Common stock ($.085* per share)				(47,850)	(47,850)
Preferred stock ($1.50 per share)				(266)	(266)
Exercise of stock options	346	34	812		846
Tax benefit from stock options			5,122		5,122
Conversion of preferred stock	791	79	4,817		4,896
Balance—January 31, 1987	282,182	28,218	191,857	1,470,418	1,690,493
Net income				627,643	627,643
Cash dividends:					
Common stock ($0.12* per share)				(67,745)	(67,745)
Exercise of stock options	37	4	452		456
100% common stock dividend	282,219	28,222	(28,222)		
Exercise of stock options	821	82	1,739		1,821
Tax benefit from stock options			9,213		9,213
Other	(147)	(15)	(4,599)		(4,614)
Balance—January 31, 1988	565,112	$56,511	$170,440	$2,030,316	$2,257,267

* Cash dividends on common stock prior to July 10, 1987, have been adjusted to reflect the 100 percent common stock dividend paid on that date.

EXHIBIT 6
Consolidated Statements of Changes in Financial Position, Wal-Mart Stores, Inc.,
and Subsidiaries (amounts in thousands)

	Fiscal Years Ended January 31		
	1988	**1987**	**1986**
Source of funds:			
Current operations:			
Net income	$ 627,643	$ 450,086	$ 327,473
Items not affecting working capital in current period:			
Depreciation and amortization	165,962	123,639	89,749
Deferred income taxes	3,198	22,432	17,922
Total from current operations	796,794	596,157	435,144
Net proceeds from exercise of options, and conversion of preferred stock	6,876	10,864	5,282
Additions to long-term debt	11,645	—	141,120
Additions to long-term obligations under capital leases	131,192	184,262	156,453
Reductions of other assets	1,522	1,300	18,609
Disposal of assets	37,341	90,920	9,913
	985,370	883,503	766,521
Application of funds:			
Acquisition of Super Saver Warehouse Club, Inc.			
Property, plant, and equipment	10,422	—	—
Other assets	231	—	—
Goodwill	50,034	—	—
Long-term debt	(20,570)	—	—
	40,117	—	—
Additions to property, plant, and equipment	527,960	403,660	350,667
Additions to property under capital leases	130,491	182,955	181,487
Reduction in long-term debt, including changes in current maturities	25,777	1,448	1,675
Reduction in long-term lease obligations, including changes in current obligations	28,348	15,339	11,134
Preferred stock conversions	—	4,902	971
Dividends paid	67,745	48,116	39,768
Additions to other assets and deferred charges	16,530	5,695	3,513
Total	836,968	662,115	589,215
Increase in working capital	$148,402	$221,388	$177,306

tripled, going as high as $78. This reflected how Sam Walton merchandised his company's stock as skillfully as he does his store. As of April 1988, 33 percent of its shares were held by institutions, and each year he invited over a hundred analysts and institutional investors to the fieldhouse at the University of Arkansas for his annual meeting. The mid-June occasion is a day-and-a-half session where investors meet top executives, as well as Wal-Mart district managers, buyers, and 200,000 hourly salespeople (called "associates"). Investors see a give-and-take meeting between buyers and district managers. "Walton also introduces his employees. They shout his name and extol him. It's a sight to behold," says a regular attendee.[8]

---

[8]Rudnitsky, "How Sam," p. 43.

EXHIBIT 6 (*concluded*)

	Fiscal Years Ended January 31		
	1988	**1987**	**1986**
Changes in components of working capital:			
Increase (decrease) in current assets:			
Cash	$ 2,798	$ (723)	$ 7,398
Short-term money market investments	(157,018)	(8,150)	165,168
Receivables	5,548	32,718	12,084
Recoverable costs from sale/leaseback	79,757	(105,250)	10,021
Inventories	620,788	642,804	284,243
Prepaid expenses	1	7,597	2,107
Total	551,874	568,996	481,021
Increase (decrease) in current liabilities:			
Notes payable	104,382	—	—
Accounts payable and accrued liabilities	306,155	301,910	286,840
Accrued federal and state income taxes	(12,060)	43,434	16,040
Long-term debt due within one year	598	(157)	(1,377)
Obligations under capital leases due within one year	4,397	2,421	2,212
Total	403,472	347,608	303,715
Increase in working capital	$148,402	$221,388	$177,306

Growth in Employee Benefits

21   The single growth characteristic in which Wal-Mart management has taken the most pride is continued development of its people. Training was seen as critical to outstanding performance, and new programs were implemented on an ongoing basis in all areas of the company. The combination of grass roots meetings, the open door policy, video, printed material, classroom, home study, year-end management meetings, and on-the-job training has enabled employees to prepare themselves for assigned advancement and added responsibilities.

22   Wal-Mart managers also try to stay current with new developments and needed changes. Wal-Mart executives each spend one week per year in hourly jobs in various stores. Walton himself traveled at least three days per week, visiting competitors' stores and attending the opening of new stores, leading the Wal-Mart cheer, "Give me a *W,* give me an *A* . . ."

23   Wal-Mart also encouraged employee stock purchases—about 8 percent of Wal-Mart stock was owned by employees. As of January 31, 1988, 5,966,382 shares of common stock were reserved for issuance under stock option plans. Under the stock purchase plan, stock could be purchased by two different methods. First, an amount was deducted from each check, with a maximum of $62.50 per check. An additional 15 percent of the amount deducted is contributed by Wal-Mart, Inc., through the Merrill Lynch stock brokerage firm. Dividends were reinvested in Wal-Mart stock unless otherwise instructed. Second, a lump-sum purchase was allowed in April, with a maximum of $1,500 and with an additional 15 percent added by Wal-Mart. For either plan, withdrawal may be made at any time, and fractional interest may be purchased because you are buying by the dollar's worth instead of by the share.[9]

---

[9]"Summary Plan Description," *Profit Sharing Plan,* February 1980, p. 4.

24   At the same time, there was a corporate profit-sharing plan that as of January 31, 1989, consisted of 5,966,382 shares of common stock. The purposes of the profit-sharing plan was to furnish an incentive for increased efficiency, to provide progressive recognition of service, and to encourage careers with the company by Wal-Mart associates. This is a trustee-administered plan, which means that the company's contributions to it were made only out of net profits of the company and were held by a trustee. The company from time to time will contribute to the plan such amounts of its net profits, usually 10 percent, as its board of directors shall determine, but not in excess of limits imposed by law.

25   Company contributions could be withdrawn only upon termination. If you terminate employment with the company because of retirement, death, or total and permanent disability, your company contribution will be fully vested. "Fully vested" means that your entire account is nonforfeitable.

26   If termination of employment occurs for any other reason, the amount that is nonforfeitable depends upon the number of years of service with the company. After completion of the third year of service with the company, 20 percent of each participant's account will be nonforfeitable for each subsequent year of service so that, after seven years of service, a participant's account will be 100 percent vested. This is shown in Table 2:

TABLE 2

Completed Years of Service as an Associate	Nonforfeitable Percentages of Company Contributions Accounts
Less than 3	0%
3	20
4	40
5	60
6	80
7	100

27   For vesting purposes, a year of service credit will not be granted for any plan year during which a participant fails to work at least 1,000 hours of service.

28   Walton is admittedly old-fashioned in many respects. Since Walton still exercises considerable control over the culture at Wal-Mart Stores, store policies reflect many of Walton's values. One of the areas in which Walton could be considered particularly old-fashioned is in the area of women. Store policies forbid employees from dating other employees without prior approval of the executive committee. Similarly, women were rare in management positions. Annual manager meetings include sessions for wives to speak out on the problems of living with a Wal-Mart manager. No women were in the ranks of top management. Walton had also resisted placing women on the board of directors. Only 12 (17 percent) women have made it to the ranks of buyers. Walton is an EEOC/AA employer but has managed to get away with "apparent" discriminatory practices because most Wal-Mart stores were located in small rural towns in the Sunbelt states (open shop).

Growth in Marketing Strategies

29   Wal-Mart implemented many marketing strategies. Wal-Mart drew customers into the store by the use of radio and television advertising, a monthly circular, and weekly newspaper ads. Television advertising was used to convey an image of everyday low prices and quality merchandise. Radio was used to a lesser degree to promote specific products that were usually of high demand.

Newspaper and monthly circulars were the major contributors to the program, emphasizing deeply discounted items. They were effective at luring customers into the store.

30   Efforts were also made to discount corporate overhead. Visitors often mistook corporate head-quarters for a warehouse, owing to its limited decorating and "show." Wal-Mart executives were expected to share hotel rooms when traveling to reduce expenses. Walton also avoided spending money on consultants and marketing experts. He prefers instead to base decisions on intuitive judgments of employees and on his assessment of the strategies of other retail chains.

31   Walton entered into the ranks of the "deep" discounters with the opening of three Sam's Wholesale Clubs in 1984. As of January 31, 1988, there were 84 Sam's Wholesale Clubs, 12 Dot Discount Drug stores, and 2 Hypermarts in 1984, with 11 distribution warehouses in operation and 4 more to be opened soon. Walton had become the nation's largest deep discounter, passing Price Club of San Diego. The "Super Center" was Wal-Mart's strategy to grow in smaller markets. Wal-Mart has been innovative in many of its marketing strategies. Since the mid-1980s Wal-Mart had advertised its "Buy American" policy in an effort to keep production at home. As such Wal-Mart buyers were constantly seeking vendors in grass roots America. As an example, Wal-Mart dropped Fuji for 3M film. Also, Wal-Mart censors products it does not like. For example, Wal-Mart has banned LPs, removed magazines, and pulled albums over graphics and lyric content, as well as stopped marketing teen rock magazines.[10]

Growth in Distribution Centers

32   Close to 77 percent of the chain's merchandise passed through 1 of 11 distribution warehouses. That percentage was more than K mart or Sears. Distributing with the newest warehouse in late 1986 gave Wal-Mart a total of nearly 6 million square feet of storage space.

33   Wal-Mart's distribution operations were highly automated. Terminals at each store were used to wire merchandise requests to a warehouse, which in turn was either shipped immediately or placed on reorder. Wal-Mart computers were linked directly with over 200 vendors, making deliveries even faster. "We spend a little over two cents for every dollar we ship out," says Walton. "For others it's around four cents. That's a 2 percent edge right there on gross margins."[11]

34   Wal-Mart owns a fleet of truck-tractors that could deliver goods to any store in 36 to 48 hours from the time the order is placed. "After our trucks drop off merchandise at our stores, they frequently pick up merchandise from manufacturers on the way back to the distribution center," says president Jack Shewmaker. "Our back-haul rate was currently running over 60 percent."[12] You don't need a computer to see this as yet another way of cutting costs.

35   Wal-Mart had one of the world's largest private satellite communication systems to control distribution. In addition, Wal-Mart pledged to install POS bar-code scanning in all of its stores by 1990. Wal-Mart computers talked directly to vendors, trimming days off the ordering process.

Management Succession

36   November 1987 was the 25th anniversary of Wal-Mart. Sam Walton named David D. Glass president and CEO and appointed himself as chairman of the board. What should Glass do to continue Wal-Mart's success? Can Glass pass both Sears and K mart in sales? Can Wal-Mart sales surpass $20 billion by 1990? (See Exhibit 7, Board of Directors.)

---

[10]Arthur Markowitz, "Wal-Mart's Super Centers," *Discount Store News* 27 (March 28, 1988), p. 12 (2).

[11]Rudnitsky, "How Sam," p. 43.

[12]Rudnitsky, "How Sam," p. 43.

EXHIBIT 7
Board of Directors

David R. Banks
President, Beverly Enterprises

Paul R. Carter
Executive vice president and chief financial officer, Wal-Mart Stores, Inc.

Hillary Rodham Clinton
Partner, Rose law firm

John A. Cooper, Jr.
President, Cooper Communities, Inc.

David D. Glass
President and chief executive officer, Wal-Mart Stores, Inc.

A.L. Johnson
Vice chairman—Sam's Wholesale Clubs, Hypermart ★USA, and Special Divisions, Wal-Mart Stores, Inc.

James H. Jones
Chairman of the board and chief executive officer, Jameson Pharmaceutical

Robert Kahn
President, Kahn & Harris, Inc.

Charles Lazarus
Chairman, Toys "R" Us, Inc.

William H. Seay
Chairman, retired, Southwest Life Insurance Company

Jack Shewmaker
Retired, Wal-Mart Stores, Inc.

John E. Tate
Executive vice president of Professional Services, Wal-Mart Stores, Inc.

James L. Walton
Senior vice president, Wal-Mart Stores, Inc.

Sam M. Walton
Chairman, Wal-Mart Stores, Inc.

S. Robson Walton
Vice chairman, Wal-Mart Stores, Inc.

Committees of the Board

Executive Committee
Paul R. Carter
David D. Glass
A.L. Johnson
Donald G. Soderquist
John E. Tate
James L. Walton
Sam M. Walton
S. Robson Walton

Audit Committee
James H. Jones
Robert Kahn
William H. Seay

Stock Option Committee
David D. Glass
Donald G. Soderquist
S. Robson Walton

Special Stock Option Committee
John A. Cooper, Jr.
James H. Jones
William H. Seay

Officers

Chairman
Sam M. Walton

President and Chief Executive Officer
David D. Glass

Vice Chairmen
A.L. Johnson
Sam's Wholesale Clubs, Hypermart ★USA, and Special Divisions

Donald G. Soderquist
Chief operating officer

S. Robson Walton

Executive Vice Presidents
Paul R. Carter
Chief financial officer

Bill Fields
Merchandise and sales

A.L. Miles
Special services

John E. Tate
Professional services

Nick White
Sam's Wholesale Club

Senior Vice Presidents
Thomas M. Coughlin
Operations—Sam's Wholesale Club

David Dible
General merchandise manager

H. "Mac" Gammon
Operations

Joseph S. Hardin, Jr.
Distribution and transportation

Joseph P. Hatfield
General merchandise manager

Harold E. Johnson
Operations

Bobby L. Martin
Information systems

Dean L. Sanders
Operations

Thomas P. Seay
Real estate and construction

Robert K. Voss
General merchandise manager, Sam's Wholesale Club

James L. Walton

Colon Washburn
General merchandise manager

Wesley C. Wright
Special Divisions

Vice Presidents
B.D. Adams
Operations

Clarence H. Archer
Pharmacy

Harryetta Bailey
Divisional merchandise manager

Stephen M. Bailey
Merchandise systems

Curtis Barlow
Real estate

Robert T. Bruce
Inventory management

Dwight A. Carney
Advertising and sales promotion

James K. Comeaux
Divisional merchandise manager

Richard Donckers
Food Retailing—Hypermart ★USA

Arthur Emmanuel
Operations

Steve Furner
Operations

Roger Lee Gildehaus
Divisional merchandise manager

David H. Gorman
Loss prevention

Harry S. Green
Operations

Michael J. Guccione
Jewelry

Steve Harig
Divisional merchandise manager

Robert L. Hart
Operations

Lewis Ray Hobbs
Divisional merchandise manager

William L. Hutcheson
Shoe Division

Pete Jasan
Divisional merchandise manager

Lolan C. Mackey
Operations

Peter C. Metzger
Imports

EXHIBIT 7 (*concluded*)

Harry Miller
  Operations
Robert J. Murphey
  Construction
Duane G. Naccarato
  Merchandise
Charles Rateliff
  Treasurer
Melvin C. Redman
  Store planning
Robert K. Rhoads
  General counsel and secretary

Charles Russell
  Operations
Leroy W. Schuetts
  Operations
H. Lee Scott, Jr.
  Distribution
Lew Skelton
  Operations
Mike Spear
  Divisional merchandise manager
Steve Tiernan
  General merchandise manager,
  Hypermart ★USA

John Tillman
  Operations
Donald E. Tripp
  General manager—Hypermart
  ★USA
P. Terry Tucker
  Divisional merchandise manager
James A. Walker, Jr.
  Controller
Jim Woodruff
  Divisional merchandise manager

B | STRATEGY IMPLEMENTATION

CASE 12

HICKORY RIDGE GOLF CLUB

1   Greg Hamilton, owner of Hickory Ridge Golf Club (HRGC), a modest nine-hole public golf course in Columbia, South Carolina, nursed his first cup of coffee of the day lost in thought. Normally, Hamilton would have been bustling around the course, preparing for the day's business. Play was generally brisk in the mornings on warm spring days, and the morning of April 19, 1989, promised to be no exception. In spite of this, Hamilton knew he had to make a decision that could have an important short- and long-term impact on the profitability and perhaps even the survival of his business.

2   In 1988, his first year of business, HRGC's revenues exceeded $116,000, although the firm suffered a loss of $17,000 (see Exhibit 1 for 1988 profit/loss statement). Cart rentals accounted for over 19 percent of revenues, second only to greens fees (see Exhibit 2 for 1988 sales breakdown). However, his fleet of nine electric carts had not been sufficient to meet 1988 demand, much less the increase in cart usage expected in 1989. Furthermore, the carts he did have were old and in need of frequent repair, which further aggravated the situation. Hamilton knew that he needed to decide whether to purchase or lease a new fleet of carts or additional carts, and, if so, from whom. However, he was unsure of where to begin. He wondered how much revenue he had previously lost due to his inadequate fleet. More important, he wondered how his decision might affect revenues in 1989. As he finished his coffee he vowed to bring up the subject with his course archi-

---

This case was prepared by Harold Valentine, OC(SS), USN, under the direction of James J. Chrisman, Assistant Professor of Management at the University of South Carolina. The case was prepared for classroom discussion and was not intended to illustrate either effective or ineffective handling of administrative situations.

604

EXHIBIT 1

HICKORY RIDGE GOLF COURSE
1988 P&L Statement

Gross receipts		$116,270
Less: Cost of goods sold	$21,079	
Gross income		$ 95,191
Expenses:		
Advertising	$ 900	
Automobile	2,353	
Depreciation	13,590	
Dues and publications	693	
Insurance	6,411	
Mortgage interest	13,459	
Other interest	2,211	
Laundry	111	
Office expense	778	
Rent on business property	1,338	
Repairs	7,532	
Supplies	13,885	
Taxes	4,905	
Meals	66	
Utilities	7,549	
Seminars	330	
Licenses	348	
Miscellaneous	15	
Total expenses		$112,801
Net profit or (loss)		($17,610)

tect/mechanic, Harold Valentine, a friend as well as trusted confidant. Hamilton knew he could count on Valentine to help him solve his dilemma.

BACKGROUND

Mr. Hamilton

3   For Hamilton, the purchase of HRGC was an important step in fulfilling a lifelong dream—to own and run a public golf course. Born on May 18, 1950, and raised in the Columbus, Ohio, area, Hamilton was introduced to golf by Arnold Adams, owner of Possum Run Golf and Swim Club. Adams gave Hamilton his first job but was far more than just an employer. He passed on his love of golf, including the conviction that it should be a game easily accessible to the general public. For several years, Hamilton spent nearly every spare moment with Adams on the course.

4   Marriage at age 21 brought many changes to Hamilton's life, including three children, but his dream to own a golf course was unchanged. His wife, Dr. Cynthia Hamilton, supported Hamilton not only emotionally but also financially through her psychiatry practice. In 1978, the couple moved to Columbia, South Carolina, and Hamilton took on the position of assistant pro at Linrick Golf Club on Monticello Road. While at Linrick, Hamilton earned his PGA assistant's license and hoped to eventually earn his PGA pro's license.

1989 to better define these needs. Price structuring at the course was changed, and alcohol use was restricted to that which was purchased on the course.

INDUSTRY ENVIRONMENT

Golf—A Booming Sport/Business

14   Golf had become a booming business and was expected to grow rapidly in the final decade of the 20th century. Nearly every authority agreed that the number of players was steadily increasing, as were the revenues these additional golfers brought in. According to *Golf Market Today*,[1] there were approximately 11.2 million golfers in the United States in 1970. As of the beginning of 1989, that figure had nearly doubled to 21.7 million, with the rate of growth accelerating over each of the past four years. Researchers from the National Golf Foundation estimated that over 30 million people would be golfing in this country by the year 2000.

15   This explosive growth was attributed, in large part, to the increased interest in golf on the part of women, the elderly, and the "Baby Boomers" (*PGA Magazine*).[2] Of particular importance was the impact women were likely to have on the future of the game. In 1989, around 25 percent of all golfers were women; yet 40 percent of all new players were women. Many of them had careers and found golf an excellent way to relax and to conduct business.[3]

16   The growth of golf also attracted the attention of the business world. *Business Week* called golf "a global phenomenon" and a "$20 billion industry with a growth rate that is nothing short of phenomenal."[4] Furthermore, the golf boom had been felt in the stock market, too, with many corporations (such as Emhart Industries, which makes club shafts, and American Brands, which makes golf shoes) seeing significant changes in their stock quotes. This growth was leading to increased corporate involvement, something which had become evident on the PGA tour, where corporate sponsorship—not to mention purses—were up.

The Lack of Facilities

17   Although the possibilities for growth seemed limitless, it appeared unlikely that supply could keep up with demand, even though both the number of courses opened and of those under construction rose significantly from 1987 to 1988. In 1987, 145 new courses were opened and 513 were under construction or in the planning stage; in 1988, 211 opened and 662 were being constructed or planned. South Carolina was tied for fifth in the nation in terms of the number of new courses opened (12), and it ranked 16th overall in total golf courses (280). The situation in some areas was becoming serious, with overcrowding becoming more and more common. Even planning for 50 percent growth over the next decade—and some believed this growth would be closer to 100 percent—the golf industry estimated that 4,000 new facilities would be necessary within the next 10 years, or an average in excess of one new course opening per day until the year 2000.

---

[1]"Golf Course Development on the Upswing in The U.S.," *Golf Market Today* 28, no. 3 (May/June 1989), pp. 3–5.

[2]"Wanted: More Golf Courses," *PGA Magazine*, March 1989.

[3]"Taking a Swing at Success," *Savvy*, April 1989.

[4]"Golf: Business Challenges and Opportunities," *Business Week*, March 27, 1989.

18   The Golf Course Superintendents Association singled out the lack of public golf courses as especially distressing in the overall facility shortage. Over 80 percent of today's players use public courses, and this figure was expected to increase. For this reason *Golf Market Today* estimated that at least 60 percent of all new courses needed to be open for public play.

Keys to Success

19   Certain aspects of running a successful course had not changed—for example, keeping a clean, well-maintained course and polite, well-trained employees.

      Nevertheless, in 1989, golf was becoming more and more a common man's game. It had become more important for the golf course owners to understand the needs and habits of a more diverse group of customers. To illustrate, some courses in Florida sought to lure in the seniors with special senior citizens discount packages, failing to consider the fact that most of their golfers were already seniors. Most of these courses were driven out of business because they failed to consider who their golfers were.

20   Diversity was also a watchword within the industry. Golfers had a fascination with gadgets: the newer, the more innovative, the more original, the better. Therefore, it was becoming more and more likely to find golf-related novelty items and gadgets in the pro shop. Along the same line, golfers were more likely to remain satisfied with their course if they were given a variety of views and shots. Courses with all or most of its holes constructed with a consistent layout bored the average golfer.

LOCAL ENVIRONMENT

The Columbia Area

21   The population of the Columbia Area (Lexington and Richland counties) had grown an estimated 11 percent between 1980 and 1988 (see Exhibit 3 for population statistics). Average area per capita income was $13,795 in 1987, which was the third highest in the state of South Carolina. Average per capita income in South Carolina was only $12,036 (see Exhibit 3).

Columbia's Golf Industry

22   The local golf scene was also changing and growing with the Columbia community. The Columbia by-pass—Interstate 326—was expected to be completed by late 1990. The by-pass would make most public golf courses in the region much more accessible to local golfers (within a 30-minute drive). There was the possibility of new competition in the local industry. Four syndicates—two from Florida and one each from Texas and California—were analyzing the potential profitability of constructing major golf complexes (of 27–36 holes each) in Columbia. Among existing local groups, Fort Jackson had received approval for an additional 18 holes, Richland County was seeking to obtain grants to build an 18- or 27-hole course southeast of Columbia, and Charwood Country Club in West Columbia was considering whether to construct 9 additional holes to complement the 9 holes, which were recently completed (which would give the club a total of 27 holes). Generally, there was a regional trend toward clubs offering a combination of memberships and pay-for-play options. Golf was also becoming more accessible to the local public, due to prices rising slower than the cost of living.

EXHIBIT 3

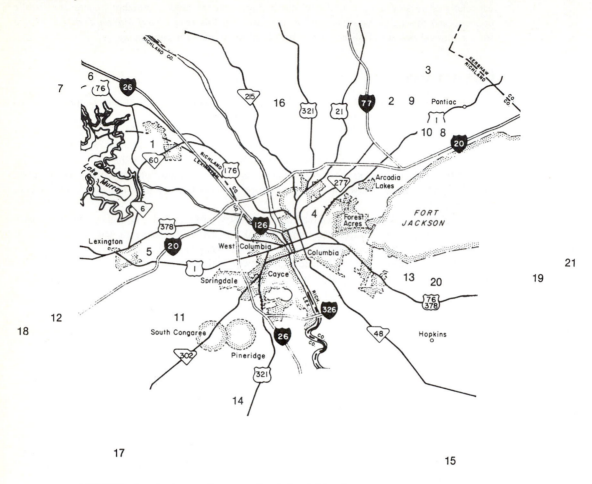

LEGEND: One inch equals approximately eight miles.

Study on Golf in Columbia

23   A study completed for Hickory Ridge Golf Club on April 20, 1989, served to further explain local conditions. This study, which targeted 210 golfers both familiar and unfamiliar with HRGC, had a margin of error of plus or minus 2 percent (see Exhibit 4). The following were the summarized findings of the study:

24   Hickory Ridge Golf Club, as well as Columbia area public golf courses, have a clientele that consists mainly of 20- to 40-year-old males who prefer to play 18 holes of golf per day. These individuals play more than 15 times per year. Of these players almost 43 percent are college students. We believe that the level of college play can be increased by sponsoring a student/professor day early during each semester. It is our finding that lower green fees coupled with good greens and fairways are the most important factors to the public golfer. Financial records revealed that weekdays hold the greatest opportunity for increased profit-

---

EXHIBIT 4
"Columbia Public Golfer": Marketing Survey Results 1989,
by Postich, Miller, and Valentine

The analysis was conducted to within minus one standard deviation and in excess of the 49th percentile for results in accordance with the previously stated requirements of 210 respondents:

1. Sixty-eight percent of the respondents were from 20 to 40 years old.
2. Fifty-six percent of the respondents drove between 5 and 15 miles to play golf.
3. Thirty-eight percent of the respondents' income was below $10,000; 28 percent of the respondents' income was between $20,000 and $30,000.
4. Eighty-three percent of the respondents located new golf courses through word of mouth.
5. Fifty-one percent of the respondents would play more golf if lower green fees were available.
6. Sixty-five percent of the respondents play golf more than 15 times per year.
7. Sixty-two percent of the respondents that were pro shop customers said that their most frequent purchase was golf balls.
8. Fifty-seven percent of the respondents said that they would prefer food items, such as hot dogs and hot sandwiches, offered in the club house.
9. Seventy-two percent of the respondents prefer to play 18 holes of golf per outing.
10. Eighty-seven percent of the respondents prefer to ride in a cart or walk with a pull cart while golfing.
11. Sixty-two percent of the respondents said that the primary determinant in the selection of a golf course is the condition of the fairways and greens.
12. Sixty percent of the respondents said that they expect to pay between $4 and $6 per round.
13. Ninety-seven percent of the respondents prefer to play with a friend or a foursome.
14. Twenty-seven percent of the respondents prefer to play on Saturdays.
15. Eighty percent of the respondents were male.
16. Thirty-four percent of the respondents were college students; 49 percent were in the work force.

---

ability. This may be accomplished by increasing league play. It should be noted that in order to avoid simply shifting weekend play to weekday play, Hickory Ridge should refrain from lowering weekday rates.

25   Our study has determined that the public golfer seeks a greater selection of golf balls and hot food. While riding carts are most preferred, a ratio of seven pull carts to 10 riding carts should be maintained in future purchases. Word of mouth is by far the most prevalent manner in which golfers learn about new courses. Therefore, road signs should be used for directional purposes only, keeping all forms of advertising within a 15-mile radius. By following these recommendations, Hickory Ridge Golf Club should continue to have a substantial increase in play.

COMPETITORS

Definition

26 In 1989, HRGC had 21 competitors in the Columbia area, of which 11 were public and 10 were private. Among those courses, only one—Sedgewood Golf Course—was located within four miles of HRGC (see Exhibits 4, 5, and 6).

Sedgewood Golf Course

27 Sedgewood Golf Course, HRGC's only local competitor, was very different in significant ways. Located four miles from HRGC, it was an 18-hole, 6,810-yard, par-72 public course, with restricted tee times on weekends and holidays. The most noticeable difference was in the price structure. A

EXHBIT 5
Course Distributions, May 1989

Private

1. Coldstream Country Club Inc., Irmo, SC
2. Columbia Country Club, Columbia, SC
3. Crickentree Golf Club, Columbia, SC
4. Forest Lake Country Club, Columbia, SC
5. Golden Hills Golf and Country Club, Lexington, SC
6. Mid Carolina Club Inc., Prosperity, SC
7. Timberlake Plantation, Chapin, SC
8. Wild Wood Country Club, Columbia, SC
9. The Windermere Club, Blythwood, SC
10. Woodlands Country Club, Columbia, SC

Public

11. Charwood Country Club, West Columbia, SC
12. Coopers Creek Golf Club, Pelion, SC
13. Hickory Ridge Golf Club, Columbia, SC
14. Hidden Valley Country Club, West Columbia, SC
15. Lake Marion Golf Club, Santee, SC
16. Linrick Golf Course, Columbia, SC
17. Paw Paw Country Club, Bamberg, SC
18. Persimmon Hill Golf Club, Johnston, SC
19. Pineland Plantation Golf Club, Sumter, SC
20. Sedgewood Country Club, Hopkins, SC
21. White Pines Country Club, Camden, SC

round of nine holes cost $7–11, depending on the day it was played, and a round of 18 holes cost $11–13. A riding cart, if used, cost an additional $9 per person for 9 holes and $18 per person for 18 holes. In comparison, on weekdays HRGC charged $4.50 for nine holes, $7 for 18, and $8 for the entire day. Rates were $1.50 higher on weekends and holidays. Carts cost $6.50 per nine holes per cart regardless of the time of week (see Exhibit 5). One notable similarity was the condition of the two courses in that both suffered from erosion and lack of complete course maintenance.

Other Facilities at Local Golf Courses

28   Also noteworthy were the conditions of other facilities offered by the competition. All courses had pro shops on the premises, and a total of 29 pro shops were in the Columbia area. These ranged from discount shops, such as Nevada Bob's, to extremely exclusive shops, such as the one at Forest Lake Country Club. Most of these shops were run by sales representatives. The biggest money tended to come from club repair and the sales of golf balls, tees, and golf gloves. The average shop was likely to stock around 30 sets of clubs, although in extreme cases local shops were known to stock in excess of 100 sets. Most stocked golf clothing, such as socks, shoes, and hats, and many also carried shirts and pants. Certain shops stocked extremely large inventories of clothing items, such as the country club pro shops.

29   Only three courses offered full restaurant/dining facilities, all of them private courses. The other operators believed that there seemed to be little profit to be made in this area at the public courses.

EXHIBIT 6

Course	Dues/Fees	Operating Hours	Closed	Tee
Private				
1	$77p/m, $210 int	7:30 AM–6:00 PM	Thanksgiving and Christmas	8m
2	N.A.	N.A.	N.A.	N.A.
3	$9,500 Equity	8:30 AM–Dark	Mondays	
4	$2,500 Equity	8:00 AM–6:30 PM		9m
5	$75p/m, $2,187 int	8:00 AM–6:30 PM	Monday, Thanksgiving, Christmas, New Year's	8m
6	$30 p/m, $750 int	8:00 AM–8:00 PM	Christmas	8m
7	$90p/m, $2,500 int*	8:00 AM–7:00 PM	Christmas	9m
8	$100p/m, $7,500 int	7:30 AM–8:00 PM	Christmas, New Year's	8m
9	$100p/m, $2,500 int	8:00 AM–8:00 PM	Monday, Thursday, Friday, Thanksgiving, Christmas, New Year's	10m
10	$105p/m, $2,000 int	8:00 AM–7:00 PM		8m
Public				
11	$6/10, $8/$12	7:30 AM–9:30 PM		8m
12	$9/$11, $9/$11	7:00 AM–Dark		10m
13	$4.50/$7, $6/$8.50	8:00 AM–Dark		Open
14	$6/$8, $12/$12	8:00 AM–Dark		8m
15	$15/$25, $15/$25	Daylight–Dark		Alt 7m/8m
16	$5.50/$8.50, $6.50/$10.50	7:30 AM–Dark	Christmas	8m
17	$10.50/$16.80, $13.65/$21	8:00 AM–Dark	Christmas	10m
18	$5.50/$11, $8/$16	8:00 AM–7:00 PM	Christmas	8m
19	$5/$10, $8/$12	7:00 AM–Dark	Christmas	8m
20	$7/$11, $11/$13	7:30 AM–Dark	Christmas	10m
21	$8/$8, $10/$10	7:30 AM–Dark		Open

Course	Pro Shop	Senior Rate	Student Rate	Restaurant	Snack Bar
Private					
1	Yes	No	No	Yes	No
2					
3	Yes	No	No	Grill	Yes
4	Yes	No	No	Yes	Yes
5	Yes	No	No	Yes	Yes
6	Yes	No	No	Yes	Yes
7	Yes	No	No	Grill	No
8	Yes	No	No	Grill	No
9	Yes	No	No	Yes	Yes
10	Yes	No	No	Yes	Yes
Public					
11	Yes	$5/$6	$5/$6	No	Yes
12	Yes	No	No	No	Yes
13	Yes	$4.50 WD	$4.50 WD	No	Yes
14	Yes	$6	$6	No	Yes
15	Yes	No	No	No	Yes
16	Yes	$4.50	$4.50/$6	No	Yes
17	Yes	No	No	No	Yes
18	Yes	No	No	Yes	No
19	Yes	Varies	No	No	Yes
20	Yes	$1 off	$1 off	No	Yes
21	Yes	Varies	No	Yes	Yes

EXHIBIT 6 *(concluded)*

Course	Lockers‡	Yardage	Par	Cart Fee (9/18)
Private				
1	No	6,155	71	$4.75/$8.40 per person
2				
3	Yes	6,471	72	$8.00/$16.00 per cart
4	Yes	6,450	72	$2.50/$5.00 per person
5	Yes	6,461	71	$5.00/$8.00 per person
6	Yes	6,600	72	$3.50/$7.00 per person
7	Yes	6,703	72	$4.75/$8.50 per person
8	Yes	6,726	72	$9.04 plus tax for 18 per person
9	Yes	6,900	72	$5.25/$10.50 per person
10	Yes	6,786	72	$4.00/$8.00 per person
Public				
11	No	6,100	72	$4/$8 per person
12	Yes	6,550	72	$4/$8 per person
13	Yes	2,807†	35†	$6.50 per cart
14	No	6,700	72	$4/$8 per person
15	No	6,615	72	Included in greens fee
16	No	7,080	73	$6/$12 per cart
17	No	6,700	72	Included in greens fee
18	No	7,050	72	$4.50/$9 per person
19	No	7,084	72	$4/$8 per person
20	No	6,810	72	$9/$18 per cart
21	Yes	6,400	72	$4/$8 per person

* Property ownership required.
† Nine-hole course.
‡ Yes indicated if plans have been set in motion to install lockers within the next year.

Only two other courses had grills. These offered hot sandwiches, hamburgers, and the like, as well as drinks and snacks, and were open during lunch and dinner hours. Fifteen other courses had simple snack bar facilities, offering hot dogs, cold drinks, chips, and candy. One course had no eating or refreshment facilities.

30   Another thing many public courses lacked was locker areas, including shower facilities. These were especially appealing to the blue-collar workers, who would often golf on the way to or from work. Although 8 of the 10 private courses offered locker areas, only 2 of the 11 public courses did so (see Exhibit 6).

CURRENT OPERATIONS (MAY 1989)

31   In practical terms, Valentine believed that HRGC was without any direct competition, because of several distinctive characteristics. First, it was the only nine-hole golf course in the Columbia area. It was also unusually level and short (2,807 yards, compared to an average 3,313 yards for nine holes in the area) for a par-35 nine-hole course, making it especially suitable for elderly and young players. Its length and absence of hills, along with the wide fairways and lack of water (which only came into play on one hole), made HRGC a good course for the beginning golfer. Besides Hickory Ridge, only six of the other area courses were open 365 days per year, and only one of

them had entirely unrestricted tee times (see Exhibit 5 for course comparisons). Overall, these factors attracted many beginners, senior citizens, and blue-collar customers to HRGC.

Fees and Sales

32   The new fee structure was designed with two purposes in mind. First, it was intended to underprice the local competition, while allowing HRGC to maintain an acceptable profit margin (between 2.5 percent and 4.0 percent). Second, it was intended to make golf accessible to as many residents of the Columbia area as possible.

33   Sales were broken down into five areas. (For a complete sales breakdown, see Exhibit 2). During 1989, the course made a total of $20,234.77. From this amount, 54.6 percent came from greens fees, 20.8 percent came from cart rentals, 11.9 percent came from snack bar and pro shop sales, 9.9 percent came from beer sales, and 2.8 percent came from pull cart rentals.

34   The marketing survey conducted by the University of South Carolina provided the impetus for many changes, especially in the areas of pricing and advertising. The price structure was entirely revamped, based on the survey's findings, with greens fees being raised from $4.00/$6.50/$7.50 (9 holes/18 holes/all day) to $4.50/$7.00/$8.00 during weekdays. Rates increased from $5.00/$7.50/8.50 to $6.00/$8.50/$9.50 during weekends and holidays. The cart rates were raised from $6.00 to $6.50 per nine per cart. Also of note was that senior citizens and student discount fees were restricted to weekdays only.

Course Operations

35   Despite all the improvements, HRGC still suffered from problems of erosion (especially in tee areas) and inconsistent conditions on the greens. Course conditions, however, were steadily improving, with new equipment allowing for more efficient use of working hours. HRGC's facilities had not changed much since Hamilton's purchase of the course. The only additions were the office built in the clubhouse and the pump house constructed near the pond. However, the existing facilities had taken on a markedly different appearance as a result of the extensive clean-up efforts.

36   Hamilton made no change regarding tee times, keeping them entirely open and making the course available on a first-come-first-served basis 365 days a year. His reason for this was that he wanted to allow the greatest number of people to tee off in the shortest amount of time possible, while providing the maximum tee-off hours possible. Hamilton wanted to prevent any unnecessary restrictions to the golfers.

37   HRGC had a full line of golf balls, a moderate selection of golf clubs (as well as some rentals), golf gloves, and other complementary items, such as socks. The shop did not carry golf shoes or clothes. After a round of golf, players could also sit back to watch the game on television with a hot chilli dog and a cold drink, before making the long trip back home.

38   In conjunction with the increase in price, Hamilton continued his efforts to make the course more playable. Clean-up was continued both on the course and in the club house, and the pro shop inventory was greatly expanded to include a full line of golf balls, as well as a medium range of club selection. (Approximately six sets at a value of approximately $2,000.)

Advertising

39   The survey had also recommended that Hamilton target certain groups, such as the elderly and the student golfer. As a result, Hamilton formulated a new advertising strategy designed to entice a greater number of college students to participate at HRGC. In hopes of catching the eye of new

students, Hamilton concentrated his advertising efforts at the beginning of each semester, reducing his efforts as final exams neared. He advertised in the *State,* and planned to advertise in the *Gamecock*. The *State* newspaper, a statewide publication, cost Hamilton $85.50 for one weekend advertisement. The *Gamecock,* the University of South Carolina's student newspaper, was only published during the spring and fall semesters. It charged $25 per week for advertisements during that period. Billboards were also employed along the main roads to bring in golfers who might not have otherwise known about HRGC. In addition, because the survey indicated that the vast majority of golfers (more than four fifths) try out new courses as a result of word of mouth, Hamilton concentrated on promoting a friendly atmosphere at HRGC. He rejected both radio and television advertising, which he had previously been considering.

Employees

40   Hamilton continued to employ Jim Alsing and Pete Peterson to operate the counter sales, while hiring John Clayton as greenskeeper and Harold Valentine as course architect/mechanic. He also billeted himself to work at the course as projects and schedules required.

41   Counter sales consisted of collecting greens and cart fees, controlling cart usage, snack bar and pro shop sales, cleanliness of their area, as well as some small administrative duties. The greens-keeper was responsible for the mowing and care of the greens, as well as reporting any agronomy problems to Hamilton. Clayton performed many other mechanical functions in caring for the course equipment, as well as mowing fairways and tees. Valentine was responsible for the direct mechanical repairs to equipment, overall course agronomy, and course alterations. (*Note:* Pay, working hours, and tenure information will not be disclosed at the request of the owner/operator.)

42   The bulk of the maintenance work fell upon Valentine and Clayton. Valentine, along with being the course agronomist and chemical specialist, worked as part-time mechanic, bringing with him 10 years of experience in that field with the navy, as well as years of experience as a young man growing up on his father's farm in Tennessee. Clayton's primary job was to maintain the greens and turf grass, along with a host of other special projects. Clayton's father, an employee at HRGC many years earlier, had helped him to develop an understanding of and devotion to the golf industry. Most special projects were contracted out to hired individual consultants as needed.

THE CART DECISION

Current Cart Situation

43   In May 1989, Hamilton's cart fleet was sorely depleted. Out of the original 14 E-Z-GO carts, only 2 were available for use. The brakes on one of those were irreparably damaged and unlikely to last much longer. Nine of the 12 recently acquired Club Car carts were also available. The other three had been rendered completely useless by cracks in the transaxles and main drive gears. The nine still in use also suffered from various mechanical problems. The fusible links on two of the carts—parts which normally last for years—were burning out about every two weeks. On a third cart, the rear support bracket for one of the shock absorbers had broken. Because the frame to which the bracket was attached was constructed of aluminum, it required a special type of welding service not available at a reasonable cost in the Columbia area.

44   There were other problems that pointed to the general deterioration of the fleet. Hamilton was beginning to recognize that extensive body damage could occur to fiberglass carts on a heavily wooded course, such as HRGC, and that fiberglass repairs were extremely expensive. On several carts, the batteries were no longer holding their charges all day, and tires were beginning to lose air overnight. Both of these problems were becoming progressively worse. Three of the 12 battery chargers had suffered complete failures in the power supply units, rendering them completely useless. In addition, none of the replacement parts ordered from Club Car had arrived, making it necessary to cannibalize parts from the three useless carts to keep the rest of the fleet operational.

45   These mechanical problems were causing trouble for Hamilton. For one thing, he had a contract to supply carts for 30 people in a golf league, which required 15 carts. On any given day he could be certain of only six to nine working carts. But even more significant was the fact that the proportion of golfers at HRGC who desired to use riding carts (the cart rental ratio) had increased. Specifically, the level of play had increased by 35.7 percent over the previous year, but the number of cart rentals had increased by 41.7 percent over the same period. The cart rental ratio had risen from 26.0 percent to 30.6 percent. More than ever, Hamilton's customers wanted to use his carts; but Hamilton had fewer and fewer carts available.

Factors to be Considered

46   Hamilton and Valentine began to investigate the various possible options to alleviate the cart crisis at HRGC. There were several options, each with its own set of important questions to consider.

47   The first alternative considered was to repair the current fleet with borrowed funds. They would have to determine the cost of repairs, and they would also have to consider the new life expectancy of the used carts if they did so. It was believed that such action would provide only four years extended operation at minimum visual improvement.

48   A second alternative was to purchase an entirely different fleet. Again, this would require borrowing funds whether they decided to buy a fleet of new carts or a fleet of used ones, as they had in 1988. In either case they would have to find whether funds were available at an affordable rate of interest.

49   A third alternative was to lease a fleet, which would require no borrowing of funds. In this situation, they would need to decide whether to purchase a maintenance agreement along with the leased fleet. Under a lease agreement, Hamilton would have final say over the number of carts to be maintained by the course, but not in how they would be used (e.g., a lease contract might refuse him the right to use the carts to do maintenance work of any kind).

50   There were also several additional questions that Hamilton and Valentine needed to consider, regardless of whether they fixed the old fleet, bought a new one, or leased a new one. First, they had to consider what types of options would be necessary to meet the expectations of the customers: sun roofs? full cart enclosures for winter golf? sweater baskets? Second, they needed to decide if they wanted to use three-wheel or four-wheel carts. Four-wheelers cause less turf damage and have a lower insurance cost, because of their greater riding stability. Third, did they want gas or electric? Gas-powered carts would require purchase of fuel and oil, and would require more daily maintenance. They were noisier and gave off fumes, and did not ride as smoothly. Electric-powered carts were heavier, causing greater soil compaction and grass deterioration while providing a smoother ride. They would also consume more electricity and would require the purchase of battery packs about every three years. Finally, they had to decide how many carts would be needed.

Visiting the Cart Companies

51   There were four regional companies that Hamilton and Valentine investigated in their attempts to answer the above questions: Melex, Yamaha, Club Car, and E-Z-GO. Each of these companies provided carts for lease and purchase.

52   Valentine was seeking a four year term agreement without maintenance agreements.

53   Valentine visited each of these firms for Hamilton. He investigated Melex in North Carolina first, then traveled to Yamaha, Club Car, and E-Z-GO in Georgia.

54   Melex had the lowest selling price: $2,800 for gasoline and $2,580 for electric. Its lease cost was $59 per month, with a residual value of $675. In addition, Melex had an outstanding distribution system and was staffed by kind and gracious sales representatives. Melex kept a full maintenance facility at Raleigh, North Carolina. The company had over 10 years of experience in the United States. The carts themselves, as well as all parts, were manufactured in Yugoslavia. Its carts were extremely similar to the previous year's model of E-Z-GO, to the point of having a plate mounted under the right fender that E-Z-GO representatives stated served no function at all.

55   Yamaha's carts were more expensive: $3,500 for gasoline, $3,200 for electric. Lease prices were $72 per month, with a residual value of $1,400. The Yamaha carts were not as aesthetically pleasing as the other models. According to one of the local courses, they had fairly poor records of holding up on rough, hilly terrain. Valentine found the Yamahas also had fiberglass bodies similar to those of Club Car. The company had served the American golf industry eight years, yet it seemed to lack adequate maintenance facilities and trained mechanical personnel in the southeastern United States. Newnan, Georgia, was the closest maintenance facility for Yamaha. The carts and parts were manufactured in Japan, a traditional trading partner with the United States.

56   Club Car's prices were more expensive than Melex, at $3,250 for the gasoline models, $2,800 for the electric, and lease prices of $71 per month, with a residual value of $450. The carts themselves showed design flaws in the differentials and electrical systems. The bodies were fiberglass. Club Car also showed a serious problem with parts availability.

57   Club Car has been in operation for approximately 30 years under various forms of management and ownership. Valentine had a difficult time determining Club Car's prices, as the personnel there were unwilling to give adequate information. According to Valentine, the company was generally uncooperative, and an abrupt cessation of communications took place after they discovered HRGC was also considering carts by E-Z-GO. The company was well established in the U.S. golf industry, and its carts and parts were made in the United States. Club Car had a service facility located only about 70 miles away in Augusta, Georgia.

58   E-Z-GO was a very sturdy cart, with a full sheet metal body and tubular frame designed to stand up to years of use and abuse. Its gas carts cost $2,900, the electric carts cost $2,680, and leasing was $59 per month, with a residual value of $675. According to Valentine, the carts themselves seemed to be mechanically sound in every area and were corrosion resistant and eye-appealing. The electric models held their charges better than those from the other three companies, and their battery chargers were the only ones which showed how long it took for batteries to charge, making it possible to predict battery replacement needs.

59   All personnel were friendly and seemed to stand behind their products. The company was very experienced in the U.S. golf industry, with 35 years already under its belt. Its carts and parts were manufactured in this country. All parts were in stock at its Augusta, Georgia, facilities.

OTHER ISSUES

60   In addition to the decision regarding the cart fleet, Hamilton had several other pressing issues to consider. Each issue would likely need to be resolved before Hamilton's goals for HRGC could be attained. When Hamilton bought HRGC, the only cooler in the snack bar was half of a whiskey barrel filled with ice. Although it was an adequate cooler, it was inefficient, because the attendant would need to reach down into the ice to find the desired brand of beer each time a drink was

ordered. Furthermore, he had to keep track of how much of each brand was on ice to be sure that he did not run out of cold cans of any one brand. Replacement cost: $1.585.

61   The clubhouse was still in need of significant renovation. Hamilton needed to discover where most of his revenues were coming from. Furthermore, as the ratio of revenues from club house activities (pro shop and snack bar) to revenues from the golf course itself increased, the need to renovate became more pressing. Renovation cost: $8,000.

62   With no mower for the rough, Hamilton was trying to use the fairway mower. This, however, did not work well on the higher, thicker rough grass. New mower cost: $1,150.

63   A new rotivator would have allowed for much more efficient aeration techniques. It would cut thin slices in the ground and be usable year round, whereas the old aerator made large holes in the turf and could only be used once per year to cut down on interference with play. Rotivator cost: $3,000.

64   The irrigation system included all tees and greens, but only on five of the nine fairways. Hamilton wanted to add irrigation to the other four fairways, even though he knew its installation would cause considerable interruption in play. Building cost: $6,000.

65   A temperature-controlled workshop was needed adjacent to the clubhouse. Because of the extreme temperatures in the metal cart shed, repair work there was almost impossible. If a new fleet of carts were bought or rented, or if the old fleet were repaired, this workshop would be mandatory. Building cost: $1,000.

66   Hamilton also owned a 15-acre, pie-shaped plot of ground adjacent to the golf course. He was considering adding a nine-hole, par-27 course there. Building cost: $75,000 minimum.

CONCLUSION

67   All of these issues weighed upon Hamilton's mind as Valentine concluded his report about the cart companies. He knew that he would need to spend money to turn Hickory Ridge Golf Course into the kind of facility he wanted it to be. He accepted that. But there were so many areas that needed attention. What should come first?

68   Again, his thoughts returned to the cart dilemma. It all seemed to revolve around his making a correct decision about the carts. If he repaired what he had, he might risk continued problems. If he leased or bought, well, that seemed like such a big step! One thing was certain: He could not ignore the problem. Every day he waited meant lost revenues and lost golfers. A golfer who decided to go somewhere else to play might never bother coming back. Hamilton had all the information he needed. He was determined to make a decision based upon this information as soon as possible, then act upon his choice, for the good of his business.

3 levels of strategy ?.?.

CASE 13

OMNI SOFTWARE & SERVICES, LIMITED

1   Jim Kilpatrick stood at a crossroads in the life of Omni Software & Services, Limited, in 1990. As he looked to the future after two years of successful break-even operations, he saw a number of alternative strategic directions that the firm can pursue, each with its own set of required resources, potential rewards, and risks.

A BRIEF HISTORY OF OMNI SOFTWARE & SERVICES, LIMITED

2   After more than a year's work on the Metis business concept, Jim came to the harsh conclusion that the venture capital community would not fund his proposal. In early 1987, he and Joe Puet— another former Policy Management Systems Corporation (PMSC) employee—dreamed up the Omni idea: they would market existing U.S. software products to insurance companies in foreign markets, drawing upon their contacts in the insurance software industry. These products would constitute a major step for international companies lagging behind the computer revolution. Omni would serve as both a distributor and unbiased advisor to its international clients, helping them select the system most useful and appropriate for them.

3   Once conceived, Omni quickly became an ongoing concern. The following timeline illustrates major developments for the company's first two years.

February 1987	Omni concept developed.
June 1987	Genelco, Inc., signed as first vendor.
September 1987	First client, Metroplitan Life, signed for consulting services.
November 1987	Metropolitan Life signs Omni's first license agreement to provide Genelco system to subsidiary in Spain.
	Second vendor signed.
Spring 1988	Penetration of Scandinavian market.
	Additional vendors signed.
August 1988	Consulting contract with UNI Forsikring in Norway.
October 1988	Gary Griggs, past international insurance company president and former EDS executive, joins management team.
January 1989	Installation contract wiht UNI to provide Cybertek products.
June 1989	Penetration of Belgian market.

This case was developed by Richard Robinson. Copyright © by Richard Robinson, 1990.

Current Business Services

4   Omni is unique in that it markets to the insurance industry on an international basis a wide range of computer software products developed by a number of different companies. Omni's suppliers each specialize in distinctive insurance software applications. In most cases, Omni has the exclusive rights for the products outside the United States.

5   Omni has products that support all of the major insurance types and applications, including traditional and nontraditional life, group and individual pension plans, accident and health insurance, workers' compensation, property, and casualty insurance and reinsurance. Omni's key advantage lies in the fact that, while any one software vendor competes in no more than one or two of the industry segments (e.g., life or accident), Omni covers the entire terrain. Because Omni does not produce its own software, it can objectively survey a client's needs and recommend the appropriate software application. The company views itself as a "problem solver," not just another purveyor of in-house products. Omni provides complete support services for its suppliers' software products. Omni has the ability to combine predeveloped software with strong professional support to offer the international market a variety of products not previously available. Acting in this capacity, Omni can serve as a "one-stop software consulting firm," providing systems integration of multiple systems.

6   Insurance application functions include marketing and sales support, proposal and illustration, the calculation of premium rates, policy and group administration, policy document printing, client billing, and claims handling. The products operate on a number of computer systems (PCs, mainframes, and miniprocessors). Omni is free of the risk of product obsolescence or the burden of product-development costs.

Vendor Terms

7   Omni's competitive advantage revolves around its exclusive portfolio of software vendors based in the United States and Canada. Contracts between Omni and vendors are negotiable within the following parameters:

1. Territory and exclusivity of representation.
2. Minimum sales volume Omni must attain.
3. Omni's ability to drop the line if a better product is introduced.
4. License fee.

8   To date, Omni has gained the following significant terms with respect to the first three factors above:

1. Exclusive representation for all territories outside North America.
2. Perpetual renewal rights for meeting minimum sales volume.
3. Reservation of rights by Omni to terminate the relationship at any time.
4. Limited liability by Omni if it does not sell the product (liability extends only to potential loss of contract).
5. Omni *may not* sell a competing product for a specific market niche as long as a vendor's contract is retained.
6. Renegotiation of a contract as Omni gains leverage.

OMNI Software & Services, Limited

Corporate Overview

CLIENTS

UNI FORSIKRING   References: Phone:
Ruselokkveien, 26   Mr. Svein Hagen - Exec. VP   472-31-5195
Oslo, Norway   Mr. Svein Flugstad - Exec VP   472-31-5950
FAX # 472-31-5987   Mr. Per Simonsen - VP   472-48-9737

UNI is the largest insurance company in Norway. It has been a client since August, 1988. OMNI currently has a team working at UNI's facilities in Oslo installing the full line of Cybertek products. The first phase of the installation began in January 1989 was completed October 1, 1989 on schedule. As a result, UNI was the first major insurance company in Scandinavia to offer an equity-based, life-insurance product, Universal Life. Additional scheduled phases will provide the support of new life and pension products and the conversion of UNI's existing life policies to the Cybertek system.

Metropolitan Life   References: Phone:
One Madison Avenue   Mr. Richard Wiseman - VP - IFM   1(212)578-4787
New York, New York   Mr. Vince Motto - Asst. VP   1(212)578-5199
FAX # 1(212)770-0705

"The Met" has selected OMNI to support its international operations. The Met became OMNI's first client in November of 1987. OMNI successfully installed the Genelco life-insurance system for The Met's Spanish company ("Génesis"). Live operation of the system commenced in Spanish in March 1988. OMNI continues to provide services and on-site support for Génesis. During 1989, OMNI has also installed the Genelco system for The Met in Seoul, Korea and Taipei, Taiwan. The Met has an aggressive international expansion program which is expected to include OMNI's participation in many new markets around the world.

Groupe Assubel   References: Phone:
Rue de Laeken, 35   Mr. Walter Vander Elst - Dir.   332-214-6034
Bruxelles, Belgium   Mr. Jean Marie Maes - Directeur   322-214-6840

Assubel is the second largest company in Belgium. Assubel has purchased The Leverage Group's life system from OMNI. Assubel plans to use this product to introduce new, equity-based life and pension products into the Belgium market during 1990. OMNI plays a major role in support of Assubel's introduction of new life-insurance products.

Additional clients include the following companies:

> Bankers Life - Manilla, The Philippines
> Equifax, Inc. - Atlanta, Georgia
> Eurosept - Paris, France
> Norske Liv - Oslo, Norway
> Samvirke Forsikring - Oslo, Norway
> Storebrand Norden - Oslo, Norway
> WASA - Stockholm, Sweden

10/89

OMNI Software & Services, Limited

Corporate Overview

OMNI'S SUPPLIERS

Supplier Companies:
  Cybertek Corporation
  Genelco, Inc.
  Erisco, Inc.
  Financial Data Planning Corporation
  Real Time Corporation
  Strategic Data Systems
  The Actuarial Network
  The Leverage Group

CYBERTEK CORPORATION

Cybertek is one of the largest life insurance software companies in the world with 1987 revenues in excess of $25 million (U.S. dollars). It was founded in 1969 by former IBM employees who were pioneers in the automation of the insurance industry. **Cybertek**'s products address the needs of life-insurance and operate on IBM micro-processors and mainframes. The November 1987 issue of Forbes magazine recognized **Cybertek** as one of the best small companies in the U.S. One in every four of the top 100 life insurance companies in the U.S. and Canada use **Cybertek**'s products.

GENELCO, INC.

Genelco is a wholly owned subsidiary of General American Life Insurance Company of St. Louis, Missouri. Genelco's products support life insurance, employee benefits, and group health. They operate on IBM System/38, IBM AS400 and Wang/VS computer hardware. **Genelco**'s Life Support Plus life administration system was recently redeveloped using the relational data base environment of the AS400 and supports traditional insurance products such as term and whole life as well as all of the advanced products such as unit/linked and universal life.

ERISCO

Erisco, a company of the Dun & Bradstreet Corporation, provides specialized software applications for the growing needs of the health and benefits industry. Founded in 1968 as a data processing services company, Erisco now supports a client base of 250+ companies throughout the United States, Canada and the U.K. The primary products offered by Erisco are:

ImpleFacts -   a fully automated software application for administering defined contribution record keeping plans;
LoanFacts -   an online system for the administration and monitoring of employee loans from defined contribution plans;
ClaimFacts -   an automated health claoms processing system;
GroupFacts -   an administration system for the group life & health insurance   business; and
CertiFacts -   a hospital preadmission concurrent review and discharge planning system.

FINANCIAL DATA PLANNING CORP. (FDP)

FDP is an association of Consulting Actuaries and other professionals, founded in 1968. It specializes in developing computer software which aids in the sale, setup and service of Employee Benefit Plans,

10/89

OMNI Software & Services, Limited

Corporate Overview

OMNI'S SUPPLIERS (Continued)

Deferred Compensation, and Salary Continuation Plans. it has offices in Miami and Boston which provide software and services to 30 of the 50 largest life insurance companies in the U.S. FDP's software products include:

> Multiple Account Allocation System (MAAS) - a fully automated system for administering Group Pension Plans; and
> Pension Partner - supports the proposal and administration of all types of pension plans, whether insured, non-insured or self-insured.

REAL TIME CORPORATION
Real Time, a $50 million company headquartered in Toronto, Canada, is a leading international supplier of insurance systems to the Property and Casualty insurance markets in the United States, Canada and the United Kingdom. Real Time's parent company, Memotec Data Inc., of Canada, is an international provider of telecommunications, networking and system integration solutions with annual revenue in excess of $360 million. REAL TIME is a well respected, financially secure corporation. Its products address the needs of general insurance and include IBM micro-processor and mainframe products.

STRATEGIC DATA SYSTEMS, INC.
Strategic Data Systems, Inc. (SDS) is headquartered in Sheboygan, Wisconsin with branch offices located in Boston, Massachusetts and Columbia, South Carolina. Strategic Data Systems, Inc. was number twenty-seven (27) in the December 1987 issue of Inc. magazine's "500 Fastest-Growing Private Companies". SDS has software products which support general insurance and operate on IBM System/38, IBM AS400, and Wang/VS computer hardware.

THE ACTUARIAL NETWORK
The Actuarial Network is a professional actuarial consulting group, located in Mequon, Wisconsin. It has expereience in several international insurance markets with advanced and traditional life insurance products. The Actuarial Network's consultants combine actuarial knowledge with computer skills to meet the modern day challenges of its clients. Their areas of expertise include: 1) Financial valuation and projection systems; 2) Product design, pricing and implementation of life insurance products; 3) Experience and profitability analysis; 4) Strategic planning for data-processing, reinsurance, and surplus management; and 5) Negotiation and implementation of reinsurance treaties. Modeling systems which operate on IBM PC and compatible equipment are supported.

THE LEVERAGE GROUP
The Leverage Group is located in Glastonbury, Connecticut. It's products focus on life insurance and especially the automation of new advanced life products. Some of the largest U.S. Life Insurance companies have licensed the products of The Leverage Group to use in evaluating and starting-up the administration of new products. The products are developed using the Cobol programming language and operate on both IBM micro-processors, DEC/VAX mini-computers and IBM mainframes.

10/89

OMNI Software & Services, Limited

Corporate Overview

SOFTWARE PRODUCTS

Life Insurance
General Insurance
Pension Insurance
Health Insurance Claims
Employee Benefit Administration

Life Insurance

Sales Proposals & Illustrations
Support (PC & Mainframe)
Agency/Company Communications
Policy Issue
Client Administration
Policy Administration
Billing & Collection
IBM PC, S/38, AS/400, Mainframes

General Insurance (Non–Life)

Sales Support
Personal & Commercial Rating
Automated Underwriting
Policy Issue
Client Administration
Policy Administration
Billing & Collections
Claims Handling & Administration
IBM PC, S/38, AS/400, Mainframes; Wang/VS

Individual & Group Pension Insurance

Health Insurance Claims Adjudication

Employee Benefit Administration

10/89

OMNI Software & Services, Limited

Corporate Overview

PROFESSIONAL SERVICES

Feasibility Studies
Requirements Studies
Implementation Support Services
On-going Support Services
Joint-Development Projects

Feasibility Studies

New and Existing Insurance Products Review
Software Alternative Evaluation
Software User and Supplier Visits
Product Demonstrations
Computer Hardware Capacity Review
Cost Justification / Benefit Evaluation
Actuarial Planning and Review

The purpose of a Feasibility Study is to document the Client's business needs and compare those needs to the capabilities of proposed systems and to assist the Client in its evaluation. A Feasibility Study Document will be prepared as a result of these services. **OMNI** and the Supplier working with the Client will identify the capacity and ability of the proposed software products to satisfy each requirement. The Feasibility Study Document will be used as the foundation of a detailed Requirements Study and will have value to the Client regardless of the future course of action. **OMNI** feels that this is a critical first step to the successful selection and implementation of any software product.

Requirements Studies

Detailed Requirements of Insurance Products
New Product Consulting
System Demonstrations
Modification Determination
Project Planning
Computer Hardware Capacity Planning
Management Consulting
New Life Product Design, Pricing and Implementation Planning

The purpose of the Requirements Study is to determine the Client's detailed requirements and specifications as they relate to the software systems. In so doing, a more accurate projection for the cost of the modification and customization of the proposed products to meet the Client's business needs would be known in advance. **OMNI** feels that this is a critical step in the successful selection and implementation of any software product and leads to a better relationship between the participating parties and a more successful implementation of the system.

The Requirements Study would result in the creation of three (3) separate documents which could

10/89

OMNI Software & Services, Limited

Corporate Overview

PROFESSIONAL SERVICES (Continued)

assist the Client's management in making the final commitment to license the proposed systems and would be used to control and management the implementation projects. These documents are as follows:

1) Management Overview Document -
   summarizing the insurance product specifications and the implementation plan including the cost, personnel and time required to implement the proposed systems,

2) Requirements Study Document -
   detailing the specifications for the insurance products and the modifications required relative to the proposed systems, and

3) Implementation Plan
   with time-lines, resource requirements, task inter-dependencies, responsibility assignments and the project management methodology to be employed.

Implementation Services

Project Administration
System Customizations
System Modifications
Methods Analysis
Interface Development
Insurance Consulting
Systems Engineering
Education and Training
Conversion Assistance

These Services provide assistance to the Client in the installation and implementation of the software products into the Client's day-to-day business operation. The objective is not just to install the software on the Client's computer, but to provide the professional services necessary for the Client to receive the benefits of the operation of the software in support of the insurance business.

On-going Support Services

Local Support Personnel
Standard Maintenance
Updates and Enhancements from Supplier
24 Hour per Day Telephone Assistance
Shared Development Projects
On-going Education and Training
Participation in User Seminars
OMNI Principal Account Responsibility

The successful implementation of the Client's software systems is essential, but the ongoing support is even more important. For this reason, there are software usage fees to ensure the continuation of support and the Client's ongoing success using the software. An Annual Usage Fee commencing

10/89

OMNI   Software & Services, Limited

Corporate Overview

PROFESSIONAL SERVICES (Continued)

after the first year following the licensing of the system is the vehicle for funding this on-going support. For this fee **OMNI** would provide the following services on an on-going basis:

1) Local support of **OMNI** employees familiar with the technical and insurance aspects of the software products.
2) Standard maintenance support as defined in the Software Usage Agreements for any problems that may occur with the system as delivered from **OMNI**;
3) The benefits of the updates and enhancements that may be developed by Supplier or **OMNI** for the products licensed by the Client;
4) The opportunity to participate with other **OMNI** and the Supplier's customers in the development of software to support new insurance products;
5) 24 hour per day Customer Assistance Centers for telephone inquiries and problem analysis;
6) The availability of on-going education and training at **OMNI** and the Supplier's offices and Customer Assistance Centers;
7) Participation in various Customer Seminars sponsored by **OMNI** and the Software Suppliers for the purpose of exchanging ideas and identifying common system enhancement requirements with other companies using the software; and
8) An assigned **OMNI** principal to be responsible for ongoing contact and to ensure the Client's satisfaction with the software and support services.

OMNI is dedicated to having a successful long-term relationship with all of its customers. The value of such relationships as sources of future references and revenue is vital to **OMNI**'s growth and success. **OMNI**'s overall support strategy is shown by the chart on the following page.

Joint Development Projects

> Project   Organization/Sponsorship
> Funding   Determination/Solicitation
> Development Planning Seminars
> Project   Planning/Management
> Product Marketing
> On-going Maintenance
> Participate Re-imbursement

There are opportunities continuously to work with insurance companies around the world to develop new software for the insurance industry. By bringing several companies with similar needs and interest together, **OMNI** can provide a valuable service to its Clients and create new product opportunities at the same time.

10/89

OMNI Software & Services, Limited

Corporate Overview

THE COMPLETE SOLUTION

LIFE INSURANCE | **GENERAL INSURANCE**

MICRO-PROCESSOR
(IBM PC & PS/2)

CYBERTEK
  SalesPro
  FIELD LINK

THE LEVERAGE GROUP
  Life Administration

FINANCIAL DATA PLANNING
  Pension Parter

EQUIFAX INSURANCE SYSTEMS

  Automated Underwriting
  Commercial Line Rating
  Personal Lines Rating

MID-RANGE PROCESSOR
(IBM S/38 & AS400)

GENELCO

  Life Administration
    Traditional Products
    Advanced Products
    Commissions
    Accounting

STRATEGIC DATA SYSTEMS

  Policy Administration
  Billing
  Personal Lines Rating
  Claims
  Open Item Reconciliation

MAIN-FRAME PROCESSOR
(IBM 9370, 4300, 3090)
(DOS & MVS, CICS, VSAM)

CYBERTEK
  Life Administration
    Traditional Products
    Advanced Products
ERISCO
  Group Pension Plans
  Employee Benefit Plans
THE LEVERAGE GROUP
  Life Administration System

EQUIFAX INSURANCE SYSTEMS

  Combined Billing System
  Universal Billing System
  Prem. Accounting/Claims
  Automated Underwriting
  Company Communications

10/89

< < 1350 Browning Road < > Columbia, South Carolina 29210 USA < > Phone (803)772-2817 < > Fax (803)772-3079 > >

CASE 14

HARLEY-DAVIDSON, INC.: THE EAGLE SOARS ALONE

1   In May 1987, Vaughn Beals, chief executive of Harley-Davidson, Inc., and Thomas Gelb, vice president of operations, made a difficult decision. They had turned Harley-Davidson around on a dime and were now poised for continued success with a fine-tuned production process and an exciting new product line. However, in a continued effort to maintain low costs, Beals and Gelb were forced to give a contract for eight electronically controlled machining centers worth $1.5 million to Japanese-owned Toyoda Machine Works. Even though the Toyoda production site for the machining centers was in Illinois, Beals would have preferred to buy from an American company. But he was constrained because of the Japanese company's ability to deliver both high quality and low price.

2   Beals was well aware of the implications of the decision. He had previously toured several Japanese motorcycle plants during Harley's turnaround. And he understood the pressure foreign competition had put on his company, as well as on other manufacturing-intensive companies in the United States. Nonetheless, the decision reflected Harley's commitment to quality and reliability, and also indicated the company's willingness to change with the competitive environment.

3   Beals and his small management team turned around a company whose product—Harley-Davidson motorcycles—embodied the American values of freedom and rugged individualism. Beals had put Harley back as the market leader in the super heavyweight (more than 851cc) motorcycle market. Harley owned 33.3 percent of that market in 1986, compared to Honda's 30.1 percent. As of August 1987, Harley had 38 percent of the large cycle market, and total company sales were expected to rise from under $300 million in 1986 to over $600 million in 1987.

4   Yet Beals knew that his company needed to diversify to stabilize performance. The Milwaukee-based company manufactured motorcycles and motorcycle accessories, as well as bomb casings and other defense products for the military. In 1986, Harley acquired Holiday Rambler Corporation, a recreational vehicle company, a business that Beals felt fit perfectly with the others, and one that was in an industry free from Japanese competitors.

5   Beals knew that, to remain strong competitively, Harley had to continue to improve both production and human resource management techniques. He also realized his company's basic product, super heavyweight ("hog") motorcycles, had the loyal customers and brand image upon which successful competitive and diversification strategies could be built. The company's non-motorcycle businesses were performing well, and the Holiday Rambler acquisition looked promising. The challenge Beals faced was how to keep the company moving down the road at high speed.

This case was prepared by Stuart C. Hinrichs and Charles B. Shrader, both of Iowa State University; and Alan N. Hoffman, Bentley College. Reprinted by permission.

This case was written to illustrate various management principles and concepts for class discussion, and was not intended to be an example of either effective or ineffective company practices. The authors thank Linda Zorzi, assistant to Vaughn L. Beals (CEO and Chairman of Harley-Davidson, Inc.); Kathryn Molling, Public Relations Director, Harley-Davidson, Inc.; and Don Wright, Vice President of Corporate Services, Holiday Rambler Corporation, for information they provided in preparing this manuscript. The authors also thank Michael Melvin and Blain Ballantine for providing helpful information. Copyright © 1987, by Charles B. Shrader.

HISTORY[1]

6   The Harley-Davidson story began in 1903, when William Harley, age 21, a draftsman at a Milwaukee manufacturing firm, designed and built a motorcycle with the help of three Davidson brothers: Arthur, a pattern maker at the same company as Harley; Walter, a railroad mechanic; and William, a tool maker. At first, they tinkered with ideas, motors, and old bicycle frames. Legend has it that their first carburetor was fashioned from a tin can. Still, they were able to make a three-horsepower, 25-cubic-inch engine and successfully road test their first motorcycle.

7   Operating out of a shed in the Davidson family's backyard, the men built and sold three motorcycles. Production was expanded to eight in 1904, and in 1906 the first building was erected on the current Juneau Avenue site of the main Milwaukee offices. On September 17, 1907, Harley-Davidson Motor Company was incorporated.

8   Arthur Davidson set off to recruit dealers in New England and in the South. William Harley completed a degree in engineering, specializing in internal combustion engines, and quickly applied his expertise in the company by developing the first V-twin engine in 1909. He followed this with a major breakthrough in 1912—the first commercially successful motorcycle clutch, which made possible the use of a roller chain to power the motorcycle. The first three-speed transmission was offered in 1915.

9   During the early 1900s, the United States experienced rapid growth in the motorcycle industry, with such firms as Excelsior, Indian, Merkel, Thor, and Yale growing and competing. However, with the exception of Harley-Davidson and Indian, most of the early U.S. motorcycle companies turned out shoddy, unreliable products. Early continued success in racing and endurance made Harleys favorites among motorcyclists. The company's V-twin engines became known for power and reliability.

10   During World War I, Harley-Davidson supplied the military with many motorcycles. By virtue of very strong military and domestic sales, Harley-Davidson became the largest motorcycle company in the world in 1918.[2] The company built a 300,000-square-foot plant in Milwaukee, Wisconsin, in 1922, making it one of the largest motorcycle factories in the world.[3]

11   In the late 1930s, Harley-Davidson dealt a strong competitive blow to the Indian motorcycle company by introducing the first overhead valve engine. The large, 61-cubic-inch engine became very popular and was thereafter referred to as the "Knucklehead." Indian could not make a motorcycle to compete with these Harleys.

12   Harley introduced major innovations in the suspensions of its cycles in the 1940s. However, in 1949, Harley first met with international competition. British companies, such as Norton and Triumph, were making motorcycles that were cheaper, lighter, easier to handle, and just as fast, even though they had smaller engines.

13   Harley-Davidson countered the British threat by making further design improvements in the engines, thereby increasing the horsepower of their heavier cycles. The changes produced in 1957, what some consider to be the first of the modern superbikes: the Harley Sportster. During the 1950s Harley also developed the styling that made it famous.

14   As the 1950s drew to a close, new contenders from Japan entered the lightweight (250cc and below) motorcycle market. Harley welcomed the little bikes, because it was thought that small bike customers would quickly move to larger bikes as the riders became more experienced. The

---

[1]David K. Wright, *The Harley-Davidson Motor Company: An Official Eighty-Year History*, 2nd ed. (Osceola, Wis.: Motorbooks International, 1987).

[2]Wright, *The Harley-Davidson Motor Company*, p. 17.

[3]Wright, *The Harley-Davidson Motor Company*, p. 17.

Japanese cycles proved to be popular with riders; however, Japanese products began to successfully penetrate the off-road and street cycle markets. In the 1960s, Japan entered the middleweight (250 to 500cc) market.

15   As Harley entered the 1960s, it made an attempt to build smaller, lightweight bikes in the United States. However, the company found it difficult to build small machines and still be profitable. As a result, Harley acquired 50 percent of Aermacchi, an Italian cycle producer, and built small motorcycles for both street and off-road use. The first Aermacchi/Harleys were sold in 1961.[4]

16   The Italian venture endured until 1978 but was never considered to be highly successful. Few took Harley's small cycles seriously, including some Harley dealers, who refused to handle them. In the meantime, Japanese cycles dominated the small and middleweight markets. Harley seemed trapped in the heavyweight segment.

17   In an attempt to expand production capacity and raise capital, Harley went public in 1965. The company merged with the conglomerate AMF, Inc. in 1969. AMF, a company known for its leisure and industrial products, expanded production capacity from 15,000 units in 1969 to 40,000 units in 1974.[5] With the expanded capacity, AMF pursued a milking strategy, favoring short-term profits, rather than investment in research and development, and retooling. The Japanese products continued to improve, while Harley began to turn out heavy, noisy, vibrating, poorly finished machines.

18   In 1975, AMF was faced with a serious Japanese threat to the heavyweight market. Honda Motor Company introduced the "Gold Wing," which quickly became the standard for large touring motorcycles, a segment Harley previously dominated. At the time, Harley's top-of-the-line touring bike sold for almost $9,000, while the comparable Honda Gold Wing was approximately $7,000.[6] Not only did Japanese cycles sell for less than comparable Harleys, but Japanese manufacturing techniques yielded operating costs that were 30 percent lower than Harley-Davidson's.

19   Motorcycle enthusiasts more than ever began to go with Japanese products, because of the cycles' price/performance advantages. Even some loyal Harley owners and police department contracts were lost. The company was rapidly losing ground, both technologically and in the market.

20   Starting in 1975 and continuing through the middle 1980s, the Japanese companies penetrated the big bore custom motorcycle market, producing Harley look-alikes with V-twin engines.[7] The Honda "Magna" and "Shadow," the Suzuki "Intruder," and the Yamaha "Virago" were representative of the Japanese imitations. In a short time, Japanese companies captured a significant share of the large cycle segment and controlled nearly 90 percent of the total motorcycle market.[8]

21   During AMF's ownership of Harley, motorcycles were strong on sales but relatively weak on profits. AMF did put a great deal of money into Harley, and production went as high as 75,000 units in 1975.[9] But motorcycles never seemed to be AMF's priority. For example, in 1978, motorcycles accounted for 17 percent of revenues but for only 1 percent of profits. AMF was more inclined to emphasize its industrial products and services.

---

[4]Wright, *The Harley-Davidson Motor Company*, p. 35.

[5]Wright, *The Harley-Davidson Motor Company*, pp. 282–83.

[6]"Uneasy Rider: Harley pleads for relief," *Time*, December 13, 1982, p. 61.

[7]Wright, *The Harley-Davidson Motor Company*, pp. 244–62.

[8]"Trade Protection: Mind my (motor) bike." *The Economist*, 264 (July 1977), 82.

[9]Wright, *The Harley-Davidson Motor Company*, p. 281.

THE TURNAROUND[10]

22 Vaughn Beals served as Harley's top manager during its last six years under AMF control. Beals was uncomfortable with AMF's short-term orientation and unwillingness to confront problems caused by imports. Consequently in June 1981, a subgroup of Harley management, including Beals, completed a leveraged buyout of Harley-Davidson from AMF. To celebrate, Beals and the management team made a Pennsylvania-to-Wisconsin motorcycle ride, proclaiming "The Eagle Soars Alone."

23 Beals knew that reversing Harley's momentum would not be easy, especially without the help of the former parent. Indeed, things began to get worse. Harley suffered its first operating loss in 1981. In 1982, many motorcycles were coming off the assembly line with defects, registrations for motorcycles were falling, and the Japanese were continuing to penetrate Harley's market segments. Company losses for the year totalled over $25 million.[11] Several Japanese companies built up inventories in the face of a declining market and engaged in aggressive price discounting.

24 Beals petitioned the International Trade Commission (ITC) for temporary protection from Japanese "dumping" practices in 1982. He accused the Japanese of dumping large quantities of bikes in the United States and selling them for prices much below what they were in Japan. The U.S. Treasury had previously found the Japanese guilty of excess inventory practices, but the ITC ruled that the practices had not adversely affected the sales of Harley-Davidson motorcycles. Therefore, no sanctions were placed on the Japanese companies. The Japanese continued price competition, and many thought Harley would soon buckle from the pressure.

25 In 1983, with the help of many public officials, including Senator John Heinz of Pennsylvania, Harley was able to obtain protection from the excess inventory practices of the Japanese. In April 1983, President Reagan, on the recommendation of the ITC, imposed a declining five-year tariff on the wholesale prices of Japanese heavyweight (over 700cc) motorcycles. The tariff schedule was as follows:

1983	45 percent
1984	35 percent
1985	20 percent
1986	15 percent
1987	10 percent

26 The effects of the tariff were mixed. Much of the Japanese inventory was already in the United States when the tariff went into effect. Dealers selling Japanese cycles sharply reduced prices on older models, which hurt the sale of new bikes.

27 On the other hand, the tariff signaled that Japanese overproduction would not be tolerated, giving Harley some breathing room and management a chance to reposition the company. Beals and others inside the company felt that the dumping case and the tariff protection helped focus the company on developing competitive strengths and on improving the production process. They also felt that the tariffs were the result of the government's recognition of Harley's overall revitalization effort, which had begun several years prior to the imposition of the tariff.

---

[10]Wright, *The Harley-Davidson Motor Company*, pp. 244–62.

[11]Dean Witter Reynolds, *Prospectus, Harley-Davidson, Inc.*, July 8, 1986, p. 8.

Improving Production[12]

28   In the early years, Harley had been successfully run by engineers. Beal's background was in engineering as well, and as president he began to focus on the beleaguered production process. Until 1982, the company used a batch production system in which only one model was produced at a time. The final line work would shift from 90 to 140 people, depending on which model was being produced on a given day.

29   To make the production system more efficient, Beals, Thomas Gelb, and others on the management team implemented what they called their productivity triad: materials-as-needed, a just-in-time inventory method; statistical process control; and employee involvement. The materials-as-needed (MAN) system stabilized the production schedule and helped reduce inventory. Production worked with marketing to make more accurate demand forecasts for each model. Precise production schedules were established for a given month and were not allowed to vary by more than 10 percent in subsequent months. A production method was adopted in which a different mix of models was produced every day. This was referred to as the "jelly bean" method.

30   Under the MAN system, Harley required its suppliers to comply with its quality requirements. Harley offered long-term contracts to suppliers who conformed to its quality requirements and delivered only the exact needed quantity for a given time period. Harley also integrated backward into transporting materials from suppliers. The Harley-Davidson transportation company made scheduled pickups from suppliers, which, in turn allowed Harley greater control over the shipments, thereby cutting costs.

31   Prior to the 1983 tariff, Beals, Gelb, and others visited several Japanese motorcycle plants and learned the importance of employee development and involvement. As a result, rigorous training programs were developed. By 1986, over one third of the employees were trained in statistical process control, the ability to sample and analyze data while performing a job. Setup times were reduced by implementing ideas gleaned from quality circles and problem-solving sessions involving workers, managers, and engineers.

32   Further improvements in the production process were made by Walter Anderson, senior production engineer, with the help of Harley employees and management. Instead of running components down straight lines, Anderson organized workers into a series of "work cells." Work cells consisted of a few workers in a small area with all the machines and tools they needed to complete a job. The work cells were often arranged in U-shaped configurations, which allowed intensive work within a cell and reduced the total movement of components through the process. The cells also improved employee efficiency and job satisfaction, in that, while workers stayed at the same work station all day, they enjoyed variety in their tasks.

33   A "simultaneous engineering" system implemented by Beals also helped to improve production. In simultaneous engineering, the design and manufacture of products were combined from the start. The process facilitated the use of statistical design control and helped generate products more efficiently.

34   Harley also invested heavily in research and development. A computer-aided design system was developed by the research and development group. The CAD system allowed management to make changes in the entire product line while maintaining the traditional styling. In 1983, the company developed a more efficient engine, and, in 1984, a new suspension. Harley was soon thereafter recognized to be an industry leader in various areas of production, including belt drive technology, vibration isolation, and steering geometry. Since 1981, the company has allocated a major portion of revenues to R & D each year.

---

[12]Rod Willis, "Harley-Davidson Comes Roaring Back," *Management Review*, October 1986, 20–27.

35   Beal's emphasis on production brought big payoffs for the company. In 1986, 99 percent of the Harleys were coming off the production line free of defects. The company also lowered its breakeven point from 53,000 units in 1982 to 35,000 units in 1986.[13] Many companies now visit Harley for seminars and advice on how to improve efficiency.

36   Perhaps one of the greatest indicators of Harley's production turnaround was evidenced through one of its oldest pieces of equipment—a huge sheet metal-forming machine known simply as "the Tool." The Tool, originally built in Milwaukee but later moved to the plant in York, Pennsylvania, was used to forge the "Fat Bob" gas tanks for all the FX and FXR series bikes. There was no operating manual nor maintenance book for the Tool, yet the company still used this old legendary machine to crank out modern, high-quality products.

37   In March 1987, Vaughn Beals appeared before a Washington, D.C., news conference and offered to give up the tariff protection that was to last until the middle of 1988. Congress praised the announcement and commended the company for its success. President Reagan even visited the York plant in celebration of the event.

Corporate Structure[14]

38   According to Beals, one of the most important contributions to the company's turnaround was the savings obtained by reducing the number of salaried staff. Staff jobs were reduced drastically by Beals as a result of his experience with leaner Japanese companies. The number of managers at each plant was reduced, and each manager was given responsibility for one function at the plant, such as hiring, operations, productivity, and so on.

39   The number of line employees was also reduced. Line employees were given responsibility to inspect products for defects, apply quality control, determine quotas and goals, and make production decisions.

40   A majority of the company's employees participated actively in quality circle programs. The quality circles were used not only to improve efficiency but also to address other issues, such as job security. An outcome of the turnaround was a growing fear among employees of being laid off. Both the reduction in staff and the increased productivity caused workers to worry about the security of their jobs. However, the quality circles came up with the idea to move some sourcing and fabricating of parts in-house. In-house sourcing made it possible for many employees, who may have otherwise been laid off, to retain their jobs.

41   Harley's corporate staff was made very lean and the structure was simple. Top executive officers were put in charge of functional areas. Under top management, the company was basically organized into two divisions—motorcycles and defense. Holiday Rambler Corporation became a wholly owned subsidiary in 1986.

Top Management[15]

42   Vaughn L. Beals, Jr., was appointed as the chief executive officer and chairman of the board of directors of Harley-Davidson Motor Company. He earned an engineering degree from the Massachusetts Institute of Technology and worked as a logging machine manufacturer and as an engine maker before joining AMF in 1975. In 1981, along with one of the grandsons of the founder and

---

[13]Willis, "Harley-Davidson Comes Roaring Back."

[14]Willis, "Harley-Davidson Comes Roaring Back."

[15]Jeff Baily, "Beals Takes Harley-Davidson on New Road," *The Wall Street Journal*, March 20, 1987, p. 39.

12 other individuals, he led the leveraged buyout of the Harley-Davidson Motor Company. He was known throughout the company for his devotion to and enthusiasm for motorcycles. He owned a Harley deluxe Electra-Glide and rode it on business trips whenever possible.

43   Harley's top management always demonstrated their willingness to take a "hog" on the road for a worthy cause. On one occasion, in 1985, Beals and product designer, William G. Davidson (known as "Willie G") led a caravan of Harleys from California to New York in an effort to raise money for the Statue of Liberty renovation. At the conclusion of the ride, Beals presented a check to the Statue of Liberty Foundation for $250,000.

44   Beals claimed that his major responsibility was for product quality improvements. On one occasion, during a business trip, Beals noticed a defect in a 1986 model's seat. He stopped long enough to call the factory about the problem. The workers and test riders, however, had already found and corrected the flaw.

45   Beals made an all-out effort to keep managerial levels in the company to a minimum. The board of directors was composed of six officers, four of whom came from outside the company. The CEO often communicates with everyone in the company through memos known as "Beals'-grams."

46   Because of the company's success, and in an effort to provide additional capital for growth, Harley went public with an offering of approximately 6 million shares in the summer of 1986. Beals owned nearly 16 percent of Harley stock, which was increasing in value.

Human Resource Management[16]

47 Harley-Davidson employed approximately 2,336 people in 1986, down from 3,840 in 1981. Under chief executive Beals, the company made great strides in developing a participative, cooperative, less hierarchical work climate. Employees wrote their own job descriptions and actively participated in on-the-job training. Employees learned that they were not only responsible for their own jobs but also for helping others learn. Performance was evaluated through a peer review program.

48   The company developed many career and placement opportunity programs as a response to employee concern over job security. Harley entered into a cooperative placement agreement with other Wisconsin unions. The company even developed a voluntary layoff program in which senior workers volunteered to be laid off first in down times to protect the jobs of newer workers. Harley offered sophisticated health and retirement benefits, and had also developed employee wellness and college tuition funding programs.

Financial Performance

49 Harley was purchased through a leveraged buyout from AMF in 1981 for approximately $65 million.[17] The buyout was financed with a $30 million term loan and $35 million in revolving credit from institutional lenders. AMF also received $9 million of securities in the form of preferred stock. In 1984, an agreement was reached between the two companies whereby the preferred stock held by AMF was cancelled and payments were to be made directly to AMF from future Harley-Davidson profits.

50   In 1985, Harley negotiated an exchange of common stock for forgiveness of a portion of the loans. The company offered $70 million in subordinated notes and $20 million in stock for public sale in 1986. The proceeds were used to repay a portion of the debt to AMF, refinance unfavorable loans, provide financing for the Holiday Rambler acquisition, and provide working capital.

---

[16]Willis, "Harley-Davidson Comes Roaring Back," pp. 20–27.

[17]Dean Witter Reynolds, *Prospectus, Harley-Davidson, Inc.*, July 8, 1986, p. 8.

51   Holiday Rambler Corporation was a privately held company until its acquisition by Harley in 1986. Holiday Rambler performed very well in its first year as part of Harley-Davidson. It had total sales of approximately $257 million through September 1987 compared with $208 million for the same period in 1986, nearly a 24 percent increase.

52   While Harley-Davidson's net sales and profitability improved during the years 1982 to 1986, net income and earnings per share fluctuated in that period. The motorcycle division's sales decreased as a percentage of the total because of the rapid increase in the defense division. In the years following the 1981 buyout, the company relied greatly on credit for working capital.

Marketing Strategy

53   Harley-Davidson's marketing efforts centered around the use of the Harley name. The company emphasized that its name was synonymous with quality, reliability, and styling. Company research indicated a 90 percent repurchase rate, or loyalty factor on the part of Harley owners.

54   Harley's marketing concentrated on dealer promotions, magazine advertising, direct mail advertising, sponsorship of racing activities, and the organization of the Harley owners group (HOG). The HOG club had enrolled 77,000 members by 1987 and permitted the company close contact with customers.

55   In addition, Harley sponsored or cosponsored organizations, such as the Ellis Island Statue of Liberty Foundation and the Muscular Dystrophy Association.

56   The company was also the first motorcycle manufacturer to offer a national program of demonstration rides. Some dealers felt the program, introduced in 1984, resulted in a large number of Harley motorcycle purchases.

57   A major form of advertising was accomplished through Harley's licensing operation. The licensing of the Harley name was very profitable and served to promote the company's image.

58   The company directed a portion of its marketing expenditures toward expanding the field sales force in an effort to assist the domestic dealer network. In some areas the sales force developed local marketing programs to train dealers.

The Harley Image

59   Few companies could elicit the name recognition and brand loyalty of Harley-Davidson. Harley's appeal was based on the thrill and prestige of owning and riding the king of the big bikes. A Harley has traditionally been known as a sturdy, powerful, macho bike, definitely not for wimps or kids, and a true bike for the open road.

60   A worrisome problem with the Harley image, however, was the perceptual connection of Harleys exclusively with "outlaw" biker groups. The negative "Road Warrior" image affected sales in some areas to such a degree that the company initiated a public relations campaign. The company gently attacked the biker image by directing much of its advertising toward young professionals. The message was that Harley-Davidson represented fun, recreation, and reliability. The company heralded the fact that famous professionals, such as Malcolm Forbes and Reggie Jackson, rode Harleys. The campaign seemed to work. More doctors, lawyers, and dentists began to purchase Harleys.

61   Harley also put tighter controls on licensing its name, ensuring that it was not used in obscene ways. Advertisements picturing Reggie Jackson and Malcolm Forbes atop their "hogs" further helped the company's image.

62   A related problem was that Harley had not attracted very many women customers. This was due to the image and to the size of the bikes. Harleys were very big and heavy. The Harley low-rider series was attracting some women customers because the bikes were lower and easier to get

on. Notwithstanding, some Japanese companies introduced smaller, lighter, low-riding, and in-expensive Harley look-alikes in a straightforward attempt to attract women buyers. Honda's "Rebel" (250cc) was one such bike that became fairly successful with women.

63   However, Harley was careful not to alienate their loyal biker customers. The company continued to promulgate its tough image and even attempted to enhance the image through certain forms of advertising in motorcycle magazines. For example, one ad pictured a group of rather tough-looking bikers and had a caption that read: "Would you sell an unreliable bike to these guys? We Don't!" Another ad showed a junkyard filled with scrapped Japanese bikes. The caption was: "Can you find a Harley in here?"

64   Perhaps the most objective indicator of the strength of the Harley image came from an unlikely source—Japan itself! Japanese companies made numerous attempts to copy Milwaukee's designs.[18] For example, Suzuki's 1987 "Intruder" (1400cc) went to great lengths to hide the radiator, because Harleys were air cooled. Some analysts felt that Japanese imitations only served to strengthen the mystique of the original. The more the Japanese tried to make look-alike bikes, the more the real thing increased in value. Beals agreed. He maintained that Harleys were built to last longer and have a higher resale than other bikes.

Diversification Strategy

65   Since the early years of the company, Harley-Davidson specialized in the heavyweight motorcycle market segment. Heavyweight bikes were divided into three categories: touring/custom, standard street, and performance motorcycles. Harley was never totally successful in building smaller bikes. Beals was even quoted at one time as saying that Harley would not build small bikes.

66   Harley's motorcycle product line was very narrow, compared with that of its competitors. The company's management thought about expanding international operations and penetrating other markets. The largest export markets for Harley were Canada, Australia, and West Germany.

67   The company purchased a small three-wheeler firm named "Trihawk" in 1984. Shortly thereafter the company realized it could not make a go of it in this market because of high start-up costs, and the project was terminated.

68   Under Beals the company moved into the manufacturing of casings for artillery shells and rocket engines for military target drones. The defense business proved to be very profitable for Harley. In an attempt to diversify the company, Beals set corporate goals to increase the level of defense-related business. The company became very active in making bids for the design, development, and manufacturing of defense products.

69   Accessories, bike parts, clothing and "leathers," and even furniture associated with the Harley name were big business for the company. Brand-name licensing and related accessories generated about as much income as did the motorcycles.

70   But Beals wanted to move the company into other businesses not related to the rather narrow motorcycle line and not in competition with Japanese companies. He felt Harley needed to diversify in order to be a truly stable performer. Thus, Harley acquired the Holiday Rambler Corporation in December 1986. Beals saw the fit as a good one, because Holiday produced recreational vehicles and was what he called "manufacturing intensive" just like Harley.

71   Holiday Rambler manufactured premium motorhomes, specialized commercial vehicles, and travel trailers. The company employed 2,300 people and was headquartered in Wakarusa, Indiana. At the time of the acquisition, Holiday was the largest privately owned maker of recreational vehicles, recognized as a leader in the premium class motorhome and towable trailer markets. In

---

[18]"Why Milwaukee Won't Die," *Cycle* 38 (June 1987), 35–41.

1986, Holiday Rambler ranked fourth in market share in the motorhome market and fifth in towable recreational vehicles. Its products were gaining share in the industry as a whole.

72   A Holiday subsidiary, Utilimaster, built truck trailers and bodies for commercial uses. The company had contracts with such companies as Purolator Courier and Ryder Truck Rentals. Other Holiday subsidiaries produced office furniture, custom wood products, custom tools, van conversions, and park trailers.

73   Even with the Holiday Rambler acquisition and with the success in defense-related products, Harley looked for other means of diversifying. In September 1986, a tobacco company purchased a license to test market Harley-Davidson brand cigarettes.

THE FUTURE

74   Because of Harley's success in the face of stiff competition, the company came to be viewed as an example of what can be accomplished by using modern production and personnel management techniques. Top management was committed to keeping the company lean and viable. Yet they knew they needed to diversify and change. Beals felt that his company needed to become as tough as its image.

75   Beals had focused his turnaround effort on the internal operating efficiency of the company. Now he needed to provide leadership for a newly acquired subsidiary and plan for growth in the defense division. He also faced the challenge of breaking the company out of its narrow market segment in its bread-and-butter division: motorcycles. Should he plan for growth and market penetration in the motorcycle industry? Or should he be content with maintaining Harley as a big bike company only?

76   Since 1903, 150 American motorcycle companies had come and gone. Harley-Davidson Motor Company, with Vaughn Beals at the helm, was the only one that survived. The eagle continues to soar alone.

EXHIBIT 1
Harley-Davidson, Inc.—Sales and Income by Business Segment

	1983	1984	1985
	(in thousands)		
Net sales:			
Motorcycles and related products	$229,412	$260,745	$240,631
Defense and other businesses	24,093	33,080	46,845
	$253,505	$293,825	$287,476
Income from operations:			
Motorcycles and related products	$ 16,513	$ 15,489	$ 9,980
Defense and other businesses	3,566	7,012	9,390
General corporate expenses	(6,606)	(6,969)	(6,457)
	13,473	15,532	12,913
Interest expense	(11,782)	(11,256)	(9,412)
Other	188	(311)	(338)
Income before income taxes, extraordinary items and cumulative effect of change in accounting principle	$ 1,879	$ 3,965	$ 3,163

Source: Dean Witter Reynolds, *Prospectus, Harley-Davidson, Inc.,* July 8, 1986. Reprinted by permission.

EXHIBIT 2
Harley-Davidson, Inc.—Consolidated Balance Sheet

	1984	1985	1986
	(In thousands, December 31)		
Assets			
Current assets:			
Cash	$ 2,056	$ 13,470	$ 27,854
Accounts receivable net of allowance for doubtful accounts	27,767	27,313	36,462
Inventories	32,736	28,868	78,548
Prepaid expenses	2,613	3,241	5,812
Total current assets	65,172	72,892	148,676
Property, plant and equipment, at cost, less accumulated depreciation and amortization	33,512	38,727	96,815
Deferred financing costs	—	2,392	4,206
Intangible assets	—	—	77,562
Other assets	523	81	1,240
	$99,207	$114,092	$328,499
Liabilities and Stockholders' Equity			
Current liabilities:			
Notes payable	$ —	$ —	$ 14,067
Current maturities of long-term debt	2,305	2,875	4,023
Accounts payable	21,880	27,521	29,587
Accrued expenses and other liabilities	24,231	26,251	62,447
Total current liabilities	48,416	56,647	110,124
Long-term debt, less current maturities	56,258	51,504	191,594
Long-term pension liability	856	1,319	622
Stockholders' equity:			
Common stock 6,200,000 issued in 1986 and 4,200,000 in 1985	42	42	62
Class B common stock, no shares issued	—	—	—
Additional paid-in capital	9,308	10,258	26,657
Deficit	(15,543)	(5,588)	(717)
Cumulative foreign currency translation adjustment	—	40	287
	(6,193)	4,752	26,289
Less treasury stock (520,000 shares) at cost	(130)	(130)	(130)
Total stockholders' equity	(6,323)	4,622	26,159
	$99,207	$114,092	$328,499

Sources: Harley-Davidson, Inc., *1986 Annual Report;* and *1987 Annual Report;* Dean Witter Reynolds, *Prospectus, Harley-Davidson, Inc.,* July 8, 1986. Reprinted by permission.

EXHIBIT 3
Harley-Davidson, Inc.—Consolidated Statement of Income

	1982	1983	1984	1985	1986
	(Year ended December 31, in thousands, except per share amounts)				
Income statement data:					
Net sales	$ 210,055	$ 253,505	$ 293,825	$ 287,476	$ 295,322
Cost of goods sold	174,967	194,271	220,040	217,222	219,167
Gross profit	35,088	59,234	73,785	70,254	76,155
Operating expenses:					
Selling and administrative	37,510	36,441	47,662	47,162	51,060
Engineering, research and development	13,072	9,320	10,591	10,179	8,999
Total operating expenses	50,582	45,761	58,253	57,341	60,059
Income (loss) from operations	(15,494)	13,473	15,532	12,913	16,096
Other income (expenses):					
Interest expense	(15,778)	(11,782)	(11,256)	(9,412)	(8,373)
Other	(1,272)	188	(311)	(388)	(388)
	(17,050)	(11,594)	(11,567)	(9,750)	(8,761)
Income (loss) before provision (credit) for income taxes, extraordinary items, and cumulative effect of change in accounting principle	(32,544)	1,879	3,965	3,163	7,335
Provision (credit) for income taxes	(7,467)	906	1,077	526	3,028
Income (loss) before extraordinary items and cumulative effect of change in accounting principle	(25,077)	973	2,888	2,637	4,307
Extraordinary items and cumulative effect of change in accounting principle	—	7,795	3,578	7,318	564
Net income (loss)	$ (25,077)	$ (8,768)	$ (6,466)	$ 9,955	$ 4,871
Average number of common shares outstanding	4,016,664	3,720,000	3,680,000	3,680,000	5,235,230
Per common share:					
Income (loss) before extraordinary items and cumulative effect of change in accounting principle	$ (6.61)	$ 0.26	$ 0.79	$ 0.72	$ 0.82
Extraordinary items and cumulative effect of change in accounting principle	—	2.10	0.97	1.99	0.11
Net income (loss)	$ (6.61)	$ 2.36	$ 1.76	$ 2.71	$ 0.93

Source: Harley-Davidson, Inc., *1986 Annual Report*. Reprinted by permission.

EXHIBIT 4
Harley-Davidson Executive Officers

Name	Age	Position	Years with Company*	Annual Compensation
Vaughn L. Beals, Jr.	58	Chairman and CEO	10	$207,217
Richard F. Teerlink	49	Vice president, Chief Finance Officer	5	$143,375
Jeffrey L. Bleustein	46	Vice president, Parts and Accessories	15	$118,387
Thomas A. Gelb	50	Vice president, Operations	21	$132,666
James H. Paterson	38	Vice president, Marketing	15	$ 95,728
Peter L. Profumo	39	Vice president, Program Management	17	$129,521

* Years with Harley-Davidson or AMF, Inc.

Source: Dean Witter Reynolds, *Prospectus, Harley-Davidson, Inc.,* July 8, 1986. Reprinted by permission.

EXHIBIT 5
Board of Directors, Harley-Davidson, Inc.

Vaughn L. Beals, Jr.	Chairman, president, and chief executive officer, Harley-Davidson, Inc., Milwaukee, Wisconsin
Frederick L. Brengel	Chairman and chief executive officer, Johnson Controls, Inc., Milwaukee, Wisconsin
F. Trevor Deeley	Chairman and chief executive officer, Fred Deeley Imports, Richmond, British Columbia, Canada
Dr. Michael J. Kami	President, Corporate Planning, Inc., Lighthouse Point, Florida
Richard Hermon-Taylor	Management consultant, South Hamilton, Massachusetts
Richard F. Teerlink	Vice president, treasurer, and chief financial officer, Harley-Davidson, Inc., Milwaukee, Wisconsin

Source: Harley-Davidson, Inc., *1986 Annual Report*. Reprinted by permission.

EXHIBIT 6
Harley-Davidson's U.S. Market Share—Super Heavyweight Motorcycles (850cc +)

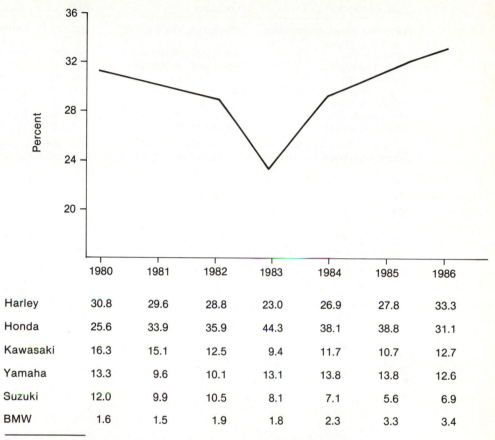

	1980	1981	1982	1983	1984	1985	1986
Harley	30.8	29.6	28.8	23.0	26.9	27.8	33.3
Honda	25.6	33.9	35.9	44.3	38.1	38.8	31.1
Kawasaki	16.3	15.1	12.5	9.4	11.7	10.7	12.7
Yamaha	13.3	9.6	10.1	13.1	13.8	13.8	12.6
Suzuki	12.0	9.9	10.5	8.1	7.1	5.6	6.9
BMW	1.6	1.5	1.9	1.8	2.3	3.3	3.4

Source: Harley-Davidson, Inc., *1986 Annual Report.* Reprinted by permission.

EXHIBIT 7
Harley-Davidson, Inc.—Facilities

Type of Facility	Location	Sq. Feet	Status
Executive offices, engineering, and warehouse	Milwaukee, Wisconsin	502,720	Owned
Manufacturing	Wauwatosa, Wisconsin	342,430	Owned
Manufacturing	Tomahawk, Wisconsin	50,600	Owned
Manufacturing	York, Pennsylvania	869,580	Owned
Engineering test laboratory	Milwaukee, Wisconsin	6,500	Lease expiring 1991
Motorcycle testing	Talladega, Alabama	9,326	Lease expiring 1988
International offices	Danbury, Connecticut	2,850	Lese expiring 1988
Office and workshop	Raunheim, West Germany	4,300	Lease expiring 1989

Source: Dean Witter Reynolds, *Prospectus, Harley-Davidson, Inc.,* July 8, 1986. Reprinted by permission.

BIBLIOGRAPHY

Harley-Davidson, Inc. *1986 Annual Report.*

Harley-Davidson, Inc., *1986 10-K Report.*

Dean Witter Reynolds, *Prospectus, Harley-Davidson, Inc.,* July 8, 1986.

CASE 15

LA-Z-BOY CHAIR COMPANY

1   One of the most widely recognized trademarks in the United States, La-Z-Boy seems to connote a relaxed, lazy atmosphere. Is the La-Z-Boy Chair Company (LZB) like the visions its trademark suggests? Hardly! Consider the percent increase in net sales and percent increase in net profit in the last six years. Exhibits 1 and 2 show the Income Statements and Balance Sheets for the years 1983 through 1988, respectively. This dramatic growth, which made LZB number three in the furniture industry and the largest producer of upholstered furniture, was achieved by acquiring four other companies as well as by internal growth. The four acquisitions are shown in Table 1, with their annual sales in the year prior to acquisition.

2   While the furniture industry sales grew by 52 percent in the last 10 years from sales of $9.7 billion in 1978 to $14.8 billion in 1987, LZB sales grew at a much faster rate of 216 percent. During the 10-year period, the top 10 manufacturers moved from 20 percent to 33 percent of the total market growing by 139 percent. During this same 10-year period, LZB moved from eighth to third place in the industry. Can this performance be continued? What can LZB do for encores?

COMPANY BACKGROUND

3   LZB was founded by Edward M. Knabusch and his cousin Edwin J. Shoemaker in 1927 as a partnership known as Kna-Shoe Manufacturing Company in Monroe, Michigan. In 1928, the first reclining chair was developed as a wooden-slat porch chair. Although the Lion Store in Toledo, Ohio, refused to handle it, the buyer suggested that if it were an upholstered chair it would have a much wider market year round. The two partners followed the suggestion and produced and patented the first "La-Z-Boy Chair" in 1929. In that same year the company was incorporated as the Floral City Furniture Company, the name selected because Monroe was then known as the "Floral City" since it was the home of the world's two largest nurseries.

4   During the depression years of the 1930s, the chair was leased to established companies on a royalty basis, with Floral City retaining the rights for Monroe County. In 1938, a new mechanism was developed which was so revolutionary that new patents had to be secured. Floral City took back the patent in 1939 and continued to manufacture chairs through 1941. La-Z-Boy Chair Company was formed in 1941 to separate the production function from the merchandising activity. Beginning in 1942 and continuing through World War II, LZB produced seats for military vehicles and naval vessels.

This case was prepared by Robert P. Crowner, associate professor of management of Eastern Michigan University, as a basis for class discussion.
Copyright © 1988 by Robert P. Crowner

EXHIBIT 1

LA-Z-BOY CHAIR COMPANY
Income Statement
For Years Ending April 30
(in thousands of dollars)

	1983	1984	1985	1986	1987	1988
Net sales	$196,973	$254,865	$282,741	$341,656	$419,991	$486,793
Costs and expenses:						
Cost of sales	136,952	167,387	191,312	235,524	289,779	352,069
Selling, general, and administrative	38,595	45,962	54,713	65,610	85,469	91,354
Interest expense	1,031	963	1,146	1,570	1,877	4,008
Total	176,578	214,312	247,171	302,704	377,125	447,431
Operating income	20,395	40,553	35,570	38,952	42,866	39,362
Other income	2,062	3,037	3,117	2,807	2,081	2,662
Income before taxes	22,457	43,590	38,687	41,759	44,947	42,024
Income taxes:						
Federal:						
Current	237	14,790	9,201	14,797	19,558	17,931
Deferred	8,717	4,010	6,508	2,809	(1,175)	(4,832)
State	732	1,505	1,619	1,143	1,900	2,444
Total taxes	9,686	20,305	17,328	18,749	20,283	15,543
Net income	$ 12,771	$ 23,285	$ 21,359	$ 23,010	$ 24,664	$ 26,,481
Net income per common share	0.69	1.16	1.17	1.26	1.34	1.45

EXHIBIT 2

LA-Z-BOY CHAIR COMPANY
Balance Sheets
For Years Ending April 30
(in thousands of dollars)

	1983	1984	1985	1986	1987	1988
Current assets:						
Cash	$ 1,115	$ 3,220	$ 2,062	$ 2,419	$ 1,393	$ 2,207
Short-term investments	14,973	25,957	18,250	13,305	21,172	14,740
Receivables	70,762	79,557	92,167	106,638	116,952	135,560
Less allowances	2,140	2,300	2,445	2,814	3,118	4,976
Net receivables	68,622	77,257	89,722	103,824	113,834	130,584
Inventories						
Raw materials	11,463	11,992	12,209	15,305	19,541	24,522
Work in process	6,740	8,965	11,630	14,771	17,143	23,323
Finished goods	4,563	5,147	4,097	5,157	8,791	18,977
Total	22,766	26,104	27,936	35,233	45,475	66,822
Other current assets	452	585	2,985	3,229	5,037	5,085
Total current assets	107,928	133,123	140,955	158,010	186,911	219,438
Other assets	500	2,572	7,726	18,095	9,488	6,737

EXHIBIT 2 *(concluded)*

	1983	1984	1985	1986	1987	1988
Fixed assets:						
Land	$ 1,954	$ 2,197	$ 2,344	$ 2,842	$ 3,586	$ 5,266
Buildings	28,853	31,316	37,314	44,088	52,782	64,637
Machinery	29,024	33,410	40,248	51,041	66,821	69,437
	59,831	66,923	79,906	97,971	123,189	139,340
Less depreciation	27,535	31,095	35,157	41,082	49,701	55,180
Net fixed assets	32,296	35,828	44,749	56,889	73,488	84,160
Goodwill						26,257
Total Assets	$140,724	$171,523	$193,430	$232,994	$269,887	$336,592
Current liabilities:						
Notes payable			$ 1,077	$ 3,682	$ 6,099	$ 10,744
Current portion of long-term debt	$ 936	$ 1,098	1,087	1,717	979	7,039
Accounts payable	10,414	10,966	15,470	11,033	20,134	16,815
Payroll	6,173	7,987	8,265	13,144	15,941	16,046
Other liabilities	4,345	4,182	6,383	7,478	10,014	13,098
Income taxes	993	4,655	1,185	2,392	7,168	1,764
Deferred income taxes	6,649	9,321	12,016	12,196	11,241	6,868
Total cur. liab.	29,510	38,209	45,483	51,642	71,576	72,374
Long-term debt	11,763	13,222	11,165	24,463	23,270	76,215
Deferred income taxes	2,136	3,474	7,288	9,917	9.687	9,238
Equity:						
Common stock, $1 par value	18,641	18,641	18,641	18,641	18,641	18,641
Capital in excess of par value	5,168	5,540	5,514	5,783	6,054	6,493
Retained earnings	73,984	92,862	108,354	124,951	142,485	161,629
Currency adjustments	(131)	(271)	(654)	(659)	(449)	320
	97,662	116,772	131,855	148,716	166,731	187,083
Less treasury shares	347	154	2,361	1,744	1,387	8,318
Total equity	97,315	116,618	129,494	146,972	165,344	178,765
Total liabilities and equity	$140,724	$171,523	$193,430	$232,994	$269,877	$336,592

TABLE 1

Burris Industries, Inc.—acquired July, 1985	$10.6 million
Rose Johnson, Inc.—acquired January, 1986	$20.0 million
Hammary Furniture, Inc.—acquired September, 1986	$22.0 million
Kincaid Furniture, Inc.—acquired January, 1988	$85.0 million

5   In 1947, chair production began again and sales grew to $52.7 million by 1970. The first out-of-state plant was built in Newton, Mississippi, in 1961. Edward Knabusch, who died in 1988, continued as president of LZB until 1972, when he was succeeded by his son Charles. Edwin Shoemaker continues to be active in LZB as vice chairman of the board and executive vice president of engineering.

SALES AND MARKETING

6   Sales and marketing are under the direction of Patrick H. Norton, senior vice president. Norton, who is 66 years old, joined LZB in September 1981, following a successful career with Ethan Allen, Inc. Exhibit 3 shows the organization chart for the upper management of LZB. In addition to the activities of advertising and sales communication, residential sales, contract sales, and sales for Burris Industries, the following activities also report to Norton: corporate interior design for Showcase Shoppes, national merchandising manager, sales and service administration, manufacturing services manager, sales and marketing research, product design, and store development for Showcase Shoppes. Norton's strategy is responsible for the dramatic expansion of LZB into the broader lines of furniture since he arrived. He believed that for LZB to continue to expand and be competitive it must offer a full line of furniture.

Sales

7   Sales are divided into two broad categories. The Residential Division, which is by far the largest segment of the business, sells a complete line of reclining chairs and other upholstered chairs, sofas and sleep sofas and modular seating groups as shown in Exhibit 4. The Burris Division sells upscale upholstered furniture to the residential market, which is complemented by an extensive line of wooden occasional tables sold by the Hammary Division. Within these divisions traditional, transitional, and contemporary styles are sold.

8   The Contract Division sells desks, chairs, and credenzas to the general business market. The Rose Johnson Division complements the contract division by providing office panel walls, chairs, and work centers.

9   Residential sales are carried out by 100 independent manufacturer's representatives who are under annual contract to sell the LZB line exclusively within their geographic area. These reps are paid by commission equivalent to 3 percent of direct shipments plus 2 percent from an incentive pool for performance against an order goal. The incentive begins when the rep reaches 70 percent of the goal and reaches the full 2 percent when 100 percent of the goal is attained. Sales in excess of the goal receive a commission of 7 percent. The established goal is based upon history and the corporate target regarding market share and growth. The rep can protest the goal. LZB's new sales strategy is to reduce the size of the exclusive territories, often limiting them to a county in populous areas. Therefore, over time, the number of reps has been increased. This is accomplished by only changing territories as existing reps retire or are dismissed.

10   The reps are managed by four regional managers—South Central, Eastern, Midwest, and Western. The regional managers spend two to three days per week on the road working with sales reps. The regional manager breaks the region's sales goal down into goals for individual sales reps. LZB has the right to interview and approve any "associates" whom the sales reps may hire to work with them.

11   The yearly sales goal is developed by using a demographic profile. Factors considered are age groups, racial groups, since minorities historically have purchased few chairs, home owner status,

EXHIBIT 3
Organization Chart, La-Z-Boy Chair Company

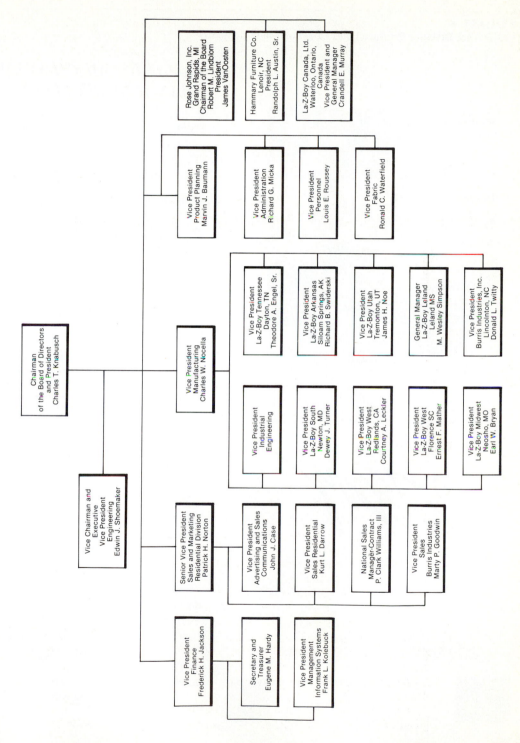

653

EXHIBIT 4
Residential Division Product Line, La-Z-Boy Chair Company

Versatile La-Z-Boy Motion-Modulars™ modular furniture, "Dreamer."

So whether you're decorating a single room or an entire house, we hope you'll make the La-Z-Boy connection. It's comfort and quality you can count on.

(Back cover) "Dreamer," Motion-Modulars™ modular furniture shown in a different configuration.

LA-Z-BOY™...MUCH MORE THAN JUST RECLINERS

Reclina-Rocker® recliner	A motion chair that both rocks and reclines. Available with an optional swivel base.
Reclina-Way® wall recliner	This motion chair can recline to a full-rest position even when placed close to the wall.
Reclina-Rest® recliner	Reclining comfort with an optional swivel base.
La-Z-Lounger® high-leg recliner	Chippendale or Queen Anne style legs give these high-leg recliners a very distinctive and elegant look.
Lectra-Lounger® power recliner	A dual-action power reclining chair with independent reclining and foot rest action; activated by pushing one or both of its power buttons.
La-Z-Rocker® swivel rocker	Swivel and rock in scaled-down comfort.
Reclina-Way® Sofette loveseat	A loveseat with two individually operated recliners for dual reclining pleasure.
La-Z-Boy Signature II™ sofa	A fully upholstered sofa or loveseat featuring the La-Z-Boy MagiCoil™ Seating System for added seating comfort.
La-Z-Boy Signature II™ sleep sofa	Engineered for seating and sleeping comfort with a Supreme Comfort™ foam or optional innerspring mattress. Easy to open and close.
La-Z-Boy Signature II™ sleep sofa with The Uni-Flex Comfort System™	Designed to provide uncompromising sleeping and seating comfort with an exclusive Supreme Elegance™ innerspring mattress, flexible side-to-side stretch decking, and a low side profile with all linkage located below the foundation surface.
Motion-Modulars™ modular seating	Flexibility with the appearance of a sofa and comfort of a recliner. Decorating options are endless, as each modular group can be individually planned for specific seating needs.
Many La-Z-Boy products feature:	**HERCULON** The Champion of Velvets **DuPont TEFLON®** soil & stain repeller

since the major market is home owners or those living in single family dwellings, and furniture dollars spent within an area. The average customer is in the middle class, with chair customers being 35 and older as contrasted with sleeper customers being younger, newly married, and renters.

12   To determine each region's goal, a regional factor is applied. Marketing Statistics, a firm located in New York, is used to obtain a buying power index for each county as a percent of the total U.S. market. A separate index is used for recliners and for sleepers. The American Furniture Manufacturers Association collects and provides information about the industry. Industrial Marketing Research in Chicago provides quarterly and annual customer surveys which are useful. Sales for LZB are about equally divided between the first and second halves of its fiscal year.

13   Distribution for LZB is divided into three major categories. General furniture dealers account for about 50 percent of sales. The Gallery Program, which currently includes about 75 stores, 25 percent of the general furniture market, and is increasing, is featured with the general dealers. Under this program, the deal must dedicate 3,500 square feet to LZB products, and LZB designs the area. The dealer is licensed on an open-end basis by location. Department stores, which do 20 percent of the total furniture business, have been a weak category for LZB. Department stores always want special pricing and LZB does not engage in discounting.

14   National accounts make up 10 percent of sales. The largest single account is Montgomery Ward, which is handled by the home office, but a 3 percent commission is paid the local sales rep for servicing the account. Most accounts are regional, such as Art Van in Detroit and Macy's.

15   LZB Showcase Shoppes, which number about 265, account for about 35 percent of sales. A Showcase Shoppe is licensed on an open-end basis by location. Location is everything—that is, the site should be located in an area where the city is growing, with a reasonable concentration of quality homes, apartments, or condominiums which are less than 15 years old within a seven-mile radius; the activity in the surrounding area should be conducive to retail activity; the street should be a heavily traveled major artery that is well known to everyone; the site should be readily visible and located near the street with maximum window frontage and should be easily accessible and convenient to shoppers; and the building should be free-standing. Small strip centers can be effective, but large strip centers or regional malls are ineffective. The minimum showroom size is 6,000 square feet, with the normal Shoppe expected to be 7,000 to 10,000, with an additional 1,500 to 2,400 square feet on site area required for warehouse, office space, and so on. An initial investment of $132,000 is typical, of which $75,000 is required for working capital and the balance for capital improvements. LZB provides the Shoppe with an operating manual, which includes advice on advertising, personnel policies, freight, service, interior design, and signage.

16   Contract sales are handled through a different group of manufacturer's reps who do not handle LZB products exclusively. These reps typically have other employees working for them. Sales of subsidiaries are handled in a manner similar to the residential sales with their own reps.

Advertising

17   John J. Case, vice president of advertising and sales communications, joined LZB in 1977 as assistant national accounts manger and progressed through several positions to his present one in 1985. He is responsible for all of LZB's national corporate advertising and public relations for the residential, office products, and Burris divisions, as well as the sales training program for dealers and sales representatives. He graduated from Michigan State University with a BA degree in telecommunications.

18   Prior to 1982, LZB spent money on corporate advertising and on retail advertising materials but had no control over its image in the local marketplace. Its corporate image and its local image were not compatible. Retail outlets bought seasonally and promoted seasonally. As a result, manufacturing was adversely affected by the two peak sales periods in May and November.

EXHIBIT 5
Sunday Supplement Advertisement, La-Z-Boy Chair Company

SALE! $399

A. "Dimension" Reclina-Rocker® recliner
A sleek and streamlined contemporary recliner. Channel stitched
and thickly cushioned. 100% acrylic cover is Scotchgard®
protected.

WESTLAND FURNITURE
■ 490 South Maple Road—Ann Arbor, Michigan 48103

EXHIBIT 6
Television Advertisement, La-Z-Boy Chair Company

LA-Z-BOY®

1 NATIONAL RECLINER SALE
  "What You're Sitting On"
2 FATHER'S DAY SALE
  "What He's Sitting On"

3 FALL SALE
  "Perfect Chair"
4 HOLIDAY SALE
  "My Wife Gave Me This One"

1

ALEX: I'll bet you're watching me from your favorite chair. The most comfortable chair in your house, huh?

Is your chair this comfortable?

The National La-Z-Boy Recliner sale is going on right now... (ALEX SNORES)

2

ALEX: Would all the dads leave the room for a second. Go on, it's okay. Now the rest of you.

(INDIGNANT) Look at what that man was sitting on. Doesn't he deserve better? Genuine La-Z-Boy recliners are on sale right now for Father's Day.

So think about it. He's a nice man.

3

ALEX: You know the designers at La-Z-Boy have been working hard to find a way to make La-Z-Boy recliners even more comfortable for you.

But, how can you improve the perfect chair?

Ooooooh. The price of course! Why didn't I think of that?

4

ALEX: Dad, this Christmas, don't hint. Just come right out and tell your family if they give you a La-Z-Boy recliner,

they'll never ever have to buy you a tie as long as you live. My wife gave me this one...

The La-Z-Boy Holiday Sale. Going on now.

657

EXHIBIT 7
Co-op Advertising Help, La-Z-Boy Chair Company

THE MOST EFFECTIVE WAY TO MAKE YOUR ADVERTISING EFFORTS REALLY PAY OFF!

This brochure contains complete information on the La-Z-Boy® co-op advertising program for 1987. The program covers most La-Z-Boy® chairs, sleep sofas, sofas, Scilette™ loveseats, and Motion-Modular™ units, and is in effect from January 1 through December 31, 1987.

The La-Z-Boy® Chair Company has remained the first name in seating comfort for over 50 years through our continuing national advertising programs. We would like you to tie in your advertising to our national campaigns because your local advertising is extremely important to our mutual sales. Your advertising tells La-Z-Boy® customers where they can buy genuine La-Z-Boy® products. With our co-operative advertising program, we can help you sell more La-Z-Boy® products through your local advertising — as well as help you pay for the ads.

CO-OP ADVERTISING FUNDS

The La-Z-Boy® Chair Company will provide you with co-op advertising funds when you meet the requirements outlined in this brochure. As a dealer, you will accrue three dollars ($3.00) on most chairs including Leather Finesse® chairs, and single Motion-Modular™ units, and six dollars ($6.00) on each Signa-ture™ sofa or sleep sofa, Motion-Modular™ sofa or sleep sofa units, and each leather covered chair invoiced to your store during the period this agreement is in effect. The amount of co-op advertising funds you accrue is available to you. Co-op funds are accrued from January 1 to December 31, 1987, but can only be applied to advertising run in the same time period. (Refer to Method of Payment.)

*Certain styles, at the discretion of La-Z-Boy® Chair Company, do not accrue co-op advertising dollars.

TERMS OF AGREEMENT

This co-op advertising program is in effect through 1987 un-less either the La-Z-Boy® Chair Company or you, the dealer, decide to terminate it. This pro-gram can be terminated by either company or dealer upon thirty (30) days prior written notice.

This brochure includes all terms and conditions of the La-Z-Boy® Chair Company advertising program. It supersedes all pre-vious co-op agreements.

This co-op agreement and any questions or disputes will be decided under the laws of the State of Michigan.

QUALIFYING ADVERTISING

The La-Z-Boy® Chair Company will reimburse you 50% of your eligible advertising expenses from the co-op funds you have accrued. For these reimbursements, you must meet the follow-ing requirements:

1. You must maintain a prominent in-store display of La-Z-Boy® Chair Company products throughout 1987.

2. The advertising must prom-inently utilize the La-Z-Boy® name in one of the following fashions.

PRINT: All print ads must contain "La-Z-Boy®" in the caption or body copy of the advertisement.

TELEVISION: The "La-Z-Boy®" name must be mentioned in the script of the commercial, and La-Z-Boy® products must be shown.

RADIO: The "La-Z-Boy®" name must be mentioned in the radio script.

BILLBOARDS: Requests for outdoor billboard posters must be accompanied by a photo of the billboard and a copy of the invoice. The "La-Z-Boy®" name must appear on the billboard.

OTHER TYPES OF ADS: Additional forms of advertising other than those described above may be eligible for co-op funds. Please contact the La-Z-Boy® Chair Company Advertising Department to receive prior approval.

4. The co-op trade products cannot appear or be men-tioned in your advertising. Competitive products are de-fined as any recliner, sofa, sleep sofa, swivel rocker or modular seating other than La-Z-Boy® Chair Company.

TRADEMARK USAGE

Proper copy of the registered La-Z-Boy® trademark is re-quired to qualify for co-op funds.

Whenever using the La-Z-Boy® name in advertising, you must adhere to the following rules:

1. **The name La-Z-Boy® must never be used as a noun.** For example: "Looking for a La-Z-Boy® chair? We have it" or "La-Z-Boy®." Looking for it? is correct.

2. **A trademark symbol must follow the registered name at least once in copy, and preferably the first time the name appears.** Since the name "La-Z-Boy®" is a regis-tered trademark, the symbol must be used on the most prominent "La-Z-Boy®" in the ad. Other registered La-Z-Boy® trademarks include Reclina-Rocker®, Reclina-Way®, Signa-ture®, Sofa, La-Z-Boy Rocker®, Signature™ sleep sofa, Leather Finesse®, Reclina-Way Settee™ and Motion Modular™.

3. **The trademark must always be used with the generic name.** Therefore "Every La-Z-Boy® chair is on sale," would be correct but "Every La-Z-Boy® is on sale" would be wrong. The simple way to remember is to think of the trademark name as a proper adjective, which de-scribes something. Also cor-rect usage would be "Reclina-Rocker® chair," "Reclina-Way® swivel rocker," "Signa-ture™ sofa," "Reclina-Way Settee™ loveseat," "Signature™ sofa, and Motion Modular™ modular seating.

4. **Trademarks should never be used in the possessive form.**

5. **Trademarks should always be used in the singular.** They aren't im-proper plurals for the La-Z-Boy® trademarks. Therefore, "Over 600 La-Z-Boy® in stock," is wrong.

Remember co-op funds will not be issued if the La-Z-Boy® trademark is used wrong.

METHOD OF PAYMENT

You will receive a credit memo from the La-Z-Boy® Chair Company for your co-op funds when the following items are received:

1. Your claim in the form of a debit memo/invoice request-ing payment.

2. A dated tear sheet (with a copy of the newspaper's invoice or the full page tear from the newspaper or other publication as it ran.

3. If you are requesting credit for radio or television advertis-ing, you must send a copy of the station invoice and a copy of the commercial, the script with the ANA/RAB or ANA/TVB documentation on the script itself.

Co-op funds will be issued at the rate of 50% of your advertising costs, that meet the above re-quirements. These co-op funds are drawn from the amount you accrue in the manner described in the section CO-OP ADVER-TISING FUNDS.

Accrued funds must be used during the period of January 1 to December 31, 1987, and funds cannot be carried for-ward into the next year. Co-op claims must be submitted to the Co-op Advertising Depart-ment, La-Z-Boy Chair Com-pany, Monroe, MI 48161 within ninety (90) days after the ad ran. **ALL CO-OP CLAIMS FOR ADVERTISING RUN IN DECEMBER 1987 MUST BE SUBMITTED BY MARCH 1, 1988.**

Any claims re-submitted for co-op must be within the designated time periods.

LA-Z-BOY

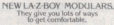

EXHIBIT 12
Influences on Buying, La-Z-Boy Chair Company

Influences on Buying

Although consumers cite price as the "most difficult" factor about buying furniture, construction, comfort and durability are considered to be stronger influences in the furniture buying decision.

	Very Important	Somewhat Important
Construction	85.3%	14.7%
Comfort	93.8	6.0
Durability	87.3	12.3
Fabric	68.0	31.0
Finish on wooden parts	64.4	32.2
Styling/design	65.2	32.9
Soil and stain resistant fabrics	67.3	30.3
Material used	65.7	31.3
Guarantee/warranty	59.1	36.1
Retailer's reputation	39.5	46.9
Size	52.6	40.9
Manufacturer's reputation	45.9	42.8
Price	59.4	35.6
Brand name	26.0	56.5
Delivery time	21.9	44.4
Decorator/designer	7.5	29.6

Shopping Activities

Before making a furniture purchase, 75 percent of consumers visited home furnishings stores to shop for ideas. It tops activities leading to a final selection. (Source: *Better Homes & Gardens*).

Shopped stores to get ideas	75.0%
Watched local newspaper ads for furniture	59.6
Looked in a Sears', Penney's, or Ward's catalog to check prices	39.4
Looked in a manufacturer's catalog I have (such as one for Ethan Allen, Pennsylvania House, etc.)	37.0
Got suggestions from friends, relatives, etc.	27.6
Clipped manufacturers' ads and tried to locate a specific piece of furniture	16.3
Telephoned different local stores about prices and brands	15.9
Talked to a decorator from a local store	13.9
Sent for manufacturers' brochures featured in magazine ad	12.0
Talked to a decorator other than one in store	7.7
Called "800" toll-free number to see what local store carried a certain brand	2.6
Other	2.4
No answer	2.6

by the end of 1986 and expected the number would increase to 5,700 by 1991. Shipments by manufacturers to galleries are expected to increase from 21 percent in 1986 to 43 percent in 1991. The increasing competition for retail floor space will require manufacturers to provide more support to the retailers.

27   According to a survey made in 1985 by *Better Homes & Gardens*, most customers (89.4 percent) shop at more than one store when buying furniture. The survey also showed that 58.2 percent of the customers took a month or more to make a purchase commitment. To get ideas before they

EXHIBIT 12 (*concluded*)

Construction features (coil construction, joint construction, etc.)	87.3%
Brand name	68.5
Finish on wood surface	61.1
Price	28.4
Salesperson's recommendation	23.1
Friends' and relatives' recommendations	22.4
Just by looks	18.3
Other	2.6
No answer	0.2

Quality Measures

Construction features are considered by consumers to be the best measure of quality of a piece of furniture.

bought, 75 percent said they shopped various stores. Decorating information was considered important to purchasers, although 90 percent said they did not hire an interior designer the last time they decorated their homes. About half admitted they needed advise. About 80 percent of married purchasers indicated that it was important for the spouse to be pleased and, therefore, they usually shopped together. Other data regarding furniture purchases are shown in Exhibits 11 and 12.

28   In a marketing research report in 1985 done by the Marketing Research Bureau, consumers raised ethical issues regarding in-store designers. They believed there was a potential conflict of interest in that the designer might be motivated by the desire to sell more furniture, rather than solving the customer's problems. The same survey indicated that the usual shopping procedure was for customers to visit their local home furnishing dealer, obtain numbers of the desired furniture, and then buy the furniture from discount outlets at a substantially lower price.

29   Unlike LZB, the competing brands of Action Chair, which is a division of Lane Chair, LZB's largest competitor, specialize in selling through department stores. Department stores like to have exclusives, which is one of the reasons LZB does not use them as dealers. Most of LZB's competitors are not fully integrated in manufacturing and typically buy their mechanisms from Leggett & Platt, Super Sagless, or Hoover.

MANUFACTURING

30   Charles W. Nocella, vice president of manufacturing, is responsible for the extensive manufacturing organization shown in Exhibit 3, which includes all plants except the Waterloo, Canada; Rose-Johnson; Kincaid; and Hammary. In addition to the activities shown, Nocella is responsible for purchasing, safety, and traffic. The plants operate quite autonomously under the direction of a vice president in each plant. The 14 plants employ about 6,650 people, with a combined floor space of 4,536,000 square feet. Much of this floor space was constructed quite recently—527,800 in 1987, 74,000 in 1985, and 120,000 in 1984, plus the additions made through acquired companies. A listing of the plants is shown in Exhibit 13, with pertinent information as of April 25, 1987.

EXHIBIT 13
Manufacturing Plants, La-Z-Boy Chair Company

Location	Floor Space (in sq. ft.)	Operations Conducted	Built	Employees
Monroe, MI	215,200	Home office, research, and development	1941	415
Newton, MS	464,200	Recliners, rockers, and hospital seating	1961	678
Redlands, CA	179,900	Assembly of recliners and rockers	1967	289
Florence, SC	407,900	Recliners and hospital seating	1969	801
Florence, SC	48,400	Fabric processing center and parts whse.	1975	19
Neosho, MO	473,400	Residential and contract furniture	1969	992
Dayton, TN	564,200	Recliners, sofas, sleepers, and modular seating	1973	1,076
Siloam Spgs., AK	189,600	Recliners and sleepers	1943	246
Tremonton, UT	402,400	Recliners and contract	1979	617
Leland, MS	153,500	Desks and contract	1985*	130
Waterloo, OT	209,800	Recliners, rockers, sofas, and contract	1979*	412
Lincolnton, NC	379,000	Upholstered furniture	1986*	299
Grand Rapids, MI	428,000	Manufacture office furniture and panels	1986*	223
Lenoir, NC	420,800	Upholstered products, case goods, and hospitality furniture	1986*	453
Praire, MS	453,800	Distribution center and small parts whse.	1986*	6
Hudson, NC	730,000	Solid wood bedroom and dining room furniture	1987*	1,427

* Year acquired as a result of purchasing a company.

The plants at Florence, Neosho, Newton, Tremonton, Leland and the Fabric Processing Center are leased on a long-term basis. All other plants are owned by LZB.

31   LZB manufacturing is characterized by backward integration. Lumber for the furniture framing is purchased from sawmills and kiln dried at the plants. LZB makes its own chair mechanisms and purchases its sleeper mechanisms from Leggett & Platt. Metal for the recliner mechanisms is purchased in coils, and the parts made at the plants. Fabric is purchased direct from the mills in large quantities to fulfill the needs of all plants. It is received, stored, and shipped from the Fabric Processing Center in Florence, South Carolina, to all plants for use in upholstering. The center

has automated storage and is controlled by computer, so little manpower is required to operate this centralized facility.

32 LZB's manufacturing philosophy could be characterized as rather conservative. LZB usually waits until a new technique is thoroughly perfected before beginning to use it. For instance, computerized cutting of fabric at the plants was only instituted within the last two years, even though the concept had been around for over 10 years. The punch presses and methods used in the pressrooms in the plants have not been updated in the last 20 years.

33 The manufacturing process is twofold, involving both wood and metal. The wooden parts are manufactured from kiln-dried hardwood lumber. The raw boards are brought into the wood room, where they go through the rip saw operation. Here, the lumber is cut into predetermined lengths, with the knot-holes and major blemishes being removed. Only the good portions of the lumber are used. An 80 percent yield is strived for, but 65 to 70 percent is normally attained.

34 Following cutting, the wood pieces go through a series of planing, squaring, and sizing operations. Then the pieces are measured and glued together, parallel to the long side to provide wood slabs, which are again trimmed and cut into the final subassembly sections. From here, the pieces go through a series of operations, which include drilling dowel holes, contouring specific shapes on band saws, and sanding. Wood assembly is the final operation, wherein the various pieces are doweled, glued, and pressed together into frames. These wooden frames are then ready for subassembly with metal parts.

35 The metal parts are produced in the punch press room, where coils and strips of unhardened steel are run through dies to produce engineered components. The metal parts are not heat-treated, because hardness is not required, but some must be painted if they will be visible on the final product. The metal parts are then riveted together as required and go to the "metal-up" department, where they are assembled. The metal parts are then combined with the wooden parts to form a subassembly ready to be upholstered in the "frame-up" department. The marriage of metal and wood working together as one unit is what has provided LZB with its quality reputation.

36 All of the plants except—Monroe, Michigan; Florence, South Carolina; and Waterloo, Ontario— are not unionized, which is unusual in the upholstered furniture industry. Factory workers have been paid on a "piece work" concept from the beginning. Typically, one employee upholsters the seat and back of a chair and a second employee does the body, since there are too many styles for one employee to do the whole chair. A base rate is paid based on local wage surveys, but each employee has the opportunity to make quite a bit more depending on the number of pieces produced.

37 Each plant employs two to four time-study engineers to keep the piece rates up to date. Normal performance by the factory employees is 150 percent of standard. In 1973, machine controlled time was changed to 150 percent to facilitate the 150 percent normal performance. The company's policy is to never retime a job just because people are making money on the standard rate. Rather, jobs are retimed when there has been a change in methods or design. A complaint procedure is in place, so anyone can grieve a rate they believe is unfair. One rule of thumb is that the rate is good if the standard for the day can be made in five hours. Employees are reluctant to change jobs, because it temporarily cuts into their incentive performance.

38 LZB is very committed to quality, which is made somewhat trickier to accomplish by the incentive program. Constant vigilance is required by supervision. Piece rates are only paid for producing the item once—employees must rework their defective production on their own time. Each part is distinctively marked by the employee, so it can be traced back to him if a quality problem develops. There is about one inspector for every 125 chairs produced per day. A typical plant produces 1,200 to 1,300 chairs per day and some produce 300 to 400 sleeper sofas per day. A rule of thumb for planning purposes is one and three quarter chairs can be produced per man day. One employee can upholster about 10 chairs per day and another employee can frame 15 per day.

39   Products are basically produced to order, with only about 2.5 percent made for inventory. There is a 14-week window used for computer scheduling in Monroe by the manufacturing services manager. Two weeks before the product is to be in its shipping box, the fabric is shipped to the plant and subsequently cut. For actual plant scheduling, order tickets are used, which are accumulated for individual items in the same style. Fabrics are grouped by a lay (40 sheets of fabric) for cutting of a given pattern. Sometimes different fabrics can be combined, but stripes and plaids have to be cut separately. The optimum layout of pieces on a sheet of fabric is determined by the pattern layout department via computer transmission from Monroe. The material is actually cut by CNC (computer numerical control) equipment in the plant. Foremen meet informally each morning at each plant to develop a mutually beneficial daily schedule. The foremen of cutting and sewing work together to balance the load in sewing. Most dealers do not want to receive an early shipment, so the shipping schedule is the controlling element.

40   As stated before, each plant operates quite autonomously and often with a unique management style. LZB does not have a strong corporate policy regarding management, but in general it is loosely knit, and with a friendly small-town atmosphere. Edward Knabusch's philosophy was "to treat people like people." The style could be said to be somewhere between participative and authoritarian, although some of the most successful plants are more authoritarian. Exhibit 14 shows the organization chart for the Dayton, Tennessee, plant as an example of a plant's organization.

PRODUCT PLANNING AND DEVELOPMENT

41   Marvin J. Baumann, vice president for product planning and development, is responsible for product development, product engineering, and the mechanical engineering and test laboratories, all of which employ 75 people. Development has been aided by product development's use of CAD/CAM. LZB is somewhat unique in its industry, in that it extensively tests its products. Recently an independent testing lab (ETL) was added to test such products as the Lectra-Lounger and the Lectra-Lift Chair.

42   All product designs are developed internally. A natural process for design is utilized; an idea is developed, the parts are framed, an approval process is followed leading to final approval, and then the design is implemented at the plants with appropriate training. New versions of the reclining mechanism are being developed, since the patent has expired. New ideas for furniture design are often found through sales and marketing techniques like consumer demand surveys, furniture markets, and travel into Europe. In fact, the most popular current style of chair is the Eurostyle, the plush overstuffed look. Competitors have the impression that LZB over-engineers its products, but LZB believes that good engineering can only result in good quality. An annual review of LZB's products with the vendors is made. Cost, styling, and convenient transportation are considered in developing a new style. The removable-back reclining chair is an example of convenient transportation, because the back can be separated from the rest of the frame, allowing more chairs to be loaded on a truck.

43   Once a style is approved, technicians use computerized pattern layout systems to generate the cutting patterns for upholstery fabrics. The objective is to minimize waste by maximizing the number of pattern pieces attainable from a given sheet of fabric. The resulting patterns become part of an electronic library store in the company's central computer. On demand, digitized cutting instructions are down-loaded to fabric cutting machines at LZB's plants. Currently, some 700 patterns are available on-line. A subsequent step will be to up-load data from the cutting machines to analyze actual efficiencies.

EXHIBIT 14
Plant Organization Chart for Dayton, Tennessee, La-Z-Boy Chair Company

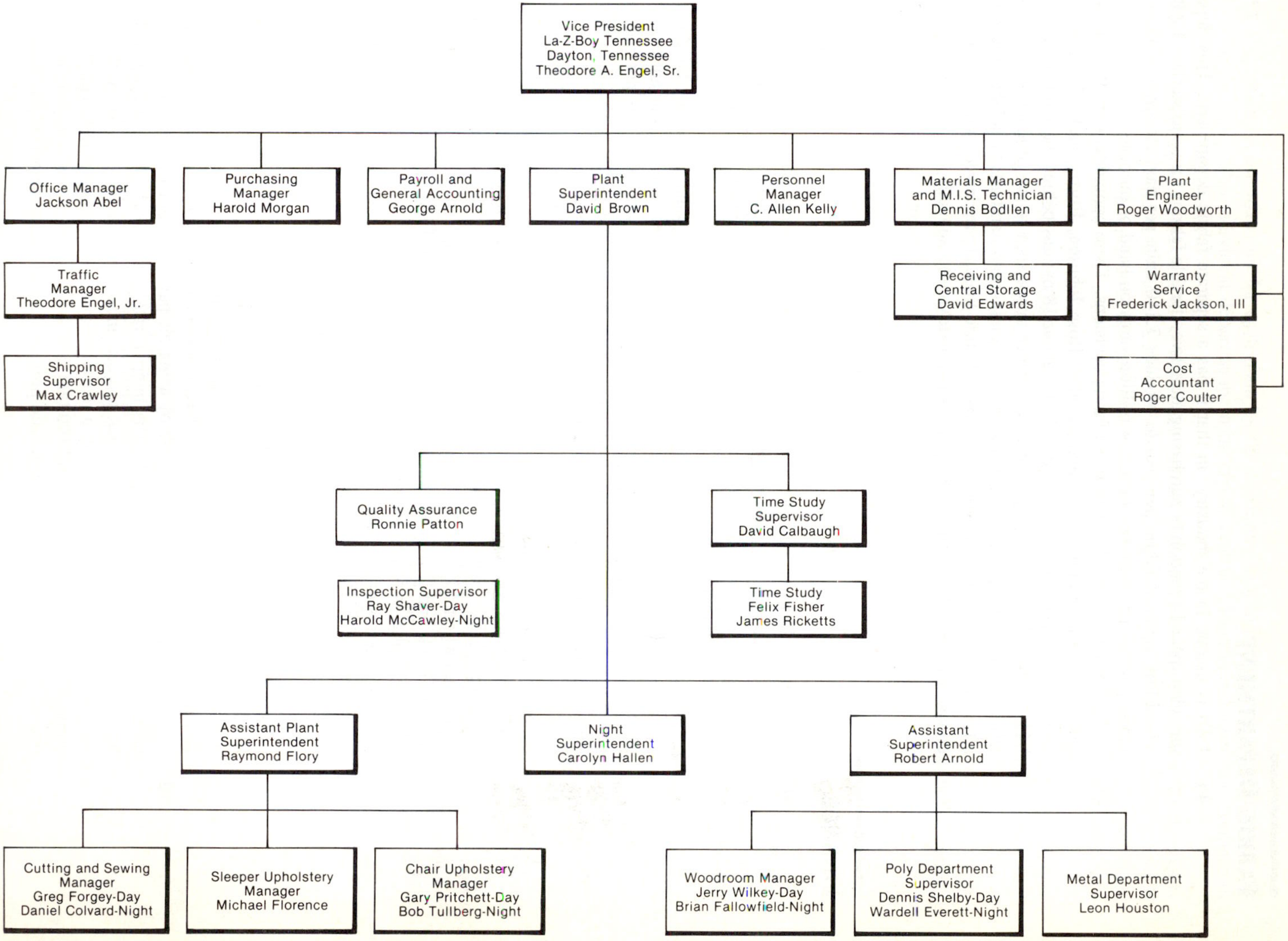

Vice President
La-Z-Boy Tennessee
Dayton, Tennessee
Theodore A. Engel, Sr.

Office Manager
Jackson Abel

Purchasing
Manager
Harold Morgan

Payroll and
General Accounting
George Arnold

Plant
Superintendent
David Brown

Personnel
Manager
C. Allen Kelly

Materials Manager
and M.I.S. Technician
Dennis Bodlien

Plant
Engineer
Roger Woodworth

Traffic
Manager
Theodore Engel, Jr.

Receiving and
Central Storage
David Edwards

Warranty
Service
Frederick Jackson, III

Shipping
Supervisor
Max Crawley

Cost
Accountant
Roger Coulter

Quality Assurance
Ronnie Patton

Time Study
Supervisor
David Calbaugh

Inspection Supervisor
Ray Shaver-Day
Harold McCawley-Night

Time Study
Felix Fisher
James Ricketts

Night
Superintendent
Carolyn Hallen

Assistant
Superintendent
Robert Arnold

Assistant Plant
Superintendent
Raymond Flory

Woodroom Manager
Jerry Wilkey-Day
Brian Fallowfield-Night

Poly Department
Supervisor
Dennis Shelby-Day
Wardell Everett-Night

Metal Department
Supervisor
Leon Houston

Cutting and Sewing
Manager
Greg Forgey-Day
Daniel Colvard-Night

Sleeper Upholstery
Manager
Michael Florence

Chair Upholstery
Manager
Gary Pritchett-Day
Bob Tullberg-Night

669

the company are posted and employees may apply for the position. Most of management has been with the LZB for an extended time, having been promoted from within.

59   Supervisory, technical, and clerical employees are paid by rating jobs, using a point factor method. Jobs are matched against common factors, such as education, related experience, mental skill, human relations responsibility, complexity and impact of work decisions, and necessity for accuracy. Employees are evaluated regularly on achievement of their department's mission statement and how the goals were achieved. To foster continued individual growth, required training is used to equip people to rotate into new positions.

60   LZB is committed to the concept of incentive pay. Factory workers are paid on a piece rate concept. Office workers are included in profit sharing and receive merit pay based on performance. Executives and middle managers receive bonuses for quality work. All employees have a comprehensive benefit plan, including paid vacations, health and dental insurance, prescription plan, including paid vacations, health and dental insurance, prescription medicine program, term life insurance, and a defined benefit retirement plan.

THE FUTURE

61   *Forbes* magazine in its February 22, 1988, issue ran an article entitled "Takeover Bait?" in which it listed LZB as 1 of 22 likely prospects for a takeover. It fits the picture of high cash reserves, low debt, a low price/earnings ratio, and a strong cash flow from operating income. Is LZB worried? Gene Hardy says such defense measures as staggered three-year terms for directors and 67 percent stockholder vote required for approval of any merger are already in place. Perhaps most important is the distribution of stock among family and friends, although a leveraged buyout could occur under the right circumstances. The price range for LZB stock for recent years is shown in Table 3.

62   As might be expected, Charles Knabusch does not wish LZB to be acquired. He said, "We are happy doing our thing, our way." His goals for the company are to continue growing while remaining profitable. But how is this to be accomplished in an industry that is becoming increasingly concentrated and with a stable but aging population?

TABLE 3

Fiscal Year	Price Range
1983	$2^5/_8$– $7^7/_8$
1984	$7^7/_8$–$12^1/_8$
1985	$6^3/_4$–$10^5/_8$
1986	$10^7/_8$–$16^7/_8$
1987	$15^5/_8$–$20^1/_8$
1988	$13^1/_8$–$22^5/_8$

CASE 16

POLAROID CORPORATION/INNER CITY, INC.

1   Bill Skelley, manager of Polaroid Corporation's Inner City subsidiary, gazed intently across his circular conference table, emphasizing his concerns with the company's future:

2   We are a forty million dollar company, just as responsible for its operations as any other profit-center firm. We assemble parts for Polaroid's cameras . . . we package film . . . we do silk screen printing. At the same time, we help people who have never before succeeded at work to develop the skills they need, to hold a job anywhere. When we finish training somebody to be productive, we place them into a mainstream job with some other employer, to make room for a new trainee here.

3   We're held responsible for the bottom line. Since 1978, we've returned more than our budgeted contribution to Polaroid headquarters. [Table 1 shows Inner City's financial statements for 1985 and 1986.]

4   Now, though, the whole economy is changing, with serious implications for us. Our history and skills lie in the manufacturing area, but all the economic growth is in the service sector: that's where the entry-level jobs are. To give our graduates a chance, we have to change the work we train them to do. We have to decide what work Inner City should take on—what new business we should go into.

5   And the low unemployment rate here in Massachusetts makes it hard to attract new trainees. Our waiting list for employment used to have a thousand to fifteen hundred names; now there is virtually no waiting list at all. A skeptic might say our whole reason for existing is obsolete.

POLAROID CORPORATION

6   Polaroid Corporation was founded in 1937 by Edwin H. Land, who continued to lead the firm until his retirement in 1980. Through those years the company was based entirely on the products of Dr. Land's inventive genius—polarized filters and instant photography. Polaroid experienced rapid growth in sales, employment, and profitability until 1978, when sales grew 30 percent over the previous year, reaching $1.4 billion with a return on equity of 13.8 percent. In 1979, however, several factors—including Kodak's penetration of the instant photography market, the failure of Polaroid's instant motion picture system, and an oil-starved economic recession—put an end to the growth. (Table 2 shows 10 years' operating results for Polaroid.)

7   From its inception, Polaroid Corporation reflected the values of its founder. The company was an innovator in participative management systems and responsiveness to community needs. In the late 1960s, autonomous worker teams were introduced in Polaroid's film manufacturing plant. When public criticism in 1970 focussed on the use of instant photography in South Africa's "Apartheid" identification pass program, Polaroid sent an employee team to investigate; supporting

This case was prepared by John A. Seeger, associate professor of management at Bentley College, and Marie Rock, senior policy analyst at Data General Corporation, as a basis for class discussion. Distributed by North American Case Research Association. All rights reserved. Permission to re-publish should be obtained from NACRA and from the authors. Copyright © 1987 by John A. Seeger.

TABLE 1

INNER CITY, INC.
Statement of Operations
For the Year Ending December 31
(dollars in thousands)

	1985		1986	
	Budget	**Actual**	**Budget**	**Actual**
Sales	$44,576	$38,457	$30,407	$35,401
Cost of sales:				
Direct material	42,078	35,857	27,666	32,595
Direct labor	490	610	536	621
Total	42,568	36,467	28,202	33,216
Other direct costs	0	0	113	154
Gross margin	2,008	1,990	2,092	2,031
Other income	0	16	0	2
Subtotal	2,008	2,006	2,092	2,033
Operating costs:				
Indirect trainee labor	646	655	860	693
Staff labor	798	793	840	746
Overhead	564	499	392	496
Total	2,008	1,947	2,092	1,935
Surplus (Deficit) from operations	0	59	0	98*

* Redistributed to parent corporation.

INNER CITY, INC
Statement of Financial Condition
As of December 31
(dollars in thousands)

	1985	1986		1985	1986
			Liabilities and Owners' Equity		
Assets					
Cash	$ 6	$ 44	Accounts payable	$ 7	$ 30
Accounts receivable:			Accrued expenses	16	42
Polaroid	558	480			
Trade—net	64	36	Total current liabilities	23	72
Other	3	5			
Inventories	544	904	Advance from parent	2,778	3,019
Prepaid expenses	4	1	Total liabilities	2,801	3,091
Total current assets	1,179	1,470			
Plant and equipment—net	99	98	Capital stock	1	1
			Paid-in surplus	24	24
Total assets	$1,278	$1,568	Retained earnings (deficit)	(1,548)	(1,548)
			Total liabilities and owners' equity	$1,278	$1,568

TABLE 2
Polaroid Corporation and Subsidiary Companies—Ten-Year Financial Summary
(Unaudited. Years ended December 31. Dollars in millions, except per share data.)

	1986	1985	1984	1983	1982	1981	1980	1979	1978	1977
Consolidated Statement of Earnings										
Net sales:										
United States	$ 964.3	$ 799.3	$ 743.5	$ 730.1	$ 752.5	$ 817.8	$ 791.8	$ 757.2	$ 817.4	$ 645.8
International	664.9	515.9	528.0	524.4	541.4	601.8	659.0	604.3	559.2	416.1
Total net sales	1,629.2	1,295.2	1,271.5	1,254.5	1,293.9	1,419.6	1,450.8	1,361.5	1,376.6	1,061.9
Cost of goods sold	921.7	756.0	735.2	698.3	769.6	855.4	831.1	876.8	778.3	575.7
Marketing, research, engineering, and administrative expense	571.8	505.6	492.6	462.1	472.6	520.8	483.9	449.4	418.2	337.3
Total costs	1,493.5	1,261.6	1,227.8	1,160.4	1,242.2	1,376.2	1,315.0	1,326.2	1,196.5	913.0
Profit and operations	135.7	33.6	43.7	94.1	51.7	43.4	135.8	35.3	180.1	148.9
Other income	18.1	28.9	39.5	32.5	45.5	49.2	25.4	13.3	20.3	19.0
Interest expense	18.6	22.3	20.9	26.5	35.5	29.9	17.0	12.8	5.9	6.4
Earnings before income taxes	135.2	40.2	62.3	100.1	61.7	62.7	144.2	35.8	194.5	161.5
Federal, state, foreign income taxes	31.7	3.3	36.6	50.4	38.2	31.6	58.8	(3)	76.1	69.2
Net Earnings	$ 103.5	$ 36.9	$ 25.7	$ 49.7	$ 38.2	$ 31.1	$ 85.4	$ 36.1	$ 118.4	$ 92.3
Earnings per share	$ 3.34	$ 1.19	$ 0.83	$ 1.61	$ 0.73	$ 0.95	$ 2.60	$ 1.10	$ 3.60	$ 2.81
Cash dividends per share	$ 1.00	$ 1.00	$ 1.00	$ 1.00	$ 1.00	$ 1.00	$ 1.00	$ 1.00	$ 0.90	$ 0.65
Selected Balance Sheet Information										
Working capital	$ 637.0	$ 697.8	$ 734.2	$ 769.0	$ 745.4	$ 749.5	$ 721.9	$ 525.9	$ 609.5	$ 589.6
Net property, plant, equipment	357.7	349.0	306.6	277.0	281.8	332.9	362.2	371.6	294.8	225.9
Total assets	1,479.2	1,384.7	1,346.0	1,319.1	1,323.6	1,434.7	1,404.0	1,253.7	1,276.0	1,076.7
Long-term debt	—	124.6	124.5	124.4	124.3	124.2	124.1	—	—	—
Stockholders' equity	994.7	922.2	916.3	921.6	902.9	958.2	960.0	907.5	904.3	815.5
Other Statistical Data										
Additions to property, plant, equip.	$ 82.9	$ 104.5	$ 82.7	$ 51.8	$ 31.5	$ 42.5	$ 68.1	$ 134.6	$ 115.0	$ 68.7
Number of employees	14,765	12,932	13,402	13,871	14,540	16,784	17,454	18,416	20,884	16,394
Return on stockholders' equity	10.8%	4.0%	2.0%	5.4%	2.5%	3.2%	9.1%	4.0%	13.8%	11.8%

that group's analysis, the company refused to supply film to the government there. In 1978, Polaroid discontinued *all* sales in South Africa.

8   Richard Lawson, director of corporate materials management and services for Polaroid and president of Inner City, Inc., commented:

9   Dr. Land believed in helping people to grow and attain their limits. He created the Polaroid philosophy, recognizing that it takes people to produce a quality product and that everyone, even the sweeper, had good ideas. Here, the sweeper has a chance to become a lab technician.

10   Our first goal is to build a company that makes a quality product we can all feel proud of. Hand in hand with this is a belief that we have to be good community members.

INNER CITY, INC.

11   Inner City, Inc., was a subcontract manufacturing firm, processing materials or assembling parts for Polaroid or other companies. Bill Skelley described his operation, as it might appear to a potential customer:

12   We tell prospective customers, "We'd like to work for you. Send us your raw materials inventory. We'll process it and send it back to you. We're located on Columbus Avenue in Roxbury, and our work force is 95 percent minority." To tell the whole story, we might add, "Most of our people are unskilled. They've been with us, on average, only a couple of months. Most have no previous work history, or they've had problems at earlier jobs. Some have served time."

13   We hire from the bottom of the labor force; our incoming trainees don't attach any importance to timeclocks or absenteeism or discipline or dress. Most just don't know what real work is, or how an employer expects them to behave.

14   When you ask prospective customers to send their work into that environment, all sorts of perceptions start running through their minds. But when they come to visit, they find our trainees obviously working hard, and they're surprised. They say, "Wow, you guys have a very efficient, neat, well-organized and clean operation! How do you do it?" We say, "That's what we expect. You can't run a place like this unless that's the order of business."

The Environment

15   Inner City occupied the top four floors of a freshly painted six-story brick and concrete building in Roxbury, a poor, predominantly black neighborhood of Boston. The building was flanked on two sides by vacant lots awaiting urban redevelopment; behind it were 19th century brick row houses, deteriorated by time and characteristic of much of historical Boston. Many houses were boarded up and abandoned, symbolizing the area's chronic unemployment—three times higher than that of surrounding neighborhoods. Across the street, bustling, dusty construction work continued on a new rapid transit line, spearhead of a major redevelopment program. According to plans for urban development, the area surrounding Inner City would eventually boast of cobblestone streets, brick walkways, and new housing.

16   When Inner City was incorporated in 1968 as a subsidiary of Polaroid Corporation, the city of Boston, along with the rest of the nation, was experiencing great social unrest. Only four years earlier, the first federal civil rights laws had been enacted. Equal employment opportunity had not yet been legislated; discrimination was commonplace in employment, housing, voting, education, transportation, and in the daily lives of many Americans. Organizations which had represented the black community since 1910 were joined by college students to protest social injustices. Often,

demonstrations intended to be nonviolent broke into rioting and destruction—sometimes initiated by law enforcement personnel, sometimes by extremists among the protesters. Press and television coverage brought the violent encounters into public consciousness.

17   Reacting to spreading social unrest and violence, President Lyndon Johnson launched a number of projects, including the War on Poverty in 1964, designed to derail the accelerating problems of the nation's youth and unemployed. Antipoverty programs, including training programs conducted by public agencies and private corporations, sprang up around the country. Still, social upheaval continued. In the mid to late 60s, several civil rights leaders and activists were assassinated, sparking even more social dissension across the country. Protesters against racism, against the Vietnam war, and against "the Establishment" marched through city streets and across college campuses, including those in Boston.

18   Riots erupted in major U.S. cities. Large areas of Rochester burned, as did Washington's black neighborhood. In Los Angeles, the vast area called Watts burned for days as snipers prevented fire fighters from entering, and looters vandalized those stores still standing; 35 died in the riot, as 833 others were injured and 3,600 more were arrested. In May of 1970, National Guard troops opened fire on students at Kent State University, killing 4 and wounding 10. Across the country, colleges closed until the following September, in sympathy with the slain students and to prevent further violence on their own campuses. Nervous civic leaders in Boston eyed the Roxbury ghetto, anticipating the worst.

The Founding of Inner City, Inc.

19   Governments, businesses, and civic minded groups of minorities and whites attempted to cope at the local level with the nationwide illnesses of racism and unemployment. At the Polaroid Corporation, black employees and the management executive committee focussed on the issues. Richard Lawson, a member of the original planning team, recalled its formation:

20   We had formed a "Volunteer Committee," where we shared ideas related to company business. At first we met on our own time. Then Polaroid let us meet on company time, and allowed us to do more and more. As the Volunteer Committee grew in size, its running became a full-time job held by elected officials who represented to management Polaroid's black employee viewpoint.

21   At this same time a movement was taking place in Washington which called for private enterprise to respond to the problem of hard-core unemployment in the nation's inner cities. We came up with the idea of establishing a small manufacturing plant in Boston's inner city, that would be a stepping stone for people coming to work at Polaroid or elsewhere.

22   I worked at Inner City during its first year, and then went back to Polaroid. From there I went to the Harvard Business School. About a year after I returned to Polaroid, Inner City was in financial turmoil. Community leaders felt the troubles resulted from mismanagement, and because I was a recent Harvard graduate, I was made manager of Inner City in 1973. Nowadays, assignments to Inner City are voluntary. Mine in '73, was not.

23   Inner City was losing $700,000 to $800,000 a year with no apparent end in sight, and turning out only about 50 graduates a year. It was costing us $9,000 to train a single graduate, far more than it would cost to send them to college. Inner City's operating systems duplicated all the overhead of the parent corporation; by simplifying things, I got the average cost down to $3,000 per graduate.

24   For the life of me, I couldn't run a business to see it lose money. And I didn't think it was right for a successful business to carry a losing business. Now we run Inner City like any business in the United States. It makes money. If it doesn't, it had better answer why. Inner City now has to answer questions like, "What did you do?" and "What do you plan to do?" [Exhibit 1 summarizes operating results for 10 years, ending in 1986.]

57 We take a couple of approaches to you as a trainee: we make you feel good about yourself initially; we tell you we expect an awful lot out of you; and we're not going to accept anything less. We say, "That's what you've got to do to be successful; now we'll help you with it. Are you willing to pay the price? That's the key question; if you are, you will be successful. If you're not, you'll probably wind up being terminated."

58 Trainee Gene Lang straddled a chair and chomped on a candy bar, hungry after working a full shift at Inner City, Inc.

59 Before I came to Inner City, I only got jobs for one thing: quick cold cash, then I'd split. But this place really turned my head around. This is a place that wants you to work, to be on time, and to learn. They said to me, "You'll learn about holding on to a job by being here on time, by following the rules, and by taking pride in yourself and your work." Well, that sounded like so much crap to me. But you get here, man, and you see the other trainees. They been here a few weeks and so you see that they really work together. And that's the key, it's family. I mean, you might have some family scraps once in a while, but everyone starts to care about each other.

60 We all start to believe in each other, that we can make it through the program and graduate so that we can work in a permanent job someplace else. There *are* exceptions, the ones who don't want to be family; they usually goof off and get canned.

61 And it's tough here. They want you to know that you can make it through the program, but it's up to you to show you supervisor that you're serious about it, 'cause they sure as hell are.

Placement

62 Inner City placed approximately 100 trainees per year in a variety of manufacturing and service settings. Since 1968, over 1,600 program graduates had been placed in 53 Boston-area companies, ranging from high technology to education to service. For the first 10 years, the firm's trainees were placed with the parent company when their skills were sufficiently developed. In the business downturn of 1978, Polaroid's hiring policy changed; after that time, all graduates were placed with other Boston-area employers.

63 An important pre-placement activity was the "mock interview," with Inner City staff members playing the role of the potential employer. Millie Muther described the trainee's view of this experience:

64 One of my people had his first mock interview just today; that's his suit hanging there in the corner. He worked until 1:00, then changed into his suit and tie in the men's room. He says, "Are you sure I look all right?" Well, his collar was folded up, so he let me fix it. He says, "Can you see me shaking? Do you know how nervous I am? Is he going to say hello first or do I say it first to him?" He just got caught up, and so nervous. They're very proud to be all dressed up and going for their first interview. Even if it's only a mock interview, it's very important to them. He went downstairs and did a super job.

65 Brian Stebbins, a college senior in a management internship program, served as an assistant supervisor to Millie Muther and described the progress of a former trainee who had experienced a successful placement:

66 You hear from former trainees every once in a while. I'm thinking of one who came back here to visit; he had had a really tough life before he came here and he had a tough beginning here, too. He was finally placed after a while. When he came back, he showed us his new bank book to show us his savings, and he wanted us to look out the window to see the car he just bought. But I remember that he had some very tough problems while he was here. We just kept telling him: "Willie, if you just keep working and do well here, you'll get a good job and you'll see a big turnaround." He came into our office one day and just broke down and started crying. He's over 40, but he broke down trying to tell us that he was a man and

TABLE 3
Individuals Hired and Placed

	1982	1983	1984	1985	1986
Number hired	248	426	479	511	460
Number placed	62	94	130	106	102

TABLE 4
Retention Rates: 1984 Study Group

Year Placed	Survey Total	Employees Still on the Job at			
		3 Mo.	6 Mo.	12 Mo.	18 Mo.
1982	57	50 (88%)	44 (77%)	42 (74%)	38 (67%)
1983	85	75 (90%)	68 (82%)	43 (52%)	17 (21%]
1984	41*	33 (80%)	28 (68%)	*	*

* Small sample: first quarter placements only; this group not on job long enough to measure beyond six months.

he wanted a job. That was heart-breaking. We kept encouraging him. We said there would be a change, but I don't think that he believed us completely until he went out and got the job.

67 Bill Skelley pointed out another placement potential for some trainees—promotion to Inner City staff positions:

68 One trainee was just made a supervisor. We found after she came here, she had graduated from college in North Carolina; she's done very well. Another former trainee handles our whole payroll system; she's taking college courses at Northeastern now. Another former trainee is doing a fine job as a crew chief on the production floor. It really helps to see someone who works beside you go up the ladder. These people are excellent role models.

Retention

69 Typically, about one quarter of the trainees entering Inner City's program graduated to "regular" full-time employment. Some 30 percent—referred to as "negative results" by the staff—were either fired or quit in the face of termination. Another large group left after a few months' training to take other, higher-paying jobs. Nongraduates, Bill Skelley pointed out, benefited from their training while employed in the program, even though they chose not to finish it. By year, the numbers of people hired and placed are shown in Table 3.

70 Retention rates for Inner City graduates in their first jobs were tracked from 1982 to 1984 and indicated a substantial success during the graduates' first several months at work. Table 4 shows that, of the total of 183 graduates covered by surveys, 158, or 85 percent stayed with their original employers for at least 90 days after placement. By the six-month point, retention had dropped only slightly to 140, or 77 percent. By year of placement, retention rates were measured as shown in Table 4.

TRAINING POLICIES

71   Inner City emphasized its commitment to preparing people for long-term employment by implementing policies that might be considered stringent in many businesses.

Suspensions

72   Unruly and disruptive behavior or refusal to work was controlled through the use of suspensions. Millie Muther described handling a trainee's refusal to cooperate—a situation which might warrant a suspension:

73   You say to yourself, "Why is that person doing that today? He is usually pretty good and has never refused to do a job." So you talk to that person and you get to the core of the problem and you solve it. It's usually a misunderstanding with someone else or a problem at home. But, if something like that continues, or is done more than once, we usually suspend them for three days because you can't refuse to do a job. You may not like to do it, but you can't refuse.

74   An example might be a trainee—Eddie—who has just been placed. He started our really well—had no problems at all. Then all at once he changed. He came in one day with a certain attitude; it just wasn't him. He still came in on time, but he wouldn't communicate. You can't place people with an attitude like that. We talked about his behavior to get at the source of his problem.

75   We had put up bars on all the six floor windows—kids were breaking in from the roof to steal film. The first day of the bars was when we saw the change in Eddie. It hadn't occurred to me that the bars would affect anyone. But Eddie had spent time in jail, and the bars had a special meaning for him. Knowing the problem helped me work with him. It made me feel pretty good when he finally did get a job—and it's a job he wants.

76   There are different ways to deal with problems. I've had people refuse to do a job; and when I've talked to them, it's because they've had this back problem, or they've had this operation, and they can't help it. If they don't speak up or communicate in the correct manner, they could wind up getting terminated. So it's another lesson for them.

Terminations

77   Continued disruptive behavior is usually a way of testing the supervisor and can lead to termination early in the program. Millie Muther described some of the tactics used by trainees, and their results:

78   They're brand new, so normally they're going to put me through the test first. If there is a change in supervision, then they're going to put the new supervisor through the test to see if they can get away with more.

79   They test you by coming back from lunch or breaks late They're supposed to punch in for morning, at lunch, and when they leave for the day, but not for breaks. So if they are late from break, the first time I usually ignore it, but after that I'll talk to them. And I'll say, "I saw you the other day when you were late. I didn't say anything because I was hoping it was just a mistake on your part."

80   I try to put the ownership back on them, and to make sure they realize that I'm not out to get them, that I want to help them. After that, they'll go on warning and then they could be terminated if their behavior doesn't improve. You stress to them that, no matter where they work, they have to come back on time, not one or two minutes late, or they're not going to keep their job. They learn eventually.

81   We terminated a man on the spot, a couple of weeks ago. He put four packs of film underneath his hat. A lot of people saw that, so you can't let him get away with it. At first, we were going to wait—to catch him red-handed leaving the floor. But we've tried that before; you get interrupted for a few seconds, and the thief is gone. So we talked it over and said he's got it under his hat, and it shouldn't be there, so let's get rid of him now. A legal department in some big company would say the film doesn't cost you much;

a lawsuit would cost a lot. But this is a training program. It's different. And even this guy has a right to appeal.

82   Trainees know up front that I'm not here to fire them. I don't fire people; I never have. I've signed the termination papers, but they've done the firing to themselves. They'll say, "I don't know why you fired me, I don't know what I did." And so you show them the record, and point out that they didn't learn by going on warning or by being talked to. There are only so many breaks I can give them.

83   There was no specific rule at Inner City regarding the number of warnings prior to termination from the program. Rules were well defined, however, regarding processes for reinstatement of trainees.

Appeals Board

84   Not all terminations were permanent; Inner City gave its trainees a second chance. The terminated trainee received an appeals letter with his or her final check. The letter stated an appeal date, typically two weeks from the termination date, and a meeting time of 3:30 P.M. According to Millie Muther, punctuality was considered to be an important indicator of a trainee's willingness to continue with the program.

85   They have to be prompt and be here by 3:30. If they're a minute late, we don't see them because it proves that they really don't want their job. Ninety-nine percent of them are here before 3:30. Right now, I have 28 people on my floor; 6 of them have gone through the appeal process. When they come back, many of them seem to be okay for a while. Then all of a sudden some of them slip back again, and they end up being terminated. In the second termination, there is no appeal.

MEETING A CHANGING ENVIRONMENT

86   Long-term corporate commitment by Polaroid was essential to Inner City's ability to meet the challenges of an ever-changing environment.

Corporate Commitment

87   The commitment of Polaroid to Inner City's survival had been evident since its inception. Bill Skelley addressed this issue:

88   When the parent company experiences difficult times—which we have gone through—it is forced to look at all facets of the company. Look at Inner City. Is it a cost or a drain on the company? If we lost a million dollars, there would be a lot of people sitting in Polaroid headquarters questioning the validity of this program. That could happen very quickly. Unemployment is 3.7 percent in this state; the lowest since sliced bread came on the board. Jobs are going begging; you have to bus people in from Timbuktu.

89   It would be easy to ask, "Why do you need Inner City any more?" The people who make those decisions must have an in-depth understanding of what is happening in the real world. Polaroid went through a 30 percent reduction in personnel, beginning in 1978 or 79. Today the company is down to about 9,000 employees, domestically—some 14,000 worldwide. It really tested the corporate commitment to have products built by temporary people at Inner City, while full-time Polaroid employees were losing their jobs.

90   Now the corporation is staying lean. Like most big companies, it hires *only* temporary people for entry-level manufacturing work. Last year they hired over 2,000 temps, and many of them came right out of Inner City's ranks. Say you were working here at $3.50 an hour, and you got a note saying, "Come to work at Polaroid and you can make $7.00 an hour." You'd say, "When do I report?" We told our people

those were only temporary jobs; they'd be let go in three to six months, and they couldn't come back here if they left. Some held on there longer than we'd expected; others were back on the streets in three weeks. But such is life.

Current Problems and Alternatives

91 Bill Skelley summarized some of the current problems and alternatives for Inner City:

92 For the first time in our history, the people we hire have options in their lives. Virtually *anyone* can get a job. Historically, our people had only us as a viable option.

93 How do we motivate people to go through training when they can go out and get a job on their own, even though it's a dead-ended job? That's what we're struggling with—trying to convince younger people today to do some long-range planning. Long-range career planning for many of them is based on next Saturday night's party. Planning for six to nine months, never mind the next couple of years, is difficult.

94 Do we have to pay them more? Then, how do we price our products competitively? And if we pay more, we create another problem: people won't want to leave here. This is an environment geared to making them feel good about themselves, and we're also convenient to their homes. So, if we raise their pay by "X" cents per hour, whatever that may be, we reduce their incentive for leaving.

95 Also, for the first time in our history, the majority of our 1986 placements were in the service sector. Now "service sector" means a lot of things. For us, it *doesn't* mean flipping hamburgers—because we won't do that. But it *could* mean working in a bank as a teller. It could mean working in a hotel as a telephone operator or a receptionist or a bell captain or a housekeeper.

96 The skill levels needed for service sector jobs are higher than for entry-level manufacturing jobs. Which means that our people have to be better prepared. To go and sit on the production line at an electronics firm as an entry-level manufacturing person is pretty basic—it's just putting the piece parts together. To go and do a comparable job in a hotel requires a lot more from you. For instance, one of our women in a housekeeping function at a major hotel has to interface with a computer five or six times a day. She's got to go to the computer and punch numbers in to find out where her next assignment is, how many towels and bars of soap she needs. And this is in an entry-level job. We have to do a better job of preparing our people.

97 We're finding a population more in need at the same time that the jobs are more demanding. There's a widening gap. The schools are at an all-time low on preparing people for the world of work. There's a 47 percent noncompletion rate in the city's schools, and even those that *do* complete aren't prepared to get a job on their own.

98 We're trying now to tailor our training program to the service sector. I think 56 percent of our graduates last year went into service sector jobs; two years ago it was 14 percent. The advantage of service sector jobs is that they are mostly in Boston; we don't run into the transportation problem we normally have. See, our people don't drive; 99 percent of them don't own a car. And if you get jobs out on Route 128 or in some distant suburb, you are limited by a transportation problem.

99 We're trying to expand our silk screening business with a new machine that more than quadruples our capacity. It teaches a specific skill. Hopefully we can place somebody in that type of business.

100 We have to look at other service-related alternatives. For example, the fulfillment business is a multibillion dollar industry. Let's say that you buy five six-packs of a soft drink and send the labels in and you get a free digital watch. Who sends you the watch? Companies don't do it themselves. We tried to do it once, but we got out of it because we weren't doing it right. Now we're looking at doing it again.

101 We're also looking at data entry. What if we set up a data entry business here? That sounds good but changes the way we approach things: it would require a higher-skilled person. It means that we would have to keep people longer. Rather than turning people over in six months it means that they're going to be here for two or three years. And if that happens, then you've got to pay them a competitive market wage. You've got to add a benefits package and you can't serve as many people. Our costs skyrocket. How do you offset those costs?

102   Another idea is an "externship" kind of program, where we place our temporary employees in a Polaroid production operation and we supervise them there. Hopefully it will be a good training tool for us. We're doing it now on a limited basis. We provide the supervisors, so we've got to make money at it.

103   We're still doing camera assembly, but some of it may be automated through robotics over the next few years, so I'm looking at products we can bring in for 1989. What happens if some of that gets automated? Then we switch to the service sector.

     We've gone through our period of rapid growth. We're plateauing now, and looking at a redirection; new growth will come out of that. Redirection could mean that we'll be out this building in a few years; I believe we'll have a new place to reside. There's going to be a *change* in direction. The world is changing around us. If we don't change with it, we limit what we can do.

CASE 17

MERCK: STRATEGY MAKING IN "AMERICA'S MOST ADMIRED CORPORATION"

1   Merck and Company is, perhaps, America's best kept corporate secret. Selected by Fortune 1,000 executives—for four consecutive years—as "America's Most Admired Corporation," Merck is hardly a household name. But, Merck knows how to compete effectively and how to do the right things right. Merck is driven by an ambition to be on the cutting edge of research and development in its industry and by an obsession with building quality into its products. This dual goal pervades every aspect of the firm's culture, managerial decision making, and organizational structure. Guided by an innovative (or, more appropriately, a visionary) chief executive officer (CEO), Merck is determined to remain the U.S. leading pharmaceutical company.

2   What does it take to build "America's Most Admired Corporation?" This case provides some clues to the secret of one of the most successful companies in modern American history. This case shows how carefully crafted strategies orchestrated by a visionary and dedicated leader can payoff well. But, to understand Merck's secrets, let us first examine how the company came into existence.

History

3   Merck's roots can be traced as far back as 1668, when the Merck family bought an apothecary in Darmstadt, Germany. More than 150 years later the Merck family decided to complement the apothecary by manufacturing its own drugs. In 1827, this decision became a reality when a manufacturing operation was opened also in Darmstadt, Germany. The Merck family brought its drug manufacturing expertise to the United States in 1887, when it opened a branch in New York. Shortly thereafter, in 1891, the Merck & Company partnership was formed in New York. Merck started manufacturing drugs and specialty chemicals in Rahway, New Jersey, in 1903. In 1908, Merck & Company incorporated in New York and later, in 1919, it sold stock to the public for the first time. By 1941, Merck & Company had established manufacturing facilities throughout the United States.

4   As Merck & Company was growing throughout the United States, another competitor, Sharp & Dohme, was following close behind. In 1845, Sharp opened an apothecary in Baltimore and later in 1860 formed a partnership with Dohme. While Merck was building expertise in manufacturing, Sharp and Dohme concentrated heavily on research. Today's Merck & Company was formed in 1953, when Merck merged with Sharp & Dohme. Other acquisitions and divestments would follow, but this merger represents what Merck stands for today, excellence in research and manufacturing of pharmaceuticals and specialty chemicals. Indeed, Merck defines its business as "a worldwide, research-intensive health products company that discovers, develops, produces, and markets human and animal health products and specialty chemicals" (annual report, 1988).

This case was prepared by Shaker A. Zahra, Bob Lewis, and Rich Hubbard of George Mason University.

INDUSTRY SEGMENTS AND PRODUCTS

5   Merck competes primarily in two industry segments: human and animal health products, and specialty chemicals. The contribution to sales for 1988 for each of these segments is presented in Exhibit 1.

Specialty Chemicals

6   The specialty chemicals group offers a wide variety of products that include: xantham gum, a biogum with various uses, including growing oil field applications; *Epi-Lock* and *Synthaderm,* polyurethane wound dressings; and several water treatment related products, including *pHree-GUARD, BoilerGUARD,* and *POL-E-Z.* In addition, the group provides special software applications to maximize the efficiency of water treatment facilities.

7   Specialty chemicals products are used in a wide variety of applications. The most common uses water treatment, food processing, and skin care. Merck entered the specialty chemicals market in 1968, when it acquired Calgon Corporation. Calgon's main business was the manufacturing of water treatment products and providing related services. In 1972, Merck strengthened its position in specialty chemicals by acquiring the Kelco company. Kelco mainly produced alginates and xanthum gum. Today, Merck's specialty chemical products comes from the Kelco Division, Calgon Vestal Labs, and Calgon Water Management Division.

8   Sales of products and services from the specialty chemicals group are made in channels of trade including industrial users, distributors, wholesalers, municipalities, and utilities. The group has been making steady gains in its segment. Exhibit 2 reflects sales of the group over the last couple of years.

Human and Animal Health Products

9   Most of Merck's income comes from the human and animal health products segment. Within this segment Merck's products can be grouped into eight primary categories, as illustrated in Exhibit 3, which lists their contributions to company sales in 1988.

10   The human products that Merck offers include therapeutic and preventive preparations, generally sold by prescription. Merck sells prescription drugs through its professional representatives (called

---

EXHIBIT 1
Merck Sales by Segment

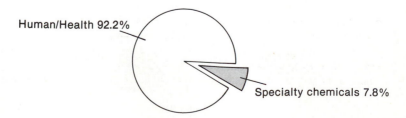

Human/Health 92.2%

Specialty chemicals 7.8%

Source: annual report, 1988.

EXHIBIT 2
Sales Trend in Specialty Chemicals Segment

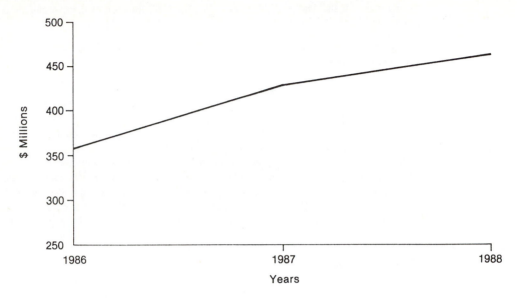

Source: annual report, 1988.

EXHIBIT 3
Product Contribution to Human and Animal Segment Sales

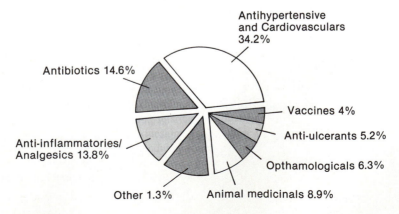

Source: annual report, 1988.

"detailmen") to drug wholesalers and retailers, physicians, veterinarians, hospitals, clinics, government agencies, and other institutions. Merck prides itself on the knowledge and competence of its detailmen. A new sales recruit can expect to be in training for two years, which includes technical training and is equivalent to that given at many medical schools.

11   The cardiovascular medications, particularly *Vasotec,* are the flagship products of the Merck line. *Vasotec,* originally developed as a blood pressure reducer, was approved in 1988 for treatment of congestive heart failure patients. Sales in 1988 for *Vasotec* alone were nearly $1 billion. *Mevacor* and *Zocor* (as yet to receive FDA approval) are two cardiovascular products with billion dollar futures, also. Both are medications used to reduce cholesterol levels, and analysts expect these two drugs to be contributing in excess of a billion dollars a year by 1990.[1]

12   *Pepcid,* a once a day treatment for peptic ulcers, has made great inroads on the once sacred grounds of Smithkline's *Tagamet. Pepcid* now contributes well over $100 million in annual sales, and is being prescribed more and more over *Tagamet* and Glaxo's *Zantac.*[2]

13   Antibiotic medications are another area where Merck's conviction to research is paying off. The product *Primaxin* currently has the broadest spectrum of antimicrobial activity of any antibiotic yet marketed.

14   Overall, Merck has 15 drugs currently producing annual revenues in excess of $100 million each.

FINANCIAL PERFORMANCE

15   The pharmaceutical industry tends to be somewhat immune to most economic conditions. Rather, demographics and public interest in health related issues, such as cholesterol reduction, are more of an influence on the industry.

16   In the late 1970s and early 80s, Merck lost its number one position in the industry to Bristol-Meyers, as the result of several of its drugs coming off patent protection.[3] Merck maintained a focus on long-term strategies, rather than managing for the short-term, by spending a significant amount of time and money to develop new products. This long-term view is credited with bringing Merck through the difficult times of the early 1980s and back to the top of the pharmaceutical industry. Table 1 presents selected financial data for the period 1978–88.

17   In addition to excellent financial performance, Merck has managed to maintain an impressive rate of growth in sales in recent years, as shown in Exhibit 4.

18   Between 1981 and 1985, as Merck's profits grew by an average of only 8 percent, the rest of the industry enjoyed rates in excess of 15 percent.[4] The reason for this gap between Merck and industry performance was simple: some of Merck's cash cow drugs were coming off patent and the company was losing sales due to increasing generic competition both domestic and abroad. Rather than seeking a quick-fix, Merck stepped up R&D to protect its long-term survival. As a result, Merck's earnings have made a strong come back and currently top the industry. Exhibit 5 depicts Merck's progressive growth and recent surge in earnings.

[1]John Byrne, "The Miracle Company," *Business Week,* October 19, 1987, pp. 84–89.

[2]Annual report, p. 28.

[3]Staff writer, "Merck; admirable, but . . .," *The Economist,* January 17, 1987, pp. 61–2.

[4]Christopher Eklund and Cynthia Green, "A Research Whiz Steps Up from the Lab," *Business Week,* June 24, 1985, pp. 87–8.

TABLE 1
Selected Financial Data (dollars in millions, except per share amounts)

	1988	1987	1986	1985	1984	1983	1982	1981	1980	1979	1978
Sales	$5,939.5	$5,061.3	$4,128.9	$3,547.5	$3,559.7	$3,246.1	$3,063.0	$2,929.5	$2,734.0	$2,384.6	$1,981.4
Materials and production costs	1,526.1	1,443.3	1,338.0	1,272.4	1,424.5	1,263.4	1,222.2	1,229.3	1,078.4	910.3	744.2
Marketing/admin. expenses	1,877.8	1,682.1	1,269.9	1,009.0	945.5	905.1	892.2	837.3	762.7	669.2	554.7
Research/development expenses	668.8	565.7	479.8	426.3	393.1	356.0	320.2	274.2	233.9	188.1	161.4
Other (income) expenses, net	-4.2	-36.0	-32.1	-17.2	9.8	25.6	27.8	2.8	5.5	10.7	15.5
Income before taxes	1,871.0	1,405.2	1,073.3	857.0	786.8	696.0	600.6	585.9	653.5	606.3	505.6
Taxes on income	664.2	498.8	397.6	317.1	293.8	245.1	185.5	187.6	238.1	224.5	198.1
Net income	1,206.8	906.4	675.7	539.9	493.0	450.9	415.1	398.3	415.4	381.8	307.5
Per share of common stock	$3.05	$2.23	$1.62	$1.26	$1.12	$1.02	$0.94	$0.89	$0.92	$0.84	$0.68
Dividends on common stock:											
Declared	546.3	365.2	278.5	235.1	224.0	210.8	207.1	196.8	178.1	150.9	132.3
Paid per share	$1.28	$0.82	$0.63	$0.53	$0.50	$0.47	$0.47	$0.43	$0.38	$0.32	$0.28
Capital expenditures	372.7	253.7	210.6	237.6	274.4	272.8	295.1	322.8	256.5	170.1	155.9
Depreciation	189.0	188.5	167.2	163.6	151.6	135.2	121.1	105.0	91.3	80.6	74.3
Year-end position:											
Working capital	1,480.3	798.3	1,094.3	1,106.6	1,076.5	734.9	860.4	744.9	847.1	782.4	689.6
Property, plant, and equip (net)	2,070.7	1,948.0	1,906.2	1,882.8	1,912.8	1,515.2	1,557.5	1,396.6	1,185.2	1,027.6	924.2
Total assets	6,127.5	5,680.0	5,105.2	4,902.2	4,590.6	4,214.7	3,655.4	3,317.2	2,907.7	2,649.1	2,278.1
Long-term debt	142.8	167.4	167.5	170.8	179.1	385.5	337.3	241.0	211.4	213.7	211.4
Stockholders' equity	2,855.8	2,116.7	2,541.2	2,607.7	2,518.6	2,409.9	2,180.2	1,978.2	1,841.6	1,645.0	1,436.3
Year-end statistics:											
Average common shares outstanding	395,640	407,055	417,978	427,561	440,670	443,661	443,899	445,857	449,742	452,551	453,439
Number of stockholders	68,500	56,900	48,300	47,000	50,200	51,800	55,200	57,000	58,700	60,600	62,900
Number of employees	32,000	31,100	30,700	30,900	34,800	32,600	32,000	32,400	31,600	30,800	28,700
Financial ratios:											
Net income as a percent of:											
Sales	20.30%	17.90%	16.40%	15.20%	13.80%	13.90%	13.60%	13.60%	15.20%	16.00%	15.50%
Total assets	20.40	16.80	13.50	11.40	11.20	11.50	11.90	12.80	15.00	15.50	14.40
Return on equity	42.26	42.82	26.59	20.70	19.57	18.71	19.04	20.13	22.56	23.21	21.41

EXHIBIT 4
Sales

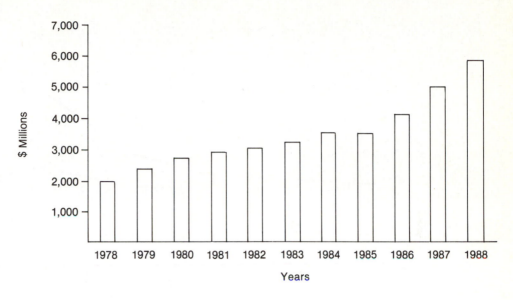

Source: annual report, 1988.

EXHIBIT 5
Earnings per Share

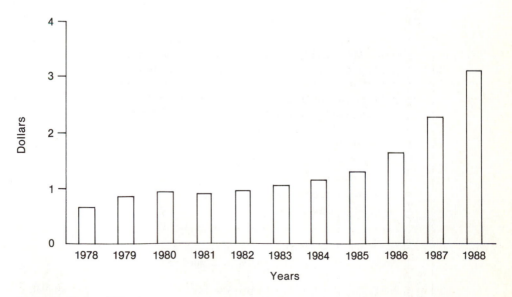

Source: annual report, 1988.

EXHIBIT 6
ROI

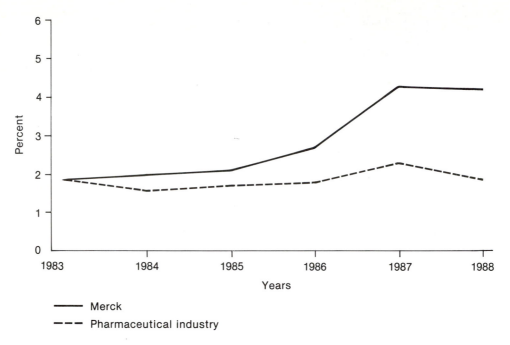

Source: Pharmaceutical Manufacturers Association, *Facts at a Glance,* 1987.

19   Clearly, Merck's ROI also has far outpaced the industry average in recent years. Exhibit 6 compared Merck and the pharmaceutical industry as a whole.

20   In addition to classic measures of performance, such as earnings growth, ROI, and net profit margin, Merck has been "America's Most Admired Corporation" four years running in *Fortune* magazine's annual feature of the same title. *Fortune* polls 8,000 top executives and financial analysts and asks them to rank companies in their industry in eight categories:

21   Quality of management.

Quality of products or services.

Innovativeness.

Long-term investment value.

Financial soundness.

Community and environmental responsibility.

Use of corporate assets.

Ability to attract, develop and keep talented people.

22   For the fourth consecutive year, Merck has received the highest cumulative score out of the 300+ largest corporations in America.

EXHIBIT 7
Percent of Sales Domestic and Foreign

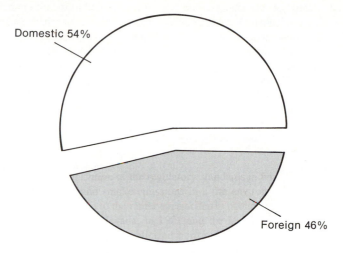

Source: annual report, 1988.

Foreign Trade Contribution

23   The pharmaceutical industry as a whole, and Merck in particular, have a favorable impact on the burgeoning U.S. trade deficit. Historically, Merck has had large favorable trade balances and, in 1988, Merck had a favorable balance of approximately $850 million. This can be attributed to Merck's aggressive global push for growth and the recent weakening of the dollar. Exhibit 7 shows both domestic and foreign sales for 1988.

MANAGEMENT

24   The current style and attitude of management at Merck & Company can be attributed directly to the efforts of the CEO, Dr. P. Roy Vagelos. Ironically, Vagelos grew up working at his parents' luncheonette that was located within walking distance from the Merck plant in Rahway. Listening to the scientists' discussions over lunch inspired Vagelos to seek a career in medicine. Vagelos worked as an intern in Merck's labs while attending medical school at Columbia University. After completing medical school, he spent the next 20 years in basic research and teaching. In 1976, he joined Merck & Company as head of the research division.

25   When Vagelos joined Merck, the research division was not productive, and "the company had not produced a big winner for a decade or more."[5] Vagelos determined that this lack of production

---

[5]Stephen Quickel, "The Drug Culture," *Business Month*, December 1987, p. 36.

was due to a lack of direction. Scrapping dubious projects, Vagelos began financing only major programs directed at discovering drugs that would cure known diseases.[6]

26   After pointing the research division in the right direction, he sought to perfect it by hiring the most talented people money could buy. He proceeded to recruit eminent university scientists. To entice these scientists, Vagelos created a "campus-like" atmosphere and offered outstanding salaries. His background as a scientist at Washington University and his other academic credentials made him credible to those he wanted to hire. Vagelos also made sure that researchers had first-rate facilities, which was often not the case in private industry. Vagelos sums up his recruiting philosophy as follows: "We don't always get our man, but we have never missed hiring someone we wanted because of money."[7]

27   Vagelos became the CEO of Merck in 1985. His management practices then spread from the research division to the entire company. Vagelos refuses to rest on his string of successes. For example, after the news on September 1, 1987, that the FDA approved the Merck drug *Mevacor,* Vagelos phoned the scientist that had headed up *Mevacor* to congratulate him. In the same conversation, he also asked the scientist how they were coming on possible substitutes. "Instead of running Merck defensively, avoiding risks and letting its current successes carry it along, he is driving the company just as hard today as he did when he became research chief 12 years ago. For all Merck's momentum, Vagelos is making sure it runs scared."[8]

28   The most significant feat that Vagelos has accomplished at Merck was gaining the respect of his employees. The employees realize that Vagelos is both a capable scientist and manager. As a result, they do not spend time second-guessing strategic decisions and instead concentrate their efforts on supporting and implementing the decisions. A significant indication of his appropriate style and capabilities as a CEO is the aforementioned fact that Merck has been "America's Most Admired Corporation" four years in a row. When the top executives from America's 300 largest corporations rate your quality of management at the top of all industries four years in a row, that indicates that you are doing something right![9]

HUMAN RESOURCES

29   Excellence in management and development of its employees worldwide is of strategic importance to Merck. Vagelos's strategy is to "hire the best, provide the best training, and encourage professional growth."[10] Merck's managers and supervisors have the responsibility to establish and maintain work environments where people are given appropriate responsibility for their jobs, understand their objectives, and feel they are treated fairly.

30   Research is the lifeblood of Merck, and the recruiting and retaining of top researchers is key to the continuing success of Merck. Merck has worked very hard to set up its labs and research divisions in such a way as to erase the stigma most academics usually associate with moving from academia to industry.[11] Merck's research labs boast an excess of 3,320 employees, representing more than 10 percent of the company's total work force. The researchers and scientists working

---

[6]Ibid.

[7]Ibid.

[8]Stephen Quickel, "Merck & Company—Sheer Energy," *Business Month,* December 1988, p. 36.

[9]Ellen Schultz, "America's Most Admired Corporations," *Fortune,* January 18, 1988, p. 36.

[10]Annual report, p. 34.

[11]Staff writer, "Giving Free Rein to Merck's Best and Brightest," *Business Week,* October 19, 1987, p. 90.

in these labs enjoy a casual atmosphere, moving around the lab grounds in white coats and jeans, while having one of the best compensation packages in the industry. Vagelos places recruiting of top researchers at the top of his priority list. For example, to recruit Leslie Iversen, a British biochemist, and one of the world's leading researchers in Alzheimer's and other neurological diseases, Merck built a 122-person neuroscience research center in Harlowe, Essex, a short distance from Iversen's home.[12]

31   In addition to active pursuit of the best employees available, Merck also takes some progressive approaches to ensure its employees' job satisfaction. The turnover rate at Merck averages only 5 percent. Flexible schedules, daycare facilities, and work-at-home arrangements are a few examples of what Merck does to create a pleasant working environment for employees. In particular, Merck has adopted changes in policy to reflect the changing demographics of the work force, more specifically the two-worker family, and the resulting need for quality daycare. For example, Merck will hold a position for new mothers and fathers who go on unpaid leave for up to 18 months after the birth of a child, six times longer than most other companies. At the company's main facilities in Rahway, employees can get daycare for their infants at facilities started by Merck, for a price based on the employee's salary level.[13]

32   Merck has also developed a fair performance appraisal system. In response to declining company performance during the early 1980s, Merck created a task force to identify factors responsible for these problems. The major conclusion of the task force was the overwhelming employee dissatisfaction with the company's current performance appraisal system and salary administration programs. In fact, the biggest single complaint was the lack of real reward distinction between the outstanding performers and those not performing as well.

33   To remedy the situation, Merck implemented a new appraisal system that evaluates employees' performance in three categories: specific job measures and ongoing duties, planned objectives, and management of people.[14] The third category, management of people, was added because employees and managers at all levels of the company felt that managers were primarily rewarded for their technical abilities, but that their managerial abilities were ignored, a common problem in technically driven companies run by technicians.

34   A distribution target for performance ratings was established to help managers rate the employees in relation to their peers. This essentially produced a two-step evaluation process; first, an employee's performance is measured against objectives and ongoing duties, and then his or her performance is compared with the performance of other employees in the same area of the company.

35   Salary guidelines have also been established that define salary ranges for each position and the level and frequency of increase that may be given for each category of performance.

ORGANIZATION AND STRUCTURE

36   Merck and Company is divided into several divisions. Merck Sharp & Dohme (MSD) is responsible for the marketing and administration of Merck's human pharmaceuticals. This division employs approximately 2,500 people. The majority of these employees are Merck's "professional representatives," who present Merck's product line of human pharmaceuticals to physicians, pharmacists, and hospitals.

---

[12]Stephen Quickel, "The Drug Culture," *Business Month,* December 1987, p. 36.

[13]Staff writer, "The Flexible Work Force; What Organizations Think," *Personnel Administrator,* August 1986, pp. 36–40.

[14]William H. Wagel, "Performance Appraisal with a Difference," *Personnel,* February 1987, pp. 4–7.

37   MSD's counterpart for the animal health markets is MSD AGVET. MSD AGVET is responsible for marketing and administration of agricultural products in addition to animal health products.

38   Merck Sharp and Dohme Research Laboratories is the division responsible for the discovery and development of compounds for both MSD and MSD AGVET.

39   Merck Pharmaceutical Manufacturing Division (MPMD) is the manufacturing arm of Merck and Company. This is the largest division, employing 5,400 people.

40   Merck and Company shows signs of backward integration in its Merck Chemical Manufacturing Division (MCMD), which produces bulk chemicals used by MPMD, in addition to making chemicals for sale to the public. Merck has a few smaller subsidiaries, such as Calgon Corporation, but the divisions outlined above represent the major business of Merck & Company.

41   Merck's divisions and departments interact frequently with each other. This is no accident. Because Merck's dedication to research is the gospel that Vagelos preaches, the company has a unique informal structure. Vagelos purposely instituted a free atmosphere so his scientists would not be restricted by formal authority. For example, a research team must sell its idea to those functional groups from whom it needs assistance on the projects. These functional groups, or units, are budgeted development money to invest in projects of their choice. "The idea is to gain greater collegiality and unity of purpose. As a consensus develops around a project, it gains support intellectually and financially from the team's members."[15] The flexibility and freedom of Merck's structure is what makes the research department, and thus the whole company, thrive.

42   A second important area that a research project must gain support from is marketing. In fact, marketing is second in importance only to research at Merck. With the advent of new products and the continued success of existing products, Merck has added sales personnel and restructured the sales force as well. Prior to 1988, Merck had 1,600 sales representatives divided into two groups. However, Merck soon realized that this organization was not adequately promoting the products. As a result, in 1988, it increased the sales force by one third and created three general groups of 550 representatives and a fourth group of 430 representatives to specialize in hospital products. Each representative in the general groups has one to three products to sell. This permits sales people to develop thorough knowledge of their products.

MANUFACTURING AND OPERATIONS

43   As mentioned earlier, Merck has two manufacturing divisions. The first is MCMD, which is responsible for producing specialty chemicals for the market and bulk chemicals used by the MPMD. Merck believes in quality. The MCMD facilities are "state of the art." For example, the Elkton, Virginia, plant uses robotic technology to ensure high quality. "This system guides a product sample through testing and returns the results electronically to the plant floor, minimizing response time and handling errors."[16] Safety is another big issue at Merck. The MCMD was recognized by the Chemical Manufacturing Association for having the best safety record of all firms having over 20 million hours of exposure.

44   This same commitment to quality and safety applies to the MPMD, as well. The MPMD produces products for direct human consumption, which makes a quality commitment a must. Since the MPMD receives almost all of its raw materials from the MCMD, management believes it is imperative that both divisions produce a quality product. The MPMD also ensures quality through

---

[15]John Byrne, "The Miracle Company," *Business Week,* October 19, 1987, p. 86.

[16]Annual report, p. 22.

state of the art technology. As an example, Merck's plant at West Point, Pennsylvania, uses a unique Vision System. This system uses computer imaging to measure the accuracy of labeling. The MPMD is starting to design new packaging techniques to make them more consumer-oriented. Merck also has instituted modular designs into both manufacturing divisions so they can be used to produce more than one product.

45 Merck has consistently invested large amounts of capital into its manufacturing divisions, which has made them the model facilities that they are today. However, this financial commitment has seemingly peaked. Merck feels that its facilities are the best available and, therefore, are starting to turn its financial attention to its research laboratories and new administrative offices. The facilities are now completely modular and, therefore, can be more productive as well as adaptive to changes in the market. Also, the new high-potency medicines do not require the complex production facilities of the past, mainly because they do not require as many different raw materials. For these reasons, management believes that reductions are possible in capital expenditures on plant facilities without compromising their productive output.

46 Merck's manufacturing focus in the future will center on five objectives. First, Merck will still ensure that preventative maintenance occurs where necessary. Second, the company will provide expansion to support new products after careful review of existing plant capacities. Third, it will maintain its commitment to clean environment and employee safety. Fourth, it will continue to look for ways to increase productivity through advances in process technology. Last and most important, Merck will continue its dedication to producing the highest-quality products possible.

MAJOR COMPETITORS

47 The pharmaceutical industry is very competitive, with no single company holding a dominant market share position. In this industry, it appears that gaining market share is not directly correlated to an increase in profitability. But, gaining market share is the result of successful product differentiation.

48 Merck's major domestic competitors include Abbott Labs, American Home Products, Eli Lilly, Johnson & Johnson, Squibb, Warner-Lambert, Syntex, and Schering-Plough. In particular, Merck is currently engaged in a fierce competition with Squibb in the anti-hypertensive market. Merck's *Vasotec* competes head to head with Squibb's highly successful *Capoten*. *Capoten* sales continue to grow at about 26 percent per year, but *Vasotec* is growing faster and is expected to exceed *Capoten's* level of sales.[17] The outcome of this battle is particularly crucial for Squibb, since *Capoten* accounts for more than 40 percent of its sales. Both drugs have exceeded the billion dollar mark in annual sales, a feat accomplished by only three other drugs.

49 The primary competition from outside the United States comes from Glaxo Holdings, Hoescht, Ciba-Geigy, each with about 3 percent of the global market, and from Sankyo, a Japanese firm. Merck's current goal is to expand its global market share, but each of the above firms use Merck's same formula, plenty of R&D, and successful product differentiation to compete.

50 In 1989, the pharmaceutical industry in which Merck competed was fiercely competitive. Exhibit 8 below shows that the top four companies accounted for nearly 25 percent of industry sales.

51 Exhibit 9 illustrates the correlation between market share and profitability as measured by return on investment (ROI).

---

[17]Susan Benway, "Don't Look Back, Squib—A Giant Is Gaining on You," *Business Week,* October 10, 1988, pp. 68–71.

EXHIBIT 8
Concentration Ratio

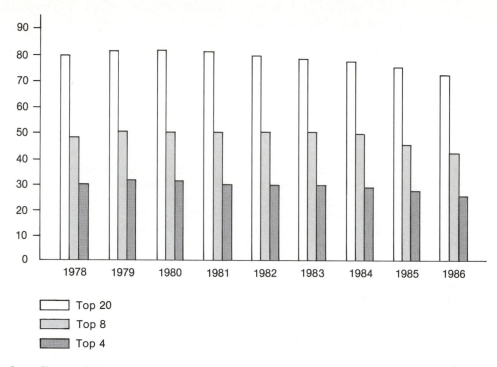

Source: Pharmaceutical Manufacturers Association, *Facts at a Glance*, 1987.

52   Instead of building market shares within the pharmaceutical industry, key competitors opted to diversify into the related health care industry. Many of these companies believed that they could better serve "The changing health care industry as a diversified supplier of health aids, from drugs to equipment."

53   The push for diversification among pharmaceutical companies began in the 1970s, intensified throughout the 1980s, and was expected to continue well into the 1990s.

54   In the 1970s, pharmaceutical companies began purchasing companies that dealt with consumer products in an effort to diversify. Several examples, Warner-Lambert bought Entenmann's, a bakery products company, and American Optical, an eyeglass manufacturer, and Squibb purchased Life-savers, a candy manufacturer. Toward the 80s, after displaying a dismal record of success with their consumer products acquisitions, many of the companies began shedding these units and investing in companies in other health care type of businesses. For example, Warner-Lambert shed Entenmann's and used the proceeds to purchase IMED Corporation, a medical technology firm.[18]

55   Finally, in the mid 80s, the pharmaceutical companies began divesting their unprofitable attempts at diversification and funneling the proceeds back into their strengths, R&D and marketing new products. Divesting these units left many companies with some hefty cash reserves. A survey of

[18]Ibid.

EXHIBIT 9
Market Share Versus ROI

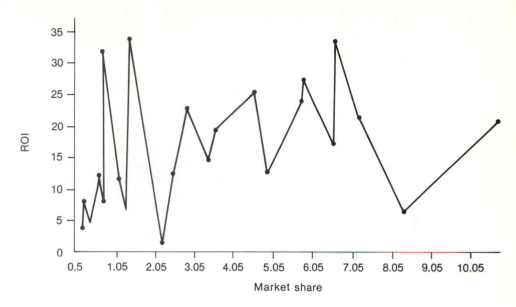

Source: Compustat.

estimated cash and liquid reserves of major pharmaceutical companies at the end of 1986 included: Merck with $1.5 billion, Bristol-Meyers with $1.3 billion, Pfizer with $1.4 billion, and Eli Lilly with $800 million.[19] This enabled these companies to invest heavily in R&D and marketing. Yet, these cash reserves, coupled with the industry's historically high profit margins, also made these companies targets for takeovers. As a result, many companies instituted stock repurchase plans as a defensive measure.

56   A summary of key acquisitions/divestitures in this time period is listed below.

57   1985 — GD Searle Corporation is bought by Monsanto.
          — Sterling Drugs is bought by Eastman Kodak.
          — Richardson Vicks is bought by Procter & Gamble.
          — Bristol-Meyers buys Genetic Systems Corporation, a developer of diagnostic and therapeutic products.
       1986 — Warner-Lambert sells off three medical equipment businesses.
          — Squibb sells off its Charles of the Ritz cosmetic and fragrance unit.
       1987 — Eli Lilly sells off its Elizabeth Arden cosmetics unit and announces stock repurchase plan.
          — SmithKline Beckman repurchases 12.6 million of its outstanding shares.

58   What is the effect of these mergers, acquisitions, and divestments on the structure of the industry? Experts do not expect significant changes in the level of concentration in the industry. Rather, they predict that these companies will have to compete differently.

---

[19]Staff writer, "Prospects Continue Strong," *Standard & Poor's Industry Surveys,* April 1987, p. H19.

Product Differentiation

59   Fierce competition in the industry is in many ways a manifestation of product differentiation, through R&D spending and marketing activities.

R&D

60   Exhibit 10 depicts the strong positive association between R&D spending and corporate ROI. While not perfectly linear, the exhibit shows that spending on R&D is associated with superior corporate financial performance.

61   Table 2 presents data on R&D spending by major companies in the industry. During the period 1983–87 Merck consistently ranked first among the 16 leading companies in terms of R&D spending.

62   Statistics on R&D indicated that spending by pharmaceutical companies was one of the highest among U.S. major industries, rising from 11.3 percent as a percent of sales, to 15.1 percent over the past decade. Statistics also show that about 70 percent of drug R&D in this country was funded directly by domestic pharmaceutical manufacturers, 10 percent by colleges and universities (often in conjunction with leading drug companies), and 20 percent by government and other sources."[20] These percentages translate to $5.4 billion spent in R&D in 1987, up from $1.4 billion in 1978.

EXHIBIT 10
R&D Expenditures Versus ROI

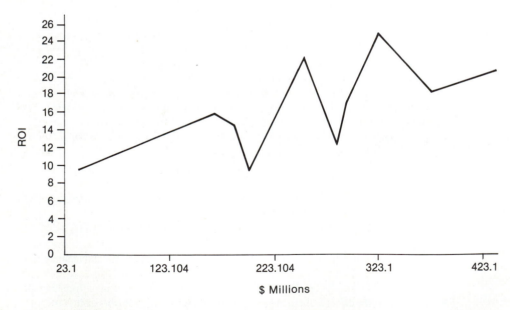

Source: Compustat.

---

[20]Staff writer, "Industry Has Prescription for Success," *Standard & Poor's Industry Surveys,* June 1988, p. H19.

TABLE 2
R&D Expenditures

| | 1986 | | 1987 | | 1983 | | 1984 | | 1985 | | Average | |
	$	Rank	$	Rank	$	Rank	$	Rank	$	Rank	$	Rank
Merck	$479.8	1	$565.7	1	$356.0	1	$393.1	1	$426.3	1	$444.2	1
Eli Lilly	427.0	2	466.3	2	293.6	2	341.3	2	369.8	2	379.6	2
SmithKline Beckman	376.9	3	423.7	3	264.7	3	279.2	3	309.6	3	330.8	3
Pfizer	335.5	4	401.0	4	227.2	5	252.3	5	286.7	4	300.5	4
Upjohn	314.1	5	355.5	6	229.2	4	258.2	4	284.1	5	288.2	5
Bristol-Meyers	311.1	6	341.7	7	185.3	7	212.4	8	261.7	6	262.4	6
American Cyanamid	278.3	8	313.6	8	214.7	6	236.8	6	250.6	7	258.8	7
Abbott Labs	284.9	7	361.3	5	184.5	8	218.7	7	240.6	8	258.0	8
American Home Prods.	227.1	9	247.3	10	161.2	10	183.7	10	217.3	9	207.3	9
Warner-Lambert	202.3	11	231.8	11	175.0	9	194.9	9	208.2	10	202.4	10
Schering-Plough	212.1	10	250.7	9	144.7	11	163.6	11	175.4	11	189.3	11
Squibb	163.0	12	221.4	12	141.7	12	150.6	12	165.7	12	168.5	12
AH Robins	51.8	15	58.4	15	40.7	13	43.4	13	52.4	13	49.3	13
Marion Labs	52.8	14	81.5	14	21.6	16	32.2	14	42.7	14	46.2	14
Rorer Group	69.7	13	81.8	13	25.7	14	29.5	15	17.9	16	44.9	15
Bausch & Lomb	25.7	16	26.5	16	23.6	15	18.2	16	21.5	15	23.1	16

EXHIBIT 11
U.S. New Drug Approvals

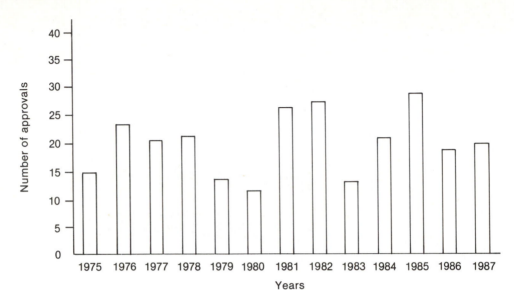

Source: Pharmaceutical Manufacturers Association, *Facts at a Glance*, 1987.

63   Industry experts considered R&D spending to be essential for effective, sustainable product differentiation. Being the first to introduce new drugs resulted in very rewarding financial performance.

64   In addition, Ronald Bond and David Lean concluded that the original seller's "persistent dominance in the face of competition from cheaper, more highly promoted substitute drugs would suggest that the product differentiation advantage of being first with a 'breakthrough' is very substantial indeed."[21]

65   Exhibit 11 illustrates the number of new drugs that received FDA approval over the last 13 years. These approvals represented a major milestone by companies achieving them and often served as a barrier to entry.[22]

Marketing and Advertising

66   Advertising is important in the pharmaceutical industry to build brand recognition with the public for proprietary drugs and to build brand recognition and loyalty with physicians for ethical drugs. In a study by Mier Statman (1981), he concluded that physicians had come to identify the drugs

---

[21]William S. Comanor, "The Political Economy of the Pharmaceutical Industry," *Journal of Economic Literature* XXIV (September 1986), p. 1188.

[22]Pharmaceutical Manufacturers Association, "Pharmaceutical Research: Delivering Value in the Cost Containment Era," 1988, p. 27.

TABLE 3
Advertising Expenditures

	1986 $	1986 % Sales	1987 $	1987 % Sales	1983 $	1983 % Sales	1984 $	1984 % Sales	1985 $	1985 % Sales	Average $	Average % Sales
Abbott Labs	$ 94.4	2.5%	$135.3	3.1%	$ 70.3	2.4%	$ 77.5	2.5%	$ 87.2	2.6%	$ 92.9	2.6%
AH Robins	95.5	12.1	109.7	12.8	64.2	11.4	72.8	11.5	86.8	12.3	85.8	12.1
American Home Prods.	441.3	9.0	447.3	8.9	409.9	8.4	412.0	9.2	408.1	8.7	423.7	8.8
Bausch & Lomb	40.1	5.7	77.3	9.2	27.8	4.9	29.3	5.5	36.5	6.2	42.2	6.5
Bristol-Meyers	820.4	17.0	918.7	17.0	651.4	16.6	743.8	17.8	775.9	17.5	782.0	17.2
Eli Lilly	49.4	1.3	29.9	0.8	47.6	1.6	49.5	1.6	47.6	1.5	44.8	1.3
Marion Labs	58.8	14.7	62.5	10.5	23.2	12.8	28.2	12.5	41.4	14.0	42.8	12.6
Merck	145.4	3.5	202.0	4.0	97.4	3.0	101.3	2.8	102.8	2.9	129.8	3.3
Pfizer	170.6	3.8	181.8	3.7	166.5	4.4	161.6	4.2	158.0	3.9	167.7	4.0
Rorer Group	40.0	4.7	49.4	5.3		N.A.	22.4	4.3	19.3	5.7	32.8	5.3
Schering-Plough	262.4	10.9	321.9	11.9	206.5	11.4	211.9	11.3	224.5	11.6	245.4	11.5
SmithKline Beckman	236.5	6.3	250.8	5.8	160.1	5.6	179.3	6.1	176.0	5.4	200.5	5.9
Squibb	117.6	6.6	151.1	7.0	105.6	6.0	111.0	5.9	119.5	5.9	121.0	6.3
Upjohn	101.4	4.4	123.7	4.9	71.8	3.6	87.3	4.0	94.1	4.7	95.7	4.3
Warner-Lambert	692.8	22.3	797.5	22.9	592.0	19.0	607.0	19.2	630.8	19.7	664.0	20.7

with specific brand names so that the original seller maintained most of his prior market position even after patent expiration."[23]

67   Pharmaceutical companies accomplished brand loyalty for ethical drugs mainly through direct selling which built strong relationships with physicians. These salesmen, the "detailmen," were a valuable source of information for physicians. In fact, the Kefauver Committee challenged the pharmaceutical industry's selling expenses, claiming they were much too high and should be cut, which would result in savings for consumers. The industry replied that significant expenditures went into training the detailmen sufficiently to become a resource to the physicians. The physicians stood behind the industry by testifying that the detailmen were in fact an integral part of their information basis and relied heavily on them to keep up with the changes in the available drugs.

68   These marketing efforts comprise approximately 20 percent of sales.[24] "Traditional product advertising in scientific journals accounts for 24 percent of advertising efforts, direct mail about 6 percent and detail staff for another 20 percent.[25]

69   Table 3 presents data on advertising expenditures by the leading 15 pharmaceutical companies during the 1983–87 period.

Industry Performance

70   During 1975–85, industry revenues grew at an annual average rate of 8 percent, as illustrated in Exhibit 12.

71   Exhibit 13 compares industry performance, measured by return on equity (ROE), to the average achieved by all U.S. industries during the 1983–88 period.

72   Exhibit 14 also compares the pharmaceutical industry to all other industries, using net profit margin as a measure of performance.

Threats

73   Merck faces several major threats in the industry. First, as mentioned, the industry is fiercely competitive. In recent years, foreign companies have posed the greatest threat to Merck. Foreign companies are not only active in marketing and distributing their products in the United States, but they are also increasingly involved in joint ventures that will solidify their competitive position.

74   Second, as of 1984, the government has undertaken many steps that may weaken industry innovativeness. The effect of government actions was to reduce the time span of patent protection, thus making it easier for other firms to manufacture generic drugs.

75   Third, the ever-rising growth of the generic drug industry is a major threat facing the industry. Firms in this industry (a few of which may also produce branded drugs) make copies of unpatented drugs and sell them under a generic name at a lower price than the branded drugs. The branded-only drug firms are vehemently opposed to generic drugs and claim that many of the generic drugs are not bioequivalent to the branded drug. In fact, "the FDA has acknowledged that, of the 6,000 marketed generic drugs listed in its *Approved Drug Products with Therapeutic Equivalence Evaluations,* about 20 percent have not been determined by the agency to be therapeutically equivalent

---

[23]William S. Comanor, "The Political Economy of the Pharmaceutical Industry," *Journal of Economic Literature* XXIV (September 1986), p. 1189.

[24]Joan Kangilaski, "Drug Companies Reach into Mixed Marketing Bag," *Advertising Age,* October 24, 1985, p. 35.

[25]Ibid.

EXHIBIT 12
Sales Growth

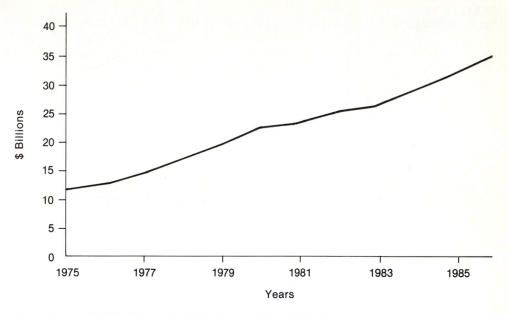

Source: Pharmaceutical Manufacturers Association, *Facts at a Glance,* 1987.

EXHIBIT 13
Return on Equity

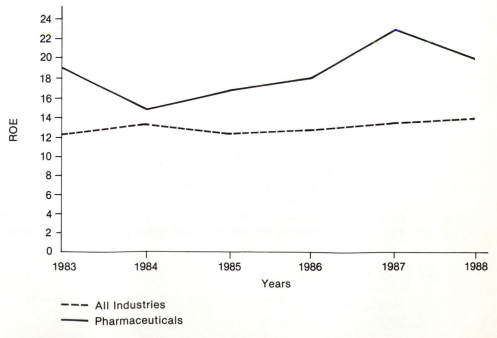

Source: *Forbes* industry analyses, 1984–89.

EXHIBIT 14
Net Profit Margin

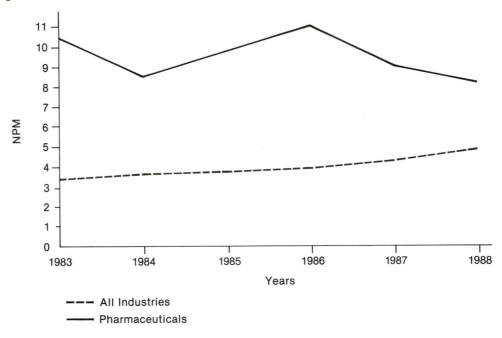

Source: *Forbes* industry analyses, 1984–89.

to the pioneer products."[26] Despite the controversy, the generic drug industry is capturing an increasingly large share of the prescription drug market without having to spend any significant amount of money in research and development. Currently, generic drugs account for about 23 percent of all prescriptions.[27]

Opportunities

76   The above threats notwithstanding, Merck is well positioned to explore many promising opportunities in the United States and abroad. Continuing its tradition of extensive R&D, Merck can target specific market groups, such as senior citizens, or continue its current strategy. Additionally, Merck's excellent reputation makes it an attractive candidate for strategic alliances in the United States or abroad. Opportunities appear limitless for Merck. Still, the question Merck must address in the 1990s is: How much emphasis should the firm give its pharmaceutical core business? Much depends on the preferences of Merck's senior executives, who so ably have created a great company.

[26]Gerald J. Mossinghoff, "Generic Drugs," Pharmaceutical Manufacturers Association.

[27]Ibid.

BIBLIOGRAPHY

Benway, Susan. "Don't Look Back, Squib—A Giant Is Gaining on You." *Business Week*. October 10, 1988, pp. 68–71.

Byrne, John. "The Miracle Company." *Business Week*. October 19, 1987, pp. 84–89.

Colford, Steven W. "CBS Readies for Prescription Drug Ads." *Advertising Age*. November 11, 1985, p. 12+.

———. "New Rx for Drug Ads." *Advertising Age*. August 7, 1985, p. 1+.

Comanor, William S. "The Political Economy of the Pharmaceutical Industry." *Journal of Economic Literature*. Vol. XXIV, September 1986, pp. 1178–1217.

Davenport, Carol. "America's Most Admired Corporations." *Fortune*. January 30, 1989, pp. 68–82.

Eckholm, Erik. "River Blindness—Conquering an Ancient Scourge." *The New York Times Magazine*. January 8, 1989. pp. 1–6.

Eklund, Christopher, and Cynthia Green. "A Research Whiz Steps Up from the Lab." *Business Week*. June 24, 1985, pp. 87–8.

Kangilaski, Joan. "Drug Companies Reach into Mixed Marketing Bag." *Advertising Age*. October 24, 1985, pp. 35–36.

Liebenau, Jonathan. "Innovation in Pharmaceuticals: Industrial R&D in the Early Twentieth Century." *Research Policy*. Vol. 14, 1985, pp. 179–87.

McCabe, E. F. "Merck Responds to Market Changes; a University Learns Its Lessons." *Management Review*. January 1987, pp. 56–60.

Mossinghoff, Gerald J. "Generic Drugs" Pharmaceutical Manufacturers Association.

Schultz, Ellen. "America's Most Admired Corporations." *Fortune*. January 18, 1988, p. 36.

Smith, Lee. "Merck Has an Ache in Japan." *Fortune*. March 18, 1985, pp. 42–46.

Staff writer. "Merck; Admirable, but . . ." *The Economist*. January 17, 1987, pp. 61–2.

Staff writer. "Giving Free Rein to Merck's Best and Brightest." *Business Week,* October 19, 1987, p. 90.

Staff writer. "The Flexible Work Force; What Organizations Think." Personnel Administrator. August 1986, pp. 36–40.

Staff writer. "Drugs Need New Boffins." *The Economist*. July 16, 1988, p. 12.

Staff writer. "Profit Outlook Remains Favorable." *Standard & Poor's Industry Surveys*. January 1975, pp. H13–H19.

Staff writer. "Steady Growth in Shipments Likely." *Standard & Poor's Industry Surveys*. July 1980, pp. H12–H18.

Staff writer. "Wall Street High on Drug Firms." *Standard & Poor's Industry Surveys*. March 1986, pp. H17–H24.

Staff writer. "Prospects Continue Strong." *Standard & Poor's Industry Surveys*. April 1987, pp. H17–H24.

Staff writer. "Industry Has Prescription for Success." *Standard & Poor's Industry Surveys*. June 1988, pp. H17–H27.

Quickel, Stephen. "Merck & Company—Sheer Energy." *Business Month*. December 1988, p. 36.

———. "The Drug Culture." *Business Month*. December 1987, pp. 36.

Wagel, William H. "Performance Appraisal with a Difference." *Personnel*. February 1987, pp. 4–7.

Waldholz, Michael. "Merck and Johnson & Johnson to Form Venture for Over-the-Counter Medicines." *The Wall Street Journal*. March 29, 1989. p. A4.

Value Line Industry Profile. "Drug Industry." *Value Line*. February 10, 1989. p. 1253.

CASE 18

NORTHERN TELECOM, INC.

1   Hall Miller, vice president of marketing for the Central Office Switching Division of Northern Telecom, Inc., looked up from the magazine on his desk to a picture of a single, snow-covered log cabin with stately mountains rising in the background. The picture reminded him of his childhood in British Columbia.

2   His eyes moved from the picture to the window, where he could see traffic already starting to pile up on the portion of Interstate 40, which ran through Research Triangle Park, North Carolina, between Durham, Chapel Hill, and Raleigh. It was mid-afternoon in March 1988 and the traffic would be bumper to bumper in another hour.

3   Hall smiled as he realized that the picture on the wall represented his perception of Northern's performance in the United States, while the impending traffic jam reminded him of the changing market conditions he felt the company would soon be facing.

4   Hall had been reviewing the results of a survey conducted by *Communications Week* in the fourth quarter of 1987. The purpose of the study was to identify purchase trends and priorities in the selection of central office telephone switching equipment. The survey respondents were primarily telephone company planners, who were directly involved with selecting and purchasing central office switches.

5   Hall was interested in the results of the *Communications Week* survey, since he wanted to use the information to prepare for the quarterly meeting of the regional marketing managers, which would be held in early April. These managers were assigned to each of the seven regions into which Northern Telecom had divided the United States for marketing purposes. It was these managers' responsibility to work with the sales force in each region to develop overall marketing strategies. They also worked on quotations and new business development in their regions.

6   Hall felt the time had come to get the group to step back and assess the overall market situation faced by the Central Office Switching Division and to identify potential changes in the division's marketing strategy.

HISTORY

7   Northern Telecom, Inc. (NTI), the U.S. subsidiary of Canadian-based Northern Telecom, Ltd. (NTL), was originally part of the Bell System. Bell Canada, the parent company of NTL, was a subsidiary of AT&T until the late 1950s, when AT&T was ordered to divest its foreign subsidiaries. Prior to that divestiture and for some time afterward, Northern Telecom was known as Northern Electric, the Canadian counterpart of AT&T's U.S. manufacturing arm, Western Electric.

This case was prepared by Lew G. Brown and Richard Sharpe. Dr. Brown is an assistant professor, Department of Management and Marketing, Joseph M. Bryan School of Business and Economics, University of North Carolina at Greensboro. Mr. Sharpe has an MBA from the University of Tennessee at Knoxville. Appreciation is expressed to Northern Telecom for its support in developing this case. This case is for classroom discussion purposes only.

8   Despite the divestiture, Northern Telecom still had a captive customer in its parent, Bell Canada; and this relationship gave it roughly 80 percent of the Canadian market. However, Northern's management realized that if it were to survive it would have to design its own equipment. Previously, Northern had made copies of telephone equipment manufactured by Western Electric. To make its own equipment, Northern would have to be able to afford the massive research and development budgets required in the telecommunications equipment industry. The Canadian market alone would not support the required level of investment. Therefore, Northern broadened its market by establishing its presence in the United States in the 1960s and 1970s as a supplier of telephone switches.

9   A telephone switch is a device that routes individual calls from the person making the call to and through the telephone network. Once in the network, the call is routed from switch to switch until reaching the person being called. Initially, Northern Telecom had sold switches known as "private branch exchanges." These private branch exchanges were switches that were owned by the customer, such as a manufacturing company or a university, and were housed in the customer's facilities. Northern also sold the telephone sets that went with its systems.

10   Manufacturing and support facilities were established in West Palm Beach, Florida; Atlanta, Georgia; Richardson, Texas; Minnetonka, Minnesota; San Ramon, California; and Nashville, Tennessee, the U.S. headquarters of NTI. Northern's first facility in North Carolina opened in the early 1970s in Creedmoor, a small community north of Durham. It still amazed Hall to think that Northern had grown from 300 people at Creedmoor to 10,000 employees in the Raleigh area in less than a decade.

DEVELOPMENT OF THE DIGITAL SWITCH

11   Throughout the 1970s, Northern Telecom, in conjunction with Bell-Northern Research (BNR), Northern's R&D equivalent to Bell Labs, developed a process known as *digital* switching. Unlike *analog* signals—a continuous wave of electrical signals varying in amplitude and frequency in response to changes in sound—*digital* signals involve sampling the human voice at a rate of 8,000 times per second and breaking it into a stream of thousands of bits of electrical pulses in a binary code. As the pulses are routed through the network, they are multiplexed, which involves coding each pulse and sending them together in streams. Because each pulse is coded, it can be sent immediately and followed by other pulses from other conversations. This allows transmission of multiple conversations simultaneously on the same line. At each telephone switch, the pulses are either routed to another switch or are multiplexed (put back together) into voice signals and sent to the appropriate terminating party for the call.

12   Digital technology offered a number of advantages over analog switching, including faster and "cleaner" transmission, lower costs per line, and decreased floor space requirements for switching equipment (a digital switch required less than 50 percent the space of an analog switch).

13   In 1970, Northern developed the SP-1, a hybrid electromechanical switch whose functions were digitally controlled. In 1975, it introduced the first completely computerized telephone switch, the SL-1. The SL-1 was a significant technological advance over the analog and hybrid switches then in use and became a platform for a high-performance product line that allowed businesses to significantly reduce their telecommunications costs.

14   With its development of the digital switch, Northern entered the central office switch market. As opposed to private branch exchanges, central office switches are located in the telephone company's facilities. The customer's telephone sets are connected directly to the telephone company's switch, rather than to its own switch located in its facilities. Thus, Northern's customer became the telephone company rather than individual businesses. Northern installed its first digital central office switch in 1979.

THE BREAKUP OF AT&T AND EQUAL ACCESS

15   Until the early 1980s, AT&T had a monopoly in the U.S. telephone market, providing local and long distance telephone service through the Bell System to more than 85 percent of the United States. Western Electric was the only supplier of telecommunications equipment to AT&T. The remaining 15 percent of the telephone service market was served by 1,200 "independent" telephone companies. Northern Telecom, along with other equipment vendors, sold its products to these independent telephone companies.

16   In 1982, through the provisions of the Modification of Final Judgment, which ordered the breakup of AT&T, AT&T divested the 22 local operating companies comprising the Bell System. Although the "new" AT&T retained the long distance portion of the business (called AT&T Communications), the newly formed Bell operating companies provided local telephone service and became distinct entities that were no longer tied to AT&T. As such, the Bell operating companies were now free to buy telecommunications equipment from other suppliers than Western Electric (renamed AT&T Technologies). For Northern Telecom and other vendors, divestiture was the end of a monopoly and the beginning of a highly competitive marketplace. Exhibit 1 shows how the 22 Bell operating companies, such as Southern Bell and South Central Bell, were grouped to form seven regional holding companies, such as BellSouth.

17   The Modification of Final Judgment also included the provision that the local telephone companies must provide exchange access to all long distance carriers (such as MCI and US Sprint) "equal in type, quality, and price to that provided to AT&T and its affiliates." To provide "equal

---

EXHIBIT 1

access," many telephone exchanges (central office switches) had to be replaced with digital technology switches. Northern Telecom was well positioned at that time for success in the U.S. central office switching market, having a product lead in digital switching and being able to compete in an open market driven by equal access.

18   Thus began an era for Northern known to some observers in the industry as "one of the great marketing successes of recent times." Northern's sales went from US$2.7 billion in 1983 to $4.2 billion in 1985, and it ranked second only to AT&T.

NORTHERN'S PRODUCTS

Hardware

19   Northern Telecom's digital central office switching components fell into four categories: systems, remotes, extensions, and lines. "Systems" equated to digital central office switches. Northern had three versions collectively known as the DMS Family (Digital Multiplex System)—the DMS-100, the DMS-100/200, and the DMS-200. The DMS-100 handled local lines only, the DMS-100/200 handled both local lines and toll trunks (trunks were lines between offices carrying long distance traffic), and the DMS-200 handled toll trunks only. Each DMS system had a maximum capacity of 100,000 lines.

20   Exhibit 2 presents a picture of a DMS-100 switch and a line card. The switch contains numbers of these line cards, one per subscriber line. The software resident in the switch and each line card allows the "programming" of each telephone served by the switch to determine which centrex features that telephone will have.

21   Exhibits 3 and 4 show Northern Telecom's U.S. installed equipment base by customer type, by product category, and sales by year.

22   "Remotes" were digital switching units that extended central office features to remote areas. Northern's remotes ranged in size from 600 to 5,000 lines. Unlike central office systems, which were housed in buildings, remotes were often constructed in environmentally controlled cabinets and placed outside on concrete platforms in areas away from central offices. In addition to extending central office features and services, most remotes had some "stand-alone" capability (i.e., if the host central office switch went out of service for some reason, calls could still be made between customers being served by the same remote). Remotes also provided a cost savings in lines by performing a line-concentrating function, since all the subscribers who were served by a remote in a particular location were wired to the remote, rather than to the central office. Thus, all the customers on the remote were served by a single pair of wires extending from the remote to the central office. Remotes could be located up to 150 miles away from their hosts.

23   "Extensions" represented hardware additions and software upgrades to existing Northern switches.

24   "Lines" were reported in thousands; thus, as of year-end 1987, NTI had over 15.5 million lines in-service. A line represented the ability to serve one customer.

Software

25   In addition to hardware, an important portion of Northern Telecom's product line was software. Northern Telecom's DMS switches were driven by both operating software (similar to DOS in a PC environment) and applications software performing specific functions (such as an accounting program to log and bill long distance calls).

EXHIBIT 2
A.   A Northern Telecom DMS-100 central office switch.

B.   A line card. Each line card serves one telephone line.

EXHIBIT 3
Northern Telecom, Inc., DMS-100 Family Installed Base by Customer Type, as of Year-end 1987

Customer	Systems	Remotes	Extensions	Lines (000)
Bell operating companies	658	248	1,106	9,841
Independent operating companies	434	1,303	1,120	5,686
Total U.S.	1,092	1,551	2,226	15,527

EXHIBIT 4
DMS-100 Family U.S. Sales by Year

Year	Systems	Remotes	Extensions	Lines (000)
1979	5			2
1980	13			75
1981	69	31	19	453
1982	51	86	41	492
1983	83	130	58	798
1984	116	210	152	1,379
1985	266	304	332	3,665
1986	235	359	604	3,962
1987	254	431	1,015	4,701
Total	1,092	1,551	2,226	15,527

Source: Northern Telecom Data.

26   Centrex (originally an AT&T brand name) had become a generic term describing any central office-based applications software package combining business-oriented voice, data networking, and control features bundled with intercom calling and offered to end users as a package. As a shared central office-based service, centrex was designed to replace applications served by equipment located at the customer's premises, such as key telephone systems and private branch exchanges. As opposed to investing in telephone switching equipment, the customer simply paid the telephone company a monthly fee per centrex line for access to a multitude of sophisticated business voice and high-speed data features. Call Forwarding and Call Waiting were examples of centrex basic voice features that had been offered to the residential market. Centrex (as an AT&T brand offering) was widespread throughout the 22 local Bell System telephone companies prior to divestiture. Centrex (as a generic product) was a major source of revenue for the telephone operating companies. The companies billed the customers each month for the features they had selected for use in their telephone systems.

AT&T'S STRATEGY

27   In the late 1970s, AT&T began what was known as a "migration" strategy, urging business customers to a private branch exchange (on-site) solution for their telecommunications needs, as opposed to a central office-based solution. Implementation of this strategy, which was designed to "bypass"

EXHIBIT 5
Meridian Digital Centrex Status—U.S.A., as of March 26, 1988 (1Q88)

	In-Service		Shipped and In-Service		In-Service, Shipped, and Firm Orders		
	Systems	Lines	Systems	Lines	Systems	Lines	Srs
Bell operating companies	594	1,610,166	696	1,956,973	757	2,087,921	44
Independent operating companies	265	292,633	280	387,810	288	401,299	6
Total U.S.	859	1,902,799	976	2,344,783	1,045	2,489,220	50

Numbers are cumulative across the page.
"SRs"—Schedule Requests; jobs not yet firm orders.
Source: Northern Telecom data.

EXHIBIT 6
Meridian Digital Centrex Major End Users

Vertical Markets	Number of Major MDC End Users	Example
Universities	35	Indiana University
Government:		
—Municipal	30	—City of Las Vegas
—State	20	—Suncom (Florida)
—Federal	11	—Senate/White House
Major businesses	50	Ford Motor Company
Airports	15	Los Angeles Airport
Banks	27	Citicorp
Hospitals	16	Marquette Hospital
Telephone companies	11	NYNEX Headquarters

Source: Northern Telecom Data.

Telephone company work to defeat

the local telephone companies, intensified during and following divestiture. Telephone companies were directly affected by this strategy, for end users began purchasing their own private branch exchanges directly from AT&T and other vendors, rather than paying the telephone company's monthly per-line fees for central office-based business services. Telephone companies did not like this migration strategy, since it threatened their revenues.

28 Northern Telecom introduced its digital centrex applications software and was able to capitalize on the resentment telephone companies felt toward AT&T. Meridian Digital Centrex (MDC), Northern's centrex software offering, was introduced in 1982, and sales grew significantly from 1985 to 1987. Exhibit 5 shows NTI's MDC statistics by customer type.

29 Telephone companies purchased Northern's MDC software for their DMS switches for the purpose of reselling to end users the business services features the applications software provided.

EXHIBIT 7
Meridian Digital Centrex Line Size Distribution

Number of MDC Lines	Number of Installed Systems of This Size
1—1,999	658
2,000—9,999	241
10,000 +	71
MDC software, no lines	75
Total in-service, shipped and on order through 1Q88	1,045

Source: Northern Telecom data.

The telephone companies often renamed the service for the purpose of developing brand identity and loyalty (much as in the same way Sears bought appliances made by Whirlpool and sold them under the Kenmore label). BellSouth, for example, used John Naismith, the author of *Megatrends*, to advertise centrex as ESSX service. Exhibit 6 provides a profile of some of the major MDC software end users by vertical markets served. Exhibit 7 provides a breakdown by line size of the Northern's DMS systems that had MDC software.

FINANCIAL PERFORMANCE

30 Exhibit 8 is a consolidated review of the financial performance of Northern Telecom Limited and its subsidiaries during the period 1979–87. As indicated, revenues for 1987 were $4.8 billion, up 11 percent from 1986. Net earnings for 1987 rose 15 percent to $329 million, up from $287 million in 1986.

31 As noted in the bottom portion of Exhibit 8, Northern Telecom Limited had five principal business areas, Central Office Switching, Integrated Business Systems and Terminals, Transmission, Cable and Outside Plant, and Other. Central office switching, Hall's division, accounted for $2.6 billion, or 53 percent of total revenues in 1987.

32 The Integrated Business Systems and Terminals group sold on-premises customer equipment, such as private branch exchanges, local area networks, data terminals, electronic and key telephone systems, residential telephones, and special applications telephone systems. Many of the products sold by the Business Systems and Terminals group were offered under the Meridian product line name.

33 The Transmission group and Cable and Outside Plant group sold digital subscriber carrier systems, microwave radio transmission systems, fiber optic systems and cable, and network management systems.

34 Exhibit 9 presents a summary of Northern's income statements by geographic area for the 1985 to 1987 period. Although sales outside of the United States and Canada represented only a small percentage of total sales, Northern had scored a major breakthrough in 1985 by landing a five-year, $250 million contract with Nippon Telegraph and Telephone (NTT) and becoming the first foreign company to sell switches to NTT.

35 NTL had 48,778 employees as of year-end 1987, and 1987 earnings per share were $1.39.

EXHIBIT 8
Consolidated 11-Year Review

Northern Telecom, Ltd., and Subsidiaries (dollars in millions)

	1987	1986	1985	1984	1983	1981	1979	1977
Earnings and related data:								
Revenues	$4,853.5	$4,383.6	$4,262.9	$3,374.0	$2,680.2	$2,146.1	$1,625.1	$1,149.7
Cost of revenues	2,895.8	2,730.5	2,078.9	2,074.1	1,713.3	1,542.5	1,117.0	821.4
Selling, general, and administrative expense	917.8	764.6	701.9	603.2	454.8	300.1	234.9	149.1
Research and development expense	587.5	474.5	430.0	333.1	263.2	151.8	117.6	64.2
Depreciation on plant and equipment	264.1	247.3	203.3	162.8	126.6	100.8	77.9	29.1
Provision for income taxes	141.5	127.9	132.8	120.3	79.3	29.8	30.3	45.5
Earnings before extraordinary items	347.2	313.2	299.2	255.8	183.2	92.1	97.4	76.3
Net earnings applicable to common shares	328.8	286.6	273.8	243.2	216.7	105.4	97.4	80.2
Earnings per revenue dollar (cents)	6.8	6.5	6.4	7.2	8.1	4.9	6.0	7.0
Earnings per common share (dollars):								
—before extraordinary items	1.39	1.23	1.18	1.06	0.83	0.45	0.53	0.48
—after extraordinary items	1.39	1.23	1.18	1.06	0.98	0.50	0.53	0.51
Dividends per share (dollars)	0.23	0.20	0.18	0.16	0.16	0.14	0.12	0.11
Financial position at December 31:								
Working capital	570.7	1,188.7	933.9	859.0	563.4	421.6	477.4	307.3
Plant and equipment (at cost)	2,345.6	1,975.2	1,737.5	1,458.0	1,152.2	829.8	602.8	356.9
Accumulated depreciation	1,084.2	877.3	672.4	591.5	506.4	355.0	237.8	184.3
Total assets	4,869.0	3,961.1	3,490.0	3,072.9	2,309.4	1,809.4	1,620.8	698.8
Long-term debt	224.8	101.1	107.6	100.2	102.3	207.5	165.0	48.0
Redeemable retractable preferred shares	153.9	281.0	277.5	293.6	—	—	—	—
Redeemable preferred shares	73.3	73.3	73.3	—	—	—	—	—
Common shareholders' equity	2,333.3	1,894.9	1,614.6	1,379.8	1,178.3	719.5	793.5	431.0
Return on common shareholders' equity	15.6%	16.3%	18.3%	19.0%	21.7%	15.7%	14.6%	19.4%
Capital expenditures	416.7	303.8	457.3	437.3	305.7	174.9	148.4	42.1
Employees at December 31	48,778	46,202	46,549	46,993	39,318	35,444	33,301	24,962

Quarterly Financial Data (unaudited) (dollars in millions, except per share figures)

	4th Qtr.		3rd Qtr.		2nd Qtr.		1st Qtr.	
	1987	1986	1987	1986	1987	1986	1987	1986
Revenues	$1,299.1	$1,314.4	$1,158.1	$1,032.2	$1,253.0	$1,067.4	$1,143.3	$969.6
Gross profit	584.9	536.1	479.1	404.5	489.9	389.4	403.8	323.1
Net earnings	140.0	132.2	69.5	66.0	77.6	64.9	60.1	50.1
Net earnings applicable to common shares	136.0	125.9	66.2	59.4	72.9	58.0	53.7	43.3
Earnings per common share	0.57	0.54	0.28	0.25	0.31	0.25	0.23	0.19
Weighted average number of common shares outstanding (thousands)	236,444	234,767	236,024	234,199	235,573	223,650	235,237	233,154

Revenues by Principal Product Lines (dollars in millions)

	1987	1986	1985	1984	1983
Central office switching	$2,577.2	$2,230.2	$2,141.3	$1,452.9	$ 981.9
Integrated business systems and terminals	1,302.0	1,284.7	1,256.6	1,162.9	985.8
Transmission	498.6	468.1	431.2	385.1	376.3
Cable and outside plant	408.2	348.4	373.4	314.9	275.5
Other telecommunications	67.5	51.5	60.4	58.9	60.7
Total	$4,853.5	$4,383.6	$4,262.9	$3,374.0	$2,680.2

(handwritten notes: "slow market"; "ROS = N/E / S"; "ROE = N/E / TA"; "347.2 17"; "313.2 46")

EXHIBIT 9
Northern Telecom Ltd., Income by Geographic Area, 1985–87
(dollars in millions)

	1987	1986	1985
Total revenues:			
United States	$3,103.0	$2,965.6	$2,967.3
Canada	2,140.3	1,771.1	1,792.8
Other	272.1	245.9	215.2
Less—inter-area transfers	(661.9)	(599.0)	(712.4)
Total all revenues	$4,853.5	$4,383.6	$4,262.9
Operating earnings:			
United States	$787.0	$674.2	$699.6
Canada	491.6	383.8	319.8
Other	(11.1)	18.8	12.0
Total all operating earnings	$1,267.5	$1,076.8	$1,031.4
Less—Research and development	($587.5)	($474.5)	($430.0)
Less—General corporate expenses	($227.6)	($188.3)	($179.3)
Net Operating Earnings	$452.4	$414.0	$422.1
Plus—Other income	36.3	27.1	9.9
Earnings before tax	$488.7	$441.1	$432.0
Identifiable assets:			
United States	$1,807.2	$1,749.6	$1,868.2
Canada	1,297.5	1,189.3	1,389.8
Other	181.1	210.1	264.2
Corporate assets*	332.4	460.3	204.6

* Corporate assets are principally cash and short-term investments and corporate plant and equipment.
Source: Northern Telecom, Ltd., 1987 annual report.

THE CHANGING MARKETPLACE

36   Hall felt that Northern's success through the 1980s had been driven by five major factors:

37   1. A sustained product development lead in digital central office switching technology (AT&T did not introduce a digital central office switch until 1983).

2. Access to a huge market that had previously been restricted due to monopolistic constraints.

3. A willingness in that new market to be served by another vendor than AT&T (AT&T had moved from the position of supplier and parent organization to that of a competitor).

4. Equal access legislation requiring product replacement of old technology exchanges with new digital switches.

5. The ability to dilute the effect of AT&T's migration strategy on the Bell operating companies by providing them with revenue-generating features in MDC applications software for the DMS.

38   Despite Northern's success, however, Hall realized that the marketplace was changing and that Northern needed to reconsider its strategy to respond to these changes.

EXHIBIT 10
Northern DMS and AT&T 5ESS System Shipments by Half Year

	Northern	AT&T
1H85	144	169
2H85	145	141
1H86	108	152
2H86	139	144
1H87	128	135
2H87	127	130

Source: Northern Telecom data; AT&T estimates.

AT&T's 5ESS

39   Demand for digital switches had exceeded supply in the early 1980s, and AT&T had not entered the digital switching marketplace until 1983, with the 5ESS switch. As a result, Northern Telecom had a substantial competitive lead in both product/feature development and in marketing its products to the telephone companies. AT&T had found itself in the unusual position of being an industry technology "follower," rather than the industry leader. Moreover, because of its monopoly position, AT&T had not been concerned previously with having to market its products.

40   Exhibit 10 compares Northern's DMS and AT&T's 5ESS shipments in half-year increments starting in 1985. Although only 13 of AT&T's 5ESS units were in-service by the end of 1983, with an additional 72 being placed in-service in 1984, pent-up demand in the telephone companies for additional products to help satisfy equal access requirements and the desire to have multiple suppliers helped sales of the 5ESS grow rapidly. Moreover, Northern experienced delivery problems in 1985, with one of its remote switch products and performance problems with a particular release of operating system software. Combined with the strong market demand for digital technology, these events helped to assure that AT&T's 5ESS would be a successful product. The U.S. telephone digital switching market became a two-supplier arena.

41   AT&T claimed to have 800 5ESS systems, 660 remotes, and 15 million lines in-service as of September, 1987 (these figures included some switches located outside the United States and some within the AT&T system itself). Northern Telecom had 1,092 systems, 1,551 remotes, and 15.5 million lines in-service as of the end of 1987.

Pricing

42   Due to equal access, demand for digital switches exceeded supply from 1982–86. During this period, delivery was the primary determinant of which vendor would be chosen. Volume sales agreements negotiated with each regional or local telephone company for multiple changeouts of old technology switches were the norm, rather than the exception. Price was not a key selection criteria.

43   However, with supply exceeding the demand for digital switches from 1986 onward, the situation had become one of competitive bidding for each switch replacement, with bidding parties offering aggressive discounts. The objective was to win the initial system even at the sake of short-term profits, for winning the switch meant additional opportunities for revenue through software and hardware upgrades and extensions.

44   In 1987, the industry average price of a digital switch was estimated at $326 per line of capacity. However, discounts of up to 30 percent on this price were not uncommon. A switch with a 20,000 line capacity might be bid in the $4.5 million range. Switch prices ranged from $1 million to $10 million, with an average price of $2.5 million.

45   Hall had concerns that the discounts the vendors were offering often resulted in the winner leaving large sums of money on the table (e.g., coming in with a bid at $500,000 less than the next lowest competitor, when all that would have been necessary to win the switch was a $100,000 discount). Moreover, Hall did not want bids to be so low that the telephone companies would refuse to accept higher bids.

The End of Equal Access

46   In addition to increased competition and pricing pressures from AT&T, other factors were affecting the market. With the completion of the equal access process, telephone company construction budgets were declining 3–4 percent annually. Along with the decline in capital budgets was a corresponding increase in the expense budgets. As a result of this shift, telephone companies were expected to allocate more budget dollars toward upgrading equipment and less toward the purchase of new switches.

The Analog Switch Replacement Market

47   Following equal access, the next major determinant of growth in the U.S. telecommunications market was replacement of analog switches. These switches were analog stored program control (software driven) AT&T switches that were installed in the late 1960s and the 1970s. Exhibit 11 shows historical information and projections of the central office switch market by technology from 1988 through 1991. As indicated in Exhibit 11, analog switches accounted for 57 million lines of the total installed base in 1987, or 46 percent of the market, compared to a total of 36 million digital lines. The "Other" category represents older analog switches, which were electromechanical switches (no software).

48   Numerous factors were involved in analog replacement, which was estimated to be a $30 billion market over the next 30 years. Unlike other switches that had to be replaced, analog switches had been upgraded to support equal access requirements, since they were software driven. With depreciation service lives of 15–20 years, they would remain in the network until the early 1990s, assuming that the depreciation rates and regulatory positions did not change (switch replacement required approval from the appropriate state public utility commission). The latest versions of these switches offered a comprehensive set of centrex features, and they were large in terms of line size (30,000 to 55,000 lines). As such, a digital replacement switch would require both sufficient capacity and an equivalent set of centrex features.

49   These analog switches were usually housed in "wire centers," which were simply buildings that housed more than one type of central office switch and were typically located in high-growth metropolitan areas. Northern had a number of strategies to establish a presence in these wire centers, in the hope that this initial presence would provide a competitive advantage when an analog switch became available for digital replacement. Other vendors were marketing adjuncts for the analog switches, which were enhancements designed to prolong their life, while these same vendors worked to develop competitive digital switches. As such, these adjuncts were basically "stopgap" measures designed to meet a particular need and to buy additional time for R&D switch development.

EXHIBIT 11
Central Office Equipment Market by Technology, Total Market

	1986	1987	Projected → 1988	1989	(Thousands of Lines) 1990	1991
Installed base:						
Digital	27,048	36,560	45,230	54,072	62,693	72,057
Analog	56,143	57,022	57,426	57,854	56,750	54,800
Other	38,175	31,322	25,613	19,826	15,933	12,293
Total	121,366	124,904	128,269	131,752	135,376	139,150
Percent:						
Digital	22.3	29.3	35.3	41.0	46.3	51.8
Analog	46.3	45.6	44.8	43.9	41.9	39.4
Other	31.4	25.1	19.9	15.1	11.8	8.8
Demand:						
Digital	10,066	9,508	8,670	8,844	8,620	9,365
Analog	1,591	881	417	429	36	0
Total	11,657	10,389	9,087	9,273	8,656	9,365
Total Bell Operating Companies						
Installed base:						
Digital	14,509	21,341	27,389	33,553	39,997	46,966
Analog	53,899	54,729	55,114	55,451	54,317	52,379
Other	25,246	20,114	15,998	11,891	9,077	6,648
Total	93,654	96,184	98,501	100,895	103,391	105,993
Percent:						
Digital	15.5	22.2	27.8	33.3	38.7	44.3
Analog	57.6	56.9	56.0	55.0	52.5	49.4
Other	27.0	20.9	17.2	11.8	8.8	6.2
Demand:						
Digital	6,904	6,832	6,048	6,165	6,443	6,969
Analog	1,530	830	385	338	0	0
Total	8,434	7,662	6,432	6,502	6,443	6,969
Total Independent Operating Companies						
Installed base:						
Digital	12,539	15,219	17,841	20,519	22,696	25,091
Analog	2,244	2,293	2,312	2,403	2,433	2,421
Other	12,929	11,208	9,615	7,935	6,856	5,645
Total	27,712	28,720	29,768	30,857	31,895	33,157
Percent:						
Digital	45.2	53.0	59.9	66.5	71.0	75.7
Analog	8.1	7.9	7.8	7.8	7.6	7.3
Other	46.7	39.1	32.3	25.7	21.4	17.0
Demand:						
Digital	3,162	2,676	2,622	2,679	2,177	2,396
Analog	61	51	32	91	36	0
Total	3,223	2,727	2,654	2,770	2,213	2,396

Source: Northen Business Information, *Central Office Equipment Market: 1987 Edition*.

ISDN

50   Beyond the replacement of analog switches, the next phase of telecommunications technology was called ISDN (Integrated Services Digital Network). ISDN would allow the transmission of voice, data, and video simultaneously over the same facilities. With existing technology, voice, high-speed data, and video had to be transmitted separately or over separate lines. While business telecommunications in 1988 were 90 percent voice and 10 percent data, this ration was predicted to move to 50 percent/50 percent. Cost, space, and time constraints would require that voice and data be integrated over one network. +

51   ISDN would also allow standard interfaces between different pieces of equipment, such as computers; and it would free end users from concerns about whether new equipment from one vendor would interface with equipment made by another vendor, which an end user might already own.

52   Although universal standards for ISDN had yet to be resolved, useful applications were already apparent. Since ISDN phones were designed to display the calling number and the name assigned to the number on a small screen simultaneous with ringing, the party being called would be able to know where the call was coming from prior to answering. This call screening ability would provide opportunities to enhance 911 services (police, fire department, rescue squad, and the like) by immediately identifying the calling party's location and other useful information (such as a known medical condition or the location of the nearest fire hydrant) and by efficiently routing both the call and the information to all parties involved. A person served by ISDN could talk to her banker while looking at her account information on a computer terminal and send data instructions to move funds, simultaneously, on the same line.

53   ISDN was flexible, in that, from any ISDN telephone jack, one could connect a computer terminal, personal computer, file server, printer, facsimile or telex machine, or video camera. Equipment could be moved to any location without having to worry if a specific kind of cable were available. The various pieces of equipment could share a common ISDN loop for data and voice transmission, reducing or eliminating the need for modems and multiplexers. Data on an ISDN network could be transmitted at a rate of up to six times faster than standard analog networks but at a comparable cost.

54   Northern was positioning ISDN as its premier Meridian Digital Centrex software offering, since it offered both business voice features and high-speed data capabilities over a single line. Northern's strategy was to "migrate" end users from MDC to ISDN, stressing that existing MDC feature capabilities could serve customer needs today while ISDN standards and applications were being developed by industry regulatory organizations and other telecommunications equipment and computer vendors. In addition, MDC integrated with ISDN, with ISDN combining existing voice and data services while adding additional new features and sophisticated applications.

55   AT&T, on the other hand, had been advertising ISDN heavily to end users and was attempting to position it as a technologically superior *replacement* to centrex, rather than as a centrex enhancement. AT&T was pursuing this strategy since BRCS, its digital centrex offering, was perceived as being much less "feature-rich" than its analog centrex systems or Northern's Meridian Digital Centrex.

56   Northern Telecom placed the first successful ISDN phone call in the United States in November 1987, and it had a number of DMS sites in-service offering ISDN capabilities. In addition, both Northern Telecom and AT&T had numerous ISDN field trials and commercial applications scheduled with telephone companies and business end users throughout the country at specific sites during the 1988–90 time frame.

COMPETITION

57   In addition to the changing market and technological environments, Northern faced a number of strong competitors. Replacement of analog switches and ISDN were two potential markets attracting other equipment companies into the U.S. digital central office telecommunications market. Also, most of the telephone companies were interested in having a third equipment supplier, in addition to AT&T and Northern Telecom, to ensure that pricing and product development remained highly competitive.

58   Another potential opportunity/threat for Northern was that the seven Regional Holding Companies (RHCs) had petitioned Judge Green to lift the restrictions barring them from providing information services, going into the long distance business, and manufacturing terminals and central office switches through direct subsidiaries or joint ventures, or both.

59   Finally, although the level of competition was increasing, the number of competitors was actually decreasing. In 1979, there had been 30 major telecommunications equipment manufacturing companies in the developed world. Estimates were, however, that this number would decrease to 15 by 1989. Some experts estimated that a firm needed a 10 percent worldwide market share to survive. The worldwide telecommunications construction market was estimated to be $109 billion for 1988, up from $100 billion in 1987, with the United States accounting for 22 percent of this market.

60   Following is a discussion of some of Northern's competitors and the inroads each had made into the Bell operating companies.

Siemens

61   Siemens, a West German conglomerate, had sales of 8 billion DMs for its telecommunications segment in 1987 (sales for the entire company in 1987 were US$20 billion). Seventy-three percent of Siemens' total sales for the year were from Germany and Europe, with 10 percent from North America.

62   The headquarters for Siemens' U.S. telecommunications division was in Boca Raton, Florida. An R&D facility was also located at Boca Raton, while manufacturing sites were located at Cherry Hill, New Jersey, and Hauppauge, New York. Siemens had 25,000 employees in the United States.

63   Siemens' digital central office offering was the EWSD. It was available in three versions: DE3, with a maximum capacity of 7,500 lines; DE4, with a maximum capacity of 30,000 lines; and DE5, with a maximum capacity of 100,000 lines.

64   Siemens had announced ambitious feature roll out plans for its offerings, promising both centrex and ISDN feature parity with both AT&T and Northern Telecom. However, whether it could effectively leapfrog the software development intervals incurred by the industry leaders remained to be seen.

65   Siemens had made inroads with five of the seven RHCs: Ameritech, BellSouth, Bell Atlantic, NYNEX, and Southwestern Bell. Siemens' progress had been based primarily on both competitive pricing and the desire of the Bell Operating Companies to increase competition in the central office switch market.

66   In spite of its recent success, industry consultants cited operational/maintenance problems with the EWSD regarding system reliability, architecture, and compliance to Bellcore standards (Bell Communications Research, or "Bellcore," was a standards organization jointly owned by the seven RHCs.) However, heavy R&D efforts were underway to resolve these issues at Boca Raton, and Siemens was fully committed to adapting its products to U.S. market specifications.

67   Siemens had a $2.1 million contract with West Virginia University to develop computer-based training courses in the operation of EWSD central office equipment. In terms of joint ventures and acquisitions, the company purchased 80 percent of GTE's foreign transmissions operations in 1986.

Ericsson

68   Ericsson, a Swedish-based telecommunications company, had consolidated international sales of US$5.5 billion in 1987. Europe and Sweden accounted for 84 percent of the geographic distribution of total sales for the year, with the United States and Canada contributing 7 percent. Like Siemens, Ericsson was attempting to crack the hold that Northern Telecom and AT&T shared on the U.S. central office switch market. Ericsson had targeted the Bell Operating Company market in BellSouth, NYNEX, Southwestern Bell, and US West.

69   Ericsson's digital central office offering was the AXE 10. Ericsson had already installed the AXE in 64 countries, had a worldwide installed base of over 11 million lines, and dominated markets in the developing world. Like Siemens, Ericsson had announced aggressive feature roll out plans (bypassing years of software development by AT&T Technologies and Bell-Northern Research), which it might not be able to deliver.

70   The AXE was manufactured in 16 countries and was being made available by Ericsson's Network Systems Division in Richardson, Texas. No plans were underway to construct manufacturing facilities for the AXE in the United States, although Ericsson was considered to have superior skills in setting up manufacturing plants in foreign countries and in training local workers for skilled jobs.

71   Ericsson had made a number of recent strategic moves intended to strengthen its position in the United States. The company had reorganized by regions to serve more effectively the RHC markets; moreover, it had reorganized marketing for the division into the functional areas of market development, marketing communications, systems engineering, and marketing systems. Plans had been announced for a Technical Training Center at the company's U.S. headquarters in Richardson, Texas. In addition, Ericsson had announced that it would be working with IBM to develop private networking capabilities.

NEC

72   NEC had $13 billion in sales in U.S. dollars for 1987, $4 billion of which was from its "communications" segment. Geographic sales distribution percentages were classified as "domestic" (Japan) at 67 percent and "overseas" at 33 percent.

73   NEC's digital central office offering was the NEAX61E. The switch was primarily an ISDN adjunct that interfaced analog systems and grew into a full central office. As such, it was basically an interim offering that was designed to extend the life of analog switches while buying time to improve the product in the hopes of having a competitive offering ready when analog replacement began. NEC claimed that the NEAX61 was serving 4.8 million lines in over 250 sites in 40 countries.

74   NEC's U.S. headquarters was located in Irving, Texas, where production of the system was scheduled to begin by mid-1988. NEC had made inroads with four of the seven RHCs—Bell Atlantic, NYNEX, Pacific Telesis, and US West.

75   The company had recently announced plans for a Switching Technology Center in Irving, dedicated to developing software for central office switches and customer premises equipment. A second facility in San Jose, California, would develop software for intelligent transport networks,

transmission systems, data communications, and network management systems. NEC claimed that it was moving its software development closer to its customers.

76   A major problem that NEC had to overcome was one of perception. NEC's first attempt to enter the U.S. market with the NEAX61 in the early 1980s met with little success. The product was highly touted, launched, and subsequently withdrawn due to numerous performance issues. Many industry experts felt that NEC was again entering the market prematurely with a product that was not powerful enough to meet U.S. requirements to support advanced business features or large capacities.

Stromberg-Carlson

77   Stromberg-Carlson was a division of Plessy, a British telecommunications corporation. Plessy had 1987 revenues of $2.45 billion from all product lines. Because Stromberg was a division, reliable data on its 1987 financial performance was not available. Stromberg-Carlson's product offering was the DCO (Digital Central Office). It was available in three versions: the DCO-CS, which was a toll version of the DCO (7,000 trunks, maximum); the DCO-SE (a 1,080 line switch designed to serve as a rural central office); and the DCO (32,000 lines, maximum). In addition, Stromberg-Carlson offered a full line of remotes, ranging in size from 90 lines to 10,000 lines.

78   Unlike Siemens, Ericsson, and NEC, Stromberg-Carlson had been a player in the U.S. telecommunications marketplace for a number of years. Stromberg was a primary supplier to the independent operating companies and was committed to maintaining strong ties with them. Stromberg's strategy was to target small to mid-size central offices (5,000–12,000 lines), focusing on rural applications. While Stromberg's lack of a large switch limited the market it could address, its niche strategy had served it well over the years, in that it could economically provide digital central capabilities in small line sizes.

79   However, Stromberg was now trying to crack the Bell operating company market as well. The company had made inroads with BellSouth and Pacific Telesis and had recently signed a volume supply agreement with South Central Bell for the 1989–90 time frame.

80   Stromberg-Carlson's U.S. headquarters and DCO manufacturing facility were located in Lake Mary, Florida (a suburb of Orlando). While Stromberg stated that it had a manufacturing capacity of 1 million lines per year at the Lake Mary facility, less than half of this capability was being used.

81   In response to its agreement with South Central Bell, Stromberg-Carlson had recently opened sales offices in Birmingham, Alabama. The company had a small installation force and was negotiating with AT&T to arrange to install some of its switches in South Central Bell.

82   Stromberg-Carlson shipped its 1,000th remote in December 1987 and placed its 2 millionth line in-service in January 1988. Two hundred switches, 400 remotes, and 400,000 lines were shipped by Stromberg-Carlson to the U.S. market in 1987.

Alcatel N.V.

83   Alcatel was established in France in 1985 as a subsidiary of Alcatel S.A. In December 1986, the firm's present name was adopted with the transfer of assets from its parent, Compagnie General d'Electricite (CGE). At the same time, CGE and International Telephone and Telegraph (ITT) combined their telecommunications activities, with ITT assuming 37 percent ownership of Alcatel. Alcatel offered digital switches, cable and fiber optic transmission networks, and radio and satellite transmission systems. 1986 sales were 10.6 million French francs.

84   The ITT deal allowed Alcatel to gain a position in West Germany, Italy, and Spain. While Alcatel had been insignificant in the world telecommunications market, the arrangement with ITT set the stage for it to become a major equipment manufacturer. Alcatel's strengths in transmission facilities offset ITT's weakness in this area. ITT contributed a dominant position in switching throughout the European market. Although the acquisition introduced Alcatel to the U.S. Market, due to ITT's presence, it was not clear what effect this would have on the U.S. market. ITT had been working unsuccessfully for several years to develop a switch for the U.S. market.

CONCLUSION

85   Musing over the status of Northern's potential competitors, Hall Miller's gaze returned to the magazine on his desk. Overall, the *Communications Week* study had given Northern high marks relative to most of the competitors. However, there were shortcomings in particular areas he wanted to address. (Exhibits 12 and 13 contain the results of the study, segmented by Bell and independent operating company respondents.)

86   In terms of the changing market and increased competition, Hall felt Northern had a competitive advantage, in that the company had the largest installed base of digital switches of any vendor. This would help generate revenue through hardware and software extensions and new features prior to the replacement of analog switches. However, Hall had seen AT&T's 5ESS shipments reach parity in a relatively short time, and it seemed that competitors were popping up everywhere. In addition, 1988 MDC sales had been sluggish. Hall felt this was largely due to customer confusion resulting from AT&T's hype of ISDN.

87   Hall glanced out the window towards the Raleigh-Durham Airport. It was 5:20 P.M., and the highway was packed with traffic. He decided that he would develop a presentation for the regional marketing managers that outlined the division's position and presented a number of possible changes in the marketing strategy that the division could consider. This would generate discussion and help the group focus on the options that needed more in-depth study before a decision could be made.

88   Hall closed the magazine and placed it, along with several other pieces of information that had been gathered for him, in his briefcase. Despite the traffic and the work, he had to get home in time for his daughter's 6 P.M. soccer game. Perhaps he would be able to work on his analysis after supper.

EXHIBIT 12
Summary of Vendor Performance Rankings by Bell Operating Company Respondents

	AT&T	Ericsson	NEC	Northern Telecom	Siemens	Stromberg-Carlson
Initial cost	3.12	3.37	3.42	3.83	3.51	3.76
Life cycle cost	3.55	3.26	3.29	3.53	3.48	3.26
Strength of financial backing	4.66	3.48	3.74	4.24	4.05	3.05
Availability	3.90	3.36	3.29	4.17	3.40	3.56
Service/support	4.07	3.21	2.97	3.39	3.22	3.50
Reliability	4.06	3.31	3.08	3.52	3.47	3.24
Delivery	3.76	3.18	2.80	3.71	3.21	3.39
Experience in industry	4.88	3.97	3.34	4.29	3.78	3.91
High-technology company	4.63	3.77	3.69	4.28	4.08	3.23
Sound technical documentation	4.32	3.24	2.67	3.50	3.37	3.10
Breadth of product line	4.07	3.24	3.14	3.90	3.33	2.80
International experience	3.19	4.08	3.83	3.58	4.20	2.64
Long-term commitment to R&D	4.44	3.81	3.83	3.99	3.91	3.04

Scale of 1–5; 5 = excellent, 1 = poor.
N = 497.
Source: *Communications Week.*

EXHIBIT 13
Summary of Vendor Performance Rankings by Independent Operating Company Respondents

	AT&T	Ericsson	NEC	Northern Telecom	Siemens	Stromberg-Carlson
Initial cost	2.40	2.67	3.70	3.67	3.12	3.96
Life cycle cost	3.24	2.74	3.17	3.71	3.04	3.61
Strength of financial backing	4.65	3.31	3.69	4.34	3.65	3.50
Availability	3.56	2.61	3.22	4.06	2.93	4.03
Service/support	3.79	2.81	2.98	3.81	3.02	3.75
Reliability	4.23	2.80	3.41	4.08	3.25	3.63
Delivery	3.46	2.61	3.16	3.83	2.91	3.80
Experience in industry	4.74	3.27	3.55	4.58	3.62	4.19
High-technology company	4.72	3.35	3.93	4.45	3.84	3.72
Sound technical documentation	4.47	2.78	2.95	4.08	3.32	3.63
Breadth of product line	4.16	2.83	3.43	4.12	3.27	3.47
International experience	3.84	3.48	4.04	3.84	4.03	3.27
Long-term commitment to R&D	4.67	3.21	3.80	4.29	3.69	3.57

Scale of 1–5; 5 = excellent, 1 = poor.
N = 1,047.
Source: *Communications Week.*

CASE 19

CHRYSLER ACQUIRES AMERICAN MOTORS

1 On March 9, 1987, Chrysler Corporation and Renault of France (a major holder of American Motors stock) signed a letter of intent under which Chrysler would buy American Motors Corporation (AMC) in a deal initially valued at $1.11 billion involving both stocks, bonds, and cash. Under the original terms of the agreement Chrysler would trade $522 million in its stock for AMC's outstanding shares, give Renault a $200 million, 10-year, 8 percent note for its AMC interest, and pay Renault $35 million in cash. Wall Street's reaction was immediate—Chrysler's stock rose $1.50 per share to $53.875 and AMC's stock rose 75.0 cents to $4.25. Soon after this initial increase Chrysler's stock experienced a serious decline. During the week of April 13 its stock fell from $54.50 to $36.375 per share. Standard & Poor put Chrysler and AMC on its credit watch, while stating "Chrysler is paying roughly $2 billion in common stock, assumed debt and other obligations, including unfunded pensions and legal contingencies. In return, it's receiving a business with questionable prospects."[1]

2 The acquisition was ultimately approved by AMC's board of directors after Chrysler "sweetened" the offer by increasing the initial offer of $4.00 of Chrysler stock for each share of AMC stock to $4.50 a share (resulting in an exchange of $595 million, rather than the initial $522 million). Wall Street's reaction was again immediate—Chrysler's stock fell $1.250 to $34.125 and AMC's stock rose 12.50 cents to $4.25. On August 5, 1987, AMC's stockholders unanimously agreed to Chrysler's terms, thus ending the turbulent and often frustrated career of American Motors and the joining of that organization to an equally crisis-ridden automobile manufacturer.

3 Cash-rich Chrysler had been looking for an acquisition for quite awhile. In commenting on the AMC move, Chrysler chairman Lee A. Iacocca said, "We believe our decision to acquire American Motors is right for both companies—not just for the immediate future, but even more so for the long haul. . . . It'll strengthen both of us in what's already a tough market."[2] Whenever doubts about the advisability of making the acquisition were ever raised, Chrysler vice president Bennett Bidwell stated, "Iacocca kept banging us over the head saying, 'This is for the long haul. This is a once-in-a-lifetime opportunity to broaden the distribution network, get a brand and a new plant and go forward. You take the pimples and the warts along with the beauty marks.' "

This case was prepared by Joseph Wolfe, Management and Marketing Department, College of Business Administration, University of Tulsa.

Joel Garrott and Tisha Rohr assisted in the preparation of this case, which employs both public and privately obtained materials. The case is intended for class discussion purposes and does not exemplify either correct or incorrect managerial actions or decisions.

[1] "Chrysler Buyout of AMC Pleases Analysts," *The Tulsa Tribune,* March 10, 1987, p. B1.

[2] Jacob M. Schlesinger and Amal Kumar Naj, "Chrysler to Buy Renault's Stake in AMC; Seeks Rest of Company," *The Wall Street Journal,* March 10, 1987, p. 3.

CHRYSLER'S HISTORY

4   The Chrysler Corporation was founded by Walter P. Chrysler in 1921 with the purchase of the ailing Maxwell Motor Company. The first car to bear his name, the 6-cylinder "70" of 1924, was something of a sensation with its four-wheel contracting hydraulic brakes and 70 mph performance. Sales of 43,000 units were reported in 1925. By 1928, Chrysler laid the foundations to rival Ford in its total volume and General Motors in the number of models and cars it produced. The firm acquired the Dodge Brothers and launched two new makes, the Plymouth Four in the low price field and the DeSoto Six at the higher end of the price spectrum. The Chrysler Corporation sold 98,000 cars in 1929 and, by 1936, the firm was selling more cars than the once-mighty Ford Motor Company. The path to sales success, however, was not without its mishaps.

5   In 1934, Chrysler brought out its Airflow designs for both the DeSoto and Chrysler cars. While featuring a welded unitary body, which was 40 times more rigid than conventional designs, head-lights mounted flush in the body, and a completely aerodynamic shape, the cars were commercial failures and the cars were hurriedly supplemented by the Airstream line in 1935. For the next 20 years, the company's styling policy was basically cautious and conservative, and the firm empha-sized a car's engineering over its appearance. Despite Chrysler's conservative styling approach, one of its major competitors had problems of its own. The Ford Motor Company was still basically a one-car company, even though it had acquired the Lincoln motorcar in 1922 and had introduced the Mercury in 1939, and it was wracked with internal management strife and external union problems. By 1946, Chrysler had over 25 percent of the American automobile market and was number two behind General Motors in both 1947 and 1948, although by 1949 Ford usurped Chrysler's spot behind GM.

6   Over the next two and a half decades, Chrysler's overall market share generally deteriorated and slipped to as low as 9.6 percent of the market in 1962 and 8.5 percent in 1981.[3] (See Table 1.) At this time the firm instituted two financial policies. The firm employed debt to cushion itself from its more violent swings in demand, and it maintained a GM-type dividend policy to sustain its attractiveness to investors.

7   In the 1960s, under the guidance of Lynn Townsend (a former accountant with Touche, Ross), Chrysler expanded worldwide, with plants in Australia, South Africa, South America, and Europe. Two acquisitions—Simca in France and Rootes Motors, Ltd., in Great Britain—were failing com-panies when they were acquired and Chrysler was unable to turn them around. Additionally, they continued to siphon needed funds from American operations, which were beginning to become inefficient producers in their major market. One consultant at the time estimated that Chrysler's production costs were 10 percent per car higher than Ford's, and Ford itself was inferior to GM in its production efficiencies.

8   Chrysler also began to suffer an image problem. Although the firm attracted the more conservative customer, Chrysler executive Eugene Cafiero noted that its buyers were a little older and they had less income. Accordingly, they purchased fewer options and they kept their cars longer. To remedy this situation, Townsend offered "hot" cars, such as the Dodge Charger and Coronet, and the Plymouth Road Runner, Satellite, Barracuda and 'Cuda, while featuring cowgirls and hoopla as part of the firm's "Dodge Rebellion" advertising campaign. Unfortunately, the average Chrysler-product customer was not rebellious and felt abandoned or scorned by the company that had courted him and her so vigorously in prior years.

9   By the 1970's Townsend was still emphasizing large cars, although there were indications that

[3]*Automotive News,* April 30, 1980, p. 15.

TABLE 1
American Market Shares by Corporation (percent)

Year	GM	Ford	Chrysler	Independents*	Imports†
1946	37.7	21.9	25.7	14.5	—
1947	41.8	21.0	21.7	15.2	—
1948	40.6	18.8	21.4	18.6	0.4
1949	42.8	21.3	21.4	14.2	0.2
1950	45.4	24.0	17.6	12.8	0.2
1951	42.8	22.1	21.8	12.8	0.4
1952	41.7	22.7	21.2	13.4	0.7
1953	45.0	25.1	20.3	9.0	0.5
1954	50.7	30.8	12.9	5.0	0.5
1955	50.7	27.6	16.8	4.0	0.8
1956	50.7	28.4	15.4	3.6	1.6
1957	44.8	30.3	18.3	3.0	3.4
1958	46.3	26.4	13.9	5.2	8.1
1959	42.1	28.1	11.3	8.3	10.1
1960	43.6	26.6	14.0	8.2	7.5
1961	46.5	28.5	10.7	7.7	6.4
1962	51.8	26.3	9.6	7.3	4.8
1963	51.0	24.8	12.3	6.6	5.1
1964	49.0	26.0	13.8	5.1	6.0
1965	50.0	25.4	14.6	3.7	6.1
1966	48.1	26.0	15.3	3.1	7.3
1967	49.5	22.1	16.0	3.0	9.3
1968	46.7	23.7	16.2	2.9	10.4
1969	46.7	24.2	15.1	2.6	11.2
1970	39.7	26.4	16.0	3.1	14.6
1971	45.1	23.5	13.7	2.6	15.0
1972	44.4	24.3	13.8	3.0	14.5
1973	44.3	23.5	13.3	3.5	15.1
1974	41.8	24.9	13.5	3.9	15.7
1975	43.3	23.0	11.7	3.8	18.1
1976	47.2	22.4	12.9	2.6	14.8
1977	46.3	22.6	10.9	1.7	18.2
1978	47.6	22.9	10.1	1.5	17.7
1979	46.4	20.3	9.0	1.6	22.6
1980	45.9	17.2	8.8	2.0	26.1
1981	44.5	16.2	8.5	1.6	27.2
1982	44.0	16.9	8.6	1.4	27.8
1983	44.1	17.1	9.2	2.1	25.9
1984	44.2	19.0	9.5	1.8	23.5
1985	42.8	19.0	11.3	1.2	25.7
1986	41.2	18.2	11.5	0.7	28.4

* Includes Crosley, Hudson, Nash, Studebaker, Packard, and Kaiser-Frazer until early 1960s, AMC alone thereafter.

† Included Austin, Bantam, Fiat, Renault, and Volkswagen in the 1950s; changed to Datsun/Nissan, Toyota, Honda, Mercedes-Benz, Volvo, Saab, and Volkswagen in the 1960s.

Source: *Automotive News,* April 30, 1980, p. 15 for 1946–79 data; Motor Vehicle Manufacturers Association of the U.S., Inc., and Ward's Automotive Yearbooks for 1980–86 data.

Americans could no longer afford to own and operate them. The company spent $450 million restyling the full-size line, while GM introduced its small-sized Vega in 1971, Ford launched the Pinto, and AMC ushered in the Gremlin. Accordingly, Chrysler possessed no small cars when the Arab oil embargo began in 1973. With sales falling to unprofitable levels, Townsend lowered Chrysler's breakeven point by firing or laying off thousands of designers and engineers. Despite these economy moves, the firm lost $260 million in 1975, and Townsend was replaced by John Riccardo, another ex-accountant from Touche, Ross.

10   Riccardo created a $5.5 billion program designed to move Chrysler into the small car market, but his plan was destined for problems and delays. New models experienced production snafus and quality control problems, and product recalls were frequent, thus destroying the firm's hard-earned reputation for engineering excellence. By 1978 Chrysler's rebuilding program appeared to be on track as its new subcompact, front-wheel-driven Omnis and Horizons were named *Motor Trend* magazine's 1978 Car of the Year. Unfortunately, *Consumer Reports* labeled the same products "Not Acceptable" and stated so on the front cover of its July 1978 issue. These cars possessed what the magazine stated was an alarming directional instability at speeds greater than 50 mph. This same steering problem caused Canadian authorities to refuse the purchase of these vehicles for government use.

11   Riccardo's building program escalated an additional $2.2 billion and sales for all Chrysler products fell drastically. Losses amounted to $204.6 million, and the company found its financial resources dwindling. To cover long-term financial operations, Chrysler prepared to issue a block of preferred stock, even though both Moody's and Standard & Poor rated the issue speculative. Merrill Lynch completed the offering with an 11 percent dividend yield, while Chrysler continued to borrow heavily from insurance companies and banks.

12   With the arrival of Iacocca in December 1978 after being fired by Henry Ford over policy differences, Chrysler began another turnaround. During the next two years, many of the firm's foreign operations were sold off for cash to keep the firm afloat until it could design and launch a new fleet of more salable cars. In August 1978, Peugeot-Citroen purchased Chrysler's European subsidiaries for $230 million in cash, and Peugeot stock representing approximately 12.5 percent of its equity. In February 1979, GM purchased Chrysler's Venezuelan assembly plants and, the following year, bought the acquisition of Chrysler's equity in Chrysler Fevre Argentine and the purchase of Chrysler do Brasil by Volkswagen.

13   With falling sales and increasing losses it appeared that time would run out before Chrysler could bring its new highly-touted K-cars (Aries and Reliant) to market in 1981. Both Riccardo and Iacocca immediately began to lobby for government assistance. In late December 1979, Congress passed its famous Chrysler Motors loan guarantee bill, which called for contributions of $462.5 and $125.0 millions from respective union and nonunion employees. Additionally, Chrysler would issue $162.5 million in stock to its workers, the federal government would waive its status as senior creditor on $400.0 million of new bank loans and on loans from state and local governments, and on loans of $100,000 or less from small suppliers. The government would also establish a board to monitor the aid package and set a 0.5 percent to 1.0 percent fee on loan guarantees of $1.5 billion.

14   Although the government had stepped in to help Chrysler, the government's aid imposed a number of strategic restrictions on the firm's operations. Chrysler had to narrow the variety and assortment of its lineup of cars, could produce only four-cylinder front-wheel-driven cars, and had to withdraw from the heavy-duty truck industry; additionally, the firm had to use all its funds for internal operations. With these restrictions on Chrysler's strategic flexibility, Iacocca accelerated the repayment of the firm's debt as soon as increased sales and profits made it possible.

15   In April 1985, Chrysler increased its holdings in Mitsubishi Motors from 15 percent to 24 percent while announcing a joint venture in which it would market a Maserati sports car built in

EXHIBIT 1
Significant Events in Chrysler's History

Year	Event
1921	Company founded by Walter P. Chrysler.
1924	Chrysler car introduced.
1928	Firm acquires Dodge Brothers; introduces Plymouth and DeSoto automobiles.
1934	Airflow designs introduced.
1936	Chrysler Motors outsells Ford Motors for first time.
1946	Chrysler market share climbs to 25.7 percent.
1948	Independents obtain 18.6 percent of the American automobile market.
1949	Ford outsells Chrysler Motors.
1954	Ford obtains its peak market share of 30.8 percent.
1959	Imported cars obtain 10.1 percent of the American market.
1962	General Motors reaches its highest market share of 51.8 percent; Chrysler's market share falls to 9.6 percent.
1964	Ford Mustang introduced; imported cars take 6.1 percent of the market.
1966	U.S. government institutes strict automobile safety regulations, mandatory recall announcements, and emissions regulations.
1967	Air Quality Act passed in Congress.
1973	Imported cars take 15.1 percent of the market; OPEC cartel created.
1974	Chrysler loses $52 million.
1975	Lynn Townsend replaced by John Riccardo; firm loses $260 million.
1976	$7.5 billion down-sizing plan initiated; Chrysler loses $206 million; independents obtain 2.6 percent of American sales; 12.6 million American cars recalled.
1978	Lee Iaccoca hired; Chrysler loses money for next three years.
1979	Chrysler obtains a $1.5 billion loan guarantee package; firm loses $1.1 billion; Japanese cars take 22.6 percent of the American market.
1980	250,000 American automobile workers on layoff; GM loses $763 million, Ford loses $1.5 billion, and Chrysler loses $1.7 billion; GM budgets $40.0–$75.0 billion for capital investment until 1985.
1983	Honda opens a plant in Ohio; Nissan opens a truck manufacturing plant in Tennessee—cars to be produced there in 1985; Chrysler repays all guaranteed loans.
1986	Acquires Gulfstream Aerospace Corporation—sales of $634.7 million.
1987	Commits $12.5 billion to a five-year product and capital spending program in core autombile business.

Italy. Ford and GM were also courting European manufacturers, as well as buying up the stock of Alfa Romeo and Lotus. One year later, Chrysler announced its intention to acquire 51 percent of Maserati, while construction was started in Bloomington–Normal, Illinois, for a joint Chrysler-Mitsubishi assembly plant. In 1987, Chrysler announced that it would acquire Lamborghini in an attempt to compete with Mercedes and Porsche in the superluxury sports car market. Exhibit 1 presents a list of selected significant dates in the firm's history.

AMERICAN MOTORS' HISTORY

16 Chrysler's acquisition of AMC marks the demise of a firm with origins dating back to 1902 and the production at Kenosha, Wisconsin, of the one-cylinder Rambler by the Thomas B. Jeffery Company. As the American automobile industry began to mature in the early 1950s, the remaining independents that had been able to survive the Great Depression sought mergers with each other as a way to salvage or forestall their dwindling fortunes. Packard merged with Studebaker in 1954, but that combination failed by 1963, although the Packard itself was discontinued in 1958; Willys merged with Kaiser-Frazer in 1952, but they folded by 1955. American Motors was created in 1954 through the merger of the Nash-Kelvinator Corporation and the Hudson Motor Company. AMC was an innovator from its inception. By design or default it did not wish to follow the "Big Three." Bill Chapin, grandson of Roy Chapin, who was the founder of Hudson Motors, and son of Roy Chapin, Jr., AMC chairman from 1967 to 1978, described AMC's philosophy accordingly:

17 AMC made a very valiant attempt to separate themselves from General Motors and Ford and Chrysler and give themselves an identity that people would recognize in the marketplace.[4]

18 In a last-ditch effort to save the company in the late 1950s, AMC dropped its large Nash and Hudson cars and focussed its attention on the Rambler, which had been resurrected as a nameplate in 1950 as a 100-inch wheelbased economy car selling for $1,808. George Romney, a past AMC chairman and the major force behind the company's switch to compact cars, recalls how the Rambler forced the other American automakers to build compacts of their own:

19 It was successful. That was before any foreign cars penetrated the market. I talked about competitors' cars as being gas-guzzling dinosaurs and we ran very newsworthy advertisements selling the cars.[5]

20 After Romney left AMC in 1962 to pursue a political career, the firm began to abandon its small car strategy when it introduced a series of large cars and a sports car called the Javelin. In 1970, trying to escape the perception that it built boring cars for older and, equally-boring motorists, AMC dropped the Rambler and replaced it with an unsuccessful line of small cars featuring cute names and unique shapes—the Pacer (fish bowl), the Gremlin (triangular), and the Hornet (square).

21 The idea of differentiating themselves from the Big Three may have been sound, but problems accompanied the execution of their stand-alone strategy. AMC had planned to put GM's rotary engine in the Pacer, but GM dropped the engine and AMC had to use one of its older six-cylinder engines instead. Accordingly, the Pacer lost the fuel efficiency it was designed to deliver, and it also had to undergo front-end design changes to accommodate its replacement engine. Additionally, the fish-bowl-shaped large-windowed Pacer was an interesting design concept, but many felt it was ugly as well as being very difficult to air condition. The triangular-shaped Gremlin also had its problems. Although the name "Gremlin" was supposed to conjure images of fun and impish delight, the word *gremlin* was also a mechanic's term for describing a troublesome engine. The era was not all bad luck for AMC, for as it acquired the Kaiser Jeep Corporation in 1970—and the Jeep proved to be the only real money maker for the company.

22 In 1979, Regie Nationale des Usines Renault (Renault) began acquiring a stake in AMC as a method for securing a stronger foothold in the huge American automobile market. Renault would ultimately buy 46.1 percent of AMC's common stock, although the venture accumulated losses from 1979 to 1986 amounting to $839 million. Although many said it was wise for Renault to unload the perennial money-losing AMC, others believe that Renault/AMC was about to have its

---

[4]"Decline of AMC Started in 1960s," *The Tulsa Tribune*, March 10, 1987, p. B2.

[5]Ibid.

EXHIBIT 2
Significant Events in American Motors' History

Year	Event
1954	American Motors created from merger of the Hudson Motor Company and Nash-Kelvinator; Nash sells 62,911 cars while Hudson sells 50,660 units.
1955	AMC sells 194,175 cars, of which 83,852 were Ramblers and 45,535 were Hudsons.
1957	Nash and Hudson cars taken out of production; Rambler only car made by AMC.
1958	186,227 Ramblers sold—ranked seventh in American autombile sales.
1959	Record profits of $60.3 million on 401,446 units.
1962	George Romney leaves AMC.
1967	Roy Chapin, Jr., becomes chairman of the board.
1970	Rambler taken out of production; Pacer, Gremlin, and Hornet introduced; acquires Kaiser Jeep Corporation.
1978	W. Paul Trippett becomes chairman of the board.
1979	Renault of France acquires 22.5 percent of AMC stock for $150 million.
1980	Renault invests $310 million more in AMC stock—has 5 of 16 seats on the board of directors.
1983	AMC sells 226,580 cars.
1984	Records first profit after 14 consecutive quarters of losses; Jose J. Dedeurwaerder named AMC president—Renault officials occupy the three most important positions in AMC.
1986	AMC sells 77,005 cars; Jeep sales are 207,514, up 14.4 percent over 1985 sales; Joseph E. Cappy becomes president and CEO; Renault chairman Georges Besse assassinated by a French terrorist group.
1987	New Renault chairman Raymond Levy says profitability to be the holding company's main goal; Chrysler buys out AMC.

best year in 1987–88, with the introduction in 1987 of three new models—the Alpine sports car and the Medallion compact, which were both made in France, and the Premier, a family-sized car built in AMC's ultra-modern Bramalea, Ontario facility. Exhibit 2 traces AMC's history since its creation in 1954.

THE AMC ACQUISITION

23   **Terms.**   Chrysler's acquisition plan calls for the purchase of 50.5 million shares of AMC common stock for the equivalent of $4.50 a share, or approximately $226 million, with a new issue of 10-year, 8 percent Chrysler bonds. Other holders of AMC common (59.3 million shares) and convertible preferred (71.3 million shares) stock would receive Chrysler common stock, with a market value of about $4, for each share of AMC stock. The price was to be based on the value of Chrysler stock shortly before the transaction closed. Chrysler, however, said it would give AMC stockholders at least 0.0687 shares of Chrysler stock for each share of AMC stock. This could have the effect of pushing the value of the proposal above $4.50 per share of AMC stock, provided Chrysler stock rises above $65.50 a share. The cost of these AMC shares would total approximately $590 million, with an additional $35 million in cash going to Renault for its interest in AMC's finance subsidiary. (See Exhibit 3.)

EXHIBIT 3
End-of-Week Stock Prices, December 1986 to August 1987

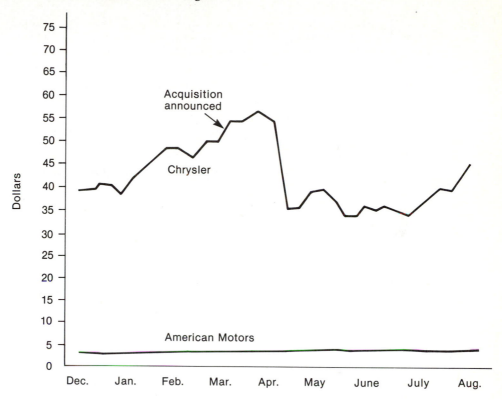

24   With the acquisition of American Motors, Chrysler must assume AMC's unfunded pension liabilities (somewhere in the area of $330 to $400 million) as well as its $767 million long-term debt. With about $25 million in transaction costs minus AMC's $120 million cash on hand, Chrysler will pay a minimum of about $2 billion for AMC. Additionally, Chrysler will agree to a profit-sharing arrangement with Renault tied to AMC's performance. If AMC's operations show a profit, Renault could ultimately receive an additional $350 million, which would result in a purchase price of over $2.3 billion. However, in the words of Robert Miller, Jr. who conducted the final negotiations for Chrysler, "The day we have to write a check for $350 million is the day we'll be laughing . . . all the way to the bank."

25   **Capacity.**   Chrysler currently has nine assembly plants, with a total capacity of 1.8 to 2.1 million vehicles per year. Because they have been running at about 100 percent capacity, Chrysler had been using AMC's Kenosha plant to assemble its Chrysler Fifth Avenue, the Dodge Diplomat, and the Plymouth Gran Fury full-sized passenger cars. Even with this subcontracted production, AMC was operating at only about 49 percent of its own full-time capacity. With the acquisition of AMC, Chrysler obtained 15 manufacturing facilities, four of which are assembly plants that add the capability of producing 796,000 vehicles to Chrysler's overtaxed production capabililty. One of the acquired assembly plants is AMC's state-of-the-art $675 million facility in Bramalea, Ontario, Canada—the most efficient automobile plant in North America. AMC's other plants—in Kenosha, Wisconsin; Brampton, Ontario; and Toledo, Ohio—are considered antiquated, and some analysts

EXHIBIT 4
Chrysler Assembly, Subassembly, and Distribution Facilities

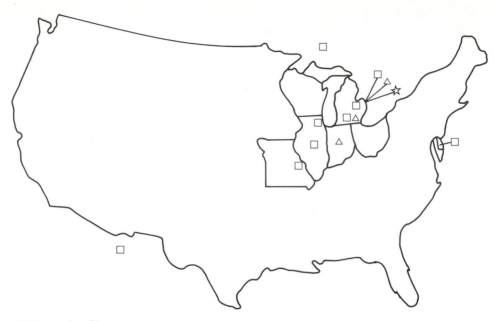

☐ Assembly Plants
   Detroit, Michigan
   Sterling Heights, Michigan
   Warren, Michigan
   Bloomington-Normal, Illinois
   Belvidere, Illinois
   Newark, Delaware
   Fenton, Missouri
   Canada
   Mexico

△ Sub-Assembly Plants
   Detroit, Michigan (glass)
   Trenton, Michigan (engines)
   Kokomo, Indiana (transmissions)

☆ Headquarters and Research and Development
   Detroit, Michigan

believe that at least parts of them will ultimately have to be shut down. Exhibits 4 and 5 present the locations of both Chrysler and AMC's major North American facilities.

26   Along with AMC's physical facilities, Chrysler also inherits its work force, which has been rather demoralized, due to the firm's dwindling profits and the continuous pressure of eminent layoffs and an unfunded retirement plan. United Auto Workers (UAW) locals at the Kenosha and Toledo plants used the threat of strikes as a lever to obtain the most lucrative contracts in the industry, including more paid vacations and a larger number of union officials on the AMC payroll. While workers at Chrysler and AMC receive approximately the same hourly wage rate, AMC's

EXHIBIT 5
American Motors Assembly, Subassembly, and Distribution Facilities

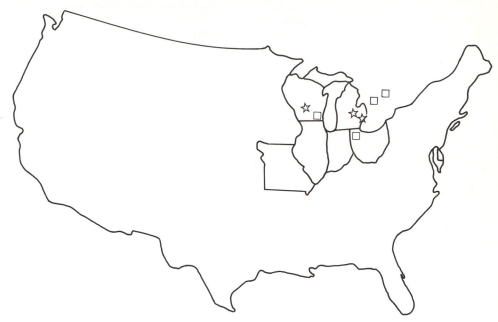

☐ Assembly Plants
    Kenosha, Wisconsin
    Toledo, Ohio
    Brampton, Ontario, Canada
    Bramalea, Ontario, Canada

☆ Administrative Offices and Research and Development
    Southfield, Michigan
    Detroit, Michigan
    Burlington, Wisconsin

labor costs are higher, due to differences in local union agreements and a relatively inefficient plant in Kenosha. In the two months preceding the acquisition, union members repeatedly resisted AMC's demands to slash wages and to make other work rules concessions, even though the firm said refusal would mean plant closings. When AMC received concessions in 1985, Toledo workers sabotaged Jeeps on the assembly line.

27   Most of AMC's 19,500 workers were delighted by the news of the buyout and felt that management was the cause of their problems. Cliff Shively, a worker at the Jeep plant, expects great things to come from the merger: "Whatever Iacocca touches turns to gold." The UAW's officialdom, which has had a long and stormy relationship with AMC in the past, is basically positive about the deal. As stated by UAW president Owen Bieber, the acquisition ". . . creates a good match that potentially points the way to a more secure future for workers at both companies."[6]

---

[6]Schlesinger and Naj, "Chrysler to Buy," p. 24

TABLE 2
American Motors' 1987 Product Line

AMC
    Eagle — 4-door $11,485
           — 4-door wagon $12,301
           — Limited $13,033

Renault
Alliance — 2-door $6,399–$7,625
         — 2-door hatchback $6,399–$8,499
         — 2-door convertible $11,099–$12,099
         — 4-door $6,599–$7,900
         — 4-door hatchback $7,250–$7,950

GTA — 2-door $8,999
     — 2-door convertible $12,899

Encore — base price $6,710

Medallion — 4-door DL $9,965
          — 4-door LX $10,479
          — 4-door wagon $10,693

Premier — $14,000 (approx.)

Alpine — $30,000 (approx.)

Jeep
Commanche — 4 wheel dr.—Short bed $9,877
           — 4 wheel dr.—Long bed $10,244
           — 2 wheel dr.—Short bed $6,995
           — 2 wheel dr.—Long bed $7,787

Wrangler — Saharah $11,995
        — Laredo $13,395
        — Base price $10,595

Cherokee — 2 wheel dr.—2 Door $10,441
        — 2 wheel dr.—4 Door $11,675
        — 4 wheel dr.—2 Door $12,415
        — 4 wheel dr.—4 Door $13,270

Wagoneer — Grand Wagoneer $24,623
        — Limited $21,926

28   **Product lines.** Chrysler acquires AMC's current product line, which, as shown in Table 2, includes AMC's Eagle, the Renault Alliance/Encore subcompact line, the newly introduced Renault Medallion, and the Jeep line, consisting of the Commanche, Wrangler, Cherokee, and Wagoneer. Additionally, Chrysler will market the Renault Alpine, a $30,000 sports car, and the Premier, both due for introduction in fall 1987. Chrysler's own product line is shown in Table 3. Table 4 provides excerpts from test reports on three of AMC's products as published by *Consumer Reports*.

29   Sales of the Alliance have been falling since its introduction in 1982, and the Encore's sales performance has also been disappointing; Chrysler officials have stated that these models will be discontinued (Table 5). The Medallion, priced at about $11,000 and the $14,000 Premier—both modern front-wheel-drive mid-size cars similar to models in the Chrysler fleet—are designed to compete against Ford's Taurus and Mercury Sable, Honda's Accord, and Toyota's Camry; the *Consumer Reports* evaluation of these four cars is excerpted in Table 6. In the short time since

TABLE 3
Chrysler's 1987 Product Line

Chrysler
Lebaron GTS — Highline $10,577
— Premium $12,192

Lebaron Formal — Sedan $11,121
— Wagon $12,669

Lebaron Coupe — Highline $11,720
— Premium $12,713

Labaron Convertible — Base $13,974

New Yorker — 4-door only $14,876

5th Avenue — 4-door only $16,446

Special-interest vehicle
Voyager Passenger Wagon — Standard Series $10,876
— Grand Series $12,216

Plymouth
Horizon America — 5-door $6,107

Sundance — Subcompact 2- or 4-door $7,999

Reliant — 2-door $8,778–9,222
— 4-door $8,778–9,222
— 4-door wagon $8,778–9,222

Caravell — 4-door sedan $10,238–10,952

Grand Fury — 4-door $11,780

Dodge

Shadow — $7,875	Charger — N.A.
Daytona — $10,025	Omni — $6,200*
Diplomat — $11,407	Aries — $6,995
Lancer — $10,482	Dodge 600 — $10,659
Ram Wagon — $12,469	Caravan — $10,887
Mini Ram Van (FWD) — $9,717	Dakota — $8,244
Ram van (RWD) — $10,047	Ram Pick Up — $8,793
Ram 50 Pick Up — $6,845	Ram Charger — $11,549
Colt — $5,899	Vista — $11,122

N.A. means not available.
* Estimated.

the introduction of the Medallion, dealers have been satisfied with its sales and are hoping that the Premier's sales will be an improvement over those of the Alliance. Chrysler itself is also concerned about sales for the Premier, because the terms of the acquisition call for a commitment by Chrysler to sell 300,000 Premiers between 1988 and 1992 or pay a penalty to Renault.

30   The Jeep line, which Iacocca calls "the best-known automotive brand name in the world," sold a record 207,514 units in 1986, capturing 4.5 percent of the American truck market. This accounts for over one fourth of the U.S. sports-utility segment of the truck market, which includes the Ford Bronco, Chevrolet Blazer, and Japanese imports, such as those made by Suzuki and Toyota.

TABLE 4
Selected Test Reports on AMC Products

AMC Eagle
Car features full-time four-wheel drive. Its old body design lacks interior room, especially in the cargo area of the wagon.*

Renault Alliance/Encore
The optional 1.7-liter 4 started easily and ran well. The 5-speed manual transmission shifted smoothly into the first four gears but awkwardly into fifth and reverse. The automatic transmission shifted smoothly. Weak acceleration with automatic and 1.4-liter 4. This front-wheel-drive car handled very well in normal driving, somewhat imprecisely at the track. Excellent braking. The front seats were very comfortable except for tall people, who needed more leg room. Most drivers wanted to sit higher; the steering wheel was to high and too horizontal. The *Alliance's* rear seat was uncomfortable for two or three; the *Encore's* rear seat was tighter and very uncomfortable for two or three. Fairly comfortable ride. Moderate noise level. Effective air-conditioning and ample ventilation, but slow, hard-to-modulate heating. Poorly designed horn control, not on steering wheel. Clear displays. Predicted reliability—much worse than average.†

Renault/Eagle Medallion
The *Eagle Medallion* offers comfort, conveniences, and performance far more impressive than those of Renault products we've tested in the past. However, every Renault model sold in this country has turned out to be relatively troubleprone. People who have owned *Renaults* probably wouldn't leap at the chance to buy another—even under another name. Although Chrysler, in its agreement with AMC, has pledged to sell and service the car for five years, buyers considering the *Eagle Medallion* must come to grips with the possibility that the car could have a short future in this country.

The best choices in the compact class remain the *Toyota Camry,* the *Mitsubishi Galant,* and *Mazda 626,* and the *Nissan Stanza.* Domestic models that have scored quite well in our tests include GM's *Buick Skylark, Oldsmobile Calais,* and *Pontiac Grand Am.*‡

* "Summary Judgements of the 1987 Cars," *Consumer Reports* 52, no. 4 (April 1987), p. 218.

† "Buying a Used Car," *1987 Buying Guide Issue* 51, no. 12, pp. 62ff.

‡ "Road Tests: Eagle Medallion, Chevrolet Corsica," *Consumer Reports* 52, no. 11 (November 1987), pp. 708–11.

TABLE 5
Unit Sales of AMC Product Line

Make/Model	1985	1984	1983
AMC			
Eagle	12,776	20,654	31,207
Renault			
Alliance	71,494	100,366	126,008
Encore	39,179	69,235	20,182
Jeep*	234,973	188,272	111,950

World Wholesale Unit Sales

	1986	1985	1984	1983
Automobiles	66,372	151,481	248,955	270,019
Jeep vehicles	221,362	240,769	193,428	113,443
Total	287,734	391,769	442,383	383,462

* Production figures, rather than unit sales.

Source: 10K reports.

TABLE 6
Selected Test Reports on Medallion and Premier Competition

Ford Taurus/Mercury Sable
Both the 3-liter V6 and the 2.5-liter 4 started and ran well. With the V6, the overdrive automatic transmission usually shifted very smoothly. With the 4, the automatic transmission shifted smoothly, but acceleration was not more than adequate. This front-wheel-drive model handled very well; the wagon version was especially competent. Fairly long stopping distances and considerable brake fade, but stops were straight. Exceptionally comfortable front seats. Excellent driving position with power seat; but without the power adjustment, the seat was too low and the steering wheel too high. Rear seat fairly comfortable for two or three. Quiet inside. Stable, tightly controlled ride on all but the bumpiest roads. Excellent climate-control system. Excellent controls and displays. Predicted reliability—worse than average, but no specific trouble spots have shown up in the first partial year.

Honda Accord
The 2-liter 4 sometimes stalled once after a cold start and occasionally hesitated while warming up. The 4-speed automatic transmission usually shifted smoothly. This front-wheel-drive car handled very well. Very good brakes. Very comfortable front seats; low, sporty-car driving position. Rear seat uncomfortable for two or three. Moderate noise level. Firm ride with good control. Excellent climate-control system. Excellent controls and displays. Predicted reliability—much better than average.

Toyota Camry
The 2-liter 4 started and ran very well. The automatic overdrive transmission shifted smoothly; it provides a choice of Power or Normal range. This front-wheel-drive model handled steadily and accurately. Excellent brakes. Exceptionally comfortable front seats. Excellent driving position, with plenty of adjustment. Rear seat very comfortable for two, comfortable for three. Moderate noise level. Smooth, soft ride. Excellent climate-control system. Excellent controls and displays. Predicted reliability—no data; new model. Previous *Camry* models have been much better than average.

Source: "Summary Judgements of the 1987 Cars," *Consumer Reports* 52, no. 4 (April 1987), pp. 225, 220, 222.

Although Chrysler has been highly successful with its innovative minivans, the company is not represented in the sports-utility segment of the truck market. Robust growth is forecast for this segment, with sales expected to increase from 732,000 in 1986 to 1.15 million in 1991. Table 7 shows the market shares obtained by the major manufacturers participating in the utility and recreational vehicle market in the United States from 1984 to 1986. Chrysler could have developed its own new vehicle comparable to the Jeep, but the investment would have ranged from $1.1 to $2.0 billion and would have taken several years.

31   Jeep, although a number of its subassemblies have been manufactured by General Motors in the past, has other problems of longer-term consequences. Refer to Table 8 for relevant information. Over $1.7 billion in product-liability suits have been filed against AMC for turnover accidents in Jeeps. Those injured claim that, among other problems, the vehicle's rollbar offers inadequate protection. Under the acquisition agreement, Chrysler assumes liability for any damages assessed up to an undisclosed ceiling, and Renault will help pay any payments above that undisclosed amount.

32   **Distribution.** Chrysler's network of 4,026 dealers would expand by about one fourth, with the addition of 1,472 AMC dealerships. Table 9 itemizes the number of franchised dealers existing in the United States by manufacturer. Chrysler executives say they will operate the AMC dealer network as a third distribution system, separate from Dodge and Chrysler-Plymouth at least temporarily, while working eventually to integrate their product development teams. Given AMC's past sales records, the strength of its dealerships is questionable. Christopher Cedergren, of J. D. Powers & Associates, a company that studies consumers' perceptions of the quality and image of

TABLE 7
Utility and Recreational Vehicle Market Shares

	1986	1985	1984
General Motors	31.2%	35.9%	36.1%
Ford	27.6	29.3	29.9
American Motors	12.9	12.9	13.5
Toyota	11.6	9.8	8.7
Chrysler	4.8	4.3	5.3
Nissan	4.1	4.9	4.6
Suzuki	3.5	—	—
Isuzu	3.2	2.4	1.1
All others	1.1	0.5	0.8

Share of U.S. Light Truck Market, 1986*

Chrysler	12.8%
American Motors	4.5%

* Includes utility vehicles.

TABLE 8
Selected Test Reports on Jeep and Similar Vehicles

The Yugo GV, the Hyundai Excel, and the American Motors Corporation's Jeep Comanche received the lowest scores in the latest round of government frontal crash tests at 35 miles per hour, suggesting an increased likelihood of head injuries to occupants of those automobiles. . . .

The government permits a vehicle a maximum score of 1,000 in the head-injury category for a 30-mph crash, but it does not set a requirement for 35-mph crashes. It is generally agreed a score exceeding 1,000 indicates a higher risk of head injury, with the potential for injury rising as the score increases.

In the safety agency's latest crash tests, which involved eight vehicles, the Jeep Comanche pickup scored 2,700 in the head-injury category on the passenger side of the vehicle. This is the highest head-injury score posted for either the driver or passenger side by any of 11 vehicles tested so far this year. The Comanche's driver-side score was 1,052. . . .

The Comanche also scored above the level thought to indicate an increased risk of chest injury to the driver. The Hyundai and Yugo had better scores on the chest-injury test.

Source: *The Wall Street Journal,* June 12, 1987, p. 40.

cars sold in the American market, addresses Chrysler's challenge in attempting to improve AMC's dealerships:

33   What [Chrysler's] got to do is to weed out the weaker dealers and bring in the stronger ones. Attracting good dealers shouldn't be all that hard now, however. I'd say that the value of a Jeep/Renault dealership is considerable higher now that it was [before the acquisition].

34   Chrysler and AMC dealers have differing views on the benefits of the merger. James Kelel, a part owner of a Renault/Jeep dealership in Detroit, says, "I see more products coming down the road in the future for us. We haven't had many products to sell for a long time."[7] Ian Steedman,

[7]Ibid.

TABLE 9
Domestic Dealerships by Manufacturer

	1986	1978	1977	1976
General Motors	11,570*	11,565	11,610	11,670
Ford	6,745*	6,723	6,722	6,712
Chrysler	4,026	4,786	4,822	4,811
American Motors	1,472	1,661	1,612	1,690
	Domestic Dealerships			
	1987	1986	1985	1984	1983
Chrysler	4,038*	4,026	4,007	3,994	3,872
American Motors	1,500*	1,472	1,562	1,624	1,709

* Estimated.
Source: 10K and stockholders' reports.

a sales representative with a Tulsa Jeep/Renault dealership concurs; "Iacocca's riding high right now—I don't see how we can lose. We'll have more stability with Chrysler backing us financially. Plus, the Fifth Avenues will be shipped for us to sell here and we need a car like that in this market."

35   On the other hand, Joel Beja, sales manager at a Hempstead, Long Island, Dodge dealership saw things differently:

36   Right now, I have ten Chrysler, Dodge, and Plymouth dealers within 15 minutes' drive from me. I'm not thrilled about AMC dealers selling Chrysler cars. We're already saturated here.[8]

BIBLIOGRAPHY

1986–87 Industry Norms and Key Business Ratios. N.Y.: Dun and Bradstreet, 1987.

1987 Almanac of Business & Industry Financial Ratios. Englewood-Cliffs, N.J.: Prentice-Hall, 1987.

"AMC Turning Over Retail Financing Line to Chrysler Corp." *The Wall Street Journal.* June 16, 1987, p. 48.

Automotive News. April 30, 1980, p. 15.

"Buying a Used Car." *1987 Buying Guide Issue* 51, no. 12, pp. 56–89.

"Chrysler Buyout of AMC Pleases Analysts." *The Tulsa Tribune,* March 10, 1987, p. B1.

"Decline of AMC Started in 1960s." *The Tulsa Tribune.* March 10, 1987, p. 2B.

Jeffreys, Steve. *Management and Managed: Fifty Years of Crisis at Chrysler.* Cambridge: Cambridge University Press, 1986.

MVMA Motor Vehicle Facts and Figures. Detroit: Motor Vehicle Manufacturers Association, 1987.

"Road Tests: Eagle Medallion, Chevrolet Corsica." *Consumer Reports* 52, no. 11 (November 1987), pp. 708–11.

Schlesinger, Jacob M. "AMC Accepts Sweetened Bid from Chrysler." *The Wall Street Journal.* May 21, 1987, p. 8.

[8]Ibid.

Schlesinger, Jacob M., and Amal Kumar Naj. "Chrysler to Buy Renault's Stake in AMC; Seeks Rest of Company." *The Wall Street Journal*. March 10, 1987, p. 3.

Standard NYSE Stock Reports, June 5, 1987. N.Y.: Standard & Poor's Corp.

Standard NYSE Stock Reports, July 21, 1987. N.Y.: Standard & Poor's Corp.

"Summary Judgements of the 1987 Cars." *Consumer Reports* 52, no. 4 (April 1987), pp. 210–229.

Ward's Automotive Yearbook. Detroit: Ward's Communications, 1984.

"Yugo, Hyundai and Jeep Model Vehicles Fare Poorly in Safety Agency Crash Test." *The Wall Street Journal*. June 12, 1987, p. 40.

Zammuto, Raymond F. *Assessing Organizational Effectiveness*. Albany: State University of New York Press, 1982.

APPENDIX A

Selected Financial Results for Chrysler Motors (000s)

Fiscal Year Ending	12/31/86	12/31/85	12/31/84
Assets			
Cash	$ 285,100	$ 147,600	$ 75,200
Marketable securities	2,394,300	2,649,900	1,624,900
Receivables	372,500	207,500	332,200
Inventories	1,699,600	1,862,700	1,625,900
Other current assets	612,500	445,800	321,700
Total current assets	5,364,000	5,313,500	3,979,900
Property, plant, & equip.	8,885,300	7,304,400	6,247,700
Accumulated depreciation	(2,767,500)	(2,664,800)	(2,534,500)
Net plant & equipment	6,117,800	4,639,600	3,713,200
Invest. & advances to subsidiaries	2,307,300	2,070,400	1,240,900
Other noncurrent assets	674,100	—	—
Deposits & other assets	—	581,800	128,700
Total assets	14,463,200	12,605,300	9,062,700
Liabilities			
Notes payable	119,800	195,300	6,700
Accounts payable	2,958,300	2,504,500	2,323,000
Current long-term debt	82,200	101,600	42,800
Accrued expenses	1,960,700	1,927,800	1,698,900
Income taxes	—	—	13,600
Other current liabilities	—	—	30,700
Total current liabilities	5,121,00	4,729,200	4,115,700
Deferred charges	712,400	690,200	21,700
Long-term debt	2,334,100	2,366,100	760,100
Other long-term liabilities	950,900	604,500	859,300
Total liabilities	9,118,400	8,390,000	5,756,800
Net common stock	229,800	153,200	123,900
Capital surplus	1,866,600	1,943,200	2,325,300
Retained earnings	3,567,500	2,153,300	921,200
Treasury stock	319,100	34,400	64,500
Shareholder equity	5,344,800	4,215,300	3,305,900
Total liabilities and net worth	$14,463,200	$12,605,300	$9,062,700

Chrysler Income Statement

Fiscal Year Ending	12/31/86	12/31/85	12/31/84
Net sales	$22,586,300	$21,255,500	$19,572,700
Cost of goods sold	18,635,200	17,467,700	15,528,200
Gross profit	3,951,100	3,787,700	4,044,500
Selling, general, & administrative expenses	1,613,100	1,576,800	1,255,000
Depreciation & amortization	543,600	263,700	554,400
Nonoperating income	563,600	422,500	195,200
Interest expense	32,700	—	—
Pretax income	2,325,300	2,369,800	2,430,300
Provision for income taxes	921,700	734,600	934,200
Extraordinary items	—	—	883,900
Net income	$ 1,403,600	$ 1,635,200	$ 2,380,000

Ratio Analysis

Fiscal Year Ending	12/31/86	12/31/85	12/31/84
Quick ratio	0.60	0.64	0.49
Current ratio	1.05	1.12	0.97
Receivables turnover	60.63	102.44	58.92
Inventories turnover	13.29	11.41	12.04
Inventories days sales	27.09	31.55	29.91
Current debt/equity	0.02	0.02	0.01
Total debt/equity	0.45	0.59	0.24
Net income on sales	0.06	0.08	0.12
ROA	0.10	0.13	0.26
ROE	0.26	0.39	0.72

Stock Information: Week Ending 7/16/87

Outstanding shares (000): 214,052
Volume: 4,140,300

High: 39.125
Average: 38.750
Low: 36.000

Market value (000): 8,294,515
EPS: 5.98
Price/earnings ratio: 6:4

Source: 10K reports.

APPENDIX B

Selected Financial Results for American Motors (000s)

Fiscal Year Ending	12/31/86	12/31/85	12/31/84
Assets			
Cash	$ 145,198	$ 143,324	$ 92,641
Receivables	230,620	224,954	154,828
Inventories	369,358	413,441	468,986
Other current assets	43,491	37,843	65,020
Total current assets	788,667	819,562	781,475
Property, plant, & equip.	1,659,092	1,398,602	1,272,252
Accumulated depreciation	(412,015)	(371,052)	(341,808)
Net plant & equipment	1,247,077	1,027,550	930,444
Invest. & advances to subsidiaries	129,512	90,007	73,471
Deposits & other assets	60,086	63,825	44,770
Total assets	2,225,342	2,000,944	1,830,160
Liabilities			
Notes payable	9,349	2,000	—
Accounts payable	303,462	275,676	236,665
Current long-term debt	16,951	155,559	200,973
Accrued expenses	289,599	323,920	286,222
Income taxes	—	—	—
Other current liabilities	136,712	59,355	73,788
Total current liabilities	756,073	816,510	797,648
Long-term debt	105,123	561,403	429,092
Other long-term liabilities	985,608	400,072	252,153
Total liabilities	1,846,804	1,777,985	681,245
Preferred stock	145	73,744	72,508
Net common stock	1,167	183,461	183,460
Capital surplus	993,537	482,632	482,631
Retained earnings	(596,055)	(498,235)	(371,694)
Treasury stock	(20,256)	(18,643)	(15,638)
Shareholder equity	378,538	222,959	351,267
Total liabilities and net worth	$2,225,342	$2,000,944	$1,830,160

American Motors Income Statement

Fiscal Year Ending	12/31/86	12/31/85	12/31/84
Net sales	$ 3,462,504	$ 4,039,901	$ 4,215,191
Cost of goods sold	2,858,284	3,504,791	3,594,229
Gross profit	604,220	535,110	620,962
Selling, general, & administrative expenses	480,047	445,265	425,501
Depreciation & amortization	155,108	136,879	114,034
Nonoperating income	23,968	12,712	28,064
Interest expense	84,352	90,941	94,022
Pretax income	(91,319)	(125,263)	(15,469)
Provision for income taxes	—	—	—
Extraordinary items	—	—	4,500
Net income	$ (92,319)	$ (125,263)	$ 19,969

Ratio Analysis

Fiscal Year Ending	12/31/86	12/31/85	12/31/84
Quick ratio	0.50	0.45	0.31
Current ratio	1.04	1.00	0.98
Receivables turnover	15.01	17.96	27.22
Inventories turnover	9.37	9.77	8.99
Inventories days sales	38.40	36.84	40.05
Current debt/equity	0.04	0.70	0.57
Total debt/equity	0.32	3.22	2.19
Net income on sales	(0.03)	(0.03)	0.00
ROA	(0.04)	(0.06)	0.01
ROE	(0.24)	(0.84)	0.06

Stock Information: Week Ending 7/16/87

Outstanding shares (000): 139,122
Volume: 2,844,000

High: 4.750
Average: 4.250
Low: 4.125

Market value (000): 591,268
EPS: −00.67
Price/earnings ratio: −6:3

Source: 10K reports and Value Line reports.

APPENDIX C

1986 Ratio Analysis of Ford and General Motors

	Ford	GM
Quick ratio	0.77	0.67
Current ratio	1.18	1.17
Receivables turnover	17.98	9.10
Inventories turnover	10.83	11.65
Inventories days sales	33.25	30.90
Current debt/equity	0.09	—
Total debt/equity	0.23	0.13
Net income on sales	0.05	0.03
ROA	0.09	0.04
ROE	0.22	0.10

Stock Information for Ford and General Motors: Week Ending 7/16/87

	Ford	GM
Outstanding shares (000)	268,400	317,810
Volume	5,073,700	4,072,900
High	107.250	85.375
Average	107.000	83.250
Low	101.000	80.500
Market value (000)	28,718,800	26,457,682
EPS	15.35	7.31
Price/earnings ratio	6:9	11:3

Source: 10K reports.

APPENDIX D

Consolidated Postacquisition 1986 Pro Forma Results (000s)

Assets:	
Cash	$ 395,298
Marketable securities	2,394,300
Receivables	603,120
Inventories	2,068,958
Other current assets	655,991
Total current assets	6,117,667
Property, plant, & equip.	10,544,392
Accumulated depreciation	(3,179,515)
Net plant & equipment	7,364,877
Invest. & advances to subsidiaries	2,436,812
Other noncurrent assets	674,100
Deposits & other assets	60,086
Total assets	16,653,542
Liabilities	
Notes payable	129,149
Accounts payable	3,261,762
Current long-term debt	99,151
Accrued expenses	2,250,299
Income taxes	—
Other current liabilities	136,712
Total current liabilities	5,877,073
Deferred charges	712,400
Long-term debt	2,639,223
Other long-term liabilities	1,936,508
Total liabilities	11,165,204
Net common stock	230,419
Capital surplus	1,798,175
Retained earnings	3,151,380
Treasury stock	308,364
Shareholder equity	5,723,338
Total liabilities and net worth	$16,653,542

Estimated Postacquisition Income Statement

Net sales	$26,048,804
Cost of goods sold	21,493,484
Gross profit	4,555,320
Selling, general, & administrative expenses	2,093,147
Depreciation & amortization	698,708
Nonoperating income	587,568
Interest expense	117,052
Pretax income	2,233,981
Provision for income taxes	921,700
Extraordinary items	—
Net income	$ 1,312,281

Looking back, Magee attributes the sales take-off after the telephone installation to corporations desiring to purchase the product, but first calling to ascertain that the company existed.

22   Although he completed the writing of version 4.0 by April of that year, it took six months to bring the product to market. He hired a technical writer to write the manual, and then typeset it himself on a Macintosh. The lack of a manual had been a big customer complaint. The product finally was shipped in October 1986. Magee professes that at that time he knew nothing about diskettes, manuals, or packaging. He learned by talking with people, and joined numerous PC user groups and actively attended meetings. He served as program director for the Atlanta PC User's Group. He also became heavily involved in the Southeastern Software Association, a group that two years later named him Software Entrepreneur of the Year.

23   That fall, Magee Enterprises exhibited at Comdex for the first time. Comdex is the computer industry's leading mega-trade show, is held semiannually, and is heavily attended by vendors, as well as users of systems. Vendors rent booths and exhibit their new products to dealers, and users are treated to elaborate demos and gimmicks to entice them to buy. Considerable press speculation takes place prior to Comdex as to whom and what will make its debut. Comdex is regarded as a barometer for the direction of the industry.

ASSOCIATION OF SHAREWARE PROFESSIONALS

24   A collection of about 150 prominent shareware authors, including Magee, formed the Association of Shareware Professionals (ASP) in spring 1987. Magee has served as founding president and as press liaison, and currently (1990) serves as vice president.

25   All of the association's meetings are conducted through CompuServe. The association has a forum in which to exchange business ideas, help individual authors, and set standards that will boost shareware's quality and credibility with the corporate buyer. Shareware distributors who display the ASP logo agree to distribute only the most current versions of shareware, to respect shareware authors' copyright requirements, and to follow an honesty-in-advertising rule. Ads must attempt to educate users about shareware and must include the statement "Shareware programs require separate payment to the authors if found useful."

26   ASP members are also expected to follow a code of conduct and representation that gives users consistency in terminology and business practices. In addition, ASP offers a list of all ASP-member products, complete with full descriptions and current version numbers, and are available on numerous bulletin boards. Consumers with complaints may go to ASP's ombudsman who manages the dispute-resolution service.

PRODUCTS

27   Automenu is a menu utility program for DOS, geared to corporate PC users who run multiple applications. It permits the user to create custom-designed menus to organize, control, and automate access to application programs, and to execute DOS commands and batch files. The menu system reduces the need for training of personnel in DOS and the finer points of computer systems.

28   Treeview was found by Magee on a bulletin board. The author agreed to sell total rights of the product. Changes were incorporated and the product's name was changed, because of a trademark conflict. In the product's first three months of sales, its sales were two and a half times the price paid for the product. When the product appeared on the market, one reviewer commented to the

effect that now we know what Magee Enterprises has been doing, they have been working on a new product—Treeview—another great product from Magee Enterprises.

29   Magee continues to look on bulletin boards for products. He states that he is only interested in a total buyout and won't consider a royalty arrangement. The company has also hired a programmer to write new programs.

PRODUCT SUPPORT

30   For technical support or electronic information, customers can call Magee Enterprises' bulletin board, The Big Peach, which operates 24 hours a day, seven days a week. About 150 calls per day are handled in this manner. The company also has one direct technical support line available for customers to call with technical questions about products. There are also two incoming 800 numbers, one designated for sales information, and the other for orders.

31   To become a registered user, the customer returns the warranty registration card included in the package. Magee Enterprises maintains a database on all registered users, and they are notified of product upgrades as they become available. In the early days, records of early users were not systematically kept and updated, and consequently, the database of early registrants is incomplete. All registered users receive a copy of the newsletter, *The Echo,* issued twice, since January 1989.

MARKETING

32   Automenu and Treeview are now distributed through a combination of dealers, distributors, direct sales, and the shareware concept. Originally, Automenu was distributed only through shareware. When corporations requested Automenu, dealers called Magee Enterprises, first having to locate the company. Consequently, Magee developed appropriate pricing and moved into traditional software distribution channels. A comparison of Magee Enterprises' market distribution between 1989 and 1990 is presented in Exhibit 1. The company will continue to increase its emphasis on more traditional marketing channels. The advertising budget for 1989 was 5 percent of sales, and plans are to increase the dollar amount of the 1990 advertising budget by 100 percent.

33   The large majority of Magee Enterprises' registered users are corporations. Only honesty motivates the user to send in the registration fee, although vendors, including Magee Enterprises, try to make it easier for managers to spot unregistered shareware. At one time, registered Automenu disks were blue and had a registration number, while shareware disks were gray with an "SW" serial number. Registered Treeview diskettes were green; and shareware diskettes were yellow. In return for the registration fee, Magee Enterprises sends the customer a manual, notice of updates and new product availability, and access to free technical support. A minimal charge is made for upgrades as they become available.

34   Magee views shareware as an important marketing concept for the company to get people to evaluate the product. Magee estimates that he gives away 20,000 to 30,000 diskettes a year. He explains that if he gives away 3,000 diskettes at a trade show and if 2 percent of the people pay, then that pays for all the disks. If 7 percent pay, that pays for his participation in the entire show.

35   The company changed its policy for handing out shareware copies of its programs beginning with the fall 1989 Comdex trade show. In the past, shareware were handed out to anyone who approached the booth. Now, employees explain the product (shareware) and impress upon the customer that the shareware diskette is an evaluation copy and if they are going to use it, they

EXHIBIT 1
Product Distribution Profile, 1989 versus 1990 (in percent)

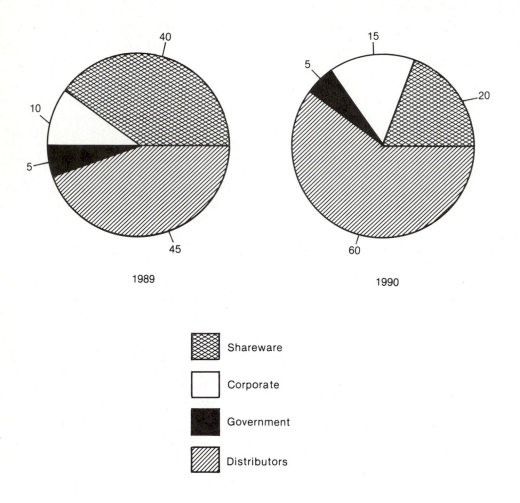

1989   1990

Shareware

Corporate

Government

Distributors

should send their registration fee. Since instituting this policy, the number of diskettes given away has decreased dramatically.

36   Magee has used a one-to-one swap with other customers as a last resort, a practice that he said makes competitors furious. Magee tells the story of purchasing agent who once called him about purchasing 500 copies of Automenu. The purchasing agent's boss was furious because rather than purchase Automenu he had purchased a competitor's product. The boss had heard that Automenu was the best product. The purchasing agent was scared he would lose his job over the incident and

---

EXHIBIT 2
Product Pricing History

	Date Price Effective	Price
Automenu	March, 1983	$20.00
	March, 1984	30.00
	March, 1986	50.00
	July, 1989	69.95
Treeview	November, 1988	$39.95
	June, 1989	50.00
	June, 1990	25.00

---

was hopeful that Magee might offer him a special price on 500 copies. Instead of charging him, Magee gave a one-to-one swap of the competitor's products in return for his promise to purchase all future copies from Magee.

Pricing

37 When questioned about how he set the price of Automenu, Magee related that someone had once told him to add up all his product costs and multiply by five. He did this and, still thinking it did not look right, decided to double the price. The product's price history is presented in Exhibit 2.

38 By early 1989, Magee considered raising the price again because major competitors were over $40. As shareware products have attained traditional commercial-level acceptance, price increases typically follow in order to better position themselves with their competitors. Magee believed that a price too low in comparison to his commercial competitors can sometimes be interpreted as a product of lesser value by the customer. This time, a market research effort was used to study the pricing issue.

39 Magee Enterprises offers site licensing as well as volume discounts for larger customers. When Tom Dickerson joined the company as head of sales, he proposed the idea of giving credit for previously purchased individual copies upon the purchase of a site license. This idea was subsequently adopted with customers of Magee products.

Public Relations

40 Magee accepts frequent speaking engagements and attends numerous trade events. Employees feel that Magee's public exposure has been a contributing factor to the company's success.

Logo

41 The company's logo has been in use since 1985, when Magee purchased it for $50 from an art student who was a little sister in his fraternity at Auburn. Since then, Magee has made good on his promise to her that, if his company ever made any money, he would take her to Las Vegas.

PRODUCTION AND PACKAGING

42   Originally Magee Enterprises subcontracted another company to mass copy the programs at a cost of about 75 cents per diskette. In 1988, two in-house diskette duplicators, one $3^1/_2$ inch and one $5^1/_4$ inch, were purchased. The company uses the duplicators to mass copy programs from a master diskette. Over the first year, the savings Magee Enterprises realized was more than three times the cost of equipment.

43   Different labels are used for registered and shareware software. The shareware label says *shareware* and gives a number to call to register. UPS picks up once a day, with 4,000 to 5,000 programs shipped per month.

44   In May 1989, while Magee was away on business, an employee failed to reorder manuals when the supply dwindled to 5,000. The order was finally placed, with only 1,800 remaining in inventory. This resulted in no product being shipped for about six weeks, throwing the company 3500 orders behind. Numerous distributors, overseas, and hundreds of one-item, end-user orders accumulated.

45   Customers were notified by mail and told of the problem. Followup letters were sent. Sample copies of the letters are included as Exhibit 3. In addition to letters, telephone calls were made to distributors throughout the crisis. One cancellation for three packages was received.

46   Compounding the problem was a switch of printers at the same time. Having used the same printer from the company's inception, Magee had recently gotten bids from several printing companies. The old printer had charged about $25,000 for 10,000 manuals, while the new printer was charging about $16,000 for 10,000 manuals. Since switching printers, the new printer did not have printing plates and was unable to do a rush job. This also delayed production.

47   Upon receipt of the manuals, the distributor's orders were shipped first. The remaining orders were shipped in the order they were received with no preference given to large orders. All employees pitched in, working both days and evenings to ship the orders. It took approximately three weeks to catch up on the backlog.

48   Since the crisis, the company changed from a manual count system to a computerized inventory system, based on orders shipped. The shipping room was reorganized. Pallets containing the minimum number of boxes, trays, sleeves, diskettes, and manuals are placed in one area with back-up inventory placed in another area to allow for visual checks. Pink paper is wrapped around pallets at the reorder point. Magee described the changes as, "We're doing very redundant checks because the people that caused the problem don't realize the devastation it caused."

49   At the time of the crisis it was rumored that a major distributor was saying that Magee Enterprises couldn't fill its orders and suggested that the customer try a different product. For the first time in the company's history, the company was forced to borrow money to cover the cash flow shortage. Fortunately, a year prior to the incident, Magee had set up a $25,000 line of credit upon which the company drew.

50   Production problems have plagued the company numerous times in the past. Magee expressed that whenever the company seemed to run out of something, it was always at a time when orders were high.

51   Early on, packaging was done by part-timers with about eight hours a week needed to fill routine orders. As volume grew, employees contributed one to two hours each week to support packaging operations. Packaging parties, in which most of the employees work three to four hours in the evening, were held every few weeks to fill large distributor orders.

52   Magee considers the product's packaging as critical, because in many instances the package may be all the customer sees of the company. Magee explains that the product is shipped in a bigger box to give the customer more perceived value, noting that if the diskette was merely shipped in the manual, customers wouldn't feel they were getting very much for their money. Both Automenu and Treeview are similarly packaged. A plastic tray holds the materials and gives the package

EXHIBIT 3
Letters to Customers

March 27, 1989

Dear Valued Customer:

Due to a production problem, your recent order for Automenu® will be delayed. We anticipate a shipment date no later than April 7, 1989. We are sorry for the delay and will ship your order before April 7th if at all possible. Your order will include three complimentary packages for your inconvenience.

If you have any questions regarding your order, please contact me at 1-800-662-4330. Thanking you in advance for your cooperation during this delay.

Sincerely,

Betty Reitz
Customer Service

April 5, 1989

Dear Valued Customer:

We recently advised you of a shipping problem with dealer orders. I regret to inform you, due to circumstances beyond our immediate control, we must delay shipping until approximately May 5, 1989.

Please accept our apologies for this delay, and if at all possible we will ship before this date. If you have any questions, please feel free to contact me at 800-662-4330.

Sincerely,

Betty Reitz
Customer Service Manager

(continued)

EXHIBIT 3 *(concluded)*

June 14, 1989

Dear Sir:

Enclosed you will find your complimentary copies of AUTOMENU® as promised in March 1989. As you will recall, Magee offered these free packages as an apology for the delay in shipping your order.

We sincerely appreciate your business and have taken steps to avoid any future supplier problems. Thank you for your patience and continued business.

If I can be of further assistance, please don't hesitate to call me at the toll-free number listed below.

Sincerely,

Betty Reitz
Customer Service Manager
1-800-662-4330

Enclosures

support. The tray contains both $5^1/_4$ and $3^1/_2$ inch diskettes, manual, color-coded warranty card, generic postage-paid comment card, and a technical support brochure.

COMPETITION IN THE SOFTWARE INDUSTRY

53   The software market may be defined in a variety of ways. International Data Corporation (IDC), a market research firm, divides the market by type of software: systems and utilities, application tools, and application solutions. Magee Enterprises' two products, Automenu and Treeview, fit the system and utilities category and are limited to a PC–DOS environment.

54   The microcomputer software market started as a cottage industry with a mix of computer aficionadas designing programs out of their homes. Today, the industry is highly competitive, with a distinct consolidation trend, dominated by a few large companies.

55   The microcomputer software market has been compared to the music and book industries, where companies compete to make the "best sellers" list. Several companies have become visible and successful based on one or two major programs. An industry expert estimates that only about ten percent of the thousands of software companies, mainstream and shareware alike, ever break a million dollars in sales. Magee is among that ten percent, primarily thanks to Automenu. Magee estimates there are about 65 products in Automenu's utility category—an easily customized menu system—and estimates the market size at 28 million personal computers, about 15–20 million of which probably have hard disks.

EXHIBIT 4
Top Ten Sellers of Utility Programs

1. Fastback Plus 2.01
   Fifth Generation Systems Inc.

2. The Norton Utilities Advanced Edition 4.5
   Peter Norton Computing

3. Automenu
   Magee Enterprises, Inc.

4. LapLink III
   Traveling Software Inc.

5. PC Tools Deluxe 5.5
   Central Point Software

6. X-Tree Professional
   X-Tree Inc.

7. Above Disc 3.0
   Above Software

8. Sideways 3.2
   Funk Software

9. Battery Watch
   Traveling Software Inc.

10. DESQview 2.2
    Quarterdeck Office Systems

Source: *PC Magazine,* October 31, 1989, p. 63.

56   Magee considers Automenu's major competitor to be Direct Access. In 1986, Direct Access received editor's choice in a software review. Automenu was not even mentioned in the article. At the time of the review, Direct Access was much smaller than Magee Enterprises, but the article catapulted Direct Access to the top.

57   Although Magee claims that Automenu has more users than does Direct Access, he notes that Direct Access's sales revenues are higher due to higher pricing. In comparing products, Magee considers Direct Access easier for the customer to use, but it lacks the flexibility that corporate America likes. Numerous software reviews list flexibility as one of the strengths of Automenu.

58   In the year following Direct Access's selection as editor's choice, Automenu made its mark in the shareware arena. Automenu was named as one of the "best-selling shareware programs for IBM PCs and compatibles" in February 1987 in *PC Week*.[4] In May 1989, it was listed by *Changing Times* magazine as the "best of the almost-free software" for menus utilities.[5]

59   The manager of departmental computing for Coca-Cola Foods in Houston found Automenu on a bulletin board a few years ago. She found it worth sharing with her colleagues and recounts "It caught on like wildfire. It saved our company a tremendous amount of time"[6]

60   The line between commercial software and shareware began to blur in 1989. In turn, Automenu enjoyed more frequent reviews by mainstream software journals. Automenu was called "The Right

---

[4]Amy Bermar. "For Shareware Authors, Honesty's Still Best Policy, But It Won't Make Them Rich," *PC Week*, 4 (February 10, 1987), p. 49(3).

[5]Charles Bermant, "In Search of Utilities Software," *Personal Computing* 12 (May 1988), p. 139(5).

[6]Ibid., p. 139.

EXHIBIT 5
Automenu Competitive Information Sheets

Menu System Comparison **Magee**	Automenu 4.5	Direct Access	Direct Net	Perfect Menu	Menu Blocks	Menu Works	Hot 3.0
Mouse Support	●			●		●	●
Required memory (kb)	32	256	256*	512	128**	256	256
Minimum resident memory to execute application (kb)	0	0	0	0	62**	3	128
Network compatible	●		●				
Screen blanker	●	●	●	●	●	●	●
Screen blanked message	●				●	●	
Password protection for menu items	●	●	●	●	●	●	
Multiple password protection for menu items	●		●				
On-line help	●			●	●	●	●
Timed execution	●					●	
Usage tracking		●	●	●	●		
Menu building facility	●	●	●	●	●	●	●
Knowledge of DOS required to set up menu	●	●	●	●	●	●	●
Maximum number of items per screen	8	20	20	20	8	9	15
Maximum number of screens per menu file	8	1	1	N/A	1	9	1
Linkable menus	●			●	●	●	●
Multiple menus on-screen							●
Encrypt menu data files	●						
Total number of possible menu selections	Unlimited	400	400	640	Unlimited	Unlimited	Unlimited
Ability to pass parameters to application	●	●	●	●	●	●	●
Ability to prompt user for input	●	●	●			●	●
Descriptions for each menu item	●			●	●		●
Available memory displayed on menu	●				●		
Time/Date displayed on menu	●	●	●	●	●	●	
Customize colors	●	●	●	●		●	●
Price	69.95	89.95	245.00		79.95	24.95	179.95

*Direct Net requires an additional 128kb with usage tracking enabled.
**Menu Blocks requires an additional 45kb with the help system enabled and another 5kb with password protection enabled.

EXHIBIT 6
Treeview Competitive Information Sheets

File Manager Comparison
Magee

	Treeview 1.1	XTree Pro	Tree86 ver. 2.0	QDos II	Norton Commander 2.0	Pathminder	Lotus Magellan
Mouse Support	●		●		●		
Multiple Directory Windows	6				2		
User Defined Keys	30						10
Prototyping (Point & Go)	●						●
EMS Support	●	●	●			●	●
Show all files on one drive	●	●	●				●
Show all files on all drives		●	●				●
Show all files in subdirectories	●						●
EGA 43/VGA 50 line support	●		●		●		
Macros	●						●
Tag files by range of dates/times	●						(1)
Tag files by filename mask	●	(1)	(1)	●	●		(1)
Modify file date/time	●						
Modify file attributes	●	●	●	●		●	
Update target directory	●						
Graphical directory tree	●	●	●	●	●	●	●
Move files across directories	●	●	●	●	●	●	●
Move files across drives		●			●		●
Built-in file viewer	●	●	●	●	●		●
Ability to hook in external viewer	●						●
Built-in editor		●		●	●	●	●
Ability to hook in external editor	●		●		●		●
Execute program	●	●		●	●	●	●
Fuzzy Search							●
Customize colors	●	●	●	●	(2)	●	(2)
Print file and/or directory tree		●	●			●	●
Maximum files per window	2515	16000	N/A	700	N/A	N/A	N/A
Required memory (kb)	256	256	256	256	256	256	512
Minimum resident memory to execute application (kb)	158	85	89	123	18	4	4
Price	50.00	129.00	89.95	79.95	89.95	89.95	199.00

(1) - Indirectly accomplished
(2) - Limited customization

COMPANY OPERATIONS

12 The sales figures for 1985 had not been unanticipated or surprising. Turnover continued to increase, and sales for 1987 reached the £2.5 million mark. Survival Aids, Ltd. was now an established, successful company that was a dominant force in its industry. The company enjoyed a national reputation, and its products were of the highest quality available. Survival Aids would continue to expand its product line and would broaden its selling techniques.

Products and Services

13 Survival Aids now sells approximately 1400 different products to outdoor enthusiasts. Most products are made by other companies for Survival Aids; however, many products are made to the company's specifications and, in some cases, the company has exclusive rights to other manufacturers' products.

14 **Products.** The following products, by major category, are sold by Survival Aids:

Protection	*Food*
Shell clothing	Rations
Footwear	Cooking equipment
Outer thermal clothing	*Tools*
Inner thermal clothing	Knives
Immediate care	Kits and accessories
Bivis, bags, blankets	Pouches and firestarters
Sleeping systems	*Survival Skills*
Location	Books and courses
Navigation, signaling	*Military*
Time	Combat clothing
Distance	Waterproofs
Light	Boots
Water	Bergens
Water purification	Webbing
Water carriers	Kits and accessories

15 **Product selection.** Products that do not sell well are usually dropped from the catalog, and new ones are added. The following criteria or policy statements were used to select new products included in the 1986 catalog:

16
    1. "No new products are to be offered for sale until they have been thoroughly tested, costed, sourced, sampled, packaged, and stocked."
    2. "We want more own/exclusive products in our own packaging but will accept certain high quality products from companies such as Tekna and Pains Wessex."
    3. "New products should have reasonable wholesale margins."
    4. "Quality has become a key feature of the company's inventory. Suppliers must be reliable, and alternative sources must be developed."
    5. "No new products may have any assembly requirement. They must be supplied ready for sale."
    6. "New products and existing products must have better instructions, labelling, packaging, and documentation in 1986."

17 **Services.** In 1982, Nick decided to begin a survival training school that would teach outdoor enthusiasts basic survival skills and would provide some exposure for the company. Initially,

EXHIBIT 2
Organization Chart of Survival Aids, Ltd., 1988

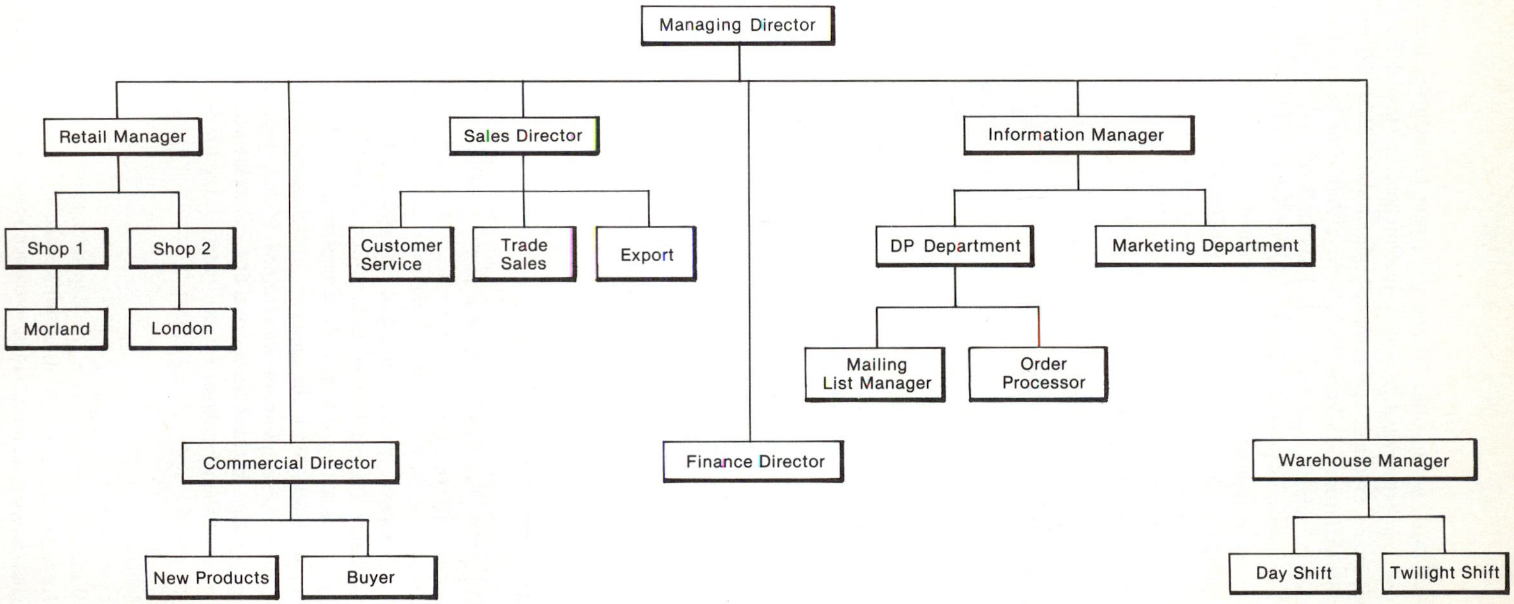

Survival Aids would offer 20 courses a year to teach the following skills: expedition training, survival, combat survival, executive development, and civil defense. Nick estimated that the survival school would eventually generate revenue of about £100,000 per year. There were other benefits to be derived from the school. First, Survival Aids employees could be exposed to outdoor activities. Second, the school could provide facilities for R & D. Third, students would be potential customers for the company's products. Finally, the school would be good advertising.

18   The training programs that were presented to people from age 14 up were somewhat successful. The programs did meet some of the established goals; however, the survival school was not sufficiently profitable to continue. The program was eventually sold to Outward Bound, another organization in the same training business. Other services, such as seminars and equipment demonstration programs, are still provided when needed.

Organization and Personnel

19   From a business with no personnel and no structure, Survival Aids has grown to a company employing 35 people that has a fairly well-developed organizational structure (see Exhibit 2). Since unemployment in the area is relatively high, it is not difficult to hire capable employees. It is somewhat more difficult to hire managers with technical skills, because of the company's rural location; however, Nick assembled a very professional staff capable of managing the company through future growth stages.

20   The company provides very comfortable working conditions, the management style is participative, and the employees are well paid. In addition to above average wages, all employees participate in a profit-sharing plan. Nick decided to set aside in perpetuity 15 percent of pretax profits for worker incentive. Employees would receive a percentage of that lump sum, based on their personal performance (graded very good, satisfactory, or unsatisfactory) and their base salary. Nick has even considered letting his managers buy stock in the company (at present, he owns 100 percent of the company's stock), because he believes that all employees should share in the success of the company.

Marketing and Distribution

21   Selling survival packs through camping and outdoor leisure shops was satisfactory in the early stages of Survival Aids' development; however, when the product line expanded, Nick realized that he should have more direct control over the selling and distribution of his merchandise. To gain this control, Nick decided that mail order selling was most appropriate for Survival Aids.

22   **Selling.**   The majority of sales of Survival Aids' products comes from mail order customers. The heaviest selling season is from September to March, when the company averages about 150 orders per week. Since the quality of merchandise is high and the products are well described in the catalog, very few items are returned. Nick expects mail order to continue to be an important source of sales, because he believes that its advantages outweigh the disadvantages. The following are some of the advantages of mail order selling for Survival Aids:

Full price paid.
Cash in advance.
Few bad debts.
Wide range of customers. No dependence on major accounts.
Lack of stock does not usually lose sale.
Cash sales and credit purchase reduce working capital requirements.

Best and sometimes only way to approach military customers.
Small items are suited for mail order.
Location is not a disadvantage.
Catalog is an easy and inexpensive way to introduce new products.
Direct contact with end user.

24   While mail order selling seemed to have several advantages over other selling techniques, it also had some drawbacks. The following are some of the disadvantages of relying on mail order selling:

Small orders may be uneconomic to process, especially if paid for by credit card.
Returns could be expensive.
Customers cannot really "examine" products before they are purchased.
It is necessary to maintain a large and growing mailing list.

25   Nick realized that Survival Aids would need to utilize more than one selling technique if it was to reach the most potential customers. In February 1986, the first Survival Shop, a retail outlet for Survival Aids products, was opened in the company's Morland facility. This shop was quite profitable, especially during the six summer weeks when many tourists visited the Lake District. To further test the profitability of retail outlets, Nick opened a shop in a major London train station in 1987. Early indications are that the shop will be profitable, leading Nick and his managers to contemplate opening additional shops in London and other parts of the country.

26   Nick had also tried some other selling techniques with varying degrees of success. The company tired contract sales (selling to the military, government agencies, and the like), but very little continuity was obtained from this method of selling. Nick identified the following problems associated with contract selling: Survival Aids does not manufacture products; contract business is not repetitive; it is time consuming; and one-of-a-kind orders do not fit into Survival Aids' system. While contract selling would be continued, it would receive very little budget support. Survival Aids had also been represented at several trade shows, usually with exposure and advertising value outweighing profitability. The company now sells through mail order, contract sales, and retail shops, and it continues to wholesale its products to independent camping shops and the NAAFI (the equivalent to U.S. military post exchanges).

27   **Competition.**   Several companies sell items similar to those offered by Survival Aids, but no single company has a product line as complete as Survival Aids'. Companies that compete do so on the basis of price, rather on quality or service. Nick is aware of a few companies that could expand their product lines to compete with Survival Aids; however, he is confident that good service and high-quality products will keep Survival Aids ahead of the competition.

28   **Advertising.**   The target market for Survival Aids is primarily military personnel and people (primarily males) interested in any outdoor activity. To attract this market, Survival Aids relies mainly on its catalogs; however, it does use other advertising media. The company advertises in weekly, monthly, and quarterly magazines, such as *Great Outdoors, Soldier,* and *Y.H.A. News.* Advertisements are also placed in other local publications. Advertising is important, but effective public relations also sells products. Survival Aids has been the subject of many news and television reports, and company employees have written numerous articles that have appeared in national magazines. Survival seminars have considerable PR value, and Nick and his managers are often asked to speak to local organizations and business schools.

29   **Catalogs.**   The lifeblood of any mail order company is its catalog. The catalog offered by Survival Aids in 1987 does not even resemble the first one published in 1980. From a simple typewritten document listing 68 items, the catalog has progressed to a full-color, 48-page annual publication describing more than 1,400 items (most manufactured in the U.K.) purchased from

200 suppliers. In 1987, Survival Aids ordered 200,000 catalogs at a cost of 0.45 each. The mailing list, with approximately 130,000 names, is actively maintained. Customers who have not purchased anything for six months are sent a "last catalog" notice. Customers who have received such notice are dropped from the mailing list if they do not make a purchase within a reasonable amount of time. People who request their first catalog are sent the latest edition, which includes incentives to recommend Survival Aids to their friends.

30   Besides being informative, the catalog is also instructive. For example, the 1987 catalog provides information about such topics as "how to keep warm in a British winter" and "what to wear in hot wet climates." The catalog has also been used to try to expand the target market. The cover of the 1987 catalog featured a woman for the first time in the company's history. The description of the cover noted that the "Front cover picture shows 22-year-old Heather Morris from Chirbury, Shropshire, taking part in Operation Raleigh. Heather was on the Black River Expedition in Honduras, in April 1985." The catalog has not been circulated enough to know whether the picture of a woman hiking through the jungle will encourage more females to buy from Survival Aids.

Automation

31   Processing customer orders, maintaining an extensive mailing list, keeping records, and several other operations eventually became too cumbersome to do manually; therefore, in 1986, a computer was purchased. The company installed a sophisticated mini-computer, which provided on-line order processing, stock control, dispatch control, marketing information, office automation, and accounting packages. So many routine functions were computerized that the company soon needed a larger, more powerful machine. Since customer service is so important to Survival Aids' continued growth, manual backup procedures are in place should the computer be unavailable.

32   The introduction of the computer created no problems for Survival Aids. The company was particularly fortunate to have on its staff a person who was interested in computers and whose expertise has grown to keep pace with Survival Aids' data processing needs. Other employees had to be trained to use the computer. Even though the employees were not computer literate, they soon learned enough about the hardware and software to function efficiently. Now most staff have terminals on their desks and four employees have completed programming courses.

Financial Information

33   For the last six years Survival Aids has been a profitable company (see Exhibit 3) with turnover nearly doubling each year and profit increasing from £5,000 to nearly £80,000 in 1987. The company's net profit for 1986 (18 months) was £29,200 (see Exhibit 4), and it had tangible assets worth £141,891 (see Exhibit 5). Finally, the source and application of funds is included in Exhibit 6.

THE FUTURE

34   Survival Aids, Ltd., has been successful and profitable since its founding. The company's sales have nearly doubled each of the past five years, with 1987 sales reaching £2.5 million and 1988 sales expected to be approximately £3.5 million. The products sold by Survival Aids are of the highest quality, management and staff are very capable, and no competitors pose a serious threat to the company. Although the company has been successful in the past, Nick is not sure that it

EXHIBIT 3
Survival Aids Ltd., Five-Year Summary

	1983	1984 (12 months)	1985	1986 (18 months)	1987 (12 months)
Profit and loss:					
Turnover	£410,648	£787,063	£1,237,847	£2,600,939	£2,584,936
Operating profit	16,726	37,339	42,669	61,570	102,100
Interest	(1,827)	(2,406)	(11,543)	(20,875)	(22,700)
Profit before tax	£ 14,899	£ 34,933	£ 31,126	£ 40,695	£ 79,400
Assets employed:					
Fixed assets	£ 22,039	£ 45,818	£ 50,233	£ 96,104	£ 141,891
Net current assets (liabilities)	2,847	(6,485)	12,524	15,336	37,584
Creditors due after more than one year	(18,576)	—	(1,883)	(19,386)	(45,130)
Deferred taxation	(1,309)	(9,338)	(9,020)	(11,000)	(11,000)
Shareholders' funds	£ 5,001	£ 29,995	£ 51,854	£ 81,054	£ 123,345

EXHIBIT 4
Survival Aids Ltd., Profit and Loss Account for the Year Ended 30 September 1987

	Year Ended 30 September 1987	Eighteen Months to 30 September 1986
Turnover	£2,584,936	£2,600,939
Cost of sales	(1,647,910)	(1,684,201)
Gross profit	937,026	916,738
Distribution costs	(86,665)	(131,809)
Administrative expenses	(748,261)	(723,359)
Operating profit	102,100	61,570
Interest payable	(22,700)	(20,875))
Profit on ordinary activities before taxation	79,400	40,695
Tax on profit on ordinary activities	(22,690)	(11,495)
Profit on ordinary activities after taxation	56,710	29,200
Extraordinary item	(14,419)	—
Profit for the financial period	42,291	29,200
Retained profit, beginning of period	55,053	25,853
Retained profit, end of period	£ 97,344	£ 55,053

will continue to grow without some changes. There are several options being considered to make Survival Aids even more dominant in its market. The following are some of those options:

35   **Retailing.**   The company has been a retailer for just over a year; however, indications are that retailing could be successful and allow Survival Aids to continue to grow. Expanding retail operations would require several changes in the company's strategies and policies.

36   **Franchising.**   If retailing proves to be successful, Nick might consider franchising his

EXHIBIT 5
Survival Aids Ltd.: Balance Sheet—30 September 1987

	1987	1986
Fixed assets:		
Tangible assets	£141,891	£96,104
Current assets:		
Stocks	489,500	353,571
Debtors	153,097	113,540
Cash at bank and in hand	503	460
Total	643,100	467,571
Creditors: Amounts falling due within one year	(605,516)	(452,235)
Net current assets	37,584	15,336
Total assets less current liabilities	179,475	111,440
Creditors: Amounts falling due after more than one year	(45,130)	(19,386)
Provisions for liabilities and charges	(11,000)	(11,000)
Net assets	£123,345	£81,054
Capital and reserves:		
Called-up share capital	£26,001	£26,001
Profit and loss account	97,344	55,053
Total capital employed	£123,345	£81,054

business. He realizes that this is a fast-growth option, and that he might lose some control of his business.

37   **Manufacturing.**   Survival Aids has always sold products manufactured by other companies; however, it might be possible and profitable for the company to begin manufacturing some of the products it sells.

38   **Expand the product line.**   It might be advantageous to offer outdoorsmen a larger variety of products. For example, Survival Aids could increase its product line to include guns, boating accessories, mountain climbing equipment, and so on. Several customers had requested these types of items in the past and Nick felt that there would be substantial demand for them in the future.

39   **Acquire other companies.**   Acquiring complimentary companies would provide instant growth and could expand the product line at the same time. For example, there is a relatively small but profitable company that manufactures tents, rucksacks, and climbing hardware. Such a company might be an attractive acquisition candidate.

40   **Sellout.**   Rather than buying another company, Nick could sell Survival Aids. He had been approached on several occasions by people who expressed an interest in buying his company. Nick could sell Survival Aids to another company and either remain as a key executive or leave and pursue other interests.

41   **Export.**   Survival Aid catalogs are now distributed in several foreign countries, and orders are received from abroad, but international sales have never amounted to more than 10 percent of total turnover. Nick is particularly interested in exporting to the United States. At one point, the company was represented at a trade show in Chicago, and an advertisement was placed in *Soldier of Fortune* magazine. Sales in the United States were too meager to justify any further selling effort; however, Nick feels that he and Survival Aids may now be ready to make a concerted effort to become established in the United States.

EXHIBIT 6
Survival Aids Ltd.: Statement of Source and Application of Funds
for the Year Ended 30 September 1987

	Year Ended 30 September 1987	Eighteen Months to 30 September 1986
Source of funds		
Profit on ordinary activities after taxation	£56,710	£29,200
Add (deduct) items not involving the movement of funds during the period:		
—depreciation	45,018	25,990
—(profit) loss on disposal of tangible fixed assets	(5,518)	1,392
—deferred taxation charge	—	1,980
Total funds from operations	96,210	58,562
Funds from other sources:		
Proceeds from disposal of tangible fixed assets	28,000	1,028
Increase in long-term portion of hire-purchase creditor	25,744	17,503
Increase in creditors falling due within one year	139,242	144,345
Total	289,196	221,438
Application of funds		
Extraordinary item after taxation	14,419	—
Purchase of tangible fixed assets at cost	113,287	74,281
Increase in stocks	135,929	183,447
Increase in debtors	39,557	5,507
	303,192	263,235
Net application of funds	£(13,996)	£(41,797)
Increase (decrease) in net liquid funds		
Cash at bank and in hand	£43	£(28)
Bank overdraft	(14,039)	(41,769)
	£(13,996)	£(41,797)

42   **Go public.**   Since Nick is the sole owner of Survival Aids, he could realize a significant profit and foster company growth by selling Survival Aids stock to the public.

43   **Do nothing.**   Nick could make no significant changes and simply let things remain as they are. Survival Aids would continue its steady growth, and there would be no pressure on the employees to "grow" and accept change.

CASE 22

SPRINGFIELD REMANUFACTURING CORPORATION

1   Salespeople desperately tried to generate new orders. Company president John Stack stated that he
had enough work for the remaining employees through August, but that he needed a "big play"
by September. Stack considered whether to lay off employees (Springfield Remanufacturing Corporation had never had a layoff) or to avoid the layoff and risk the financial stability of the
corporation. A dejected Stack noted, "I guess we will find out if we mean what we say—we'll
show them the numbers—we'll see."

FORMATION OF THE COMPANY

2   On February 1, 1983, after nearly three years of rumors and frustration, the financially troubled
International Harvester (IH) sold one of its last remaining diesel engine and engine component
remanufacturing operations as part of its turnaround strategy. IH needed to do something because
of its $4 billion debt load and $1.6 billion in operating losses. During a depressed truck and farm
economy, the corporation was seeking answers to its troubles. Therefore, it decided to sell the
Springfield plant and four other parts-remanufacturing centers. IH's sale of the Springfield, Missouri,
facility marked the end of IH's remanufacturing activities but not the end of their troubles. IH later
sold its Farm Division to save its Truck Division, and the firm later reorganized as Navistar.

3   The Springfield Remanufacturing facility employed 171 workers at the time of the sale. It was
originally meant to be sold to Dresser Industries, a major customer of the plant, despite the fact
that SRC's employees had had a bid on the table to purchase the company. When negotiations
with Dresser broke down in December 1982, employees of the firm began to consider forming
their own company. Springfield Remanufacturing Corporation (SRC) was the result of these discussions when, two months later, employees obtained financing from the Bank of America in San
Francisco. The company and the 68,000-square-foot plant was bought from IH by a group of 13
employees for approximately $7 million at three percentage points above the prime rate. The plant's
assets provided enough collateral so the employees did not have to give the lender any of the equity
in the firm.

4   Twelve of these new owners were former employees and managers of IH at the plant. The 13th
was Don McCoy, the controller of the IH division of which the Springfield plant was part. President
of the new corporation was John P. (Jack) Stack, who had previously been plant manager. Stack
and the other 12 owners decided to broaden the ownership of the new corporation through an
employee stock ownership program. As former employees were rehired, they decided to set aside
each year a portion of the corporate earnings to buy some of the company's unissued stock. This
stock would then go into a trust fund for workers. The employee stock ownership plan (ESOP)
was greeted with enthusiasm. Foreman Joe Loeber noted, "It added a little incentive to know you're

This case was prepared by Professors Charles Boyd and D. Keith Denton of Southwest Missouri State University as a basis
for class discussion and not as an illustration of effective or ineffective handling of an administrative situation. Copyright ©
1987 by Charles Boyd and D. Keith Denton.

working for your own future and not just the other guy's. Everybody's excited." The managers owned shares of stock and signed an agreement that the corporation would issue shares of stock directly into the ESOP. Thus, the ESOP became the vehicle for employee ownership of the firm.

5   Stack and other management realized the plant's future lay outside of IH. He noted, "We were really different. IH employees were normally represented by Untied Auto Workers and the Springfield plant wasn't." As early as two years before the actual sale, local management at the Springfield plant submitted a bid for the plant that was not given serious consideration by IH. A year later, a more detailed plan was submitted but again was rejected.

6   The day after the sale, SRC brought back 30 of its former IH employees and increased its employment by 30 a day until most of the original employees were back. When SRC started business, it had signed up 60 percent of the old customers. Before the sale, it had $10 million in sales of parts for construction equipment, another $7 million for farm equipment, and $3 million for trucks.

7   On February 1, 1983, Jack Stack issued a news release stating that the new firm would remain in Springfield and would continue to be a major rebuilder of diesel engines, injection pumps, water pumps, and other engine components. The news release noted that SRC would be a supplier of remanufactured engines and engine components to IH's agricultural equipment and truck dealers.   *Product*

8   The news release, like the news about the IH sale of the Springfield facility, did not tell the whole story about this unique situation. It was no secret that many of IH's manufacturing facilities had suffered from abrasive employee-management relations. When Jack Stack arrived at the facility four years before the eventual sale, the employees were on the verge of forming a union and the company was running behind production schedule. Stack was sent from IH headquarters and given six months to straighten out the problem at the plant or close it.

9   Stack called a meeting with all employees and "begged" them to give him and his team a chance to change things. He promised to listen, and he promised change. The employees agreed to give   *labor*   him a chance. The union election was scheduled for March 10; this gave Stack two months to win over the employees. Stack won the election as over 75 percent of the employees voted in favor of management over the union.

10   Management's relations with employees began to change. There were better human relations, better communications, and better cooperation. Three topics were emphasized to the employees: safety, housekeeping, and quality. Statistical measures for these three activities were developed by management and taught to the employees. Eventually, the employees were taught about costs and profits. Data were graphed, kept updated, and posted in prominent places within the plant. As a result, employees became very goal-oriented. Stack commented: "You've got to have an enemy to have a team. If you can set that enemy outside your organization and declare what that enemy is, that's the unifying factor behind the whole organization."

11   So such things as safety problems and quality rejects became the enemy, and improving performance in these areas became the employees' goals. As a result, the organization's efficiency   *miss.*   and effectiveness improved dramatically.

12   One year later, production was up 30 percent. By June 1984, the facility had become the "best" of the outside firms performing remanufacturing work for IH. It had remained profitable during the time that similar facilities had been losing money.

13   Several programs that Stack and others started during this time were given credit for helping turn things around. One of these is the Quality of Work Life (QWL) program, in which employees analyze and propose solutions to organizational problems. They had also formed small employee groups, known as quality circles, that were used to make the plant more efficient and productive. Innovative approaches were also used. For example, when IH imposed a wage freeze, the QWL group decided to go to a flex-time, four, 10-hour/day week. This saved employees money on transportation and lunches and reduced absenteeism by giving workers a day off so they could take care of personal business.

METEORIC RISE

14   The rise of SRC from the ashes of IH was almost immediate and profound. The success did not go unnoticed by the news media. Several articles on the success of SRC were written, and the firm was featured in an issue of *INC* magazine. A television documentary by PBS was aired during the fall of 1987.

15   During 1984, SRC increased sales by 20 percent to $15.5 million. A year later business increased by 40 percent to $23 million in sales, and 100 employees were added to the payroll to bring total employment to 225.

16   In one year they remanufactured 2,500 engines, and in two years of operation the firm had warranty returns averaging less than 1 percent. SRC's customers included Ingersol-Rand, J.I. Case, Dresser Industries, and International Harvester.

17   A red-letter day for SRC came in April 1985, two years after its formation, when SRC announced that it had received a contract from General Motors (GM) to remanufacture 15,400 5.7 liter V-8 diesel engines for GM's Oldsmobile Division. There are about 1.5 million GM cars in service powered by the 5.7 liter engine. GM decided to subcontract the remanufacturing of these engines, because daily demand had stabilized at a level which GM management no longer considered justifying the plant space it had devoted to the remanufacturing. GM ceased production of the 5.7 liter diesel engine a week prior to signing the contract with SRC. The volume of SRC's work was expected to slowly decrease as the cars powered by the 5.7 are taken out of service over time.

18   Lee Shroyer, marketing manager, said the contract could mean 40 new jobs in Springfield and 60 new jobs at a satellite operation in the nearby community of Willow Springs. With this contract, SRC became the first company to be named as an authorized engine rebuilder for GM. The three-year contract was expected to be worth $40 million to SRC. An SRC manager stated, "We should continue to work with GM as long as we can maintain their quality and safety requirements and I don't see any problem with that." With this new business, 1985 sales were expected to exceed $30 million.

19   Because of this new business, additional fixtures, tooling, jet sprays, and new arrangements were made in the Springfield plant to improve the flow of materials. To accommodate increased business, SRC needed a new building. In May, 1985 they secured an additional building in Willow Springs, a small town 70 miles away. Stack expected to be turning out 5 engines per day by mid-May and 125 per day by November. By November they expected to employ 75 people and eventually employ 150 after 2 years.

REASONS FOR SUCCESS

20   SRC's 40 percent growth rate did not come by accident. The firm would not have received the GM contract if it did not turn out extremely high-quality products. Stack noted that a remanufacturing or recycled assembly is 30 to 40 percent the price of a new one, which means lower inventory carrying cost for the original equipment manufacturer (OEM) customer. SRC warranties are as good or better than those of a new product. Less than 1 percent of its products are returned for any reason—the industry average is 6 percent. Some of the products are guaranteed to be delivered within 48 hours. Within the industry, SRC has some of the best warranties, lowest cost, and highest reliability. During recent years, SRC experienced almost a 400 percent growth in business, and a 5 percent decrease in overhead cost. This growth occurred despite the depressed agriculture and construction industries.

21   Its success is built on at least four ingredients: Jack Stack, the charismatic and thoughtful president; a very capable management team; a positive philosophy toward employees; and employee ownership. Stack is the visionary who keeps the company focused on its objectives and clearly believes in his management style. Stack is complemented by those around him. Mike Carrigan, vice president of production, is a self-confessed "pack rat" who totally understands the production process. He is always looking to improve methods of operation and reduce waste. He would much rather fix what he has rather than buy something new. He seems ideally suited to this recycling work. Gary Brown, the human resources manager, likewise knows the personnel function and knows what kind of people SRC is looking for. Both Brown and Carrigan say there are two types of people—competitive and noncompetitive ones. They look for the competitive "hungry" ones. The ones who like to win, who like to compete, and who are interested in self improvement.

22   At SRC, it tries to maximize its people. It spends a great deal of time trying to cultivate an air of trust and openness between people. Stack noted, "There's not a financial number our employees don't know or have access to." They conduct weekly meetings with employees, where they go over the business, including financial statements, operating income, profits, losses, assets, liabilities, and other financial figures. All employees may not know or understand all the financial figures, but they know the figures are available. They do know what each department contributes and costs the company. Stack has been quoted as saying, "We teach them about finance and accounting before we teach them how to turn a wrench."

23   Management at SRC also tries to make work "fun." The managers are constantly setting standards for direct and indirect labor and then try to make "games" out of achieving results. These games are set up so employees understand what is needed and have incentives and rewards given. A popular phrase around SRC is STP-GUTR (Stop The Praise—Give Us The Raise). SRC pays employees a sizable bonus if quarterly financial goals are met. Winning at the "game" is based on an employee's ability to save labor and/or material cost. Some employees at the plant receive as much as 12 percent of their salary in bonus money. Employees also receive cash payments for suggestions that save the company money. When safety goals were met, insurance money refunded to SRC was used to purchase gifts of appreciation.

24   SRC also practices a decentralized-participative style of management, where it tries to push decision making down to the lowest level. Employees and first-line supervisors are encouraged to take on new tasks. For example, most supervisors "adopt" an area outside their supervisory area. One supervisor may be in charge of controlling chemical costs, ranging from solvents to "white out" correction fluid. Another supervisor may be in charge of all plant abrasives. Management at SRC believes it teaches everyone the value of cooperation and makes them better at communicating and persuading, since they must convince others outside their area to control costs in their "adopted" area. Of course all of these programs are enhanced because of ESOP. It is not someone else's business, it's theirs.

Marketing Concept

25   SRC fills a market niche, with the OEM being the customer. The marketing concept is simple and straightforward. Diesel engines are usually employed in trucks, earth-moving equipment, and other types of "workhorse" applications in which these engines labor daily under heavy strain. Because of this heavy usage, vital engine parts eventually break down, and the user must either purchase an entirely new piece of equipment, have the engine repaired, or have the engine or its major components rebuilt. The first option is often passed up, due to the very high expense of purchasing an entirely new piece of equipment. Each of the other two options requires the services of a firm that either builds or repairs engine components. This is known as the *aftermarket*.

26   Most firms in the engine or automotive aftermarket compete against the OEM company that originally built a particular engine component by offering their own repair service or replacement part. As a result, the OEM loses market share in the aftermarket. The distinctive difference of

40   But during the period from November 1986 to February 1987, several significant changes occurred at General Motors (GM): the $700 million payoff to Ross Perot, a huge stock buyback, and continued competitive problems in the automobile market. And what happened to GM was important to SRC, since 50 percent of SRC's business was with GM during 1986. In April 1987, GM notified SRC that it would need 5,000 fewer engines from the firm during 1987 than previously planned. To SRC, this means 50,000 manhours, or 25 percent of its 1987 business.

41   Fortunately, SRC moved six months ago from remanufacturing diesel engines exclusively to also remanufacturing gasoline engines. The firm began remanufacturing 30 gasoline engines per day for Chrysler in February 1987, and later began remanufacturing them for GM, too. This new business helps cushion the blow from the loss of GM's diesels, but not nearly enough. It is clear that SRC will have to work hard for new business during 1987; it cannot be the year of concentrating on customer enhancement which Stack had hoped it would be.

42   By early June 1987, Springfield Remanufacturing Company (SRC) had responded to the situation with an increased attrition rate from its 400-person work force. During the past six months, 43 employees had been terminated: 20 for performance reasons, the rest voluntarily. Still no layoff program has been instituted, but time is running out. Stack's "big play" has to come soon. He wonders what options are available, what will be the effect of my actions?

EXHIBIT 1

Springfield Remanufacturing Corporation and Subsidiary
Consolidated Balance Sheets

	January 25, 1987	January 26, 1986	January 27, 1985	January 29, 1984
Assets				
Current assets:				
Cash	$ 50,082	$ 13,584	$ 20,597	$ 316,688
Trade accounts receivable, less allowances for doubtful accounts	2,237,471	3,184,409	2,098,321	2,547,771
Inventories	9,230,828	10,451,968	8,055,556	9,514,189
Prepaid income taxes	—	—	—	298,200
Prepaid expenses and other current assets	32,637	37,875	39,826	48,645
Total current assets	11,551,018	13,687,836	10,214,300	12,725,493
Property, buildings, and equipment	2,244,519	1,905,348	669,177	291,043
Total assets	$13,795,537	$15,593,184	$10,883,477	$13,016,536
Liabilities and Stockholders' Equity				
Current liabilities:				
Notes payable	$ 383,658	$ 2,677,195	$ 2,526,557	$ 7,141,616
Accounts payable	3,867,352	5,825,521	2,661,636	1,907,233
Accrued contribution to employee stock ownership trust	—	521,011	413,510	—
Income taxes payable	363,340	47,000	—	—
Other current liabilities	1,211,717	900,450	771,721	727,954
Current portion of long-term debt	358,533	309,002	297,280	10,006
Total current liabilities	6,184,600	10,280,179	6,670,704	9,786,809

EXHIBIT 1 *(concluded)*

	January 25, 1987	January 26, 1986	January 27, 1985	January 29, 1984
Excess of net assets acquired over cost	$ 786,710	$ 1,573,420	$ 2,360,129	$ 3,146,838
Long-term debt	2,537,874	1,317,522	1,126,922	43,377
Deferred income taxes	10,000	34,000	—	—
Total liabilities	9,519,184	13,205,121	10,157,755	12,977,024
Stockholders' equity:				
Class A Common Stock, voting, par value $0.10 per share, 1,500,000 and 500,000 shares authorized, 1,140,000 and 500,000 issued and outstanding	114,000	50,000	50,000	50,000
Class B Common Stock, nonvoting, par value $0.10 per share, 10,000,000 and 1,000,000 shares authorized, 1,984,500 and 541,500 shares issued and outstanding	198,450	54,150	51,000	50,000
Additional paid-in capital	603,300	124,365	5,100	—
Retained earnings	3,688,114	2,159,548	619,622	(60,488)
Treasury stock, at cost	(327,511)	—	—	—
Total equity	4,276,353	2,388,063	725,722	39,512
Total liabilities and stockholders' equity	$13,795,537	$15,593,184	$10,883,477	$13,016,536

EXHIBIT 2

**Springfield Remanufacturing Corporation
and Subsidiary
Consolidated Statements of Earnings**

	January 25, 1987	January 26, 1986	January 27, 1985	January 29, 1984
Net sales	$37,937,498	$27,818,322	$23,976,808	$16,347,600
Cost of goods sold	30,864,793	23,766,826	20,696,029	13,420,229
	7,072,705	4,051,496	3,280,779	2,927,371
Gain (loss) on disposal of inventory	(2,229,765)	115,138	—	—
Gross margin	4,842,940	4,166,634	3,280,779	2,927,371
Operating expenses:				
Selling, general, and administrative	2,850,189	2,570,828	2,158,463	2,826,165
Contribution to employee stock ownership trust	706,216	521,011	419,610	—
Interest	442,039	597,462	798,305	948,403
	3,998,444	3,689,301	3,376,378	3,774,568
	844,496	477,333	(95,599)	(847,197)

(continued)

CASE 23

THE ARTISAN'S HAVEN

THE DECISION TO GO INTO BUSINESS

1   John and Katie Owen were confronted with a serious problem in 1973. John was fired from his job with a large chemical company in Trenton, New Jersey, for which he had worked for 33 years. The Arab oil embargo had caused a recession in the U.S. economy, and the nation was bracing itself for anticipated high inflation. After working for one company for so long and giving the firm his best years, John was emotionally upset over his dismissal. It was not as though he had made a big mistake or that he had done anything wrong. He was simply one of the older employees whom the company wanted to replace with younger, more energetic people. The recession gave the firm the opportunity it needed to make wholesale changes in personnel.

2   Finding a job during a recession is not easy, and, for a 55-year-old man whose experience is limited to one industry, it is almost impossible. John felt helpless. He did not know what to do, and his frustration turned into anger as he realized for the first time in his working life that he was just a pawn in a great game of corporation chess. After several weeks of fear, anxiety, and doubt, John reached a major turning point in his life. He knew that he never wanted to work for anyone or for any firm again.

3   The decision not to work for others was a major one, but John still did not know what to do. Should he retire? If he did, it would not be a comfortable retirement. Should he start his own business? If so, what kind of business should it be? He knew that he did not want to be involved with chemicals. Even before he was fired, John had begun to have reservations about producing dangerous chemicals and dumping harmful waste into rivers. But his pay was good, and he did not have the time or the inclination to think about these deep questions too seriously. It was more important to John to pay his bills, to take nice vacations, and, in general, to have fun.

4   Although John likes to take credit for the idea, Katie is the one who suggested that he consider opening a store to sell arts and crafts. John's hobby for many years had been making gold jewelry, and he had become a very good goldsmith. Katie was an amateur interior designer, and she also enjoyed doing cross-stitch and making dried floral arrangements. Starting a business to sell something they enjoyed making and knew something about seemed like a very good idea. In addition, John and Katie could work together in this kind of business, and Katie had always wanted to spend more time with John.

5   In 1974, they opened their first store in Trenton, and it was very successful. Their location was excellent, and their merchandise was high quality. Everything they did just seemed to work, and, by 1980, the Owens owned six stores in New Jersey and Pennsylvania.

6   In 1980, John and Katie were both 62 years old, and they were more secure financially than they had ever been. When John lost his job with the chemical company, his net worth had been

Copyright © 1987 by Neil H. Snyder. This case was written by Neil H. Snyder of the McIntire School of Commerce at the University of Virginia and by Brooke Garrett, a graduate of the McIntire School, who is now with Signet Bank.

about $150,000, and almost all of it was tied up in his house and furnishings. His income at the time was comfortable, but not great. Now, his net worth was in excess of $1 million, and John and Katie could do many of the things they had always dreamed of doing. One thing they had dreamed of doing was retiring to a nice southern town and enjoying life.

7   So, at age 62, John and Katie decided to sell their stores in New Jersey and Pennsylvania and move to Athens, Georgia. A couple with whom they were very close had moved to Athens several years before, and John and Katie had visited them several times. They liked the town, they liked the University of Georgia, they liked the people, and they liked the climate. The move just seemed like the right thing to do.

MOVING TO ATHENS, GEORGIA

8   John and Katie settled into their new way of life in Athens very quickly. They joined a local church that consumed a fair amount of their time. Katie got actively involved in the Christian Women's Club. John joined the Lion's Club and was able to contribute a great deal of time to many of its projects.

9   However, one thing was missing. While they were in business, John and Katie had enjoyed making decisions and watching the bottom line of their income statement change to reflect the quality of their judgment. None of their activities in Athens provided the same sense of excitement and satisfaction that owning and operating a business had provided. After a year, John asked Katie about opening a business in Athens, and Katie agreed.

STARTING OVER AGAIN

10   In the fall of 1981, the Owens opened The Artisan's Haven in downtown Athens directly across the street from the University of Georgia, and the community responded enthusiastically. The store sold handmade gold and silver jewelry, pottery, dried floral arrangements, woodcrafts, and various other handmade objects. Upon entering the store, customers were overwhelmed by the quality of the merchandise. It looked like it could have come out of a magazine like *Country Living* or *Southern Living*. All of the merchandise was made with great care and attention to detail.

11   Part of the immediate success of the new store was due to the popularity of arts and crafts at the time. But the Owens themselves were the main attraction. John and Katie seemed to be more relaxed about life and the rapport they developed with their customers was nothing short of amazing. They offered classes to teach their customers how to make many of the items sold in the store. Katie became an interior decorator whose advice was sought by many prominent and influential people in the community. John organized the artists and crafts people in the northeast Georgia area into a guild. As a result of their work, the Owens developed a large, wealthy customer base and an excellent supply of high-quality goods to sell.

DEMOGRAPHICS OF ATHENS

12   The population of Athens and Clarke County, the county surrounding Athens, is approximately 83,000 people. Twenty-one percent of the residents are professionals, and almost a third of them are students at the University of Georgia. A recent study of household incomes in Athens revealed the following (see Table 1):

TABLE 1

Household Income*	Number of Households*
Greater than $50,000	4,719
$35,000 to $49,999	6,426
$25,000 to $34,999	7,691

*An average household in Athens is composed of 2.5 people.

COMPETITION

13   The Artisan's Haven has no direct competition in Athens. Traditionally, few residents in the community have shown much interest in high-quality goods and services. Cultural events, such as plays and musical shows, are occasional attractions. Until very recently, the best restaurants in town were steak houses that catered primarily to students, and there were fast-food chains and small locally owned operations. Big events in Athens that set it apart from other communities in the area are University of Georgia football games and fraternity and sorority parties.

14   However, things in Athens are changing, and the wealthier residents in the community are beginning to pay attention to their quality of life. The only stores selling products that compete with The Artisan's Haven include jewelry stores, department store chains, and a few lower-end specialty shops. These stores are not considered direct competitors, because the quality of their merchandise is inferior to the quality of the merchandise sold in The Artisan's Haven. The store's closest direct competitors are in Atlanta, the state's capitol about 70 miles away, and many of Athens' wealthier residents go there routinely to shop.

MANAGEMENT AND PERSONNEL

15   John and Katie own and operate their store. In addition, they make many of the products they sell. The Owens have been very fortunate to get to know two retired upper-middle-income women who are looking for opportunities to stay busy doing things they enjoy. These two women work part-time for the Owens for nominal wages. Besides being excellent employees, their friends visit them in the store, and many of them have become regular customers.

16   The Owens' most important employee is Rachel Thompson. She is 57 years old. They first met her when she was a customer in the store. After they got to know her, they discovered that Rachel's hobby was interior decorating and that most of what she bought was for friends' homes. She was not paid for any of this work. When she was approached by the Owens, Rachel was more than delighted to accept their offer of employment. Rachel's primary responsibility is to work with Katie on interior decorating jobs and to wait on customers in the store. She works about 20 hours a week.

17   Madeline Murray lives next door to the Owens. She is 53 years old and a very skillful crafts-woman, who developed her talent by doing the needlework in her home and the homes of her children, relatives, and many friends. The Owens first bought needlework from her by the piece, because it was impossible for Katie to do all of the cross-stitching and to wait on customers all day. After it became obvious to the Owens that Madeline enjoyed working with and being around them and that they enjoyed her, they invited her to join them at the store. Her job was to do needlework for sale in the store and to work with customers who wanted custom-designed needle-work made for their homes. Madeline also works about 20 hours a week.

18   Rachel and Madeline are like part of the family. Customers frequenting The Artisan's Haven sense the warmth and friendliness of everyone in the store, and they tell John and Katie regularly how enjoyable it is to shop there.

MARKETING

19   When the Owens first opened the store in Athens, their marketing efforts targeted local residents, tourists, and students. They used radio and newspaper advertising primarily. After several months of operation, they surveyed their customers to evaluate the effectiveness of their promotion effort. Not surprisingly, they learned that word of mouth and the Owens themselves were by far the most effective forms of advertising. Additionally, they learned that students were not attracted to their store in large numbers, because of the prices of the goods sold and because they were not furnishing homes in which they intended to live for lengthy periods. Tourists did not flock to the store, either, because Athens is not known as a tourist attraction.

20   The Owens decided early on that The Artisan's Haven did not need extensive print or broadcast media support. However, they did continue to run an occasional radio spot or ad in the local newspaper.

ORGANIZATION

21   The Owens incorporated The Artisan's Haven in the beginning, because they wanted to limit their liability. They were not certain about their options in this area, so they contacted an attorney who helped them make a choice about how to incorporate. They learned that there are major differences between a Subchapter C corporation and a Subchapter S corporation. Both offer several important features, such as continuity of life, centralization of management, limited liability, and easy transferability of interest. The S corporation is usually preferred by small business owners, because it is treated like a partnership for tax purposes.

22   Although the Owens could have incorporated The Artisan's Haven as an S corporation, they chose the C corporation. The C corporation allowed the Owens to deduct certain fringe benefits, like medical and health insurance, and to shelter earnings for later use. Because of their age, these were important issues to the Owens.

    The major disadvantage of a C corporation is double taxation. The Owens were not as concerned about this issue as the others, because they were able to pay themselves attractive salaries that were tax deductible expenditures.

FINANCE

23   Exhibits 1, 2, and 3 contain pertinent financial information for The Artisan's Haven. The income statement shown in Exhibit 1 indicates that the largest expenses for the Owens are wages, travel, and rent. The 1981 data is a little misleading, because the store was in operation for only half the year. Travel is a major budget item, because the Owens travel a great deal to visit crafts people and art shows. Advertising in 1981 was a large expense item, because the Owens were establishing their name and reputation.

EXHIBIT 1

THE ARTISAN'S HAVEN
Consolidated Income Statements for the
Period Ending January 31, 1986

	1981	1982	1983	1984	1985	1986
Sales	$16,610	$55,673	$78,736	$105,928	$123,683	$153,186
Cost of sales	8,305	27,837	35,968	43,441	60,201	75,806
Gross profit	8,305	27,836	42,768	62,487	63,482	77,380
Expenses:						
Rent	3,900	7,800	7,800	7,800	7,800	7,800
Wages to officers	10,000	11,000	15,500	20,000	25,000	50,000
Other salaries	0	0	0	4,526	9,688	10,803
Utilities	434	612	712	862	1,002	1,165
Advertising	35,000	2,000	2,000	2,000	2,000	2,000
Travel	391	774	933	1,171	1,394	1,654
Supplies	649	835	971	1,175	1,366	1,589
Insurance	145	560	560	560	560	560
Depreciation	168	535	535	535	535	535
Interest	0	278	278	278	409	409
Total expenses	50,687	24,394	29,289	38,907	49,754	76,515
Profit before tax	(42,382)	3,442	13,479	23,580	13,728	865
Tax	0	0	0	0	5,805	423
Net income	$(42,382)	$ 3,442	$13,479	$ 23,580	$ 7,923	$ 442

EXHIBIT 2

THE ARTISAN'S HAVEN
Consolidated Balance Sheets
As of January 31, 1986

Assets	1981	1982	1983	1984	1985	1986
Cash	0	$ 68	$ 5,823	$16,532	$22,018	$20,996
Inventory	$18,000	26,262	30,651	35,398	40,782	62,168
Prepaid expenses	2,089	1,973	1,862	2,239	2,355	2,451
Total current assets	20,089	28,303	38,336	54,169	65,155	85,615
Long-term assets:						
Equipment	4,675	4,675	4,675	5,752	5,752	7,860
Furniture	3,897	3,897	3,897	3,897	3,897	4,623
Less: Acc. dep.	168	703	1,238	1,773	2,308	2,843
Total p, p, & e	8,404	7,869	7,334	7,876	7,341	9,640
Total assets	$28,493	$36,172	$45,670	$62,045	$72,496	$95,255

EXHIBIT 2 *(concluded)*

Assets	1981	1982	1983	1984	1985	1986
Liabilities & Stockholders' Equity						
Current maturities	$ 278	$ 278	$ 278	$ 278	$ 278	$ 597
Accounts payable	2,122	7,899	10,211	14,447	17,901	21,870
Accrued expenses	1,093	1,240	1,829	1,942	2,068	2,189
Total current liab.	3,493	9,417	12,318	16,667	20,247	24,656
Long-term debt	47,382	45,695	38,813	27,259	26,207	34,115
Total liabilities	50,875	55,112	51,131	43,926	46,454	58,771
Stockholder's equity:						
Common stock	20,000	20,000	20,000	20,000	20,000	30,000
Retained earnings	(42,382)	(38,940)	(25,461)	(1,881)	6,042	6,484
Total equity	(22,382)	(18,940)	(5,461)	18,119	26,042	36,484
Total liab. & equity	$ 28,493	$ 36,172	$ 45,670	$ 62,045	$72,496	$95,255

EXHIBIT 3
The Artisan's Haven, Sales by Quarter

Year	Quarter	Sales by Quarter	Total Sales
1981	3	$ 3,246	$16,610
	4	13,364	
1982	1	3,080	55,673
	2	10,397	
	3	4,512	
	4	37,684	
1983	1	5,511	78,736
	2	17,321	
	3	8,663	
	4	47,241	
1984	1	9,533	105,928
	2	25,422	
	3	10,595	
	4	60,378	
1985	1	10,021	123,683
	2	32,033	
	3	14,841	
	4	66,788	
1986	1	12,195	153,186
	2	44,906	
	3	17,961	
	4	78,124	

A MAJOR DECISION POINT

24   In July 1987, John Owen suffered a massive heart attack, and he was told by his doctors to restrict his activities significantly. Before the heart attack, John and Katie had discussed the possibility of selling the business. Now Katie was certain that she wanted to sell it.

25   Four months before the heart attack, a local entrepreneur named Don Lassiter, who was in the business of buying and selling businesses, had approached the Owens about buying The Artisan's Haven for his wife. They had told him no. At the time, the Owens were in no hurry to sell; but John's physical condition had caused Katie to become very anxious. She was concerned that John would want to keep the business and literally work himself to death. She was also worried that she could not take the pressure of running the business and taking care of John. Katie wanted to sell the business, and the sooner the better. When she raised the issue with John, he agreed.

26   Once they decided to sell The Artisan's Haven, John and Katie needed to determine how much the business was worth and if Don Lassiter still wanted to buy it. There were other issues to be considered, too. For example, Lassiter might not be the only potential buyer. How would they contact other people who might be interested in their business?

27   Although they had gone through the process of selling a business several years before, neither John nor Katie knew much about the intricacies of calculating the value of a firm. They had relied heavily on their accountant, who was a close friend, to help them in that deal. The Owens were very knowledgeable about arts and crafts and people, but not finance.

28   The more they thought about it, the more they realized that a multitude of decisions had to be made. John told Katie that any buyer would require them to sign an agreement not to compete. Neither of them objected to that stipulation. Also, there was a question about how much time John and Katie were willing to work with the new owner(s), and in what capacity, after the business was sold. Both of them were uncertain about how to approach this question, and this was not the kind of question they could rely on a financial advisor to answer.

29   How many more questions would they need to answer? John and Katie did not know.

CASE 24

HAZLETON LABORATORIES CORPORATION

INTRODUCTION

1   The recent growth of Hazleton Laboratories Corporation (HLC), a globally disbursed and complex firm, was so phenomenal that, in 1990, the company underwent a second major organizational restructuring in two years. However, because the explosive growth in sales from $87 million in 1986 to $170 million in 1990 was forecasted to continue, Hazleton's CEO Donald Nielson, wondered about the need for still further organizational restructuring to meet the needs of the company's expanded international marketplace.

OVERVIEW

2   Hazleton Laboratories Corporation was founded in 1968. Headquartered in Herndon, Virginia, a suburb of Washington, D.C., the company's mission was to provide the highest quality in scientific services and products to organizations engaged in life sciences research. This area of research focused on products, processes, and diseases affecting man and the environment. The company grew to become one of the world's largest providers of biological and chemical research services and a major supplier of laboratory animals. A description of Hazleton's major facilities as of 1990 is provided in Table 1.

TABLE 1
Hazleton Facilities

The following discussion elaborates the services and products of each of Hazleton's North American, European, and Japanese locations.

Washington, D.C.

The suburbs of Washington, D.C., were the sites of three units of Hazleton Laboratories America (HLA). The majority of the laboratory facilities and the operational and scientific management were located in Vienna, Virginia, with additional animal laboratory facilities in Rockville, Maryland, and additional laboratory facilities in Kensington, Maryland. The Washington facilities had approximately 700 personnel and 340,000 square feet of laboratory and administrative space.

All Hazleton laboratories had their dossiers accepted by the Japanese ministry of agriculture, forestry, and fisheries and after inspection of its toxicology program by the Japanese ministry of health and welfare, the Washington laboratories were awarded an "A" rating. The immunotoxicology capabilities of the staff, coupled with the experience and facilities dedicated to primate toxicology, provided support to investigate the toxicology needs of biotechnology. The Washington laboratories served as the North American center for inhalation toxicology studies conducted by Hazleton. In addition, the laboratories participated in the

(continued)

This case was prepared by Professor John A. Pearce II of George Mason University and Sherry S. Chaples. Development of this case was sponsored by a Funds for Excellence grant from the State Council of Higher Education for Virginia.

TABLE 1 *(continued)*

National Toxicology Program for over 15 years and support basic research of investigators at the National Cancer Institute.

Due to HLA–Washington's location, it had ready access to the regulatory agencies. Coupled with its interaction with Hazleton's regulatory affairs personnel, this allowed them to provide total toxicology services to their clients. In addition to the offices in Washington, the Regulatory Affairs Division had offices in Harrogate, England; Paris, France; and Tokyo, Japan.

Vienna, Virginia

The Virginia facility was the original Hazleton toxicology laboratory. This laboratory, accredited by the Toxicology Laboratory Accreditation Board, was one of the first contract laboratories to automate the collection of study data. Its Immunochemistry Division provided biotechnological and chemistry services especially in the areas of development and testing.

Rockville, Maryland

Hazleton acquired this facility from Litton Bionetics, Inc., in September 1985. The laboratory's 100-person staff provided safety evaluation and toxicology studies to governmental and commercial clients since the early 1960s. The labs were housed in an 88,000-square-foot, state-of-the-art building specifically designed as a dual-corridor barrier facility operation. They had also participated for many years in the National Toxicology Program. The labs also supported basic research by investigators at the National Cancer Institute.

The Rockville Laboratories became an extension of the Vienna campus, adding needed capacity for both commercial and governmental clients. This division also provided specialized support in the field of inhalation toxicology.

Kensington, Maryland

This facility, which was acquired in 1985 from Litton Bionetics, became the Molecular Toxicology Division of Hazleton. Recognized as a world leader in molecular toxicology, the division had a staff of 80, occupying about 24,000 square feet of laboratory space. Laboratory operations consisted of both testing and research programs. In addition, the labs conducted studies that monitored human populations for genetic effects and others that analyzed possible effects on the immune system. Sponsors of their ongoing research programs included government agencies, private foundations, and associations, as well as selected research programs funded by the company. The capability in biotechnology services was also established at this location, and this capability fast became a major growth area for the corporation.

Madison, Wisconsin

The Hazleton Laboratory in Madison, Wisconsin, was located on a 26-acre site and provided services to its clients in the areas of chemistry, toxicology, and clinical sciences. Over 700 scientists and associated personnel worked in the 250,000 square feet of laboratory and office space to support the testing needs of the food, pharmaceutical, and chemical industries. This facility served industry in various chemical, toxicology, and biomedical disciplines since the company was founded.

The Chemistry Division at this location provided analytical testing services that included the determination of nutrient content of foods and feeds, identification of hazardous compounds in the environment, studies of metabolism and of the environmental fate of compounds, and of the migration of packaging components into foodstuffs.

The Madison Toxicology Division provided a full range of preclinical toxicology services that included all phases of classical toxicity testing. These tests were run in all the standard laboratory species, as well as in chickens, ducks, quail, and domestic livestock.

The resources included more than 75,000 square feet of animal and support facilities. Animal surgery capabilities within this group enabled the staff to conduct studies that required specialized surgical procedures. Additional facilities were available that allowed them to conduct domestic livestock programs in a variety of species, with specialization in dairy cattle studies.

TABLE 1 *(continued)*

Hazleton's clinical sciences provided clinical evaluation services in the areas of drug and personal care product development, OTC and consumer product evaluation, dental research, and biological and analytical chemistry testing services. Hazleton operated clinical facilities in the United States and in United Kingdom.

West Palm Beach, Florida

The Clinical Research Unit in West Palm Beach, Florida was composed of 24 individual subject rooms, sample collection rooms, and a laboratory with state-of-the-art equipment to process samples for analysis.

Hazleton's West Palm Beach facility provided OTC product testing services for evaluating the safety and efficacy of cosmetic and proprietary products and the advertising claim substantiation of a product.

The Florida clinic also conducted dental studies and studies of the dermatological and health care products, such as sunscreen lotions, shampoos, cosmetics, and antiperspirants.

Denver, Pennsylvania

Hazleton Research Products (HRP) operated in five locations in the United States. Its headquarters and small animal breeding facilities were located in Denver, Pennsylvania. Its other facilities were located in Cumberland, Virginia; Reston, Virginia; Alice, Texas; and Kalamazoo, Michigan.

HRP was engaged in the breeding, importation, and sale of animals used exclusively for research. The animals were used to study the products of pharmaceutical and biotechnology and often were the final step in testing before compounds were introduced into human beings. This lab was also equipped to provide a variety of special services for client's research needs, including blood typing, opthalmic testing, clinical chemistry, hematology, pathologic support services, and provides anti-sera production.

Harrogate, England

Headquarters of Hazleton Europe were at Harrogate in Yorkshire, England. The Harrogate laboratories employed over 400 scientists and support staff, who provided a full array of toxicology and chemistry services in a 180,000-square-foot facility. Their pharmaceutical and agrichemical company clients employed this facility to meet the requirements for registration of candidate materials anywhere in the world.

The metabolism staff worked with a fully computerized laboratory data capture and management system. Staff at the Madison, Wisconsin, laboratories was involved since the system had applicability at both sites.

In toxicology, the Harrogate laboratory was the European center for all inhalation toxicology studies conducted by Hazleton. This laboratory specialized in nose-only exposure for the international toxicology market.

Chemistry and metabolism capabilities in Harrogate mirrored those of the Madison, Wisconsin, laboratories and regular cross-transfer of technology assists both units. Multinational clients took advantage of similar support on both sides of the Atlantic.

Leeds, England

The Hazleton Medical Research Unit was located at Springfield House, Leeds, adjacent to both the university medical school and general infirmary. This 48-bed facility opened in May 1986 and conducted studies in healthy volunteers, including safety and tolerance, drug metabolism studies, drug interactions, and postmarketing product support.

Support services were also offered in conjunction with the studies they conducted and on a "stand alone" basis to clients who are conducting their own clinical trials. Shipment of biotechnological products and other samples from single and multicenters was organized by Hazleton from any location in the world. Analysis of samples, coupled with data transmission where required, provided facility extension to Hazleton's clients.

Lyon, France

Hazleton France offered capabilities in toxicology and chemistry to domestic and international clients from the outskirts of France's second largest city, Lyon. Hazleton France had an internationally trained

(continued)

TABLE 1 *(concluded)*

staff of 120 scientific, technical, and administrative personnel, who operated more than 88,000 square feet of laboratory and support facilities. This facility grew due to its strategic location and its international focus of the industry. Hazleton France was also the Hazleton center for acute toxicology.

Munster, West Germany

Hazleton Deutschland was located in Munster, West Germany, home of one of Germany's largest universities. Acquired in 1980, this laboratory was recognized worldwide as a leader in the field of primate reproduction studies. Clients from Europe, North America, and Japan used Hazleton Deutschland for those types of specialized research efforts.

The laboratory staff of 65 scientists and technicians operated in 40,000 square feet of modern laboratory space. The animal areas consisted of 26 primate rooms and 32 small animal rooms, which accommodated over 1,000 primates and up to 15,000 rodents.

Hazleton Deutschland served as the central laboratory for the performance of all primate reproduction studies in Hazleton. Technical links were maintained between this laboratory and other Hazleton facilities. This ensured that their clients benefited from shared technology development and scientific input.

Tokyo, Japan

Japan was a major market for Hazleton services and products, because of Japan's large pharmaceutical and chemical industries that served those markets worldwide. Requirements for Hazleton services by Japanese clients reached then-record levels in 1985 and caused Hazleton to open this liaison office in Tokyo. Staffed by Hazleton employees, Nippon Hazleton coordinated with Japanese clients the services of all Hazleton laboratory facilities. This provided Hazleton's Japanese clients direct access to their services and also facilitates communications in English or Japanese.

Other services provided by Nippon Hazleton included:

- On-site assistance in protocol development and regulatory affairs.
- Assistance to off-shore clients serving the Japanese market.
- Expeditious coordination of communication between Hazleton Laboratories and Japanese clients.
- Professional representation of Hazleton Laboratories in other Far East nations.

Paris, France

The Paris office reported to the Lyon, France, office. It operated similarly to Tokyo, in that it was also a liaison office that provided access to Hazleton's services worldwide.

---

3   Hazleton's clients included research institutes; manufacturers of pharmaceutical, chemicals, food, cosmetics, and biotechnology; other industrial companies; scientific research labs; and government agencies. The company employed 2,600 scientists, technicians, and administrative personnel who conducted operations in the United States, England, France, Japan, and West Germany. Although Hazleton was not a household name, thousands of popular consumer products were developed or tested by the company, particularly in the areas of cosmetic and drugs (prescription and over the counter). Moreover, many processed foods were tested or had their contents labeled by Hazleton.

4   In addition to research, product development, and testing, Hazleton also provided regulatory affairs consulting services. All industries served by Hazleton must meet regulatory and testing requirements before their products were distributed to the public. The Environmental Protection Agency (EPA), Food and Drug Administration (FDA), European Economic Community (EEC), and Organization for Economic Cooperation and Development (OECD) were just some of the

agencies that require compliance with their regulations prior to releasing products. Because of the high impact nature of their work, more than 100 scientific papers were written, published, and presented worldwide by Hazleton's researchers each year.

DESCRIPTION OF HLC'S ACTIVITIES

5   Hazleton Laboratories Corporation was divided into five major types of activities that provided the various services and products needed to meet the needs of its clients. These activities were: toxicology, chemistry, human clinicals, animal products, and regulatory affairs.

Toxicology

6   Toxicology was concerned with the effects of daily exposure to potentially poisonous materials on humans in the home, workplace, and environment. In the toxicology laboratories, a battery of specialized tests were administered to various species of laboratory animals.

7   Professionals from a variety of disciplines were utilized to conduct the experiments and analyze the results. These tests lasted a few hours or continued throughout the animal's entire lifetime and revealed such findings as developmental and reproductive malformations, tumors, lethality, irritations, or other undesirable effects. Hazleton Laboratories established industry standards for excellence in toxicology studies. It was the first independent contract laboratory whose procedures were accredited by the Toxicology Laboratory Accreditation Board.

8   The areas of focus within this division included: acute, subchronic, chronic, oncogenicity, reproduction, inhalation, contract pathology, genetics, in vitro teratology, and immunotoxicology.

Chemistry

9   Chemistry determined the composition and chemical properties of various substances. This set of activities offered a wide range of in-house and contract services, such as formulations, metabolism, nutritional, pesticides, pharmaceutical, pharmacokinetics, and trace analysis. Hazleton's chemists verified the purity of test substances and determined their stability and concentration in the food and water of test animals, analyzed animal tissue or cultures after they were tested in other departments, provided government and industry with an understanding of the chemical behavior and residual environmental effects of particular products, and provided testing or analysis of how organisms were protected from disease.

Human Clinicals

10   Human clinicals conducted clinical investigations that analyzed the blood and urine of people that participated in studies conducted at Hazleton's facilities. Physicians, nurses, technicians, and medical assistants worked with pharmaceutical companies and regulatory agencies to determine the safety and effectiveness of new drugs and nutritional programs. A diverse population of human volunteers was carefully monitored to assess such effects as product efficacy, photosensitivity, and phytotoxic reactions.

11   This set of activities offered a wide range of services, including design and implementation of test protocols, data reduction and statistical analysis, and substantiation of advertising claims.

Animal Products

12   Animal products bred purpose-bred mongrels and beagles, rabbits, guinea pigs, and primates for laboratory use. The division also imported primates from various parts of the world. These animals are primarily used by the pharmaceutical, chemical, and agricultural industries for testing new drugs or chemicals before approval for marketing. In addition to offering animals for research, Hazleton was equipped to provide a variety of special services, which include antisera production, blood typing, ophthalmic testing, clinical chemistry, hematology, and pathology support services. Hazleton's laboratory units were the largest client for Hazleton's animal products.

Regulatory Affairs and Quality Assurance

13   Because all of the industries served by Hazleton were required to meet some type of regulatory requirement before they could market their products, Hazleton's regulatory affairs and quality assurance operations complemented the company's emphasis on providing its clients with a product development package. This package enabled Hazleton's clients to be served from product inception, through market release, to maintaining its marketability. Hazleton personnel provided knowledge of national and international regulations, as well as skills in such areas as strategy design, petition preparation, and liaison assistance and counsel with regulatory agencies. Hazleton took great pride in maintaining constant contact with such agencies around the world as EPA, FDA, EEC, OECD; in designing test standards; and in helping to develop guidelines for regulatory approval.

THE MULTIDISCIPLINED NATURE OF HAZELTON

14   Most of Hazleton's laboratories were multidisciplined—that is, when testing was completed in one area of activity, the services of another area of activity were often required to complete the analysis. Toxicology, one such discipline, usually referred to animal testing, and ultimately, to human testing. Animals were administered a compound to determine whether it caused a toxic reaction. If the compound did not cause adverse reactions, or if the toxic level was at a very high dose level, the compound could then be tested on humans. Toxicology was, therefore, safety testing, not efficacy testing. Hazleton conducted toxicology in five locations, two in the United States and three in Europe. Each toxicology laboratory housed several thousand rats and mice and several hundred dogs, primates, and rabbits.

15   The compounds were administered in a variety of ways: injection, inhalation, capsule, oral interbation, oral gavaging, or mixing the dose directly in the feed or water. Testing usually began with short-term studies that demonstrated at which dose level a significant reaction began. Dose levels were then decreased until no effect appeared. At this dose level, the animals were monitored for long-term effects. The animal was then sacrificed and a total necropsy was performed. Such tissues as the heart, lungs, liver, kidneys, and pituitary glands were removed and examined.

16   For manufacturers of pesticides, Hazleton conducted residue studies. The pesticide was sprayed on crops, which were then harvested, taken to the laboratory, ground up, and tested for pesticide level. The testing was crucial because, if the pesticide level reached a critical level, the crops could not be sold.

17   Finally, in the chemistry labs, Hazleton obtained samples of blood or urine from animals or human beings and conducted analytical profiles. Metabolism chemistry involved measuring the air and performing tests on excreta and urine to determine what happened to the compound once it got into the system of the animal or human. Environmental chemistry involved obtaining samples

of effluent in waste soil and liquids and performing content analyses. Nutritional chemistry involved testing for and establishing safe levels of chemicals in food products for the majority of the largest companies in the United States. Different foods were analyzed and labeled according to the FDA regulations.

18   The chemistry laboratories resembled traditional chemistry laboratories, while both the animal and human clinics resembled hospitals. In the human clinic there were even cardiac care centers where a patient's heartbeat could be monitored by doctors and nurses on a 24-hour basis.

HISTORY OF THE COMPANY

19   Under the direction of Donald Nielsen, the company president since 1968, Hazleton acquired numerous companies, facilities, and product lines within the life sciences industries. In fact, in its 22-year history, the company had successfully completed 20 corporate mergers. Most notable was its acquisition of Raltech Laboratories in 1982, which expanded Hazleton's United States operations by 50 percent.

20   In April 1987, HLC was acquired by Corning, Inc., in an exchange of stock. Top executives at Hazleton cited the following reason for the merger: Hazleton's growth plans for the future required additional capital and greater expertise in international business operations; and these growth factors could be supplied by Corning. The merger would also provide Hazleton shareholders with an investment in a larger and more diversified enterprise, as well as expanding the laboratory science business of both companies. Additionally, this merger demonstrated Corning's commitment to a growth strategy in a technology-based industry, devoid of Japanese competition, in which they could quickly become a world leader—laboratory services.

21   Following the finalization of the merger, Hazleton became a subsidiary of Corning, with Hazleton's common stockholders receiving approximately one-half share of Corning for each share of Hazleton common stock. Although Hazleton was to benefit from Corning's technology and financial resources, Hazleton continued to operate as an independent subsidiary. Corning's confidence in Hazleton's management, philosophy, and policies were evidenced by Hazleton's continued self-management, with Donald Nielsen as CEO and all his top managers, who averaged 15 years of experience, remaining in key positions.

STRATEGY, STRUCTURE, AND THE FUTURE OF HAZLETON

22   In a presentation to the top management team in September 1989, Nielsen stated that to ensure the growth of the company an organizational restructuring was required that was compatible with the firm's principles (as provided in Figure 1) and its successful strategy. He stated:

23   The strategy dictates that we think globally, we act locally and globally; we cultivate fewer, but larger clients; we provide more services to each client; we have a closer relationship with each client; we develop new and creative information systems to track the progress of multiple studies, in multiple line disciplines which may be performed at multiple sites; and that we concentrate on clients not markets.

24   To accomplish the above requires some changes in the way we operate. Over the next few years we need to bring all of Hazleton together so we act and think as one unit and our clients worldwide can be comfortable that any Hazleton unit will meet their requirements. The client needs to become more assured that dealing with Hazleton will positively assist in accomplishing their worldwide development requirements.

25   We intend to gain a competitive advantage by stressing quality in everything we do, and by developing a true compound development capability through mega-sites.

FIGURE 1
Hazleton Labs' Business Principles

> In January 1989, Donald Nielsen established and distributed the following business principles, which were still in effect at the end of this case:
>
> *Business*
> - To provide superior scientific services and products that add value to organizations engaged in life sciences research.
>
> *Mission*
> - To help clients bring to market safe and effective new products and to maintain the marketability of existing products.
> - To serve clients by providing services and products that may be needed to meet their own internal research or regulatory requirements, or both.
> - To provide superior scientific services and products as quickly and economically as possible, commensurate with high quality and regulatory compliance.
>
> *Strategy*
> - To develop and sell worldwide those scientific services and products needed by the industries we serve to move their new products from the basic research stage through to the regulatory approval stage. Hazleton will also provide those scientific services necessary to keep existing products from falling out of compliance.
>
> *Goals*
> - To provide superior services and products to those clients we have the privilege of serving.
> - To provide all employees with the opportunity to grow and develop to their full potential in a safe and attractive working environment.
> - To provide our shareholders with an above-average rate of return on their investment.
> - To be a good neighbor.

ORGANIZATIONAL STRUCTURE

26   Growth during the first 20 years of the life of the company centered on an acquisition strategy, whereas from 1985 to 1990 the strategy shifted to concentrated growth and a global focus. The major challenge that the company faced was the design and activation of an appropriate organizational structure to accompany its recently adopted corporate strategy.

Pre-1989 Structure

27   Figure 2 presents the Hazleton organizational structure prior to 1989. At that time, the company was an organization of fairly independent entities that operated under the direction of a centralized management team, which felt the need for little communication or coordination among locations. Each location had an established client base and operated almost exclusively to satisfy its individual performance objectives.

28   Over a period of a few years in the mid-1980s, the marketplace forced the company to accept a global organization toward marketing, production, and customer service or risk its market position. A key impetus for change was Hazleton's need for coordinated efforts on large-scale contracts that

FIGURE 2
Pre-1989 HLC Organizational Chart

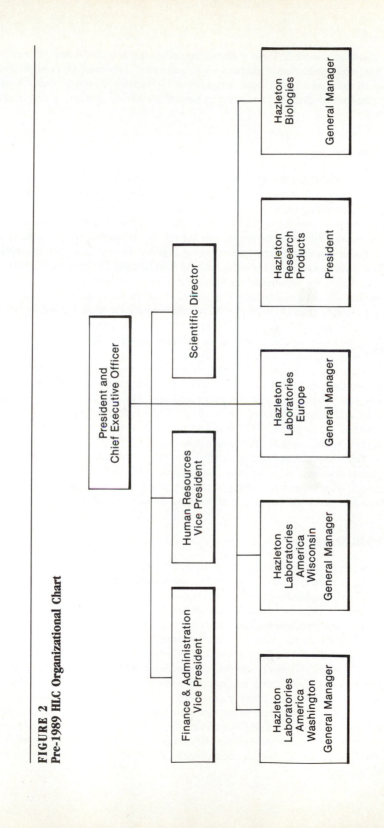

it had been awarded. These multimillion-dollar contracts demanded the inputs from several labs. Thus, while globalization had been a long-range goal of the company, competitive market conditions forced an unanticipated rapid acceleration of Hazleton's growth plans. Realizing the need for organizational changes to reflect it dynamically evolving strategy, a new structure was created in 1989.

1989 Structure

29   Figure 3 illustrates the structure as it was redesigned in 1989. This modified matrix format was the company's first attempt to incorporate a global focus into its operations.

30   The operating units or labs were still independent. However, functional SBUs were created in an attempt to coordinate the functional areas of the company. Each locations's general manager was responsible for costs, profits, lab utilization, and contract acquisition.

31   Under this arrangement, the company experienced problems with its organizational structure, most notably in three areas. First, coordination between facilities was lacking. When one location did not have the facilities to accommodate all phases of a contract, the general manager needed to contact other labs individually to negotiate an allocation of the work. Also, if a lab was contacted by a client for specific work and the lab did not have the needed capability or capacity, the search for an appropriate location would be necessary. This process of matching resources with client needs was complicated further if the job was highly varied, thus requiring the use of multiple Hazleton facilities.

32   Second, the functional SBUs did not work well, especially in the area of toxicology. There was no coordination between the two vice presidents handling this functional area. As a result, there was little consistency on a companywide basis. The company did learn, however, that a global functional area, as operated in chemistry, worked much better. For example, through the amalgamation of chemistry, HLC was able to condense the time frame for bringing a compound to market, thereby substantially reducing costs.

33   Third, the managerial role conflict was substantial under the modified matrix structure. The general managers were too busy managing their lab operations to fully carry out their functional duties. With local issues taking precedence, the net result was that GMs were attempting to keep their labs full at the expense of attention to company's global goals.

1990 Structure

34   In an announcement in November 1989, Nielsen presented a reorganization of the company for 1990, in a further effort to integrate communication elements into the structure and to split the functional responsibilities from lab responsibilities. Figure 4 shows the relationships between the company's revised organizational chart and the functions carried out at each location.

35   The new structure established a vice president for marketing and business development, who was responsible for global marketing strategy, literature, and coordinating major programs. Reporting to him was the Regulatory Affairs Department, which addressed changing global conditions. Two directors of development (pharmachemicals and food, and chemicals and agrichemicals) were responsible for monitoring and responding to industry needs. R&D spending, new compounds in development, and new client requirements were just some of the areas they oversaw.

36   Also directly reporting to the vice president of marketing and business development were the key client executives. These executives were assigned to large clients and were responsible for the clients' programs within Hazleton. In addition, they had dotted line reporting responsibility to the labs where the programs were being conducted. These client executives were not physically located at headquarters.

FIGURE 3
1989 HLC Organizational Chart

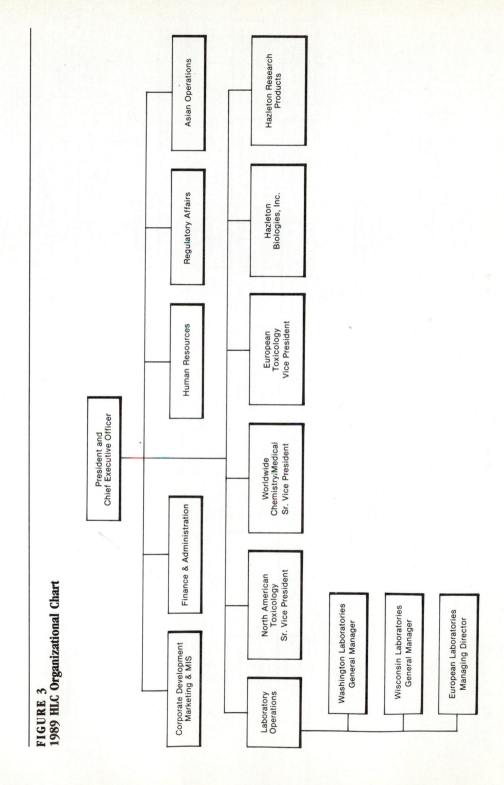

FIGURE 4
1990 HLC Organizational Chart

FIGURE 4
1990 HLC Organizational Chart

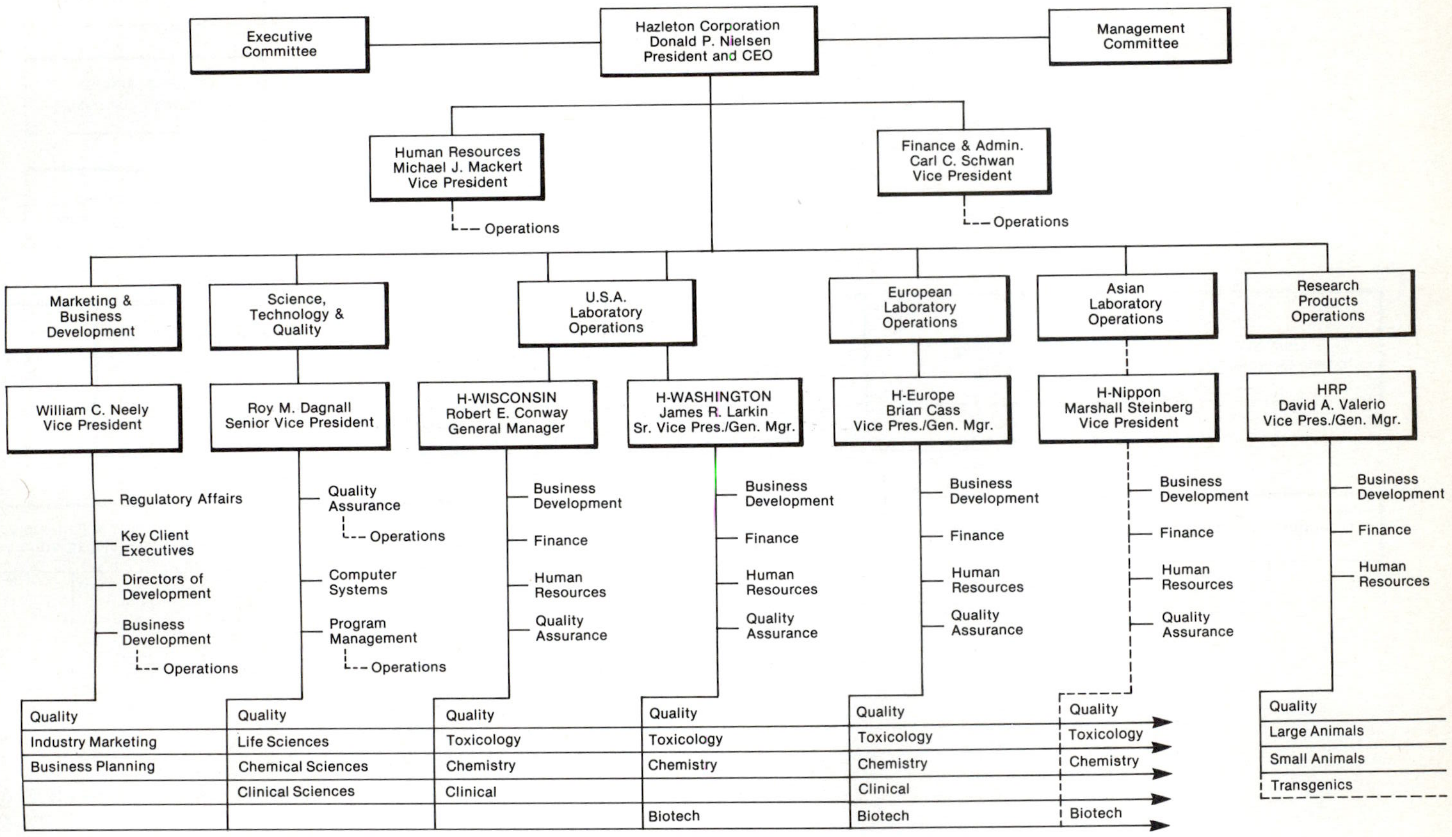

37   The other newly established global functional division was the Science, Technology, and Quality Division. The vice president who headed the division was responsible for ensuring that the best available technology was being employed everywhere in the corporation. Such technology enabled the company to maximize productivity and standardize reporting. Like the vice president of marketing and business development, the VP of science, technology, and quality had global and across-boundaries authority and responsibility, yet lacked line manager authority.

38   The general managers of the laboratories also faced changes in their responsibilities—they were no longer fully independent managers. Those general managers who had succeeded in large part due to an entrepreneurial style were faced with culture shock when their power to negotiate client projects placements was removed. On the other hand, they recognized the need for greater interdependency among the company's labs. They knew that Nielsen's intent was not trying to decrease entrepreneurial spirit but to add the global dimension.

39   Under the general managers, each lab was operated as a profit center. Eventually, the labs were expected to be treated as factories or production centers—and measured on the efficiency of their production facilities. However, half of the GM's bonus was based on the achievement of the corporate goals. This was done to convince the GMs that they needed to be concerned with more than the profitability of their own operations.

40   In addition to overseeing operations, the GMs assisted in the selling function, which was done more inside the lab than outside. The business development person went out and called on a client, but the customer did not generally do business until he or she visited the lab. The general manager was a critical sales agent in such initial visits.

41   The organizational chart reflected other, more subtle, changes as well. For example, as of 1990, there were business development representatives at each location. They reported directly to the lab general manager, with dotted line responsibility to the vice president of marketing and business development. Since approximately 85 percent of business was still locally obtained, capturing business for their own lab was the primary responsibility of the business development representatives. However, the company established a bonus program, which provided incentives for the business development people to find or to develop clients that utilized labs beyond their home labs.

42   The final responsibility for placement of work was to be handled differently. If clients had a preference for a particular lab, the company attempted to accommodate their requests. If they could not place the work where the clients wanted, Hazleton would try to convince the clients to do it at another location so the work could be started immediately. The clients had the option to wait until their first preference lab (or even specific scientist) had open time periods. In general however, placement problems stemming from individual client preferences seldom arose, since major program clients typically required and expected multisite lab capability.

43   The major difficulties with work placement occurred when a specific lab did not have the functional capability to carry out a particular stage of a study or when the lab was being fully utilized. Then the business development executive, who was responsible for deciding work placement, contacted other labs by telephone to determine companywide utilization levels. The company was working on a computer network system to facilitate this process. Essentially, then, the marketing and business development executives decided where such overflow work was placed.

44   Nielson experienced some resistance from his management team to these changes in authority and responsibility. Interpersonal conflicts among the new functional vice presidents and the general managers were a particular problem. There were also heightened sensitivities over coordination and communication needs since information flowed from the study director to the program manager to the key client executives to the client, or the reverse. Nielsen tried to resolve the disputes by stressing the need for more centralization and focus on the company's global market goals.

45   Although not shown in the chart, reorganization was also used to reinforce the importance of a global company focus, the Incentive Compensation Plan changed over the years, as reflected in the following table:

Year	Percent of Bonus Tied to	
	Corporate Goals	Local Goals
For general managers		
1987	0	100
1988	25	75
1989	50	50
1990	50	50
For business development executives and scientists		
1988	0	100
1989	25	75
1990	25	75

ORGANIZATIONAL ISSUES

46   Hazleton's organizational structure was becoming more centralized. However, the company remained complex as a result of the number of services and products it provided, in combination with its span of worldwide locations. Hazleton was considering what the next step should be to restructure the company so it could accomplish its global mission and goals.

47   A new organizational structure, if there was one, would need to address a number of specific issues:

a. Was more centralization necessary? Specifically, how should the company coordinate information and the receipt of contracts from its multiple entry points (i.e., business development, client executives, and multiple scientists all working with the same client)?

b. With the movement toward a more global focus in serving the world market, was the 1990 structure best? Or should the company be set up by markets served (e.g., drug companies, agricultural chemical companies)?

c. Should each facility become specialized in one functional or subfunctional area?

d. Some key client executives and industry specialists were also business development executives. Thus, reporting lines were sometimes confusing. How could this problem be eliminated?

e. Since the primary selling function was removed from the general manager's responsibilities, GMs could claim that the business development managers or key client executives were not doing the job of keeping the labs fully utilized. Would the GMs be justified in this claim?

f. Should the marketing and business development personnel continue to be the people to assign work? Or should the power revert back to the originating lab?

g. Should marketing and sales become a centralized function (with a single entry point to the company) or should they continue to be conducted at the individual lab level?

h. Who should be the point of contact for status reporting and answering customers' questions? As of 1990, clients were contacting company officials at multiple levels (the lab that obtained the contract, the lab doing the work in question, and the GM). Also, when one location could not handle a particular job and the job was placed at another lab, which lab should be ultimately responsible for this client and who should the client contact for contract updates?

 i. Who should be responsible for the companywide utilization rates of all labs?

 j. Who should be responsible (key client executive, program manager, and so on) when one lab of a multiple location study failed in its task?

 k. To what extent would any proposed change extinguish the entrepreneurial spirit of the location or the firm as a whole?

 l. Would it be better to continue an incremental structure change policy or to incorporate all changes into the structure at one time?

48 In essence, the challenge for the corporation is to answer the question: What are the best organizational structure and coordinating mechanisms for Hazleton Laboratories Corporation?

CASE 25

MAKHTESHIM CHEMICAL WORKS: AN ISRAELI CHEMICALS COMPANY SEEKING U.S. MARKET ENTRY

1 "To say that we are unhappy with our progress to date would be an understatement," admitted Ilan Leviteh, vice president of Makhteshim Chemical Works, a small Israeli specialty chemicals company. Now, in 1987, Makhteshim faced a key decision: "Our penetration of the U.S. market has not gone well, and we have to decide what to do about it. We have to be here," he emphasized. "The U.S. market is just too important."

2 Makhteshim's management still saw the large U.S. market for flame retardant chemicals as an inviting opportunity for expansion. Although the managers believed Makhteshim had a strong technology and an excellent manufacturing cost position, they were frustrated by the company's inability to establish a significant position in the U.S. market.

3 For the last three years, M&T Chemicals (M&T), a U.S. company, had marketed the F-2000 series of brominated polymeric flame retardants for Makhteshim. If Makhteshim wanted to exercise its cancellation option in its contract with M&T for the sale of its flame retardant product line in the United States, it had to do so soon. Should Makhteshim cancel and find a new U.S. representative, or should it try to continue working with M&T in the hopes that sales performance would improve? Another major U.S. flame retardant company has asked Makhteshim to produce a generic product for it. Could Makhteshim enter into some sort of joint arrangement for that product, as well as the F-2000 line? Or, should Makhteshim just expand its New York office, and do the marketing and sales jobs itself? Faced with several alternatives, Makhteshim was determined to reassess its entry strategy in this vital market.

MAKHTESHIM CHEMICAL WORKS

4 Makhteshim Chemical Works was established in Israel in 1952. Makhteshim is the majority shareholder of Agan Chemical Manufacturers. Makhteshim-Agan is the chief chemical producer within Koor Chemicals, Ltd., the chemical division of Koor Industries, Ltd.

5 Koor Industries, Ltd., is Israel's largest industrial manufacturing firm. Koor Industries, had worldwide sales of over $2.1 billion in 1986 and ranked 262nd on the Fortune 500 list of non-U.S. companies. It has over 100 manufacturing facilities and over 180 marketing, financial, and commercial companies within the group.

6 Makhteshim Chemical Works and Agan Chemical Manufacturers, Ltd., are both parts of the chemical branch of Koors Industries. They operate three manufacturing facilities in Israel employing 1,750 workers.

This case was prepared by Patricia P. McDougall of Georgia State University, Earl H. Levith of Edlon Products, Inc., and Kendall J. Roth of the University of South Carolina. Mr. Levith served as the 1985–86 director of the Fire Retardant Association. The authors wish to thank Dr. William R. Sandberg for his helpful comments.

TABLE 1
Makhteshim-Agan Export Percentages

	Sales Dollars	Production
Export	$112,000,000 (70%)	90%
Local markets	48,000,000 (30%)	10%

TABLE 2
Makhteshim-Agan Main Product Groups

Product	Percentage of Revenues
Agrochemicals and household pesticides	87.0%
Fine chemicals and intermediates	5.0
Polyester and flame retardants	3.0
Photographic chemicals	2.0
Industrial chemicals	3.0
Total	100.0

7   Outside Israel, Makhteshim and Agan operate somewhat as a joint company—Makhteshim-Agan—sharing offices, staffs, and communication facilities. The agricultural chemicals sales and marketing forces of the two companies are joined in the United States; however, they are not joined for the nonagricultural chemicals in the United States.

8   Makhteshim-Agan has three regional sales offices, which are located in Europe, the United States, and Brazil. The company attains distribution of its products in 65 countries through more than 40 distribution centers on five continents. Sales in Israel account for only 10 percent of Makhteshim-Agan's production. Sales in 1985 were $160 million, with export sales accounting for 70 percent of the sales dollars (see Table 1). The distribution of sales among the company's main product groups is shown in Table 2.

9   In Israel, Makhteshim Chemical Works and Agan are run as basically two different companies, each with separate headquarters and staffs. They compete with each other and other Koors subsidiaries for the resources from the parent company. Agan deals primarily in agricultural chemicals and household pesticides. Makhteshim, on the other hand, produces agricultural chemicals, fine chemicals,[1] flame retardants, polymer intermediates, and other industrial chemicals. Because of their different product focuses, the marketing approaches and operating philosophies of these two organizations are different.

10   The agricultural chemical business tends to be more tightly focused, with fewer suppliers competing in a relatively homogeneous marketplace for chemicals. The number of customers tends to be smaller and more stable, and ongoing relationships can be built up on the business side of

---

[1]Fine chemicals are specialty chemicals made in very small volumes. They are usually used in complex reactions, have high profit margins, and are extremely expensive. For example, a fine chemical may be made in a 50-gallon batch and sell for $20 per pound, while a commodity chemical would be made in a continuous process and may sell for $20 per ton.

customer companies. Because Agan sells primarily chemical compounds of known technology and enjoys widespread recognition for providing quality products, there is little need for interaction between Agan's R&D staffs and the customers' technical people. In most parts of the world, Agan's technical people generally limit their contacts to demonstrating the application of herbicides and pesticides, along with general agrochemical techniques. Thus, Agan has developed a marketing approach that does not require great technical sales expertise, but relies on price. This strategy has been successful for Agan.

11   Makhteshim, on the other hand, sells a diverse product line in many markets. One common element in these markets is its strong technological orientations. Makhteshim's management believes the company enjoys a strong technological position based primarily on its work in bromine and phosgene chemistry. The managers consider Makhteshim's technical staff to be of excellent qualilty and its laboratory facilities to be "world class." They have backed these resources with an $80 million capital investment program begun in 1986 and are confident that Makhteshim does fine technical work when it is aware of a problem or an issue confronting a customer industry. Nonetheless, Makhteshim has been successful in its European and Far East markets using a "low-cost" strategy; and Makhteshim's sales force in the European and Far East markets has been Israeli nationals who compete primarily with low prices.

12   A second common element in Makhteshim's markets is the incorporation of the chemicals, such as flame retardants, into the customer's end product. In this environment the customer's technical staff (who specify the components of the end product) play a key role in the purchasing decision. In the flame retardant industry, suppliers typically hire technically trained salespeople, because competitive pressures require that salespeople be familiar with the product technology and the various issues facing the customer's industry. Knowledge of a customer's technology and the nature of its end product are also important, since rival sellers of flame retardants often used alternate technologies to perform the same function.

13   In the opinion of its management, Makhteshim operates at a disadvantage on this second element. The company's technical staff members are not part of its marketing program. Instead, they remain in their laboratories, with limited interaction with customers or industry peers, tending toward isolation from industry issues and trends. Their contacts with Makhteshim's sales force are limited, generally consisting of responding to the latter's requests for specific technical information. Management believes that this state of affairs makes it difficult for the technical staff to develop an overall picture of industry trends or an understanding of how staff members might make better commercial use of their technical skills.

14   Some elements of Makhteshim's management believe the company has failed to recognize opportunities and to obtain the resources required to implement its own strategy, because many of its overseas activities are combined with Agan. Instead, Makhteshim had been forced to adopt a low-cost strategy that limits the resources committed to its technical sales function and to the regulatory and political conflicts that surrounded some of its products. Sometimes this has meant bringing new products to market with limited technical support.

15   In entering the U.S. market, Makhteshim attempted to overcome this shortcoming by arranging for M&T to market its F-2000 flame retardant product line. Although flame retardant products comprise less than 5 percent of Makhteshim's sales, these products are highly profitable.

16   While M&T is not considered by industry sources to be one of the strongest players in the flame retardant marketplace, it is considered to have a good technical staff that calls regularly on customers and would easily be able to handle the F-2000 line. M&T is a specialty chemicals company. Industry sources describe its technical department as "competent" and "credible" but lacking technological leadership. M&T's good cost position is viewed as its primary competitive advantage, with its products marketed primarily on the basis of price. One industry expert referred to M&T's product line as "copycat products," and noted that the deal with Makhteshim afforded M&T the opportunity

to buy into a high-tech line. M&T manufacturers its own product line, which includes Thermoguard. In some respects Thermoguard is competitive with Makhteshim's F-2000 flame retardant product line. M&T simply added the F-2000 product line to its own narrow flame retardant product line and tried to sell it as an additional product. No major emphasis was given to the F-2000 line.

17 Makhteshim had expected to gain a significant (>15 percent) market share of the U.S. flame retardant market within its first two years, but the product has thus far not achieved a major end user conversion. M&T's position is that Makhteshim expected too much too soon. M&T points to a recent major customer order as a breakthrough in the marketing program. Although the initial order was small, M&T attests that the fact the customer has developed a new product line based on Makhteshim's product offers the potential of continuing sales for a long time.

18 While Makhteshim is committed to the U.S flame retardant market, the Israelis are increasingly concerned about the style and cost of doing business in the U.S. marketplace. They are unfamiliar with a large sales force. They are not use to large bills for dinners, tend to stay in less-expensive hotels, and control entertainment expenses tightly.

19 As the deadline for exercising its cancellation option in M&T's contract approaches, Makhteshim's management is reassessing its basic strategy in the U.S. flame retardant market. In particular, some now doubt the efficacy of distributor marketing when it is not backed with knowledge of the market and strong support from their own manufacturing operations. All recognize that any decision for more resources will undergo intense scrutiny by Koor management, and will be questioned vigorously by other groups within Koor, who are all competing for the same limited resources. A clear consensus is at present not available.

APPENDIX

U.S. FLAME RETARDANT INDUSTRY NOTE

20 The flame retardants industry in the United States is an $850 million dollar business, growing at annual rates in excess of 15 percent per year (see Tables 3 and 4). The purpose of flame retardants is to slow down the development and spread of a fire, allowing sufficient time for people to react to the fire situation. Flame retardants are used in a multitude of end use applications, from electrical wire insulation, connectors, and circuit boards to carpet backing, children's clothing, plywood paneling, and plastic plumbing. With the continuing increase in the use of new materials, and new

TABLE 3
U.S. Sales of Flame Retardant Substances, 1986

	Pounds (millions)	Sales (dollars in millions)
Organic:		
Chlorinated	100	$ 70
Brominated	150	260
Inorganic:		
Aluminum trihydrate	400	80
Antimony oxide	40	60
Other	350	380
Total	1,040	$850

Source: Interviews with industry experts.

TABLE 4
Flame Retardant End Use U.S. Market Growth Rates

	Percent
Carpet backing	(5)%
Wire/cable	>15
Unsaturated polyester	8–10
Thermoplastics	6–10
Flexible PVC	>10
New applications/polymers	>20

Source: Interviews with industry experts

applications for existing materials, industry experts predict that the U.S. flame retardant chemical industry will grow to over $2 billion by the year 2000.

U.S. Flame Retardant Industry Characteristics

21   The flame retardant industry is a high-profit and value-added industry, and it has three major characteristics. It is (1) created by regulation. (2) driven by technology, and (3) sustained by supplier commitment.

22   The flame retardants industry is *regulation created*. Few consumers of flame retardants would use them if they were not required to do so. Flame retardants add cost to the end product, change and degrade properties of the base polymer, and are generally inconvenient to use. However, with the increasing rash of highly publicized fires taking their toll in both lives and property, and the increasing use of polymers in critical applications, flame and fire retardants are increasingly demanded by building codes, insurance regulators, the military, large consumers, and government bodies at all levels.

23   Standards have been set by Underwriters Laboratories, the U.S. military, the states of California and New York, Factory Mutual, the EEC, and a multitude of countries around the world. For example, laws have been passed in California regulating mattresses sold in the state. In 1987, New York passed laws requiring testing and registration of plastic products containing flame retardants used in New York. The upholstered furniture industry has accepted standards governing its products. The VIC (Verband Chemische Industrie, Germany's principal industry trade group) has announced that its members would stop further development of plastics containing poly brominated diphenyl oxides until a toxicity issue is resolved.[2]

24   While Israel was successful negotiating a free trade agreement with the United States, a notable exception to this success was in the area of bromine chemicals and flame retardant chemicals. Industry sources have described Israeli testimony and efforts as "surprisingly" poor.

25   Most industry analysts foresee increasing regulation as a certainty, with more and more governmental entities concerning themselves with the issues of smoke emissions and toxic gasses from plastics in fires. It has been estimated that the cost of compliance with current and proposed regulations, in the United States alone, will be in the amount of hundreds of millions of dollars. As a consequence of this governmental involvement, political issues have overwhelmed technology, creating a severe threat to some products and technologies and a golden opportunity for others.

---

[2]Makhteshim's F-2000 series has received full clearance on toxicology and would not be affected by this action.

EXHIBIT 1
Flame Retardant Producers' Distribution Chain

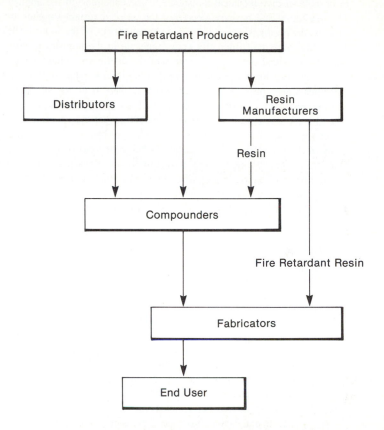

26   The flame retardants industry is *technology driven*. The customers for flame retardants have a single objective—to meet a specific flame retardant performance requirement at the lowest possible cost, giving them a competitive advantage in a specific application. They are relatively indifferent to the product or technology that gives them this level of flame retardant performance. However, the flame retardant user has a variety of performance requirements, which they are attempting to satisfy simultaneously. Thus, a product that gives them flame retardancy alone, but degrades other performance characteristics they are trying to achieve, is unacceptable. For example, aluminum trihydrate (ATH) is an inexpensive flame retardant for wire insulation. However, to reach a high level of flame retardancy, so much ATH must be used in the wire that the wire becomes stiff and difficult to bend. Unless this can be overcome with other additives. ATH will not be the product of choice in wire insulation, no matter how well it performs as a flame retardant.

27   The flame retardant manufacturers must be aware of and be able to address the properties of the total polymer system. They must know the effects of their products on the polymer, the interaction of their products with other additives and modifiers, and the total system cost and performance characteristics. This usually results in a close working relationship between the flame retardant manufacturer and the customer. The technical people of the customer, those actually

developing new products for the marketplace, must feel comfortable that the flame retardant supplier understands his or her problems and can help solve them. The flame retardant supplier is expected to be able to give technical assistance to the customer on the application of his or her products. The marketing and business people of the flame retardant supplier are expected to know the end users of the products and to know the characteristics of the industry being served by his customer. They, too, must be sufficiently knowledgeable in the industry technology to understand and deal with the technical issues. An example of the distribution chain can be found in Exhibit 1.

28   The third major characteristic of successful flame retardant businesses is the importance of the customer's perception of a long-term *commitment* from the supplier. A customer's new products may require years of research to develop. They are highly proprietary and rarely patentable. It can take at least a year and easily over $200,000 to get the necessary UL or MILSPEC certifications before the product can be sold for a specific application. Often, a flame retardant supplier will run many of the tests for his or her customer before the customer will submit them for official testing. Once the official testing is completed (usually a UL test is required), it can take an additional year or more before the customer certifies the product and incorporates it into a product line. A customer will not likely undertake the development of a new product with a supplier that the customer feels lacks either the commitment or staying power to assure the new products continued availability.

Flame Retardant Industry Situation

Marketing

29   The flame retardant industry is a specialty chemicals business that sells a performance characteristic, rather than a chemical product. Sales of products for flame retardant purposes to the polymers industry in the United States in 1986 were on the order of $850 million, with an industry growth rate in excess of 15 percent. Pricing levels ranged from a low $0.15 per pound in aluminum trihydrate to specialty fluoropolymers costing $15.00 to $20.00 per pound. Halogen flame retardants (chlorine or bromine based) are typical in the wire/cable markets, and are priced in the $2.25 to $2.75 per pound range. Synergist (e.g., antimony oxide) costs around $1.90 (see Table 5). Operating profit in the flame retardant specialty additives business is high, typically running 20–40 percent on sales.

30   A key point to understand, however, there is no universal flame retardant for all polymer systems. Each flame retardant system will have performance advantages and disadvantages in any particular polymer system. For example, halogenated systems (bromine or cholorine in combination with antimony oxide as a synergist) have been the primary flame retardant systems in polypropylene, polyethylene, and nylon in the United States, due to their ability to withstand the high processing

---

TABLE 5
Flame Retardant Product Pricing (1986)

Type	$/Lb.	
Flourine compounds	$15.00 /	$20.00
Chlorine/bromine compounds	0.50 /	3.05
Phosphorus compounds	1.10 /	1.80
Antimony	1.50 /	1.90
Aluminum trihydrate	0.10 /	0.30

Source: Interviews with industry experts.

temperatures required. Phosphorus systems have served a similar market in Europe, along with bromine and chlorine. Aluminum trihydrate has been used primarily in carpet backing and some wire/cable applications, due to its low cost relative to halogens and its acceptable performance characteristics. Opportunity in the flame retardant industry depends on the performance of the given technology in a particular application.

Key Marketing Trends

31   Currently, three trends are radically changing the character of the industry and redefining the opportunities available to the participants. These are:

Increasing politicization.

Industry consolidation.

Technological change.

32   There is *increasing politicization* of the regulatory standards in which the flame retardants industry must function. Toxic gas and smoke emissions in a fire environment are becoming critical to the nontechnical community, due to the rather spectacularly publicized deaths in recent hotel fires. The MGM Grand Hotel in Reno, Nevada, in 1981 and the DuPont hotel fire in Puerto Rico in 1986 are particularly vivid examples of publicized horror. The public is demanding a "safe" fire environment and is demanding that technology provide a solution. Some flame retardant systems may be regulated out of existence, not on the scientific merits of their products but on the political issues at hand. Primarily at risk are some brominated products, which are also under attack in Germany as dioxin creators. All halogen based systems are at risk, due to their high smoke levels and their evolution of acid gasses.

33   The second major trend is that of recent industry consolidation. As can be seen from Table 6, major players are consolidating their strengths.

34   Finally, the issue of market obsolescence, due to technological change, will have a profound effect on certain market segments. Ten years ago, Occidental Chemical sold several million pounds of its product, Dechlorane® Plus to the polypropelyne market. Today, less than one 10th of that amount is sold in that segment. This is due to new polymers being used in the previous applications and to engineering redesigns to remove the need of flame retardancy altogether. A similar situation is occurring in carpet backing, as major carpet manufacturers are conducting research and development to make the carpet fiber itself flame retardant.

TABLE 6
Industry Consolidations

Buyer	Acquired
Great Lakes Chemical	Velsicol
Ethyl Corporation	Saytex
	Dow
Tenneco	Albright & Wilson
Albright & Wilson	Mobil
Anson, Inc.	McGean Rehco, Inc.

Technology

35   Technology, brought to play in the marketplace, is considered by most industry experts to be the single most important factor of success in the flame retardant business. New regulations for smoke and toxic gas emissions require technological improvements in existing products. The acid gasses (HCl, HBr) that develop during a fire not only pose a threat to lives but may do considerable damage to expensive electronic equipment. When a New York City telephone switching station burned, over $50 million of equipment was destroyed, not by flames but by the acid gasses released in the fire. Also, because halogens act primarily in the vapor phase, large amounts of smoke are generated, hampering escape from the fire. For these two primary reasons, regulators and consumers are driving the flame retardant industry away from halogen systems. Aluminum trihydrate is the main beneficiary of this effect, because its primary mechanism is that of a heat sink in the early stage and later decomposing into innocuous water vapor.

36   New polymers are constantly being brought to market, replacing other construction materials (wood, metal), as well as other polymers. With these new polymers come increasing challenges for flame retardancy. Some of these challenges are higher processing temperatures, polymer and copolymer compatibility, and smaller particle size for thinner sections.

37   The flame retardant companies are addressing these technology issues with significant research programs in surface modifications and coatings, fine particle grinding technology, encapsulation techniques, concentrates, and chemical/matrix modifications. Industry association, such as the Fire Retardant Chemical Association (FRCA) and the Society of Plastics Industry (SPI), as well as groups of individual producers, are addressing the questions of regulation and toxicity.

Manufacturing

38   Manufacturing plants for fire retardant chemicals tend to be small (annual capacities of 10–50 million pounds) and flexible. Several products are made using the same equipment. Their $5–$20 million capital cost is considered low by chemical industry standards. The plants often require specialized equipment, and production is usually campaigned, resulting in significant inventory levels. A plant's location is usually not a factor in competition, because transportation costs, even from overseas, are small relative to value added. For example, Occidental's Dechlorane^R Plus sells for approximately $2.60 per pound. Transportation, duty, and handling costs to most parts of the world rarely exceed $0.05 per pound. Product quality and consistency, however, are critical. Raw materials tend to be a small part of the overall cost of the products (15–25 percent). While a strong raw materials base may be a competitive advantage, it is not a requirement for success.

Other Key Points

39   Several other key points must be made to understand the current industry situation. First, the flame retardants business is a *worldwide business,* both in terms of markets and producers. Companies based in West Germany, Israel, and Japan have established strong marketing presences in the United States, just as U.S. companies have done overseas. Applications technology is the name of the game, and technology transfers are rapid and efficient.

40   Second, while the industry is large in dollar terms, it is a *very small industry* in people and organizational terms. Everyone in the industry knows everyone else, what they are doing, and with whom they are doing it. There are very few secrets for very long. This requires that market participants have strong leadership, with clearly defined plans and objectives because execution of plans must be clean and sure. False starts or hesitation in execution can cause the loss of an opportunity or of a competitive position.

41   Finally, the *rapid change* of the rules by which the industry has lived for the last 30 years has thrown it into confusion. Managers who are used to dealing with technical performance issues are somewhat at a loss in dealing with political regulatory bodies. Newer managers seem to face these issues more effectively. However, industry management is currently in a generational transition and remains for the most part ill equipped to deal in this new arena. Thus, companies that can deal with the public policy makers have an opportunity to influence regulation in the direction most beneficial to their products and technologies.

CASE 26

HARCOURT BRACE JOVANOVICH

1   In late 1987, William Jovanovich, CEO of Harcourt Brace Jovanovich, found himself at the helm of a firm whose future could at best be described as uncertain. Having fended off unwanted suitors for some time, Jovanovich had also saddled his firm with an enormous debt burden. HBJ's financial worries were exacerbated by a trend toward globalization and consolidation of the book publishing industry. HBJ was faced with some tough choices as it finished the 1980s and entered the 1990s.

COMPANY BACKGROUND AND DESCRIPTION

2   Originally incorporated as Harcourt, Brace & Co. in 1919, the company adopted its current name in 1970. It consists of three business segments: publishing, Sea World Enterprises, and communications and services. Acquisitions have played a major role in HBJ's growth.

3   Historically, the company's strength has been in publishing; the fifth largest book publisher in the country, its primary publications include textbooks, professional journals, and general fiction and nonfiction books. In addition, HBJ publishes and scores aptitude tests and has operations that manufacture and sell school and office graphic supplies. During recent years, however, the firm has retreated somewhat from its publishing emphasis. In 1980, book publishing accounted for 52.4 percent of sales and 61.5 percent of operating profit. In 1985, these figures had declined to 39.4 percent and 35 percent, respectively.[1]

4   Sea World Enterprises operates three marine theme parks in Cleveland, San Diego, and Orlando. It also owns and operates Cypress Gardens, a botanical garden in Winter Haven, Florida. A fourth Sea World was scheduled to open in San Antonio in 1988.

5   HBJ's Communications and Services Division operates two ABC-affiliated VHF TV stations; publishes farm, business, and professional periodicals; sells accident, health, and life insurance; and operates book clubs.

RECENT DEVELOPMENTS

6   In 1986, HBJ reversed its recent trend away from book publishing and purchased CBS's Educational and Professional Publishing division for $500 million. The acquisition, which included Holt, Rinehart & Winston and W.B. Saunders, made HBJ the largest U.S. Publisher of elementary and high school textbooks and of medical books.[2] Analysts characterized the acquisiton—to the chagrin

---

[1]Peter W. Barnes and Roger Lowestein, "Harcourt Brace to Buy CBS's Book Division," *The Wall Street Journal,* October 27, 1986, p. 4.

[2]Barnes and Lowestein, "Harcourt Brace to Buy CBS's Book Division," p. 4.

This case was prepared by V. L. Blackburn and C. B. Shrader, Iowa State University.

of Peter Jovanovich, the CEO's son—as a "strategic about-face."[3] Jovanovich maintained that HBJ had been internally developing its book publishing segments all along and suggested that "analysts only look at what you buy, not what you do."

7 Early in 1987, HBJ made a $50 per share bid for Harper & Row, topping Theodore L. Cross's bid of $34 per share. Rupert Murdoch was also drawn into the battle, and the spoils finally went to his company, News Corporation, Ltd. In the face of HBJ's offer for Harper & Row and its acquisition of the CBS division, rumors abounded that the company was attempting to take on debt to make itself a less likely takeover target.

MANAGEMENT

8 William Jovanovich has held the position of chief executive officer for more than 32 years. He joined the company as a salesman in 1947 and by 1955 had been promoted to his current position. A succession of number-two people have come and gone during his tenure, prompting questions about his management style and potential successor. Asked whether his management style is too

---

EXHIBIT 1
HBJ Directors (showing principal corporate affiliations)

Theodore M. Black	President, Walter J. Black, Inc.
J. Wiliam Brandner	Executive vice president, Office of the President, and treasurer, Harcourt Brace Jovanovich, Inc.
Ralph D. Caulo	Executive vice president, Office of the President, Harcourt Brace Jovanovich, Inc.
Trammell Crow	Founder of Trammell Crow Co.; director, Fidelity Union Life Insurance Co., Dallas
Robert L. Edgell	Vice chairman, Harcourt Brace Jovanovich, Inc.
Paul Gitlin	Partner, Ernst, Cane, Berner & Gitlin, Attorneys
Maria C. Istomin	Artistic director, John F. Kennedy Center for the Performing Arts, Washington, D.C.
Walter J. Johnson	President, Walter J. Johnson, Inc.
Peter Jovanovich	Executive vice president, Office of the President, Harcourt Brace Jovanovich, Inc.
William Jovanovich	Chairman and chief executive officer, Harcourt Brace Jovanovich, Inc.
Eugene J. McCarthy	Senator from Minnesota (1958–1970); writer and lecturer
Peter J. Ryan	Partner, Fried, Frank, Harris, Shriver & Jacobson, Attorneys
Virginia B. Smith	Former president, Vassar College; director, Marine Midland Banks, Inc., and Marine Midland Bank, N.A.
Jack O. Snyder	Executive vice president, Office of the President, Harcourt Brace Jovanovich, Inc.
Michael R. Winston	Vice president for academic affairs, Howard University

---

[3]"HBJ to Buy CBS Text Unit for $500 million," *Publishers Weekly*, November 7, 1986, p. 12.

autocratic, Jovanovich replies that the suggestion is "a *People* magazine notion that has nothing to do with corporate structure. There's no communal way to run a company. If there's a strong number-two man, he goes out and becomes number one elsewhere."

9   The son of an immigrant coal miner, Jovanovich now surrounds himself with the trappings of his position. A *Forbes* columnist reported seeing in Jovanovich's office five briefcases with his initials, a Tiffany desk set, and a facsimile set of Leonardo drawings. By way of justification for multiple office locations, Jovanovich observed "I like edifices."

10 Current speculation suggests that Jovanovich hopes to pass the reins to his son, Peter, who has been named to the office of the president and holds a seat on HBJ's board. Both William and Peter have attempted to quash any such rumors. William Jovanovich has gone so far as to say that there is no question of succession, since he is not retiring. His current contract runs through 1989. Exhibit 1 details HBJ's officers and directors and their corporate affiliations.

GENERAL TRENDS IN THE PUBLISHING INDUSTRY

11 The book publishing industry generates approximately $10 billion in yearly sales, with the top six firms accounting for approximately 30 percent of industry revenues. Although the industry has historically been fragmented, it has faced increasing consolidation in recent years. In particular, 1986 was a banner year, with book publishing acquisitions totaling more than $2 billion.[4] The largest of these acquisitions are shown in Exhibit 2. Although acquisitions and consolidation are expected to continue, analysts foresaw that the industry would still be characterized by fragmented specialty publishing, even if six or seven firms held a significant portion of the market.[5]

12 Explanations for the acquisition fever are numerous. The most controversial argument casts publishing acquisitions in terms of ego gratification: publishing executives want to have acclaimed literary artists under contract, because this enhances their own importance. The value of backlists provides probably the most compelling justification for acquisitions. Backlist books by well-known authors, such as Hemingway and Fitzgerald, sell well (in predictable quantities) year after year, with little advertising or sales support. Also, by combining manufacturing, distribution, and sales force efforts, some publishers are able to increase revenues through mergers without realizing commensurate cost increases. Finally, mergers provide a means of jumping traditional entry barriers and expanding the acquiring firm's scope of publishing interests.[6]

13 A related trend is the gradual globalization of the industry, characterized primarily by foreign entry into the U.S. markets through both internal expansion and acquisition. Saturation of the European market, the value of the dollar relative to foreign currency, and the internationalization of literary artistry are contributing factors.[7] As shown in Exhibit 2, Bertelsmann and International Thompson, incorporated in West Germany and Britain, respectively, have recently acquired U.S. companies, as has News Corporation, Ltd., a British firm.

14 When HBJ, Addison-Wesley, Macmillan, Houghton Mifflin, and McGraw-Hill were rumored to be potential takeover targets in 1987, the consensus was that European firms were the most likely and viable threats.

---

[4]Robert J. Cole, "Bids for Harper & Row Spur Publishing Stocks," *The Wall Street Journal,* March 13, 1987, p. D2.

[5]Cole, "Bids for Harper & Row Spur Publishing Stocks," p. D2.

[6]Katherine Bishop, "The Battle of the Booksellers," *New York Times,* March 17, 1987, p. D1.

[7]*Standard & Poor's Industry Survey,* October 1987.

EXHIBIT 2
Largest Book Publishing Acquisitions of 1986

Property	Buyer	Price (in millions of dollars)
Scott, Foresman	Time	$520
CBS book publishing operations	Harcourt Brace Jovanovich	500
Doubleday & Co.	Bertelsmann AG	475
South-Western Publishing	International Thomson	270
Silver Burdett	Gulf & Western	125

Source: Reprinted by permission of *The Wall Street Journal,* © Dow Jones & Company, Inc., 1987. All rights reserved.

THE BATTLE FOR CONTROL OF HBJ

15   On May 18, 1987, British Printing and Communications Corporation made a $44 per share offer for HBJ. This $2 billion offer officially launched the battle for control of HBJ and pitted Robert Maxwell, the socialist CEO of BPCC, against William Jovanovich.[8] Jovanovich immediately characterized the "sudden, unsolicited offer" as "preposterous, both as to intent and value."[9]

16   To date, the offer represented the largest bid in the active publishing acquisition market. Most analysts, however, believed that it was too low and that additional suitors might be enticed to enter the fray, offering between $50 and $60 per share. In reaction to the offer and in anticipation of a bidding war, HBJ's share price rose $16.125 the day after the announcement, closing at $46.63.

17   Analysts speculated that Jovanovich would rely on the low bid price and Robert Maxwell's background to justify any defensive moves. After World War II, Robert Maxwell held the position of CEO of Pergamon Press. During an attempted takeover bid, Saul Steinberg found that Pergamon's profits had been significantly overstated. The ensuing investigation by the British government led to Maxwell's being stripped of his board position. He regained this position in 1974 and claimed he was cleared of all previous charges.[10]

18   In fact, at the time of the bid for HBJ, Jovanovich did refer to Maxwell's background, saying that "Maxwell's dealings since he emerged from the mists of Ruthenia after World War II have not always favored shareholders—as Mr. Saul Steinberg can attest."[11] Jovanovich also seemed offended by the fact that the bid was being made by a much smaller company. In 1986, HBJ earned $74.8 million on revenues of $1.3 billion, and BPCC earned $135 million on $775 million in revenues; thus, BPCC was approximately 60 percent the size of HBJ in terms of sales.

---

[8]Edwin McDowell, "Maxwell's Harcourt Bid Ends," *New York Times,* May 29, 1987, p. D1.

[9]"HBJ Rejects Maxwell's $1.7 Billion Bid," *Publishers Weekly,* May 29, 1987, p. 18.

[10]"HBJ Rejects Maxwell's $1.7 Billion Bid," p. 18.

[11]"HBJ Rejects Maxwell's $1.7 Billion Bid," p. 18.

The Defense

19   In defense against the hostile bid, Jovanovich took immediate, drastic action to ensure his continued control of HBJ. A complicated recapitalization plan was announced, which increased HBJ's debt to nearly $3 billion. The plan entailed paying a special dividend of $40 per share, at a total cost of $1.6 billion, on July 31. In addition to the cash payment, shareholders received a fraction of a share of new preferred issue with a face value of $13.50, although its market value was estimated at closer to $10 and the value of the existing common stock was expected to drop.[12] HBJ also began a share repurchase program and by the last week in May had bought back 4.8 million shares at a cost of $265.2 million.[13]

20   Like all recapitalization plans, HBJ's basically resulted in substituting the majority of equity for debt. Also, the combined effect of the share repurchases and the issuance of new preferred stock placed approximately 30 percent of the voting rights in the friendly hands of management, directors, employees, and the First Boston Corporation.

21   Maxwell reacted by filing suit as a shareholder to block the plan. (At the time of the takeover bid, BPCC owned 460,600 shares, or almost 2 percent of HBJ's outstanding common stock. It also held $9.49 HBJ debentures.) In the suit Maxwell charged that the planned dividend was illegal under New York state law, since it exceeded by $1 billion HBJ's surplus available for dividends, and the law precludes paying dividends in excess of surplus. The suit claimed that HBJ ended 1986 with a $500 million surplus, lost $34 million in the first quarter of 1987, and would spend $330 million for share repurchases. In addition, Maxwell charged that the issuance of new equity classes and common stock share repurchases would relegate common stockholders to a minority position when control was effectively shifted to management. The net result, according to Maxwell, did not differ substantially from a leveraged buyout.

22   At 8:30 A.M. on June 8, Maxwell also attempted to win an injunction to prevent the recording of dividend payments on that date or any other specific date. Under HBJ's indenture contract, subordinate debentures are convertible into common stock at the price in effect at the time of conversion.[14] Maxwell filed this injunction to prevent the dividend payment until HBJ provided full disclosure to holders of convertible debentures (totaling $200 million) issued in March 1986.

23   The judge in the Manhattan district court denied Maxwell's request, indicating that the filing had not been made in a timely manner and that disputes regarding debenture conversion were already being dealt with in a Florida state court. In Florida, Sun Bank, the trustee for debenture holders, was simultaneously involved in litigation with HBJ in an attempt to clarify the conversion price. The Manhattan judge suggested that any further claims Maxwell had as a debenture holder should be handled in conjunction with the Sun Bank case.[15]

24   In June, BPCC itself made a $1.03 billion rights issue. Maxwell indicated at the time that the proceeds could be used to make a further offer for HBJ if the Florida courts blocked the recapitalization plan. Even if the plan succeeded, however, British analysts believed that BPCC's new financing would allow them to top HBJ's offer. If not, the proceeds from the sale of rights gave BPCC the "resources and flexibility to pursue other opportunities for international expansion."[16]

---

[12]John Marcom, Jr., and Clifford Krauss, "British Printing Drops Its Offer for Harcourt," *The Wall Street Journal,* May 29, 1987, p. 4.

[13]"Maxwell Sues to Block HBJ's $3 Billion Plan," *Publishers Weekly,* June 12, 1987, p. 23.

[14]"Judge Rules against Maxwell, Clearning HBJ Proposal," *Publishers Weekly,* June 19, 1987, p. 25.

[15]"Judge Rules against Maxwell," p. 25.

[16]Barbara Toman, "British Printing Sets $1.03 Billion Issue; Maxwell Sees New Harcourt Bid Possible," *The Wall Street Journal,* June 17, 1987, p. 12.

25   On July 27, Robert Maxwell announced that BPCC was ending all litigation against HBJ and would soon be bidding for a different U.S. publishing company. In conceding defeat, Maxwell stated that, although "BPCC did not achieve its ultimate goal of acquiring HBJ, we are pleased that our efforts have greatly benefited the shareholders of HBJ which included BPCC."[17] On the day of the announcement, Houghton Mifflin, Macmillan, and McGraw-Hill stock prices rose in anticipation of possible bids from Maxwell. William Jovanovich did not make a public statement regarding BPCC's withdrawal announcement.[18]

Analysts' Evaluation

26   The recapitalization plan announced by HBJ was one of the first of its kind. Analysts immediately began to discuss the implications of such bold defensive tactics. American corporations have become increasingly assertive in their reactions to hostile takeover attempts, as Exhibit 3 shows; it briefly describes some of the more widely used defenses.

27   One of the more popular approaches has been the leveraged buyout. Usually implemented by executives of the target firm, this entails making the company private, using debt secured by its future cash flows and assets. This defense has been criticed by William Jovanovich and others as posing conflicts of interest for managers, who are not subjected to public scrutiny regarding the firm's performance after it becomes privately owned.[19] However, leveraged buyouts legally put the company "into play" (up for sale), which obligates the officers to sell to the highest bidder.

28   The defense used by HBJ has been termed the "leveraged recapitalization." Like the leveraged buyout, it requires incurring enormous debt loads. In addition, those characteristics that make a firm a good candidate for leveraged buyout also make it a good candidate for leveraged recapitalization. These characteristics include a strong market position, steady cash flows that can be used

---

EXHIBIT 3
Descriptions of Takeover Defenses

Poison pill
The issuance of securities that can be converted to cash, notes, or equity of the acquirer.

Pac Man
Attempting to acquire the threatening firm.

Leveraged buyout
Usually implemented by management; making the firm private by using loans secured by its assets and future cash flows.

Sale of valued assets
Selling off those assets that are of the most interest to the acquiring firm, thereby reducing the company's value as a target.

Self-tender
A share repurchase that reduces the number (percent) of shares available for purchase by the potential acquirer.

---

[17]"Maxwell Concedes Defeat in HBJ Takeover, Aims at Other U.S. Firms," *Publishers Weekly*, August 7, 1987, p. 309.

[18]"Maxwell Concedes Defeat in HBJ Takeover," p. 309.

[19]Marcom and Krauss, "British Printing Drops Its Offer for Harcourt," p. 4.

to service and pay debt, a low debt position prior to the buyout or recapitalization, and undervalued assets that can be sold at a profit to pay debt. Unlike buyouts, recapitalizations do not legally put the firm into play, so management is absolved of its responsibility to sell to the highest bidder. Critics maintain that, as a result, managers are able to gain control of the firm's equity for bargain prices without making a personal investment.[20]

29   Analysts have also criticized leveraged recapitalizations as adding to shareholder risk. Shareholders have so far fared well; Harcourt's share closed up $9 immediately following the announcement. Investment analysts fear, however, that shareholders will become overly optimistic in light of such early success and fail to recognize the potential for disaster. As long as operating earnings meet expectations, stockholders will continue to reap the benefits of recapitalization. When operating margins fall even slightly below expectations, though, stock prices will fall dramatically. Even the slightest economic downturn can precipitate heavy losses for such highly levered firms. In addition, recapitalized companies put themselves at risk of rising interest rates and reduced financial and competitive flexibility.

30   It is too early to judge the long-term consequences of the leverage recapitalization. Any shortfall spells disaster for shareholders and creditors, although management has relatively little to lose from a financial standpoint.

HARCOURT'S FUTURE

31   Ivan Obolensky, a partner with Sterling, Grace and Company, has expressed concern for HBJ's future. "I don't understand where all the euphoria is coming from. Jovanovich has succeeded, but there's no room for error in meeting his projections."[21]

32   For the second quarter of 1987, Harcourt Brace Jovanovich reported a net loss of $70.8 million versus a net income of $10.9 for the same quarter of 1986. Revenues increased 31 percent to $408.7 million for the second quarter of 1987, from $312 million for the second quarter of 1986. For the total first six months of 1987, HBJ suffered a loss of $98.5 million versus a profit of $3.5 million for the preceding year. These figures clearly point to the high price HBJ has paid for its independence. Prior to the announcement, HBJ shares sold for $10.25.

33   The success of HBJ's recapitalization plan and in fact HBJ's survival are contingent on the company's ability to achieve its extremely ambitious sales and profit projects. Estimates included in the plan called for a net income of $23 million in 1987 (before preferred dividends) and $33 million in 1988. Projections called for more than doubling 1986 revenues—$2.2 billion by 1989. Harcourt officials hastened to point out in SEC filings of second quarter losses that the majority of HBJ's sales and income are realized during the third quarter of the year.[22]

34   Additional documents filed with SEC in August 1987 outlined specific plans to reduce costs. They called for a 5 to 10 percent reduction in staff over the next year, which translated into a loss of 800 to 1,600 positions. This announcement came on the heels of a July cut of 38 positions in the trade division, 18 of which were in customer service. HBJ also planned to cancel all philanthropic activities through 1988, freeeze some wages, and sell executive perquisites, including company-owned planes and condominiums.

---

[20]McDowell, "Maxwell's Harcourt Bid Ends," p. D1.

[21]McDowell, "Maxwell's Harcourt Bid Ends," p. D1.

[22]Charles F. McCoy, "Harcourt Posts 2nd-Period Loss of $70.8 Million," *The Wall Street Journal,* August 17, 1987, p. 7.

35   HBJ faces some difficult times as a consequence of its overriding commitment to fend off Robert Maxwell's takeover. Although William Jovanovich probably succeeded in making HBJ an unappealing target for other hostile bids, the total cost of independence is yet to be determined. In the face of growing competition and increasing consolidation in the publishing industry, HBJ has sacrificed its financial flexibility and possibly weakened its future competitive position. Its very survival hinges on its ability to generate cash flows from operations or sales of assets sufficient to service and pay debt.

EXHIBIT 4
Selected Balance Sheet Data

	Year Ended December 31				
	1986	**1985**	**1984**	**1983**	**1982**
Current assets	$ 458,595,579	$ 285,971,699	$238,531,740	$223,357,459	$198,358,817
Current liabilities	246,642,452	128,866,757	125,281,691	108,728,882	86, 833,396
Working capital	211,953,127	157,104,942	113,250,049	114,628,577	111,525,421
Current ratio	1.9 to 1	2.2 to 1	1.9 to 1	2.1 to 1	2.3 to 1
Long-term debt	790,277,858	222,302,939	128,260,571	113,776,471	110,347,903
Total assets (including HBJ insurance)	2,413,295,148	1,380,857,091	578,707,473	497,233,931	443,780,242
Shareholders' equity	531,477,176	305,906,617	211,946,792	183,593,090	165,500,998
Book value per common share	$13.48	$8.95	$7.42	$6.73	$6.08
Number of common shares outstanding	39,418,557	34,174,239	28,551,444	27,270,927	27,229,143

Per share amounts, the number of common shares outstanding, and dividends prior to 1986 were restated to reflect the three-for-one stock split in 1986.

EXHIBIT 5
Consolidated Sales and Revenues
By Sources, 1986–1982

	1986		1985		1984		1983		1982	
	Amount	%	Amount	%	Amount	%	Amount	%	Amount	%
Educational Publishing	$ 450,013,149	34.6%	$400,585,206	40.5%	$355,780,595	47.1%	$227,315,275	49.4%	$273,774,531	46.9%
Informational Publishing and Services	278,412,316	21.4	247,935,638	25.0	213,581,836	28.3	177,901,179	26.9	168,101,646	28.8
	728,425,465	56.0	648,520,844	65.5	569,362,431	75.4	505,216,454	76.3	441,876,177	75.7
Parks	223,239,856	17.2	170,388,155	17.2	143,181,982	19.0	129,366,819	19.5	118,980,621	20.4
Insurance	331,549,863	25.5	171,576,097	17.3	42,226,887	5.6	28,093,385	4.2	22,758,135	3.9
Corporate	16,889,605	1.3	—	—	—	—	—	—	—	—
	$1,300,104,789	100.0%	$990,485,096	100.0%	$754,771,300	100.0%	$662,676,658	100.0%	$583,614,933	100.0%

EXHIBIT 6
Consolidated Statements of Income (not including HBJ insurance)
For the Years Ended December 31, 1984, 1985, and 1986

	1984	1985	1986
Sales and revenues	$712,544,413	$818,908,999	$968,554,926
Costs and expenses:			
Cost of sales	324,651,146	373,097,973	431,093,075
Selling and editorial	200,008,650	236,427,716	274,068,904
General and administrative	111,859,452	120,993,166	143,640,104
Relocation costs*	6,624,678		
Income from operations	73,862,358	107,260,294	151,507,156
Interest expense	13,326,603	18,544,415	21,718,605
Income (loss) before taxes	60,535,755	88,715,879	129,788,551
Income taxes (credit):			
Federal	19,225,150	29,926,863	47,632,000
State and local	6,831,140	8,242,000	11,681,000
Net income	$ 34,479,465	$ 50,547,016	$ 70,475,551
Net income per share of common stock	$1.23	$1.62	$1.91

* In 1982 the company charged to income $27,700,000 as the estimated costs of relocating its headquarters during the years 1982, 1983, and 1984. The estimate included the costs relating to moving employees and office equipment, the training and recruiting of new employees, employee severances (net of actuarial gains which arise from these terminations), and fees to consultants. The company's relocation was completed during 1984. The actual costs of relocation exceeded the original estimates by $6,624,678 ($0.12 per share), owing in part to changes in operations between offices in California (San Diego and San Francisco) and Orlando; also, duplicate rents and wages during the period of moving were considerably higher than anticipated.

EXHIBIT 7
Consolidated Statements of Income
For the Years Ended December 31, 1983, 1982, and 1981

	1983	1982	1981
Sales and revenues	$648,827,041	$575,254,594	$539,296,454
Costs and expenses:			
Cost of sales	297,820,715	271,261,955	251,160,186
Selling and editorial	181,336,740	163,653,634	143,369,330
General and administrative	108,035,640	102,248,290	92,283,937
Relocation costs	—	27,700,000	—
	587,193,095	564,863,879	486,813,453
Income from operations	61,633,946	10,390,715	52,483,001
Relocation costs (net)	—		
Interest expense (net)	10,276,507	12,647,026	12,839,113
Income (loss) before taxes on income	51,357,439	(2,256,311)	39,643,888
Income taxes (credit):			
Federal	17,570,000	(6,811,000)	11,893,000
State and local	6,311,000	1,261,000	3,996,000
	23,881,000	(5,550,000)	15,889,000
Net income	$ 27,476,439	$ 3,293,689	$ 23,754,888
Net income per share of common stock	$3.03	$0.36	$2.70

EXHIBIT 8
Consolidated Income from Operations
By Sources, 1986–1982

	1986		1985		1984		1983		1982	
	Amount	%	Amount	%	Amount	%	Amount	%	Amount	%
Educational Publishing										
	$ 53,935,046	35.6%	$ 35,746,372	33.3%	$36,719,971	49.7%	$26,128,447	41.7%	$14,038,775	128.0%
Informational Publishing and Services										
	39,953,557	25.0	31,903,349	29.7	27,587,668	37.4	21,574,211	34.4	14,398,610	131.3
	91,888,603	60.6	67,649,721	63.0	64,307,639	87.1	47,702,658	76.1	28,437,385	259.3
Parks										
	40,089,435	26.5	34,240,931	31.9	24,033,525	32.5	19,207,692	30.7	18,148,471	165.5
Insurance										
	31,754,313	21.0	18,870,150	17.6	4,461,871	6.0	4,707,578	7.5	98,560	.9
Corporate										
	(12,225,195)	(8.1)	(13,500,508)	(12.5)	(12,315,999)	(14.3)	(8,975,747)	(14.3)	(8,018,753)	(73.1)
Relocation Costs										
	—	—	—	—	(6,624,678)	(8.9)	—	—	(27,700,000)	(256.6)
	$151,507,156	100.0%	$107,260,294	100.0%	$73,862,358	100.0%	$62,642,181	100.0%	$19,965,663	100.0%

CASE 27

FOOD LION, INC.

HISTORY OF THE FIRM

1   In 1957, three Winn-Dixie employees opened their first supermarket in Salisbury, North Carolina, under the name Food Town. Co-founders Ralph Ketner, Brown Ketner, and Wilson Smith all had considerable retail experience in the grocery industry; however, Food Town struggled in its early years. Various marketing gimmicks were implemented (the company gave away trading stamps and even free automobiles), but the stores failed to win the loyalty of customers. In fact, Ralph Ketner had to close 9 of the 16 stores during the first 10 years of operation. He blamed much of this failure on the underpricing techniques of Winn-Dixie. By 1966, only seven Food Town stores remained.

2   In response to the problem, Ketner adopted the idea of slashing prices on all items sold in the stores. He realized that a drastic increase in volume would be necessary to make this approach work and keep the company afloat. The company theme of LFPINC ("Lowest Food Prices in North Carolina") became popular as both customers and sales increased greatly. Sales rose 54 percent to $8.9 million and profits rose 165 percent to $95,000 in the first year under the new policy.[1]

3   In 1970, the company went public. Etablissements Delhaize Freres et Cie, a Belgium grocery chain, purchased 47.6 percent of the stock in 1974. Today, Delhaize controls 50.6 percent of the voting stock and has 5 of the 10 seats on the board of directors.[2] The company changed its name to Food Lion in 1983, to avoid confusion with another similarly named chain. Also, the company began implementing its expansion program.

4   Today, Food Lion has expanded into eight states, from Delaware to Florida, and is considered to be one of the fastest growing retail grocers in the country (see Exhibit 1). Food Lion president and CEO Tom E. Smith explains, "Our goal is to bring extra low grocery prices to as many people in the Southeast as possible."[3]

5   Food Lion has 27,000 employees, and it continues to operate conventional size stores (21,000–29,000 square feet) and to offer discount prices. The company remains committed to expansion throughout the Southeast and has avoided moving into the sales of general merchandise in its stores. A food consultant's comments highlight the company's success in the aforementioned areas. He states that Food Lion is "probably the best example of commitment to a format and operating style

---

[1]Richard Anderson, "That Roar You Hear Is Food Lion," *Business Week,* August 24, 1987, p. 66.

[2]Ibid., p. 66.

[3]1987 Food Lion, Inc., Annual Report, p. 1.

EXHIBIT 1
Store Distribution

Location	Number of Stores	Percent of Total
North Carolina	233	49.1%
Virginia	112	23.5
South Carolina	74	15.6
Tennessee	29	6.1
Georgia	19	4.0
Florida	6	1.3
Delaware	1	0.2
Maryland	1	0.2
Total	475	100%

Source: Standard & Poor's Stock Report, p. 3905

in the industry today. And although it is a conventional store operator, it also stands as an excellent practitioner of niche marketing. The stores aren't fancy, but beat everyone on price, and the company doesn't make many mistakes."[4]

Ralph Ketner

6   Since co-founding Food Lion, Ralph Ketner has continued to be a force behind its success. In 1968, it was his idea to adopt the strategy of discount pricing and his LFPINC theme that promoted the company. He acted as chief executive officer until 1986, when he passed the reins to president Tom Smith. Despite resigning as CEO, Ketner still exerts considerable influence over the operation of Food Lion. He remains chairman of the board of directors and plans to retain this position until 1991. In addition, Delhaize signed an agreement in 1974 to vote with Ketner for 10 years. This agreement was later extended and will be in effect until 1989.[5]

Tom E. Smith

7   President and CEO Tom E. Smith is very much responsible for Food Lion's growth and success. This is largely attributed to his involvement with the company since his youth. At age 17, Smith began as a bag boy at Food Lion's first store. He attended night school at Catawba College and graduated in 1964 with an A.B. degree in business administration. He spent the next six years working for Del Monte, then he was hired as Food Lion's sole buyer. Smith developed the successful strategy of stocking fewer brands and sizes than his competitors. He also took advantage of wholesaler specials by purchasing large volumes at discount prices. He was named VP for distribution in 1974, and later became executive VP in 1977. His continued success in these areas led to his promotion to president in 1981, at the age of 39. In 1986, he was named CEO.

8   Smith views himself as a planner, who carefully molds the company's growth while keeping a close eye on the operations. This style has enabled him to react to and resolve any problems quickly

---

[4]Richard DeSanta, "Formats: Growing Apart, Coming Together," *Progressive Grocer,* January 1987, p. 37.

[5]"Ketner Gives Up Food Lion Reins," *Supermarket News,* January 6, 1986, p. 18.

and effectively. He has been a primary reason for Food Lion's constant commitment to its overall strategy of discount pricing and cost reduction. Smith has also became well-known through his participation in over 50 percent of the Food Lion commercials. This media exposure has brought him recognition not only in the Southeast but as far away as San Francisco and even Scotland from visiting customers.[6] These commercials portray Smith as a hard-working and very trustworthy manager.

FOOD LION'S ATTITUDE TOWARD SOCIAL RESPONSIBILITY

9   Food Lion is recognized as a corporate neighbor, and it takes pride in performing charitable acts. In 1986, the company received the Martin Luther King Award in recognition of its humanitarian efforts. Food Lion received the award after providing a series of commendable projects. Most notable was the donation of trucks to aid the southeastern farmers during the drought last year. These trucks enabled the farmers to transport hay from Indiana. Also, the company was cited for providing equal opportunity employment and for establishing express lanes for handicapped customers.[7]

INDUSTRY

10   Several trends in the supermarket industry may be cause for concern for many retail grocers. During 1987, there was a decline in the percentage of disposable income spent for food at home. After discounting inflation, real sales did not increase from 1986. As Exhibit 2 shows, food-at-home spending accounted for more retail sales than any other category in 1983. However, slow growth has caused a reduction in this percentage, leaving food stores in second place behind auto dealers. Another interesting trend has been the growth in sales of eating and drinking establishments during this same period.

11   The grocery industry is also experiencing competition from other types of stores. Discount department and drug stores are starting to sell more packaged foods. Many fast-food restaurants continue to sell a larger variety of prepared foods for takeout. Sales from specialty shops, which concentrate on one particular type of food, have increased as well. Wholesale clubs have also been of concern to retail grocers. These clubs have been effective at luring many customers away from conventional supermarkets. Supermarkets stressing discount prices have been hurt most by the emergence of the wholesale clubs.

12   In response to the trends, most grocery chains are stressing the idea of one-stop shopping. New store formats and product offerings are abundant. These ideas are an attempt to obtain a product mix that stresses higher margined items and services, as well as creating an atmosphere that causes consumers to view the supermarket as more than a place to buy groceries. Such items as flowers, greeting cards, videocassettes, and drugs are appearing more frequently in many supermarkets. There has also been a greater emphasis on stocking perishables.

13   Clearly, the biggest trend in the industry is the use of bigger stores. Several experts believe that the increased size is necessary to provide the variety that many consumers desire. One chain president expressed this sentiment: "Customer satisfaction starts with the store design: one-stop

---

[6]"That Roar You Hear Is Food Lion," p. 65.

[7]1986 Food Lion, Inc., Annual Report, p. 4.

EXHIBIT 2
Division of U.S. Retail Sales

Division of Sales	1983	1984	1985	1986	1987*
Food stores	22.0%	21.1%	20.6%	20.4%	20.3%
Eating & drinking	9.9	9.6	9.7	10.0	10.1
Drug & proprietary	3.5	3.4	3.4	3.4	3.6
General merch.	11.1	11.0	10.9	10.7	11.0
Furniture & appl.	4.6	4.8	5.0	5.4	5.5
Auto dealers	19.8	21.6	22.6	22.9	22.2
Hardware & lumber	4.4	4.7	4.8	5.2	4.7
Clothing	5.3	5.3	5.4	5.5	5.8
Gas stations	8.5	7.8	7.3	6.1	5.7
All others	10.9	10.7	10.4	10.4	11.2

*First six months.
Source: Bureau of the Census (revised) 1987.

EXHIBIT 3
Chain Executives' Opinions on Prospects for New Formats

	Excellent	Good	Fair/Poor
Superstores	56%	36	8
Combination	38	53	9
Convenience stores	26	39	35
Super warehouse	22	39	39
Hypermarkets	10	33	57
Specialty	8	37	55
Wholesale clubs	6	30	62
Conventional	4	35	59
Warehouse stores	1	17	79

Source: *Progressive Grocer*, April 1988

shopping, complete service departments, and integrating a drugstore and pharmacy into the store."[8] Much of this trend is a result of the massive increase in working women. The greater number of dual-income families, single parents, and singles living alone also contribute to the growth in one-stop shopping. Time and convenience are two characteristics often desired by consumers in the groups above.

14   The one-stop shopping concept has resulted in several new store formats. Combination stores offer consumers a variety of nonfood items. These stores can be as large as 35,000 square feet, and 25 percent of the space is devoted to nonfood and pharmacy items. Superstores are similar to the combination stores, in that they offer a wide selection of general merchandise items. These stores are all greater than 40,000 square feet and are thought to be the strongest format for the near future. Exhibit 3 shows chain executives' views on the prospects for the various formats that exist today.

[8]"Retail Operations: The New Basics," *Progressive Grocer*, September 1987, p. 56.

15   The newest and largest of the formats is the hypermarket. Currently, 55 of these stores exist in the United States. The typical hypermarket ranges in size from 125,000 to 330,000 square feet and requires $25 million to $50 million in sales per year just to break even.[9] Normally, 40 percent of the floor space in hypermarkets is devoted to grocery items, and the remaining 60 percent is used for general merchandise. Their success depends on a variety of factors. Freeway access, population density, and visibility are all key variables that contribute to a hypermarket's success. A majority of the stores are run by companies that are not U.S. food retailers. For example, Wal-Mart has opened several stores under the Hypermarket USA name. Also, Bruno's, a retail grocery chain, is teaming up with K mart to build a store in Atlanta.[10]

16   Because of the trend to expand store size, the number of stores declined for the first time in years. However, the larger store sizes resulted in an increase in actual square footage. Many small units have been closed, due to the openings of larger stores. In many market areas, there continues to be too many stores and too few customers to support them. This is going to be an even bigger concern, given the advent of the combination stores and hypermarkets, since they tend to attract customers from a wider area than the conventional stores.

17   Although the majority of retailers believe that the bigger stores are necessary to be successful in the future, a large group believes the industry is going overboard in its attempt to provide one-stop shopping. Chain executive Carole Bitter believes that the emphasis on size is unfounded. "There has been an ego problem in the industry that has led to overbuilding and has driven up store sizes and has increased the number of formats."[11] Proponents of conventionals claim that the larger stores are too impersonal to be attractive to everyone. They also believe that many consumers desire the conventional type of store, and that this format will continue to be successful. Although many consumers claim that they want more service departments, studies have shown that the shoppers are not willing to pay enough for such departments to make them profitable. Exhibit 4 reveals what the average shopper desires. One-stop shopping capabilities rates only 26th on the list.

EXHIBIT 4
Store Attributes Desired by Consumers

Rank	Characteristic
1	Cleanliness
2	All prices labeled
3	Low prices
4	Good produce department
5	Accurate, pleasant clerks
6	Freshness date marked on products
7	Good meat department
8	Shelves kept well stocked
9	Short wait for checkout
10	Convenient store location

Source: *Progressive Grocer*, April 1988.

---

[9]David Rogers, "Hypermarkets Need Something Special to Succeed," *Supermarket Business*, May 1988, p. 26.

[10]Ibid., p. 26.

[11]"Retail Operations: The New Basics," p. 62.

COMPETITION

18 In recent years, competition in the Southeast has become quite intense. Previously, this area was characterized by predominantly conventional stores. Combination and superstores were scarce. However, many retailers realized that the Southeast was a prime location for the newer formats. In 1984, Cub Foods opened three large modern stores in the Atlanta area in an attempt to challenge Kroger's dominance in the Southeast. This move marked the beginning of several competitive shakeups in the South.

Kroger

19 Kroger operates 1,317 supermarkets and 889 convenience stores in the South and Midwest. In 1987, sales were nearly $18 billion. More than 95 percent of the floor space is either new or has been remodeled during the past 10 years.[12] This is a result of the chain's move to larger combination and superstore formats. Kroger has not been as successful as it would like. The company realizes a net profit margin of approximately 1 percent. This is partly due to its new outlets cannibalizing its existing stores and has caused same store sales comparisons to be relatively flat.[13]

20 In response to the disappointing profit margins, Kroger is planning to decrease its capital spending plans by about $300 million. It is hoped that this will reduce interest costs as well as keep start-up expenses down. Also, the firm is cutting corporate overhead 20 percent. As for future store designs, Kroger is considering the curtailment of the new super-warehouse stores. These stores combine low grocery prices with high-priced service departments and have not appealed to a large segment of the market. Furthermore, the company is planning to reduce store remodeling in mature market areas.[14]

Winn-Dixie

21 Winn-Dixie is the fourth largest food retailer in the country, with sales of nearly $9 billion. The chain operates 1,271 stores in the Sunbelt area, with the heaviest concentration of stores located in Florida, North Carolina, and Georgia. During the past few years, Winn-Dixie has been hurt by the influx of competition in the Southeast. As a result, profit margins have dipped to just over 1 percent. Net income also declined in 1987. Management points to a lack of investment in new stores and a rather slow response to competitors' underpricing methods as the main reasons for the decline in profits.[15]

22 Management has adopted several new strategies to combat the competition. Foremost is the move to larger store formats. In the past, the chain operated mostly conventional stores and depended on operating efficiencies to realize sizable profits. However, management believes that it is now necessary to alter the stores in response to changing consumer needs. At the end of 1987, the average supermarket was 27,700 square feet. There are approximately 250 new stores in the 35,000 to 45,000 square foot range, and they are expected to account for nearly half of all sales in the

---

[12]*Standard & Poor's Standard Stock Reports.* p. 1318.

[13]*Value Line Investment Survey.* 1987, p. 1511.

[14]Ibid., p. 1511.

[15]*Standard & Poor's.* p. 2491

next five years.[16] The units in the 35,000 square feet category are combination stores, which are operated under the Winn-Dixie name. The 45,000 square foot stores employ the superstore format and use the name "Marketplace." Emphasis is being placed on service departments as well as on price sensitivity.

23   Other changes involve management. Last year, the company eliminated a layer of management, which resulted in 60 layoffs. The firm is also adopting a decentralized strategy, which divides the company into 12 operating units. Each division is allowed to develop its own procedures and image. It is hoped that this will help the stores cater more effectively to the consumers in each market area.

Lucky Stores

24   Lucky operates nearly 500 supermarkets throughout the country. The majority of these are located in California; however, the chain does operate 90 stores in Florida. In 1986, Lucky began a major restructuring. This resulted in the sale of all the nonfood businesses. Also, the company has concentrated on increasing the store size to enable the sale of more service and nonfood items. The average size of the stores at the end of 1986, was 31,000 square feet.[17]

25   At the end of the year, there was much speculation that American Stores Company would begin to pursue an unsolicited tender offer for all outstanding shares of Lucky common stock. American Stores is a leading retailer in the country and operates mostly combination food and drug stores.

Bruno's

26   Bruno's operates approximately 100 supermarkets and combination food and drug stores in the Southeast. This chain pursues a strategy of high-volume sales at low prices. Another strategy involves the use of four different formats under various names. "Consumer Warehouse Foods"

EXHIBIT 5

	Kroger	Lucky	Winn-Dixie	Bruno's	Food Lion
No. of stores	2,206	481	1,271	111	475
Employees	170,000	44,000	80,000	10,655	27,033
Sales ($ mil)	17,660	6,925	8,804	1,143	2,954
Sales/employee	103,881	157,386	110,049	107,265	109,267
Net profit ($ mil)	246.6	151	105.4	31	85.8
Net profit margin	1.4	2.2	1.2	2.7	2.9
Gross margin	22.4	25	22	20.8	19.2
Current ratio	1.1	.83	1.65	1.63	1.41
Return on equity	24.5	46.3	15.2	15.4	25.3
Return on assets	5.5	11.8	7.9	10.3	10.6
Lt debt/equity	0.69	0.38	0.03	0.04	0.26
Earnings per share	3.14	3.92	2.72	0.79	0.27
Avg. P/E ratio	15.1	10.2	13.9	23.1	35.3

---

[16]"Winn-Dixie Strategy," *Supermarket News*, March 3, 1987, p. 12.

[17]*Standard & Poor's*, p. 1387.

stores are relatively small warehouse type stores, which emphasize lower prices and reduced operating costs. "Food World" stores are large supermarkets, which offer a variety of supermarket items at low prices. "Bruno's Food and Pharmacy" stores promote the idea of one-stop shopping through the combination store format. Finally, "FoodMax" stores are superwarehouses, which offer generic and bulk foods in addition to the national labels.[18]

26   The company is also well-known for its innovative forward buying program. Bruno's is able to purchase goods at low prices because of its 900,000 square foot distribution center, which houses excess inventory. This strategy has been very successful, and the company boasts one of the highest operating (4.8 percent) and net profit margins (2.7).[19] (See Exhibit 5.)

EXPANSION AT FOOD LION

27   Food Lion has continued to grow and expand in the Southeast. During 1987, the chain opened 95 new stores while closing only 8, bringing the total of 475. With the exception of four supermarkets, Food Lion operates its stores under various leasing arrangements. The number of stores has grown at a 10-year compound rate of 24.1 percent.[20] With this expansion has come impressive growth in both sales and earnings over the same period (see Exhibit 6). The firm has attained 29.7 percent sales and 30.9 percent earnings compounded over the past 10 years.[21]

28   The existence and further development of distribution centers serve as the core for continued expansion. At the end of 1987, four such centers had been completed. These are located in Salisbury and Dunn, North Carolina; Orangeburg County, South Carolina; and Prince George County, Virginia. Two additional centers are planned, for Tennessee and Jacksonville, Florida. These distribution centers enable Food Lion to pursue expansion using its "ink blot" formula. In this strategy,

EXHIBIT 6
Growth and Expansion (dollars in thousands)

Year	Number of Stores	Sales	Net Income
1987	475	$2,953,807	$85,802
1986	388	2,406,582	61,823
1985	317	1,865,632	47,585
1984	251	1,469,564	37,305
1983	226	1,172,459	27,718
1982	182	947,074	21,855
1981	141	666,848	19,317
1980	106	543,883	15,287
1979	85	415,974	13,171
1978	69	299,267	9,481

Source: Food Lion annual reports.

[18]Ibid., p. 3358M.

[19]John Liscio, "Beefing Up Profits," *Baron's,* May 25, 1987, p. 18.

[20]1987 Food Lion, Inc., Annual Report, p. 9.

[21]Ibid., p. 9.

new stores are added to an existing market area to saturate the market. "If anyone wants to go to a competitor, they'll have to drive by one of our stores," explains CFO Brian Woolf.[22] Despite the emergence of new stores, cannibalization has not been a problem. In fact, same-store sales increase approximately 8 percent annually. When Food Lion enters a new area, the strategy of underpricing the competitors is employed. Such a strategy has caused average food prices to decline 10–20 percent in some parts of the country.[23] Every new store is constructed no further than 200 miles from a distribution center. With continued expansion, new distribution centers whose radiuses overlap an existing distribution territory are erected to keep down warehouse and transportation costs.

29   Moreover, Food Lion continues to employ a "cookie-cutter" approach to its new stores. Rather than purchase existing stores, the firm much prefers to build new ones from scratch. All the stores fall into the conventional store category. The majority are 25,000 square feet and cost only $650,000 to complete. These stores emphasize the fruit and vegetable departments. Approximately 40 percent of the new stores are 29,000 square feet and contain a bakery/delicatessen. These are placed after careful consideration is given to the demographics and psychographics of the area. Normally, new stores turn a profit within the first six months of operation. In comparison, most competitors construct slightly larger stores, which cost over $1 million to complete.[24]

30   The standard size of the stores has allowed the company to keep costs down while sticking to basics. Aside from the bakery departments, Food Lion has stayed away from service departments, such as seafood counters and flower shops. Such departments are often costly, due to the increase in required labor. Also, Food Lion has remained a retail grocery chain, shunning the idea of moving into the general merchandise area. This structure has prompted Food Lion to be compared to both Wal-Mart and McDonald's.

31   With the steady increase in stores over the past 10 years comes an increase in the need for quality employees. In an interview last March, Smith expressed concern over the high dropout rate of high school students.[25] Food Lion relies heavily upon recent graduates, and the current trend may signal a decline in the quality of the average worker. Food Lion has responded to the labor problem by setting up an extensive training program for its 27,000 employees. These programs range from in-store training at the operational level to comprehensive training programs for potential managers. In addition, the firm continues to offer programs at headquarters to upgrade the work of the upper staff. Management is also attempting to increase the use of computers within the company. More specifically, Smith is hoping to utilize computer systems to handle much of the financial reporting aspects in the individual stores in an attempt to lessen the need for more employees.

ADVERTISING

32   Rather than employ costly advertising gimmicks, such as double-coupon offers, Food Lion's advertising strategy combines cost-saving techniques with an awareness of consumer sentiment. Smith is the company's main spokesman, appearing in over half of the television commercials. Not only has this method kept advertising expenses down but has also made the public aware of both Smith and his discount pricing policy. By producing most of the ads in-house and using only

[22]"Beefing Up Profits," p. 19.

[23]"Food Lion's Roar Changes Marketplace," *Tampa Tribune,* April 5, 1989, p. 1.

[24]"That Roar You Hear Is Food Lion," p. 65.

[25]"Food Lion, Inc.," *The Wall Street Transcript,* March 28, 1988, p. 88890.

a few paid actors, the cost of an average TV spot is only $6,000. Also, the company policy of keeping newspaper ads relatively small results in annual savings of $8 million. Food Lion's advertising costs are a mere 0.5 percent of sales, one fourth of the industry average.[26]

33   The content of the ads is another reason for Food Lion's success. Many of the TV spots feature some of the cost-cutting techniques used by the firm. One theme often mentioned at the end of an ad states "When we save, you save." Another commonly used theme states "Food Lion is coming to town, and food prices will be coming down." Before moving into the Jacksonville, Florida, area, Food Lion launched a nine-month advertising campaign. Many of these ads focused on innovative management methods that permit lower prices to be offered in the stores. For example, one ad demonstrates how a central computer is used to help control freezer temperatures. Other ads attempt to characterize Food Lion as a responsible community member. One such spot describes the importance that management places on the preventive maintenance of its forklifts and tractor-trailers.

34   Smith has also used the media to react to potential problems. For instance, Winn-Dixie launched an advertising attack against Food Lion reminding customers how competitors have come and gone. The company countered with an ad featuring Tom Smith in his office reassuring consumers. "Winn-Dixie would have you believe that Food Lion's low prices are going to crumble and blow away. Let me assure you that as long as you keep shopping at Food Lion, our lower prices are going to stay right where they belong—in Jacksonville."[27] Smith also reacted quickly to a possible conflict in eastern Tennessee in 1984. Several rumors circulated that linked the Food Lion logo to Satanic worship. In response, Smith hired Grand Ole Opry star Minnie Pearl to appear in the Tennessee advertisements until the stories disappeared.[28]

INNOVATIONS

35   The grocery industry is characterized by razor-thin margins. While most retail grocery chains have failed to introduce new innovations in the industry, Food Lion has employed several techniques that enable the firm to offer greater discounts on nearly all its products. These innovations help Food Lion to realize a profit margin of nearly 2.9 percent, twice the industry average. Many of the innovations are ingenious cost-cutting ideas. CFO Woolf explains the company credo of doing "1,000 things 1 percent better."[29] Such a philosophy has resulted in keeping expenses at 14 percent of sales. This represents only 66 percent of the industry average.

36   Examples of the ideas are abundant. Rather than purchase expensive plastic bins to store cosmetics, Food Lion recycles old banana crates. These banana boxes are also used for storing groceries in warehouses. These innovations save the company approximately $200,000 a year.[30] Furthermore, the firm utilizes waste heat from the refrigerator units to warm part of the stores. Also, motion sensors automatically turn off lights in unoccupied rooms. Costs are further reduced by Food Lion's practice of repairing old grocery carts, rather than purchasing newer and more expensive models. Perhaps the greatest savings can be attributed to the carefully planned distribution system. This system allows management to take advantage of wholesalers' specials. The centralized

---

[26]"That Roar You Hear Is Food Lion," p. 65.

[27]"Food Lion, Winn-Dixie in Animated Squabble," *Supermarket News*, September 14, 1987, p. 9.

[28]"That Roar You Hear Is Food Lion," p. 66.

[29]Ibid., p. 65.

[30]"Ad Series Heralds First Florida Food Lion," *Supermarket News*, March 2, 1987, p. 12.

buyout-and-distribution technique allows products for all stores to be purchased at one volume price.

37   Moreover, labor costs remain lower than those of many competitors. Smith is vehemently opposed to the use of unionized labor. Despite protests from the United Food and Commercial Workers International Union, claiming that Food Lion's wages are well below union standards, management has continued to please its workers and avoid unionization. In fact, Smith believes its employees benefit package is unequaled in the industry. A profit-sharing plan linking an employee's efforts in making Food Lion profitable with wealth accumulation for the future is already in use. Plans to improve long-term disability insurance benefits are underway.[31] In contrast, several other chains have experienced problems solving labor union problems. For example, a month-long strike by Kroger's Denver-area employees resulted in concessions on wages, benefits, and work rules. Safeway employees were also given quick concessions after threatening to close down several stores.[32]

38   Other innovations are designed to increase sales. Food Lion often sells popular items, such as pet food and cereal, at cost in an attempt to draw more customers into the stores. The company makes $1 million a year selling fertilizer made from discarded ground up bones and fat. Lower prices are also feasible, due to the policy of offering fewer brands and sizes than competitors. The company has increased its private label stock, which now includes at least one unit in every category. These two methods allow the company to price its national brand products below many competitors' private brands. As mentioned earlier, the smaller store size and sale of mostly food items have contributed to the high profit margin realized by the company.

FINANCE

39   Food Lion's sound financial structure has enabled the company to continue expanding without becoming overextended or burdened with heavy debt repayments. The firm's capital structure consists of 26 percent long-term debt and 74 percent equity (see Exhibit 7). The majority of growth has been financed through internally generated funds. The company does not want to grow at the expense of profits. With careful planning, Food Lion has been very successful in this area, and it has been able to maintain very impressive margins throughout the expansion period.

40   The growth in Food Lion's stock prices also reflects the sound financial position of the company. This growth illustrates the continued confidence of investors in the future productivity of the firm. In response to the rapid rise of stock prices, management has declared two stock splits since late 1983, when the two separate classes of stock were formed from the previous single class. These splits are designed to keep the price of the stock low enough to be attractive and affordable to all investors. Exhibit 8 shows the adjusted stock prices beginning in 1983, when the two classes were formed.

41   Furthermore, the per share data reveals the success Food Lion has achieved over the past decade (see Exhibit 9). These figures also illustrate investors' desire for Food Lion stock. More specifically, the price/earnings ratio indicates how much investors are willing to pay for a dollar of the company's earnings. In 1987, Food Lion's P/E ratio was the 83rd highest of all the companies listed in the Value Line Investment Survey.

---

[31] 1986 Food Lion, Inc., Annual Report.

[32] *Value Line Investment Survey*. August 28, 1987, p. 1501.

EXHIBIT 7
Financial Ratios

Year	Operating Margin	Net Profit Margin	Return on Assets	Return on Equity	Percent Lt Debt of Cap.
1987	6.8%	2.9%	14.2%	32.4%	26.0%
1986	6.9	2.6	14.1	29.8	24.0
1985	6.3	2.6	14.4	29.1	20.5
1984	6.3	2.5	13.6	30.2	22.8
1983	5.9	2.4	13.0	28.3	25.9
1982	5.6	2.3	15.7	28.1	18.0
1981	6.7	2.9	18.1	32.3	12.4
1980	5.9	2.8	17.7	33.4	15.5
1979	6.7	3.2	20.0	39.0	19.0
1978	6.9	3.2	19.5	38.3	22.8

Source: 1987 Food Lion annual report.

EXHIBIT 8
Adjusted Stock Prices

	Class A		Class B	
	High	Low	High	Low
1983:				
IV	$2^1/_8$	$1^5/_8$	$2^1/_8$	2
1984:				
I	$1^5/_8$	$1^3/_8$	$1^3/_4$	$1^3/_8$
II	$1^5/_8$	$1^3/_8$	$1^5/_8$	$1^1/_2$
III	$1^7/_8$	$1^3/_8$	$1^7/_8$	$1^1/_2$
IV	$2^1/_4$	$1^7/_8$	$2^3/_8$	$1^7/_8$
1985:				
I	$2^5/_8$	$2^1/_8$	$2^7/_8$	$2^1/_4$
II	$3^1/_8$	$2^1/_4$	$3^1/_8$	$2^3/_4$
III	3	$2^3/_4$	3	$2^7/_8$
IV	$3^3/_4$	$2^3/_4$	$3^3/_4$	$2^7/_8$
1986:				
I	$4^1/_2$	$3^3/_8$	$4^7/_8$	$3^3/_8$
II	$6^1/_8$	$4^1/_8$	$7^1/_8$	$4^7/_8$
III	$7^1/_4$	$5^1/_2$	9	$6^7/_8$
IV	$6^1/_8$	5	$7^3/_8$	$5^7/_8$
1987:				
I	$7^5/_8$	$6^1/_8$	$8^1/_2$	$6^3/_8$
II	$8^1/_8$	$6^1/_8$	$8^1/_2$	7
III	$12^1/_4$	$7^3/_4$	13	$8^1/_4$
IV	$13^3/_8$	$7^3/_4$	$14^1/_4$	8

Source: Food Lion annual reports.

EXHIBIT 9
Per Share Data

Year	EPS	P/E Range	Dividends	Payout Ratio
1987	.27	54–22	$.04^1/_8$	15%
1986	.19	47–17	$.01^7/_8$	9
1985	.15	25–15	$.01^1/_4$	8
1984	.12	20–12	$.00^3/_4$	6
1983	.09	28–19	$.00^3/_4$	8
1982	.07	32–12	$.00^3/_4$	9
1981	.06	17–10	$.00^5/_8$	9
1980	.05	13–9	$.00^1/_2$	9
1979	.05	17–9	$.00^1/_2$	9
1978	.05	11–5	$.00^1/_8$	4

Source: *1988 Standard & Poor's Corp.* p. 3906

FUTURE

42   Next week, Tom Smith is meeting with the board of directors to discuss and present his ideas for the next few years. Given the recent troublesome trends in the grocery industry, as well as the increasing competition in the Southeast, he is reviewing the future strategy of Food Lion. Foremost in his mind is the extent to which Food Lion should continue to expand operations of its conventional stores in this area. He is also pondering movement into other market areas. Smith wants to be sure that the company will be able to finance future growth without greatly changing its current capital structure. Although the current success of Food Lion is quite impressive, Smith realizes that other grocery chains have experienced problems by not responding to the changing environment. He wants to be certain that this does not happen to Food Lion.

CASE 28

CINEPLEX ODEON CORPORATION

1   In mid-February 1989, Jack Valenti, head of the Motion Picture Association, reaffirmed the film industry's basic health by citing 1988 movie theater attendance figures surpassing 1 billion people for the seventh year in a row. While this magnitude translated into box office revenues of over $4.4 billion, there are indications the industry is in a state of both absolute and relative decline. It is also undergoing a restructuring that is fundamentally changing the nature of competitive practices for those in the film exhibition business. In the first instance, a lower proportion of America's aging population attends the movies each year, partially due to the use of VCR's for film viewing, the presence of television in both its broadcast and cable versions, and to other uses of the consumer's leisure time dollars. In the second instance, a great degree of owner concentration is occurring, due to separate actions by both the Hollywood producers of films and their exhibitors.

2   Despite the apparent decline of the motion picture theater as the major supplier of America's needs for mass entertainment, the Toronto-based firm of Cineplex Odeon has quickly become North America's second largest and most profitable theater chain through a series of shrewd and adventuresome acquisitions while creating a large number of up-scaled, multiscreened theaters in key cities and market areas. With 482 theaters and 1,809 screens in 20 states, the Washington, D.C., area, six Canadian provinces, and the United Kingdom, the firm posted record sales of $695.8 million and profits of $40.4 million in 1988 while standing on the verge of developing and operating more than 110 screens in the United Kingdom by 1991. Central to Cineplex Odeon's success is the firm's driven and often-abrasive chairman, president, and CEO, Garth Drabinsky. It is against the backdrop of the industry's fundamental changes and basic decline that Drabinsky must chart his firm's future actions to insure its continued growth and prosperity.

THE MOTION PICTURE THEATER INDUSTRY

3   The motion picture theater industry (SIC 783) has undergone a number of radical transformations since its turn of the century beginnings. The first movies were shown in cramped and hastily converted storefront locations called *nickelodeons,* so-named for their five-cent admission charges. Their numbers grew rapidly because the costs of entering this industry were relatively low and a plentiful supply of films was available in both their legal and pirated versions. By 1907, it was estimated the United States had about 3,000 movie theaters, mainly concentrated in the larger cities. Rural areas were serviced by traveling film shows, which made their presentations in the local town meeting hall.

4   The typical show lasted only 15 to 20 minutes, augmented by song slides or lectures. As the film medium's novelty declined, audiences began to clamor for more lavish and ambitious productions using recognizable actors and actresses. Feature-length movies replaced one-reel short subjects and comedies in the middle to late 1910s, and the theater industry's greatest building

---

This case was prepared by Joseph Wolfe of the University of Tulsa.

period began. Opulent, specially built structures soon became the focal point of every major city's downtown area. Often possessing more than 5,000 seats, they came complete with a pit orchestra and vocalists and chorus, baby-sitting facilities, elevators and grand staircases to a heaven-like balcony, numerous doormen, and a watchful and attentive fleet of uniformed ushers.

5   By the mid-1920s, over 19,000 theaters were in operation, and Hollywood's film producers began what was a continuing attempt to control via acquisitions the first-run exhibitors of their films. The battle was initially waged between Paramount and First National, but soon Loew's (MGM), Fox, and Warner Brothers joined in, with First National being the major loser. By 1935, the twin realities of the Great Depression and the advent of sound films caused the number of theaters to plummet to about 15,000. Because of the nation's bleak economic outlook, many theaters had become too run-down or too costly to convert to the greater demands of sound films. Many Americans also substituted radio's free entertainment for their weekly lemming-like trek to the movies. Surviving theaters introduced the double feature to create more value for the entertainment dollar, while obtaining the major source of their profits from candy, soft drinks, and popcorn sales.

6   During World War II, motion picture attendance and Hollywood's profits reached their all-time highs, with about 82 million people a week going to the nation's 20,400 theaters. This pinnacle did not last long, however, as postwar incomes were spent on new cars, television sets, and homes built in the newly emerging suburbs. Motion picture attendance began its precipitous fall in 1947, with attendance reaching its all-time low of 16 million per week in 1971. The number of theaters followed the same downward trend, although a steady increase in the number of drive-in theaters temporarily took up some of the slack. (See Exhibit 1.)

7   The postwar period also saw the effects of the government's 1948 Consent Decree. By the early 1940s, Hollywood's five major studios had obtained control or interests in 17 percent of the nation's theaters. This amounted to 70 percent of the important large city first-run theaters. Although certain studios were stronger in different parts of the country—Paramount dominated New England and the South, Warner Brothers the mid-Atlantic region, Loew's and RKO the New York–New Jersey area, and 20th Century-Fox the western states—each controlled all stages of the distribution chain from its studios (manufacturing), its film exchanges (wholesaling), and its movie theaters (retailing). Under the Consent Decree the studios could either divest their studios and film exchanges or get rid of their movie theaters. Hollywood chose to sell the cinemas, thereby opting to control the supply side of the film distribution system.

8   In an effort to arrest the decline in attendance and to counter the relatively inexpensive and convenient medium of black-and-white television in the 1950s, the film studios retaliated by offering movies that dealt with subject matter considered too dangerous for home viewing, shown in formats and hues beyond television's technical capabilities. Moviegoers heard the word "virgin" uttered for the first time, women "with child" actually looked pregnant, rather than merely full-skirted, and couples were shown in bed together without having to put one foot on the floor. From 1953 to 1968, about 28 percent of Hollywood's films were photographed and projected in a bewildering array of widescreen processes, such as Cinerama, CinemaScope, RegalScope, SuperScope, Technirama, VistaVision, Panavision, Techniscope, and even three-dimensional color.

9   As movie attendance stabilized in the mid-1980s to a little more than 20 million patrons per week, two new trends have established themselves in the movie theater business. The first has been the creation of multiple screened theater sites, while the second trend has been Hollywood's reacquisition of theaters and theater chains as part of a general consolidation within the industry. Many theater chains have rediscovered the glitz and glamor of old Hollywood by either subdividing and rejuvenating old theaters or by constructing multiplexes from scratch in suburban malls and shopping districts. The economies of multiple screened operations are compelling at the local level. Rather than needing a separate manager and projectionist for each theater, a number of variously sized auditoriums can be combined and centrally serviced. Box office operations and concession

EXHIBIT 1
Number of U.S. Movie Theaters
Selected years, 1923–1989

Year	Theaters	Drive-ins	Total	Screens
1923	15.0		15.0	
1926	19.5		19.5	
1929	23.3		23.3	
1935	15.3		15.3	
1942	20.3	0.1	20.4	
1946	18.7	0.3	19.0	
1950	16.9	2.2	19.1	
1955	14.1	4.6	18.7	
1965	9.2	4.2	13.4	
1974	9.6	3.5	13.2	14.4
1980	9.7	3.6	13.3	17.6
1981	11.4	3.3	14.7	18.0
1984	14.6	2.8	17.4	20.2
1985	15.1	2.8	17.9	20.7
1986	16.8	2.8	19.6	22.8
1987*	17.9	2.8	20.7	23.6
1988*	18.1	2.7	20.8	24.3

* Estimated.

Sources: Joel W. Finler, *The Hollywood Story* (New York: Crown Publishers, 1988), p. 288; "The Motion Picture Rides into Town, 1903," *The Wall Street Journal,* February 7, 1989, p. B1; *1989 U.S. Industrial Outlook* (Washington, D.C.: U.S. Department of Commerce/International Trade Administration, 1989), p. 57–1.

stands can also be centrally managed and operated. The availability of a number of screens at one location also yields programming flexibility for the theater operator. A "small" film without mass appeal can often turn a profit in a room seating only 300 people, while it would be unprofitable and would be lost in a larger auditorium. Having a number of screens in operation also increases the likelihood the complex will be showing a hit film, thereby generating traffic for the other films being shown at the site. Having multiple screens also allows the operator to outfit various rooms with different sound systems (the THX System by Lucasfilm versus the standard 4-track optical stereo system) and projection equipment (at least one 70mm 6-track magnetic sound projector in addition to the usual 35mm projector), thereby offering the very finest possible viewing.

10   The second trend toward consolidation is occurring at all levels of the film distribution chain. A number of studios have recently purchased major theater chains after sensing a relaxation of the enforcement of the Consent Decree (in 1984, the Justice Department offered advance support to any studio financing a lawsuit to reenter the movie theater business) plus their promise to limit their ownership to less than 50 percent of any acquired chain. MCA, owner of Universal Studios, has purchased 49.7 percent of Cineplex Odeon, the Cannon Group has purchased the Commonwealth chain, and United Artists Communications purchased the Georgia Theatre Company, the Gulf States and Litchfield chains, and—in 1988 alone—the Blair, Sameric, Commonwealth (from the Cannon Group) and Moss theater chains. Gulf & Western's Paramount Studios purchased Trans-Lux, Mann Theaters, and Festival Enterprises, while Columbia and Tri-Star (owned by Coca-Cola) bought the Walter Reade and Loews chains. On the retailing side, Cineplex Odeon has purchased the Plitt, RKO, Septum, Essaness, and Sterling chains, Carmike Cinemas has purchased Stewart & Everett,

while AMC Entertainment purchased the Budco Theatres. Through these actions and others the top six chains now own nearly 40 percent of America's screens. This is a 67 percent increase in just three years.

11   Wholesaling operations have been drastically reduced over the years on a scale unnoticeable to the public but very significant to those in the business. When filmgoing was in its heyday, each studio operated as many as 20 or so film exchanges in key cities across the country. Hollywood's studios have since closed many exchanges, until they are now operating only five to eight branch offices each. Paramount recently merged its Charlotte and Jacksonville branches into its Atlanta office, while Chicago now handles the business once serviced by its Detroit, Kansas City, Des Moines, and Minneapolis branches. As observed by Michael Patrick, president of Carmike Cinemas, "as the geographical regions serviced by these offices increase, the ability of smaller exhibitors to negotiate bookings is diluted relative to the buying power of the larger circuits."[1]

COMPETITIVE CONDITIONS

12   Despite the glamor associated with Hollywood, its start, its televised Academy Award Show, and such megahits as *Who Framed Roger Rabbit?*, *Rain Man*, and *Batman*, theater operators are basically in the business of running commercial enterprises dealing with a very perishable commodity. A movie is a merchandisable product made available by Hollywood and various independent producers to commercial storefront theaters at local retail locations. Given the large degree of concentration in the industry, corporate level actions entail the financing of both acquisitions and new construction, while local operations deal with the booking of films that match the moviegoing tastes of the communities being served.

13   To the degree a movie house merely retails someone else's product, the theater owner's success lies in the quality and not the quantity of products produced by Hollywood. Accordingly the 1987–88 Christmas season did not produce any blockbusters, while 1987's two big hits were *Beverly Hills Cop II* and *Fatal Attraction,* and 1986's hits were *Top Gun, Crocodile Dundee*, and *The Karate Kid, Part II*. Under these conditions of relatively few real moneymakers, the bargaining power shifts to the studios, leaving the exhibitors with more screens than they can fill with high-drawing films. Although the independent producers (the "indies")—such as the DeLaurentis Entertainment Group, New World, Atlantic, Concorde, and Cannon—are producing proportionally more films every year and the majors are producing fewer, their product is more variable in quality and less bankable. Additionally, theaters often pay a premium for the rights to exclusively show first-run movies in a given area or film zone, such as the May 1989 release of *Indiana Jones and the Last Crusade*. This condition hurts the smaller chains especially hard, because they do not have the resources to outbid the giant circuits.

14   Marketing research conducted by the industry has consistently found young adults are the prime consumers of motion picture theater entertainment. This group is rather concentrated but not organized. A study by the Opinion Research Corporation in July 1986 found those under the age of 40 accounted for 86 percent of all theater admissions. Frequent moviegoers constitute only 21 percent of the eligible filmgoers, but they account for 83 percent of all admissions. A general downward attendance trend has been occurring, as shown in Exhibit 2, where 43 percent of the population never attended a film in 1986. The long-term demographics also appear to be unfavorable,

---

[1]Michael W. Patrick, "Trends in Exhibition," in Wayne R. Green (ed.), *The 1987 Encyclopedia of Exhibition* (N.Y.: National Association of Theatre Owners, 1988), p. 109.

EXHIBIT 2
Frequency of Attendance by Total Public, Ages 12 and Over

Attendance	1986	1985	1984
Frequently	21.0%	22.0%	23.0%
Occasionally	25.0	29.0	28.0
Infrequently	11.0	9.0	8.0
Never	43.0	39.0	39.0
Not reported	0.0	1.0	2.0

Frequently: At least once a month.
Occasionally: Once in two to six months.
Infrequently: Less than once in six months.

Source: *1988 International Motion Picture Almanac* (New York, Quigley, 1988), p 29A.

EXHIBIT 3
U.S. Population by Age Group for 1980, with Projections for 1990 and 2000

Age Range	Year	Number (in millions)	Percent of total	Percent Change
5–17	1980	47.22	20.7%	
	1990	45.14	18.1	−4.4%
	2000	49.76	18.6	10.2
18–24	1980	30.35	13.2	
	1990	25.79	10.3	−15.0
	2000	24.60	9.2	−4.6
25–44	1980	63.48	27.9	
	1990	81.38	32.6	28.2
	2000	80.16	29.9	−1.5
45–64	1980	44.49	19.5	
	1990	46.53	18.6	4.4
	2000	60.88	22.7	31.1
65 and over	1980	25.71	11.3	
	1990	31.70	12.8	23.3
	2000	34.92	13.0	10.2

1980 total: 227,705,000.
1990 total: 249,675,000.
2000 total: 267,955,000.

Adapted from U.S. Department of Commerce, Bureau of the Census, *Statistical Abstract of the United States, 1985* (Washington, D.C.: Government Printing Office, 1985), pp. 26–27.

because America's population is moving toward those age categories least likely to attend a movie. Those 40 and over make up only 14 percent of a typical theater's admissions, while they account for 44 percent of the nation's population. Those from 12–29 years of age make up 66 percent of admissions, while accounting for only 36 percent of the population.[2] (See Exhibit 3.)

15   It appears that certain barriers to entry into the motion picture theater industry exist. Economies

[2]Presented in *1988 International Motion Picture Almanac* (N.Y.: Quigley Publications, 1988), pp. 29A–30A.

EXHIBIT 4
Average Operating Results for Selected Motion Picture Theater
Corporations, By Asset Size, 7/84–6/85

Operating Results	Smaller-sized		Middle-sized		Larger-sized	
Revenues	$224,171	100.0%	$4,476,042	100.0%	$151,545,455	100.0%
Cost of operations	93,917	41.9	1,780,066	39.8	54,707,909	36.1
Operating income	130,254	58.1	2,695,976	60.2	96,837,546	63.9
Expenses:						
Compensation of officers	6,788	3.0	150,647	3.4	2,121,636	1.4
Repairs	5,497	2.5	74,134	1.7	2,438,504	1.6
Bad debts	170	.1	4,196	.1	82,661	.1
Rent	32,195	14.4	315,841	7.1	11,489,901	7.6
Taxes (excluding federal tax)	12,904	5.8	179,881	4.0	5,689,843	3.8
Interest	8,045	3.6	117,216	2.6	8,031,999	5.3
Depreciation	8,866	4.0	269,122	6.0	8,954,959	5.9
Advertising	16,004	7.1	152,745	3.4	5,689,843	3.8
Pensions and other benefit plans	—	—	42,662	1.0	771,504	.5
Other expenses	70,971	31.7	1,682,992	37.6	55,245,207	36.5
Net profit before taxes	(31,186)	(13.9)	(293,460)	(6.6)	(3,678,421)	(2.4)
Current ratio	1.0		1.3		0.7	
Quick ratio	0.6		1.0		0.5	
Debt ratio	140.6		52.9		74.2	
Asset turnover	3.0		1.3		1.0	

Source: L. Troy, *Almanac of Business and Industrial Financial Ratios* (Englewood Cliffs, N.J.: Prentice-Hall, 1988), p. 332.

of scale are present, with the advantage given to operations concentrated in metropolitan areas, where one omnibus newspaper advertisement covers all the chain's theaters. As shown in Exhibit 4, the largest chains in the United States lost the least during the period of July 1984 to June 1985. Based on these results, scale economies appear to exist in the areas of operating costs, executive compensation, advertising, and rental expenses. Those choosing to enter the industry in recent years have done so through the use of massive conglomerate-backed capital. The possibility that an independent can open a profitable movie theater is very remote. "There's no way the small, independent operator can compete against the large screen owners these days," says John Duffy, cofounder of Cinema 'N' Drafthouse International, of Atlanta, Georgia.[3] (See Exhibit 5.) As a way of carving a niche for himself, Duffy's chain charges $2.00 for an "intermediate run" film but serves dinner and drinks during the movie, thereby garnering more than $5.00 in food revenue, compared to a theater's average $1.25 per admission.

16   Despite attempts by various theater owners to make the theater-going experience unique, customers tend to go to the most convenient theater that is showing the film they want to see at the time best for them. Accordingly, a particular theater chain enjoys proprietary product differentiation to the degree it occupies the best locations in any particular market area. Additionally, the cost of

---

[3]Quoted by Peter Waldman, "Silver Screens Lose Some of Their Luster," *The Wall Street Journal,* February 9, 1989, p. B1.

EXHIBIT 5
North America' Largest Theater Circuits

Circuit	Headquarters	Screens
United Artists Communications	Denver, Col.	2,677
Cineplex Odeon	Toronto, Canada	1,825
American Multi-Cinema	Kansas City, Mo.	1,531
General Cinema	Chestnut Hill, Mass.	1,359
Carmike Cinemas	Columbus, Ga.	742

Source: 10-Ks and various stockholders' reports for 1988.

building new facilities in the most desirable areas has increased dramatically. Harold L. Vogel, of Merrill Lynch, Pierce, Fenner and Smith, has observed the average construction cost comes to over $1 million per screen in such areas as New York or Los Angeles.[4]

17   Just as the motion picture was a substitute for vaudeville shows and minstrels at the turn of the century, radio and now television have been the major somewhat interchangeable substitutes for mass entertainment in America. Most recently cable television, pay-per-view TV, and videocassettes have eaten into the precious leisure time dollar. It has been estimated that 49.2 million homes now subscribe to cable television, 19.0 million homes have pay-per-view capability, and 56.0 million homes have a VCR, with 20.0 percent of those homes having more than one unit. The greatest damage to theater attendance has been accomplished by videocassettes, which deliver over 5,000 titles to viewers, at a relatively low cost, in the comfort of their own living rooms. As Sumner Redstone, owner of the very profitable National Amusements theater chain, says, "Anyone who doesn't believe videocassettes are devastating competition to theaters is a fool."[5]

18   Although the motion picture medium has been characterized as one that provides visual mass entertainment, those going to movies must ultimately choose between alternative forms of recreation. In that regard skiing, boating, baseball and football games, books, newspapers, and even silent contemplation vie for the consumer's precious time. Exhibit 6 shows the movie theater industry has declined in its ability to capture both America's total recreation dollars or its thirst for passive spectator entertainment. During the period from 1984 to 1987, the greatest increases in consumer recreation expenditures were for bicycles, sports equipment, boats, pleasure aircraft, and television and radio equipment and their repair.

19   Different marketing strategies are being employed in an attempt to remain viable in this very competitive industry. Some chains, such as Cinemark Theaters and Carmike Cinemas, specialize in $1 or low-price second-run multiplexed theaters in smaller towns and selected markets. In a sense they are applying Wal-Mart's original market strategy of dominating smaller, less-competitive rural towns. Others, such as General Cinema, United Artists Communications, and AMC Entertainment, favor multiplexed first-run theaters in major markets. Within this group, AMC Entertainment has been a pioneer as a multiscreen operator. It opened its first twin theater in 1963 and its first quadplex in 1969. As of mid-1988, AMC was operating 269 complexes with 1,531 screens, with most of its expansion in the Sunbelt. General Cinema has been diversifying out of the movie theater business through its nearly 60.0 percent interest in the Neiman Marcus Group (Neiman-

---

[4]Harold L. Vogel, "Theatrical Exhibition: Consolidation Continues," in Wayne R. Green (ed.), *The 1987 Encyclopedia of Exhibition* (N.Y.: National Association of Theatre Owners, 1988), p. 62.

[5]Quoted by Stratford P. Sherman, "Movie Theaters Head Back to the Future," *Fortune*, January 20, 1986, p. 91.

EXHIBIT 6
Motion Picture Exhibitors' Share of Entertainment Expenditures
Receipts as a Percent of Total for Selected Years 1929–1989

Year	Consumer Expenditures	Recreation Expenditures	Spectator Expenditures
1929	0.94%	16.6%	78.9%
1937	1.01	20.0	82.6
1943	1.29	25.7	87.6
1951	0.64	11.3	76.3
1959	0.31	5.6	61.0
1965	0.21	3.5	51.2
1971	0.18	2.7	47.7
1977	0.56	5.8	34.8
1983	0.16	2.4	41.9
1986	0.14	1.9	37.3
1987	0.14	1.8	36.9
1988	0.13	1.8	36.5
1989*	0.13	1.7	36.1

* Estimated by the casewriter.
Sources: Joel W. Finler, *The Hollywood Story* (New York: Crown Publishers, 1988), p. 288; U.S. Bureau of Economic Analysis, *Survey of Current Business,* July issues; and U.S. Bureau of the Census, *Statistical Abstract of the United States: 1989* (109th ed.) (Washington, D.C.: U.S. Government Printing Office, 1988).

EXHIBIT 7
Per Screen Admissions, Capital Expenditures, and Operating Profit Margins
Selected Years, 1979–1987

Item	1979	1981	1983	1985	1987
Tickets sold (000,000)	1,121	1,067	1,197	1,056	1,086
Average admission per screen	65,575	58,422	63,387	49,936	47,797
Capital expenditures (000,000)	$19.0	$57.4	$77.6	$164.0	$515.7
Profit margin	9.3%	9.1%	11.7%	11.6%	8.8%

Source: Peter Waldman, "Silver Screens Lose Some of Their Luster," *The Wall Street Journal,* February 9, 1989, p. B1

Marcus, Contempo Casuals, and Bergdorf Goodman) and 18.4 percent interest in Cadbury Schweppes. Most recently, General Cinema sold off its soft drink bottling business to PepsiCo for $1.5 billion to obtain cash for investments in additional nontheater operations.

20   A great amount of building has occurred in the theater industry in the past few years. Since 1981, the number of screens has increased about 35 percent, but the population proportion attending movies has actually fallen. Additionally, the relatively inexpensive days of "twinning" or quad-plexing existing theaters appears to be over, and the construction of totally new multiplexes is much more expensive. Exhibit 7 shows that operating profit margins peaked in 1983 at 11.7 percent, and they have fallen dramatically since then as the industry has taken on large amounts of debt to

finance the construction of more and more screens, now generating 24.6 percent fewer admissions per screen. Many operations are losing money, although certain economies of scale exist and labor-saving devices have allowed industry employment to fall slightly, while the number of screens has increased substantially. The Plitt theaters were money losers before being acquired by Cineplex Odeon, and AMC Entertainment lost $6.0 million in 1987 and $13.8 million in 1988 on theater operations. Carmike was barely profitable in 1986, and General Cinema's earnings from its theater operations have fallen for the past three years, although the operation's assets and sales have been increasing. Generally speaking, about half the nation's motion picture theaters and chains have been unprofitable in the 1980s, while numerous chains have engaged in the illegal practice of "splitting," wherein theater owners in certain markets decide which one will negotiate or bid for which films offered by the various distributors available to them.

THE CINEPLEX ODEON CORPORATION

21   Today's exhibition giant began in 1978 with an 18-screen complex in the underground garage of a Toronto shopping center. Garth Drabinsky, a successful entertainment lawyer and real estate investor (see Exhibit 8), joined with the Canadian theater veteran Nathan Aaron (Nat) Taylor in this enterprise. After three years and dozens of new theaters, Cineplex entered the American theater market by opening a 14-screen multiplex in the very competitive and highly visible Los Angeles Beverly Center. Despite the chain's growth, it was only marginally profitable. When the fledgling chain went public on the Toronto Stock Exchange in 1982, it lost $12.0 million on sales of $14.4 million.

22   Cineplex nearly went bankrupt but not through poor management by Drabinsky or Taylor. Canada's two major theater circuits, Famous Players (Paramount Studios) and the independent Odeon chain, had pressured Hollywood's major distributors into keeping their first-run films from Cineplex. But in 1983, Drabinsky, who as a lawyer had written a standard reference on Canadian motion picture law, convinced Canada's version of the U.S. Justice Department's antitrust division that Famous Players and Odeon were operating in restraint of trade. Armed with data gathered by Drabinsky, the Combines Investigative Branch forced the distributors to sign a consent decree, thus opening all films to competitive bidding. Ironically, without the protection provided by its collusive actions, the 297 screen Odeon circuit soon began to lose money, whereupon Cineplex purchased its former adversary for $22 million. The company subsequently changed its name to Cineplex Odeon.

23   In its development as an exhibition giant, the chain has always been able to attract a number of smart, deep-pocketed backers. Early investors were the since-departed Odyssey Partners, and, with a 30.2 percent stake, the Montreal-based Claridge Investments & Company, which is the main holding company of Montreal financier Charles Bronfman. The next major investor was the entertainment conglomerate MCA Incorporated, of Universal City, California. MCA purchased 49.7 percent of Cineplex's stock (but is limited to a 33.0 percent voting stake because of Canadian foreign-ownership rules) in January 1986 for $106.7 million. This capital infusion gave Cineplex the funds to further pursue its aggressive expansion plans. As Drabinsky said at the time, "There's only so much you can do within the Canadian marketplace. It was only a question of when, not where, we were going to expand."[6] In short order the company became a major American exhibitor by acquiring six additional chains. Some rival and fearful exhibitors, because of Drabinsky's quest

---

[6]Quoted by David Aston in "A New Hollywood Legend Called—Garth Drabinsky?" *Business Week*, September 23, 1985, p. 61.

for growth via the acquisition route, have been tempted to call him Darth Grabinsky. (See Exhibit 8.)

24   Despite these rumblings, Cineplex Odeon has reshaped the moviegoing experience for numerous North Americans. Many previous theater owners had either let their urban theaters fall into decay and disrepair or they had sliced their larger theaters into unattractive and sterile multiplexes. Others had built new but spartan and utilitarian facilities in suburban malls and shopping centers. When building their own theaters from either the ground up or when refurbishing an acquired theater, Cineplex pays great attention to making the patron's visit to the theater a pleasurable one. When the Olympia I and II Cinemas in New York City were acquired, a typical major renovation was undertaken. Originally built in 1913, the theater seated 1,320 and was billed as having "the world's largest screen." New owners subsequently remodeled it in 1939 in an art deco style, and in 1980 it was renovated as a triplex, with a fourth screen added in 1981. As part of Cineplex's renovation, the four smaller auditoriums were collapsed into two larger 850-seat state-of-the-art wide-screened theaters featuring Dolby stereo sound systems and 70mm projection equipment. Its art deco design was augmented by postmodern features, such as marble floors, pastel colors, and neon accents.

25   Whether through new construction or the renovation of acquired theaters, many Cineplex cinemas feature entranceways made of terrazzo tile, marble, or glass. The newly built Cinema Egyptien in Montreal has three auditoriums and a total seating capacity of 900. It is replete with mirrored ceilings and hand-painted murals rendered in the traditional Egyptian colors of Nile green, turquoise, gold, lapis lazuli blue, and amber red. Historically accurate murals measuring 300 feet in length depict the daily life and typical activities of the ancient Egyptians. (See Exhibit 9.) Toronto's Canada Square office complex features a spacious, circular art deco lobby, with a polished granite floor and recessed lighting highlighted by a thin band of neon encircling the high domed ceiling. On the lobby's left side, moviegoers can snack in a small cafe outfitted with marble tables, bright red chairs, and thick carpeting. In New York City the chain restored the splendor and elegance of Carnegie Hall's Recital Hall as it was originally conceived in 1981. The plaster ceilings and the original seats were completely rebuilt and refinished in the gold and red velvet colors of the great and historic Carnegie Hall.

26   Just to make the evening complete, and to capture the high profits realized from concession operations, patrons of a Cineplex theater can typically sip *cappucino* or taste any of the 14 different blends of tea served in Rosenthal china. Those wanting heavier fare can nibble on croissant sandwiches, fudge brownies, carrot cake, or a *latte macchiato,* while freshly popped popcorn is always served with real butter. In-theater boutiques selling movie memorabilia to add to the dollar volume obtained from the moviegoer were created but discontinued, due to unnecessarily high operating costs.

27   This glamor does not come cheaply, because the chain usually charges the highest prices in town. For those in a financial bind, the American Express credit card is now honored at many of the chain's box offices. Cineplex broke New York City's $6 ticket barrier by raising its prices to $7, thus incurring the wrath of Mayor Ed Koch, who marched in picket lines with other angry New Yorkers. Cineplex's action also caused the New York state legislature to pass a measure requiring all exhibitors to print admission prices in their newspaper advertisements. When justifying the increased ticket price, Drabinsky said the alternative was "to continue to expose New Yorkers to filthy, rat-infested environments. We don't intend to do that."[7] Instead of keeping prices low, $30 million was spent refurbishing Cineplex Odeon's 30 Manhattan theaters to attract better-paying customers. Another unpopular and somewhat incongruous action, given the upscale image engendered by each theater's trappings is the running of advertisements for Club Med and California

---

[7]Quoted by Richard Corliss, "Master of the Movies' Taj Mahals," *Time,* January 25, 1988, pp. 60–61.

EXHIBIT 8
Cineplex Odeon Theater Acquisitions

Odeon
Plitt Theatres
RKO Century Warner Theaters
Walter Reade Organization
Circle Theatres
Septum
Essaness
Sterling Recreation Organization
Maybox Movie Centre, Ltd.

raisins before its films. Regardless of the anger and unpopularity created among potential patrons, Cineplex is not interested in catering to the "average" theater patron. Rather than trying to attract the mass market, the theater chain aims its massive and luxurious theaters at the aging Baby Boomers, who are becoming a greater portion of America's population.

28 Over the years, Cineplex Odeon and Garth Drabinsky have received high marks for their creative show business flair. As observed by theater industry analyst Paul Kagan, "Garth Drabinsky is both a showman and a visionary. There were theater magnates before him, but none who radiated his charisma or generated such controversy."[8] These sentiments are reiterated by Roy L. Furman, president of Furman Selz Mager Dietz & Birney, Inc., one of Drabinsky's intermediaries in the Plitt acquisition. "Too many people see the [theater] business as just bricks and mortar. Garth has a real love for the business, a knowledge of what will work and what won't."[9] When a new Cineplex Odeon theater opens, it begins with a splashy by-invitation-only party, usually with a few movie stars on hand. Besides his ability to attract smart investors, Drabinsky believes moviegoers want to be entertained by the theater's ambience as well as by the movie it shows. Accordingly, about $2.8 million (about $450,000 per screen) is spent when building one of the chain's larger theaters, as opposed to the usual $1.8 million for a simple no-frills sixplex. "People don't just like coming to our theaters," says Drabinsky, "They linger afterward. They have another cup of *cappuccino* in the cafe or sit and read the paper. We've created a more complete experience, and it makes them return to that location."[10] He later expanded on this observation, saying, "This company has attempted to change the basic thinking. We've introduced the majesty back to picture-going."[11]

29 Drabinsky dates his fascination with the silver screen to his childhood bout with polio, which left him bedridden much of the time from the ages of 3 to 12. His illness also imbued him with a strong sense of determination, and this resolution has helped to drive Cineplex Odeon forward. No one speaks for the company except Drabinsky, and he logs half a million miles a year visiting his theaters and otherwise encouraging his employees. The energetic CEO likes to drop by his theaters unannounced to talk with ushers and cashiers, and he telephones or sees 20 to 25 theater managers a week. His standards are meticulously enforced, often in a very personal and confron-

---

[8]Ibid., p. 60.

[9]Aston, "A New Hollywood Legend," p. 62.

[10]Quoted by Alex Ben Block, "Garth Drabinsky's Pleasure Domes," *Forbes*, June 2, 1986, p. 93.

[11]Mary A. Fischer, "They're Putting Glitz Back into Movie Houses," *U.S. News & World Report*, January 25, 1988, p. 58.

EXHIBIT 11
1988 Per Capita Attendance Rates

United States	4.4%
Great Britain	1.4
Canada	2.8
France	1.9
West Germany	1.9
Italy	1.6

Source: "Movies 'Held Firm' Last Year," *Tulsa Tribune,* February 16, 1989, p. 9C

EXHIBIT 12
Cineplex Odeon Corporation
Unaudited First Quarter Consolidated Statement of Income
(in thousands of U.S. dollars)

	1989	1988
Revenue:		
Admissions	$ 85,819	$ 80,389
Concessions	26,657	24,082
Distribution, post production and other	70,033	28,782
Sale of theater properties	5,731	1,600
Total revenue	188,240	134,853
Expenses:		
Theater operations and other expenses	133,158	97,733
Cost of concessions	5,085	4,466
Cost of theater properties sold	5,837	550
General and admin. expenses	8,035	6,310
Depreciation and amortization	11,207	7,923
Total expenses	163,322	116,982
Income before the undernoted	24,918	17,871
Interest on long-term debt and bank indebtedness	12,257	9,138
Income before taxes	12,661	8,733
Minority interest	978	—
Income taxes	968	727
Net income	$ 10,715	$ 8,006

Source: *First Quarter Report 1989,* pp. 12–13.

37   There is also a question about whether Cineplex can continue its current growth rate via acquisitions and debt financing. The cost of acquisitive growth may become more expensive, because many of the bargains have already been obtained by Cineplex or other chains. The early purchase of the Plitt Theater chain in November 1985 cost about $125,000 per screen, although the bargain price for Plitt may have been a one-time opportunity, because it had just lost $5 million on revenues

EXHIBIT 13

CINEPLEX ODEON CORPORATION
Consolidated Statement of Income
(in thousands of U.S. dollars)

	1988	1987	1986	1985
Revenue:				
Admissions	$355,645	$322,385	$230,200	$ 84,977
Concessions	114,601	101,568	71,433	24,949
Distribution, post production and other	156,372	61,216	30,846	7,825
Sale of theatre properties	69,197	34,984	24,400	6,549
	695,815	520,153	356,989	124,300
Expenses:				
Theatre operations and other expenses	464,324	371,909	258,313	89,467
Cost of concessions	21,537	18,799	13,742	5,980
Cost of theatre properties sold	61,793	21,618	11,690	2,736
General and admin. expenses	26,617	17,965	15,335	5,701
Depreciation and amortization	38,087	23,998	14,266	3,678
	612,358	454,289	313,346	107,562
Income before the undernoted	85,457	65,864	43,643	16,738
Other income	3,599	—	—	(330)
Interest on long-term debt and bank in-debtedness	42,932	27,026	16,195	3,961
Income before taxes, equity earnings, pre-acquisition losses and extraordinary item	44,124	38,838	27,148	13,107
Income taxes	3,728	4,280	6,210	3,032
Income before equity, earnings, pre-acquisition losses and extraordinary item	40,396	34,558	21,138	8,075
Add back: Pre-acquisition losses attributable to 50% interest Plitt not owned by the corporation	—	—	1,381	—
Equity in earnings of 50% owned companies	—	—	—	1,021
Income before extraordinary item	40,396	34,558	22,519	10,374
Extraordinary item	—	—	—	9,096
Net income	$40,396	$34,558	$ 22,519	$ 10,374

Source: Company annual reports for 1987 and 1988.

EXHIBIT 14
Cineplex Odeon Corporation
Unaudited First Quarter Consolidated Balance Sheet
(in thousands of U.S. dollars)

	1989	1988
Assets:		
Current assets:		
Accounts receivable	$ 229,961	$ 151,510
Advances to distributors and producers	18,334	26,224
Distribution costs	9,695	10,720
Inventories	7,781	7,450
Prepaid expenses and deposits	6,756	5,505
Properties held for disposition	23,833	25,557
Total current assets	296,360	226,966
Property, equipment, and leaseholds	844,107	824,836
Other assets:		
Long-term investments and receivables	35,169	130,303
Goodwill (less amortization of $3,545; 1988—$2,758)	53,589	53,966
Deferred charges (less amortization of $8,456; 1988—$7,724)	30,222	27,100
Total other assets	118,980	211,369
Total assets	$1,259,447	$1,263,171
Liabilities and Shareholders' Equity		
Current liabilities:		
Bank indebtedness	$ 37,185	$ 21,715
Accounts payable and accruals	98,876	107,532
Deferred income	38,167	21,967
Income taxes payable	3,726	5,651
Current portion of long-term debt and other obligations	12,174	10,764
Total current liabilities	190,128	167,629
Long-term debt	625,640	663,844
Capitalized lease obligations	14,213	14,849
Deferred income taxes	10,920	10,436
Pension obligations	6,847	6,326
Stockholders' equity:		
Capital stock	284,533	283,739
Translation adjustment	12,473	13,348
Retained earnings	88,571	77,856
Total equity	385,577	374,943
Total liabilities and shareholders' equity	$1,259,447	$1,263,171

Source: *First Quarter Report 1989*, pp. 14–15.

EXHIBIT 15
Cineplex Odeon Corporation
Consolidated Balance Sheet (in thousands of U.S. dollars)

	1988	1987	1986
Assets:			
Current assets:			
Accounts receivable	$ 151,510	$ 42,342	$ 20,130
Advances to distributors and producers	26,224	10,704	4,671
Distribution costs	10,720	10,593	4,318
Inventories	7,450	8,562	6,978
Prepaid expenses and deposits	5,505	4,683	4,027
Properties held for disposition	25,557	22,704	16,620
Total current assets	226,966	99,588	56,744
Property, equipment, and leaseholds	824,836	711,523	513,411
Other assets:			
Long-term investment and receivables	130,303	49,954	14,292
Goodwill (less amortization of $2,758; 1987—$1,878)	53,966	52,596	40,838
Deferred charges (less amortization of $7,724; 1987—$1,771)	27,100	12,015	6,591
	211,369	114,565	61,721
Total assets	$1,263,171	$925,676	$631,876
Liabilities and Shareholders' Equity			
Current liabilities:			
Bank indebtedness	$ 21,715	$ 20,672	$ 30
Accounts payable and accruals	107,532	74,929	47,752
Deferred income	21,967	755	—
Income taxes payable	5,651	4,607	1,926
Current portion of long-term debt and other obligations	10,764	5,965	6,337
Total current liabilities	167,629	106,173	55,945
Long-term debt	663,844	449,707	317,550
Capitalized lease obligations	14,849	14,565	15,928
Deferred income taxes	10,436	13,318	11,142
Pension obligations	6,326	4,026	3,668
Minority interest	25,144	—	—
Stockholders' equity:			
Capital stock	283,739	289,181	212,121
Translation adjustment	13,348	1,915	(3,591)
Retained earnings	77,856	46,791	19,113
	374,943	337,887	227,643
Total liabilities and shareholders' equity	$1,263,171	$925,676	$631,876

Source: Company annual reports for 1987 and 1988.

of $111 million during the nine months ending June 30, 1985. To get into the New York City RKO Century Warner Theaters chain in 1986, Cineplex had to pay $1.9 million per screen, while it paid almost $3.0 million a screen in 1987 for the New York City-based Walter Reade Organization. Overall, Cineplex Odeon paid about $276,000 each for the screens it acquired in 1986, and some are questioning the prices being paid for old screens, as well as the wisdom of expanding operations in what many see is a declining and saturated industry. A past rule of thumb has been that a screen should cost 11 times its cash flow; but some experts feel a more reasonable rule should be 6 to 7 times its cash flow, given the glut of screens on the market. The changing effects of Cineplex's acquisition and debt structure since 1984 have been summarized in Exhibit 10.

38   Given the nature of the North American market and Cineplex Odeon's penchant for growth, it is currently implementing a planned expansion into Europe. Cineplex is scheduled to build 100 screens in 20 movie houses throughout the United Kingdom by 1990, and it has further plans in Europe and Israel for the early 1990s. Exhibit 11 lists the comparative per capita motion picture attendance rates found in various European countries. Other exhibitors are also interested in bringing multiscreened theaters to Europe. In addition to Cineplex's plans, Warner Brothers, American Multi-Cinema, Odeon, and National Amusements have announced their intentions of opening a total of more than 450 screens in the United Kingdom, with further theaters scheduled for later dates.

39   While few deny the attractiveness of the theaters owned and operated by Cineplex, the firm may have overextended itself both financially and operationally. (See Exhibits 12, 13, 14, and 15). Is Cineplex Odeon on the crest of a new wave of creative growth in North America and Europe, or does it stand at the edge of an abyss? Is consolidation or a thorough review of past actions in order? What next moves should Garth Drabinsky and Cineplex make to continue the firm's phenomenal success story?

SELECTED REFERENCES

Finler, Joel W. *The Hollywood Story*. New York: Crown, 1988.

Gertner, Richard, ed. *1988 International Motion Picture Almanac*. New York: Quigley, 1988.

Green, Wayne R., ed. *Encyclopedia of Exhibition*. New York: National Association of Theatre Owners, 1988.

Hall, Ben M. *The Best Remaining Seats: The Story of the Golden Age of the Movie Palace*. New York: Bramhall House, 1961.

Harrigan, Kathryn Rudie. *Managing Mature Businesses*. Lexington, Mass.: Lexington, 1988.

———. "Strategies for Declining Industries." *The Journal of Business Strategy*. Vol. 1, no. 2 (Fall 1980), pp. 20–34.

Musun, Chris. *The Marketing of Motion Pictures*. Los Angeles: Chris Musun Company, 1969.

1988 International Motion Picture Almanac. New York: Quigley, 1988.

1989 U.S. Industrial Outlook. Washington, D.C.: U.S. Department of Commerce/International Trade Administration, 1989.

Tromberg, Sheldon. *Making Money, Making Movies*. New York: New Viewpoints/Vision Books, 1980.

Troy, L. *Almanac of Business and Industrial Financial Ratios*. Englewood Cliffs, N.J.: Prentice-Hall, 1988.

U.S. Bureau of the Census. *Statistical Abstract of the United States: 1989*. 109th ed. Washington, D.C.: U.S. Government Printing Office, 1988.

U.S. Department of Commerce. Bureau of the Census. *Statistical Abstract of the United States, 1985*. Washington, D.C.: Government Printing Office, 1985.

Waldman, Peter. "Silver Screens Lose Some of Their Luster." *The Wall Street Journal*. February 9, 1989, p. B1.

CASE 29

THE WALT DISNEY COMPANY FILMED ENTERTAINMENT DIVISION

1   Thoughts from Walt Disney:

2   The idea of Disneyland is a simple one. It will be a place for people to find happiness and knowledge. It will be a place for parents and children to share pleasant times in one another's company: a place for teachers and pupils to discover greater ways of understanding and education. Here the older generation can recapture the nostalgia of days gone by, and the younger generation can savor the challenge of the future. Here will be the wonders of Nature and Man for all to see and and understand. Disneyland will be based upon and dedicated to the ideals, the dreams and hard facts that have created America. And it will be uniquely equipped to dramatize these dreams and facts and send them forth as a source of courage and inspiration to all the world.

3   Disneyland will be something of a fair, and exhibition, a playground, a community center, a museum of living facts, and a showplace of beauty and magic.

4   It will be filled with the accomplishments, the joys and hopes of the world we live in. And it will remind us and show us how to make those wonders part of our own lives.[1]

HISTORY OF WALT DISNEY[2]

5   Walt and Roy Disney opened the Disney Brothers Studio in 1923, with a camera, two employees to paint and ink the animations, and a contract for *Alice in Cartoonland*. Shortly afterward they had their first big success with a new star named Mickey Mouse, who appeared in *Steamboat Willie*. In 1929, the Walt Disney Company was incorporated. By 1931, the Mickey Mouse Club was formed and soon had an enrollment of over a million members. Mickey Mouse had become well known all over the world, and this new popularity brought with it a new source of income to the Disney enterprise. When the great Depression hit, the Disney brothers realized that the economic basis for cartoons was deteriorating. The theaters were forced to offer more entertainment to lure customers, and the theaters had little left in their budgets for short subjects (cartoons). Although maintaining cartoons as a sustained source of cash, Disney decided to branch into feature film productions. In December 1937, *Snow White* had its premiere and grossed over $8 million.

6   During Walt's trips to Europe and his travels through the United States, he developed the desire to build an amusement park. Tivoli Gardens in Copenhagen, became his inspiration. He decided to create a park that was spotless, brightly colored, and modestly priced, with festive music, excellent food and drink, and warm courteous employees. Walt opted to finance his new project with television contracts, due to the studio's volume of debt. The studio's decision to enter the

---

[1]Bob Thomas, *Walt Disney: An American Tradition* (New York: Simon and Schuster, 1976), pp. 246–47.

[2]Ibid.

television industry created quite a stir in the movie industry, which blamed television for the decline in theater attendance.

7   Disneyland was a great success, with attendance exceeding projections by 50 percent, prompting Walt to create an entire new "community," Disney World, designed for total family enjoyment.[3] He wanted full control of the environment and plenty of room for expansion. The state of Florida was chosen because it was already attracting a large number of tourists, and it was east of the Rockies, ensuring that the new park would not cannibalize Disneyland's audience. Disney wanted to maintain the beauty and ecology of the natural Floridian environment and to set an example of good development in planning, water control, pollution prevention, and conservation.

8   Before his community could become a reality, Walt Disney died on December 15, 1966. Shortly after his death, Roy issued a statement assuring Disney's employees and stockholders that the company would continue operating according to the guidelines Walt had established. Disneyworld opened on October 1, 1971, but the company soon ran into problems. Disney's secret formula since Walt's earlier years was its continuous list of creative, fresh, and new ideas. However, after he died, no new concepts were developed, and the old characters became stale. Even when, 10 years later, the company began planning Tokyo Disney and the Epcot Center (Experimental Prototype Community of Tomorrow), management relied on the meticulous blueprints Walt had prepared before this death.

9   In 1979, the firm attempted to shift the target of some of its movies and theme parks away from children, and toward teenagers and adults. Although the reaction at the theme parks was positive, Disney's theater releases, like *Watcher in the Woods, Midnight Madness,* and *The Black Hole,* were box office bombs.

10   Epcot, which cost $1 billion to build, was opened in 1982. The following year marked the opening of Tokyo Disney and the start of the cable television channel, the Disney Channel. Although this growth added new life to Disney, it ladened the firm with debt. The firm issued 1.1 million new shares of stock in an effort to retire loans from Epcot Center and offset a portion of the $33 million lost by the motion picture segment.

11   To increase its success in the film industry, Disney established its Touchstone subsidiary to serve the adult segment of the market but retained the Walt Disney Productions label for the family feature segment. The approach was a simple one: keep the old Disney fans with the traditional Disney family entertainment and attract new followers by introducing the Touchstone productions. Unfortunately, this strategy did not solve Disney's problems, and Disney continued to experience failures at the box office and soon became the object of takeover attempts.

Mickey Held Hostage[4]

12   In 1984, Disney fought two takeover battles. The first takeover attempt was led by Saul Steinberg. Steinberg has increased his Disney holdings to 12.2 percent of the firm and had set his sights on a 49 percent ownership. Disney increased its debt volume by acquiring the Arvida Corporation (which it sold again in 1987) and began proceedings to purchase Gibson Greetings, Inc. The firm eventually paid Steinberg $325.3 million for his stake in the company.

13   The second takeover attempt was led by Irwin Jacobs, who built his holding to 7.7 percent of the company. Jacobs sought to take control and dismantle Walt Disney, separating the film segment from the remaining "profitable" divisions of the corporation. The Bass family (a major stockholder) bought Jacobs out so the Walt Disney Company could remain in tact, believing that the firm would

---

[3]Leonard E. Zehnder, *Florida's Disney World: Promises and Problems* (Tallahassee, Fla.: Penisular Publishing, 1975.

[4]John Taylor, *Wall Street, the Raiders, and the Battle for Disney* (New York: Knopf, 1987).

lose its unique character if portions of it were sold. However, the board of directors yielded to pressure from Roy Disney and the Bass family and made changes in the company. Ronald Miller, CEO, a 30-year employee, was ousted and Michael Eisner, former president and chief operating officer of Paramount Pictures, was brought in to turn the company around.

THE AMERICAN FILM INDUSTRY[5]

What Makes a Film a Hit?

14   A film's profitability is based on the public's reaction to the film and on the studio's costs. Many factors can influence the public's perception, including actors/actresses, producers, directors, technology, and storylines. It is possible that any one of these factors can make or break a film; however, in most cases, it is a few uniquely talented actors, writers, and directors that have the greatest impact on the end product. For this reason, competition for these individuals is intense.

15   Technological advancements are incorporated into productions from the moment they are made available. This is mainly an effort on the part of the studios in the industry to become innovators for special effects. But these advancements are rarely enough to create a box office hit on their own.

16   The increased costs for "dazzling" technological effects and blockbuster talent have made film production very expensive. In response to these expenses, studios have tried to lower costs through long-term contracts to ensure the participation of talented actors, writers, or directors (a revival of the old "studio system"), through limited partnerships (which provide outside financing and, in turn, reduce risk), and through the production of sequels or films that are based on popular shows of the past, such as *Star Trek I, II, III, IV,* and *V.*[6]

The Life Cycle of a Motion Picture

17   A moviemaking venture is a risky financial investment, because there are no guarantees of success and there is a lengthy time lag before revenues are generated. (Exhibits 1 and 2 examine the costs involved in making a motion picture. Exhibit 3 traces the life cycle of a motion picture.) Accounting rules have given the studios some leeway. Most production expenses are not recognized immediately but are capitalized as inventory on a balance sheet. When revenues are finally generated, the studios begin to realize the costs on their income statements. However, these rules do not help a studio that produces a box office bomb. Because they are unable to develop a fail-proof formula for success, firms have tried to combat the revenue-generating time lag. Their primary method of reducing this period is through branching into various distribution channels (see Exhibit 3).

18   The initial success of a film is judged by a theater audience. It is through this market that the studios receive their first source of revenue. Leasing agreements, on a flat fee or a percentage of gross receipts basis, are made with theaters prior to their review of a film. Films are usually released during the summer months and at Christmas time (see Exhibit 4). A successful production can run for as long as six months before losing its appeal. It is during these release periods that most industry advertising is done. Stars from movies will make appearances to promote the upcoming motion pictures. Few movies can recover from a poor initial showing. "For big action/adventure

[5]References for the history of the film industry include: Don Pember, *Mass Media History* (Chicago: Science Research Associates, 1980);   "Hollywood: Legend and Reality," *USA Today,* July 1987, pp. 44–59; and   Brian D. Johnson, "Hollywood Hits 100," *Maclean's,* June 8, 1987, pp. 32–35.

[6]Laura Landro, "Formula Films: Sequels and Stars Help Top Movie Studios Avoid Risks," *The Wall Street Journal,* June 6, 1989, p. A1.

EXHIBIT 1
How the Production Dollar is Divided

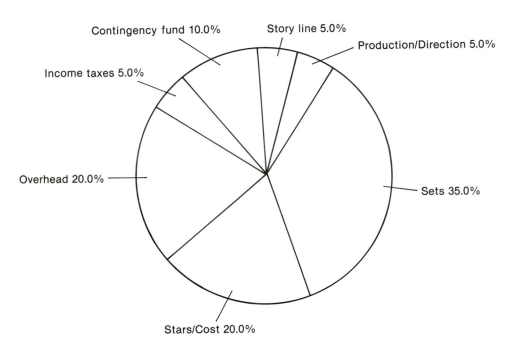

An Average Production Budget

Contingency fund 10.0%   Story line 5.0%
Income taxes 5.0%   Production/Direction 5.0%
Overhead 20.0%   Sets 35.0%
Stars/Cost 20.0%

films, it is considered mandatory to play to overflow crowds from the start. Studios must generate a sense of excitement during the film's first two weeks."[7]

19   An unsuccessful film at the theater will become an addition to a studio's library, from where it may eventually be revived for a television audience. However, successful productions will be re-released in home video markets. Videocassette rental establishments have become increasingly popular as the development of VCRs has made videotapes more affordable. Revenue in this market is received then the video outlet buys the cassettes. These outlets are then entitled to whatever revenue they can generate from their purchase. Many firms have also released video productions of their films to be sold to the public, usually at a lower price than those offered to the rental outlets.

20   The next step in the revenue generation cycle is cable, network, and syndicated television. In these markets, the studios offer motion picture hits by themselves or in combination with less-successful films as a package deal. In addition, studios have begun to concentrate on the further development of the made-for-television market, which includes films series, miniseries, and pilot productions. To take further advantage of the movement toward home entertainment, studios have begun to purchase cable stations to provide them with an audience and an efficient means to showcase their new releases.

21   A successful production may find its way overseas, and foreign sales represent 20 to 30 percent

[7]Richard Turner, "Fox's Gamble on Release of 'The Abyss': Film Isn't Easy to Market, Has No Major Stars," *The Wall Street Journal*, July 26, 1989, p. B1.

EXHIBIT 2
History of Production Costs

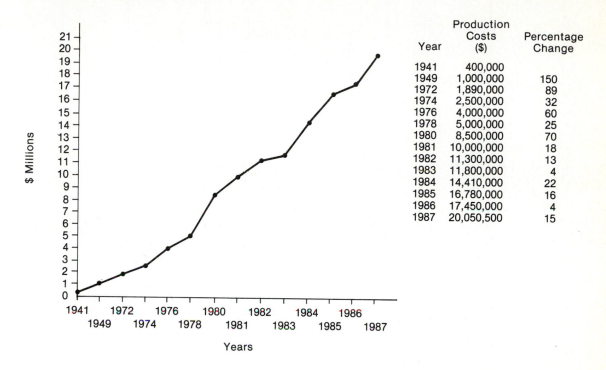

Year	Production Costs ($)	Percentage Change
1941	400,000	
1949	1,000,000	150
1972	1,890,000	89
1974	2,500,000	32
1976	4,000,000	60
1978	5,000,000	25
1980	8,500,000	70
1981	10,000,000	18
1982	11,300,000	13
1983	11,800,000	4
1984	14,410,000	22
1985	16,780,000	16
1986	17,450,000	4
1987	20,050,500	15

of American filmmakers' gross revenue. The need to export entertainment has arisen from declining theater attendance in the United States.[8] In spite of declining attendance, theater audiences remain the most important testing ground for new releases.

22   The final market for film productions is pay-per-view television, by which consumers order specific programming at a particular time to be watched on their home television. The project is new and is only available to approximately 10 million homes in the United States.

Industry Trends[9]

23   Film studios must adapt to changes if they are to remain profitable. This is demonstrated in the development of the standard length of a theater production, which is between 83 and 96 minutes. This time span is not only an acceptable length to sit in a theater comfortably, but it is also the

---

[8]Peter Waldman, "Silver Screens Lose Some of Their Luster Growth Comes Amid Worries of a Shakeout," *The Wall Street Journal,* 1989.

[9]References for film industry trends include: "Movie Industry Faces Retrenchment," *Standard & Poor's Industry Surveys,* November 29, 1984, pp. L15–L21; "Industry Recession Persists," *Standard & Poor's Industry Surveys,* February 6, 1986, pp. L17–L21; "Movie Business Picks Up Steam," *Standard & Poor's Industry Surveys,* March 26, 1987, pp. L17–L26, L51; "Appetite for Movies Strong," *Standard & Poor's Industry Surveys,* March 10, 1988, pp. L17–L26, 49; "Diversification Boosts Revenues, Selection," *Standard & Poor's Industry Survey,* March 16, 1989, pp. L17–L25, L47; and Jane Klain, ed., "Statistics: Motion Picture Industry," *International Motion Picture Almanac* (New York: Quigley Publishing, 1989).

EXHIBIT 3
Life Cycle of a Motion Picture

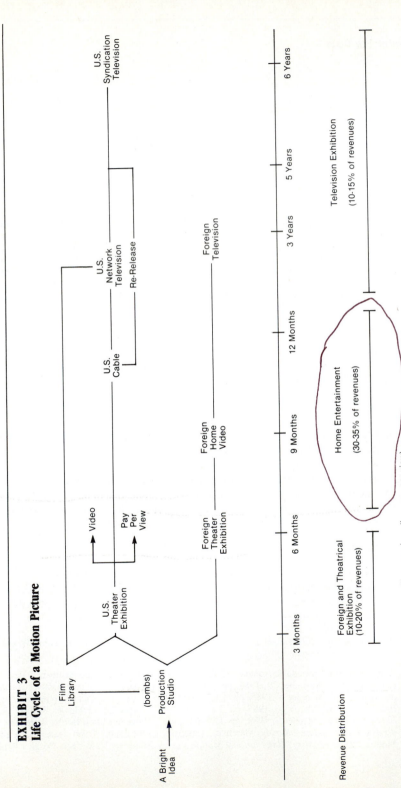

*The remaining revenue if generated from ancillary services (i.e., pay-per-view).

EXHIBIT 4
Monthly U.S. Film Attendance, 15-Year Average

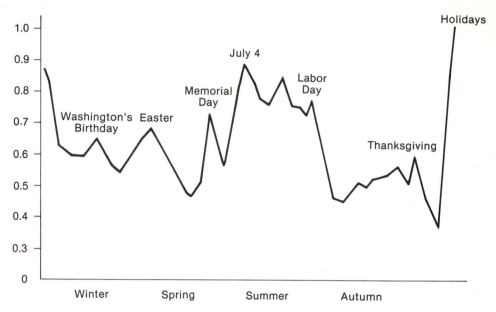

Source: Gulf & Western, Inc.

perfect length for filling a television time slot in prime-time programming. Therefore, the same product, with a little editing, can generate revenue from several sources.

24   Adaptability can also be seen in the industry's reaction to the decline in theater attendance. In 1988, attendance dropped 3 percent, to 1.08 billion. This drop was primarily attributed to the increased popularity of home video and cable television. The industry's response was forward integration into these new markets and increased production of theater releases to fuel these markets.

25   As the studios step up production, the theaters have begun to build multiplex theater complexes. These complexes contain several theaters to offer their customers a variety of recent films. To combat the declining attendance figures, the new theaters have been built to only a 10th of their original size (see Exhibits 5 and 6). Seeing this trend, some studios have begun to invest in theater ownership. Examples of this effort are Columbia Pictures' acquisition of Loew Theaters and the Paramount and Warner ownership of Cineamerica.

26   Production companies are also learning to adapt to government regulations. (The industry's rating system—G, PG, PG-13, R, X—is a self-imposed standard that the studios developed.) In addition to being used as an exciting theme for a feature film (i.e., *The Front Page.*), government regulations can also have a tremendous impact on the operations of the industry. The governmental trend of late is a relaxed attitude toward mergers, which has allowed conglomerates to once again take control of production firms. Due to these mergers, production firms today are not only in the business of making movies. they are publishing books and magazines and producing records.

27   The government is taking a stricter stance on the issue regarding the licensing of films to exhibitors. Production studios can currently obtain distribution contracts (licenses) without allowing theaters to preview the productions. However, some states have now begun to enact legislation

EXHIBIT 5
Yearly Percent Change in Screens

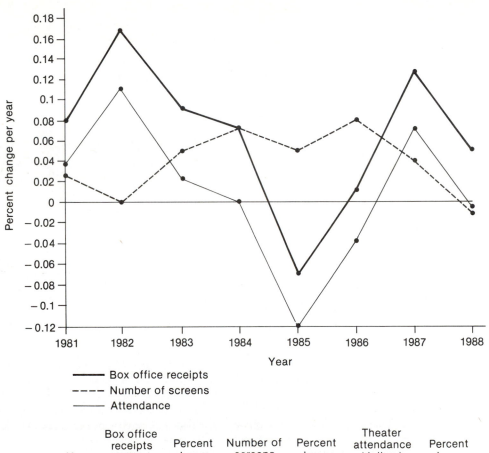

Year	Box office receipts (dollars)	Percent change	Number of screens	Percent change	Theater attendance (dollars)	Percent change
1980	2.749	0	17,590	0	1.022	0
1981	2.966	7.89	18,040	2.56	1.060	3.72
1982	3.453	16.42	18,020	−0.11	1.175	10.85
1983	3.766	9.06	18,884	4.79	1.197	1.87
1984	4.031	7.04	20,200	6.97	1.199	0.17
1985	3.749	−7.00	21,147	4.69	1.056	−11.93
1986	3.778	0.77	22,765	7.65	1.017	−3.69
1987	4.253	12.57	23,555	3.47	1.089	7.08
1988	4.458	4.82	23,234	−1.36	1.085	−0.37

that will prohibit this licensing before the theater owners have had the opportunity to screen the movie. This will mean that the firms will have to change their distribution strategies.

28   As the studios begin to think about expanding into the ownership of television stations, they will have to conform to FCC regulations that govern the quantity of programming that the networks can produce, and the number of stations that can be owned by one entity. A single entity can own no more than 12 stations or reach an area of 25 percent of U.S. viewers.

EXHIBIT 6
Domestic Theatrical Movie Industry

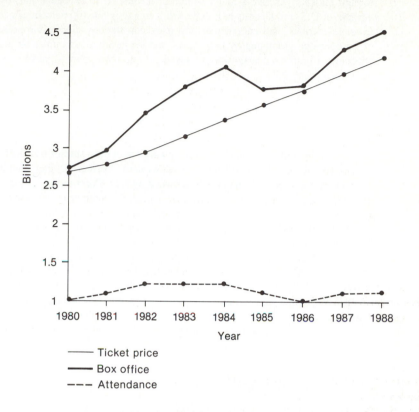

Domestic Theatrical Movie Industry

Year	Box Office Receipts*	Theater Attendance	Ticket Price*	Number of Screens
1980	2.749	1.022	2.691	17,590
1981	2.966	1.060	2.779	18,040
1982	3.453	1.175	2.937	18,020
1983	3.766	1.197	3.146	18,884
1984	4.031	1.199	3.361	20,200
1985	3.749	1.056	3.550	21.147
1986	3.778	1.017	3.714	22,765
1987	4.253	1.089	3.907	23,555
1988	4.458	1.085	4.110	23,234

*Revenues in billions of dollars.

29   Many firms are concentrating on how they can penetrate the European Community (EC) when it opens in 1992.[10] The entertainment industry has already formed a strong foothold overseas and foreign markets generate a major source of income. It is expected that, by mid-1990, available airtime for U.S. productions in Europe will increase by 60–100 percent as a result of new satellites, fewer restrictions, and unprepared local television stations. Some Europeans fear the domination of European programming by U.S. firms, and the desire to set quotas on non-European television programs. Limits on non-European television to no more than 40 percent of all broadcasting time have been proposed.

COMPETITION

30   As in the time of the old "studio system," ownership of most studios is in the hands of conglomerates. Paramount pictures is owned by Gulf & Western, Warner Brothers Studios is a part of Time-Warner, and Twentieth Century Fox is owned by New Corporation. These owners give the studios the ability to weather most of the movie industry's downturns; however, several "single focus" organizations have remained profitable (see Exhibit 7). Firms within the entertainment industry are constantly attempting to discover a theme that will appeal to the masses and become a box office hit. These companies know that the public's perception of a film, regardless of its critical reception, will make or break their revenue possibilities. Studios also realize that, with no brand loyalty, and the unique character of each new project, their films must compete with each film that is released on the market. This means that studios are not only competing with other production studios they are also competing with themselves. The strong competitors in the industry, with their huge financial and marketing resources, have an enormous influence on the system. It is not difficult to understand how this industry has become a battleground for continual creative innovations.

TIME WARNER INCORPORATED[11]

31   Warner Communications, Inc., is attempting to create a total entertainment center through its multiple subsidiaries, which include Warner Brothers and Lorimar Telepictures, Warner Home Video, Warner Brothers Television, and Warner Elektra Atlantic Corporation, both domestic and international. In addition, Warner has entered the music and publishing industries with Warner, Electra, Asylum and Atlantic, *Mad Magazine, DC Comics,* and Warner Books.

---

[10]"Some Support Is Seen within EC for Quotas on Outside TV Shows," *The Wall Street Journal,* July 19, 1989, p. B1.

[11]References for the Warner Corporation include: Paul M. Barrett, "Time and Warner Back Merger Plan before House Panel," *The Wall Street Journal,* 1989; Jose Cordova, "Warner Communications Unit Buys 20% in Big Hispanic Magazine," *The Wall Street Journal,* February 15, 1989, p. B8; Tom Graves, "Additional Media/Entertainment Combinations Likely," *Value Line,* March 15, 1989; Laura Landro, "Creating a Giant: Time and Warner Seek to Fend off Global Rivals but Risk Putting Themselves in Play," *The Wall Street Journal,* March 6 1989, p. A1; Joanne Lipman, "Time-Warner Deal May Yield One-Stop Shopping Possibility," *The Wall Street Journal,* March 7, 1989, p. B7; Linda Sandler, "Time-Warner Deal Fuels Run-up in Other Media Issues but Terms Dissappoint Some Time Holders," *The Wall Street Journal,* March 7, 1989, p. C1; Randal Smith, and Laura Landro, "Time-Warner Pact Seems Likely to Clear Any Antitrust Hurdles," *The Wall Street Journal,* March 13, 1989, B6; and *Warner Communications, Inc. Annual Report,* February 1988.

Show Industry comparison

EXHIBIT 7
Profitable "Single Focus" Organizations (dollars in thousands)

Orion Pictures Corporation	1988	1987	Year Ended 1986	1985	1984
Current assets	$693,791	$608,748	$461,388	$407,511	$278,621
Other assets	35,192	30,279	32,928	28,440	23,579
Short-term liabilities	70,982	43,888	37,692	33,894	25,046
Total liabilities	576,387	504,281	382,149	281,856	213,869
Shareholders' equity:					
Common & preferred stock	159,832	158,780	136,904	139,268	76,187
Retained earnings	(7,236)	(18,955)	(24,737)	14,827	12,144
Total revenues	426,948	327,638	198,122	223,025	154,728
Total costs & expenses	411,424	314,900	235,589	214,326	145,066
Net income	$ 12,159	$ 9,833	$(31,862)	$ 6,619	$ 7,332

Paramount Pictures Corporation					
Current assets		$ 730,400	$ 570,000		
Other assets		10,024,700	8,698,900		
Short-term liabilities		4,171,600	3,716,200		
Total liabilities		9,822,400	8,466,500		
Shareholders' equity:					
Common & preferred stock		199,200	199,200		
Retained earnings		736,000	623,600		
Total revenues		1,777,500	1,687,300	$1,459,900	
Total costs & expenses		1,453,400	1,397,800	1,208,900	
Net income		$ 196,400	$ 176,600	$ 155,400	

Warner Communications, Inc.					
Current assets	$1,768,500	$1,647,700	$1,389,333		
Other assets	2,829,800	2,224,600	1,834,119		
Short-term liabilities	1,533,000	1,415,900	1,083,896		
Total liabilities	2,807,100	2,394,800	2,050,932		
Shareholders' equity:					
Common & preferred stock	1,256,600	1,250,000	1,122,825		
Retained earnings	534,600	227,500	49,695		
Total revenues	4,206,100	3,403,600	2,848,324		
Total costs & expenses	748,100	592,400	492,671		
Net income	$ 423,200	$ 328,100	$ 185,795		

32   Warner Brothers is the primary source of financing for most of their productions. However, they have recently begun to use limited partnerships (to respond to the increasing number of competitive forms of entertainment). These partnerships provide funding and lessen the financial risk involved with producing films.

33   In a further effort to reduce risk, Warner Brothers is involved in a joint venture with Columbia Pictures Industries, Inc. Together these companies operate the former Warner Brothers and Columbia studio properties and production facilities under the joint management of both parties. The studio plant and facilities are rented to third-party motion picture and television production companies.

34   Globalization in the industry has forced Warner to maintain a powerful overseas distribution network. Recently Warner contracted with Disney to act as its international distributor for Disney and Touchstone pictures.

35   Warner has a film library composed of cartoons and feature films produced by Warner Brothers since 1949, and films produced by others but licensed to Warner Brothers for television or home video markets.

36   In 1984, Warner began a movement to return to its core business of communication and entertainment. This move prompted the sale of such assets as Atari, Warner Cosmetics, Franklin Mint, and Panavision. Warner's next move was the acquisition of Cineamerica, which owns and operates movie theaters in the United States. Warner is also constructing multiplex cinemas in Europe and has plans for the development of a motion picture studio in Brisbane, Australia.

37   On July 14, 1989, Time and Warner merged to capitalize on Warner's international distribution network and on Time's direct marketing skills. Their goal is to form a "product pipeline" for Warner's film production. With Time's cable and television network divisions (American Television & Communication Corporation, HBO, and Cinemax) and Warner's production capacity, the new company will obtain stronger bargaining power and greater control in filling air time. Their involvement in publishing and filmed entertainment will facilitate the transformation of books into motion pictures. The merger has caused some concern. There is a fear that this new firm will have the power to lock out competitors and raise prices. From Time and Warner's perspective, the merger will put a strain on the top management groups. Time is a conservative company that will have to learn to adapt to the creative style of Warner.

PARAMOUNT PICTURES CORPORATION[12]

38   Paramount Pictures and its subsidiaries constitute the Motion Pictures and Television operations of the Entertainment and Communication Group of Gulf & Western. The company finances its own and independent productions of motion pictures. In 1987, Paramount swept the box office with three of the year's top film releases: *Beverly Hills Cop, Fatal Attraction,* and *The Untouchables.*

39   In the late 1970's Paramount had a dismal market share of 10 percent, ranking last among the industry's major competitors. This trend was reversed when Michael Eisner joined Paramount as president and chief operating officer. By 1978, Paramount experienced 18 months of continuous box office hits, such as *Saturday Night Fever, Grease,* and *Heaven Can Wait.* Paramount placed a concerted effort on identifying quality performers in the industry, engaging in long-term contracts with successful actors and actresses, and, most important, reviewing the quality of the storylines of their scripts.

40   Paramount invests in projects that provide continuing returns over extended periods in the future. These projects should either have prospective sequels or have the potential to be successful in other media. Gulf & Western's ownership of Simon & Schuster, a publishing company involved with consumer, educational, and professional information, helps the company create a production pipeline. Paramount also recreates past successful themes, such as *The Untouchables,* a movie based on the classic television series that aired from 1959 to 1963.

41   Paramount's marketing approach is to expand its distribution channels and target a wide audience in terms of market segments served and geographical expansion. Paramount's television subsidiaries create programming, such as TV series and game shows for distribution to commercial networks, and to cable, home video, and foreign markets. As a result of the increase in first-run syndication television stations, Paramount has engaged in a joint venture to sell advertising time, on a barter

---

[12]References for Paramount Pictures, Inc. include: *Gulf & Western Annual Report 1987,* March 1988, pp. 4–19; Laura Landro, "Gulf & Western Plans to Sell Finance Firm, Build a Media Giant," *The Wall Street Journal,* April 10, 1989, p. A1.

basis, to these stations. Paramount will provide programming at low or no cost to these stations in exchange for commercial time during their programs.

42   In an effort to stay competitive, Paramount made a hostile offer to Time to break the merger between Time and Warner. After heated court hearings, Paramount finally dropped its hostile bid for Time, Inc., but continues the search for another entertainment takeover target. There have been rumors that the Walt Disney company might be a Paramount target.

ORION PICTURES CORPORATION

43   Orion Picture Corporation and its subsidiaries are engaged in the financing, production, and distribution of motion pictures for theaters, network television, cable, and home video markets. The company and its subsidiaries also finance, produce, and distribute television programming.

44   Orion's management believes that production stability builds trust and quality for the organization. President and CEO Eric Pleskon states, "We will be able to reconfirm our tradition of distributing pictures of quality and sound commercial value, produced at reasonable cost."[13]

45   Orion distinguishes itself from its competitors through its independent distributing division of specialized foreign or English-language motion pictures. Films distributed by this division include such releases as the recent academy award winner *Au Revoir, Les Enfants* (*Goodbye, Children*). The Orion Pictures Distribution Corporation promotes and licenses theatrical motion pictures domestically and in Canada.

46   To compete more effectively, the company decided to enter the home video distribution market. For this purpose the Orion Home Entertainment Corporation was created. This newly created subsidiary eliminates the presale of films to third parties. This may mean less financial support from third parties, but the inflows from the company's distribution video rights more than compensate for the loss.

47   To hedge against financial exposure, Orion does not engage in the production or coproduction of theatrical motion pictures unless certain strategically defined participants are present. These include leading actors, directors, and independent producers committed to the project.

48   In the television market, Orion provides programming for network and syndication stations. In addition, it maintains exclusive licensing agreements in cable television with Showtime/The Movie Channel to further expand its opportunities for revenue.

49   Orion is actively pursuing the trend towards international expansion. As government control in broadcasting decreases and the number of private stations increases, Orion's international division has successfully negotiated contracts in Europe and Australia.

WALT DISNEY COMPANY

50   When Michael Eisner arrived at Disney in 1984 he faced several problems. The Walt Disney Company had just escaped two takeover attempts. These events had cost Disney both in terms of increasing debt and in sending stockholders a message that they were not all treated equally (after the greenmail offer to Steinberg). The poor performance of Disney's film division caused many to

---

[13]*Orion Pictures Corporation 1988 Annual Report*, May 1988; and *Orion Pictures Corporation 1987 Annual Report* May 1987.

believe that Disney should stick to cartoons and theme parks and forget about motion picture production.

51   Within five years, Eisner was able to work his "magic" and put Disney back on track. He realized that Disney had a wealth of assets, with its film library and real estate, and that these assets were not being utilized to their fullest potential. Eisner also perceived that the company could not continue to operate on the philosophy of doing it "just like Walt would have." The company had to have the ability to change and grow as the world around it changed, without losing sight of Walt's basic values.

52   At the time Eisner came to Disney, few thought there would be a fit between his background and the culture of the company. But his family-oriented style and outpouring of ideas allowed him to make a successful transition from Paramount to Disney. He was able to develop new concepts while maintaining the traditional values of Disney. Roy Disney referred to him as "a genuine idea man." Eisner claimed, "My primary interest is ideas."[14]

53   The Walt Disney Company and its subsidiaries have always been determined to provide the highest-quality family-oriented entertainment in all three of its business segments: theme parks and resorts, filmed entertainment, and consumer products. In 1984, Michael Eisner set a few additional goals. A decision was made to concentrate on the growth of shareholders' value. This was to be achieved through internal growth of existing businesses, and external expansion, through related acquisitions, that would strengthen the existing businesses. The growth would be financed with Disney's strong debt capacity. Eisner stated that "the strategic use of Disney's cash flow is the primary strength of the company."[15] Specifically, Disney sought to achieve a growth in stockholder earnings of 20 percent annually over a five-year period and to maintain a 20 percent return on equity.

54   A second goal was to achieve an effective utilization of Disney's assets. This meant increased film releases from its film library of classics, further development of its real estate holdings, and taking advantage of opportunities for merchandising its character licenses.

Disney Subsidiaries

55   Although the Walt Disney Company is composed of several diverse segments, the company closely integrates its three divisions. For example, the motion pictures create characters that become the basis for fun rides at the theme parks and for hot-selling items in the Disney Stores. By implementing this strategy, Disney successfully portrays the common theme of fun and educational family entertainment throughout the company. However, each segment is responsible for maintaining and expanding its own market share. Walt Disney Imagineering and Disney Development departments provide planning, real estate development, show design, engineering support, production support, project management, environment support, and research and development services for all three of the Disney subsidiaries.

Theme Parks and Resorts

56   The Theme Parks and Resorts Division operates the Disney attractions. Assets include the Disneyland theme park and hotel and other attractions in California and the Walt Disney World resort in Florida, which includes the Magic Kingdom, Epcot Center theme park, Disney MGM studio

---

[14]Stephen Koepp, "Do You Believe in Magic," *Time,* April 25, 1988, p. 73.

[15]*Walt Disney 1988 Annual Report.*

tours, hotels, villas, shopping villages, conference centers, and recreational facilities (camping, golfing, water skiing, tennis, sailing, swimming, and horseback riding).

57   Internationally, Disney receives royalties from the Tokyo Disneyland theme park and Euro Disneyland. Oriental Land Company, Ltd. (an unrelated Japanese corporation), owns and operates the Tokyo theme park. In Europe, Disney is an equity investor for EuroDisneyland. Here Disney receives management fees as the operator of the facilities.

58   Hotel construction and the addition of entertainment complexes will be the primary direction for the theme parks and resorts in the coming years. Disney's chief financial officer, Gary Wilson, a former Marriott Corporation executive, states that hotels are a top priority. Examples of this emphasis can be seen in the newly constructed Caribbean Beach Resort, in the early construction of the Walt Disney Dolphin and Swan luxury hotels, and in the proposed Disney Yacht Club and Beach Club with its own lighthouse. Expansion of theme parks include plans for a new water park, Typhoon Lagoon, continual enhancements at the Epcot Center, and the startup of EuroDisneyland. The attraction expansions, which increase attendance, and price increases have contributed to a steady increase in theme park revenues, as is shown by the 11 percent increase in 1988 revenues. Disney's total theme park attendance in 1988 was the second highest in its history, although it was 5 percent below the record levels set in 1987.

59   The theme parks and resorts generate a major source of revenues for the firm. These revenues are used to invest in other divisions. For example, they provide a strong capital base for the start of Disney's consumer products segment. The primary purpose of Disney's theme parks and resorts is to provide financial security and stability to the company.

Consumer Products

60   Walt Disney licenses and distributes the name Walt Disney, its characters, literary properties, songs, and music to manufacturers, retailers, printers, and publishers. Disney produces audio products for the children's market, and film, audio, and computer software for the educational market. In addition, this segment operates the Disney Stores, which provide retail outlets for Disney's merchandise throughout the United States.

61   The first Disney store opened in California and soon after nine others followed from coast to coast. The colorful, theatrical stores are usually filled with customers and have sales which, at $1,000 per square foot, often surpass the national average for retail outlets by four times. To promote the other operations of Disney, the stores sell tickets to the parks, promote films, and showcase upcoming events by means of television monitors. The company plans to continue the expansion of its retail outlets, with plans for 100 stores by 1992. Overseas retail outlets are also being considered.

62   The acquisition of ChildCraft, a catalog marketer of children's products, opened a new distribution channel for Disney's educational toys and increased the revenue from consumer products by 25 percent. ChildCraft also added a manufacturing capability for wooden play equipment and schoolroom furniture to Disney's operations.

63   The Walt Disney Company has been successful with consumer products for several reasons. It is utilizing aggressive advertising to promote its films and theme parks, which are the origin for their merchandise. The characters are continually enhanced with contemporary designs and quality improvements. And Disney is helped further by the increased buying power of the Baby Boom generation.

64   In the United States, Disney represents 12 percent of all licensed character merchandise. The merchandise categories include apparel, toys, housewares, stationery, and domestic items. Disney is currently fighting to protect the copyrights of its 3,000 licenses from unauthorized use. Within the United States, Disney has filed 17 suits in seven states, naming more than 700 defendants for

copyright infringements. Outside the United States, Disney has brought 78 different actions to enforce its rights.

Filmed Entertainment

65   Disney's filmed entertainment subsidiary produces motion pictures, animated motion pictures, and original television products for distribution to theatrical, television (including network and first-run syndication markets), and home video markets. Certain programs are also syndicated by Disney internationally. These programs are televised in Australia, Brazil, Canada, China, France, Germany, Italy, Japan, Mexico, Spain, and the United Kingdom. The company also invests in programming for the Disney Channel. The company markets and distributes its products throughout the United States, but foreign distribution companies are utilized in all other countries.

66   In 1984, an effort was made to put the film division back on track. Jeffrey Katzenberg (chairman) and Richard Frank (president) were recruited from Paramount for the job. These two men were instrumental in setting the following goals: the division would make a conscious effort to employ the industry's top talent for writing, directing, and production and obtain these individuals at the lowest cost possible. It would attempt to produce 10 to 12 Touchstone features and three to four family movies each year. Disney would escalate production of animated features. And the film library would be more effectively utilized by releasing several classics each year.

67   Within four years, the film division had accomplished all four goals. In 1987, *Roger Rabbit* was released. It grossed $150 million and become the top attraction in theaters. Critics remarked that *Roger Rabbit* was an "ingenious melding of animators' ink and human flesh that reminded you thrillingly that, even after a century, the movies have not exhausted their magic."[16] In 1987, Disney captured 20 percent of total box office receipts with hits like *Good Morning Vietnam, Three Men and a Baby,* and *Big Business.* It was the first studio to release three films back to back, in a 12-month period, with revenues of more than $100 million each. In addition, the Home Video Division released *Cinderella,* which sold more than 7 million copies.

68   Disney's accomplishments at the box office can be attributed to Jeffrey Katzenberg. The production activities of the studio are performed under very stringent budgets. "We watch every single solitary nickel," says Katzenberg. Disney produces the majority of its films in-house. This approach helps the firm control costs, because the studios do not pay the high markup prices that usually accompany prepackaged deals of the top known talent.

69   A second major element of the cost control efforts of the division is its recruiting tactics. Disney seeks talented actors, such as Tom Selleck, Bette Midler, and Robin Williams, whose careers have either been temporarily derailed or who have not been able to demand the kind of compensation their talent should demand in the industry. The company then signs these actors to multiproduction contracts at fixed salaries. This strategy not only helps control costs but is also Disney's attempt to assure the quality of its productions.

70   In addition to these contracts, the studio also gives talented actors the opportunity to produce or direct their own pictures. Eisner encourages the interaction between gifted writers, producers, directors and actors and the Imagineering group. This association is an attempt to create a "Hollywood" influence in their theme parks and vice versa. Eisner has said that "it's basically the same business. An attraction in one of our parks is like a film in that it has to have a theme and tell a story. And I know a good story always has a beginning, middle, and end."[17]

---

[16]Quote from Charles Champlin, columnist for the *Los Angeles Times;* quoted in the 1988 Walt Disney annual report.

[17]Charles Leerhsen, "How Disney Does It." *Newsweek,* April 9, 1989.

MARKETING[18]

71   As Eisner introduced new employees into the marketing area, Disney's marketing activities became more assertive. Robert Levin, former Needham Harper Worldwide senior vice president, was hired as marketing chief for films. Among some of Levin's changes were extra television commercial time to promote Disney's movies and an accelerated release schedule for Disney's classic cartoons and films. Levin also explored the possibility of one company exclusively promoting each film. Successful associations were achieved with Coca-Cola, McDonald's, and Procter & Gamble. The division was able to reach the individual consumer more directly through these consumer products. These aggressive and innovative marketing campaigns helped to place the company (in 1988) as industry leader for the first time in its 65-year history, with a box office market share of 19 percent.

72   Disney has become more competent in integrating its entertainment facilities. For example, the company acquired commercial time during the *Disney Sunday Movie* to advertise feature film releases, consumer products, and new theme park attractions. An extra benefit of this strategy is Disney's ability to supervise the products being associated with the company's image. This same philosophy is practiced with the Disney Channel and Disney Home Videos, which feature clips of upcoming attractions. This intertwined effort has reduced the company's overall advertising budget and has helped the company reach its audiences more effectively than through a multimedia campaign.

73   Disney has set out to aggressively market the productions of its film division, as shown by Disney's increased volume of television commercial time for its syndicated shows. "Once you've got the product, you've got to let people know about it. . . . We are a consumer company and marketing is at the top of the list," according to Eisner.[19]

74   One of Disney's most effective efforts is its ability to generate good will. Disney receives relatively minimal negative press coverage. This is not by accident but a result of professional media handling. Disney provides reporters, photographers, and media technicians with guest tickets for transportation, accommodations, and events. This promotes new attractions and good will.

Disney Dollars[20]

75   Disney's financial performance during the Eisner era has been sensational (see Exhibit 8). Annual revenues have increased by 150 percent since 1984, profits have increased fivefold, and the stock price has quadrupled its 1984 value. Financing for Disney's major investments is a relatively simple task. The company is able to raise large sums because of its favorable image and leverage position. Isgur, a Paine Webber analyst, comments, "It's the Disney magic—people couldn't conceive that Mickey Mouse would give them a bad deal."[21] The division seeks ways to reduce financial risk through limited partnerships and by reducing the time cycle for the return on its investments. Disney has entered into negotiations with Silver Screen Partners, through whom the company can obtain funding for its productions. In addition, its diversification into home video, television, and the Disney Channel allows Disney to collect returns on its investments in a shorter time.

---

[18]Pamela Ellis, "Hi Ho, Hi, Ho," *Marketing and Media Decisions*, September 1986, pp. 52–64.

[19]Ibid.

[20]Andrea Garbor, and Steve Hawkins, "Of Mice and Money in the Magic Kingdom," *U.S. News & World Reports*, December 22, 1986, p. 44.

[21]Koepp, "Do You Believe in Magic?", p. 73.

EXHIBIT 8
Eisner's Financial Performance

THE WALT DISNEY COMPANY AND SUBSIDIARIES
Year Ended September 30
(dollars in millions)

	1988	1987	1986	1985
Assets:				
Cash & short-term investments	$ 344	$ 70	$ 39	$ 35
Accounts & notes receivables	821	318	241	173
Taxes on refundable income	—	—	—	60
Merchandise inventories	123	93	85	84
Film production costs	175	230	182	102
Real estate inventories	—	214	221	229
Entertainment attractions & other property:				
Attraction, buildings, and equipment	2,794	2,728	2,531	2,414
Accumulated depreciation	(938)	(812)	(702)	(600)
Total	1,856	1,916	1,829	1,814
Projects in progress	266	106	144	95
Land	25	27	28	29
Total	2,147	2,049	2,002	1,937
Other assets	197	147	128	119
Total assets	$ 3,806	$ 3,121	$ 2,897	$ 2,740
Liabilities:				
Accounts payable	$ 464	$ 340	$ 270	$ 240
Income taxes payable	123	97	59	24
Borrowings	585	547	823	862
Unearned deposits & advances	193	201	172	179
Deferred income taxes	596	518	388	279
Total liabilities	1,961	1,702	1,712	1,584
Stockholders' equity:				
Preferred shares:				
Authorized—300 shares outstanding	307	283	256	360
Retained earnings	1,538	1,136	929	796
Total shareholders' equity	1,845	1,419	1,185	1,156
Total liabilities and shareholders' equity	$ 3,806	$ 3,121	$ 2,897	$ 2,740

Income Statement ($000,000)

	1988	1987	1986	1985
Revenues:				
Theme parks and resorts	$ 1,834	$ 1,524	$ 1,258	$ 1,097
Filmed entertainment	876	512	320	245
Community development	167	305	315	204
Consumer products	—	130	123	110
Total	2,877	2,471	2,015	1,656
Cost and expenses:				
Theme parks and resorts	1,285	1,120	1,002	912
Filmed entertainment	745	460	286	242
Community development	70	263	250	162
Consumer products	—	58	66	56
Total	2,100	1,901	1,604	1,372

EXHIBIT 8 *(concluded)*

	1988	1987	1986	1985
Income before corp. expenses:				
Theme parks and resorts	$ 549	$ 404	$ 256	$ 186
Filmed entertainment	131	52	34	2
Community development	97	42	66	42
Consumer products	—	72	56	54
Total	777	570	411	284
Corporate expenses:				
General & administrative	70	66	50	60
Net interest	29	41	52	42
Investment & interest income	(49)	—	—	—
Total	50	107	102	101
Income before income taxes & unusual charges	726	462	310	183
Unusual charges:	—	—	—	166
Income before taxes & accounting change	726	462	310	17
Income taxes (benefit)	334	215	136	(5)
Total				
Income before accounting change	392	247	174	22
Cumulative effect of change in accounting for investment tax credits	—	—	—	76
Discontinued operations	52	—	—	—
Net income	$ 444	$ 247	$ 174	$ 98
Earnings per share:				
Income before accounting change	3.23	1.82	1.29	0.15
Cumulative effect of change in accounting for investment tax credits	—	—	—	0.53
Total	$3.23	$1.82	$1.29	$0.68
Average number of common and equivalent shares outstanding	137.80	135.80	134.80	143.40

Human Resources

76 Michael Eisner and his new recruits brought the company diversity in both education and training. This talent base was a major requirement for Disney's development of exciting and profitable ideas. As Disney profited from its successful projects, morale was boosted. For example, Disney's animation department, which had been constantly overlooked by the rest of the company, suddenly received new emphasis and gained an optimist view that was likened "as palpable as the aroma of popcorn coming from the popper in the lobby."[22] The different departments and divisions interact with as little corporate bureaucracy as possible in an effort to affirm Eisner's belief that Disney employees are "basically hardworking family people."

77 But all employees are not satisfied with Walt Disney's policies. Disney's cost control mechanisms emphasize stringent budgets and low employee compensation. Disney can be "terrible to negotiate with," says actor Tom Selleck. But Eisner feels that management must keep a close hold on costs. "You've got to get hysterical and pretend you're playing with your own money."[23]

---

[22]"Eisner." *Current Biography Yearbook 1987*, p. 155.

[23]Koepp, p. 73.

IS DISNEY LOSING CONTROL OF MICKEY?

78   Is Disney in danger of saturating the market by "overplaying" its characters? Many believe that Disney's recent campaign to fully utilize its assets and make Disney a common household name is actually tarnishing Disney's image. It is believed that this action will saturate Disney's market, which is already limited, because most children grow up and out of Disney. Disney's management claims that the company has closely monitored the demand for its products. These executives feel that it is not possible to reach a saturation point. As one child grows out of Disney, another reaches the age where he or she can be enchanted by Walt Disney products. If parents grew up with Disney, it is almost guaranteed that their children will also watch Disney productions. There are also many individuals who never grew out of their fondness for Disney. However, according to Frank Wells, "We want to stop well short of the saturation point, not wait for the public to tell us that we've crossed the line."[24]

79   Michael Eisner called a special meeting of top Disney executives to discuss the recent suit filed against Disney by its own stockholders. The suit was provoked by the intensive takeover talks that were flooding the industry. The lawsuit claimed that Disney's officers and directors breached their duties by preventing unwanted takeover attempts. The plantiffs felt that Disney should "take all appropriate steps to expose itself to the marketplace."[25] This action made Eisner realize that it was now more important than ever for Disney to come to a decision about its direction.

80   Several questions needed to be answered. Should Disney continue with its current concentration on technological advancements in its films? *Roger Rabbit*'s technologically superior production left many wondering what would come next. Can and should Disney remain a focused organization in an industry that is rapidly diversifying? There is little doubt that this question would be answered for Eisner if he would consider a Disney acquisition. But Disney executives wondered if the company could survive such an action without being dismantled.

81   Disney appears to have come full circle from its position in 1984, as rumors have been spreading of pending takeover attempts. It is now up to the Walt Disney Company to prove that it learned from its past. In four years it climbed up from the bottom of the film industry to one of its premier performers. The question for Eisner was how to keep the momentum going.

---

[24]David J. Jefferson, "Walt Disney Co. Sued by 2 Holders Over Rights Plan," *The Wall Street Journal*, July 31, 1989, p. B3.

[25]Ibid.

CASE 30

GENERAL MOTORS CORPORATION

1   Founded by William C. Durant and incorporated on October 13, 1916, General Motors (GM) is the largest manufacturer of automobiles in the world. As of December 31, 1987, GM had 209 manufacturing facilities in the United States and 32 in other countries, 11 service parts distribution centers, 15 Electronic Data Systems facilities, and 24 Hughes Aircraft facilities (see Exhibit 1 for partial organization chart). General Motors produces a variety of vehicles ranging in type from pickup trucks to highway tractors under the product lines of Chevrolet, Buick, Pontiac, Oldsmobile, and Cadillac.

2   In addition to passenger vehicles, the corporation has diversified throughout the years into providing products and services for defense and various other nonautomotive industries. The defense products produced by GM include military vehicles, radar and weapon control systems, guided missile vehicles, and defense satellites. The nonautomotive products produced are comprised of the design, installation, and operation of business information and telecommunication systems; the design, development, and manufacture of locomotives; and specialized automated production and test equipment. In 1987, automotive products represented 88 percent of sales and 89 percent of the profits. Defense products represented 8 percent of the sales and 9 percent of the profits, and nonautomotive products represented 4 percent of sales and 2 percent of total profits. The United States accounted for 48 percent of net income, Europe 34 percent, Latin America 12 percent, Canada 1 percent, and other overseas sales 5 percent. The major increase in sales for the 1987 period were concentrated in Europe.

THE MANAGEMENT

3   The basic scheme for General Motors operations was developed by Alfred P. Sloan in the 1920s. Sloan developed a decentralized structure with GM's five car divisions, forcing them to compete against each other. General Motors had 14 layers of management.

4   In 1981, Roger Smith became GM's chairman and faced a tremendous challenge. General Motors' market share and total sales were declining. Furthermore, in 1980, GM lost $762 million; its first lost since 1921. These problems stemmed from Americans' views toward GM of making unsafe products that polluted and congested cities and of selling look-alike cars. Many of the safety criticisms were quickly translated into strict laws and regulations for establishing safety standards. In addition, there were volatile swings in demand between large and small cars in the 1970s, and during these years GM focused not on large cars but on fuel efficient cars. When gasoline prices fell in the early 1980s, consumers rushed to buy larger cars. GM responded by keeping many of its larger cars in production, which led to a multitude of models and high production costs.

5   In facing the challenge of being CEO, Smith was very optimistic. Looking forward, Smith

This case was prepared by Dr. Walter Greene of University of Texas–Pan American at Edinburg, Texas.

D Competitive Industry Analysis

Industry Definition

1   This case focuses on the hardware component of the personal or microcomputer industry in the United States. The computers designed and manufactured by this industry are used by business, home, educational, and government segments of the market. As the decade of the 1980s draws to a close, the size of the U.S. market for microcomputers exceeds $23 billion.

2   The term *microcomputer* covers many different types of machines: personal computers, inexpensive computers for playing games, and expensive workstations used primarily for computer-assisted design and manufacturing (CAD/CAM). The characteristic that unifies these computers is their use of a central processing unit (CPU) in a microchip.

History of the Industry

3   In 1969, Dr. Ted Hoff, an engineer at Intel Corporation, designed a silicon chip that contained arithmetic and logic circuits for a calculator. The chip was called a *microprocessor*. This innovation laid the foundation for the microcomputer industry.

4   Following a 1974 article in *Radio Electronics* that described how to build a personal computer using a microprocessor, $500 kits that could be used for this purpose became available. Thousands of these kits were sold to hobbyists, and computer clubs sprang up in many cities. Two young

This case was developed by Shaker A. Zahra and John A. Pearce II of George Mason University. The assistance of C. Besore, S. Birmingham, G. White, and J. Young is appreciated.

members of one of these clubs, Steve Jobs and Steve Wozniak, designed and built a single-board computer. After Wozniak's employer, Hewlett-Packard (HP), rejected the computer, Jobs and Wozniak showed it to members of their club. They all wanted to buy one, and a local computer store ordered 50. These machines, called Apple® I, were built in Job's parents' garage.[1] Due to demand, Jobs and Wozniak organized themselves as a company and a year later, in 1977, they delivered the first Apple II computer. By the end of 1977, Apple, Commodore, and Radio Shack all had microcomputers on the market. Several other companies started building microcomputers and the industry was born. These first-generation computers were 8-bit machines that used a CP/M operating system.

5   In the early years, microcomputers were viewed as toys for hobbyists. But, in 1979, Dan Bricklin and Bob Frankson created the first electronic spreadsheet program, VisiCalc®.[2] When released, it only worked in the Apple II. This quickly made the Apple II an important business tool.

6   Realizing the potential of the market, IBM introduced the personal computer (PC) in 1981. Because of IBM's name and reputation, the company soon gained the largest market share in the industry.[3] The IBM® Personal Computer, which used 16-bit technology provided by the Intel 8088 microprocessor, represented the second generation of microcomputers.

7   Attracted by the industry's high-growth rate, other manufacturers began to enter the market. New entrants included COMPAQ®, AT&T, Xerox, Digital Equipment Corporation (DEC), Data General, and Wang. By 1983, IBM PC-1 compatibles and other microcomputers began to flood the market. By the end of 1984, there were 350 companies around the world producing micro-computers. This growth in the number of competitors coincided with a slump in demand that caused many companies to go bankrupt or exit the market; many others laid off employees or reduced their operations. Employment in the computer industry as a whole decreased 9 percent in 1985 and 7 percent in 1986. The slump was further exacerbated by the entry of low-priced Asian clones into the U.S. market. A weak domestic economy, low capital spending, disenchantment with micro-computers, and continued difficulties in networking contributed to a persistently lower rate of growth in demand for industry product.

8   In 1984, around 53 percent of all new nonhome PCs were bought by first-time purchasers. In 1985, the rate had dropped to 48 percent, and in 1986 to 37 percent. This trend of replacement was expected to continue. Yet, there was still room for the industry to expand. In 1985, 84 percent of the 6.1 million public and private enterprises had no microcomputers. In 1986, 72 percent of almost 7 million workplaces still had none.

INDUSTRY DYNAMICS

Products

9   Using the IBM as a standard, microcomputers were classified into three broad categories: IBM, IBM-compatibles, and non-IBM-compatibles. Compatibles included a wide range of products from inexpensive clones to sophisticated high-performance machines that did everything an IBM machine could do and, often, more.

10   Some companies elected to offer microcomputers that were not compatible with the IBM standard. Their goal was to maintain compatibility with other computers in their own product lines.

---

[1]Apple is a registered trademark of Apple Computer, Inc.

[2]VisiCalc is a registered trademark of Lotus Development Corporation.

[3]IBM is a registered trademark of IBM Corporation.

EXHIBIT 1
Capabilities of Currently Used Machines

Generation	Microprocessor Intel	Bus	Example
2	8088	8-bit	IBM PC
	8086	16-bit	COMPAQ Deskpro Model 2
3	80286	16-bit	IBM Personal Computer AT
4	80386	32-bit	COMPAQ Deskpro 386
			IBM PS/2

Source: DataPro Research Corporation, *Analysis from DataPro's Microcomputer Lab,* May 1987.

These companies included HP, AT&T, and DEC. However, due to the power of the IBM standard in the marketplace, even these companies had introduced machines with IBM-compatible features.

11 Microcomputers had been further categorized with respect to the degree of portability into "desktops," "transportables," and "lap portables" or "laptops." Desktops offered the most storage capacity and the largest screen of the types and were, therefore, the heaviest and least portable of the three. Desktop vendors included IBM, COMPAQ, Apple, and HP. Transportables, sometimes called *portables*, were distinguished from lap portables in that they were designed to be moved from one location to another, while lap portables were used en route. Transportables usually required an AC power source and used the standard 5.25-inch diskette drives. Lap portables or laptops ran on batteries, used 3.5-inch diskette drives, and were the lightest of the three model types. Lap portable vendors included Toshiba, NEC, and Zenith. COMPAQ was the major vendor of transportables. These different classes of microcomputers used a wide range of technology, as shown in Exhibit 1.

Segments

12 The microcomputer market included four segments: the business segment, the educational segment, the home segment, and the government segment.

The business segment was important because of the high profit potential and the number of computers sold per organization. These high margins attracted the major computer companies. These larger companies had mainframes or minicomputers installed in target businesses. In addition, the larger competitors had the manufacturing capacity required to better meet large customers' needs. Companies that excelled in this sector were IBM, COMPAQ, Apple, AT&T, HP, and Wang.

13 Toward the end of the 1980s, there were notable differences in the level of microcomputer usage based on business sectors. For example, almost all companies with more than 1,000 employees had PCs. In contrast, only 20 percent of the companies with fewer than four employees had PCs. In the banking, finance, and insurance industries, 55 percent of all sites had PCs. On the other hand, retail trade businesses and small service businesses had only a 15 percent penetration rate, the lowest in the business segment. Finally, large corporations accounted for less than one fifth of the total PCs installed in the business market.

14 The value of the educational segment was in its long-term potential. Even though this segment yielded lower margins than the business segment, the early contact with the user was believed to generate long-term brand loyalty. As a result, most manufacturers gave this segment special attention. They charged lower prices and donated equipment and software. This marketing strategy also helped in stimulating derived demand for use at home. The prominent companies in the educational segment were Apple, Tandy, IBM, and Zenith. The penetration rate of the educational segment was estimated at 41 percent.

15   The typical home computer user owned a Commodore Model 64 computer and used it primarily to play games and for educational purposes. The majority purchased the microcomputer in computer or department stores. Apple and Commodore were the major vendors for the home computer market. Both companies encountered severe competition from the clones that offered IBM compatibility. Overall, sales to the home computer segment were predicted to increase, because of rising computer literacy and the availability of brand names at lower prices.

16   The federal government constituted a segment distinct from the business segment, because government agencies had different needs and procurement processes. Major suppliers for this segment were Zenith Data Systems, IBM, Unisys, COMPAQ, and GRID systems. Sales to the federal government were $2 billion in 1985, $2.2 billion in 1986, $3.1 billion in 1987, and estimated at $3.3 billion for 1988. Sales to this segment were expected to grow throughout the 1990s. The 150,000 microcomputers owned by the government were predicted to increase to 500,000 by 1990, with large purchases in multimillion dollar amounts. However, these large purchases stimulated competition among microcomputer manufacturers; increased competition was reflected in pressure to lower prices.

17   In both the business and government segments, there was an important factor that affected demand on microcomputers: the trend toward systems integration. Assembly of complete systems that incorporated microcomputers and were designed to perform the buyer's specific functions was becoming an increasingly important criterion in the purchase decision. Integrated systems were sometimes assembled with equipment from several manufacturers, which permitted the vendors to give the buyers the best price for the required performance.

FORCES ON COMPETITION

Rivalry in the Industry

Key Competitors

18   Exhibit 2 lists the top 10 U.S. companies based on the revenue derived from microcomputer sales. Total revenue from data processing products and services for each company is also included in the exhibit to provide insight into the resources that were potentially available to pursue microcomputer production and marketing efforts.

Three Strategic Groups

19   Microcomputer manufacturers evolved into three groups: the top, middle, and bottom tiers. Manufacturers at the top tier were involved in the development of advanced technology and the introduction of unique new products. Included in this group were IBM, COMPAQ, Apple, AT&T, DEC, and HP. Because IBM was in this tier and was the recognized standard in the industry, other makers in the top tier were concerned with what IBM did. However, each of the competitors strove to stay at the forefront in technology. Most manufacturers in this group provided extensive support programs for their products and targeted very large organizations (typically the Fortune 500 businesses) as lucrative customers for custom-designed organizationwide installations, which often included supporting communications. Often there was strong brand loyalty among top-tier customers. Even Apple, which historically targeted educational and home markets, had recently found corporate sales and networking attractive. New technology allowed Apple's computers to be compatible with IBM, DEC, and AT&T systems.

20   The middle tier included such manufacturers as Leading Edge, NCR, and Commodore. These firms generally took advantage of available technology and spent "just enough" on research and development (R&D) to add some additional features to create an improved product at a lower price

EXHIBIT 2
Top 10 U.S. Microcomputer Companies According to Revenues in 1986

Company	Company Sales	Company Revenue
IBM	$5,650	$49,591
Apple Computer, Inc.	1,781	2,031
Tandy	997	1,560
Unisys Corp.	800	9,431
COMPAQ Computer Corp.	625	625
AT&T	600	2,085
Zenith Electronics Inc.	548	1,900
Commodore International Ltd.	525	800
Hewlett-Packard Co.	450	4,500
Xerox Corp.	400	2,100

Source: "The Datamation 100," *Datamation,* June 15,1987.

than top-tier leaders. They often targeted large businesses in the Fortune 2,000 group. The major competitive focus for middle-tier manufacturers was a combination of price and performance. A major improvement that middle-tier vendors featured was higher operating speed. Oddly enough, the middle-tier manufacturers were often pleased to see the top-tier manufacturers leap to new technological advances, because it widened the competitive gap between the two levels. Middle-tier competitors provided reasonably good support but not as strong as in the top tier. There was only moderate brand loyalty among middle-tier customers.

21   The bottom tier included numerous small manufacturers whose spending on innovation was modest. They used reverse engineering to develop copies of IBM machines already on the market. This group was fragmented. Blue Chip, Hyundai, Samsung, and Tatung were typical of this group. They competed strictly on the basis of price and compatibility with other machines. The bottom-tier companies did not attempt to compete in the corporate community; their customers were typically small businesses and home buyers. Further, they offered little or no after-purchase support. Barriers to entry at the bottom tier were minimal, because parts could be copied quickly without prohibitive R&D costs. Although manufacturers in this group had pressed for government protection from imports, there were no legal barriers to entry from overseas suppliers, except for recent action to halt the importation of Japanese microchips.

22   The major differences among 10 major competitors in the strategic groups are examined in Appendix A.

Barriers to Entry

23   Rivalry among existing companies was only one element in the competitive situation that characterized the industry in the late 1980s. Companies also sought to erect and maintain barriers to entry or mobility through several means, as follows:

Differentiation

24   The goal of microcomputer vendors was to be IBM-compatible. In the top and middle tiers, differentiation was crucial to distinguish look-alike products from each other. To compete effectively, these companies provided more features, faster operating speeds, or value-added services.

EXHIBIT 3
Cost of Components of PC XT Compatibles

Component	Cost		
Black-and-white screen (Taiwan)	$ 75	to	$100
Controller cards	65		70
ROM/BIOS chip	10		15
Main circuit card (U.S., Taiwan)	75		150
Metal chassis and cover	35		85
Keyboard (U.S., Taiwan, or Thailand)	20		50
Floppy disk drive (Japan)	60		60
Power supply (Hong Kong or Taiwan)	30		100
Total	$370		$630

Source: Geoff Lewis, "The PC Wars: IBM vs. The Clones," *Business Week,* July 28, 1986.

These actions created barriers to entry into these top tiers. IBM hoped to use proprietary technology to a greater extent in the future to pull away from the pack of clones.

25   In the bottom tier, however, PCs were considered generic products. Although some companies, such as Aesthetics Technology, attempted to differentiate their products by providing aesthetic differences such as unique paint finishes, woodgrain covers, and company logo, low cost was the key success factor in this tier.

Capital and Market Cost

26   Low costs and low prices were fairly easy to achieve for clone makers because of readily available parts. Exhibit 3 shows that the bottom-tier clone could be produced for under $400. Although not the primary focus of the top two tiers, costs were nonetheless becoming increasingly important because decreasing market prices reduced profit margins.

Economies of Scale

27   As with most emerging industries, economies of scale were not apparent in the early years of the microcomputer industry. However, as the industry evolved and prices became increasingly competitive, companies attempted to achieve economies of scale through automation in manufacturing. Several companies (e.g., IBM, Apple, and COMPAQ) also initiated programs to improve productivity and reduce costs of operations. Additional economies of scales were expected to result as further market penetration was achieved.

Concentration Ratios

28   Exhibit 4 shows the 10 U.S. companies with the largest market shares based on the number of units sold. Companies not listed had less than a 1 percent market share. As Exhibit 4 shows, the same four companies have occupied the top four positions since 1983. However, Apple's, Tandy's, and Commodore's shares decreased significantly as IBM's increased. Tandy and Commodore were expected to lose additional shares as competition intensified. In contrast, COMPAQ was expected to achieve one of the top four positions in the near future. Exhibit 5 shows the market shares of

EXHIBIT 4
Market Share for the Top 10 Companies

Company	Market Share During			
	6/30/83	1/1/85	1/1/86	1/1/87
IBM	10.4	28.8	37.1	39.4
Apple	28.9	28.6	21.9	19.7
Tandy	26.6	9.3	9.9	7.7
Commodore	8.3	7.2	4.3	3.7
COMPAQ	0.1	1.8	3.2	3.5
AT&T	—	0.1	0.8	2.7
DEC	1.6	2.0	2.6	1.9
Zenith	1.5	0.9	1.3	1.6
Hewlett-Packard	4.9	1.6	1.5	1.4
Wang	0.3	2.2	1.7	1.2

Source: Mark Ludvig, COMTEC Market Analysis Services/Gartner Group (Stamford, Connecticut), October 8, 1987.

the top four microcomputer vendors. As can be seen, the market was highly concentrated with the top four companies having a 70.5 percent concentration as of January 1, 1987.

Barriers to Exit

29 The shakeout in the microcomputer industry that began in 1984 forced many firms to exit the marketplace, including Eagle Computer, Inc.; Gavilan Computer Corporation; and Osborne Computers.

30 There were, however, some barriers to the exiting industry. Often, microcomputers were one of an array of businesses within a corporate portfolio. It would be difficult to imagine, for example, IBM or AT&T pulling out of the microcomputer industry. Each of these firms marketed its microcomputers as one of a wide range of other products. In fact, both IBM and AT&T announced changes in their strategies to achieve stronger positions in voice/data networking and work group systems, using microcomputers as key elements. IBM acquired a telecommunications business, Rolm, in order to be a strong competitor in networking. Moreover, it was no secret that AT&T lost money in its computer business every year since it introduced its first microcomputer in 1984. Yet, the company made emphatic official statements that microcomputers were a major element of its long-term plans.

Buyers

31 As the microcomputer industry became more established, the microcomputer user became more sophisticated and demanding. As a result, there was pressure on manufacturers to give users what they wanted, rather than what makers chose to build. Users became quite capable of discerning the comparative advantages and disadvantages of available systems, and this put more power in the users' hands. Manufacturers also recognized that practical considerations motivated the purchase of minicomputers. As a result, sellers offered custom-configured microcomputers, with cards, hard disks, and other devices installed by the users' special requirements.

EXHIBIT 5
Market Share and Concentration Ratios

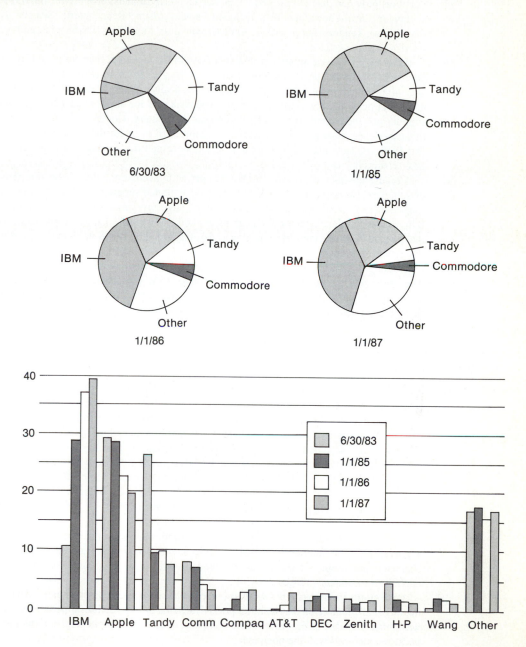

Suppliers

32   Suppliers provided microchips, boards, power supplies, cabinets, disk drives, monitors, cards, and keyboards. Well-known suppliers included Faraday (main circuit board), Seagate Technologies (hard disks), Tandom (floppy disks), Amdek (monitors), Keytronics (keyboards), and AST Research (cards).

33   Most suppliers were small and undiversified, which increased their vulnerability to microcomputer manufacturers' decisions. For example, to be chosen as an IBM supplier, a small supplier was often required to increase its capacity drastically. When it financed this growth through additional debt, there was often a severe dependence of the supplier on IBM for survival. If the supplier lost the contract it was likely to go out of business. Computer Memory, Inc. (CMI), had this experience when it won the contract to supply hard disks for the IBM Personal Computer AT. But IBM was not satisfied with CMI's performance and discontinued its contract. CMI was not able to survive.

34   Because the microcomputer industry was driven by technology that changed rapidly, the power of suppliers was weakened. Rapid obsolescence inhibited suppliers from dedicating themselves to long-term technological leadership that required large investments in research. To maintain flexibility, most suppliers licensed their products to other suppliers. This provided them with royalties and assured them that their technology was the standard. This licensing, however, further weakened the power of a single supplier.

35   Although suppliers did not hold much power, they could cause problems for manufacturers when they did not deliver on time. For example, IBM was unable to meet the demand for the Personal Computer AT, because of delays in the delivery of parts. COMPAQ took advantage of this situation and captured some of IBM's market share.

MARKETING PRACTICES

36   To achieve their goals, microcomputer manufacturers used a variety of marketing practices to reach customers. Media advertising was important to most sizable vendors. Computer, technical, and business publications were major print vehicles for microcomputer ads. Makers in all competitive tiers used advertising in computer publications to reach broad national markets. A useful advertising technique was the product review in computer publications. Manufacturers usually allocated machines to be tested by technical writers, hoping for favorable product reviews. Newspaper advertising was also used, but these ads tended to be more logically focused and were often placed by retailers or distributors on a cost-sharing basis with the manufacturer. Manufacturer reimbursement for newspaper advertising placed by retailers sometimes went as high as 75 percent for brand-exclusive ads.

37   Radio and television were also popular advertising channels in microcomputer marketing. Most TV watchers were familiar with IBM's television commercial that featured a Charlie Chaplin-like character, and Apple's commercials that ended with a bite being taken out of the multicolored apple in the company's logo.

38   Promotions of various types were also used to increase microcomputer sales. The customer was the target of promotions that featured price reductions on the machines, peripheral equipment that was either included in the price of the computer or offered at reduced prices, and extra software packages included with the computer.

39   Dealers were also the recipients of promotional benefits, especially from the largest manufacturers. Price cuts and volume discounts were often offered to move machines that were no longer the latest in technology or to simply increase sales. Promotions also provided dealer and salesperson

incentives. Dealers could be offered free financing, deferred payment periods, or preferred financing rates during promotional campaigns.

40   In addition to these marketing techniques, some manufacturers maintained their own sales forces. IBM was probably the most well-known manufacturer that fielded its own salespeople. Manufacturers' sales representatives had the advantage of training in the specific features of the maker's equipment. They had a direct line to the company for support, and they usually were aware of new products that the company planned to introduce and how these products could improve a customer's system. Manufacturers' sales personnel were generally targeted toward corporate accounts, government customers, large educational school systems, and major distributors.

PRICES

41   In the PC industry, competition increasingly focused on price. Some experts expected prices for hardware to decrease 11 percent annually in the future, pressuring manufacturers to reduce cost, seek efficiencies, or emphasize differentiation.

42   Prices were an indicator of the popularity of available models, although manufacturers had been known to reduce prices drastically, to push weak products and to eliminate excess inventory. IBM discovered that this could sometimes create an unexpected backlash when it drastically reduced prices on its PC line to reduce inventory. Potential buyers interpreted this drop in prices as a signal of an impending new product introduction and postponed purchases.

DISTRIBUTION

43   Channels of distribution were especially important in the microcomputer industry. Making the product available to the customer was a crucial phase of the sales process, yet distribution had been termed a major bottleneck in the industry. Methods of distribution included direct sales, retail sales, mail order, and mass merchandisers.

44   Direct sales was a major channel that was used primarily by large manufacturers for sales to volume customers. A direct sales force offered many support services that included educating customers and keeping them informed of recent developments in the product line.

45   The local retailer was one of the earliest distribution channels for microcomputers. In fact, over the years, stores and other resellers accounted for as much as 60 percent of IBM and COMPAQ sales. Many of these outlets were independently owned, while others were extensions of the manufacturer, such as Tandy's Radio Shack retail outlets.

46   Chain retailers were an important arm of the retail channel. These stores usually carried microcomputers from a number of manufacturers, as well as peripherals and software. Businessland, Inc., and Computerland Corporation were the largest of the chain retailers.

47   A variant in the retail channel was the value-added reseller (VAR). These specialized retailers purchased individual computer products, assembled and enhanced the products, and resold the package as a solution to a specific customer need.

48   The chain from retailers back to the manufacturer included distributors, both independent or company owned. ATARI® was an example of a manufacturer that had its own distributor.[4] In

---

[4]ATARI is a registered trademark of ATARI, Inc.

1986, independent retailers who sold AT&T machines were successful in getting AT&T to authorize its first distributor.

49   Increased user familiarity with and knowledge of various manufacturers' machines had given rise to a unique retail channel that would have been considered unacceptable a few years ago— the mail-order retailer. The emergence of this channel was also indicative of the level of confidence the public had in microcomputers, for there was little service or support provided by the mail-order merchant. The primary appeal of mail-order buying for the sophisticated microcomputer buyers was low price.

50   Another channel of distribution that had opened up as a result of growing user sophistication was mass merchandising through such organizations as Sears and K mart. These retail outlets were used primarily by home computer brands, such as Atari and Commodore.

SUBSTITUTES

51   Programmable calculators, typewriters, and word processing equipment were the potential substitutes for the microcomputer in the office environment. Consumers who sought word processing capabilities found programmable typewriters a popular substitute. Competition was rising from consulting firms, accounting firms, and electronic information-processing businesses. These firms were targeting smaller companies that did not want to invest the time, money, and anxiety in developing microcomputer systems or in training their staff to use microcomputers.

52   However, the microcomputer industry encountered the fiercest competition from mainframe computer producers and, more importantly, minicomputers. Businesses were sometimes choosing minicomputers over microcomputers, when the latter would suffice, because of the problem associated with networking numerous microcomputers. Experts expressed optimism that the threat from these related products would decrease as the integration of mainframes, minicomputers, and microcomputers continued.

ENVIRONMENTAL FACTORS

53   Technological changes and new product announcements presented both opportunities and threats for firms in the microcomputer industry. New technology, such as the Intel 80386 chip, presented the possibility of setting new standards for the industry. These new standards would weed out some firms while giving others a chance to increase market share. New product announcements had the same effect. For example, IBM's 1987 spring announcement of its Personal Systems/2 line and its new marketing emphasis on connectivity in the corporate arena posed severe threats for organizations with IBM PC-compatible machines. New products under development by these firms had to be modified if they were to continue to be compatible. Design modifications cost these companies millions.

54   With the large number of companies vying in the market and the wide range of potential applications, some firms found niching to be a worthwhile competitive strategy. Apple, for example, found the desktop-publishing niche to be a fertile market. Another profitable niche was the $1.5 billion market for engineering workstations. These workstations were high-powered, memory-intensive desktop microcomputers that were used for design and engineering applications. Such stations were forecasted for a 30 percent annual growth over the next five years. Apollo Computer, Sun Microsystems, and DEC held positions superior to IBM in this sector. The laptop microcomputers represented another niche worth about $500 million a year in sales and was expected to

grow rapidly in the next five years. A manufacturer who wanted to avoid confrontation with IBM could do so in this niche.

55   The market for network microcomputers connected via a communications channel was believed to be a growth area by both AT&T and IBM. The concept extended earlier office automation systems and made use of database sharing among the network of microcomputers, so that each terminal was a powerful workstation, rather than just a read-only machine. Since communications were key elements in the network approach, AT&T saw its long experience and core business in telecommunications as an advantage. IBM felt strongly about the potential in networking and, as a result, had acquired Rolm, a communications firm.

56   A related strategy to office automation was the "work group" approach. This consisted of groups of products (including microcomputers) that provided the capabilities needed to perform required tasks, including word processing, electronic mail, graphics, administrative functions, and computing. Companies that pursued the work group approach to office automation were said to provide "total solutions" to the needs of the customers.

57   The global nature of competitive forces also presented new opportunities for U.S. firms. Foreign markets represented potential growth in sales and offered new niches for meeting the needs of a varied customer base. However, increasing competition from the foreign producers continued to pose severe threats for the domestic industry.

58   The use of microcomputers in the educational segment was expected to continue to increase. First, microcomputers now had an established role in the teaching function of schools. Colleges, high schools, and even middle schools provided courses on how to use the microcomputer. Students found that the introductory course merely prepared them for a succession of courses in which use of the computer was essential. Second, microcomputers were now considered invaluable in the management and administration of schools and school systems.

59   Government use of microcomputers was also growing. Desktop machines were in all departments of the federal government. State and local governments were using microcomputers as well.

60   Businesses continued to find microcomputers helpful in a wide range of commercial applications. As in the education field, business uses of microcomputers included both the performance of primary business functions and management tasks. Understandably many of the leading companies in the markets targeted this segment to achieve further penetration.

61   The desire to protect technological contributions to the design of computers and related products resulted in the emergence of intellectual property law. The objective was to safeguard against the illegal counterfeiting or the use of the intellectual material represented in the product. The Counterfeit Access Device and Computer Fraud and Abuse Act of 1984 was one attempt to achieve this protection. This law was primarily aimed at illegal access to computer databases and the commission of criminal fraud. Moreover, the Racketeer Influenced and Corrupt Organizations Act of 1970 (RICO) could also be used to prosecute software piracy if fraud in the infringement of copyrights or misappropriation of trade secrets was proven.

THE FUTURE

62   The structure of the industry was projected to be different by the year 2000. One scenario predicted the consolidation of the current computer industry sectors into one dominant segment that offered opportunities for no more than 60 to 70 companies. An alternative scenario suggested that by the turn of the century the industry would consolidate and only five or six companies would survive. Increased advertising expenditures, services, reduced manufacturing costs and prices, and sophisticated technology used by major companies were expected to force the lower-tier clone companies out of their niches.

63   Foreign competitors were expected to continue their assault in domestic and international markets. Offering less expensive but powerful models, the success of the producers concerned even the most established companies in the microcomputer industry. So real was the threat of competition from foreign manufacturers that some leading U.S. corporations formed alliances with selected foreign partners or developed divisions for international marketing. These efforts resulted in increased shipments of about 5 percent annually of U.S. computers to foreign markets.

64   In summary, the 1970s witnessed the birth of the minicomputer industry and the proliferation of new start-ups that offered novel products and services. In the 1980s, the industry experienced a major shakeout, redefinition of industry boundaries, and revision of the competitive tools emphasized by key competitors. To survive in the 1990s and beyond, minicomputer companies were being challenged to innovate, differentiate, and further segment the market.

APPENDIX A

Profile of Major Competitors in the Microcomputer Industry, 1988

65   *International Business Machines (IBM)* was considered the most successful organization in the microcomputer industry. It ranked number one in mini, micro, and mainframe sales by the Datamation 100 in 1987. IBM ranked fourth among Fortune 500 firms. Its operations spanned information handling systems, equipment, and services. Data processing machines and systems, telecommunications systems and products, information distributors, office systems, typewriters, copiers, education and testing materials, and related supplies and services were some of its major products, which it leased or sold. Recently, IBM had acquired Rolm Communications Systems, which increased its capabilities in the software-driven cable telephone market.

66   IBM entered the microcomputer arena in 1981 through its Entry Systems Division (ESD), a part of the company's Information Systems Technology Group. It introduced its PC line of microcomputers and the PC-DOS® operating system, which revolutionized the industry.[5] IBM quickly gained market share leadership and established industry standards for what was then an emerging, fragmented industry. Because of its status in the computer mainframe market and its company resources, IBM had a competitive advantage from the beginning. The company used a variety of distribution channels, such as value-added sellers, retailers, and its own product centers. By the end of 1985, IBM held approximately 26 percent of the market of installed microcomputers. Revenues from the PCs accounted for almost $6 billion, or 11 percent of IBM's total revenues.

67   As IBM clones hit the market in large numbers, competition greatly intensified. Clones offered better, cheaper, and more responsive products. Severe competition, combined with an economic downturn in sales of microcomputers, led to a major slump in sales for IBM. IBM found itself faced with decreasing sales, increasing costs, and aging technology.

68   Accusations against IBM of not listening to the customer, being slow to respond to changing technology, and being too large to be innovative had been made by many inside and outside the company. However, IBM was determined to regain its lost market share. To combat its problems, IBM reduced the costs of its AT® and XT® machines (introduced in 1984 and 1983, respectively), released approximately 13,000 of its 400,000 employees, and invested $23 billion in plant automation over a five-year period. IBM also placed more emphasis on direct selling by its sales force. In June 1986, IBM sold its 81 IBM Product Centers to Nynex Corporation, because of the concern that they were detracting from the productivity of IBM's direct sales force and were leading to an

---

[5]PC-DOS is a registered trademark of Microsoft Corporation.

overdistribution of IBM products. IBM felt that it would have more control over its distribution channels by beefing up its direct sales force.

69   As of 1988, IBM's goal was to become the lowest cost producer in the industry while meeting the changing needs of the customer. In April 1987, IBM released its new line of microcomputers, the Personal System/2. It also released a new operating system, OS/2 in 1988. Its Systems Application Architecture (SAA), which was planned for completion by 1991, was designed to provide a software system to be used on all IBM computers. Initial indications suggested that these strategic moves were paying off; sales and revenues were rising.

70   *Apple Computer, Inc.* sold peripherals, software, and operating systems. In 11 years, the company that started in a garage had grown to be a $1.9 billion company. In fact, many credited Apple with popularizing microcomputers, because of its introduction of the first packaged system. Apple's traditional strength had been the educational market and, to a lesser extent, the home market. Since the first Apple was delivered in 1977, the company had been very successful. It had since introduced different products, including the Macintosh®.[6] It also had such failures as the Lisa®, the first Apple targeted to the business market.[7]

71   Apple saw its first quarterly loss in mid-1985. To improve its position, Apple laid off 20 percent of its employees (1,200 jobs), consolidated manufacturing into three facilities (Fremont, California, Cork, Ireland, and Singapore), and closed three other manufacturing plants. The company was restructured from three divisions into one, and from one organized by product lines to one organized by markets. These efforts allowed the company to reduce its cost structure from break-even sales of $450 million in fiscal year 1984 to $350 million in fiscal 1985. In 1985, a fight between founder Steve Jobs and John Sculley, then president of Apple Computer, Inc., led to Jobs's resignation from the company. In January 1986, Apple introduced the Macintosh Plus and entered the desktop publishing market. In 1987, profits rose 41 percent to $217.5 million, from $154 million the previous year. Sales also rose 40 percent to $2.66 billion in 1986, from $1.9 billion in 1987. These results reflected the Macintosh's increasing popularity. Apple had no long-term debt as of June 1987. It had more than $600 million in cash reserves.

72   Apple manufactured personal computers in two main lines: the Apple and the Macintosh. In 1986, the Macintosh (Mac) line outsold the Apple II line for the first time; but sales of the Apple II remained high, due to abundant software for educational and home use. Apple also sold peripherals, such as the LaserWriter Plus, under its own name, which allowed the company to enter the desktop-publishing niche. It also opened the door for Apple to enter the business market. Although the Macintosh had only 7 percent of business computer sales in 1987, there were strong signs that its popularity was increasing rapidly. The company was fairly confident that allowing users to use MS-DOS® and Unix® in the Apple computers would allow the company to increase its market share in the business market.[8]

73   Apple had moved from a heavy emphasis on advertising its image to a strategy designed to help its sales at the retail level. The budget for direct response advertising was increased and direct mail was used. The advertising strategy emphasized ease of use and the improved power of the machine. To make sure its machines were easy to use, Apple's software developers used a single set of commands so, once a person learned them, the commands could be used in other packages.

74   To improve the quality of distribution, Apple cut 600 stores from its 2,600 authorized dealers. In its effort to promote personal selling, Apple included a clause in the dealer's contract that

---

[6]Macintosh in a registered trademark licensed to Apple Computer, Inc.

[7]Lisa is a registered trademark of Apple Computer, Inc.

[8]Unix is a registered trademark of Lotus Development Corporation.

prohibited the dealer from selling Apple products through mail-order. Moreover, the company recognized the importance of direct sales in serving the business segment and placed 40 salespersons to work with dealers who served corporate customers. In addition, Apple set up a 30-person sales force to penetrate the government segment.

75   *COMPAQ Computer Corporation* was founded in February 1982 by three former Texas Instruments engineers. COMPAQ's sales reached $625.2 million in 1986, despite the slowdowns and market uncertainties that had plagued the microcomputer industry since 1984. The company's ability to weather the industry slump was attributable to its strengths in technology, manufacturing, distribution, and management, and its maintenance of a high degree of compatibility with IBM products. COMPAQ was listed as a Fortune 500 company in 1986, only four years after its founding, and was one of the most profitable organizations in the PC industry, ranking second only to IBM in sales of PC-compatible products.

76   COMPAQ entered the PC market in November 1982 with the COMPAQ Portable and has introduced a steady stream of new products since then. The Portable gained immediate recognition and dealer support due to its strong compatibility with the IBM PC and the fact that IBM was unable to meet the demand for PCs at the time. Furthermore, IBM did not have a portable on the market until 1984. The COMPAQ line of portables was expanded by the Portable Plus in October 1983, the Portable 286 in April 1985 (later discontinued), the Portable II in February 1986, the Portable III in February 1987, and the Portable 386 in September 1987. The Portable Plus enhanced the basic portable by adding a 10MB hard disk. The Portable II and III systems were both compatible with the IBM Personal Computer AT. Each successive portable had been reduced in size and was functionally improved over previous models.

77   COMPAQ's strategy centered on providing a wide range of high-quality, innovative products, which were fully compatible with their IBM counterparts. Its strategy, according to the COMPAQ president, Rod Canion, was to "challenge IBM in performance and features, but not in price." An example of this strategy in action was the Deskpro Model 2 that was one of the first systems to use the Intel 8086 microprocessor and maintain compatibility with the IBM Personal Computer XT.

78   One of the COMPAQ's major strengths was its distribution network. Its network included over 2,900 authorized COMPAQ Computer Centers worldwide. This dealer-oriented program was more extensive than IBM's. As a result, COMPAQ was able to penetrate the major computer retailers when IBM was unable to meet PC demand. COMPAQ provided the dealers with the answer when it introduced the Portable that used "off-the-shelf" IBM software. COMPAQ then took advantage of this foothold by strengthening its dealer relationships. By having no direct sales force to compete with dealers, COMPAQ had ensured dealer loyalty.

79   Most of the 2,900 COMPAQ Computer Centers provided training and maintenance. COMPAQ also offered third-party warranties through a division of 3M. Since this warranty service was nationally coordinated, dealers were able to compete more aggressively with other vendors' direct sales and service forces. COMPAQ offered a Major Accounts Sales Program to dealers in response to dealers' needs for training to better solicit and service major accounts from Fortune 1,000 firms. COMPAQ also offered a 38 percent profit margin to dealers, higher than IBM's 32 percent margin. The lack of a direct sales force, however, limited the company in dealing with large corporate accounts.

80   In 1987, COMPAQ showed signs of departing from its original strategy of following IBM at every turn. The introduction of the COMPAQ Deskpro 386 and the Portable 386 indicated that COMPAQ was now ready to depart from its traditional follower role. The Deskpro 386 was compatible with the original IBM standard, and IBM had set out in a new direction of proprietary technology. However, COMPAQ was betting that it would be left with a sizable residual market

demanding IBM PC-compatible products to support their substantial past investments in IBM equipment and compatible software.

81   *AT&T* entered the microcomputer market in 1984, after the divestiture of AT&T's regional telephone companies. The corporation expected its extensive resources (revenues of $34.1 billion in 1986) and well-known name to move its microcomputers into major prominence in the market. Unfortunately, its PC 6300 sales during the first two years were disappointing despite a large and costly advertising compaign. AT&T had achieved only a 2 percent share of the microcomputer market in 1987, and the corporation was reported to have lost over $800 million in the process of establishing its position.

82   AT&T chose to have its first machines made by the Ing. C. Olivetti Company of Italy. The initial microcomputer, called the 6300, was IBM compatible. Unfortunately, the 6300 sold poorly and managed to gain only 1 percent of the market, despite a reported advertising budget of $100 million. AT&T subsequently incorporated a unique operating system of its own development called Unix in a 6300 Plus machine that also operated IBM PC programs. AT&T believed that the Unix system, previously used in large-scale systems, would be successful in the microcomputer environment. AT&T then contracted with Convergent Technologies to manufacture the 7300 machine, called Unix PC. Again, this offering did not sell well.

83   By the end of 1986, AT&T announced massive cuts and write-downs in staff, operations streamlining, and asset/inventory valuations. AT&T's chairman insisted, however, that the firm was not pulling out of any major market segment. New changes in AT&T's strategy were considered. Vittorio Cassoni was installed as senior vice president of Data Systems in November 1986. His stated goals for the microcomputer segment centered on AT&T's development as a leader in the PC work group area of business and for its recognition as a superior supplier of the high end of the PC market.

84   *Tandy* was considered a quality supplier, especially among the low-cost dealers. Its greatest strengths were its low-cost distribution channels and its nationwide service and customer support. By building most of its computers' components, Tandy offered an IBM compatible at low prices. Also, Tandy avoided dealer margins by owning its own retailers. As a result, it had a 60 percent gross margin, compared to COMPAQ's gross margin of 42 percent. To provide better customer service and improve its image, Tandy set up a separate marketing organization, the Business Product Division. This unit was to spearhead future efforts to penetrate the business segment.

85   *Zenith Data Systems (ZDS)* established a strong, stable position, primarily in the educational and governmental sectors, despite the fact that it was not highly visible in the industry. With increasing sales in each of the last five years, ZDS contributed close to 21 percent of Zenith's total sales. ZDS's strategy offered a broad line of IBM-compatible products. In addition, it used a "seeing" strategy in both the government and educational segments and secured small contracts to establish contacts that made it easier to win larger contacts later on.

86   *Commodore*, whose traditional segment was mainly in the home segment, found survival in the industry difficult, owing to strategic and financial problems. It attempted to improve its position by focusing its efforts on two versions of the Amiga computer. Model 500 was aimed at the home and educational market and sold for $600. Model 2000 sold for about $2,000 and was targeted at the business segment. Commodore also emphasized its powerful graphics, sound capabilities, and an add-in board that allowed the computer to run IBM-PC and compatible software.

87   *Hewlett-Packard* was highly visible in the PC marketplace, although its dollar sales ranked below many of the other major vendors. One of the company's strengths was its orientation toward solving problems in the office environment, rather than merely offering individual, stand-alone products. Representative of this focus was the HP Personal Productivity that integrated its Touch-screen and Portable PCs with the HP 3000 minicomputer to provide a complete office system.

Despite its earlier attempts at using proprietary versions of MS-DOS to differentiate from IBM, HP succumbed to IBM's strength with the release of the Vectra PC. The Vectra PC, fully compatible with the IBM Personal Computer AT, offered advantages of faster operating speed and lower price than the Personal Computer. HP devoted more than 11 percent of sales to R&D.

88   *Digital Equipment Corporation (DEC)* entered the microcomputer area in 1980 with its Rainbow series machines. These machines failed for two reasons. First, the original model was an 8-bit machine that used CP/M, at the time when this type of machine was nearing obsolescence. The company later reintroduced the Rainbow as a 16-bit machine, but it was not IBM-compatible. Second, the Rainbow was a closed system and most buyers wanted the flexibility offered by IBM and compatibles. DEC did not gain a significant market share with these machines and had difficulties in marketing and distributing. It first elected to market through several channels: independent retailers, industrial distributors, DEC's Digital Business Centers, and a direct sales force. Later, the company decided to market each model through a specific channel. This resulted in confusion among customers about where to buy each model. The company's newest attempt to enter the field was extending its VAX architecture downward into the desktop and workstation market segment via the MicroVax and the VAXstation.

89   *Wang* followed a strategy of concentrating on services, voice and data integration, and systems integration to boost its role and visibility in the microcomputer market. It formed a joint marketing agreement with Apollo Computers and Sun Microsystems Incorporated to enter the CAD/CAM market.

CASE 32

COMPAQ COMPUTER CORPORATION

COMPANY HISTORY

1   COMPAQ Computer Corporation of Houston, Texas, was incorporated in February 1982. The company's three founders, J. Rod Canion, James M. Harris, and William H. Murto, were formerly engineers at Texas Instruments (TI). Starting a microcomputer company was not at the top of their list of ideas. Earlier inspirations included opening a Mexican restaurant, building circuit cards for expanding the capacity of IBM Personal Computers, and developing a beeping device for locating lost personal items. But building an IBM-compatible portable computer was the idea that won them the needed seed money from venture capitalists Benjamin Rosen and L. J. Sevin, co-owners of Sevin Rosen Management Company.

2   In the business plan submitted to Rosen and Sevin, the name of the company was Gateway Technology, Inc. Rosen's first impression of the plan was that it was extremely optimistic. He could not accept that a start-up company could achieve $35 million in sales in its first year, and $198 million in its second year by selling a portable IBM-compatible personal computer as was forecast in the plan. He told them to rethink their projections to make them more realistic. The name of the company was later changed to COMPAQ Computer Corporation in honor of its first suitcase-sized portable machine.

3   With an initial $1.5 million in funding from Sevin and Rosen, the three engineers started what would become one of the most successful companies in U.S. history. First-year sales reached $111.2 million. In the second year, sales were $329 million, almost triple those of the first year and far surpassing the estimates in the business plan. Rod Canion, the company's president, led COMPAQ with a single, consistent game plan—to build microcomputers that were totally compatible with the original industry standard set by IBM and the IBM PC and PC XT. Canion recognized the power of IBM in the marketplace with the creation of software. Realizing that success in the microcomputer industry greatly depended on the availability of software, it seemed that the best way to enter the industry in 1982 was to produce IBM-compatible products.

4   When IBM entered the emerging microcomputer industry in 1981, hundreds of companies followed. Although some of these companies were already established in closely related industries, such as mainframe computers, minicomputers, or electronics, a large number consisted of small companies formed by entrepreneurs who saw a chance to capitalize on the demand created by IBM. IBM's large size and power in the industry enabled it to command support for software and peripherals companies, setting product standards, and expending large amounts of money and effort on promotion. However, its bureaucratic structure made it slow to react to a rapidly changing market. Furthermore, IBM's open-architecture approach to the design of its earliest microcomputers meant that they were easily copied. By offering an IBM look-alike machine, a small company could take advantage of software created for the IBM PCs without being subject to the overhead costs for product development and manufacturing that IBM was bound to incur due to its size.

This case was prepared by Shaker A. Zahra, Jackie Young, and John A. Pearce II of George Mason University.

The Future

54   At the end of 1987, COMPAQ was well positioned in its segment. Armed with several promising new products, the firm's top-management team felt confident that the company was indeed on the frontier of a high-growth industry. Indeed, the limitless opportunities included introducing a laptop minicomputer, applying new findings on artificial intelligence, and linking minicomputers and telecommunication. Moreover, the company segmented the market further to pinpoint additional areas to penetrate.

55   Management was also aware of the need to shift the strategy from "follow the leader" to being an innovative competitor. IBM, alarmed at COMPAQ's success, responded by emphasizing the proprietary nature of its recent product introduction. As a result, COMPAQ found it difficult to imitate IBM's products and to generate its own innovative ideas.

56   This serious change in focus came at a time when price competition was widespread in the industry. The effect of this competition was felt in the reduced profit margins of COMPAQ and its dealers. So, at the time when the company should have increased its research, development, and advertising activities, the company had to find new approaches to retain its dealers.

57   As management explored new ways to redefine COMPAQ's competitive advantage, one trend in the minicomputer industry was clear. COMPAQ could not duplicate its initial success without finding a solid foundation on which to reformulate its strategy.

CASE 33

AT&T MICROCOMPUTERS

OVERVIEW

1   AT&T's microcomputer business was begun in 1984, at a time that coincided with a corporate restructuring that resulted from a federal court-ordered breakup of the original firm. Although AT&T's lost its seven regional Bell Telephone operating companies in the divestiture, it gained the right to engage in business areas not previously open to it under antimonopoly statutes. This change permitted AT&T to enter the microcomputer industry, a market that was relatively new, profitable, bathed in high-tech glamor, and seemingly insatiable.

2   AT&T's familiarity with electronics and technological product development, the public's familiarity with its name, and the company's image of dependability were valuable assets. Additionally, starting the business line within a corporation with revenues of more than $30 billion eliminated problems of financial resources for this new venture. These factors made AT&T's entry into the minicomputer industry very promising.

3   By 1984, AT&T had established a presence in the overall computer industry with its development of the Unix operating system. Moreover, AT&T had the technological expertise and the complementary communications linkage necessary to acquire a large share of the profitable microcomputer and office automation markets. In addition, AT&T had a cadre of experienced executives who were capable of managing the computer business. Also, the firm had an experienced sales force that could market its microcomputers. Indeed, the new Computer System Division was considered of the caliber of organization that could compete successfully with IBM. In fact, challenging IBM was AT&T's primary goal for its computer business. Arrangements were made with Ing. C. Olivetti & Company of Italy to manufacture the microcomputers that AT&T would sell under its name, and the new business was launched.

4   Despite its early promise, by the end of 1986 AT&T had managed to become only eighth in world microcomputer sales. With about 10 percent of the dollar sales of IBM it was far behind its supplier, Olivetti, which ranked third.

5   One reason for this disappointing performance was the drastic slump in microcomputer sales beginning in 1984 when AT&T entered the market. After a 51 percent growth rate from 1983 to 1984 for U.S. manufacturers, sales growth declined to 12 percent by the end of 1985, then to 9 percent by the end of 1986. Yet, two years later, the company's position in the industry had not improved. Indeed, whether AT&T should continue its efforts in this market was then a matter of serious debate among industry analysts.

This case was prepared by Shaker A. Zahra, George White, and John A. Pearce II of George Mason University.

FINANCIAL PERSPECTIVE

6 As one of America's leading corporations, AT&T had ample financial resources to establish a microcomputer business. However, AT&T planned its entry so as not to require investment in manufacturing plant and equipment by choosing to have its machines made by Olivetti. Although AT&T did not publish financial data on its individual businesses, consolidated corporate data in Exhibits 1 and 2 showed a solid financial footing during the period from 1984 to 1986.

7 Estimates of the dollar value of AT&T's microcomputer sales were $200 million in 1984, $500 million in 1985, and $600 million in 1986. For comparison purposes, Exhibit 3 shows the sales for the top 10 industry competitors in 1986.

8 There were signs, however, that the situation would improve. Vittorio Cassoni, the senior vice president who headed Data Systems, announced in April 1987 that computer revenue would be at least equal to the 1986 results, and that losses would be cut to one third of the 1986 figure. Cassoni also predicted that the computer business would be profitable within two years. Indications in early 1988 were that the computer business was meeting or exceeding those financial goals.

BUSINESS STRATEGY

9 When AT&T entered the microcomputer business in 1984, its strategy was to rival IBM in the high end of the PC-compatible market. In fact, industry analysts supported this forecast by predicting that IBM and AT&T would be the survivors of the micro sales slump that began that year.

10 AT&T shaped its strategy at the outset to take advantage of the industry's recognition that IBM compatibility was the evolving standard. Other micro makers who had used operating systems different from IBM were learning, at great expense, that they would have to change and follow the leader to survive. However, AT&T's machines did not sell well enough to pose a threat to IBM. Consequently, AT&T found itself competing against all the other top-tier IBM-compatible microcomputers for a minor share of the market while IBM safely retained its leadership.

11 In 1985, AT&T altered its strategy. Its next products, the 6300 Plus and Unix® PC machines, used the AT&T-developed Unix operating system. This action was taken in an attempt to establish a new standard that would either compete with or supplant the MS-DOS system used in IBM PCs. Although the Unix system had been popular with programmers and was successful in mainframes and minicomputers, it was not well accepted by microcomputer users. In fact, it was widely considered to be user unfriendly. The 6300 Plus machine survived only because it operated MS-DOS as well as Unix software.

12 The Unix PC, or Model 7300 machine, was released in 1985. It was intended to challenge IBM in voice/data networking. IBM had recently acquired the Rolm telecommunications firm as implementation of a strategy of taking over a major portion of the office automation market for voice/data workstations and networks. Because of AT&T's leadership in telecommunications, it was believed that the combination of AT&T communications and the Unix PC would be highly competitive with IBM in this business area. However, because the Unix system was not accepted in microcomputers, AT&T's challenge to IBM was not successful.

13 Next, leaked reports and rumors emanating from an AT&T high-level strategy meeting in 1986 dealt the microcomputer business a serious blow. Statements in an internal memo to management personnel after the meeting were especially damaging. The memo cited three priorities: strengthening and enhancing the profitability of AT&T's core business of telecommunications, deploying a "new generation of networking solutions," and establishing a "major position" internationally. Further, the memo implied that AT&T might not stay with an IBM-compatible approach. The memo led to speculation that AT&T was about to withdraw from the microcomputer market. Dealers were

EXHIBIT 1

AT&T
Consolidated Balance Sheet
(dollars in millions, except per share amount)

	1986	1985	1984
Sales and revenues:			
Sales of services, net of access charges	$19,108	$17,393	$15,781
Sales of products	10,178	11,235	10,189
Rental revenues	4,801	5,789	7,217
Total operating revenues	34,087	34,417	33,187
Operating costs and expenses:			
Cost of services	8,954	9,097	8,984
Cost of products	7,196	7,066	6,405
Cost of rentals	2,099	1,936	2,100
Selling, general, and administrative expenses	11,071	11,104	11,216
Research and development expense (B)	2,278	2,228	2,188
Provision for business restructuring	2,157	—	—
Total operating costs and expenses (C) (D) (E)	33,755	31,431	30,893
Operating income	332	2,986	2,294
Other income—net (F)	402	252	525
Interest expense (H)	613	692	867
Income before income taxes	121	2,546	1,952
Provision for income taxes (G)	(193)	989	582
Income before cumulative effect of a change in depreciation method	314	1,557	1,370
Cumulative prior years' effect (to December 31, 1985) of a change in depreciation method (E)	(175)	—	—
Net income	139	1,557	1,370
Dividends on preferred shares	86	110	112
Income applicable to common shares	$ 53	$ 1,447	$ 1,258
Weighted average common shares outstanding (millions)	1,071	1,058	1,010
Earnings per common share before cumulative effect of a change in depreciation method	$ 0.21	$ 1.37	$ 1.25
Cumulative prior years' effect of a change in depreciation method (E)	(0.16)	—	—
Earnings per common share	$ 0.05	$ 1.37	$ 1.25

EXHIBIT 2

AT&T
Consolidated Statements of Funds Flow
(dollars in millions)

	1986	1985	1984
Funds (cash and temporary cash investments) at January 1	$2,214	$2,140	$ 5,312
Sources of funds:			
From operations:			
Net income	139	1,557	1,370
Depreciation	3,925	3,232	2,778
Net (increase) decrease in working capital detailed below	2,661	13	(1,836)
Noncurrent portion of provision for business restructuring	1,159	—	—
Deferred income taxes—net	(391)	855	777
Less: Equity investment income in excess of dividends	24	23	20
Other adjustments for noncash items	359	61	12
Total from operations before cumulative prior years' effect of a change in depreciation method	7,110	5,573	3,057
Cumulative prior years' effect of a change in depreciation method	175	—	—
Total from operations	7,285	5,573	3,057
From external financing:			
Increase in long-term debt, including capital leases	729	141	171
Issuance of common shares	64	671	1,225
Increase in short-term borrowing—net	108	—	—
Total from external financing	901	812	1,396
From other sources:			
Divestiture cash flow settlements (R)	—	—	175
Sales to affiliate of long-term receivables net (J)	—	408	—
Total from other sources	—	408	175
Total sources of funds	8,186	6,793	4,628
Use of funds:			
Additional to property, plant, and equipment—net (R)	3,629	4,178	3,462
Dividends paid	1,381	1,374	2,327
Retirement of long-term debt	1,893	569	427
Increase (decrease) in investment—net	(31)	402	76
Increase in other assets	477	123	435
Decrease in short-term borrowing—net	—	22	446
Redemption of preferred shares	545	37	29
Other—net	(96)	14	598
Total uses of funds	7,798	6,719	7,800
Funds (cash and temporary cash investments) at December 31	$2,602	$2,214	$ 2,140

(continued)

EXHIBIT 2 *(concluded)*

	1986	1985	1984
Working capital components (excluding cash and temporary investments, debt maturing within one year, dividends payable, and deferred income taxes)			
(Increase) decrease in net receivables	$1,123	$ 420	$(5,105)
(Increase) decrease in inventories	1,027	(139)	(1,141)
(Increase) decrease in other current assets	9	119	286
Increase (decrease) in accounts payable	(309)	(142)	2,778
Increase (decrease) in payroll and benefit liability	300	85	388
Increase (decrese) in other current liabilities	511	(330)	958
Net (increase) decrease in working capital	$2,661	$ 13	$(1,836)

EXHIBIT 3
Sales by the World's Top 10 Microcomputer Companies in 1986

Rank	Company	Sales (in millions)
1	IBM	$5,650.0
2	Apple Computer	1,781.0
3	Olivetti	1,267.6
4	Tandy	977.0
5	Unisys	800.0
6	NEC	697.0
7	COMPAQ Computer	625.2
8	AT&T	600.0
9	Toshiba	581.5
10	Zenith Electronics	548.0

Source: *Datamation*, June 15, 1987, p. 31.

irate over the effect of these rumors on sales. Adding fuel to the fire was the announcement about massive financial and personnel restructuring. For awhile, AT&T's efforts in the microcomputer business appeared to lack necessary focus. The vice president in charge of the computer business at that time, James Edwards, summed up his concerns about this situation by stating that ". . . we were rapidly moving headlong into probably the most competitive business in the world, without knowing exactly what we were doing."

14   The furor created by these events became so intense that it was necessary to the chairman and chief executive of AT&T, James E. Olson, to clarify the situation. Olson stated that corporate restructuring efforts did not mean AT&T was about to withdraw from any of its major market segments. Olson described the cutbacks as part of a long-term strategy to strengthen AT&T's core businesses to be successful in the targeted data network and global markets. Furthermore, Olson explained that the plans were expected to cover four to five years.

15   This statement was followed in early 1987 by a press conference in New York with Vittorio Cassoni, senior vice president heading the Data Systems Division. Cassoni's statements reassured

the public that AT&T was firm in its commitment to the microcomputer line, that micros were a basic ingredient in its plans regarding workstations, and that PCs were as strategically important to AT&T as any other product line.

16   In late 1987, Cassoni gave an interview in which he admitted that AT&T's strategy in microcomputers had not been as clear as it should have been. He went on to articulate the strategy as follows:

- To continue with Intel/IBM-compatible technology and add functions to that capability.
- To provide a microcomputer work group product line and be recognized as one of the leaders in office automation work group systems.
- To look for networking synergies between AT&T's computer product line and its communications capabilities and leverage off the recognized AT&T strength in communications.
- To be recognized as a superior supplier of the high end of the microcomputer market.

17   With a comprehensive microcomputer strategy finally in place, AT&T offered products that were considered stronger than previous models in their capabilities. These products were aimed at information management specialists who used networked microcomputers. Most of the models were clearly targeted against similar IBM products. These moves led one market researcher to predict that AT&T was readying itself for a "limited challenge" against IBM and Digital Equipment Corporation (DEC) in 1990.

MARKETING

18   Marketing in a competitive environment was not familiar to AT&T when it began offering microcomputers for sale. For decades the telephone giant had enjoyed a virtual monopoly, and its corporate culture was permeated with a confidence resting on a near "take it or leave it" mentality. Although the people in AT&T professed to understand that their marketing now took on a new dimension called *selling,* the realization was not easy to implement. Nowhere in the corporation was this lack of a selling orientation to marketing more dramatically demonstrated than in its microcomputer business.

19   When it entered the microcomputer market, AT&T indicated that it intended to be a major force in the industry. In fact, there were expectations that AT&T with its great financial resources would challenge IBM. AT&T's first product (the PC 6300) was manufactured by Olivetti of Italy and was labeled with the AT&T logo. The PC 6300, a fully IBM-compatible machine, was sold through authorized independent dealers supplied directly by AT&T and through the telephone business sales force. Despite the fanfare accompanying the 6300's introduction, sales were a disappointing 30,000 units in 1984, representing only 1 percent of the market. The advertising budget for this rather modest achievement was reported to have been over $100 million.

20   In 1985, AT&T introduced a new machine made by Convergent Technologies and called the *Unix PC Model 7300.* This computer incorporated the Unix System V operating system, developed by AT&T, rather than the MS-DOS system used in the IBM PC. Although Unix had proved to be a very capable system with mainframes and minicomputers, its potential in microcomputers was not realized. The initial version of the Model 7300 was not IBM-compatible, could read MS-DOS data but not run it, and was not compatible with the AT&T 6300 machine. Sales of the Unix PC Model 7300 were about 10 percent of AT&T's projections.

21   Late in 1985, AT&T introduced yet another machine, the PC 6300 Plus. While the new microcomputer also used the Unix operating system, it was modified to run MS-DOS software, making it AT&T's challenger to the IBM PC AT. The 6300 Plus proved to be a valuable addition

to the AT&T line, but marketing support floundered. By late 1986, AT&T's marketing problems centered on five areas: public relations personnel were not briefed on products; salespeople were not given details of product announcements until after the fact; many products were not announced at all; products were announced but not shipped promptly; and there were no aggressive efforts to have software written for the Unix PC. Again, AT&T's lack of experience in a competitive environment may have been the cause for this incoherent approach to marketing its microcomputers.

22   In October 1986, AT&T moved aggressively into a price-cutting and sales-incentive campaign designed to respond to dealer complaints. Dealers wanted attractive pricing, marketing support from AT&T, and product supplies consistent with promotions. Prices on machines were cut as much as 30 percent, dealers were given points redeemable in training programs and other marketing expenses, and salespersons were given cash bonuses for meeting sales objectives. Dealers were even given 60-day free financing, up to 180 days to pay, and preferential credit lines for stocked products to improve availability of microcomputers for sale. As a consequence of these moves, AT&T's sales reached 3.2 percent market share for 1986.

23   While the 1986 marketing campaign was under way, AT&T announced yet another product development program, this time with Lucky-Goldstar in South Korea. In a move to market a machine in the low tier, AT&T planned to have Lucky-Goldstar build low-cost IBM-compatible microcomputers to be sold under the AT&T name by late 1988. Another attractive feature of a Korean built machine was the prospect of higher profit margins than AT&T was achieving on the Olivetti micros.

24   Distribution experienced some erratic shifts during the early years of AT&T's microcomputer business. For more than two years, AT&T's distribution channels for microcomputers were simple and tightly controlled. The AT&T company sales force and authorized microcomputer retailers, supplied directly by AT&T, sold AT&T micros. The retail dealers were required by AT&T to commit to large annual purchase programs and carry heavy inventories.

25   After continued complaints about these requirements for dealers, AT&T authorized its first distributor in late 1986. Soon after this change, AT&T announced that it would turn over small- and medium-sized microcomputer accounts exclusively to dealers, and that it would handle only large customer network sales through its own sales force. Plagued with continuing complaints from dealers about shipping and billing mistakes, AT&T announced that dealers would be supplied directly from Olivetti.

26   An additional change to affect the marketing of microcomputers came in a 1987 reorganization. For the first time, the internal computer sales force became accountable to the head of Data Systems.

ORGANIZATION

27   AT&T's corporate organization underwent some important changes since the "new" AT&T's emergence. Starting in 1984, AT&T had six major functional activities, as shown in Exhibit 4: AT&T Communications, AT&T Information Systems, AT&T Network Systems, AT&T Technologies, AT&T Bell Laboratories, and AT&T International Business. The computer business including microcomputers, was initially placed under AT&T Technologies. However, a few months later the Computer Systems Division was realigned to AT&T Information Systems.

28   The Computer Systems Division, headed by a group vice president, was dependent on other parts of the AT&T organization for major support. AT&T Technologies provided systems development support for AT&T's computers, and another part of the organization had responsibility for marketing computers, along with an array of other information management products and systems

CASE 34

APPLE COMPUTER, INC.

THE FORMATIVE YEARS

1   With the advent of electronic kits to build microcomputers, computer clubs sprang up in many cities. One of these clubs was the Homebrew Computer Club in Menlo Park, California. In 1976, Stephen G. Wozniak, one of its members, wrote a BASIC programming language for a new microprocessor sold by MOS Technology. He then designed a computer to run it and shared the design with some of his friends, one of whom was Steve Jobs. Jobs saw the potential of the computer and encouraged Wozniak to sell the design to other hobbyists. On April Fool's day, 1976, Wozniak and Jobs formed a business and called it the Apple Computer Company. These microcomputer pioneers were in their early twenties.

2   Selling Jobs's Volkswagen van and Wozniak's two programmable calculators, they raised $1,350 to finance the new company. With the money, Jobs and Wozniak designed and built a single-board computer, which had no keyboard, case, sound, or graphics, and called it the Apple I. One of the early computer retail stores, The Byte Shop, ordered 50 boards. By the end of that year, the board was sold through 10 retail outlets, and Apple had started its meteoric ascent.

3   Although originally sold only to knowledgeable hobbyists, Steve Jobs saw the possibility of developing a similar product for the general public. For this purpose, Wozniak developed a second computer, superior to the Apple I. This second microcomputer model included a keyboard, power supply, color graphics capability, and a BASIC operating language, all in a plastic case. In 1976, Apple's first formal business plan was developed by A. C. "Mike" Markkula, who became Apple's first chairman of the board in 1977. The company aimed to reach a sales level of $500 million in 10 years, an amount that was exceeded in 1982.

4   In 1977, the company was incorporated by Jobs, Wozniak, and Markkula. The latter invested $250,000 in the company. Later, venture capitalists provided an additional $3 million. The Apple logo was designed by the Regis McKenna Advertising Company and an advertising campaign began. Although initially aimed at hobbyists, it later targeted the general public through the use of ads in consumer magazines. The Apple II was shown in the first West Coast Computer Faire. Its success was immediate, with many dealers signing up to sell the microcomputer. That same year, Apple began shipping its computers to Europe. By the end of 1978, Apple had more than 300 dealers.

5   The introduction in October 1979 of VisiCalc, the first electronic spreadsheet program, quickly made the Apple II an important business tool. People other than computer specialists now had a reason to use the microcomputer. Of the 13,000 Apple IIs sold by September 1980, approximately 19 percent were purchased to run VisiCalc. More programs and add-ons were created for the Apple microcomputer and the company continued to be successful. In spite of technical problems with a

---

This case was prepared by Shaker A. Zahra, Celia Besore, and John A. Pearce II of George Mason University.

new computer, the Apple III, every share offered in the initial public stock offering in December 1980 was sold within minutes.

6   In 1981, Apple restructured the top-management team. Mike Scott, Apple's president since February 1977, was named vice chairman, Mike Markkula became Apple's president, and Steve Jobs replaced Markkula as chairman. In that year, Apple launched the first of their Apple Expos and began to air commercials with well-known personalities as spokesmen, such as Dick Cavett.

7   Apple's position in the market was so strong that, when IBM entered the microcomputer industry in August 1981, Apple ran a full-page ad in *The Wall Street Journal* welcoming them. Little did Jobs know that IBM would take Apple's number one position. Jobs miscalculated the value of the industry to the giant; at the time, the market was approximately $1.4 billion and he thought IBM would not be interested.

8   By December 1982, Apple became the first personal computer company to reach the $1 billion annual sales rate.

IN SEARCH OF LEADERSHIP

9   The year 1983 marked a major turning point in the life of the company. Apple became the youngest company ever to enter the Fortune 500 list; it ranked number 411. During 1983, John Sculley, formerly Pepsi-Cola's president, joined Apple as its new president and CEO. Jobs ended what has been described as an intense courtship with the now-famous pitch: "Do you want to spend the rest of your life selling sugared water or do you want a chance to change the world?" Jobs became chairman of the company and executive vice president in charge of the Macintosh Division.

10   Early in 1984, Apple introduced its new product line, the Macintosh. A predecessor of this microcomputer, the Lisa, was unsuccessful. The Lisa used innovative technology, but it was expensive (about $9,995), did not have enough software, and was not compatible with any other microcomputer. The Lisa did, however, introduce most of the features of Apple's new flagship product, the Macintosh. The user-friendly Macintosh offered a new operating system, greater memory and speed than competitors, and an enhanced graphics package.

11   After years of prosperity, 1985 was Apple's most difficult year. Wozniak resigned in February to start a company called CL9 (Cloud Nine) to produce infrared, remote control devices. He felt he had nothing to do in Apple since he was not interested in management and he had disagreements with Jobs. In fact, he had begun to separate himself from Apple after surviving a near fatal plane crash in 1981. In 1983, after fully recovering from the accident, Wozniak returned to work in the Apple II Division. Although the Apple II line was the company's "cash cow," Apple did not pay it a great deal of attention. The emphasis was on work for Job's new pet project, the Macintosh. After Wozniak publicly criticized Apple's management, he left the company permanently.

12   The exit of Wozniak was not Apple's only problem. The first quarterly loss in 1985 was Apple's first as a public company. Although the firm had higher sales than ever before, dealer inventory was high, even though Apple was producing only at approximately 12 percent of capacity. Analysts attributed some of the problems to strategic mistakes made by Apple. The Macintosh XL computers, for example, were considered to have insufficient memory capacity. Rather than trying to find efficient distribution channels, Apple had tried to use a costly direct sales force for the low-margin personal computers. In spite of the already strong dominance of IBM in the microcomputer industry, no serious effort was made to make possible communication with IBM computers.

13   To improve its financial position, Apple laid off 20 percent of its employees (1,200 jobs), consolidated manufacturing into three facilities (Fremont, California; Cork, Ireland; and Singapore),

and closed three other manufacturing plants. The company was restructured from three divisions into one, and from a company organized along product lines to one organized according to markets. Combining the two divisions (the Apple Division and the Macintosh Division) also helped to improve morale problems that had arisen from the preferential treatment given the Macintosh Division at the expense of the Apple II Division. These steps helped the company to reduce its cost from a break-even sales of $450 million in fiscal year 1984 to a break-even sales of $350 million in fiscal 1985.

14   After the reorganization, Jobs was left with no direct day-to-day control responsibilities. A power struggle between founder Jobs and president Sculley led to Jobs's resignation. However, Job's departure was not a peaceful transition. Jobs informed Apple's board of his intention to create a new company to produce microcomputers for universities. At first, Apple was interested in acquiring a 10 percent stake. However, when the board heard that Jobs was taking five top Apple employees with him, the directors became alarmed. Apple feared that Jobs's major reason for starting his company was revenge. For this reason, Apple filed a suit before the Santa Clara County Superior Court on September 22, 1985. The issue was whether Jobs had engaged in unfair business practices when he recruited five employees for his new company while still the chairman at Apple, and whether he had taken proprietary information with him when he left. Jobs responded that the employees had approached him independently, and that he had given Sculley the names of these employees while still employed at Apple. Jobs also reiterated that he had no intention to compete with Apple. However, this new computer was aimed at universities, a segment identified by Apple as users of the Macintosh. In fact, one of the persons that left the company with Jobs, Dan Lewin, was responsible for setting up Apple's marketing program for selling Macintoshes to colleges.

15   The lawsuit Apple brought against Jobs was later settled privately after Jobs agreed to allow Apple to inspect products developed by the new company 60 days before introduction. While other companies might have been greatly troubled led by such a major transition, Apple's performance remained solid. Its net profit margin, which had decreased to 3.4 percent in 1985, jumped to 8.1 percent in 1986. At the beginning of 1987, Apple was ranked number one by *Forbes* in both corporated profitability and five-year average sales growth. Apple also ranked number four in five-year average earnings per share.

APPLE TODAY

16   The departure of two of Apple's three founders signaled the end of an era in the life of the organization. Sculley's reign brought the introduction of many professional management principles. Change centered on the decision-making process, making it more group than individual based. As a result, power became diffused throughout the firm. Although Sculley retained considerable power as chairman, CEO, and president, decisions were not centralized.

17   Although still concerned with growth, Apple placed greater emphasis on efficiency and a strong return on investment. This was accompanied by increased reliance on the company's new reporting and review procedures to control costs. Also, a new forecasting model similar to those used by soft drink makers had been introduced. The engineering department was replenished with people from Hewlett-Packard, Tandem, ATARI, and IBM. Candidates from MBA programs were increasingly sought and hired. Finally, new techniques, such as direct-mail marketing, reducing prices, and making use of other computer manufacturers' direct sales forces, were introduced to help penetrate the business segment.

MISSION, GOALS, AND STRATEGY

18 Apple's enduring mission was to "bring the power of computing to individuals" by making it accessible and affordable. Apple pursued this mission by following an innovation strategy. This strategy was refined in the mid-1980s to reflect the need to provide connectivity with industry standards. As Sculley said, "Apple's original goals of 'one person, one computer,' was transformed into 'one person, one computer, transparently and elegantly connected to the world.'"

19 Apple's business philosophy centered on three ideas:

1. *Computers as a way of life.*   Apple aimed to provide computers to use at home, school, and work.

2. *Accessible and affordable technology for individuals.*   Apple's intent was to provide computing power to individuals: the "one person, one machine" philosophy cited earlier. Although Apple placed increased emphasis on sales to the business sector, its approach was still to target individuals within the business, and let them promote Apple's product to their management. Adoption of Apple's products often occurred because one employee "fell in love" with it and promoted it among the colleagues.

3. *Apple was an exciting place to work.*   Apple's internal working environment was evolved around creativity, innovation, teamwork, achievement, and responsible risk taking. To this purpose, Sculley tried to maintain an atmosphere of informality in the organization to attract creative people needed for his company. This was complemented by a structure and controls to maintain creativity and innovation within the bounds of profitabililty.

20 Sculley defined his role as being an impresario whose task was to nurture the creativity of his artists-employees. As an impresario, Sculley challenged the creativity of his employees while at the same time providing the resources and support needed. He encouraged some amount of contrarian thinking, because he believed that dissent stimulated discussion, prompted others to make more perceptive observations, and ultimately improved decision making.

21 Apple attempted to differentiate itself from the rest of the microcomputer vendors. It competed by offering an alternative, excellent product to what was available in the marketplace. Its ease of use, superior graphics, and sound capabilities made Apple's computers the preferred microcomputers of many users.

22 Apple's computers were traditionally closed systems, unlike open systems, such as the IBM Personal Computer, which provided slots to plug in add-on cards and to make interface specification public. Apple reconsidered that strategy, because the availability of add-on products from third-party vendors increased the popularity of a computer. Through the use of add-ons, Apple's new machines, the Mac II and SE, could also use Unix and MS-DOS, which in turn assisted Apple in competing in the business segment. Apple also gave its computers the ability to share data with mainframes and minis. An add-in board for the Mac provided connection to Ethernet, the most popular local area network, which allowed the Macintosh to communicate with the DEC and IBM PC worlds.

23 Apple's entry into the business segment was through a backdoor approach. Rather than aiming its computers at all sections of an organization. Apple targeted areas in companies that could make use of its graphics capabilities. One of these areas was publishing. Businesses found that once Apple's Macintoshes appear in an office, they tend to proliferate. Users claimed that the easy use of Apple products cut costs and training time and improved efficiency. To make sure its machines were easy to use, Apple's strategy revolved around having all of its software developers use a single set of commands so, once a command is learned, it can be used in many packages.

24 To make sure its computers had enough available software, Apple established an independent

software company named Claris. This company was active in developing, publishing, and marketing software.

25   Recognizing the importance of connectivity with other computer systems, Apple established alliances with other computer vendors, such as DEC, the second-ranked minicomputer seller. This alliance was an answer to IBM's new Systems Application Architecture (SAA), which was a direct result of IBM's new strategy of cross-system compatibility. Under this alliance, a wide range of software became available that could be run under DEC's VAX computers and Apple's Macintosh computers.

26   To reiterate its commitment to innovation, the R&D budget was increased by 30 percent in 1987, and a Cray Supercomputer was acquired to speed up product developments. These steps were considered integral parts of Apple's strategy of innovation to meet the demands of the market it had created.

MARKETS

27   Exhibit 1 shows shifts that occurred in the market share of the top 10 companies in the microcomputer industry from 1983 to 1987. Although Apple's market share decreased by 10 percent in approximately four years, the company still had strong market share with 19.7 percent. Apple achieved this share total by competing in five segments: the education segment, the consumer segment, the business segment, the government segment, and the international segment.

Education Segment

28   Apple's traditional target was the educational market and, to a lesser extent, the home market. Apple was the leader in the educational market with a 65 percent share. Apple's strategy to penetrate this market was to donate free systems, form consortia with schools and universities, sponsor research projects, and ensure compatibility within each family of computers. The company's main competitors in this segment were IBM, Tandy, and Zenith. IBM attempted to increase its market share in this segment with the introduction of its PS/2 Model 25. Through the use of robotics in

EXHIBIT 1
Market Share for the Top 10 Companies

Company	6/30/83	1/1/85	1/1/86	1/1/87
IBM	10.4	28.8	37.1	39.4
Apple	28.9	28.6	21.9	19.7
Tandy	26.6	9.3	9.9	7.7
Commodore	8.3	7.2	4.3	3.7
COMPAQ	0.1	1.8	3.2	3.5
AT&T	—	0.1	0.8	2.7
DEC	1.6	2.0	2.6	1.9
Zenith	1.5	0.9	1.3	1.6
Hewlett-Packard	4.9	1.6	1.5	1.4
Wang	0.3	2.2	1.7	1.2

Source: Mark Ludvig, COMTEC Market Analysis Services/Gartner Group.

manufacturing the "old" technology (8086 microchip), IBM produced an inexpensive machine that it could discount further, if needed. To better defend itself from IBM's attack in this segment, Apple hired the former marketing director of IBM's Academic Information Systems Group.

Consumer Segment

29   Apple's strength in the education segment helped generate sales in the consumer market, since families wanted to have the same computer at home that their children used at school. Apple fostered loyalty to its products in the consumer market by actively working with independent groups, such as the Apple Computer Clubs and the Apple User Group. The computers most purchased in this segment were the Apple IIc and the Apple GS. Apple's competitors in this segment included IBM, Commodore, ATARI, and Tandy.

Business Segment

30   Apple's penetration of the business segment began in 1984, when it introduced its Macintosh computers. However, it was not until 1986 that Apple started to succeed, based on its introduction of the Macintosh Plus, sophisticated software, and peripherals. As mentioned before, Apple followed a backdoor strategy, in that it made use of one application, desktop publishing, to enter the business segment. By 1986, there had been 50,000 Macintosh publishing systems sold. A major part of the appeal of these systems was their reasonable price ($17,000 for a complete system). Unfortunately for Apple, the competitive advantages of the Macintosh Plus were quickly countered by IBM. Although IBM had not scheduled delivery of its Operating System/2 (OS/2) until almost mid-1988, it began shipping in December 1987. Since this new system gave the PS/2 some of the critical capabilities of the Macintosh, Apple had to work hard to sell its microcomputers to this segment.

31   Apple competed on the basis of features and performance, rather than price, since most of its systems tended to be expensive. It emphasized ease of use with sophisticated computers. As a result, Apple has identified four horizontal application areas to market: desktop publishing, desktop presentation, desktop communications, and engineering/scientific applications. These applications have been targeted to penetrate two segments: health care and government offices.

Government Segment

32   The government segment was composed of the federal, state, and local governments. Because of the sales potential in this segment, Apple's goal was for government sales to account for 10 percent of total revenues. However, in 1988, government sales accounted for only 1 percent of Apple's revenue. The company was fairly confident that allowing users to use MS-DOS and Unix in the Macintosh computers would allow it to increase market share in this important market. Apple was using computer dealers, value-added resellers, systems integrators, and direct sales in its effort to penetrate this segment where its main competitors were IBM, MS-DOS compatibles, and Zenith.

International Segment

33   Apple had served the international market since 1979, first through independent distributors (Eurapple) and later through the creation of the Apple Computer International. It had 15 wholly owned subsidiaries and served about 80 countries through licensed distributors. Sales in the international segment accounted for approximately 25 percent of Apple's revenues. Apple's strategy in this market was to make use of local talent, to adapt the product to the country, and to produce software that could be easily adapted to foreign languages.

MARKETING

Products and Prices

34 Apple manufactured personal computers under two mainlines: the Apple and the Macintosh. The Apple line included the Apple IIc, the Apple IIe, and the Apple IIGS. The Macintosh line included the Macintosh Plus, the Macintosh SE, and the Macintosh II. In 1986, the Macintosh line outsold the Apple II line for the first time, but sales of the Apple II remained high because of abundant software for educational and home use. Apple also sold peripherals under its own name, such as the LaserWriter Plus. The laser printer allowed Apple to enter and conquer the desktop publishing niche. It also opened the door for Apple to enter the business market. Although the Macintosh achieved only 7 percent of business computer sales at the beginning 1987, there were signs that its share would soon increase. In a survey done by Techtel Corporation, the Mac II and the Mac SE were the second most-mentioned computers considered for purchase. Kidder, Peabody & Company estimated that Apple had increased its share in the Fortune 1,000 market to 9 percent because of the Mac.

35 Nearly one half of the 1 million Macintoshes that Apple had installed were sold in 1987. These machines were produced at a rate of 65,000 to 70,000 a month in Apple's highly automated California factory.

Promotion

Advertising

36 In 1976, Apple retained Regis McKenna Advertising to handle its advertising. Apple's was represented by Chiat/Day Advertising when Chiat acquired McKenna in early 1981. In 1986, Apple moved its advertising to BBDO, who had previously handled its overseas advertising. The change in advertisers corresponded to a shift in positioning by Apple from projecting itself as a company selling hardware and dazzling technology to one selling solutions.

37 In 1984, Apple spent $100 million on advertising, which ranked 94 among the *Advertising Age's* "100 Leading National Advertisers." In 1985, it spent less ($65 million) in an effort to improve profit margins. Apple has moved from a heavy emphasis on advertising its image to one designed to help sales at the retail level. The budget for direct response advertising was increased and direct mail was used. The advertising strategy was to emphasize the ease of use and the power of the machine.

38 Since its first product introduction at the West Coast Computer Faire, Apple was known for its innovative presentations of products through the use of event marketing and publicity campaigns. For example, in October 1986, the press was invited to the Plaza Hotel in New York to preview Apple's newest TV commercials. Apple also became known for its imaginative commercials, such as the "1984" commercial aired during the SuperBowl, which portrayed IBM as Big Brother, and the controversial "Lemmings" commercial done for the 1985 SuperBowl, which showed business following IBM over a cliff.

Promotions

39 Apple offered same-day repair services, low-cost extended warranties, regional support centers, and credit purchase plans. The company also promoted independent users groups, such as the International Apple Core, computer literacy programs, computer club competitions, the Apple University Consortium, and computer training scholarship programs.

Distribution

40 Apple divided the U.S. market into three regions—West, Central, and East—for the purpose of its sales organization. Each region was structured to handle its own training, service, distribution, and selling operations. In addition, to have better control and access to the marketplace, Apple decentralized its distribution system. Three full-service support centers for receiving and processing customer orders were established in Chicago, Illinois; Charlotte, North Carolina; and Sunnyvale, California. Two centers that handled distribution only were established in Dallas and Boston.

41 Traditionally, Apple utilized dealers and retail outlets, such as Businessland, as its main distribution channels. In 1980, Apple had the largest distribution network in the industry, with 800 independent retailers in the United States and Canada and with 1,000 outlets overseas. A year later there were 3,000 Apple dealers worldwide. To improve the quality of distribution, Apple reduced the number of authorized dealers to 2,000 in 1986. In its effort to promote one-to-one selling, Apple included a clause in the dealer's contract that prohibited the dealer from selling Apple products through mail order.

42 To support dealer specialization and consumer satisfaction, Apple offered many programs, such as the Education Dealer Program, the Advanced Desktop Publishing Program, and a co-op advertising and marketing program called *AppleFund*.

43 Apple emphasized direct sales to reach the educational segment. Recognizing the importance of direct sales to serve the business segment, Sculley placed 40 salespersons to work with dealers that serve corporate customers. He developed a National Accounts channel to service 75 large corporations. Sculley also set up a 30-person government sales force to penetrate the government segment.

44 Value-added resellers (VARs) became important distribution channels for microcomputer companies that wanted to reach the business market. Value-added resellers typically bought computer equipment, packaged it with applications software, and resold it in a vertical market. Apple, traditionally, followed a strategy of closed architecture. Because of this strategy, it was almost impossible to change the basic system; therefore, most value-added resellers were not interested in developing products for Apple. This strategy changed when Apple introduced the "open" Macintosh SE and the Macintosh II. Because of the popularity of these computers, Apple developed nearly 200 authorized resellers that add considerable value to its computers. Apple also used VARs to break into vertical markets. Some examples of the activities carried out by VARs included adapting the Mac for manufacturing uses, such as cell controllers, factory floor terminals, and data analyzers, and producing a shielded Tempest version to sell to defense and intelligence organizations.

Manufacturing

45 From its inception, Apple used such state-of-the-art manufacturing techniques as computer integrated manufacturing, automated storage and retrieval, flexible automation procedures, robotics, and just-in-time inventory. To make the latter effective, Apple developed long-term supplier partnerships to supply zero-defect, on-time delivery. Most parts had backup sources, thus restricting the power of a single supplier. Through the efficiency of this system, Apple's was able to produce a Macintosh computer every 25 to 30 seconds in the Fremont, California, facility. This facility produced the computers in the Macintosh line, in addition to peripherals. Its Singapore plant produced all the computers in the Apple II family. The Irish factory produced the international versions of the Apple II.

and third-party developers sold software and hardware that allowed the Macintosh to communicate with other microcomputers, minicomputers, and mainframes. Some industry observers estimated the Macintosh's share of the expert systems market would quickly grow from a level of 10 to 40 percent. Just as the expert systems required fast processors, they also required a large memory.

53   The dramatic growth and great promise of the Macintosh, however, also highlighted one of Apple's major weaknesses—an overreliance on the Macintosh for more than half of its revenues and earnings.

54   As he pondered the future, Apple's CEO and president Sculley was well aware of IBM's rising stakes in the microcomputer business, the competitive threats introduced by new strategies in the industry, and the need to retain the entrepreneurial quality in Apple's culture. His company that changed the rules of the competitive game in the microcomputer industry was still on the frontier, and it was still very determined to remain there.

CASE 35

THE FINANCIAL SERVICES INDUSTRY

INDUSTRY DEFINITION

1   It could be claimed that the financial services industry traces its beginnings to the invention of money in ancient times. However, the industry's all-encompassing label, *financial services,* is relatively new. The name has evolved in direct market response to consumer demand for more comprehensive servicing of financial needs. Clearly, consumers are becoming less and less interested in drawing fine historical product lines among those institutions with which they transact their financial business. In keeping with a growing demand for time-saving convenience and comprehensive one-step supermarket-type service, members of various financial institutions have responded by offering customers a wider range of traditional financial services, as well as innovative new packages. The lines of demarcation between traditional industries, such as banking, insurance, and real estate, are rapidly disappearing.

2   A working definition of the financial services industry is that group of institutions that provides four categories of service:

1. Obtaining funds for those who wish to invest them—includes underwriting, investment banking services, brokerage services, and the provision of loans.
2. Providing income-earning outlets for those with funds to lend or invest—includes deposit services, brokerage activities, money market funds, mutual funds, life insurance, and pension funds.
3. Payments services—includes traditional payments services, as well as credit cards, bill-paying services, and cash management services.
4. Advice on the best way to get the services needed in the first three categories.

This definition clearly emphasizes the importance of focusing on customer needs, as opposed to individual products, product lines, or specialized institutions.

3   The list of institutions that could legitimately be members of the financial services industry is lengthy. As a general categorization, these institutions can be divided into one of two classifications—banks and nonbanks. While membership in the bank category is fairly obvious, participants in the nonbank group include insurance companies, mutual savings banks, finance companies, investment companies, real estate investment trusts (REITs), savings and loan associations (S&Ls), pension funds, and credit unions. In light of the dynamism of the current financial environment, the line of demarcation between banks and nonbanks is rapidly growing less clear.

This case was prepared by John A. Pearce II of George Mason University, J. Kay Keels of Louisiana State University, and Sondra K. Patrick of George Mason University.

BANKS

4   The banking system in the United States has been called a dual system for two reasons. First, banks are categorized as either state or national banks, depending upon their charter. Second, banks are classified by their association with the Federal Reserve System (the Fed) as either members or nonmembers.

5   In the case of distinction by charter, "dual" is a misnomer for the system, because there are actually 50 different banking systems for state-chartered banks. One of the major differentiating factors among state systems deals with the establishment of bank branches. Some states allow no branches at all, while some states permit branching statewide. A related and very sensitive issue in the banking community has been the prohibition nationwide of any interstate branching.

6   Membership in the Fed is another characteristic that separates banks. All federally chartered banks were required to join the Federal Reserve System when it was established in 1913. State banks were permitted to join if they wished to do so. Recently, the number of member banks has declined as state banks have exercised their option to withdraw, and national banks have circumvented the membership requirement by applying for state charters.

NONBANK FINANCIAL INSTITUTIONS

7   Since the end of World War II, nonbank financial institutions have grown in number, in resources, and in importance to the financial community. By the end of 1973, nonbank financial institutions collectively held 24 percent more assets than commercial banks. The two largest holders of these assets were S&Ls and life insurance companies. Although such institutions as insurance companies and saving and loan associations are familiar to most consumers, many nonbank financial institutions are less well known. Case appendixes A–D provide financial information on the 25 largest diversified financial companies, the 25 largest saving institutions, the 25 largest life insurance companies, and the 50 largest banks in the United States.[1]

8   *Insurance companies* can be divided into two major categories: life insurance companies and property-casualty insurance companies. The first life insurance company was begun well over two centuries ago and was called the *Corporation for Relief of Poor and Distressed Presbyterian Ministers and of the Poor and Distressed Widows and Children of Presbyterian Ministers*. Today some of the largest corporations in the United States are life insurance companies, and Americans hold over $1 trillion worth of life insurance. The huge policy reserves (excess of premiums charged over benefits paid) accumulated by these life insurance companies make them legitimate members of the financial services industry in at least two ways. First, the reserves are invested by the insurance firms, and these investment earnings are used to reduce the premiums a policyholder pays. In this way, the earnings on reserves act as a kind of interest-earning savings account. Second, with such tremendous sums of money to invest, life insurance companies become big lenders, principally in the form of domestic corporate bonds and mortages.

9   As is also true with life insurance companies, property-casualty insurance companies are primarily guided in their investment decisions by the major goal of safety of principal, followed closely by income maximization and liquidity requirements. Life insurance policies must always eventually pay in full whereas property-casualty companies only pay on a fraction of their policies. Further, payment requirements are much more predictable for life insurance companies than for

---

[1]Doris E. Harless, *Nonbank Financial Institutions* (Federal Reserve Bank of Richmond, October 1975).

property-casualty firms. For these two reasons, investment patterns for the two types of companies differ, property-casualty companies investing much more heavily in bonds and common stocks.

10   The first *mutual savings bank* was established in Scotland in 1810, but the idea spread quickly, and in less than a decade two savings banks had been founded in the United States. The majority of these institutions is still concentrated in a five-state area in New England and the Middle Atlantic region. The primary purpose of mutual savings banks is to invest collectively the savings of small investors. All mutual savings banks are state-chartered, state-supervised, nonstock, deposit institutions. Earnings from investments are credited to investors' accounts as interest. Mutual savings banks are restricted by most states in their investment and lending activities to an approved list of securities and loans.

11   Once considered to be only a small step up from the neighborhood "loan shark," *finance companies* are now beginning to take their place as full-fledged members of the financial services industry. In the past, these companies were identified primarily by their lending practices—direct or indirect lending or the purchasing of accounts receivable—and by their particular customer groups' needs, for such services as sales financing, consumer financing, or commercial financing. However, as is characteristic of the entire industry, services are becoming much more diversified and the lines of demarcation increasingly blurred.

12   *Investment companies* primarily serve small investors by pooling their collective funds and investing those funds in a wide variety of securities. The types of portfolios managed by investment companies vary a great deal, some investing principally in stocks; some, in bonds; and some companies maintaining a "balanced" portfolio of common stock, preferred stock, and bonds.

13   *Real estate investment trusts* (REITs) allow individuals and institutions an opportunity to hold interest in real property and mortgages. Funds from the REITs share sales are pooled and used to make mortgage loans and to acquire property. Earnings consist mostly of interest on loans or rent from owned property. REITs are publicly held, and shareholders are generally small individual investors.

14   The concept of a *savings and loan (S&L) association* was born in 1831 when a group of citizens met at an inn and drew up articles for the first cooperative home-financing society in the United States, the Oxford Provident Building Association of Philadelphia County. Each member of the association contributed some savings, and, when his name was drawn from a hat, he could borrow money to buy a home. Today, besides being lending institutions, S&Ls serve nonborrowing customers with a variety of savings options, including the interest-bearing NOW accounts, in which savers are allowed to write negotiable orders of withdrawal (NOWs), instruments that are functionally the same as checks. The granting of the right to S&Ls to offer personal checking services brought the S&Ls into closer competition with banks, another example of the diversification occuring within the financial services industry.

15   *Pension funds* are established primarily to pay retirement benefits. The two major types of pension funds are public, the largest of which are government pension plans, and private. Private pension funds are either insured or noninsured. Noninsured pension funds are usually separate financial entities, whereas insured ones are not. Two main services of funds for private, noninsured pension funds are employer contributions and investment income. Pension fund investment practices have leaned heavily toward common-stock portfolios.

16   Every *credit union* requires four essential features: (1) a group of people, (2) a common interest, (3) pooled savings, and (4) loans to each other. It is a cooperative self-help thrift and loan society composed of individuals bound together by some common tie. Credit unions, under state or federal charter, are member-owned, member-operated, and member-controlled. Purchased ownership shares resemble savings accounts, and dividends are paid to members from loan and investment income. Loan privileges are extended to members only.

EXHIBIT 1 *(concluded)*

Date	Event	Impact
1934	Securities Exchange Act of 1934	Required registration of brokers and dealers handling securities; created SEC
1940	Investment Company Act of 1940	Protected shareholders of investment companies
1945	McCarran-Ferguson Act	Delegated regulation and taxation of casualty-property insurance companies to state authorities
1956	Bank Holding Company Act	Brought all bank holding companies under supervision of Federal Reserve
1958	Welfare and Pension Plans Disclosure Act	Regulated disclosure of information and financial condition
1960	Introduction of negotiable certificate of deposit (CD)	Allowed banks to compete openly for corporate funds
1960	Amendments to Internal Revenue Code	Granted tax-exempt status to REITs
1966	Interest Rate Adjustment Act	Established interest-rate ceilings for S&Ls
1969	Consumer Credit Protection Act	Federal Regulation of consumer lending
1970	Investment Company Amendments Act of 1970	Established new standards for management fees and mutual fund sales charges
1973	Bill passed by Connecticut General Assembly	Paved way for S&Ls to offer checking services with demand deposits
1974	Employee Retirement Income Security Act of 1974	Pension reform legislation
1980	Depository Institutions Deregulation and Monetary Control Act	Provided for the phase-out of Regulation Q

supply fell by 33 percent, producing the Great Depression and bringing to a close the free banking era.

21   At the beginning of the cartel banking era, the prime concern was for the safety and stability of each bank. The appropriate solution according to regulations was to limit the amount of risk and competition to which any bank could be exposed. The Banking Act of 1933, also known as the Glass-Steagall Act, was supposed to be such a safety measure. For the first time in banking history, the industry was divided into commercial and investment banking segments, each type to be regulated by a separate body. The Securities and Exchange Commission (SEC), created by the Securities Act of 1933 and the Securities Exchange Act of 1934, was to regulate investment banking. Further segmentation occurred as the Bank Holding Company Act of 1956 brought all holding companies under the supervision of the Federal Reserve Board. Amendments to this act in 1970 further restricted banks to prevent them from entering other areas of financial business. The Banking Act of 1935, along with all the other legislation, further solidified the cartel-like nature of the industry. New bank charters were granted, subject to a test of demonstrated need. The 14,000 banks that survived the Great Depression were indeed a protected cartel.

22   Since the New Deal legislation began the cartel era, the industry has continued to be a cartel,

but one that has become increasingly weaker. One of the first weakening agents was the negotiable certificate of deposit (CD), which was introduced in 1960 to allow commercial banks to compete more effectively for corporate funds that were being lost to securities markets, due to rising interest rates. Banks were suddenly thrust into the business of liability management.

23   Liquidity crunches resulted in the Interest Rate Adjustment Act of 1966, allowing ceilings on time-deposit interest rates. This act allowed thrift institutions to pay higher rates than commercial banks.

24   Yet another threat appeared in 1979 as interest rates once again soared above the Regulation Q ceilings. The newest competition for consumer deposits came in the form of the money market mutual fund. Many banks and especially thrifts were hit hard by this new competition. The result was the Depository Institutions Deregulation and Monetary Control Act of 1980, which called for the gradual phasing out of the Regulation Q ceilings. By late 1982, free and open price competition for deposits was virtually a fact.

PORTER'S FIVE INDUSTRY FORCES

25   The five major forces which drive competition in the financial services industry and which shape the nature of the industry are shown in Exhibit 2. To analyze the financial services industry, each of these five forces will be examined.

The Threat of Entry

26   The possible entry of new participants into an industry can be determined by a unique set of factors that determines the significance of threats of entry into a particular industry. At least six factors affect who provides financial services and how they are provided. Consideration of these factors would affect entry decisions by potential competitors. The six factors are: (1) characteristics of services offered and the demand for them, (2) relative importance of the customer's price versus nonprice considerations, (3) risk, (4) economies of joint production and distribution, (5) regulations, and (6) federal government participation.[2]

27   One important characteristic of financial services that determines production and distribution is the place where the service falls on the continuum between mass-produced services and unique, tailored services. Automobile loans are an example of a mass-produced service. By contrast, a uniquely tailored service would be the private placement of a debt issue. To those institutions offering services at the mass-production end of the continuum, advantages of an economies-of-scale barrier would exist. At the tailored-service end of the continuum, barriers associated with product differentiation would be present.

28   One increasingly important nonprice consideration in the financial services industry is convenience. Institutions have sought to sell convenience through such tactics as longer hours, credit cards, bill-paying services, and automatic tellers. A second important nonprice consideration is advice, a selling point used extensively in life insurance companies, brokerage and investment banking firms, and bank trust departments. Other nonprice trade-offs are liquidity and insurance against loss. The specialized nature of advice leads to a product-differentiation barrier, while the growing importance of convenience is related to the switching-cost barrier.

---

[2]P. Michael Laub, "Banks and Financial Services," in *The Future of the Financial Services Industry* (Conference Proceedings, Federal Reserve Bank of Atlanta, June 3–4, 1981), pp. 62–76.

EXHIBIT 2
Forces Driving Financial Services Industry Competition

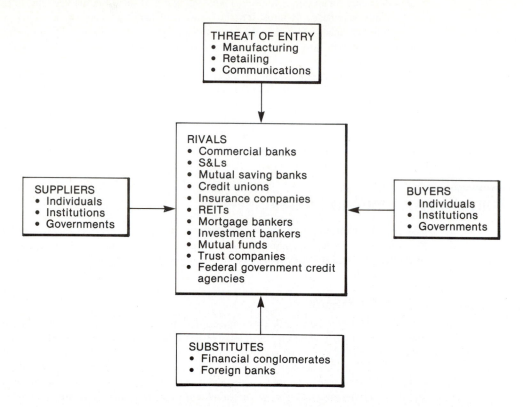

29   There are four types of risk that could affect who offers financial services: (1) interest-rate risk, (2) default risk, (3) liquidity risk, and (4) portfolio risk. *Interest-rate risk* arises because of the fluctuation of the general interest-rate level, and the mismatch of maturity dates of assets and liabilities. *Default risk* is the risk that a loan will not be repaid. *Liquidity risk* refers to the risk that an institution will not be able to produce sufficient cash to meet its obligations at a specified time. *Portfolio risk* is concerned with the uncertainty of the rate of return on a managed portfolio. A potential entrant's attitude toward risk could suggest a sizeable entry barrier in terms of capital requirements.

30   The joint economies of production and distribution factors result from the growing demand among customers to have more financial services sold together. This trend toward the consolidation of larger and larger packages of financial services suggests at once several barriers to entry available to those firms capable of offering multiple services, as well as serious substitute threats to more traditional single-service firms. (Substitutes will be addressed more fully in a later section.) In addition to economies of scale, some nonscale cost advantages include proprietary product technology and the experience curve, since many potential entrants are in businesses outside the realm of traditional financial services. Favorable locations might also prove to be a barrier, since traditional industry participants, like insurance, real estate, and finance companies, often have nationwide

EXHIBIT 3
New Entrants into the Financial Services Industry

Company	Company Acquired	Industry	Year Acquired	Purchase Price ($ millions)
American Can	Voyager Group	Insurance	1983	$ 45
	PennCorp Financial	Insurance	1983	295
	Transport Life	Insurance	1982	152
	Associated Madison	Insurance	1981	127
Ashland Oil	Integon	Insurance	1981	238
BAT Industries	Eagle Star	Insurance	1984	1,300
Crown Central	Continental Amer. Life	Insurance	1980	32
Ethyl	First Colony	Insurance	1982	270
General Electric	Employers Reinsurance	Insurance	1984	1,075
National Steel	United Financial	Thrift	1980	241
RCA	CIT Financial Corp.	Consumer finance	1980	1,500
St. Regis	Colonial Penn	Insurance	1984*	590
	Dependable Insurance	Insurance	1983	46
	Drum Financial	Insurance	1981	51
Sear Roebuck	Coldwell Banker	Real estate	1981	202
	Dean Witter	Brokerage	1981	610
Xerox	Van Kampen Merritt	Investment banking	1984	150
	Crum & Forster	Insurance	1982	1,600

* Acquisition pending.
Source: *Business Week*, August 20, 1984, p. 54.

networks of offices. Joint economies of product and distribution could lead to entry barriers created by more favorable access to distribution channels. Finally, these joint economies certainly suggest the possibility of entry barriers posed by capital requirements.

31   The final two service-affecting factors of regulations and federal government participation are directly related to the government policy entry barrier. Three types of regulatory restrictions that significantly affect the financial services industry are: (1) rate restrictions, (2) powers restrictions, and (3) locational restrictions. *Rate restrictions* include those placed on rates charged to users of funds, as well as those paid to providers of funds. *Powers restrictions* involve the limitation of services that can be offered. *Locational restrictions* refer to those affecting such banking practices as branching and interstate banking. Other regulatory considerations include capital and reserve requirements and disclosure statements. By its very imposing size and by the broad range of its financial activities, the federal government has a profound effect on the structure of the financial services industry. Not only is it a regulator, but also a customer and a supplier to the industry, as well as an industry participant.

32   The primary mode of entry into the financial services industry recently has been by acquisition. Citing such reasons as synergy, entry into fast-growth glamor markets, or sources of steady cash flow to balance seasonal swings, many retailing and industrial firms have scrambled to get into financial services. Exhibit 3 illustrates the diversity of participants that had entered the industry by the early 1980s.

EXHIBIT 4 *(concluded)*
Nonbank Financial Companies

Company	Sales 2d Quarter 1987 ($ millions)	Change from 1986 (%)	6 Months 1987 ($ millions)	Change from 1986 (%)	Profits 2d Quarter 1987 ($ millions)	Change from 1986 (%)	6 Months 1987 ($ millions)	Change from 1986 (%)	Margins 2d Quarter 1987 (%)	2d Quarter 1986 (%)	Return of Common Equity 12 Months Ending (6-30)	Price/ Earnings Ratio (7-24)	12 Months Earnings per Share
Industry composite	$38,207.1	12%	$76,838.6	13%	$1,625.1	–7%	$3,743.8	13%	4.3%	5.1%	13.1	12	3.21
Aetna Life & Casualty	5,535.0	12	10,661.7	9	225.9	42	407.9	36	4.1	3.2	13.8	8	7.08
American Express	4,253.2	17	7,954.9	13	47.9	–87	204.4	–62	1.1	9.9	13.6	20	1.73
American General	1,587.0	8	3,237.0	11	125.0	–1	273.0	8	7.9	8.5	11.5	11	3.74
American National													
Insurance	233.8	8	453.7	9	23.4	–4	45.2	–9	10.0	11.3	5.8	13	2.85
Bear Stearns (8)	596.3	7	1,274.9	7	44.7	6	104.3	17	7.5	7.6	24.7	8	2.06
Chubb	927.2	21	1,803.5	20	91.5	71	170.2	72	9.9	7.0	16.7	8	7.07
Commercial Credit	227.8	–9	447.4	–10	23.6	71	42.9	73	10.4	5.5	6.0	26	1.12
Edwards (A. O.) (10)	133.3	3	285.9	16	10.9	–16	27.8	7	8.2	10.0	19.8	11	2.49
Farmers Group	300.5	8	596.3	8	62.5	17	119.4	14	20.8	19.1	15.7	13	3.29
Federal National													
Mortgage Assn.	2,425.3	–9	4,960.8	–7	62.0	32	118.4	45	2.6	1.8	10.9	14	2.85
Fireman's Fund	1,109.4	14	2,027.8	17	–158.8	NM	–92.2	NM	NM	4.5	–0.4	NM	–0.12
First Boston	707.8	–4	1,667.0	1	–13.2	NM	63.0	–31	NM	2.9	14.6	10	4.23
First Capital Holdings	444.3	NM	665.2	NM	11.3	269	21.4	307	2.5	11.3	37.3	9	1.43
General Re	854.6	10	1,736.1	17	118.9	64	230.8	79	13.9	9.4	14.5	14	3.71
Hall (Frank B.)	96.6	–3	202.2	1	–0.6	NM	5.6	–46	NM	4.5	–51.2	NM	–0.54
Hartford Steam Boiler	106.2	10	207.2	10	13.6	17	26.7	25	12.8	12.1	23.0	12	2.42
Home Group	588.1	7	1,184.4	11	–34.2	490	65.6	941	5.8	1.1	8.6	9	2.03
Hutton (E. F.) Group	848.3	27	1,719.3	23	–17.3	NM	19.4	–19	NM	NM	–13.8	NM	–3.60

Kemper	956.3	12	53.7	45	109.4	69	5.6	4.3	12.7	10	3.12
Lincoln National	1,733.5	23	66.5	25	125.4	20	3.8	3.8	10.7	10	5.07
Marsh & McLennan	539.1	19	78.9	22	171.8	32	14.6	14.2	39.1	15	3.85
Merrill Lynch	2,441.9	5	83.3	-9	192.0	8	3.4	3.9	16.1	8	4.47
Morgan Stanley Group	830.7	20	62.4	37	126.7	22	7.5	6.6	26.3	8	8.88
Paine Webber Group	637.6	5	17.6	146	52.8	45	2.8	1.2	11.1	11	2.94
Rothschild, Unterberg											
Holding	124.1	19	-7.7	NM	3.7	-82	NM	7.2	-8.8	NM	-1.02
SAFECO	680.2	4	57.6	35	111.8	41	8.5	6.5	13.2	11	2.83
St. Paul	822.8	9	77.9	202	147.9	194	9.5	3.4	16.0	9	5.18
Student Loan Marketing											
Assn.	372.7	12	44.6	24	87.1	23	12.0	10.8	31.5	23	3.60
Torchmark	398.4	2	47.8	-12	96.5	-5	12.0	13.8	20.7	10	2.79
Transamerica	1,950.9	25	90.3	31	183.0	61	4.6	4.4	14.4	10	4.25
Travelers	4,112.1	16	113.9	24	222.7	30	2.8	2.5	10.3	9	4.85
U.S. Leasing											
International	116.7	9	7.4	15	15.1	24	6.4	5.9	11.3	11	4.34
USF&G	1,167.1	11	99.0	88	193.9	88	8.5	4.9	21.5	8	4.67
USLICO	126.3	-1	6.6	-13	14.1	5	5.2	5.8	9.2	12	2.12
USLIFE	312.2	7	19.9	-3	36.3	-3	6.4	7.2	8.4	10	3.91

Note: NM = not meaningful.
Source: *Business Week*, August 17, 1987, pp. 104–11.

Rivalry

33 The intensity of rivalry in an industry is the result of at least eight interacting factors:[3] (1) numerous or equally balanced competitors, (2) slow industry growth, (3) high fixed or storage costs, (4) lack of differentiation or switching costs, (5) capacity augmented in large increments, (6) diverse competitors, (7) high strategic stakes, and (8) high exit barriers. Several of these factors are clearly at work in the financial services industry, although some of these factors become difficult to track because industry participants seem to be rapidly changing. When acquisitions such as those noted in the previous section change the nature of an industry's participants, rivalry is naturally affected.

34 The presence of numerous or equally balanced competitors suggests the notion that a firm should "only pick on someone its own size." Within the financial services industry, participants are certainly numerous. The banking segment alone has over 14,000 members. To examine the "equally balanced" part of this factor, perhaps the industry's "elite" could serve as an example. In its 1987 report on the performance of the nation's top 900 corporations, *Business Week* listed 50 bank and bank holding companies and 35 nonbank financial companies that together comprise over 9 percent of all firms listed (see Exhibit 4). By virtue of such national prominence, the entire list might be considered "equally balanced" on a very crude national scale. This list, however, yields to even finer gradations of competitive groupings. Using 1987 second-quarter sales in ranking, half of the bank and bank holding companies listed (25 firms) fall into a $100 million to $400 million category, while the other half is at $500 million and above. Even further, firms that reported sales over the billion-dollar mark numbered 11, the top 6 of which represented a span of over $2 billion in sales to less than $7 billion. Concerning nonbank financial companies, 22 out of 35 showed second-quarter 1987 earnings above $500 million, while the top 5 firms' earnings spanned a $2 billion to $6 billion range. It appears that industry participants at various size levels face numerous equally strong competitors.

35 Slow industry growth has also been listed as a contributor to intensified rivalry. From 1973 to 1983, the diversified financial and the commercial banking sectors ranked near the bottom in service sector growth, being far outstripped by the retailing, diversified service, and transportation sectors. This slow growth environment continued through 1987 for financial service organizations (see Exhibit 5). The most recent decline is dramatic and signals a turn in the economy away from consumer-oriented and service sectors to merchandising and manufacturing sectors. Rivalry is intense because market share can only be increased by stealing it from one's competitors (see Exhibit 6).

36 Financial services are expected to grow well into the 1990s in spite of periodic setbacks. Fierce competition will definitely be beneficial to borrowers but disastrous to small or inefficient financial companies. With declining profits, many financial companies will be forced into mergers or driven out of business, while consumers and chief financial officers will benefit from the offering of many new services.[4]

37 As competition for the consumer's dollar increases, the effort to attract the consumer's attention usually intensifies. The seriousness of such effort is often gauged in terms of advertising expenditures. In 1988, the top 10 financial service advertisers will have spent over $112 million annually, a figure which will continue to escalate throughout the 1990s. With so many name changes, mergers, and acquisitions, advertising for name recognition has become increasingly important. Large companies are expanding their financial services to attract a greater share of an individual's financial activities. These services include the creation of brokerage companies, discount brokers, savings and loans, commercial banks, catalog companies, and insurance companies. As the financial services

---

[3]Michael E. Porter, *Competitive Strategy* (New York: Free Press, 1980).

[4]Gary Hector, "The Money Game Will Get Brutal," *Fortune,* February 2, 1987, pp. 42–44.

EXHIBIT 5
Winners and Losers in Second-Quarter Profits

The Industries

The Sharpest Gains		The Deepest Drops	
	% Change from Second Quarter, 1986		% Change from 1986's Second Quarter
Airlines	1,225%	Banks	Less
Appliances	310	Metals and mining	Less
Leisure time	154	Oil service and supply	Less
Tire and rubber	92	Savings and loan	−56%
Special machinery	62	Trucking	−33
Paper and forest products	56	Nonbank financial	−7
Electrical and electronics	37	Natural resources (fuel)	−7
Textiles and apparel	35	Telecommunications	−4
Nonfood retailing	33	Conglomerates	−3
Chemicals	32	Publishing/TV	0

All-industry average: −24%

The Companies

Who Made the Most		Who Lost the Most	
	Millions of Dollars		Millions of Dollars
Ford	$1,498	Citicorp	$2,585
IBM	1,178	Chase Manhattan	1,378
Exxon	1,150	Manufacturers Hanover	1,373
General Motors	980	BankAmerica	1,136
General Electric	720	Chemical New York	1,103
AT&T	596	First Chicago	698
Du Pont	504	J. P. Morgan	586
Philip Morris	476	Mellon Bank	566
Chrysler	429	Bankers Trust	554
Sears, Roebuck	390	First Interstate	470

Data: Standard & Poor's Compustat Services, Inc.

Source: *Business Week,* August 17, 1987, p. 101.

industry expands, the need for financial advisers and statistical experts, as well as marketing, sales, and operations managers, will increase.[5]

Substitute Products

38   A rash of innovative new products arising from industry participants posed a threat to some of the traditional financial services. As was noted earlier, banks began issuing CDs in the 1960s, thrifts were allowed to open NOW accounts in the 1970s, and the idea of a cash management account

---

[5]Tony Wainwright, "Beyond Advertising: Financial Services Take Fast Track" *Advertising Age,* January 19, 1987, p. 34.

EXHIBIT 6
Yardstick of Management Performance

| | | Profitability | | | | | Growth | | | | | | |
| | | Return on Equity | | | Debt as % of Equity | Net Profit Margin | Sales | | | Earnings per Share | | | Earnings Stability |
Company	% In Segment Sales/Profits	Rank	5-Year Average	Latest 12 Months			Rank	5-Year Average	Latest 12 Months	Rank	5-Year Average	Latest 12 Months	
Financial companies													
Student Loan	•/•	1	40.0%	28.3%	1925.6%	10.1%	4	29.8%	11.0%	2	54.2%	25.9%	very high
H&R Block	57/81	2	23.7	21.8	2.0	9.7	5	16.3	24.6	5	8.8	4.8	very high
Southmark	76/85	3	22.7	12.3	175.8	13.6	1	99.3	5.9	1	110.4	−29.2	very high
Equifax	•/•	4	22.1	26.4	19.5	4.0	8	8.6	14.4	4	9.2	40.5	average
American Express	•/•	5	17.5	24.1	122.3	7.8	3	37.1	10.2	7	3.7	77.1	low
Integrated Resources	61/60	6	15.7	1.1	118.2	4.1	2	47.9	26.2	6	7.5	−76.1	low
Household International	49/68	7	12.1	13.7	368.3	5.6	11	−7.2	−57.0	3	9.3	6.4	average
Gulf & Western	45/61	8	7.9	11.7	74.6	6.4	12	−13.8	11.7		NM	2.7	NM
Beneficial Corp	52/•	9	5.2	def	404.1	def	10	−5.9	0.0		NM	P-D	NM
Commercial Credit	76/58	10	3.4†	1.5	215.3	1.3	9	5.5‡	−13.7		NM	−69.4	NM
Cigna	39/PD	11	1.9†	def	9.4	def	7	10.2	4.4		NM	P-D	NM
Fedl Natl Mortgage	•/•	12	def	11.3	3930.8	1.4	6	14.8	6.1		NM	D-P	NM
Medians			13.9	12.0	149.1	4.9		12.5	8.2		5.6	2.7	
Exchange houses													
First Boston	•/•	1	26.9%	18.5	43.3%	5.1%	2	32.6%	27.0%	1	18.9%	11.3%	average
Salomon	18/68	2	20.9	19.1	151.6	2.2	7	3.9	−5.9	2	−0.9	91.9	very low
Paine Webber Group	•/•	3	19.4	13.8	130.9	3.0	6	16.3	26.5	3	−5.9‡	84.6	very low
EF Hutton Group	74/DP	4	17.3	2.9	36.7	0.8	4	23.5	9.2	5	−17.4	−75.3	average
Merrill Lynch	87/85	5	15.0	13.9	162.2	3.8	5	17.2	34.2	4	−11.0	64.1	low
Bear Stearns Cos	•/•		NA	37.1	45.0	5.7	1	51.1‡	5.1		NA	4.9	NA
Morgan Stanley	•/•		NA	49.7	57.9	7.4	3	30.7†	NA		NA	NA	NA
Medians			19.4	18.5	57.9	3.8		23.5	17.9		−5.9	11.3	
Commodity traders													
Salomon	81/31	1	20.9%	19.1	151.6%	2.2%	1	3.9%	5.9%	2	−0.9%	91.9%	very low
Commercial Metals	63/20	2	8.7	10.5	25.9	1.6	3	−4.7	−13.1	3	−10.3	49.5	average
Kay	65/52	3	7.4	19.7	74.0	1.8	2	−2.3	37.5	1	37.6‡‡	181.7	average
Medians			8.7	19.1	74.0	1.8		−2.3	−5.9		−0.9	91.9	
Industry medians			16.5	13.9	120.3	3.9		15.6	9.2		−0.9	8.9	
All-industry medians			12.6	13.0	46.0	3.9		7.1	3.9		−0.9	2.8	

• = 90 percent or more. DP = segment deficit, total profit. PD = segment profit, total deficit. D-P = deficit to profit. P-D = profit to deficit. def = deficit. NA = not available. NM = not meaningful. †Four-year average. ‡Four-year growth. ‡‡Three-year growth.

Source: *Forbes* 139, no. 1 (January 12, 1987).

(CMA) was introduced by Merrill Lynch in the early 1980s. Even the brokerage business was not exempt, as was demonstrated by the rise of discount brokers in the 1970s.

39   Three environmental shocks tended to affect the financial system and led to product innovations: (1) changes in technology, (2) changes in demand, and (3) changes in public regulation. Technological demands on the financial services industry had intensified, particularly in the 1980s. National electronic networks made it apparent that, as the last shackles of banking regulation were shed, many of the financial industry giants would be poised and ready to enter into nationwide banking. Further, changing demands, especially for increased convenience and the bundling of financial services, would continue to challenge the industry to create more innovative services.

40   The threat of substitutes is not confined just to current industry participants, however. Given the nature of acquisitions in the industry, precedent had been set for some powerful new entrants into the industry. Already financial institutions had begun to redefine themselves as information and communications companies. It easily followed that communications companies might begin to redefine their self-images as consumer companies. The door was opened for an AT&T or an IBM as potential suppliers of financial services.

41   The threat of substitute services existed not just on a national basis but on an international scale as well. Until the passage of the International Banking Act of 1978, foreign banks were virtually unrestricted in the establishment of full-fledged banks in this country.

Buyers

42   Customers of the financial services industry can be basically separated into three groups: (1) individuals, (2) institutions, and (3) governments. The consumers of the 1980s were more affluent, more sophisticated, more interest-rate sensitive, and were less loyal to specific institutions than in the past. Although a number of circumstances might contribute to the bargaining power of buyers, only two seem particularly relevant to financial service customers: (1) price sensitivity and (2) availability of full information. Fluctuating interest rates and rising inflation contribute to financial customers' price sensitivity. Buyer power is enhanced, because financial services customers demand more from every dollar they invest. The trend toward increased advertising among financial service industry participants served to make consumers more sophisticated and better informed.

Suppliers

43   There are basically two categories of resources for the financial services industry: funds and personnel. Funds are not only the industry's input but are also its output. All of the statements made above about the industry's customers pertain equally to the industry's suppliers for, in many cases, they are the same. However, supplier power tends to be a mirror image of buyer power. Two contributors to supplier power deserve mention: (1) lack of substitutes and (2) the importance of the product as an input. Since there are no substitutes for funds, and since funds are the industry's only input, supplies of funds do wield some power.

44   The second basic resource in the financial services industry is its personnel. Although the following statements were made with respect to banking in particular, they easily apply to all segments of the industry.

45   Quite simply, people are *everything* in banking. . . . People are the principal competitive weapon a bank has. . . . A bank is not strong by virtue of its buildings, machines, name, or money. Pure and simple, it is its people that count—for everything. . . . Banking . . . is almost always a personal service—people-

to-people business. Whether we sell our service, get our price, or develop a quality product, is totally dependent on people. Our people often *are* the service we sell. They are selling themselves and their ability to provide services.[6]

THE FUTURE OF THE FINANCIAL SERVICES INDUSTRY

46   Much has been written and there has been much speculation about the shape of the financial services industry in the future. There are at least eight major environmental determinants that could play a role in the industry's future: (1) consumer demand and preference, (2) technological developments, (3) regulatory uncertainty, (4) new institutional arrangements, (5) increase in competition, (6) increasing global orientation, (7) increasing diversity of products, and (8) increased volatility of economic events. Since consumers, regulations, new institutional arrangements, and increased competition have been treated elsewhere, the following brief discussion notes the remaining four factors.

47   Electronic technology already plays a key role in the industry, and the progression of more sophisticated links between data processing and communications hints at future possibilities that almost defy imagination. Some major forces sure to play a part include satellites, digital communications, and the home computer.

48   As is true of many other industries, the orientation in financial services is becoming increasingly global. This globalism can be attributed to technology, growing per capita wealth, and economic volatility. Electronic impulses and satellite transmissions are oblivious to national boundaries. It seems almost unnatural to confine financial activities to one country any more. Many products, such as the American Express and Visa cards and traveler's checks, have indeed already become universal.

49   The increasing diversity of products has led to the "supermarket" approach to financial services, as evidenced by such giants as Sears. Throughout the 1980s, the typical affluent American household dealt with about 20 different financial vendors and purchased nearly 40 different products and services.

50   Volatility of economic events has become an expected norm. Changing interest rates, fluctuations in the money supply, the consumer price index, and variations in the gross national product have made the nation, institutions, and consumers very information-sensitive.

51   Those financial services institutions that thrive and prosper beyond the 1990s and into the 21st century will likely have found ways to deal effectively with these environmental elements. By that time, these same forces may well have drastically changed the players in the game.

[6]Elbert V. Bowden, *Revolution in Banking* (Richmond, Va.: Robert F. Dame, 1980).

APPENDIX A

The 25 Largest Diversified Financial Companies

Rank 1986	Rank 1985	Company	Assets ($000)	Revenues ($000)	Revenues Rank	Net Income ($000)	Net Income Rank	Stockholders' Equity ($000)	Stockholders' Equity Rank
1	1	Federal Nat'l Mortgage Ass'n (Washington, D.C.)	$100,406,000	$10,540,000	5	$ 183,000	25	$1,593,000	13
2	2	American Express (New York)	99,476,000	14,652,000	4	1,250,000	1	5,726,000	1
3	•	Salomon (New York)	78,164,000	6,789,000	10	516,000	7	3,454,000	6
4	3	Aetna Life & Casualty (Hartford)	66,829,900	20,482,900	1	1,043,100	2	5,697,200	2
5	4	Merrill Lynch (New York)	53,013,471	9,606,349	7	454,349	8	2,875,514	8
6	6	CIGNA (Philadelphia)	50,015,800	17,064,100	2	817,300	3	4,875,000	3
7	5	First Boston (New York)	48,618,206	1,309,765	33	180,555	26	958,780	23
8	7	Travelers (Hartford)	46,299,600	16,046,600	3	545,800	5	4,705,800	5
9	•	Morgan Stanley Group (New York)	29,190,361	2,463,484	24	201,250	23	797,571	25
10	8	Bear Stearns Cos. (New York)	25,939,440	1,188,951	35	89,474	35	651,435	31
11	9	E. F. Hutton Group (New York)	25,921,257	3,504,927	16	(90,286)	49	733,484	28
12	11	American International Group (New York)	21,022,868	9,704,119	6	795,827	4	4,867,797	4
13	10	Leews (New York)	19,024,309	8,625,988	8	545,503	6	2,916,624	7
14	12	Student Loan Marketing Ass'n (Washington, D.C.)	18,232,065	1,376,785	32	144,559	29	654,805	30
15	15	Lincoln National (Fort Wayne)	16,243,838	5,998,713	12	284,392	12	2,196,594	12
16	13	Transamerica (San Francisco)	16,181,783	7,119,688	9	267,541	14	2,304,362	11
17	14	Paine Webber Group (New York)	14,725,750	2,384,720	25	71,599	37	633,365	33
18	16	Continental (New York)	13,623,225	6,002,273	11	449,632	9	2,550,894	9
19	•	Household International (Prospect Height, Ill.)	13,206,600	3,825,400	14	208,600	22	1,161,600	21
20	21	Fleet Financial Group (Providence, R.I.)	11,690,346	1,207,513	34	136,744	30	770,654	26
21	17	Kemper (Long Grove, Ill.)	9,735,091	3,329,897	17	201,110	24	1,423,530	18
22	19	Fireman's Fund (Novato, Calif.)	9,178,000	3,699,000	15	228,000	18	1,560,000	16
23	20	USF&G (Baltimore)	8,935,991	4,336,783	13	296,330	11	1,576,161	14
24	23	General Re (Stamford, Conn.)	8,676,600	3,175,200	22	328,700	10	2,413,100	10
25	22	St. Paul Cos.	7,627,082	3,181,587	21	217,114	20	1,440,565	17

Source: Fortune 115, no. 12 (June 8, 1987), p. 204.

965

APPENDIX B

The 25 Largest Savings Institutions

Rank 1986	Rank 1985	Company	Assets ($000)	Deposits ($000)	Deposits Rank	Loans ($000)	Loans Rank	Net Income ($000)	Net Income Rank
1	1	Federal Corp. of America (Irvine, Calif.)	$33,952,994	$16,929,388	3	$11,650,995	6	$ 95,369	9
2	3	Great Western Financial Corp. (Beverly Hills, Calif.)	27,630,183	18,130,530	2	21,970,955	1	300,786	2
3	2	H. F. Ahmanson (Los Angeles)	27,592,294	21,687,190	1	18,680,570	2	300,604	1
4	4	CalFed (Los Angeles)	21,552,900	15,486,500	4	15,912,600	3	164,400	5
5	5	Meritor Financial Group (Philadelphia)	18,447,272	12,676,100	5	15,515,724	4	22,920	34
6	6	GLENFED (Glendale, Calif.)	16,387,444	11,660,817	6	13,140,320	5	88,295	11
7	12	Great American First Savings Bank (San Diego)	13,064,815	8,877,414	7	8,877,743	7	93,745	10
8	7	Golden West Financial Corp. (Oakland)	12,435,350	7,698,523	9	7,986,984	9	183,808	4
9	10	Gilbralter Financial Corp. (Beverly Hills, Calif.)	12,248,615	6,001,205	14	4,773,050	16	49,077	19
10	9	Home Federal Savings & Loan Ass'n (San Diego)	12,074,620	8,562,059	8	1,232,040	49	103,358	7
11	8	First Federal of Michigan (Detroit)	11,271,916	5,047,913	18	4,778,940	18	73,023	12
12	11	CityFed Financial Corp. (Palm Beach, Fla.)	10,728,053	5,857,240	16	7,022,032	10	37,524	23
13	16	Columbia Savings & Loan Ass'n (Beverly Hills, Calif.)	10,222,652	5,192,585	17	1,817,752	41	193,526	3
14	14	Crossland Savings (New York)	10,095,697	6,876,465	11	8,251,452	8	101,232	8
15	15	Coast Savings & Loan Ass'n (Los Angeles)	9,725,362	5,931,131	15	5,508,974	14	50,377	16
16	13	Imperial Corp. of America (San Diego)	9,597,240	6,063,147	13	5,783,466	13	50,340	17
17	•	Empire of America Federal Savings (Buffalo)	9,095,241	7,352,759	10	6,803,587	11	66,638	14
18	•	Dime Savings Bank of New York (Garden City)	8,366,595	6,691,224	12	6,355,896	12	130,612	6
19	19	TCF Banking & Savings (Minneapolis)	6,517,650	3,405,961	24	2,735,217	28	21,401	38
20	19	United Financial Group (Houston)	6,464,869	3,101,427	30	1,680,699	43	(36,250)	48
21	22	ConTrust Savings Bank (Miami)	6,142,788	3,400,244	25	3,385,492	22	55,906	15
22	20	Western Savings & Loan Ass'n (Phoenix)	5,547,105	3,813,475	21	2,995,312	24	30,171	24
23	18	Carteret Savings & Loan Ass'n (Morristown, N.J.)	5,537,547	4,165,587	19	4,536,160	17	46,091	20
24	23	Homestead Financial Corp. (Burlingame, Calif.)	5,492,380	2,538,168	36	1,831,453	40	29,445	25
25	24	Washington Mutual Savings Bank (Seattle)	5,392,597	3,293,169	27	2,739,297	28	70,654	13

Source: *Fortune* 115, no. 12 (June 8, 1987), p. 206.

APPENDIX C

The 25 Largest Life Insurance Companies

Rank 1986	Rank 1985	Company	Assets ($000)	Premium and Annuity Income ($000)	Rank	Net Investment ($000)	Rank
1	1	Prudential of America (Newark)	$103,317,115	$17,380,277	1	$6,221,946	2
2	2	Metropolitan Life (New York)	81,581,350	12,148,965	2	6,705,678	1
3	3	Equitable Life Assurance (New York)	48,577,698	5,500,913	4	2,733,134	5
4	4	Aetna Life (Hartford)	42,957,155	10,506,887	3	3,130,175	3
5	5	New York Life	29,793,627	3,477,186	7	2,412,632	6
6	8	Teachers Insurance & Annuity (New York)	27,887,103	2,654,607	13	2,778,127	4
7	6	John Hancock Mutual Life (Boston)	27,213,497	4,173,912	5	1,406,348	10
8	7	Travelers (Hartford)	27,210,137	4,023,926	6	2,371,822	7
9	9	Connecticut General Life (Bloomfield)	24,806,504	2,896,639	11	1,544,123	8
10	10	Northwestern Mutual Life (Milwaukee)	20,187,343	2,934,270	9	1,439,008	9
11	11	Massachusetts Mutual Life (Springfield)	18,027,848	2,487,919	14	1,338,391	12
12	12	Principal Mutual Life (Des Moines)	16,993,647	3,112,712	8	1,391,709	11
13	13	New England Mutual Life (Boston)	12,827,256	2,769,876	12	1,019,988	13
14	14	Mutual of New York	11,248,982	2,197,790	15	723,087	16
15	19	Executive Life (Los Angeles)	9,870,910	1,615,782	21	800,593	15
16	15	Mutual Benefit Life (Newark)	9,837,863	1,634,881	19	891,052	14
17	16	Connecticut Mutual Life (Hartford)	8,934,017	1,763,712	17	645,224	18
18	17	State Farm Life (Bloomington, Ill.)	7,485,062	1,224,966	29	657,372	17
19	18	IDS Life (Minneapolis)	7,301,941	1,213,298	31	580,540	19
20	21	Variable Annuity Life (Houston)	6,614,424	1,004,512	36	562,186	20
21	20	Nationwide Life (Columbia, Ohio)	6,444,987	1,013,129	35	386,565	24
22	26	Aetna Life & Annuity (Hartford)	5,610,053	986,995	37	312,460	30
23	24	Continental Assurance (Chicago)	5,601,469	1,488,613	25	178,575	49
24	25	Pacific Mutual Life (Newport Beach, Calif.)	5,515,535	1,457,421	26	438,057	22
25	30	New York Life & Annuity (Wilmington, Del.)	5,481,656	1,489,552	24	483,440	21

Source: *Fortune* 115, no. 12 (June 8, 1987), p. 208.

APPENDIX D

50 Largest U.S. Banks

	Assets 12/31/87 ($ mil.)	Deposits 12/31/87 ($ mil.)	Deposits Change from 1986 (%)	Deposits Interest/ nonint. (%)	Deposits For- eign (%)	Loans 12/31/87 ($ mil.)	Loans Change from 1986 (%)
1. Citicorp	$203,607	$119,561	4%	87/13%	53%	$138,085	5%
2. Chase Manhattan	99,133	68,578	4	74/26	49	67,979	3
3. BankAmerica	92,833	76,290	−7	77/23	24	64,508	−13
4. Chemical New York	78,189	55,509	42	78/22	29	49,800	26
5. Morgan (J. P.)	75,414	43,987	2	84/16	68	30,631	−12
6. Manufacturers Hanover	73,348	45,176	−1	81/19	50	55,617	−1
7. Security Pacific	72,838	45,551	0	77/23	16	51,628	1
8. Bankers Trust New York	56,521	30,220	2	78/22	62	26,184	−10
9. First Interstate Bancorp	50,927	37,570	−5	70/30	5	32,777	−5
10. First Chicago	44,209	31,538	17	81/19	47	28,012	10
11. Wells Fargo	44,183	32,320	−2	80/20	5	36,791	0
12. Bank of Boston	34,117	22,472	3	79/21	27	24,757	3
13. First Republicbank	33,211	25,491	59	76/24	8	24,104	63
14. Continental Illinois	32,391	19,624	9	83/17	52	20,067	−3
15. PNC Financial	31,433	20,348	16	80/20	6	17,117	10
16. Mellon Bank	30,525	21,548	0	80/20	13	20,199	−14
17. Bank of New England	29,475	22,767	7	78/22	10	22,054	16
18. NCNB	28,915	19,550	6	80/20	7	17,087	8
19. First Union	27,629	17,425	2	77/23	7	15,388	10
20. Suntrust Banks	27,188	22,493	6	75/25	1	18,410	9
21. First Bank System	26,850	15,799	−3	82/18	14	13,290	−11
22. Marine Midland Banks	25,453	17,303	−1	80/20	18	21,011	12
23. Fleet/Norstar Financial Group	24,531	17,531	12	77/23	7	16,399	25
24. Irving Bank	23,534	15,152	−1	70/30	37	15,129	8
25. Barnett Banks of Florida	23,451	20,167	6	84/16	0	17,023	14
26. NBD Bancorp	23,354	18,166	9	77/23	8	13,235	6
27. Bank of New York	23,065	17,126	13	73/27	28	16,271	18
28. Republic of New York	22,388	14,839	37	94/6	51	5,581	28
29. Sovran Financial	21,233	16,667	11	81/19	1	13,745	12
30. Norwest	20,747	13,644	−3	78/22	3	12,896	−3
31. Citizens & Southern	20,444	14,974	7	71/29	0	12,996	12
32. MCorp	20,228	16,632	−5	81/19	3	13,289	−11
33. First Wachovia	19,342	14,342	4	72/28	3	12,341	5
34. Banc One	18,730	14,478	8	81/19	1	12,934	12
35. Midlantic	17,792	13,638	1	73/27	1	13,079	13
36. MNC Financial	16,658	11,241	13	80/20	12	11,570	17
37. First Fidelity Bancorp.	16,241	12,070	0	72/28	1	10,287	14
38. Hartford National	15,691	11,580	6	75/25	6	10,078	20
39. Corestates Financial	15,036	10,301	−3	68/32	7	10,131	4
40. National City	14,912	11,427	10	79/21	4	9,924	9
41. U.S. Bancorp	13,353	9,522	20	78/22	0	8,669	22
42. Southeast Banking	12,842	9,518	0	78/22	4	8,242	10
43. Fidelcor	12,650	8,869	−2	82/18	13	7,472	14
44. Keycorp	11,596	9,379	14	77/23	0	7,557	24
45. National Westminster Bank USA	11,539	9,539	9	78/22	19	8,216	12
46. Valley National	11,300	9,736	−2	79/21	0	7,926	1
47. Shawmut	10,803	7,576	−2	71/29	2	7,339	7
48. Signet Banking	10,724	7,625	14	84/16	2	6,760	13
49. Harris Bankcorp	10,556	7,754	2	67/33	20	5,999	5
50. Ameritrust	10,334	7,755	−3	83/17	3	7,111	−1

APPENDIX D (*continued*)

	Performance						Market Value	
	Oper. Income 1987 ($ mil.)	Net Income 1987 ($ mil.)	Change from 1986 (%)	Return on Assets 1987 (%)	Lever-age, 1987	5-Year Aver. Growth EPS (%)	3/11/88 ($ mil.)	Rank
1. Citicorp	$ – 1,138.0	$ – 1138.0	NM%	– 0.62%	29.9	NM%	$6,246	1
2. Chase Manhattan	– 928.0	– 894.8	NM	– 0.97	27.7	NM	2,142	11
3. BankAmerica	– 986.0	– 955.0	NM	– 1.02	35.4	NM	1,553	21
4. Chemical New York	9,103.0	– 853.7	NM	– 1.23	29.1	NM	1,342	26
5. Morgan (J. P.)	83.3	83.3	– 90	0.09	16.6	– 18.2	6,125	2
6. Manufacturers Hanover	– 1,168.4	– 1,140.2	NM	– 1.55	30.2	NM	1,325	28
7. Security Pacific	21.0	15.7	– 97	0.00	23.2	– 53.8	3,296	4
8. Bankers Trust New York	1.2	1.2	– 99	0.00	21.6	– 51.2	2,608	8
9. First Interstate Bancorp	– 563.4	– 556.2	NM	– 1.09	20.3	NM	2,041	13
10. First Chicago	– 570.7	– 570.7	NM	– 1.37	25.0	NM	1,308	30
11. Wells Fargo	58.6	50.8	– 81	0.06	23.6	– 17.8	2,776	6
12. Bank of Boston	11.9	19.7	– 92	0.02	19.8	– 33.5	1,516	22
13. First Republicbank	– 656.8	– 656.8	NM	– 2.44	24.4	NM	53	178
14. Continental Illinois	– 609.5	– 609.5	NM	– 2.03	23.4	NM	833	39
15. PNC Financial	166.7	204.8	– 28	0.73	15.5	8.6	3,445	3
16. Mellon Bank	– 844.0	– 844.0	NM	– 2.65	23.9	NM	749	42
17. Bank of New England	122.2	140.5	– 33	0.51	19.5	6.0	1,993	14
18. NCNB	146.3	166.9	– 16	0.62	18.7	7.8	1,691	19
19. First Union	265.7	283.1	2	1.10	15.0	20.2	2,291	10
20. Suntrust Banks	282.1	282.8	17	1.11	16.1	13.8	2,850	5
21. First Bank System	54.9	49.6	– 76	0.15	21.6	– 8.4	1,337	27
22. Marine Midland Banks	– 427.9	– 408.8	NM	– 1.72	23.4	NA	NA	NM
23. Fleet/Norstar Financial Group	159.4	185.1	– 23	0.76	15.3	6.5	2,440	9
24. Irving Bank	– 193.3	– 193.3	NM	– 0.82	26.0	NM	983	35
25. Barnett Banks of Florida	195.5	195.6	12	0.89	17.9	25.3	1,981	16
26. NBD Bancorp	154.6	162.2	– 3	0.72	17.6	14.6	1,579	20
27. Bank of New York	93.7	103.4	– 33	0.43	20.6	0.4	956	36
28. Republic of New York	– 15.8	33.0	– 78	0.09	21.1	– 19.4	1,310	29
29. Sovran Financial	212.1	217.4	15	1.10	16.3	14.4	1,937	17
30. Norwest	– 30.6	– 29.8	NM	– 0.20	18.0	NM	1,238	31
31. Citizens & Southern	151.6	157.8	1	0.81	18.6	12.6	1,506	24
32. MCorp	– 261.2	– 258.3	NM	– 1.30	20.3	NM	117	168
33. First Wachovia	166.2	176.6	– 9	0.97	14.7	12.5	2,053	12
34. Banc One	203.5	208.9	5	1.18	12.8	13.6	2,664	7
35. Midlantic	161.0	161.5	9	0.96	15.7	8.8	1,512	23
36. MNC Financial	148.2	148.8	21	0.99	16.9	15.3	1,167	33
37. First Fidelity Bancorp.	46.5	48.5	– 59	0.27	17.9	0.3	1,981	15
38. Hartford National	125.4	125.4	7	0.88	17.4	15.1	1,708	18
39. Corestates Financial	151.1	162.3	10	1.04	15.4	13.4	1,493	25
40. National City	90.0	96.9	– 28	0.68	16.1	15.9	1,208	32
41. U.S. Bancorp	108.5	108.5	43	0.90	14.9	9.2	1,044	34
42. Southeast Banking	38.0	38.4	– 56	0.26	19.5	– 4.5	723	44
43. Fidelcor	37.7	37.7	– 59	0.20	20.6	– 9.6	NA	NM
44. Keycorp	67.2	80.0	– 10	0.72	16.4	12.8	746	43
45. National Westminster Bank USA	– 214.6	– 212.0	NM	– 1.86	21.4	NA	NA	NM

(*continued*)

APPENDIX D *(concluded)*

	Performance						Market Value	
	Oper. Income 1987 ($ mil.)	Net Income 1987 ($ mil.)	Change from 1986 (%)	Return on Assets 1987 (%)	Lever- age, 1987	5-Year Aver. Growth EPS (%)	3/11/88 ($ mil.)	Rank
46. Valley National	−45.1	−44.4	NM	−0.41	16.8	NM	572	58
47. Shawmut	22.5	33.5	−57	−0.33	16.2	−2.0	1,708	18
48. Signet Banking	12.2	23.5	−73	0.22	18.4	−5.8	767	40
49. Harris Bankcorp	41.8	42.6	−37	0.40	15.2	10.5	NA	NM
50. Ameritrust	−10.9	−10.1	NM	−0.10	12.8	NM	703	48

Source: *Business Week,* April 4, 1988, pp. 94–95.
NA = not available.
NM = not meaning.

CASE 36

BANKAMERICA CORPORATION

BankAmerica is taking decisive steps to return to sustained operating profitability.

Its principal objectives are to be the prime provider of retail and wholesale banking services in the western United States and to be a preeminent provider of integrated wholesale financial services throughout the world.[1]

1   Indeed, this is a significant statement by the third largest multinational bank in the United States, a bank that has experienced a sizable decrease in its asset base and earnings as a result of questionable management decisions (see Exhibit 1).

2   A number of questions have arisen with regard to the future strategy of the bank for the next decade; more specifically, the following issues confronted the bank: the impact of or need for mergers, the continued disposal of assets, the role of the bank with respect to international lending activities to underdeveloped countries, and the need for improved control and accountability by its lending officers—all crucial questions faced by a once formidable retail and wholesale banking giant.

ORGANIZATIONAL STRUCTURE

3   BankAmerica is structured around three profit centers: (1) Retail Banking, (2) World Bank, and (3) Seafirst Corporation. Another division, BankAmerica Systems Engineering, serves to provide technological and research support to the various divisions.

Retail Banking

4   The customer coverage of this unit is extensive and includes many offices; all are located in California: (a) 895 branches, (b) 156 convenience banking centers, (c) 30 home loan centers, (d) 8 consumer loan centers, and (e) 12 real estate loan centers. An additional 30 private banking offices are located worldwide.

5   The division provides a wide array of products, such as consumer loans, loans to small- and medium-sized businesses, deposit services, mortgage banking, employee benefit trust services, traveler's checks, business services, payment services, and insurance. Several other customer-oriented services were provided during 1986; for example, personal checking account customers could receive a refund of up to six months' service charges if they were dissatisfied with the service. Another key service was furnished by automatic teller machines (ATMs), whereby operating hours were increased and the bank's Versatile cardholders could have easy access to their accounts in

---

[1]This case was developed from various Bank of America annual reports and 10-Ks.

This case was prepared by Randall White of Auburn University at Montgomery, Alabama.

EXHIBIT 1
Rankings of the Top 25 U.S. Commercial Banks by Assets, as of
June 30, 1987 (dollars in billions)

1.	Citicorp	$194.4
2.	Chase Manhattan	98.9
3.	BankAmerica	97.0
4.	Chemical New York	78.4
5.	J. P. Morgan	74.7
6.	Manufacturers Hanover	73.8
7.	Security Pacific	64.7
8.	Bankers Trust	54.7
9.	First Interstate Bank	51.8
10.	Wells Fargo	44.7
11.	First Chicago	41.7
12.	First Republicbank	34.4
13.	Continental Illinois	33.4
14.	Mellon Bank	33.2
15.	Bank of Boston	30.5
16.	First Bank System	28.4
17.	PNC Financial	28.2
18.	Bank of New England	27.1
19.	First Union Corp.	25.8
20.	SunTrust Banks	25.6
21.	NCNB Corp.	24.9
22.	Marine Midland Banks	24.4
23.	Irving Bank Corp.	24.2
24.	NBD Bancorp.	22.6
25.	MCorp.	22.2

Source: *Standard & Poor's Industry Surveys,* August 20, 1987. The profit figure for BankAmerica was obtained from *Business Week,* April 17, 1987.

47 states and Canada with Great Britain and Japan coming on-line during 1987. Cardholders could also pay for retail purchases at over 1,800 California outlets in addition to their gas and supermarket needs, the latter being recently instituted through a test market in Bakersfield, California. The bank's VISA cardholders could also receive cash advances from some 10,000 VISA ATMs in the United States and several countries overseas, such as Great Britain, France, Spain, Hong Kong, Australia, and Japan. Another innovative approach was to provide *Preferred Banking* status to their affluent customers such that this targeted clientele would be provided an array of financial and other services.

World Bank Division

6   This division focuses on major corporated clients, financial and other institutions, and governments worldwide. It extended its International Bank System (IBS)—this was an integrated, real-time global database network stretching from Europe to Hong Kong, Panama, and Puerto Rico, with other locations in the United States and Asia scheduled for 1987.

7   A few of the services provided by this division included its role as lead manager for a $475 million syndicated loan agreement to finance the largest open pit mine in China's Shanxi Province,

in addition to opening its third office in Guangzhou Guangdong Province. The division also arranged syndication for a $210 million Malaysian rural water supply project and also concluded its first amortized interest-rate swap totaling $10 million in India.

Seafirst Corporation

8   Acquired in 1983 and publicized as the "West Coast's biggest interstate banking acquision," this division is the parent for Seafirst Bank, which is located in Washington state, where it is a major force in the Pacific Northwest. Although plagued by bad oil loans, which resulted in a $337 million loss in 1985—many of which were bought from similarly troubled Penn Square Bank in Oklahoma— Seafirst Bank reported an increase in profits from $29.1 million in 1985 to $62 million in 1986. Its core businesses are consumer and business customers, totaling about 800,000 in the Northwest. About 158 branches serve their clientele in the region with a staff that "is courting customers with a vengeance and giving competitors fits."

BankAmerica Systems Engineering

9   Dealing principally with managing, developing, and applying management information systems technology throughout the bank, the division has centers located in England, Hong Kong, New York, San Francisco, Los Angeles, and Concord, California, where a new $160 million Technology Center was constructed.The majority of its activities are focused on technological projects designed to monitor and control costs on a worldwide basis, as well as to improve productivity and the quality of services and products to its clients.

LOAN PORTFOLIO

Domestic Loans

10   The U.S. domestic picture looked bleak due to an oversupply of commercial real estate office space in major regional areas, in addition to falling agricultural commodity prices and land values. Rising consumer indebtedness and personal bankruptcies added more fuel to the depressed California market. Consumer losses for 1985 and 1986 included credit card losses totaling $145 million and $166 million, respectively; however, management was confident of an overall decline in net credit losses for 1987.

Foreign Loans

11   In its international lending activities, BankAmerica exposed itself to a broad range of country risks ranging from political to legal to cultural factors. It has, however, attempted to assess these risks in its lending activities to less-developed countries (LDCs) by looking at that nation's debt position and its ability to service that debt, in addition to its foreign exchange reserves and its infrastructure. The country's past credit performance and compliance to loan restrictions imposed by the International Monetary Fund (IMF) and the World Bank (WB) are also looked at.[2] Last, the corporation also set up a loan "exposure limit for each country to ensure that the international portfolio is well diversified" (Annual Report).

---

[2]IMF is primarily a lending organization, while the World Bank provides funds for a variety of incountry projects.

The Domestic and Foreign Loan Picture

12 The data reflects a diversified portfolio, consisting of retail lending primarily in real estate on the West Coast, in addition to commercial loans for small to large businesses, governments, and financial institutions both domestically and abroad. As shown in Exhibit 2, the two major loan categories are domestic and foreign loans. With respect to domestic loans, the *total volume*—which is comprised of real estate, consumer installment, through lease financing—amounted to $53.061 million in 1986, compared to $48.450 million in 1982, an increase of $4.611 million or 9.5 percent.

EXHIBIT 2
Loan Outstandings for Years Ended December 31, 1982 to 1986 ($ millions)

	1986	1985	1984	1983	1982
Domestic loans:					
Real estate	$17,847	$19,887	$19,882	$19,368	$18,067
Consumer installment	12,570	14,375	13,348	11,648	9,499
Commercial and industrial	18,258	20,616	20,813	18,450	15,874
Agricultural	1,175	1,610	1,966	2,136	1,828
Financial institutions	2,209	1,580	1,532	1,066	1,257
Lease financing	1,002	1,501	1,868	2,015	1,925
Foreign loans	20,894	24,757	25,637	27,674	28,177
Total loans	$73,955	$84,326	$85,046	$82,357	$76,627

Source: Bank of America annual reports, 1982–86.

EXHIBIT 3
Allowance for Possible Credit Losses for Years Ended December 31, 1984 to 1986 ($ millions)

	1986		1985		1984	
	Allowance	Percent of Loan Outstandings	Allowance	Percent of Loan Outstandings	Allowance	Percent of Loan Outstandings
Domestic loans:						
Real estate	$ 393	2.20%	$ 117	0.59%	$ 69	0.35%
Consumer installment	258	2.06	226	1.57	91	0.68
Commercial and industrial	452	2.47	300	1.45	198	0.95
Agricultural	141	11.99	107	6.65	30	1.53
Financial institutions	32	1.45	12	0.75	3	0.20
Lease financing	8	0.84	14	0.92	16	0.87
Foreign loans	752	3.60	744	3.01	225	0.88
Total domestic	2,036	2.75	1,520	1.81	632	0.74
Unallocated	136	—	64	—	371	—
Total loans	$2,172	2.94	$1,584	1.88	$1,003	1.18

Note: The allowance for possible credit losses is allocated by applying loss factors to the related loan outstandings and from estimates of probable future losses. These factors include general economic conditions; deterioration in credit concentrations or pledged collateral; international lending risk; historical loss experience; and trends in portfolio volume, maturity, composition, delinquencies, and nonaccruals.

Source: Bank of America annual reports, 1984–86.

Total foreign loans, on the other hand, declined from $28.177 million in 1982 to $20,894 million in 1986 (about $7,283 million), an approximate drop of 26 percent. This declining condition in foreign loans can be attributed to a number of factors, such as the economic decline faced by many less-developed countries accompanied by falling commodity prices as many LDCs were commodity producers of oil and other price-sensitive commodities.

13   With respect to foreign loans, Exhibit 3 reflects a 234 percent increase in "Allowance for credit

---

EXHIBIT 4
Net Credit Losses as a Percent of Average Loan Outstandings for Years Ended December 31, 1984 to 1986 (dollars in millions)

	1986		1985		1984	
	Net Credit Losses	Percent of Loan Outstandings	Net Credit Losses	Percent of Loan Outstandings	Net Credit Losses	Percent of Loan Outstandings
Domestic loans:						
Real estate	$ 244	1.26%	$ 173	0.86%	$ 39	0.20%
Consumer installment	279	1.99	238	1.68	128	1.05
Commercial and industrial	345	2.05	279	1.54	330	1.88
Agricultural	72	5.50	152	8.70	78	3.77
Financial institutions	6	0.31	2	0.14	1	0.13
Lease financing	14	1.10	43	2.75	29	1.53
Foreign loans	459	1.89	712	2.84	302	1.13
Total loans	$1,419	1.75%	$1,599	1.91	$907	1.10

Source: Bank of America annual reports, 1984–86.

EXHIBIT 5
Nonaccural, Restructured, and Past Due 90 Days or More Loans for Years Ended December 31, 1981 to 1986 (dollars in millions)

	1986	1985	1984	1983	1982	1981
Nonaccrual loans:						
Domestic	$2,628	$1,741	$1,484	$1,905	$1,395	$ 814
Foreign	1,339	1,416	1,805	1,178	392	138
Subtotal	3,967	3,157	3,289	3,083	1,787	952
Restructured loans:						
Domestic	44	247	192	154	258	263
Foreign	20	19	26	77	359	8
Subtotal	64	266	218	231	617	271
Past due (90 days or more) loans:						
Domestic	242	406	657	554	729	145
Foreign	43	37	84	577	149	230
Subtotal	285	443	741	1,131	878	375
Total	$4,316	$3,866	$4,248	$4,445	$3,282	$1,598

Source: Bank of America annual reports, 1981–86.

losses," from $225 million in 1984 to $752 million in 1986. The foreign loans allowances were 35 percent of the overall total allowances—$2,172 million—for 1986. Domestic loans also indicate an increasing overall trend with regard to "Allowance for credit losses," except for lease financing. This increasing allowances picture is (a) real estate—470 percent, (b) agricultural—370 percent, (c) consumer installment—184 percent, (d) commercial and industrial—128 percent, and (e) financial institutions—967 percent. Hence, the overall total allowances rose significantly from $1,003 million in 1984 to $2,172 million in 1986, a 117 percent increase.

14   Foreign loans in Exhibit 4 show a sizable increase in net credit losses from $302 million to $712 million (about 135 percent) from 1984–85, followed by another loss—although substantially less—from $302 million to $459 million (approximately 52 percent) from 1984–86. Total "net credit losses" also reflect this trend—76 percent in 1984–85 (i.e., from $907 million to $1,599 billion) and 56 percent in 1984–86 (i.e., $907 million to $1,419 billion).

15   Although loans are usually covered at the principal balance outstanding, a number of domestic and foreign loans were put in a nonaccrual basis when 90 days or more past due which, ultimately, reduced current years earnings (see Exhibit 5). In essence, then, interest income from these loans can only be recorded when the funds are received. At the same time, it is still management's decision on placing loans in a nonaccrual basis if the loan is properly secured or is undergoing a loan renewal. Additionally, nonaccrual loans may be restored to an accrual status if the loan is current with respect to interest and principal and if future prospects look promising.

16   Again referring to Exhibit 5, restructured loans, on the other hand, are loans that are renegotiated

---

EXHIBIT 6
Cross-Boarder Outstanding Exceeding 1 Percent of Total Assets (Note 1)
for Years Ended December 31, 1983 to 1986 (dollars in millions)

	1986	1985	1984	1983
Brazil:				
Total cross-border outstanding (Note 2)	$2,741	$2,799	$2,721	$2,484
Cross-border outstanding as a percent of total assets (Note 3)	2.6%	2.4%	2.3%	2.0%
Mexico:				
Total cross-border outstanding (Note 2)	$2,500	$2,583	$2,689	$2,741
Cross-border outstanding as a percent of total assets (Note 3)	2.4%	2.2%	2.3%	2.3%
Venezuela:				
Total cross-border outstanding (Note 2)	$1,260	$1,450	$1,508	$1,641
Cross-border outstanding as a percent of total assets (Note 3)	1.2%	1.2%	1.3%	1.3%

Notes:
1. Cross-border loans are denominated in a currency other than that of the borrower's country, thus incurring additional risk as a lack of foreign exchange, whereas local currency loans are repaid in the borrowing country's currency.
2. Cross-border outstandings reported in prior periods have been restated for . . . Mexico.
3. Cross-border outstandings include the following assets, primarily in U.S. dollars, with borrowers or customers in a foreign country: loans, accrued interest, acceptances, interest-earning deposits with other banks, other interest-earning investments, and other monetary assets. . . . Management reported that no other country had nonaccrual, restructured, or past due 90 days or more loans exceeding 10 percent of cross-border outstandings as of 12/31/86.

Source: Bank of America annual reports, 1983–86.

for a variety or reasons, such as borrower financial difficulty or other concessionary terms as a reduction or deferral of interest or principal payments. Finally, loans past due 90 days or more—the so-called problem workout loans—are those in which management doubts that the borrower will be able to meet the loan repayment terms.

17   Exhibit 6 displays the foreign loan exposures to three Latin American countries. For example, where the exposure exceeded 1 percent of total assets, Brazil's exposure has increased *from* 2 percent in 1983 to 2.6 percent in 1986, while Mexico, on the other hand, declined *from* 2.3 percent for both 1983 and 1984 *to* 2.2 percent in 1985, then edged upward in 1986 to 2.4 percent. Venezuela declined *from* 1.3 percent for both 1983 and 1984 *to* 1.2 percent for 1985 and 1986, respectively. Hence, Exhibit 6 suggests that the bank has taken some steps to monitor and control its foreign loan exposure, although the overall picture remains alarming.

CONTROL AND ACCOUNTABILITY

18   In its attempt to closely monitor lending activities and to stress individual loan accountability on the part of credit officers, the corporation replaced its loan committee approval system and centralized lending at designated locations. Moreover, experienced loan officers exercised close control over credit officers to ensure conformance with established credit standards and to minimize risk exposure. Additionally, special asset groups were established to focus on problem loans and industries. In essence, problem loan monitoring and collecting was separated from loan making, thus enabling the corporation to continue to improve credit quality. Finally, new training programs for credit officers were set up in addition to personnel incentives.

EXHIBIT 7
Net Gain on Sales of Assets for Years Ended December 31, 1984 to 1986
(dollars in millions)

	1986	1985	1984
Assets:			
Banca d'America e d'Italia (Note 1)	$236	—	—
Headquarters (Note 2)	77	$310	—
Finance America and BA			
Financial Services Corp. (Note 3)	—	180	—
Other assets (Note 4)	98		$65
Total assets	$411	$509	$65

Notes:
1. Sold for $603 million in December 1986.
2. Sold its 50 percent interest in Los Angeles headquarters for $310 million, resulting in a $77 million gain during third quarter 1986; an additional pretax gain of $114 million has been deferred and will be recognized over its 14-year lease obligation. In the third quarter of 1985, sold its San Francisco World Headquarters for $660 million, from which a pretax gain of $310 million was obtained; similarly, an additional $237 million was deferred and will be recognized over its 10-year lease obligation.
3. In the fourth quarter 1985, it sold two wholly owned finance subsidiaries for $434 million.
4. Various other overseas branches (about 45) in 14 countries were either sold or consolidated.
Source: Bank of America annual reports, 1984–86.

DISPOSAL OF ASSETS

19   As part of its restructuring program, the corporation found it imperative to divest several segments of the business to streamline and reduce its asset base, improve operating efficiency, and, equally important, enhance its capital strength (see Exhibit 7). The net effect of these divestitures was to reduce its total asset base from $118.5 billion in 1985 to $104.2 billion in 1986.

20   Although its primary and capital ratios exceed regulatory guidelines,[3] the corporation plans to

EXHIBIT 8
Primary and Total Capital for Years Ended December 31, 1984 to 1986
(dollars in millions)

	1986	1985	1984
Capital components:			
Stockholders' equity	$4,038	$4,547	$5,119
Subordinated capital notes	1,141	1,198	799
Minority interest	10	8	9
Allowance for possible credit losses	2,172	1,584	1,003
Primary capital	7,361	7,337	6,930
Secondary capital—qualifying debt	1,245	931	914
Total capital	$8,606	$7,337	$6,930
Capital ratios:			
Primary capital	6.92%	6.11%	5.84%
Total capital	8.09	6.88	6.61

Notes:
  Primary capital ratio = stockholders' equity plus the allowance for possible credit losses, minority interest in equity of consolidated subsidiaries, and subordinated capital notes divided by total assets plus the allowance for possible credit losses.
  Total capital ratio = primary capital plus certain qualifying intermediate- and long-term debt, divided by total assets plus the allowance for possible credit losses.
  Source: Bank of America annual reports, 1984–86.

EXHIBIT 9
Personnel Staffing and Operating Units for December 31, 1982 to 1986

	1986	1985	1984	1983	1982
Full-time equivalent staff (Note 1)	68,497	78,067	83,638	86,104	81,008
Operating units:					
Domestic branches (Note 2)	1,053	1,059	1,103	1,231	1,085
Foreign:					
Branches	66	103	113	116	119
Representative offices	17	17	15	17	17

Notes:
1. Full-time equivalent is a measure equivalent to one full-time employee working on a standard day and is based on the number of hours worked in the given month.
2. Includes Bank of America NT&SA and Seattle First National Bank.

[3]Regulators now view capital as a sign of a bank's strength, and they require banks to maintain capital levels of at least 5.5 percent to 6.0 percent of a bank's assets.

continue divestiture of additional assets in 1987. For example, the Consumer Trust Services, in addition to issuance of equity and debt securities (which will be sold under a December 1986 agreement for $100 million) will generate a pretax gain exceeding $80 million. According to management, despite the sale it will still be able to furnish trust services to its institutional clientele. The Charles Schwab Corporation—a well-known discount brokerage service—will also be sold and should post a pretax gain of about $120 million in the first quarter of 1987. Overall, the net effect of past and future divestment should provide additional liquidity to the corporation (see Exhibit 8). In a similar manner, staffing would also be affected (see Exhibit 9).

MERGER

21 Initiating a persistent strategy for a takeover of BankAmerica, First Interstate Bancorp (FI) filed a registration statement with the SEC covering a $3.23 billion bid for BankAmerica. (See Exhibit 10 for a chronology of events.) According to *The Wall Street Journal,* A. W. Clausen, chairman and CEO of BankAmerica, had sent a letter on December 15, 1986, to Joseph J. Pinola, First Interstate's chairman and CEO, which stated:

> You appear to be following a calculated plan to create a situation in which you can dictate a takeover of BankAmerica on your terms at some future time when our alternatives might be restricted. . . . It is our duty to our shareholders, and indeed to the banking community, to prevent you from creating such a situation.

Clausen also accused Pinola of being "reckless" and suggested that the bank "may take First Interstate to court" as a result of their "comments about BankAmerica's financial status condition." Twice previously, BankAmerica urged Pinola to "pull back, pending an internal strategic review."

22 Another BankAmerica source stated that First Interstate's move would undoubtedly:

> force the board into a much more hard and hostile attitude than had First Interstate waited. . . . It needn't have been that way. I'm going to pretend that BankAmerica was eager to be acquired. But it was certainly possible for the board to reach an independent decision that a merger was in the best interests of the institution.
>
> . . . a friendly transaction isn't out of the question. But given the personalities and the rivalries, I'd be very surprised if it all ended up sweetness and light.

According to Hill, First Interstate increased its bid to $3.39 billion, which was quickly rejected by the bank's board to allow the corporation to continue with its internal strategic review. In fact, the board later authorized management to "take such actions as might be 'appropriate' to fend off 'unilateral action' by First Interstate." Thus, continuation of the takeover effort by FI could be construed as hostile in light of the board's statement. Sources close to FI indicated the likelihood of a proxy contest in which case FI could offer its own slate of directors supportive of a takeover while, at the same time, allow FI's slate to obtain more conclusive data regarding BankAmerica's financial health. Last, shareholders' support "for a new board potentially would be less confrontational and disruptive." In that light, "individuals own more than half of B of A's 154 million common shares. Traditionally loyal, they might ignore Pinola's bid to buy their holdings."

23 Nevertheless, BankAmerica did apparently succeed at preventing the unwanted takeover by First Interstate. According to Carson's report in February 1987:

> Joe Pinola may be down but not out. Granted, in ending his 18-month bid to acquire BankAmerica Corp., the scrappy chairman of First Interstate Bancorp failed to pull off the biggest bank merger in history. But the way he sees it, BankAmerica had shed so many key assets over the past few months that it bore no resemblance to the bank he originally sought. Anyway, Pinola has other plans for First Interstate now.

EXHIBIT 10
BankAmerica—A Chronology of Events

January	1981	Under Tom Clausen, reports record earnings of $643 million for 1980.
April	1981	Sam Armacost succeeds Clausen, who moves to World Bank; bank reports first quarterly earnings decline in 14 years.
December through December	1981 1984	Shows a declining trend in net income: $457 million in 1982, $390 million in 1983, $346 million in 1984.
July	1985	Announces second-quarter loss of $338 million and begins first layoffs.
August	1985	Bank cuts its dividend for first time in 53 years.
September	1985	Headquarters Tower sold for $660 million (see "Disposal of Assets" covered in case and Exhibit 7).
December	1985	Reports a loss of $337 million.
January	1986	Suspends dividends.
February	1986	Weill proposes to raise $1 billion for the bank in return for Armacost's job.
March	1986	Board rejects Weill's offer and appoints Armacost to a newly created position as chairman and CEO of Bank of America (B of A), the principal unit of the parent, BankAmerica; Cooper is elected president of B of A.
August	1986	Poelker, chief financial officer, and Schwab, a director, resign.
October	1986	First Interstate proposes merger; board replaces Armacost; Prussia (at the time, chairman of the parent, BankAmerica) resigns; Clausen is rehired as chairman of the parent; Cooper is elevated to president of the parent, in addition to his position as president and CEO of B of A. Citicorp expresses interest in a takeover at BankAmerica.
November	1986	Citicorp drops bid.
December	1986	Reports a loss of $518 million.
January through April	1987 1987	Resignations: McLin (who engineered the acquistions of Seafirst Corporation and the Charles Schwab Company); Appelgarth, a senior VP. First Interstate's merger bid is dropped.
May	1987	Cooper resigns.

Source: Adapted from *Business Week,* October 27, 1986, p. 109.

In a similar vein, Schmitt also reported on FI dropping its bid to acquire BankAmerica, again quoting Pinola that the "continuing dismemberment of this institution no longer justifies our current offered price." Schmitt also reported the FI was "deferring all actions" but would "continue to monitor closely the activities of the company."

24   Citicorp also indicated takeover attempts. The New York–based banking giant, with assets exceeding $194 billion and profits exceeding $1 billion (see Exhibit 1) expressed a desire to acquire all or part of BankAmerica's assets, particularly the latter's California retail bank branches. Citicorp sought to get regulatory approval "to convert BankAmerica to a thrift that could be merged into its California thrift unit, Citicorp Savings." However, industry sources claimed Citicorp was no longer interested in the total acquisition due to several factors as sales of several of the bank's

> desirable assets to pay for loan losses, the possibility of continued loan-portfolio deterioration . . . , the problems of assuming more Third World debt, dilution of Citicorp's own earnings, and other considerations.

Nevertheless, Citicorp was believed to be still interested in about 200 of BankAmerica's 900 California bank branches.

25   The Citicorp move was presumably influenced by a recent California statute enacted September 1986 allowing New York banks to buy California businesses effective January 1, 1991. There was also another move by a California legislator to propose a legislative bill that would expedite the entry of "major New York banks, including giant Citicorp, to acquire BankAmerica sooner than the current 1991 date."

RAISING EQUITY

26   The continuing divestments and merger battle with First Interstate brought about a different tactic, in which BankAmerica found it necessary to raise capital to shore up its shrinking capital base. Initially, it made a public offering of securities backed up with credit card receivables valued at $250 million. This novel approach would be a means to raise needed funds.

> The securities will represent an interest in a larger pool of credit card receivables and will pay only interest for 18 months. After that, they will pay interest and principal, with principal payments divided on a fixed percentage basis between investors in these securities and the rest of the pool.

27   Subsequent to this offer, the corporation's board authorized management to raise equity capital and "take all appropriate steps to deter First Interstate's hostile advances." These included so-called poison pill provisions (e.g., bylaw changes, such as expanding the board membership with friendly individuals or issuing additional stock to dilute the share price or create a new class of stock) or litigation. Although FI intended to continue its merger pursuit, BankAmerica's chairman and CEO Clausen indicated that "I'm not impressed with the management capability of First Interstate." (It should be mentioned that FI's present management consisted of several BankAmerica former employees, including Pinola.) Moreover, Clausen claimed that the corporation anticipated improved earnings in 1987 (this, too, has been disputed by many analysts who have followed the merger battle); however, he admitted that dividend payments, which were discontinued in 1986, would not be paid in 1987. He also indicated that the board had turned down an offer to sell some of its problem loans, which totaled about $4 billion.

28   Shortly thereafter, BankAmerica filed with the SEC a shelf registration letter to cover approximately $1 billion in securities. There were no specific terms mentioned or a selling date or if the securities would be placed publicly or privately. The corporation reported, however, that it was very liquid and had no funding problems and claimed that

> there are a number of potential institutional investors who would be interested in acquiring equity securities in a private placement, including some overseas investors. But that shouldn't be construed as meaning that any company would be taking a significant ownership position in BankAmerica.

Faced with this continuing battle to remain independent, the corporation was dealt a severe blow as its credit ratings were downgraded by Moody's Investors Service, Inc. About $5.5 billion of both long- and short-term debt and its preferred stock were affected. Approximately $4.7 billion of its senior debt were lowered to "speculative grade" for the first time. Reasons cited by Moody's were the increased levels of problem assets, especially the Latin American debt problems; however, the rating service added that the corporation had substantial marketable assets as its main unit, Bank of America NT&SA (B of A), had an excellent customer franchise and a substantial deposit base.

29   Nevertheless, after the successful attempt at preventing the unwanted takeover by First Interstate, the bank decided to focus on shielding itself from future takeovers and to protect its board members from shareholder lawsuits. It was apparently becoming increasingly difficult to attract qualified board members. Moreover, it had faced an increasing number of customer and shareholder lawsuits due to its large losses and the rejection of FI's bid.

30   The bank reported in a proxy statement for the annual meeting on May 28, 1987, that the SEC had approved its shelf registration statement regarding issuance of $1 billion in securities. However, its declining stock price precluded it from selling equity and debt issues at favorable rates. Yet, it was able to sell $100 million of capital notes—regulations allowed it to count the notes as a part of capital—its first underwritten debt offering since July 1984. The 12-year notes offered a fixed rate for the first three years, after which investors could switch to another fixed or floating rate for each subsequent 3-year term. This presumably allowed the bank to cut costs and attract investors. But, the notes were rated below investment grade by Moody's and offered a yield that exceeded the going market rate, when compared to similar offerings by other banks.

31   It also attempted to raise $1 billion in capital from Japanese investors who, apparently, bought a part of the $100 million issue. Japan was considered a prime target for the bank's securities, due to the rising U.S. trade deficit and the fact that BankAmerica was a large postwar lender to Japan. However, investment banking sources indicated that Japanese investors were wary about the bank's securities, due to its financial problems.

MANAGEMENT

32   The staggering losses over the last two fiscal years increased the pressure on top management. In mid-1985, the optimistic strategy outlined by Samuel H. Armacost, its president, was not working as problem loans in agriculture, shipping, real estate, and foreign investments were draining management time and resources to cope with them. The second quarter loss of $338 million in 1985 was a

> direct result of BankAmerica's decision to increase its loan-loss reserves by a stunning $892 million, one of the biggest set-asides in banking history and nearly equal to the bank's total reserve balance at the beginning of the quarter. The decision was strongly influenced by federal regulators, who recently completed a regularly scheduled audit of the bank.

33   This action validated the fears of many both inside and outside the bank, with analysts forecasting even higher losses and loss provisions for 1986. Importantly, continuation of dividend payments was in jeopardy, which would impact on the bank's widely dispersed shareholders despite the huge cost-cutting measures. (See Exhibit 11.) It seemed likely that layoffs could occur, "something the Bank has avoided for 80 years."

34   In early 1986,[4] Sanford I. Weill—former president to American Express and presently chairman and CEO of Commercial Credit Company—sought to "buy" Armacost's job by raising "$1 billion in new equity for the bank in exchange for the chief executive position." After responding that it had "no interest in considering you (Weill) as a candidate," the bank immediately named Armacost to the newly created position of chairman and CEO of Bank of America—the principal unit of the parent, BankAmerica Corporation—who the bank felt could bring the much sought turnaround to fruition. Armacost would rely heavily on Thomas W. Cooper, the newly elected president and chief operating officer of Bank of America, who had the reputation of being a "tough and extremely budget-conscious manager." Cooper, who joined Bank of America in 1985 in the new Payments

---

[4]In terms of a chronology of events, Weill's offer to "buy" Armacost's position of chairman and CEO of Bank of America occured *prior* to Joseph Pinola's (chairman of First Interstate Bancorp) dropping his merger bid. At a director's meeting held on March 2–3, 1986, BankAmerica's board rejected Weill's bid on March 3 and subsequently elected Armacost to the new position of chairman and CEO of Bank of America. The following day, March 4, "Weill withdrew his bid."

EXHIBIT 11

BANKAMERICA CORPORATION
Selected Financial Data
For Years Ended December 31, 1981–1986
($ millions, except per share data)

	1986	1985	1984	1983	1982	1981
Operating results:						
Net interest revenue on a taxable-equivalent basis	$ 3,850	$ 4,119	$ 4,044	$ 3,509	$ 3,075	$ 2,885
Less: Taxable-equivalent adjustments	57	77	124	155	168	169
Net interest revenue	3,793	4,042	3,920	3,354	2,906	2,686
Provision for credit losses	2,004	2,180	861	658	508	326
Noninterest revenue	2,352	2,145	1,603	1,347	1,185	995
Noninterest expense	4,491	4,434	4,208	3,537	3,057	2,706
Income (loss) before income taxes, extraordinary item, and cumulative effect of accounting change	(350)	(427)	454	505	526	649
Provision for (benefit from) income taxes	168	(90)	108	114	131	202
Extraordinary item	—	—	—	—	31	—
Cumulative effect of accounting change	—	—	—	—	31	—
Net income (loss)*	(518)	(337)	346	390	457	447
Financial condition and capital (at 12/31):						
Net loans	71,783	82,742	84,043	81,327	75,957	73,125
Total assets	104,189	118,541	117,680	121,176	122,405	121,269
Deposits	82,205	94,211	94,048	95,751	94,407	94,369
Debt†	4,609	5,387	4,619	2,429	2,109	1,716
Stockholders' equity	4,038	4,547	5,119	5,136	4,596	4,102
Primary capital	7,361	7,337	6,903	6,180	5,279	4,728
Total capital	8,606	8,268	7,844	7,147	5,972	5,407
Earnings (loss) per common share:						
Income (loss) before extraordinary item and cumultive effect of accounting change	(3.74)	(2.68)	1.77	2.18	2.60	2.98
Extraordinary item	—	—	—	—	0.20	—
Cumulative effect of accounting change	—	—	—	—	0.21	—
Net income (loss)	(3.74)	(2.68)	1.77	2.18	3.01	2.98
Stock data:						
Dividends declared	—	1.16	1.52	1.52	1.52	1.50
Book value at year-end	21.49	24.96	28.74	28.87	28.58	27.32
Preferred stock dividends	59	71	78	63	5	—
Common stock dividends	—	177	229	229	224	221
Dividend payout ratio on common stock			85.88	69.72	50.50	50.34
Average common shares outstanding	154,276,853	152,299,548	150,668,137	150,346,295	150,207,852	150,099,703
Common stockholders of record at year-end‡	138,254	148,200	160,231	161,023	164,822	165,093

(continued)

EXHIBIT 11 *(concluded)*

	1986	1985	1984	1983	1982	1981
Financial ratios:						
Rate of return on:						
Average earnings assets	(0.51)%	(0.32)%	0.33%	0.37%	0.44%	0.47%
Average total assets	(0.45)	(0.28)	0.29	0.32	0.38	0.40
Average common stockholders' equity	(16.28)	(9.74)	6.10	7.63	10.77	11.17
Average stockholders' equity	(12.15)	(6.84)	6.68	7.82	10.75	11.17
Ratio of average stockholders' equity to average total assets	3.74	4.16	4.30	4.06	3.54	3.54
Primary capital ratio	6.92	6.11	5.84	5.06	4.29	3.88
Total capital ratio	8.09	6.88	6.61	5.85	4.85	4.44

* Assumes that change in accounting policy is applied retroactively. If the accounting change had not occurred, net income for 1982 would have been $426 million, or $2.81 per common share, and 1982 rates of return would have been as follows: on earnings assets, 0.38 percent; total assets, 0.33 percent; common stockholders' equity, 9.29 percent; and stockholders' equity, 9.30 percent.

† Includes intermediate-term debt, long-term debt, and subordinated capital notes.

‡ Common stockholders of record at January 31, 1987, were 137,436.

Source: Bank of America annual reports 1981–86.

Processing Division, had already validated his tough reputation by reducing the division's staff to 20,000, a 20 percent decline, in addition to placing a hiring freeze and cutting several top executives. In fact, according to several bank insiders:

> Armacost, who has spent his entire career at B of A, is letting Cooper take the painful actions that he found too painful to execute himself. "Sam has always been reluctant to get out the sword," . . . "Tom has been willing to cut through bone and lose some joints to save the body."[5]

35 Some major differences were also reported between the Armacost and John Poelker faction (Poelker was Bank of America's chief financial officer) and the Cooper and Prussia combine— Prussia was chairman of BankAmerica, the parent corporation—in terms of how to restore earnings. Poelker eventually resigned; Prussia remained with BankAmerica.

36 In late August 1986, Charles Schwab, chairman of the parent's discount brokerage unit and reputedly a strong critic of Armacost, resigned from the board shortly after Poelker's resignation as chief financial officer. Poelker, who was hired to institute badly needed credit controls, served with the parent company about five months; four other top executives also resigned. Inevitably, this exodus of key executives led to a loss of credibility on Wall Street and with regulators.[6] Comparisons to the ill-fated fiasco of Continental Illinois Corporation arose; however, it appeared that B of A's large deposit base would be a major deterrent to any banking panic.

37 In October 1986, and after considerable pressure, the board replaced Armacost as chairman with A. W. (Tom) Clausen, the former chairman and CEO of the parent who departed in 1981 for the World Bank—Clausen was not approved for another term at the World Bank by the Reagan

[5]The above comments are attributed to W. Mack Terry, a former B of A senior vice president who resigned in June 1986.

[6]These turn of events occured *prior* to the downgrading of BankAmerica's credit ratings by Moody's Investors Services, Inc.

administration. (Clausen was Armacost's mentor.) Prussia "took early retirement at the same time Armacost resigned." Interestingly, 8 of the 11 inside directors were appointed by Clausen; the board membership was later increased to 17.

38   Clausen had been characterized as being aloof, autocratic, and one who wanted to exercise tight control over the bank's operations; this was in sharp contrast to Cooper's bluntness. Cooper was elevated to president of the parent holding corporation, in addition to his present position as chairman and CEO of B of A, the parent's main unit. Clausen, it should be noted, had been generally perceived by many who claimed that he was responsible for much of the bank's problems—which began during his reign.

39   Several significant departures of key executives followed Clausen's appointment. Stephen L. McLin, the investment banker who engineered the profitable acquisition of Seafirst Corporation and the Charles R. Schwab Company and the lucrative sale of the parent's consumer finance and Italian subsidiaries, resigned to become president of America First Financial Corporation. Paul V. Appelgarth, a senior vice president of B of A, also resigned to join American Express Travel Related Services Company. And, more importantly, the parent's president, Thomas A. Cooper—who became the victim of a presumably fierce internal power struggle with Clausen—resigned in May 1987. Cooper, who had implemented massive cost cuts in his two years with BankAmerica, was seen by many to be a key figure in the bank's restructuring efforts after large losses were incurred by the bank in 1985 and 1986.

40   In view of these top-management changes, the following might shed some light on the management turmoil:

> What little is known of Clausen's longer-term strategy only heightens concern about B of A's future. Asked by one potential investor what he might do if he had more resources, Clausen spoke eloquently of lending more money to Latin American countries. While what might go over well at a World Bank meeting, it doesn't inspire hope in those looking for signs that B of A's fundamental ills are being cured.

41   An action that would later affect BankAmerica in 1987 was Citicorp's decision to increase its loan-loss reserve to $3 billion; this would result in a staggering loss of $2.5 billion for the second quarter of 1987 and an estimated loss of $1 billion for 1987. Citicorp made the decision in response to its large Third World loan portfolio. BankAmerica now faced increased pressure to do something.

42   In response to Citicorp's action, Clausen said in a speech that the corporation was "moving in the right direction and getting up a full head of steam." In the meantime, Chase Manhattan Corporation followed Citicorp's move by adding $1.6 billion to its loan-loss reserve, which would also result in an estimated $1.4 billion loss for the second quarter of 1987 and $850 million for the year. Chase's decision increased its loan-loss reserve to $2.7 billion or 4.1 percent of its total loans, most of it due to foreign loan problems.

43   The following day, Clausen again reiterated that the bank would not boost its reserve to take care of its troubled foreign loans, adding that "We continue to monitor conditions carefully." He also argued that the bank's "loan-loss reserves are appropriate" and he saw "no fundamental change in the economics of the situation." Of course, any increase in its reserve position would bring about another year of huge losses. However,

> its (BankAmerica) assertion about the adequacy of its foreign-debt reserves increasingly is contradicted by the actions of many other banks, a contradiction it will have to justify to bank regulators, the Securities and Exchange Commission and its outside auditors, Ernst & Whinney.

44   Shortly thereafter at a special meeting, the bank raised its loan-loss reserve by $1.1 billion for its problem Third World loans. This latest action would bring about a $1 billion second quarter loss for 1987 and increase its loan-loss reserve to $3.3 billion, which is 4.8 percent of total loans (see Exhibits 12, 13, and 14). During this period, several other banks—Manufacturers Hanover,

EXHIBIT 12

BANKAMERICA CORPORATION
Consolidated Balance Sheet
For Years Ended December 31, 1985–1986
(in millions of dollars)

	1986	1985
Assets		
Interest-earning deposits	$ 3,917	$ 7,937
Investment securities (market value: 1986—$5,595; 1985—$5,858)	5,702	5,948
Trading account assets	3,230	3,148
Federal funds sold and securities purchased under resale agreements	3,496	1,751
Loans (net of unearned income)	73,955	84,326
Less: Allowance for possible credit losses	2,172	1,584
Net loans	71,783	82,742
Cash and noninterest-earning deposits	9,116	7,637
Premises and equipment	1,892	1,950
Customers' liability for acceptances	1,985	3,791
Accrued interest receivable	744	1,214
Other real estate owned	476	470
Other assets	1,875	1,953
Total assets	$104,189	$118,541
Liabilities		
Domestic deposits:		
Interest-bearing	$ 43,851	$ 47,693
Noninterest-bearing	18,336	16,586
Foreign deposits:		
Interest-bearing	18,722	28,480
Noninterest-bearing	1,296	1,452
Total deposits	82,205	94,211
Federal funds purchased and securities sold under repurchase agreements	3,031	2,810
Commercial paper	182	839
Other short-term borrowings	4,215	3,135
Liability on acceptances	1,985	3,791
Accrued interest payable	547	858
Other payables and accrued liabilities	3,337	2,963
Intermediate-term debt	2,606	3,333
Long-term debt	862	856
Subordinated capital notes	1,141	1,198
Total liabilities	100,151	113,994
Stockholders' Equity		
Preferred stock	709	709
Common stock, par value $1.5625 (authorized: 200,000,000 shares; issued: 1986—155,566,222 shares; 1985—153,990,425 shares)	243	241
Additional paid-in capital—special preferred	—	8
Additional paid-in capital—common	965	945
Retained earnings	2,225	2,802
Cumulative translation adjustments	(90)	(145)
Common stock in treasury, at cost (1986—622,668 shares; 1985—575,168 shares)	(14)	(23)
Total stockholders' equity	4,038	4,547
Total liabilities and stockholders' equity	$104,189	$118,541

Source: Bank of America annual reports, 1985–86.

EXHIBIT 13

BANKAMERICA CORPORATION
Consolidated Statement of Operations
Years Ended December 31, 1984–1986
(in millions of dollars)

	1986	1985	1984
Interest on loans	$ 7,982	$ 9,342	$ 10,022
Loan fees	508	456	431
Interest and dividends on investment securities:			
Taxable interest	419	451	531
Nontaxable interest	37	51	63
Dividends	6	7	8
Interest on trading account assets	241	195	131
Interest on deposits	626	854	1,090
Interest on federal funds sold and securities purchased under resale agreements	195	217	307
Net leasing revenue	117	162	212
Total interest revenue	10,131	11,735	12,795
Interest on deposit liabilities	5,375	6,501	7,809
Interest on other short-term borrowings	430	535	698
Interest on intermediate-term debt	367	387	255
Interest on long-term debt	83	82	80
Interest on subordinated capital notes	83	98	33
Total interest expense	6,338	7,693	8,875
Net interest revenue	3,793	4,042	3,920
Provision for credit losses	2,004	2,180	861
Net interest revenue after provision for credit losses	1,789	1,862	3,059
Trading account profit and commissions	67	36	51
Investment securities profit	79	30	11
Foreign exchange trading profit	141	170	117
Deposit account service charges	332	304	274
Merchant fees on credit cards	195	167	162
Brokerage commissions	214	133	91
Other fees and commissions	670	663	648
Net gain on sales of assets	411	509	65
Other revenue	243	133	184
Total noninterest revenue	2,352	2,145	1,603
Personnel	2,341	2,210	2,156
Net occupancy-premises	513	462	441
Equipment-rentals, depreciation, and maintenance	385	388	342
Nonrecurring loss from escrow and trust operations	—	—	95
Other expense	1,252	1,374	1,174
Total noninterest expense	4,491	4,434	4,208
Income (loss) before income taxes	(350)	(427)	454
Provision for (benefit from) income taxes	168	(90)	108
Net income (loss)	$ (518)	$ (337)	$ 346
Net income (loss) applicable to common stock	$ (577)	$ (407)	$ 267
Average number of common shares outstanding (amounts in thousands)	154,277	152,300	150,668
Earnings (loss) per common share	$ (3.74)	$ (2.68)	$ 1.77
Dividends declared per common share	—	1.16	1.52

Source: Bank of America annual reports, 1984–86.

EXHIBIT 14

BANKAMERICA CORPORATION
Consolidated Balance Sheet
For Years Ended December 31, 1985–1986
(in millions of dollars)

	1986	1984
Assets		
Interest-earning deposits (with parent and subsidiaries: 1986—$180; 1985—$76)	$ 3,620	$ 7,552
Investment securities	5,306	5,527
Trading account assets	3,056	3,078
Federal funds sold and securities purchased under resale agreements	2,868	1,499
Loans (net of unearned income) (to parent and subsidiaries: 1986—$437; 1985—$783)	64,413	74,871
Less: Allowance for possible credit losses	1,936	1,401
Net loans	62,477	73,470
Cash and noninterest-earning deposits	8,134	6,802
Premises and equipment	1,654	1,724
Customers' liability for acceptances	1,895	3,576
Accrued interest receivable	673	1,118
Other real estate owned	402	390
Other assets	1,521	1,434
Total assets	$91,606	$106,170
Liabilities		
Domestic deposits:		
Interest-bearing	$38,137	$ 42,303
Noninterest-bearing	16,537	14,671
Foreign deposits:		
Interest-bearing (with parent and subsidiaries: 1986—$1,303; 1985—$1,165)	20,025	29,645
Noninterest-bearing	1,299	1,456
Total deposits	75,998	88,075
Federal funds purchased and securities sold under repurchase agreements (with parent and subsidiaries: 1986—$1,105; 1985—$1,813)	3,540	4,233
Commercial paper	8	115
Other short-term borrowings	2,492	2,119
Liability on acceptances	1,895	3,576
Accrued interest payable	424	702
Other payables and accrued liabilities	2,193	2,019
Intermediate-term debt	115	87
Long-term debt (issued to parent: 1986—$210; 1985—$210)	260	271
Subordinated capital notes issued to parent	900	900
Total liabilities	87,825	102,097
Stockholders' Equity		
Common stock, par value $31.25 (authorized: 35,000,000 shares; issued and outstanding: 34,338,956 shares)	1,073	1,073
Additional paid-in capital	1,100	1,100
Retained earnings	1,699	2,045
Cumulative translation adjustments	(91)	(145)
Total stockholders' equity	3,781	4,073
Total liabilities and stockholders' equity	$91,606	$106,170

See notes to consolidated financial statements.

Source: Bank of America annual reports, 1984–86.

Security Pacific Corporation, Norwest Corporation, 2nd Bank of Boston Corporation, in addition to Citicorp and Chase—have "added a total of almost $6 billion to loan-loss reserves."

45   These series of actions have seriously hampered BankAmerica's ability to attain profitability in 1987 and, more significantly, guaranteed a third consecutive year of losses. In spite of this debacle, the bank still maintained that sources (including ex-B of A officers) contended that the bank would have to dispose of more assets, even its profitable Seafirst Corporation, "or it will wither away until it is acquired by another big bank." Rumors suggested Citicorp, in which a merger of these two giants appeared possible in light of the government's interest in supporting large national banks (i.e., a superbank) to compete with large foreign banks. Alan Greenspan, the recently appointed chairman of the Federal Reserve Board, was reportedly responsive to large banks.

CASE 37

MERABANK

1   MeraBank is one of the oldest and largest financial institutions in the Southwest. Formerly First Federal Savings and Loan, MeraBank changed its name, creating a new corporate identity to support and enhance its strong commitment to customer service and to facilitate new strategic thrusts. Now, MeraBank must consider the impact of its name and identity change, its expansion and repositioning strategies, and its basic services marketing challenges.

BACKGROUND

2   On January 1, 1986, First Federal Savings and Loan of Arizona gave banking a great new name, MeraBank. The rich history of First Federal was a foundation and catalyst for the emergence of MeraBank.

Brief History of MeraBank

3   Arizona was a frontier state in 1925 when State Building and Loan opened its doors for business. State Building and Loan was a forward-thinking company, an enthusiastic group of business people determined to grow with the needs of the nation's newest state. In 1938, the company became First Federal Savings and Loan and continued to grow, becoming the state's oldest and largest thrift.

4   First Federal was an appropriate name for this innovative company that achieved a long list of "firsts." For example, First Federal was the first Arizona savings and loan to open a branch office. This was achieved in 1948 when a branch office was opened in Yuma. First Federal was the first savings and loan in Arizona to exceed a billion dollars in assets. It was the first savings and loan to acquire other savings and loans with the acquisitions in 1981 of American Savings in Tuscon, Mohave Savings in northern and northwestern parts of Arizona, and the acquisition in 1982 of Mutual Savings in El Paso, Texas. After becoming a public company in 1983, First Federal was the first Arizona savings and loan to be listed on the New York and Pacific Stock Exchanges.

5   In 1984 and 1985, First Federal's growth accelerated, primarily due to the injection of capital from the stock conversion. The company progressed with its mission clearly defined—to be a leading real estate-based financial institution in the Southwest. To achieve its mission, activity centered on diversification with a real estate focus. Three companies were acquired—Realty World, a realty franchising business; First Service Title, a title and escrow service; and F.I.A. Associates, an investment consulting and advisory company. Consumer loan operations were expanded through-out eight western states. In 1985, the company changed its charter from a savings and loan

This case was prepared by Michael P. Mokwa, John A. Grant, and Richard E. White of Arizona State University, in cooperation with MeraBank and the First Interstate Center for Services Marketing at Arizona State University. The help of Robba Benjamin, Margaret B. McGuckin, and Barry Iselin of MeraBank is gratefully acknowledged.

association to a federal savings bank. First Federal officially became MeraBank on January 1, 1986.

6   In December 1986, MeraBank was acquired by Pinnacle West, formerly AZP, Inc. Pinnacle West is Arizona's largest corporation. Pinnacle West is a diversified group of subsidiaries that includes: Arizona Public Service Company, a public utility; Suncor Development Company, a real estate development company; El Dorado Investment Company, which invests through limited partnerships in private companies with significant growth potential; and Malapai Resources Company, which locates and develops fuel and uranium reserves. MeraBank with its $6.3 billion in assets and banking presence could be expected to improve short-term earnings and growth potential for the diversified Pinnacle West.

MeraBank's Business Lines

7   Throughout all of its changes, MeraBank has positioned itself as a family-oriented financial institution, capitalizing on its real estate expertise. For over 15 years, MeraBank has set the pace in residential mortgage lending in Arizona, with a market share nearly double that of its closest competitor. The company also has been a significant originator and syndicator of commercial real estate development and construction loans on a national basis. As illustrated in Exhibit 1, MeraBank's

---

EXHIBIT 1
MeraBank's Areas of Operation

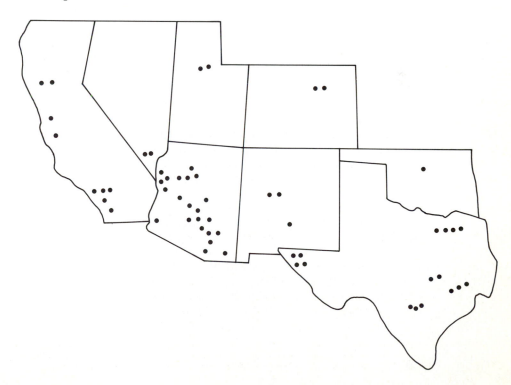

operations span eight western states. It is the 25th largest thrift in the United States, the largest thrift in Arizona, and the second largest financial institution in Arizona.

8   MeraBank has five major business lines: (1) retail banking; (2) consumer lending; (3) real estate lending and mortgage banking; (4) corporate banking; and (5) real estate development.

9   MeraBank has a well-established retail banking presence. The company offers the convenience of 78 branches, including 9 in Texas. Aside from MeraBank's commitment to the Texas region, expansion is being planned for other geographic areas in the Southwest. MeraBank's core products relate to checking and savings, but utilization of electronics and the potential for cross-selling are providing new opportunities in retail banking. Currently, MeraBank is a part of the largest ATM (automatic teller machine) system in the state of Arizona.

10   Phoenix is the largest and strongest area of operation for MeraBank's retail banking. MeraBank's market penetration is nearly 18 percent in Phoenix, which is significantly greater than in the smaller metropolitan areas of Tuscon and El Paso. The Phoenix area accounts for over 45 percent of the bank's business, while Tuscon is about 10.4 percent and El Paso is 8.8 percent. Other parts of Arizona account for 12.8 percent of the business, other areas of Texas are 4.1 percent, and other states are 18.2 percent. By reaching 15 percent of the Arizona market, MeraBank has a 7.1 percent share of the total deposit market. Exhibit 2 illustrates MeraBank's position in the total deposit market in comparison with other Arizona financial institutions. The exhibit shows each major competitor's share of the total deposit market. Valley National Bank (VNB) is the leader, followed by First Interstate Bank (FIB), The Arizona Bank (TAB), Western Savings (WS), MeraBank (MB), United Bank (UB), Pima Savings (PS), Great American Savings (GAS), Southwestern Savings (SWS), Chase Bank (CH), and CitiBank (CB).

11   In consumer lending, MeraBank offers customers a variety of secured and unsecured loans, including home equity lines of credit, car loans, RV loans, and boat loans. Credit cards and lines of credit are also important dimensions of the consumer lending package. MeraBank views consumer

EXHIBIT 2
Consumer Banking—Total Deposit Market Share by Competitors, Third Quarter 1987

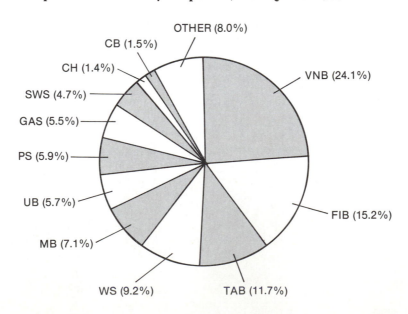

lending as an expansion area and has opened new consumer lending offices, called MeraFinancial Services Corporation, in key expansion areas of Colorado, California, and Texas. The bank's goal in this area is to create as large a consumer loan portfolio as possible, commensurate with sound underwriting. The consumer lending group has instituted a detailed program of monthly loan reviews that will keep management well informed on the status of the portfolio and how it is meeting underwriting standards.

12   A strong core of MeraBank's expertise lies in real estate financing. The mortgage lending operations originate and service more loans in Arizona than any other finance company. Exhibit 3 illustrates MeraBank's dominance in the residential mortgage market by looking at the largest of Arizona's counties. Additionally, Meracor Mortgage Corporation offices operate in Arizona, California, Colorado, Nevada, New Mexico, Texas, and Utah. They handle residential, commercial, and construction loans. A further presence of MeraBank in the real estate lending market is the marketing of its realty brokerage office franchises. Meracor Realty Corporation holds the license for a large segment of the West and Southwest, having franchised more than 135 Realty World offices. Realty World brokers can offer MeraBank mortgages and services to clients, enabling the bank to reach new customers without adding its own branch office. Through ReaLoan, a computerized mortgage application system, a home buyer and broker can use a computer terminal to analyze the dozens of mortgages available through MeraBank.

13   In 1985, MeraBank expanded into title insurance. This service was designed to provide customers with title insurance and escrow services from national title insurance companies. Further expansion of the mortgage banking business is sought as MeraBank continues to pursue a program of nationwide lending to strengthen its position as a major force nationally in commercial and construction lending. F.I.A. Associates, the bank's real estate advisory and management company, manages over $1.5 billion in real estate properties and is viewed as a way of diversifying in the real estate business through institutional investors.

EXHIBIT 3
Consumer Banking—New Residential Mortgages, Maricopa County, Third Quarter 1987

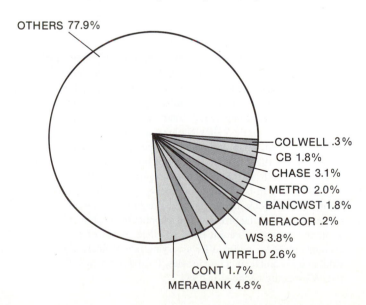

14   Corporate banking provides both deposit and lending services to companies throughout the Southwest. MeraBank offers corporate clients a variety of deposit, checking, and lending services as well as financing, secured by accounts receivable and inventory. The bank finances equipment acquisition and plant expansions as well. Cash management accounts and high-yield bonds are products that were designed to meet the needs of the corporate banking customers. Corporate banking is a new area for savings institutions, and the bank is branching into this new and challenging business prudently.

15   MeraBank is also a significant competitor in real estate joint ventures, which include the marketing and property management of joint venture projects. This fifth business line, real estate development, is achieved through Meracor Development Corporation, the bank's joint venture and development company. Meracor activities focus on the management of profitable, high-quality projects in Arizona, and to a lesser extent in Texas, California, Colorado, and New Mexico. Management has made a strategic decision to reduce dependence on this area and to limit the size of joint venture development in the future to assure that MeraBank retains a conservative level of leverage.

The Competitive Market Environment

16   Competition in financial markets is expanding and intensifying as many new institutions are entering and as traditional market and service boundaries are eroding. The basic financial market in Arizona, MeraBank's largest area of operations, can be segmented fundamentally into (1) banks and (2) savings and loans. Information about MeraBank's major competitors in each of the segments can be found in Exhibit 4. In 1985, savings and loans totaled about 24 percent share of the Arizona deposit market, while banks maintained the largest overall market share with 70 percent of the deposits.

17   With product deregulation, savings and loan institutions have been given freedom to expand much more into consumer banking services. This has allowed saving and loan institutions to compete directly with the banks, which has resulted in a blurring of the distinction between banks and savings and loan institutions. Through mergers and acquisitions, which have taken place as a result of geographical deregulation, larger national and international bank holding companies have moved into the Arizona competitive environment and made their presence known. Of the six largest banks in Arizona, four changed hands in 1986. The two largest banks that have not changed hands during this period are Valley National Bank and First Interstate Bank.

18   Despite increased competition and activity, total deposits in the Arizona market have begun to decline. Arizona's deposit base increased by $11.2 billion from 1983 to 1986, reaching a peak of $33.4 billion. However, in 1987, total deposits declined from 1986. The leading financial institutions saw a stable or declining market share trend. First Interstate's market share dropped from 19 percent to 15.4 percent, while Valley National and MeraBank's market share declined 2.5 and 1.4 points, respectively. All major competitors experienced a positive annual growth rate between 1983 and 1986. But, in 1987, all but two competitors had a drop in the average deposit per branch from the first quarter of 1987 through the third quarter of 1987.

19   The decline in bank deposits appears to stem from consumers' desire for higher return investments. As the stock market enjoyed a record bull market period in the first three quarters of 1987, conservative banking products had a continuing decline. Certificates of deposits (CDs), which offer a guaranteed rate of return for a specified period of deposit time, declined while money market accounts (MMA), which offer a varying rate of interest with no time commitment on the deposit, exhibited a dramatic increase in sales. Passbook savings (PB) and interest-bearing checking accounts (NOW) steadily declined in 1987.

EXHIBIT 4
Major Competitors: Arizona Financial Market—1986 (dollars in billions)

Competitor	AZ Branches	Assets	Loans	Deposits
Banks:				
Valley National	272	$10.7	$7.3	$9.2
First Interstate	183	6.5	4.3	5.7
Arizona Bank	119	4.5	3.2	3.8
United Bank	47	2.7	1.8	2.2
MeraBank	68	6.3	5.1	4.0
Savings and loans:				
Western Savings	82	5.5	3.0	3.8
Great American	NA*			
Southwest Savings	50	2.1	1.7	1.5
Pima Savings	28	2.6	1.8	1.3

* Arizona operations combined with parent company.

The Major Competitors

20   In the Arizona market, the most formidable competitor has been Valley National Bank, with nearly $10 billion in assets. Valley National remains as the only bank that is headquartered in Phoenix. Valley has 277 branches in Arizona. Valley National's 24.1 percent share of the total deposit market is maintained with 25 percent of the branches. Valley National's strategy seems centered on intense penetration and physical presence, supported by regional expansion.

21   Valley National is also the leader in the Arizona market for electronic banking and is planning further expansion. At present, the Valley National debit card is the one most widely accepted in the Arizona market and can be used to make purchases at grocery stores, service stations, convenience stores, and even department stores. This electronic funds transfer card has become known as a POS (point of sale). It allows a debit of the customer's bank account as payment for a purchase. The POS is expected to be expanded into more retail outlets by Valley National.

22   In the lending end of the business, Valley National has instituted a Loan by Phone program. The bank promises answers to loans in 30 minutes. These are some of the services that Valley focuses on in its advertising to create its image as "The Leader in Your Banking Needs."

23   First Interstate Bank has been very close in asset size to MeraBank but has over twice as many branch locations in Arizona. First Interstate has 15.2 percent of the deposit market share and 16.4 percent of the branches. The bank is also involved in POS capability, with its debit card being accepted at all but grocery store locations. First Interstate is an affiliate of First Interstate Bancorp, which is the eighth largest retail banking organization in the nation. First Interstate is a relatively new name for a long-standing competitor. Its advertising theme is "Serving Arizona for 110 years." First Interstate customers are the highest users of the automatic teller machines (ATMs) in Arizona, and First Interstate plans to continue to expand its ATMs, POS, and branches to stay on the leading edge in convenience banking.

24   The Arizona Bank is another competitor close to MeraBank in asset size, with just under $5 billion. The Arizona Bank, with 126 branches in Arizona, was acquired in October of 1986 by Security Pacific Corporation, the sixth largest bank holding company in the United States. The bank's image is tied closely with the state it serves. To convey an Arizona image, a native American Indian is used in the bank's logo, with the slogan "The Bank Arizona Turns To" and "Count on

Us." The bank's plans include expansion of more branches in the Phoenix metropolitan area and some outlying communities.

25   The United Bank of Arizona has been a smaller competitor, with only 47 branch operations. It has maintained over $2 billion in assets. United Bank has a 5.7 percent share of the total deposits, with only a 3.9 percent share of the branches. United Bank was acquired by Union Bancorp in January of 1987. Union Bancorp is a holding bank in Los Angeles, a subsidiary of Standard Chartered PLC, an International Banking Network. United Bank has had the fastest percentage growth in assets, deposits, and loans of all major Arizona banks in the last five years. The bank's focus has been on responsiveness to the needs of middle-market growing businesses. This is reflected in the advertising theme, "Arizona's Business Bank for over 25 Years." Citicorp has been very interested in United Bank and would like to acquire it to enhance its own presence in Arizona.

26   In the savings and loan segment, the largest competitor has been Western Savings, with approximately $5.8 billion in assets. Headquartered in Phoenix, Western Savings has begun expansion into Tuscon and Flagstaff. In its major markets, Western Savings has located branch offices in popular grocery stores. To develop the image as "The Foresight People," Western Savings plans to continue to expand products and services. The company experienced about a 2 percent drop in CDs but has seen an increasing volume of retail deposits. Western Savings is the only thrift currently involved in POS. It has only been able to have its POS card accepted by about 200 Mobil service stations.

27   Great American, though substantially smaller, has been agressively expanding in the Phoenix area, following a similar location strategy to that of Western Savings. Headquartered in San Diego, the company plans continued expansion in the Phoenix area, targeting high-income growth markets. Great American has experienced the largest increases in the MMAs and has seen a strong increase in the volume of retail deposits in the last year. The company presents itself in the image of a bank, trying to stress Great American, "Your Advantage Bank."

28   Southwest Savings is a smaller institution, with 53 branch operations. It has been an independent and closely held organization. Southwest has committed itself to serving the growing senior citizen population in Arizona. Southwest Savings has experienced the industry trend in product performance, with about a 2 percent drop in CDs, while MMAs were up sharply. However, overall total deposits have been down.

29   Pima Savings has operated out of Tuscon, where it has a 40 percent share of the total savings and loan deposits in Pima County. Pima Savings has a 5.9 percent market share of the total deposits in Arizona, with only 3.7 percent of the total branches. Pima Savings has seen continued growth in total deposits and in CDs. The company is viewed in the industry as the investment rate leader. Pima is rapidly expanding branches in the Phoenix area, frequently using Safeway grocery stores as outlets. Pima is owned by Pima Financial Corporation, which is a subsidiary of Heron Financial Corporation, a U.S. holding company for one of Europe's largest privately owned companies.

30   Other major competitors in the Arizona financial market began to arrive with reinstatement of interstate banking in 1986. Among the newest financial institutions are: Citibank, which took over Great Western Bank & Trust of Arizona and is a subsidiary of Citicorp, the largest bank holding company in the United State; and Chase Bank of Arizona, a division of Chase, the second largest holding company in the country. Chase took over the former Continental Bank. These acquisitions should have an impact on the Arizona financial market in the near future. Interstate banking has provided the opportunity for the acquisitions of Arizona's financial institutions by out-of-state companies and could continue to be a factor in the competitive environment. Also considered as competitors in some segments of MeraBank's lines of business are insurance companies, finance companies, investment companies, money market funds, credit unions, and pension funds. Overall, many organizations are entering financial service markets.

THE NAME AND IDENTITY CHANGE

31   In 1985, the total population of Arizona was 3.2 million. The state had experienced a five-year increase in its total population, an increase of nearly 25 percent. Growth had been projected to continue. MeraBank's other dominant market, Texas, also had been growing. In 1985, it had a much larger population than Arizona, over 15 million people. At that time, First Federal operated 12 offices located throughout Texas in El Paso, Dallas, Austin, Houston, and Fort Worth.

32   Even though First Federal was well positioned in its highly competitive markets, banking deregulation and legislative changes were opening doors to interstate banking and to charter changes for thrift institutions. New products and services would soon be available, and a significant challenge confronted First Federal. Although First Federal offered a full range of products and services, most consumers perceived banks to be better—more full-service and service oriented—than savings and loans.

33   First Federal perceived a new change as a necessity, but the corporate priorities in 1985 were complex. The company hoped to demonstrate superior financial performance, while making customer service its most effective marketing tool. Moreover, the company hoped to protect its current market share from the threat of new competition, while increasing retail banking coverage in Texas and expanding beyond Arizona and Texas.

34   The board of directors had been considering a name change since the company went public in 1983. The name First Federal was a very common name in financial institutions. There were over 89 First Federals in Texas alone. If expansion was to be considered, the company needed a name it could grow with. Aside from expanding under one name and distinguishing itself to stockholders, the board wanted to include the word "bank" in its name and position itself as a bank in the market.

35   A market research company from New York was retained to help determine what the new name and bank image should be. However, the board felt the process would be easy, simply changing some signs and forms. The board decided that the First Federal logo could be maintained by simply changing the name to FedBank. The board dismissed the market research team, and, by 1984, it was ready to make the change. In August, a new senior vice president was given the task of implementing the name change. The initial step was to check out regulations regarding the use of the word "bank" in the name of a chartered savings and loan association. However, it was discovered in the legal search that the proposed use of Fed in the new name would violate federal law. There is a regulation banning private organizations from using a name that sounds like a federal agency. In this case, the proposed FedBank name was very similar to the federal bank known as the "Fed."

36   The task of changing the name would have to start over. The first market research company had left with some ill feelings. So in 1985, a new consulting firm, S & O Consultants, from San Francisco, was contracted for the project. S & O specialized in corporate identity. It had recently done the name change for First Interstate Bank in Arizona and was familiar with the financial institution market in the area.

The Project Objective

37   Objectives were established at the beginning of the project. The primary objective was to select a name that conveyed a positive image and new identity. The name needed to be legally available in all 50 states. It needed to fit all the business lines—everything from the title company to retail banking to real estate joint ventures. A distinctive identity was to be developed as well. The First Federal logo was very similar to other existing corporate identities and offered little value to the company as an identity. The new name needed to create excitement and set the tone for continued innovation and leadership. It needed to increase the employee's morale and help generate new

business. However, the company did not have unlimited resources. So a very important objective was to accomplish everything within a strict, tight budget, and a short time frame.

The Process

38   Distinct phases were identified in the change process. First, the name itself had to be generated and selected. Second, the logo and identity surrounding the name had to be developed. Third, the identity needed to be communicated in a clear and concise way, and finally, evaluation must be undertaken.

39   Selecting the name was the first step. Criteria for the new name were established. These included implying stature and strength, being distinctive, memorable, and easy to pronounce. All the criteria were ranked and weighted in terms of perceived importance. The criteria of conveying a service-oriented bank and of implying stature and strength were ranked as the two most important criteria for the new name.

40   After a positioning statement was developed for the name itself, the process of generating the name began. Over 800 names were evaluated and critiqued. The top 20 names were further evaluated, using a mathematical scoring system, and all the top 20 names were legally searched in all 50 states. The evaluation of the final five that were considered is shown in Exhibit 5.

41   An early favorite was Merit Savings Bank. However, this name was being used elsewhere, particularly in California. And it was associated with a brand of cigarettes. However, the name had some interesting roots. After an arduous series of executive interviews, brainstorming sessions, and stormy meetings, a consensus was reached. The name MeraBank was selected.

42   In phase two, the logo and identity were developed. The company desired a design that would uniquely identify it and reach across all its business lines. The logo had to be instantly recognizable, even before the name was seen. The company wanted something that would emphasize a commitment to comprehensive financial services. The logo would have to be modern, make a strong retail statement, and incorporate a taste of Southwestern imagery, but not limit the bank to Arizona.

43   Choices were narrowed, and focus-group testing began. Focus-group reaction favored a multicolored logo. Group participants described the identity as "progressive," "modern," and "large." Obviously, this met the company's objectives. The colors were described as being "attractive" and "Southwestern." The vibrant yellow-gold and orange-red of the sunrise with the royal purple of the mountains were well-understood Southwestern images.

44   Several modifications were made to the logo, based on focus-group work. For example, the company has had a substantial senior citizen customer base. The seniors expressed some very strong dissatisfaction with the proposed typeface. They perceived the logo as very contemporary, but the typeface was perceived as very different and too modern. What resulted was a new and much more conservative typeface with the same multicolored contemporary logo. Perceptions were much more favorable.

45   Effective communication of the name and imagery were vital to establishing the identity and accomplishing performance-oriented objectives. A strategic decision was made to communicate the change from the inside out. To accomplish this, a large task force was assembled internally to cover literally every aspect of the identity change. The name-change task force began working in July of 1985. It included a project manager, seven project leaders, and 30 employees. The task force was responsible for the signage, forms, merchant notification, employee notification and promotion, media notification and promotion, and customer notification and promotion.

46   To direct and guide the task force, several objectives and strategic thrusts were outlined. The first objective was to gain employee awareness and enthusiasm for the name change. Employee support was essential to communicate the name from the inside out. A second objective of the task

EXHIBIT 5
Summary of Name Choice Legal Search

	Estimated Probability of Successful Federal Registration	Prior Federal Registration	Prior State Registrations (if yes, how many states)	Prior Incidence of Litigation	Incidence of Common-Law Usage
Firstmark Savings Bank	5%	Yes, to FIRST-MARKCORP, for "consumer, commercial, and industrial financing"	Yes, 15 states	Yes, successfully precluded a savings and loan from use	Irrelevant
Interprise Savings Bank	50%, based upon similarity in sound to "ENTERPRISE"	No, but ENTERPRISE BANK is registered as ENTERPRISE LOANS	No, yes for ENTERPRISE in 2 states (incl. Calif. & Texas)	No	(1) ENTERPRISE S & L in Long Beach, Calif. (2) ENTERPRISE BANCORP in San Francisco, Calif.
Landmark Savings Bank	5%	Yes, to (1) SIGNAL LANDMARK for "residential and commercial construction" (2) LANDMARK PRIME LINE for "services"	Yes, 11 registrations in financial services category 10 registrations in real estate-related category	Yes	Numerous examples are: LANDMARK NATIONAL BANK (Denver) LANDMARK NATIONAL BANK (Dallas) LANDMARK THRIFT & LOAN (San Diego) LANDMARK REAL ESTATE (San Diego)
Merit Savings Bank	50%	No, but design mark registration of MERRITT COMMERCIAL S & L (Maryland), MERITLINE (product of CALIF. FIRST BANK OF SAN FRANCISCO)	No	No	Numerous examples are: (1) MERIT S & L (Los Angeles: 5 branches $280 million asset) (2) MERIT FINANCIAL in Denver, Dallas, and Houston
Pace Savings Bank	50%	No, but 3 similar word marks are registered: 1) PACE PLAN (product of COMMONWEALTH BANK in Penn.) 2) PACECARD (product of NATIONAL BANK OF COMMERCE W. VA.) 3) PACESETTER (product of NATIONAL BANK OF TULSA (Okla.)	Yes, as a word mark in Illinois and as initials (P.A.C.E.) in New Jersey	No	Not a common name for financial services and real estate but used by: 1) PACE MORTGAGE in Denver 2) PACE CO. REAL ESTATE in San Diego 3) PACE FINANCIAL MANAGEMENT in Dallas

force was to develop a graphic plan and standards manual that clearly spelled out the proper representation and usage of the new logo. A high priority was given to the delicate task of communicating the change to primary stakeholders, including board members and the stockholders. A major undertaking involved identification and revision of all forms. The effort uncovered the opportunity to reduce by 30 percent the number of forms used.

47   The task force also needed to develop an advertising campaign and related promotions for customer notification. A TV spot would provide only 30 seconds to communicate the new identity; a billboard would provide less time. A very complex message had to be refined to its strongest, simplest components. Also, the task force needed to develop branch employee training and information sessions, including the revision of the branch operations manual. Finally, the task force had to be prepared to handle any of the legal questions that could arise concerning the name change. Thus, one of the task force members was a staff attorney.

48   The plans to generate employee awareness and enthusiasm were initiated within tight time and resource constraints. The task force knew that employee support was essential to market acceptance. The name, but not the logo, was first announced to all employees at the company's big 60th birthday celebration in September 1985. Further internal communication was initiated through a new publication called *The MeraBanker*. The employee campaign even included a "mystery shopper" who went into the field asking employees questions about the name change.

49   A customer-awareness program began in November with a teaser advertising campaign. By December, more than 1,200 stationery forms and collateral pieces had been redesigned and printed. On January 1, 1986, the new signs and the major campaign theme, "First Federal Gives Banking a Great New Name," were unveiled. Throughout the customer awareness program, the *MeraBanker* term was consistently used for name and identity-related internal communication.

50   Extensive work was done with the press. Hundreds of press releases were sent out. Early releases included a question-and-answer piece that did not include the full identity. Later in the program, the logo, the name, and the advertising campaign were released to the press.

51   MeraBank wanted its identity to be comprehensive and wanted to maintain the integrity and power of the identity. So for the first time in the company's history, a graphic standards manual was developed to state how and for what purposes the logo could be used. This was necessary to determine proper use for advertising, promotions, and brochures, as well as use on checks, credit cards, debit cards, ATM cards, all banking forms, and annual reports. MeraBank even changed its hot-air balloon.

Results of the Name Change

52   The impact of the name change was very positive. Employees were enthusiastic about the change, and the name change scored extremely well on the mystery shopper quizzes. Over 96 percent of all employees answered questions about the new name correctly. The extensive amount of employee involvement in the name change stimulated a renewed sense of pride in the company. Moreover, the name change was the catalyst generating a new orientation: employees and management perceived themselves as a bank.

53   Market studies were undertaken to determine consumer response. Consumers were positive about the new name. Over two thirds recalled the new name, their primary source being television advertising. Fifty-five percent of consumers could identify the new name as MeraBank, and very few people perceived the name change as negative. Overall post-name change advertising was perceived as more meaningful than previous advertising. In fact, advertising recall doubled and achieved a significant breakthrough in terms of consumer scoring.

54   The new advertising was very successful in promoting the new MeraBank image. When surveys

were conducted after the name change, people began to list MeraBank in the bank category and not with the savings and loan institutions. The ad campaign also helped to promote the trial of MeraBank. Of those surveyed who were likely to try MeraBank, most were impressed with the name change advertising and rated it as being very meaningful to them. Those who were willing to try MeraBank described the company as "progressive" and having a "high level of customer service."

55   A year after the name change, MeraBank's assets were up 20 percent, and its advertising recall was up almost 100 percent. MeraBank's retail banking and mortgage lending market share had dropped slightly. This was planned through new pricing strategies, which were undertaken to reduce the overall cost of funds. MeraBank, now positioned as a bank, lowered interest rates, getting these more in line with bank competitors versus savings and loan competitors.

THE NEW MERABANK

56   MeraBank began thinking of itself as a bank after the name change. Customers, employees, and the financial market began to refer to MeraBank as a bank, not as a thrift. However, changing the charter and creating new advertising campaigns were just the beginning. A complete repositioning in the market would be necessary to educate, attract, and serve "bank" customers. Changes in products, advertising, service, and facilities would be needed to complete the identity metamorphosis.

57   Several strategic changes occurred in conjunction with the name change. Advertising positioned MeraBank directly against the banks. Management dropped interest rates on savings deposits to bring them in line with bank rates. In the six months following the name change, the six-month CD rate dropped 1.1 percent. Through December 1987, the overall interest expense had been reduced by over $20 million as a result of this strategy. Interest rates and fees on credit cards were increased to be aligned with the pricing policies of banks. Customer service did not appear to suffer as a result of these changes. The number of total retail households served by MeraBank increased by 9 percent the first six months after the name change. By December 1987, the number of households served was up 22 percent.

The Marketing Group

58   Overall, changes were initiated to build a new corporate culture, emphasizing service and measuring performance against both banks and thrifts. Strategy implementation became the major responsibility of the marketing group. As a result of the successful name change, the senior vice president of marketing was promoted to executive vice president and chief administrative officer in charge of marketing, human resources, and long-range planning. She recruited a new senior vice president for the marketing group.

59   Headed by a senior vice president, the department is organized into four major divisions. The first division, Market Planning, Research, and Development, works on analyzing and segmenting the market and on keeping an accurate account of MeraBank's position in the financial market. Marketing Services develops and manages products, promotions, advertising, and print production for the company. Corporate Communications is responsible for public relations activities audio/visual productions, and employee communications. The fourth division, Directing Marketing, oversees direct-mail campaigns, telemarketing, customer service, and training. Though the reporting structure is set clearly, the functions interface frequently, and informal relationships appear to be very cooperative.

Consumer Market Segments

60   The primary demographic factors related to financial product usage appear to be age and income. Financial consumers for the banking industry often are segmented, using these two criteria. Segments with the strongest potential for heavy financial product usage are: mid-age middle-income; mid-age affluent; preretired middle income; preretired affluent; and retired high income groups. These segments represent 57 percent of the Phoenix Metropolitan population and 47 percent of the Tucson area.

61   Using segmentation profiles as a base, MeraBank has begun to target its distribution system as well as its products and communication efforts toward specific market segments, in particular more affluent population segments. A profile of MeraBank's customer segments appears in Exhibit 6. A major indicator of MeraBank's commitment to reach new segments and serve new needs can be

---

EXHIBIT 6
Market Segmentation Profiles

Communication efforts to sell specific products/packages can be directed specifically to segments by learning more about financial styles of these groups.

Mid-Age, Middle Income—These households will be hard to target as an entire segment, because they are widely distributed across all financial styles and thus vary greatly in their attitudes toward financial matters. Households in this segment are family oriented. Much of their financial behavior is focused on protecting their families and planning for their children's future.

Mid-Age, Affluent—A large portion of this segment are Achievers and have the most-in-command financial style. They are likely to be receptive to marketing approaches that appeal to their self-image as successful, knowledgeable, and decisive people.
Households in this segment are value sensitive. They are receptive to distinctive product features and are able to make price/feature trade-offs. While households in this segment are price sensitive, they are willing to pay for services that they don't have time for, especially the dual-earner households. They have positive attitudes toward using electronics and are likely to own computers and other electronic/high-technology products.

Preretired, Middle Income—Half of the households in this segment are Belongers. Their financial style is predominantly more safe and simple. Many of these households will be receptive to marketing approaches that stress traditional, conservative values and emphasize the safety of the institution. In their efforts to minimize taxes and accumuluate funds for retirement, these households will require conservative, lower-risk products.
Many of these households are shifting their focus away from their children to their own future retirement. Though the family is still important, these households' goals are changing as they enter a new life stage. They place a high value on the reputation of the financial institutions they use and on having trust in them.

Preretired, Affluent—The financial styles of the preretired affluent households are predominantly most in command and most comfortable. They are oriented toward the present and are concerned about retaining their present lifestyles during their retirement. They are sophisticated in their approach to financial matters. These households like having access to people that they perceive as competent, but they are receptive to using the telephone for financial dealings.

Retired, Higher Income—Households in this segment are the more safe and simple and prefer to keep their financial affairs uncomplicated and are generally unexperimental. Other households, called *most comfortable,* are sophisticated in their approach to their financial affairs. They view themselves as prosperous and financially secure. They highly value security and involvement in financial affairs. These retired households are likely to be receptive to social seminar-type events, because they have the time to attend and the interest in learning.

seen in its direct marketing budget, which increased 200 percent from 1985 to 1986. As a result of the repositioning effort and the move to targeting, the total households that were served increased 15 percent, to well over a quarter of a million households.

Service and Product Development

62   MeraBank launched two new retail banking services since the name change: the Passport Certificate Account and the Working Capital Account. These new accounts have brought in new deposits at a time when total deposits have been declining. Many existing product lines, such as CDs, have seen a decline in sales. MeraBank has suffered a loss of about 2 percent of its CD deposits. Passbook savings accounts have also been on a decline. However, MeraBank has increased its share of interest-bearing checking accounts—a conventional "bank" product, despite increases in the minimum balance of the NOW account from $100 to $500. Similarly, an increase in credit card fees has had only a minimal effect on the number of credit card accounts and card usage.

63   The Passport Certificate is targeted to the 55+ age group. The advertising campaign has used primarily newspapers. The core product is very traditional, a certificate of deposit. But the CD is augmented with free checking as well as free and discounted travel services, such as car rentals, insurance; even a 24-hour travel center is included. The account is made more tangible by giving each customer a wallet-sized passport card with the account number and the package benefits included.

64   The Working Capital Account is targeted to the affluent, middle-aged market segment. It is patterned after a money market account. It is a liquid investment with a very high yield tied to the one-year Treasury bill. The account requires a high minimum balance of $10,000 but permits unlimited access to the money. The investor can gain a high-yield CD rate but maintain checking privileges and access to the money. Once again, newspaper was the primary advertising medium for the product. The Working Capital Account provides its subscribers with monthly statements of the investment and the checking accounts. The account is the only product of its type in the Arizona market. In the first nine months after introduction, it generated a half billion dollars.

65   MeraBank has a strong commitment to customer service and convenience that goes beyond the traditional branch structure. The direct marketing division supervises the operations of Meratel, which is a customer service hotline and "telephone bank." Customers can open an account, obtain information, or transact business by calling 1-800-MERATEL. This convenience to customers has been well received. Call volume increased 300 percent during the year following the name change, from 75,000 calls in 1986 to 266,000 calls in 1987. To further improve the level of service performance, MeraBank has initiated direct marketing campaigns to retail customers, contacting them by mail and telephone. The intention is to expand this operation and begin a regular program of calling retail customers to enhance convenience.

66   MeraBank's management believes that its success is dependent on the capabilities and performance of employees. The company is recruiting and developing employees who are more sales oriented. Employees are expected to produce superior levels of performance, be customer oriented, have high standards of integrity, and work in unison with a team spirit. To ensure these service standards, a comprehensive training program has been instituted for the sales staff, with an incentive compensation system for frontline personnel. The commission program has resulted in doubling the cross-sales ratio at the front line. The training process has also been revised to reflect more product training and to amend a thrift vocabulary by incorporating banking terms. Periodically, the company will sponsor a contest to encourage high-quality service and improve morale. Internal newsletters provide employees with communication and inspiration to maintain quality service.

67   Community service also is an important orientation at MeraBank. In 1987, MeraBank contributed

over $1.2 million to charity, and many of its employees work in behalf of civic and charitable endeavors. Contributions are divided among worthy cultural, civic, educational, health, and social welfare programs. In one project, MeraBank teamed with Realty World brokers to create a "Dream House." This project benefits victims of cerebral palsy. Strong community spirit is perceived to be a direct expression of MeraBank's service philosophy and culture.

Advertising and Promotion

68   Advertising and promotional strategy play a key role in positioning MeraBank. Following the name change, advertising objectives emphasized creating awareness and educating the public to the new identity. These objectives have evolved to emphasize increasing both deposits and branch traffic. The initial name-change campaign required an increase in promotional expenditures. However, the current advertising budget is only slighly more than it was for First Federal Savings. The primary media used are television and newspaper, while radio is used to a lesser extent. TV advertising is targeted at the 35+ age customer, while newspaper ads are aimed at an older 55+ customer. Direct-mail and billboard campaigns are used less often, but have been effective for some products.

69   MeraBank television advertising has incorporated the new identity of the institution, while maintaining the First Federal campaign theme of "We'll Be There." This theme has been used since 1985, and there are no plans to change the theme for general TV ads. However, MeraBank has tried to develop more sophisticated messages and imagery in the ads. Also, it runs special promotional campaigns, using television as the primary media. For example, MeraBank has become involved in an advertising campaign promoting CDs and a contest linked with ABC television stations and the 1988 Winter Olympics.

70   This campaign capitalized on patriotic interest in the Olympics and offered a free trip to the games in Canada as the grand prize. The winner of the contest was announced at the halftime of the 1988 Super Bowl. Additional prizes were large interest rates on CDs with MeraBank. TV, newspaper, and direct mail were utilized in this campaign. The campaign also included a contest for employees. Employee Olympics were held to spur interest in the promotion and to encourage outstanding service. Employees were able to nominate peers for sportsmanship, team spirit, and customer service.

Merchandising and Facility Management

71   Extending the emphasis placed on promotion, MeraBank has given more attention to branch merchandising. The entire point of sale "look" has been revised to reflect the new corporate identity. Signage, brochures, and point of purchase material incorporate the company logo and identity color scheme. Though thought has been given to a standardized interior appearance, there is not a uniform branch configuration. However, the newer and remodeled facilities reflect an interior design that is more open and modular in construction. Partitions are utilized to provide a flexible lobby setup. Both interior decor and career apparel that would embody MeraBank's corporate identity through style and color schemes have been under serious consideration. The basic design and exterior of branch locations also are under review.

72   MeraBank has essentially three prototypes for branch facilities: (1) a large regional center; (2) an intermediate size complex; or (3) a small shopping center style. However, a pilot project is being undertaken with the Circle K convenience stores. A MeraBank branch and Circle K convenience store are sharing the same building. Though no direct internal connection was made between the bank and store, the two facilities share a parking lot and the same foundation. This approach is viewed as a way of saving on construction costs for new branches as well as providing added security to the customers who use the ATM machine outside of the branch, because the

convenience store is always open. It is not, however, regarded as an expansion strategy into retail grocery outlets—a strategy that has been popular with competitors.

73   MeraBank is planning a new corporate headquarters. The new office building is being designed based on a careful study of the company's history and image. The building is to personify the new positioning thrust and corporate culture of MeraBank.

Emerging Technology

74   MeraBank belongs to an automatic teller machine network that provides its customers with the most extensive coverage of any financial institution in Arizona. Expansion of the ATMs and a nationwide hookup are being planned. This could lead toward a future where most banking transactions could be done electronically at home using a computer terminal. Home banking appears to be a long-term technological goal of the banking industry.

75   The current trend in convenience bank merchandising is electronic fund transfers. Electronic fund transfers are used by many banks in the Phoenix area in the form of a debit card, POS. Though it looks like a credit card, it is used to facilitate payment at retail locations. Using the POS, a transaction is automatically debited to an account. While POS has been limited to market tests in most states, penetration in Arizona has been substantial.

76   A recent survey found the overall rate of POS acceptance to be 26 percent among financial service customers. The response varied by age groups. Younger age brackets had higher usage ratings. While the ratings may not seem impressive, they are when compared with the early ratings of ATM acceptance. Investment in POS technology is very high. However, market penetration might generate transaction volumes that reduce transaction costs considerably. Though many of the larger financial institutions have been involved in POS, MeraBank is taking a conservative stance toward electronic technology and is waiting to see how others fair before they follow.

Profitability Perspectives

77   Examining the profit picture at MeraBank, it is easiest to consider loans as the assets of the bank and deposits as the liabilities. A key to profitability is the diversity of the bank's assets and liabilities. MeraBank attempts to spread its investment risks and not invest too heavily in any one particular business line. Currently, the retail banking, consumer lending, real estate lending, and mortgage banking lines of business contribute most significantly. Corporate banking contributes to a lesser extent. On a limited basis, the real estate development line is profitable.

78   MeraBank is very competitive on consumer loans, such as auto loans, student loans, RV, and boat loans. Home and mortgage loans are a particular strength. The home equity loan is the fastest growing loan in the Arizona market. Commercial loans are a smaller segment of MeraBank's loan operations. Given that commercial interest rates vary on a case by case basis, it is difficult to generalize profitability in this line of business.

79   One area of consumer loans that could be developed into a more profitable position is credit cards. Profit in this area relates to volume and use of the card. Since the name change, MeraBank has offered the first year of the card with no fee but has added a $15 annual fee for each year after the first. The interest rate paid by the customer is 17.9 percent, which is comparable to other Arizona banks. Anyone may apply for a MeraBank credit card. The program is not tied to a deposit in the bank. Changes in the credit card program have brought MeraBank in line with the pricing policies of the major banks. However, credit card customers decreased when the changes were initiated. This is not thought to be a long-term setback.

80   On the liability side of the balance sheet, MeraBank offers several products that vary widely in their profit contribution. Certificates of deposit are the most profitable deposits. A bank can

guarantee a certain return on the deposit, then pool them together and invest them at a higher rate. Passbook savings accounts would rank second in profitability potential. Low interest rate returns are the sacrifice for demand deposit accounts. Other less-profitable deposit products would be IRAs, followed by money market accounts. The least-profitable deposit account is the interest-bearing checking account, which serves as a loss leader to attract customers and to "cross-sell" other more profitable accounts. Automatic teller cards and point of sale cards also are only marginally profitable and serve mainly as loss leaders.

81   Financial planning, sales of securities, estate planning, administering trust, and private bankers are services provided by many major banks. These services are very competitive in the Arizona market and require experienced personnel with established performance. However, MeraBank has not expanded into these areas. Though these services have been studied, MeraBank views them as marginally profitable and does not consider them as a hedge against the risk of any loan segment going soft.

Expansion

82   The objectives of reaching new consumers and offering convenience to all consumers drive the expansion of branch locations. Since the name change, new branches have been added in the existing service areas of Arizona and Texas, and further penetration of these states is being actively pursued.

83   Other expansion efforts seem to be evolving within the current eight-state Southwest region that already is served by divisions of MeraBank. The Southwest imagery that is projected in the corporate identity should fit well into such states as Colorado and California. Moreover, MeraBank management believes that the identity and the imagery of its logo would be acceptable to all parts of the country in any future expansion.

FUTURE CHALLENGES

84   MeraBank is no longer a small building and loan. It has grown in sophistication. MeraBank aspires to continue its tradition of innovation and leadership. The financial services market will become more complex and turbulent. Diversification and expansion present significant opportunities, but also tough questions. MeraBank envisions establishing and sustaining a competitive advantage in terms of its consumer service and service marketing strategies across its business lines and diverse geographic markets. With many different facilities, employees, and markets, setting appropriate objectives while creating the best strategies and programs to service its markets will be challenging.

85   MeraBank envisions using its identity as a means to powerfully exhibit who it is as a company and to provide evidence of its marketing presence. MeraBank believes that its identity can differentiate it from competitors and provide a distinct position in the market to generate sales and performance. The firm recognizes the problems of being a service provider with many intangibles to manage and market. Its identity must be considered all the way throughout service design, development, and delivery.

86   Increasingly, MeraBank has begun to consider fundamental service marketing challenges, such as making its services more tangible for its publics; controlling its service quality; developing its service culture; enhancing the productivity of its service encounters and environments; and protecting its new identity. MeraBank's new management orientation and renewed employee enthusiasm have generated a new strategic thrust and uncovered new challenges.

CASE 38

THE AIRCRAFT MANUFACTURING INDUSTRY

Introduction

1   Over its relatively short history, the aircraft manufacturing industry (SIC 3721) has evolved into a symbol of American ingenuity and outstanding technological leadership. However, in the 1980s the industry came under attack on several fronts from foreign manufacturers.

2   This case reviews the evolution of the aircraft manufacturing industry, industry products, forces of competition, the structure of existing strategic groups, and trends that may impact the industry's future performance.

HISTORY OF THE INDUSTRY

3   The civilian aircraft industry grew out of technology initially demonstrated in 1903, but the market did not fully develop until after World War II. The technologies of aeronautical control and aerodynamic lift were brought together by the Wright brothers using a small wind tunnel and model flying machines. After success with gliders, they eventually achieved the first powered-controlled flight on December 17, 1903. Although four successful flights were completed, there was little interest on the part of the public, and an instant market did not develop for the aircraft.

4   It took the Wrights four years to convince the army to buy one aircraft. By 1917, seven other companies were building aircraft for the World War I military market. After producing less than a thousand aircraft in 1917, more than 14,000 were produced in 1918.

5   The initiation of airmail service in the 1920s resulted in instrumented, all-weather aircraft. These developments provided the impetus for successful commercial air transportation in the 1930s. An aircraft market was soon developed to provide models for business, agricultural, forest service, photography, surveying, and private use. In 1929, 5,414 civilian aircraft were produced.

6   Technology continued to improve over the decades. Markets grew rapidly until the 1980s, when the U.S. commercial aircraft portion of the industry faced a decline in growth coupled with greater foreign competition. Over most of the industry's history, between three and five U.S. companies competed fiercely. Added to this competitive arena in the 1980s were the products of the European Airbus Industrie consortium.

This case was prepared by Shaker A. Zahra and John A. Pearce II of George Mason University, with the assistance of Frank R. Denton; Daniel C. Hurley, Jr.; Gregory A. Nalepa; Ronnie L. Schelling; and Eric D. Schilling.

INDUSTRY DEFINITION

Products and Shipment

7   In 1988, the aircraft industry consisted of establishments that provided two broad categories of products: primary and secondary. *Primary products* included complete military and civilian aircraft as well as aeronautical services. These products represented 84.2 percent of industry shipments. *Secondary products* represented 12.9 percent of industry shipments. These products included research and development of airframe or aircraft prototypes and/or modification on a fee or contract basis. Miscellaneous receipts for such activities as merchandising or contract work, including certification to meet legally required standards for airframe design, represented approximately 2 percent of industry shipments.

8   Table 1 provides figures on the value of industry shipments between 1982 and 1987, and basic information regarding employment and earnings in the industry.

TABLE 1
Overview of Aircraft Industry Shipments and Basic Information (in millions)

Year	1982	1983	1984	1985	1986	1987
Value of sales	$28,047	$30,522	$28,453	$33,034	$35,947	$37,394
Value of sales (1982)	$29,047	$28,079	$25,224	$29,760	$31,340	$31,450
Total employees (000)	275	251	233	251	259	261
Production employees (000)	139	121	116	124	129	130
Hourly earnings	$12.91	$13.60	$14.05	$14.35	$14.38	—

Source: *U.S. Industrial Outlook*, 1987.

TABLE 2
A Breakdown of Aircrafts Products in the Civilian and Military Markets

	Total Aircraft		Civilian Aircraft — Large Transport		Civilian Aircraft — General Aviation		Civilian Aircraft — Helicopters		Military	
Year	Units	Value	Units	Value	Units	Value	Units	Value	Units	Value
1975	16,918	$ 9,355	285	$ 4,006	14,056	$1,033	838	$266	1,739	$ 4,050
1976	17,865	9,001	217	3,155	15,451	1,226	821	324	1,376	4,296
1977	19,392	9,092	159	2,672	16,904	1,488	984	352	1,354	4,580
1978	19,881	10,179	241	4,308	17,811	1,781	833	371	996	3,719
1979	19,302	15,028	376	8,030	17,048	2,165	1,041	403	837	4,430
1980	14,660	18,845	383	9,793	11,877	2,486	1,353	674	1,047	5,892
1981	11,860	20,157	388	9,731	9,457	2,920	953	636	1,062	6,870
1982	6,248	19,266	236	6,254	4,266	2,000	587	365	1,159	10,647
1983	4,407	25,232	262	8,493	2,691	1,470	401	269	1,053	15,000
1984	3,931	25,754	188	6,343	2,431	1,681	376	330	936	17,400
1985	3,620	31,496	273	9,375	2,033	1,435	384	506	930	20,180
1986	2,980	34,370	310	11,500	1,380	910	365	460	925	21,500
1987	2,830	34,900	340	12,400	1,225	890	370	510	895	21,100

Source: U.S. Department of Commerce, *U.S. Industrial Outlook*, 1987—Aerospace, 37–4.

9   Table 2 provides a breakdown of the industry's primary products in the two major segments: civilian and military markets. In 1988, the industry's products included: *(a)* large transports, classified as capable of carrying 50 or more passengers or large amounts of cargo; *(b)* general aviation aircraft for personal and business uses, which included transport of fewer than 50 passengers, and specific applications (e.g., cropdusting, photography, surveying, or fire fighting), and *(c)* helicopters.

10   Although the number of large transports sold during the 1980s fluctuated, their value increased more than threefold. In the same period, the number of general aviation aircraft sold decreased by more than 90 percent, although only 10 percent in terms of value.

11   While the number of helicopters sold fell less sharply than the general aviation sector, the value nearly doubled over this period. The number of military aircraft sold decreased by half but increased more than five times in value.

Markets and Customers

12   From its origins, markets for the products of the industry were international, with the exclusion of the Eastern bloc countries and the Soviet Union. About 70 percent of military aircraft were sold to U.S. military services, with the remainder sold through direct contract or foreign military sales (FMS) administered programs to allies or approved customers.

13   By the mid-1980s, sales of commercial transport aircraft were split between the domestic U.S. and export markets. The same was true of other civil aircraft production, as shown in Table 3.

14   Buyers of transport aircraft consisted primarily of passenger and airfreight airline companies. Important markets for these aircraft were located in North America, Europe, and the newly developing countries of Asia

15   General aviation airplanes (all civil craft except scheduled air carriers) were marketed internationally for personal, government, and corporate use. General aviation markets were traditionally located in North and South America plus Europe. However, American manufacturers faced home-

TABLE 3
U.S. Civil Aircraft Production—Calendar Years 1974–1985

Year	Domestic Shipments			Export Shipments		
	Trans-ports	General Aviation	Heli-copters	Trans-port	General Aviation	Heli-copters
1974	91	9,903	433	241	4,268	395
1975	127	10,804	528	188	3,268	336
1976	64	12,232	442	158	3,218	315
1977	54	13,441	527	101	3,469	321
1978	130	14,346	536	111	3,471	368
1979	176	13,177	570	200	3,878	459
1980	150	8,703	841	237	3,178	525
1981	132	6,840	619	255	2,617	453
1982	111	3,326	333	121	940	254
1983	133	2,172	187	129	519	216
1984	102	2,013	143	83	425	233
1985	126	1,545	239	152	484	137

Source: Aerospace Industries Association of America, *Aerospace Facts and Figures,* 1986/1987, p. 30.

grown competition in this declining market by makers in Europe, Canada, and, to an increasing extent, in South America.

16   Total aircraft sales more than doubled between 1979 and 1987. Furthermore, during the 1975 to 1987 period, military and commercial transport segments jockeyed for the largest dollar share of the industry, with military sales holding a commanding lead from 1982 onward. Meanwhile, shares of helicopter and general aviation products declined steadily, as shown in Table 2.

17   Factors that depressed the general aviation and helicopter segments included increased liability costs, the general economic downturn in the early 1980s, cutbacks in sales to lesser-developed countries due to debt crises, and the saturation of markets with used equipment that had a long projected useful life.

18   The large transport sector also suffered some declines due to the economic downturn of the early 1980s. Also, the deregulation of domestic airlines led to a rationalization of fleets, which temporarily lowered sales to these companies.

19   The military sector continued to be the largest segment of the industry, with over 60 percent share of industry sales in 1987. This growth reflected the Reagan Administration's defense buildup policy.

INDUSTRY STRUCTURE

20   Industry statistics in 1988 showed that the U.S. four- and eight-firm concentration ratios for the aircraft manufacturing industry were 67 percent and 82 percent, respectively. Not surprisingly, this structure resulted from a combination of factors, which included high entry barriers, patented technology, unpatented but secret know-how, large capital requirements, and economies of scale available to the manufacturers.

Entry Barriers

21   Capital investment and mastery of technology constituted the two principal barriers to entry in the aircraft industry. The large capital investment required to build the aircraft represented a formidable hurdle. For example, in 1982, the aircraft industry's (SIC 3721) capital expenditures for new buildings and other structures and for new machinery and equipment amounted, respectively, to $237.5 million and $602.8 million. As another example, the value of the industry's total inventories as of the end of 1981 and 1982 was $15.770 billion and $19.328 billion, respectively.

22   Technological innovations represented another major barrier. Developments in airframe design, engine technology (e.g., the new "high-performance bypass engine"), airfoil design, and avionics, each posed significant challenges to those already in the industry, and especially for potential entrants. Many of the high-tech components of modern aircraft were protected by patents and licensing agreements. However, the unpatented, secret know-how learned in producing these complex products posed equally significant barriers.

23   The economies of scale enjoyed by experienced aircraft and component manufacturers presented yet another barrier to entry. For example, manufacturers of large transport aircraft typically sought to amortize fixed costs over some minimum or "break-even" number of units, usually in the hundreds of units. Transport sales averaged only about 240 units per year throughout the 1980s. The need to break even in an established oligopolistic competition was thus a significant barrier to entry for a potential competitor.

Foreign Competition

24   In the 1980s, the *large transport* segment encountered stiff competition from foreign producers. While Boeing and McDonnell Douglas retained 78 percent of revenues from this segment, Airbus Industrie's (Airbus) share rose to 17 percent. British Aerospace and Fokker accounted for the remaining 5 percent. Indeed, in 1988, the threat of Airbus was becoming very real. After 10 years of producing only wide-body aircraft, the A300 and A310, Airbus launched the 150-seat, A320 narrow-body aircraft starting in 1984.

25   Airbus planned to introduce two additional aircraft in the near future—the A330, designed to accommodate more than 300 passengers on short- to medium-range routes, and the A340, planned to carry 250 passengers over longer ranges. Although Airbus relied chiefly on non-U.S. markets for its sales, penetration of the U.S. market increased in the late 1980s.

26   The development of Airbus's A340 was particularly noteworthy, because it was designed to compete head to head with McDonnell Douglas's MD-11. This action alarmed Boeing and McDonnell Douglas. Both companies testified before Congress that Airbus Industrie received billions of dollars in subsidies from its sponsoring governments, and that it sold its aircraft below cost. Boeing estimated that Airbus had lost between $8 billion and $10 billion since its creation in 1969. Airbus survived only because of the support it received from its consortium members. This support was continued, because Airbus was viewed as a symbol of European technological leadership, and because Airbus was successful in creating jobs and European governments were used to the concept of generating jobs through subsidies.

27   In 1988, the *general aviation* segment was also undergoing major structural changes. The United States was the acknowledged largest market in the world for business and recreational aircraft. Three out of every four turbine-powered general aviation airplanes registered in the free world were located in the North American market. This large market attracted competition from foreign manufacturers, who gained a strong foothold in the U.S. general aviation market. In fact, foreign producers were especially successful in penetrating the high-priced business aircraft market. Meanwhile, there was less foreign competition in the recreational aircraft market.

28   In response, U.S. producers altered their corporate strategies to combat tightened market conditions. Several major manufacturers became subsidiaries of large, more diversified corporations. This enabled them to weather business downturns and to maintain effective research and development programs.

29   Producers in the United States placed much of the blame for depressed sales on excessive product liability insurance costs, which inflated airplane prices. Domestic aircraft manufacturers remained liable for the safety of their products as long as the equipment was in service, sometimes more than 30 years. In fact, U.S. general aviation manufacturers advocated a federal "statute of repose" that would shorten the number of years for which they were vulnerable to product liability claims.

30   Although foreign manufacturers were also vulnerable to U.S. laws governing product liability, they had two advantages over U.S. producers. First, they were not subject to U.S. laws for aircraft sold outside the U.S. market. Second, the foreign airplane fleet was much smaller and newer than the U.S.-produced fleet. This fact usually resulted in lower insurance premiums for offshore manufacturers.

31   The growing U.S. regional airline industry was also attracting many foreign producers of commuter aircraft. By the end of the decade of the 1980s, several foreign manufacturers attempted to expand into the 20- to 60-seat market. This move was viewed as discouraging domestic producers from investing in large commuter aircraft development. Foreign producers were willing to pursue this expensive and risky market to achieve a dominant position by using an expanding line of new equipment.

32   The prevalence of foreign manufacturers in this market segment reflected government financial support for foreign competitors. Foreign nations often targeted aircraft sectors for rapid development to enhance their industrial prestige and technological progress.

Leverage of Aircraft Manufacturers with Suppliers

33   Aircraft manufacturers, as producers of a complete product that was ready for use, had a decided bargaining advantage over their suppliers whose products consisted of components that must be installed in the finished aircraft. Given the high degree of concentration within the civil transport sector, and little credible threat of forward integration by component manufacturers, aircraft manufacturers enjoyed greater leverage with their suppliers than most other manufacturers.

34   The bargaining power in each segment followed slightly different patterns, however. Large transport manufacturers dealt from a position of strength with aerospace suppliers. As mentioned in the industry definition, the finished goods of these manufacturers were the major market for output of the other aerospace industries. This was also true for producers of military aircraft, although the process in this segment was often muddied by government procurement rules. Manufacturers of general aviation products were usually smaller than firms in the other segments, and their power with suppliers was noticeably low.

Leverage of Aircraft Manufacturers with Buyers

35   Manufacturers of large transports competed for the same market segment, principally the large commercial airlines. Government sales constituted an almost negligible percentage of their sales.

36   With the recent arrival of Airbus Industrie as a full-line competitor, competition for the commercial segment increased. Boeing and Airbus shared the same basic strategy, products, and customers, and thus their struggle was intense. As a result of this rivalry, the leverage of aircraft manufacturers over the buyer airlines slipped somewhat, with fiercer price competition aimed at achieving break-even shares.

37   The producers of military products were locked in a relationship with the government that was not easily defined along competitive/cooperative and buyer/seller lines. There was no clear indication of how much leverage these producers had over their major buyer, the U.S. government.

38   Manufacturers of small aircraft and helicopters had a declining amount of influence over their buyers. The buyers were purchasing a well-established product, and because of the relatively high price, it was advantageous for the buyer to shop around and remain well informed. Buyers knew what was available in the market and they also had a ready substitute available—the large supply of used aircraft that had a long service life.

COMPETITION WITHIN INDUSTRY: PROFILE OF STRATEGIC GROUPS

39   The overall aircraft industry had three principal strategic groups: firms that produced a full range of aircraft (so-called strategic group A), companies that manufactured military aircraft as part of a defense portfolio (strategic group B), and companies that produced smaller, general- or specific-purpose aircraft (strategic group C). Exhibit 1 shows differences among the three strategic groups based on two criteria: breadth of product offerings and the segment served. Exhibit 2 provides a more detailed description of these strategic groups. Exhibit 3 shows how the three groups differed in the various elements of their strategies.

EXHIBIT 1
Strategic Group Map

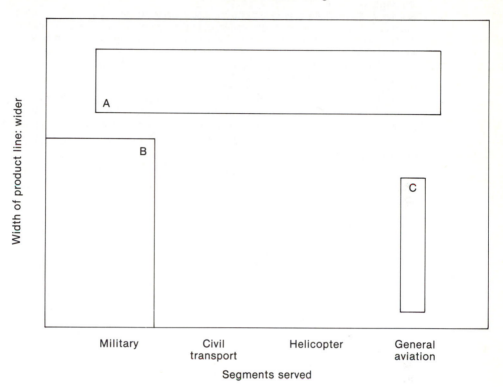

Aircraft manufacturing

Width of product line: wider

A

B

C

Military Civil transport Helicopter General aviation

Segments served

A LOOK INTO THE FUTURE

40 As the U.S. aircraft manufacturing industry prepared for the 1990s, there was a growing sense of uneasiness because of the ever-rising foreign competitive threats. Other concerns included the following:

1. Government financing or support for their own domestic producers in violation of the spirit of the free trade agreements increased the prospect of trade barriers against aviation products.
2. Gramm-Rudman-Hollings budget cuts in the United States could affect the federal research and development spending outlays and could curtail the ability of U.S. manufacturers to compete with foreign firms.
3. Incremental costs of technological development in the industry could continue to rise. Such rises in costs would be difficult to justify based on actual new product or process improvements.

EXHIBIT 2
Profile of Three Strategic Groups in 1988

Strategic Group A

Boeing, McDonnell Douglas, and Airbus Industrie were the top three transport airframe manufacturers in this group. Each produced a full range of aircraft; however, Boeing offered the greatest variety of aircraft models (six). Airbus Industrie announced in the mid-1980s that it planned to offer five models.

During the 1980s, competition within this group became increasingly spirited, especially as the major air carriers began replacing their second-generation, long-range transports with newer aircraft possessing vastly improved fuel efficiency, avionics, and smaller crew requirements. Competition in this strategic group was altered by the ownership interests of European governments in the Airbus Industrie consortium. The factors that intensified competition were the entry of Airbus; the slowdown in the transport market; the rise of strategic stakes for maintaining technology leadership; and high exit barriers, both emotional and political. Overall, strategic group A was fiercely competitive.

Strategic Group B

Competition within this group centered on the production of military aircraft, with the major buyers involved in special, strategic relationships with producers. These firms accepted their high mutual interdependence, and they often cooperated with each other in joint ventures or multiple procurement relationships with the government. These practices severely limited competition within the group, compared to that in other groups. Because of the large capital investments needed, entry from outside the group was unlikely. Thus, competition was limited to rivalry among the existing members of this group.

Strategic Group C

The general aviation producers were intensely competitive with each other for two reasons. First, this group had the lowest entry barriers in the industry in terms of capital requirements and technological sophistication needed. Second, products of each producer were generally good substitutes for one another. The unit growth in this segment had actually been negative, so the companies had to compete in a shrinking market. However, many of the firms had strategic reasons for not exiting the industry. As a result, this group experienced intense rivalry.

EXHIBIT 3
Strategic Group A in 1988

Major players: Boeing, Airbus Industrie, McDonnell Douglas.
Geographic markets: Free world.
Customers: Wide range of civilian and government customers.
Products: Wide range, covering all but smaller civilian airplanes.
Company size: Large corporate entities, possibly diversified into electronics and aerospace.

Marketing:
1. Commerical markets segmented into long- versus short-haul aircraft; also into seating capacity, etc.; similar approach to other product/buyer segments.
2. Head-to-head competition with others in group for market share.
3. Strong price competition.
4. Long-term contracts normal, with multiple deliveries/negotiated options.

Specialization:
1. Maintained wide product lines.
2. Served wide geographic markets.
3. Served multiple-customer segments (civil and military).

Brand identification:
Exposure to industrial and military buyers through trade magazines; limited consumer brand image development.

EXHIBIT 3 *(continued)*

Channels:
Sold primarily through own sales force or through an owned subsidiary (push marketing).

Product quality:
Consistently high quality, certified through government standards.

Technological leadership:
Sought after as a group and within the group. Perception of Airbus as the industry leader.

Vertical integration:
Full forward into sales, limited backward. Components from independent suppliers.

Cost position:
Economies of scale available, leading to market share competition through price competition. Eventual winner able to invest profits of dominant position to maintain significant barriers to entry and mobility. Boeing currently led in this area.

Service:
Engineering follow-up services included as part of original sale. Other services (e.g., financing part of the competitive basis of the industry).

Relationship to parent:
Companies large, diversified entities; however, aircraft manufacturing still central business.

Key factors of success:
Market share, width of product line, and technological leadership.

Strategic Group B in 1988

Major players: Grumman, Rockwell, General Dynamics, Lockheed, Northrup, LTV Aerospace.
Geographic markets: Free world.
Customers: U.S. and free-world military.
Products: Attack and fighter aircraft, bombers, electronic warfare and earily warning planes, reconnaissance/observation aircraft, cargo/transport aircraft.
Company size: Large, diversified in various defense projects and products.

Marketing:
1. Buyer U.S.G. or approved foreign military.
2. Competition limited with firms often sharing in cooperative development and production of systems or airframes.
3. Marketing done in highly politicized atmosphere, and success depended on knowledge of military and political influences on procurement.

Specialization:
Companies operated in several of the product areas listed above. Interests defined by the flow of defense expenditures (current and anticipated). Little involvement in civilian aircraft production.

Brand identification:
Limited, but some mass market image advertising takes place.

Channels:
Indirect pressure on Congressional/Pentagon defense planners to maintain programs and purchases.

Product quality:
High quality a key feature of the group. Performance to predetermined specifications part of all contracts.

Technological leadership:
Very important in this segment. Much of the federal R&D budget "invested" in these companies to maintain their capabilities.

Vertical integration:
Low. Companies mostly horizontally diversified to various weapons systems projects.

(continued)

EXHIBIT 3 *(concluded)*

Cost position:
Limited cost competition, few product substitutes, very high unit costs and prices. Questions raised about these companies' willingness to invest to reduce costs because of "compensation" received on cost-plus contracts.

Services offered:
Contractual long-term performance and parts availability services commonly offered.

Relationship to parent:
The Strategic Business Unit manufacturing airframes often one of many weapons or electronic development entities in a diversified company. Focus on portfolio of defense systems to milk current and future defense contracts.

Key factors of success:
Technological ability and skill in marketing in the specialized market.

Strategic Group C in 1988

Major players: Beechcraft, Cessna, Gates Learjet, Piper, Gulfstream.
Geographic markets: Free world.
Customers: Recreational, business, agricultural, and unscheduled commuter operations.
Products: Smaller civilian aircraft.
Company size: Small, previously independent entities, nearly all of which were recently acquired by a larger corporation due to capital needs.

Marketing:
1. Fragmented industry with seriously depressed markets.
2. Competition within group and with some of the product offerings of group A members.

Specialization:
1. Narrow product lines.
2. Differentiated on performance and image.

Brand identification:
1. Well known in consumer and corporate markets.
2. Exposure in trade press and word of mouth.

Channels:
Varied distribution, with some leasing, some sales by manufacturer or by independent distributors or brokers.

Product quality:
Generally lower than other segments but certified for relevant market.

Technological leadership:
Previously very important, but depressed markets limited the base for R&D on major new products. Focus on use of R&D to keep product current and differentiated from others.

Vertical integration:
Varied from none to moderate.

Cost position:
Few economies of scale available, especially with a depressed market. Few long-term prospects for mass production, combined with quality standards, led to hand assembly with some customizing available. Costs per unit rising.

Service:
Gaining importance, since service varied by company and used as a factor in differentiation.

Pricing:
Competitive due to excess capacity.

Relationship to parent:
Most of these competitors bought in the last decade after previously surviving as independents. They now served as an SBU instead of as an independent corporation.

Key factors of success:
Product differentiation, segmentation, and technological expertise tempered with strict cost control.

4. Costs and dangers of air travel (air traffic control and air safety issues) were predicted to limit demand by making industry products more expensive to buy and risky to operate.
5. The pending repeal of certain investment tax credits was expected to have a measurable effect on buyers in the general aviation segment and some effect in the market for large transports.

41   These threats were not taken lightly by firms in the industry. However, there were several good reasons to be optimistic about the future of the industry.

42   Demand for air travel was expected to increase at a rate of 5 to 10 percent annually. Most industry analysts believed air traffic growth would rebound from the recession of the early 1980s. This growth was expected from both the business and nonbusiness segment of the population. In the nonbusiness area, improving economic conditions were predicted to result in continued increases in per capita disposable income, which, in turn, should favorably affect the growth of air travel for personal reasons, especially for leisure.

43   The business segment of the population was of particular importance to the airlines and, therefore, to the aircraft manufacturers, because it was the full-fare, bread-and-butter portion of their revenue base. As the U.S. economy improved, there was every reason to expect that both domestic and international business travel would grow. Although some observers believed that telecommunications technology (specifically teleconferencing and other telecommunications advances) may have a negative effect on business airline travel, there were widespread disagreements about the potential impact of these substitutes.

44   Future demand of air cargo services was expected to rise, because of improved speed of delivery by reduced business inventory costs. Many businesses were attempting to lower inventory costs and using some form of a just-in-time system. Businesses felt it was economically cheaper to order items when needed and to pay a premium to have them air-shipped than to pay the high-inventory carrying costs.

45   Foreign competition was anticipated to have a great impact on the future of U.S. aircraft manufacturers. Airbus Industrie was expected to develop a family of aircraft that will compete directly with the U.S. manufacturers. It was also expected that the Japanese and Soviets would enter the market in the next 20 years and provide further competition, which may create a small shift in the distribution of market shares in international markets.

46   Industry analysts and aircraft manufacturers believed that the demand from the military segment would continue to grow. In 1988, new programs for missile defense systems in space have been announced; the B-1 and Stealth aircraft programs were going ahead; post-space shuttle NASA programs were being considered. Moreover, agreements on nuclear arms control were expected to force signatories to find new ways to compete militarily. Therefore, prospects for steady increases in R&D and defense production over the next decade were predicted to provide the civil side of the industry a substantial base on which to cushion its own frequent ups and downs. Besides a stable economic base, military applications were predicted to generate unprecedented breakthroughs and improvements in aerospace technology.

CASE 39

MCDONNELL DOUGLAS CORPORATION

BACKGROUND

1   James S. McDonnell, Jr., incorporated his company as the McDonnell Aircraft Corporation on July 6, 1939. The firm's founder was referred to as "Mr. Mac," because of the strict control he used over the company's operations. To him, the company's major goal was to produce aircrafts for the U.S. government market. At the time the company was formed, most aircraft sales to government agencies were for airmail transportation or for agricultural purposes. But just preceding World War II, the company's emphasis shifted toward military aircraft production at a time when the entire civil aircraft industry was mobilized to meet military needs.

2   After World War II, most companies began to make civilian versions of their wartime transport aircraft to take advantage of the expanding commercial market for air travel. However, McDonnell Aircraft continued to operate primarily in the military segment of the rapidly growing aerospace industry. Mr. Mac's narrow business mission prevailed until 1967, when the company merged with the Douglas Aircraft Company. The horizontal merger combined one of the top defense contractors with a company whose principal line of business was manufacturing large commercial transports.

3   Organizationally, James McDonnell remained as the chairman and CEO while Donald Douglas, owner of the Douglas Aircraft Company, was given the presidency of the newly formed Douglas Aircraft Division. The name changed to the McDonnell Douglas Corporation (MDC) to reflect the merging of the two firms.

4   In general, both parties welcomed the merger. The Douglas Company was losing market share to Boeing and Lockheed. The company was also considered the highest cost producer among its major competitors. The McDonnell Company had the needed cash flows to sustain the Douglas Company. On the other hand, Mr. Mac recognized that remaining solely as a defense contractor left the McDonnell Company highly susceptible to the shifting priorities of defense agencies. Furthermore, Mr. Mac hoped to capitalize on government-funded R&D efforts that could be transferred to the large commercial transport segment, as Boeing did throughout the 1950s.

5   During the 1970s, McDonnell Douglas continued to broaden its business through backward integration. For example, the company formed the McDonnell Douglas Automation Company to develop and provide the company with computer-aided design and manufacturing (CAD/CAM). Because of the technology push that characterized the aerospace industry since its conception, the company hoped to reap significant rewards by having these applications developed at significant cost savings. Likewise, the company formed what is now known as the McDonnell Douglas Electronics Company through a series of acquisitions. The electronics group was expected to develop the sophisticated electronic systems, used in both commercial and military aircraft, which gave the company better control over the quality of these systems.

This case was prepared by Shaker A. Zahra, Greg Nalepa, and John A. Pearce II of George Mason University.

EXHIBIT 1
McDonnell Douglas Corporation Organization

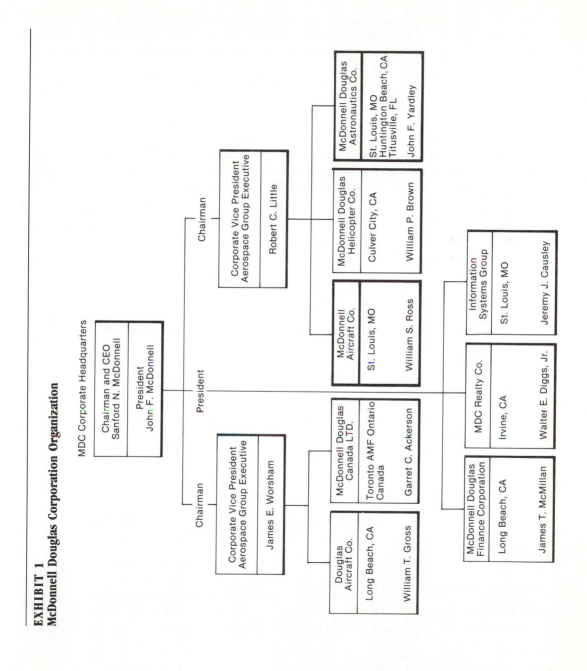

6   The company refined its business concept through forward vertical integration. Its wholly owned subsidiary, the McDonnell Douglas Finance Corporation, was formed to provide financing to major commercial airlines.

7   The company also used unrelated or conglomerate diversification to expand its business into unrelated areas of real estate, computer information systems, health care services, and energy systems. However, the firm remained closely tied to the aerospace industry, where 90 percent of its revenues were generated.

8   After Mr. Mac's death in 1980, his nephew, Sandy McDonnell, took over as chairman and CEO. John McDonnell, Mr. Mac's son, was promoted to president of the company and was placed in charge of all the businesses that fell outside of the aerospace industry. Exhibit 1 shows the MDC organizational structure.

9   To survive in the dynamic aerospace industry, the company had to increase its administrative innovation. The top-management team, supported by John McDonnell, began to emphasize five critical maxims: strategic management, human resources management, participative management, ethical decision making, and quality/productivity. These maxims became the crux of the post-Mr. Mac corporate culture.

10   MDC's business concept expanded. The company's major business lines included military, commercial transport aircraft, and space and missile systems and information. Exhibit 2 provides sales and earnings for each of these major business lines from 1984 to 1986.

11   The military line included combat products, such as the F-15 Eagle, the F/A 18 Hornet, and the AV-8B Carrier II (the advanced vertical takeoff fighter). In 1983, MDC expanded the military aircraft segment of the industry by acquiring Hughes Helicopter, Inc. A key factor in this purchase was the acquisition of the AH-64 Apache Helicopter manufactured by the Hughes Company for the U.S. Army. Since the Hughes Company was expected to be a major competitor in the LHX (the Light Helicopter experimental program that in the 1990s was to replace the U.S. Army's existing helicopter inventory), this acquisition was crucial to the future of MDC's military diversification.

12   The large transport business line included three principal aircrafts: the MD-80, the DC-10, and the KC-10 (a military tanker-cargo version of the DC-10). In 1982, noting Boeing's commanding lead and Airbus's competitive growth, some MDC board members urged the company to quit the commercial transport business. Other members urged the opposite, favoring to invest heavily in a new commercial aircraft. A compromise was reached by developing the next generation of DC-

---

EXHIBIT 2
MDC's Sales and Earnings by Business Line (dollars in millions)

Line	Sales and Other Income			Earnings		
	1986	1985	1984	1986	1985	1984
Combat aircraft	$ 6,050.3	$ 6,067.5	$5,358.5	$405.2	$526.9	$483.0
Transport aircraft	3,518.9	2,785.2	2,152.8	104.7	102.3	56.7
Space systems and missiles	2,012.9	1,660.5	1,419.9	75.1	74.0	36.2
Information systems	1,189.8	1,104.5	888.1	(69.7)	(109.3)	(45.3)
Net earnings of MDEC	34.6	29.7	40.5	34.6	29.7	40.5
Operating revenues/ earnings	$12,806.5	$11,647.4	$9,859.8	$549.9	$623.6	$571.1

Source: MDC's Annual Finance Statement, December 31, 1986.

9s, called the *MD-80*. To remain competitive with Boeing and Airbus, MDC also developed the MD-11, a descendant of the DC-10.

13   MDC's space and missile line produced the Harpoon and Tomahawk cruise missiles. These products placed the company in the lead in the tactical missile field, which accounted for almost 50 percent of the space and missile sales. MDC also positioned itself to capture a larger share of the future space market. In 1985, the company won a five-year defense contract for building a ground-based nonnuclear missile for intercepting incoming ballistic missiles. The program, known as HEDI, was developed as an integral part of the U.S. Strategic Defense Initiative. MDC also collaborated with NASA for preliminary design work on a major portion of the U.S. manned space station.

14   In 1987, MDC ranked 17th in the information industry among U.S. manufacturers. Principal products in this segment included health systems, CAD/CAM systems, network systems, and payment systems. Exhibit 2 shows that this business line has been the least profitable. In fact, the Information Systems Group (ISG) scaled down operations in 1985 by curtailing new product development. In addition, the ISG reorganized to better control costs which were very high compared to revenues.

Financial Performance

15   MDC developed a strong financial position. As Exhibit 3 shows, sales per share and cash flow per share have increased steadily throughout the 1980–87 period. These figures indicated that the company was capable of generating the necessary internal revenues to pursue key investments in plant, property, and equipment.

EXHIBIT 3
Financial Analysis of MDC

Item per Share	1980	1981	1982	1983	1984	1985	1986	1987
Sales	158.40	191.75	190.32	205.51	241.40	284.66	312.08	335.00
Cash flow	6.38	8.44	10.26	12.46	17.30	18.99	18.74	20.85
Earnings	3.85	4.44	5.44	6.91	8.10	8.35	6.24	7.50
Dividends received	0.90	1.06	1.24	1.42	1.62	1.84	2.08	2.32
Capital spenditure	7.41	8.67	8.28	16.07	15.27	12.88	15.21	15.85
Book value	39.49	42.93	47.24	52.39	58.55	65.34	70.12	74.90
Total sales	6,066.3	7,384.9	7,331.3	8,111.9	9,662.6	11,478.0	12,661.0	13,750.0
Operating margin	2.3%	4.5%	5.6%	5.9%	7.3%	7.7%	7.1%	7.0%
Net profit ($ mil.)	144.6	176.6	214.7	274.9	325.3	336.7	252.5	305.0
Net profit margin	2.4%	2.4%	2.9%	3.4%	3.4%	2.9%	2.0%	2.2%

Source: Value Line Investment Survey, July 17, 1987.

CIVILIAN AIRCRAFT COMPETITION

16   MDC operated in an intensely competitive environment, both in civilian and military aircraft production. In the commercial aircraft segment, the company had two key competitors: Boeing and Airbus Industrie. The competitive battle in this market was fought with technological leadership, market share, and varied product line. In the 1980s, however, MDC was viewed as a follower, not a leader, in technological advances and leadership, with a market share that dropped as low as 18 percent.

17   The major competitive emphasis turned into a battle for market share, where price and financing arrangements played a decisive role in sales competitions. Questionable financing and leasing arrangements developed to allow airlines to return the aircraft on short notice, with only nominal interest penalties. This left the producer with an unwanted inventory of used aircraft. These types of practices put a downward pressure on profit margins.

18   Two competitors dominated the aircraft market: Boeing and Airbus.

19   Boeing, like MDC, was well diversified within the aerospace industry in both military and space programs. However, Boeing's major line of business was the production of large commercial transports. This segment of its business constituted 60 percent of the total sales, compared to MDC's 27 percent. Boeing, therefore, relied heavily on the large commercial transport segment and spent heavily in R&D and investments in plant, property, and equipment.

20   Boeing's success began in 1952 when the company pioneered jet engine technology for the B-52 bomber. This enabled the company to apply advanced technology to the highly successful commercial Boeing 707 airplane. The company then enjoyed steady growth in revenue and market share. Boeing spent $795 million for new plants and equipment in 1986. In 1987, the company was the leader in the large transport business, with 55 percent of the market.

21   Boeing's commanding industry lead enabled the company to make great strides in research and development while maintaining a low-cost position. In 1986, Boeing's operating margin in the production of commercial transports was 4.2 percent, compared to MDC's 3 percent. This low-cost position gave the company a strong competitive advantage against price wars.

22   Airbus was established in the late 1960s as the aircraft development, production, and marketing arm of a consortium of European aircraft-producing nations. Each member of the consortium, whether government owned or not, received financial assistance in the form of government loan guarantees or interest-free loans. These loans were intended to encourage aircraft design and development and cover a portion of the production costs.

23   From its conception, Airbus had the dual objective of reducing European reliance on U.S.-built aircraft and of becoming a major supplier to the world's airline system. Because of substantial government subsidies, Airbus was able to aggressively price its aircraft in an attempt to capture market share. Both MDC and Boeing later testified before Congress that Airbus used the subsidies to sell its aircraft below costs. Boeing in fact argued that Airbus had lost between $8 billion and $10 billion in its first 20 years of operations.

MILITARY AIRCRAFT COMPETITION

24   Competition in the military aircraft segment was not as open as in the commercial aircraft area. The Department of Defense (DOD) had a vested interest in maintaining the status quo of the companies that produced these aircraft. As a result, DOD had a tendency to keep each company solvent. For example, legislation to pass the R&D costs to producers did not result in the elimination

of any of the price defense contractors. Instead, DOD encouraged a teaming arrangement, where companies awarded major contracts would spread the risks by sharing the costs of R&D with one another.

25 In the military aircraft industry, MDC had many competitors. The most important ones were Northrop, Lockheed, General Dynamics, Grumman, and Boeing.

26 Northrop relied heavily on defense contracts, which accounted for 88 percent of its total sales. In 1983, Northrop decided to produce and finance the F-20, a derivative of its popular F-5 fighter plane. DOD showed little interest in the company's new plane and did not place any orders. Northrop was also unsuccessful in selling the F-20 to friendly foreign governments; therefore, the company sustained huge losses, estimated at between $400 million and $500 million.

27 Lockheed derived about 87 percent of its sales from the U.S. government. In addition, the company was involved in submarine warfare, fleet ballistic missiles, rocket boosters, shipbuilding, and ocean mining. Although sales had declined from about $2 billion in 1985 to about $200 million in 1987, it was projected that Lockheed (backed by Boeing and General Dynamics) would be awarded the contract in the late 1980s for a large defense project called the *Advanced Tactical Fighter (ATF)*.

28 General Dynamics (GD) faced problems with its military aircraft, the F-111 and F-16. GD relied extensively on government sales, which accounted for 87 percent of total sales. GD's primary business, however, was naval shipbuilding, not military aircraft production. GD participated on a team with Boeing and Lockheed to build a prototype for the new ATF program in the 1980s, even though they were to terminate aircraft production by 1990.

29 Grumman Corporation was the largest domestic producer of carrier-based aircraft, including military aircrafts. Sales to DOD accounted for about 80 percent of the company's sales for aircraft, truck bodies, canoes, and special-purpose vehicles.

30 Boeing's total sales to the military accounted for only 33 percent of the company's total sales. Boeing managed, however, to garnish the Airborne Warning and Control System (AWACS) program, an advanced derivative of the company's 747 commercial aircraft. In addition, Boeing manufactured the E-6A submarine communications aircraft for the U.S. Navy. Teamed with Bell Helicopter, Boeing was awarded a $1.7 billion contract to build six flying prototypes of the V-22 helicopter (a tilt-roto helicopter sold to all branches of DOD). Although Boeing concentrated on the military transport segment of the industry, the company positioned itself to become a viable competitor in the fighter aircraft segment that MDC dominated.

31 The competitive lines in the military segment were drawn with the future in mind. Most industry observers expect MDC's business concept to remain relatively unchanged. The company had strong ties to both the large commercial transport and military aircraft segments of the aerospace industry. In 1986, MDC decided to launch the MD-11 series of commercial transports. The decision to proceed with the development of the MD-11 proved to be a costly mistake. The new aircraft faced competition from Airbus's new A-340 series and Boeing's 767 and 747 aircraft. MDC expected to incur expenses between $2.5 to $3 billion during the first six years of MD-11's production. Because MDC's two major competitors had aircraft to fit the 260- to 320-seat capacity of the MD-11, MDC found itself having to compete on price. Boeing endured this price competition, because it was the largest market shareholder and lowest cost producer in the industry. Airbus also endured, because it received large government subsidies and was, therefore, somewhat protected from market fluctuations in price.

32 Many industry observers believed that Airbus was trying to force MDC out of the large transport industry. Instead of competing with the two powerful competitors, MDC considered retrenching from the large transport segment and canceled development of the MD-11. In addition, slower DOD spending and increased program competition forced MDC to expand its commercial aircraft

manufacturing business at an inopportune time. Because of the squeeze on profit margins in the military aircraft segment, MDC relied more heavily on debt to finance the MD-11.

33   Because MDC was in a strong competitive position in the military segment of the industry, producing military aircraft remained the company's "cash cow." Since its position within the defense industry was secure, MDC's major decision focused on whether to subsidize its large transport production or to invest in other, more profitable lines of business.

CASE 40

AIRBUS INDUSTRIE: A WAVE OF THE FUTURE

Like Americans, we Europeans are fiercely proud of our independence. We resent being told what industry we should be in or out of. We do not appreciate being told that we should stick "to building trains and things like that," as was hinted at recently by one of our competitors. Imagine the outcry if a European had remarked that the United States should stick to bottling soft drinks, or producing episodes of "Dallas" or "Dynasty" simply because you are good at "things like that."

— Jean Pierson, CEO & president, Airbus Industrie

HISTORY

1   In the two decades following World War II, U.S. companies produced most of the free world's commercial aircraft, with British manufacturers making noticeable, but unsustained, inroads into the near U.S. monopoly. During the early 1960s, however, the majority of Europe's aircraft manufacturers began to study projects relating to a high-capacity, short- or medium-range commercial transport. This was potentially a very large market since about 70 percent of the world's air traffic flew routes less than 2,500 nautical miles.

2   Intent on seizing this opportunity, the aircraft industries of France, West Germany, and Great Britain entered into a preliminary agreement in 1967, defining the design of the airframe and engines of an aircraft to meet the immediate need. One airframe and one engine manufacturer were selected from each country to implement the agreement. The airframe participants were Sub-Aviation (France), Hawker Siddeley Aviation (Great Britain), and Deutsche Airbus (a joint company formed within the Germany aircraft manufacturing industry). The aircraft engine manufacturers included SNECMA of France, Rolls-Royce of Great Britain, and MTU of Germany. The British government and Rolls-Royce withdrew shortly thereafter to concentrate on participation in Lockheed's L-1011 aircraft. Hawker Siddeley Aviation, however, remained associated with the Airbus consortium.

3   The initial project, designated the A300 (denoting the objective seating capacity), had the advantage of meeting the needs of a market gap that had been neglected by the U.S. manufacturers. The project also gave the Europeans a decided 10-year technological lead over their major U.S. rivals.

4   In September 1967, the French government created a new form of business entity, known as a "Groupement d'Intérêt Économique" (GIE). Its purpose was to satisfy the member companies' desires to retain freedom to pursue certain ventures independently while working together on the Airbus project.

5   Airbus Industrie was formally established under French law on December 18, 1970, using the GIE business arrangement. It reflected the need for European companies to band together, both to design a broad product line of advanced design transport aircraft and to market these aircraft

This case was prepared by Shaker A. Zahra, Daniel C. Hurley, Jr., and John A. Pearce II of George Mason University.

effectively against established competition in a highly competitive market. The members of Airbus Industrie were:

1. Société Nationale Industrielle Aerospatiale SA of France, known as Aerospatiale: 37.9 percent interest.
2. Deutsche Airbus GmbH: 37.9 percent interest.
3. British Aerospace PLC: 20 percent interest.
4. Construcciones Aeronauticas SA (CASA) of Spain: 4.2 percent interest.

6   Interestingly, the French government owned over 97 percent of the shares of Aerospatiale. The British government and private investors held equal 48.43 percent portions of British Aerospace interest, with the company's employee holdings at 3.14 percent. The Spanish government owned a 100 percent interest in Construcciones Aeronauticas.

EXHIBIT 1
Airbus Industrie Membership

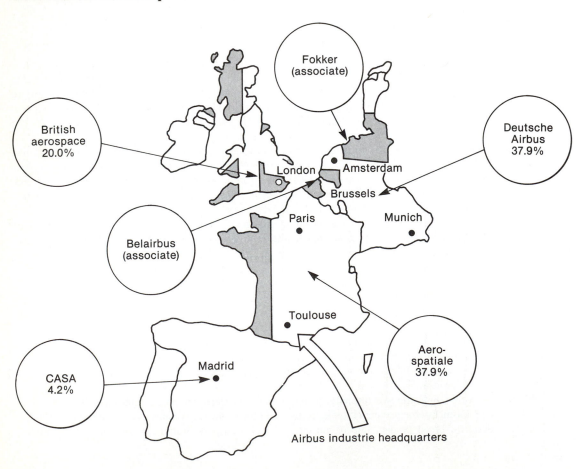

Source: Airbus Industrie, *Briefing,* 1985, p. 8.

EXHIBIT 2
Interrelationships among the Airbus Consortium Members

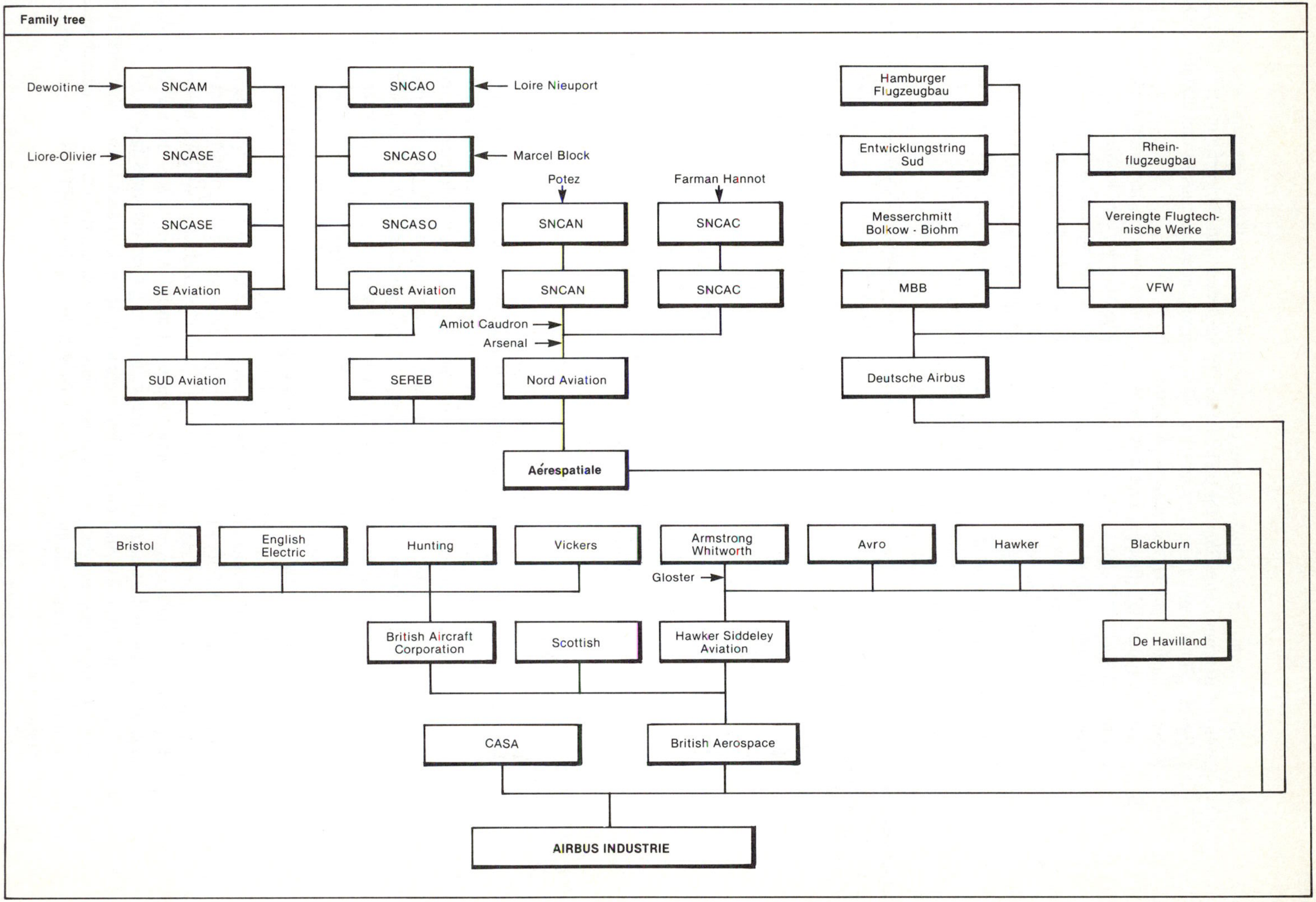

Family tree

7   Airbus Industrie also had two associate members: Fokker NV of Holland and The Belairbus group of Belgium, providing for participation by the Dutch and Belgian aircraft industry. Exhibit 1 depicts primary and associate members of the Airbus Industrie consortium. Exhibit 2 shows the interrelationships among Airbus's membership.

8   Airbus Industrie's first product was the A300, a twin-engine wide-body commercial transport having a 240- to 350-seat capacity. It went into scheduled service in May 1974. In April 1983, Airbus Industrie's second aircraft, a smaller but more technologically advanced A310 (210- to 265-seat capacity), entered service. The A320 entered scheduled service in 1988, expanding Airbus Industrie's product line into the 135- to 179-seat, single-aisle market.

9   With the arrival of the 300-seat capacity, medium- and long-range A330 and A340 models, Airbus Industrie completed its five-model product line. It appeared that by the early 1990s Airbus would compete directly with Boeing's full-range family of aircraft.

MISSION AND GOALS

10   The long-term objectives of Airbus Industrie centered on achieving a sufficient volume of business to become self-sustaining and profitable. Practically speaking, this translated into a goal of obtaining an overall 30 percent market share worldwide for aircraft with seating capacity of greater than 100 seats by the mid-1990s.

11   Pursuing these objectives and goals, Airbus Industrie adopted an outlook of designing aircraft to meet the needs or airlines worldwide. As a result, Airbus Industrie placed equal emphasis on revenue generation and reduced operating costs.

CORPORATE STRATEGY

12   Airbus adopted a strategy based on product differentiation combined with low price. The company sought to differentiate itself from the other commercial aircraft manufacturers by emphasizing technological innovations in airframe design, engine technology, airfoil design, new materials, and advanced digital avionics. In fact, Airbus Industrie developed an impressive list of technological accomplishments. These included twin engine, twin-aisle configuration, advanced rear-loaded airfoil, full flight regime autothrottle, and automatic wind-shear protection. Other innovations were a digital autoflight system and a two-man cockpit on a wide-body, advanced cathode ray tube cockpit displays with an electronic centralized aircraft monitor, and electronic signaling of all secondary control. Plans for future innovations included a second-generation digital autoflight system, fly-through controller, and side-stick controller.

13   These many achievements intensified concern in the United States regarding its declining technological leadership. For example, former astronaut Charles (Pete) Conrad was quoted in the August 3, 1987, issue of *Time* magazine as saying, "The U.S. industry is falling behind. It disturbs me that the highest technology commercial ship about to fly is the A320—not a U.S.-made plane. In this world, technology sells airliners, and we have to get off our butts fast."

14   Airbus Industrie has also championed techniques leading to significant reductions in operating costs, using lighter weight, composite materials incorporating the variable camber feature already mentioned and, particularly, in designing aircraft that required only two crew members on the flight deck.

15   In addition to its strategy of technology-based differentiation, Airbus Industrie simultaneously embarked on a unique pricing system. The company set prices that were based on its costs but were comparable to prices charged by its principal competitor, Boeing. For example, Airbus Industrie sold aircraft for as low as $35 million to $40 million. This price was well below the going market rate of $50 million to $60 million. Consequently, some competitors complained that prices charged by Airbus Industrie did not cover either the development and production costs or any profit. Airbus Industrie explained that its aircraft were priced to show a profit once the particular model's "break-even point" was reached. Airbus Industrie's explanation was challenged because of the practice of some European governments by providing massive subsidies to the consortium.

16   Unlike its successful strategy of differentiation, Airbus Industrie's pricing created considerable controversy not only within the civil aviation community but also at the international level. These practices prompted the U.S. government to question whether Airbus Industrie's aircraft partners were benefiting unfairly from European government subsidies, in violation of the General Agreement on Tariffs and Trade (GATT).

17   In response to these allegations, Airbus Industrie introduced new production methods, which resulted in more efficient operations. For example, in contrast to conventional systems employing stationary shipbuilding techniques, Airbus Industrie made use of the excellent production facilities of its members and pioneered a system of "production sharing," involving prefabrication of complete subassemblies in which final assembly represented only a small portion of the total work on the airframe.

18   Aerospatiale was designed to manufacture the flight deck, the forward fuselage sections, the center fuselage/wing box section below the cabin floor, the lift dampers, and the engine pylons. MBB produced the major fuselage sections, the rudder, and the tailcone. British Aerospace manufactured the main wing box; Belairbus the slats; Fokker the ailerons, wing tips, main landing gear doors, and leg fairings; and MBB the flaps, spoilers, and flap track fairings. MBB also assembled the complete wing. CASA supplied the tailplane and elevators, the nose landing gear doors, and the forward cabin entry doors.

19   The completed subassemblies were flown by Super Guppy cargo aircraft to Toulouse, France, for final assembly and painting. The completed aircraft was tested at Hamburg, West Germany. There the aircraft was provided with customized internal furnishings. These production innovations saved time, reduced costs, and helped maintain quality. Approximately six weeks elapsed between the arrival of the subassemblies and the departure of the completed aircraft. Nearly 96 percent of the construction work was completed before the subassemblies were flown for final assembly.

20   Because of the close association with their respective governments and because of the European political tradition of state-supported or socialized industry, the parent governments provided the major portion of the investment capital and developmental financing. The size of this support was estimated at between U.S. $9 billion and U.S. $12 billion for the period from 1970 to 1987. These subsidies occurred in various forms, including direct grants, no-interest loans, deferred-payment loans, and government-guaranteed commercial loans. Most loans were tied to airplane sales, with a loan installment payment being made when each aircraft was sold.

21   Various European officials defended these subsidies as permissible under the GATT Agreement on Trade in Civil Aircraft. They suggested that these subsidies did not "distort the market," 70 percent of which was controlled by Boeing. Further, they pointed out that subsidies were equivalent to the U.S. government's practice of supporting U.S. manufacturers through military contracts.

22   Although both Boeing and McDonnell Douglas drafted petitions for relief under the unfair trade provisions of the Trade Act of 1974, neither filed a petition with the U.S. government, because they feared that the sanctions that would result could disrupt the market. For example, more than 30 percent of the construction of a Boeing 767 involved non-U.S. components, and this figure was

CASE 41

BEECH AIRCRAFT CORPORATION

INTRODUCTION

1   Beech Aircraft Company, a wholly owned subsidiary of the Raytheon Company, was founded in 1932 by Walter H. Beech and Mrs. O. A. Beech in Wichita, Kansas. Walter Beech, having acquired some aviation experience in World War I, had come to Wichita in 1919 to join the Wichita Aircraft Company. An advocate of building aircraft with lasting structures, he and Lloyd Stearman soon left the company to form the Travel Air Company, which subsequently became part of the Curtiss-Wright Corporation. After many years, Beech left an executive position at Curtis-Wright to pursue his dream of owning his own company and building his own aircraft.

2   Beech introduced a twin-engine executive transport in 1937 that stayed in production until 1966. This business aircraft became the model for subsequent Beech aircraft, and business aircraft became the major market niche that Beech pursued. With the executive in mind, Walter Beech designed an aircraft that had a cockpit, cabin space, cargo capacity, and comfort. He also built basic military training aircraft, military aerial targets, portions of space vehicles, and airframes for Bell Helicopter. In 1947, Beech introduced a cabin biplane that was in production until 1984.

3   The Raytheon Company acquired Beech Aircraft Company in 1980. Raytheon was a defense contractor that designed and manufactured electronic systems, subsystems, equipment, and components. In addition to the Beech acquisition, Raytheon diversified into energy services, heavy construction equipment, textbook publication, and major household appliances.

4   Prior to the merger, Walter Beech held extensive discussions with General Dynamics and Sperry Corporation. However, Beech's board of directors favored Raytheon for several reasons. First, Raytheon had an interest in and appreciation for the dynamics of the general aviation industry. Second, Raytheon had an outstanding reputation in the industry for supporting research and development activities. Third, Raytheon's past track record showed an understanding on its part of the special needs of acquired firms. These firms were provided with guidance and general directions without being subsumed into the existing corporate structure. This quality was viewed as particularly important in the case of Beech Aircraft, because the company wanted to retain as much of its entrepreneurial vigor and narrow industry focus as possible.

5   Raytheon proved to be true to Beech's anticipations. It maintained the original organizational structure of the Beech Aircraft Company. Furthermore, Beech was permitted to follow its philosophy of building comfortable, capable aircraft for businesses and executives.

6   In 1988, Beech had a president and chief executive officer, 17 vice presidents, and 4 other officers. These included executive vice presidents for operations and marketing, senior vice president, and vice presidents for product marketing, manufacturing, aerospace programs, material and production, operations administration, controller, industrial relations, procurement, chief engineering, sales and marketing services, government relations, and quality assurance. The large

This case was prepared by Shaker A. Zahra, Frank Denton, and John A. Pearce II of George Mason University.

number of vice presidents not only recognized all areas for their contribution to success, but also enabled a vice president to interface and deal with customer concerns.

7   These officers were in charge of the day-to-day operations. They set prices and marketing goals and initiated changes in the company to reduce costs and increase profitability. Their policies were subject to the approval of Raytheon's senior corporate staff.

8   In 1988, Beech Aircraft Company's seven wholly owned subsidiaries functioned as independent profit and loss centers. These included: (1) Beech Acceptance Corporation, for financing and leasing; (2) Beechcraft AG, for European sales and support; (3) Travel Air Insurance, for aircraft liability insurance; (4) Beech Holdings, for marketing support; (5) Beech International Sales, for export sales; (6) Beech Aerospace Services, for supporting missile target drones and Beech military aircraft; and (7) Scaled Composites, for designing and building composite aircraft scale models to support advanced airframe development. Beech also owned 10 sales companies operating in 34 locations.

STRATEGY

9   Beech continued its tradition of building aircraft designed for the needs of businesses and executives throughout the 1980s. Providing comfortable cabins and using engines large enough to obtain basic rated performance for all operating and certified weight conditions were top priority. The business jet acquired from Mitsubishi was a prime example of this dedication to an idea. The cabin was redesigned to provide spacious seating and work space for four executives. A couch was installed to carry additional passengers or to hold additional baggage. New engines were installed and an additional fuel tank was made standard. Further, the aircraft was certified for a heavier payload, and previous weight restrictions at high-altitude airports were eliminated. As a result, Beech's product was considered the fastest jet in its payload class.

10   A second product innovation was the Composite Beech Starship I. It was designed to provide seven reclining, swivel seats; stereo headsets; work tables; toilet compartments; refreshment galley; and storage for hanging bags and coats. These refinements were designed in response to the growing emphasis on business and executive travel.

11   A third innovation was Beech King aircraft. This aircraft was introduced to meet executives' needs for a pressurized, high-altitude plane with more flexibility and capability in inclement weather and crowded airspace conditions. Because affordable, small, fuel-efficient jet turbofan engines were available to meet these needs, Beech added the Beech Jet. The modified Mitsubishi Jet offered business customers a higher-speed aircraft at affordable rates.

12   Although Beech Aircraft Company was continually researching product innovations, it continued to update and improve its existing models. For example, the Beechcraft Bonanza, introduced in 1947, was revamped in 1987. In other cases, larger engines were used in existing aircraft.

13   Although innovation and improved product quality served as the cornerstone of Beech's strategy, there was evidence that the company was changing its strategy by using price as a competitive weapon. In 1987, Beech met the lack of sales for its Beechcraft Bonanza with a 20 percent reduction in price. Industry analysts considered this a turning point in Beech's competitive strategy. Price reduction was seen as evidence of the company's growing concern over the increased competitiveness of the industry.

14   Reverting to reduction in prices was accompanied by increased emphasis on reducing costs. This meant closing several facilities and laying off production and support personnel. The company also initiated reductions in the number of airports maintaining Beech servicing facilities. These actions were taken in response to Beech's declining sales, rising costs, and increasing uneasiness over the modest rate of growth of the general aviation market.

EXHIBIT 1
Active Executive and Business Aircraft, 1980–1984

	Active Aircraft		Thousands of Hours Flown	
Year	Executive	Business	Executive	Business
1980	14,860	49,391	5,332	8,434
1981	18,582	47,716	6,190	8,122
1982	15,735	47,873	4,983	6,861
1983	17,064	45,025	5,241	5,959
1984	16,675	47,098	4,773	6,635

15   Between 1980–84 Beech witnessed a dramatic decrease in the number of aircraft sold. This involved over 1,200 units in 1980 declining steadily to 288 in 1985. As Exhibit 1 shows, Beech's sales experienced the beginning of a traumatic deline in 1982. These declining sales reflected a persistent trend in the industry that resulted from the recession of the early 1980s.

16   Another factor behind the continual decline in the general aviation segment was the increased rate for liability insurance. In some cases, manufacturers were held liable for any defect or malfunctioning in their aircraft for as long as 30 years. After Beech's merger with Raytheon, Beech developed a novel solution to the liability problem. Through Raytheon, Beech was able to "self-insure" its products for up to $30 million. This action was expected to improve company sales.

17   In 1988, Beech built a new production facility in Wichita, capable of supporting future composite aircraft at an investment of over $140 million. Beech also invested in composite productivity. This was achieved through developing a filament wound production technique that was faster and less labor intensive than the existing approach of laying up the composite material by hand on the molds. In addition, Beech also invested $250 million in its new Starship I.

18   In summary, the principal components of Beech's strategy remained unchanged throughout the 1980s. Innovation, product improvement, and increased attention to convenience and comfort served as the foundation of the company's strategy. These were supplemented by increased attention to competitive prices and active involvement by Beech in selected areas of interest.

MARKETS AND PRODUCTS

19   Throughout its history Beech emphasized the business executive as its primary consumer. This broad market definition was maintained after the company's merger with Raytheon. The King Air, a major revenue producer for over 20 years, the new Beech Jet, and the Starship I had each been positioned to cover the business market. The Baron was promoted for the executive who had "arrived." The Bonanza offered a little more airplane for the businessperson or executive who could afford it.

20   With the advent of the 1980s, Beech recognized that companies had difficulty explaining the high expenses for company aircraft to their stockholders. Therefore, Beech concentrated on smaller firms whose executives could make a decision to purchase an aircraft without having to justify their choices. The higher performance combined with more space and greater weight-carrying capability made these planes especially suited for oil companies and other growing corporations. The emphasis was on smaller aircraft to meet the needs of smaller businesses—the Beech Aircraft Company met the needs.

21   By introducing several models of smaller planes in the late 1980s, Beech attempted to build on the growing small business segment of the economy. In fact, company officers expected this to be one of the fastest-growing areas. Market efforts were directed at emphasizing the utility of the small aircraft to the small business owner. This service was not only a business necessity but a sign of distinction.

22   The declining general aviation aircraft market resulted in the sale of many two- and three-year-old aircraft. This trend placed considerable pressure on the prices of new aircraft. Beech responded by improving product quality and enhancing the performance of its aircraft.

COMPETITION

23   The 1980s witnessed a persistent, strong trend toward increased industry concentration. For example, in 1985, three companies, Beech, Cessna, and Piper, delivered 84 percent of the U.S. general aviation shipments; of that, Beech contributed 14 percent. Pressured by declining sales (Exhibit 1), an intense rivalry was created among existing companies in the industry. Although "jockeying for position" was the key characteristic of competitive moves, Exhibit 2 shows that market shares remained fairly stable.

24   Several trends affected the balance among key competitors in the general aviation industry. First, with declining sales, rivals found it attractive to pursue new opportunities outside the industry, as Beech Aircraft had. Second, mergers with well-established, financially solid companies occurred with greater frequency. For instance, Piper Aircraft was acquired by an investment company. Later, Piper ceased aircraft production and was restricted to selling existing inventory.

25   The change in Piper's status left Beech Aircraft Company face to face with two competitors: Cessna and Learjet. Like Beech, Cessna had the backing of a major company, General Dynamics, that provided necessary funds to update designs, upgrade facilities, and develop new models. Moreover, Cessna's strategic moves paralleled those of Beech in terms of reducing costs and using prices as a means of generating sales. Beech and Cessna differed fundamentally in their business philosophies. Beech pursued a strategy that centered on an image of building superior-quality products, while Cessna attempted to generate a higher sales volume by following the low-cost option.

26   The second competitor was Learjet. Like its two rivals, Learjet was acquired. The merger agreement in September 1987 with Integrated Resources, Inc., stipulated that Learjet would be permitted to operate as an autonomous business entity. Soon after the merger took place, though, Integrated Resources sold an important portion of Learjet that specialized in providing service facilities. This left the company with two primary divisions: aerospace and aircraft. Like Beech, Learjet appeared determined to remain a viable competitor in the business segment of the general aviation market. In fact, Learjet redesigned its planes, improved its existing models, and extended its markets in the United States and abroad. Because the revamping efforts proved to be less successful than anticipated, the company lost over $40 million in a single joint venture that was intended to enhance product development.

27   Despite the similarities in the moves taken by each firm, the efforts stressed by Beech, Cessna, and Learjet remained distinctive. Beech's products catered to businesses that desired more room, more comfort, and higher-payload aircraft. In contrast, Cessna's products stressed affordability. In terms of the existing business fleet, Beech was considered the stronger of the two companies. Understandably, the competition between the two firms was fierce. Cessna's creation of a business jet challenged Beech's market position. In response, Beech purchased the rights to a similar jet from Mitsubishi and made improvements to provide a clear competitive advantage over Cessna.

EXHIBIT 2
Number of Aircraft Sold by Key Competitors, 1980–1985

Year	Ayers	Beech	Cessna	Learjet	Piper
1981	59	1,242	4,680	138	2,495
1982	25	526	2,140	99	1,048
1983	9	402	1,219	45	661
1984	NA	411	978	33	664
1985	NA	288	881	33	538

NA = data not available.

Learjet's products covered a wide spectrum. They were known for their relatively competitive prices, higher speed, and comfort. As a result, industry analysts predicted that competition between Learjet and Cessna would be intense. In effect, the two companies locked into a long-term battle for market share in a declining industry.

28   Competition in this segment of the industry became global in scope. Piaggio, of Italy, introduced a new business aircraft that was lighter, with an unusual structural design made mostly of aluminum. This move signaled serious interest on the part of foreign competitors to penetrate the market with lower costs and up-to-date designs. In response, Beech designed a composite airframe and a novel avionics package. In addition, the company was successful in shortening production hours over the foreign competitors. Beech had learned to cut other costs by extracting more favorable terms from its suppliers.

THE FUTURE

29   While Beech had remained faithful to its original mission, its business environment had changed a great deal. First, there was a decline in demand for general aviation products that was expected to persist in the 1990s. This decline was due in part to the increased interest of major commercial airlines in targeting the business travelers.

30   Second, there was growing competition from domestic and foreign producers. Learjet had shown strong interest in the executive-business aircraft segment and had taken numerous steps to improve its performance. Cessna seemed intent on protecting its current market share. Learjet, Cessna, and Beech were active in product and process innovations to differentiate their products and reduce costs. The dynamics of competition were changing for two additional reasons: the increasing presence of international competition, and the takeover of industry participants by larger firms. These acquisitions provided these companies with additional funds for product development and testing.

31   Third, as industry sales continued to decline, operating costs rose steadily, because of rising labor cost and increased marketing efforts to differentiate brands in the industry. Beech responded to this trend by cutting costs and investing approximately $500,000 on graphite composite technology. These monies included capital investment in facilities and equipment, development costs for the Starship I, and initial production costs. In turn, these improvements were expected to reduce labor costs by lowering weight and reducing operating costs.

32   Finally, Beech sales were impacted by a lack of pilots. Prior to the 1980s, there had been an abundance of pilots who sought jobs flying company aircraft. But, by the late 1980s, many of these pilots were reaching retirement and replacements were hard to find. Younger pilots preferred

EXHIBIT 3
An Overview of Raytheon's Key Financial Indicators

Item	1982	1983	1984	1985	1986	1987	1988
Sales ($ millions)	5,513	5,937	5,995	6,408	7,308	7,775	8,400
Operating margin (%)	10.5	9.7	9.9	10.9	10.8	11.0	11.0
Net profit margin (%)	5.8	5.1	5.7	5.9	5.4	5.8	5.7
Earnings per share ($)	3.78	3.55	4.02	4.60	5.10	6.10	6.80
Cash flow per share (%)	6.07	6.11	6.09	7.54	8.52	10.20	10.90
Long-term debt ($ millions)	67.9	99.1	85.5	74.8	48.7	45.0	50.0

the higher income and shorter hours available from major airlines. An example of the impact of limited pilot availability on Beech's business pertained to the Starship I. Beech originally designed the Starship I for 12,500 pounds takeoff weight, a weight for which it was permissible to fly with only one pilot. The takeoff weight was raised to 14,000 pounds and, as a result, required two pilots. Industry analysts expected this change to have an adverse effect on sales of the company's Starship I.

33   Although these trends were expected to impact Beech's business adversely, industry analysts believed that the future of Beech was intertwined with Raytheon's. Since the merger, Raytheon provided effective leadership, organization, and capital for Beech to pursue its goals in the general aviation market. With rising competitive pressures and declining sales, some expected Raytheon to direct Beech into a different direction, since Raytheon produced a wide range of electronic equipment, military missiles, and chemical and nuclear plants; engaged in geophysical exploration; and manufactured household appliances. Moreover, nearly 50 percent of Raytheon's sales were derived from governmental contracting.

34   Raytheon had three alternatives regarding the future of Beech Aircraft. The first called for additional support for Beech in its continuing competitive battle with Cessna and Learjet. This option was plausible in view of the well-balanced portfolio and strong financial position of the Raytheon Company. Exhibit 3 provides an overview of key financial figures for Raytheon between 1982 and 1988.

35   The second possibility for Raytheon was to make Beech more active in defense contracting. This option was attractive, because it brought Beech's mission closer to the thrust of Raytheon's dominant business concept.

36   The third alternative was to divest Beech. Indeed, some industry analysts questioned whether or not there was a future in the general aviation industry. The competitive battle between Beech, Cessna, and Learjet raised the cost of acquiring and maintaining market shares so high that financial gains were elusive.

CASE INDEX

INDEX